ADOLESCENCE

PAUL S. KAPLAN

The State University of New York at Stony Brook and
Suffolk County Community College

Houghton Mifflin Company   Boston New York

FOR ZACHARY AHARON AND DAVID RAFAEL,
FUTURE ADOLESCENTS

V. P. & Publisher: Charles Hartford
Senior Sponsoring Editor: Kerry Baruth
Senior Development Editor: Bess Deck
Editorial Assistant: Caryn Yilmaz
Senior Project Editor: Aileen Mason
Editorial Assistant: Liliana Ritter
Senior Production/Design Coordinator: Jodi O'Rourke
Senior Manufacturing Coordinator: Priscilla Bailey
Senior Marketing Manager: Katherine Greig
Senior Designer: Henry Rachlin

Printed in the U.S.A.

Library of Congress Control Number: 00-133791

ISBN: 0-395-90823-X

1 2 3 4 5 6 7 8 9 -DOW- 07 06 05 04 03

Brief Contents

Preface   xvii

Part I Exploring Adolescence

1 The World of Adolescence   1

2 The Scientific Approach to Adolescence   26

Part II Physical and Cognitive Development

3 Physical Development   60

4 Cognitive Development   94

Part III The Contexts of Development

5 Families   136

6 Peers   178

7 The School Experience   214

8 The Media   254

Part IV Social, Moral, and Personality Development

9 Self-Concept and Identity Formation   296

10 Love and Sex   342

11 Moral Development, Values, and Religion   384

12 Work and Career Development   416

Part V Challenges to Adolescent Development

13 Stress and Psychological, Physical, and Learning Problems   452

14 Drug Use and Violence   494

Epilogue   532

Appendix: Review Questions   A-1

Glossary   G-1

Credits   C-1

References   R-1

Name Index   NI-1

Subject Index   SI-1

CONTENTS

PREFACE   xvii

PART I   EXPLORING ADOLESCENCE

1   THE WORLD OF ADOLESCENCE   1

WHAT IS YOUR OPINION?   1

ADOLESCENCE: A FRAME OF REFERENCE   1
A Time Frame That Varies   1
Rites of Passage   1   *Achieving Autonomy*   3
Broad and Narrow Socialization   4
Dispelling the Myths   6

MODERN VIEWS OF ADOLESCENCE   7
20th-Century Changes in Views in Adolescence   7
Adolescents View Themselves   8
Adults View Teens   8
In the Eyes of the Law   10
Psychologists View Adolescents   11
■ FOCUS: Curfews: A Protection or an Infringement of Rights?   12

THEMES OF ADOLESCENCE   13
Theme 1: Adolescence Is a Time of Choices, "Firsts," and Transitions   13
Theme 2: Adolescence Is Shaped by Context   14
■ PERSPECTIVE 1: We Don't Like What You're Listening To!   15
■ PERSPECTIVE 2: I Should Be Treated Like Everyone Else   16
Theme 3: Adolescence Is Influenced by Group Membership   16
Theme 4: The Adolescent Experience Has Changed over the Past 50 Years   19
Theme 5: Today's Views of Adolescence Are Becoming More Balanced, with Greater Attention to Its Positive Nature   23

HAS YOUR OPINION CHANGED?   23

CHAPTER SUMMARY AT A GLANCE   25

2   THE SCIENTIFIC APPROACH TO ADOLESCENCE   26

WHAT IS YOUR OPINION?   27

THEORETICAL APPROACHES TO ADOLESCENCE   27
What Is a Good Theory?   28
How Theories Differ from One Another   28

PERSPECTIVES ON ADOLESCENCE   29
Psychoanalytic Conceptions of Adolescence   29
Erikson and Identity   32
Havighurst's Developmental Tasks   33
Cognitive Changes in Adolescence: Jean Piaget's Theory   34

The Information-Processing Approach   35
The Behavioral Approach: You Are What You Learn   36
Social Learning Theory   37

■ PERSPECTIVE 1: Encouraging a Friend   38

The Ecological Approach   39
Eclecticism   43

RESEARCH INTO ADOLESCENCE   43
Research Designs   43
Cross-Sectional Designs 43   *Longitudinal Designs* 44
Sequential Designs 45
Research Methods and Data Collection   46
Observation 46   *The Case Study* 46   *Questionnaires and Surveys* 47
The Use of Correlations 48   *Experimental Research* 48   *Quasi-Experimental Methods* 49

■ FOCUS: MISTAKES, MISUNDERSTANDINGS, AND MISCALCULATIONS   50

Research in Other Cultures and Subcultures   51
Reviewing the Research: The Internet   52

ETHICAL STANDARDS AND DILEMMAS   54
Informed Consent   54
Deception   56
Confidentiality   57

HAS YOUR OPINION CHANGED?   57

■ PERSPECTIVE 2: Breaching Confidentiality   58

CHAPTER SUMMARY AT A GLANCE   59

PART II   PHYSICAL AND COGNITIVE DEVELOPMENT

3   PHYSICAL DEVELOPMENT   60

WHAT IS YOUR OPINION?   61

PUBERTAL CHANGES   61
The Growth Spurt   61
The Female Adolescent Develops   62
Menstruation 63

■ PERSPECTIVE 1: Help for the Single Dad   64

Secondary Sex Characteristics 64
The Male Adolescent Develops   65
The Developing Brain   65

THE BIOLOGICAL BASES FOR BEHAVIOR AND DEVELOPMENT   67
What Causes Puberty?   68
Hormones and Behavior   69

■ FOCUS: THE EMOTIONAL SWINGS OF ADOLESCENCE: MYTH OR REALITY?   70

Genetic Influences on Behavior   71
Misunderstandings About Genetics 72   *Determining Genetic Contribution* 72
Genetic Factors and Social Behavior 74   *Temperament* 75   *Why Am I So Different from My Siblings?* 76

THE INTERPLAY OF PHYSICAL DEVELOPMENT AND EXPERIENCE   78
The Secular Trend: Taller, Earlier, and Heavier   78
Environmental Factors and Pubertal Timing   79

Psychological Reactions to Pubertal Timing: Early and Late Maturation   80
Early and Late Maturation in Males 80   *Early and Late Maturation in Females* 81
■ PERSPECTIVE 2: I'm Ready; You're Not   82

THE HEALTH OF TODAY'S TEENAGERS   83
Rating Adolescent Health   83
The Increasing Concern over Adolescent Health Practices   84
Nutrition   84
Teenagers and Body Image 85   *Body Image and Eating Habits* 86   *Obesity* 88
Physical Activity   88
HAS YOUR OPINION CHANGED?   88
Sleep: Why Are Teens So Tired?   89
PLACING ADOLESCENT PHYSICAL DEVELOPMENT IN PERSPECTIVE   91
THEMES   92
CHAPTER SUMMARY AT A GLANCE   93

COGNITIVE DEVELOPMENT   94

WHAT IS YOUR OPINION?   95
DEVELOPMENTAL APPROACHES   95
Piaget on Adolescent Cognitive Development   95
Organization: Schemata and Operations 96   *Adaptation: Assimilation and Accommodation* 96   *Influences on Development* 96   *The Early Stages of Cognitive Development* 96   *The Stage of Formal Operations* 97
■ PERSPECTIVE: Come Down to Earth   99
Piaget and Education 100   *Critique of the Concept of Formal Operations* 101
Going Beyond Formal Operations 101
Vygotsky's Sociocultural Theory   103
Social Interaction and the Transmission of Skills 103   *The Zone of Proximal Development* 103   *Vygotsky's Influence on Education* 104
Piaget and Vygotsky Reconsidered   107

INFORMATION PROCESSING   109
Information Processing in Adolescence   110
Attention 110   *Speed of Processing* 110   *Memory* 111   *Automaticity* 112
Strategy Use 112
Metacognition   112
Self-Regulation   113

APPROACHES TO INTELLIGENCE   115
The Stanford-Binet and Wechsler Tests   115
Intelligence Testing in Adolescence   116
Controversies Surrounding Intelligence Testing   117
The Origins of Intelligence 117   *Culture and Intelligence* 118   *Is Intelligence One Quality or Many?* 119

USING COGNITIVE ABILITIES   123
Critical Thinking   123
Creativity   125
Decision Making   126
■ FOCUS: THE ISSUE OF COMPETENCY   128

SOCIAL COGNITION   129
Looking at Others   130
Taking Another Person's Perspective   130
Adolescent Egocentrism   131

PLACING ADOLESCENT COGNITIVE DEVELOPMENT IN PERSPECTIVE   133
HAS YOUR OPINION CHANGED?   133
THEMES   134
CHAPTER SUMMARY AT A GLANCE   135

PART III   THE CONTEXTS OF DEVELOPMENT

5   FAMILIES   136

WHAT IS YOUR OPINION?   137

THE ADOLESCENT-PARENT RELATIONSHIP   137
The Changing Relationship   138
Achieving Emotional Autonomy   139
  Four Components of Emotional Autonomy 139   *Attachment Theory and Emotional Autonomy* 139
The Development of the Adolescent-Parent Relationship   141
Power and Cohesiveness   143

PARENTING STYLES   145
Four Different Styles of Parenting   145
Changes in Parenting Style in Adolescence   146
Culture and Parenting Style   147

COMMUNICATION AND CONFLICT   149
■ PERSPECTIVE 1: I've Heard It All Before   149
Communication with Parents and Peers   149
■ FOCUS: ADOPTED CHILDREN IN ADOLESCENCE   150
  The Generation Gap 151
Conflict at Home   152
  Why Does Conflict Occur? 152
■ PERSPECTIVE 2: Postal Inspection   154
  Family Conflict in Other Cultures 155   *The Adaptive Nature of Conflict* 157
  Positive Conflict Management 157
Mothers and Fathers: Gender Differences in Communication and Conflict with Adolescents   158

OTHER FAMILY RELATIONSHIPS   159
Sibling Relationships   160
  Patterns of Sibling Interaction 160   *When Parents Treat Siblings Differently* 162
■ PERSPECTIVE 3: They Love Her More   162
Adolescent-Grandparent Relationships   162

THE CHANGING AMERICAN FAMILY   164
Single-Child Families   165
Maternal Employment   166
Divorce   167
  Adolescents and Divorce 169   *Preventing the Problems* 170
Single-Parent Families   171
Stepfamilies   172
How Families Work Is More Important Than How They Are Structured   175

PLACING FAMILY RELATIONSHIPS IN PERSPECTIVE   175
HAS YOUR OPINION CHANGED?   175
THEMES   176
CHAPTER SUMMARY AT A GLANCE   177

6 PEERS 178

WHAT IS YOUR OPINION? 179

THE PEER GROUP 179
Changes in Interpersonal Relationships 179
The Functions of the Peer Group 181
Conceptualizing Peer Relationships 182

FRIENDS 183
The Many Benefits of Friendship 183
Conceptions of Friendship 184
Forming Friendships 185
   Similarity 185   *Selection and Socialization: Choosing Friends* 186
Friendship and Gender 187
Communication and Conflict 187

CLIQUES AND CROWDS 189
Cliques 189
Crowds 190

POPULARITY AND UNPOPULARITY 192
Who Are the Popular Teens? 192
■ PERSPECTIVE 1: Is He Really My Friend? 193
Who Are the Unpopular Teens? 194
   Rejected Adolescents 194   *Neglected Adolescents* 195   *Why Are Some*
   Adolescents Disliked? 195   *Consequences of Rejected and Neglected Status* 196
Bullying 197
Enhancing Social Skills 199

ROMANTIC RELATIONSHIPS 200
Dating 200
   The Dating Process 201   *Dating Roles* 203   *Parental Reaction to Dating* 203
■ PERSPECTIVE 2: Do They Have to Know Everything? 203
Conflict in Romantic Relationships 205
■ PERSPECTIVE 3: I Can't Leave Him 205
■ FOCUS: PARTNER VIOLENCE 206

BEHAVIORAL AUTONOMY AND CONFORMITY 206
The Dynamics of Peer Pressure 207
The Extent of Peer Pressure 208
Conformity to Peers: The Parental Dimension 210

PLACING PEERS IN PERSPECTIVE 211

HAS YOUR OPINION CHANGED? 211
THEMES 212
CHAPTER SUMMARY AT A GLANCE 213

7 THE SCHOOL EXPERIENCE 214

WHAT IS YOUR OPINION? 215

MIDDLE SCHOOL 215
Transition to Middle School 215
■ PERSPECTIVE 1: Why the Change? 218
The Wrong Fit? 218

HIGH SCHOOL 220
Transition to High School 220
Rating the Schools 222
Achievement in High School 223

■ FOCUS: "OF COURSE WE HAVE COMPUTERS!" 224

Minority Group Youth and Achievement 224   *Gender and Achievement* 227
Pervasive Disengagement 228

ENHANCING THE SCHOOL EXPERIENCE 230

Principles of Learner-Centered Education 230
Motivation to Learn 231

Intrinsic and Extrinsic Motivation 232   *Attribution Theory: Why Did I
Succeed or Fail?* 233   *Goal Setting and Self-Evaluation* 234
Motivation Reconsidered 236

The Parental Role 237
Teacher Expectations 239
Tracking 241
School Choices 242

■ PERSPECTIVE 2: A Community Divided 243

The Transition to College 243

DROPPING OUT 245

■ PERSPECTIVE 3: Standards for the Football Team 248

PLACING THE SCHOOL EXPERIENCE IN PERSPECTIVE 250

HAS YOUR OPINION CHANGED? 251
THEMES 252
CHAPTER SUMMARY AT A GLANCE 253

THE MEDIA 254

WHAT IS YOUR OPINION? 255

THE MEDIA AND THE TEEN 257

The Teenager as Consumer 257
Mechanisms of Influence 258
The Cohort Effect and Teenage Culture 260

THE COMPUTER REVOLUTION: EMAIL AND THE INTERNET 261

Adolescents as Internet Users 262
Uses of the Internet 263
Dangers in Paradise 264

Computer Use and Social Relationships 264   *Dangerous Liaisons* 265
Styles of Thinking 266   *The Internet and Homework: Currency, Relevancy,
and Truthfulness* 266   *Overuse of the Internet* 266

■ PERSPECTIVE 1: Does He Ever See the Daylight? 266

VIDEO GAMES 267

Video Games and Gender 268
You Missed One of the Monsters: Video Games and Aggression 269
Video Games, Prosocial Behavior, and Social Skills 271
The Overuse of Video Games 271
Video Games and Adolescents: A Summary 272

MUSIC AND RADIO 273

The Meaning of Music 273
The Controversial Face of Music 273

■ PERSPECTIVE 2: Why the Obsession? 275

Music Videos 277

■ FOCUS: CENSORSHIP, WARNING LABELS, AND RATING SYSTEMS 278

TELEVISION AND THE MOVIES 281

Violence on Television and in the Movies 282
Fantasy and Sex in the Media 283
Stereotypes 285

Television Talk Shows   286
Advertising   287
Western Influences on Other Societies   288
The Influence of Movies and Television: A Final Word   289
■ PERSPECTIVE 3: Legal Responsibility   289

Magazines   289
Placing the Media in Perspective   292
Has Your Opinion Changed?   293
Themes   294
Chapter Summary At a Glance   295

Part IV   Social, Moral, and Personality Development

Self-Concept and Identity Formation   296

What Is Your Opinion?   297
Basic Concepts Related to the Self   297
Self-Concept in Adolescence   300
Developmental Changes in the Self-Concept   300
Acting Phony: Which Is My Real Self?   302
Is the Self-Concept Stable?   303
The Real and Ideal Selves   303

Self-Esteem in Adolescence   304
Trends in Self-Esteem   307

■ PERSPECTIVE 1: I Just Can't Do It   309

Self-Esteem in Adolescents from Minority Groups   310
Self-Esteem: Can There Be Too Much of a Good Thing?   311
Self-Esteem and Aggression 311   *Unstable Self-Esteem* 312   *Baseless Inflated Self-Esteem* 313   Causes of Inflated Self-Esteem* 313
Self-Esteem, the Self-Concept, and Cognitive Development   313
Improving Self-Esteem   315

Identity   316
Theories of Identity Formation   318
Exploration and Commitment: Erikson on Identity   318
The Four Identity Statuses   320
Identity Foreclosure 320   *Identity Diffusion* 321   *Identity Moratorium* 321

■ PERSPECTIVE 2: Just Puzzled   321

Identity Achievement 322
Do Males and Females Take Different Paths to Identity Formation?   323

■ FOCUS: Squeaky Wheels and Nails That Stick Out: The Self and Culture   324

Concerns About Identity Status   326

Gender Roles   327
Gender Stereotypes   327
Sex Typing: A Developmental View   328
Gender and Voice   330
How Gender Roles Develop: A Focus on Process   331
The Learning Theory Approach 332   *Role Models* 333
The Cognitive View 333   *Biological Contributions* 334

ETHNIC/RACIAL IDENTITY 335
The Process of Exploration 336
Forming a Racial/Ethnic Identity 336
Separation, Assimilation, Integration, and Marginality 337

PLACING THE SELF-CONCEPT AND IDENTITY FORMATION IN PERSPECTIVE 339

HAS YOUR OPINION CHANGED? 339
THEMES 340
CHAPTER SUMMARY AT A GLANCE 341

LOVE AND SEX 342

WHAT IS YOUR OPINION? 343

PHYSICAL DEVELOPMENT AND SEXUALITY 343
Physical Changes and Adolescent Sexuality 343
Masturbation 344

DATING, LOVE, AND SEX 345
Dating 345

■ PERSPECTIVE 1: Dating Kevin 345

Love 346
What Is Love? 346   *Styles of Love* 348   *Two Views of Intimacy* 349
The Link Between Love and Sex 351

SEXUAL ATTITUDES AND BEHAVIOR 352
The Revolution in Sexual Attitudes 352
The Evolution of Adolescent Sexual Behavior 354

■ PERSPECTIVE 2: Love, Sex, and Commitment 354

Motives for Intercourse 355
Personal Values 355   *Peer and Partner Pressure* 355   *Family Influence* 356
The Media 357
Contraceptive Use 358
Sexual Orientation: Homosexual Behavior 360

SEX EDUCATION 364
Sex Education at Home 364
Sex Education in the Schools 364

■ PERSPECTIVE 3: What Did You Find? 365

■ FOCUS: DO PARENTS HAVE THE RIGHT TO KNOW THAT THEIR DAUGHTER IS SEEKING AN ABORTION? 366

Sexually Transmitted Infections 368
Chlamydia 368   *Gonorrhea* 369   *Syphilis* 369   *Genital Warts* 369
Herpes Simplex 370   *Acquired Immune Deficiency Syndrome (AIDS)* 370
Preventing the Spread of Sexually Transmitted Infections 371
Teenage Pregnancy 372
Teenage Mothers and Their Children 374   *A Different Look at Teenage Pregnancy and Parenthood* 375   *The Father* 376   *The Extended Family* 377
Programs to Prevent Adolescent Pregnancy 377
Forced Sexual Behavior 378
Sexual Harassment 379

PLACING ADOLESCENT SEXUALITY IN PERSPECTIVE 381

HAS YOUR OPINION CHANGED? 381
THEMES 382
CHAPTER SUMMARY AT A GLANCE 383

11 MORAL DEVELOPMENT, VALUES, AND RELIGION 384

WHAT IS YOUR OPINION? 385

APPROACHES TO MORAL DEVELOPMENT 386
Piaget's Theory of Moral Reasoning 387
Kohlberg's Theory of Moral Reasoning 387
Level 1: Preconventional Moral Reasoning 388 *Level 2: Conventional Moral Reasoning* 388 *Level 3: Postconventional Moral Reasoning* 388 *At What Stage of Moral Development Do Teens Reason?* 389 *Is Moral Reasoning Related to Moral Behavior?* 390 *Do Males and Females Reason Differently About Moral Issues?* 390 *Criticisms of Kohlberg's Theory* 392
Moral Behavior 393
Morality and Emotion 394
Freud and Morality 394 *Empathy* 394
Morality and Culture 395
Putting It All Together 396

THE SPIRITUAL DIMENSION 398
Stages of Religious Development 398
Adolescents and Religion 399
■ PERSPECTIVE 1: My Beliefs Have Changed 400
Religious Values and Behavior 401
■ FOCUS: Cults 402

PROSOCIAL AND ALTRUISTIC BEHAVIOR 402
Activism and Volunteering 405
Prosocial Behavior and Gender 405
The Emergence of the Moral Adolescent 407

MORAL EDUCATION 409
Values Clarification 409
Kohlberg's Approach to Moral Education 410
The Teaching Approach 411
■ PERSPECTIVE 2: How Do We Do It? 411
Home and Community Involvement 412
Problems with Moral Education 413

PLACING MORAL DEVELOPMENT IN PERSPECTIVE 413

HAS YOUR OPINION CHANGED? 413
THEMES 414
CHAPTER SUMMARY AT A GLANCE 415

12 WORK AND CAREER DEVELOPMENT 416

WHAT IS YOUR OPINION? 417

WORKING ON THE CLOCK 417
Adolescents Consider the World of Work 417
The World of Work Today 418
The Adolescent with a Job 419

VOCATIONAL CHOICE 423
The Life-Span, Life-Space Approach to Careers 423
Holland's Typology 424
Career Choice 426
■ PERSPECTIVE 1: Hamlet on the Edge 427

GENDER AND CAREER CHOICE 428

Women's Career Choices 428

Encouragement to Enter Male-Dominated Occupations 429

Occupational Stereotypes 430　*Background Factors and Vocational Choice* 430

An Emphasis on Interpersonal Goals 430　*The Issue of Balance* 431

Men and Career Choice 433

MINORITY GROUP MEMBERSHIP AND CAREER CHOICE 435

Explaining the Trends 435

Career Choice Among African Americans and Latinos 437

Career Choice Among Asian Americans 438

Career Choice Among Native Americans 439

A Plan of Action 440

THE FORGOTTEN 42 PERCENT 442

■ PERSPECTIVE 2: I Don't Know What to Do 442

The Transition Between School and Work 442

Employers and High School Graduates 443

■ FOCUS: CAREER AND TECHNICAL EDUCATION: SALVATION OR TRAP? 444

Apprenticeship 445

Youth Unemployment 448

PLACING VOCATIONAL CHOICE IN PERSPECTIVE 449

HAS YOUR OPINION CHANGED? 449

THEMES 450

CHAPTER SUMMARY AT A GLANCE 451

PART V　CHALLENGES TO ADOLESCENT DEVELOPMENT

13 STRESS AND PSYCHOLOGICAL, PHYSICAL, AND LEARNING PROBLEMS 452

WHAT IS YOUR OPINION? 453

STRESS 453

Is Adolescence a Particularly Stressful Period of Life? 454

Why Be Concerned About Stress? 455

Gender, Minority Status, and Stress 455

The Nature of Stressors 456

■ PERSPECTIVE 1: With a Little Help from a Friend 457

Stress-Resilient Adolescents 457

Temperament and Personality 458　*Social Orientation and Social Support* 458

Hobbies and Activities 458　*Family Relationships* 458　*Internal Locus of Control* 458　*Coping Style* 458　*Self-Esteem* 458　*Helping Others* 459

Self-Regulation 459　*Intelligence and Cognitive Skills* 459

A Model for Stress Resilience 459

Long-Term Outcomes for Stress-Resilient Adolescents 460

Coping with Stress 461

INTERNALIZING BEHAVIORS AND DISORDERS 463

Shyness 464

Social Phobia 465

Depression in Adolescence 466

Prevalence of Depression in Adolescence 467　*What Causes Depression?* 468

Gender Differences in Depression 472　*Treatment for Depression* 473

■ PERSPECTIVE 2: I Won't Go   473

Suicide   474

EATING DISORDERS   476

Anorexia Nervosa   477

■ PERSPECTIVE 3: I'm Not Starving Myself   477

Bulimia   478

Treatment Options   478

COPING WITH CHRONIC ILLNESS   480

■ FOCUS: YOUNG AMERICANS WITH DISABILITIES   482

LEARNING DISABILITIES   482

What Is a Learning Disability?   482

The Social and Emotional Functioning of Adolescents with
    Learning Disabilities   484

Secondary and Postsecondary Education   485

ATTENTION-DEFICIT/HYPERACTIVITY DISORDER   488

Symptoms of ADHD   488

Life with ADHD   489

■ PERSPECTIVE 4: On Medication   489

Treatment of ADHD   490

PLACING ADOLESCENTS WITH SPECIAL NEEDS IN PERSPECTIVE   491

HAS YOUR OPINION CHANGED?   491

THEMES   492

CHAPTER SUMMARY AT A GLANCE   493

14

DRUG USE AND VIOLENCE   494

WHAT IS YOUR OPINION?   495

DRUG USE   495

The Extent of Drug Use in the United States   496

Appreciating the Dangers of Drugs   497

TOBACCO AND ALCOHOL   498

Cigarette Smoking   498

   Patterns of Cigarette Smoking   499   *The Image of the Smoker*   500

Alcohol   501

The Gateway Drug Effect Theory   502

OTHER DRUGS   504

Marijuana   504

■ PERSPECTIVE 1: Sibling Action   505

Cocaine and Crack   506

Heroin   506

Methamphetamine   506

The Club Drugs   507

PREDICTORS OF DRUG USE AND DRUG ABUSE   508

Individual Characteristics   508

   Biological Factors in Drug Use   509

Family Relations   510

Peers   511

Protective Factors Against Drug Use   512

Drug Education   512

■ PERSPECTIVE 2: Answer the Question!   514

VIOLENCE AND DELINQUENCY 516

Types of Violence 517

Is Aggression a Stable Trait? 519

The Causes of Violence 520

Individual Factors: Personality 520   *Individual Factors: Biological* 520
Individual Factors: Cognitive 521   *Family Processes and Relationships* 522
Peer Factors 523   *Community Factors* 523

■ FOCUS: GANGS 524

Predicting Violence 524

Protective Factors Against Violence 525

Can Violence Be Curbed? 526

■ PERSPECTIVE 3: The Witness 527

Lost Boys 527

The Link Between Drug Use and Violence 529

PLACING DRUG USE AND VIOLENCE IN PERSPECTIVE 529

HAS YOUR OPINION CHANGED? 529

THEMES 530

CHAPTER SUMMARY AT A GLANCE 531

EPILOGUE 532

SOCIETIES ARE BECOMING MORE PLURALISTIC 534

TECHNOLOGY DIFFERENTIATES GENERATIONS 534

GENDER ROLES CONTINUE TO EVOLVE 535

FAMILY STRUCTURES ARE MORE VARIED AND FLUID 535

ADOLESCENTS MUST COMPETE IN A GLOBAL MARKETPLACE 536

ACHIEVING BALANCE 536

APPENDIX: REVIEW QUESTIONS A-1

CREDITS C-1

GLOSSARY G-1

REFERENCES R-1

NAME INDEX NI-1

SUBJECT INDEX SI-1

PREFACE

What first comes to mind when the word "teenager" or "adolescent" is mentioned? For far too many people, images of teenagers who are in trouble, confused, or aggressive spring first into consciousness. The general tone when people discuss adolescents is often negative, and this negativity is echoed in the press because so much of what is reported about adolescents involves violence and drug abuse.

Adolescents seem to be a group in crisis. Even professionals who work with adolescents or who study adolescent behavior may inadvertently contribute to this youth-in-crisis mentality by focusing on adolescents who are failing in school or who have serious psychosocial problems. For example, there are literally hundreds of studies of aggression in adolescence, but far fewer on the subjects of helping others and cooperation. The problem-oriented focus is understandable. After all, it reflects the public's concerns. However, focusing on problems also contributes to an atmosphere of negativity.

Countering this one-sided negative perception is one of several strategies used in this text to provide an in-depth and well-rounded understanding of the adolescent experience. I also strive to present multiple, and sometimes conflicting, points of view in the field. Finally, the text is organized around five key themes that draw together the sometimes disparate points of view and provide a context for understanding adolescence in the past, present, and future.

A POSITIVE APPROACH

One of the purposes of this book is to present research on adolescence in a more positive light. Most adolescents cope very well with the stressors they encounter. Most adolescents do not abuse drugs, nor are they violent. Most adolescents look toward the future with hope and optimism, believing they will succeed and create a satisfying life in adulthood. This is not to say that the problems adolescents face are not real. They are. However, the journey through adolescence is usually negotiated successfully. This text will certainly present the problems and challenges adolescents face, but it will take a more balanced approach, emphasizing the positive adjustments and coping mechanisms that adolescents use.

EXAMINING THE COMPLETE PICTURE

This book will also present readers with many issues and controversies that surround the period of adolescence. Issues such as the effect of curfews on adolescent after-school behavior, the extent of peer group influence, the influence of both printed and electronic media, and the effect of employment on high school students do not allow for easy, pat conclusions. This text presents research on all sides of an issue, and seeks to encourage readers to discuss these issues and to consider their own opinions.

There is a difference between indoctrination and education. One of the dictionary meanings of the word "indoctrinate" is "to imbue with a partisan opinion or point of view." Indoctrination occurs when a student is brought to believe that there is only one way to think. Sometimes, this is accomplished by presenting research showing only one point of view. Education, on the other hand, can be defined in terms of the acquisition of knowledge or skills. Education, in the broadest sense, requires presenting research on issues from multiple points of view and allowing readers to form and consider their own viewpoints.

One reason simple conclusions are not always possible is that the adolescent's environment is a complicated place. In some ways, today's adolescent faces the same problems adolescents have faced in the past, such as the need to form an identity and to become emotionally and behaviorally autonomous. In other ways, the situation has changed. The world of the adolescent, today, is increasingly technologically sophisticated, competitive, and multicultural.

THEMES OF THE TEXT

This text develops five themes that provide a context for understanding the adaptive power of adolescents as they confront challenges and changes in themselves and in their societies.

1. Adolescence is a time of choices, "firsts," and transitions.

Adolescence is a transitional phase between childhood and adulthood. The adolescent encounters many new experiences and must cope with many new challenges.

2. Adolescence is shaped by context.

Adolescents are enmeshed in multiple levels of the environment. The family continues to be a potent force in adolescent development, but the neighborhood, school, political and legal systems, culture, and media also influence adolescents, sometimes in obvious ways and sometimes in very subtle ways. This contextual approach allows for a wider view of the adolescent experience. This text will present a number of current theoretical approaches but the contextual view will be prominently displayed, allowing the reader to consider multiple sources of influence.

3. Adolescence is influenced by group membership.

Group membership influences development and behavior. For example, whether one is male or female certainly influences one's outlook, perception of role, and behavior. Being a member of a minority group also influences the adolescent experience. Of course, the extent to which group membership influences the course of adolescence varies. However, an understanding of the adolescent experience requires an appreciation of cultural and subcultural group influence on the individual.

Today, there is a new appreciation for the importance of culture in development. There are two ways to cover this area. One is to devote a full chapter to cultural and subcultural influence. Another way, and the way I chose to cover the material, is to explore the importance of group membership within each area, within each chapter. I chose this path for two reasons. First, it allows for better integration of the material within the course. It is easier to appreciate the specific influences of gender on vocational plans or of minority group status on identity formation when the information is presented as an integral part of the chapters covering vocation or identity formation. Second, group membership is one influence among many, and its importance varies with acculturation and identification with the subculture. The adolescent experience of an African American in the United States may differ somewhat from that of white adolescents, but many of the basic concerns are the same.

4. The adolescent experience has changed over the past 50 years.

The world is changing at a very fast rate. Technological changes, including those in the media, seem to happen almost daily. Western nations are also more pluralistic than they have been in the past, with people of many cultures and religions living and working together. The world is also a more competitive one, where more education and skills are required.

5. Today's views of adolescence are becoming more balanced, with greater attention to its positive nature.

This shift reflects one of the major reasons for writing this text. Slowly, a more balanced approach to adolescence is taking shape, one that does not deny the challenges of adolescence but that emphasizes how adolescents successfully approach and master these challenges.

THE STRUCTURE OF THIS BOOK

The text is divided into five major parts. The first two parts of the book discuss the basics of adolescent development. After an introductory chapter, we continue with a discussion of theories of adolescence and ways of conducting research. Chapters covering physical and cognitive development follow.

Part Three offers four chapters that bring the adolescent's environment into sharper focus. Separate chapters cover the family, the peer group, the school, and the media. Providing a separate chapter on the media represents a unique departure from traditional texts. The influence of the media is so great in Western society that it deserves a full chapter of coverage.

The fourth part of the book presents four of the most basic considerations for adolescents. Separate chapters cover each of the following topics: self-concept and identity development; love and sex; moral development, values, and religion; and work and vocational choice.

Part Five offers two chapters dealing with specific challenges that adolescents face. One chapter covers stress as well as such psychological problems as anxiety and depression. The final chapter in the text focuses on drug use and violence.

PEDAGOGICAL FEATURES

This text offers an integrated learning system to help students master the material and to encourage them to think about the issues and questions that surround the study of adolescence.

What Is Your Opinion? and
Has Your Opinion Changed?

The What Is Your Opinion? survey opens each chapter, engaging students' interest by challenging them to express their preconceptions about chapter topics. Then, at the end of the chapter, students revisit their opinions in the matching Has Your Opinion Changed? survey, helping them to see where learning more about a topic may have changed or broadened their perspectives, or confirmed their original beliefs.

Key Terms

Key Terms are in bold in the text and are defined in a marginal glossary. I have limited the number of key terms. Although some terms are obviously required in order to understand the field, there has been a proliferation of terms in many books, making courses more often exercises in vocabulary than in concepts and ideas. The most important key terms are placed in bold; other terms that may be less important but are still new are italicized.

Focus

A Focus box in each chapter covers an applied issue or area of concern in depth. For example, Focus boxes cover cults, gangs, the self in different cultures, partner violence, censorship, and the question of parental notification for abortion, among other topics. These Focus boxes offer detailed coverage of applied topics, with an emphasis on multiple perspectives supported by current research. Whether through independent reading or through discussion of the Focus boxes in class, students learn to synthesize their own conclusions on topics that have generated sometimes conflicting research findings or societal points of view.

At A Glance

At A Glance charts are clear and concise visual summaries of each section of the text, highlighting the key points and topics for the section. Intermediate review materials provided immediately after a section of text may be more educationally sound than review materials provided only at the end of a chapter.

Perspective

Perspective boxes in each chapter highlight real-life experiences of different types of people: students, parents, caregivers, teachers, and others. Each case offers two perspectives: that of an adolescent facing an issue and that of another individual such as a parent, teacher, or friend. Questions at the end of the Perspective box require students to think critically about how they would deal with the problem or challenge, incorporating their own life experience with concepts they have learned in the text. Additionally, the feature often challenges students to take the perspective of someone other than the adolescent, helping students prepare for situations that they are likely to encounter as parents, teachers, or other professionals.

Placing ___ in Perspective

Placing ___ in Perspective is the last text section of every chapter, beginning in Chapter 3. This section places the area under study into the total context of adolescence. For example, Placing Self-Concept and Identity Formation in Perspective allows students to see how self-concept and identity formation fit into the overall life of the adolescent, providing a broad context for the topic as a capstone for the chapter.

Themes

Themes boxes at the end of the chapter summarize how chapter material relates to each of the five main themes of the text. Like the Placing ___ in Perspective feature, the Themes boxes provide a larger structure in which students can see how the topics they have studied in detail in the chapter fit into a larger and interconnected study of adolescence.

Chapter Summary At A Glance

Chapter Summary At A Glance tables at the end of each chapter bring together the major points from each of the sectional At A Glance tables in the chapter. Chapter Summary At A Glance is a quick review tool for key concepts from each section of the text. It also includes the key terms for each section, with page references to where those terms can be found in the book.

Review Questions

Review Questions for each chapter appear in the appendix and provide a built-in study guide and review tool for students. Questions are categorized into two levels: Level 1 questions are multiple choice; Level 2 questions require longer answers.

TEACHING AND LEARNING RESOURCES

A full range of teaching and learning resources supports the text.

For the Instructor

Instructor's Resource Manual with Test Bank

The *Instructor's Resource Manual with Test Bank* is a complete teaching resource.

Chapter Outlines are provided for quick review or lecture preparation.

Learning Objectives are included for each chapter.

"Put It in Writing" activities are writing-response activities that can be used as a quick snapshot of student learning, understanding, and engagement with a particular topic. Activities ensure that students have learned and can apply information about key topics from the chapter and are designed to be completed and tabulated quickly in class, or before the next class period.

Supplementary Activities provide a variety of resources for in-class discussion, or for independent work, as they are designed to stimulate discussion. Activities can be started in class and completed outside of class.

Critical Thinking Exercises are supplemental exercises that encourage students to research topics on their own, using Web or traditional research tools. Some exercises are media-focused; some focus more on self-reflection. Exercises provide a set of framework questions for each activity to help students think critically about each topic.

Studying Themes Activities are optional student activities to explore how the themes of the text are applied in each chapter.

Media Connections are lists of movies, books, journal articles, and/or Web sites that relate to key points in the chapter.

Printed Test Bank is the print version of the questions that are available within the computerized testing software program. The Printed Test Bank includes multiple-choice and essay questions for all chapters, with complete answer keys.

Instructor's Resource ClassPrep CD-ROM with Computerized Test Bank

ClassPrep CD-ROM contains all the content of the *Instructor's Resource Manual,* plus PowerPoint presentations for each chapter and other teaching tools. Selected art and tables from the text are also available for use in PowerPoint.

Computerized Test Bank, included on the ClassPrep CD-ROM, offers multiple-choice and essay questions. Test questions are keyed to pages in the student text and reflect the content of the learning objectives that appear in the *Instructor's Resource Manual* and in the *Study Guide.*

Instructor's Web Site offers all the content of the *Instructor's Resource Manual* and ClassPrep CD-ROM (except testing materials), plus live links to the sites listed in the Media Connections lists for each chapter. Password protected.

For Students

Study Guide

The *Study Guide* offers several resources to help students master the content of the text and the course.

Learning Objectives are provided for each chapter.

Chapter Summaries, which are prose summaries prepared by Paul Kaplan, highlight key points in each chapter.

Sample chapter tests offer sample multiple-choice and essay questions for each chapter, based on the learning objectives for the text. Complete answer keys are provided. These sample tests are available only to students using the *Study Guide;* they do not appear in other student ancillary materials.

Student Web Site

Students can access a number of review and exploration materials on the password-protected Web site.

Learning Objectives are provided for each chapter.

Chapter Summaries prepared by Paul Kaplan help students recall key topics from the chapters.

ACE self-quizzes allow instant practice and feedback.

NetLab exercises and **Thinking Critically and Evaluating Research activities** challenge students to apply their knowledge.

Live links are provided to selected articles and research on the Web.

ACKNOWLEDGMENTS

Writing a text requires a great deal of help from others. My developmental editor, Joanne Tinsley, was a great help, offering useful suggestions, wonderful feedback, and encouragement. I also thank Kerry Baruth, senior sponsoring editor at Houghton Mifflin, for his support and enthusiastic leadership. I greatly appreciate the work of two excellent and talented professionals, Senior Development Editor Bess Deck and Senior Project Editor Aileen Mason, who worked tirelessly to bring this project into publication. I acknowledge the work of copyeditor Mary Berry, photo researcher Ann Schroeder, art editor Charlotte Miller, proofreader Norma Frankel, and indexer Bernice Eisen. Editorial assistants Nirmal Trivedi, Caryn Yilmaz, and Liliana Ritter provided essential help as well. I am very grateful for the help of Doreen Munna and Dolores Perillo of the Suffolk County Community College library who helped me obtain the many sources that were required in the writing of this text.

The ancillary team crafted an exceptional collection of resources to accompany the text. I am grateful to Annie McManus of Parkland College for creating the *Instructor's Resource Manual* and PowerPoint presentations, as well as for her contributions to the *Study Guide*. I thank Christine Vanchella, South Georgia College, who wrote test and quiz questions for the Test Bank, for the student Web site, and for the *Study Guide*. She also updated and enhanced the NetLabs, Thinking Critically, and Evaluating Research activities for the student Web site. Development Editor Rita Lombard and Editorial Assistant Caryn Yilmaz pulled the supplements package together.

I express my gratitude to the following reviewers who offered constructive feedback. It was my very good fortune to receive valuable comments and suggestions from them:

William M. Bukowski, *Concordia University*
Cheryl A. Camenzuli, *Hofstra University*
Elaine Cassel, *Marymount University*
Richard Chiles, *Jackson State University*
Michael Cunningham, *Tulane University*
Lena K. Ericksen, *Western Washington University*
Daniel Fasko, Jr., *Morehead State University*
Wanda Franz, *West Virginia University*
Albert Gardner, *University of Maryland*
Carol S. Huntsinger, *College of Lake County*
Michelle L. Kelley, *Old Dominion University*
Kenyon C. Knapp, *Troy State University*
Ellen M. Long, *Juniata College*
Joseph G. Marrone, *Siena College*
Jerry A. Martin, *University of North Florida*
Christine McDonald, *Indiana State University*
Annie McManus, *Parkland College*
Doug Needham, *Redeemer College*
Maribeth Palmer-King, *Broome Community College*
Elizabeth Pemberton, *University of Delaware*
James D. Reid, *Washington University, St. Louis*
Jane P. Sheldon, *University of Michigan, Dearborn*
Lee Shumow, *Northern Illinois University*
Sharon E. Stein, *Ferrum College*
Terry Hunkapiller Stepka, *Arkansas State University*
Rob Turrisi, *Boise State University*
Mike Tyler, *Florida Gulf Coast University*

Alexander Vazsonyi, *Auburn University*
Elizabeth C. Vozzola, *Saint Joseph College*
Rob Weisskirch, *California State University, Fullerton*
Lisa Whitfield, *North Central College*
Christine Ziegler, *Kennesaw State University*
Joan Zook, *State University of New York, Geneseo*

Finally, I would like to thank my wife Leslie, whose patience and understanding allowed me to spend the vast amount of time working on this text.

P. S. K.

1

THE WORLD OF ADOLESCENCE

WHAT IS YOUR OPINION?

ADOLESCENCE: A FRAME OF REFERENCE
- A Time Frame That Varies
- Broad and Narrow Socialization
- Dispelling the Myths

MODERN VIEWS OF ADOLESCENCE
- 20th-Century Changes in Views of Adolescence
- Adolescents View Themselves
- Adults View Teens
- In the Eyes of the Law
- Psychologists View Adolescents
  FOCUS: Curfews: A Protection or an Infringement of Rights?

THEMES OF ADOLESCENCE
- Theme 1: Adolescence Is a Time of Choices, "Firsts," and Transitions
- Theme 2: Adolescence Is Shaped by Context
  Perspective 1: We Don't Like What You're Listening To!
  Perspective 2: I Should Be Treated Like Everyone Else
- Theme 3: Adolescence Is Influenced by Group Membership
- Theme 4: The Adolescent Experience Has Changed over the Past 50 Years
- Theme 5: Today's Views of Adolescence Are Becoming More Balanced, with Greater Attention to Its Positive Nature

HAS YOUR OPINION CHANGED?

CHAPTER SUMMARY AT A GLANCE

I remember sitting around at a family gathering when I was 17 years old or so. Everyone was discussing the "best age." My uncle, then in his 50s, pined for the days when he had been 18, felt strong and vital, had a quick mind, felt free, and looked toward the future with hope and optimism. He remembered his active social life, his adventures with his friends, and the feeling of freedom and invincibility.

I agreed that mine was the best age, but I felt less conviction than my uncle. I, too, enjoyed the increased freedom, but I was also worrying about two difficult midterms the next day, a term paper that was due in a week, and my uncertain relationship with my girlfriend. I didn't know what I wanted to be, what to believe in, or what major to choose.

Adolescence is a time of change. It is a time of growth, learning, and questioning. Often, it is a period of contrasts. One day everything seems to be going well, and the next day nothing seems to be going right. Adolescence is a time of considering the future while dealing with the challenges of an ever-changing present.

In this chapter, we will examine the nature of the adolescent experience and take a brief look at its recent history. Then we will consider five recurring themes that we will encounter as we investigate the many changes and challenges of adolescence.

ADOLESCENCE: A FRAME OF REFERENCE

Adolescence is the period of life between childhood and adulthood. The word *adolescence* comes from the Latin word *adolescere*, which means "to grow up." Typically, adolescence begins with the onset of puberty, which technically refers to the time at which an individual is first able to reproduce. Today, the term **puberty** is more often used to refer to all the physical changes that occur during the early part of adolescence, including changes in body composition of fat and muscle; changes in the respiratory and circulation systems, which result in greater strength and endurance; and changes in the nervous and endocrine systems (Graber, Petersen, & Brooks-Gunn, 1996). Equally important in understanding the concept of adolescence is knowledge of the psychological and social experiences of the individual during this transitional period.

Adolescence is often divided into three parts: early, middle (or mid), and late adolescence (Blos, 1962). Various psychologists use different boundaries, and for our purposes, *early adolescence* is the period between the beginning of puberty through age 14 and is marked by extensive and rapid physical change. *Middle adolescence* is from the ages of 15 through 17 and roughly corresponds to the high school years. *Late adolescence* begins at age 18, and exactly when adolescence ends remains a source of controversy.

A Time Frame That Varies

The criteria used to determine the end of adolescence and the beginning of adulthood depend upon the individual's society and culture. Some societies determine the time at which someone takes on adult responsibilities by providing a ceremony that bestows adult responsibilities and privileges on the person. Other societies take a different approach, allowing a more individualistic answer to the question of when adolescence ends and adulthood begins.

Rites of Passage In many societies, adolescents participate in **rites of passage,** ceremonies that celebrate the transition from one stage of life to the next and publicize the fact that the individual has arrived at a new moral, spiritual, or philosophical enlightenment. These ceremonies often involve some separation from society, some preparation or instruction from an elder, a public

WHAT IS YOUR OPINION?

Please place the number best reflecting your opinion next to each of the following statements. We will return to this questionnaire at the end of the chapter so you can determine if your opinions have changed.

1 — Strongly Agree
2 — Moderately Agree
3 — No Opinion
4 — Moderately Disagree
5 — Strongly Disagree

_____ 1. Most adolescents are well behaved, respectful, and helpful.

_____ 2. Most of the problems adolescents experience are due to poor parenting.

_____ 3. A person in Western society becomes an adult at age 18.

_____ 4. Considerable turmoil and significant conflict with parents are inevitable in adolescence.

_____ 5. Adolescents are influenced by the negative media stereotypes of them.

_____ 6. The media have too much influence over teenagers today.

_____ 7. African American, Latino, Native American, and Asian American teens have significantly different experiences compared with Caucasian teens in the United States.

_____ 8. Adolescents today lead fundamentally different lives than adolescents did 50 years ago.

_____ 9. An effective way to fight teen crime is to institute a curfew from 11 P.M. to 6 A.M.

_____ 10. Teens over the age of 15 years should be tried as adults if they have committed a felony.

adolescence The transitional stage between childhood and adulthood.

puberty Physical changes involved in sexual maturation as well as other body changes that occur during the early adolescent years.

rite of passage A ceremony or ritual that marks an individual's transition from one status to another.

1

enactment of specified traditions, and a welcoming back to society with some acknowledgment of the changed status (Delaney, 1995).

Many traditional and preindustrial societies have such rites of passage. The physical changes marking the beginning of puberty act as a signal that it is time to recognize sex differences and define gender roles. In fact, it is not unusual for societies to separate boys and girls at the beginning of the pubertal growth spurt. Ceremonies for girls are often tied in with menarche (the first menstrual period). About half of all preindustrial societies have such ceremonies. The Wadadika Paiute (a Native American tribe) of Oregon, for example, isolate a girl in a "menstrual" hut for a month, and her mother or grandmother instructs her about menstruation and valued physical and social traits. She cares for herself and learns her role, then puts on a new dress and returns home. The seclusion allows her to be free from her daily tasks in the family and other worldly concerns (Whiting & Whiting, 1991). In many of these societies, although menarche is considered the end of childhood, marriage is considered the beginning of adulthood (Whiting, Burbank, & Ratner, 1986). The gap between childhood and adulthood, called *maidenhood,* is often relatively short, but it does exist.

Ceremonies for boys are common as well. Some Native American tribes, for example, take each 14- or 15-year-old male to a sweat lodge, where his body and spirit are purified by the heat. A medicine man advises and assists the boy with prayers. The adolescent is then brought to an isolated spot, where he fasts. He prays, reflects on the medicine man's words, and awaits a vision that reveals to him his path of life as a man in society (Heinrich, Corbine, & Thomas, 1990).

Males of the Kota people in Africa paint their face blue, which they view as the color of death, as part of their traditional rite of passage into adulthood. This symbolizes the death of childhood, and people in their village will pretend not to recognize them until they have completed their transformation into adulthood (Schaeffer & Lamb, 1995). This rite of passage is now taking place at a later age so that they can complete schooling.

Some rites of passage involve an ordeal to prove one's abilities. For example, part of the rite of passage for males in the Masai tribe in Africa involves fending for themselves in the wild and experiencing a painful initiation ceremony (Hendry, 1999). Some rites of passage for boys and girls involve physical mutilation and are being increasingly criticized by individuals, many of whom are from different cultures and consider such practices as inhumane (Haviland, 2003).

Some religious groups also offer rites of passage that show the individual's willingness to take on the religious responsibilities. For example, Roman Catholic and many Protestant denominations have confirmation ceremonies. Most Jewish boys celebrate a bar mitzvah and some Jewish girls a bat mitzvah, which indicate their change of status as they take on adult religious responsibilities. Some Latinos may celebrate the quinceañera (fifteenth birthday). This celebration of an adolescent girl's coming of age is part of their ethnic heritage (Andersen & Taylor, 2002).

Industrialized societies offer a number of secular transitions that are similar to rites of passage. For example, obtaining a driver's license may be considered a rite of passage because it is a significant event in the lives of many teens. Adolescents prepare for a driving test, attend classes, and pass a test; and to some extent their status changes, as driving signifies physical independence from parents. Yet getting a driver's license requires no moral or philosophical enlightenment signifying a change in the recipient's relationship to society or the individual's future goals.

High school graduation, in many respects, is another rite of passage. Adolescents in school are

Many societies have traditionally had rites of passage, which are specific ceremonies that mark the transition from one stage of life to the next. Is high school graduation a rite of passage for American adolescents?

isolated from the rest of society for a good part of the day and are taught by teachers who are older and specially chosen by society. The graduation ceremony, with its special dress, pomp, and formal setting, may be thought of as a transition (Delaney, 1995). But not all adolescents graduate or attend their graduation. More important, the teacher-student relationship lacks the moral and spiritual function so prominent in rites of passage, and graduation does not always strengthen the bond with society. These rites of passage are very weak compared with the rites in more traditional societies.

Achieving Autonomy   No universal rite of passage exists in Western societies to signify the adolescent's change of status from adolescence to adulthood. When does adolescence end and adulthood begin in Western societies? Some might suggest a particular age—but what age? For example, in the United States, the voting age is 18, but drinking alcohol is not legal until 21. The age at which one is legally responsible for criminal behavior (that is, when one is treated as an adult by the criminal justice system) differs from state to state. Only a very weak case can be made for using any particular age.

Because using a rite of passage or a specific age to measure the end of adolescence and the beginning of adulthood does not work in Western societies, the key may be found in the concept of *autonomy*, or being capable of an independent existence. Two different types of autonomy are important. **Emotional autonomy** is a state of developing special, intimate relationships with others outside the family. **Behavioral autonomy** involves acting in a manner that shows control of one's impulses and accepting responsibility for one's behaviors. If acting in a personally responsible manner in which risk taking and reckless behavior are minimized is used as the criterion, adulthood might not be reached until at least the early 20s (Jonah, 1986). Of course, individual differences are common; some 18-year-olds show mature behavior, and some 25-year-olds behave recklessly. Despite this variation, however, the achievement of emotional and behavioral autonomy seems to mark the dividing line between adolescence and adulthood.

Parental recognition of autonomy can be part of the process of change from adolescence to adulthood. Blos (1979) argued that one facet of attaining an adult status is an acknowledgment by the same-sex parent that one has achieved adult status. This confirmation, which Blos called "the blessing," can take many forms. Bjornsen (2000) asked 281 male and female college students whose average age was 22 years the following two questions regarding their relationship with the same-gender parent: (1) "Was there a time when your parent did something or said something to you that meant that you were 'all grown up' or had reached maturity?" and (2) "Was there a time when you *wanted* your parent to do something or say something to you that meant that you were 'all grown up' or had reached maturity?"

Bjornsen placed the responses into seven different categories: (1) rite of passage (my parents told me I was all grown up when I turned 18, started college), (2) puberty (experienced first menstruation, started dating), (3) respect for adolescent (told me/other people how responsible I was, trusted me), (4) recognized decision-making ability (told me I could/had to make my own decisions, gave me adult privileges), (5) recognized specific skills (household finances, adult chores), (6) financial responsibility (expected me to pay for myself), and (7) always treated me as grown up (throughout my life I have been treated with respect, like an adult). The majority of males (71.3 percent) and females (71.7 percent) stated that they had received the parental blessing from their same-gender parent. As shown in Table 1.1, males were more likely than females to have received a blessing regarding decision-making abilities, specific skills, and financial responsibilities. Females were more likely than males to have received a blessing regarding a rite of passage, pubertal changes, increased respect, or always being treated an adult. The majority of respondents who had not received a blessing stated that they wished their parent would have acknowledged their grown-up status (respect) or their decision-making abilities. Many participants wrote sensitive and powerful stories of the blessing they received or wanted to receive. The data suggest that receiving

Emotional autonomy (the development of very close relationships with others outside the family) and behavioral autonomy (acting in a reputable manner by controlling one's own impulses and accepting responsibility) are two of the most important aspects of adolescence.

emotional autonomy   The development of special, intimate relationships with others outside the family.

behavioral autonomy   Acting in a manner that shows control of one's impulses and accepting responsibility for one's behaviors.

Table 1.1

**Survey of Adolescents (by Gender) Who Received
or Wanted Acknowledgment of Reaching Adulthood**

Type of Parental Confirmation	Received Acknowledgment		Wanted Acknowledgment	
	Male (%)	Female (%)	Male (%)	Female (%)
Rite of passage	22.1	26.6	—[a]	7.1
Pubertal growth	5.2	9.7	5.9	7.1
Respect	13.0	20.2	47.1	50.0
Decision making	37.7	26.6	41.2	32.1
Skills	10.4	8.1	—[a]	3.6
Finances	10.4	3.2	5.9	—[a]
Always treated as an adult	1.3	5.6	—[a]	—[a]

[a]Less than 1%.

Source: Adapted from Bjornsen (2000).

some acknowledgment from parents toward the end of adolescence may be an important step in the transition to adulthood.

Broad and Narrow Socialization

Western cultures, as noted, allow individuals great latitude in both when and how to make the transition to adulthood. This individuality makes it difficult to designate a particular age, an age range, or even a particular event as determining the beginning of adulthood (Arnett & Taber, 1994). This is not so in more traditional cultures, which extend less individual freedom to teenagers and expect greater conformity. The differences between Western and more traditional cultures are reflected in the cultures' socialization practices. **Socialization** is the process by which new members of a society are instilled with the fundamental elements of their culture.

Cultures can be divided into those that practice broad versus narrow socialization (see Table 1.2). Cultures characterized by **narrow socialization** value tradition, conformity, obedience, and fitting into family and society. Deviations from these expectations are discouraged and often punished, and all members of the culture are expected to adhere to particular traditions (Arnett, 1995b). In contrast, cultures characterized by **broad socialization** encourage independence, individualism, and self-expression, allowing people to take many different routes on the odyssey to adulthood. Developing an individual identity is a for-

Table 1.2

Comparison of Broad and Narrow Socialization

Some societies practice broad socialization, giving each member a great deal of freedom, whereas others practice narrow socialization, giving each member more structure.

Broad Socialization	Narrow Socialization
Emphasis on individuality	Emphasis on how one fits into the group
Importance of individual identity	Importance of group identity
Less pressure to conform to societal standards	More pressure to conform to societal standards
Encouragement to pursue own personal desires	Encouragement to follow path that will bring honor and prestige to the family
Agents of socialization often conflict	Agents of socialization more often present a unified front
Greater self-reliance	Greater reliance on group

socialization   The process by which new members of a society are instilled with the fundamental elements of their culture.

narrow socialization   Child-rearing procedures and societal beliefs that encourage conformity to traditional values and family loyalties and de-emphasize individualism.

broad socialization   Child-rearing procedures and societal beliefs that encourage individual choice and freedom rather than conformity to traditional values.

midable challenge, and these cultures offer adolescents many choices. In fact, societies using broad socialization practices constantly remind their older members about the need to give choices to their youth. Broad socialization promotes a wide range of social and psychological developmental paths, and people are allowed and encouraged to pursue their own preferences to a great extent.

Western societies have very broad socialization practices. Adolescents receive little occupational training or schooling within the family. Long periods of formal education are required, and marriage is delayed. Western society emphasizes developing one's own identity, following one's own path to happiness and self-fulfillment, with less emphasis on tradition. All these factors typically increase the age at which an individual reaches emotional and behavioral autonomy. The end of adolescence is individually defined and involves achieving independence and autonomy in many areas of life. Most young people consider themselves adults when they live on their own and can support themselves financially. This entails taking on greater responsibility for their own maintenance and making their own decisions. Of course, as adolescents proceed through the stage, they take on more responsibilities, but it does not usually approach full independence.

The transition to adulthood is gradual and sometimes ambiguous, defined more by individual circumstances than by societal agreement. Consider the increasing trend of late adolescents returning home from college after graduation and staying with their parents, perhaps because of financial constraints. They may live autonomous lives, have their own intimate relationships, and show responsibility for their behavior; however, they do not take on the typical trappings of adulthood, including living independently and being completely financially independent.

Socialization, beyond influencing the duration of adolescence, affects the actual experience of adolescence. Societies that practice broad socialization often find their agents of socialization in conflict. For instance, adolescents may be encouraged by their peers to dress in a particular manner, while parents discourage it (Arnett, 1995b). An adolescent with some acting talent may be encouraged by peers or even teachers to seek out advanced education in the theater arts and perhaps even pursue an acting career, while parents may want their child to follow a different, more secure career path. Movies and music videos encourage sexual behavior, which parents may discourage. Youth from societies practicing narrow socialization do not experience as much conflict. Peers often support the more traditional ways of behaving and acting, sometimes ostracizing those who stand out. The contradictory forces operating in Western societies create more anxiety and confusion for the teen compared with more traditional societies, in which less conflict in direction appears.

Societies practicing narrow socialization often emphasize group goals; group achievements; and meeting social, familial, and group expectations. Cultures practicing broad socialization emphasize the importance of individual achievement and of developing a unique, personal identity. With the contradicting social agents and the emphasis on the development of the self in cultures practicing broad socialization, it is no wonder that many adolescents become anxious about the future or wonder about where they fit into society (Arnett, 1995b).

Traditional societies also give adolescents more supervision and less freedom to make their own decisions. Adolescents in Western societies, in contrast, are asked to find their individual identity and their place in society with much less adult supervision or externally imposed discipline or guidelines. These broad socialization practices encourage people to make up their own minds about what is right and wrong, and they lack the clear uniform

Cultures can be divided into those that practice narrow versus broad socialization. Those that practice narrow socialization, such as many more traditional Asian societies, value tradition, conformity, obedience, and fitting into the family. Cultures that practice broad socialization encourage independence, individualism, and self-expression.

standard of conduct governing relations among people of more traditional societies. Broad socialization, then, leads to greater individualism but provides less guidance and restraint of sensation-seeking impulses.

Dispelling the Myths

The story of adolescence is one of change—of how adolescents negotiate the long and increasingly complex passage to adulthood. But as we investigate various aspects of the adolescent experience, we will need to dispel many myths and counter many stereotypes about what it means to be an adolescent. No other group, with the possible exception of the elderly, is subject to so many overgeneralizations projected in newspapers and movies.

Some professionals who work with troubled adolescents inadvertently add to these stereotypes by generalizing from their clinical experiences. Older adolescents often believe these stereotypes as well. For example, college students and many professionals still hold to the idea that adolescence is a period of continuous turmoil, when fights with parents are bitter and relationships are poor. Certainly more conflict with parents occurs in adolescence than in the earlier childhood years (Arnett, 1999), but research evidence disputes the idea that adolescence is a period of continuous storm and stress (Holmbeck & Hill, 1988). That traditional view has given way to a view of adolescence as a period of life in which people gradually achieve independence within the context of a changing family relationship (Grotevant, 1998).

Some evidence shows that mental health professionals are slowly giving up the older conception of adolescence, but many still hold fast to those ideas (Stoller et al., 1996). It is clear from public opinion surveys, though, that the general public's attitudes change even more slowly (Public Agenda, 1997). Although

AT A GLANCE 1.1 ADOLESCENCE: A FRAME OF REFERENCE

KEY POINT: The period of adolescence forms the bridge between childhood and adulthood.

SUPPORTING POINTS	EXPLANATION
Puberty involves physical changes leading to sexual reproduction, as well as other body changes that lead to physical maturity.	All body systems, including the respiratory, circulatory, and nervous systems, show important changes during puberty.
Adolescence is the period between childhood and adulthood.	Adolescence is often divided into early adolescence (puberty through age 14), middle adolescence (ages 15–17) and late adolescence (ages 18 and older).
Rites of passage can mark the beginning of adulthood.	Many societies have rites of passage from adolescence to adulthood. No universal rite of passage exists in technologically advanced Western societies.
Controversy exists over when, exactly, adolescence ends.	No definite age can be given as to when adolescence ends. No one event experienced by every adolescent marks the entrance into adulthood. The times for achieving emotional autonomy (independent, intimate social relationships) and behavioral autonomy (controlling one's own behavior and taking responsibility) differ greatly among people.
Societies practicing broad socialization give their adolescents a great deal of freedom, and they emphasize independence and individualism. Societies practicing narrow socialization emphasize conformity, tradition, and fitting in. This focus leads to an emphasis on cooperation and fitting into the group.	Western cultures generally practice broad socialization and emphasize individual achievement and self-actualization. This leads to more risk taking and less guidance and self-control.

the problems of adolescent drug use, violence, and stress-related problems cannot be minimized (see "Stress and Psychological, Physical, and Learning Problems" and "Drug Use and Violence"), a more positive view should reign. The problems and challenges of adolescence are real, but a crisis-based perception of adolescence is inadequate. Most adolescents are optimistic about their future; they are not drug abusers, nor are they violent. To date, too little research has been done on adolescent prosocial (helping) behavior, including the behavior of adolescents who volunteer for community service (Eisenberg, 1990). This text will offer a more balanced approach and consider both healthy development and the difficulties adolescents may experience. *(For a review of this section, see At A Glance 1.1.)*

MODERN VIEWS OF ADOLESCENCE

20th-Century Changes in Views of Adolescence

Although authors and scholars have written about adolescents for centuries, systematic research on the period of adolescence did not really begin until the 20th century (Petersen, 1991). The first scientific approach is credited to G. Stanley Hall (1904), who summarized the available research in two volumes. Hall argued that urban industrial society forced adolescents to leap, rather than grow, into maturity. At the beginning of the 20th century, the demands of the family and work dominated the lives of young people, just as they had throughout history. Few attended high school, and most began working by age 16 or 17. In the United States in 1900, only 11.4 percent of young people 14 through 17 years old were attending secondary school, and by 1920 the percentage was only 15.4. Adolescents routinely left school without graduating to enter the world of work, and women took on household responsibilities or became workers in a few restricted occupations (Mirel & Angus, 1986). Women, especially in lower-income groups, were expected to marry early and have many children; females' life paths were more rigidly defined and their activities much more regulated than those of men. The double standard of sexuality, in which men were allowed or even encouraged to engage in sexual behavior but women were criticized for it, was much stronger than it is today. Widespread and often violent racial discrimination in education and employment dramatically narrowed the choices of African American youth. Other groups were subjected to discrimination as well.

In the first part of the 20th century, then, most Americans believed that it was beneficial for young people to enter the world of full-time work early and help their families with what they earned. Work was viewed as essential for shaping character and values. Until the 1930s, most children received only 8 years of schooling. However, changes were brewing. Technological innovations and moral outrage at the working conditions for young workers, and most important, the Great Depression, changed everything. Millions lost their jobs or could not find work. By 1931, adolescent workers had virtually disappeared from the work force (Mirel & Angus, 1985). The percentage of teens who were in high school jumped, mainly because there was nowhere else for them to go unless they milled around aimlessly, as many did. By 1932, as many as 300,000 teens had left home and were wandering around the country. The lack of employment left a mark on those adolescents, who came to prize a steady job and income as they matured (Elder,

Most adolescents before the Great Depression received little schooling and were expected to take their place working in industry, sometimes in terrible conditions for little money. The main reason for change was the disappearance of jobs due to the Great Depression, but technological improvements and moral outrage at working conditions also reduced teenage employment. Today, almost all adolescents attend and graduate from high school.

1974, 1980). With unemployment high and child labor less acceptable, school seemed the obvious answer to the "youth problem"; by the 1939–1940 school year, more than 73 percent of 14- to 17-year-olds were in high school (O'Neil & Sepielli, 1985). With the exception of the period from 1940 to 1944 (World War II), enrollment continued to grow. By 1950, 82 percent of all teens between ages 14 and 17 were in school. Today, practically all adolescents attend high school, and most graduate.

Thus, for most of their adolescence, teens are segregated from adult society; they begin full-time work at a much later age and spend more time with peers (Mirel, 1991). These peer group associations become important in socialization, influencing values, loyalties, and codes of conduct. Teens isolated from the "real" world see themselves as different, having much more in common with one another than with people of other ages. Distinctive hairstyles, special clothing, and use of slang arise. The social role of adolescents, outside the role of consumer, is very small (Gilbert, 1985). The role of the family, which once taught most of the skills needed to live in society (such as vocational skills), is often superseded by the school.

The 20th century, then, brought a shift for adolescents from centuries of domination by home and work to a world dominated by high school and the increasing importance of the peer group (see Figure 1.1). The change from being producers to being important consumers marks a turning point in the history of adolescence, as does the shift from bearing the burdens of premature adulthood to confronting the reality of greater age segregation in the prolonged period between childhood and adulthood. As we will see in "The School Experience," the mission of the secondary school to both educate students in academic areas and participate in their moral growth is controversial. The need for extensive schooling, the increasing options for women and members of minority groups, and the increasing age for marriage are ongoing trends.

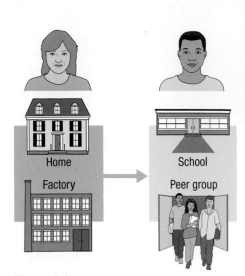

Figure 1.1
The Changing Lives of Adolescents
Although the home remains a vital element of the adolescent's environment, the importance of the school and peer group have increased greatly over the past 100 years.

Adolescents View Themselves

Today's adolescents have a very positive view of themselves and their generation. One survey of 9- to 17-year-olds found that 83 percent describe themselves as happy and 62 percent, as confident (Schwartz, 1997). Most adolescents see their relationships with their parents positively as well. Only a third say their parents don't know how to communicate with them. Only 11 percent of all adolescents think parents who care more about their jobs than their children are common, whereas 27 percent of the adults feel such job-centered mothers are common, and 35 percent think such fathers are common (Russell, 1997).

Adults View Teens

Many adults today possess a less-than-positive view of adolescents. One public opinion poll found widespread negative attitudes toward teenagers (see Table 1.3). When asked what first comes to their minds when they think about today's teens, two thirds of Americans use adjectives such *as rude, irresponsible,* and *wild.* Relatively few see teens in a positive light, such as describing them as *smart* or *helpful* (Public Agenda, 1997). Half the adults surveyed believe that teens get into trouble because they have too much free time, and more than 40 percent believe that teens have poor work habits and lack self-discipline. Relatively few see parents as good role models, half say they spoil their children, and many believe parents are doing a worse job of parenting than their parents did a generation ago.

There is evidence that this negative attitude represents a change from 50 years ago. As shown in Figure 1.2, when the responses of adults in the year 2000 are compared with those in 1949 on the question of whether young people have more or less common sense than they had a generation ago, many more respondents in the recent study believed teens lack common sense than those in the earlier study (Gallup, 2000).

It is easy for people with negative attitudes toward adolescents to find specific examples that validate their beliefs and then generalize from these exam-

Table 1.3

The Public's View of Teenagers

A public opinion poll asked the following question: "Now I'm going to describe different types of teenagers and ask if you think they are common or not. How about teenagers who _____? Are they very common, somewhat common, not too common, or not common at all?" *Teenagers* were defined for respondents as being 13 to 17 years old.

Teenagers who . . .	Percentage of Respondents[a] Saying "Very Common"					
	General Public	*Parents*	*Parents of Teens*	*African American Parents*	*Hispanic Parents*	*White Parents*
Face social problems like drugs, gangs, or crime	62	66	62	71	72	64
Get into trouble because they have too much free time	50	51	45	63	61	49
Have poor work habits and lack self-discipline	41	40	43	49	46	38
Lack good role models	36	36	35	43	34	36
Are wild and disorderly in public	30	33	30	49	43	31
Are lively and fun to be around	29	25	24	35	26	25
Are friendly and helpful toward their neighbors	12	10	12	16	14	10
Treat people with respect	12	9	9	17	11	8

[a]Sample sizes: general public = 2,000; parents = 763; parents of teens = 162; African American parents = 367; Hispanic parents = 340; white parents = 596.
Source: Adapted from Public Agenda (1997).

Figure 1.2
Do Young People Have More or Less Common Sense?

In general, would you say that young people today are more levelheaded and have more common sense than young people did, say, 25 years ago, or not as much? A poll of adults in the year 2000 found that adults today think young people do not have as much common sense as people did 25 years ago. A similar poll given in 1949 had opposite results. The exact results are shown here.

Source: Adapted from Gallup News Service (2000).

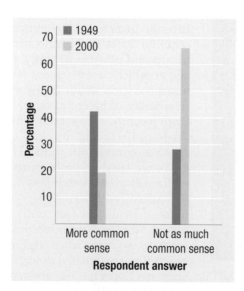

In a recent poll, half the adults believed teens get into trouble because they have too much free time, 40 percent thought adolescents lack self-discipline, and two thirds thought adolescents are rude and irresponsible. Why does the adult public have such a negative view of adolescents?

ples. They focus on news stories that reflect the negative stereotypes they hold about teenagers. Every article about a violent teen, a pregnant adolescent, or a reckless act of driving by a young person cements their beliefs. Adolescents who help out at shelters for the homeless or aid other people in need are rarely mentioned by the news media, and if noticed at all, they are quickly dismissed as exceptions.

Even adults who do not possess negative attitudes toward adolescents believe certain myths or subscribe to stereotypes—for example, that adolescents are basically unstable, out of control, ruled by hormones, bound to do anything their peers suggest, and in constant conflict with their parents (Lesko, 1996). As we shall see, research study after research study show that these stereotypes aren't true. Adolescents, generally, are a hopeful, well-adjusted group with good interpersonal relations and strong connections to their families (Grotevant, 1998).

Adults often forget that adolescence is a transitional period between childhood and adulthood. As with any transition, new challenges arise, and new skills must be developed to deal effectively with them. This development entails some trial and error. For example, compare the way you interact with people of the other gender now and when you were 13 or 14 years old. You may believe that the way you deal with problems and challenges now is the way you always did, and forget just how much you have learned.

In the Eyes of the Law

The legal view of the adolescent is controversial and confusing. The age at which an adolescent obtains some adult privileges, such as driving a car, differs among states and throughout the world (Leiter, 1997). Although the age when one can get married without parental permission is 18 in almost all states, the minimum age for marriage with parental permission differs widely.

Variations in other rights are common (Hempelman, 1994). A minor who intentionally injures another person or damages property may be held liable for the act at age 14, and even earlier in certain courts. The legal age of emancipation, the ability to enter into contracts, and the ability to consent to medical treatment differ among the states. In addition, the question of whether the many adolescents who come in contact with the judicial system are to be treated as adults or treated more leniently as minors is important. Their legal status is tied into the question of whether adolescents should be perceived as older children or younger adults.

At what age should an adolescent be considered legally an adult? Many legal questions surround the period of adolescence.

Thirty years ago, children and adolescents who committed crimes, and even some who were arrested for truancy or running away from home, were tossed into adult jails, where they were abused and exposed to adult criminals. Congress passed the Juvenile Justice and Delinquency Prevention Act of 1974, which required states to separate adolescents and children from adults in jails and prisons. Recently, though, a movement to reduce the age at which an adolescent is considered an adult for trial purposes has successfully transformed the law and reduced the confidentiality of juvenile records (Children's Defense Fund, 1998). Until recently, a 17-year-old, like a 17-day-old, was a legal infant (Melton, 1991), and the child became an adult in the eyes of the criminal court at 18 years. However, many younger juveniles today are tried in adult courts. In general, the law provides for no transition between infancy and adulthood.

Adolescents have some, but not all, the constitutional protections of adults. In fact, until a Supreme Court ruling in 1967, minors were not accorded due process, and only in the past 30 years or so have such rights as double jeopardy and proof beyond a reasonable doubt been validated for minors. The Supreme Court has not given all rights to juveniles; for example, they may not always have the same right to a jury trial because of the uncertainty about the meaning of *trial by peers* when juveniles are involved. Privacy rights—including access to contraception; freedom from unreasonable searches and seizures; and the right to political expression in school, including whether principals have the right to censor school newspapers—continue to be major sources of concern.

It is easy to state that adolescents should be accorded the same privacy rights as adults. However, consider the case of a high school administrator who believes that a student has a gun in his locker. Should the school have to get a warrant to search for the gun? If adolescents were accorded the same rights as adults, the school would have to get the warrant; at this time, the school does not need one. Although the United States Supreme Court has recognized minors' rights to some privacy, it has permitted states to infringe on these rights to a greater extent than for adults. The Court has permitted states to limit minors' privacy rights whenever a "significant state interest" can be demonstrated rather than using the stricter "compelling interest" standard. Some advocates for adolescents argue that the Court's rulings are too often based upon the idea that adolescents are incompetent and especially vulnerable. One of the more controversial issues is whether communities have the right to legislate curfews for minors to curb crime and protect teens from becoming victims of violence (see "Focus: Curfews: A Protection or an Infringement of Rights?").

There is also a debate over the rights of parents of adolescents. For example, given that parents have the responsibility to support their adolescent children, do they have the right to know if their adolescent child has received an abortion or is receiving contraceptives at the school nurse's office? Conflicts between the rights of parents and adolescents are very difficult to resolve.

It is difficult to predict how the legal status of adolescents will change in the future. Adolescents have been given some, but not all, constitutional protections. After sensational crimes, states often lower the age of majority, at least as far as responsibility for criminal acts is concerned. Questions concerning the right to free speech (especially in schools), privacy, and parent rights are areas of some confusion, and people who deal with these questions often hold seemingly inconsistent views. For example, those who claim adolescents should have equal rights with adults and equal constitutional protections often argue that adolescents still deserve lesser penalties when they commit a criminal act and should not be subject to capital punishment because they are so young. Those who believe adolescents should not have complete constitutional protections often argue that they should be treated as adults when they commit criminal acts.

Psychologists View Adolescents

The adolescent is affected by many agents of socialization and other forces, some of which—such as the law—are beyond the teen's influence. However, it is inaccurate to view the adolescent as simply buffeted by parents, peers, and teachers. As shown in Figure 1.3, psychologists today view adolescents as being influenced by, and at the same time influencing, other people, a concept called **reciprocal interaction** (Bell, 1968; Kim et al., 2001).

Adolescents influence others by the way they act and how they approach interpersonal interactions. Consider two adolescents faced with the same situation—for example, asking a teacher to reconsider a grade in high school. One takes an aggressive, accusatory, angry stance, arguing that the teacher had no right to give him that grade; the other quietly and with logic points out the teacher's errors. The teacher may act defensively toward the first individual but show greater understanding and tolerance toward the second.

Adolescents influence, and sometimes create, their own environments. They choose which websites to visit, which music to listen to, and often which activities to engage in. They select and are selected by other adolescents as friends. The amount of choice they have increases with age, with older adolescents having more choice than younger adolescents. They are actively involved in creating their own lives.

Each individual enters an interaction with a different background and perhaps a different set of expectations. A teenage girl who has experienced the painful breakup of her parents and a number of unsatisfying relationships with boys may approach an interaction differently from an adolescent who was raised in a happy, intact family and has had mostly positive experiences in dating. Individual differences are integral to the nature of the adolescent experience.

A number of important points stand out clearly from our discussion of broad versus narrow socialization and the modern look at adolescence. First, adolescents face many individual choices and are expected to follow paths that will lead to a personally fulfilling life. Second, adolescents in the latter half of the 20th century and into the 21st century spend a great deal more time preparing

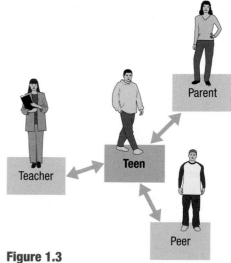

Figure 1.3
Reciprocal Interaction
Parents, teachers, and peers affect, and at the same time are affected by, one another.

reciprocal interaction The idea that the individual is influenced by others and at the same time may influence others.

FOCUS Curfews: A Protection or an Infringement of Rights?

Across the United States, curfews for adolescents are popular. Even though juvenile crime has declined significantly, many people still view crime as being out of control, and they want to curb it. Most Americans favor a curfew, and that support does not vary much by race, ethnicity, or even age of those surveyed. For example, a 1994 survey of adult residents of Cincinnati, Ohio, showed they favored a curfew, as did 77 percent of juveniles surveyed in the District of Columbia. Although those opposed to a curfew often raise the specter of racism, support for curfews is found in the African American community as well. Three quarters of the African American residents of Mobile, Alabama, supported a proposed curfew, and curfews have been proposed by African American and white mayors and city council members alike (Crowell, 1996).

Many American cities have had curfew laws for decades, and the number has increased significantly (Sheperd, 1996). The 1996 Anti-Gang and Youth Violence Act provides financial support to local communities for curfews and antitruancy laws. Law enforcement agencies also support these efforts, although their enforcement is sporadic. The hours of curfew and the exact prohibitions differ widely. Most provide a number of exceptions, allowing juveniles who work or are attending a planned social function to stay out past curfew. Most cities have later curfew hours on Friday and Saturday evenings.

On the surface, curfews seem reasonable. If teens are not permitted to congregate in public places during the late evening hours, crime and teen victimization should decline. Unfortunately, the evidence for the effectiveness of curfews to reduce crime is mixed. Authorities in some cities that vigorously enforce a curfew claim that it has resulted in a marked reduction of crime and teen victimization (Bilchik, 1995; Sharp, 1996). In Dallas, for example, a curfew, combined with extensive police patrols and truancy enforcement, has significantly reduced gang violence where simple saturation policing without a curfew did not (Fritsch, Caeti, & Taylor, 1999).

Other authorities note that curfews may be less effective than they seem, because they may simply shunt crime to other hours and may be dealing with only a small part of the problem. For example, violent crimes committed by juveniles are most frequent between the hours of 3 and 4 P.M., and about a third of all violent crimes take place between 3 and 7 P.M.; less than 20 percent of violent juvenile crime occurs during curfew hours (Sickmund, Snyder, & Poe-Yamagata, 1997).

The effectiveness of curfews is not the only controversy. The United States Supreme Court has consistently maintained that constitutional protections extend to adolescents, but it has also allowed states and localities to place restrictions on the constitutional rights of juveniles that would not be legal if applied to adults. Juvenile curfews are often challenged in the courts for various reasons. The First Amendment to the U.S. Constitution includes the right of free association, and the Fourteenth Amendment requires equal protection under the law, which one could argue is not being shown if curfews apply only to juveniles. Although one might think that curfews would be challenged on the basis of these constitutional rights, most challenges actually involve the question of the right of the local community to infringe upon the parents' rights to raise their children as they see fit, without undue governmental interference (Hemmens & Bennett, 1999; Nalin, 2001). Some argue that because most states hold parents responsible for their children and adolescents, curfews interfere with parental rights.

Whereas some state and federal courts have upheld the legality of curfews, other courts have considered them unconstitutional. It is clear that the courts are unwilling to declare that age is in the same category as race and religion—that is, that any discriminatory treatment based on it is considered illegal. Although every citizen is entitled to equal protection, not all differential treatment due to age is illegal; it is only illegal to treat people differently without what the courts consider a valid reason.

The Supreme Court has noted that children and adolescents need special protection and that the states need not give all rights to adolescents. Government may infringe on adolescents' rights because of (1) the vulnerability of children and adolescents; (2) the inability of juveniles to make important decisions in a mature, intelligent manner; and (3) the importance of parental guidance in child rearing (*Bellotti v. Baird,* 1979). In other words, although children and adolescents share some constitutional protections with adults, there are times when it is legal to discriminate on the basis of age.

The issue of the legality of curfews will continue to be argued until the Supreme Court makes a final decision on the matter. The Court may strike down curfews as unconstitutional or rule that curfew laws are constitutional when written in a particular way. No one yet knows. What is clear, though, is that many cities have adopted curfews, and most law enforcement personnel, adults, and even teens are in favor of curfews.

The legality of curfews, as well as of other issues, hinges on the answers to questions like the following: Are teenagers more vulnerable to negative peer influence? Do they make poor decisions? What is the extent of parental power and influence? These questions have not yet been fully answered in the research literature, and the answers may provide valuable information for government officials responsible for public policy.

At a Glance **1.2** Modern Views of Adolescence

KEY POINT: Scientific interest in adolescence is relatively recent, but the existence of a period between childhood and adulthood has been recognized for some time.

SUPPORTING POINTS	EXPLANATION
The greatest change in adolescence beginning in the 20th century is that almost all adolescents attend high school.	Almost every adolescent today attends high school. The average adolescent spends more time with other adolescents and less time with adults. Adolescents are an important consumer group.
Today's adolescents have a positive view of themselves and their future, but many adults perceive adolescents negatively.	Adolescents are hopeful about their future. Many adults see adolescents as rude and irresponsible, mostly blaming the parents.
The legal status of adolescents is a matter of controversy, and court decisions have been inconsistent.	The age at which adolescents are accorded rights and privileges differs. Adolescents may be allowed to drive at age 16, but not drink alcohol legally until age 21. Adolescents have not been given the same privacy rights as adults.
Each adolescent has unique experiences, and each individual both affects and is affected by others.	The term *reciprocal interaction* is used to describe the phenomenon in which an adolescent both is affected by and affects others. Each individual enters adolescence with a different background and will have unique experiences that will influence development.

for their adult role in schools in which they are more isolated from the adult world than in the past. The transitional stage of adolescence is much longer, and teens receive more freedom and less direction than they did years ago or still do in more traditional societies. Third, adolescents are more confident and hopeful about their future and their own lives, while their elders may hold a more negative view of them. Fourth, Western societies do not know whether they want to treat adolescents as irresponsible children or responsible young adults. Finally, adolescents are individuals who help create their own environment and should not be seen as living solely in a world created by others. *(For a review of this section, see At A Glance 1.2.)*

Themes of Adolescence

As we examine the many changes and challenges that arise during adolescence, we will use five themes. These themes bring adolescence into sharper focus, give greater continuity to the discussion, and help organize the voluminous information available on adolescence.

Theme 1: Adolescence Is a Time of Choices, "Firsts," and Transitions

Adolescence is, by definition, a transitional stage—the stage between childhood and adulthood. A *transition* is a period of passing from one condition, form, stage, or activity to another. A transition connotes change and impermanence. These changes occur in every aspect of life, including the physical, cognitive, social, moral, interpersonal, and intrapersonal (within oneself) dimensions. Understanding the nature of these changes during adolescence is an important step in appreciating the nature of adolescence.

If adolescence is a time of change, it is natural to find that it requires adjustments and adaptations. Adolescence can be perceived as a series of "firsts" (Siegel & Shaughnessy, 1995). It is the time of one's first dance, first date, first crush, first sexual experience, and first job, as well as a time of creating new relationships and thinking about the future. It is a time of looking at the world in a new and different way, of discovering who one is and what one wants to be. It is a time of experiencing, for the first time, the intense feelings that come from deeper, more intimate relationships.

Theme 2: Adolescence Is Shaped by Context

What is the best way to view the adolescent experience? A number of approaches to understanding adolescence are discussed in detail in the chapter titled "The Scientific Approach to Adolescence." We will use each of these approaches at appropriate times, as each of them add something to our understanding of adolescence. We will emphasize a relatively recent perspective—the *contextual* and more specifically the ecological view—that sees the adolescent as enmeshed in a complex environment with many layers.

Consider for a moment the adolescent as being at the center of a circle. The first, and most important, context surrounding the teen is the family. Parents serve as models, guides, and teachers; they reinforce the adolescent's desirable behaviors (helping younger siblings, getting good grades) (see Table 1.4). Even though adolescents spend less time with their parents and family and more time with peers than when they were younger, parents continue to function as models. If parents are active in giving to the community, adolescents are more likely to do so as well. If parents drink alcohol to excess or smoke cigarettes, adolescents are much more likely to do so. Parents also create the atmosphere in the home, encouraging particular communication patterns. Parents help make the rules, but these rules must change to keep pace with the developmental needs of the adolescent. You can't use the same rules with a 13-year-old and a 17-year-old.

Adolescents also exist in a peer context. Everyone accepts the idea that the peer group gains influence during the teen years. Teens turn toward the peer group for support and guidance more often than they did when they were younger. Friendships become more important, and the advent of romantic relationships brings a qualitative change to certain teen relationships. Adolescents spend more time with friends, often are found in cliques or crowds, and have deeper and more intimate friendships. Some believe that as adolescents spend less time with parents, peers and cliques may fulfill their emotional needs, and

Table 1.4

How Do Parents Influence Their Adolescent Children?

Although peer group influences increase during the adolescent period, parental influence continues to be strong. Parents affect their adolescent children in the following ways.

Function	Description	Example
Models	Adolescents may imitate parental behavior.	Parents who smoke are much more likely to have adolescent children who begin to smoke.
Reinforcers/punishers	Parents praise or punish their adolescent child's behavior.	Parents verbally or nonverbally react to their adolescent's achievements or lack of achievements.
Create home atmosphere	Each home has a different feeling; some are filled with tension, others with acceptance.	A home with an atmosphere of acceptance and good relationships helps adolescents develop their interpersonal skills and identity.
Teachers	Parents sometimes actively instruct their adolescent children.	Parents teach particular skills and contribute to their adolescent's knowledge in some areas.
Provide emotional support	Parents give their adolescent children a sense of safety and support.	After a hard day, parents offer love and affection.

By taking an ecological view, we see the adolescent enmeshed in many layers of environment. An adolescent in a poverty-stricken, crime-ridden neighborhood and an adolescent living in a quiet, safe, wealthier area have different experiences and may look at the world in a different manner.

their acceptance and rejection may be even more important (Adler, 1999).

Teenagers' days are organized around attendance at middle school and high school. Part-time jobs may also structure their day. It is only in the last several generations that high school attendance and graduation have become the norm. The school context is not only a location in which formal instruction takes place; it is also a place where teens meet their friends and form groups, helping teens learn how to deal with the complexities of interpersonal relationships. The basic structure of the secondary school differs from the elementary school as students travel from class to class; have many different teachers; and as we will see in "The School Experience," are treated differently. Teenagers are influenced by teachers, what they learn in school, and the social setting of the school.

The adolescent is also enmeshed in a community context. Imagine being raised in a rural community in which everyone knows one another and you may not even lock your doors. Consider how that experience would differ from being raised in an economically depressed area of a large city, a working class suburb, or a wealthy area of the city. The experience of a teen raised in a poverty-stricken area will differ from that of a teen raised in a wealthy suburban or rural area. A teen raised in an area in which drug sales and violence are common may develop a different outlook on life than a teen raised in an area in which there is very little crime. Where one lives and the school one attends typically depend upon one's financial status. Children living in poverty often are exposed to more violence. Poverty affects every area of life.

Adolescents are also surrounded by a media context, including radio, television, music, the Internet, email, and print media, which all serve as sources of information and deeply influence the adolescent. Adolescents spend hours a day listening to music and watch television for at least another 2 hours. Most popular music recordings are bought by adolescents, and adolescents watch more movies than any other age group in the population (Arnett, 1995a). More adolescents are comfortable with computer-related technology than are older adults. Questions about how the media influence the lives of teenagers will be the focus of the chapter "The Media."

PERSPECTIVE 1

WE DON'T LIKE WHAT YOU'RE LISTENING TO!

SETTING THE SCENE: Lydia is a 15-year-old sophomore in high school who loves to listen to music. Her favorites are heavy metal and some alternative music. She always seems to be listening to music, and she spends most of her money on new CDs.

PARENTS: We know that her music is important to her, but some of the lyrics are filthy and promote violence. There is no respect or love in these songs. One song about a beating seems to glorify, rather than condemn, violence. Another song is about a sexual assault. The songs seem to hold out little hope. We're concerned about the influence that these lyrics and the glorification of violence may have on Lydia. We're thinking of taking some kind of action. Perhaps we can keep her from buying these recordings, but we don't see how. She is beginning to dress differently as well—somewhat punk.

LYDIA: First, I like the beat and the music; I don't care that much about the lyrics. I don't think sexual assault or violence is acceptable. I don't think what I listen to is any of my parents' business. I even use earphones so the music won't bother them. As far as how I dress, that is also my business. I admit that how I act may be their concern, but the way I dress and what I listen to should be up to me.

QUESTION: If you were Lydia's parents, would you be concerned? If so, what would you do? Do her parents have the right to limit the music she listens to? Does Lydia have the right to dress the way she wants, wear whatever makeup she wants, and wear her hair according to her own desires, or should her parents have a say in these things?

PERSPECTIVE 2

I SHOULD BE TREATED LIKE EVERYONE ELSE

SETTING THE SCENE: A famous baseball player is arrested for possession of marijuana. He could get up to 6 months in jail for possession, but most commonly the sentence is community service. The judge gives the athlete a short jail sentence, telling the ball player that he is a role model and should act the part.

BASEBALL PLAYER AT NEWS CONFERENCE: *The judge is wrong. I should receive the same sentence as anyone else. The only people I need to explain myself to and be a role model to are my children, not the fans. I get paid for what I do on the baseball field.*

JUDGE: *You are a role model whether or not you choose to be, by the very nature of your job. All those commercials you do—the endorsements—are linked to your status as a role model.*

QUESTION: Do you agree with the baseball player or the judge, and why?

The media influence is difficult for parents to control. Forbidden magazines can be bought and hidden or borrowed in school from a friend; programs can be taped for later viewing or watched at a friend's home. The media in the United States and most Western countries reflect the idea of broad socialization discussed earlier. They are fragmented and allow expression of a great many attitudes and ideas, some of which are contradictory. Some echo pessimism and hopelessness, some the anger and angst of adolescence, and some the hopefulness and positive experience of love. The media also present adolescents with models. Athletes, movie stars, and recording artists all may influence teenagers by what they wear and say, and how they behave. The extent of the influence of these models is a matter of controversy, as is the question of whether successful public figures, as role models, should have a greater responsibility for their actions.

The adolescent is also raised in the context of a particular culture or subculture. An adolescent raised in Japan encounters a different set of values and attitudes, and has a different life experience, than a teen raised in Argentina. One's general outlook on life and priorities are prescribed by one's culture. Some cultures socialize their children and adolescents to feel closer to their families of origin, whereas others emphasize more independence. For example, Chinese culture sees the individual as embedded in a more collective context; it emphasizes the importance of a harmonious society with a well-structured network of interpersonal relationships and the need to fit into this structure and perform one's duties and responsibilities. Chinese society does not conceive of individuals as isolated, separate entities but regards them as a part of a social network with specific rules governing relationships (Lam, 1997). The division of cultures into those that practice narrow versus broad socialization, as noted previously, brings the question of the universality of the adolescent experience to the forefront. Although we will deal mostly with adolescence in Western cultures, it is important to remember that the Western conception of adolescence is not the only one available.

The importance of culture is now well established, although psychologists are interested in the similarities, as well as differences, among cultures. Few cultures today remain isolated from Western technology. Many traditional societies have been changed as they adopt certain Western models, such as universal schooling, technology, and some conception of individual rights. Eastern industrial societies such as Japan adapt these Western institutions and tools within the context of some of their traditional beliefs. Cultural influence, though, is reciprocal; Eastern philosophy, religion, and ways of looking at the world also influence Western thought and culture. Immigrants from Asia carry along their culture and traditions as they settle in Western societies, and their ideas and philosophy of life may influence society as well.

Many adolescents are also members of subcultures. Complex societies are made up of a number of groups, each of which differs in attitudes, child-rearing strategies, beliefs, and communication patterns. If these minority groups differ significantly from the dominant culture and think of themselves as different, they are considered *subcultures* (Light, Keller, & Calhoun, 1994). Group membership is so important that we will considered it as a separate theme.

Theme 3: Adolescence Is Influenced by Group Membership

Group membership may define one's point of view and change one's life experiences. The simplest example involves gender; the experience of male and female teens differs. Not only are many male and female teens treated somewhat differ-

The United States, as well as many Western nations, has grown more diverse. The experience of adolescents from minority groups is both similar to and different from that of adolescents from the majority group.

ently by their parents but also people expect males and females to display different behaviors.

Group membership also includes subcultures. The principal minority groups within the United States are African Americans, Latinos, Asian Americans, and Native Americans. Each subculture exists within a larger, dominant culture rather than being completely apart from it. Appreciating the values, child-rearing strategies, and attitudes of a particular group is vital to understanding the context in which adolescents develop. The subcultural identity influences the social setting of the home (the way it is set up) and the social customs (the way boys and girls are treated) (Pachter & Harwood, 1996). Subcultural membership also influences customs regarding child care, as some cultures expect a child to be more or less independent. Finally, subcultures also influence the attitudes and values of caregivers. When Puerto Rican and Anglo mothers were asked about the most desirable traits to instill in their children, Puerto Rican mothers stressed qualities reflecting respect and social abilities, whereas Anglo mothers generated more individualistic descriptions, such as self-confidence and independence (Harwood, 1992).

The experiences of many minority group adolescents differ from those of majority group adolescents. Perhaps the most important difference is found in the rates of poverty. African American, Latino, Native American, and some groups of Asian American adolescents are much more likely to grow up and live in poverty than are white adolescents. This poverty translates into worse schooling, more violent neighborhoods, and fewer resources. For instance, many middle-class and upper-income teens do not worry about where their tuition is coming from, but teens with fewer resources must do so. White adolescents also may live in poverty, of course, but the percentage living in poverty is higher among minority groups.

Another difference for many minority group adolescents is the experience of prejudice and discrimination. Some adolescents experience discrimination personally, whereas others are well aware of their group's history of difficulty with the system. Some adolescents from groups historically subject to discrimination may not believe that they can break out of the cycle of poverty and violence.

A third area of difference for minority group adolescents is the major challenge of identity formation. Minority group members not only face the standard challenge of developing a personal identity but also must determine how they relate to their group and how they wish to fit into the overall society. One middle-income African American youth once asked me to think about how he feels

Minority groups often use different child-rearing strategies based upon cultural prescriptions about how children should act and be raised, as well as their current circumstances.

when he enters a restaurant and is the only African American there. Sometimes, stereotypes get in the way. For instance, one Latino young man from an upper middle class family found that shop owners assumed him to be poor and paid no attention to him when he was looking at, for instance, an expensive sweater. How to integrate some identification with one's group with full participation in the opportunities of the overall society is often a difficult challenge for young people.

A fourth area of difference is found in the family experiences of minority group adolescents. For instance, multigenerational families are somewhat more common among African Americans than in the general public, and grandparents are typically more involved in child rearing. The African American family is often extended, with many people helping to raise the child (Garcia-Coll, Meyer, & Brillon, 1995; Smith, 1995). Older children often help take care of their younger siblings and have child-care responsibilities.

Many African American youngsters are accustomed to a high-energy, fast-paced home with a great deal of concurrent stimulation and extensive kinship networks that offer a source of strength and comfort. Within this context, traditional values typically stress interdependence, security, establishing a positive self-image and racial identity, and perseverance in the face of adversity (McAdoo, 1991). The family socializes children to deal with prejudice. Organized religion and spirituality are often important sources of inspiration. African American parents may use a stricter, more authoritarian form of discipline, which may be necessary for the safety of children raised in neighborhoods wracked by violence and poverty (Kelley, Sanchez-Huckles, & Walker, 1993). The contextual view is especially useful here. African American parents of adolescents growing up in a dangerous area use functional child-rearing strategies that differ from middle-class techniques. They promote self-reliance, resourcefulness, the ability to manipulate situations, mistrust of people in authority, and the ability to ward off attack (Ogbu, 1992).

Latino adolescents are united by a common language but may differ in customs and the strictness of their families (Wasserman et al., 1990). Latino families often emphasize sharing and cooperation rather than competitiveness. The individualism and competition of American schools may conflict with the child's learning at home (Delgado-Gaitan & Trueba, 1985). A sense of family pride and loyalty is also nurtured. The Latino idea of individual dignity not based upon economic status differs from that of the general society (Garcia-Coll et al., 1995).

Traditional Latino role expectations demand that men be virile, somewhat aggressive, and protective of women—the machismo attitude (Bigner, 1994). *Machismo* actually refers more to the male's responsibility to the family, as family loyalty supersedes individual interest. Older children often have child-care responsibilities. The roles of mother and father are clearly defined, with the father being more authoritarian and the mother more involved in child rearing, although this role is changing (Garcia-Coll et al., 1995). Latino parents emphasize the importance of proper demeanor and a sense of pride (Harwood, 1992), and they endorse stricter standards than other parents.

Asian American children, especially those with parents from the Pacific Rim, experience a very different child-rearing regimen. Asian American children are typically taught to think of family first and to subjugate their own desires and concerns. For many Asian Americans, individual behavior reflects either shame or pride on the family (Morrow, 1987). Asian American families stress that the individual is secondary to the family. Anger and displeasure are to be avoided, and social customs demand strict adherence. Communication is often indirect, and outward displays of emotion are not encouraged, except with infants (Slonim, 1991). Asian Americans are accustomed to a fairly structured, formal setting. Common features of Asian American child rearing include parental control; obedience; discipline; an emphasis on education; filial piety, and respect for elders; and a desire to minimize conflict and respect obligations and tradition (Lin & Fu, 1990). Asian American children are taught that through hard work, moral living, and diligence, they will fulfill their potential and make their families proud.

Native American tribes differ widely. More than five hundred tribes are recognized by the federal government, making it difficult to talk about a common culture. Native Americans, though, are often raised in collective, cooperative, noncompetitive social networks (Harrison et al., 1990). Responsibilities for child rearing are shared among caring adults, including extended family members. Native Americans place great value on age and life experience, and parents often seek advice from older family members or elders. Children are often treated somewhat permissively, and there is less interference in the affairs of others and regulation of activities than in families of European backgrounds (Williams, 1979). Being part of a group and blending in are important virtues, whereas asserting one's individuality is not encouraged (Nazarro, 1981). Sharing is an important value learned early, and people in authority are supposed to share (Lewis & Ho, 1979). Strong extended family structures are common, although not as prevalent as they were years ago. Patience is a virtue; Native American children learn this lesson at a young age and will wait for their turn without being assertive.

These descriptions are general, of course, and not every member of these groups will have these experiences. Often, people in a particular minority group differ greatly. Latinos, for example, come from many different countries, and people from Puerto Rico differ from those who come from Chile. The U.S. Census Bureau's "Asian" category covers seventeen countries, and the Immigration Service counts more than twenty-nine countries (Edmondson, 1997). In addition, just as not all minority group families are poor, adolescents in these homes also differ in the extent to which these descriptions apply. Latino and Asian American teens whose families have more recently immigrated to the United States will show traditional attitudes and values more than those who have been in the country longer.

Theme 4: The Adolescent Experience Has Changed over the Past 50 Years

Is the experience of an adolescent in the early years of the 21st century different from what it was in 1960? The answer seems to be yes and no. Certainly, some aspects of the adolescent experience are similar. Adolescents at both periods of time have had to face the consequences of physical and cognitive (intellectual) changes. For instance, adolescents both then and now have had to adapt to their newfound sexuality and freedoms.

Sometimes, specific events that occur may significantly affect the lives of an entire generation. How might the terrorist attacks of September 11, 2001, change the way adolescents view the world?

Although many of the developmental tasks of adolescence probably haven't changed much, the context in which adolescents meet these challenges certainly has. Each of the contexts discussed earlier has changed significantly over the past 50 years. The world of adolescents today differs substantially from the world of their parents and grandparents when they were adolescents. People are influenced by the economic and technological events of the day. The context in which an adolescent lives is also defined by the historical time in which the teen is living. The generation of the very late 1960s and early 1970s was greatly affected by the Vietnam War, and the present generation of adolescents will certainly be affected by the terrorist attacks of September 11, 2001. The effect of growing up in a particular generation or historical time is called the **cohort effect.**

The typical family in the 21st century differs greatly from the traditional family in the middle of the 20th century, the family with a mother who was a homemaker and a father employed full-time. In fact, only about 12 percent of American children today live in such families because of the increase of both employment among mothers and single-parent families due to divorce or parenthood outside marriage (Hernandez, 1997). In 1940, only 10 percent of the mothers were employed, whereas today the figure stands at more than 60 percent (U.S. Census Bureau, 2001). Many of today's adolescents have grown up in a home in which they have been more independent, often taking on responsibilities at an early age and making some of their own decisions. Many have been latchkey or self-care children who do not have a parent or other older person waiting for them when they come home from school. One of the defining features of such situations is an emphasis on independence training beginning at an early age; for example, many of these children are used to making their own meals.

About 20 percent of all children now live in single-parent families, which have increased with the rise in the number of divorced and unmarried parents. Approximately 1 million divorces take place a year, and if trends continue, more than half of all American children will spend some part of their childhood in a

cohort effect   The effect of growing up in a particular generation.

single-parent household before their 18th birthday. Many single parents remarry, and stepfamilies are common.

With either a single parent or both parents employed, the present-day adolescent is also less closely monitored. Teens spend more time today with friends than they did years ago, and parents appear to be even more concerned about the possibility of bad peer influences, perhaps because teens are less well monitored. Romantic relationships and sexual experimentation are occurring somewhat earlier, and concerns about the spread of sexually transmitted infections and teen pregnancy are greater.

The high school today differs greatly from what it was years ago. American schools seem to waffle between being more student centered (emphasizing choice, personal development, health, and citizenship) and more content centered. World events often cause a swing from one emphasis to the other. The Soviet sputnik space program in the late 1950s caused a distinct change in the curriculum to emphasize math and science courses, followed in the late 1960s and 1970s by a greater emphasis on personal development and choice. In the aftermath of an influential report in the early 1970s called "A Nation at Risk," the pendulum swung back, and slowly a more stringent curriculum was formulated and followed. This trend has continued into the early years of the 21st century. High school students today are more likely to find stricter requirements—especially in math, science, and foreign languages—and less choice in courses.

Other aspects of high school have changed as well. Violence in the schools has become a national concern, and the high school's responsibility to develop moral individuals is debated. Another concern is the achievement of adolescents, especially those raised in poverty and belonging to minority groups.

The adolescent in the early 2000s has a greater choice of media than adolescents 50 years ago. Many have cable television with dozens of stations. Increasing numbers have access to the World Wide Web and its incredible amount of information (Cravatta, 1997). The use of chat rooms and the Internet is expanding significantly, bringing with it questions about security, privacy, and the ability of teens to obtain just about any information they want, including information from racist or violent websites. Although the influence of the media on adolescents is controversial, there is no doubt that adolescents of this generation are exposed to many different types of media with many more messages than previous generations.

The demographics of adolescence are also changing. The United States has about 31 million people aged 12 to 19 years, accounting for more than 10 percent of the population; that number will increase to 35 million by 2010 (Kantrowitz & Wingert, 1999; U.S. Census Bureau, 2001). Many of these teens will belong to minority groups, and the percentage of African Americans, Latinos, Asian Americans, and to a lesser extent, Native Americans will increase substantially in the 21st century (see Table 1.5). Today, Latino youth are the

Table 1.5

Resident Population of the United States (Percentage of the U.S. Population)

The percentage of the U.S. population belonging to minority groups will increase substantially in the coming years.

Year	White (non-Latino)	African American	Native American	Latino	Asian American
2000	71.4	12.2	0.7	11.8	3.9
2010	67.3	12.5	0.8	14.6	4.8
2020	63.8	12.8	0.8	17	5.7
2030	60.1	13.0	0.8	19.4	6.7
2040	56.3	13.1	0.8	21.9	7.8
2050	52.8	13.2	0.8	24.3	8.9

Note: The U.S. Census Bureau uses a low, medium, and high set of projected figures. These figures are taken from the medium series.

Source: Data from U.S. Census Bureau (2001).

largest ethnic group in the country and will be an increasing percentage of the population (Miller, 2003). Today about 71 percent of the U.S. population is white, but by 2050 only about 53 percent will be white. The United States is becoming more diverse every year (Wellner, 2002), and interactions between teens of different ethnic and racial backgrounds will increase because of both numbers and the fact that an increasing number of minority group members are moving to the suburbs and wealthier areas of cities.

A few short years ago, the concept of American society as a melting pot was popular—that is, minority groups were believed to melt into American society as they took on the values of the dominant culture. Because the melting pot does not seem to explain our society today (if it ever did), many psychologists and educators look at the United States (and many other Western societies) in terms of *cultural pluralism*, in which a number of cultural groups exist side by side. This new perspective has the advantage of encouraging an appreciation of just how an individual's culture affects behavior and development.

The cohort effect shows itself, then, in the changes in family structure, women's roles, the school, the demographics of the United States, and technological change. Adolescents today face challenges that differ somewhat from those encountered by previous generations. Their world is much more diverse, technologically sophisticated, and competitive. Today's adolescents have had less supervision and more independence at an earlier age. At the same time, some of the developmental challenges facing adolescents, such as adapting to a changing body and developing an identity, remain similar. The challenges facing the adolescent today, then, are both similar to, and different from, those faced

Today, a new movement in psychology, called *positive psychology*, emphasizes the study of well-being, happiness, satisfaction, and originality. It emphasizes health rather than illness. What is motivating these adolescents to give of their time to help others?

by adolescents of previous generations. When investigating adolescent development, it is wise to keep in mind the cohort effect, the differences between generations.

Theme 5: Today's Views of Adolescence Are Becoming More Balanced, with Greater Attention to Its Positive Nature

Challenges and changes can be viewed in many ways. Each challenge in adolescence has multiple implications and can be viewed positively or negatively. For instance, the physical changes that lead to sexual maturity and sexuality can be seen as a positive force or in terms of the problems of adolescent pregnancy and the spread of disease. The increase in autonomy can be seen in terms of positive self-discovery or as a threat to the social harmony of the family.

Research studies show that the majority of children and adolescents adapt well to the challenges they face (Grotevant, 1998). There is certainly a relationship between exposure to multiple stressors and maladjustment, but the relationship is only modest, and many children and adolescents exposed to difficult environments adapt to them (Dubow et al., 1991). Youth who function well while experiencing significant stressors are called *stress resistant* or, more recently, *stress resilient* (see "Stress and Psychological, Physical, and Learning Problems"). At one time, these youth were singled out as the exceptions, but 25 years of research has yielded the surprise that resilience is relatively common (Masten, 2001). Resilience depends upon the type and amount of stress encountered and the youth's resources for handling the challenges. This does not mean that these resilient adolescents do not experience their share of problems, such as depression and anxiety, which they certainly do compared with youth from less stressful environments (Luthar, 1991). However, compared with others in their stressful environments, they show fewer such problems than one might expect, and many are functioning well.

It is fair to say that psychology in general, and adolescent psychology in particular, has often focused on illness and problem behavior rather than mental health and the development of positive emotions and behaviors. There is a great deal of research on drug abuse, teenage pregnancy, violence, and delinquency, along with studies on how to curb and prevent these problems; there is much less study of how children and adolescents become socially competent, compassionate, motivated individuals (Larson, 2000). This is understandable, as psychology has often stressed healing, and adolescent psychology has concentrated on the prevention and treatment of these problems (Seligman & Csikszentmihalyi, 2000). Psychology traditionally has not focused on what actions lead to well-being and how to build positive qualities.

The emphasis of psychology may be changing. A new movement, sometimes referred to as *positive psychology*, seeks to emphasize the study of well-being, contentment and satisfaction, hope and optimism, interpersonal skills, originality, future mindedness, altruism, and other positive qualities. This is not the first time psychology has embarked on such a quest. An older movement, *humanistic psychology*, emphasized personal choice, realizing one's potential, the importance of subjective experience, and developing one's distinct human potential. Unfortunately, the humanistic movement did not amass a significant scientifically based research base, and the emphasis on the self encouraged self-centeredness. Positive psychology, as it is now envisioned, will grow through the use of scientific research and will look at healthy and reciprocal interpersonal relationships (Seligman & Csikszentmihalyi, 2000).

This text will take a positive and optimistic view of adolescent changes and challenges. After all, most adolescents are happy, healthy, and optimistic and have good interpersonal relationships with their families and others. This does not mean that they have no problems, doubts, or anxieties, but no one is immune to these. We will certainly examine them, but we will emphasize the positive adaptation that most adolescents make to the challenges that confront them.

Development is not always a smooth process, and progress toward autonomy is rarely without incident, misstep, or controversy. If we see these challenges in terms of opportunities for growth and appreciate the fact that so many experiences are new, then we emerge with a more positive view of adolescence. It is not a view that turns away from the obvious problems that adolescents face, nor a view that fails to appreciate the dangers that may arise; instead, it is a more balanced and positive view of an exciting and challenging period in each of our lives. *(For a review of this section, see At A Glance 1.3.)*

AT A GLANCE 1.3 THEMES OF ADOLESCENCE

KEY POINT: Five themes will be followed throughout this text.

SUPPORTING POINTS	EXPLANATION
Adolescence is a time of choices, "firsts," and transitions.	Adolescence is a time of one's first romantic relationship, of making one's first major life decisions, and of receiving one's first taste of independence.
Adolescence is shaped by context.	The adolescent's life is affected by multiple layers of environment, including parents, siblings, peers/friends, school, neighborhood, the media, culture, and the legal system.
Adolescence is influenced by group membership.	Many adolescents today are members of minority groups. The largest minority groups in the United States are African Americans, Latinos, Asian Americans, and Native Americans. Adolescents from minority groups may have different experiences than their European American peers. The experience of female adolescents differs from that of male adolescents.
The experience of adolescence has changed over the past 50 years.	The cohort effect is the influence of growing up at a particular historical time. Compared with the world of teenagers 50 years ago, the world of adolescents today is more technologically sophisticated and competitive. It contains a less stable family structure and a greater number of choices.
Today's views of adolescence are becoming more balanced, with greater attention to its positive nature.	Historically, research has focused on the problems of adolescence, including violence and teenage pregnancy. The possible negative implications of sexual maturation have been well researched. Recently, a more balanced view of adolescence, focusing on how most adolescents develop into healthy, happy individuals, has been advanced. This more balanced view does not ignore the difficulties adolescents face. Some adolescents are considered resilient; that is, they adjust well to difficult environments.

CHAPTER SUMMARY AT A GLANCE

KEY TOPICS	KEY POINTS	
Adolescence: A Frame of Reference	The period of adolescence forms the bridge between childhood and adulthood. (*At A Glance 1.1, p. 6*)	**KEY TERMS** *adolescence (p. 1)* *puberty (p. 1)* *rite of passage (p. 1)* *emotional autonomy (p. 3)* *behavioral autonomy (p. 3)* *socialization (p. 4)* *narrow socialization (p. 4)* *broad socialization (p. 4)*
Modern Views of Adolescence	Scientific interest in adolescence is relatively recent, but the existence of a period between childhood and adulthood has been recognized for some time. (*At A Glance 1.2, p. 13*)	*reciprocal interaction (p. 11)*
Themes of Adolescence	Five themes will be followed throughout this text: 1. Adolescence is a time of choices, "firsts," and transitions. 2. Adolescence is shaped by context. 3. Adolescence is influenced by group membership. 4. The experience of adolescence has changed over the past 50 years. 5. Today's views of adolescence are becoming more balanced, with greater attention to its positive nature. (*At A Glance 1.3, p. 24*)	*cohort effect (p. 20)*

Review questions for this chapter appear in the appendix.

2

THE SCIENTIFIC APPROACH TO ADOLESCENCE

WHAT IS YOUR OPINION?

THEORETICAL APPROACHES TO ADOLESCENCE
- What Is a Good Theory?
- How Theories Differ from One Another

PERSPECTIVES ON ADOLESCENCE
- Psychoanalytic Conceptions of Adolescence
- Erikson and Identity
- Havighurst's Developmental Tasks
- Cognitive Changes in Adolescence: Jean Piaget's Theory
- The Information-Processing Approach
- The Behavioral Approach: You Are What You Learn
- Social Learning Theory
  Perspective 1: Encouraging a Friend
- The Ecological Approach
- Eclecticism

RESEARCH INTO ADOLESCENCE
- Research Designs
- Research Methods and Data Collection
  FOCUS: Mistakes, Misunderstandings, and Miscalculations
- Research in Other Cultures and Subcultures
- Reviewing the Research: The Internet

ETHICAL STANDARDS AND DILEMMAS
- Informed Consent
- Deception
- Confidentiality
  Perspective 2: Breaching Confidentiality?

HAS YOUR OPINION CHANGED?

CHAPTER SUMMARY AT A GLANCE

Imagine that part of your job involves working with adolescents. You may be a teacher, a social worker, a counselor, or even a business executive who would like to sell your products to adolescents. You are introduced to a group of adolescents and must proceed from there to efficiently and effectively fulfill your obligations. How would you know what to expect? How would you go about finding out more about this group of adolescents?

Today, we are fortunate to have theoretical approaches that can help us understand adolescents. A **theory** is a systematic statement of underlying principles that describe a particular phenomenon—in our case, adolescent development. Theories of adolescent development are useful tools for understanding the nature of adolescent development.

Developmental theories perform many useful functions. First, they provide a framework for understanding the challenges a person typically faces at a particular time of life and predict the next step in development. In that way they offer social scientists a way of predicting what will happen next. Second, theories can relate one fact to another. For example, the theorist Jean Piaget argues that adolescents develop the ability to deal with abstractions. We also know from our conversations with teenagers that they are more interested in the nature of God and developing their own philosophy of life than are younger children. Piaget's theory can be used to link one fact with the other and to predict that adolescents who can use abstract concepts will be more likely to focus on developing a meaningful philosophy of life. Third, theories can help us form questions for further study. Adopting a theory leads to asking particular questions. For example, a theory that emphasizes the importance of role models would ask questions about the role models available in a teen's life; in contrast, a theory that emphasizes the importance of reinforcement would ask questions about what kind of reinforcers are present in an adolescent's environment. A theory that emphasizes the importance of finding a personal identity would ask questions about how this search occurs, whereas a theory that emphasizes the importance of the biological changes in an adolescent's life would ask questions about how hormonal changes influence the adolescent. To answer these questions scientifically, a researcher must conduct a well-designed research study.

A knowledge of research methods is necessary not only for designing studies but also for evaluating the information that surrounds us. If you have ever used the Internet to find information, you may have been overwhelmed by the amount of data available. How can you tell which information is valuable and which is not? If you have a knowledge of research methods, you can see through the half-truths and incorrect assumptions and conclusions.

This chapter begins with an introduction to the nature of theories, including a discussion of how to tell a good theory from a bad one. It then reviews the prominent theoretical approaches to adolescence. Each theory is useful in its own way, and has its strengths and weaknesses. The chapter continues with an analysis of various research methods. Finally, it looks at the ethical dilemmas most frequently encountered by researchers.

THEORETICAL APPROACHES TO ADOLESCENCE

Eight theoretical approaches to adolescent development will be presented in this chapter. Many theories are needed, because no single theory can serve as an adequate framework for every area of interest. What if you were interested

theory A systematic statement of underlying principles that explain a particular phenomenon.

27

in how adolescent thought processes differ from those of younger children? You would seek a theory that focuses on these changes rather than one that theorizes about the changing relationship between teenagers and parents. This does not mean that a particular theory that emphasizes cognitive development would not help us understand other facets of development, such as social development. Indeed, changes in adolescent thought processes influence how teens think about, and behave toward, their friends and family.

What Is a Good Theory?

How do you know which theory to use? Theories are really not right or wrong, but *useful* or *less useful*. If two theories might be applicable to understanding a particular behavior, you would adopt the one that was most useful—that is, the theory that was better at helping you understand present behavior and predict future behavior.

Good theories are also *inclusive;* that is, they cover a considerable amount of ground. A theory that is useful for understanding how adolescents' interpersonal relationships change should cover as many of these relationships as possible. In addition, ideally, a theory's main ideas can be *tested*. Each theory should lead to testable questions that confirm the way the theory operates. This may seem simple, but it actually is not. Some theories, such as those of Sigmund Freud, are difficult to test because the central concepts have not been defined in a way that allows empirical (statistical) scientific testing (Cairns, 1998).

Theories should also be *economical*—that is, introduce as few new terms as possible to explain behavior—and be *clear* and *concise*. New terms should be defined precisely and understandably, and their meaning should not be open to debate. Good theories also spark a great deal of research and offer a different way of viewing and predicting behavior.

How Theories Differ from One Another

Theories differ from one another in a number of dimensions. For example, they often differ in *scope*. Some emphasize social development, others cognitive development. In addition, theories may differ in their explanation of the *basic cause of behavior*. Some theories, such as Piaget's theory, view behavior change as arising from internal factors (factors within the individual); other approaches, such as behavioral theory, emphasize external factors (social forces outside the individual); and still others, such as the ecological approach, focus on the interaction between internal and external factors.

Perhaps the most obvious difference among theories is their stand on whether development is best understood as *discontinuous* or *continuous*. Theorists arguing for discontinuous development believe that people develop in stages, and each stage is qualitatively different from the others. Each stage shows a qualitative leap in ability. Progression from stage to stage occurs in a sequential, unvarying order, and each person passes through the same stages. Stages cannot be skipped, and development is always forward, but people may enter or leave a particular stage at different times (see Table 2.1). Freud, Erik Erikson, and Piaget are prominent stage theorists, and each proposes a stage that corresponds to adolescence.

Other psychologists argue that development is a more continuous process, and they do not agree with the concept of stages. For example, neither behaviorists nor social learning theorists posit any stages. These psychologists see development as occurring in smooth, small steps explained by looking at past achievements. They see no stages but rather gradual development. (*For a review of this section, see At A Glance 2.1.*)

Table 2.1

Classic Stage Theories

Stage theories share some common features:

1. Stages are sequential.

2. No stages are skipped.

3. Development occurs in the forward direction, and no regression occurs.

4. Each stage shows a qualitative change in abilities.

5. There are individual differences in the age at which children enter and leave any particular stage.

AT A GLANCE   **2.1** THEORETICAL APPROACHES TO ADOLESCENCE

KEY POINT: Theories of adolescence involve systematic statements of principles that are helpful in describing and predicting adolescent behavior.

SUPPORTING POINTS	EXPLANATION
Theories help understand, explain, and predict adolescent behavior.	Theories help psychologists link one behavior to another, explain the origins of behavior, and predict behavior.
Good theories are useful for understanding and predicting behavior.	A good theory is inclusive, leads to testable hypotheses, introduces as few new terms as possible, and spurs research.
Theories differ in their view of the causes of behavior, their use of stages, and their scope.	Theories differ from one another in scope; some deal with social development, whereas others deal with personality development. They differ in their view of the cause of behavior; some theories view motivation as arising from within the individual, whereas others see it as originating from social forces outside the individual or as a combination of the two. Some theories use stages, and others do not.
Some theories argue for discontinuous development, whereas others view development as a continuous process.	Some theories view behavior as occurring in a discontinuous stagelike sequence. Stages are sequential, and each stage is qualitatively different from the others. Individuals may enter and leave a stage at their own rate. Other psychologists view development as a continuous process in which progress is made in small steps explained by past achievements.

PERSPECTIVES ON ADOLESCENCE

The first modern theoretical perspective on adolescence was advanced by G. Stanley Hall, who emphasized the biological aspects of adolescence. Hall's 1904 two-volume encyclopedic work, titled *Adolescence: Its Psychology and Its Relations to Physiology, Anthropology, Sociology, Sex, Crime, Religion, and Education*, summarized what was known about adolescence at the time. The first volume reviewed physical and motor development; physical and mental diseases associated with adolescence; sociological, criminal, and cross-cultural studies of adolescence; sexual development; and historical material. The second volume discussed sensory and voice changes; the evolution of emotions; religious experience; and social, intellectual, and educational foundations. Hall's work was instrumental in sparking interest in the field, and some of his ideas continue to influence the field today (White, 1994).

The distinctive physical changes that occur during adolescence lead to a basic psychological imbalance, according to Hall, who first used the phrase *storm and stress* to describe adolescence. Adolescence as a time of conflict is a theme of the early views of adolescence, to which we now turn.

Psychoanalytic Conceptions of Adolescence

Psychoanalytic thinking is based upon the work of Sigmund Freud. Freud (1923/1961, 1933) argued that later behavior, including behavior in adolescence, is linked to earlier experiences that have been repressed (that is, that have remained buried in the *unconscious* beyond normal awareness). Motives arise from the unconscious, that portion of the mind that is beyond normal awareness. The unconscious consists of thoughts, drives, and memories of which the individual is unaware but that may influence behavior. For example, a person may experience sexual difficulties because of traumatic sexual experiences in childhood that the individual does not remember. Adolescents and adults may not truly be aware of their motives or wishes because they may be unacceptable to

G. Stanley Hall is considered the "father of the study of adolescence." His work summarizing the research on adolescence served as a starting point for psychologists interested in adolescence.

Sigmund Freud emphasized the influence that biological factors have on adolescent development. His daughter, Anna Freud, focused on the importance of the ego and the defense mechanisms.

society or to the individual and are unconscious. An adolescent showing anger to his teacher, for example, may not be aware that the anger comes from feelings that he cannot express toward a parent.

Freud emphasized the basic conflict that occurs when urges confront a world that allows only partial gratification. The mind consists of three parts (Freud, 1923/1961, 1940/1949). The *id* is the source of all wishes and desires and cannot tolerate delay. It wants everything immediately. The *ego*, which is partly conscious, is responsible for dealing with reality and satisfying the needs and desires of the id in a socially appropriate manner. The ego must understand the consequences of the act. As the child matures, the ego becomes better able to delay gratification and balance the desires of the id and the constraints of the third construct, the *superego*. The superego is analogous to one's conscience and acts as an internal gyroscope. It contains the *ego ideal*, which is the moral code of the individual, gained from one's parents. A great deal of anxiety can arise when desires of the id come into conflict with societal and superego restraints. In fact, Freud (1923/1961) wrote that the ego is "a poor creature owing service to three masters." These masters—the id, the superego, and the external world—can be powerful, so the ego must have a great many ways of dealing with these unpleasant or unacceptable realities.

One of Freud's controversial, and often misunderstood, ideas involves infantile and childhood sexuality. Freud did not believe that children experience adult sexual feelings. For Freud, sex is similar to what might be called *bodily pleasure* or *sensuality*, which he considered a positive force. Freud called the sexual energy the *libido*, and the libido is found in different portions of the body as the child grows and matures.

Freud described human development in terms of psychosexual stages (see Table 2.2). A person's personality is determined by his or her experiences in early childhood. During the stage covering adolescence, known as the *genital stage*, the increase in sexual hormones causes the individual to gradually look for relationships with the other gender. Freud believed that from puberty onward, the individual's great task is to become free from emotional dependency on parents. A son must relinquish the exclusive emotional tie to his mother and find a deep relationship with another female. He must resolve his rivalry with his father and free himself of his father's domination. A daughter must separate from parents and establish her own life. This is not an easy task (Freud, 1905/1953). Puberty is a period in which sexual instincts are dramatically heightened; this new sexuality creates stress and conflict that require adaptations and adjustments, resulting in emotional imbalance and conflict.

Whereas Freud emphasized the id and instinctual processes, later psychoanalytic thinkers emphasized the importance of the ego. Freud's youngest child, Anna Freud, became a great psychologist in her own right and was one who emphasized the importance of the ego. She further developed the idea of defense mechanisms. Sometimes, if the ego is threatened, it will protect itself by using a **defense mechanism,** an automatic and unconscious method of reducing anxiety and unpleasant, unacceptable feelings. For example, a young adolescent boy introduces himself to a girl and asks her out, but the girl refuses. His friends are watching. The boy may *rationalize,* or make up an excuse, arguing that when he spoke with her, it became obvious that they would not enjoy each other's company; or days later he may simply *deny* that the incident had occurred.

Anna Freud (1958, 1963) focused on the contradictions in adolescent behavior, noting the swings between imitation of others and searching unceasingly for one's own identity and between being dependent on parents and rebelling against parents. She emphasized the importance of the adolescent's striving for autonomy from parents. Sometimes, this emotional separation can be difficult,

defense mechanism An automatic and unconscious strategy that reduces or eliminates feelings of anxiety or emotional conflict.

Table 2.2

The Psychosexual Stages

Freud describes human development in terms of psychosexual stages. The experiences of an individual during these stages, especially the first three, determine the individual's later personality. Personality characteristics arise from receiving either not enough or too much gratification during these stages. In either case, the individual may become fixated—that is, the individual does not progress normally from one stage to the next and continues to seek gratification in these earlier ways, resulting in particular personality characteristics and behaviors.

Age	Stage	Description	Personality Characteristics
Birth–18 months	Oral	Emphasis is on sucking and taking things in or biting and chewing.	Characteristics include being suggestible, acquisitive, and dependent, or sarcastic and argumentative.
18 months–3 years	Anal	Gratification comes from expelling feces, toilet training, and coming to terms with societal controls.	Characteristics include being very orderly, stingy, stubborn, and miserly, or being messy, rebellious, aggressive, prone to emotional outbursts, tardy, and overly generous.
3–5 (or 6) years	Phallic	Interest in genital areas. Oedipus conflict involves sexual feelings for the opposite-sex parent, along with a wish to rid oneself of the same-sex parent. The Oedipus complex is resolved through identification with the same-sex parent and repression of feelings toward the opposite-sex parent, and is responsible for gender-role conceptions.	Characteristics depend on defense mechanisms used and can include being vain/contemptuous, flirtatious/shy, proud/humble, and brash/bashful.
5 to 6 years–adolescence	Latency	Sexuality is hidden.	
Adolescence	Genital	Puberty leads to the emergence of adult sexuality and mature relationships.	

with adolescents not admitting any dependence, pride, or love in their parents and sometimes taking the opposite attitude. The adolescent's desire for autonomy and striving for independence often conflict with their actual state of dependence on parents, leading teens to deride and be critical of their parents. Anna Freud also noted that the ego must deal with sexual impulses as well.

These feelings are difficult to deal with, so adolescents defend themselves against their impulses in many ways. Anna Freud emphasized two especially important defense mechanisms used by adolescents: intellectualization and asceticism (A. Freud, 1936/1946). **Intellectualization** involves dealing with emotional difficulties on an intellectual, often abstract, plane. Adolescents may take a very abstract, nonpersonal attitude toward sex and aggression, for example. They may develop elaborate theories of love, family, and authority to avoid directly facing the emotional difficulty (Crain, 1992). **Asceticism** is characterized by self-denial—avoiding pleasure. This may indicate a fear of sexuality or at least a defense against sexual feelings.

The teenage years, then, are marked by turbulence and the use of defense mechanisms. The adolescent experiences ambivalent feelings, showing behaviors that alternate between such extremes as excessive independence and clinging dependence.

Normally, as time passes, adolescents adjust to their biological impulses as their ego and superego change to allow for mature forms of sexual expression as well as their developing independence. However, sometimes these biological impulses may overwhelm the ego, leading to impulsiveness and a desire for continuous and immediate gratification. On the other hand, the ego may react to these impulses by denying them and becoming very rigid and defensive.

A more recent thinker in the psychoanalytic tradition, Peter Blos (1962, 1967, 1979), focused on two themes in his study of adolescence. First is the importance of the *de-idealization* of the parent as the adolescent-parent relationship develops

intellectualization A defense mechanism, often used by adolescents according to Anna Freud, in which people take a detached, abstract attitude toward an area of emotional difficulty.

asceticism A defense mechanism, often used by adolescents according to Anna Freud, in which people use excessive self-denial and pleasure-avoiding tactics to deal with emotionally difficult impulses.

into a more equal footing. A second theme is *individuation* as the adolescent continues the process of developing as a distinct individual.

Modern psychoanalytic literature focuses on the adolescent's striving to mature, describing adolescence as a period of advancement, regression, and reorganization in which the individual works through internal conflicts and problems with others (Blos, 1967; Clarkin, 1997). Adolescence is viewed as a turbulent period during which adolescents give up their childish dependence and attachment to parents and emerge as independent and unique individuals.

In sum, psychoanalytic thought emphasizes the importance of sexual awakening, turbulent parent-child relationships, and the need to give up childhood attachments and become a unique individual. Stress and conflict in family situations, which are viewed as natural and typical, lead to individuation and a modification of relationships with parents. The use of defense mechanisms, the importance of physical changes, and breaking away from parents are important concepts in understanding adolescents.

One difficulty with the Freudian conception of adolescence is the perpetual conflict that Freudians see as natural. Recent literature questions the extent of conflict within families and, most important, questions the inevitability and necessity of such conflict (Grotevant, 1998). Perhaps one reason psychoanalysts view adolescence as a time of continuous conflict is because they are clinicians dealing with teens in trouble, and they generalize the turmoil they see in these adolescents to all adolescents (Clarkin, 1997). Freudian theory is also difficult to test empirically, making research very difficult to conduct.

Erikson and Identity

Psychoanalytic theory emphasizes the turmoil caused by biological factors and places much less emphasis on the social areas of life (Viney, 1993). Many theorists sought to amend this, the most influential being Erik Erikson, who deemphasized the importance of biological factors and sexual motivation in favor of a search for a personal identity (Erikson, 1963, 1968). The unconscious becomes less important than the conscious ego.

Erikson argued that each individual proceeds through eight stages of development from cradle to grave. Each stage presents the individual with a crisis, and at each stage a particular personality component becomes the focus of development (see Table 2.3). The crisis arises from a combination of socialization demands from others and the person's attempt to respond to these challenges, influencing those around him (Waterman & Archer, 1990). If a particular crisis is handled well, the outcome is positive. If it is not handled well, the result is negative. Few people emerge from a particular stage with an entirely positive or negative outcome. A healthy balance must be struck between the two poles, although the outcome should tend toward the positive side of the scale. People can reexperience these crises during a later life period, but they usually take place at particular periods in one's life. The resolution of one stage lays the foundation for negotiating the next stage (Baltes, Lindenberger, & Staudinger, 1998).

Each of Erikson's descriptions of the psychosocial stages uses the term *versus*. However, it is better to think of the outcomes in terms of a continuum, with an individual's status lying somewhere between the two extremes. The psychosocial crisis of adolescence, for example, is *identity versus role confusion*. Forming a coherent identity is the basic theme of Erikson's writings on adolescence. Adolescents must tentatively answer such questions as, Who am I? Where do I belong? and What do I want to do with my life? An adolescent's success in forming an identity depends in part on the success the adolescent has coping with

Erik Erikson received his training directly from Anna Freud. Erikson made a unique contribution to the study of adolescence in emphasizing the importance of forming a unique and stable identity during this period of life.

Table 2.3

Erikson's Psychosocial Stages

Stage	Crisis	Resolution	Poor Resolution	Strength
Infancy	Basic trust vs. mistrust	Confidence in satisfaction of needs	Rage due to uncertainty of satisfaction	Hope
Early childhood	Autonomy vs. shame and doubt	Independence stemming from self-control	Estrangement due to being controlled	Willpower
Play age	Initiative vs. guilt	Acting on desires, urges, potentials	Conscience restrains pursuits	Purpose
School age	Industry vs. inferiority	Absorption in "tool world"	Skills and status inadequate	Competence
Adolescence	Identity vs. role confusion	Confidence in one's sameness seen by others	Previous identity developments fail	Fidelity
Young adulthood	Intimacy vs. isolation	Fusing identity with another	No close relationships	Love
Adulthood	Generativity vs. stagnation	Guiding the next generation	Arrest of ripening process	Care
Old age	Integrity vs. despair	Emotional integration	"Time is short"	Wisdom

Source: Allen (1994), p. 169.

the demands of the previous stages. For example, the psychosocial crisis of infancy involves basic trust versus mistrust. Infants should develop a feeling that they live among people who care, that their needs will be taken care of, and that the world is a safe and secure place. Basic mistrust reflects a more pessimistic view of the world as an unsatisfying, dangerous, insecure place. The psychosocial crisis of early childhood (toddlerhood) is autonomy (being someone on my own) versus shame and doubt. The outcome of this stage may affect the attainment of identity formation through the belief that one is capable of choosing one's identity rather than having it imposed (Waterman & Archer, 1990).

During adolescence, people investigate various alternatives for their personal and vocational futures and develop a sense of who they are and want to be. The adolescent with a solid, stable sense of identity formulates a satisfying plan and gains a sense of security. Adolescents who do not may develop role confusion and seem aimless and adrift. Those with a solid sense of identity are less susceptible to peer pressure, have higher levels of self-acceptance, are optimistic, and believe they are in control of their future, whereas those without a sense of identity can be described in the opposite manner (Hamachek, 1988).

In sum, Erikson's emphasis on identity is certainly his most important contribution to the study of adolescence—one so profound that for many individuals, *identity crisis* is a familiar term. Erikson also reminds us that the search for identity varies in different cultures and is bounded by the society in which the adolescent is developing. His theoretical treatment opened a new conceptual way of looking at adolescence that has led to much research.

Criticisms of Erikson's theory are in some ways similar to those of Freud's theory. It is difficult to test the theory. Some of Erikson's psychosocial crises are vague and general. In addition, Erikson argues that each stage has one major psychosocial crisis, but there is no reason to believe that this is the case.

Havighurst's Developmental Tasks

Whereas Erikson's psychosocial stages are broad conceptions (which is one criticism of his work), Robert Havighurst (1972) looked specifically at what tasks children and adolescents must successfully complete. Havighurst acknowledged the strong influence that Erikson had on his ideas. He believed that during each stage of life, people must deal with challenges, or **developmental tasks,** to feel positive about themselves and satisfied with their lives. Different developmental tasks arise at different times of life. Just as in Erikson's theory, according to

developmental tasks Challenges that arise at specific ages, the successful completion of which leads to positive outcomes.

Havighurst the outcomes of earlier tasks influence the way children and adolescents deal with later tasks. Successfully dealing with a task leads to happiness and social approval, whereas failure leads to unhappiness and difficulty with others. The eight major developmental tasks for adolescents follow:

- Achieving new relations with age mates of both genders.
- Achieving a masculine or feminine social role.
- Accepting one's physique and using the body effectively.
- Achieving emotional independence from parents and other adults.
- Preparing for marriage and family life.
- Preparing for an economic career.
- Acquiring a set of values and an ethical system as a guide to behavior and developing an ideology.
- Achieving socially responsible behavior.

In sum, Havighurst's developmental tasks show that it is possible to list age-related tasks that are somewhat more specific than Erikson's psychosocial crises. Individuals must successfully meet these tasks during adolescence. Critics, however, have pointed out that the tasks are rooted in a mainstream, middle-class, socially conservative philosophy. For example, not everyone wants to marry, and "preparing for marriage" may not be required for happiness. The definition of "socially responsible behavior" may be debated as well.

Cognitive Changes in Adolescence: Jean Piaget's Theory

Whereas Freud and Erikson were interested in personality development and Havighurst concentrated on listing specific tasks necessary to successfully negotiate adolescence, Jean Piaget's professional life was spent studying cognitive, or intellectual, development. Piaget ably demonstrated that children do not think like adults, and he outlined the qualitative differences among how children of different ages think. For Piaget (1970), development involves the change and reorganization in the way people deal with their environment.

Development is defined by four principal factors. *Maturation* refers to genetic factors influencing development; *social transmission* refers to formal learning; *experience* involves the person's unique and personal interactions with the environment, which Piaget believes is most important; and *equilibration* explains how people change their ideas and behavior. Adolescents seek a balance between what they know and what they are experiencing. When adolescents are faced with a situation that calls for a new and different analysis, they enter a stage of disequilibrium leading to a change in thinking and behavior. Consider an adolescent who believes he is good in science and wants to be a chemist. After doing well in a few early courses he has difficulty in chemistry, math, and physics, and he is not enjoying these subjects. He experiences a difference between what he knows (I'm good in science, and enjoy it) and what he is experiencing (I'm not as good as I thought in this area, and I'm not enjoying it). To resolve this discrepancy, he may reconsider his chosen career field or recommit himself to the same field, but with a greater understanding of the difficulty.

Piaget carefully described the process by which children develop their cognitive skills. The last and, according to Piaget, final stage of cognitive development, called the *stage of formal operations*, develops within adolescence. Adolescents develop the ability to understand and use abstractions, consider realities other than the one in which they are living, and use scientific reasoning. They become impressed by possibilities over reality. We will examine the stage of formal operations in depth in "Cognitive Development."

In sum, Piaget sees development in terms of changes in the way people deal with their environment. He emphasizes the qualitative differences between the thinking of adolescents and younger children. The fact that adolescents think differently leads to new ways of looking at problems and challenges. For example, adolescents who can deal with abstractions are now able to create their own moral and value system based upon their own ideas and principles and divorced from any one situation. Piaget's explanations have led to a significant amount of research.

Although Piaget's work is monumental, criticisms have arisen. For example, Piaget may have underestimated the importance of formal learning (what someone is taught). In addition, as we shall see in the chapter on adolescent cognitive development, some of Piaget's concepts are vaguely defined.

The Information-Processing Approach

Piaget's theory is not the only one discussing cognitive development. Some researchers emphasize the importance of how people bring in information and process it. These information-processing researchers emphasize the differences between adolescents and younger children (as well as older adults) in such areas as attention, memory, and problem solving, allowing these information-processing abilities to be seen in a developmental context. For example, adolescents process information much faster than younger children, giving them a great advantage. An adolescent who can process information faster can accomplish more, finish a task more quickly, and be ready for the next one.

Jean Piaget argued that adolescents become capable of understanding abstractions and using scientific reasoning.

Information-processing specialists look at each of these processes in depth, trying to understand just how individuals deal with the information that surrounds them in the environment. These theorists often use the computer as an analogy to the workings of the human mind, but this does not mean that they see human beings as computers or robots. The computer analogy helps explain how children and adolescents solve problems and use information. What we type into the computer (the input) is roughly similar to information we obtain from the environment through our senses. In a computer, some operations are performed on the information according to a program, and the information is encoded and stored in a way that is retrievable. Similarly, some processes must occur in the mind that enable the individual to attend to a particular stimulus, organize it, and remember it so it can be used in the future. The information that is retrieved and used by a computer if the proper command is given is the output. In human beings, the output could be some motor activity such as throwing a football, or it could be verbal, such as coming up with the answer to a math problem. Finally, an individual receives feedback, information indicating whether the movement or answer was effective. Human beings also have an upper-executive program that coordinates activities and guides purposeful behavior, which is similar to the title of a computer program. For example, an executive program in human beings titled *shooting a basketball* would entail many movements and adjustments.

In sum, information-processing theorists follow information through a system to learn how it is encoded, processed, and retrieved. They look at cognition on a very detailed level, investigating the processes of perception, attention, representation, memory, and retrieval. This approach allows psychologists to delve more deeply into the same phenomena that interested Piaget.

Information-processing theory is not without critics, however. For example, no one yet knows how far the computer analogy can be taken. In addition, psychologists do not know whether the step-by-step analysis of subprocesses needed to understand information processing is possible. Furthermore, this approach pays little attention to individual differences, which remains an important aspect of adolescent development (Cairns, 1998).

The Behavioral Approach: You Are What You Learn

The theories of Piaget, Freud, and Erikson, as well as information-processing theories, all deal with processes that lie within the mind. Some psychologists argue that behavior can be understood best without considering what is going on within the mind (Skinner, 1953, 1974). These psychologists, called **behaviorists,** emphasize the importance of studying observable behaviors instead of mental processes, and they argue that people act in a particular way because they have learned to do so. The most prominent behaviorist was B. F. Skinner.

Behaviorists believe that behavior is learned, mostly through **operant conditioning,** the process by which behavior is governed by its consequences. If the consequences of a behavior are pleasant, the behavior is more likely to recur; if not, the behavior is less likely to recur. Suppose a teenage boy would like to meet a girl in math class. He introduces himself and uses a line to begin a conversation, which fails. According to this theory, he would be less likely to try the same approach again; if it succeeded, he would be more likely to try it again.

Any event that increases the likelihood that a behavior that preceded it will recur is called a **reinforcer.** As children mature, the nature of the reinforcers changes. For instance, stickers and stars may be effective reinforcers for younger children, but they typically are not effective for adolescents. An ice cream cone may be effective for a younger child but not for an adolescent with 10 dollars in her pocket who can easily buy a sundae.

The sources of reinforcement also change. Parents are the most important reinforcers for young children, whose world is narrowly defined. As children become adolescents and proceed through the period, the evaluations of friends become very important, sometimes competing with those of parents, and, in some areas, mixed messages result. Friends may reinforce a teen for using slang or cursing, whereas parents may not approve of this communication style. As we will discuss in "Peers," friends and parents do not always reinforce adolescents for different behaviors. However, it is clear that there are many sources of reinforcement.

The theories of behaviorists, such as Skinner, differ from the theories we have so far investigated in three important ways (Crain, 2000). First, the other theories discuss internal events—that is, thinking, perception, and reasoning, processes that occur within the mind. Behaviorists argue that psychologists can understand and predict behavior when only overt behaviors—those behaviors

Peers are a major source of reinforcement during adolescence.

behaviorists Psychologists who focus on observable behavior and explain behavior in terms of the processes of learning, emphasizing the importance of the environment in determining behavior.

operant conditioning The learning process in which behavior is governed by its consequences.

reinforcer Any event that increases the likelihood that a behavior that preceded it will recur.

that we can see—are examined. Behaviorists certainly understand that people have ideas, feelings, and hunches, but they do not believe these phenomena cause behavior (Catania, 1998). These hunches have to come from experiences with the world, and psychologists should look at people's past experiences.

Second, behaviorists do not believe in the concept of stages, or periods when people organize their experiences in qualitatively different ways. Freud suggested five stages; Erikson, eight; and Piaget, four. Behaviorists argue that stages are not necessary to understand behavior and that the environment shapes behavior in a gradual, continuous fashion rather than a discontinuous fashion.

Third, and most important, is the source of change. Behaviorists see the source of change as external; a change in behavior occurs when reinforcers change. Psychologists who offer a more developmental model argue that changes are motivated from within. That idea does not mean that the social environment is unimportant. Rather, many of these theorists look at how people of different ages perceive the information from outside sources and act on it.

In sum, behaviorists remind us of the importance of learning. Behavioral theory is based on clearly defined principles and concepts. What we learn in childhood forms the basis of the behavioral repertoire, but reinforcement and punishment are ongoing processes and become much more complicated in adolescence.

Although few would question the importance of learning, notice that behaviorists do not refer to thought processes, memory, or any other intellectual processes; they seem to see adolescents as the sum total of reinforcers and punishers. Some critics believe that reference to mental events (thought processes) is necessary to best understand behavior, and without investigating these processes, behavioral theory yields only a partial understanding of behavior.

Social Learning Theory

People also learn by observing others; they do not have to be directly reinforced or punished to change their behavior. If a younger teen notices his brother staying out late and coming in after curfew with no consequences, we would expect him to be influenced by what he has seen. Adolescents are more altruistic if they observe people they respect who give or donate their time to worthy causes. The pioneer in understanding observation learning is Albert Bandura (1982, 1986).

Children and adolescents imitate the models they see around them. Parents, teachers, and older siblings serve as models, as do others who adolescents may admire, such as athletes and musicians. There is great concern about the behaviors modeled on television programs and in the movies—violence, for example—which may influence children and adolescents.

Sometimes adolescents imitate directly, and the source of their behavior is readily available. Teens who directly model their dress after a music star are obvious examples. Adolescents, though, also learn general ideas from watching others—for example, that particular behaviors are acceptable or unacceptable. Teenagers do not imitate everyone they see. Models who are regular associates or peers who are personally engaging or prestigious or who are seen as especially credible gain attention. Models who are successful, competent, and powerful are also effective.

Social learning theorists divide behavior into two different processes: learning and performance. Teens may learn something, either through direct reinforcement or through observing others. However, whether they exhibit the behavior (performance) depends partly on **self-efficacy**, the belief about what one can and cannot do in a particular situation. Judgments of self-efficacy, whether accurate or not, affect one's choice of activities (Bandura, 1986, 1994). Adolescents who believe a task is within their capabilities will attempt it, whereas they will avoid activities that they believe exceed their capabilities (Bandura, 1982).

Self-efficacy is a central concept of social learning theory. Self-efficacy affects just how much effort an adolescent will expend on a task. People with a high

Albert Bandura extensively studied observation learning and provided a unique social learning perspective.

self-efficacy The belief about what one can and cannot do in a particular situation.

PERSPECTIVE 1

ENCOURAGING A FRIEND

SETTING THE SCENE: Grace's friend Susan is a vivacious, talkative, confident individual, except in math. She is a good math student, but she is not planning to take any more mathematics past the sophomore year of high school. She tells you that she doesn't feel that she can do well in math, despite the fact that she has already done fairly well.

GRACE: *Susan tutors me in math, but she does not believe she is good in math. The same thing happens in art, where she draws beautifully but does not believe she can succeed. She seems to need encouragement, but I'm afraid that if I encourage her and she fails, she will be in a worse situation than before.*

SUSAN: *I just don't think I can do well in advanced math. Sure, I've done all right up to now, but when I compare myself with those math geniuses, well, I don't measure up.*

QUESTION: Should Grace encourage Susan to continue taking math? What can be done about Susan's lack of self-efficacy in areas where she has shown some ability?

degree of self-efficacy put more effort into a particular task than those who have a low degree of self-efficacy. Self-efficacy is dependent upon the task. A teen may have a high degree of self-efficacy in solving math problems, a low degree of self-efficacy concerning giving a speech in front of the class, and a moderate degree of self-efficacy in ability to perform well on the soccer field.

Self-efficacy judgments arise from past experiences, observations of others, verbal persuasion, and one's physiological state (Bandura, 1982). Past experience in similar situations is one key to success, raising one's sense of self-efficacy, whereas repeated failure may lower it. People are also affected by watching others succeed or fail. Sometimes they can be persuaded that they can or cannot do something, although raising unrealistic expectations through persuasion can undermine self-efficacy. People may also rely on information from their physiological state. A teen may interpret feelings of nervousness before doing something as a sign of uncertainty, and this may negatively affect self-efficacy (see Table 2.4). A teen's judgment of self-efficacy may be a key to understanding some behavioral choices. For example, research demonstrates that how much students study depends more on self-efficacy than on actual ability (Zimmerman, Bandura, & Martinez-Pons, 1992).

In sum, social learning theory is one of the more popular approaches today. It emphasizes the importance of the models that surround adolescents, an area of keen public interest. In addition, the concept of self-efficacy may hold a key for understanding why some adolescents try harder than others when faced with certain challenges. The main criticism of the theory is that it lacks a developmental basis; that is, there seems to be little difference in the process by which a teenager versus a younger child observes, interprets the information, and chooses to behave in a certain way.

Table 2.4

Self-Efficacy

Self-efficacy is the extent to which individuals believe they can successfully perform a behavior related to a particular task. It answers the question, Do you think you can do it? Self-efficacy is determined by four factors.

Determinant	Explanation	Expansion
Past experiences	Past successes and failures	If you have successfully performed the behavior earlier, you expect to be able to do so again. If you have failed at the same or a similar task, you have a lower sense of self-efficacy.
Models	Other people who have successfully performed the task	People see that others who are similar to themselves or have less skill than they do are successfully performing the behavior: "If they can do it, so can I!" People may also see others with greater skills failing and say to themselves, "If they couldn't do it, how can I?"
Encouragement	People who encourage others to do something	A teacher encourages a student by telling her that she can succeed. This may be useful if a person with the skills needs a little help, but convincing someone without the necessary skills is counterproductive.
Physiological feedback	Evaluation of how one feels when given a task	An individual who experiences excessive nervousness before giving a speech in class may interpret this feedback as indicating a lack of ability to perform the task.

Adolescents with a high degree of self-efficacy believe they can do something and are more likely to try.

The Ecological Approach

One objection to all these theoretical perspectives is that they do not take into account the whole context of the adolescent's world. They seem to view the individual almost in isolation from the total environment. *Ecological theory*, first proposed by Urie Bronfenbrenner (1979, 1986; Bronfenbrenner & Morris, 1998), suggests that people live their lives enmeshed in many different environments at the same time (see Figure 2.1). Bronfenbrenner uses the analogy of a set of Russian dolls, each inside the other. People both affect and are affected by these multiple layers of environment. Ecological theory systematically links these environments to one another. A number of different environmental systems operate simultaneously.

The *microsystem* consists of the immediate interactions of the teen and the environment. This face-to-face interaction may occur in the home or at school (Bronfenbrenner & Crouter, 1983). The microsystem includes where the teen lives, the people in the home, and the activities they do together. A younger child's microsystem is limited to just the home, family, school, or child-care services, but teens have more interactions with many more people outside the family, including a more extensive peer group.

The *mesosystem* involves the interrelationships among two or more settings in which the person actively participates. For example, the teen's mesosystem includes the relationship between the parents and the school and between parents and the teen's peer group. The entry of a teen into a new setting causes changes in other settings. For example, the teen's attendance in school may affect the pattern of activities and interactions occurring within the family (Bronfenbrenner & Crouter, 1983). Perhaps the teen is a member of a school team that requires the parents to change their schedules to transport the adolescent to and from the activity.

The *exosystem* involves settings in which the teen is not actively involved, at least at the present time, but that still affect the family and adolescent, such as a parent's place of work, a class attended by older or younger siblings, parents' networks of friends, and even the activity of the local school board. Sometimes, elements of the exosystem

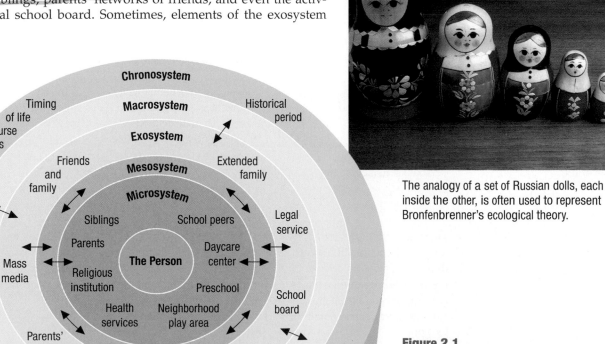

The analogy of a set of Russian dolls, each inside the other, is often used to represent Bronfenbrenner's ecological theory.

Figure 2.1

Bronfenbrenner's Ecological Theory of Development

Urie Bronfenbrenner views the individual as enmeshed in many layers of environment.

Source: Adapted from Kopp & Krakow (1982), Figure 12.1.

AT A GLANCE   2.2 PERSPECTIVES ON ADOLESCENCE

KEY POINT: Each theoretical perspective has a distinct message and approach that help psychologists better understand adolescence.

THEORY	BASIC PREMISES	STRENGTHS	WEAKNESSES
Freud's psychoanalytic theory, with additions by other theorists who followed him, views adolescence as a time in which biological drives lead to a search for relationships with people of the other gender and a desire to free oneself from emotional dependency on parents.	• Personality and later behavior are determined by early experience. • Motives arise from unconscious thoughts, drives, and memories. • Children develop through a series of stages called the *psychosexual stages*. The last stage, the genital stage (in which the mature sex drives arise), occurs during adolescence. • The ego may adopt a defense mechanism when overwhelmed by anxiety. • Peter Blos emphasized the de-idealization of parents and the striving for individuation.	• Psychoanalytic theory emphasizes the importance of sexual awakenings. • Freud focuses on the importance of giving up childhood ties and creating new, meaningful relationships. • The use of defense mechanisms is a valuable explanation for some behavior.	• The perception of adolescence as a time of continuous and inevitable conflict does not match recent research. • The theory is difficult to test.
Erikson's psychosocial theory views human development as occurring in eight stages, each of which has possible positive and negative consequences.	• People proceed through eight developmental stages from birth through old age. • The adolescent stage emphasizes the development of personal identity. • Cultural factors are important to development.	• Development is seen in terms of the life span. • The concept of identity is a cornerstone of our understanding of adolescence. • Emphasizing culture helps us understand adolescence in many groups.	• The theory is difficult to test. • The theory is too general. • The focus on one psychosocial crisis per stage is questionable.
Havighurst's developmental theory lists specific developmental tasks or challenges that must be met to negotiate each stage of life.	• Specific developmental tasks exist for children and adolescents. • Successful completion of developmental tasks results in personal satisfaction and growth.	• Developmental challenges in this theory are more specific than those mentioned in other approaches.	• Some tasks, such as preparing for marriage, may not be required for successful completion of adolescence. • The tasks may represent mainstream, middle-class values.
Piaget's theory of cognitive development is the most popular approach to understanding how adolescents reason differently from younger children.	• There are differences between how children and adolescents think. • Development is defined by maturation, social transmission, experience, and equilibration. • During the stage of formal operations adolescents can use abstractions, consider alternative realities, and use scientific reasoning.	• Piaget outlines the qualitative ways that adolescents' thinking differs from younger children's thinking. • The work is monumental in scope. • The theory has led to a significant amount of research.	• Piaget may have underestimated the importance of formal learning. • Some concepts are vaguely defined.

AT A GLANCE 2.2 PERSPECTIVES ON ADOLESCENCE (CONTINUED)

THEORY	BASIC PREMISES	STRENGTHS	WEAKNESSES
Information-processing theory emphasizes the basic processes underlying cognitive development, including attention, perception, representation, processing, and retrieval.	• The theory emphasizes the way people take in and process information. • Adolescents and younger children differ in attention, memory, and problem solving.	• The theory looks at cognitive processes such as attention and memory in great detail. • The theory offers comparison of how different age groups process information.	• The step-by-step analysis of subprocesses needed to explain information processing may not be possible. • The theory pays little attention to individual differences.
The *behavioral approach* views behavior as determined by what an individual learns in a particular environment.	• The theory studies observable behaviors. • Behavior is learned. • People develop gradually and continuously. • The source of change is external; that is, behavior changes as reinforcers in the environment change.	• The theory emphasizes the importance of learning. • The adolescent's environment is seen as more complicated than the child's. • The theory is clear and precise, with well-defined terms .	• The theory lacks attention to internal, cognitive processes such as thinking and memory. • The theory may yield only a partial picture of behavior.
Social learning theory postulates that people learn through observing others and that behavior is regulated by self-observation, during which people evaluate what they can and cannot do successfully.	• Adolescents learn by observing others. • People model themselves after individuals who are effective in getting things done. • Behavior is divided into learning and performance. • Self-efficacy, the belief about what one can and cannot do, is an important factor determining behavior.	• The theory emphasizes the importance of models that surround adolescents. • The concept of self-efficacy is important to understanding behavior.	• The theory lacks a developmental basis. The process of observation learning is not seen as differing among people of varying ages.
Bronfenbrenner's ecological theory contends that an individual's entire environment must be taken into consideration if his or her behavior is to be understood.	• Adolescents live their lives enmeshed in many layers of environment. • Layers of environment that seem removed from the adolescent, such as the parents' workplace and economic and political systems, may affect development. • Transitions bring about changes in roles, which change how people think, act, and are treated.	• The theory encourages a wider view of the context in which adolescents live. • Political and economic systems are important in the adolescent's environment. • The focus on transitions singles out important life changes as altering adolescents' roles.	• The theory is very complex, requiring an in-depth investigation into the many contexts of development. • It may not be practical to look at each level of the environment when conducting research.

directly affect the teen, as when the school board increases class sizes. The exosystem may also indirectly affect the teen by creating changes that affect the parents' lives; for example, a generous increase in parents' salaries may translate into greater opportunities for the adolescent to travel. The insecurity that a parent may experience at work may negatively affect parent-child interactions.

The *macrosystem* is composed of the ideology or belief system inherent in social institutions, including ethnic, cultural, and religious influences and existing economic and political systems. For example, people in the United States live under an economic and political system that differs from that of people living in other countries. These differing social customs, ideologies, and economic systems affect the social institutions of the country and, therefore, the adolescent. The availability of health care may influence whether a teen in need can receive psychological treatment. The laws of the state determine how adolescents who run afoul of the law will be treated. Changes in social structure may also affect adolescents. Both the increased mobility of families and the change in women's status influence the adolescent and the other systems. Within each society, a number of different microsystems, mesosystems, exosystems, and macrosystems operate, depending on social class, ethnicity, and religious grouping.

Finally, there is the chronosystem, which Bronfenbrenner (1989) describes as the dimension of time. The environment changes over time. Developmental changes are often triggered by life events or experiences, for example, the birth of a sibling or a severe illness that restricts functioning. Whatever the origin of these events, they alter the relationship between person and environment.

The time dimension can operate in two ways. First, certain events may occur at a specific time in life. You may be the oldest child, and whether your next sibling was born when you were 2, 3, 5, or 8 years of age may make a difference in how you react to the sibling, as well as in your continuing relationship with him or her. Second, events occur within a historical time frame. A female adolescent in the early 2000s is much more likely to believe that her future involves both employment and a family than a female adolescent in the 1950s.

Ecological theory emphasizes the importance of looking beyond the current environment and appreciating the relationships between systems. An adolescent's success in high school depends not only on the way the teen is taught but also on the relationship between the school and the home and the parents' attitude toward education. It also depends on the decisions made by others, such as state authorities, who never even interact with the adolescent.

Ecological theory also looks at the transitions that occur, such as entering middle school or entering the world of work. These transitions may alter social roles, which may influence how people are treated, how they act, how they feel, and how they think. For example, entering the world of work often means gaining independence and taking on the new responsibilities of a worker. Transitions also change the nature of the individual's relationship with a particular system. For example, the transition to middle school means that the middle school changes from an exosystem to a microsystem and a mesosystem, and moving to another country involves changing macrosystems.

In sum, as Bronfenbrenner's theory suggests, to truly understand adolescents, we must appreciate the entire context of their lives. Each individual's life is embedded in a series of multilevel contexts. The most immediate context is the family, but other contexts (such as the school, peer group, neighborhood, religious institution, and political system under which the adolescent lives) are important as well. The different facets of the environment affect one another. The functioning of an individual, then, is the product of interactions between the person and the many facets of the environment that continually emerge and change over time (Fisher & Lerner, 1994).

The contextualization of development is one of the most prominent theoretical changes influencing the study of adolescence, but it has been criticized as being very complicated. Certainly, taking the entire environment into account is beneficial, but consider how difficult it would be to consider all the environmental elements when conducting research. Therefore, researchers using ecological theory often focus on one aspect of the environment, be it the microsystem, mesosystem, exosystem, or macrosystem. Whether we can ever gain a total understanding of the individual in such a complex environment remains open to question.

Eclecticism

So which theory of adolescence is best? Which theory should we use? Actually, we will use all these theoretical approaches to better understand different aspects of adolescent behavior. This *eclectic* approach chooses the theory that is most useful for analyzing the behavior under analysis. For example, Piaget's ideas may be most interesting concerning cognitive development; Erikson's theory for understanding the search for identity; and the ecological approach, for understanding the total environment of the adolescent.

Theory guides research. Say a researcher wants to examine aggression. Adopting a behavioral perspective would lead to asking questions involving what reinforcers and punishments exist in the environment and the past experience of the adolescent. Adopting a social learning approach would lead to an analysis of the models available and the nature of the observation learning. Each of these questions can be researched by conducting studies that are specially designed to answer them. Theories also allow a researcher to interpret results and suggest further questions for research. *(For a review of this section, see At A Glance 2.2.)*

RESEARCH INTO ADOLESCENCE

The scientific study of adolescence is based upon the use of research methods and designs that have shown their effectiveness for generations. Consider the daunting task for someone who wants to discover just how much conflict really exists between parents and their adolescent children, what adolescents believe about smoking, or what effect sex education courses have on the sexual behavior of adolescents. The development of scientific methods of research allows researchers to use tried and true ways to find the answers to these and other questions. These methods allow others to *replicate*—that is, to duplicate— what has been done or to expand upon the results in an organized way. This means that the description of the study, how the participants were chosen, and the methods used must be precise enough to allow others to follow it exactly or alter it in some predetermined manner. Say you conducted research on the nature of adolescent-peer conformity in dress, and your participants were 14-year-olds. Others might be interested in looking at 16- or 18-year-olds or measuring conformity in other areas, such as conformity to antisocial behavior.

Research Designs

Researchers in adolescence often want to research change over time, such as changes in feelings of loneliness or in attitudes toward helping others. There are three major approaches to measuring change over time; each design has advantages and disadvantages.

Cross-Sectional Designs In a **cross-sectional design,** two or more groups of different-aged participants are compared on some measure, such as self-concept. For example, gifted female third, fifth, and eighth graders were questioned about their self-concepts using the Piers-Harris Self-Concept Scale, an eighty-item self-report questionnaire. Each item requires a yes/no answer, and scores range from 0 to 80 (1 point for each yes answer). The older girls were less positive about themselves than the younger girls (Klein & Zehms, 1996).

cross-sectional design   A research design in which people at different ages are studied to obtain information about changes in some variable.

This result raises a number of issues concerning the extent of the decline in self-concept and whether it is found in girls who are not academically gifted. Researchers using the cross-sectional design compare people of different ages on a particular variable. Participants of all age groups can be studied at about the same time. These studies provide a glimpse into differences in behavior or attitudes among groups of people of different ages.

The cross-sectional research design has definite strengths. It is relatively simple and economical with respect to time. Participants are seen once, and there is usually no need to keep contact with them, which would require a staff. In addition, there is no chance that practice effects will confound the results. For example, if you were following the same people over time to measure changes in problem-solving skills, you might administer a similar test at each testing session; any improvement could partially be due to practice and similarity of tests. This practice effect does not occur with cross-sectional designs.

The cross-sectional design also has its weaknesses. By its very nature, the cross-sectional design in this case requires an assumption that when the fifth-grade girls are eighth graders, they will answer the self-concept questions in the same way as the group of eighth graders did during our study. This assumption cannot be demonstrated easily and always remains a problem with cross-sectional designs. In addition, it is assumed that all three groups of girls are basically similar and can be directly compared. They may well differ on some unknown quality (Miller, 1998). Despite these weaknesses, however, cross-sectional studies are very valuable.

Longitudinal Designs   Another approach to measuring change over time is to follow the same group of participants for a specified time, periodically evaluating them. Using this **longitudinal design,** researchers can readily see the stability or change in a particular quality over a period of time. For example, a number of studies have followed boys with attention-deficit/hyperactivity disorder (ADHD) from childhood to adolescence and from adolescence to adulthood to discover to what extent the impulsiveness, hyperactivity, and other problems associated with this disorder change or remain the same (Mannuzza et al., 1991). These studies find that some children with ADHD no longer fit the diagnostic category in adolescence. For those who do, some reduction in symptoms occurs, although the individuals may continue to experience adjustment problems, especially if they had significant conduct problems in childhood.

Longitudinal studies have a number of strengths. Because they follow the same group of children or adolescents, it is possible to evaluate changes in a particular aspect of development, such as attitudes toward parents or anxiety over interpersonal relationships, over whatever period of time interests the researchers. Some longitudinal studies go on for many years, whereas others test participants over a briefer period of time, for example, a year. Because longitudinal studies measure the *same* participants over time, the question of whether the groups being compared are equivalent becomes moot. In a longitudinal study, we do not have to question whether a group of 12-year-olds is similar to a different group of 18-year-olds, because those 12-year-olds actually became those 18-year-olds.

Longitudinal designs also have their weaknesses. A researcher may begin with 100 young adolescents as participants but, when ready to test them again years later, may find only 45 participants willing to continue the study. *Attrition*—that is, dropping out of the study—can be a significant problem. In studies of youth with ADHD, for example, as many as 50 percent of the participants drop out, because adolescents and young adults tend to move around a great deal and cannot be contacted easily. It is difficult to determine whether those who do not return for later testing are similar to those who do return. In addition, it takes a considerable amount of work, time, and money to keep contact with participants in longitudinal studies. Finally, because participants may be taking a similar test a number of times, they may improve simply due to practice. One way to remedy this problem is to use different forms of the same test,

longitudinal design   A research design in which participants are followed over an extended period to note developmental changes in some variable.

for example, using different numbers on mathematics tests. However, developing alternate forms is often very difficult.

Sequential Designs   Sometimes, researchers use more complex **sequential designs,** which combine cross-sectional and longitudinal designs. For example, a researcher may begin with groups of 13- and 16-year-olds, comparing them on their views of religion in a cross-sectional manner. After 2 years, the researcher may compare the groups again, but in two ways. Now the original groups of 13-year-olds and 16-year-olds are 15 and 18 years old, respectively. The researcher may compare these groups longitudinally, for instance, comparing the same group of children at 13 years old and then 2 years later, at 15 years of age, and comparing the responses of the group of 16-year-olds who are now 18 years old. The researcher may also compare these participants again cross-sectionally, comparing the first group, who are now 15-year-olds, to the second group, who are now 18-year-olds. Figure 2.2 graphically displays all three research designs.

Sequential designs have the advantage of flexibility, allowing a researcher to look at changes both cross-sectionally and longitudinally. However, the design is very complicated, and one group may have a much greater dropout rate than the others. The design also requires a great deal of time and has the same practicality disadvantages as the longitudinal approach.

Research studies using any of these designs must be evaluated in terms of the time period they are investigating. A cross-sectional study of the attitudes toward work of 15-, 17-, and 19-year-olds conducted in 1985 may be interesting,

Figure 2.2
Research Designs
Researchers may use cross-sectional studies in which participants of different ages are compared at the same time; longitudinal studies in which data is gathered from the same group of participants over a period of time; or sequential studies that combine elements of cross-sectional and longitudinal studies.

Cross-sectional studies: Participants of various ages are compared at the same time.

Longitudinal studies: Data is gathered from the same participants over a period of time.

Sequential studies: A sequential design combines elements of cross-sectional and longitudinal designs.

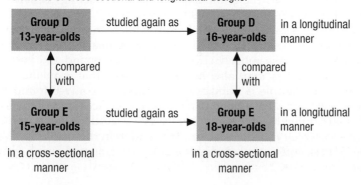

sequential designs   Research designs that combine elements of both cross-sectional and longitudinal research designs.

but is time bound. Longitudinal and sequential studies are also bound by time, because what may be true at the time the study was conducted may or may not be true today. A longitudinal study of alcohol consumption in the 1980s, for example, cannot possibly take into consideration the many ensuing legal and societal changes, including the rise in the legal drinking age from 18 to 21 years.

Research Methods and Data Collection

Psychologists have formulated a number of different methods that structure their research and data collection. Each of these methods has both strengths and limitations.

Observation   Observation is a common method of gathering information. For example, researchers may observe adolescent mothers to determine the nature of their interactions with their infants (Higginson, 1998) or observe adolescents with disabilities to note how they deal with their environment (Zacijek-Farber, 1998).

Although observation seems simple enough, it poses complex problems. First, the researcher cannot observe everything and must define exactly what behavior to observe. Two researchers may define a concept differently. For instance, how would you define *aggression?* Some might simply define it in terms of pushing, shoving, and hitting, whereas others might also include yelling and threatening. If two observers differed in their definitions of *aggression,* the observer with the broader definition would observe a great deal more aggression than the observer with a narrower definition. The results of research studies using different definitions may not be directly comparable. Researchers must use an **operational definition**—that is, a definition presenting the behavior under study in terms of observable operations or characteristics that can be measured. The use of operational definitions allows all observers to measure the behavior in question in the same manner. For example, a researcher may define *intelligence* in terms of an adolescent's score on a particular standardized intelligence test.

Second, the very presence of someone watching may influence participants to act differently. Some participants may try to present themselves in their best light, whereas others may do the opposite. Observers may try to solve this problem by being as unobtrusive as possible or by making repeated observations, hoping the adolescents will get used to their presence. Finally, observation can be useful if it is done systematically and objectively, but it cannot tell us anything about cause and effect.

The Case Study   A method that allows a researcher to gather data on one individual rather than a group is the **case study** approach. The exact methods researchers use to gather data may differ. A researcher may observe the individual, talk to others who know the person, or speak with the individual. For instance, consider the case study of an 18-year-old rape victim in China. The victim related the experience, described how she felt years later, and talked about its influence on her during a relationship years later with a married man. The researcher explored the crime and its resulting feelings in terms of the society and culture (Gil & Anderson, 1999).

Case studies allow a researcher on adolescence to concentrate on one individual, whereas most other research studies deal with groups of adolescents. This allows a researcher to more fully understand an individual's experience. Case studies may also point out factors that may then be tested using groups. For example, a number of case study narratives found that many alcoholic teens have an alcoholic parent; have easy access to both alcohol and other drugs; and often have mothers who suffer from depression or other adjustment problems, which causes a feeling of alienation in their children (Vaughn & Long, 1999). These interesting findings can be investigated using groups of adolescents.

operational definition   A definition that describes a behavior or a concept in a way that can be measured.

case study   A method of research in which one person's progress is followed for a period of time.

Case studies, though, are by their very nature time-consuming, as a psychologist must question, observe, and/or test one participant at a time. In addition, one cannot generalize from a case study or even a few case studies very easily. The teenager under study may not be typical of other teens in the same situation. For example, if you were conducting a case study of a teenage alcoholic, it would be difficult to determine whether her experience was similar to that of other teenage alcoholics. Case studies can be very useful, adding a dimension to understanding teenagers' experiences, as long as people recognize their limitations.

Questionnaires and Surveys The **survey** approach, which uses questionnaires or interviews, is especially useful when trying to obtain a great deal of data about many adolescents. The approach would be useful for determining, for example, adolescents' attitudes toward religion or their parents' rules. You would ask many adolescents to fill out a questionnaire and perhaps then break the data down by age, gender, socioeconomic status, and race/ethnicity. A survey on cigarette advertising was conducted among 10- to 14-year-olds in a mostly low- to middle-income Latino area of Brooklyn, New York. Relatively few students in this age group smoke (research shows that smoking increases significantly throughout junior high school and, especially, in high school). The students were asked questions about their major reasons for beginning to smoke, their major sources of information, and cigarette advertising. They were also asked if their parents smoked and whether their parents had given them advice not to smoke (Sun et al., 1998). The survey was very specific, as it included only students attending an urban junior high school. Could the researchers conclude that their findings are typical nationally or even statewide? The answer is no, and these researchers, indeed, made that clear. Students who smoked cited curiosity and imitating peers as major reasons for smoking, and most preferred a brand that was highly promoted in ads. Most said that their parents were the most significant source of information and urged them not to smoke.

At what age do you think adolescents should be allowed to drink alcohol? Research using questionnaires often can answer questions concerning the attitudes, beliefs, and behavioral practices of adolescents.

There are times, however, when a researcher may want to extend findings to a much larger group. Say you wanted to find out how adults perceive teens today. You could randomly select adults nationally and ask them to fill out questionnaires or answer an interviewer's questions. That is exactly what was done in a survey of adults and young people conducted by the nonprofit agency Public Agenda (1997). Two thousand telephone interviews with adults and six hundred interviews with teens were conducted using a random sample of U.S. households. Each household had an equal chance of being contacted, even those with unlisted numbers. Some of the results can be found in Table 1.3.

One can extend the findings of a survey only if the *sample* (the people interviewed) accurately reflects the *population* (the larger group to which you want to extend your findings). The extent to which the sample is representative of the population determines whether such a generalization is appropriate.

Questionnaires and interviews can be very useful in gathering a great deal of data on a group of people. They often accurately measure people's opinions or the frequency with which people behave in a particular way. Results of surveys can often be used to change policy. For example, if the students in a particular school believe that race relations is a major problem that is not being addressed, it might turn the school's attention to this problem.

Questionnaires have their limitations. Obviously, some people may not tell the truth even though the questionnaires are anonymous. Second, the wording

survey A method of study in which data are collected from a number of people through written questionnaires or oral interviews.

of the questions must be fair and impartial. For example, if you are studying methods of punishment, using the terms *spank* or *beat* or the phrase *physical methods of punishment* may yield different results. Most important, though, is the previously mentioned problem of sampling. If a researcher wants to generalize from sample to population, the sample must be representative (that is, reflect the nature of the population).

The Use of Correlations   What factors relate to high or low achievement in high school? Is watching televised aggression related to violence in adolescence? Some research studies are conducted with the goal of finding a relationship between two variables but do not attempt to determine cause and effect. Consider a researcher who has a sample of sixth- through tenth-grade students and measures how much violent television the adolescents watch and then collects a measure of aggression for the same sample. What relationship would you expect to find between watching violence and showing aggression? Psychologists use the term **correlation** to describe the statistical relationship between two variables (Ray, 1997). A *positive correlation* occurs when high scores on one variable are related to high scores on another variable and low scores on one variable are related to low scores on another variable. In other words, as television viewing of violence increased, so would aggression. In contrast, a *negative correlation* or *inverse correlation* means that high scores on one variable are related to low scores on the other, or low scores on the first variable are related to high scores on the second.

Correlations allow for prediction. For example, if a positive correlation is found between watching violent television and aggression, we could predict that people who watch more violent programming would be more aggressive. However, the ability to predict depends on the strength of the correlation. A perfect positive correlation is 1.00, no correlation at all is signified by 0, and a perfect inverse correlation is −1.00. When the hours of viewing televised violence were measured along with aggressive behavior, a positive correlation in the range of .2 to .3 was found (McLeod, Atkin, & Chaffee, 1972). This is a modest correlation, meaning that although there is a relationship between watching violence and later behaving aggressively, many children do not behave aggressively after watching violence. Television viewing is one factor, but other factors may be involved, such as background, being angry even before viewing the violence, and inhibitions against violence.

Studies that use correlations are often misinterpreted; indeed, this misinterpretation is one of many mistakes made when people read studies in psychology (see "Focus: Mistakes, Misunderstandings, and Miscalculations"). Correlations tell us only whether there is a relationship, the direction of that relationship, and the strength of the relationship. Notice that in the study of television viewing and aggression, no attempt was made to control the amount of television viewing, that is, to restrict viewing for some participants or encourage it for others. The correlation obtained does not tell us anything about cause and effect. We cannot tell from this study whether television viewing caused aggression, because it is possible that more aggressive adolescents simply choose to watch more aggressive programming. In addition, some other factor—perhaps parental models or child-rearing methods—may underlie both watching aggressive television and violent behavior.

Experimental Research   A researcher who wants to make definite causal inferences must use an **experimental study.** Such studies emphasize *control.* Basically, all factors are held constant except for the variable or variables that the researcher chooses to study. The variable that is manipulated is called the **independent variable,** and the variable that will serve as the outcome measure is called the **dependent variable.** For example, what is the effect of seeing a video of a model smoking or not smoking a cigarette on adolescent perceptions of personality characteristics? The independent variable would be whether the model smoked in the video, and the dependent variables would be ratings of

correlation   A term denoting the statistical relationship between two variables.

experimental study   A research strategy using controls that allows the researcher to discover cause-and-effect relationships.

independent variable   The factor in a study that will be manipulated by the researcher.

dependent variable   The factor in a study that will be measured by the researcher.

Table 2.5

Adolescents View Smokers and Nonsmokers

Adolescents in the experimental group viewed a video segment with the female model smoking, whereas the control group viewed the same video segment with the same female model not smoking. Predict how the experimental and control groups would differ on the following qualities.

The model who smokes will be seen as more _____.

_____ A. outgoing

_____ B. certain of herself in a crowd

_____ C. popular

_____ D. sophisticated

_____ E. intimidated by other people

_____ F. admired by other teens

_____ G. attractive

_____ H. manipulated by other people

_____ I. emotional after breaking up with her boyfriend

Source: Adapted from Jones & Carroll (1998).

---

various personality characteristics, such as dependence, extroversion, or responsibility.

The participants must be randomly assigned to either the experimental group or the control group. Random assignment ensures that each participant has the same opportunity to be a member of the experimental group and control group and makes the experimental and control groups as similar as possible. If participants were allowed to choose whether they wanted to be in the experimental or control group, the groups would not be similar at the beginning of the study. The researchers then expose the experimental group to the treatment, but not the control group, and measure the differences between the groups.

In a study conducted by Brett Jones and Marie Carroll (1998), members of a group of 17- to 24-year-old undergraduates were first given a general health questionnaire and then randomly divided into an experimental and a control group. Both groups were shown the same video of an attractive 19-year-old female student talking on the telephone, receiving a male visitor, conversing with him, and then getting a phone call. The experimental group saw the young woman smoking during the last part of the video, whereas the control group saw a nonsmoking model. After viewing the 10-minute video, both groups were asked questions about the young woman in the video. Table 2.5 lists the social characteristics tested. Check off the characteristics on which you believe the experimental and control group would differ.

The experimental group saw the smoker as significantly more outgoing, more sophisticated, less easy to manipulate, and less emotionally upset if she were to break up with her boyfriend. No significant differences between the groups were found on the model's characteristics of being certain about herself, being intimidated by others, being admired or attractive, or being popular. Young females associate smoking with greater freedom and sophistication, characteristics emphasized in many smoking ads.

Quasi-Experimental Methods Often, perfectly designed experimental studies cannot be conducted. In such cases **quasi-experimental studies** may be used (Ray, 1997). These studies do not involve random assignment of participants to conditions but rather compare groups that already exist or measure

quasi-experimental study A research design used when sufficient control over the variables under study is lacking. Because of the lack of control, definitive statements about cause and effect cannot be made.

Every day, we see research results being applied to our daily lives. Manufacturers make claims for products they sell in stores or advertise on television. Research results may be discussed on popular talk shows. Rarely are these claims subjected to critical scrutiny. Even newspapers that report scientific accomplishments rarely give enough information to determine how research was conducted and who served as participants in studies. The eight questions that follow can help you ask the proper questions and not fall into the trap of mistake, misunderstanding, and miscalculation in assessing research results.

1. Who Participated in the Study?

One area to look at when assessing a researcher's findings is who participated in the study. A study of how college students see their future is interesting, but before we can generalize to all adolescents, we must get representative feedback from the almost half of all adolescents who do not go on to college immediately upon high school graduation. In a study of overweight individuals who are following a particular diet, we might ask ourselves whether these individuals were male or female and how overweight they were.

2. Whose Adolescence Is It?

If you just read books about life in the 20th century, you might believe that everyone in the 1960s marched for causes, and everyone in the 1980s was selfish. It is more interesting to discuss and investigate college students involved in the civil rights movement than to look at students who did not participate in civil rights protests. One of the problems of discussing adolescence is to choose whose adolescence you wish to examine. The experience of a white, middle-class adolescent attending college will differ greatly from the adolescence of a Latino female growing up in poverty who does not attend college.

3. How Were the Treatment and Control Groups Created?

Your school offers a special three-session program on test taking and studying. You read in the school newspaper that students who took the program did better on their final exams than a group of students who did not take it. The person offering the program states that this is "proof" that it works. It sounds great, but is the claim accurate?

The program may or may not have helped. We don't have an answer, at least from this study. **Selection bias** operated in this study; that is, the initial groups were not equivalent (Miller, 1998). The students who volunteered for the training may have been more motivated or more dissatisfied with their grades than the control group subjects. Although the results of the study are interesting and suggestive, they do not lead to the conclusion that the staffer made.

The best way to solve the problem of selection bias is to first ask for volunteers and then randomly assign the volunteers to the treatment and control groups. That way, the chances are much greater that both groups will be equivalent when the study starts.

4. What Other Influences Are Operating?

What if you truly believed that attending a three-session program would improve your test-taking skills? Could this belief have influenced how well you did on your exam, independent of the value of the program? The idea that one's expectations can influence one's behavior is known as the **self-fulfilling prophecy.** Perhaps the students who attended the sessions truly believed they would do better on their exams. In that case, they may have acted differently—studied more, paid more attention to lectures, or simply possessed more confidence when they took their exams.

The researcher might consider giving the members of the control group something to do as well so that they, too,

selection bias The assignment of initially nonequivalent participants to the groups being compared.

self-fulfilling prophecy The concept that a person's expectations concerning some event affect the probability of the event's occurrence.

changes that occur within a single group of people before and after some event transpired or some treatment was administered (Leary, 1995). No control group is used here, sometimes because one simply may not be available. The interpretation of quasi-experimental studies is sometimes difficult. For instance, perhaps a school finds that it has a definite drug problem through conducting a series of questionnaires, and it decides to begin an extensive drug education program. At the end of the term, a significant reduction in drug use occurs. Does this mean that the decline was due to the program, or might it have happened anyway? To find out, perhaps we could compare the drug use rates with those of another school with a similar student population. We might also compare the rates of drug use with surveys conducted at the school in earlier years. Although quasi-experimental studies are not the equal of well-designed randomized controlled experimental studies, they can offer some evidence about the success or failure of a program.

expect to do better. At times, it is not just expectations but also the feeling that participants are being treated specially that may lead to a change in behavior. Only by equalizing expectations and the feeling of being treated specially can we be certain that the nature of the program caused the improvement.

5. How Did the Experimenter Define the Terms?

Why might two researchers studying the same thing disagree on their findings? One reason is that researchers might define their terms differently. Consider the researcher investigating couple violence. How should *couple violence* be defined? Should it be considered only as physical violence (slapping or pushing) or as both physical and emotional violence (threatening, derogatory comments, or screaming)? Obviously, the way researchers define their terms will influence the results.

6. Where Did You Read About It?

People often do not remember where they read or heard something. Over time, people accord information received from less-than-expert sources greater credibility than it is worth. Social psychologists sometimes refer to this as the **sleeper effect**—the delayed increase in the pervasive impact of a less-than-credible source (Brehm & Kassin, 1996). The sleeper effect reliably occurs when the source of material is not seen until after a message has been read. Imagine that as you are skimming through a magazine, you see an article about the influence of rap music on adolescents. If you notice that the author is someone with an obvious bias against rap music, you may continue to skim the article but take the author's known bias into consideration. However, what if you first read the article and then notice the author? You probably read it with a more open mind, and the information has a better chance of staying with you.

7. Was That a Correlation?

What if a study finds that adolescents who listen to heavy metal music are more likely to engage in reckless behavior (Arnett, 1991b)? This finding does not mean that listening to heavy metal *causes* the reckless behavior. Other factors may explain the relationship. For example, people who take risks and are reckless may be more likely to listen to heavy metal music. Or a different factor—perhaps being raised in a particular home situation—may underlie the likelihood of both listening to heavy metal and being reckless. There are many possibilities, but the important point is that the correlation does not offer evidence of cause and effect.

8. What About My Own Experience or That of Others?

Personal experience is valuable. It is one way of knowing. The problem is that people too often generalize from their own experiences. They may reason, "Because it happened to me, then it must be true for everyone," or "My experience is the typical experience." A teenager may have had a poor experience in a particular class and believe that everyone has had that experience. Often, such generalizations are validated by the bias of paying attention to others who have had the same experience and dismissing those who have had different experiences. We rarely realize that our experiences may be atypical or at least not as widely shared as we believe.

The interpretation of research can involve many other problems as well, but this brief sketch should encourage you to ask questions about how research was conducted. In a world now filled with information, this skill helps people become more educated consumers of research and information, as well as less likely to fall into the trap of mistake, misunderstanding, and miscalculation.

Research in Other Cultures and Subcultures

Conducting any research is difficult, but performing research in other societies or among subcultures within one's own society presents unique challenges. Such research is important, however, if we are to extend our understanding of the adolescent experience past our own borders or to individuals in minority groups. Some researchers even argue that unless we look at other cultures and subcultures, a serious, systematic attempt to understand human behavior and development is not possible, perhaps because our own cultural biases get in the way (Heron & Kroeger, 1981).

Cross-cultural studies and studies conducted using participants from various subcultures help us extend our theoretical approaches. For example, are the developmental tasks described by Havighurst the same or different in various cultures? Cross-cultural studies also widen our perspective, increase under-

sleeper effect A delayed increase in the persuasive impact of a noncredible source.

Research on children and adolescents in other cultures allows psychologists to more fully understand the nature of cultural influence on development and behavior, often widening our horizons and understanding of childhood and adolescence.

standing among people, and possibly reduce prejudice. We sometimes think that the way things are done in our homes and communities is the only way possible, and cross-cultural research can show different ways problems are handled.

Cross-cultural research can also present problems. For example, devising measuring instruments that can be used across cultures is difficult, as is accurate translation, for it is not always easy to translate one language exactly into another, with its connotations and expressions. When research participants are members of minority groups, trusting the researcher may become an important concern. In addition, a concept in one culture or subculture may have a different meaning in another. For example, achievement in dominant Western culture is an individualistic concept, whereas in other cultures and in some Western subcultures it is a group ideal. Despite problems arising from cross-cultural research, it makes a valuable contribution to understanding the adolescent experience all over the world.

Reviewing the Research: The Internet

Prior to conducting their studies, researchers must find out what is already known about their area of interest. Such a review of the literature allows researchers to verify that their proposed study is based on solid research. It also allows them to make *hypotheses,* or educated guesses, about what may occur in the study. Sometimes researchers conduct extensive reviews of the research, for example, looking at how adolescents spend their time in work and leisure across the world (Larson & Verma, 1999). Students also review research as they write papers on particular subjects.

Research reviews are much easier today because of the existence of databases and abstract services. Internet-based material is also popular. However, there are many misconceptions about research using the Internet. First, many people believe that if something is on the Internet, it is true. That, quite simply, is not the case. Just about anyone can place something on the Internet, and it may be picked up by a search engine. In contrast, a journal article typically is first subjected to a peer review, in which other psychologists or educators critique the article before the author revises it (Rothenberg, 1998). Second, people believe that anything on the Internet is recent. Internet-based material may give the date of its posting but often may not indicate when it was first written. Third, many students believe that just about everything of value can be found readily on the Internet. This is also not true. Most journals and books are not found on the Internet. Finally, material on the Internet is often disjointed and fragmentary and

AT A GLANCE   **2.3** RESEARCH INTO ADOLESCENCE

KEY POINT: Psychologists use a number of different research designs and methods to structure their scientific research.

RESEARCH DESIGN	DESCRIPTION	STRENGTHS	LIMITATIONS
Cross-sectional	Groups of people of different ages are compared on some measure.	Is relatively simple and economical. No problem with practice effects, because tests are given only once.	The assumption that the groups being compared are similar is a problem.
Longitudinal	The same group of participants is followed for a time.	Is good for evaluating changes over time. Because only one group is used, the problem of comparing participants in different groups is not present.	Participants dropping out may be a concern. It is difficult to keep in touch with participants.
Sequential	Longitudinal and cross-sectional designs are combined.	Can look at change from both cross-sectional and longitudinal viewpoints.	The design is complicated. One group may have a much greater dropout rate than another.

RESEARCH METHOD			
Observation	Participants are observed in particular context.	Systematic and objective observation may yield important information.	Participants may act differently than they otherwise would because they are being observed. The researcher must carefully define the behavior being observed.
Case study	One individual is questioned or observed.	Emphasizes the experience of one person, allowing for great detail.	The researcher cannot easily generalize the results to larger groups of people.
Survey and questionnaire	Participants are interviewed or asked to fill out a questionnaire.	Allows collection of data on many people in a relatively short time.	Some samples are not representative of populations. Wording may be biased.
Use of correlations	Researcher determines statistical relationships between two variables.	Allows for prediction.	Studies designed to find the relationship of one variable to another do not allow for explanation of cause and effect.
Experimental study	Researcher randomly assigns participants to experimental or treatment group(s) and manipulates independent variable so that it is the only difference between the two groups.	Allows for cause-and-effect explanations of variables in an experiment.	The study is difficult to design due to the need for random assignment of participants to experimental and control groups.
Quasi-experimental study	A method used when using adequate controls is impossible. For example, a researcher may not be able to randomly assign participants to different groups.	Is sometimes necessary when sufficient control over the variables under study is lacking.	Problems in interpretation arise. These studies do not allow definitive statements about cause and effect.

may not offer important information, such as how a particular study was conducted or even who the authors were.

The Internet can be a convenient source of information, of course, and more will be said about it in "The Media." Yet using the Internet exclusively may lead to a partial coverage of material that may or may not be accurate, complete, or well documented. It is important to keep these factors in mind when looking at research published on the Internet.

A further concern is research conducted over the Internet, which raises questions of safety and privacy. Any personal information, such as a Social Security number, given over the Internet may go to unscrupulous people. In addition, most studies conducted on university campuses have to be approved by institutional review boards to ensure that they meet ethical requirements. Surveys or other research conducted over the Internet, in contrast, offer participants no real protections. *(For a review of this section, see At A Glance 2.3.)*

ETHICAL STANDARDS AND DILEMMAS

Researchers have much to consider as they design their experiments. Each research design and method has its strengths and limitations. Researchers must also consider a number of ethical problems and have developed research standards that ensure the participants' safety from physical and psychological harm and spell out the participants' rights, such as the right to withdraw from the study. Researchers have a responsibility to pursue important research goals, but they also have the responsibility to protect the participants in their studies.

Many professional groups, as well as the U.S. government, have specific rules concerning the treatment of participants in research studies. The American Psychological Association and the Society for Research in Child Development have published extensive standards for the ethical treatment of participants in research. They are similar in most respects. In addition, institutional boards of review at most universities independently review proposed plans for conducting research before any study is performed. These review boards also publish their own sets of ethical guidelines, which follow closely the federal and professional sources.

One cardinal rule is that participants must not be harmed by their involvement in the research. In addition, the researcher must obtain the informed consent of all participants. The researcher must tell participants of their rights to withdraw from the research and to refuse to answer any questions they choose. Participants have the right to confidentiality and to be told of the results of the research. Unfortunately, ethical dilemmas still arise, and well-meaning people can disagree on whether some aspect of a research study is ethical. Dilemmas often emerge in the areas of informed consent, deception, and confidentiality.

Informed Consent

Participation in a research study must be voluntary, and researchers must obtain informed consent for each participant. Notice that the requirement states not just *consent* but *informed consent*. Researchers must give participants enough information to understand the nature of the experiment and make a reasoned decision about participating (Leary, 1995). According to the American Psychological Association's ethical standards (1992), the language must be nontechnical and understandable, and potential participants must understand that they are free to participate, decline, or withdraw. They must be informed of any significant factors that may influence their decision to participate, such as risks, possible discomfort, or any limitations on confidentiality. Researchers need not tell the participant their hypotheses (what they think the study may find), as this would bias the participant's behavior and is not needed by the potential participants to determine whether they wish to volunteer for the study.

Potential participants who are minors (under 18 years old) require the permission of their parent or guardian to participate in research studies (King & Churchill, 2000). Researchers must also enlist the voluntary cooperation of older children and adolescents (6 to 17 years old), in addition to obtaining parental permission.

Institutional Review Boards may waive the requirement for informed consents, either because the research involves minimal risks or obtaining the permission is impossible. For example, counting the number of teenagers using a park or observing whether more teenage boys or girls order a salad in the college cafeteria does not require permission. However, if people are observed under circumstances in which they would expect privacy, permission is necessary (Leary, 1995).

The need for parental approval when dealing with teenagers can be problematic. Consider a researcher who wants to conduct a study on the sexual behavior of sophomores in high school and is fully willing to discuss what types of questions will be asked, guarantee confidentiality, and tell participants that they do not have to answer any particular question that they find objectionable. Some parents refuse permission, arguing that they do not want their adolescent children (16-year-olds) to participate in the study. Because these teens are minors, the school requires parental notification and approval, even if the teenagers are willing to participate. Most parents, though, simply don't return the forms—a common problem. In one school in which a survey on drinking and drug use was being conducted, only 17 of 100 parents returned the forms, even though there was no evidence that the parents not returning the forms objected to the study (Lane, 1995).

Some researchers claim that teenagers have the ability to decide for themselves whether to participate in a research study, especially a study that uses anonymous questionnaires. After all, important research cannot be conducted when researchers face willing teenagers but wary parents. They point to the fact that under certain circumstances, a young teenager can give consent to medical treatment (for example, if he or she is chronically ill and knows a great deal about the condition) and may elect to have an abortion without parental notification in some states. These researchers argue that *passive parental consent* (that is, adolescents can participate if they want to as long as their parents do not actively oppose participation) rather than *active parental consent* (that is, the parent must sign the consent form) should be sufficient at times.

Almost all studies require parental permission, but there are some exceptions. For example, some Institutional Review Boards may allow passive consent for some studies involving an evaluation of a curriculum modification or questionnaires on nonsensitive topics (University of Texas, n.d.). At times Institutional Review Boards may even waive requirements for parental consent for research on sensitive topics where parental involvement would not be in the best interest of the child, for example, neglected or abused children. When a decision is made to waive parental consent, special safeguards must be in place to protect the child's rights and interests. Another possible exception is conducting research on the effects of abortion. The teen who has had an abortion may not have informed her parents of her actions, and just seeking such parental consent might place the participant at risk.

Another significant problem with informed consent is how much information the potential participant requires to make a reasoned decision. For example, telling an adolescent that he would be observed to see how much he helps others might significantly affect his behavior. Omitting information that may not be vital to the decision to participate in the study, a practice called *incomplete disclosure,* may in a strict sense be seen as violating the rule of informed consent. However, incomplete disclosure or, as we will soon see, actual deception may be necessary if the topic is important (a subjective criterion) and there is no other way to gather the information. The researcher must convince an independent review board that incomplete disclosure (or actual deception) is justified. The researcher must still inform participants of potential risks and must make full disclosure at the earliest opportunity after the study is completed. The researcher and the independent review board must be convinced that incomplete disclosure will not result in any harm (Miller, 1998).

Deception

Consider a hypothetical researcher who wants to study the influence that knowing one's intelligence score would have on academic self-efficacy and occupational aspirations. The researcher asks for individuals to volunteer for a study supposedly investigating the relationship between intelligence scores and a measure of problem solving. A few days after taking an intelligence test, the participants are given their scores. However, some participants are told lower scores than they truly obtained, some are told higher scores, and some are told the truth. Some participants are very concerned and unhappy, whereas others are surprised and impressed. Before the researcher gave the intelligence tests, she administered questionnaires concerning the participants' study skills, future plans, and academic self-confidence. Two weeks later, she interviewed the participants again and administered the questionnaires a second time.

AT A GLANCE 2.4 ETHICAL STANDARDS AND DILEMMAS

KEY POINT: Researchers face ethical dilemmas in their research and are bound by ethical standards advanced by both governmental agencies and professional organizations.

SUPPORTING POINTS	EXPLANATION
The American Psychological Association, the Society for Research in Child Development, and the federal government have issued ethical standards for researchers.	The standards established by these groups are similar and spell out the rights of participants and responsibilities of researchers.
Colleges and universities have their own committees that look over proposals for research and determine if they are ethical.	These committees ensure that studies conducted under the auspices of their schools conform to accepted ethical standards.
Researchers must obtain informed consent from participants.	Participants must be informed as to the nature of the study and be told of such rights as the right to withdraw from the study. Teens under 18 years old also require their parents' permission to participate in a study.
Some research requires the researcher to deceive the participant in some way to obtain the necessary information for the study.	Deception may be allowed if the study is deemed important and there is no other way to gather the data. Under no circumstances is deception allowed in discussing the risks, if any, of a study.
The participant has the right to confidentiality.	The participant's individual responses are held confidential.
Under certain specific circumstances, the promise of confidentiality may be broken.	If responses indicate that a participant is in danger or needs serious help, the researcher will report this to parents or the school as is considered appropriate.

Is such a study ethical? No ethical problem is more controversial than deception. It is used most commonly in psychological research simply to prevent participants from learning the real purpose of the study so their behavior will not be affected. Other forms of deception include using a confederate who poses as another participant and provides false feedback or gives false information (Leary, 1995). Researchers who use deception claim that if participants were told everything, their responses would change. For example, if we were studying sexism or racism, telling the participants that fact might suppress sexist or racist statements.

In contrast, some experts argue that deception is wrong for two reasons. First, it is morally and fundamentally wrong to use deception; the ends do not justify the means. Second, widespread deception may cause public distrust of behavioral scientists, and people who enter studies may wonder whether they are being told the truth (Baumrind, 1985). Studies on participants' reactions to deception show that more than 90 percent understand the need for it and do not seem to mind being misled (Christensen, 1988). Some participants may be more injured than others, however. The use of deception may influence those participants who already perceive themselves as rejected or alienated or who have deep reservations about authority figures (Fisher & Tryon, 1988).

Both the American Psychological Association and federal guidelines state that deception should not be used in research unless absolutely necessary. Deception is never justified if it might increase risk or discomfort or lead to an unpleasant experience, circumstances that might influence whether participants would be willing to volunteer for the study. Participants must be informed as soon as possible about any deception used (American Psychological Association, 2002, Principle 8.07C). A debriefing clarifies the study and sometimes helps participants determine what they may have learned about themselves (Holmes, 1976a, 1976b). Participants leave with an understanding of what was being studied and how their participation contributed to knowledge in the field. Any false information the participants were given must be corrected. Researchers also must take care to reduce any stress induced by the study.

Confidentiality

Another ethical concern involves the confidentiality of the information obtained in the study. Parents who give permission for their children to participate in the study may want to know how their children answered particular questions. Although parents are informed of the results of the study itself, their children's responses remain confidential. Some evidence exists that children may fear that their parents will find out how they responded in a study, even if the researcher tells them that their responses are confidential (Abramovich et al., 1991). There is no evidence on this question from studies of teenage participants, but for them confidentiality is probably as much a concern or perhaps an even greater concern.

Confidentiality is a serious concern when the type of information being collected is sensitive and personal—for example, a psychologist studying sexually transmitted infections (Rosnow et al., 1993). Interviews on sexual conduct may involve participants telling researchers very embarrassing personal information or even admitting illegal activities (Rathus, Nevid, & Fichner-Rathus, 2000). Questionnaires are anonymous, and interviewers may not know the true names of the subjects. Published work never discloses the identity of the participants. Most psychological studies involve groups of people, and responses are grouped so no single participant's answers are identifiable and confidentiality is protected.

Sometimes a researcher must violate the ethical standard of keeping a participant's responses confidential. What if the researcher uncovers something that should be reported either to parents or school authorities for the good of the

Please place the number best reflecting your opinion next to each of the following statements. Then compare your opinions now with those you held before reading the chapter.

1 — Strongly Agree
2 — Moderately Agree
3 — No Opinion
4 — Moderately Disagree
5 — Strongly Disagree

_____ 1. Good theories about adolescence make it easier to understand the developing adolescent.

_____ 2. The most important developmental changes that occur during adolescence are found in the physical realm.

_____ 3. Adolescents think and reason very differently from preadolescents.

_____ 4. Adolescents are more influenced by what they see their parents do than by what their parents say.

_____ 5. Observation is basically too subjective a method of research to yield important insights into the adolescent experience.

_____ 6. Case studies that study one individual cannot help us understand much about adolescence, because the individual's experience may not be typical.

_____ 7. The research reported on the Internet is the most professional and up-to-date research (or information) available.

_____ 8. Deceiving potential participants in a study by giving false information about the purpose of the study is unethical and should not be practiced by researchers.

_____ 9. Teenagers should be allowed to volunteer to take part in research studies on their own, without their parents' permission.

_____ 10. Under no circumstances should the confidentiality promise in a research study be broken.

PERSPECTIVE 2

BREACHING CONFIDENTIALITY?

SETTING THE SCENE: Interviews are being conducted with young adolescents concerning the changes in their relationship with their parents. Consent forms have been obtained from both parents and adolescents. During one of the interviews, a participant, Don, reports that his parents sometimes tell him that the family would be better off without him, and they hit him severely when he has done something wrong. They constantly punish him by isolating him in his room for long periods of time. Don seems somewhat depressed and afraid of his parents.

INTERVIEWER: I don't know what to do! Is this information substantial enough to breach confidentiality and report to the child abuse agency?

DON: I was promised confidentiality. I love my parents and don't want them to get in trouble. If the interviewer reports it, things will get worse for me.

QUESTION: If you were the interviewer, what would you do?

child or teenager? For example, what if a teenager scores very low on a test of cognitive development or shows something on a personality inventory that may indicate the need for intervention (Miller, 1998)? What if a researcher determines that a teenager has an emotional disorder, such as depression, but the adolescent is afraid of a parent's being informed (Cicchetti & Toth, 1998)?

Deciding what to do in such situations can be difficult. According to the Society for Research in Child Development's "Ethical Standards for Research with Children" (1990), when investigators, in the course of gathering information, become aware of something that jeopardizes a child's well-being, they have the responsibility to discuss it with parents, guardians, or the school to obtain the necessary help. The ultimate goal is the welfare of the participant (Cicchetti & Toth, 1998).

It is possible to reduce the conflict between confidentiality and the welfare of the adolescent. For example, consent forms may note that if a particular cognitive impairment or problem is found, it will be reported to the school. Such a limitation on confidentiality given as part of the consent form certainly helps researchers decide how to proceed. At other times, it may be possible to design the study so the problem does not arise at all. For example, anonymous questionnaires make it impossible to know who answered them.

Ethical issues continue to be hotly debated. The researchers' need to conduct studies that have the potential to help people must be balanced with the participants' rights. Most research studies in psychology are not harmful and raise few ethical dilemmas, but some are potentially harmful or might raise ethical questions. It is in these cases that sensitivity and understanding are most required. Researchers must be guided by humane principles and practices advocated by professional organizations, independent review boards, and governmental agencies—guidelines that allow them to conduct scientifically valuable and valid research in an environment where participants can be confident that their rights will be respected. *(For a review of this section, see At A Glance 2.4.)*

CHAPTER SUMMARY AT A GLANCE

KEY TOPICS	KEY POINTS	
Theoretical Approaches to Adolescence	Theories of adolescence involve systematic statements of principles that are helpful in describing and predicting adolescent behavior. (*At A Glance 2.1, p. 29*)	◄— **KEY TERMS** *theory (p. 27)*
Perspectives on Adolescence	Each theoretical perspective has a distinct message and approach that help psychologists better understand adolescence. (*At A Glance 2.2, p. 40*)	◄— *defense mechanism (p. 30)* *intellectualization (p. 31)* *asceticism (p. 31)* *developmental tasks (p. 33)* *behaviorists (p. 36)* *operant conditioning (p. 36)* *reinforcer (p. 36)* *self-efficacy (p. 37)*
Research into Adolescence	Psychologists use a number of different research designs and methods to structure their scientific research. (*At A Glance 2.3, p. 53*)	◄— *cross-sectional design (p. 43)* *longitudinal design (p. 44)* *sequential designs (p. 45)* *operational definition (p. 46)* *case study (p. 46)* *survey (p. 47)* *correlation (p. 48)* *experimental study (p. 48)* *independent variable (p. 48)* *dependent variable (p. 48)* *quasi-experimental study (p. 49)* *selection bias (p. 50)* *self-fulfilling prophecy (p. 50)* *sleeper effect (p. 51)*
Ethical Standards and Dilemmas	Researchers face ethical dilemmas in their research and are bound by ethical standards advanced by both governmental agencies and professional organizations. (*At A Glance 2.4, p. 56*)	

Review questions for this chapter appear in the appendix.

3

PHYSICAL DEVELOPMENT

WHAT IS YOUR OPINION?

PUBERTAL CHANGES
- The Growth Spurt
- The Female Adolescent Develops
  Perspective 1: Help for the Single Dad
- The Male Adolescent Develops
- The Developing Brain

THE BIOLOGICAL BASES FOR BEHAVIOR AND DEVELOPMENT
- What Causes Puberty?
- Hormones and Behavior
  FOCUS: The Emotional Swings of Adolescence: Myth or Reality?
- Genetic Influences on Behavior

THE INTERPLAY OF PHYSICAL DEVELOPMENT AND EXPERIENCE
- The Secular Trend: Taller, Earlier, and Heavier
- Environmental Factors and Pubertal Timing
- Psychological Reactions to Pubertal Timing: Early and Late Maturation
  Perspective 2: I'm Ready; You're Not

THE HEALTH OF TODAY'S TEENAGERS
- Rating Adolescent Health
- The Increasing Concern over Adolescent Health Practices
- Nutrition
- Physical Activity
- Sleep: Why Are Teens So Tired?

PLACING ADOLESCENT PHYSICAL DEVELOPMENT IN PERSPECTIVE

HAS YOUR OPINION CHANGED?

THEMES

CHAPTER SUMMARY AT A GLANCE

Look at pictures of yourself from early adolescence through age 20 in your photo album. If you have pictures taken about the same time each year, perhaps school pictures, you will immediately notice the physical changes. Consider how you look now and how you looked then. We tend to forget the process that led up to our present-day appearance and physical attributes. We may forget how we reacted when we realized that some physical characteristic did not measure up to our standards, and we wished to be taller, better developed, or have different facial features. We often forget the doubts and feelings we experienced during the transition from childhood to adolescence to adulthood, and sometimes we fail to empathize with young teens going through this process.

This chapter begins with a discussion of the very noticeable physical changes of adolescence. Most of these changes occur early, during *puberty*, but they continue throughout adolescence. The chapter then looks at the biological mechanisms that cause these changes to occur. It continues with a discussion of how genetic factors not only underlie physical development but also contribute to personality and social development. The physical changes that occur in adolescence raise a number of social and psychological issues, for example, the effects of early and late maturation. The chapter concludes with an analysis of the health status and health habits of teenagers today in the areas of nutrition, physical exercise, and sleep.

Even though all adolescents progress through similar physical changes, each experiences the changes as uniquely challenging. Each adolescent develops physically within his or her own environment, specific culture, and subculture and is exposed to a different set of peers and parents. The importance of each teen's subjective experience of physical development should not be lost in any description of the general sequence of events and coping styles used by adolescents.

PUBERTAL CHANGES

The physiological changes that occur during adolescence are often divided into primary and secondary characteristics. Body changes directly related to sexual reproduction, including maturation of the testes in males and of the ovaries in females, are called **primary sex characteristics.** Changes that are not directly related to reproduction but that distinguish boys from girls, such as beard growth in males and breast development in females, are called **secondary sex characteristics.**

The sequence of changes in adolescence is predictable, but the timing of the changes varies considerably from person to person. For example, the average age of the first menstrual flow among American teens is approximately 12.8 years (Tanner, 1990), but a girl may begin menstruating any time between ages 10 and 16.5 years and still be within the typical range.

The Growth Spurt

A spurt in growth, both in height and weight, is a clearly noticeable early change. The rate of growth during this period is exceeded only by growth during the prenatal stage and the first year of life (Wagner, 1996). The average girl experiences her growth spurt about 2 years earlier than the average boy, so girls in the beginning of adolescence are generally taller and heavier and have larger muscles than boys (Tanner, 1970). The growth spurt begins between ages 8.7 and 10.3 years for girls and between ages 10.3 and 12.1 for boys (Malina, Bouchard, & Beunen, 1988).

WHAT IS YOUR OPINION?

Please place the number best reflecting your opinion next to each of the following statements. We will return to this questionnaire at the end of the chapter so you can determine if your opinions have changed.

1 — Strongly Agree
2 — Moderately Agree
3 — No Opinion
4 — Moderately Disagree
5 — Strongly Disagree

_____ 1. Menarche (the onset of menstruation) is a pivotal crisis in the life of a young girl.

_____ 2. It is unhealthy for a girl to engage in so much exercise that it delays the onset of puberty.

_____ 3. Parents should place greater restrictions on girls who mature early, because they are more likely to date and be influenced by older teens.

_____ 4. The increase in emotionality in adolescence is caused by increases in hormones.

_____ 5. Genetic factors become less important as possible explanations for behavior and development as a person matures.

_____ 6. People can learn to deal with the fact that they are slow at doing something or get angry easily.

_____ 7. Adolescents are more health conscious today than adolescents were a decade or two ago.

_____ 8. Teenage girls' eating problems are mainly due to the influence of the media, which glorify "thinness" and make being heavy a social stigma.

_____ 9. People often overestimate the importance of being thin.

_____ 10. Most teenagers understand the importance of nutrition and exercise.

primary sex characteristics Body changes directly associated with sexual reproduction.

secondary sex characteristics Physical changes that distinguish males from females but are not associated with sexual reproduction.

Typically, an adolescent girl experiences her growth spurt well before the average adolescent boy, so 12-year-old girls are actually taller than 12-year-old boys.

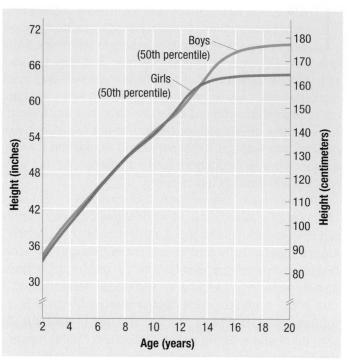

Figure 3.1
The Growth of Boys and Girls from Age 2 to 20 Years
At one point in early adolescence, the typical girl is taller than the average boy, but the average boy soon surpasses the average girl.
Source: Centers for Disease Control and Prevention (2000a), pp. 20, 21.

Figure 3.1 shows the typical increases in height (Centers for Disease Control, 2000a). Notice that the typical girl is slightly shorter than the average boy until adolescence. She surpasses him after 11 years, because a girl's growth spurt takes place so much earlier than a boy's. Between the ages of 13 and 14 years, the typical boy again becomes taller than the typical girl, as his growth spurt has now started and the girl's has nearly ended. This pattern can be seen clearly in the curve showing velocity of growth in Figure 3.2. Except for some small differences in the earliest years, no differences in velocity of growth are found from early in childhood until adolescence. Like the beginning of the growth spurt, the peak rate of growth is much earlier for girls than for boys. In addition, the average boy grows about 4 inches (103 centimeters) a year, compared with the average girl's 3½ inches (90 centimeters) per year (Tanner, 1990).

Weight also increases (see Figure 3.3) and shows spurts, with the peak velocity in weight increase about 6 to 9 months after the peak velocity in height increase. Leg length, as a rule, reaches its peak first, with trunk length about a year later. All structures grow during this time, but not at the same rate. The hands and feet reach adult size first, causing many adolescents to complain about having hands or feet that are too big. (Adults can tell them that when they are fully grown, their proportions will be correct.)

Within each gender, some children experience the beginning of their growth spurt earlier than others. An early-maturing boy may begin his spurt at 9 years, whereas a late-maturing boy may not begin his until age 13 (Tanner, 1991). Generally, girls reach their adult height sometime between 15 and 16 years and boys, between 16 and 17½ years, although individual differences can be found (Brooks-Gunn & Petersen, 1984).

The Female Adolescent Develops

In girls, the appearance of breast buds is the first sex characteristic to appear (at about 10½ years) (Brooks-Gunn & Reiter, 1990). When the growth spurt is at its

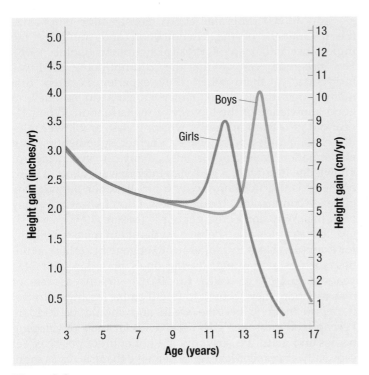

Figure 3.2
The Pubertal Growth Spurt
The typical girl begins her growth spurt much earlier than the average boy, and her growth spurt ends much earlier.

Source: Adapted from Tanner (1990), p. 14. Reprinted by permission of the publisher from *Fetus into Man: Physical Growth from Conception to Maturity* by J. M. Tanner, p. 14, Cambridge, MA: Harvard University Press, Copyright © 1978, 1989 by J. M. Tanner.

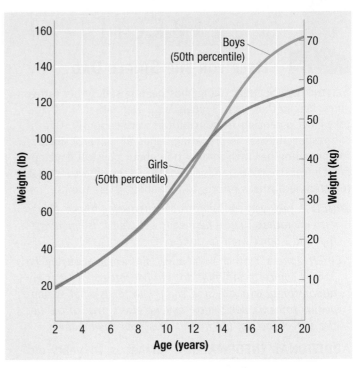

Figure 3.3
Weight Gain for Boys and Girls Between Ages 2 and 20 Years
Girls are a little heavier than boys in early adolescence; however, this situation changes between ages 13 and 14, when boys become heavier and remain so throughout adolescence.

Source: Centers for Disease Control and Prevention (2000a), pp. 18, 19.

maximum, changes in the genital organs occur, including maturation of the uterus, vagina, labia, clitoris, and breasts. When physical growth slows considerably, **menarche** (the onset of menstruation) takes place. *Menstruation* refers to the cyclic shedding of the uterine lining, which results in vaginal bleeding about 2 weeks after an egg is released from an ovary and is not fertilized. At menarche, a number of other changes in fat and muscle composition also occur. Following menarche are further changes in body shape and voice. Menarche follows the peak velocity in height increase, the age at which the most rapid growth occurs. A girl can expect to grow about 1 to 3 inches (3 to 7 centimeters) after menarche and to undergo considerable physical development; changes in body shape and facial features may occur in almost fully grown girls (Brooks-Gunn & Reiter, 1990).

Menstruation At one time, menarche was viewed as creating complex adjustment problems for girls. But research in the 1980s and 1990s found that most teenage girls do not have intense reactions to menarche; instead, most girls find it only mildly stressful (Koff & Rierdan, 1995). Some report mild physical distress, apprehension, and an immediate desire for privacy. Girls also may feel pride as they reach a developmental milestone. Girls who are less prepared or who begin menstruating very early are the most likely to evaluate the experience negatively. Typically, any negative feelings pass quickly.

Perhaps one reason for the milder reactions to menarche today is that most female adolescents receive at least some information about what is happening (or is about to happen) to them. When a group of ninth-grade girls was asked about their preparation for their first menstrual experience, almost all said they were either "well prepared" or "somewhat prepared" (Koff & Rierdan, 1995). Mothers provide daughters with most of the information about menarche; other females, mostly girlfriends, rank second in providing information; and health education classes and health providers rank third.

menarche The first menstrual cycle.

PERSPECTIVE 1

HELP FOR THE SINGLE DAD

SETTING THE SCENE: Janet has been raised by her father since her mother died 3 years ago. Her father, Ned, has taken his parenting responsibilities very seriously. One of the responsibilities is preparing Janet for puberty, including providing her with information about physical development, menstruation, and sexuality. Janet, however, has rejected her father's efforts to talk about these topics.

JANET: *I feel very uncomfortable discussing these things with my father. I know he means well, but it is embarrassing, and I don't want to do it.*

NED: *If Janet's mother were alive, she would probably be Janet's source of information. I'm her father, and it is my responsibility to make sure she understands what is happening to her. I don't know anyone else I trust to tell her the correct facts of life in an honest and open manner.*

ADDITIONAL INFORMATION: Janet is 11 years old and is a relatively popular, happy child.

QUESTION: What should her father do?

Educational programs about menstruation emphasize the naturalness of the phenomenon and minimize the importance and extent of physical symptoms (Golub, 1993). Few girls today can say that they did not know what was happening to them when they experienced their first menses (menstrual flow). However, girls do not have a good knowledge of the biology of menstruation. When 11-year-old girls from primarily working class and lower middle class families were asked whether statements about menstruation were true or false, many showed a lack of knowledge (see Table 3.1). When interviewed, about a third of the girls did not know why a girl gets her period. One girl even commented, "I don't know. I don't know why they need this. Why don't boys get one?" (Moore, 1995, p. 94).

Teenage girls often believe myths about menstruation—for example, that it is dangerous to engage in certain activities, such as swimming, during one's period. When 14½-year-old girls were asked to discuss various aspects of menstruation, they seemed to find it embarrassing or to feel it causes them to become weak and should be hidden. Perhaps the messages girls receive about their developing bodies and maturing sexuality are not entirely positive. Yet especially after menarche, girls perceive themselves as more womanly, accept their bodies as feminine, and begin to reflect on their reproductive capabilities (Koff & Rierdan, 1991). Menarche is one sign of maturity, and they are pleased to be seen as more adult.

Secondary Sex Characteristics Girls receive much less information about secondary sex characteristics, such as breast development and changes in body shape, than about menarche. However, breast development is one of the more public aspects of physical development. Both family and peers tend to comment upon breast development, which often embarrasses girls, many of

---

Table 3.1

How Much Do 11-Year-Old Girls Know About Menstruation?

Before you read further, test your knowledge about menstruation. Cover the answer column, and answer "true" or "false" to each statement. As you will see when you look at the answer column, most young girls know something about menstruation, but their knowledge is incomplete.

Statement	Answer	Percentage Correct
1. Changes in a girl's routine, such as going on holidays, can cause changes in her menstrual cycle.	True	21.2
2. It is normal to put on weight at the time of puberty.	True	64.7
3. Girls usually reach puberty before boys.	True	87.1
4. Periods come approximately every 28 days, but they may be much longer when they are just starting.	True	82.4
5. Everyone can tell when a girl is having her period.	False	78.2
6. It is dangerous for a girl to go swimming when she is having her period.	False	40.0
7. Female athletes in heavy training and ballet dancers sometimes stop menstruating.	True	25.9
8. Menstruation (periods) cleanses the body of dirty blood.	False	18.8
9. Menstrual blood comes from the uterus, which is the place in a woman's body where babies grow.	True	72.9
10. Menstrual blood comes from the bladder.	False	44.7
11. All girls get cranky before their periods.	False	28.2

Source: Adapted from Moore (1995), Table 1, p. 94.

whom wish for greater privacy (Brooks-Gunn et al., 1994). Some discussion of physical development occurs with mothers, but a great deal of discomfort surrounds any discussion of it with fathers, who are often seen as having negative attitudes toward these changes in their daughters. Girls learn next to nothing about puberty from their fathers, and less than 15 percent of all girls tell their father when they reach menarche.

The Male Adolescent Develops

The initial sign of sexual development in boys is the onset of testicular growth, which occurs at about 11 to 11½ years. The growth spurt in boys does not begin until about a year later, after considerable development of the sex organs has taken place. The voice deepens, and facial hair appears. Muscles develop, in part because of the secretion of testosterone, and the heart and lungs increase dramatically, as does the number of red blood cells. In contrast to girls, boys may not achieve the maximum growth spurt until they have developed nearly adult-sized genitalia (Brooks-Gunn & Reiter, 1990). The trunk and legs elongate after these changes. Leg length reaches its adult proportions before body breadth. The last growth change is a widening of the shoulders.

Psychologists know little about the meaning of puberty to boys. Is the occurrence of *ejaculation,* the expulsion of semen from the penis, as significant for boys as menarche is for girls? Although two-thirds of a sample of young adolescent boys did admit to having been a little frightened when they first ejaculated—a response in some ways comparable to girls' response to menarche—they also reported stronger positive responses than negative ones. Boys receive little information about ejaculation from any source. In fact, boys may actually know more about menarche than about ejaculation, because many health education classes routinely cover menarche (Gaddis & Brooks-Gunn, 1985). Boys are very reluctant to discuss the experience with parents or even friends, and when they do, it is in the form of humor. Perhaps this secrecy is due to the link between ejaculation and *masturbation* (the stimulation of one's own genitals for pleasure), a relationship that does not exist for menarche (Brooks-Gunn & Reiter, 1990).

The Developing Brain

One physical development during adolescence that has received attention from researchers only recently is the maturation of the brain. Most research in brain development focuses on the early, formative years of childhood. In fact, for many years scientists believed that the brain basically finished its development by puberty and then more or less settled into its adult status in both structure and function. One exception to this concept of brain stability that has been known for many years is that myelinization—the process by which neurons are surrounded by a fatty covering, a *myelin sheath*—continues throughout adolescence. The myelin sheath insulates a part of the neuron called the *axon,* allowing impulses to travel faster and more efficiently, thus improving coordination. Myelinization explains why teenagers show faster reflexes than preschoolers. The process of myelinization is not complete at adolescence and continues through early adulthood (Kalat, 2000).

Recently, some researchers have begun to look at other neurological changes that occur during adolescence, and their findings challenge the idea that the brain basically reaches stability at adolescence. The brain overproduces in terms of the number of brain cells and connections between cells. At specific times, these neurons and the connections between them are pruned. In other words, the brain actively organizes and reorganizes itself, using some cells and connections and not others. The cells and connections that are not used disappear according to a "use it or lose it" principle (Landau, 2000). Scientists have known for some time that this process occurs in infants and toddlers, but new research shows that a pruning of these connections may occur during adolescence as well (National Academy of Sciences, 2001). The **prefrontal cortex,** a part of the brain responsible for planning and decision making, undergoes a growth spurt at about age 9 or 10

prefrontal cortex   The part of the frontal lobes of the cortex responsible for executive decision making and planning.

Research into adolescent brain structure and functioning shows that adolescents are more likely to use a "gut reaction" rather than analyzing the experience more thoughtfully.

years, when neurons create many new connections; the pruning begins during early adolescence. The implications of this pruning are under study today, but pruning seems to be associated with more efficient brain operation.

Another aspect of brain development during adolescence is the regulation of emotional experience. Adolescence is a time of emotional challenges in the areas of social anxieties, early romantic relationships, academic pressures, and the need to balance short- and long-term goals. When people experience an emotion, they use their cognitive skills to guide, inhibit, or modify that emotion or their reaction to the emotional experience. For instance, teenagers may feel angry when friends criticize their appearance and may react "without thinking," whereas adults may better evaluate why the friends criticized their appearance and moderate their reactions, deciding not to show them in their facial expressions or voices.

New research shows that parts of the **cerebral cortex** that have connections to areas in the brain responsible for emotional experience may mature during adolescence, especially early adolescence (Dahl, 2001). Scientists explain the development of emotional regulation by referring to two important brain structures, the *amygdala* and the prefrontal cortex. The amygdala processes emotional information on a basic level, giving the person a "gut feeling," whereas the prefrontal cortex is responsible for analyzing experience and rational decision making. Some evidence exists that especially in early adolescence, the prefrontal cortex is still not functioning as it will later in life; thus, the young adolescent reacts to emotional experience on a more basic level, being less capable of analyzing experience and making rational judgment. This means that many young teenagers may be overwhelmed by their "gut reactions" to emotional experience, possessing less than an adult's ability to modulate emotions.

The primacy of the amygdala for analyzing emotions was shown in a study that asked adolescents between 11 and 17 years old to discriminate among different facial expressions while their brains were scanned using functional magnetic resonance imaging, a technique that records brain functioning. In an earlier, similar study, adults exhibited activity mostly in their frontal lobes of the cortex. The adolescents, especially the younger adolescents, showed greater amygdala functioning; in other words, they relied more on the amygdala than the frontal lobes. The adolescents made many more mistakes as well; for example, they characterized facial expressions that showed fear as sadness, anger, or confusion. A progressive shift from dependence on the amygdala to increased use of the prefrontal cortex occurred with age (Baird et al., 1999). Younger teens, then, may read social signals, such as facial expressions, incorrectly and react in a less thoughtful manner than older teens and adults.

The continuing development of the prefrontal cortex may mean that young teenagers do not yet have the neurological ability to make the soundest judgments or to regulate their emotions in an adult manner. Early adolescents may not access critical memories and lessons that may be needed to make a mature judgment. Certainly good judgment is learned, but the immaturity of the brain of young teens may be a limiting factor.

The way the adolescent brain develops may have implications for answering questions about abnormal functioning as well. For example, the symptoms of attention-deficit/hyperactivity disorder, including attentional difficulties, impulsiveness, and sometimes hyperactivity, often moderate in adolescence (see "Stress and Psychological, Physical, and Learning Problems"). Some research points to the pruning of connections between neurons in a part of the brain called the *striatum* as a possible explanation for this moderation in symptoms (Teicher & Ito, 1996).

This new wave of brain research shows that the adolescent brain is still developing, a work in progress. The finding that some of the last parts to mature

cerebral cortex The outer surface of the cerebrum, responsible for sensory and motor functions as well as higher mental processes.

AT A GLANCE **3.1** PUBERTAL CHANGES

KEY POINT: The physical changes that occur during puberty affect every area of development.

SUPPORTING POINTS	EXPLANATION
The sequence of physiological changes in puberty is predictable, but the timing of the changes varies from individual to individual.	Psychologists can predict what change will occur next but not exactly when it will occur.
Girls experience their growth spurt about 2 years earlier than boys.	As a group, girls mature earlier than boys.
Most girls experience only mild apprehension toward menarche, and these feelings pass quickly.	The relatively mild psychological reaction to menarche today is due to better education concerning the physical changes in puberty.
The growth spurt in males does not occur until a number of other physical changes have taken place, for example, the development of the penis.	The growth spurt in females takes place much earlier in the sequence of physical changes than it does in males.
The process by which neurons become coated by a fatty covering, the myelin sheath, continues throughout adolescence.	The continuation of myelinization during adolescence implies that adolescent reactions to stimuli will be faster and the workings of the neurons somewhat more efficient than in younger children.
Scientists have found a spurt in the development of connections between neurons in the brain prior to adolescence, as well as some pruning of these connections during adolescence.	The exact implications of this pruning of connections between neurons are under study, but many psychologists believe the pruning leads to more efficient brain functioning.
The prefrontal cortex is relatively immature in early adolescence and matures during adolescence.	Early adolescents may not have the same ability to modulate emotional response or make rational decisions as older adolescents and adults.

are linked to both rational decision making and emotional regulation implies that the young adolescent may lack some of the abilities necessary for controlling emotion and conducting rational analysis in social situations.

At the same time, we should not overinterpret this research as implying that adolescents are not responsible for their actions or cannot learn self-control. The research shows only that there may be limitations to their abilities, especially in early adolescence. In addition, scientists are just beginning to understand brain-behavior relationships, which are often very complex, and we should guard against using the results of preliminary research as the basis for explaining social behavior. *(For a review of this section, see At A Glance 3.1.)*

THE BIOLOGICAL BASES FOR BEHAVIOR AND DEVELOPMENT

Conventional wisdom ascribes the cause of the physical changes of puberty to both biological and genetic factors. For example, genetic factors explain much of the timing and course of physical development. Normally, people look for *direct effects*—that is, some biological cause for a particular behavior, such as the biological trigger for puberty or the direct influence of hormones on behavior. It is important to remember, however, that biological factors can also *indirectly* influence behavior. Some aspect of physical development, such as the extent of breast development, may influence both other people's reactions to the teen and the adolescent's behavior.

What Causes Puberty?

Three structures form a system that is primarily responsible for puberty: the *hypothalamus* (a part of the brain); the *pituitary gland,* a small gland at the base of the brain; and the *gonads,* or sex organs—the testes in males and the ovaries in females. These structures secrete **hormones,** chemical substances produced in one part of the body that travel to another, where they elicit responses (Chiras, 1993). The hypothalamus produces chemicals known as *releasing factors* or *gonadotropin-releasing hormone;* the bloodstream carries these chemicals to the pituitary gland, stimulating it to produce substances called *gonadotropins,* which stimulate the gonads (sex organs). In late middle childhood, concentrations of these gonadotropins, which include luteinizing hormone (LH) and follicle-stimulating hormone (FSH), begin to increase. The pituitary gland secretes them in bursts or pulses. These hormones induce the ovaries to produce female sex hormones (estrogens) and the testes to produce male sex hormones (androgens), which in turn stimulate the gonads to produce sperm in males and mature ova in females. The sex hormones produced by the gonads cause the pubertal changes in the body.

The changes that take place during adolescence, then, are largely determined by hormones, one group of which is the sex hormones. Estradiol (a potent estrogen) is a sex hormone secreted by girls' ovaries in response to FSH and LH. It begins to increase after age 9 or 10 years, and the increase continues until a girl is about 13½ or 14 years old (Must et al., 1992). Testosterone is the primary sex hormone stimulated by LH and FSH in boys. At about age 10, testosterone levels begin to rise at night. Testosterone concentrations can increase as much as 20 times their initial levels between ages 10 and 17 years, with the greatest increase occurring between 12 and 14 years.

Beginning about 2 years before puberty, the hypothalamus also stimulates the pituitary gland to produce a hormone that causes the adrenal glands to increase production of the hormones dehydroepiandrosterone (DHEA) and dehydroepiandrosterone sulfate (DHEAS). The metabolism of adrenal hormones leads to the production of weak sex hormones. The hypothalamus-pituitary-adrenal system is important because it contributes to the development of secondary sex characteristics. For example, the adrenal glands' production of DHEA and DHEAS is responsible for pubic and axillary hair (Cutler, 1991). In fact, the increase in adrenal hormones is the earliest sign of hormonal maturation (Buchanan, Eccles, & Becker, 1992a).

The adrenal hormones may also play an important part in sexual attraction (McClintock & Herdt, 1996). Research indicates that 10 years is the average age at which the first sexual attraction occurs, which is somewhat earlier than first thought, and certainly before the significant increase in gonadal hormone production (Pattatucci & Hamer, 1995). This first sexual attraction seems to occur when the adrenal glands are producing high levels of DHEA, which is metabolized into both testosterone and estradiol.

Testosterone, along with the adrenal hormones, stimulates the development of male primary and secondary sex characteristics, including growth and development of the male reproductive system, muscle development, enlargement of the testes and penis, bone growth, growth of body hair, deepening of the voice, and sweat gland activity. Estrogens are responsible for the development and maintenance of the female reproductive organs, breast development, and changes in body fat distribution. Although males and females produce both estrogen and testosterone, males produce more testosterone and females more estrogen. During adolescence, the sex hormones are secreted into the bloodstream in great quantities.

hormones   Chemical substances secreted by one organ that control the function of another organ.

Hormones and Behavior

The relationship between hormonal action and the physical changes that define puberty, such as the growth spurt and primary and secondary sex characteristics, is well established. The relationship of hormones to adjustment and emotional experience, in contrast, is open to question (see "Focus: The Emotional Swings of Adolescence: Myth or Reality?").

Hormones may influence teenagers' emotional experience and behavior in a number of ways. First, there may be a direct link between hormone levels and moods or behaviors. Indeed, high levels of several hormones secreted during adolescence are associated with higher levels of depressive emotion and aggressive mood (Susman et al., 1987)

Second, it may be the rapid rise in hormone level, rather than the absolute level of hormones, that necessitates a difficult adjustment and thus leads to depression or moodiness. In early adolescence, for example, low concentrations of hormones such as gonadotropins and sex hormones are replaced by higher concentrations. A mood or behavior change may reflect an adaptation to the change in hormone levels rather than a response to the absolute hormone level itself (Brooks-Gunn & Warren, 1989). If so, by middle or certainly by late adolescence, teens probably have adapted to these higher concentrations. Some evidence supports this line of thinking. For example, estrogen is related to higher levels of feelings of well-being in adult females but to higher levels of depression during the hormone's most rapid rise in early adolescence (Brooks-Gunn & Warren, 1989). Perhaps adult females have adapted to the higher levels of hormones. Another finding supporting the adaptation hypothesis is that higher levels of hormones for one's age are associated with more negative moods (Nottelmann et al., 1987). Adolescents who have to deal with higher-than-typical levels of hormones may have more difficulty doing so. Adaptation to hormonal change may be difficult if a teen's concentrations rise earlier or higher than is typical in development and the teen does not have the time to gradually adjust to these hormone levels (Susman et al., 1987).

A third possible explanation for a linkage between emotional experience and hormonal action is that the irregular or cyclical nature of hormone secretion may cause mood swings or increased emotionality. Indeed, hormonal fluctuation is significant in early adolescence (Buchanan et al., 1992a). Teens often complain of having less energy and more fatigue than other age groups, and adolescents experience more extreme swings in alertness, drowsiness, and tiredness (Larson, Csikszentmihalyi, & Graef, 1980). The fatigue may be a consequence of the adjustment to fluctuations or increases in hormone levels (Sonis et al., 1985).

Fourth, complex interactions between teens' hormone levels and environmental stressors may result in greater mood swings and emotionality (Buchanan et al., 1992). Teens with higher levels of hormones or significant fluctuations who are faced with greater environmental stressors, such as pressure from parents or schools, may experience greater mood swings. Evidence for this hypothesis comes from research showing that adolescents with serious preexisting psychological problems are at a greater risk for developing depression than adolescents with just higher hormone levels and no preexisting problems (Paikoff, Brooks-Gunn, & Warren, 1991). Perhaps depressive problems are more likely to occur in young adolescents who already have serious family or personal problems. The level of hormones or the rapid increase in hormonal level, then, becomes just one stressor among many.

Last, it is possible that physiological changes arising from hormonal action elicit comments from others, which then affect the teen's self-confidence and moods. For example, a slight change in energy level, fatigue, sleepiness, or irritability may cause parents or friends to treat adolescents differently or subject them to criticism, which in turn may influence their behavior. Of course, any and all these possibilities might explain the influence of hormones on behavior and emotional experience (Paikoff, Brooks-Gunn, & Warren, 1991).

The Emotional Swings of Adolescence: Myth or Reality?

"Puberty brings on a period of increased emotionality, mood swings, and negative moods." If you agree with this statement, you are in good company. The Greek philosopher Aristotle described the adolescent as "passionate, irascible and apt to be carried away by impulse." G. Stanley Hall, the psychologist most responsible for our modern interest in adolescence, believed it was natural to experience intense emotional reactions during adolescence. Anna Freud argued that puberty brought with it significant increases in drives that overwhelm the adolescent's ability to cope. When these drives are combined with issues of independence and dependence, the result is emotional instability (A. Freud, 1962). These attitudes are not confined to Western philosophers. Confucius believed that adolescence was a time of great emotional upheaval. The Gesuii tribe of Kenya, which is fairly typical of many tribes, groups young male youths and early adults into a warrior class, which is considered to be made up of high-spirited, aggressive individuals who are potential troublemakers (Larson, 1991).

How truthful is the popular wisdom that teenagers are more emotional or moody? If moodiness is defined in terms of intensity and fluctuations in mood, then moodiness may be more characteristic of adolescents than adults, but not more than children (Csikszentmihalyi & Larson, 1980). Teens do report wider daily mood variability than adults, including higher highs and lower lows (Larson, Csikszentmihalyi, & Graef, 1980), but their emotional variability is no greater than that of children (Larson, 1991). Adolescents 16 to 19 years old report experiencing more intense emotions than older members of the same family (Diener, Sandvik, & Larsen, 1985). These strong emotional states don't last very long, however; they dissipate within half an hour, whereas adults' states last longer. Adolescents, then, experience more extreme states, but they are more transient (Larson et al., 1980).

Furthermore, not all evidence points to increased moodiness, especially after early adolescence. For example, researchers found no age-related changes in parents' reports of their children's moodiness between ages 14 and 16 (Achenbach & Edelbrock, 1981). A study of teens in fifth through eleventh grades found a constant frequency, duration, and intensity of moods (Stapley & Haviland, 1989). Other studies found a small increase in mood variability for girls between fifth and ninth grades and none for boys (Larson & Lampman-Petraitis, 1989). When slight differences are found on scales measuring stubbornness, being sullen, or being irritable, younger children tend to score higher than adolescents. There is some evidence, then, for greater moodiness, especially during early adolescence, but it seems that this moodiness does not become more pronounced with age (Boice, 1990). Although some moodiness is typical, extreme variability and negativity are signs of maladjustment (Larson et al., 1990).

One major change in adolescent emotional experience on which there is considerable agreement is the increase in mildly negative emotions (Brooks-Gunn & Reiter, 1990). As teens mature between fifth and ninth grades, they report fewer extremely positive moods and more moderately negative moods (Larson & Lampman-Petraitis, 1989). There is a downward shift in average daily mood, and they report more moderate states. The largest difference occurs in extremely

The possible hormonal link to irritability and aggression has received considerable attention. The relationship between testosterone and aggression is fairly well established in animals (Susman & Dorn, 1991). In human beings, though, the relationship appears more complicated. Testosterone levels are related to some emotional dispositions such as anger, anxiety, sadness, less impulse control, and some aggressive behavior (Susman et al., 1987). Levels are also linked to a particular type of aggression, response to provocation, rather than to general aggression (Olweus, 1986; Olweus et al., 1980). Under conditions of threat or unfair treatment, boys with higher testosterone concentrations are more likely to respond with aggression (Olweus et al., 1988). The link between testosterone level and behavior is more potent for adolescents with a history of aggression, such as boys prone to provocation or delinquency due to personality characteristics. Some researchers claim that higher levels of testosterone in adolescence are related to an aggressive style only if the aggression confers a dominant status on the individual (Schaal et al., 1996). In fact, one study found a relationship between testosterone level and social dominance, but not between testosterone level and physical aggression (Tremblay et al., 1998). The link between testosterone and aggression is not found in girls (Susman et al., 1987), perhaps because social pressure not to be aggressive inhibits aggression (Paikoff, Buchanan, & Brooks-Gunn, 1991).

Not all research shows a link in males between hormone levels and aggression, and the linkage remains controversial (Consantino et al., 1993). In addition, positive emotions. Ninth-grade boys and girls used the extreme positive scale point about half as often as they did in fifth grade. In addition, older girls reported a greater frequency of mildly negative and mildly positive states, whereas older boys reported more frequently experiencing only mildly negative states.

When scales measuring the states of unhappiness, sadness, or depression are administered to adolescents, increases in these states are frequently found (Larson & Lampman-Petraitis, 1989). Gender differences exist, too, with depression being more common among teenage girls than teenage boys (see "Stress and Psychological, Physical, and Learning Problems") (Csikszentmihalyi & Larson, 1984). Studies suggest that adolescents, especially girls, may be more vulnerable to depressive emotions than during the childhood years.

The interpretation of research evidence on emotional experience and expression in adolescence is complicated by the importance of the context. Between the fifth and seventh grades, teens report less intense positive emotions when in the presence of their family members and more positive emotions when with friends (Flannery et al., 1994). By ninth grade, emotions become somewhat more positive with family members, at least for boys (Larson & Richards, 1991).

These findings challenge the idea that adolescence is a time of greatly increased emotionality, but they do not suggest that it is a time of decreased emotionality. Adolescence may be thought of as a plateau in which the emotional variability of childhood is sustained, but shown in different ways (Larson & Lampman-Petraitis, 1989). Although the majority of daily states are still positive, adolescents rate them as somewhat less positive than do younger children.

There are two explanations for this difference. First, perhaps younger and older youth interpret similar internal and external experiences differently. Adolescents may become more critical and discerning in their reading of emotional cues and less willing to label experiences as positive in the extreme; they become more conservative in labeling emotions. The second explanation is that these changes may reflect real differences in adolescents' emotional experiences in everyday life; the downward shift in average emotional state actually occurs. Possible causes include an increase in stress, interpersonal problems, becoming more sensitive to criticism from others, and hormonal changes. A relationship exists between negative life events and negative or variable moods, and if stress increases, some increase in negative moods may accompany this increase. Perhaps the reason for the change in perception is not as important as the fact that adolescents perceive fewer occasions in which they feel on top of the world and more occasions when they feel mildly negative.

Adolescence may be a time of emotional variability and intensity, at least compared with adulthood. As adolescents proceed through the stage, they experience more mildly negative states. Although the evidence is not complete, adolescents probably also tend to be somewhat moodier. However, most studies on the topic compare adolescents with adults rather than with children. The increase in emotionality and fluctuations in negative and positive moods reflect the many changes in the lives of teenagers. This emotionality is not a sign of storm and stress but rather reflects the uncertainty, excitement, and challenges experienced by adolescents (Larson, 1991).

most theoretical perspectives, including social learning theory and behaviorism, argue that aggression is a learned behavior. Cognitive studies, which will be discussed in "Drug Use and Violence," find that how people interpret the information they receive is also related to aggression. Perhaps hormonal action has a predisposing effect, but hormone level alone cannot explain aggression or social dominance in human beings.

Summarizing the influence of hormones on behavior, and especially on emotionality, is difficult, given our incomplete knowledge. The research available certainly shows that hormones may have both direct and indirect influences on moods and energy levels. But the influence of hormones is modified and mediated by family, school, peer, gender role, and personality factors, which interact with biological factors (Buchanan et al., 1992a). The impacts of these complex interactions are difficult to untangle, and further research is necessary for a complete picture of the influence of hormones on behavior to emerge.

Genetic Influences on Behavior

Almost everyone is willing to attribute the timing and course of physical development to biological factors directed by one's genes. However, most people resist the idea that genetic factors influence personality, social behavior, or cognitive development, attributing these areas solely to environmental factors such as the family, peers, and teachers. As we will see, both environmental and genetic factors are involved in physical and social development.

Misunderstandings About Genetics   Part of the difficulty in understanding genetic influence is due to a lack of knowledge about how genetic factors operate. First, many people believe that an individual who possesses a gene for a particular trait is certain to show that trait. In most cases, having a particular gene may *predispose* an individual to showing a trait (make it more likely that the person will show the trait), but environmental factors determine whether the individual actually exhibits the trait. For example, if genetic endowment contributes to alcoholism or aggressiveness, a person with such genes would have a greater chance of developing alcoholism or showing aggressiveness, but environmental factors would play crucial roles.

Many people also incorrectly believe that if genetic factors underlie a trait, the trait cannot be altered. However, if genetic factors underlie a trait, such as intelligence, it does not mean that an individual's intelligence cannot be modified through environmental means, such as an intensive training program. Genetic factors do not imply immutability. For example, although there may be limits to the degree to which we can increase intelligence through environmental manipulation using our current knowledge, there is no doubt that it can be increased. Nothing is as damaging as the belief that genetic involvement means that some characteristic is carved in stone.

Another common misunderstanding is that genetic factors are more important in infancy than in adolescence or adulthood. The activity of genes is ongoing, and genes can turn on and off at different ages in response to environmental events (Plomin, 1991).

Determining Genetic Contribution   Keeping in mind the need to avoid potential misunderstandings about the role of genes in determining behavior, we turn now to an examination of what we actually know about the influence of genes on behavior and how we know it. How can scientists determine the extent to which genetic factors are responsible for a characteristic or a behavior? It isn't as easy as it might seem. Consider the following: In a given family, the father, mother, and two children are quite overweight. Going back a few generations, you find that almost everyone in the family is overweight. Can you conclude from this evidence that obesity is genetic? The answer is no. Environmental, rather than genetic, factors may be responsible for the characteristic. The children may have learned how to eat from their parents. The parents may have modeled poor early habits or encouraged their children to overeat.

Trying to separate the possible environmental (learning) factors from the genetic involvement is difficult and requires the use of specific research methods. The term **heritability** is used to describe what proportion of the differences *among people* in a given population on a particular characteristic is caused by genetic factors (Cipriani, 1996). Heritability, then, involves variations in populations, not within individuals (Dolan & Molenaar, 1995). Two methods useful for determining heritability are twin studies and adoption studies.

TWIN STUDIES   Twin studies are based upon the fact that **monozygotic twins** (identical twins, who develop from one fertilized egg) have 100 percent of their genes in common, and **dizygotic twins** (fraternal twins, who develop from the fertilization of two different eggs by two different sperm), like all other siblings, share on the average only 50 percent of their genes. A simple method for evaluating the heritability of a trait is to find the extent to which one twin's having the trait means the other twin will have it also. The degree of agreement between traits in twins is called the **concordance rate.** If pairs of monozygotic twins show the trait much more often than pairs of dizygotic twins, some genetic influence can be assumed. If a trait is completely caused by genetics, the concordance rate is 1.00 in identical twins and .50 in fraternal twins (Cummings, 1995). For example, identical twins correlate about .90 for height and fraternal twins, about .45

heritability   The proportion of the measured differences among people in a given population on a particular characteristic that is due to genetic factors.

monozygotic twins   Twins who develop from one fertilized egg and have an identical genetic structure.

dizygotic twins   Twins resulting from the fertilization of two eggs by two different sperm and whose genetic composition is no more similar than any other pair of siblings.

concordance rate   The degree of similarity between twins on a particular characteristic.

Identical twins (above) share 100 percent of their genes, whereas fraternal twins (below) share an average of 50 percent of their genes.

Table 3.2

Concordance Rates in Monozygotic (MZ) and Dizygotic (DZ) Twins

Notice the significant differences between the values for monozygotic (identical) twins and dizygotic (fraternal) twins on some attribute. These differences show some genetic involvement in the trait.

| | Concordance Values | |
Trait	MZ	DZ
Blood type	100	66
Eye color	99	28
Hair color	89	22
Epilepsy	72	15
Diabetes	65	18
Cleft lip	42	5

Source: Cummings (1994), Table 3.2, p. 417.

(Pike & Plomin, 1996) (see Table 3.2 for other traits). A mathematical formula allows for a quantitative estimate of heritability from such data.

Sometimes it is possible to compare pairs of twins reared apart with other twin pairs raised together, which offers additional data. When both identical and fraternal twins raised together or apart were compared as adults, the identical twins had almost identical body mass (a measure of weight corrected for height), whether reared apart or together. Fraternal twins varied much more than the identical twins, even if they were reared together (Stunkard, 1990).

One difficulty with twin studies is that parents may treat identical twins more similarly than fraternal twins. If this is so, the higher concordance rates between identical twins on a characteristic might be the result of a more similar environment than that experienced by fraternal twins (Reiss, 1993).

ADOPTION STUDIES Researchers also study adopted children and their parents to determine genetic influence. Consider a child of parents with a particular body mass adopted by parents with a significantly different body mass. Will the child's body mass be more similar to that of the adoptive or the biological parents? Researchers who compared adopted children's body mass (thin, medium, overweight, or obese) with the body mass of both their biological and their adoptive parents found a clear relationship between adoptee body mass and the body mass of the biological parents (Stunkard et al., 1986). There was no relationship between adoptee body mass and the body mass of adoptive parents.

Adoption studies are often criticized because parents may treat an adopted child differently than a biological child (Reiss, 1993), thus introducing into the research an environmental variable, parental treatment, that might explain any differences. In addition, it is frequently difficult to find information about the biological fathers of adopted children (Nigg & Goldsmith, 1994). Most studies offer a great deal of information about mothers and very little about fathers, providing only a partial genetic picture of the children.

It is clear that twin and adoption studies cannot give us all the definitive answers to questions about the extent of genetic contributions to development. However, they are useful estimates of genetic contribution. In addition, these studies show the importance of the environment. For instance, the Texas Adoption Project found that the intelligence scores of adopted children were more similar to their biological than adoptive parents. However, the relationships were all quite low, and most of the variability was not the result of genetic influences but of socioeconomic factors, such as neighborhood, friends, and schools (Cummings, 1994).

Genetic Factors and Social Behavior   It is easy to understand how genetic factors may influence physical development—for example, through hormonal action—but how can one's genetic endowment influence social behavior and personality? We know of no genes for social behaviors, such as friendliness and kindness. If genetic factors influence these behaviors, they must do so through physiological means or indirectly through how others react to a particular characteristic. The search for possible ways in which genetic and environmental factors interact continues. One theoretical model, the *genotype/environment interaction model,* suggests three different genetic/environmental effects, or ways in which genetic endowment and environmental factors interact to determine social behavior: passive, evocative, and active (see Figure 3.4) (Scarr & McCartney, 1983).

The first way these factors can interact is through *passive effects*, in which parents provide a rearing environment that is in itself affected by the parents' genes. For example, verbal ability is in some measure affected by genetic factors, and parents both pass on genes for this ability and create an environment in which this ability can be developed. The environment created by the parents is in part shaped by their genetic endowment. The importance of passive effects declines as children, and especially adolescents, gain more freedom and have a greater opportunity to choose their own activities.

The second type of genotype/environment effects, called *evocative effects,* include the various responses that people with different genetic endowments evoke from other people. For example, sociable, easygoing adolescents receive different reactions from others than do tense adolescents. Attractive teens receive different feedback than unattractive teens. The importance of evocative effects continues throughout life.

The third kind of genotype/environment effects, *active effects,* represent the teen's selective attention to, and learning from, aspects of the environment that are influenced by the person's genes. People seek out environments they find comfortable and stimulating. They actively select elements from the environment to pay attention to and learn about. This is sometimes called *niche picking* or *niche building.* These selections are related to the individual's motivation, personality, and intellectual ability, all of which are partially affected by one's genetic endowment. Active effects are the most powerful connection between people and environment. For example, someone who enjoys athletics pays attention to all kinds of athletic stimuli, selecting athletic activities, participating in them, and thus becoming a better athlete.

People help create their own environment. This adolescent's athletic talents encourage him to choose athletics as an important part of his day.

Figure 3.4
How Do Genetic Factors Affect Social Behavior?
Sandra Scarr and Kathleen McCartney (1993) suggest three ways in which genetic and environmental factors may interact to determine social behavior.

Passive effects: The child is influenced by the type of environment the parents provide, which may depend partially upon the intelligence level of the parents, which is partly genetic.

Evocative effects: This child's sociable manner, which may be partially related to temperament, may evoke a friendly response from others.

Active effects: Adolescents are allowed greater freedom to pursue their own interests and create their own world. Some of these choices may be partially determined by abilities that are influenced by genetic factors.

Temperament   The influence of genetic endowment and its interaction with environmental factors are shown in the research on temperament. Each child is born with a **temperament,** or individual style of responding to the environment. According to the classic work in the field, most children fit into three general types: easy, slow to warm up, and difficult (Thomas, Chess, & Birch, 1970). Children with "easy" temperaments are generally happy and flexible, and they get along with most people. Children who are "slow to warm up "are somewhat inhibited and do not respond well to changes in the environment, but their reactions are not intense. They exhibit a low activity level and have a tendency to withdraw from new stimuli. "Difficult" children are intense, demanding, and inflexible.

Critics of this approach note that only about two-thirds of all children fit directly into one of these three categories, and the use of the "difficult" category can easily lead people to think in negative terms. Other researchers have proposed different ways of conceptualizing temperament. One method suggests that temperament comprises three characteristics: emotionality, activity, and sociability. *Emotionality* refers to strength of arousal shown by infants in response to events. *Activity* is the expenditure of energy and movement, and *sociability* is the child's desire for rewards and being with other people (Buss & Plomin, 1984). The advantage of this system is that all children can be measured on these dimensions. No matter which approach is used to conceptualize temperament, all elements describing temperament have substantial genetic involvement (Goldsmith, Buss, & Lemery, 1997). A child's temperament influences how people react to him or her, which shows the importance of evocative effects. The child with an easy temperament is more likely to garner positive comments than the difficult child.

For our purposes, the important issue is how temperament may influence *adolescent* behavior. The extent to which temperament changes or remains stable is an issue, especially after infancy. Evidence exists both for moderate stability and for change (Kagan, Arcus, & Snidman, 1993; Park et al., 1997).

It is somewhat difficult to conduct longitudinal studies of temperament. We cannot expect children to show their temperament in the same way as they mature. For example, at age 2 months a child who is easily distractible will stop crying for food if rocked, and at 2 years will stop a tantrum if another activity is suggested. The underlying characteristic of distractibility is present, but with

temperament   An individual's style of responding to the environment.

age, different behaviors will be shown. One study found evidence of temperament styles observed at 3 years that were still evident in the behaviors of late adolescents at age 21, showing a continuation of temperament into, and in fact throughout, adolescence (Newman et al., 1997). In this study, observers (using a different category system) rated the behavior of about a thousand 3-year-old children and placed each child into an appropriate temperament category. Children assigned to the "well-adjusted" group showed adequate self-control and task persistence, were self-confident, and did not become overly upset if a task was too difficult. "Undercontrolled" children were irritable, impulsive, and not persistent on tasks; could not sit still; and were inattentive. "Inhibited" children were shy and fearful, offered little spontaneous communication, and lacked self-confidence.

When tested at age 21 years, some interesting continuities were found in the areas of adjustment, interpersonal conflict, and social reputation. Individuals in the well-adjusted group at 3 years continued to be described within the average range in adjustment, had minimal amounts of conflict, and had excellent peer relationships. Those rated "inhibited" at 3 years had smaller social support networks, had problems communicating with others, and were seen as not being very good at getting things done when they were 21 years. Young adults in the inhibited group, though, showed little antisocial behavior and still maintained reasonably good romantic and work relationships. Young adults who had been placed in the "undercontrolled" group at 3 years experienced a great deal of conflict in their interpersonal relationships, reported more antisocial behavior, and were not perceived by others as conscientious. The correlations between temperament group and later behavior were positive, but were not extremely strong, showing evidence for continuity but also some evidence for change.

The concept of temperament may be somewhat important in understanding the behavior of adolescents (Chess & Thomas, 1984; Nitz & Lerner, 1991). On the one hand, two adolescents may have similar intelligence scores and interests, yet they may differ significantly on the quickness with which they move and the ease in which they approach a new environment (Thomas & Chess, 1991). Temperament reflects behavioral style. On the other hand, two adolescents may have similar temperaments, but their abilities or motivations may differ.

Temperament, in itself, does not determine the level or quality of psychological functioning. What is most important is how well the teen's temperament fits with the environment. The **goodness-of-fit model** argues that the better the fit between the temperament and task, the more successful a teen will be. Say demands are made on a teenager for quick adaptation to change, such as participation in a new group; this challenge can be met by a child with the temperamental attributes of quick adaptability, but a child who adapts more slowly may find that the task is more difficult and causes greater anxiety.

The goodness-of-fit model may explain, and even predict, why some teens have difficulty in one setting and not another. An adolescent's temperament may fit some situations well and others not so well. Teachers may want students to show little distractibility, whereas parents may want their teens to be able to move easily from one activity to another (for example, from watching television to eating dinner). Adolescents who have a poor fit with the demands of their parents in childhood continue to show this poor fit throughout adolescence (Chess & Thomas, 1984). Adolescents whose temperaments match the demands of parents and peers have higher social competence and academic achievement, and their parents view them positively (Nitz & Lerner, 1991).

Adolescents need to appreciate the nature of their temperament. Teens who find that they get too angry at minor annoyances or who withdraw from social situations even when they would be accepted must understand the nature of their behavioral orientation and cope with it. A teen who is slower and more deliberate may need to begin an assignment earlier. Adolescents who know they can explode with intense anger can learn ways to reduce the problem.

Why Am I So Different from My Siblings? If genetic factors are so important in physical development and play a part in the personality and social areas of life, how can two children with the same parents be so different? The

goodness-of-fit model A way of analyzing how adolescents with different temperaments adapt to their surroundings; the model states that an adolescent adapts best when there is a match between the individual's temperament and the demands of the social environment.

AT A GLANCE   **3.2** THE BIOLOGICAL BASES FOR BEHAVIOR AND DEVELOPMENT

KEY POINT: Genetic and hormonal factors directly and indirectly influence development and behavior.

SUPPORTING POINTS	EXPLANATION
The hypothalamus, pituitary gland, and gonads (sex organs) are responsible for pubertal changes.	The end result of the hypothalamus–pituitary gland–gonadal system is the production of the male and female sex hormones, which are responsible for many pubertal changes.
The hypothalamus–pituitary gland–adrenal gland system also influences physical development.	The weak sex hormones produced by the adrenal glands seem to affect the development of some secondary sex characteristics, such as pubic hair.
Hormones may influence emotional experience in many ways.	Some research finds a direct relationship between hormone levels and greater emotionality, less impulse control, and aggression when provoked, although the relationship is complex. Other research suggests the rapid increase in hormones or hormonal fluctuation may influence emotionality or that high hormonal levels may be merely one additional stressor in a teen's life.
To determine the extent of genetic influence on a particular trait, scientists use twin studies and adoption studies.	Twin studies measure the extent of agreement between pairs of twins on a particular trait. Adoption studies measure the similarity between an adopted child and the biological and adoptive parents on some characteristic.
Genetic factors may interact with the environment to influence social behavior in three ways: by having passive, evocative, and active effects.	Passive effects indicate that parents' genetic endowment influences the way parents construct the child's environment. Evocative effects operate when some characteristic of the child that is influenced by biological factors, such as appearance, causes a reaction in others. Active effects operate when an individual chooses one activity over another because of superior abilities or interests, which may be influenced by genetic factors.
Temperament describes an individual's style of responding to the environment.	One system of measuring temperament describes children as easy, slow to warm up, and difficult. Another system measures emotionality, activity, and sociability. Other systems are also used. There is evidence for moderate stability in temperament, but also evidence for some change.
Temperament itself may be less important than how its characteristics fit in with environmental requirements.	The goodness-of-fit model maintains that an individual should show the best adjustment when temperament meshes with environmental demands.
Despite the fact that two siblings share the same parentage, they should be expected to show markedly different interests, abilities, and behaviors.	Siblings share, on average, half their genes, which means that half their genes are not held in common. Some shared environmental influences (such as living in the same family) exist; however, many more nonshared environmental influences (such as unique experiences with parents, at school, and with friends) affect children's behavior.

answer is easy to understand. Genetic influences may be divided into shared and unshared genetic influences. Shared genetic influence is the percentage of genes that two children share, which averages 50 percent for siblings. That means that an average of 50 percent of each sibling's genes are not shared. Although siblings possess some genes in common, they are also genetically different from each other. Environmental influences can be divided into two categories, First, **shared environmental influences** are those shared by siblings, including child-rearing strategies, socioeconomic variables, and parents' personalities (Pike & Plomin, 1996). Second, **nonshared environmental influences** include the individual's unique experiences, such as being treated differently from one's siblings, different school experiences, and peer relationships. Even shared features of the environment are experienced differently by siblings. After all, siblings are born at different times, their parents may be more or less at ease with their roles, and

shared environmental influences
Environmental factors, such as socioeconomic status or parental child-rearing styles, that are shared by siblings.

nonshared environmental influences
Environmental factors that are unique to the individual.

the family may be in different financial positions as the children develop. Also, many factors usually considered shared may affect children in the same family differently. For example, divorce is obviously a shared experience by children in the same family, but it may affect siblings differently (Pike & Plomin, 1996).

Nonshared environmental influences are more important in the areas of personality, cognitive ability, and psychopathology than are shared environmental influences (Plomin, 1994; Saudino & Plomin, 1996). Nonshared environmental influences often work to make siblings in the same family more different from each other than similar (Dunn & Plomin, 1990; Plomin, 1994a). For example, many studies show that agreeableness, conscientiousness, and emotional stability are somewhat influenced by one's genes. Genetic variance in personality traits account for between 22 and 46 percent of the total, whereas shared environmental influences contribute between 0 and 11 percent, and nonshared environmental influences account for between 44 and 55 percent (Loehlin, 1992). The greatest contributors to personality traits are the individual's unique experiences.

As we have said, half the genes of siblings who are not identical twins are not the same, and this type of nonshared inheritance can account for some behavioral differences as well (Plomin & Daniels, 1987). Siblings may be more similar to each other genetically than cousins or nonrelated people, but their genotypes also differ greatly from each other. When we look at both shared and nonshared environmental influences and genetic dissimilarity, it is obvious that variations in sibling behavior should be expected. In other words, the richness of genetic and environmental interaction should make us expect people in the same family to act differently, even if genetic factors underlie a particular trait. People often overestimate sibling similarity in both environmental and genetic aspects of life and underestimate the importance of nonshared qualities of both. *(For a review of this section, see At A Glance 3.2.)*

THE INTERPLAY OF PHYSICAL DEVELOPMENT AND EXPERIENCE

Genetic and environmental factors interact to determine physical attributes and physical abilities. Thus, an analysis of both genetic and environmental factors is necessary to explain physical development and appreciate how physical development may influence other areas of life, including social relationships and personality.

The Secular Trend: Taller, Earlier, and Heavier

In the past 150 years or so, each new generation has been taller and heavier than the preceding one, and each grows to maturity more rapidly (Eveleth & Tanner, 1990). In addition, each new generation has entered puberty at a slightly earlier age. These, as well as other, developmental tendencies toward earlier maturation, are known collectively as the **secular trend.** Since 1900, children each decade have been growing taller at the rate of approximately 1 centimeter and heavier by half a kilogram (1.1 pounds) (Katchadourian, 1977).

Menstruation is also starting earlier. Between 1880 and 1970, the age of menarche averaged some 3 to 4 months earlier per decade, although the decline was greater in some decades than in others (Tanner, 1990). The same trend is found across all industrialized nations (see Figure 3.5). For instance, between 1840 and 1850, the average age of menarche in Denmark was 17.2 years, whereas today it is less than 13 (Tanner, 1991b). In Japan, the decline in age of menarche has been steep; between 1950 and 1975 it declined about 1 year per decade (Eveleth & Tanner, 1990). A recent study of girls in India found a lowering of the age of menarche by an average rate of 6 months per decade in the last 3 decades in some areas (Bagga & Kulkarni, 2000). Secondary sex characteristics, such as

secular trend   The trend toward earlier maturation today compared with past generations.

breast enlargement and the appearance of pubic hair, are also appearing at younger ages, as is the peak adolescent growth spurt (Herman-Giddens et al., 1997). The secular trend is likely due to an improvement in nutrition, a decline in growth-retarding illnesses during the first 5 years of life, and better medical care.

In the last 20 years, the trend toward earlier maturation has slowed in what has been called a "stabilization" (Eveleth & Tanner, 1990, p. 170). However, this stabilization may not apply to all areas or groups. A recent study found that adolescent girls today are taller than those studied 20 years ago. Women's average height has risen from 5 feet 3 inches in 1980 to 5 feet 4⅜ inches in the mid-1990s (Temple, 1997). Another study found that after a pause in the 1950s and 1960s, the trend for people to become taller returned for both boys and girls born between 1973 and 1992 (Freedman et al., 2000). The greatest increase in height was found for African American boys between 5 and 8 years old and for both African American boys and girls between 9 and 12 years old. In addition, although the onset of menses in Caucasian girls has remained stable over the past decades, the age at which African American girls experience menarche is still declining (Herman-Giddens et al., 1997). Nutrition and health factors may still be influencing these trends as improvements in health care and nutrition continue in the African American community.

Environmental Factors and Pubertal Timing

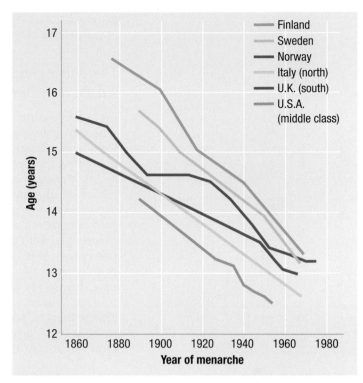

Figure 3.5

Secular Changes in Age of Menarche from 1860 to 1980

The average age of menarche has been declining for many years.

Source: Tanner (1990), p. 160. Reprinted by permission of the publisher from *Fetus into Man: Physical Growth from Conception to Maturity* by J. M. Tanner, p. 160, Cambridge, MA: Harvard University Press, Copyright © 1978, 1989 by J. M. Tanner.

Taken together, genetic, nutrition, and medical factors still do not account for all the variation in physical development among teenagers in the same population. Research points to environmental influences as additional factors determining pubertal timing (Belsky, Steinberg, & Draper, 1991). For example, very intensive physical training can delay puberty and menstruation (Warren et al., 1991). Delayed menarche is a common characteristic of some groups of athletes, with delays of 1 or 2 years reported for gymnasts, figure skaters, dancers, and runners. Typically, mothers and daughters show some similarity in age of menarche (Brooks-Gunn, 1991). However, when girls enrolled in dance company schools were compared with girls who did not attend such schools, a relationship between the mother's and daughter's age of menarche was found only for the nondancers, not for the dancers (Brooks-Gunn & Warren, 1988).

Studies of physical stress, such as malnutrition and disease, generally find that these stressors delay puberty—including menarche—perhaps allowing the body to channel its resources into survival rather than the physical changes of puberty (Surbey, 1998). Psychosocial factors have also been implicated in determining the timing of menarche. A number of research studies find a relationship between familial stress and earlier onset of puberty (Ellis & Graber, 2000). For example, family conflict and father's absence in childhood predict a moderately earlier age of menarche (Moffitt, Belsky, & Silva, 1992). Better family relations, including lack of conflict, the presence of the father, and lower amounts of stress are associated with later onset of menarche (Graber, Brooks-Gunn, & Warren, 1995). Not all results are consistent, though (Susman, 1997). Stress may well have different effects depending on the kind of stress and the individual's stage of puberty. Stress may affect youngsters at different stages of pubertal development differently (Susman et al., 1989). At present, the hormonal pathways that might explain the relationship between family situations and pubertal timing are not well understood. Our understanding of both hormonal regulation and the interaction between the hypothalamus-pituitary-adrenal system and the hypothalamus-pituitary-gonadal system is poor. Environmental factors may influence the timing of puberty, but the situation is certainly not well understood.

Psychological Reactions to Pubertal Timing: Early and Late Maturation

Most adolescents are neither very early maturing nor very late, but fall somewhere in between. They develop along with the majority of their peers. Some teenagers, though, mature either quite early or very late, and this experience may affect their personality and interpersonal relationships (see Table 3.3).

It is not difficult to define early or late maturation statistically, but it is the *perception* of being early or late that may affect an adolescent's psychological experiences. For instance, female ballet dancers, who can objectively be considered later developers, do not think of themselves that way because they compare themselves with other ballet students (Gargiulo et al., 1987). The individual's perception of maturational status depends not only on the objective status of development but also on comparisons with friends. Adolescents actively compare themselves with others.

Early and Late Maturation in Males   Early-maturing males have a substantial social advantage over late-maturing males. Adults rate early maturers more positively than late maturers. Early-maturing boys are considered more

Table 3.3		
Early And Late Maturation		
Most teenagers are neither early nor late maturing, but the experience of early or late maturation can affect the adolescent.		
Timing of Maturation	**Female**	**Male**
Early maturation	• Is more popular and dates earlier and more often	• Is considered more masculine and attractive
	• Is more vulnerable to peer pressure	• Is more popular and self-confident
	• Is more likely to get into trouble in school, use drugs, and engage in early sex	• Is somewhat more likely to show behavior problems in school
	• Has lower grades	• Becomes less active, less curious, and more submissive with age
	• Experiences more emotional distress	
	• Has a less positive body image	
Late maturation	• Experiences less pressure to engage in antisocial conduct	• Is considered tenser, more childish, and more attention seeking
	• Is more poised and assertive	• Is considered more rebellious, yet dependent
	• Has a body image that is more consistent with current trends (taller and thinner)	• Is more assertive, flexible, and insightful in adulthood
	• Has fewer problems with parents	
	• Has more time to adjust to changes and challenges	

Being early or late in development can influence an individual's personality and experiences in adolescence.

masculine, more attractive, and better groomed. They also have advantages in athletic competition, which may lead to popularity and increased self-esteem. Boys who mature early tend to be taller, stronger, more athletically oriented, and generally more popular than late-maturing boys. They have greater expectations for being independent (Spencer et al., 1998). They have more self-confidence and are more satisfied with their physical appearance. These advantages continue into early adulthood.

The picture is not entirely positive, though, as early-maturing males are also more likely than their later-maturing peers to show behavioral problems at school, to be truants and delinquent, and to use drugs (Andersson & Magnusson, 1990; Duncan et al., 1985). Early-maturing boys may form friendships with older boys and may be drawn into such behaviors. In addition, early-maturing boys become less active, more submissive, and less curious as they progress through adulthood, especially in middle age (Peskin, 1973). All in all, however, early maturation is usually considered a social advantage for boys.

Late-maturing boys are considered tense and childish, and they are seen as always seeking attention (Brooks-Gunn, 1988). Peers perceive them as bossy, restless, less attractive, and having less leadership ability. Late maturers are also viewed as more rebellious and dependent, demonstrating a basic conflict in their personalities. They have a difficult time adjusting in adolescence (Alsaker, 1992). Some may compensate for their feelings of inadequacy by acting out. However, others may develop coping and interpersonal skills that help them throughout life. In fact, late maturers are often more assertive, flexible, and insightful, especially as they proceed through middle age, whereas early-maturing boys become more conforming and rigid.

Early and Late Maturation in Females Early-maturing girls are more optimistic about their future, are more popular with boys, and date both more often and earlier than later-maturing girls (Gargiulo et al., 1987; Simmons & Blyth, 1987). They are also more vulnerable to peer pressure to perform antisocial acts or take risks compared with on-time and late-maturing peers (Ge, Conger, & Elder, 1996). Perhaps one reason for the tendency for early-maturing girls and, to some extent, early-maturing boys to take more risks in sexual expression and drug use is that these young teens are less cognitively mature and show less mature reasoning powers (Orr & Ingersoll, 1995). Early-maturing girls are more independent, but also more likely to be delinquent, use drugs, and misbehave in school (Aro & Taipale, 1987; Koff & Rierdan, 1993). Despite the fact that intelligence tests measure no differences in cognitive ability, early-maturing girls have lower grades than average-maturing girls (Spencer et al., 1998). They are more likely to associate with older girls when compared with late-developing or on-time girls, and they experience more pressure to have early sexual intercourse and break rules; indeed, they are more likely to engage in sexual intercourse at an earlier age (Magnusson, 1988).

One major difference between the experiences of boys and girls is that young teenage girls who are well developed can make themselves look older, whereas even well-developed boys tend to look their age.

One basic difference between early-maturing boys and girls may account for the greater dangers that seem to surround early-maturing girls: Early-maturing boys still look their age. Few people will confuse a 14-year-old early-developing boy with a 17-year-old. This is not the case with an early-developing teenage girl. By using makeup, adopting a more mature hairstyle, and dressing in a certain manner, she often can look older than she is. Thus, people may attribute greater social maturity to early-maturing girls than they really have (Caspi et al., 1993). In addition, girls, unlike boys, prefer to go out with those who are the same age or older than they are. Early-maturing girls may be flattered by the attention of older boys. Parents may not feel that their daughters are ready to

PERSPECTIVE 2

I'm Ready; You're Not

SETTING THE SCENE: Naseem is constantly at odds with her parents. She feels her parents are not allowing her to grow up.

NASEEM'S PARENTS: *We know that Naseem feels that we are too strict, but we don't think she is ready for some experiences. Although she is just 14, she looks 18. When she does her hair, puts on her makeup, and dresses up, she attracts boys who are 17 and 18, and we don't feel she can handle the pressures of dating older boys. Most of her friends are older. We also don't think she should be dressing the way she does or wearing so much makeup.*

NASEEM: *My parents just don't want me to grow up. I can handle myself. I know the facts of life. Most of my friends are older; I just don't have anything in common with girls my own age. Why can't my parents trust me? I know they don't like the way I do my hair or makeup or the way I dress, but that's the way my friends do it. My parents can't stop me from growing up.*

QUESTION: Last week, Naseem's parents noticed a number of pamphlets on birth control in their daughter's room, sticking out of her backpack. They didn't say anything, but they are concerned. They know she is friendly with older boys, especially one boy, Tom. If you were Naseem's parents, what would you do?

date an older boy at this age, and this situation may lead to considerable conflict between the adolescent girl and her parents.

Early-maturing girls also admit to experiencing more frequent and intense emotional distress than do average-maturing girls (Ge et al., 1996). A comparison of the level of psychological distress between early-maturing girls and on-time and late-maturing girls in grades 7 through 10 found that the mean level of distress for early-maturing girls was only slightly higher in grade 7, but the mean differences became greater at grades 8, 9, and 10. It seems that early maturation forces girls to confront stressful environments and expectations before they are truly psychologically prepared for such challenges.

Early-maturing girls also tend to have a poorer body image and to be less satisfied with many of their physical characteristics than later maturers (Duncan et al., 1985). Some early-maturing girls are somewhat heavier than their peers and may not conform to cultural values of thinness (Attie & Brooks-Gunn, 1989). Later-maturing girls tend to be somewhat taller and thinner, more nearly approximating the cultural ideal of beauty in Western society. Most of these differences are significantly reduced or even nonexistent by 10th grade.

Early-maturing girls who date at a young age may not be able to cope with the typical disappointments and rejections and are more vulnerable to depression (Graber et al., 1994). Early-maturing girls are also at a somewhat greater risk for anxiety disorders, such as phobias and panic disorders, along with depression and eating disorders (Hayward et al., 1997).

Despite the possible negative consequences of early maturation among girls, many early-maturing girls do not have behavioral problems. Early maturation may be most difficult for girls with a history of such problems. A comparison of early-maturing, on-time, and late-maturing girls found an increase in problem behaviors for the early-maturing girls. When early-maturing girls with a history of problem behavior were compared with those who did not have such a history, only the girls with a history of problems showed an increase in behavioral problems (Caspi & Moffitt, 1991). The early maturers without a history of behavioral problems were no different than on-time maturers. Early maturation, then, is a stressor that magnifies individual differences that exist even before adolescence.

Late-maturing girls are more likely to show higher levels of self-doubt, but they are under far less social pressure than early-maturing girls. Because girls mature about 2 years earlier than boys, later-maturing girls may develop along with their male peers. Late-maturing girls are more gregarious, poised, and assertive. In general, early-maturing girls and late-maturing boys seem to have the most adjustment problems (Graber et al., 1997).

Pubertal timing may influence how parents deal with their adolescent children. Parents perceive less conflict with early-maturing sons than with moderate- or late-maturing sons. In contrast, early-maturing daughters are perceived to be a source of more stress and anxiety for their parents than late-maturing daughters and on-time maturers (Savin-Williams & Small, 1986). Perhaps part of this stress comes from difficulties in monitoring early-maturing girls dating older boys. The early-maturing boy is less likely to date and be involved with older teenage girls. *(For a review of this section, see At A Glance 3.3.)*

AT A GLANCE   3.3 THE INTERPLAY OF PHYSICAL DEVELOPMENT AND EXPERIENCE

KEY POINT: Genetic and environmental factors interact in a complex manner to determine the behavior of the individual.

SUPPORTING POINTS	EXPLANATION
The secular trend describes the tendency for successive generations to enter puberty at an earlier age. It also refers to other trends, such as the fact that people are becoming taller.	The secular trend exists because of improvements in nutrition and medical care. There is evidence that it is leveling off or may have stopped in many developed societies.
Environmental factors may influence the timing of puberty.	Extreme physical exercise may delay the onset of puberty. Stress, as in poor family situations, may influence pubertal timing, but the hormonal mechanisms responsible are not yet well understood.
Early maturation is an advantage in males, whereas late maturation in males appears to be a disadvantage.	Early maturing boys are more attractive and more confident. Later-maturing boys are seen as childish and dependent.
Early maturation in females is considered a disadvantage.	Although early-maturing girls may be more popular, they are also more vulnerable to peer pressure, the use of drugs, having sex early, and getting lower grades. Later-maturing girls have the advantage of maturing with the boys in their grade and show fewer adjustment problems.

THE HEALTH OF TODAY'S TEENAGERS

In the past 25 years, people in developed countries have come to realize that choices in eating, exercise, sleep, and drug taking help determine their health status and significantly influence their psychological functioning. This section first will look at the state of adolescent health and then investigate the choices adolescents make in nutrition, physical activity, and sleep. Behavioral risk factors, including drug taking and violence, will be discussed in "Drug Use and Violence."

Rating Adolescent Health

The health of most adolescents is objectively good from a medical standpoint, and most adolescents, when asked, state that their health is excellent or good. African American and Latino adolescents are less likely than Caucasian adolescents to report having excellent or very good health, although more than a majority say they have good or excellent health. They are also less likely to have health insurance, and about one in seven adolescents is uninsured. Minority group youth have a higher frequency of chronic illnesses, probably due to their higher rates of poverty. One suggestion to improve medical services, especially for traditionally underserved adolescents, is to bring doctors to the schools through school-based health centers (Lieu, Newacheck, & McManus, 1993). Another suggestion is for doctors dealing with teenagers to discuss psychosocial and behavioral concerns more with their adolescent patients.

The basic doctor-patient relationship changes during adolescence. In childhood, the doctor essentially talks to the parent about the child's health. In adolescence, teenagers become active participants in their own health maintenance behaviors and assume responsibility for discussing health issues with the doctor.

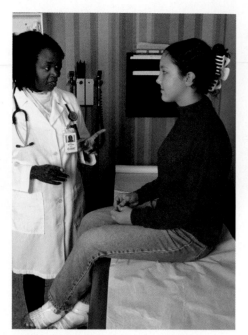

The doctor-patient relationship changes in adolescence as privacy issues arise and adolescents become active participants in making health decisions.

It is important to schedule time for private conversations between the doctor and the adolescent patient. These private conversations reflect the increasing freedom and responsibility to make one's own decisions in all areas of life, including health, that arise during adolescence.

The Increasing Concern over Adolescent Health Practices

Although most adolescents are healthy, there is still need for concern. The health problems of adolescents are mainly, but not exclusively, in the behavioral areas, including poor levels of physical fitness, poor nutrition, drug taking, violent behavior, and early sex (Carnegie Council, 1995).

The relationship between behavior and health is obvious in some cases, such as drinking and traffic accidents. In other cases, the consequences of poor health habits may not be evident for many years; for example, smoking, lack of exercise, and poor eating patterns may take their toll only later. Furthermore, teenagers in high-risk groups do not change their behaviors. Teenagers who were found to be at risk for later heart disease due to high blood pressure, obesity, and family history consumed saturated fats and large amounts of salt, were not exercising, were drinking alcohol, and were smoking cigarettes with no thought to their future health status (Adeyanju, 1989). Young people's health is more often jeopardized by their own risky behaviors than by disease (Moore, Gullone, & Kostanski, 1997; Wilson & Joffe, 1995).

What is the nature of adolescent health choices? How well do adolescents eat? How much do they exercise? Do teens get enough sleep? We will consider each of these issues in turn.

Nutrition

The recommended daily allowances for most vitamins and minerals, especially calcium, increase during the teenage years (Barr, 1994). In fact, nutrition needs are greater during adolescence than during any other time of life, with the exception of pregnancy or lactation (Whitney & Rolfes, 2002). Eating patterns among teens are variable, and no single pattern is found. Some teenagers have good diets, whereas the diets of others are deficient. In less developed countries or those with long, ongoing wars, malnutrition may be a significant problem. In the United States and developed countries, nutrition problems are most likely to involve particular vitamin or mineral deficiencies, overeating, nutrition imbalances, and poor food choices (Freedland & Dwyer, 1991).

Many adolescents do not consume the recommended levels of vitamins, minerals, and dietary fiber, and their diets contain too much fat—about 20 percent more than recommended (Levine & Guthrie, 1997). Table 3.4 shows the results of one study of the adequacy of adolescent nutrition intake in the United States (Munoz et al., 1998). As you can see, relatively few adolescents consume enough fruit or vegetables. This consumption pattern may place teens at risk for developing later health problems. Teenage girls are especially likely not to meet the recommended dietary allowances for calcium, iron, magnesium, and zinc. Teen boys, who eat more than girls, nevertheless are often deficient in calcium and dietary fiber. Teens tend to consume a high-fat diet and have a sedentary lifestyle (watching more sports on television than participating in them), factors that may contribute to the increase in obesity found in teens today.

Eating patterns, such as eating a good breakfast, are often formed early in life and continue through adolescence (Nicklas et al., 1993). The most common nutrition problems are skipping breakfast and snacking excessively (Hertzler & Frary, 1989). Adolescent girls are more likely to skip breakfast than teenage boys, but both groups tend to skip lunch (Shaw, 1998). They compensate by snacking on food that is often not very nutritious. Skipping breakfast is a special

Table 3.4

Percentage of Adolescents Who Meet the Recommended Number of Servings for Four Food Groups

Food Group	Male (%)	Female (%)
Dairy products	49	22
Fruits	17	19
Vegetables	50	21
Grains	43	21

Source: Data from Munoz et al. (1998).

problem, because eating breakfast is related to better attention and academic progress. Teenagers who live in poverty skip breakfast more often, but lack of money does not seem to be the reason (Bidgood & Cameron, 1992). Rather, the most common reason is not liking to eat particular meals and lack of time (Singleton & Rhoads, 1982).

Peers also influence a teenager's eating patterns. If an adolescent's friends perceive drinking milk as childish and choose soft drinks instead, skip meals, or snack on the run, these patterns influence others in the group. Many factors influence the food choices of adolescents, but nutrition value is far down the list, with food cravings, taste, time, and convenience being much more important (Neumark-Sztainer et al., 1999). Nevertheless, nutrition is important in adolescence, not only for health reasons but also because eating affects one's weight and body image.

Teenagers and Body Image The primary concern of adolescents, especially in early adolescence, is their body (Emmons, 1996). A positive view of one's body is related to self-esteem, self-confidence, popularity with the other gender, and assertiveness (Hesse-Biber, Clayton-Matthews, & Downey, 1987). Adolescents place more importance on body image and feel more negatively about their bodies than do older people (Cash, Winstead, & Janda, 1986). Physical attractiveness correlates with greater participation in extracurricular activities, as well as positive peer and teacher ratings and relations (Duke-Duncan, 1991). A disparity between perceived body image and ideal body image may lead to dissatisfaction with one's physical appearance, causing lower self-esteem, social anxiety, and self-consciousness (Smith, Handley, & Eldredge, 1998).

A natural part of pubertal development for females is an increase in body fat, whereas the weight gain for males is mostly an increase in muscle mass (Richards, Casper, & Larson, 1990). Partly because of this increase in fat, girls are much more likely to experience problems with their body image than boys and are generally less satisfied with their bodies (Galambos, Almeida, & Petersen, 1990). For example, although 81 percent of the girls in one study were assessed to be within the ideal weight range or even underweight, 78 percent wanted to weigh less, and only 14 percent were satisfied with their current weight (Eisele, Hertsgaard, & Light, 1986). Many more girls consider themselves overweight than really are overweight (Pritchard, King, & Czajka-Narins, 1997). This dissatisfaction with body weight is so common in U.S. girls that it is sometimes called a "*normative discontent,*" meaning that it is typical of teenage girls in American society (Foster, Wadden, & Vogt, 1997; Rodin, 1993). Teenage girls often misperceive how they look, thinking they weigh more or are larger than their actual measurements. The cultural ideal for women in Western societies equates thinness with success and beauty, but this conflicts with improvements in nutrition and health care, which have made the average female somewhat heavier than she was just 25 years ago (Furnham, Titman, & Sleeman, 1994).

Satisfaction with one's body is based upon cultural considerations. Caucasian females tend to show greater discontent with their bodies and want a lower body weight than do African American females (Emmons, 1996; Pritchard et al., 1997). Latino and Asian females share some of the preference for thinness (Cash & Henry, 1995; Joiner & Kashubeck, 1996). African Americans and people from the Caribbean value a somewhat larger body size, and normal-weight females in these cultures are less likely to consider themselves overweight (Coogan et al., 1996). Socioeconomic status also influences body satisfaction. Females from higher income groups are more likely to desire to be thinner than girls from lower income groups (Duncan et al., 1985).

As adolescence proceeds, male body image tends to improve somewhat, whereas female body dissatisfaction increases. Caucasian girls and boys were assessed at 13, 15, and 18 years of age on measures of satisfaction and

Most teenage girls, even if their body weight is within the normal range, still believe they need to lose weight. This normative discontent for weight may lead to unhealthy eating habits.

dissatisfaction with various parts of the body, overall body image, and physical attractiveness. There were no significant gender differences in overall body dissatisfaction at 13 years, although more girls than boys were dissatisfied with their body build. By 15 years and again at 18 years, however, clear differences were present, with girls more dissatisfied than boys (Rosenblum & Lewis, 1999). Satisfaction with weight and body image is based not only on objective criteria but also on subjective evaluation. Individuals who believe they are farther from their ideal than they really are (looking at their objective weight status) feel worse about themselves than those who may actually have a larger difference in objective weight status from their ideal but do not consider themselves as having that much disparity (Cash & Hicks, 1990). The labels that individuals assign themselves have major implications for body image. When football players, swimmers, and nonathletes were sampled, for example, the percentage of body fat was negatively related to body image for nonathletes but not for athletes, who compare themselves with their peers and do not feel overweight (Huddy, Nieman, & Johnson, 1993). It may be that athletes feel good about their bodies despite higher weights, or that their body image is more closely tied to athletic accomplishments, such as winning football games, than to physical attributes.

Body Image and Eating Habits Without question, most high school girls—obese and nonobese alike—have a powerful fear of obesity. Between one-half and two-thirds of all high school girls in the United States are on a diet at any particular time. Furthermore, most of these diets are unnecessary, because the majority of female dieters of all races and ethnic groups are not overweight (Cauffman & Steinberg, 1996). The Centers for Disease Control (1991) estimated that 62 percent of all girls and 28 percent of all boys in grades 8 and 10 had been on a diet in the past year. Male dieters set preferred weights closer to their actual weights than did female dieters, especially Caucasian females, who want an average weight much lower than their reported weight (Emmons, 1996). Most of this dieting involves adopting a low-fat or low-calorie diet, eating less, and perhaps increasing physical activity—behaviors that usually can be considered healthy (French, Perry, et al., 1995). However, a substantial number of adolescents use dangerous and unhealthy activities, such as fasting or fad diets, to reduce weight.

These unhealthy weight loss practices have been reported by girls as young as 9 years old (Berg, 1992). Body image views may be formed at puberty, and dissatisfaction with one's body and dieting may be present even before puberty begins (Sands et al., 1997). About a third of all 9-year-olds and more than half the 10-year-olds in one study reported fear of becoming fat and perceived themselves as overweight, even though they were not (Mellin, Irwin, & Scully, 1992). Extreme weight concern in these young girls is predictive of symptoms of eating disorders later on, including anorexia nervosa and bulimia (Killen et al., 1994). Anorexia nervosa is an eating disorder involving self-starvation that is potentially fatal, whereas bulimia involves bingeing and purging behaviors in which an individual eats large amounts of food and then induces vomiting. Anorexia nervosa and bulimia will be discussed in detail in "Stress and Psychological, Physical, and Learning Problems." In middle school (5th through 8th grades), concerns about weight are even more prevalent, and extreme weight control behaviors are sometimes found (see Table 3.5) (Childress et al., 1993). These behaviors and attitudes are associated with depressive symptoms, lower self-esteem, and feelings of inadequacy and worthlessness (Killen et al., 1994; Lewinsohn et al., 1993).

Some of the adolescent girls' obsession with weight is based upon girls' perception of social attitudes. Females are more stigmatized by being overweight than males. When students in high school were questioned about their attitudes toward weight and dating, male students were less tolerant of overweight partners than were female students (Sobal, Nicolopoulos, & Lee, 1995). In addition, many models in magazines and television are ridiculously thin, and teenage girls often believe they have to measure up to an impossible cultural stereotype. Pictures of very thin models in magazines influence their ideas about the perfect body shape; these photos convince many teens that they are fat and must diet (Turner et al., 1997). About half reported that they wanted to lose weight because of a magazine picture, although only 29 percent were actually overweight. Yet each gender distorts the opinions of the other. When shown pictures of girls with different body types, nearly twice as many girls as boys chose the thinnest female figure as the most attractive, and twice as many boys as girls chose the heaviest male figure as attractive (Cohn, Adler, & Irwin, 1987). This same misconception appears in college students; college women exaggerate male preference for female thinness, and males underestimate female preferences for male thinness (Cash & Henry, 1995).

Males have largely been ignored in this analysis of problems with body image. However, recent findings indicate that males are also falling victim to body image difficulties (Davis et al., 1996). Some male wrestlers have engaged in very unhealthy dieting, and runners show an intense concern for weight control and a tendency toward disordered eating patterns (Parks & Read, 1997).

Another major problem among male adolescents is the increased use of drugs to develop greater muscle density and improve athletic performance. The prescribed cultural stereotype for attractiveness in males, and especially male athletes, is a very angular, muscular body. Athletic competition is highly competitive, and athletes often look for a competitive edge. To reach the goals of greater muscularity and improved athletic performance, some males use nutrition supplements of dubious effectiveness and anabolic steroids (Wang & Yesalis, 1994). Anabolic steroids are drugs derived from the male sex hormone testosterone, which is responsible for the development of male characteristics and lean body mass. Athletes may take anabolic steroids to stimulate muscle mass despite the long-term risks and side effects, which include breathing difficulties, skin problems, elevated heart rate, risk of heart disease, and aggressiveness and hostility, to name just a few. Anabolic steroids are dangerous and, indeed, illegal

Table 3.5

Middle School Students' Desire to Lose Weight and Ways of Achieving Weight Loss

A sizable percentage of fifth through ninth graders want to lose weight, and some use dangerous methods to do so.

Item	Gender	
	Female[a]	Male[b]
Wanted to lose weight*	55.0	28.5
Felt looked fat*	54.5	27.8
Afraid of weight gain*	32.5	13.0
Dieted*	42.6	19.7
Fasted*	11.2	6.0
Vomited*	5.6	3.9
Exercised*	37.8	27.3
Used diet pills*	3.6	1.1
Used diuretics	2.2	0.8
Used laxatives	2.3	0.7
Binged*	6.5	26.3

[a]*n* = 1,599. [b]*n* = 1,530.
*Statistically significant difference between males and females.
Source: Adapted from Childress et al. (1993), Table 2.

Please place the number best reflecting your opinion next to each of the following statements. Then compare your opinions now with those you held before reading the chapter.

1 — Strongly Agree
2 — Moderately Agree
3 — No Opinion
4 — Moderately Disagree
5 — Strongly Disagree

_____ 1. Menarche (the onset of menstruation) is a pivotal crisis in the life of a young girl.

_____ 2. It is unhealthy for a girl to engage in so much exercise that it delays the onset of puberty.

_____ 3. Parents should place greater restrictions on girls who mature early, because they are more likely to date and be influenced by older teens.

_____ 4. The increase in emotionality in adolescence is caused by increases in hormones.

_____ 5. Genetic factors become less important in possible explanations for behavior and development as a person matures.

_____ 6. People can learn to deal with the fact that they are slow at doing something or get angry easily.

_____ 7. Adolescents are more health conscious today than adolescents were a decade or two ago.

_____ 8. Teenage girls' eating problems are mainly due to the influence of the media, which glorify "thinness" and make being heavy a social stigma.

_____ 9. People often overestimate the importance of being thin.

_____ 10. Most teenagers understand the importance of nutrition and exercise.

substances (National Academy of Sports Medicine, 1992; Ropp, 1992). Male athletes also take a myriad of other performance-enhancing substances. Most have not been the focus of much controlled research, and the future consequences of their consumption are unknown. The use of steroids by adolescents is significantly related to their use by friends, usually other athletes (Yarnold, 1998).

Obesity Depending on the definition of obesity, estimates for the number of all teenagers who are obese range from 10 to 15 percent, and some estimates are higher (Brown, 2002). Obesity has increased among teenagers over the past 20 years, probably because they are less active than they were. Obesity is a problem in minority group youth as well as majority group youth (Will et al., 1999).

Obese teenagers face many problems. For one, they have more difficulty developing a coherent identity (Shestowsky, 1983). Obesity also creates social problems for the teen. Because our society's view of beauty and attractiveness is equated with being thin, the obese person is out of step with current fashion. Obese teens are more likely to be rejected, especially in dating situations, and are often teased. Overweight boys have lower self-esteem in the athletic domain and overweight girls, in the social domain (Mendelson & White, 1985). Obesity causes youngsters to feel more self-conscious about their weight, and such feelings translate into low body esteem, which in turn may erode global self-esteem (Mendelson, White, & Mendelson, 1996).

The long-term consequences of obesity can be severe. The relative risk of death from all causes, and death from coronary heart disease in particular, is about twice as high in individuals who have been overweight in adolescence than in people who are lean. The relative risks of dying from stroke and colon cancer later in life are also higher.

Most studies, though, do not find that obese people are at risk for major psychological problems (Friedman & Brownell, 1995). Self-esteem is not singly dependent on weight, either. Some obese people have high self-esteem. Some overweight teens even develop a good physical self-image, often by improving their grooming, becoming more assertive, or engaging in activities in which they show talent and success.

Obese children become obese teens, and obese teens become obese adults (Epstein, 1987). This progression probably has a number of reasons. For example, parental supervision of eating habits wanes during the teen years as the adolescent gains personal freedom. Social and academic pressure may lead to increased caloric intake. Many students use food to quiet their anxiety, and the less physically active life many older teens lead runs counter to the more active life of childhood (American Athletic Union, 1989). Even though many teenagers are less active, their diets may be high in fat and sugar, and they do not cut back on their consumption of these foods (Carruth & Goldberg, 1990).

There is no easy cure for obesity. Certainly, nutrition information is needed, because teens eat an enormous amount of junk food, and their diets are often rich in starch but deficient in basic nutrients. In addition, some teens use crash diets, semistarvation, or fad diets in a desperate attempt to lose or maintain weight. These approaches can cause physical damage, especially to the kidneys, and they are not effective in the long run. Perhaps a combination of increased physical activity under a doctor's supervision, nutrition information, a reduction in the consumption of junk food, and psychological support provided by a peer group and family members can help the obese teen lose weight and keep it off. However, long-term weight loss is difficult, and the battle against fat is lifelong.

Physical Activity

The benefits of physical activity are substantial at all ages. Exercise plays an important part in physical and psychological health (Potvin, Gauvin, & Nguyen, 1997). Physical inactivity is a risk factor for obesity and chronic disease such as cardiovascular disease later in life (Savage & Scott, 1998). Physical activity reduces mortality rates later on, promotes weight loss, and plays a role in preventing obesity. Exercise also helps people cope with stress. Adolescents who are more active have higher levels of self-esteem and see their bodies more positively (Calfras & Taylor, 1994; Morris & Summers, 1995).

Unfortunately, far too many adolescents are physically inactive (Epstein et al., 1999). A study of middle school students in grades 7, 8, and 9 found that 25 percent of the males and 41 percent of the females were considered sedentary, whereas about a third of the boys and girls were rated as active (Savage & Scott, 1998). Over one-third of adolescent males said they participated in vigorous physical activity less than twice a week, and almost half of adolescent females reported levels of activity below nationally recommended guidelines in middle school. Physical activity declines as the years of adolescence roll by (see Figure 3.6). Adolescent girls, in particular, tend to be sedentary, especially after puberty, and they participate in fewer sports (Freedland & Dwyer, 1991). Activity and fitness levels of American youth generally have deteriorated significantly over the past two decades.

One reason for the lack of activity is that enrollment in high school physical education classes falls drastically from ninth to twelfth grades (Elias, 1994). Physical activity is tied to team sports in many high schools. Teens who don't qualify for varsity teams—about 70 percent who try out in junior high, and then 70 percent of the teens on junior high teams when they get to high school—tend to abandon sports, along with other kinds of physical activity (*CQ Researcher*, 1997). Many high school students see being active and fit as the province of the athletes. In fact, even those who make the team often don't stay very active after graduating from high school. Once teens learn to drive, they walk and bicycle less. In addition, computer activities and television time cut into physical activity. Barriers to exercise include time problems and social factors, such as having no one to exercise with (Myers & Roth, 1997). Some physical education classes are changing from emphasizing competitive sports to focusing on activities such as walking, running, and bicycling, possible sources of physical activity after adolescence.

Some adolescents exercise in health clubs, but they are really the exceptions. Although more teens are joining health clubs, many do not go, and those who do go often engage in more socializing than exercising (*CQ Researcher*, 1997).

Males and females may exercise for different reasons. A survey of undergraduate men and women who exercise found that men exercised more for health and fitness reasons, whereas women exercised more for weight and appearance reasons (Smith, Handley, & Eldredge, 1998).

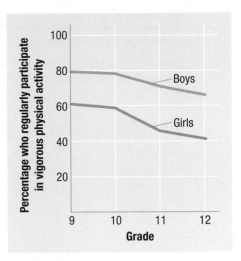

Figure 3.6
Regular Participation in Vigorous Physical Activity by High School Students, 1995
As adolescents proceed through the high school years, they are less likely to be physically active.

Source: Centers for Disease Control (1995). National Youth Risk Behavior Survey.

Sleep: Why Are Teens So Tired?

The amount of sleep adolescent boys and girls between the ages of 10 and 18 years get each night declines substantially, from about 10 hours during middle childhood to less than 7.5 hours at age 18 (see Table 3.6) (Wolfson & Carskadon, 1998). Optimal sleep time for adolescents is about 9.2 hours, which is about the same amount of time that teenagers say they need when asked (Carskadon, Harvey, & Duke, 1980). Teens go to bed later and rise earlier on school days (Manber et al., 1995). Almost half the high school students go to bed after midnight on school nights, and 90 percent do so on weekends (Carskadon & Mancuso, 1988). When they have to get up earlier—for example, for an early-starting school day instead of a late-starting one—they do not adjust their bedtimes, so they get less sleep (Allen, 1992). Teens today get about 1.5 hours less sleep than their great-grandparents did, perhaps due to greater academic and social pressures (Harris, 1995).

Teenagers sleep less than elementary school children for many reasons. Parents become much less likely to demand or even suggest specific bedtimes as the years of adolescence pass by. Adolescents also like staying up later, using the later time to watch television, study, and socialize. Adolescents cite social and academic pressures and earlier starting times in high school as the main reasons for staying up later and getting less sleep. However, the adolescent preference for later bedtimes and to sleep later into the morning if they have a chance,

Table 3.6

Self-Reported Sleep Patterns in Adolescents

Adolescents say they need a little more than 9 hours per night of sleep to function most effectively. As teenagers progress through the adolescent years, the amount of sleep they get declines.

Type of Night	Age	Girls			Boys		
		Bedtime	*Rise Time*	*Sleep Time*	*Bedtime*	*Rise Time*	*Sleep Time*
School nights	10	9:30	7:15	9 hr 45 min	9:09	7:00	9 hr 51 min
	11	9:30	7:05	9 hr 35 min	9:40	7:00	9 hr 20 min
	12	9:45	6:55	9 hr 10 min	9:50	7:05	9 hr 15 min
	13	10:06	6:50	8 hr 44 min	10:28	7:00	8 hr 21 min
	14	10:10	5:56	7 hr 46 min	10:16	6:15	7 hr 59 min
	15	10:24	6:05	7 hr 41 min	10:43	6:27	7 hr 44 min
	16	10:52	6:13	7 hr 21 min	11:08	6:38	7 hr 30 min
	17	10:58	6:26	7 hr 28 min	11:14	6:45	7 hr 31 min
	18[a]	1:15 A.M.	8:18	7 hr 3 min	1:30 A.M.	8:36	7 hr 6 min
Weekend nights	10	10:25	8:10	9 hr 45 min	10:22	7:45	9 hr 23 min
	11	10:22	8:25	9 hr 3 min	10:50	7:45	8 hr 55 min
	12	10:55	8:35	9 hr 40 min	11:05	8:35	9 hr 40 min
	13	11:20	8:45	9 hr 25 min	11:42	8:45	9 hr 3 min
	14	11:57	9:14	9 hr 17 min	12:06 A.M.	9:12	9 hr 6 min
	15	12:11 A.M.	9:24	9 hr 13 min	12:27 A.M.	9:25	8 hr 58 min
	16	12:28 A.M.	9:21	8 hr 53 min	12:44 A.M.	9:37	8 hr 52 min
	17	12:39 A.M.	9:21	8 hr 42 min	12:51 A.M.	9:29	8 hr 38 min
	18[a]	2:48 A.M.	10:39	7 hr 51 min	2:43 A.M.	10:40	7 hr 57 min

[a]From college freshmen.
Source: Carskadon (1990), Table 1, p. 6.

Most adolescents admit they do not get sufficient sleep. The lack of sleep is due to staying up later and getting up earlier on school days.

called a *delayed phase preference,* may also have a physiological basis (Carskadon, Veira, & Acebo, 1993).

Teenagers know they are not getting enough sleep (Andrade et al., 1993). When asked, 87 percent said they needed more sleep than they get (Wolfson & Carskadon, 1998). Teenagers are well aware that they are often tired in school and show signs of fatigue.

Many people think that adolescents do not really need as much sleep as preadolescents. However, teenagers actually require as much, or even more, sleep than when they were younger (Carskadon, 1990). Even when sleeping as much as younger adolescents, older teenagers report being sleepy and tired during the day (Carskadon et al., 1980). Sleep is especially important at a time of rapid physiological change, and some modifications in the brain's electrical activity during sleep in adolescence may signal organizational changes in the brain (Harris, 1995).

The constant fatigue experienced by teens may lead to lack of attention in school and poor academic performance. Teenagers getting less sleep report greater levels of depressive moods, and insufficient sleep may be one source of the irritability and moodiness that some adolescents show (Wolfson & Carskadon, 1998). More sleep, earlier bedtimes, and later weekday risings are associated with better grades.

AT A GLANCE **3.4** THE HEALTH OF TODAY'S TEENAGERS

KEY POINT: Teenagers make many health-related choices that influence their well-being, especially in the areas of nutrition, physical exercise, and sleep.

SUPPORTING POINTS	EXPLANATION
Although most adolescents are in good physical health, there is room for concern.	Health concerns revolve around nutrition, physical fitness, lack of sleep, violence, and drug use. Even when young people are at risk for future physical ailments, they do not change their behaviors.
Specific nutrition deficiencies in adolescents in developed countries have been noted.	Teens may not be getting enough calcium or consuming sufficient amounts of fruits and vegetables.
Females are more likely to have a poor body image than are males, and many who are within the normal range of weight consider themselves overweight.	The tendency of female adolescents to consider themselves overweight when they aren't is so common that it is called the *normative discontent* for weight. Female teenagers often want to live up to an impossible physical ideal.
Obesity is a major problem among teenagers.	Obesity has increased among teenagers probably because of a decline in physical exercise. Obese teens often have social problems and difficulties with their self-image.
Teenagers become more physically inactive as they age.	Adolescents become more physically inactive as they drive more, spend less time in physical education classes, and spend considerable time watching television and playing computer games.
Teenagers do not get sufficient sleep.	Adolescents require about 9 hours of sleep a night. Most do not get enough sleep because they stay up later and get up earlier on school days than they did when they were younger. Lack of sleep may lead to inattentiveness in school, as well as accidents.

Studies linking lack of sleep with poorer academic performance and moodiness use correlations, and the direction of effects can be questioned. Greater amounts of sleep may help students perform better, but students who do better in school may tend to sleep more. Perhaps a third factor, such as personality characteristics or stress, may be involved. For example, adolescents who are more anxious or have greater problems handling stress may sleep less. Lack of sleep may even be dangerous, as many teenagers drive, and being sleepy at the wheel may lead to accidents (Carskadon, 1990).

Part of the increased freedom of being a teen is staying up later. However, research suggests that teens are not getting enough sleep and often say they are tired, and that this lack of sleep may be associated with academic and behavioral problems. These research results can be used to help teenagers and their parents understand the importance of sleep during this period of life. *(For a review of this section, see At A Glance 3.4.)*

PLACING ADOLESCENT PHYSICAL DEVELOPMENT IN PERSPECTIVE

It is easy to recite a list of physical changes that occur in adolescence, but it is just as important to appreciate the subjective experience of each adolescent who is coping with these changes. Adolescents face many challenges, and it would be folly not to take seriously the adjustments associated with, for example, changing body image. Yet most adolescents cope well with the challenges.

THEMES

THEME 1 **Adolescence is a time of choices, "firsts," and transitions.**	● The physical changes that occur during puberty can be regarded as a transition to adulthood. ● The level of sex hormones increases substantially, and adolescents experience mature sexual feelings for the first time. ● Adolescents have more responsibility for their own nutrition choices than they did as children. ● Adolescents must adjust to the physical changes that occur in adolescence. ● Adolescents have choices in physical fitness.
THEME 2 **Adolescence is shaped by context.**	● The reactions of family members and friends to adolescents' physical development influence the way adolescents react to their changing bodies. ● Early or late pubertal timing may interact with feedback from others to influence the adolescent experience. ● Culture and environment influence an adolescent's nutrition choices.
THEME 3 **Adolescence is influenced by group membership.**	● The pubertal experience of boys and girls differs. ● The trend toward earlier maturation and increased height may still be operating among some minority group youth, including African American adolescents. ● Although teenagers from minority groups are generally in good health, fewer rate their health as "excellent" compared with teenagers from European American backgrounds. ● Caucasian females are more likely to experience eating difficulties than are African American females. ● Girls are more dissatisfied with their bodies than are boys.
THEME 4 **The adolescent experience has changed over the past 50 years.**	● Girls today receive more information about the pubertal changes that are occurring, or are about to occur, than did girls 50 years ago. ● The secular trend, which involves the tendency toward earlier puberty and taller growth, is generally leveling out, although some changes continue. ● Adolescents are less physically active today than years ago. ● Adolescents get less sleep today than their grandparents did.
THEME 5 **Today's views of adolescence are becoming more balanced, with greater attention to its positive nature.**	● Rather than considering menstruation a seriously adverse experience, psychologists today realize that most girls show only mild reactions to menarche. ● Instead of viewing the brain as fully formed and functional, modern neuroscience notes changes in structure and function that occur during adolescence. ● Years ago, any characteristic that was ascribed largely to genetics was considered unchangeable. Today, psychologists understand that genetic influence does not imply immutability. ● Whereas psychologists once viewed temperament as creating difficulties or challenges in adjustment, today they believe that it is the fit between temperament and the challenges of the environment that determines the need for adjustment.

Much of the difficulty and uneasiness teens experience is due to the novelty of these challenges and the lack of experience younger teens have in dealing with social situations. It takes experience, patience, knowledge, and understanding from others to accept oneself and to feel confident about one's physical self and abilities. Although they cannot change their height or physical characteristics, teenagers can do much to improve their health status, physical abilities, and appearance. Their health habits in the areas of nutrition, exercise, and even sleep are largely under their control. Research shows that good habits start early; children who eat well and exercise tend to continue doing so in adolescence. For those who don't develop good health habits in childhood, there is still time to change. With education, encouragement, and opportunity, teenagers can adopt better health habits that will lead to better health and longer, happier lives.

CHAPTER SUMMARY AT A GLANCE

KEY TOPICS	KEY POINTS	KEY TERMS
Pubertal Changes	The physical changes that occur during puberty affect every area of development. *(At A Glance 3.1, p. 67)*	← *primary sex characteristics (p. 61)* *secondary sex characteristics (p. 61)* *menarche (p. 63)* *prefrontal cortex (p. 65)* *cerebral cortex (p. 66)*
The Biological Bases for Behavior and Development	Genetic and hormonal factors directly and indirectly influence development and behavior. *(At A Glance 3.2, p. 77)*	← *hormones (p. 68)* *heritability (p. 72)* *monozygotic twins (p. 72)* *dizygotic twins (p. 72)* *concordance rate (p. 72)* *temperament (p. 75)* *goodness-of-fit model (p. 76)* *shared environmental influences (p. 77)* *nonshared environmental influences (p. 77)*
The Interplay of Physical Development and Experience	Genetic and environmental factors interact in a complex manner to determine the behavior of the individual. *(At A Glance 3.3, p. 83)*	← *secular trend (p. 78)*
The Health of Today's Teenagers	Teenagers make many health-related choices that influence their well-being, especially in the areas of nutrition, physical exercise, and sleep. *(At A Glance 3.4, p. 91)*	

Review questions for this chapter appear in the appendix.

4

COGNITIVE DEVELOPMENT

WHAT IS YOUR OPINION?

DEVELOPMENTAL APPROACHES
- Piaget on Adolescent Cognitive Development
  Perspective: Come Down to Earth
- Vygotsky's Sociocultural Theory
- Piaget and Vygotsky Reconsidered

INFORMATION PROCESSING
- Information Processing in Adolescence
- Metacognition
- Self-Regulation

APPROACHES TO INTELLIGENCE
- The Stanford-Binet and Wechsler Tests
- Intelligence Testing in Adolescence
- Controversies Surrounding Intelligence Testing

USING COGNITIVE ABILITIES
- Critical Thinking
- Creativity
- Decision Making
  FOCUS: The Issue of Competency

SOCIAL COGNITION
- Looking at Others
- Taking Another Person's Perspective
- Adolescent Egocentrism

PLACING ADOLESCENT COGNITIVE DEVELOPMENT IN PERSPECTIVE
HAS YOUR OPINION CHANGED?
THEMES
CHAPTER SUMMARY AT A GLANCE

Do you view the world differently than you did 10 years ago? Do you reason about problems differently? Your first response to these questions is probably "of course," but if you tried to list the differences between how you think today and how you reasoned about problems years ago, you would likely have difficulty explaining them. When I ask my students these questions, they often answer, "I'm more mature"; explaining what they really mean by *more mature,* though, is difficult for them.

Cognitive (intellectual) changes in adolescence are just as important as the physical changes discussed in "Physical Development," but they are far less apparent. Everyone notices growth spurts and changes in appearance, especially during puberty. It is far less obvious to any observer that teenagers look at the world and reason about their experiences differently than they did before.

This chapter discusses several approaches to understanding the changes that occur in thinking and intellectual abilities during adolescence. Of the developmental approaches, Jean Piaget's view conceptualizes the development of cognitive abilities across a series of stages—the last of which covers adolescence—and this view emphasizes the qualitative leap in the adolescent's ability to think. Lev Vygotsky's sociocultural theory emphasizes the social nature of cognitive development, a view that has gained many adherents over the past decade. The information-processing approach delves into areas such as memory and problem solving, noting how adolescents differ from younger children in these abilities. Other approaches focus on the concept of intelligence, including the testing of intelligence in childhood and adolescence.

The chapter next discusses how adolescents use their newly acquired intellectual skills to critically analyze material, creatively deal with problems, and make decisions. Cognitive advances significantly affect social behavior as well, and the final portion of the chapter examines how this occurs.

DEVELOPMENTAL APPROACHES

Two prominent developmental approaches, one advanced by Jean Piaget and the other by Lev Vygotsky, offer very different views of cognitive functioning as it changes with age and experience.

Piaget on Adolescent Cognitive Development

Piaget spent his entire adult life investigating the changes in the way children and adolescents think and deal with problems. In his studies, Piaget used the *clinical method;* he presented children of different ages with a problem and observed how they dealt with it, often directly questioning them along the way. This method of mixing observation with self-report allowed Piaget to gain great insight into the children's and adolescents' cognitive processes as they worked on the problems. However, because he did not adhere to the strict procedures of scientific research, such as the use of control groups, Piaget's method also left his findings vulnerable to the criticism discussed in "The Scientific Approach to Adolescence."

Piaget viewed cognitive development as the individual's continuous adaptation to changes in the environment. He focused on the different ways in which children and adolescents deal with the challenges and problems of life. Two of the most important concepts in Piaget's theory are *organization* and *adaptation.* Children must organize their knowledge in a way that makes it useful. They must also adapt or adjust to their ever-changing environments.

Organization: Schemata and Operations Suppose you give a child a ball. The child looks at it, tries to pick it up, pushes it around, and kicks it. The child uses various methods to explore the object. Piaget used the term **schema** to describe an organized system of actions and thoughts that are useful for dealing with the world. Schemata (plural for *schema*) are tools for learning about the world. They can be generalized, and children develop new schemata as they mature.

Very young children's schemata are physical, such as picking something up with one hand or stroking an object. As children mature, these schemata become more symbolic and mental. For example, a 9-year-old who is shown an 8-ounce glass and an 8-ounce cup understands that they hold the same amount of liquid, even though the glass is taller and appears to have more milk in it. Piaget used the term **operations** for these organized, logical mental processes.

Adaptation: Assimilation and Accommodation The active interaction with the environment that impels developmental progress can be explained in terms of two processes: assimilation and accommodation. **Assimilation** is the process by which new experiences are incorporated into one's already existing schemata (Piaget & Inhelder, 1969). For instance, a teenager who knows music well may hear a song and easily place it in a particular musical category, for example, classic rock. Despite the fact that each recording has its own style and differs from the others in many aspects, it can be comfortably placed in a particular category. **Accommodation** is the process by which one alters existing schemata to fit new experiences. For example, when the music-savvy teen hears a recording that does not seem to fit into any known categories, she will need to add a new musical category to her knowledge base. Accommodation creates new ways of dealing with or categorizing a situation. Through assimilation and accommodation, people understand and adapt to the changing world around them.

Influences on Development As noted in "The Scientific Approach to Adolescence," Piaget believed that four factors influence development. *Maturation,* the first influence, is the unfolding of the genetic plan—essentially, the genetic influence on development. *Social transmission* is formal learning, for example, parents teaching their children how to hold a spoon or sew. Experience involves the active daily personal encounters that people have with their environment. Finally, **equilibration** is the process by which we seek a balance between what we know and what we are experiencing at the time. Equilibration is Piaget's mechanism for explaining change. A child who believes one thing but experiences something mildly different enters a state of *disequilibrium.* For example, consider a young child faced with the two rows of checkers shown in Figure 4.1, each with the same number but one spread wide apart and the other closer together. Originally, the child believes that the longer row has more, because it extends further. This child is satisfied with his decision and is in a state of equilibrium, even though his judgment is incorrect. Eventually, the child begins to realize that the longer row is less dense than the shorter one and concludes that this row may have fewer objects. The two beliefs, which cannot be held at the same time, lead to a state of disequilibrium. The child resolves this state by taking into consideration both the length and the density, thus developing a new, more advanced state of equilibrium (Flavell, Miller, & Miller, 2002).

The Early Stages of Cognitive Development Piaget argued that children develop their cognitive skills in four distinct stages, the last of which occurs during adolescence (Inhelder & Piaget, 1958). During the first stage, or *sensorimotor stage* (lasting from birth through ages 18 to 24 months), infants learn about their world using their senses (such as vision and hearing) and their motor abilities (such as stroking, pushing, and grabbing). Infants develop two important understandings. They develop an appreciation of *object permanence*, the awareness that things do not disappear even though they may be out of sight. For instance, a 6-month-old infant will not search for a bottle after it is completely

Even though each song has its differences, a knowledgeable adolescent shows assimilation by placing a song into a particular category.

schema A method of dealing with the world that can be generalized to many situations.

operation An internalized action that is part of the individual's cognitive structure.

assimilation The process by which information is altered to fit into one's already existing schemata.

accommodation The process by which an individual alters existing schemata to fit new information.

equilibration The process by which people seek a balance between what they know and what they are experiencing.

hidden from view under a blanket, but an 8-month-old infant will. Infants in this stage also begin to develop an ability to understand *symbols,* or the idea that one thing can stand for another (for example, a paper plate for a hat).

During the second stage, or *preoperational stage* (which lasts from ages 2 to 7 years), children can use symbols and understand some language. Their limitations are obvious, though. At the beginning of the stage, children exhibit *animism,* attributing the characteristics of living things to nonliving things. For instance, if his older brother stepped on his teddy bear, a young preschooler may believe that the teddy bear felt pain. Children at this age are *egocentric;* they believe, in essence, that the world revolves around them, and they do not understand that other people may view the world differently. They believe that everyone is experiencing the world the way they are.

Another important limitation of preschoolers is their inability to understand *conservation,* the idea that things can change their appearance and still be the same. Piaget's classic experiment on conservation involves showing children of various ages two tall containers, filling them with an equal amount of fluid, and then asking if the amount of fluid in the two containers is the same or different. The child says the amount is the same. The experimenter, in full view of the child, then pours the fluid from one of the tall containers into a wide, squat container (so the water level is much lower) and asks the question again. This time, the preschool child typically believes that the tall container holds more liquid than the squat container (see Figure 4.2). The child does not understand that the amount of fluid in each container is still the same. If the experimenter then pours the fluid from the squat container back into the original tall container and again asks if the amount of fluid in the two tall containers is the same or different, the child will again say they are the same. A child at the preoperational stage does not see the discrepancy in his or her answers.

During the third stage, called the *stage of concrete operations* (which lasts from about ages 7 to 11 years), children are no longer animistic or egocentric, nor are they fooled by most conservation problems, such as the one described above. Children at this stage still exhibit limitations, however, such as the inability to deal with abstractions. For instance, if you ask young elementary schoolchildren to explain the meaning of the proverb "People in glass houses shouldn't throw stones," they will probably give a literal answer or even answer with a question such as, "Why would anyone live in a glass house?"

The Stage of Formal Operations Piaget's final stage of cognitive development is the **stage of formal operations** (beginning at about 11 years). Five major cognitive changes occur during this stage and are described in the following sections. All the changes rarely, if ever, take place before adolescence, and all develop gradually throughout the period (Moshman, 1998). The gradual development of these cognitive abilities means that older adolescents show them more frequently than younger adolescents.

1. Separating the Real from the Possible As adolescents enter the stage of formal operations, they become less bound to reality. They can separate themselves from their present reality and think about other alternatives. Many younger children in the stage of concrete operations consider their present reality the only one available; it is the only one they know. They may complain that another child can stay up later, but they have no overall consideration of that child's different reality. Adolescents, in contrast, can separate themselves from their present situation and think about a better family life, a better neighborhood, or a better world. They are not limited by their present situation.

Because adolescents can look at other possible lifestyles and parent-child relationships and ask why their own lives cannot approach the others, it is no wonder that many teens are less satisfied with their family lives than when they were younger. It is not only the striving for independence that causes this dissatisfaction, but the adolescent's newly developed ability to consider different realities, some of which may be idealizations. This emphasis on possibilities is so

Figure 4.1
An Example of Equilibration
At first, the young child believes that the top row has more checkers, because it extends further. According to Jean Piaget, a more mature child becomes aware that the top row is less dense and enters a state of disequilibrium, resulting in an ability to take into account both number and density.

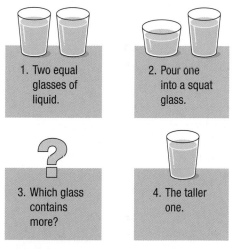

Figure 4.2
Conservation
Young children do not understand that two 8-ounce containers—one tall and one squat—hold the same amount of liquid, because the containers do not look the same.

stage of formal operations Jean Piaget's last stage of cognitive development, in which a person develops the ability to deal with abstractions in a scientific manner.

important that Piaget argues that the direction of thinking between reality and possibility reverses in this stage (Piaget & Inhelder, 1951/1975). Reality becomes secondary to what is possible. Adolescents are often entranced by politicians or social reformers who describe a vision for a better country or world. Their ability to see alternative realities causes them to ask why poverty or racism exists, or why resources cannot be dedicated to feed the hungry in other lands and eliminate starvation throughout the world.

2. Hypothetical-Deductive Logic. Another important characteristic of formal operational thinking is **hypothetical-deductive logic,** which involves the ability to form hypotheses explaining a particular phenomenon, deduce from these hypotheses what should or should not happen, and test these deductions in a scientific manner (Flavell et al., 2002). This logic allows adolescents to understand the scientific method, appreciating the need to control all variables except one (Overton, 1991). Adolescents can think more scientifically, devising strategies for solving problems and then systematically testing these possible solutions. The ability to use hypothetical-deductive logic allows adolescents to think critically, analyze arguments, and detect strengths and weaknesses (Klaczynski & Narasimham, 1998).

Adolescents also can imagine hypothetical situations, such as supposing that there were no poverty, or that people could fly, and then reason from these premises. Markovits and Vachon (1989) tested 10-, 13-, 15-, and 18-year-olds on their ability to reason using *if-then* premises. Some of the premises were factually accurate ("If one hits a glass with a hammer, the glass will break"), whereas other premises were factually inaccurate ("If one hits a glass with a feather, the glass will break"). One of the premises was abstract ("If one heats a BYV, one will produce an XAR"). The researchers then asked participants to make deductions from these premises. For example, they offered the premise "If one hits a glass with a feather, the glass will break," told participants that they came across a broken glass, and asked them if the glass was hit with a feather or was not hit with a feather. None of the 10-year-olds and only some of the 13-year-olds could accept contrary-to-fact premises. Furthermore, these younger students could not logically deduce anything from an abstract premise. The 15- and 18-year-olds, in contrast, had no difficulty accepting contrary-to-fact premises and reasoning from them, although they were more accurate in their deductions with the factually correct premises. These older adolescents were also able to deal with abstract premises. Piaget argues that adolescents can make deductions that are

The ability to use hypothetical-deductive logic allows adolescents to understand and use scientific reasoning.

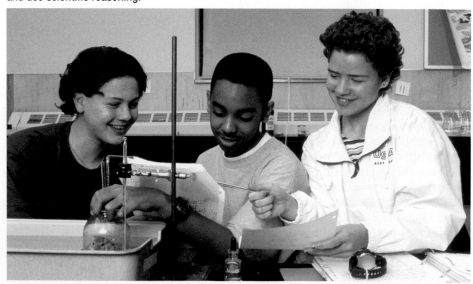

hypothetical-deductive logic The ability to form a hypothesis, scientifically test it, and draw conclusions using deductive logic.

no longer simply related to reality; they can reason about hypothetical statements and propositions that may never occur (Piaget & Inhelder, 1951/1975).

The use of hypothetical-deductive logic can even lead to a reduction in prejudice. Often, racial and religious prejudices are based upon personal experience; that is, one or two bad experiences can cause someone to create a general rule that "explains" those experiences (Klaczynski & Gordon, 1996a). Appreciating the fact that a few experiences do not indicate a rule can lead to better relations with others.

3. COMBINATIONAL LOGIC.   **Combinational logic** involves the ability to generate all possible combinations from a group of possibilities. For instance, Piaget and Inhelder (1958) presented children of various ages with five jars of a colorless liquid and asked them to find which combination of the chemicals would produce a yellow liquid. As preoperational thinkers, preschoolers simply made a mess of the situation, combining the chemicals at random. Elementary schoolchildren, who are in the stage of concrete operations, understood the task completely and combined the chemicals but did not approach the task with any scientific strategy. The adolescents, in contrast, used formal operational thinking; they formed a scientific and logical strategy, combining liquids from tubes 1 and 2, then from 1 and 3, and so on.

Adolescents use combinational logic to generate multiple solutions to a problem and combine properties of objects or events to solve complex tasks. An adolescent planning a party can imagine all her friends in different situations and generate different outcomes about each possible combination. This ability may lead to better social planning (deciding who to invite and pair with whom), but it may also generate anxiety about how some combinations of friends will get along (Kahlbaugh & Haviland, 1991).

The ability to use combinational logic also allows adolescents to generate many life goals and combine them into distinct possibilities, both compatible or incompatible. For example, an adolescent may want to become a lawyer, join the Peace Corps, and delay having a family, and the teen may be aware of which possibilities can coexist and which cannot. Empirical studies show that by 13 years of age, 80 to 90 percent of adolescents can do this (Byrnes, 1988; Overton & Byrnes, 1991).

4. ABSTRACT, SYMBOLIC THOUGHT.   Piaget considered the development of abstract symbolic thought to be the most important cognitive advancement during the formal operational stage. A fundamental change occurs between 13 and 15 years of age, as adolescents develop the ability to understand abstract principles involved in concepts such as justice, individual rights, and freedom of speech and religion, which have been nothing more than catch phrases until now. Unlike children in the stage of concrete operations, who focus on the real world, adolescents develop the ability to compare propositions and ideas on a much higher level, divorced from the reality of a situation. Abstract thought also allows adolescents to develop internal systems of overriding principles and values, and to defend these values when appropriate. For example, adolescents may defend the idea of equality, and this ideal acts as a principle that defines their belief system.

The ability to deal with abstractions also allows teens to interpret abstract sayings and gain meaning from them. If you ask adolescents about a political cartoon or the saying "You can lead a horse to water, but you can't make him drink," their answer will be divorced from the reality of what is shown in the

PERSPECTIVE

COME DOWN TO EARTH

SETTING THE SCENE   Steven is a politically aware junior in high school. He has very firm opinions rooted in a belief in democracy, fairness, and individual rights.

STEVEN'S FATHER: *We are constantly arguing about political and economic issues. Steven is idealistic, which is fine, but he seems not to understand the real world. The other day Steven went to a job interview dressed in jeans and a tee shirt. When I told him that was unacceptable for an interview, he told me that the boss should only be concerned about whether he can do the work, not what he looks like. Steven wants to eliminate poverty, and his answer is simply to tax everyone and give money to the poor. I try to tell him this won't work, but it does no good.*

STEVEN: *My father seems to have lost his ideals. He is happy just to let things stand as they are. I'm not. I believe that things should change, and I hope to contribute to that change by becoming more involved politically.*

QUESTION   Is Steven's "lack of reality" a problem? Should Steven's father continue to try to get Steven to face what his father calls "the real world"? If so, how should Steven's father approach his son?

combinational logic   The ability to produce all possible alternatives to answer a question.

cartoon or the literal words of the proverb. Adolescents can think about the meanings of cartoons and adages that are divorced from any one case.

5. THINKING ABOUT THINKING.   The ability to use abstractions is a characteristic of formal operational thinking that allows adolescents to reflect on their own thought patterns. They can analyze their own opinions and beliefs and think critically about them. They become interested in how their thoughts develop and in the thoughts of others, often analyzing, or sometimes overanalyzing, them. Piaget used the term *reflective thinking* to describe this critical analysis of one's own thinking and the construction of a theory of one's ideas. This type of thinking can be seen in adolescents' reflections on their religious beliefs, which may now vary from their parents' beliefs (Spilka, 1991b). The basic elements of Piaget's formal operational thought can be found in Table 4.1.

Piaget and Education   Piaget's ideas have many educational implications. The first implication is that children and adolescents are active thinkers who construct their own understanding of what occurs around them. A learner, then, is an active participant trying to understand the world, not a passive individual who merely listens and takes in what the teacher says. Piaget himself emphasized the importance of presenting the learner with situations that are experiments in the broadest sense. Learners should try things out to see what happens, manipulate things, pose questions, and seek their own answers; they also should reconcile what they find at one time with what they find at another and compare their findings with those of other learners (Duckworth, 1964). Piaget believed that educational activities should promote active discovery, a concept that leads to an educational philosophy in which teachers structure the material so that learners can discover things on their own.

Another major implication of Piaget's ideas involves applying our knowledge of how children and adolescents think to the learning process. Adolescents can plan and conduct experiments using scientific logic. They also can follow a logical argument and notice an illogical conclusion that someone may suggest. Adolescents can understand and use abstractions, allowing them to discuss advanced, theoretical subjects. Because adolescents can separate the real from the possible, they are able to identify different paths—for example, paths open to a president facing a foreign policy crisis. They can also consider different possibilities in a story or novel. Adolescents see alternative courses of action that could have been followed.

Table 4.1

The Stages of Formal Operations

Characteristic	Explanation	Example
Combinational logic	The ability to find all the possible alternatives	When asked what the president could have done in a certain situation, a teenager will produce a great many alternatives, some real and some impractical. If given five jars of colorless liquid and told that some combination will yield a yellow liquid, an adolescent will use an efficient and effective strategy that will produce all possible alternatives.
Separating the real from the possible	The ability to separate oneself from the real world and consider different possibilities; the ability to accept propositions that are contrary to reality	A teenager can imagine other realities and lifestyles and think about what could be rather than what is. A teenager can readily discuss propositions such as "What if all human beings were green?"
Using abstractions	The ability to deal with material that is not observable	An adolescent understands higher-level concepts such as democracy and liberty, as well as the abstract meanings of proverbs.
Hypothetical-deductive reasoning	The ability to form hypotheses and use scientific logic	A teenager uses deductive logic to test a hypothesis.

Source: Kaplan (2000), p. 482.

Adolescents can discuss political cartoons and the more abstract meaning of music or art. They can appreciate the conflicts between society and the individual. For example, asking elementary school students in the stage of concrete operations to describe what an author may have had in mind when writing a story will not work because it requires them to hypothesize about intentions, which is very difficult for them, especially if these intentions are more abstract. This exercise certainly would be appropriate for most adolescents, however.

Critique of the Concept of Formal Operations   Not all adolescents, and not even all adults, reason at the formal operational level. Between 40 and 60 percent of all adults from Western cultures use formal operational thinking (Neimark, 1975, 1982). About 60 percent of older adolescents use formal operational reasoning when appropriate, a bit higher than the measure for adults (Keating, 1991). Many people, then, do not use formal operations. In many more-traditional societies, few people reach the stage of formal operations (at least as tested by standard tests), although systematic logical thinking certainly is used (Weisfeld, 1999). Studies show that people in non-Western cultures generally perform more poorly on tasks that require formal operational reasoning (Dasen & Heron, 1981). The ability to conserve and other concrete operational abilities certainly are needed in everyday life, but most people get along very well without using abstractions or imagining other realities. Perhaps Piaget's stage of formal operational reasoning, then, is applicable only to adolescents from technological societies, who receive a great deal of formal education and therefore have a great deal of practice using formal operational reasoning. Although the other three stages postulated by Piaget seem to be universal, the same cannot be said about formal operations, which cannot be seen as a characteristic of adolescent thought around the world.

In addition, even people who have the ability to reason at the formal operational level may not do so on every task that requires it. A teen may use formal reasoning when dealing with a mathematical problem in school, for example, but not when trying to discuss a political idea with a parent. People do not perform as well when faced with very abstract problems, problems of unfamiliar content, or problems with which they have had no experience. Piaget (1972) speculated that formal operational reasoning is theoretically available to most adolescents and adults, but they do not always use these abilities due to lack of familiarity with the content of the task. In fact, the problems Piaget used when testing the participants in his research often involved reasoning about the physical sciences, problems that may not be familiar to some people. Generally, older adolescents are further along in their development of formal operational abilities than younger adolescents (Rutter & Rutter, 1993).

Such evidence led Piaget (1972) to reevaluate some of his ideas, and he agreed that education, vocational interests, and one's culture determine performance on tests that require formal operational abilities. Cross-cultural evidence shows this nicely. For example, a study of Africans who play a complex board game in which players try to capture seeds found that the players need to anticipate possible moves and calculate very complex defensive and offensive moves—strategies that require the type of logical thinking typical of formal operations (Retschitzki, 1989). The experts in this game, however, do not do well on standard Piagetian tests of formal operations. Although they have a great deal of experience with formal operations in this context, they do not have much experience with the type of problems that Piaget used.

Going Beyond Formal Operations   Piaget argued that cognitive abilities undergo no additional qualitative changes after the stage of formal operations, but some psychologists disagree (Rybash, Roodin, & Hoyer, 1995). Beginning in late adolescence and continuing into young adulthood, new and qualitatively different types of reasoning, collectively called **postformal operational reasoning,** may be found. Characteristics of such reasoning include an emphasis on practicality and context; an acceptance of contradiction in the

postformal operational reasoning   Any qualitatively different reasoning style that goes beyond formal operational reasoning and develops during late adolescence and early adulthood.

world; and **relativistic reasoning,** the appreciation that an individual's knowledge depends on his or her subjective experiences and perspective. Older adolescents and young adults no longer see the world in simple terms of right and wrong with little in between. Instead, they see things as relative. Such thinking recognizes the subjective character of human knowledge—the idea that other people may not interpret the same events in the same way.

When adolescents first begin to understand that others may not see the world the way they do and that not everything is known or, indeed, capable of being known, they begin to use and overuse phrases such as "I can't tell" and "It depends" to answer questions, as well as to say things like "Everyone has a right to his or her own opinion" (Leadbeater, 1991). They begin to doubt that there are any real answers to anything. This "rampant relativism" may be one of the costs of becoming a critical thinker (Keating, 1990, p. 70). Finally, people commit themselves to a particular viewpoint while accepting the relative nature of truth. They accept that some views are simply better researched or based on better evidence than others. Thus, college students often progress from a belief in absolute truth to a belief in full relativism to a more balanced position (Perry, 1981).

Relativistic thinking is readily apparent in teenagers who question everything, and especially their parents' values and ethics. For example, parents may believe it is wrong to live with a boyfriend or girlfriend before marriage. Adolescents may see this as a debatable point and argue with their parents' absolute beliefs. They may argue that it may be wrong for their parents but not for them. Parents may get tired of finding all their beliefs questioned and their cherished values debated. The lack of certainty that comes with relativism can be difficult for adolescents as well. It may take quite a while before adolescents can accept the basic nature of relativism, yet commit themselves to some viewpoint. One way to distinguish adolescence from childhood is to watch for the emergence of relativism and skeptical doubt. In turn, adolescence can be distinguished from adulthood by a change from rampant skepticism to a new view that recognizes that by sharing social experience and engaging in creative argument, we can obtain some understanding of truth, although always understanding that we are fallible (Lapsley, 1990).

Postformal operational reasoning also emphasizes practicality and context. An adolescent using formal operational reasoning to look at a problem, such as poverty in the United States, would consider all the alternatives (combinational logic), deduce the action that is theoretically best, and advocate it. Older adolescents and young adults using postformal operational reasoning would take into account both the political context and practical features, such as available resources (Labouvie-Vief, 1980, 1984). Postformal thinkers seek a balance between what is best and what is practical at the time. The alternative they choose may not be the best theoretically, but it is a realistic compromise considering the multiple constraining factors and one that balances the rights and needs of each group. Again, it is easy to see how a young teenager thinking abstractly and logically might be impatient about solving social problems and fault older people who are thinking in a more practical manner.

A third factor in postformal operational reasoning is the understanding that contradiction can occur and, indeed, is a basic part of the world. Many adolescents, flushed with the ability to use hypothetical-deductive logic, see hypocrisy everywhere. For example, they might find it difficult to integrate the knowledge that a person they admire in the public sector may have cheated on his wife or be a terrible father. The understanding and acceptance of contradiction ("I can both like and dislike another person at the same time") is first evident in late adolescence. For example, middle adolescents are often concerned about the conflicting labels they place on themselves. How can they be both honest and dishonest in what they say and do? How can they be both selfish and giving? These basic contradictions may cause teenagers to feel phony. Later in adolescence, however, they can accept contradictions in their own character and do not seem to mind them. They successfully integrate their seemingly conflicting characteristics and actions into a coherent whole.

relativistic reasoning   Reasoning that involves an appreciation of the fact that knowledge depends on the individual's subjective experiences and perspective.

The discovery of postformal operational reasoning does not lessen the importance of Piaget's discoveries about how adolescents think. It simply adds a piece to the puzzle of how people deal with the challenges they face in their daily lives.

Vygotsky's Sociocultural Theory

One of the troublesome concerns when discussing cognitive development is the lack of attention paid to the different contexts in which it unfolds. For example, adolescents in Western society are expected to go to school, choose an occupation, and achieve autonomy while maintaining a positive relationship with their family. In contrast, for adolescents in many more-traditional societies, schooling is more an apprenticeship, one's choice of occupation is narrow, and remaining dependent on the family is common.

To address this concern, psychologists have turned to Lev Vygotsky's (1962, 1978) sociocultural approach to cognitive development (Baltes, Lindenberger, & Staudinger, 1998). According to Vygotsky, behavior and development cannot be understood without an appreciation of the cultural, historical, and social context that defines and influences the individual. People acquire ways of thinking and behaving that allow them to live in a particular culture. Culture provides the tools that enable people to solve problems. Some cultural tools are physical, such as those used to plant and harvest crops; others are psychological, such as language (Crain, 1992). Psychological tools that aid thinking and behavior, such as speech, writing, and numerical systems, are called *signs*.

Culture also determines the types of skills that adults must teach their children and adolescents. In our culture, for example, reading is an important skill that adults teach to their children, and sex education is considered important for adolescents. Cultures differ in the tools they use, and the tools available to the individual depend on the culture and the historical point in time. A culture emphasizing memorization, for example, would require different skills than one emphasizing concepts and scientific reasoning.

Social Interaction and the Transmission of Skills   Vygotsky was interested in how cultures transmit ways of thinking and behaving from one generation to another. He argued that this transmission occurs through social interaction between the child or adolescent on one side and parents, other adults, and more expert peers on the other. Children and adolescents are taught concepts, skills, and ways of thinking through dialogues with adults and more advanced adolescents. These social interactions both mirror an individual's culture and form the basis of his or her mental processes.

According to Vygotsky, all cognitive processes begin with social interactions that are later internalized. Therefore, mental functioning can be understood only by looking at the social processes and cultural foundations from which they arise. This position is contrary to the position of other psychologists, such as Piaget, who argue that mental functioning arises from within the child, and that such processes as thinking, memory, and attention apply exclusively to the individual. Vygotsky takes the opposite position—that cognitive processes such as thinking begin as active social interactions, which then shape the mind. For example, a parent may model a particular type of thinking and engage in a question-and-answer session with her child. The child next has a "conversation" with himself. For example, after being shown where to find something, the child may ask himself, "Now where can I find the answer?" Eventually, what was first overt and social becomes internalized, and the child can perform the behavior without any help. The emphasis on the social origins of mental processes is one reason for Vygotsky's current appeal; he focuses much more on teaching and formal instruction than did Piaget.

The Zone of Proximal Development   To understand how people learn through social interactions, consider the following scenario. Two adolescents, Mohammed and Alan, are given a task to perform, and neither can do it by himself. A competent adult guides each teen, trying to help each one understand and master the task. With such help, Mohammed is able to succeed, but Alan is not. Are both functioning on the same level? Some people would say yes, because neither was able to perform the task independently, but Vygotsky would argue that the two teens were quite different. Mohammed's potential in this task at this moment is much greater than Alan's. Mohammed is on the verge of learning this material, whereas Alan is not. A static view of cognitive ability would rate them both equally, but Mohammed can do so much more with adequate help than Alan can. Vygotsky (1978) used the term **zone of proximal development** to describe the difference between a child's actual development when working alone and his or her level of potential development when problem solving with the guidance of a competent partner. The more expert partner may teach through prompts, cues, modeling, explanation, asking leading questions, discussions, and many other techniques (Miller, 1993). Vygotsky claimed that education should be based not upon what individuals can do by themselves but upon their potential as shown by what they can do with the help of a guide. Individuals are active participants as they move through the zone of proximal development.

Vygotsky's Influence on Education Three important elements of Vygotsky's theory are influencing education today. First, Vygotsky emphasized the importance of an expert—be it a teacher, parent, or older child—helping to gradually instruct a younger child or adolescent. Second, the expert often offers the adolescent a considerable amount of structure and then, little by little, gives the learner less outside help. Third, Vygotsky's idea of the zone of proximal development tells teachers to go slightly beyond where students are comfortable and help students learn. As students learn about their world, they become more aware of it and more in control.

Lev Vygotsky emphasized the importance of the interaction between an experienced guide and a learner.

Vygotsky emphasized the importance of formal learning, but he also understood that children learn some things by themselves outside of school, often through discovery (Vygotsky, 1962). In their daily lives, for example, children discover the location of various things in the house or the fact that you push the button on the television set to turn it on. Vygotsky called these *everyday concepts.* In fact, children learn speech so easily that Vygotsky believes that they must be biologically programmed to do so; it requires little or no parental instruction. However, according to Vygotsky, children by themselves do not usually learn other sign systems (for example, reading and writing) or abstract concepts such as the laws of physics (which Vygotsky called *scientific concepts*). People learn these things through formal instruction, often in school. It would take much longer for people to learn these skills by themselves, and many simply would not be able to do so. Instruction is necessary and, indeed, impels development. For example, children may spontaneously develop the idea of what a cat looks like and how it acts because they have seen and played with one. Children require formal instruction, though, to learn where the cat fits into the animal kingdom, how many different types of cats there are, and how cats differ from other animals. Without this formal instruction, their conceptual world would be small and incomplete.

Scientific concepts offer people broader frameworks in which to view their own world and gain awareness and control of their environment. For example, people most often use grammatically correct language and know a great deal about their native language, despite having little formal training. Yet they are largely unaware of why they are using particular words or grammatical constructions until they learn to write. Writing requires much more effort than

zone of proximal development The difference between a person's actual developmental level as determined by independent problem solving and the higher level of potential development as determined by problem solving under adult guidance or in cooperation with more capable peers.

speech; the writer must reflect on sentence construction. Scribner and Cole (1981) presented literate and illiterate adults with sentences that were both grammatical and ungrammatical. Both the literate and the illiterate groups recognized which sentences contained grammatical mistakes, but only the literate group understood why the sentences were wrong. They had greater awareness of language. Teachers generally agree that children require instruction to learn, although the teacher must remember that the learner is actively involved in learning. Teachers also know that you cannot teach concepts of every level to a student. An individual who cannot add and subtract cannot be taught algebra, for example.

Educational methods that reflect Vygotsky's ideas are becoming more popular in schools. These ideas include scaffolding, cooperative learning, and reciprocal teaching.

SCAFFOLDING   Scaffolding is a temporary structure that gives the support necessary to accomplish a task. An effective teacher offers this structure by defining the activity and demonstrating the skills necessary to complete a task. Parents often use scaffolding as adolescents learn important skills, such as how to drive a car. At first, the parent offers a considerable amount of instruction, and the driving setting is relatively simple (perhaps an empty parking lot).Then, as the adolescent becomes somewhat more skilled, the parent decreases the amount of instruction and offers the new driver experience in more demanding driving situations.

Teachers use scaffolding in a similar manner. They sometimes simplify problems by breaking them into component parts so that learners encounter only one part at a time. The teacher focuses the learner's attention on each element of the task as it becomes relevant. Teachers also may use scaffolding to teach thinking and decision-making skills. The scaffolding, here, is a skeletal framework of thinking procedures, such as a checklist of steps necessary to make the thinking procedure explicit. Students use the scaffolding to steer themselves through the steps as they carry them out. This scaffolding allows students to concentrate on applying rules to complex procedures without memorizing the steps.

Three types of cognitive scaffolding are shown in Figure 4.3. The first is a *procedural checklist*, which lists the mental steps necessary to make a decision. A second type, called *process scaffolding*, consists of a series of questions that take the individual through the procedure. A third type, called a *graphic organizer*, uses charts and diagrams that promote the same thing (Beyer, 1998). Scaffolding works because it gives students the proper structure and support, and then, as the student becomes more familiar with the task and does not need the help, it can be dismantled.

A good example of scaffolding is found in learning to drive. At first, the teacher gives a great deal of instruction and restricts where the learner can drive. When the driver has more experience, the teacher offers less direction and allows a wider variety of driving experiences.

scaffolding   A temporary educational aid used to help students learn material. Once students are proficient, the scaffolding is slowly dismantled.

A procedural checklist for decision making

- Identify a choosing opportunity.
- State the problem/goal.
- State the criteria of the "best"choice/decision.
- List the possible alternative choices.
- List the possible consequences of selecting each alternative.
- Evaluate each consequence in terms of the criteria identified above.
- Select the alternative that best meets the identified criteria.

Process-structured questions for decision making

1. What do you want to make a decision about?
2. What do you want to accomplish by making this decision?
3. How will you know when you have made the "best" choice?
4. What are all the alternatives you have to choose from?
5. What are the possible consequences of each alternative—long range as well as short range?
6. What are the pluses and minuses of each consequence?
7. Which alternative is "best"? Why?

A graphic organizer for decision making

Figure 4.3
Scaffolding for Student Learning
Three types of scaffolding are the procedural checklist, process scaffolding, and graphic organizer. Scaffolding offers students structure. As students become more proficient, the scaffolding can be dismantled gradually.
Source: Beyer (1985).

Situation/opportunity:		
Problem:	Goal/criteria:	
Alternatives:	Consequences/costs/etc.:	Evaluation:
Decision:	Reasons:	

In cooperative learning, students help each other create a product, but they are evaluated separately on their contributions.

cooperative learning Learning strategies that require students to work together to achieve some common goal.

COOPERATIVE LEARNING The use of **cooperative learning** techniques has become very popular. In cooperative learning, two or more students work together to accomplish an academic goal (Slavin, 1984, 1990). The students must work together to create a single product, but individual accountability is also emphasized (Morgan, Whorton, & Gunsalus, 2000). Often, this means that slightly more advanced students explain and help less advanced classmates to grasp concepts. This strategy conforms well to Vygotsky's zone of proximal development. It is probable that when one student has mastered a skill, most of the other students will find that skill in their zone of proximal development; that is, they are on the verge of learning it. Because cooperative learning requires a great deal of collaboration, it also may improve relationships among students and even among groups of students of varying backgrounds (Slavin & Cooper, 1999). As students work toward academic goals in a group, they learn to respect and depend upon one another.

Teachers today use a number of cooperative learning strategies. For example, in team accelerated instruction (TAI), students are placed in heterogeneous teams, but they work on individualized curriculum materials at their own levels and rates. Students are encouraged to help each other and to check each other's work. Teams receive certificates based on the number of units completed and the accuracy of all team members' assignments (Lindauer & Petrie, 1997). Cooperative learning is a strategy that continues to evolve as new ways to implement the cooperative approach are being developed (Williams, 1996). Part of the strategy's success is due to its flexibility and use of peers as teachers.

Table 4.2

Reciprocal Teaching

Reciprocal teaching is a technique that aims to help students develop their reading skills through summarizing, questioning, clarifying, and predicting.

Summarizing	Questioning
Students are asked to do the following:	Students are asked to identify the different questions instructors might ask:
• Delete minor and unimportant information.	• Questions about details.
• Combine similar ideas into categories and label them.	• Questions about cause and effect.
• State the main idea when the author provides one.	• Questions that compare and contrast.
• Invent the main idea when the author does not provide one.	• Questions about the main idea.
	• Questions that call for inference.

Clarifying	Predicting
Students are asked to find and identify words or concepts that are obscure, ambiguous, or hard to understand.	Students are asked to think about what they already have been told in their reading and what they predict the author will explain next.

Source: Adapted from Hart & Speece (1998).

RECIPROCAL TEACHING   Another teaching technique based upon Vygotsky's ideas, *reciprocal teaching,* involves a dialogue between students and teachers to discover the meaning of a written passage (Palincsar, 1986; Palincsar & Brown, 1984). The goal of reciprocal teaching is to produce thoughtful readers who can use appropriate strategies and monitor their comprehension to be effective, independent readers. The approach uses four strategies: summarizing, questioning, clarifying, and predicting (see Table 4.2).

The teacher begins by reviewing the strategies with the students and enters into a discussion about the reading selection, asking students to consider what information they have about the topic and predict what they will learn. The teacher models the use of these four strategies, but with time gives more responsibility to the students to use the strategies while providing feedback and coaching, a form of scaffolding. After a few sessions, one of the students acts as the teacher. The student teacher then asks a question, which is answered by the other students, summarizes the answers, asks for elaboration on the summary, and leads a discussion aimed at clarifying the meaning of the passage. The group finally discusses predictions about what might happen next, and a new student teacher appointed.

Studies show that reciprocal teaching can be very successful with high school and community college students (Hart & Speece, 1998). Poorer readers often show the most impressive gains. In the words of one student, "All through high school I had problems in comprehension, but in reciprocal teaching I used summarizing, questioning, clarifying, and predicting and I now feel I can understand what I read" (Hart & Speece, 1998, p. 677).

Piaget and Vygotsky Reconsidered

Both Piaget and Vygotsky have greatly influenced how psychologists look at cognitive development and education. However, they approached cognitive development from different points of view. Piaget viewed the motivation for development as coming from within the individual; the child is a naturally curious individual striving to understand the world. For Vygotsky, development depends upon social interactions, through which children learn how to think

AT A GLANCE 4.1 DEVELOPMENTAL APPROACHES

KEY POINT: The theories of Jean Piaget and Lev Vygotsky offer explanations of how children's and adolescents' cognitive abilities change with age and experience.

THEORY	SUPPORTING POINTS	EXPLANATION
Piaget's theory	Four factors influence development: maturation, social transmission, personal experience, and equilibration.	*Maturation* refers to the genetic factor in development. *Social transmission* refers to formal learning. *Personal experience* refers to an individual's interaction with the environment as the person actively seeks to understand the world. *Equilibration*, Piaget's mechanism for explaining change, is the process by which individuals seek a balance between what they know and what they are experiencing.
	People develop their cognitive abilities in four stages: sensorimotor stage, preoperational stage, stage of concrete operations, and stage of formal operations (which begins in adolescence).	In the sensorimotor stage (0–18 to 24 months), children learn about their world through their senses and motor abilities. In the preoperational stage (2–7 years), children are egocentric, believing that everything revolves around them. Children cannot understand conservation; they judge everything on the basis of appearance. In the stage of concrete operations, (7–11 years), children are no longer egocentric and can conserve.
	Adolescents negotiate the stage of formal operations.	In the formal operations stage (11+ years), adolescents can • separate the real from the possible • use hypothetical-deductive logic and combinational logic • understand abstractions and think about their own thoughts
	Piaget did not believe any qualitative changes beyond formal operational reasoning took place.	Some psychologists describe *postformal operational reasoning*, in which an individual reasons on a more practical level, using context and relativism, and accepting life's contradictions.
Vygotsky's sociocultural theory	The cultural context is most important to understanding children's and adolescents' cognitive development.	The basic unit of developmental study should be the individual within a cultural context.
	Cultures actively transmit skills through social interactions with people who are more competent.	Children and adolescents learn how to think and behave through active interactions with adults and more-expert peers.
	The zone of proximal development is the difference between a child's actual development when working alone and the level of potential development shown with the guidance of a competent partner.	Teaching is most effective if it is within the zone of proximal development, aimed at one small level above where children are presently functioning.
	Cultures present material in an organized, carefully constructed manner.	Scaffolding is a structure provided to help a learner successfully perform a skill; the structure is then reduced as the learner progresses.

and what to do. Piaget emphasized the importance of discovery; a child is basically a scientist testing hypotheses in the world and discovering things. He argued that a teacher, parent, or guide engineers an environment in which the child can make an impact on his or her world. The adult's responsibility is to provide a stimulating environment. Vygotsky argued that children require, and in fact receive, instruction from more experienced people. He also believed that teaching, to be effective, requires an understanding of how the child is presently functioning and what the child needs to know.

Piaget and Vygotsky disagreed on the need for formal teaching. Piaget (1969) did not emphasize formal instruction and instead focused on discovery. Vygotsky emphasized the importance of formal learning as impelling development forward. It is through active teaching that children learn the skills necessary to thrive in their culture. Vygotsky, therefore, was interested in how cultures transmit skills to their young. He described important concepts, such as the zone of proximal development, that make such transmission possible. Children are carefully taught what their cultures deem necessary.

Both Piaget and Vygotsky argued that learning can occur in a social context, but for different reasons. For Piaget, adolescents interacting socially with one another are encouraged to change as they find that their thoughts or ways of doing something are different from, and perhaps not as effective as, those of other adolescents. The learner realizes that a change is required, and the motivation for change occurs within the individual as he or she enters a state of disequilibrium. For Vygotsky, in contrast, parents and older peers acting as teachers present material in an organized manner within the individual's zone of proximal development, thereby producing learning and change. *(For a review of this section, see At A Glance 4.1.)*

INFORMATION PROCESSING

Both Piaget and Vygotsky built impressive theories, but neither discussed basic processes necessary for learning to occur. Another theoretical approach, called the **information-processing theory,** focuses on the ways in which people take in information, process it, and then act on it. An information-processing approach to adolescent cognition analyzes such processes as attention, perception, memory, and the response system.

Several basic premises underlie the information-processing view. First, people must process information, that is, do something to information to make it useful. A person taking the SAT examination, for example, would certainly be lost if the letters and numbers on the paper made no sense. The symbols must be processed to have meaning.

Second, people have a limited capacity to process information; people have only so much mental space in which to operate. If you are trying to listen to the words of a song on the radio and read a text at the same time, your attention is divided, and some of what is sung or read will be lost.

A third premise of the information-processing view is that some behaviors are so well learned that they require very little attention; they become almost automatic. If you have been typing for many years, it takes very little attention to touch the right keys. You can type "without thinking," and this ability allows you to concentrate on the content of what you are typing.

Fourth, people use strategies to solve problems and process information meaningfully. For example, if you were told to remember the contents of an article, you might outline some of its main features, try to relate it to what you already know, and rehearse the material in your own words.

Finally, according to an information-processing view, information moves through a system (see Figure 4.4). Information first enters *sensory memory,* which is of very short duration. If not processed further, the information is lost; if it is attended to, it enters *short-term memory.* The capacity of short-term memory is

information-processing theory An approach to understanding cognition that delves deeply into the way information is taken in, processed, and then acted upon.

Figure 4.4
An Overview of the Information-Processing System
Source: Leahy & Harris (1997).

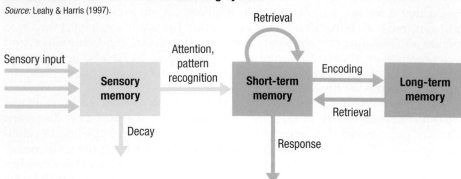

small (7 pieces of information for most adults), and the storage lasts only 30 seconds or so. Material in short-term memory includes what we are thinking about at the moment, and it comes from sensory information and previously learned information retrieved from long-term memory. The individual may keep the material in short-term memory and begin the process of *long-term memory* through some type of rehearsal. Long-term memory has a huge capacity, and material can be stored for a very long time.

Information-processing approaches also emphasize the importance of **metacognition,** or being aware of, and consciously regulating, the process by which one learns. For example, a person studying for a history test must be aware of what she knows and does not know, so she can exert more effort in the areas she does not know. She also must be able to choose the best method for studying. Some people seem capable of using their information-processing skills to learn by themselves, whereas others don't seem to be able to coordinate these skills to reach their goals. Individuals who can do so are often referred to as **self-regulated learners.** Self-regulated learners adopt their own learning goals, choose learning strategies that are appropriate, actively monitor their learning, and change strategies when appropriate.

Information Processing in Adolescence

The differences between the cognitive abilities of children and adolescents can be explained in terms of the information-processing resources available at different ages. Information-processing abilities improve significantly between early childhood and later childhood and then gradually throughout adolescence. Compared with younger children, adolescents have superior ability in the areas of attention, speed of processing, memory, automaticity, and strategy use.

Attention You are in a large lecture room for a 3-hour class. The professor is interesting, but the classroom is warm, and an undercurrent of talking continues. How long can you pay attention? Can you screen out the distractions? **Attention span** is the length of time an individual can attend to a stimulus, whereas **selective attention** is the extent to which a person can choose to attend to one particular stimulus over others. Between early and middle adolescence, significant improvements occur in both these areas of attention. Ten-year-olds show a significantly greater attention span and selective abilities compared with 4-year-olds. Gradual improvements are found throughout adolescence, although they are not as significant as the improvements that take place during childhood (Manis, Keating, & Morrison, 1980). Thus, teenagers can concentrate for a longer period of time and can voluntarily direct their attention where they want it despite competing stimuli.

Speed of Processing One of the most significant age-related changes in information processing is the speed at which teens can process material (Fry &

metacognition The conscious monitoring and regulation of the way people approach and solve a problem or challenge.

self-regulated learners Students who are self-motivated, actively select educational goals, choose ways of meeting challenges, monitor their progress, and change strategies when appropriate.

attention span The time during which an individual can focus psychological resources on a particular stimulus or task.

selective attention The ability to concentrate on one stimulus and ignore extraneous stimuli.

Attention is a crucial part of the learning situation. *Attention span* is the amount of time you can pay attention to a stimulus, whereas *selective attention* is the ability to screen out competing stimuli.

Hale, 1996). Kail (1991) analyzed many published studies on processing speed that included both a group of adults and a comparison group of younger people. The results show that speed of processing increases rapidly during childhood and continues to improve, although at a slower pace, during adolescence. Adolescents and young adults are not just faster processors than younger children; they are also faster than middle-age or older adults (Kaplan, 1998). This advantage in speed of processing is found across tasks, so adolescents can process more material in less time than younger or older people.

Memory   Changes in sensory memory are relatively minor between children and adolescents, but adolescents have an advantage in the speed at which they accumulate and transfer visual information (LeBlanc, Muise, & Blanchard, 1992). Perhaps this is because adolescents are better able to concentrate on the information, so it is transferred from sensory memory to short-term memory more efficiently (Bjorklund, 1995). The amount of information that can be actively processed in short-term memory is also greater (Fry & Hale, 1996). The typical 5-year-old can recall four or perhaps five numbers after a single presentation, but adolescents and adults can retain seven (Schneider et al., 1993). The increase in processing speed allows adolescents to use their short-term memory more efficiently and increases the rate of **rehearsal.** The faster one can rehearse, the more memories one can rehearse, the more information one can keep actively in memory, and the more one can remember (Baddeley, 1986; Bjorklund, 1995). However, rehearsing does not mean merely repeating something over and over to oneself. Two different types of rehearsal are often discussed. **Maintenance rehearsal** involves saying something over and over, whereas **elaborative rehearsal** involves making sense of what is being learned by relating it to something already in memory. For example, when asked to learn Vygotsky's zone of proximal development, it is best to relate the concept to something that has meaning to the individual. Elaborative rehearsal is more effective in transferring short-term memories into long-term memory (Schunk, 1996).

According to the information-processing view of cognition, long-term memories are laid down in patterns called *networks*, where various concepts are connected to each other in a meaningful manner. Strong associations are found between related concepts, weaker ones between loosely related concepts, and no associations at all between others. For example, what comes to mind when you think about George Washington? Perhaps you come up with the fact that he was the first president, a Virginian, and the father of the country, or that the capital of the United States is Washington, DC. A bit less strongly related is the fact that his wife's name was Martha and that he was a farmer. Completely unrelated would be the fact that the Anaheim Angels won the World Series in 2002. Long-term storage is a dictionary organized by meaning.

rehearsal   Rehearsal involves reviewing or repeating information to retain it in memory.

maintenance rehearsal   A memory strategy consisting of simple repetition of information.

elaborative rehearsal   A memory strategy that involves attending to the meaning of information or relating information to what is already known.

The strength of one's knowledge base plays an important role in determining how one processes information. New memories are related to previous memories. The richer the network of memories in a particular area, the easier to relate a new incident to an older one. For example, if you knew a great deal about coins because you were a collector, you would find it easier to understand a complicated article about how coins are minted than if you did not know anything about coins. The more you know, the easier it is to find "handles" on which to relate one fact to another. Adolescents have a greater amount of knowledge and richer networks than younger children.

Automaticity Adolescents also have an advantage over young children because by adolescence, many behaviors are familiar and thus require less processing capacity. The amount of effort required to execute various tasks declines (Case, 1998). Processing is more efficient, and it becomes possible to do more than one task at a time. As each new skill is mastered and practiced, it becomes more automatic and does not require as much processing or attention. This frees processing space for other tasks.

Strategy Use Adolescents are also more familiar with memory strategies, such as rehearsal and classification, than are younger children. Perhaps more important, adolescents are more aware of what strategies are needed to complete a task. For example, adolescents may understand that different study strategies are necessary in English and in biology. They may use one rehearsal strategy to better remember terms when studying biology, but another strategy in English—for example, after reading assigned short stories writing a summary of the plot and the characters. Adolescents, then, can direct their attention and choose their strategies more efficiently than younger children.

Metacognition

Suppose an adolescent is given a biology assignment to learn and label the bones of the hand. What is the best way for her to proceed? And how will she know that she has mastered the material? She has many choices in determining how to complete the assignment. The choice of strategy may depend on the type of assignment and her knowledge of her own abilities in the area. As has been mentioned, information-processing specialists refer to one's understanding of how one learns as *metacognition*. It is sometimes simply described as knowing about knowing or thinking about thinking (Ferrari & Sternberg, 1998).

Metacognitive abilities improve with age, and older children and teenagers have a more realistic and accurate picture of their own cognitive abilities and limitations than younger children (Short, Schatschneider, & Friebert, 1993). When asked to guess how many items from a list they know, teens are much more accurate than younger children, who tend to overestimate what they know.

Adolescents also better understand what is required to successfully complete a task. In one study, students in the first, third, fifth, and seventh grades were told to learn one of two sets of paired words (for example, *bad-dog*). Material was considered easy if the pairs were related (for example, *cloudy-day*) and difficult if they were not related (for example, *sunny-desk*) (Defresne & Kobasigawa, 1989). Younger children did not study the more difficult material longer, whereas the fifth and seventh graders did. The researchers suggest that younger students did not realize that learning the more difficult material required more time and effort. This finding holds only if people have enough time to study, however. If they are under time pressure, older students devote more time to the easier material, because they believe that this strategy is superior. After all, they would garner some points by knowing at least the easier material (Son & Metcalfe, 2000).

Metacognition requires the ability to reflect upon the state of one's knowledge and understand what one must do to successfully learn. Suppose one teacher tells you to read a very difficult, detailed selection, whereas another teacher tells you to read a story and just get the gist of it. To accomplish both successfully, you must be aware that each task requires a different learning strategy, understand how much you know about each task, choose an appropriate strategy, and monitor your progress.

Self-Regulation

Possessing good metacognitive skills helps individuals learn effectively and efficiently. According to information-processing specialists, though, some students are disciplined and motivated, and they seem almost able to educate themselves. They don't require any external inducements to learn. As noted earlier, these students are often referred to as *self-regulated learners.* They set their own goals and are acutely aware of their present state of knowledge and where they want to be. Self-regulated learners generate academic goals on their own and are internally motivated (Schunk & Ertmer, 2000). Other students, in contrast, need external direction and rely on what others tell them to do. Self-regulated learners also use motivational strategies to keep themselves on task, for example, rewarding themselves for learning difficult material. Self-regulated students feel in control of their own learning and capable of success. Table 4.3 shows the many different strategies used by self-regulated learners.

Table 4.3

Self-Regulated Learning Strategies

When measuring the extent that a student uses self-regulating learning strategies, students are asked to describe their learning strategies. Statements are then placed in categories that describe each self-regulated learning strategy.

Categories of Strategies	Definitions
1. Self-evaluation.	Statements indicating student-initiated evaluations of the quality or progress of their work; e.g., "I check over my work to make sure I did it right."
2. Organizing and transforming.	Statements indicating student-initiated overt or covert rearrangement of instructional materials to improve learning; e.g., "I make an outline before I write my paper."
3. Goal–setting and planning.	Statements indicating student setting of educational goals or subgoals and planning for sequencing, timing, and completing activities related to those goals; e.g., "First, I start studying 2 weeks before exams, and I pace myself."
4. Seeking information.	Statements indicating student-initiated efforts to secure further task information from nonsocial sources when undertaking an assignment; e.g., "Before beginning to write a paper, I go to the library to get as much information as possible concerning the topic."
5. Keeping records and monitoring.	Statements indicating student-initiated efforts to record events or results; e.g., "I took notes of the class discussion" or "I kept a list of the words I got wrong."
6. Environmental structuring.	Statements indicating student-initiated efforts to select or arrange the physical setting to make learning easier; e.g., "I isolate myself from anything that distracts me" or "I turn off the radio so I can concentrate on what I am doing."
7. Determining self-consequences.	Statements indicating student arrangement or imagination of awards or punishment for success or failure; e.g., "If I do well on a test, I treat myself to a movie."
8. Rehearsing and memorizing.	Statements indicating student-initiated efforts to memorize material by overt or covert practice; e.g., "In preparing for a math test, I keep writing the formula down until I remember it."
9–11. Seeking social assistance.	Statements indicating student-initiated efforts to solicit help from peers (9), teachers (10), and adults (11); e.g., "If I have problems with a math assignment, I ask a friend to help."
12–14. Reviewing records.	Statements indicating student-initiated efforts to reread tests (12), notes (13), or textbooks (14) to prepare for class or further testing; e.g., "When preparing for a test, I review my notes."
15. Other.	Statements indicating learning behavior that is initiated by other persons, such as teachers or parents, and all unclear verbal responses; e.g., "I just do what my teacher says."

Source: Zimmerman & Pons (1990), p. 618.

Students who use more self-regulatory strategies report higher levels of motivation, self-efficacy, and achievement (Pintrich & De Groot, 1990). High achievers, in turn, report setting learning goals that are more specific for themselves, using more strategies to learn, monitoring their own learning progress more frequently, and more systematically adapting their efforts on the basis of learning outcomes (Zimmerman, Bonner, & Kovach, 1996). In comparison with others, these students are more aware of what they are doing, how they are doing it, and the rate of their progress. They observe their own performance. Obviously, self-regulation is a continuum; some students show a high level of self-regulation, some have a medium level, and some show little self-regulated learning. Also, a student may regulate some dimensions of learning but not others.

Unfortunately, many students do not engage in effective self-regulatory activities (Pintrich & Schrauben, 1992). However, these students can be taught the skills necessary to be self-regulated learners. The strategic content learning (SCL) approach involves a range of activities that change students' attitudes, as well as improve metacognitive abilities and monitoring practices. SCL instruc-

AT A GLANCE 4.2 INFORMATION PROCESSING

KEY POINT: Information processing is an approach to understanding cognition that focuses on the ways in which people take in information, process it, and then act on it.

SUPPORTING POINTS	EXPLANATION
People must do something to information to make it meaningful.	Without some mental processing, letters and numbers would mean nothing to people.
People have a limited capacity to process information.	Individuals doing two things at the same time must divide their attention and cannot process information as well as they could if they concentrated on just one thing.
Many behaviors are so well learned that they are almost automatic and take very little processing capacity.	As decoding words becomes almost automatic, reading requires less processing space, allowing a person to pay greater attention to the meaning of passages.
People use strategies to deal with challenges.	People use a variety of strategies to deal with problems, including rehearsal and classification.
Information flows through a system.	Sensory memory has a very short duration and a small capacity. If attended to, the information is transferred to short-term memory, which has a short duration (about 30 seconds) and a small capacity (about 7 items). If rehearsed, the information enters long-term memory, which has a huge capacity; material may be stored there for very long periods.
Adolescents process material differently than younger children.	Adolescents' attention span is better than that of younger children. Adolescents have superior selective attention abilities; they are less prone to distraction. They process information faster; more cognitive processes are well learned, requiring less processing space. Adolescents use different strategies than children and are more likely to tailor their learning strategies to the requirements of the task.
Metacognition is the ability to reflect on what one is learning.	Adolescents are more likely than younger children to know that they understand something and to appreciate the fact that they may not know something.
Some students use very effective learning strategies and are self-regulated.	Self-regulated learners adopt their own learning goals, choose learning strategies that are appropriate, actively monitor their learning, and change strategies when appropriate.

tors help students engage in each of the cognitive processes required for success—for example, analyzing the task, setting appropriate goals, evaluating approaches to learning, and monitoring and changing strategies, if necessary. Over a number of sessions, instructors encourage students to try out, monitor, and modify approaches to learning. After such help, students develop better metacognitive knowledge about self-regulatory processes and have more positive perceptions of their self-efficacy, their belief about whether they can or cannot succeed at a task (Butler, 1998). *(For a review of this section, see At A Glance 4.2.)*

APPROACHES TO INTELLIGENCE

Another way of looking at cognitive development is to examine the concept of intelligence, which, as we will see, has many meanings. Some psychologists use the **psychometric approach,** which relies on sophisticated statistical methods to isolate and measure the skills thought to reflect the concept of intelligence. Most standardized intelligence tests are targeted at school-age populations. A high correlation, about .60, exists between school achievement and performance on standardized intelligence tests. An even higher correlation, between .70 and .90, exists between scores on standardized achievement tests and those on intelligence tests (Kubiszyn & Borich, 1987). That is, students who score very high on intelligence tests are likely to do better in school and on standardized achievement tests. Intelligence tests, then, have predictive power in the area of academics, and students who score very low on them may have difficulty in school. However, notice that the correlations are not perfect, meaning that other factors, including motivation, background, and work habits, affect school performance.

The Stanford-Binet and Wechsler Tests

In the early 1900s, the French government asked psychologist Alfred Binet to create a test to identify students who could not benefit from traditional education. Binet used a series of tests that measured a sample of children's abilities at different ages. If a child had less knowledge than the average child of the same age, the child was considered less intelligent. If the child knew more, the child's intelligence was said to be higher. Binet used the term *mental age* to describe the age at which the child was functioning. Later, psychologist William Stern introduced the idea of an *intelligence quotient,* or *IQ,* calculated by taking the mental age of the child, dividing it by the child's chronological age (age since birth), and then multiplying by 100 to remove the decimal. For example, a student who had a mental age of 12 and a chronological age of 10 would have an IQ of 120; if the student were 10 years old but had a mental age of 9, he would have an IQ of 90. The problem with the concept of the IQ is that it assumes a straight-line (linear) relationship between age and intelligence. This relationship does not exist, especially after age 16.

Today, we use a statistically sophisticated way of calculating the intelligence score, called a *deviation IQ.* This method compares a child's performance with the average performance of a large group of children. The average is still 100. Suppose a psychologist administers an intelligence test to every 13-year-old child in the United States. What would the distribution of scores look like? Most scores would cluster around the middle, with fewer scores on each extreme. More than two-thirds of all children have intelligence scores between 84 and 116, and very few (less than 5 percent) have scores above 132 or below 68. Far fewer people have very low or very high intelligence scores than average intelligence scores (see Figure 4.5).

Intelligence tests must be updated continually to remain useful. Many test items lose their usefulness as society changes, and different knowledge may be required. For example, the term *computer* would have had no meaning in 1905,

psychometric approach The approach to intelligence emphasizing mental testing using standardized intelligence tests.

Figure 4.5
**The Normal Curve and Scores on
Intelligence Tests**
Approximately 68 percent of all people score
between 84 and 116 on an intelligence test.
Many fewer score at the extremes.

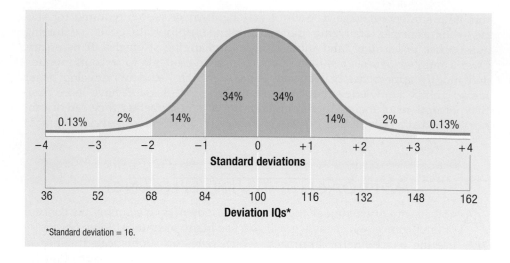

*Standard deviation = 16.

Scores on intelligence tests are positively related to academic achievement, but they have raised many important issues.

when the first edition of Binet's scale was developed, but today it takes on great importance. The original Binet test has gone through a number of revisions and today is called the Stanford-Binet Intelligence Test. It is presently in its fourth edition (Walsh & Betz, 2001). The Stanford-Binet measures four different cognitive areas: verbal reasoning, abstract/visual reasoning, quantitative reasoning, and short-term memory.

Beginning in the late 1930s, David Wechsler developed another set of individualized intelligence tests. Today, the Wechsler group of tests includes three separate intelligence tests that can be administered to people from age 3 through adults. The Wechsler Intelligence Scale for Children (WISC) can be used to test the intelligence of elementary school children and early and middle adolescents. The Wechsler Adult Intelligence Scale (WAIS) is used with older adolescents and adults. The Wechsler tests divide intelligence into two categories: verbal and performance. The verbal subtests measure such abilities as vocabulary and detecting similarities, whereas the performance subtests measure nonverbal skills, such as completing pictures and putting together puzzle pieces (Wechsler, 1991). The test can also yield a composite, or total, intelligence score. The newest edition of the WISC, its third edition, was published in 1991, and the newest adult version, the WAIS, appeared in 1997. The average score on both the Stanford-Binet and the Wechsler tests is 100.

Intelligence Testing in Adolescence

What happens to intelligence test scores in adolescence? Many studies find moderate stability for intelligence scores beginning at about age 5 years, and by age 10 years the evidence for stability is even stronger (McCall, Applebaum, & Hogarty, 1973; Moffitt et al., 1993; Wohlwill, 1980). Yet this finding presents a paradox. Although intelligence scores remain relatively constant, cognitive abilities certainly improve with age. The average 17-year-old knows more, can solve more-complex problems, and has greater skills than the same individual at 8 years old. This would seem contradictory, but it really isn't.

Intelligence test scores are based on comparisons with other people. *Norms,* or averages, are calculated from painstaking research, and how an adolescent performs on a test is determined by how he or she compares with these norms. The IQ is, in fact, a representation of a person's standing relative to his or her age group at a particular time. If various test takers are rank ordered on their general intelligence test scores beginning at age 10, the rankings will remain relatively consistent throughout adolescence (Bjorklund, 1995).

Intelligence scores can change, however, if a child's environment significantly improves or declines. For example, a child may enter a special program designed to improve cognitive functioning. In contrast, a decline in the quality of the home environment may adversely affect a child's skills. Because a very significant change rarely occurs, intelligence scores do not fluctuate very much for most children and adolescents; however, the possibility should be kept in mind (Moffitt et al., 1993).

Controversies Surrounding Intelligence Testing

Intelligence testing is controversial. Three issues that continue to be debated are the origins of intelligence, the effects of culture on intelligence testing, and the question of whether intelligence is one quality or many.

The Origins of Intelligence   How much of the difference among people's intelligence as measured by a standardized intelligence test is due to genetics? How much is due to the environment? The nature-nurture argument has been going on for many years.

The existence of a genetic component in intelligence is now well accepted (Petrill et al., 1996). The Louisville Twin Study compared identical twins, fraternal twins, and nontwin siblings (Wilson, 1977, 1983). The correlation between intelligence scores of the siblings was similar to that of the fraternal twins, which would be expected, because the two groups share about 50 percent of their genes. The intelligence scores of the identical twins were most similar, as they share 100 percent of their genes. For example, the correlation between intelligence scores of identical twins at age 15 was .88, whereas the correlation between intelligence scores for fraternal twins was .54. When identical and fraternal twins separated in infancy and reared apart were followed, 60 percent of the variance in intelligence was associated with genetics (Bouchard et al., 1990). Most studies attribute about 50 percent of the variance in intelligence among people to genetics, which means that half the differences are due to environmental factors (Cowan, Powell, & Cowan, 1998; Grigorenko, 2000).

There is ample evidence that environmental factors are crucial. For example, correlations between intelligence scores of individuals on the basis of their degree of genetic relationship certainly show that the more genetic similarity, the more similar the intelligence score (Plomin & Petrill, 1997). Yet the data can be viewed in another way: Individuals who are reared together show greater IQ similarities than those raised apart. For example, identical twins reared together and fraternal twins reared together are more similar in intelligence than identical twins raised separately and fraternal twins raised separately.

Other evidence for environmental influence comes from studies showing that intelligence scores can be raised. In a study by Skeels (1966), a number of children with mental retardation were removed from the sterile setting of an orphanage and allowed to live in a better environment with older children, who also had mental retardation. The younger children's intelligence test scores improved an average of 29 points, and one child's intelligence score actually rose by more than 50 points. The group that stayed in the depressing environment of the orphanage was found to have even lower intelligence scores than when the study began.

Psychologists know that certain environmental factors influence intelligence scores. A large study of more than 26,000 children found that the best predictors of intelligence are the family's socioeconomic status and the mother's level of education (Broman, Nichols, & Kennedy, 1975). Children born into poverty face a greater chance of perinatal and birth problems and malnutrition, and they may not have many books or access to computers. These families may find that survival is their primary aim. Families with more resources can afford to give their children a more stimulating atmosphere. The second factor, the mother's education level, is important because children spend so much time with their mothers, and less educated mothers may not provide the optimal stimulation for children. Better educated parents may be better able to provide an atmosphere conducive to encouraging the development of the intellect. It is fair to conclude, then, that there is adequate evidence for both genetic and environmental factors in intelligence. The exact way in which they interact requires more study.

Culture and Intelligence   The most controversial issue surrounding intelligence testing is whether standardized intelligence tests are biased against children from some minority groups (Hickson, Blackman, & Reis, 1995; Laosa, 1996). This became a legal question in a 1971 federal lawsuit filed by a group of parents of African American children who had been placed in classes for children with mental retardation. The parents claimed that the placements were discriminatory, because they were based on intelligence tests that were culturally biased. The court ruled in their favor, and this famous decision, *Larry P. v. Riles,* meant that intelligence tests could no longer be used as the sole basis for placing children in special classes (Rothstein, 1995).

Children and adolescents from various groups do not score equally on standardized intelligence tests. In the United States, Asian Americans score higher on intelligence tests as a group than white Americans, who score higher than African Americans (Neisser et al., 1996). The question is, why?

One significant reason is poverty. A greater proportion of African Americans and some groups of Latinos live in poverty. Children raised in poverty environments experience less cognitive stimulation and may not fully develop their intellectual skills. Middle-class children visit museums more frequently, are read to by their parents more often, and are encouraged to develop their verbal skills by answering in full sentences. Studies report that poverty and home environment explain the overwhelming majority of this difference. In fact, when poverty and home environmental variables are controlled, differences between African American and white children on intelligence test results are narrowed considerably and all but eliminated (Brooks-Gunn, Klebanov, & Duncan, 1996).

Standardized intelligence tests measure general cultural knowledge taught by middle-class parents (Scarr, 1981). Tests are formulated by middle-class psychologists and designed to predict achievement in schools that emphasize the dominant culture. Minority group youth, especially those raised in poverty, have different experiences. Consider a question on an older version of a standardized intelligence test: A child is asked, "What would you do if you were sent to buy a loaf of bread and the grocer said he did not have any more?" Professionals constructing the test thought the answer "go to another store" was reasonable, and it is. Yet more than a quarter of all children from minority groups said they would go home, a seemingly incorrect answer. When asked why they answered this way, the children told the investigators there were no other stores in the neighborhood (Hardy et al., 1976).

If poverty is a primary reason for group differences in intelligence testing, then better economic circumstances should lead to higher intelligence scores. Indeed, the differences in intelligence scores between African Americans and whites have narrowed, which is attributed to the higher education level of African American parents as they have gained greater access to educational and vocational opportunities (Jencks & Phillips, 1998; Nisbett, 1998).

Poverty, though, is not the only concern. Vocabulary may also cause problems for some adolescent learners for whom English is not the primary language (Kaplan, 1996). In addition, sometimes cultural norms influence the behavior of adolescents in a classroom, leading to beliefs that these adolescents are not bright. For example, some Latino immigrants teach their children and adolescents to respect the teacher's authority rather than express their own opinions, and this emphasis may lead to a negative academic assessment. Listening with respect, a very dignified behavior in one culture, may lead to a negative evaluation in a school setting where asserting oneself is the valued mode of communication (Greenfield, 1997). In addition, children and adolescents from the majority culture may be very comfortable with a testing setting, the format of the test, and the types of questions asked, whereas children from various minority cultures may not be as comfortable (Duran, 1989).

Recently, another possible reason for group differences in intelligence scores has been postulated. Steele (1997; Steele & Aronson, 1995) argues that just the idea of measuring intelligence can have a negative effect on scores of adolescents from some minorities who have been stereotyped as scoring lower and being less intelligent. This is called a **stereotype threat,** the threat of confirming, as a characteristic of oneself, a negative stereotype of one's group. As a consequence of the stereotype threat, whenever minority group youth encounter a test of academic ability, they perceive it as a risk, fearing they will confirm the stereotype. This depresses test performance. In one study, African American and white college students were given a test composed of very challenging items from a standardized test. Students from both racial groups were randomly assigned to one of three test conditions: stereotype threat condition, in which the test was described as diagnosing verbal ability; a control condition, in which participants were told that the test was only a research tool; and a control-challenge condition, in which the test was described as being a research tool, but participants were told to take it seriously. Very small differences were found for the control and control-challenge conditions, but African Americans scored much lower than whites in the stereotype threat condition. Steele and Aronson suggest that the stereotype threat caused problems in information processing, as participants spent more time doing fewer items. Just the threat of being at risk for confirming a stereotype can lead to poor performance.

Not all psychologists believe that intelligence tests discriminate against children from minority groups. Proponents of intelligence testing argue that the problem with intelligence tests is the way they are used, not their construction or what they indicate. The tests do predict, albeit not perfectly, academic success across ethnic groups (U.S. Department of Education, 1993). Proponents point out that children who do not score well on intelligence tests are less likely to do well in school. Thus, criticizing the messenger, the test, is not helpful. The problem with intelligence tests, in the end, may have less to do with whether or not the tests are technically fair and more to do with the way they are interpreted. Opponents of the use of intelligence tests often emphasize the negative social outcomes of testing, such as the overrepresentation of students from minority groups in special education programs. They argue that analyzing the consequences of test use is as important as determining whether the tests are technically fair (Laosa, 1996).

A major problem lies in the definition of *intelligence* used by the general public and some educators. The type of intelligence measured by intelligence tests relates to academic skills, but not to what many people often regard as intelligence, such as common sense or being able to solve problems in everyday life. Intelligence tests do not measure adaptation to life or interpersonal skills—a fact readily admitted even by those who prepare the tests (Wechsler, 1991). The controversy over intelligence testing shows no sign of abating, and its use will continue to be debated by experts and the general public far into the future.

People should recognize, however, that standardized intelligence tests do demonstrate past learning and understand that they are not global measures of functioning but just narrow measures related to school achievement. Intelligence tests do not measure overall learning potential in every area, but they do have some power in predicting how well children will do in the schools as they are now structured (U.S. Department of Education, 1993).

Properly used, intelligence tests can be a source of diagnostic help for teachers. Test scores should make up only part of an assessment and be used with other sources of information to obtain a more complete picture of a child's functioning.

Is Intelligence One Quality or Many? Is intelligence a single entity, or are there many different types of intelligence? British psychologist Charles Spearman (1904) observed that school grades in different subjects, such as

stereotype threat The threat of confirming as a characteristic of oneself a negative stereotype of one's group.

Table 4.4

Howard Gardner's Theory of Multiple Intelligences

Gardner has proposed that people can differ on 10 different intelligences.

Type	Description	Examples
Linguistic	Language skills, including reading, writing, and communicating with words	Writers, orators
Logical/mathematical	The ability to reason and calculate, as well as to think things through logically and systematically	Engineers, scientists
Musical	The ability to make or compose music	Musicians
Visual/spatial	The ability to think in pictures, to visualize a future result	Architects, sculptors, sailors
Bodily/kinesthetic	The ability to use the body skillfully to create products	Athletes, craftspeople, dancers
Interpersonal	The ability to work effectively with others and to understand others' moods and intentions	Teachers, therapists, salespeople
Intrapersonal	The ability to understand one's own feelings; self-analysis and reflection	Philosophers, counselors

Note: Recently, Gardner proposed three other intelligences: *naturalist,* which involves the ability to recognize flora and fauna and the natural world and to use this information; *spiritual;* and *existential.* These categories await further research.
Source: Adapted from Gardner (1987, 1993, 1998).

English and math, were positively correlated; that is, students who achieved high grades in one subject were likely to receive high grades in many subjects. To Spearman, this finding indicated the existence of a general factor, or *g.* Because the correlations weren't perfect, Spearman noted that specific abilities (known as *s*) also existed. In other words, each individual domain had specific skills associated with it. Spearman, however, emphasized the importance of the general, or *g,* factor. This idea did not go unchallenged; psychologist Louis Thurstone (1938) argued for the existence of seven separate mental abilities, or *primary mental abilities,* including verbal comprehension, word fluency, number facility, memory, perceptual speed, reasoning, and spatial visualization. This controversy continues, but a number of recent theories have expanded our conception of intelligence and added to the debate.

GARDNER'S THEORY OF MULTIPLE INTELLIGENCES   Howard Gardner (1983, 1987, 1993) defines *intelligence* as "an ability to solve problems or to fashion a product which is valued in one or more cultural settings" (1987, p. 25). According to Gardner's **theory of multiple intelligences,** many different types of intelligence exist: linguistic, logical/mathematical, musical, visual/spatial, bodily/kinesthetic, interpersonal (social skills), and intrapersonal (the understanding of one's own feelings and needs). Later Gardner (1998, 1999) added three more kinds of intelligence: naturalist (the understanding of the natural world and the ability to use this knowledge productively), spiritual (a concern with spiritual issues), and existential (the ability to address questions of our existence and meaning of life) (see Table 4.4). The last three are less well researched at this point (Gregory, 2000). People differ on the extent to which they possess these intelligences. An individual may excel in art and not be sensitive to the needs of others, and a person with outstanding interpersonal skills may not pass science class. In addition, different professions require different combinations of various types of intelligence; for example, a good salesperson needs good verbal skills and interpersonal skills.

Gardner believes that most intelligence tests, which measure only linguistic and logical/mathematical intelligence, are insufficient. For example, an individual who is adept at dealing with others or can fashion a product by hand shows intelligence of a different sort than that measured by standard tests. Gardner believes that schools should encourage a wider range of abilities than standard-

theory of multiple intelligences   A conception of intelligence advanced by Howard Gardner, who argues that there are ten different types of intelligence.

ized intelligence tests would indicate. Some schools have adopted Gardner's definition and focus on developing children's and adolescents' abilities in all these areas, and they recognize that any one type of intelligence is not necessarily superior to any other type (Murray, 1996).

Gardner's theory has been criticized because some of the intelligences he proposes, such as interpersonal and intrapersonal, are difficult to test. In addition, some question whether Gardner's categories are truly intelligences or, instead, are specific talents or skills.

STERNBERG'S TRIARCHIC THEORY OF INTELLIGENCE
Robert Sternberg (1985; Ferrari & Sternberg, 1998; Sternberg, 1988) proposes the **triarchic theory of intelligence,** which argues for the existence of three kinds of human intelligence: analytic, creative, and practical. *Analytic intelligence* includes the skills required to do well on standardized intelligence tests and school-related subjects. These skills involve some of the information-processing skills described earlier, such as attention, memory, and metacognitive abilities. *Creative intelligence* is the ability to use one's experience to formulate novel ideas and problems. *Practical intelligence* is the ability to size up situations, figure them out, and do what is required to adapt to their demands. Practical intelligence also involves the social skills required to cope with everyday demands, manage one's emotions and behavior, and deal with others effectively.

These intelligences are separate. Standardized intelligence tests measure analytic intelligence, which is related to success in school. However, measures of practical intelligence are better at predicting success on the job. Creative intelligence is a distinct form of intelligence, but people seem to need at least an average level of analytic intelligence to find creative solutions to problems (Sternberg, 1985).

As is the case with Gardner's multiple intelligences, people differ on Sternberg's three intelligences. Some people who do not get high scores on measures of traditional intelligence may do better on tests of creative or practical intelligence (Sternberg, 1996b). Sternberg suggested that individuals taught in a way that is compatible with their strongest intelligence will learn better. For instance, a person high in practical intelligence might learn better with hands-on materials and demonstrations. Like Gardner, Sternberg argues that school curriculum should include skills related to all three types of intelligence. Critics of Sternberg's theory, however, note that it is very difficult to measure practical intelligence or creative intelligence.

EMOTIONAL INTELLIGENCE If you were asked to list the skills required to create a successful marriage or lead a satisfying life, it is unlikely that *intelligence* as defined by today's standardized intelligence tests would be high on your list. Other factors, such as social skills, being able to express oneself and manage conflict, and the ability to delay gratification would probably be higher on the list.

Some psychologists argue that the importance of personal and interpersonal abilities has been underestimated for too long. *Emotional intelligence,* according to Salovey and Mayer (1990, 1997), is the ability to perceive, understand, and regulate one's emotions effectively. Doing so involves a number of abilities. For example, recognizing one's own emotions and those of others is a key to better interpersonal relationships. Someone with a high emotional intelligence would recognize jealousy and be in a position to manage it. The ability to use knowledge about emotions effectively requires understanding what others are experiencing and using that knowledge to improve one's relationships with others. For

Is artistic ability a type of intelligence? Howard Gardner, who formulated the theory of multiple intelligences, believes it is.

triarchic theory of intelligence A theory of intelligence postulating three types of intelligence: analytic, creative, and practical.

example, when you can recognize a friend's emotions, you can then empathize with your friend (that is, understand how your friend feels) and tailor your responses to the individual's emotions. Realizing that your friend is unhappy because he failed the same test you did so well on might lead you not to celebrate too much in front of him. Self-regulation is an important skill in controlling impulses. If you feel that you are becoming angry with someone, for example, you might consider your words more carefully. Self-regulation also facilitates one's thinking process, as the inability to manage one's feelings can interfere with clear thinking.

Daniel Goleman (1995), whose book *Emotional Intelligence* made the concept popular, notes that such abilities as self-regulation, self-awareness, impulse control (delaying gratification), self-motivation, empathy, being able to handle one's emotions, and possessing social skills are more accurate predictors of success

AT A GLANCE 4.3 APPROACHES TO INTELLIGENCE

KEY POINT: The measurement of intelligence through standardized intelligence tests is controversial.

SUPPORTING POINTS	EXPLANATION
Scores on intelligence tests relate to academic success.	The correlation between scores on intelligence tests and grades is about .60. This correlation is high, but it shows that other factors, such as motivation and work habits, are also important.
The first standardized intelligence test was devised by Alfred Binet and now is called the Stanford-Binet Intelligence Test.	The Stanford-Binet Intelligence Test measures verbal reasoning, abstract/visual reasoning, quantitative reasoning, and short- term memory.
The Wechsler Intelligence Tests allow the measurement of intelligence from age 3 years through adulthood.	The Wechsler tests measure both verbal and performance intelligence.
Scores on intelligence tests often stay stable throughout adolescence.	Unless some major change occurs in an adolescent's environment, stable intelligence test scores can be expected. If an environmental change occurs, scores may change.
Both genetic and environmental factors influence intelligence.	Current research ascribes about 50 percent of the differences between people on intelligence to genetic factors and the other 50 percent to environmental factors. Intelligence scores can be raised if the environment is improved.
Some authorities believe that standardized intelligence tests are unfair to children and adolescents from minority groups.	Some authorities claim that intelligence tests are unfair to minority group children, who may have different experiences than their middle-class peers.
There is a debate as to whether intelligence is a single entity or there are many types of intelligence.	Charles Spearman emphasized the importance of general intelligence. Louis Thurstone believed there were seven different types of intelligence, called *primary mental abilities*.
Howard Gardner argues that there are ten different types of intelligence.	Gardner argues that standard intelligence tests measure only a small amount of true intelligence.
Robert Sternberg postulates three types of intelligence.	Sternberg's triarchic theory of intelligence describes three different types of intelligence: analytic, practical, and creative.
Emotional intelligence has become a popular concept.	Emotional intelligence encompasses a group of skills—such as delaying gratification, managing conflict, and controlling one's impulses—that may be related to positive outcomes in adulthood.

than standardized IQ measures. Self-regulation, in this context, involves examining your goals and devising a strategy for getting you what you want. For example, if you wanted to become a high school teacher, you would realize that studying and some sacrifice were required. You would need self-discipline to study while others might be watching a movie. Indeed, being able to modulate one's own emotions and be sensitive to the feelings of others allows the formation of strong emotional bonds and leads to greater success in careers, marriage, and child rearing (Salovey & Mayer, 1997).

Emotional intelligence, according to Goleman, can be taught and nurtured if people become aware of its qualities and understand its importance to learning and life. People can learn to manage their anger, delay gratification, and empathize with others. It is important to understand that standardized intelligence scores and emotional intelligence are not exclusive. People often believe that people with a high IQ lack people skills, but this is not the case (Adelson, 1996). People with high standardized intelligence scores can also be sociable and sensitive.

Not everyone accepts the idea of emotional intelligence, and there is no accepted way of measuring it. However, the idea does broaden how we can look at the concept of intelligence. *(For a review of this section, see At A Glance 4.3.)*

USING COGNITIVE ABILITIES

Each of the approaches to cognitive development we have discussed—the developmental approaches, the information-processing approach, and the concept of intelligence—has much to offer psychologists in their quest for understanding adolescent cognitive abilities. Adolescents use these cognitive abilities in their daily lives in the areas of critical thinking, creativity, and decision making.

Critical Thinking

You've already spent $1,200 on repairs for your old car, and you find you need to put in another $1,000 to fix it again. Should you do it? On one side, you've already put a great deal of money into the car; on the other side, there is no guarantee that if you do, it will not need more money later on. This is one example of how critical thinking can be crucial in real-world decisions. Educators agree that critical thinking should be a major part of the educational experience (Kuhn, 1999).

Defining critical thinking is not easy, but one commonly used definition views **critical thinking** as "reasonable and reflective thinking concerning what to do or believe" (Norris & Ennis, 1989). A critically thinking person makes inferences, states assumptions, and analyzes arguments (Gadzella & Penland, 1995). Critical thinking skills include assessing the reliability of a source; distinguishing between fact and opinion; identifying assumptions; and recognizing bias, fallacy, and irrelevance (Halpern, 1998). Some researchers link the metacognitive skills discussed earlier to the formation of critical thinking skills (Kuhn, 1999). For example, understanding what one knows and how one knows it and effectively using strategies may form the foundation of critical thinking skills. Critical thinking requires an individual to question the truthfulness of information and reflect on personal beliefs. Critical thinking should not imply negative thinking or seeking to find fault with everyone.

The capacity for critical thinking increases substantially in adolescence. Teenagers can process information faster than younger children, and many basic processes are automatic (teens already know the multiplication table and how to decode words without much conscious thinking). This ability frees processing capacity for other purposes. Teens also have more knowledge than younger children. It is difficult to critically analyze a historical event, for example, if you don't understand a simple outline of what happened. Teenagers can better

critical thinking   Reasonable and reflective thinking concerning what to do or believe.

understand and use scientific logic, although they need training in this area. They also realize that other alternatives are available, as well as that the way things are done and what is said are not necessarily the same. Younger children often believe that their parents and the government are larger-than-life figures who are almost always right. Teens know better. Their use of strategies to obtain information is superior, and they can monitor their own thoughts (Keating, 1990). Cognitive advancements, then, may give adolescents an advantage over children in critical thinking, but they may not always use these skills.

Critical thinking can be taught through the use of questioning techniques, and evidence shows that such training is badly needed (Savage, 1998). For example, evaluating Web-based information is an important educational issue today. In one study, the U.S. presidents were listed on a website in the wrong order. Later, students were shown the names of the presidents in the correct order in a reference book. Students were more likely to believe that the on-line list was correct (Minkel, 2000). When adolescents use the Web, they analyze the sites in terms of personal appeal and novelty rather than authority (Shiveley & Van Fossen, 1999). They need to learn that a very important aspect of analyzing information is checking the author's credentials. Web users should also learn how to look for bias, analyze the content's validity, and analyze the clarity of the points made. Table 4.5 lists the important questions that need to be answered when judging Web-based information.

Table 4.5

Evaluating Web-Based Information

The Internet is a very popular place to find information, but is that information valid? Here are some questions to ask about information you find on the Web.

Authorship/Source	Objectivity/Bias	Validity of Content
1. Who is providing the information?	1. If the site deals with controversial issues, is more than one side of the argument presented?	1. Does the author describe the method used to develop the site? If so, is the method reasonable?
2. Is the author or organization listed?	2. Does the author or organization clearly state potential biases?	2. Was the site subjected to peer review?
3. What is the author's authority (expertise) to write on the subject?	3. Is the site on the server of an organization with a vested interest in the issue, such as a political party?	3. Does the author provide verifiable statistics or data?
4. Does the author provide detailed background information supporting his or her authority?	4. Do advertisements appear on the Web page? How might these ads influence the author or indicate a bias?	4. Does the author use a recognizable style manual to quote material?
5. Is this a research paper, scholarly result, or personal opinion?		
6. Is the site supported or funded by a particular organization or institution?		
7. Was the information subject to any review or scrutinized by experts?		

Bibliography/Reference Links	Currency	Quality of Writing
1. Does the document contain a bibliography?	1. When were the data in the document collected?	1. Is the text well written? Is it concise? Is the central thesis clear?
2. Does the author provide a list of reference links to related topics?	2. When were the data in the document first published?	2. Does the site contain indications of hasty or incomplete preparation (spelling errors, poor grammar)?
3. Are readers informed about the types of references to which they will be linked?	3. Is the document updated regularly?	3. Are the data clearly presented (tables, charts) and easily interpreted?
4. What are the link selection criteria?	4. When was the last update?	4. Is the text free of jargon, or are terms undefined?

Source: Adapted from Shiveley & Van Fossen (1999).

Teaching critical thinking is a four-step procedure. First, the teacher must nurture a positive attitude toward critical thinking, as critical analysis requires effort and a willingness to engage and persist.

Second, students need instruction and practice in critical thinking skills. These skills include understanding how cause is determined, recognizing and criticizing assumptions, giving reasons to support a conclusion, and using analogies to solve problems (Halpern, 1998).

Third, adolescents need to learn how to transfer critical thinking skills from one situation to another. Teachers may demonstrate how a skill can be used in many situations. For example, the case of the car repair at the beginning of this section is sometimes called the *sunk costs problem*. The problem may be used not only to decide whether to repair an old car but also to analyze whether to spend millions of dollars more on a missile system that does not work simply because so much money has already been spent on it, or to decide whether your friend should marry a longtime girlfriend just because they've already spent so many years together. All three incidents involve allotting resources just because considerable money or time has been previously spent. The key to each dilemma is the understanding that what is relevant in all three situations is what is occurring now, not what happened in the past or what might happen in the future. The decision about car repair, for example, should be based upon whether the car is now worth the repair price. This skill at analyzing problems can be taught to adolescents.

The last step in teaching critical thinking is the use of a metacognitive component to direct and assess thinking. Doing so tells us whether we have solved the problem or should switch strategies. It may entail looking at the situation after making a decision and analyzing whether it worked.

Teaching critical thinking is an emerging educational priority (Broadbear & Keyser, 2000). It has special relevance for adolescents, who must decide what to believe and arrive at decisions in a logical manner.

Creativity

Suppose you were asked to judge school science projects using the criterion of creativity. How would you go about doing so? **Creativity** refers to novel behavior that is appropriate to solve the problem at hand. Just because an approach is different, however, does not automatically make it creative. Let's say your kite is caught in a tree. You come up with the novel idea of throwing a baseball at it; you break the kite but do bring it down from the tree. Your approach was novel, but it was not appropriate. It did not solve your problem of bringing the kite safely back to the ground. Creativity requires responses that are both novel and appropriate (Eisenberger & Cameron, 1998). It is difficult to use appropriateness as a criterion when evaluating something like a painting or a musical score, so it is often difficult to define what is or is not creative. Is every painting a work of creativity? Perhaps it is, because it is the expression of the artist. Alternatively, you might ask if the work breaks any new ground or shows you something different.

Creativity can be found on both the individual and the societal levels. Creative products, such as Thomas Edison's light bulb or record player, may change the lives of everyone on the planet. This kind of creativity is sometimes called *Creativity* (with a capital C). Creativity can also be seen in average people's attempts to solve their everyday problems (Cropley, 1999), which is sometimes referred to as *creativity* (with a lowercase c). (Csikszentmihalyi & Epstein, 1999). Creativity is not the sole province of the brilliant. In fact, scores on intelligence tests are poor predictors of creativity. Although people with low intelligence do tend to show low creativity, little relationship is found between intelligence and creativity for people with at least average intelligence (Pychova, 1995).

Creativity often is examined as a type of thinking, according to J. P. Guilford (1967), a pioneer in the field. **Convergent thinking** involves arriving at an answer when given a particular set of facts. It is measured by IQ tests, which require individuals to solve well-defined problems that have one correct answer.

creativity Novel behavior that is appropriate to solve the problem at hand.

convergent thinking A type of thinking in which people solve problems by integrating information in a logical manner and arriving at a single answer.

Is all art creative? Creativity is often determined by novelty and appropriateness, but the second criterion is difficult to use with art or music.

Convergent thinking is oriented toward deriving the single best answer using available information. **Divergent thinking,** which is related to creativity, involves seeing new relationships between things or viewing a problem in a new way that is still appropriate to the situation. Divergent thinking leads to no agreed-upon solutions and requires an individual to generate new ideas and multiple answers from the available information. These answers are new, at least in the experience of the person now working on the problem.

Creativity may require more than divergent thinking, though. Other necessary components may include content knowledge, the ability to communicate, and the ability to critically analyze situations. Content knowledge is important in creativity, because it is difficult to be creative in any field without an understanding of the basics. Communication skills are needed for effective interaction with others and exchanges of ideas. Critical analysis of goals and strategies is also important. A person who has, say, twenty possible avenues to explore must perform some critical analysis so as to explore only the most promising avenues. In fact, a positive relationship exists between creativity and critical thinking (Gadzella & Penland, 1995).

Creativity is a special concern in adolescence. Teenagers have improved cognitive skills, such as realizing that there can be more than one answer to a problem. They also have more knowledge about specific topics, are more aware of the strategies they can use, have greater attentional abilities, and can think abstractly. They can show greater motivation and persistence, a characteristic of adult creativity that appears to be very important for creative work (Olszewski-Kubilius, 2000). However, they also have an increased desire to fit in and not be different. A teenager may want to solve a problem a different way, but may not see it as desirable. Teenagers fear being singled out or being rejected by the group. Creative individuals, however, often must follow their own path rather than the conforming, traditional path. Teens need to develop strategies for handling the anxiety that comes with thinking differently. Being creative, seen in this way, is a personal decision (Sternberg, 2000).

People develop their creative abilities, in part, by working with creative individuals. In addition, if adolescents are reinforced for approaching problems in new ways and playing with ideas, they think more creatively. Teachers have definite ideas about what classroom environments enhance or inhibit creativity (Fleith, 2000). They believe that giving students choices, using cooperative groups, and offering open-ended activities enhance creativity. In contrast, they feel that drilling and too much teacher control hinder creativity.

Fostering creative thinking is important in both schools and the workplace, and many companies now offer creativity training to their workers (Gundry & Kickul, 1996). Although not everyone will or can be Creative (with a capital C), everyone has the ability to be creative (with a lowercase c). Unfortunately, as children proceed through school, they become less likely to solve problems in novel ways, looking for safe answers (Mildrum, 2000). Some reorganization of the classroom is necessary if students are to be encouraged to develop their skills, use them to solve problems creatively, and invent new products in the future.

Decision Making

Adolescents must often make important decisions. The nature of these decisions differs from the kinds of decisions younger children make. What do I want to be? What do I stand for? What do I believe in? What path do I wish to follow? The

divergent thinking A type of thinking marked by the ability to see new relationships between things that are still appropriate to the situation.

decisions of adolescents are more oriented to the future. A young girl may want to work with dinosaur fossils, but as she approaches adolescence and then college age, she knows she must begin to look not only at her love of fossils but also at her ability in the sciences, where she'd like to work, and what schools offer the best choices. This future orientation is encouraged by the development of the formal operational ability to consider possibilities.

The adolescent develops some effective tools for making decisions. Hypothetical-deductive logic; a more impressive knowledge base; the ability to use abstractions; and improvements in attention, memory, and processing speed all combine to give adolescents decision-making tools that are not available to younger children. In addition, the ability to plan improves in adolescence (Kreitler & Kreitler, 1987).

Two developmental trends appear in decision making. First, adolescents are better decision makers than younger children. Second, older adolescents make better decisions than younger adolescents. A better decision is defined in terms of how it is made—that is, discovering alternatives, carefully analyzing them, and examining the possible consequences.

When adolescents and young adults were given hypothetical dilemmas about medical treatment (for diabetes and epilepsy) and psychological treatment (for depression and bed wetting), the 14-year-olds and adult experts made decisions similar in reasonableness of the outcome of choice, understanding of the facts, and analysis of the decision-making process (Weithorn & Campbell, 1982). In fact, most studies on important choices do not find significant differences between adults and adolescents (Moshman, 1993). By age 14 years or so, adolescents can consider options, weigh pros and cons, and make and defend their choices.

However, younger adolescents are somewhat less able to take multiple factors into consideration. Younger adolescents, being less developmentally advanced, are more concerned with appearance and fitting in. For example, in the study above, younger adolescents who were questioned about medical treatment decisions for epilepsy were more likely to reject the use of medication because of adverse cosmetic side effects, such as excessive hair growth. This is in keeping with younger adolescents' greater concern with appearance. Developmental differences may be found when factors that are more important to people of a particular age are involved.

AT A GLANCE 4.4 USING COGNITIVE ABILITIES

KEY POINT: The adolescent's abilities to think critically, be creative, and make decisions improve during adolescence as cognitive abilities develop.

SUPPORTING POINTS	EXPLANATION
Critical thinking involves reasonable and reflective thinking concerning what to do or believe.	Critical thinking improves in adolescence because processes are automatic, adolescents have a greater knowledge base, they realize that many more alternatives are available, and they can better monitor their thoughts and ideas.
Creativity refers to behaviors that are novel and appropriate.	Creativity often involves divergent thinking, that is, seeing new relationships between things and generating new ideas. Adolescents have advantages in creativity, as they understand that there is often more than one answer to a problem, have a better knowledge base and better analytical skills, and can use abstractions. However, they also may fear standing out and doing things differently.
Adolescents are faced with many important decisions that may have consequences for their future.	Adolescents have a greater capacity to make decisions due to their ability to use hypothetical-deductive logic, a more impressive knowledge base, the ability to use abstractions, and improvements in information-processing ability.

Are adolescents competent at making important decisions? This practical issue bears directly on how adolescents are treated. Unfortunately, if one looks for guidance from various court decisions, only confusion results, as the decisions are contradictory. In 1988, for example, the U.S. Supreme Court reasserted the school's right to control the content of student publications. In *Hazelwood v. Kuhlmeier*, the Court addressed a case in which a high school principal censored articles concerning divorce and adolescent pregnancy in the school newspaper even though the articles were not obscene, disruptive, or libelous. The Supreme Court stated that schools can prohibit the publication of items unsuitable for "immature" audiences because of the possibility that adolescents will come to believe that these positions are advocated by the school. In another case *(Board of Education v. Megens)*, however, the Court declared that groups of students who wanted to hold a Bible study club could do so. The school cited concerns about students believing that the school authorities advocated a particular religion or feeling pressure to join the group. The Court decided that if any outside group is allowed to use school facilities, religious groups have the same right. The Court declared that students could easily understand this legal point and would not believe that any particular religious viewpoint was being advocated. The two rulings are obviously inconsistent.

This inconsistency is found in the general public as well. I often ask students whether a 16-year-old girl who wants breast implants should be allowed to obtain them without parental permission. The answer is often no. When I ask whether a 16-year-old girl who wants an abortion without parental permission should be able to have one, the answer is often yes. The same individual who favors the death penalty for youthful offenders convicted of a crime on the grounds that the offenders are responsible for their actions is often against adolescent girls receiving an abortion without parental permission on the grounds that the girls don't fully understand what they are doing. Furthermore, a person who argues that adolescent girls should have the right to receive an abortion without parental permission often sees youthful offenders as immature and requiring special treatment and understanding.

Are adolescents mature enough to be free to choose, as well as to suffer the consequences of their actions and choices? Concerning the school newspaper issue, psychologists found that tenth graders understood that the school was not endorsing a point of view if articles were published or religious groups were permitted to use school grounds (Dunkle, 1993). It seems that high school students understand these issues very well, but many younger teens do not. When seventh graders, eleventh graders, and college students were interviewed about the nature of civil rights,

Generally, young adolescents (12 to 14 years old) are less competent than older adolescents and adults in making decisions (see "Focus: The Issue of Competency"). They are less able to create options, use less information, are less able to identify risks and benefits, and are less able to analyze the credibility of information (Furby & Beyth-Marom, 1992). When seventh and eighth graders, tenth graders, and twelfth graders were questioned about what decisions people in various situations should make, the older adolescents mentioned more of the possible risks, whereas the younger adolescents overlooked the possible negative consequences (Lewis, 1981).

Adolescents can experience a great deal of stress while making important decisions. Galotti and Kozberg (1996) asked high school students on three occasions in their junior year to complete measuring instruments concerning the decision-making process involved in determining which college to attend. They also asked participants to use their own words to describe this process and how they felt about their decision. The researchers used essays, in addition to the more standardized rating scales, to allow students to express themselves more freely. The researchers first read a sample of essays to develop a list of themes or dimensions—for example, activity level, type of criteria used, to what extent parents were involved, and level of certainty and anxiety. They then coded all the essays on these dimensions.

Both the rating scales and the analysis of the essays paint a similar picture. As the junior year progressed, students' sense of certainty and readiness to make the decision increased. They were more comfortable with their approach and confident of their ability to make the "right" decision. In contrast, students' ratings of stressfulness and difficulty remained constant over the year. In other the eleventh graders were similar to college students in their explanations, but the seventh graders were somewhat different in their understanding of abstract civil rights (Helwig, 1997).

Mature logical reasoning requires the ability to distinguish the form of an argument from its content. This ability is a form of abstract judgment that begins to develop in early adolescence and continues to evolve throughout adolescence (Moshman, 1993). For example, understanding the concept of intellectual freedom requires the ability to distinguish the right to express oneself from agreement or disagreement with the content of that expression. In one study that tested for this ability, fourth graders could not understand the difference, seventh graders understood it only if they received instruction in the area, and college students easily understood that the argument about intellectual freedom was independent of the truth status of what the person was saying (Moshman & Franks, 1986).

The development of reasoning skills and education itself depends on having opportunities to consider different points of view, freely interact with others, and reflect on one's ideas. The evidence shows, however, that elementary school students do not have these abilities, and junior high school students are just developing them, which is why they require some instruction. This reflects Vygotsky's zone of proximal distance concept. Junior high school students, who are just developing formal operational thinking, are helped significantly by instruction in the area. From this research it

is easy to argue that at least in high school, an open intellectual atmosphere is best, and students can understand the difference between the right to say something and the underlying truth of what is being said (Moshman, 1993). Secondary schools, especially high schools, should be more like universities than like elementary school with respect to academic freedom (Moshman, 1998).

What about adolescent competency to make decisions in other areas? It is fair and reasonable to argue that the criteria for maturity need not be the same for all behavioral domains. For example, a more stringent criteria for maturity might be used for potentially harmful behaviors, such as owning a handgun or smoking cigarettes, than for the expression of beliefs. Some restriction on behavior is more justifiable than any restriction on ideas or on the legal freedom of expression. In addition, the restriction of particular rights by parents because they believe their child is less mature or has some difficulty is certainly more justifiable than allowing government to make these decisions. The adolescent-as-adult view, then, is strongest regarding intellectual freedom and weaker in the area of behavioral autonomy.

The question of adolescent competency to make decisions will continue to be debated, both in the public forum and in the courts. Psychological research clearly may help the courts and the legislature make rules in this area based on an understanding of how adolescents think rather than personal bias or guesswork.

words, despite being more confident of their abilities over time, students experienced just as much stress. They often felt overwhelmed by the sheer amount of information and the short time to process it and make the decision. The researchers suggest that parents, teachers, and counselors assist students in determining a decision-making strategy and managing the information overload. *(For a review of this section, see At A Glance 4.4.)*

SOCIAL COGNITION

So far, we've examined different ways of approaching adolescent cognitive abilities including Piaget's theory, Vygotsky's theory, the information processing approach and using standardized intelligence testing, and looked at adolescent thinking and decision making. Cognitive advancements also affect how we act in social situations. Psychologists use the term **social cognition** to describe the ways people perceive, interpret, and use information about themselves and others to make sense of their social world (Shantz, 1983). Children and adolescents actively think and reason about the social environment that surrounds them. They are not simply passive receivers of information. They interpret other people's behavior and predict how their own behavior may influence others. Their social relationships are influenced by their cognitive abilities. For example, how people interact with others depends on how they understand the nature of interpersonal relationships, the accuracy with which they interpret others' behavior, and how they apply information gained in previous situations to what they are doing now.

social cognition   The ways in which people perceive, interpret, and use information about themselves and others to make sense of their social world.

Piaget believed that the same cognitive skills that are involved in analyzing social experiences are involved in understanding the physical world of nonliving things, but there are important differences between interactions with animate versus inanimate objects (Flavell et al., 2002). People have motives and intentions that are sometimes difficult to understand, whereas a pen or a television does not. People also experience emotions that may influence how they act. In addition, the relationships among people are reciprocal; one individual says something and the other individual responds, which may alter the original ideas. Social cognition focuses on how cognitive abilities influence social interactions, viewed from the perspective of the individual. Vygotsky takes a different approach, as he was mostly interested in the reverse of the process—that is, how social experiences influence cognitive development. Vygotsky's theory focuses on how cultures teach their children what to think and how to think. Children are first guided by adults, and the responsibility gradually shifts more to the children, who internalize ways of thinking.

Psychologists studying social cognition are interested in how cognitive abilities influence behaviors, including how adolescents perceive others and how they take another person's perspective. Other behaviors of interest to these psychologists—such as moral development and aggression—will be examined in later chapters.

Looking at Others

Teenagers think more abstractly about people's characteristics than younger children do. They can focus on personal traits, especially traits that explain overt behavior; for example, they might talk about another person as the "athletic type" or a "neat freak." They infer the existence of traits from specific behaviors. Adolescents create for themselves an abstract theory relating different psychological and personality characteristics to one another, and they begin to understand how these behaviors might affect future behavior. They take the context of behavior into account and consider deeper, complex causes of behavior that are hidden to the individual, such as the fact that the person fears failure (Livesley & Bromley, 1973). In short, adolescents develop the capability of looking at people from a complex, rather than a simple point of view.

Teenagers also use psychological comparisons, for example, noting that Richard is more selfish than Juan. Younger children do not use these types of comparisons. Between the ages of about 7 and 10 years, children begin to use psychological constructs (Billy is conceited) and to compare others behaviorally (Philippe is quieter than Sam) (Barenboim, 1982). The use of psychological comparisons begins at 12 years and increases through age 14, whereas the use of behavioral comparisons declines. Comparing people's traits or characteristics requires the ability to use abstractions, an ability that begins in early adolescence and continues to improve with age.

Taking Another Person's Perspective

Taking the perspective of others is a key to being able to empathize with another individual. It also allows greater understanding of what others are going through and permits a deeper intimacy. If a friend is having a difficult time, being able to understand the friend's emotions and predict his or her reactions may help us say the "right thing." This ability certainly influences our relationships with others.

Developing the ability to take another person's perspective can be viewed according to a five-stage model first described by Robert Selman (1980) (see Table 4.6). In the earliest stage, stage 0, children know that other people are different and have thoughts, but they think that other people's thoughts and feelings are the same as their own. In stage 1, children realize that people can have different perspectives that can lead to different actions. They know that motives

Table 4.6

Robert Selman's Stages of Self-Other Understanding

Adolescents are capable of comparing a view to the prevalent attitude in the society.

Stage	Age (Years)	Type of Understanding
0	3–6	Egocentric: the child has no awareness that others may interpret the same situation differently.
1	5–9	The child recognizes different perspectives but cannot relate them to one another.
2	7–12	The child can reflect on another person's point of view but still cannot consider his or her own and another's perspective simultaneously.
3	10–15	Different perspectives can now be considered simultaneously. One's own viewpoint can be reflected on from that of another person.
4	12–adult	Specific points of view can be compared with those prevalent in society generally, i.e., with an abstraction (the "generalized other").

Source: Selman (1980).

can differ. But children have great difficulty keeping more than one view in mind at once, and they focus on one perspective at the expense of another. In stage 2, children realize that other people can evaluate their actions. They realize that their own perspective may not be the only valid one, and they begin to judge themselves in terms of how others view them. Children, though, cannot simultaneously coordinate their own perspective with that of another person. A child may understand what she wants and what her brother desires but not be able to coordinate the two to form a compromise.

In stage 3, beginning at about 10 to 12 years, mutual role taking emerges, in which children can take two points of view into account at the same time and understand that others can take their perspective. In stage 4, which begins between about 12 and 15 years, adolescents can take a detached view of a relationship or problem and see it from the perspective of a neutral third person, be that a teacher, parent, or general society. For instance, they can understand how a parent may view their relationship with a teacher. Adolescents can compare their views with those of society at large (Bjorklund, 1995). This increases their capacity and tendency to observe themselves, which leads to a greater self-consciousness, more monitoring of their feelings and behaviors, and an increasing tendency to anticipate how others will react to them.

Adolescent Egocentrism

Adolescents often look at themselves in the mirror and imagine what others will think about them. Adolescents can think about thoughts, both their own and those of others. However, although teens can understand the thoughts of others, they fail to differentiate between the objects toward which the thoughts of others are directed and the objects that are the focus of their own thoughts (Buis & Thompson, 1989). Because teens are concerned primarily with themselves, they believe everyone else is focusing on them, too, and that others are as obsessed with their behavior and appearance as they are. The inability to differentiate between what one is thinking and what others are thinking constitutes what David Elkind (1967) calls **adolescent egocentrism.** According to Elkind, this leads to two of the more popular conceptions of adolescent thought processes, the imaginary audience and the personal fable.

adolescent egocentrism   The adolescent failure to differentiate between what one is thinking and what others are considering.

AT A GLANCE 4.5 SOCIAL COGNITION

KEY POINT: Social cognition describes the ways in which people perceive and interpret information about themselves and others.

SUPPORTING POINTS	EXPLANATION
Adolescents are capable of seeing others in a more complex fashion.	Adolescents are capable of making psychological comparisons—for example, deciding that Julie is more selfish than Preeti, and Lee is more responsible than Ken.
Adolescents can take the perspective of others from the point of view of a third party.	Robert Selman explains the development of perspective in terms of five stages. In the last stage, adolescents can appreciate how a peer may understand their relationship with a teacher or a romantic partner, and they can compare their views with those of society at large.
David Elkind argues that adolescents show a type of egocentrism in which they fail to differentiate between the objects of their own thoughts and the objects of others' thoughts, leading to the imaginary audience and personal fable.	The imaginary audience is the adolescents' belief that they are the focus of attention and are being evaluated by everyone, leading to self-consciousness. The personal fable is the adolescents' belief that they are special and invulnerable.

Teenagers often feel that they are constantly being evaluated by others, leading to feelings of extreme self-consciousness.

imaginary audience   A term used to describe adolescents' belief that they are the focus of attention and are being evaluated by everyone.

personal fable   Adolescents' belief that their experiences are unique and original.

Elkind (1985) argues that teenagers create an **imaginary audience,** believing that everyone is looking at and evaluating them. They then anticipate these reactions. The people in this "audience" are real but the audience is imaginary, because most of the time the adolescent is not the focus of attention. Adolescents believe that they will be the object of attention and concern, and that others are preoccupied with their behavior and appearance. The imaginary audience phenomenon leads to self-consciousness (girls are more self-conscious than boys) and to adolescents' penchant for privacy (Peterson & Roscoe, 1991). Adolescents' self-consciousness stems from the conviction that others are seeing and evaluating them in the same way that they see themselves. The desire for privacy may come from either what Elkind calls a *reluctance to reveal oneself* or from a reaction to being constantly scrutinized by others. Privacy becomes a vacation from evaluation. Teens who score high on a scale that measures the imaginary audience may not do well in school because they are so self-conscious and have to protect their self-concept by creating excuses for poor performance or failure (Montgomery et al., 1996). The imaginary audience is a natural part of development that diminishes greatly by later adolescence. Predictably, self-consciousness also declines from midadolescence to late adolescence.

A second thought process arising out of adolescent egocentrism is the **personal fable,** teenagers' belief that what they are thinking and experiencing is unique, original, new, and special. Teenagers who believe that they are unique may also believe they are immune to harm, contributing to risk taking. Some sexually active adolescents explain their lack of using contraception with some variation of "I thought I (or my partner) couldn't get pregnant" (Quadrel, Fischoff, & Davis, 1993). Adolescents consider themselves less vulnerable to negative events than adults (Smith, Gerrard, & Gibbons, 1997).

Elkind sees these phenomena as inevitable outcomes of the development of formal operations. The emergence of formal operational abilities and adolescent egocentrism leads to errors in thinking that result in the imaginary audience and personal fable. The imaginary audience results from too little differentiation of the self from others—a lack of sufficiently separating what others are thinking and what is really happening. The personal fable, in contrast, represents an overdifferentiation of the self from others—that is, failing to see similarities in experiences of self and others, leading to feelings of uniqueness and invulnerability (Lapsley, 1991).

The imaginary audience and personal fable seem to explain some interesting facets of adolescent behavior, but some criticisms are raised. The imaginary audience and personal fable are present not only in adolescents but in adults as well (Quadrel et al., 1993). In addition, research linking adolescent egocentrism to formal operational thinking has been contradictory, with some studies finding such a link and some either no link or a very weak one (Rycek et al., 1998).

The personal fable as an explanation of adolescent risk-taking has also been criticized. Many adolescents can discriminate risky behaviors from safer ones and understand the negative consequences of their behaviors (Alexander et al., 1990; Dolcini et al., 1989). Some studies find little or no differences between adolescent and adult understanding of the consequences of a particular risky action, such as driving while drunk (Beyth-Marom et al., 1993).

In addition, there are other ways to explain adolescent risk taking. Adolescents may recognize the risks but continue their risky practice because the immediate benefits seem far more attractive than the fear of possible negative consequences in the future (Moore, Gullone, & Kostanski, 1997). Ignoring the negative consequences may be a show of bravado or courage. Risk taking may show independence by not conforming to standards of older people (Lavery et al., 1993). Another possible explanation is adolescents' desire for sensation seeking, which is higher in adolescents than in adults (Arnett, 1992). Adolescents may also take risks as a way of dealing with feelings of inadequacy to gain inclusion into a group (Gonzalez et al., 1994). No single explanation is sufficient to explain risk taking. It is not clear how much the personal fable may contribute to risk taking, and other factors including sensation seeking or the need to show independence also may be involved. Risk-taking behavior is complicated, and its complete understanding is not yet within our grasp. *(For a review of this section, see At A Glance 4.5.)*

PLACING ADOLESCENT COGNITIVE DEVELOPMENT IN PERSPECTIVE

From a cognitive viewpoint, are adolescents adults or children? This chapter has demonstrated the impressive gains in cognitive abilities in adolescence. Adolescents develop the ability to use abstract thought, and they can understand rights and responsibilities divorced from any particular, concrete example. Their information-processing capability improves, as does their knowledge base. However, they lack experience working with these abilities, and the fact that their developmental concerns (desire for independence and acceptance, as well as self-consciousness about appearance) may influence their decisions can cause problems. A 16-year-old seeking to have breast implants or taking steroids, for example, may be more interested in being accepted and fitting in than in the long-range health effects of the action. Indeed, adolescents may make different decisions than adults because of their developmental concerns. But it can also be argued that adults do not always make the right decisions, and that their developmental concerns influence their judgment as well.

The evidence is clear, though, that adolescents are closer to adults in their thinking and reasoning than they are to younger children. The evidence also

HAS YOUR OPINION CHANGED?

Please place the number best reflecting your opinion next to each of the following statements. Then compare your opinions now with those you held before reading the chapter.

1 — Strongly Agree
2 — Moderately Agree
3 — No Opinion
4 — Moderately Disagree
5 — Strongly Disagree

_____ 1. Adolescents are too critical of their parents and of society in general.

_____ 2. Scores on standardized intelligence tests in adolescence do not relate to success in life.

_____ 3. Adolescents who are "book smart" are rarely "street smart."

_____ 4. Standardized intelligence tests discriminate against adolescents from minority groups.

_____ 5. Adolescents who are good in one subject usually do well in most academic areas.

_____ 6. Adolescents usually make wise decisions about important issues in their lives.

_____ 7. Adolescent criminal offenders should be treated differently than adult offenders, because the adolescents' thinking is not as clear as it will be when they are adults.

_____ 8. A 16-year-old girl who wants to have an abortion without telling her parents should be allowed to have one.

THEMES

THEME 1 Adolescence is a time of choices, "firsts," and transitions.	• Adolescents' newfound abilities to use abstractions, think about alternatives, and reason scientifically open up new avenues for exploring ideas. • Adolescents develop the ability to think of different realities and to appreciate the many different paths their lives can take. • The improved information-processing abilities of adolescents allow them to concentrate on more complicated problems. • The decisions of adolescents are more oriented to the future and have greater potential consequences than those of children. • Adolescents become more concerned about how others are seeing them, and they often believe that others are always evaluating them. • Adolescents can understand how a third person may view them—for example, how a parent may view their relationship with a sibling—which allows for greater interpersonal understanding.
THEME 2 Adolescence is shaped by context.	• Jean Piaget argued that formal operational reasoning is the highest stage of cognitive development, but this may not be so in all cultures. • An adolescent's environment determines the type of experiences he or she will have, and these experiences in turn influence the person's cognitive abilities. • Lev Vygotsky argued that one can understand development only by taking into account the entire environmental context. • Intelligence scores are sensitive to environmental changes; if the environment significantly improves, scores on standardized intelligence tests may improve as well. • Creative thinking is encouraged or discouraged by people in the environment.
THEME 3 Adolescence is influenced by group membership.	• Lev Vygotsky believed that cultures transmit their ways of thinking through social interactions between older and younger people. Various groups may look at the world differently. • Adolescents from various groups may have differing experiences, which may affect how they score on standardized intelligence tests.
THEME 4 The adolescent experience has changed over the past 50 years.	• What adolescents are expected to know changes over the generations. For example, computer skills are considered a necessity today. • Critical thinking skills are more important today than in years past because adolescents are surrounded by so much information and so many attempts to influence their behavior.
THEME 5 Today's views of adolescence are becoming more balanced, with greater attention to its positive nature.	• Adolescent idealism, once considered a source of weakness, is now considered a source of strength leading to a search for new solutions to problems. • Rather than viewing the adolescent as dominated by emotion, researchers realize that adolescents can use their newly developing critical thinking abilities to analyze information. • Rather than seeing adolescents as incapable of making good decisions, researchers today appreciate both the similarities and the differences in the decision-making process of adolescents and adults.

shows that their decision-making skills are not completely formed, so they may require some limitations on behavior, especially in early and middle adolescence, in areas of potential harm. Still, the unique reasoning of adolescents—for example, in terms of idealism—has value in itself. It can lead to new, creative ideas and solutions to social problems. Adolescents should indeed reason and see the world as adolescents, somewhat differently from the way their middle-age parents do. Looking at all the research, adolescents deserve to be treated more like adults than children.

CHAPTER SUMMARY AT A GLANCE

KEY TOPICS	KEY POINTS	KEY TERMS
Developmental Approaches	The theories of Jean Piaget and Lev Vygotsky offer explanations of how children's and adolescents' cognitive abilities change with age and experience. *(At A Glance 4.1, p. 108)*	*schema (p. 96)* *operation (p. 96)* *assimilation (p. 96)* *accommodation (p. 96)* *equilibration (p. 96)* *stage of formal operations (p. 97)* *hypothetical-deductive logic (p. 98)* *combinational logic (p. 99)* *postformal operational reasoning (p. 101)* *relativistic reasoning (p. 102)* *zone of proximal development (p. 104)* *scaffolding (p. 105)* *cooperative learning (p. 106)*
Information Processing	Information processing is an approach to understanding cognition that focuses on the ways in which people take in information, process it, and then act on it. *(At A Glance 4.2, p. 114)*	*information-processing theory (p. 109)* *metacognition (p. 110)* *self-regulated learners (p. 110)* *attention span (p. 110)* *selective attention (p. 110)* *rehearsal (p. 111)* *maintenance rehearsal (p. 111)* *elaborative rehearsal (p. 111)*
Approaches to Intelligence	The measurement of intelligence through standardized intelligence tests is controversial. *(At A Glance 4.3, p. 122)*	*psychometric approach (p. 115)* *stereotype threat (p. 119)* *theory of multiple intelligences (p. 120)* *triarchic theory of intelligence (p. 121)*
Using Cognitive Abilities	The adolescent's abilities to think critically, be creative, and make decisions improve during adolescence as cognitive abilities develop. *(At A Glance 4.4, p. 127)*	*critical thinking (p. 123)* *creativity (p. 125)* *convergent thinking (p. 125)* *divergent thinking (p. 126)*
Social Cognition	Social cognition describes the ways in which people perceive and interpret information about themselves and others. *(At A Glance 4.5, p. 132)*	*social cognition (p. 129)* *adolescent egocentrism (p. 131)* *imaginary audience (p. 132)* *personal fable (p. 132)*

Review questions for this chapter appear in the appendix.

FAMILIES

WHAT IS YOUR OPINION?

THE ADOLESCENT-PARENT RELATIONSHIP
- The Changing Relationship
- Achieving Emotional Autonomy
- The Development of the Adolescent-Parent Relationship
- Power and Cohesiveness

PARENTING STYLES
- Four Different Styles of Parenting
- Changes in Parenting Style in Adolescence
- Culture and Parenting Style

COMMUNICATION AND CONFLICT
- Communication with Parents and Peers
  Perspective 1: I've Heard It All Before
  FOCUS: Adopted Children in Adolescence
- Conflict at Home
  Perspective 2: Postal Inspection
- Mothers and Fathers: Gender Differences in Communication and Conflict with Adolescents

OTHER FAMILY RELATIONSHIPS
- Sibling Relationships
  Perspective 3: They Love Her More
- Adolescent-Grandparent Relationships

THE CHANGING AMERICAN FAMILY
- Single-Child Families
- Maternal Employment
- Divorce
- Single-Parent Families
- Stepfamilies
- How Families Work Is More Important Than How They Are Structured

PLACING FAMILY RELATIONSHIPS IN PERSPECTIVE

HAS YOUR OPINION CHANGED?

THEMES

CHAPTER SUMMARY AT A GLANCE

E veryone has some opinion about the relationship between parents and their adolescent children. If you were asked which of the following statements most accurately reflects the experience of the typical teenager, which would you choose?

- I get along with my parents fairly well. We have our disagreements, but we work out most things all right.

- My parents and I have one fight after another. They understand nothing about me. I try to have as little contact with them as possible.

This chapter examines the most important influence on adolescent behavior: the adolescent's family. It begins by answering the question just posed: What is the nature of the adolescent-parent relationship? The chapter continues with a look at various skills that parents may need when their children are adolescents, and shows how parenting practices may differ from culture to culture. Perhaps the area of greatest concern is communication, which the text examines from the viewpoint of both adolescents and parents. But parents are not the only family members who influence adolescents, and relationships with siblings and grandparents are also discussed. Finally, few adolescents today grow up in a two-parent family structure in which the father is employed and the mother is a full-time homemaker. The last portion of the chapter investigates the effect of the changing family structure.

One important point must be raised before examining family relationships in adolescence: Each person in a relationship affects the other. When investigating how parents communicate and interact with their adolescent children, it is natural to focus on parental behavior. When examining family interactions from the adolescents' point of view, it is natural to focus on adolescents' communication and behavior. As discussed in "Introduction to Adolescence," though, the concept of reciprocal interaction notes that each party to an interaction affects the other. Parents' communications affect adolescent behaviors, and adolescents' communications and behaviors affect their parents' actions. A parent who is highly critical may cause an adolescent to react with sarcasm or even avoid contact, which may lead to the parent's becoming even more negative. On the other side, an adolescent who violates curfew repeatedly or who gets into trouble in school may cause parents to adopt a stricter stance, including greater monitoring and less freedom, which in turn may cause the adolescent to become angry and noncommunicative. The fact that each person in a relationship affects the other must be kept in mind when examining all interactions and relationships within the family.

THE ADOLESCENT-PARENT RELATIONSHIP

M any movies and television programs depict parents as being out of touch with their teenagers' needs and desires, with poor relationships and intense conflict as the norm. These media portray parents as unwilling to cede control to adolescents who are pressing for the right to make their own decisions. Indeed, some psychologists view adolescent-parent conflict as inevitable as teens develop emotional autonomy; that is, they develop deep relationships outside the family, move away from their parents emotionally, and develop their own identity. These psychologists see this distancing from the family as functional, and a necessary step in the adolescent's development (Jani, 1997).

Researchers have challenged this popular view of the adolescent-parent relationship because it simply does not agree with research evidence on the

WHAT IS YOUR OPINION?

Please place the number best reflecting your opinion next to each of the following statements. We will return to this questionnaire at the end of the chapter so you can determine if your opinions have changed.

1 — Strongly Agree
2 — Moderately Agree
3 — No Opinion
4 — Moderately Disagree
5 — Strongly Disagree

____ 1. Adolescent-parent conflict is necessary if teenagers are to attain the increased independence and autonomy they desire.

____ 2. Parents faced with an increasing desire for independence from their adolescent children relax their monitoring too quickly, allowing the teenagers too much freedom too soon.

____ 3. Mothers and fathers should strive to be friends with their adolescent children.

____ 4. By age 20 or so, the relationship between parents and their children should be on a completely equal basis.

____ 5. Parents should unconditionally accept their adolescent children's viewpoints without criticizing these opinions.

____ 6. Most conflict is caused by parents' unwillingness to accept the fact that their adolescent children are older, are more mature, and need their independence.

____ 7. Parents should strive to treat all their children in the same manner.

____ 8. As long as the parents' marital relationship is not abusive, it is better for children if their parents stay together, even if they are not happy, than if they divorce.

____ 9. All factors being equal, children and adolescents are better off in a stepfamily than in a single-parent household.

____ 10. Stepparents should have the same parental rights as biological parents.

If "storm and stress" is so natural in adolescence, how can we explain the polls finding that 90 percent of all adolescent girls are "very happy" with their relationship with their mothers?

subject. The view that adolescence is filled with inevitable parent-child conflict leads to two logical hypotheses. First, if intense conflict is normal and natural, most adolescents should label their relationships with their parents as strained and filled with conflict. However, not one research study using adolescents from nonclinical environments reports high levels of conflict as being typical of adolescent-parent relationships (Offer & Schonert-Reichl, 1992).

The results of a recent poll of teenage girls and their parents illustrate this point nicely (Elias, 1998). Ninety percent of the adolescent girls and their mothers reported being "very happy" with their relationship. Ninety-seven percent of the girls said they were close to their mothers. Mothers considered their daughters to be their friends, and three-quarters said their daughter's approval was very important to them. Most mothers in a different national survey indicated that they have a good time or a pleasant experience with their teenager almost every day (Chadwick & Heaton, 1996; Sweet & Bumpass, 1988). Studies consistently find that adolescents report positive attitudes and emotions toward both parents and relatively low levels of negative emotions (Phares & Renk, 1998). When teens were asked how well they got along with their parents, over half answered "very well"; 44 percent, "fairly well"; and only 4 percent, "not well at all" (Bezilla, 1993).

Second, if intense and prolonged conflict is required for autonomy, then logically, those adolescents who report intense and prolonged conflict should be autonomous and well adjusted. Yet research evidence shows that adolescents who report close relationships with their parents and moderate amounts of conflict are *better* adjusted than adolescents who have little conflict or whose relationships are characterized by continuous conflict (Phares & Renk, 1998). Well-adjusted adolescents are still firmly connected with their families. And those with better relationships are less likely to show behavioral problems. In the relatively rare cases where high levels of conflict are reported, adolescent adjustment is poor and behavioral problems common (Montemayor, 1986). In fact, high levels of conflict are related to poor self-esteem, maladjustment, and depression in adolescents (Shek, 1998; Smetana, 1996; Smetana, Abernathy, & Harris, 2000).

To deny that there is real conflict between parents and adolescents, however, would be incorrect (Arnett, 1999; Teare et al., 1995). Conflict certainly occurs during adolescence, but it does not necessarily lead to a reduction in feelings of closeness or love. In contrast, pretending that adolescence is a smooth, seamless period of development in which parent and adolescent continue to enjoy a relationship devoid of conflict requires ignoring the research evidence.

The Changing Relationship

The most current model of the adolescent-parent relationship, and the one that best matches the research evidence, views the relationship in terms of a transformation of power in which parents and teenagers continually renegotiate their relationship as the adolescent continues along the path to adulthood. This renegotiation takes place while the adolescent remains connected to the family (Grotevant, 1998). This new view considers *interdependence,* rather than complete emotional autonomy or continued dependence, as the most common way in which adolescents negotiate adolescence. A balance is continuously being constructed between adolescent independence and family cohesion (closeness), between separation and connection, and between conflict and harmony (Baumrind, 1991a). Although conflict may increase, the parents and adolescents usually maintain their emotional bonds (Smetana et al., 2000). Adolescents continuously seek to redefine their relationship to their parents so it is consistent with their developing sense of self and their individual needs and expectations for the future (Jory et al., 1996; Tubman & Lerner, 1994).

In addition, parents are an integral part of this renegotiation. Parents expect more "mature," responsible behavior from their adolescents. Most parents fully realize that their relationship with their adolescent children must change, and that their adolescents both require and must be given more freedom and a greater say in decisions that affect them. The gradual encouragement of adolescent participation in family decision making shows adolescents that their views are important and is linked to lower levels of reliance on peers and a more positive self-concept (Fuligni & Eccles, 1993; Holmbeck & O'Donnell, 1991). However, parents are also concerned about protecting their adolescents from harm, and this protective function, so basic to the parenting role, sometimes conflicts with the adolescents' desire for autonomy.

Achieving Emotional Autonomy

In Western culture, adolescence is a time of becoming autonomous. One type of autonomy already mentioned, emotional autonomy, involves shifting away from emotional dependency on parents and forming new and close relationships with others. Certainly, older adolescents are less emotionally dependent on their parents, have developed other intense emotional relationships, and don't perceive their parents as their only source of comfort. They realize that their parents aren't always right and do not know everything, and adolescents may believe that their experiences are very different from those their parents had. Adolescents do not believe their parents have, or should have, the type of power they possessed when these adolescents were children. Yet adolescents do not freeze their parents out of the picture. Nineteen-year-old adolescents report feeling just as close to their parents as do fourth graders (Hunter & Youniss, 1982). This feeling of closeness is important, for adolescents who are emotionally autonomous and who feel close to their parents are better adjusted than those who are emotionally autonomous but feel distant or detached from their parents (Ryan & Lynch, 1989).

Four Components of Emotional Autonomy   The development of emotional autonomy continues throughout adolescence and into early adulthood. One study followed four components of emotional autonomy—(1) nondependency (a reduction in childish dependence on, but not absolute freedom from, parental influence), (2) de-idealization (not seeing parents as all powerful), (3) individuation (a sense of being an autonomous, responsible human being), and (4) seeing parents as people—in a sample of fifth graders through their ninth-grade year. As Figure 5.1 illustrates, the first three components showed impressive increases as adolescents proceeded through the teenage years (Steinberg & Silverberg, 1986). The only measure that did not show this significant increase was "seeing parents as people," which may develop later in adolescence and even early adulthood (Smollar & Youniss, 1985).

The delay in seeing their parents as people may interfere with the adolescents' development of a more tolerant relationship. Adolescents may not yet accept their parents as people with their own foibles, strengths, and weaknesses, who can perhaps be forgiven if they make mistakes. Perhaps one reason, though certainly not the only one, for the improvement of relationships with parents in early adulthood is the understanding that parents are people and an acceptance of them as such.

Attachment Theory and Emotional Autonomy   Adolescents do not achieve emotional autonomy overnight, nor does it develop in a vacuum. The nature of the adolescents' relationships with others may be influenced by the relationship they have developed with their parents. This relationship begins in infancy, as parent and child form emotional bonds with each other. This early

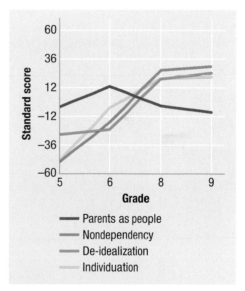

Figure 5.1

Age Differences in Four Aspects of Emotional Autonomy

This graph shows changes in four aspects of emotional autonomy between fifth and ninth grades. Notice the impressive gains in non-dependency, de-idealization, and individuation, but the delay in seeing parents as people.

Source: Steinberg & Silverberg (1986).

parent-child relationship may become the model for future relationships, and it can deeply affect the emotional well-being and interpersonal relationships of the child and, later, the adolescent.

Psychologists use the term **attachment** to describe the emotional tie that one person forms with another, the tie that binds them together in space and endures over time (Ainsworth, 1974). According to a pioneer attachment researcher, John Bowlby (1969), attachment is a product of evolution and ensures survival, because it leads to protection of the child by the caregiver and encourages healthy development. The infant is not born with a natural affinity to the caregiver; this affinity is learned through interaction with the caregiver (Waters & Deane, 1982).

Children who have not formed this early attachment can have a host of developmental problems, including the inability to form satisfying relationships with others (Rutter, 1979). However, almost everyone forms some attachment to their caregiver, so the question is one of the quality of this attachment.

Psychologists use a number of techniques to measure the quality of children's attachment to their caregiver. These techniques include naturalistic observation and an experimental technique called the *strange situation,* which involves placing a young child with a parent in a room and observing his or her behavior as the parent leaves for a short time and then returns for a reunion. A structured questionnaire, called the Adult Attachment Interview, has also been developed to measure attachment quality in older adolescents or adults by asking specific questions about how participants perceive their early relationship with their mother.

Attachment patterns in very young children are often categorized as *secure attachment* and *anxious attachment,* which consists of *anxious/avoidant attachment* and *anxious/ambivalent attachment.* (Some, but not all, psychologists use another anxious attachment category called *anxious disorganized/disoriented attachment.*) Young children who are classified as *securely attached* have the most satisfying relationship with their caregiver, using the caregiver as a source of comfort and security. Children showing *anxious/avoidant attachment* do not use their caregiver as a base for exploring the environment, and when frightened, they do not find much comfort in their relationship. Children classified as showing *anxious/ambivalent attachment* show a great deal of anxiety; they have an intense, yet unsatisfying relationship with their caregiver, and the caregiver's inconsistent behaviors lead to anxiety about the true nature of the relationship. Many studies show that securely attached children have advantages over anxiously attached children in many cognitive and social areas of development (Colin, 1996).

But what about attachment in adolescence? Attachment does not end in infancy or early childhood. Children maintain emotional bonds to parents across childhood and into adulthood (Kerns, Klepac, & Cole, 1996). Both children and adolescents continue to rely on caregivers for encouragement and comfort in times of stress. The nature of the attachment behavior may change, however. Young children who are stressed may run to their caregivers for a hug. Adolescents, in contrast, may find availability—which is determined by the belief that parents are open to communication, accessible, and supportive—to be most important. Adolescents continue to derive support from parents and use their parents as secure bases from which to explore challenges in many areas (Colin, 1996).

The quality of attachment can change if there is some significant alteration, good or bad, in the child's environment. For example, a parent may experience a prolonged psychiatric problem that adversely affects parenting behaviors. Excluding such changes, however, stability may be expected. Indeed, a number of recent studies find considerable stability in classification of attachment from infancy to early adulthood. Waters and colleagues (Waters, Merrick, et al., 2000) followed a number of white, middle-class infants who were seen in the strange situation at the age of 1 year and then were given the Adult Attachment Interview 20 years later. More than 70 percent of the participants received the same secure or anxious attachment rating in early adulthood as they did in child-

attachment An emotional tie that binds people together over space and time.

hood. About 40 percent of all the children who had experienced a negative change in their home environment changed attachment categorization. Other studies show this combination of continuity in attachment category and altered status due to change in circumstances in many other populations (Hamilton, 2000; Weinfield, Sroufe, & Egeland, 2000). This consistency may be explained in two ways (Waters, Weinfield, & Hamilton, 2000). The relationship achieved in early childhood may be resistant to change, except for major changes in life. Alternatively, basic parental caregiver behavior may remain stable over time.

A number of studies relate security of attachment to more positive outcomes in adolescence. For example, a 20-year longitudinal study found that secure attachment as measured in childhood predicts better social outcomes in later childhood, adolescence, and adulthood (Waters, Merrick, et al., 2000). Recent studies find that security of attachment is related to competence in peer relationships, lower amounts of depression and anxiety, and less delinquent behavior (Allen et al., 1998; Cooper, Shaver, & Collins, 1998; Sund & Wichstrom, 2002). Secure attachment is related to better social skills, which affect adolescents' competence in friendships (Engels et al., 2001). Among college students, secure individuals are considered more agreeable and extroverted (Shaver & Brennan, 1992). Self-esteem is higher in adolescents considered secure (Feeney & Noller, 1991). Adolescents considered securely attached are more responsive and less critical with peers (Kerns et al., 1996).

Adolescents with secure relationships with their parents, then, establish and maintain better interpersonal relationships than those who are anxiously attached. A secure relationship may provide the atmosphere necessary for adolescents to explore their environment, and that exploration includes new social relationships. Securely attached adolescents may learn a more cooperative and responsive style of interaction within the caregiver-child relationship, which may generalize to peer relationships (Kerns et al., 1996). The internalized model of adolescent-parent relationships may lead children and adolescents to choose relationships that offer them greater responsiveness and, at the same time, act in a way that evokes such responses (Thompson, 1998). Anxiously attached children and adolescents may become more dependent or hostile, and the negative reactions of others may confirm their expectations that people are unreliable or hostile. In this way, attachments may create internal models or ideas about relationships that function as filters influencing how adolescents perceive the behavior of other people. Finally, it may be difficult for adolescents to go beyond poor ongoing parent-child relationships to establish new, satisfying relationships with others (Gavin & Furman, 1989). Securely attached youths, then, are more likely to explore new opportunities for growth with confidence and competence than anxiously attached youth (Colin, 1996).

The Development of the Adolescent-Parent Relationship

The relationship between adolescents and their parents gradually changes. During early adolescence, the relationship often is typified by an adolescent pushing for independence and parents placing restrictions on this independence. A parent may require the young adolescent to call periodically when the teenager is at the mall shopping with friends. More autonomy gradually is ceded, but it is laced with conditions. The relationship between parents and adolescents lacks the symmetry that it will have later. Young teens have some additional freedom, but not as much as they want. Conflict is not uncommon, but often families find ways to avoid the conflict rather than confronting and resolving their difficulties (Hill & Holmbeck, 1987). As noted in "Physical Development," mothers are especially concerned about monitoring their early-developing daughters, who naturally want more freedom and less restriction. In fact, generally, daughters are monitored more closely than sons (Dishion & McMahon, 1998).

During middle adolescence, especially toward the end of the period (16 or 17 years), family relationships often show some improvement. Parents acknowledge the adolescents' changing status and give them more room to grow. In fact, most middle adolescents report feeling "close" or "very close" to parents at this time (Greenberger, 1984).

In later adolescence, the relationship continues to change. Parents understand that their adolescents are more autonomous, even if the adolescents remain dependent financially and receive emotional support from parents. Fewer arguments occur over everyday matters. However, neither parents nor adolescents ever see the relationship as completely equal, nor does either side see equality as desirable. Even when adolescents and their parents consider their relationship "excellent," neither side believes complete equality is desirable. The disagreements in later adolescence may be substantial in one or two areas as parents realize the limits of their power to change their adolescent's decisions or behavior. For example, it may be difficult for parents to accept the fact that their daughter is living with her boyfriend. After hours of arguments that fail to dissuade their daughter, the parents have relatively few options: accept the cohabitation, cut off all financial support, or reject the child. Generally, though, the relationship between parents and their late adolescent children improves somewhat. However, the presence of a few significant issues may interfere with this relationship.

As adolescents develop, they consider different dimensions of parenting as important. When preadolescents (8 to 9 years of age), 14- to 15-year-olds, and 17- to 18-year-olds were asked to describe a "good parent," developmental differences were found (Megan, 1994). Figure 5.2 shows the percentage of the sample agreeing with statements reflecting eight elements of good parenting. Notice that preadolescents did not perceive parents as friends, as democratic, or as allowing much privacy or autonomy. It was important to them that their parents expressed their feelings, assumed the authority role, and bought them things. They appreciated the leisure time spent with their parents. The 14- to 15-year-olds viewed their parents as educators and authority figures, but they emphasized the importance of understanding, support, and the expression of feelings. Shared leisure time was rarely mentioned. Privacy became a concern as well, and respect and trust became important. Parents were no longer just valued as gift givers. The 17- and 18-year-olds perceived support as an important parental quality, but privacy and autonomy were high on their lists as well. A good parent was understanding and supportive, and the concept of parent as friend entered the picture.

Parents of the 14- to 15-year-olds, in contrast, did not see the good parent in these terms. Parents believed that good parents carried out their responsibilities (Megan, 1994). Good parents were seen as educators and authority figures who

Figure 5.2
What Makes a Good Parent? The Developmental Perspective in Three Age Groups
Preadolescents and adolescents disagree on what makes a good parent. Adolescents consider privacy, trust, and support as more important.

Source: Megan (1994).

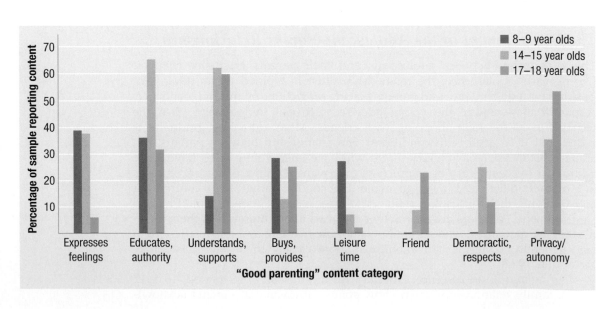

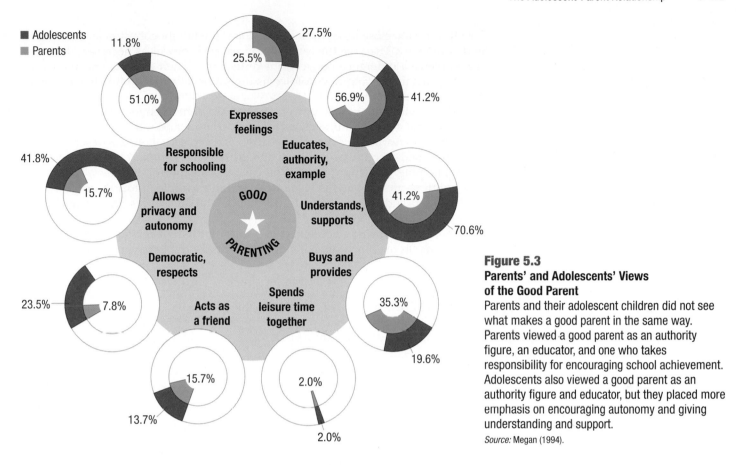

Figure 5.3
Parents' and Adolescents' Views of the Good Parent
Parents and their adolescent children did not see what makes a good parent in the same way. Parents viewed a good parent as an authority figure, an educator, and one who takes responsibility for encouraging school achievement. Adolescents also viewed a good parent as an authority figure and educator, but they placed more emphasis on encouraging autonomy and giving understanding and support.
Source: Megan (1994).

provide understanding and support, as well as people who provided for their children's material needs and took responsibility for their children's schooling (see Figure 5.3). Perhaps the most important lesson from these studies is that as adolescents progress through these years, what they think they need from their parents changes, and these different perceptions may influence how they evaluate their parents' behaviors toward them (Baumrind, 1991b).

This evaluation is most likely to be positive, and families function more effectively when they avoid extremes. That is, the family must avoid enmeshing or smothering adolescents, which would not allow their individuality to develop. At the same time, family members must avoid becoming so separate and disengaged from each other that no family cohesion or solidarity remains (Steinberg & Silverberg, 1986). The mature adolescent shows a balance between individuality and connectedness with family. Studies show that close, but not smothering, family relationships enhance resistance to peer pressure.

Power and Cohesiveness

The change in the adolescent-parent relationship is reflected in adolescents' perceptions of family cohesiveness, intimacy, and power. As adolescents progress from the sixth to twelfth grades, they see a decline in family cohesiveness (that is, being close to one another) and in their connectedness to the family. At the same time, they see more equivalence in power, although they still view parental power as greater. Both parents and adolescents portray the ideal family as being high in cohesion and having moderate power differences between parents and their children, as well as having equality of power between parents (Feldman & Gehring, 1988).

The decline in family cohesion coincides with the decreasing amount of time spent with parents and the increase in peer involvement and independence. Adolescents do not see the weaker family cohesion as desirable and often wish for more family closeness. Adolescents, then, see family cohesion as compatible with autonomy. They see the reduction in parental power as necessary, but they still perceive a difference between the authority of their parents and their own standing within the family. Adolescents do not believe that complete equality of power is desirable.

Along with changes in power and family cohesiveness come changes in other aspects of family life, such as intimacy, control, and nurturance. The *control function* involves being told what to do. The *intimacy function* describes self-disclosure and empathy, sensitivity and trust. The *nurturance function* refers to giving, helping, and supporting. When changes in control, intimacy, and nurturance with peers and parents were measured in a sample of fourth, seventh, and tenth graders and college students, developmental differences became noticeable (Hunter & Youniss, 1982).

The control function is greatest in adolescent-parent relationships across all age groups. In other words, parents try to control the behavior of their adoles-

AT A GLANCE 5.1 THE ADOLESCENT-PARENT RELATIONSHIP

KEY POINT: The nature of the parent-child relationship changes during adolescence.

SUPPORTING POINTS	EXPLANATION
Early theorists viewed parent-adolescent conflict as normal, natural, and necessary for adolescents to develop autonomy, but recent research questions whether intense adolescent-parent conflict is either common or leads to autonomy.	Research results show that most adolescents report good relationships with their parents and do not report prolonged, intense conflict. Adolescents reporting moderate amounts of conflict are best adjusted.
The most recent model of adolescent-parent relationships sees them in terms of a gradual renegotiation of power that occurs in a warm family relationship.	Adolescents and their parents gradually renegotiate the power balance, with adolescents gaining power and autonomy within a warm family relationship.
Emotional autonomy involves becoming less emotionally dependent on parents and developing other close relationships.	Emotionally autonomous adolescents who feel close to their parents are better adjusted than emotionally autonomous adolescents who do not feel close to their parents.
The quality of adolescents' attachment to parents may influence their interpersonal relationships with others, as well as their emotional development.	Adolescents remain emotionally attached to parents, although behaviors that show this attachment may differ and be less frequent. The attachment with caregivers creates a model of interpersonal relationships. Adolescents with secure attachments have better interpersonal relationships and better adjustment.
Power relationships change with age.	Early adolescence is a time of pushing for greater power, whereas a greater balance is achieved by the end of the middle adolescence and continues into late adolescence.
Concerns about power and autonomy decline over adolescence, whereas concerns about family cohesiveness increase.	A decline in cohesion is due to parents' spending less time with adolescents, adolescents spending more time with peers, and the adolescent desire for more independence.
Control, intimacy, and nurturance change over adolescence.	Parents want to control their adolescent children more than peers do at all ages. Nurturance remains higher for parents than peers throughout adolescence. Parent-teenager intimacy declines until late adolescence, after which it increases.

cent children at every age much more than friends do. The attempts at control decline, though, especially in later adolescence. The intimacy function is greater for parents at fourth grade; it is surpassed by peers by tenth grade. By mid to late adolescence (seventh to tenth grades), friendship patterns become more intimate, and the intimacy function decreases for parents, although it later increases. This later increase in parental intimacy demonstrates that the growing intimacy with peers need not interfere with intimacy with parents. In fact, adolescents with many same-sex friends, higher self-esteem, lower risk taking, and greater interest in school report greater intimacy with parents (Field et al., 1995). The nurturance factor remains very high throughout adolescence in the parent-teenager relationship. Although this helping function increases for friends, it never surpasses the level of helpfulness for parents.

The restructuring of relationships, especially during early and middle adolescence, does not leave parents out in the cold, There is evidence that adolescent-parent relationships that are generally good improve throughout adolescence, as long as there are no major outstanding issues in late adolescence. The increase in autonomy does not mean complete disengagement from parents, and this autonomy is gained or granted in an atmosphere of connectedness with the family (Hill, 1987). The rules change and self-management increases, but the family continues to play an important part in the adolescent's life (Alessandri & Wozniak, 1989). *(For a review of this section, see At A Glance 5.1.)*

PARENTING STYLES

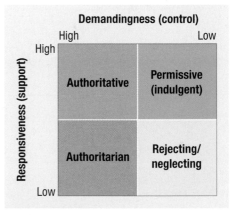

Figure 5.4
Parenting Styles
The four parenting styles—authoritative, authoritarian, permissive, and rejecting/neglecting—differ on the qualities of responsiveness and demandingness.

Families do not enter the period of adolescence with a clean slate. More than a decade of parenting precedes adolescence. Psychologists who observe parents interacting with their children frequently notice definite stylistic differences. Some parents are more rule based; some are more lenient; some have better communication than others; and some, unfortunately, ignore their children. These parenting styles are apparent very early in the parent-child relationship.

Parenting styles are perceived in terms of two factors: responsiveness and demandingness (Baumrind, 1989; Maccoby & Martin, 1983). **Responsiveness** refers to parental warmth, acceptance, provision of comfort and support, consideration of the needs of the child, and recognition of the child's achievements, as well as using a reasoning approach to discipline (Baumrind, 1989; Jackson & Foshee, 1998; Maccoby & Martin, 1983). **Demandingness** refers to the extent to which parents set firm rules and limits, expect responsible behavior from their child, monitor and supervise their child, and maintain structure in the child's life. *Involvedness* is sometimes used as a distinct third factor and at other times placed under the responsiveness factor.

Four Different Styles of Parenting

Four different parenting styles have been isolated, and they show different levels of responsiveness and demandingness (see Figure 5.4) (Baumrind, 1967, 1978, 1980; Maccoby & Martin, 1983). **Authoritarian parenting** is shown by parents who control their children's conduct by establishing rules and regulations. They require obedience and often threaten punishment if a child does not respond quickly. Authoritarian parents are quite demanding but not very responsive.

Permissive parenting (sometimes called **indulgent parenting**) characterizes parents who do not make many demands on their children. They value communication with their children and depend on their children to regulate their own activities. They try to reason with their children, but they do not stress conformity to rules. These parents emphasize self-regulation (Fagot, 1995). Permissive parents are noncontrolling and nondemanding, but relatively warm.

responsiveness The extent to which parents express warmth, consider the needs of their child, and use a reasoning approach to discipline.

demandingness The extent to which parents set firm rules and expect responsible behavior from their children.

authoritarian parenting A style of parenting in which parents rigidly control their children's behavior by establishing rules and valuing obedience while discouraging questioning.

permissive (indulgent) parenting A style of parenting marked by open communication and a lack of parental demand for good behavior.

The authoritarian parent is very demanding but not very responsive to the adolescent's needs.

Rejecting/neglecting parenting describes the style of parents who are essentially not engaged with their children; the parents are neither responsive nor demanding. They reject their children, neglect them, or both. They do not monitor their children's activities and provide little or no structure. Parents using **authoritative parenting** encourage verbal questioning, explain the reasons behind family policies, and set limits. They value both autonomy and discipline, and they are both demanding and responsive.

In early childhood, middle childhood, and adolescence, the children of parents who use the *authoritative style of parenting* generally are the most self-reliant, independent, self-controlled, and contented. They have higher levels of self-esteem, better impulse control, higher levels of adjustment, and higher school achievement (Ballantine, 2001; Paulson, 1994). Adolescents raised by authoritative parents perceive the school atmosphere and their teachers more positively (Paulson, Marchant, & Rothlisberg, 1998). They are socially competent and prosocial, and they show less anxiety and less aggression (Baumrind, 1991b). Children of authoritarian parents, in contrast, are discontented, withdrawn, and distrustful. They are generally less competent, less prosocial, and more conforming, and they often lack self-confidence (Baumrind, 1984). They may do well in school and may not exhibit deviant behavior, however, depending on the extent of the parental authoritarian behavior (Baumrind, 1989; Dornbusch et al., 1987; Jackson & Foshee, 1998; Lamborn et al., 1991). Some authoritarian parents are very intrusive, try to manage every aspect of their adolescent's life, and don't allow any independence, whereas others simply may set down a limited number of inflexible rules, allowing some freedom in other areas. Adolescents raised by intrusive authoritarian parents are more likely to show high levels of anxiety and depression. In addition, children and adolescents whose parents use harsh and abusive discipline have very poor outcomes (Weiss et al., 1992).

The children of permissive (indulgent) parents are not self-reliant, self-controlled, or achievement oriented, and they show high levels of anxiety and depression (Baumrind, 1991a). They report a strong sense of self-confidence, but also higher rates of deviant behavior, including substance abuse and school misconduct. They are often disengaged from their school (Lamborn et al., 1991).

Children of rejecting/neglecting parents are the worst off of any of the groups; they show the most behavioral and emotional difficulties and the least prosocial behavior (Baumrind, 1991a; Schaffer, 1996). Especially when compared with children raised in authoritative homes, these children show low levels of self-control and self-esteem, poor academic achievement, and much higher levels of antisocial behavior and drug use (Jackson & Foshee, 1998).

Adolescent developmental progress, then, is delayed by very directive, officious parents, parents who are unengaged, and those who are completely undemanding. Developmental progress is enhanced when parents balance responsiveness and demandingness.

Changes in Parenting Style in Adolescence

The advantages for children raised by authoritative parents continue throughout adolescence (Adamczyk-Robinette, Fletcher, & Wright, 2002). Teenagers raised by authoritative parents judge parental authority as fair and legitimate and are less likely to disregard parental authority. They are more likely to accept parental monitoring and rules, and they are relatively less susceptible to peer influence (Baumrind, 1978). This is important because parental monitoring, which involves parents' knowledge of where their children are and what they are doing, is related

rejecting/neglecting parenting A style of parenting in which uninvolved parents neither show warmth nor demand age-appropriate, responsible behavior from their children.

authoritative parenting A style of parenting in which parents establish limits but allow open communication and some freedom for children to make their own decisions.

to a number of positive outcomes, including less substance abuse and less delinquency (Dishion & McMahon, 1998). Much of this monitoring is based on the communication between parents and their adolescents—that is, adolescents telling their parents where they are and what they are doing, rather than parental tracking (Kerr & Stattin, 2000). Adolescents are more likely to talk with their parents about their plans when parents show warmth, acceptance, and interest.

Normally, parenting style does not change much. If parents were authoritative when their children were younger, they remain so as the children become teens. Some changes in responsiveness and demandingness do occur, though. When ninth and twelfth graders and their parents were questioned about their demandingness, responsiveness, and parental involvement, some interesting differences, as well as continuities, were found.

Adolescents reported that their mothers' and fathers' demandingness did not change from ninth to twelfth grades, but that mothers and fathers were less responsive to them in twelfth grade than they had been in ninth grade. Adolescents perceived no change in their parents' values or attitudes toward school or achievement, but both mothers and fathers showed less interest in their schoolwork in twelfth grade. Mothers and fathers agreed; they also reported lower levels of responsiveness and interest in schoolwork, as well as less involvement in school functions in twelfth grade than in ninth grade. Parents also did not see any changes in their values or attitudes toward achievement, but they did believe, contrary to their adolescents' perceptions, that they were not as demanding of their children in twelfth grade as in ninth grade (Paulson & Sputa, 1996). These changes are understandable in light of increasing autonomy. The reduction in parental responsiveness is consistent with the lower levels of family cohesion noted by twelfth graders as compared with ninth graders (Feldman & Gehring, 1988). Although both parents and adolescents agree that there is a decline in parental involvement, adolescents rate the absolute level of parental involvement lower than do their parents (Schwarz, Barton-Henry, & Prjzinsky, 1985).

Culture and Parenting Style

Authoritative parenting, in which parents actively explain the reasons for their rules and are willing to discuss these rules with their adolescent children, is rare in non-Western cultures. In these societies, unquestioned acceptance of rules is the norm; parents do not explain their rules or discuss the reasons behind them. Children in these societies are much less likely to question parental authority (Whiting & Edwards, 1988). Non-Western parents, like authoritarian parents, are high in demandingness. However, they do not appear to be low in responsiveness. The family shows closeness and maintains strong emotional bonds. Perhaps responsiveness and demandingness are shown differently in these cultures. In fact, a parenting style in which demandingness is high but responsiveness may be shown in other ways is called *traditional.* Responsiveness may be shown through caring behavior, a strong sense of commitment to one another, and self-sacrifice.

Such differences in parenting styles exist in minority groups within the United States and other Western countries as well. For example, Chinese and other East Asian parents often rate quite high on scales measuring authoritarianism and restrictiveness and low on authoritativeness (Chao, 1994). Among American middle-class children of European descent, this parenting style is related to a lack of achievement, but Asian children do very well in school under this type of parenting (Chao, 2001; Dornbusch et al., 1987). In some Asian societies, the strictness and desire for obedience is seen in terms of care and involvement, which is especially useful for educating the child in the self-discipline necessary for academic and vocational success. In Chinese families, mothers and fathers may express warmth differently. Mothers may express warmth by showing sensitivity to the child's emotional well-being and problems and providing social support. Fathers, in contrast, may show warmth by guiding and assisting children in learning skills necessary to fit into society, as well as by providing support in achieving academic success (Chen, Liu, & Li, 2000).

African American families often have somewhat stricter discipline that is not associated with behavior problems, such as aggression, and is positively related to school achievement (Baumrind, 1993; Deater-Deckard et al., 1996; Dornbusch et al., 1987). These more restrictive methods of discipline must be seen in a different context. In fact, greater restrictiveness is found in samples of white parents living in high risk environments; this restrictiveness may be interpreted in terms of protection and caring (McElhaney & Allen, 2001). This is also true in many Latino families, where respect is most important, and it is not considered necessary to explain rules. Many studies of parenting style have not considered the cultural context of parenting. It is possible that a style in which greater demandingness is shown may not always be seen by parents or children as indicating a lack of warmth. This holds only for discipline that is not abusive, for abusive, harsh dicipline leads to negative outcomes in every group (Deater-Deckard et al., 1996).

Research on every ethnic group in the United States and groups in dozens of other nations shows that children and adolescents respond positively when they feel loved by their parents, which involves supportiveness, caring, nurturance, and comfort; they respond negatively if they feel unloved by their parents (Rohner & Veneziano, 2001). Yet the way in which parents show caring may differ from culture to culture, and psychologists must be sensitive to cultural differences in order to draw the correct implications from the evidence.

Parenting style is a useful concept and has led to valuable insights, but a number of problems stand out. First, a large percentage of parents, sometimes close to 50 percent, do not neatly fit into the categories of parenting styles (Jackson & Foshee, 1998). Second, studies often assign parents to groups (authoritarian, authoritative, permissive, or rejecting/neglecting) on the basis of their relative standing within a sample, not on the basis of predetermined cutoff points. Thus, a parent may be authoritarian within a particular sample, but the parent is authoritarian only in relationship to other parents in the sample. This limits the ability to generalize from the results of the studies. Third, the behaviors of children and adolescents may influence parenting style. Adolescents who do not comply with parental requests may cause their parents to adopt a stricter, more authoritarian form of discipline, and adolescents who are seen by their par-

AT A GLANCE 5.2 PARENTING STYLES

KEY POINT: The style of parenting used in adolescence affects adolescents.

SUPPORTING POINTS	EXPLANATION
Two dimensions underlie parenting styles: responsiveness and demandingness.	*Responsiveness* refers to warmth and encouraging communication, whereas *demandingness* refers to setting and enforcing limits and rules.
Four different parenting styles have been discovered: authoritarian, permissive (indulgent), rejecting/neglecting, and authoritative.	Authoritarian parents rate high in demandingness but low in responsiveness, whereas permissive parents rate high in responsiveness and low in demandingness. Rejecting/neglecting parents rate low in both responsiveness and demandingness, whereas authoritative parents rate high in both responsiveness and demandingness.
Generally, adolescents thrive under an authoritative system of parenting.	Studies generally show that authoritative parenting is superior to the other types.
Cultural differences may influence the effects of parenting style on adolescents.	Authoritative parenting seems to be superior for European American middle-class children. Some African American, Asian, and Latino parents show a more demanding style of parenting that emphasizes sacrifice and caring, which is now called traditional.

ents as acting in a mature, responsible manner may be given more freedom, and parents may be more responsive to their requests. Fourth, both demandingness and responsiveness are used to describe parenting style, and psychologists do not know which of these dimensions produces the results (or whether both do) (Jackson & Foshee, 1998). Some elements of a particular dimension may be more important than others at various stages of development. *(For a review of this section, see At A Glance 5.2.)*

COMMUNICATION AND CONFLICT

Communication and conflict are important in any relationship (Jackson et al., 1998). It is easy to understand the crucial nature of communication as parents and adolescents continuously renegotiate their relationship. At the same time, the way they handle conflict will influence the course of the relationship.

Communication with Parents and Peers

When adolescent-parent communication is good, families are closer, are more loving, and show flexibility in solving family problems (Barnes & Olson, 1985). Good communication between parents and their teens helps adolescents become more sensitive to the ideas and feelings of others (Grotevant & Cooper, 1986; Noller & Callan, 1986). It fosters both a sense of individuality and a connectedness within the family. A lack of good communication, in contrast, is associated with poorer conflict resolution, feelings of frustration, and escalation of arguments (Jackson et al., 1998). When communication is good, delicate subjects can be handled with understanding and sensitivity (see "Focus: Adopted Children in Adolescence").

Communication with peers differs greatly from communication with parents during adolescence. Parents are more directive and share their wisdom, whereas communication with peers is often less directive and involves more give and take (Hunter, 1984) (see "Peers" for more discussion on communication with peers). This communication difference may spring from the parent-child relationship, which by its very nature is dominated by parents (Fuligni & Eccles, 1993). Parents may not like to listen to adolescents in the process of formulating their own values and opinions, especially if their children are taking positions that differ from theirs. Parents may counter these unwanted views with a long lecture, which is usually an ineffective method of communication. Parents concentrate more on explaining their own viewpoints than on trying to understand their children's views (Hunter, 1985).

PERSPECTIVE 1

I'VE HEARD IT ALL BEFORE

SETTING THE SCENE: Carlos is 16 years old and has one sister who is much younger than him. He has always had a good relationship with his parents, but lately he does not seem to have much patience for his parents, especially his father.

FATHER: *He is so young. I just want to give him the benefit of my experience, try to prevent him from making the same mistakes I did. Is that so wrong?*

MOTHER: *Carlos sometimes says such strange things that it frightens me. He once said that he would like to join the circus and travel right after high school, instead of going on to college. He is in mostly honors courses, and he has the ability. I just want him to see the big picture.*

QUESTION: How can this family improve its communication?

Parents tend to spend more time explaining their own views than listening to the views of their adolescent.

FOCUS   Adopted Children in Adolescence

Most adoptions occur when children are quite young, and experts today encourage parents to tell their children that they are adopted at a very early age. Adopted children sometimes ask about their biological parents, and such curiosity is natural and expected. Adoptive parents often tell the child something about the biological parents, if they know anything. Of course, what adoptive parents tell a child depends on the child's age and maturity.

A small number of children are adopted when they are adolescents. Those children often find that they must adjust to a new family at the same time that their adolescent status causes them to try to separate from that family. They may not have lived in the family long enough to acquire a sense of belonging and connection or to feel secure before they begin the process of leaving (McNamara, 1998). One adolescent complained that it was difficult to think about leaving, because he had just arrived.

Families face a number of challenges as their adopted children become adolescents. As they approach adolescence or are in the earliest stage of adolescence, adopted children may become somewhat more defensive and self-conscious about their status. They become more sensitive to how others see them (Schooler, 1998). Negative remarks, or even an offhand comment, may wound the child. Beginning at about age 10, and certainly by early adolescence, being accepted by peers becomes a primary motivation, and many adopted children choose not to talk about their status to others. They just don't want to appear different.

The conflict between teens and their parents that occurs as they renegotiate their relationship may lead adolescents to fantasize about their biological parents (van Gulden & Bartels-Rabb, 1998). They may fantasize that their biological parents were perfect, rich, and beautiful, but that some terrible event occurred so that they could not raise a child. These fantasies may begin as early as 7 years, but they intensify during adolescence. Adolescents sometimes tell others about their fantasies, even if their adoptive parents have told them contrasting information. A gentle challenge may be needed, such as privately saying, "What a wonderful story! It would have been nice if that were true. It would be fun to have a birth mother who was famous. That's certainly an easier story to share with friends" (van Gulden & Bartels-Rabb, 1998, p. 48). Sometimes these fantasies are simply an easy way for adolescents to deal with conflict with the adoptive parents—that is, fantasizing that the birth parents would be more understanding or more trusting and would allow them to do what they wanted. The fantasies may also be a way adolescents deal with negative emotions, such as anger toward the birth parents for "giving" them away, which they now may see as a rejection. Adoptive parents must understand that extolling the birth parents may be a teen's way of concealing feelings of loss, hurt, and rejection (Kunstal, 1996). The teen may even communicate these feelings through misbehavior.

During adolescence, the nature of the questions that adopted children ask their adoptive parents changes, and they may not accept the vague answers that satisfied them when they were younger. For example, younger children may be satisfied with a simple answer to a question about their past, such as "Your mother could not take care of you because she was sick." A teenager may ask more searching questions and be dissatisfied with generalities. The adopted child might know that she was abused by her birth parents, but as an adolescent she might try to find out why, a question that rarely can be answered. Sometimes the answers may complicate communication. When talking about moral issues, for example, how can parents deal with the fact that the child was born to a young unwed teenager (Schooler,

Much parental communication is delivered in the form of criticism. This is unfortunate, because criticism leads adolescents to avoid communication. Good communication requires family members to listen to each other and to express views with clarity and self-assertion yet flexibility, openly showing respect and sensitivity for the other party (Rathunde, 1997). Children and adolescents who perceive that their parents show less warmth are less likely to talk with their parents or to solve problems effectively (Herman & McHale, 1993). Parents who support their adolescents by creating an atmosphere that fosters respect for the opinions of others, mutuality, and tolerance, make it possible for their adolescents to explore identity alternatives (Grotevant & Cooper, 1986). Surveys show a pattern of fairly good communication between parents and teenagers (Chadwick & Heaton, 1996). Over half of all teens say their parents talk with them about problems, respect their opinions, and rarely miss events that are important to the teen (Moore, 1992). Adolescents, though, do perceive problems in communication more clearly than parents do. Teenagers see significantly less openness and more problems in intergenerational communication than they do in communication between peers (Barnes & Olson, 1985).

1998)? Adolescents may question the motives behind their adoption. The increasing interest in their own history and teenagers' newly developed ability to understand multiple motives lead to many searching questions about their past (Elliott, 1996).

Sometimes, these questions represent less of an inquiry into the adolescents' adoption than an awakening of their need to forge a personal identity, part of which may involve their biological/genetic inheritance (Schooler, 1997). Most nonadopted children, for example, can understand where they get their hair color from, but adopted teens cannot readily do so. They may have questions involving family talents or concerns about genetic illnesses or behavioral tendencies, such as anger or withdrawal (Schooler, 1997; Van Gulden & Bartels-Rabb, 1997). This identity search has been controversial, especially when adoptions are transracial (that is, children of one race are adopted into families of another race). However, despite arguments that transracial children might have more difficulties, research shows otherwise. Assessments of these children show that they do well and that their identity problems are no more severe than those of other adolescents (Vroegh, 1997). African American children raised by white families show a solid identity with African Americans.

Another challenge faced by both parents and their adopted teenagers involves adolescents' possible attempts to find their biological family and learn more about their history. If a child is adopted from another country, the desire to know more about it and perhaps even visit the country is even greater (Piper, 1998). Among a sample of adopted adolescents, most said yes when asked, "If possible, would you like to meet your birth mother and birth father?" (Benson, Sharma, & Roehlkepartain, 1994). A significant gender difference exists, however. A much higher percentage of girls (70 percent) than boys (57 percent) wanted to do so. This difference might reflect girls' greater interest in family relationships, an increased desire to know where their physical traits come from, or questions concerning genetic transmission of diseases or traits.

A movement to enable adopted children to find their biological parents more easily is unfolding in some states. In 1998, the voters of Oregon approved a measure giving adopted individuals who are 21 years old or older the right to their original birth certificate, which shows the names of their birth parents (Levy, 1999). Oregon joins Alaska and Kansas as the only states to allow this access; all other states have sealed their adoption records. The practice of sealing such records, however, dates only from the middle of the 20th century, before which these documents were available. Some authorities argue that making these certificates available to adopted older teens violates the confidentiality agreement with biological parents and that improving voluntary adoption registries would serve the same purpose without exposing the biological parents to an unwanted experience. Others argue that adopted children should have the right to discover their history.

It is easy to overinterpret the importance of adoption to a child's identity. Only about 27 percent of the adopted adolescents in one study noted that having been adopted was a big part of how they think about themselves (Benson et al., 1994). Asked how often they think about their adoption, 28 percent said once a week or more, whereas 52 percent said either "never" or "less than once a month." There is little doubt that adopted children have more questions to ask when they become adolescents, but it is also clear that most adapt and function well (Benson et al., 1994). They integrate what is known about their past with their present circumstances and continue to have good relationships with their adoptive parents.

The Generation Gap We sometimes assume that adults and adolescents are separated by a generational chasm that makes it almost impossible for them to get along or understand each other. The concept of the **generation gap,** the differences in attitudes between generations, has often been accepted as fact without supporting evidence. Teenagers and their parents are certainly products of different time periods. It is not unreasonable to expect the cohort effect (see "The World of Adolescence") to operate, so we might assume that teens and parents would see things differently and disagree in many areas.

The results of studies may surprise you, however. When high school seniors were asked, "How closely do your ideas agree with your parents' ideas about particular subjects?" the results showed much perceived agreement between the students and their parents (Bachman, Johnston, & O'Malley, 1993). When undergraduate students and their parents were asked to note their feelings on a number of issues, such as racism, war, sex, and drug use, and also to choose statements that mirrored the other person's view, the differences were only a matter of degree (Lerner et al., 1975). One generation agreed or disagreed more strongly with a particular position than did the other generation. The popular

generation gap The differences in attitudes among various generations.

term *generation gap,* used to denote what is seen as the ever-widening gap between the standards, values, and opinions of the generations, is more apparent than real, then, and differences are often more a matter of intensity than anything else. In the area of sex, though, qualitative differences do exist, with adolescents holding different, and much more permissive, views than parents (Chand, Crider, & Willets, 1975; Elias, 1997a).

The evidence also shows that adolescents and their parents sometimes misperceive the opinions of the other. Parents see their adolescents' views as closer to their own, and adolescents are more likely to think that their views are much different from those of their parents. Parents, then, underestimate differences, and teens overestimate them. This difference may reflect a lack of communication in some areas. Parents may not truly understand where their children differ from them, and adolescents may not be listening to their parents' views. Perhaps parents and their children are not actually talking very much. Some evidence for this idea comes from a study showing that adolescents know little about their parents' values or why their parents reason about an issue the way they do (Brody, Moore, & Glei, 1994). Parents assume that they have communicated their priorities and values, even when they have not actively discussed them. When parents show warmth to their adolescent children, discuss issues and values with them, listen to their views, and allow teenagers to have substantial input in family decision making, adolescents perceive their parents' values more accurately and are more likely to agree with these values (Brody et al., 1994).

An alternative explanation of why parents and adolescents sometimes misperceive each other's opinions is that both sides are motivated to misperceive the other. Parents are motivated to view their adolescent children as being closer to them in attitudes and beliefs than they really are. Adolescents are motivated to emphasize the differences between themselves and their parents to enhance their sense of individuality. Remember that this motivation to misperceive also occurs in parenting style. Parents often perceive themselves to be higher in demandingness, responsiveness, and involvement in schoolwork and school functions than their adolescents perceive them to be (Paulson & Sputa, 1996).

Conflict at Home

Fewer than 10 percent of all families report serious relationship difficulties involving chronic and escalating levels of conflict and repeated arguments over serious issues (Paikoff & Brooks-Gunn, 1991). And a sizable proportion of these problems represent issues that have followed the family into adolescence and remained unsolved (Collins, 1990). Arguments between parents and their adolescents occur at a rate of about one every 3 days (Montemayor, 1982). Conflict is greatest in early adolescence and at the beginning of middle adolescence. Changes in pubertal status in early adolescents are associated with increased moodiness, dissatisfaction, and aloofness, and these characteristics may raise the level of tension in the home and thus promote parent-child conflict (Tubman & Lerner, 1994). Adolescents' communication, especially between mother and son, involves less conflict as early adolescence passes.

Why Does Conflict Occur? Many factors influence the nature and frequency of conflict in the home. The area of disagreement depends, in some measure, on what parents and their adolescent children consider important. For example, some parents do not try to influence their adolescent's choice of college major or vocation, so conflict would not occur in this area. Consider two adolescents who decide to major in theater in college. The parents of one adolescent, although fully cognizant of the limited probabilities of success in the field, accept their teen's decision, whereas the other family does not accept the idea and refuses to help pay for the child's college tuition if the adolescent majors in this field. Obviously, more conflict will occur in the second child's home on the vocational issue. At the same time, there may be other areas in which more conflict occurs in the first child's home, for example, religious beliefs and practices.

Generally speaking, not all areas are equal candidates for conflict (Smetana & Asquith, 1994). Both parents and children see some personal issues, such as what programs to watch on television and what clothes to wear, as determined by the adolescent to a great extent; with age, however, adolescents become even more definite in their beliefs that these issues are beyond the bounds of parental authority (Smetana, 2000). Adolescents from many backgrounds share the belief that personal issues are their own business, but that parents are entitled to more say in safety issues and conventional issues (for example, respect for older people and how to act in social situations) (Fuligni, 1998). As adolescents mature, however, fewer issues are considered the legitimate province of parental concern. Large discrepancies are often found between the judgments of adolescents and their parents on personal safety and friendship, and many of the more serious battles involving autonomy are fought over these issues. Adolescents often reason about these conflicts differently than their parents. They see them as issues of personal jurisdiction, whereas parents treat them as issues of social convention—that is, ways of behaving that give structure to situations (Smetana, 1988). Adolescents are more likely to see these conflicts as tests reflecting their developing autonomy and individuality (Smetana, 1995). Generally, as teenagers mature, they see more areas of their lives as being under their own rightful control, and they resent too much interference by parents in more and more areas (Smetana, 1988, 1989, 2000).

A study of African American middle-class families reported similar findings concerning the areas of conflict, but two-thirds of the mothers believed that they should retain authority to regulate personal issues, whereas only one-third of the young adolescents agreed with that idea (Smetana, 2000). This finding might indicate a potential for considerable conflict, but two differences stand out from similar studies of European American adolescents. First, the scope of what is deemed personal is more limited among African American than European American adolescents. That is, they view fewer issues personal. Second, the African American families in this study believed that children and adolescents had a greater obligation to comply with all types of rules, whether or not they were seen as legitimate—a finding that nicely matches the research on parenting styles. This finding is consistent with cross-cultural studies of Asian American and Latino American families that find that adolescents in these groups have a greater obligation to respect family rules than do European American adolescents (Fuligni, Tseng, & Lam, 1999). In other words, African American families believe that adolescent children should obey the rules even if adolescents think their parents should no longer be making rules in this area, and these families place a greater emphasis on obedience and respect for the judgments of elders within the family.

Most family conflicts occur over everyday details of family life, such as who should do the chores, curfews, and the time to do homework (Lauresen & Collins, 1994). Conflicts surrounding school, family relations, and money also occur. This is true across different ethnic and minority groups. Disagreements over complex or moral aspects of behavior are rare, even though moral issues are considered the legitimate concerns for parents in all societies. More than 90 percent of parents in one survey claimed that they have not had disagreements with their adolescent children over topics such as sex or drugs (Barber, 1994a). This does not mean that parents and adolescents necessarily agree on these topics, or even that parents approve of their children's conduct in this area. It is more probable

Many conflicts occur over basic, everyday issues, such as who should do the chores.

that they do not discuss these topics. Adolescents hide their behaviors or do not discuss them with their parents to reduce the possibility of conflict.

Certain activities, by their very nature, may cause some stress and conflict (Dowdy & Kliewer, 1998). Dating is a context for sexual behavior, causing many parents to monitor teenagers in a more restrictive way than adolescents think reasonable. Dating may bring other issues to the forefront, such as curfews, friendship, and time spent with the family. These issues may be flashpoints for difficulties between parents and their adolescent children, especially daughters. This type of conflict is greatest in early, and especially middle, adolescence and becomes much less an issue in later adolescence.

Another factor affecting conflict is the degree to which parents and their adolescent children differ on an issue. Parents seem to have a band of comfort. That is, they will tolerate a range of differences in behavior, but major conflict will occur if adolescents go beyond that range. This band of comfort will differ according to the issue. For instance, consider an adolescent who frequently dresses and wears her hair and makeup in ways that her parents do not think are especially flattering. Conflict would depend on the importance of that area to the parents, as well as the extent of the differences and the acceptable range of behavior. It may be acceptable to some parents for their middle adolescent daughter to dye her hair blonde, for example, but the same parents might be more critical of green or blue hair.

Conflicts may also arise from differences in expectations, as adolescents expect greater freedom at earlier ages than their parents think is wise (Collins, 1990; Holmbeck & O'Donnell, 1991). Teenagers hold a different timetable for their independence than that of their parents (Collins et al., 1997). Adolescents often argue that they are old enough to go to a concert with their friends, spend their money the way they want to, or spend their leisure time doing what they want.

These conflicts, which are most likely to occur during early adolescence and the beginning of middle adolescence, partially arise from the common belief of adolescents that they are older and more mature than their age.

When sixth-grade males and their parents were asked to decide the ages at which they expected to engage in certain behaviors, their estimations were usually earlier than those of their parents (see Table 5.1). However, the adolescents and parents agreed on the order in which the behaviors should be allowed (Feldman & Quatman, 1988). A study of Dutch adolescents found that both boys and girls are likely to believe they are ready for particular experiences before their parents think they are (Dekovic, Noom, & Meeus, 1997). The differences are found in many areas of functioning and are most significant in early adolescence. The researchers point out that these discordant expectations can lead to conflict. Parents' views and behaviors change slowly, and parents relinquish control over daily matters in a more deliberate fashion than their teenagers think is appropriate (Goodnow, 1988; Smetana & Asquith, 1994).

Minority group families generally report lower levels of conflict and disagreement than white families. Many more white (non-Latino) parents than African American or Latino parents report conflict over chores. African American and Latino parents report significantly higher expectations for their adolescents to conform to parental authority. Again, this finding meshes nicely with the research on parenting style, which finds that African American and Latino families are more demanding, and parents expect and allow less questioning of rules. It may also be that adolescents from these cultures are raised with family responsibility and chores, and they accept their responsibilities more readily than adolescents from white, non-Latino backgrounds (Barber, 1994a).

PERSPECTIVE 2

POSTAL INSPECTION

SETTING THE SCENE: Terika is an only child, and her family lives in a middle-class area of a major city. She has an early curfew even on non-school nights, which is enforced rigidly, and her parents open her mail.

TERIKA: *They shouldn't open my mail. I think they also listen in on my phone converstaions. I have no privacy. I resent that.*

BOTH PARENTS: *We admit we are strict. We think other parents are too lax. Yes, we look at her mail because we want to know what is going on. We don't listen in on her telephone conversations, but we want to know who she is talking to. As long as she lives in our home, she must follow our rules. We see too many teens going the wrong way.*

QUESTION: In your opinion, do Terika's parents have the right to open her mail? Why or why not?

Table 5.1

When Should Adolescents Be Allowed to Participate in Specific Activities?

Adolescents generally believe they should be allowed to do things before their parents believe they should. This table shows the average age at which teenagers and parents believe activities should begin or when children should be allowed to participate in them.

Item	Age, per Child	Age, per Parent
Choose hairstyle even if your parents don't like it	14.8	14.1
Choose what books, magazines to read	13.2	14.3
Go to boy-girl parties at night with friends	14.8	13.9
Not have to tell parents where you are going	17.2	18.9
Decide how much time to spend on homework	13	15
Drink coffee	16	17.5
Choose alone what clothes to buy	13.7	14.7
Watch as much TV as you want	14.3	14.7
Go out on dates	15.4	16.1
Smoke cigarettes	20.3	20.5
Take a regular part-time job	16.2	16.6
Make own doctor and dentist appointments	17.4	17.9
Go away with friends without any adults	15.8	18.5
Be able to come home at night as late as you want	17.7	19.4
Decide what clothes to wear even if your parents disapprove	15.8	16
Go to rock concerts with friends	16.1	17.3
Stay home alone rather than go out with your family	14.5	15
Drink beer	18.9	19.3
Be able to watch any TV show, movie, or video you want	15.3	17.4
Spend money (wages or allowance) however you want	13.4	14.1
Stay home alone if you are sick	13.2	14.2

Source: Adapted from Feldman & Quatman (1988), Table 1, p. 333.

Family Conflict in Other Cultures Classic work in anthropology clearly shows that conflict during adolescence is not found in all cultures (Mead, 1928). However, conflict during this period of life is found in most cultures, be they industrial and individualistic, or more traditional and collectivist (Schlegel & Barry, 1991). Culture may determine the extent and content of the conflict. Most research looks at middle-class adolescents from European American backgrounds. In the United States, teenage autonomy is considered the norm. Most parents say that their number one child-rearing desire is to teach children to think for themselves rather than to obey. Children raised to be individualistic would be expected to seek autonomy and, consequently, to have battles over autonomy-related issues. Children raised in more collectivist cultures, which value interdependence, might experience conflict in different areas. For example, issues that are treated as personal decisions by American teens are often seen as moral obligations or duties by adolescents in India (Miller & Bersoff, 1992).

Sometimes cultures may clash, causing special difficulties. Consider an adolescent whose parents have immigrated to the United States from a more collectivist culture, for example, China. This family may experience a great deal of conflict, as the parents may continue to value their traditional beliefs while the teen takes on more American ideas. Indeed, conflicts between Chinese American adolescents and their immigrant parents often involve differences in the way the two cultures evaluate behaviors. For example, Chinese American parents expect

Imagine what it is like for an adolescent whose parents spent most of their lives in another culture. The adolescent probably has adopted many aspects of the new culture, but the parents may be deeply rooted in their native culture.

their children and teens to be more passive and obedient, whereas American culture encourages children and adolescents to be more active, independent, and self-sufficient (Yew, 1987). Yet often, Chinese American youth understand the differences in values and may even subordinate their wishes to their parents, concerned because they see the need to develop an ethnic identity or keep harmony (Yau & Smetana, 1993).

Descriptions of different parenting styles and areas of conflict in minority groups must take into account the effects of acculturation. Acculturation involves the changes that take place when a person from one culture must adapt to living in a different culture. Children and adolescents acculturate faster than adults (Szapocznik & Kutines, 1980). Children growing up in Japan, China, or Venezuela, then, may understand their families' stricter parenting styles, but children from these countries growing up in the United States may have more difficulty. In fact, one source of conflict between immigrant youth and their parents is the Americanization of the adolescent children. Immigrant children are more likely to look at their families in terms of the American family they see on television and perhaps in their friends' homes. The younger they are when they immigrate to the United States, the more the children are affected by their experience in their adopted country.

The ideal American family, as shown on television today, consists of parents who show sensitivity, open and honest communication, flexibility, and forgiveness. Although the structure of these families has changed as single-parent families and stepfamilies have become more common, the culturally prescribed closeness, emotional intimacy, and honest and open communication patterns are clear. However, immigrant families might differ from these ideals. Traditional Asian families stress a duty, responsibility, obedience, and commitment to the family that supersedes self-interest. American families are more democratic in decision making. Asians in their native lands associate parental strictness with warmth and concern, and the absence of strictness is a sign of neglect (Rohner & Pettengill, 1985).

A study of children of Korean immigrants living in the United States found that they view parental strictness negatively, as do American children from European backgrounds (Rohner & Pettengill, 1985). Interviews with Korean and Vietnamese late adolescents who were raised in the United States since early childhood found the tendency to judge parenting style in terms of Western values. These adolescents criticized their parents for lack of interest in their well-being and for not expressing love. In Southeast Asian society, however, love is shown instrumentally by taking care of others and sacrificing, not through verbal expression. These Americanized adolescents had difficulty communicating with their parents and wished their parents were less strict, had given them more freedom, were less traditional, and were more communicative. Many were unhappy that conversations with their parents were lecture oriented and stressed obedience. Yet the adolescents still identified with their responsibility to their parents and planned to care for them when they became elderly. It is interesting to note that Asian adolescents compared themselves with the ideal American family rather than with conflict-ridden American families. They constructed a model of family life as loving, harmonious, and egalitarian, whereas they characterized Asian families as distant and overly strict (Blinn-Pike, 1999).

The Adaptive Nature of Conflict   The typical level of conflict does not seem to undermine the quality of the parent-child relationship in adolescence or the attachment between adolescent and parents (Holmbeck, Paikoff, & Brooks-Gunn, 1995). Conflict may be a natural component of any close relationship and may serve as a signal that there are issues that must be settled (Holmbeck et al., 1995). Conflict functions as a catalyst for change and realignment in family relationships (Dowdy & Kliewer, 1998). It may lead to a better understanding of the differences between people who love each other, as well as enable each side to practice effective conflict resolution and reasoning skills (Holmbeck & Hill, 1991). Conflict, if examined properly, may also serve to bridge the generation gap (Holmbeck & O'Donnell, 1991). Finally, conflict may allow adolescents to differentiate themselves from their parents and aid in the renegotiation process that allows them to maintain a close relationship with parents and satisfy their needs at the same time (Holmbeck et al., 1995).

Positive Conflict Management   Whether conflict injures the relationship between parents and teens depends on the nature of the communication during conflict and the response to the disagreement. A link exists between problem-solving deficits, poor communication skills, and higher levels of adolescent-parent conflict (Grace, Kelley, & McCain, 1993). When parties to a conflict discuss a subject with an emphasis on an issue rather than a person, each side may better understand the other's point of view. However, when every issue is made personal, bitterness may result. For example, name calling, always bringing up the past, and refusing to discuss an issue injure a relationship. More positive ways of handling conflict include clearly explaining one's side, showing an appreciation and understanding of the other person's beliefs, and keeping one's emotions under some control. One reason why conflict subsides somewhat in later adolescence is because late adolescents use compromise more often than middle adolescents; middle adolescents use attack strategies more often than late adolescents (Reese-Weber, 2000).

How parents respond to disagreements with their adolescents is important in determining whether conflict will be damaging. A lack of responsiveness or a refusal to recognize differences followed by an inappropriate response may harm a relationship. Inappropriate responses may escalate the level of conflict or cause adolescents to experience frustration at their lack of power to influence decisions in the home that affect them. Parents who react to differences with their children with anger, sarcasm, or scorn, who make no adjustments, or who are coercive may find their relationship strained. However, a conflict must be seen in the context of the total relationship between the teen and parents (Cooper, 1988). When a conflict occurs in the context of a cohesive, satisfying adolescent-parent relationship, it is less likely to be damaging. That same conflict in an already poisoned and hostile atmosphere, however, can take on a life and an agenda of its own.

The style of conflict resolution used by a parent or adolescent seems stable across relationships. Adolescents who use attack strategies (yelling, or doing or saying things that hurt the other) tend to do so with both siblings and parents, and teens who use compromise strategies tend to use them with both siblings and parents (Reese-Weber, 2000). This stability is found in adolescent conflicts with parents, teachers, and romantic partners (Sternberg & Dobson, 1987).

Parents may influence their adolescent children's conflict management skills in two ways. First, parents who listen to others and compromise when appropriate are modeling these practices. Second, parents may actively teach their children how to defuse situations and communicate more effectively.

After a discussion of the issues in conflict, parents and adolescents may be able to resolve their differences, agree to disagree, or compromise. This scenario is more likely if their relationship is good, if they express themselves clearly, and if they show understanding of the other person's point of view.

Mothers and Fathers: Gender Differences in Communication and Conflict with Adolescents

The traditional role of the mother as almost sole caregiver and of the father as exclusive breadwinner has obviously changed over the past 40 years. The women's movement and civil rights struggle that took hold in the 1960s opened many more opportunities to women. Women entered college, the work force, and the professions. Many mothers found themselves in the dual role of worker and caregiver. This dual role, in turn, affected the father's role. A mother who works 35 hours per week and comes home to two children who require care may expect the father to provide more of that care and do additional housework. Fathers, who in the 1950s were told that they were simply role models whose relationship with their children was important to their children's emotional well-being, were now under greater pressure to provide actual care for the children. Until the 1960s and 1970s, the popular press had relatively few articles on fathers, and nothing on the influence of father love or caring (Rohner & Veneziano, 2001).

Fathers today are more involved with their children and do more of the housework than in the past (Gottfried, Gottfried, & Bathurst, 1995). Men's average contributions to housework and child rearing have about doubled since 1970, whereas women's contributions have decreased by a third. The level of paternal care has shifted even since the middle 1980s, and men contribute nearly one-third to this activity in dual-earner families (Parke, 1995). Yet it is wrong to go overboard and talk about equal participation in child rearing. Mothers still provide the large majority of child care, and fathers are still far less involved than mothers.

Adolescents spend more time with their mothers than their fathers, although the absolute amount of time spent with parents declines during adolescence. Adolescents see their mothers as more involved with them than their fathers, and mothers see it the same way (Richardson et al, 1984). Adolescents also perceive mothers to be more responsive than fathers (Paulson & Sputa, 1996). Adolescents report that they talk more with their mother than their father, and most teens, particularly girls, see their mother as more understanding and accepting, and their father as more judgmental, more willing to impose authority, and less willing to discuss emotional and personal issues (Jackson et al., 1998; Youniss & Smollar, 1985).

At the same time, mothers report more intense discussions and a greater number of conflicts than fathers (Almeida & Galambos, 1991). This difference can be explained by the greater amount of interaction and involvement mothers have with their adolescents, as well as the different topics they may discuss. Father-adolescent discussions often center around issues—for example, school achievement—and often are characterized by the exercise of authority. Adolescents view fathers as being more distant than mothers.

These differences do not mean that fathers do not have significant effects on their adolescents. Regardless of the degree of paternal involvement, fathers' acceptance of, and closeness to, adolescents encourages academic achievement (Forehand & Nousiainen, 1993). A father's involvement with his children is related to greater social maturity and better adjustment (Gottfriend, Bathurst, & Gottfried, 1994, 1988). Most adolescents say they are satisfied with the communication with their parents, although they are much more satisfied with their communication with mothers than fathers (Jackson et al., 1998).

AT A GLANCE 5.3 COMMUNICATION AND CONFLICT

KEY POINT: Communication and the ability to handle conflict effectively are related to better family relationships.

SUPPORTING POINTS	EXPLANATION
Communication with parents and peers differs.	Communication with parents is more directive and has less give and take than communication with peers.
Adolescent-parent communication is generally good.	Most adolescents say that they speak with their parents often and can confide in them.
Adolescents are more likely to see problems in adolescent-parent communication than are parents.	Although adolescent-parent communication is generally good, teens are more likely to believe that intergenerational communication is less open than are their parents.
Adolescents perceive better communication with their mothers than their fathers.	Adolescents see their mothers as more accepting and their fathers as more critical.
The generation gap, the supposed gap in attitudes between generations, is not as great as is often assumed.	Studies find that differences between adolescents and their parents on issues are often a matter of degree.
Parents and adolescents often do not know each other's positions on issues.	Parents often believe that their adolescent children's beliefs are closer to their views than they really are. Adolescents believe their views vary much more from their parents' views than they really do.
Conflict between parents and adolescents involves many issues.	Conflict may occur because adolescents believe they are ready for more autonomy than their parents do.
Anthropological studies show that conflict is not inevitable during the adolescent years.	Some cultures report little conflict between teenagers and parents.
Gender differences in both communication and conflict occur.	Fathers are more involved with the family today than years ago, although mothers still have the greater responsibility for child rearing. Adolescents have more contact and communication with their mother than their father. They report more conflict with their mother than their father, although they are more satisfied with the communication with their mother.

Adolescents' interactions with their mothers and fathers may differ, but both have an important part to play in the development of adolescents. We are just beginning to appreciate the importance of paternal nurturance and the impact that fathers have in families (Parke & Buriel, 1998), as well as how changing social norms may influence family relationships and interaction patterns. Fathers may become more involved with their children at all ages as changes in society and the family continue. (*For a review of this section, see At A Glance 5.3.*)

OTHER FAMILY RELATIONSHIPS

In the midst of the considerable interest in all aspects of the parent-teenager relationship, other familial relationships are often forgotten. Primary among these are relationships with brothers and sisters, as well as grandparents.

Sibling Relationships

More than 80 percent of all American children have one or more siblings (Eisenberg & Mussen, 1989), and 77 percent of all adolescents report that their siblings are an important influence in their lives (Blyth, Hill, & Thiel, 1982). When early adolescents were asked to rate members of their family, their best friend, and their teacher, adolescents rated their siblings as very important on a number of qualities (see Figure 5.5) (Furman & Buhrmester, 1985).

Patterns of Sibling Interaction Evaluations of sibling interactions often revolve around sibling rivalry, which is understandable. Conflict is more common among siblings than any other family members. But sibling relationships involve more than conflict. Siblings serve as sources of counsel, play together, are companions, and fill definite psychological needs. They often help one another (Brody et al., 1985). There is even evidence that they can provide the support and affection that may not be forthcoming from parents (Dunn & Kendrick, 1982; Kurdek & Fine, 1995). When early adolescents are isolated and lack friends, they

Figure 5.5
Adolescents Rate Their Relationships with Others
Adolescents were asked to rate their mother, father, grandparents, teacher, friend, and sibling on a number of dimensions. Notice that they rated the sibling relationship as being a bit more important than the relationship with the friend. Also notice that conflict with siblings is much higher than conflict with any other individual.

Source: Adapted from Furman & Buhrmester (1985).

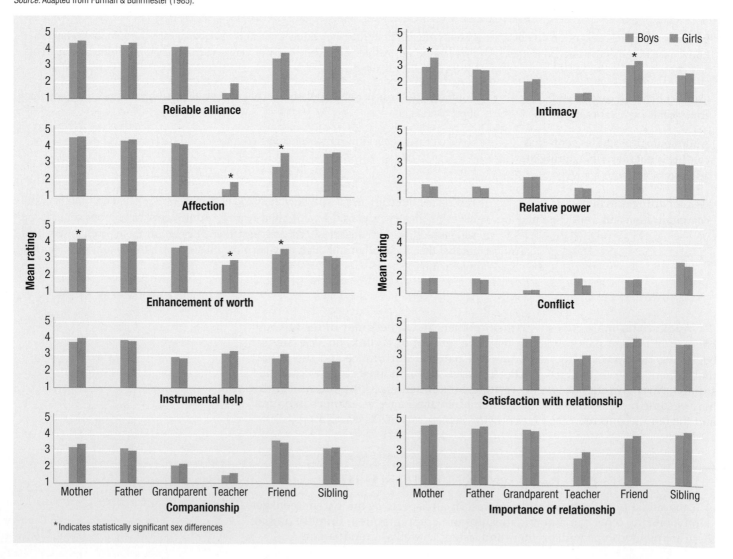

*Indicates statistically significant sex differences

may receive important support from their siblings (East & Rook, 1992).

Siblings in high-conflict homes who report receiving emotional support from their brothers and sisters are better adjusted than children in such homes who report low sibling support (Caya & Liem, 1998). Sibling support acts as a buffer to the stresses within a home filled with conflict (Jenkins, 1992; Kempton et al., 1991). The sibling relationship, then, may have protective functions. Siblings who have experienced hard times together share a unique family history and, often, family secrets. Their shared status of helpless victims in a high-conflict family solidifies a permanent bond. In fact, siblings sometimes seek each other out during parental quarrels and discuss family problems with each other rather than with outsiders (Jenkins, Smith, & Graham, 1989).

Despite the importance of sibling relationships, however, adolescents are somewhat less satisfied with these relationships than with other family relation-

How would your life be different if you had more or fewer siblings?

ships. Perhaps the extensive conflict is the reason; the mixture of feeling close to a sibling and experiencing sustained conflict with the individual is unique. Generally, siblings who are older are more likely to be sources of aid, and same-sex siblings, especially those close in age, are sources of intimacy and companionship. Sometimes these relationships resemble friendships, but the high levels of conflict often distinguish them from other friendships.

Sibling interaction in earlier life is predictable. Older children initiate more prosocial and combative behaviors, and younger children imitate more (Abramovitch et al., 1986; Vandell & Bailey, 1992). Older siblings clearly dominate younger ones. These distinctions lessen over time. Although conflicts occur, prosocial and play-oriented behaviors constitute the majority of the interactions.

Sibling relationships change in adolescence. When students in the third, sixth, ninth, and twelfth grades were asked to rate their relationships with their siblings, three age-related differences were found. First, sibling relationships become more egalitarian and less based upon power with age. Nurturance (as well as dominance) directed toward younger siblings declines by early adolescence, which probably indicates that older siblings see their early-adolescent siblings as more competent and independent and not as much in need of the protection they afforded them earlier. The relative differences in their ages becomes less important, resulting in less dominance (Buhrmester & Furman, 1990).

Second, as children grow older, sibling relationships become less intense. Ratings reflecting the intensity of the relationship decline on every dimension, including power and warmth/closeness. To some extent, this decline in intensity is due to the reduction in the amount of time spent with siblings. The decline may also be due to the availability of closer friendships and romantic relationships, meaning that siblings have less need to invest emotionally in their siblings. Yet these declines in intimacy and warmth are relatively modest, and emotional attachment remains strong throughout the adolescent years, despite the decline in companionship.

Third, conflict declines, although older and younger siblings do not agree on this. Younger siblings report that conflict with older siblings declines steadily with age, whereas older siblings do not perceive this decline in conflict (Buhrmester & Furman, 1990). Adolescents who are younger siblings report greater admiration for, and intimacy with, older siblings than older siblings report toward younger siblings. Younger siblings look up to, and value interacting with, older brothers and sisters, whereas older siblings do not and may see younger siblings as annoying. This attitude may be part of the adolescent older siblings' struggle to become independent and distance themselves from their family, whereas younger siblings may want to seem grown up and identify with their older siblings.

When Parents Treat Siblings Differently When parents are more affectionate toward one child than the other, jealousies can grow, and fewer helpful interactions between siblings occur (Volling & Belsky, 1992). Children may compare the attention and interest parents show to each sibling and remember preferential treatment. Even in adulthood, people remember, and can tell stories of, unfair treatment by their parents (Baker & Daniels, 1990).

Siblings are very sensitive to differential treatment. Even small differences in parental negativity may influence a child's adjustment. It is not whether the differential treatment really occurs that is important, but the child's perception of the situation. A child's perception of having received less parental love or attention than a sibling can adversely affect the child's behavior (Monahan et al., 1993).

Unequal treatment by parents of siblings, however, does not always lead to problems. The perception of unequal treatment and the consequences of this treatment differ according to children's understanding of why their parents treat their siblings differently. For example, children often feel it is appropriate to set different bedtimes for their younger or older siblings or to visit a room more often because a little one is afraid of the dark. Yet siblings will not accept differential parental treatment in complimenting children when they have performed equally well (Kowal & Kramer, 1997). In one study, 76 percent of all elementary school children who believed differential treatment existed did not see it as unfair, because they saw it in terms of sibling needs (Reid, Ramey, & Burchinal, 1990).

Parents, though, often know that they are treating their children differently. They may perceive one child as being more mature, having "better" friends, doing better in school, or needing more or less monitoring than another child, without regard to age or gender. If parents believe one child requires more monitoring, they may provide it for that child and give greater freedom to the other child, who they perceive as more mature.

PERSPECTIVE 3

THEY LOVE HER MORE

SETTING THE SCENE: Taneesha is 14 years old and Patrice is 15 and a half. Patrice is doing barely passing work and has some friends who have been in trouble. Taneesha is a honors student.

MOTHER: *We admit we give Patrice more attention, but she needs it. She has a great many problems, and we are trying to be understanding, yet firm. We guess Taneesha doesn't see it that way. Taneesha is bright and doing well in school. We appreciate that, but Patrice just needs more of our time than Taneesha does.*

FATHER: *And Taneesha exaggerates everything. We do expect more from her, because she can do it. We give each child what we think she needs, but Taneesha is so sensitive.*

QUESTION: Should these parents change their parenting strategy and begin to treat each child exactly the same, or should they continue to give each girl what they think she requires?

Adolescent-Grandparent Relationships

An impressive 44 percent of adolescents say that their grandparents are special figures in their lives (Moore, 1992). Contacts between grandparents and grandchildren are relatively frequent (Smith, 1995). Relationships are influenced by number of grandchildren, distance that they live from each other, whether the grandchildren's parents are divorced, the quality of the relationships parents have with grandparents, the age of grandparents and grandchildren, and the health of grandparents (Miller & Bengtson, 1991). If parents encourage a relationship, it is more likely to develop. If parents have a good relationship with their own parents, it is more likely that the children will be close as well (King & Elder, 1995; Matthews & Sprey, 1985). If grandparents live closer, it is easier to spend time with them (Hodgson, 1992). Grandparents must also encourage the relationship by communicating with their grandchildren and making time for adolescent grandchildren. Some grandparents call their grandchildren, whereas others expect their grandchildren to initiate the communication because of their status as grandparents. Children may be directly influenced by their grandparents through frequent contacts with them and the social support they provide (Block, 2002). They also may be affected indirectly through advice grandparents give to parents about discipline and punishment (Tomlin & Passman, 1989).

Adolescents' relationships with their grandparents vary. Some adolescents have very extensive contact with their grandparents, some see their grandparents only at family celebrations, and others have little contact. Adolescents do not see their grandparents as authority figures but as people who provide support.

Grandparents are not seen as authoritarian figures. Fewer than half ever discipline their grandchildren, mostly because the grandparent role is largely limited to providing assistance, and a norm of noninterference with the nuclear family is enforced (Miller & Bengtson, 1991). Culture has a significant influence on the roles grandparents play in the lives of their grandchildren. Historically, grandmothers have been important figures who provide support and cultural continuity in families and act as supplementary or surrogate parents (Smith, 1995). A study of African American and white grandmothers found differences in perceived parenting attitudes, behaviors, and involvement. African American grandmothers gave more help to, and received more help from, grandchildren than did white grandmothers. African American grandfathers both expected to have more contact with their grandchildren and actually did see them more often than did white grandfathers (Kivett, 1993). They felt closer to their grandchildren as well.

About 5 percent of all American children live with their grandparents, who have either total or partial responsibility for their upbringing. An increase has occurred across all ethnic groups, but it has been particularly significant in the African American community, where 13.5 percent of all African American children live with their grandparents, whereas 6.5 percent of all Latino children do so, and 4.1 percent of all Caucasian children do (see Fuller-Thompson & Minkler, 2000). In some inner cities, the proportions are substantially higher. About half these grandparents provide child care, and over half a million are raising their grandchildren without help ("Grandparents who care," 1995). Many grandparents are called upon to help daughters who bear children out of wedlock (Apfel & Seitz, 1991), a situation discussed in more detail in "Love and Sex." The growth of single-parent families, lack of affordable housing, teenage pregnancy, and drug addiction are factors that sometimes cause grandparents to take in their children and grandchildren (Burton, 1992). During such emergencies, grandparents take on the clear role of surrogate parent, or at least helper (Smith, 1995). Grandparents may reduce the impact of family disruption caused by drug abuse, divorce, or single parenthood (Solomon & Marx, 1995).

Children living with a grandparent generally do well (Soloman & Marx, 1995). The grandmother, who may also be poor, typically carries almost the whole burden. When grandfathers are present and involved, children are more obedient and healthier, and they benefit from the presence of a warm, accepting male role model. Studies show that children raised by their grandparents are not at a disadvantage when compared with children from single-parent families. These children are less likely to show behavior problems in school than children raised by single parents, and they show about the same number of behavior problems as children raised in nuclear families. Children in nuclear families are

AT A GLANCE 5.4 OTHER FAMILY RELATIONSHIPS

KEY POINT: Extended family relationships influence adolescent development.

SUPPORTING POINTS	EXPLANATION
Siblings can influence adolescents in many ways.	Siblings act as confidants, give social support, and act as models.
The relationship between older and younger siblings is predictable.	Older siblings dominate younger siblings, and younger siblings imitate more. Sibling relationships become more egalitarian and less intense with age.
Under most circumstances, greater parental affection toward one sibling causes jealousy and resentment, and it injures sibling relationships.	If children understand why parents treat siblings differently (e.g., one child stays up later because he is older), differential treatment may not adversely affect sibling relationships.
Grandparents may influence their adolescent grandchildren.	Grandparents may influence their adolescent grandchildren directly through their relationship or indirectly through the advice that they give to the parents.
Most adolescents do not see their grandparents as authoritarian figures.	The relationship between most grandparents and their adolescent grandchildren is warm, and grandparents provide assistance to their grandchildren.
Some grandparents raise or help raise their grandchildren.	Children raised by their grandparents do well compared with children raised in single-parent families, and they show the same number of problems as children raised in nuclear families. Children in nuclear families, however, achieve more in school.

more academically successful; they repeat fewer grades and are better students. However, children raised by their grandparents are equal in achievement to those raised in single-parent families. Their health is about equal to children in intact families and somewhat superior to those raised in single-parent families. The only area of concern for children raised by their grandparents, then, is academics. Lower academic achievement may be caused by excessive absences that began prior to a divorce (Larson, 1990/1991). Or grandparents, who often raise grandchildren under difficult circumstances, may consider the development of good character and behavior patterns more important than academic achievement and thus focus their attention there. *(For a review of this section, see At A Glance 5.4.)*

THE CHANGING AMERICAN FAMILY

If you watched a situation comedy originally televised in the 1950s, you would notice that most of the families shown included an employed father, a full-time homemaker mother, two or three children, and a dog, all living a middle-class life. Today, this is not the case. The number of single-parent families has increased substantially (Ensign, Scherman, & Clark, 1998). The most common reason children and adolescents live in single-parent families is divorce. Each year about 2 percent of all children living in the United States face parental divorce (Emery & Forehand, 1994). If divorce trends continue, more than half of all American children will spend some time in a single-parent household before their 18th birthday. Children and adolescents may also live in a single-parent family because their mother was never married or because a parent died.

Most divorced mothers and fathers remarry, and many children and adolescents experience a series of transitions from intact family to single-parent family to stepfamily. In addition, more families in developed nations are choosing to

The most common reason for living in a single-parent home is divorce. Divorce may deeply affect adolescents, but most adjust to the change in their family.

have only one child. Whether or not children or adolescents grow up in an intact family, a stepfamily, a single-parent family, or a family without siblings, most of their mothers are employed.

Single-Child Families

About 10 percent of all marriages result in the birth of one child, and the trend toward having a single child is increasing, not only in the United States but also around the world. In a recent poll, 42 percent of Russians sampled said that under the current poor economic climate they wanted a single child (ITAR/TASS News Agency, 2001). China instituted a one-child policy in 1979. Their policy encourages young people to marry later, birth control information is readily available, and economic incentives favor having one child (Choi & Kane, 1999).

Concern for the "only child" (the child with no siblings) is widespread and goes back many years. G. Stanley Hall, considered the father of the scientific study of adolescence, believed that being an only child was a "disease in itself" (Rosenberg & Hyde, 1993). Traditionally, the concern centers on three issues. First, only children might have interpersonal difficulties because they do not have ongoing social experiences with siblings. Second, only children might be spoiled by parents and develop personality problems, perhaps being more selfish (Falbo & Poston, 1993). Third, being an only child might affect academic performance.

Much research on only children comes from China because of its national policy supporting one-child families. The research evidence shows that only children are more advanced cognitively and show superior achievement when compared with children with siblings (Wan et al., 1994; Yang et al., 1995). The results of Chinese studies comparing the personalities of only children and children with siblings are less consistent. Some studies find only children to be more selfish, more egocentric, and more likely to refuse another child's request (Jiao, Ji, & Jing, 1986, 1996). Other studies, however, find no differences (Chen, Rubin, & Li, 1995; Falbo & Poston, 1993). Only children have a normal personality structure and well-developed interpersonal skills (Falbo & Poston, 1993). Some studies have even found advantages, as only children are less anxious, less fearful, and less likely to be depressed (Wan et al., 1994).

At one time, people pitied the "only child." Recent research, however, shows that only children do quite well.

A review of Western studies yields similar results: Only children have higher intelligence scores and do not have higher rates of maladjustment than children with siblings. Only children have good relationships with their parents. Mothers spend more time with them, engaging them in more conversation and giving them more information (Falbo & Polit, 1986; Polit & Falbo, 1987). There is no evidence that only children are spoiled, and their personality attributes are generally positive. The review finds that only children differ from children with siblings on only two dimensions—self-esteem and achievement—and they score higher on both.

Another study of 150,000 adults and children found that only children are better educated, score higher on IQ tests, and develop better social skills than children from larger families (Blake, 1989; Travis & Kohli, 1995). The magnitude of these differences is not great when only children are compared with children who have one or two siblings, but the differences become progressively greater as family size increases (Furman, 1995). The superiority in achievement may be due to increased parental attention and receiving a larger portion of the family resources. For example, only children are more likely to be read to by parents and to take music, dance, and art lessons (Blake, 1989). They also are more likely to be involved in extracurricular activities. Some studies find minor differences in personality; for example, children with siblings develop thicker skins from teasing and squabbling and thus are less sensitive.

Most research compares only children with children with siblings, but only children may not make up a homogeneous group. Psychologists interviewed children with no siblings when they were in junior high school, when in senior high school, as early adults, and then as middle adults. Each time, the psychologists were asked to describe the participants, and three distinct patterns arose (Rosenberg & Hyde, 1993). Members of the normal, well-adjusted group of only children were talkative, poised, assertive, and not fearful. Children in the impulsive, acting-out group were self-indulgent, undercontrolled, and dissatisfied. Members of the third group, labeled *first bornish,* were very controlled, detail oriented, very dependable, and productive—characteristics that match descriptions of firstborn children with siblings. These descriptions were stable over the years, although the firstborn category for males was somewhat less stable, for unknown reasons. Treating only children as a homogeneous group, then, may mask some important differences. Adolescents in each of these categories may have experienced different parenting styles, or temperament may interact with parenting style to create an individual's personality. More research is needed in this area.

Being an only child does not appear to have negative social consequences, and academic achievement is superior. Only children are as well adjusted as children with siblings. It would not be surprising if the negative stereotypes of the only child became less prevalent as the percentage of families in Western societies with one child increases and research continues to show few differences.

Maternal Employment

The overwhelming majority of mothers with teenage children are employed. Although some mothers return to work almost immediately after giving birth, others wait varying amounts of time. Most mothers are in the labor force before their children are adolescents.

Much of the research on the influence of maternal employment on children's social and academic achievement involves younger children. Daughters of mothers who work and are valued in the labor force have less stereotyped ideas about gender roles (Parke & Buriel, 1998). No significant differences in personality or adjustment are found for sons of mothers with lower socioeconomic backgrounds who are employed compared to sons whose mothers are full-time homemakers. The only negative finding that occasionally arises is that some middle-class boys whose mothers work do not show the same academic achievement as boys whose mothers are not employed (Lerner & Abrams, 1994). However, this finding is not reported in all studies, and when detected, it is only found if the mother is employed full-time and is relatively uneducated. It seems that educated mothers compensate for the lack of time with their children when they come home from work and on weekends.

The results of research on maternal employment and adolescents depend on the cohort being studied. Some of the older research found a relationship between poorer school achievement and maternal employment status in adolescence (Bronfenbrenner & Crouter, 1983). Current studies, however, show no differences in academic achievement between adolescents whose mothers are employed and those whose mothers are not (Armistead, Wierson, & Forehand, 1990; Crouter et al., 1990; Paulson, 1996). Employed mothers of adolescents are happier and more satisfied, and they are more likely to encourage independence in their children than are nonemployed mothers. Their daughters are more outgoing and motivated. Their adolescent sons show good social and personality adjustment, family relations, and interpersonal relations at school, and they subscribe to fewer sex role stereotypes. Maternal employment is not related to delinquency, but inadequate monitoring and supervision is (Lerner & Hess, 1991; Vander Ven et at., 2001). For both employed and full-time homemaker mothers, higher rates of problem behavior are related to inadequate supervision. It may be

Most studies today find little difference between parent-child interactions when the mother is or is not employed—a change from the findings of years ago. Today, with most mothers employed, the situation is so common that it has become the norm.

more difficult for two working parents to monitor their children, but many succeed. Alternatively, a mother who is a full-time homemaker may not monitor her children adequately, even though she has the opportunity to do so.

The fact that modern scholarship either finds no differences or even some advantages for those who work whereas older research showed more problems is explained by the cohort effect. Mothers who were employed 40 years ago, when few mothers were in the labor force, may have been forced to work outside the home because of dire economic situations. Their participation in the work force was statistically unusual, and perhaps they felt guilty about being away from their children or were rebuked by neighbors. Although many women today seek employment because of economic considerations, women are more likely to be professionals and career oriented. Maternal employment, especially when children are teens, is now the norm. The experience of mothers and adolescents years ago may not match the experience of families today. We may also be comparing two different samples; older samples may have been biased toward socioeconomically deprived families, whereas modern studies may include a more privileged, better educated group.

One objection to research on maternal employment is that it is too large a variable. Many factors influence the effects of maternal employment on children and adolescents. For example, a mother's satisfaction with working and her attitudes toward employment are important factors in the influence of employment on her family. In fact, role satisfaction is more important than employment status (Lerner & Galambos, 1986). The more satisfied a mother is with her role, the more likely she is to interact positively with her children, leading to a higher-quality relationship and better outcomes (Lerner & Hess, 1991). Mothers who believe that what they are doing is best for their children, whether it is choosing employment or staying at home, display more positive parenting characteristics than those who do not believe this.

Women who are not satisfied with their role show more negative moods and fewer positive behaviors toward their children (MacEwen & Barling, 1991). Employed mothers who believe working has negative effects may feel guilty and frustrated about being away from their children; they may find it difficult to say no or to discipline their children. It is not a mother's employment status that influences adolescent achievement, but her attitude toward, and satisfaction with, that role. When mothers report little role difficulty and high role satisfaction, their children report better outcomes. In contrast, mothers with high role conflict and low role satisfaction show more punishing and rejecting parenting behaviors, which relate to poor outcomes (MacEwen & Barling, 1991).

A father's attitudes toward his wife's working may also play a part, because the father's attitudes may influence how much support he shows the mother and perhaps how much he shares the duties at home. Adolescents perform more poorly in school when their mother's and father's attitudes toward maternal employment are inconsistent with their mother's employment status. These adolescents show less interest in their work and value achievement less.

Differences among children of employed and nonemployed mothers are disappearing, however. Cultural attitudes are more positive, and mothers feel less guilty about being employed. Other factors, such as the quality of supervision, the nature of the parent-child interactions, and family attitudes, are more important than the employment status itself.

Divorce

Divorce is not an event but rather a process that continues to influence a child or adolescent throughout the years (Goodman, Emery, & Haugaard, 1998). Divorce itself brings about many changes. The child probably has much less contact with the noncustodial parent, and financial problems may force the family to move or reduce their standard of living. Most children do not see these changes as positive, even years after the divorce (Wallerstein, Corbin, & Lewis, 1988; Wallerstein, Lewis, & Blakeslee, 2000).

Most children and adolescents find divorce painful, and their early reactions may include anger, depression, and guilt (Weinraub & Gringlas, 1995). Parent-child relationships change during or after divorce, if not both. The custodial parent, usually the mother, becomes stricter and more controlling, whereas the other parent becomes permissive and more understanding, although less accessible. Parents' discipline practices become less consistent and less effective, and parents do not monitor their children as well (Forgatch, Patterson, & Skinner, 1988; Hetherington & Clingempeel, 1992). Financial problems may force the family to move to a new neighborhood, altering the child's daily routine (Hines, 1997).

Many children and adolescents recover well after the initial period, but some do not (Hetherington, 2002). Some show reasonably good adaptation in the early stages and then show delayed effects. Many of the initial reactions become less severe or disappear in 12 to 18 months (Hetherington, 1993; Portes et al., 1992). However, the long-term effects can be significant. A longitudinal study of children whose parents had divorced during middle childhood showed that half had improved functioning, and about one-fourth had become significantly worse (Kelly & Wallerstein, 1976). Children whose parents divorce evaluate their families more negatively than do children from intact families (Parish, 1991; Richardson & McCabe, 2001). Wallerstein (1987) followed children whose parents were divorced when they were in middle childhood and found that as teenagers, a majority expressed sadness and neediness, as well as an increased sense of vulnerability. Even though it had been 10 years since the divorce, these adolescents spoke sadly of their loss of the intact family, and especially of the lack of contact with their noncustodial parent. They expressed a great concern about being betrayed in relationships and were very anxious about personal commitments.

Studies in other Western cultures also find that children in single-parent families have more doubts with respect to future marriage and family life. They are more active in forming relationships with people of the other gender, but are more critical of these relationships. They are also more critical of their marriages and get divorced more often (Kinnaird & Gerrard, 1986). Even after controlling for differences in backgrounds, studies find that females from single-parent families leave home at a younger age, cohabit more often, break up relationships more often, and have a more negative opinion of their personal relationships (Ensign et al., 1998; Spruijt & de Goede, 1997). Compared with children from intact families, children who have ever lived in a mother-only family complete fewer years of schooling, are less likely to receive high school diplomas, fall behind in high school more often, and are less likely to enter college (Evans, Kelley, & Wanner, 2001; Graham, Beller, & Hernandez, 1994).

It is not difficult to find studies showing that children and adolescents from divorced families do not compare favorably with children from intact families in many areas. However, the magnitude of these differences is modest, and there is no evidence for extensive mental health problems for children from divorced families (Amato & Keith, 1991; Goodman, 1998). Most children and adolescents successfully cope with the difficulties (Hetherington & Kelly, 2002). The problems are not inevitable (Goodman et al., 1998; Peterson, 1997).

In fact, many children of divorced parents do quite well. Recently, the results of three longitudinal studies by researcher E. Mavis Hetherington involving 1,400 families were discussed in *For Better or for Worse: Divorce Reconsidered* (Hetherington & Kelly, 2002). Hetherington found relatively good adjustment for most children after divorce. The outcome of divorce depends on many factors, including parenting skills, the level of support both adults and children receive, and the individual's willingness to face new challenges. Although Hetherington appreciates the possible destructiveness of divorce, she argues that both the popular press and academic writing have exaggerated its negative effects. Divorce may be positive as when it ends child abuse in a marriage, and according to Hetherington, it may provide opportunities for personal growth, especially for women and girls. She notes that the first 2 years are very difficult, but that despite the problems, most mothers provide the support their children need for healthy development.

Adolescents and Divorce Much more research exists on the effect of divorce on adolescents whose parents divorced 5 or 10 years before than on those whose parents divorce during the adolescent years. This research bias is understandable, because most divorces take place before the children enter adolescence (Cooney & Smyer, 1991). Adolescents experiencing parental divorce certainly have the classic immediate reactions to divorce, but some differences are also evident.

One difference between adolescents' and younger children's experience of divorce lies in adolescents' ability to understand more about what is going on in the home. Younger children can be sent to bed before an argument breaks out and may be less aware of the substantive issues that divide their mother and father; adolescents are much more likely to be aware of what is dividing their parents. They also know that they didn't cause the divorce and are less likely to blame themselves. Their more advanced cognitive skills allow them to understand the multiple causes of the divorce and to appreciate their parents' complex motives and emotions that led to the divorce (see "Cognitive Development") (Hetherington, Anderson, & Stanley-Hagan, 1991). They may be mature enough to offer support to their parents (Hetherington & Anderson, 1987).

Adolescents more often blame their fathers for the divorce, and father-daughter relationships tend to deteriorate following divorce (Kaufmann, 1987). College-age women are twice as likely as college-age men to report prolonged anger in response to the divorce of their parents and to direct that anger more at their fathers than their mothers, even if their mothers initiated the divorce (Cooney et al., 1986; Kaufmann, 1987). College-age women worry more about their mother's than their father's future and provide much more emotional support to their mother.

A relatively small group of adolescents welcome the divorce of their parents, as they have experienced discord for many years and believe their homes will be somewhat less stressful and discordant. However, most adolescents experience stress and feelings of loss when their parents divorce. Many adolescents have difficulty coping with anger, often showing sadness, acting-out behaviors, emotional and social withdrawal, and anxiety about the future (Cooney & Smyer, 1991).

Adolescents are also more capable than younger children of insulating themselves from their parents' difficulties through peer relationships. They can better put their feelings into words and discuss them with their friends, who are better able to understand and give emotional support. Yet these adolescents may become more susceptible to peer influence (Coughlin & Vuchinich, 1996). Although most divorced parents can and do give their adolescent children the emotional support they require, some are not able to do so, which may increase the adolescents' dependence on peers. Adolescents whose parents divorce report more friends who use drugs and are involved in more antisocial behavior (Neher & Short, 1998). Perhaps these adolescents are more susceptible to pressure from friends to engage in deviant behavior.

Two factors become significant when analyzing adolescents' concerns about the divorce of their parents during this time: outside relationships and financial resources. First, one of the key changes in adolescence is the development of close relationships outside the family. As the years roll by, adolescent relationships with peers become more intimate. Self-disclosure is a common staple of these relationships. Adolescents whose parents divorce during this time are keenly aware of the failure of their parents' relationship and wonder about the stability of their own relationships. They are more concerned than other adolescents about such issues as faithfulness and trust (Wallerstein & Blakeslee, 1989). Rejection and fear of betrayal are relatively common in adolescents, but these feelings are greater among teenagers whose parents have recently divorced.

Adolescents may ask whether relationships really can work or whether marriage really lasts a lifetime.

These adolescents see relationships as riskier than do children from intact families (Johnston & Thomas, 1996). When adolescents whose parents divorced when they were adolescents were questioned 6 years later, the only significant effect found involved the security of attachment to romantic partners (Summers et al., 1998); the study found no significant differences in adjustment, including interpersonal competence, emotional distress, academic achievement, or delinquency. These teens must work through not only their newly formed relationships with peers but also the changing and often chaotic relationships in their home. Some of these adolescents may fear entering into any deep relationship. Others may desperately seek out a relationship to provide the intimacy and attention now missing in the home or to act as a buffer against the problems of the home.

The second significant factor when analyzing adolescents' concerns about the divorce of their parents during this time is the possible reduction in the family's financial resources, which may endanger the adolescents' future plans. For example, consider the high school junior whose parents told her that they could no longer afford to send her to the private college she had been planning to attend; having to support two households did not allow for expensive college tuition payments. Despite the fact that the divorce of her parents was not filled with discord (it was what you might call a "friendly" divorce), she felt angry and bitter toward her parents. Adolescents are more concerned about their future academic and vocational opportunities than are younger children (Hetherington et al., 1991). At the same time, adolescents may feel angry with themselves and ashamed because they are thinking "selfishly" at a time of crisis.

One additional difficulty when divorce occurs during adolescence is that some parents use their younger teens as confidants, explaining their deepest problems, feelings, and even dating and sexual activities with their adolescents. This behavior makes inappropriate emotional demands on younger teens (Hetherington et al., 1991).

Preventing the Problems Blaming the problems that children and adolescents sometimes show totally on the divorce itself may be unfair. Research evidence clearly shows that family turmoil, whether or not it ends in divorce, creates difficulties for children and adolescents (Emery, 1982; Nelson et al., 1993). Family conflict has a negative impact on children's and adolescents' self-esteem, educational attainment, relationship with their parents, later marriage experience, and psychological adjustment (Ensign et al., 1998). Troubled behavior described by parents and teachers is often incorrectly considered the consequence of divorce. The problems often are actually caused by family turmoil and were present long before the divorce occurred (Block, Block, & Gjerde, 1986; Katz & Gottman, 1998).

Many research studies that compare children who have experienced the divorce of their parents with children from intact families have not controlled for family turmoil, a serious difficulty that makes interpretation of such research more complicated. This does not mean that the divorce process causes no difficulties; it is indeed stressful and leads to increased family disruption and problems (Forehand, Armistead, & David, 1997).

Some children and adolescents are more adversely affected by the family turmoil and divorce than others. Because some children recover faster than others, psychologists have searched for and found a number of factors that reduce the long-term impact of divorce (see Figure 5.6).

One factor is the nature of the postdivorce situation. In fact, postdivorce stressors have a greater influence on children's and adolescents' mental health than does the divorce itself (Sandler, Tein, & West, 1994). Postdivorce adjustment is much better if parents can cooperate after divorcing (Bronstein et al., 1994). If parents continue to quarrel after the divorce, the children will suffer (Berger,

Parents

- Cooperate after the divorce.
- Don't use the children as pawns.
- Support each others' parenting efforts when possible.
- Both parents maintain a good relationship with their children.

Other family and friends

- Provide social support.
- Provide opportunities for communication.

Other

- Their standard of living is not reduced too much.
- A new, stable family routine is created.

Figure 5.6
Recovering from Divorce
There is much parents, family, and friends can do to help children and adolescents recover from their parents' divorce.

1995). Children and adolescents have a much more difficult time coping with stress when there is a great deal of conflict between parents after the divorce (Portes, Haas, & Brown, 1991). Unfortunately, according to one study, about 50 percent of all parents continue to argue after the divorce (Stark, 1986).

Children and adolescents of all ages do better when their parents maintain a warm relationship with them (Dunlop & Burns, 2001; Richardson & McCabe, 2001). When adolescents were divided into three groups—divorced/good relationships with parents, divorced/poor relationships with parents, and intact/good relationships with parents—adolescents from families with divorced parents but with a good relationship with at least one parent showed no more cognitive or behavioral problems than those in the intact/good relationships group. These good relationships buffered the adolescent against the problems of divorce (Wierson et al., 1989). The relationship with the noncustodial parent is important as well. Children who report more positive and warm social interactions with noncustodial fathers obtain higher scores on achievement tests in school (Coley, 1998). The outcome is better if the noncustodial parent takes a positive interest in the child than if that parent is disengaged (Barber, 1994b). Unfortunately, evidence shows that contact declines and adolescents have less positive relationships with noncustodial fathers.

Adjustment problems are also less severe if there social supports are available (Sammons & Lewis, 2001; Silitsky, 1996). It is important for the adolescent to have a family member to talk with. Unfortunately, many of the significant adults in the adolescents' life are affected by the divorce. It may not be as easy for a grandparent, uncle, or aunt to visit the child if the custodial parent does not wish the contact to continue. Family friends and family members may take sides or be forced to take sides. Social supports may be weakened at a time when they are more important than ever (Weinraub & Gringlas, 1995).

Children and adolescents also do better and recover more quickly if the divorce does not significantly reduce their standard of living. If financial resources become strained, which is very common, the resultant parental stress can lead to less adequate parenting and bitterness and anger in adolescents. For example, custodial parents may be forced to increase hours at work to compensate for the financial difficulties, making it more difficult to adequately monitor their adolescents. A structured and satisfying family life can reduce the problems brought on by reduced living standards, however. Children and adolescents need some stability in their lives, and having solid, predictable family routines helps greatly.

Children and adolescents will show fewer adverse effects of a divorce and recover more quickly if their parents can be civil to each other after the divorce, support each other's parenting efforts, and don't use the children as pawns. Additional positive factors are a minimization of financial problems and the establishment of family routines.

Single-Parent Families

Many children and adolescents spend time in a single-parent family. When the parents are divorced or the child's mother and father did not marry, the extent of the contact with the noncustodial parent can vary greatly. Some noncustodial parents rarely or never see their children; others see them often. Sometimes other adults fill the void. African American children and adolescents, who are statistically more likely to reside with a single parent than are white children, often have grandparents or other extended family members who provide emotional support (USDHHS, 1996). They may have less access to biological fathers but more contact with other adults.

Many single parents report problems that may affect their children and adolescents. Single parents claim that financial difficulty is their number one postdivorce problem (Amato & Partridge, 1987). About half of all single-parent families live in poverty, whereas 1 in 10 two-parent families does (McLanahan & Booth,

1991). Even if the mother and children in a single-parent family do not fall into poverty, their standard of living declines significantly. One reason for low income is lack of child support payments, even from those who can pay (Sorenson, 1997). As mentioned, single mothers often must increase the number of hours they work to improve their financial situation, which makes supervision of their children difficult. Single mothers often emphasize independence rather than extended dependency (McLanahan & Booth, 1989). Children in single-parent families often must grow up faster; they often have more say in family decisions and more freedom (Smetana et al., 1991a). Single parents perceive themselves as able parents, but they report more child-rearing stresses, especially in monitoring and control (Hetherington, 1993).

Despite these problems, the change to a single-parent family sometimes can improve the atmosphere of the home. A home filled with violence will be less violent. A home fraught with emotional conflict will see the conflict reduced. The reduction in tension leads to a better atmosphere and improved functioning (Weiss, 1989). Children do better in a happy one-parent family than in a conflicted two-parent family (Goodman et al., 1998).

Stepfamilies

Life in a single-parent household is often a temporary condition, as about two-thirds of divorced women and three-quarters of divorced men eventually remarry. Children in a stepfamily face many transitions in family structure. Many have experienced a change from an intact family to a conflicted family to a single-parent family to a stepfamily (Spruijt & de Goede, 1997). These children must adjust to a new set of rules, and the stepparent and biological parent must learn to share the children with the other biological parent, who lives elsewhere. In addition, stepparents may have their own children, so children may need to learn to live with stepbrothers and stepsisters. On the positive side, the remarried mother often experiences a financial improvement and gains additional emotional support (Hetherington & Stanley-Hagan, 1995).

In the period following a remarriage, children must accept the remarriage and resign themselves to the fact that their biological parents will not be getting back together again. Children may resent a new stepparent's attempts to discipline them and feel that the entrance of the new parent threatens the relationship they have with their biological parents (Hetherington, Hagan, & Anderson, 1989). Stepparent-child relationships are somewhat more detached and conflicted, as well as less warm, than relationships of children with their biological parents (Bray & Berger, 1993). Stepparents encounter problems with legitimacy in controlling children's behavior (Ihinger-Tallman & Pasley, 1987). They often make some initial attempts to control, but when these attempts fail, they withdraw and become more disengaged and less involved (Hetherington, Cox, & Cox, 1982; Thomson et al., 1992).

Individual differences in adjustment to the remarriage of a custodial parent are marked (Crosbie-Burnett & Giles-Sims, 1994). Some children adjust well; others have more problems. Most younger children eventually form a reasonably good relationship with a competent stepparent, but adolescents may have more difficulty. Younger children become attached to, and benefit from, stepparents more easily than adolescents, who may actively challenge the new family (Hetherington et al., 1989). Children entering adolescence at the time of the remarriage have a particularly difficult time with this transition (Hetherington et al., 1991). Early adolescents in remarried families often report increased levels of problem behaviors, including

Stepfamily relationships present many challenges.

aggression and noncompliance, as well as increasing amounts of anxiety, withdrawal, and depression (Hetherington & Clingempeel, 1992). Remarried families with adolescents are more likely to be conflicted, and disengagement between stepfather and stepchildren is common (Hetherington et al., 1991). Despite these problems, only about one in five children has a bad relationship with a stepparent (Elias, 1997a).

Daughters seem to have more difficulty than sons in adjusting to the remarriage of their custodial mothers (Hetherington, Arnett, & Hollier, 1988; Hetherington & Stanley-Hagan, 1995). Girls have more success adopting to a stepmother family than a stepfather family (Clingempeel & Segal, 1986). The longer girls live in the stepmother household, the fewer adjustment problems they have and the more positively they view it. In stepfather situations, increases in conflict are not unusual. In fact, over time preadolescent boys in families with stepfathers are more likely than girls to show improvements in their adjustment. Perhaps girls develop a very strong relationship with their mothers during the time their mothers are unmarried and see the entrance of the new male stepparent as a threat to this relationship. Perhaps the presence of a male increases the tension in the family more for a daughter than for a son.

Controversy surrounds just how well children in stepfamilies do, and the research results are mixed. Some evidence does not indicate a "marital benefit" for children, despite the improved financial position. These studies find that children in stepfamilies have about the same number of adjustment problems as children in single-parent families and more adjustment problems than children in intact families, although the differences are modest (Demo & Acock, 1996; Hanson, McClanahan & Thomson, 1996). Studies comparing adolescents in stepfamilies with those in intact families often show lower educational attainment (Astone & McLanahan, 1991; Hetherington, 1993). Studies also often, but not always, show lower general well-being of adolescents in stepfamilies (Dronkers, 1993; Furstenberg, 1987; Hetherington, 1993). Other research paints a more positive picture. A number of studies comparing children in stepfamilies with those in nuclear families find little or no difference in adjustment or cognitive functioning (Clingempeel & Segal, 1986). In some cases, the presence of a stepfather reduces some of the negative effects of divorce for boys, and males score higher both on measures of cognitive development and on measures of adjustment (Hetherington, 1993; Oshman & Manosevitz, 1976).

Two factors may explain these findings. The first factor is the degree of conflict in the stepfamily. Problems are greatest where the biological parent and stepparent disagree on a number of matters. When they agree, the outcomes are better (Spruijt & de Goede, 1997). Second, parenting skills and style also explain differences in outcomes. Most, but not all, studies find that stepparents are less active both in the control and support dimensions than parents in nuclear families (Astone & McLanahan, 1991). Many stepparents use a disengaged style, characterized by low support and monitoring, sometimes combined with significant criticism and negativity (Crosbie-Burnett & Giles-Sims, 1994; Hetherington & Clingempeel, 1992). Perhaps they use this style because some stepchildren, especially adolescents, do not accept them as parental figures and may show hostility toward their stepparents. Stepfathers of early adolescents often become less involved and feel more alienated with time (Hetherington & Clingempeel, 1992).

Research studies find that two types of parenting relate to positive outcomes in stepfamilies. Consistent with the research on intact families, the best-adjusted adolescents in stepfamilies have parents who use the authoritative style of parenting (Fine & Kurdek, 1992; Golish, 2000). Studies also find positive outcomes when biological mothers are the primary disciplinarians and stepfathers either are minimally involved in discipline or support the mother's initiatives (Bray, 1988; Crosbie-Burnett & Giles-Sims, 1994). Warmth and responsiveness are most important for adolescents. Unfortunately, the disengaged style so commonly found yields the lowest levels of adjustment, along with high rates of withdrawal, unhappiness, and resentment.

When stepparents use the authoritarian parenting style, their stepchildren show more adjustment problems, mainly because adolescents resent the heavy-handed use of discipline without warmth and support. The support dimension seems to be more important than the control dimension for stepparents (Bray, 1988). Stepparents are better off if they initially leave the discipline to the biological parent, or simply support the discipline used by the biological parent, while striving to build a positive relationship with their stepchildren (Visher & Visher, 1990).

The stepfamily situation is complicated. Although stepfamilies face many adjustments, research shows that living in a stepfamily can be a positive, negative, or neutral experience, depending on the quality of the relationship between parents and children.

AT A GLANCE 5.5 THE CHANGING AMERICAN FAMILY

KEY POINT: The American family is changing as single-child families, maternal employment, divorce, single-parent families, and stepfamilies become more common.

SUPPORTING POINTS	EXPLANATION
The structure of the American family has changed.	More American children and adolescents have experienced the divorce of their parents and live in single-parent families and stepfamilies than in the past. Most mothers are employed, and more children and adolescents are growing up as "only children."
More families are having one child.	Only children do better in school and show no greater rates of maladjustment.
Most mothers are employed before their children are teenagers.	Daughters of mothers who are employed have less traditional gender expectations. Adolescents whose mothers are employed do as well as those whose mothers are not employed. Employed mothers are more likely to encourage early independence. Recent studies find no significant differences in adolescent behavior due to maternal employment status.
Divorce affects both children and adolescents.	Early reactions to the divorce of parents are usually negative, including withdrawal, acting out, anxiety, or depression. Custodial parents become stricter, and noncustodial parents become more permissive but less available.
Compared with younger children, adolescents show both similarities and differences in how they experience divorce.	Compared with younger children, adolescents can better understand the reasons for the divorce of their parents. They are less likely to blame themselves and more able to discuss their experience. However, they are just as likely as younger children to show immediate emotional and behavioral reactions. Adolescents are more concerned about relationship issues and having the family resources available to support their future plans.
The long-term effects of divorce depend on many factors.	Some children and adolescents show improvements a year or so after a divorce, whereas some do not. Those who improve have received social support, have divorced parents who can act civilly to each other, and have not been as adversely affected economically.
Adolescents living in single-parent families face additional challenges.	The most common problem for single-parent families is finances. Also, single-parent families do not monitor their adolescents as well.
Building a relationship and giving support are most important for stepparents.	Many stepparents are either minimally involved or try to use an authoritarian style; neither works well. Supporting the biological parent's discipline practices and building a solid relationship with the stepchildren are important things stepparents can do to help their stepchildren develop.
How a family functions is more important than its structure.	Research finds much variability in the parenting of single parents and stepparents, and generalizations may be unfair.

How Families Work Is More Important Than How They Are Structured

It is tempting to use family structure, such as intact, single parent, or stepfamily, as a variable determining outcome. There is no doubt that single-parent families and stepfamilies face unique challenges. Single parents often must do everything by themselves and may not have the support of the other parent. Yet many single parents claim that the lack of strife since the divorce and the improvement in the home atmosphere make it all worthwhile. Stepfamilies involve a complex web of relationships and require many adjustments, and as shown, the research is contradictory and filled with controversy.

Some authorities emphasize the difficulty that parents in single-parent and stepparent families have in control and supervision (Dornbusch et al., 1987). These authorities reason that single parents have less time and energy to monitor their children and that stepparents find discipline, control, and monitoring difficult because of their position in the family. Some research studies do conclude that single parents are less likely to monitor the behavior of their adolescents (Astone & McLanahan, 1991; Matsueda & Heimer, 1987) and are more permissive (Acock & Demo, 1994). Yet the differences are often small, and these findings do not apply to some aspects of control (Bulcroft, Carmody, & Bulcroft, 1998). For example, single-parent families often place earlier curfews on their adolescents because the parent perceives a higher level of vulnerability. The research on stepparents is more diverse, and some shows that stepparents do not differ in control significantly from parents in intact families (Acock & Demo, 1994: Kurdek & Fine, 1993). Again, variability is the rule. Stepparents are somewhat more ready to leave their children alone, but no differences are found in household rules or curfews.

It is probably unfair to make generalizations concerning how children in stepfamilies or single-parent families fare. Some single-parent families and stepfamilies function well; others do not. The same could be said about intact families. Although single-parent families and stepfamilies offer unique challenges, what goes on within the family is much more important than the structure of the family itself (Demo, 1997; Spruijt & de Goede, 1997). *(For a review of this section, see At A Glance 5.5.)*

PLACING FAMILY RELATIONSHIPS IN PERSPECTIVE

Our examination of the adolescent-parent relationship ends on a positive note. Although conflict certainly occurs, the relationship between adolescents and their parents is essentially positive. The adolescent's striving for independence occurs in the context of remaining connected with the family. This is good news for parents, who were once told incorrectly that adolescents considered them essentially obstacles to the satisfaction of their need for autonomy. Rather, research today finds that adolescents see their parents as partners who emotionally support their teenage children while gradually allowing them greater freedom. Although the movie industry might portray it differently, good adolescent-parent communication and a feeling of connectedness with parents are no longer considered unusual. Although disagreements will occur and the very nature of the adolescent-parent relationship will change, the emotional bonds that unite the generations will remain strong.

The research on parenting styles and communication shows that parents and adolescents have many choices to make. They must find ways to communicate effectively and compromise, try to understand each other's positions, and be flexible and open to new ideas. Research also shows that the structure of the family, whether it be an intact family, a single-parent family, or a stepfamily, is

Please place the number best reflecting your opinion next to each of the following statements. Then compare your opinions now with those you held before reading the chapter.

1 — Strongly Agree
2 — Moderately Agree
3 — No Opinion
4 — Moderately Disagree
5 — Strongly Disagree

_____ 1. Adolescent-parent conflict is necessary if teenagers are to attain the increased independence and autonomy they desire.

_____ 2. Parents faced with an increasing desire for independence from their adolescent children relax their monitoring too quickly, allowing the teenagers too much freedom too soon.

_____ 3. Mothers and fathers should strive to be friends with their adolescent children.

_____ 4. By age 20 or so, the relationship between parents and their children should be on a completely equal basis.

_____ 5. Parents should unconditionally accept their adolescent children's viewpoints without criticizing these opinions.

_____ 6. Most conflict is caused by parents' unwillingness to accept the fact that their adolescent children are older, are more mature, and need their independence.

_____ 7. Parents should strive to treat all their children in the same manner.

_____ 8. As long as the parents' marital relationship is not abusive, it is better for children if their parents stay together, even if they are not happy, than if they divorce,.

_____ 9. All other factors being equal, children and adolescents are better off in a stepfamily than in a single-parent household.

_____ 10. Stepparents should have the same parental rights as biological parents.

not as important as what goes on within the home. Parents and adolescents share responsibility for determining how the family functions. Although alternative family structures certainly offer unique challenges, adolescents and parents still actively make decisions that can make the home pleasant or fill it with conflict and tension. Above everything else, current research offers a more realistic and hopeful view than the contradictory and negative one that it replaces.

THEMES

THEME 1 **Adolescence is a time of choices, "firsts," and transitions.**	• The striving toward emotional and behavioral autonomy requires new ways of dealing with family members. • Power relationships change in adolescence as adolescents gain power. • Adolescence is a time of changing communication patterns with parents.
THEME 2 **Adolescence is shaped by context.**	• The development of emotional and behavioral autonomy is shaped by many aspects of the family, including parenting style. • Anthropological research shows that adolescence need not be a time of storm and stress, as there are cultures in which adolescence is not seen as a time of continuous and intense conflict. • Adolescents from immigrant families often face an adolescence influenced by both the traditional values of their culture and the more liberal, individualistic values of U.S. culture. • The nature of the adolescent's family experiences depends on sibling and extended family relations.
THEME 3 **Adolescence is influenced by group membership.**	• The influence of parenting style on adolescent development depends on the subculture. Some groups show a culturally prescribed stricter form of discipline showing caring combined with a willingness to sacrifice for the child, which may lead to positive outcomes. • Minority group families have lower levels of conflict and disagreement, probably because they stress obedience to parents. • Sons and daughters have different patterns of communication and conflict with their mothers and fathers.
THEME 4 **The adolescent experience has changed over the past 50 years.**	• Adolescents today are more likely to have experienced the divorce of their parents. • Adolescents today are more likely to have spent some part of their childhood or adolescence in a single-parent family. • Adolescents today are more likely to have stepparents and stepsiblings. • Adolescents today are more likely to have both parents employed.
THEME 5 **Today's views of adolescence are becoming more balanced, with greater attention to its positive nature.**	• Whereas earlier theoretical approaches emphasized intense conflict with the family as being necessary for adolescents to gain autonomy, modern approaches argue that gaining autonomy requires a gradual renegotiation of the relationship while remaining connected to the family. • Rather than see communication as poor in adolescence, newer research demonstrates that family members often rate communication as good. • Rather than see the only-child family as essentially dysfunctional, modern studies find definite advantages to being an only child. • Whereas single-parent families or stepfamilies were once viewed as inherently flawed, modern research emphasizes that it is how a family functions rather than its structure that is most important.

CHAPTER SUMMARY AT A GLANCE

KEY TOPICS	KEY POINTS	
The Adolescent-Parent Relationship	The nature of the parent-child relationship changes during adolescence. *(At A Glance 5.1, p. 144)*	← **KEY TERMS** *attachment (p. 140)*
Parenting Styles	The style of parenting used in adolescence affects adolescents. *(At A Glance 5.2, p. 148)*	← *responsiveness (p. 145)* *demandingness (p. 145)* *authoritarian parenting (p. 145)* *permissive (indulgent) parenting (p. 145)* *rejecting/neglecting parenting (p. 146)* *authoritative parenting (p. 146)*
Communication and Conflict	Communication and the ability to handle conflict effectively are related to better family relationships. *(At A Glance 5.3, p. 159)*	← *generation gap (p. 151)*
Other Family Relationships	Extended family relationships influence adolescent development. *(At A Glance 5.4, p. 164)*	
The Changing American Family	The American family is changing as single-child families, maternal employment, divorce, single-parent families, and stepfamilies become more common. *(At A Glance 5.5, p. 174)*	

Review questions for this chapter appear in the appendix.

6

PEERS

WHAT IS YOUR OPINION?

THE PEER GROUP
- Changes in Interpersonal Relationships
- The Functions of the Peer Group
- Conceptualizing Peer Relationships

FRIENDS
- The Many Benefits of Friendship
- Conceptions of Friendship
- Forming Friendships
- Friendship and Gender
- Communication and Conflict

CLIQUES AND CROWDS
- Cliques
- Crowds

POPULARITY AND UNPOPULARITY
- Who Are the Popular Teens?
  Perspective 1: Is He Really My Friend?
- Who Are the Unpopular Teens?
- Bullying
- Enhancing Social Skills

ROMANTIC RELATIONSHIPS
- Dating
  Perspective 2: Do They Have to Know Everything?
- Conflict in Romantic Relationships
  Perspective 3: I Can't Leave Him
  FOCUS: Partner Violence

BEHAVIORAL AUTONOMY AND CONFORMITY
- The Dynamics of Peer Pressure
- The Extent of Peer Pressure
- Conformity to Peers: The Parental Dimension

PLACING PEERS IN PERSPECTIVE
HAS YOUR OPINION CHANGED?
THEMES
CHAPTER SUMMARY AT A GLANCE

Everyone agrees that the influence of the peer group increases dramatically in adolescence, and many people see this increase as adversely affecting the teenager. They view the peer group as leading the adolescent into rebellion, risk taking, and poor study habits, and they blame the group for many of the behaviors that both parents and the general public find objectionable. The peer group is an easy target for critics who would prefer to categorize adolescents as those who blindly follow peer initiatives instead of people with minds of their own who make their own decisions. Parents might find it easier to blame the peer group for their teen's alcohol abuse or poor grades in school than to look elsewhere. The peer group has gained a bad reputation (Brown, 1990; Urberg, 1999).

Yet there is another view. The peer group serves as a sounding board. It helps teens in their transition from almost total dependence on parents to an adult independence of thought and action. It serves as a training ground for adult interpersonal relationships, including intimate relations. The peer group is not a single entity that presents the adolescent with a uniform set of expectations. Instead, multiple peer influences operate, helping adolescents prepare for the more complex world of adulthood, with its numerous and conflicting influences (Berndt, 1996). Rather than preventing adolescents from reaching their potential, the peer group often encourages adolescents to develop their abilities. This more positive view minimizes the negative impact of the peer group, emphasizing its positive value.

This chapter examines the research on the peer group as we seek to understand the influence of the peer group on adolescents. The chapter begins with a discussion of the changes in the nature and functions of the peer group in adolescence. It then looks at friendship in adolescence, investigating why adolescents are friends with some of their peers but not others; it also looks at various aspects of friendship, including communication and conflict. The chapter then looks at adolescent cliques and crowds and why some adolescents are popular while others are not. It explores the adolescent's new world of romantic relationships and dating. The chapter's investigation of the major areas of interpersonal functioning will allow us to appreciate the true influence of the peer group on adolescents through a discussion of behavioral autonomy and conformity.

THE PEER GROUP

Relationships with age mates do not suddenly appear during puberty. Younger children have friends and acquaintances and play in small groups. However, the nature of interpersonal relationships changes significantly during adolescence.

Changes in Interpersonal Relationships

Adolescents' interpersonal relationships differ in at least five ways from what they were during the elementary school years. First, adolescents have an increased desire to spend time with their peers, develop peer relationships, and engage in peer-oriented activities. Peer relationships become more important during adolescence (Bush, Weinfurt, & Iannotti, 1994). The amount of time adolescents spend with the family group declines (see Figure 6.1). Time spent with people outside the family increases dramatically (Csikszentmihalyi & Larson,

WHAT IS YOUR OPINION?

Please place the number best reflecting your opinion next to each of the following statements. We will return to this questionnaire at the end of the chapter so you can determine if your opinions have changed.

1 — Strongly Agree
2 — Moderately Agree
3 — No Opinion
4 — Moderately Disagree
5 — Strongly Disagree

_____ 1. Teenagers can become too dependent on their friends.

_____ 2. Teenagers basically conform to their peer group, doing whatever the group dictates.

_____ 3. Teenage girls are more ready for emotionally intimate relationships than teenage boys of the same age.

_____ 4. Cliques are harmful because they exclude some teens and thus lead to divisions within the school.

_____ 5. You can tell a great deal about a teen if you know the crowd (for example, "preppies" or "nerds") to which the teen belongs.

_____ 6. Parents have the right and responsibility to try to influence the nature of their adolescent child's dating relationships.

_____ 7. A man or a woman who is slapped by a dating partner should never see that individual again.

_____ 8. Early dating is harmful for teens.

_____ 9. Peer pressure to conform is a definite threat to the mental and physical health of adolescents.

_____ 10. Teen culture is essentially anti-establishment and antiparent.

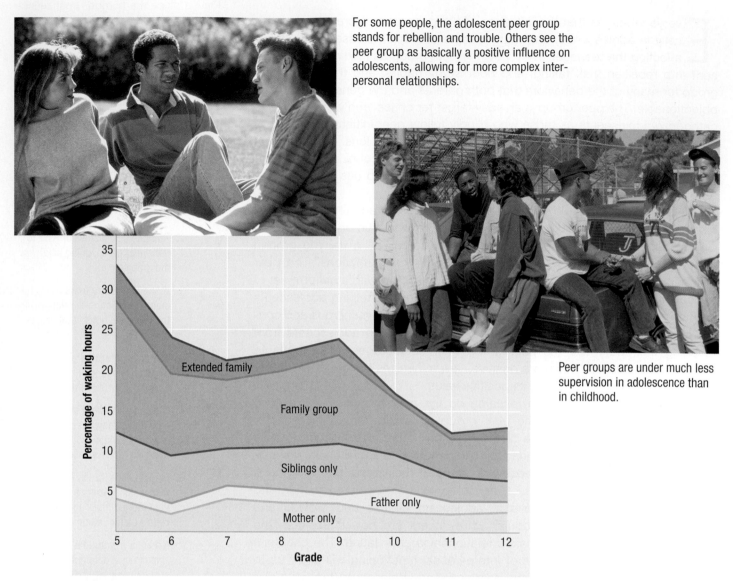

For some people, the adolescent peer group stands for rebellion and trouble. Others see the peer group as basically a positive influence on adolescents, allowing for more complex interpersonal relationships.

Peer groups are under much less supervision in adolescence than in childhood.

Figure 6.1
Age Differences in Amount of Time Adolescents Spend with Family Members
The percentage of time spent with family declines during the early adolescent years.
Source: Larson et al. (1996).

1984). Even if the time spent with peers in classrooms is not counted, high school students spend much more time with peers than younger children or older adults do (Csikszentmihalyi & Larson, 1984; Larson et al., 1996). This change occurs relatively early in adolescence, and American teens spend more time with their friends than do teens in other cultures, such as Japan (Savin-Williams & Berndt, 1990).

Second, adolescent peer groups and friendships are more autonomous and are under less adult supervision. Many of these groups and dyads (two-person relationships) function without much interference from parents or teachers. Compare this with groups of young children who are constantly kept under the watchful eye of an adult and must stay closer to home. Many peer groups cut across neighborhoods (Brown, 1990). The telephone and email provide privacy for teens as well, and teens expect, and are given, more privacy than younger children.

Third, adolescents no longer define their peer relations solely in terms of friendships but rather by their membership in groups. Adolescents frequently interact in cliques or crowds. They often come together as groups to walk to school, talk, and generally interact with one another. Adolescents have a larger web of peer relationships than they did as younger children (Collins & Repinski, 1994).

A fourth change in adolescent interpersonal relationships is the growth of relationships with teens of the other gender. Although most interactions among peers are clearly with adolescents of the same gender, an increase in the amount of time spent with members of the other gender is obvious. Many young elementary school students, especially males, go through a period in which segregation is common. In early adolescence (if not before, for some), mixed groups begin to appear. Other-gender friendships begin to develop (Blyth & Foster-Clark, 1987; Buhrmester & Furman, 1987). These friendships continue to expand throughout the adolescent years. High school freshmen spend 44 percent of their time in same-gender peer groups and 4 percent in interactions with adolescents of the other gender, whereas high school seniors spend 21 percent of their time interacting in same-gender groups and 24 percent of their time interacting with the other gender (Csikszentmihalyi & Larson, 1984).

Fifth, along with these cross-gender friendships come romantic relationships. These relationships are qualitatively different from friendships and play an important part in adolescence. One of the most significant developmental changes in adolescence is the emergence of new patterns of social interactions, including dating (Sanderson & Cantor, 1995).

These five changes transform the relatively simple childhood peer group structure and interactions into a more complicated peer group structure in which same-gender and other-gender adolescents interact in more complex ways.

The Functions of the Peer Group

The peer group fulfills many valuable functions. Peers help support adolescents at a time when they are challenged with many new experiences and are striving for independence (Youniss & Smollar, 1985). Because their peers are negotiating the same pressures and stresses, adolescents feel they understand what they are experiencing. Supportive friendships also enhance adolescents' self-esteem and help them cope with stress (Hartup, 1993). Adolescents often turn to their friends for advice and comfort (Fuligni & Eccles, 1993). By early adolescence, teens perceive their same-sex friends as major sources of emotional support, and by midadolescence, they are turning to friends quite frequently for emotional support (Furman & Buhrmester, 1985). Romantic partners also provide some emotional support, as does a clique (Hansell, 1985).

Peers also help adolescents develop their identity and move away from parents (Coleman, 1961). As adolescents do so, they end their total dependence on parents, and the peer group encourages the development of emotional autonomy. Psychoanalytic scholars argue that pubertal changes cause increased conflict and distancing from parents, which in turn cause teens to look elsewhere to have their needs fulfilled (Blos, 1979; Freud, 1923/1961). As adolescents separate from their parents, they naturally turn to friends and peers (Blos, 1979). As discussed in "Families," recent research shows that the change in adolescent-parent relationships can best be understood in terms of a transformation, with both parents and peers serving important functions in the areas of trust, intimacy, and communication (Collins, 1990; Grotevant & Cooper, 1985). During this transformation the adolescent remains connected with parents and family while at the same time expanding friendship networks and using friends as confidants (Feiring & Lewis, 1993).

Peers also enable a teen to develop a deeper form of intimacy that will be needed in adulthood. The influential psychologist Harry Stack Sullivan (1953) viewed close same-sex friendships as setting the stage for intimacy in heterosexual relationships later in adolescence. Intimate conversations with close friends increase adolescents' sense of worth and improve their understanding of others. Intimate friendships are critical for the development of high self-esteem and the ability to understand others. Whereas Sullivan proposed that the increase in inti-

Psychologist Harry Stack Sullivan viewed same gender friendships as setting the stage for the intimate relationships that are found later in adolescence and in adulthood.

macy begins to occur between the ages of 8 and 10 years, most psychologists believe that intimacy first becomes truly important during the early adolescent years (Buhrmester & Furman, 1987).

The peer group also helps adolescents improve their social skills. As teens interact with close friends, new situations arise and require compromise and understanding. Adolescents develop the ability to communicate more effectively, to understand others' points of view, and to learn how their verbal statements affect others. This improved communication leads to more accurate self-evaluation through comparisons with others (Rubin, 1980). Jean Piaget argued that interactions with peers were critical to the development of a mature sense of right and wrong and more effective relations with others. Peers also serve a corrective function by providing feedback and practice in considering others' perspectives.

Popular stereotypes may see peer relations as essentially dangerous, but most studies find that it is the absence of peer involvement that may place an individual at greater risk for maladjustment and that should concern parents and teachers (Durkin, 1995). Adolescents who have close relationships with peers experience less anxiety and depression (Buhrmester, 1992). In fact, the best early predictor of adult adjustment is not intelligence scores, school grades, or even behavior in the classroom but the ability of children and adolescents to get along with their peers (Parker & Asher, 1987). Adolescents who are generally disliked, aggressive, and disruptive and who cannot establish a place for themselves in the peer culture are developmentally at risk. Having friends and peer acceptance are related to school competence, higher self-esteem, and better adjustment (Hartup, 1983; Vernberg, 1990).

Conceptualizing Peer Relationships

Peer relationships operate on many levels, and a study of three main levels is useful. First, *dyads* are close friends and romantic partners. Second, *cliques* are groups of individuals who interact frequently on a face-to-face basis. The third level is *crowds*, large groups of people more loosely bound together by similar interests or status (Brown, 1989, 1990). Most adolescents—90 percent, in one

AT A GLANCE 6.1 THE PEER GROUP

KEY POINT: The nature of peer relationships changes in adolescence.

SUPPORTING POINTS	EXPLANATION
The nature of the peer group changes in five distinct ways during the adolescent years.	Adolescents spend more time with their peers than they did earlier in childhood. Peer groups are under less adult supervision. Adolescents develop relationships within cliques and crowds. Relations with adolescents of the other gender increase. Romantic relationships begin.
The adolescent peer group has many functions.	The peer group supports the adolescents' drive for independence. It enhances self-esteem and gives emotional support. The peer group helps adolescents form an identity. It fosters the process of gaining emotional autonomy from parents and achieving more intimate relationships. The peer group also helps adolescents develop social skills.
The peer group operates on many levels.	Adolescents form deep friendships with other adolescents. They also belong to cliques (small groups) and to crowds (larger groups).

study—see themselves as belonging to cliques or crowds, which are not under adult direction (Palmonari, Pobeni, & Kirchler, 1989). *(For a review of this section, see At A Glance 6.1.)*

FRIENDS

A peer and a friend are not the same. The term **peer** indicates anyone of similar status, whereas **friendship** connotes a positive, reciprocal relationship. Adolescents attending a particular high school have many peers, but they may or may not have many friends. Adolescents report that spending time with their friends is their most enjoyable activity. Friends talk to each other regularly and consult on both daily issues and personal problems (Savin-Williams & Berndt, 1990). Adolescents invest a good deal of energy in their friendships (Berndt & Perry, 1990).

The Many Benefits of Friendship

Having good friends has many psychological benefits. Teens with friends are more socially competent, cooperative, altruistic, and self-confident (Hartup, 1993). Having friends can reduce the tension and difficulties involved in changing from a smaller to a larger school, for example, from elementary school to middle school and then from middle school to high school (Simmons, Burgeson, & Reef, 1988) (see "The School Experience"). Having stable peer relationships promotes positive mental health and adjustment (Epstein, 1983b). Adolescents who have satisfying and harmonious friendships report positive self-esteem and relatively little loneliness (Barrera, Chassin, & Rogosch, 1993). These advantages are found across racial and ethnic groups (Chassin et al., 1986). Adolescents with close friendships also seem to develop a positive view of classmates in general and assume that they are viewed positively. Success in the peer arena is linked to better interpersonal relationships in adulthood, as well as psychological health (Giordano et al., 1998). Unpopular adolescents often find that having just one good friend may be a sufficient buffer from the isolation and low self-esteem that may result from unpopularity (Bishop & Inbertditzen, 1995).

Not all friendships, though, are of the same quality. More supportive friendships are likely to yield greater psychological benefits. Believing that one's

Friends often support one another in times of trouble.

peer   Anyone of similar status.
friendship   A positive, reciprocal relationship between two people.

friends are not supportive is related to depression, low self-esteem, and school-related problems, especially for girls (Kurdek & Sinclair, 1988). Adolescents who perceive their friendships as more supportive are more popular, socially competent, more strongly motivated to achieve, and more involved in school, and they exhibit fewer behavioral problems (Hartup, 1993).

Friends provide many types of support. They provide information, advice, and guidance on personal problems. Friends also help with homework or lend money when necessary. They often bolster each other's self-esteem, share their joys and successes, and support each other during troubled times (Furman & Buhrmester, 1992). Supportive friendships enhance feelings of well-being and belonging (Berndt & Savin-Williams, 1993).

One problem with many of the studies linking friendship with positive qualities and outcomes is that they are based on correlations. Friendships may indeed help teens develop positive qualities, but perhaps teens who have many positive qualities also find it easier to make and keep friends. For example, adolescents with low self-esteem who are lonely, anxious, and depressed may not be great companions and thus may have more difficulty making friends (DuBois et al., 1992).

Conceptions of Friendship

The conception of friendship changes as children mature. Preschoolers consider a friend anyone with whom they are playing at the time; to be a friend means to be able to play. These friendships are relatively unstable. Children in elementary school judge friendship in terms of particular psychological traits, such as honesty, caring, and sharing, which provide the basis for behaving in a particular way. Reciprocity, equality, and cooperation are all important (Parker & Gottman, 1989). Adolescents agree with elementary school children that friendship involves mutual liking, frequent positive interactions, and helping (Berndt, 1987), but they add a number of elements to their definition.

When children of various ages are asked to describe friendships, the terms *intimacy, trust,* and *commitment* are found more often among early adolescents than among younger children (Newcomb & Bagwell, 1996). For example, one young teenager being interviewed stated, "I can tell Karen [her friend] things and she helps me talk. If we have problems in school, we work them out together. And she doesn't laugh at me if I do something weird—she accepts me for who I am" (Berndt, Hawkins, & Hoyle, 1986). It is difficult to believe that a younger child would utter this statement.

When early adolescents are asked how they know someone is their friend, they often say that a friend shares problems with them, understands them, and will listen when they talk about things (Berndt & Perry, 1990). Younger children do not describe their friendships in terms of intimate self-disclosure or mutual understanding. Early adolescents also regard loyalty and faithfulness as important, and they talk about these ideas frequently (Berndt & Perry, 1990). They come to define friends as individuals with close mutual relationships, who help each other with emotional and personal difficulties and who are open and sensitive to each other's needs (Eisenberg & Harris, 1984).

Comments about shared feelings, self-disclosure, and intimacy in friendships appear during the transition to adolescence and thereafter increase steadily for both boys and girls (Furman & Buhrmester, 1992; Shulman et al., 1997). When adolescents are asked to describe relationships with their best friends, statements about self-disclosure and intimacy increase between the ages of 11 and 17 (Sharabany, Gershoni, & Hofman, 1981).

Commitment is another aspect of friendship often mentioned by teens but rarely by younger children. A friend is a person who sticks by you when you are in trouble and who doesn't drop you as soon as something goes wrong (Goodnow & Burns, 1988). Adolescents emphasize mutual trust, loyalty, and exclusivity as central to friendships (Youniss & Smollar, 1985). Friends know one another's feelings and preferences, and they support each other emotionally and materially. They discuss secret things with each other, exchange ideas, and share confidences in a secure environment (Shulman et al., 1997).

Adolescents' intimate relationships with friends change as they continue through adolescence. The earliest intimate relationships involve shared experiences and communication, but the adolescents show an inability to accommodate individual differences (Selman, 1989). One partner imposes his or her will on the other and controls the friend. A greater degree of equality exists in middle adolescence, but commitment issues remain difficult. Gradually, a type of intimacy emerges in which individual differences are not only tolerated but also encouraged and appreciated along with commitment. Respect for friends increases as adolescents mature, as does a desire to balance individuality and relatedness. Control and conformity in friendship decline. Older adolescents insist on individuality within their intimate relationships, whereas younger adolescents emphasize conformity and sharing ideas (Shulman et al., 1997). The ability to balance closeness and individuality heralds a mature form of friendship intimacy that does not emerge until later adolescence (Selman, 1989).

Friendship intimacy has benefits, but the importance of intimacy can be overstated. For example, no correlation exists between early levels of intimacy and mental health measured in adulthood. Nor does lack of intimacy in friendship relate to later criminal activity or spousal abuse. A positive correlation does exist between intimacy with friends during adolescence and intimacy with friends during adulthood (Giordano et al., 1998). Looking only at intimacy in relationships, then, does not give any information about later prosocial or antisocial values or behaviors.

Forming Friendships

Most adolescents have one or two best friends and several close or good friends (Hartup, 1993). Early adolescents describe four or five people as "best friends," but the number gradually declines during middle and late adolescence (Reisman & Shorr, 1978). With increasing age, adolescents become more selective about whom they name as friends (Urberg et al., 1995). Friendships are more stable in adolescence than in childhood, and stability increases from early to late adolescence (Epstein, 1983a; Hartup, 1993).

Similarity One factor in friendship formation is similarity. Adolescents' friends are often similar in age, race, grade level in school, values toward school, interests, and academic aspirations. This similarity allows for an easier exchange of feelings and ideas (Eshel & Kurman, 1994; Hartup, 1993). For example, serious drama or music students may find they can discuss issues of interest in a more detailed manner with others interested in the same thing. The areas of greatest similarity among friends are school-related attitudes or achievement, as well as behaviors such as smoking, drug use, dating, and religious practice (Hartup, 1993). Personality characteristics are not as similar among friends. Friends do not have to be similar in every area (Hamm, 2000).

Some similarity occurs because of demographic and geographic reasons. Most teens live a relatively segregated life, as neighborhoods often lack a mix of racial or socioeconomic groups. Adolescents are likely to come into contact and start friendships with people they meet more often and those who are available. White students have more African American friends when the percentage of African Americans is higher in

Adolescents with the same interests are often drawn together.

the school (Schofield, 1991), as the chance for contact is greater. Adolescents from higher-level socioeconomic groups have the resources to attend expensive concerts and meet others of their same socioeconomic level.

Selection and Socialization: Choosing Friends   Two other possible explanations for similarity in friendship are selection and socialization (Ryan, 2001; Urberg, 1999). *Selection* involves actively choosing friends. Consider an adolescent in and out of school, surrounded by many adolescents of similar age. The adolescent may actively choose to spend time with some adolescents rather than others by accepting or refusing invitations from other adolescents.

Socialization, in this context, refers to the extent to which adolescents are influenced by their friends to adopt attitudes and behaviors in order to remain in a group or continue a friendship. The group or friend uses reinforcement and punishment, or the threat of punishment, to create group standards and maintain attitudes. For example, an adolescent may complain about school because her friends are doing so and her complaints are reinforced by the group.

Adolescents may select other adolescents who are similar to them. Two adolescents who share the same interest in sports will find they enjoy attending or participating in the same events together. Teenagers are drawn to others who are similar in attitudes and interests. Friends may also reinforce each other for particular behaviors—for example, for drinking or dressing in a particular way, or even for liking a particular recording artist. This reinforcement is a form of socialization.

Psychologists have questioned whether selection or socialization is most important in determining friendship. Do adolescents select friends who are similar to themselves, or do some adolescents reinforce others to dress or act in a particular way? Perhaps both selection and socialization act together.

Psychologists interested in peer influence often face the problem of differentiating between selection and socialization. Do friends influence a teen to change attitudes and behavior, or do teens simply choose friends who feel and act the same way they do? Both psychologists who favor selection influences and those who favor socialization influences can produce evidence for their position. People who drink, smoke, or show high levels of aggression seek each other out, as do people who show high or low levels of school achievement (Cairns et al., 1988). Teenagers who internalize distress—that is, experience a great deal of depression and anxiety—choose friends who show similar levels of internalized distress (Hogue & Steinberg, 1995). Friends also reinforce and shape each others' behavior. Adolescents reinforce their friends in a number of areas, including aggressive behavior, antisocial activities, and educational aspirations. Those who behave in accordance with societal rules often socialize their peers to do the same (Hartup, 1993).

Both selection and socialization forces operate, often together. For example, adolescents who are aggressive form relationships with other aggressive children, and these adolescents then influence each other through modeling and reinforcement. Drug users both select other users as friends and influence each other to continue their use of drugs (Fletcher et al., 1995).

Psychologists debate the relative importance of selectivity and socialization. Some argue that they are equally important. A longitudinal study of stable friendships similar in drug use, political ideology, delinquency, and educational aspirations found that selection and peer influence were equally responsible for the similarity between friends (Kandel, 1978a, 1978b). More recent research, however, suggests that the strength of socialization forces may have been overestimated and the contributions of selection underestimated in accounting for similarity among peers (Aseltine, 1995; Berndt & Keefe, 1995; Urberg, Degirmencioglu, & Pilgrim, 1997). According to this research, similarity among friends in cigarette smoking, alcohol abuse, and substance abuse seems to be due more to selection than to influence (Ennett & Bauman, 1994; Urberg, Degirmencioglu, & Tolson, 1998). Adolescents choose new friends who are similar to their existing friends, and these similarities predate the friendships. This finding does not mean that socialization effects are unimportant, as even a low level of influence across years may have a cumulative impact (Berndt & Keefe, 1995). Socialization forces seem to maintain behaviors and attitudes, making change more difficult.

Friendship and Gender

Friendships between adolescent males more often reflect interests in shared activities, whereas female friendships tend to involve the supportive, emotional, and intimate aspects of relationships (Eshel & Kurman, 1994; Fischer, Sollie, & Morrow, 1986). Boys and girls are both aware that girls' relationships are more intimate than boys' friendships (Bukowski & Kramer, 1986). Girls' assessments of friendships show greater increases in intimacy between early and late adolescence, and boys do not report reaching as high a level of self-disclosure as girls. Both the frequency of intimate conversations and the intensity of intimacy differ (Blyth & Foster-Clark, 1987; Buhrmester & Furman, 1987; Camarena, Sargiani, & Peterson, 1990). Girls show a greater willingness to self-disclose and talk about their problems. Girls value intimacy with friends more than boys do and see it as more important as a basis for friendship. Perhaps one reason for this difference is that beginning very early in life, girls are more overtly socialized to see interpersonal relationships as important. Males express themselves through separateness and autonomy, looking at friendships in terms of shared activities, whereas females perceive relatedness as most important and emphasize emotional closeness and disclosure.

Communication and Conflict

Adolescent communication with friends differs from communication with parents (Hunter, 1985). Communication with friends involves more mutuality, more sharing, and fewer orders. Friendships, unlike parent-child relationships, are voluntary associations based on equality. Much of the communication between younger teens consists of gossip, which increases during middle childhood and remains high throughout adolescence (Gottman & Mettetal, 1986).

Friends realize that conflict will occur but believe that commitment will see the friendship through the hard times. Friends manage conflict effectively, which is necessary if the friendship is to survive. Adolescent friends are more likely to use negotiation rather than power assertion to settle their disputes (Laursen, 1993). This negotiation may occur because friendships are based on equality, although true equality is not seen until middle adolescence (Hartup, 1993). Children and younger adolescents perceive that they have to yield to their friends more than older adolescents do.

Conflicts between friends in adolescence are based on violations of rules that underlie relationships, such as untrustworthy acts, lack of sufficient attention, disrespectful acts, unacceptable behavior, and inadequate communication (Collins & Repinski, 1994). Conflict is more common among friends than among acquaintances, but friendships often survive this conflict (Youniss & Smollar, 1985). In the course of a day, a typical high school student participates in an average of seven disagreements with various individuals (Laursen, 1989, as cited in Laursen, 1993). Children at all ages understand that conflict can injure a relation-

Figure 6.2
Conflict Resolution Strategies in Adolescent Relationships
Adolescent-parent conflicts are most often resolved either through power assertion or disengagement. Conflict resolution between close peers is more likely to be solved through negotiation, whereas adolescent conflict with others is most likely to be solved through either power or negotiation.
Source: Adapted from Laursen (1993).

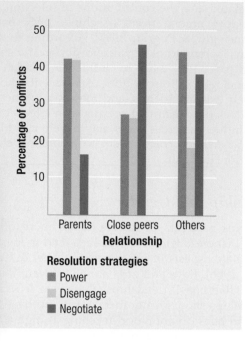

Close friends and romantic partners prefer to use negotiation and bargaining. The use of power assertion, as shown here, is more likely to injure the relationship.

ship, but the awareness that conflict management involves a resolution that is satisfactory to everyone does not develop until adolescence (Selman, 1980). Adolescents are somewhat more flexible in their resolutions; they are more pragmatic, try to avoid harming fragile relationships, and submit when necessary (Laursen, 1993).

Disagreements with parents and with friends differ (see Figure 6.2). Close friends more frequently engage in negotiation than in power assertion, whereas disagreements with parents involve more power assertion than negotiation (Laursen, 1993). Close friends report fewer "winner" or "loser" outcomes, and they have more conflicts in which there was "no outcome" than they report with parents or others. Although conflict with either parents or friends is most likely to leave the relationship unaffected, a greater percentage of conflicts negatively affect parent-adolescent relationships than relationships with friends.

The differences are due to the nature of the relationships. Peer relationships are voluntary; family relationships are not. Peer relationships are built around almost equal power; family relationships are not. Adolescents also have a greater fear that they can destroy a friendship than a family relationship. They seem to feel that by avoiding power assertion, they can reduce the chances that a dispute will injure or end the relationship. Given the option, close friends and romantic partners prefer negotiation and bargaining to resolve differences (Cowan, Drinkard, & MacGavin, 1984; Youniss & Smollar, 1985). *(For a review of this section, see At A Glance 6.2.)*

AT A GLANCE 6.2 FRIENDS

KEY POINT: Close friendships promote adolescent development, and the nature of friendship changes in adolescence.

SUPPORTING POINTS	EXPLANATION
The concept of friendship changes in adolescence.	Adolescents conceive of friendship in terms of intimacy, trust, and commitment. Shared feelings and self-disclosure are important. Late adolescents see friendship in terms of closeness, while they value their individuality.
Friendships are often based on similarities.	Most adolescents choose friends who are similar in income, ethnicity, gender, interests, and aspirations. Adolescent friends also reinforce one another's attitudes and behavior.
It is difficult to determine whether selection or socialization is more important in determining friendship.	Selection and socialization are both important, but recent evidence emphasizes the importance of selection. Adolescents may select friends similar to themselves, and these friends may then reinforce particular attitudes and behaviors. Socialization influences may then act to maintain the friendships.
Male and female friendships differ.	Male friendships often reflect shared interests, whereas female friendships emphasize the supportive, emotional aspects of friendship. Female friendships show more intimacy and self-disclosure.
Communication with friends differs significantly from communication with parents.	Communication with friends is marked by mutuality, less lecturing, and more sharing. Adolescents are more likely to use negotiation than power to settle disputes with each other, whereas parent-child disputes often are settled using power assertion.
Adolescents are more adept at handling conflict in friendships than are younger children.	Adolescents have a greater commitment to their friendships than do younger children.

CLIQUES AND CROWDS

Two types of groups first form during adolescence: cliques and crowds (Cairns et al., 1988). **Cliques** are relatively small, tightly knit groups of friends who spend considerable and sometimes exclusive time with one another (Brown, 1989, 1990). **Crowds** are larger groups loosely bound together by shared interests or status.

Cliques

Cliques are pervasive in adolescence (Ennett & Bauman, 1996). They are usually not large, averaging about five members and ranging in size from three to ten members, at least in high school. Best friends are usually in the same clique (Urberg et al., 1995). Some teens who are not actively clique members are friends of clique members and participate in some of their social activities. These teens, sometimes called *liaisons*, have friends in different cliques and have no allegiance to any one clique (Shrum & Cheek, 1987). They often provide communication between cliques. Some teens do not belong to any clique in school and are sometimes called *isolates*, but these independent adolescents do have friends (see Figure 6.3).

An analysis of social networks shows that the percentage of teens of each status differs significantly. One study of ninth graders found between 38.5 and 49.1 percent were clique members, between 27 and 31.4 percent were isolates, and

clique Small group of people who interact very frequently and develop close relationships with one another.

crowd A large group of teens who are tied together by interests and often can be recognized by dress, behavior, or both. Members of crowds may or may not have substantial interaction with one another.

Figure 6.3
Social Network Friendship Patterns: Cliques, Liaisons, and Isolates
Adolescents were asked to list their closest friends. A special computer program that analyzed the information produced this pattern of cliques, liaisons, and isolates.
Source: Ennett & Bauman (1996).

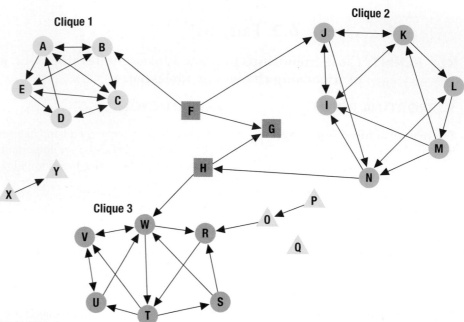

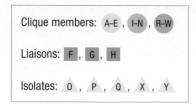

When adolescents talk about their friends, they often mean their clique. Cliques are small, tightly knit groups.

between 18.4 and 41.2 percent were liaisons (Ennett & Bauman, 1996). Clique members and isolates generally remain the same, but liaisons often become members of a clique at a later time. Adolescent girls are more likely to be clique members and adolescent boys, isolates. Cliques tend to be homogeneous in gender and socioeconomic status (Shrum & Cheek, 1987; Shrum, Cheek, & Hunter, 1988). Adolescents often use the term *my friends* to refer to both their clique at school and the liaisons (Hartup, 1993). Cliques often have leaders, with some members being more central to the clique and others on the periphery (Hansell, 1985). Cliques may add members, and some teens may drop out of a clique.

Cliques become more organized and stable with time, as an observation of junior high school students showed. Few stable cliques existed in sixth grade, and no clique appeared to have more status than any other. The cliques in seventh grade were more stable, and a hierarchy began to emerge. By eighth grade a stable hierarchy was found. The formation of cliques could be seen in the cafeteria. The sixth graders had flexible seating patterns; few groups sat together regularly, and sixth graders would sit with a variety of different children. Seating patterns among seventh graders were more stable, with students sitting in the same group for a month at a time. High-status groups, such as cheerleaders or student council members, sat together. Students also were stratified by socioeconomic status, with middle-class adolescents on one side and groups of working-class and lower-socioeconomic-status adolescents on the other. By eighth grade, seating arrangements were stable throughout the year, and popular groups of cheerleaders, athletes, and student council members merged to form a single group. Very few students from middle-class backgrounds sat on the other side of the cafeteria and vice versa (Eder, 1985). As found in other research, being a friend of a clique member was sometimes enough for admission to the clique, at least during lunch.

Crowds

Teens are also members of larger and looser groups, called *crowds.* Some crowds are collections of cliques (Dunphy, 1963), whereas other crowds are groups of individuals from different cliques who share certain interests (such as athletics) and norms (such as drug use or high levels of aggression) (Brown, 1989). The names of these crowds differ across schools and generations. Common crowd categories include "preppies," "populars," "jocks," "nerds," "druggies" or "burnouts," and "skaters." At times additional groups may arise, such as "punks," "hippies," and "politicos." Their orientation may change as well. For example, in the 1960s the politicos (those who are very politically oriented) were essentially antiestablishment, whereas in the 1990s they were more supportive of the political system.

Membership in crowds is often based on interests and defining characteristics. For example, the populars often participate in particular extracurricular activities, such as basketball teams, student government, yearbook staff, and cheerleading, and they have higher levels of self-esteem than members of less popular groups such as the nerds or burnouts, who do not participate in such valued activities. Populars are visible in school, and most students know their names, or at least who they are (Kinney, 1993). Some teens are not members of any crowd and are sometimes called "normals," an obviously inadequate term. Members of crowds are attracted to one another by common interests, activities, and attitudes toward school.

Membership in crowds may result from a combination of choosing and being chosen. For example, social class may be involved in membership in certain crowds, especially among higher-status girls who wear particular clothing (Eder, 1985). Some high school students are identified as associating with ethnically defined crowds, such as "rappers." Crowd affiliation defines who one is in the eyes of the peer group. A relationship exists between self-esteem and the social status of one's crowd (Brown & Lohr, 1986), and teens are well aware of their crowd's status.

Sometimes crowd affiliation is obvious, as people in some groups dress or look the same. For example, individuals identifying with punk dress and wear their hair in a particular way. Many adolescents, however, defy labeling and float among crowds that differ greatly from one another (Brown, 1990). Group norms in a crowd are based on the ways members express themselves and their desired activities. For example, preppies participate in sports and extracurricular activities, often dress in a particular way, and pay attention to academic issues (England & Petro, 1998). Members of crowds may not interact with each other extensively, as their numbers may be too large (England & Petro, 1998).

Crowd formation begins early. When students are asked to name the major crowds in school, the proportion of responses that fall into typical crowd categories climbs from 80 percent in sixth grade to 95 percent in ninth grade and then falls steadily through twelfth grade. By eighth and ninth grades, crowd labels such as "jocks" and "nerds" are in place (Brown, 1990). The importance of crowd affiliation seems to decline with age (see Figure 6.4) (Brown, Eicher, & Petrie, 1986).

The percentage of teens who give positive reasons for belonging to a crowd declines as adolescents mature, and by age 18 it is lower than the percentage of teens who give reasons opposing crowd membership. Females rate crowd affiliation more highly than males, but not by much. The importance of belonging to a crowd varies with one's membership status. Adolescents who belong to a crowd feel it is more important than those who do not, and marginal members consider membership even more important, probably because they are trying to get into a crowd. Teens not identifying with a crowd do not value crowd affiliation as much. Positive reasons for belonging focus on social support, friendship, and activities. Negative aspects of crowd membership include demands for conformity and the time it takes to remain in a crowd. With age, concerns about conformity become more important. Younger teens express more satisfaction with the group's ability to give support, foster friendship, and facilitate social interaction, whereas older students are more concerned about conformity and are confident that they don't need to belong to a crowd to have good friendships. Crowds appear to be an intermediate step in the development of autonomy and identity (Brown, Eicher, & Petrie, 1986; Newman & Newman, 1976).

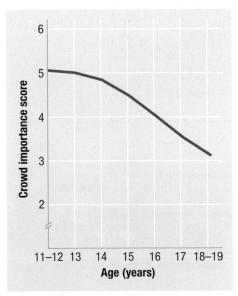

Figure 6.4
How Important Is Your Crowd?
When adolescents of various ages were asked to rate how important it was to belong to their crowd, the importance of the crowd declined with age.

Source: Adapted from Brown, Eicher, & Petrie (1986).

AT A GLANCE   **6.3** CLIQUES AND CROWDS

KEY POINT: Adolescents belong to cliques and crowds, which influence their attitudes and behaviors.	
SUPPORTING POINTS	**EXPLANATION**
Cliques are small, tightly formed groups.	Many adolescents belong to cliques ranging from three to ten people. Some adolescents, called *liaisons,* are friendly with clique members but do not actively belong to the clique.
Crowds are larger, looser groups of adolescents than cliques.	Membership in crowds is based on interests and attitudes. Members may dress or engage in particular activities to show they are part of a crowd.
Crowd membership begins early.	Identification with a crowd increases through ninth grade and declines thereafter.
Adolescents view crowd membership as having both positive and negative aspects.	The positive aspects of crowd membership involve social support and friendship, whereas the negative aspects involve conformity and time pressures.

Movement from crowd to crowd is not easy, and not all crowds are equally receptive to new members (Eder, 1985). Reputation seems important. Adolescents seeking to change crowds (or cliques) often find that despite changes in behavior, interests, and appearance, they are not accepted because of their reputation. For example, a student belonging to the druggies who goes through rehabilitation and changes his behavior may find that he is still not accepted because of his reputation. *(For a review of this section, see At A Glance 6.3.)*

POPULARITY AND UNPOPULARITY

Write down the first names of three fellow students who you thought were popular and three who were unpopular in junior or senior high school. What, if anything, did the popular students have in common? What did the unpopular students have in common?

The most common way to measure popularity is to ask children or adolescents themselves about it. The many approaches that use peer-based methods to evaluate social standing are referred to as **sociometric techniques.** The *nomination technique* asks adolescents to name a certain number of well-liked peers and, sometimes, classmates they do not like very much. The *rating scale technique* asks adolescents to rate each of their classmates on a scale of liking (Durkin, 1995). *Paired-comparison techniques* present adolescents with the names of two classmates and ask them to choose which they like best. Because all pairs are presented, the technique yields an overall measure of liking.

Research conducted on popularity finds five different statuses. **Popular adolescents** frequently receive many very favorable ratings and few unfavorable ones. **Controversial adolescents** receive many nominations on both extremes, that is, many very favorable and many very unfavorable ratings. **Rejected adolescents** receive few favorable ratings and many very unfavorable ones. **Neglected adolescents** receive few favorable or unfavorable ratings. **Average adolescents** are generally accepted but receive few extreme ratings.

Who Are the Popular Teens?

Numerous studies show that possessing athletic ability and team membership, being a cheerleader, having money, being fashionable, and being physically attractive and well groomed are related to popularity (Parkhurst & Hopmeyer,

sociometric techniques   A group of techniques used to measure friendship status and popularity.

popular adolescents   Adolescents who receive many very favorable ratings from other adolescents and very few unfavorable ratings.

controversial adolescents   Adolescents who receive many very favorable and very unfavorable ratings from other adolescents.

rejected adolescents   Adolescents who receive many very unfavorable ratings from other adolescents and few favorable ratings.

neglected adolescents   Adolescents who receive few favorable or unfavorable ratings from other adolescents.

average adolescents   Adolescents who are generally accepted, but receive few extreme ratings from other adolescents.

1998). Popular children and adolescents show higher levels of sociability and lower levels of aggression and withdrawal (Newcomb, Bukowski, & Pattee, 1993). Personal characteristics leading to popularity often include social dominance, which involves the ability to command others' attention, compliance, deference, and respect (Dong et al., 1996). Adolescents who show social dominance are leaders, show self-confidence, and demonstrate the ability to win disputes (Eder & Kinney, 1995). Physical domination, which may be an important factor in social dominance in childhood, becomes much less important in adolescence (Brown, 1989; Eder, 1985). Social dominance in adolescence is more a function of physical attractiveness, admired abilities, fashion and grooming, money, poise, being involved in prestigious groups and activities, and associating with others who have these abilities or characteristics (Brown, 1989; Eder, 1985). Many teens seek to be involved in athletics, to be part of a popular clique or crowd, to be a friend of a popular individual, or to dress more fashionably to improve their status and become more accepted and popular (Brown, 1989). These activities lead to greater social dominance (Parkhurst & Hopmeyer, 1998).

Social dominance is related to popularity, but the relationship is far from perfect, so other factors must be involved (Parkhurst & Asher, 1992). Adolescents must become socially dominant without offending others or becoming disliked; that is, they must have the requisite social skills to coordinate these goals. Socially dominant individuals may not be popular if their behaviors are not acceptable. For example, teens who are least liked at school often start fights and arguments and are generally disruptive. They are socially dominant, but their behavior interferes with relationships and activities. Although social dominance plays a part in popularity, it is probably also important to be considered cooperative, trustworthy, and even kind. However, many teens argue that popular students are not necessarily kind or trustworthy (Parkhurst & Hopmeyer, 1998). Being popular is not the same as being liked, and not all popular students are liked.

Studies of cheerleaders in junior high school demonstrate the difference between having a high social status and being well liked (Eder, 1985; Eder & Kinney, 1995). At the beginning of seventh grade, newly chosen cheerleaders were not only popular but also well liked. Many girls sought them out as friends to gain the prestige that comes with friendship with individuals who have a high social position. As time went by, the cheerleaders became more choosy about who they associated with, for two reasons. First, there are limitations on just how many meaningful time-consuming social interactions a person can have; second, they feared that interacting with lower-status girls would damage their own standing in their clique or crowd. Thus, the cheerleaders narrowed their associations. Other students considered them to be "stuck-up," and they became more disliked. At this point, few girls sought out these cheerleaders for new friendships, and though still considered popular by other students, they were in fact disliked by many. Students in high-status groups often ignored friendly initiations from students in other groups, giving the impression that they were rude. Some popular girls were considered generally stuck-up, but some were considered friendly when they were not with other members of the group. Popular girls do not necessarily dislike less popular girls. Rather, they may be concerned with keeping their status and with their friends' reactions to their associations with less popular girls. This may be especially true in relation to former close friends. Some cheerleaders in the study were aware of how they were perceived by others, and those who wanted to be both popular and well liked made

PERSPECTIVE 1

IS HE REALLY MY FRIEND?

SETTING THE SCENE: Greg and Carlos, who are in junior high school, have been friends since early elementary school. Greg's athletic talents have propelled him into the most popular group, whereas Carlos, who is quieter, more studious, and nonathletic, finds he is not a member of any real group. Carlos feels that Greg has less time for him.

CARLOS: *I thought we were friends. When Greg needs help on his homework, he calls me and I help him, but in school he pays no attention to me. Outside of school, things are a little better, but not what they were. When Greg needs something he doesn't hesitate to call, but he doesn't seem to know me when he isn't in need.*

GREG: *I like Carlos, but I now have other friends and interests. Carlos doesn't. Should I give up my new friends? I think Carlos and I can still be friends, but just not as close as we were. Sure, I call Carlos when I need help with some homework or project, but he doesn't do my work or anything like that.*

QUESTION: What should Carlos do? He feels that if he says no to helping Greg, it will end the friendship. If he keeps helping Greg but gets little in return, he'll feel he is being used.

a special attempt to say hello to other students or to interact with girls not in their group.

Many of these popular girls were aware that they were disliked but did not perceive themselves as being stuck-up, nor did they believe that their close friends saw them this way. Two seventh-grade girls (D and C) spoke to an interviewer (R) about this:

R: You say that a lot of girls envy cheerleaders.

D: Yeah: A lot of 'em get close friends. But then others, they think that they're stuck-up and they get to hate us (nervous giggle) and say all this stuff.

C: And like they start rumors and stuff. And say they don't like us and stuff.

D: And in slambooks, "Who are your enemies? Cheerleaders, Number 21" or somethin'. (Laughs) [Slambooks are notebooks with questions to which students respond and then sign a number instead of their name. These informal questionnaires were very popular in this school.]

R: Is that really hard on you all when that happens?

D: Well it makes us feel bad because, well, we don't really think we're stuck-up. But like we have one big group, you know, that like we're all good friends with. And then the others, I guess they just feel that the cheerleaders and basketball and football players all just kind of hang around together. And then if you're not in something like that or you don't make it, then you just think that, you know, well, that we're *stuck-ups* (embarrassed emphasis on last word, then laughs) or something. (Eder, 1985, p. 162)

Popular teens have more close friends; engage more frequently in activities with their friends; and live in a richer, more varied, and more rewarding social environment than rejected or neglected adolescents (Franzoi et al., 1994). They live in different worlds. Populars know and value their status, believing that others envy them. For example, one junior high school girl noted, "As a popular, [we] always had that one group—we had all the good-looking girls and that is the one [group] that everybody wanted to be in. At lunch we would sit at our own table [but] if you go out to lunch with the wrong person, rumors would go around that you went to lunch with a geek" (Kinney, 1993, p. 27). This represents a negative side of popularity—being afraid to sit with a lower-status person and having to continue to keep up an appearance to remain in the group.

Who Are the Unpopular Teens?

Unpopular adolescents are a heterogeneous group (French, Conrad, & Turner, 1995). They include adolescents who are aggressive, socially withdrawn, or not sociable or who show combinations of these characteristics (Rodkin et al., 2000). Often, unpopular teens are placed in one of two groups: *rejected adolescents* and *neglected adolescents*. Rejected adolescents are rarely nominated by their peers as friends and are actively disliked. Many show high levels of aggression, others are extremely withdrawn, still others are aggressive and withdrawn (Rodkin et al., 2000). They show poor attitudes toward school (including low attendance and achievement), and discipline problems. Neglected teens are rarely nominated as best friends, but they are not actively disliked. Members of this group show little problem behavior but are not physically attractive, do not seem to have similar interests as other teens, and are not involved in activities socially valued by other adolescents. The evidence points to very different outcomes for these two groups.

Rejected Adolescents   Research on rejected teens is substantial. Teens who engage in antisocial and aggressive behavior tend to be unpopular and rejected by many teens, although they are frequently members of cliques and crowds. Many of these teens come from homes in which they are reinforced for aggressive behavior and do not learn adequate social skills or prosocial behavior. Their rejection by teens in other groups, combined with low parental supervision and low grades, leads them to congregate with one another during late childhood and early adolescence. The group then reinforces their delinquent activities and may even encourage them to drop out of school (Patterson, Reid, & Dishion, 1992). Many of these boys are aggressive. Some of these girls are also aggressive, but many are not. They are rejected because they consistently break the rules and violate norms.

Not all aggressive adolescents are automatically rejected; about one-half are (Coie et al., 1995). Individuals who are aggressive and are not rejected are able to control their aggression and use it strategically to gain what they want at particular times. It seems that some aggressive behavior can be used in a way that does not always disrupt social relations, although the aggression is not sanctioned by peers (Pope & Bierman, 1999). Individuals who are both aggressive and unpopular often use aggression in a global manner, merely as a reaction to frustration or any assumed provocation (Coie & Lenox, 1994). They show many angry outbursts (Bierman, Smoot, & Aumiller, 1993).

Rejected aggressive teens are emotionally volatile, hyperactive, disruptive, and argumentative, and they engage in emotionally escalating arguments (Pope & Bierman, 1999). They are less sociable, and they are viewed as lacking positive social traits (Newcomb et al., 1993). Their behavior is inflexible and impulsive, and they show poor planning and problem-solving skills. They have difficulty attending to others' needs and communications. Many show high levels of negative emotions, are irritable and inattentive, and cannot regulate their own behaviors (Bierman et al., 1993). Some nonaggressive boys are also rejected because of this antisocial behavior pattern of irritability and inattentiveness (Bierman et al., 1993). Not all rejected children and adolescents are aggressive, impulsive, disruptive, or uncooperative, though. Some rejected children are shy and withdrawn (Cillessen et al., 1992).

Neglected Adolescents The other group of unpopular teens are neglected teens (Newcomb et al., 1993). Many of these teens have poor social skills (Coie, 1990); in fact, they show less sociability than average children and adolescents (Newcomb et al., 1993). They engage in less social interaction and have fewer positive interactions than average children and adolescents. Some are overly sensitive to comments or have learning problems. Others do not seem to have the same interests as their fellow teens. Neglected teens conform very well to the rules and sometimes are viewed as oriented more toward adults than toward their fellow teens. Conformity to rules and unpopularity may be related at both ends; both students who continually break rules and those who follow them with blind acceptance and conform may be less popular (White, 1989). Neglected children and adolescents are not well known by their peers. They do not show greater amounts of depression, and many have a best friend.

Many teens who are neglected in middle or junior high school change their status in high school, where a wider variety of students and groups are available. Earlier group boundaries disintegrate somewhat, especially during the junior and senior years of high school. Some neglected and even some rejected students join existing groups, whereas others develop their own groups. Those who "go mainstream" take advantage of their opportunities, often through participation in school activities. They feel better about themselves in high school than in junior high (Kinney, 1993).

Why Are Some Adolescents Disliked? Reasons for disliking others change somewhat with age. In one study, preschoolers, elementary school children, preadolescents (11-year-olds), and adolescent males (age 18, called *young adults* in the study) were asked to nominate children they disliked more than anyone else (called *enemies*) and to note why (see Table 6.1). The percentage of 18-year-olds citing aggression declined dramatically, probably because there

Table 6.1

Why Do Adolescents Dislike Other Adolescents?

Children and adolescents who were asked to nominate others they did not like and to state their reasons displayed interesting developmental changes. Disliking others because they are aggressive declined substantially with age, probably because young adults encounter fewer aggressive people. For adolescents, the most common reasons were negative character evaluations (being mean), acting less than genuine, and aberrant behavior. Only the adolescents in the sample cited disloyalty and not being able to confide in someone.

Dimension	Age			
	Preschool	*Primary Grade*	*Preadolescent*	*Young Adult*
Aggression (e.g., "He hits me")	56	50	61	22
Aberrant behavior (e.g., "He talks too loudly")	19	56	67	50
Rule violation (e.g., "He runs in the hallways")	31	19	11	—
General play (e.g., "He doesn't play with me")	19	13	11	22
Lack of helping (e.g., "He gets me into trouble")	—	38	50	22
Negative evaluation (e.g., "He is mean")	—	13	33	61
Lack of character admiration (e.g., "He gets in trouble")	—	19	22	28
Lack of genuineness (e.g., "He thinks he is great")	—	19	28	61
Nonacceptance (e.g., "He makes fun of me")	—	13	28	33
Disloyalty (e.g., "He can't be trusted")	—	—	—	33
Intimacy potential (e.g., "You can't confide in him")	—	—	—	33

Source: Hayes, Gershman, & Halteman (1996).

were fewer aggressive 18-year-olds. However, dislike due to negative character evaluations (being mean) or not being genuine increased substantially, and two categories—disloyalty and lack of intimacy potential—appeared (Hayes, Gershman, & Halteman, 1996).

Consequences of Rejected and Neglected Status The long-term outcomes for rejected and neglected adolescents differ. Children and adolescents with rejected status show more aggressiveness and disruptive behaviors, report greater feelings of dissatisfaction, and show more academic problems compared with average and neglected children and adolescents (Ollendick et al., 1991; Parker & Asher, 1987). Their status is also more stable than that of neglected children and adolescents.

Ollendick and colleagues (1992) asked fourth graders to rate how much they liked to play with or would like to play with each of their classmates and then asked for the names of their three best friends. Five years later, when in ninth grade, many of the students were evaluated on academic performance, social behavior, and adjustment. Rejected children were perceived by their peers in fourth grade as less likable and more aggressive. In ninth grade, their teachers noted that they showed more conduct problems, attentional difficulties, and aggression compared with popular peers. They failed more subjects and were more likely to commit delinquent offenses. The researchers concluded that rejected adolescents make up a group that is at risk for poor outcomes.

Controversials—those who are well liked by some students and disliked intensely by others—showed a similar pattern to the rejected children in the study of Ollendick and colleagues (1992). They demonstrated academic and behavioral difficulties, but teachers viewed them as less conduct disordered than rejected children. Controversials, like rejected adolescents, are considered at risk. Some are aggressive, but they show greater social skills and sociability (Newcomb et al., 1993).

Neglected children and adolescents, though, fared much better, according to Ollendick and colleagues (1992). Although they were less well liked than average or popular children and somewhat more withdrawn than their popular peers, teachers did not perceive this. Neglected students were no more likely to fail grades or commit a delinquent offense than average or popular students. They displayed few indications of academic, behavioral, or social maladjustment at a 5-year follow-up.

Most teens do not belong to the ultrapopular or the unpopular group but are somewhere in the middle. They have a set of good friends and find their interpersonal relationships satisfying. Research shows, though, that the rejected and controversial groups are at risk for poor outcomes (French et al., 1995), but the outcome for teens in the neglected group is more positive.

Bullying

Do you remember a student in primary or secondary school who always insulted, teased, or threatened other students or started fights? These students are described as *bullies*. **Bullying** is a specific type of aggression in which (1) the behavior is intended to harm or disturb others; (2) the behavior occurs repeatedly over time; and (3) there is an imbalance of power, with a more powerful person or group attacking a less powerful one (Pace, 2001). The bully may be physically or psychologically more powerful, and the aggression may be verbal (name calling or threatening); physical (hitting), or psychological, sometimes called *relational* (spreading rumors or purposely excluding others) (Nansel, Overpeck, et al., 2001). If two adolescents of equal strength quarrel or fight, it is not considered bullying.

Gender differences exist among bullies. Boys are more likely to threaten physical force and actually use physical violence, whereas girls are more likely to spread malicious rumors, exclude other girls from social activities, belittle others, or tease (Crick & Bigbee, 1998; Shure, 2000). Adults often fail to notice the use of these more psychological and manipulative tactics (Bullock, 2002; Casey-Cannon, Hayward, & Gowen, 2001). Gender differences in bullying may exist because of the greater sanctions against physical violence for girls. In addition, teasing and exclusion may be very effective strategies that injure the social goals of other girls, such as establishing close ties. These goals are often more important for females than males (Crick & Bigbee, 1998). One Australian study, however, found that both boys and girls considered relational aggression as more hurtful than physical aggression (Rigby & Bagshaw, 2001).

Bullying is common. A national study of more than 15,000 students in grades 6 through 10 found that 29.9 percent of the students in the sample either were bullies or were being victimized by bullies once or twice during the semester or once a week or more (Nansel, Simons-Morton, & Scheidt, 2001). Bullying is more frequent in grades 6 through 8 than in grades 8 through 10.

Bullies often pick on the same victim over and over (Perry, Kusel, & Perry, 1988). Victims are often socially isolated and lack social skills (Hoover, Oliver, & Hazier, 1992). They are more anxious and lonely, and they appear more vulnerable (Crick & Bigbee, 1998; Leff, 1999). They are submissive and easily give in. Other students tend to avoid victims when they are being bullied. Perhaps these observers fear becoming victims themselves or the loss of social status that may come from befriending a victim. Many victims are bullied by more than one person at school, making school a terrible experience for them.

Not all victims fit this profile, however. Some individuals are both bullies and victims. They are emotional and impulsive, often bullying others and at the same time being victims of bullying (Nansel, Simons-Morton, & Scheidt, 2001).

Bullying is not typical childish or adolescent behavior. It is intended to harm others, who usually have done nothing at all to the bully. What causes someone to use bullying tactics? Some bullies may believe they are gaining the respect of others through intimidation. By being a bully and getting what they want, they may achieve and maintain dominance in their own small set of friends (Pellegrini, Bartini, & Brooks, 1999). Other bullies may have a need to gain

bullying Repeated, intentionally harmful actions by a more powerful child or group against another child.

control, often because of a troubled home situation (Curtner-Smith, 2000). Their parents are often indifferent and use inconsistent discipline, combining hostility with laxness. When they do punish their children for misbehavior, the punishments are often harsh and punctuated with emotional outbursts (Olweus, 1994a). The climate of the family is angry and hostile, with little parental involvement. Bullies may be relieving their frustration by taking it out on another, less powerful individual. Bullies often show conduct problems in school and are more likely to drink alcohol and smoke. Whatever the cause of bullying, it persists because it is immediately rewarded, as when a bully gets to keep the money extorted from another student or gains a higher status with others in the group (Eron, 1998). Perhaps because they have momentarily succeeded using aggression, bullies believe in aggression and have a positive attitude toward it (Menesini, Melan, & Pignatti, 2000).

Bullying can have both immediate and long-lasting effects for both the bully and the victim (Pace, 2001). Bullies are often rejected by others, yet they are not isolated. In fact, bullies often report that it is easy to make friends, and they are not anxious (Salmon, James, & Smith, 1998). They do form friendships, but mostly with other bullies or aggressive students. They seem unaware or unconcerned about their unpopularity with nonaggressive students. They may misperceive their position in the peer group, not realizing how their bullying limits their social contacts. In fact, bullies often name other bullies as friends, and they in turn are named by other bullies as friends (Pellegrini et al., 1999). This limited circle of aggressive friends may reinforce bullying.

School bullying predicts serious antisocial behavior in late adolescence and early adulthood (Eron, 1998). Former male bullies are four times more likely to show criminal behavior than nonbullies and by age 24 years, 60 percent of former bullies have at least one criminal conviction, and 35 to 40 percent have three or more convictions (Olweus, 1992). The fact that bullies are successful in getting what they want probably interferes with their learning how to interact properly with others, leading to long-term problems.

Victims of bullying often feel sad and rejected (Casey-Cannon, Hayward, & Gowen, 2001). They may even avoid school or develop physical symptoms (Juvonen, Nishina, & Graham, 2000). The situation may improve for victims in high school, however. In fact, often in high school these adolescents find a peer group into which they fit, even if it consists of youth of similar status (Huttunen et al., 1996). Still, the experience of being victimized and rejected may remain, and victims are more likely to show adjustment problems such as depression in adulthood (Olweus, 1993).

Bullies who are also bullied show the worst outcomes. They display the poorest psychological functioning (Haynie et al., 2001). They are socially isolated, have low school achievement, and display many problem behaviors.

Some interventions to stop bullying work, reducing bullying 30 to 50 percent in schools (Olweus, 1994a, 1994b). Unfortunately, they are not used extensively in the United States. Many adults, including educators, do not believe that bullying is a problem, believing that "boys will be boys" (Nansel, Simons-Morton, & Scheidt, 2001). These adults, along with an institutional apathy toward bullying, create an atmosphere in which bullies feel secure enough to continue bullying others. Bullying is thus an institutional problem, not just a problem for the victim (Green, 2001; Olweus, 1993). Successful interventions concentrate on changing attitudes toward bullying among everyone in the school environment. These interventions increase everyone's awareness of bullying and the problems it presents, require greater teacher and parent involvement and supervision, require the formation of clear rules about what behaviors are or are not permitted, and create strong social norms against bullying while providing support and protection for victims (Olweus, 1991). The consequences of bullying for both the bully and the victim can be serious, and efforts must be made to counter bullying.

Adolescents who show unrestrained aggressive behavior are often rejected by other adolescents.

Enhancing Social Skills

Social relationships are very important in adolescence, so it is reasonable to assume that adolescents who are unpopular or who lack friends need help. Programs to help children and adolescents improve their social status usually assume that these individuals lack social skills or self-confidence (Bierman & Furman, 1984). Social skills training programs teach appropriate group-entry strategies, empathy for others, prosocial yet assertive ways of getting what is wanted, and a variety of communication skills. One such program, the Skillstreaming method, breaks down each skill into specific behaviors and uses modeling, role playing, performance feedback, and training in generalizing these skills to many different situations. It divides fifty skills into six categories: beginning social skills, advanced social skills, skills for dealing with feelings, skill alternatives to aggression, skills for dealing with stress, and planning skills. Individuals learn each skill through specific steps (Merrell & Gimpel, 1998).

Although there is little doubt that these skills can be taught, learning them frequently does not change the status of children and teens (Goldstein & Pentz, 1984). In exploring the reason behind this lack of status change, one can question the extent to which these teens actually use the skills in the course of an average day. However, lack of skills use does not seem to be a factor, because the behavioral patterns do change but the status often remains (Hymel, 1986). Reputation is one reason. When rejected and neglected boys behaved just as popular children did, peer responses to the rejected and neglected boys still were not as posi-

AT A GLANCE **6.4** POPULARITY AND UNPOPULARITY

KEY POINT: Popularity and unpopularity are determined by many factors.

SUPPORTING POINTS	EXPLANATION
Popularity is determined by many characteristics.	Teens who are popular have athletic ability, are physically attractive, and are socially adept.
The key to popularity in adolescence is social dominance.	Socially dominant teens engage in high-status activities, dress fashionably, command attention, and have good social skills. Socially dominant teens control situations without resorting to violence.
Unpopular adolescents fall into two categories: rejected and neglected.	Rejected adolescents may show high levels of aggressive, antisocial behavior, whereas rejected teens may lack social skills.
Many, but not all, aggressive adolescents are rejected.	Teens who use aggression strategically and occasionally to obtain what they want may not be rejected, but adolescents who use aggression globally, impulsively, and inflexibly are rejected.
The long-term outlook is different for rejected and neglected children and adolescents.	Rejected children and adolescents often retain their status and are frequently in trouble with school authorities. Neglected children and adolescents, in contrast, often find their own groups in high school and are not much different from typical children or adolescents.
Bullies intentionally hurt others, pick on victims who are weaker, and show these behaviors over a long period of time.	Male bullies tend to use threats and physical violence, whereas female bullies are more likely to start rumors or taunt others. Research finds negative outcomes for both the bully and the victim.
Social skills training may help unpopular students.	Programs that build social skills can be useful. However, poor social skills are not the only reason for unpopularity, so social skills training will not help everyone.

tive as responses to the popular boys (Dodge, 1980). Even placing reputation aside, sociability and social skills are not the only factors related to success in the interpersonal world; status, appearance, academic performance, athleticism, and attractiveness to the opposite sex play important roles in interpersonal relationships among adolescents (England & Petro, 1998). Some of these factors are easier to modify than others. For example, in addition to behavior training, attention to grooming and personal appearance might be helpful, as people often associate attractiveness with competence. Of course, in a perfect world, it would be best to educate people as to the falseness of friendship based on physical appearance and surface traits, but it also would be unrealistic to believe that they are not important.

The problem of reputation is much more difficult to solve. As we have noted, high schoolers seem more open to differences than junior high schoolers. Many unpopular middle school students have solid friendships in high school. Social skills training thus can help and may be useful over the long term, especially if the program includes opportunities to use the new skills. *(For a review of this section, see At A Glance 6.4.)*

ROMANTIC RELATIONSHIPS

Three of the major developmental tasks of adolescence—(1) forging a unique identity, (2) building relationship skills and developing intimacy, and (3) adjusting to new sexual desires and impulses—are played out in the context of a romantic relationship (Feldman & Gowen, 1998). Romantic relationships involve dating, romance, a more intimate type of communication, and sexual activity. Dating and romance mean much more than sexual activity; they involve a new and deeper kind of intimacy and involvement with another individual. For that reason, dating is covered in this chapter on peer relations rather than in "Love and Sex."

Romantic relationships are tentative and somewhat awkward at the beginning of adolescence, becoming less strained later on. As adolescence continues, teens spend more time with the other gender. However, some anxiety about romantic relationships remains. In fact, although adolescents experience time spent with other-gender partners very positively, time spent thinking about romantic partners is far less positive (Richards et al., 1998). They may miss the other individual and think about the less pleasant aspects of the relationship.

Dating

Dating can be viewed as a process during which adolescents practice and experiment with heterosexual relationships (Feiring, 1996). Adolescents who are homosexual also date during this time, and their experiences offer similar opportunities for forming close relationships (see "Love and Sex" for information about homosexual relationships). Interest in friendships with the other gender increases by junior high school, especially among girls, although friendships with members of the other gender rarely constitute a majority of best friends (Savin-Williams & Berndt, 1990).

Romantic relationships involve fascination, sexual attraction, and exclusiveness, qualities not indicative of friendships. Romantic relationships also feature an integration of many behaviors that involve affiliation, attachment, caregiving, and sexuality. Romantic friendships do not supplant same-gender friendships, although same-gender best friendships and romantic relationships are perceived by late adolescents and early adults as equally intimate and supportive (Furman & Buhrmester, 1992; Sharabany et al., 1981).

When middle school and senior high students were asked to fill out a questionnaire about dating, 27 percent of the eighth graders, 39 percent of the tenth graders, and 63 percent of the twelfth graders were actively dating (Quatman et al., 2001). Many adolescents have had the experience of going steady with a particular partner sometime during their middle years of adolescence (Thornton, 1990).

Dating affords an opportunity to interact and learn about others and to try out different relationships (Cox, 1990). The new social role, that of the opposite-sex partner, is challenging. Later in adolescence and continuing into early adulthood, dating becomes somewhat more serious because the possibility of mate selection enters the picture. Dating is fraught with anxiety, and disappointment and rejection are common (Greenberg et al., 1989).

The Dating Process Individuals who are dating progress from situations in which other-sex peers are present, to mixed-sex group activities, to group dating in which couples see each other in a group context, to going out alone on a date (Feiring, 1996). By age 15, most teens have had some experience dating and have engaged in some sexual experimentation. Adolescents in romantic relationships may further develop social skills that were learned and maintained in same-gender relationships involving intimacy and communication.

Relatively little research is available on dating in early and middle adolescence (Dowdy & Kliewer, 1998). Most 15-year-olds asked about their dating relationships had already had at least one relationship with a boyfriend or girlfriend, but were not currently dating. These relationships were short, averaging 4 months. Within that time, contact was relatively frequent. The teens saw and talked with each other almost daily; telephone calls were common, with the average call being 60 minutes long. Although brief, the relationships were intense. Most of these early relationships arise out of a peer group context, with group activities being more prominent than dyadic activities. When asked what they liked in their partners, a large percentage of boys chose physical attractiveness. Girls were more likely to mention intimacy and support (Feiring, 1996).

Most dating takes place within one's own racial, ethnic, and religious group, but this pattern is slowly changing. Interracial dating is increasing; although less than 5 percent of all U.S. marriages are interracial, surveys demonstrate a more liberal attitude toward it than in the past. When university students completed an anonymous questionnaire, about half reported they were open to an interracial relationship, and about a quarter said they had dated

Although in the past most dating occurred within one's own racial and ethnic group, a change toward more interracial and interethnic dating is taking place.

Table 6.2

First Date Scripts for Hypothetical and Actual Dates

	Hypothetical Date	
	Woman's[a] Script	*Man's[b] Script*
	Tell friends and family	Ask for date
	GROOM AND DRESS[c]	Decide what to do
	BE NERVOUS	**WORRY ABOUT APPEARANCE**
	Worry about appearance[d]	Prepare car, apartment
	Wait for date	**PICK UP DATE**
Man:	**PICK UP DATE**	MEET PARENTS/ROOMMATES
	Welcome date to home	Engage in courtly behavior (open door)
	Introduce to parents, etc.	**Leave**
	Leave	**Confirm plans**
	Confirm plans	**Get to know and evaluate date**
	Get to know and evaluate date	**TALK, JOKE, LAUGH**
	TALK, JOKE, LAUGH	**EAT**
	GO TO MOVIES, SHOW, PARTY	Pay
	Eat	Make out
	Accept/reject date's moves	**TAKE DATE HOME**
Man:	**Take date home**	Ask for another date
	Tell date had a good time	**KISS GOODNIGHT**
	Kiss goodnight	**Go home**
	Go home	

	Actual Date	
	Woman's Script	*Man's Script*
	Groomed and dressed	**PICKED UP DATE**
	Was nervous	Met parents/roommates
Man:	**Picked up date**	**Left**
	Introduced to parents, etc.	Picked up friends
Man:	Engaged in courtly behavior (opened doors)	**Confirmed plans**
	Left	**TALKED, JOKED, LAUGHED**
	Confirmed plans	**WENT TO MOVIES, SHOW, PARTY**
	Got to know and evaluate date	**ATE**
	TALKED, JOKED, LAUGHED	**Drank alcohol**
	Enjoyed date	Initiated sexual contact
	WENT TO MOVIES, SHOW, PARTY	Made out
	ATE	**TOOK DATE HOME**
	Drank alcohol	**Asked for another date**
	Talked to friends	**KISSED GOODNIGHT**
	Had something go wrong	**Went home**
Man:	**Took date home**	
Man:	**Asked for another date**	
Man:	Told date will call her	
Man:	**Kissed date goodnight**	
	WENT HOME	

[a]$n = 74.$ [b]$n = 61.$ [c]Capital letters indicate that the action was mentioned by at least 50 percent of the subjects per script. [d]Bold type indicates that the action was mentioned for both the woman's and the man's script.
Source: Rose & Frieze (1993), pp. 504–505.

When men and women were asked about a hypothetical or actual date, the results were hardly surprising. Men were proactive, planning and making certain everything was ready, while women were reactive, reacting to the plans and the activities.

someone of another race (Knox, Custis, & Zusman, 2000). These adolescents and early adults do not have a lower identification than those who date within their own race exclusively (Mok, 1999). Dating between teens of different religions is also increasing.

Dating can be viewed in two major ways, which were first described by Erik Erikson (1950). Some adolescents are primarily interested in finding someone with whom to share intimate thoughts and feelings, whereas others are more interested in using dating as a means to achieve independence from family and explore different roles and identities. Not all adolescents are ready for the former, and they date merely to explore a different side of themselves, gain new experiences, and engage in sexual activity (Sanderson & Cantor, 1995).

Dating Roles Teenagers understand well, and generally agree on, the roles they are to play in a dating situation (Rose & Frieze, 1989). Psychologists use the term **script** to define the sequence of events that occur in a particular setting. For example, if you were asked what occurs when you eat at McDonald's (the script for eating at McDonald's), you could easily name the actions (enter the building, get on line, order your food, and so on). Scripts give events predictability, as well as provide a sense of security.

When college freshman were asked about dating scripts, their answers showed a strong degree of gender typing (see Table 6.2) (Rose & Frieze, 1989, 1993). The men described their roles as proactive initiating the date, planning the date, opening doors, and starting sexual interaction (kissing goodnight, making out). Women saw their roles as reactive, focusing on responding to the male's overtures. The freshmen expected men to perform four to five male gender–typed actions (asking for the date, planning it, displaying considerate behavior, and initiating physical contact), whereas their expectations for women included only one female gender–typed action (being concerned about appearance). Men's scripts are somewhat more rigid, which perhaps accounts for the greater anxiety men have about dating (Himaki et al., 1980); it is easier to do something wrong if you have to plan rather than react. People sometimes talk about the changing roles of men and women, but no dramatic changes are apparent in the early stages of dating. These scripts function to make dating somewhat easier than would a more open process, which would be more conducive to anxiety and error.

Parental Reaction to Dating Parents often underestimate the importance of dating to adolescents (Kandel & Lesser, 1972). The initiation of romantic relationships significantly changes parent-teen relationships, and conflict increases. Rules about curfew and friends in the home become more important to parents and more frustrating to teens. Some of these problems revolve around the question of how much parents should control the dating. Adolescents are likely to view their relationship and sexuality as their own business. Parents may believe they have a right to influence these areas, because both the relationships and the sexual behavior that accompanies them may have long-term effects on adolescents (Smetana & Asquith, 1994).

Adolescents who are currently dating report more frequent conflict with parents than nondaters, and younger teens have more conflict over this issue than older teens. Female daters report more intense conflict with their parents than male daters, but the differences are surprisingly small. Short-term relation-

PERSPECTIVE 2

DO THEY HAVE TO KNOW EVERYTHING?

SETTING THE SCENE: Janine is a 16-year-old girl who attends a high school that even she claims is "rough." She has been dating for about a year.

JANINE: *The problem is that my parents ask me so many questions about the boys I date. They insist the boy has to come in and meet them, rather than allowing me to meet him somewhere else. They insist on speaking with him, and they ask me questions about the date. My curfew is 11:00, and I think that is too early.*

JANINE'S PARENTS: *She is so secretive. What's wrong with meeting the boy your daughter is dating? Yes, she has to tell us where she is going, but again what is wrong with that? We believe that her curfew is reasonable, and it will be extended to 12:00 when she is 17. If she calls us we will sometimes, but not always, give her special permission to stay out later. Yes, we do want to know where she is and with whom, because we believe this is part of our responsibility as parents. We also must admit we haven't liked all the boys she's dated. The other questions about the date, such as whether she had a good time or likes the boy, are just asked to show interest.*

QUESTION: Should Janine's parents modify their approach and rules for dating?

script A structure that describes an appropriate sequence of events in a particular situation.

ships bring more intense conflict than longer-term relationships. Perhaps as time passes, parents know their adolescent's romantic partner better and accept him or her.

Dating norms in other cultures differ, sometimes drastically, from norms among most Americans. A survey of college students from a U.S. midwestern state university and a Chinese university in Shanghai showed dating behaviors and attitudes that varied greatly (Tang & Zuo, 2000). American college students held more liberal attitudes toward who initiates a date, dated younger, dated more frequently, and were more likely to develop a sexual relationship. Chinese students dated later, dated less frequently, and were less likely to develop a sexual relationship. American students in this sample had their first date during their 14th year, whereas the average age for Chinese students' first date was 18 years. Social pressure to date is greater in the United States, and the ability to have dates indicates popularity. In China, however, dating in junior high or even high school is considered somewhat unusual, and opportunities for dating are more limited. American society encourages dating, whereas Chinese society frowns on it.

People who immigrate to the United States bring many cultural ideas from their country of origin. As they live in the United States longer, they—especially the children—take on more of the social customs of the country. This process may lead to parent-child conflict. A study of Indian American families found that mothers and fathers did not approve of dating, especially for their daughters. Sons showed a greater acceptance of dating than daughters, many of whom also believed they should be allowed to date. Even parents who let their adolescent children date admitted separate standards for sons and daugh-

AT A GLANCE 6.5 ROMANTIC RELATIONSHIPS

KEY POINT: Adolescents begin to form romantic relationships, which differ from other close relationships.

SUPPORTING POINTS	EXPLANATION
Romantic relationships are formed for the first time in adolescence.	Romantic relationships involve a deeper form of intimacy and involvement with another person. Sexuality is one aspect of romantic relationships.
Romantic relationships differ from close friendships.	Romantic relationships involve fascination, sexual attraction, and exclusiveness.
The male and female roles in dating are well defined.	Males initiate the date, plan the date, and initiate sexual activity. The woman's role is more reactive and involves responding to the man's dating behaviors. The male role is more rigid than the female role.
Dating, especially for early and middle adolescents, may lead to increased conflict in the home.	Arguments about curfews and other aspects of dating occur in the home because parents view these details as their legitimate concerns, whereas adolescents feel dating is their own business.
Conflict in romantic relationships is common, and adolescents deal with this conflict in many ways.	The most common ways adolescents deal with conflict are attack, seeking peer support, distraction, avoidance, and compromise.
Partner violence is a significant problem in romantic relationships.	The physical, emotional, and psychological consequences of dating abuse can be serious.

ters. Of the Indian American adolescents, 60 percent favored both dating and choosing one's own partner. A quarter of all the girls wanted to date but did not because of parental disapproval, whereas half were dating without their parents' knowledge (Dasgupta, 1998). A full 80 percent of the boys were dating. One reason for these cultural attitudes against female dating is the emphasis on sexual chastity before marriage in Indian culture; dating is seen as similar to, or leading to, sexual activity. Adolescents, though, did not see it that way.

Conflict in Romantic Relationships

Conflicts among adolescent romantic partners are frequent (Laursen, 1995). There are five ways to reduce conflict: (1) getting mad and attacking, (2) seeking support from peers, (3) seeking distraction, (4) withdrawing and thereby avoiding the problem, and (5) compromising. Avoidance and compromise are the two most common ways to deal with conflict (Collins & Laursen, 1992), with compromise being the most common. The use of avoidance increases with age, whereas the use of social support declines (Compas, 1987a; Lindeman, Harakka, & Keltikangas-Jarvinen, 1997).

Culture may also affect how people deal with conflict in romantic relationships. A cross-cultural study comparing Israeli and German youths found that German youths were more likely to use social support when dealing with such conflicts, whereas Israeli youth were more likely to engage in compromise. Avoidance was least common for both groups (Seiffge-Krenke & Shulman, 1990).

Conflicts within romance may be new to adolescents, but they turn to behaviors they use in handling disagreements in other areas of life. Individuals who use overt anger and even violence in friendships are likely to do so in romantic relationships, and dating violence is a serous problem (Feldman & Gowen, 1998) (see "Focus: Partner Violence"). People who are withdrawn or depressed are more likely to use avoidance or distraction when faced with conflict. Those who often use humor and are altruistic are more likely to turn to compromise and social support (Malik, Sorenson, & Aneshensel, 1997).

Romantic relationships are not always healthy. Some adolescent females with very poor family relationships and personality problems may begin to date early, have sex early, and generally try to use their romantic relationships to compensate for their disappointing family relationships (Hazan & Zeifman, 1994). These adolescents do not focus their attention on education or work, and they choose friends and romantic partners with problems in these areas as well (Cairns et al., 1988). These adolescent females date men who are much older, are often unemployed, have poor family lives, and are involved in antisocial behavior (Pawlby et al., 1997).

Dating involves a good deal of anxiety, and breakups are rarely easy. However, these relationships are an important part of adolescence; they help individuals develop the types of skills that will be required in long-term romantic relationships in adulthood. (*For a review of this section, see At A Glance 6.5.*)

PERSPECTIVE 3

I CAN'T LEAVE HIM

SETTING THE SCENE: Trina is an 18-year-old college student who has been dating Ziad for about a year. Trina admits that they argue often and sometimes hit each other. She finds this is happening more and more. Although Ziad is more physical, Trina also slaps him. She kept this problem from her parents until recently, when they questioned her about a bruise and she admitted what had happened.

TRINA: *I know things have gotten worse, but I can't leave him. He does it mostly when he drinks, and he has promised to control his drinking. He says he'll try harder not to become so physical, and I'll try not to egg him on or slap him. I know things aren't right, but we love each other, and that's all that matters. I know we can work it out. It's not as if we beat each other up all the time.*

ZIAD: *I love Trina. Things just get out of hand. I never want to hurt her. I don't think things are that bad, really. Her parents are overreacting. I just sometimes get angry, and things just happen. A lot of my friends have the same thing, and their girlfriends understand. I guess I'll try harder.*

PARENTS: *We are, frankly, disturbed at this pattern. We just want Trina to leave him. We don't allow him in the house. We don't know what to do. We are thinking of threatening to not pay her tuition if she doesn't stop seeing him.*

QUESTION: Why does Trina stay with Ziad? What advice would you give her parents?

Physical violence within dating relationships is common, with an incidence ranging from about 20 percent to more than 50 percent (Simonelli & Ingram, 1998). A study of 7,500 adolescents in romantic relationships found that a third reported some psychological or physical aggression (Halpern et al., 2001). Between 20 and 30 percent of college students report physical violence in their current relationship (White & Koss, 1991). Most of this violence involves pushing, grabbing, and slapping, but 1 to 3 percent of the college students sampled report beatings and assaults with objects (Arias, Samios, & O'Leary, 1987). While 43.1 percent of college women in one study said they had experienced physical violence on a date, 91.2 percent reported psychological abuse such as insults, threats, or damage to possessions (James et al., 2000; Neufeld, McNamara, & Ertl, 1999).

It may be surprising, but females are as likely, and some studies say even more likely, to engage in dating violence as men (M. L. Clark et al., 1994; Katz, Kuffel, & Coblentz, 2002). Couple violence is frequently bidirectional, and teenage boys and girls are as likely to report being perpetrators as victims (Vivian & Langhinrichsen-Roholing, 1994). However, women are more likely to resort to dating violence in self-defense. Additionally, women are at greater risk for sustaining injury, because they are usually physically smaller and weaker than men (Bookwala et al., 1992; Feiring et al., 2002).

Many researchers object to the perspective of mutual abuse, because the consequences of physical violence are so much greater for women than men. Also, defining *violence* to include fairly minor acts leads to the false impression that men and women use aggression equally. When one focuses on more serious acts of aggression, fear, and injury, the problem of male-on-female violence is much greater than female-on-male violence (Langley, Martin, & Nada-Raja, 1997). However, it would be wrong to imply that only male-on-female violence occurs in dating relationships.

The psychological effects of dating violence other than rape are rarely discussed, because there is much more interest in date or acquaintance rape, which will be discussed in the chapter "Love and Sex." One study found that about 15 percent of the men and 31 percent of the women experiencing abuse reported major emotional trauma from the violent experience (Makepeace, 1986). Women who experienced at least one incidence of physical violence in a dating relationship after age 16 reported greater levels of psychological distress than women who had never experienced violence (Coffey et al., 1996).

Dating violence probably has multiple roots and grows out of the violence and aggression that surrounds adolescents. Abusive men often were exposed as children to their fathers physically abusing their mothers (Ronfeldt, Kimerling, & Arias, 1988). Those who grow up in violent homes are more likely to move from verbal aggression to physical aggression (Stets, 1991). Some women who tolerate abuse were physically abused themselves as children (Malik, Sorenson, & Aneshensel, 1997).

Males are more likely to inflict violence against a dating partner when they have witnessed parental violence, believe that male-female dating violence is justified, use alcohol and drugs, are recipients of dating violence, and are in conflict-ridden relationships. Females are more likely to be violent toward a dating partner when they believe that female-to-male dating violence is justifiable and that male-to-female violence is not justifiable ("It's OK for me to hit you, but not for you to hit me"). These women experience

BEHAVIORAL AUTONOMY AND CONFORMITY

If you ask adults what most concerns them about teenage peer groups, they will name peer pressure and conformity. Peer pressure, or pressure to think or behave along peer-prescribed guidelines, is a hallmark of adolescence (Clasen & Brown, 1985). Peer pressure establishes and maintains group norms and loyalties. Many adults stereotype adolescents as being slavishly devoted to a unified norm and buckling under intense and unyielding peer pressure. They argue that peer groups lead adolescents into the use of alcohol, other illegal drugs, and delinquent behavior (Barrett, Simpson, & Lehman, 1988; Brook, Whiteman, & Gordon, 1983). Coleman (1961), in a classic study of ten midwestern high schools, concluded that adolescents face considerable pressure to be popular and belong to a crowd that represents a subculture with norms and values contrary to those encouraged by adults.

more conflict in dating relationships, are recipients of dating violence, and tend to use alcohol or drugs (O'Keefe, 1997). Exposure to weapons and violent injury in the community also predict more dating violence (Malik et al., 1997), and contact with aggressive peers increases the risk of inflicting dating violence for both males and females (Gwartney-Gibbs, Stockard, & Brohmers, 1987). Finally, some aggression is an attempt to gain power. Abuse is related to lack of satisfaction with relationship power, rather than to the amount of power itself (Ronfeldt et al., 1998).

Some account for male violence in terms of Western society's patriarchal values and the view that men use force to maintain their social advantages over women (Dobash et al., 1992). In this view, *patriarchal terrorism* occurs when a man uses abuse as a control tactic (Johnson, 1995). However, this societal view, although interesting, is weakened by evidence showing that men with nontraditional attitudes toward sex roles are actually more likely to use physical aggression toward women than men with traditional attitudes (Bookwala et al., 1992). Additionally, most men see violence against women as unacceptable (Arias & Johnson, 1989) and do not engage in such violence.

A model for understanding dating violence advanced by Riggs and O'Leary (1989) holds some promise. The model proposes two general categories of variables that influence violence: contextual and situational. Contextual variables include parental aggression toward the child, prior use of aggression, personality factors, and emotionality. Situational variables are more immediate and act as triggers; they include stress, alcohol use, the partner's use of aggression, conflict in the relationship, and expectations of a positive outcome from the violence. Contextual variables increase the likelihood of the situation's becoming violent, whereas situational factors act as the triggers.

Efforts to end dating violence can be categorized into primary and secondary prevention. Primary prevention stops the first instance of abuse before it happens. Secondary prevention occurs when abusers cease being violent and victims stop being victimized (Foshee et al., 1998; Foshee et al., 1996). Overall, programs designed to change attitudes about dating violence show mixed results (Hilton et al., 1998). One promising program, the Safe Dates Program, uses school and community-based activities to address primary prevention by changing norms, decreasing stereotypes, and improving conflict management. Safe Dates promotes secondary prevention by changing beliefs and by informing adolescents about the services available for victims and perpetrators of abuse. An evaluation found that adolescents in the Safe Dates program reported 25 percent less psychological abuse, 60 percent less sexual violence, and 60 percent less physical violence perpetrated against their current partner than participants in the control group. Help-seeking increased substantially, and both dating partners received this help.

Dating violence is a serious problem, but many teens do not see it that way. In one study, 44 percent of the girls stayed with their boyfriends after moderate violence (slapping), whereas 36 percent stayed after severe violence (choking or punching) (Elias, 1997b). Programs need to communicate that even minor violence or abuse is unacceptable (Bethke & de Joy, 1993). Teens at risk for perpetrating severe violence need special help, and targeting them may be the most effective way to reduce dating violence (Hilton et al., 1998). It is clear, though, that both perpetrators and victims require help so that the incidence of dating violence can be reduced and the victims can better deal with its emotional consequences.

The Dynamics of Peer Pressure

How can a friend or a clique create pressure to conform? What type of power do peers exert? Social scientists have discovered five different bases for power. The first basis is *coercive power*—that is, threatening or punishing, and thus almost forcing the adolescent to do something. Coercion is relatively uncommon (Berndt, 1996). Peer pressure usually is much subtler. Another basis for power is *reward power.* Teens are rewarded by their friends for doing something, such as conforming to dress, grooming, and music preferences, as well as attitudes toward school. Teens receive positive feedback or at least avoid negative feedback. A third basis is *referent power.* Adolescents may conform to the suggestions and behaviors of others they admire. They look up to others who have traits they consider desirable, and they often try to emulate them. A fourth power base is *expert power.* An adolescent who sees another teenager as an expert in a particular area, such as fashion or music, may conform on that basis. The last type of power base is *legitimate power*—that is, the exercise of power given to someone by the society, such as a parent or a teacher. Legitimate power is not a factor in peer group pressure and adolescent conformity. Peer influence is based mostly on reward power, referent power, and expert power (in certain areas); only occasionally is coercive power a factor (Savin-Williams & Berndt, 1990).

It is incorrect to blame peer pressure for antisocial behavior. Peer influence does not cause a teen to "turn bad"; rather, aggressive children gravitate to one another and form friendships before adolescence (Cairns et al., 1988). Group norms certainly reinforce and encourage aggressive behaviors, but they do not cause the aggression. Antisocial peer groups do not redirect the behavior patterns of members but rather reinforce predispositions that predate group membership.

The Extent of Peer Pressure

Are adolescents as conforming as many adults believe? In Western cultures, adolescence is a time of achieving behavioral autonomy, the ability to show control of one's impulses and to accept responsibility for one's behavior. It is also a time of achieving emotional autonomy, that is, shifting away from total emotional reliance on parents.

Early adolescents become more behaviorally autonomous in relation to their parents but less behaviorally autonomous in relation to friends (Fuligni et al., 2001). As adolescents become more emotionally autonomous and idealize their parents less, they depend somewhat less on them and more on their peers. This shift is accompanied by increased susceptibility to peer influences (Steinberg & Silverberg, 1986). Some argue that adolescents simply switch their dependence on parents to dependence on peers, but this is not really the case. Most research shows susceptibility to peer influence peaks either during early adolescence or in the beginning of middle adolescence. Some research suggests that susceptibility to peer pressure increases substantially as youngsters move through early adolescence, peaking at age 14 or so and declining thereafter. But conformity to antisocial acts peaks a bit later, during the early part of middle adolescence (ninth grade or so) before declining (Berndt, 1979). Other research does not show such a decline in early or middle adolescence for peer pressure toward misconduct (Clasen & Brown, 1985).

One way to investigate peer influence is to ask adolescents how they would respond if their friends urged them to do something they did not want to do. Between middle childhood and middle adolescence (age 15 or so), willingness to comply with friends' suggestions increases; a decline then occurs (Brown, Clasen, & Eicher, 1986; Steinberg & Silverberg, 1986). Some research finds a peak in susceptibility to friends' influence, as well as in responsivness to friends' support, then, in middle adolescence (Berndt, 1996). At these times, the greatest number of arguments between parents and children take place. Peer conformity at these ages may simply reflect the fact that emotional autonomy develops before behavioral autonomy. Adolescents who are transforming their relationship with their parents before they are ready to become behaviorally autonomous may use the peer group to fill the void. Late adolescents demonstrate more behavioral autonomy, showing more independence from both parents and friends.

Thus, adolescents, especially individuals in the early and the beginning of the middle years of adolescence, are more conforming. However, conformity is not limited to adolescents; adults show it, too. Adolescents may be more conforming, though, because they evaluate fewer situations negatively. When asked if they would do something their peers pressured them to do, they often say yes because they do not see the behaviors as wrong.

Best friends have a much greater influence on adolescents than do casual friends or the crowd (Berndt, 1996). In the areas of smoking, drinking, and other drug use, the influence of best friends is greater than that of other friends, and other friends' influence is greater than that of peers in general (Berndt, 1996).

Although peer influence is usually seen as promoting risk taking, peers actually influence each other both in favor of and against risky behaviors. For example, peers may influence adolescents to use or not to use drugs and alcohol, and to achieve or not to achieve in school (Berndt & Keefe, 1995; Mounts & Steinberg,

1995). Friends also influence nutrition, sexual behavior, and physical activity (Millstein, Petersen, & Nightingale, 1993).

Many people see peers as exerting pressure in one direction and parents in another. Yet peers and parents may exert influence in the same direction, connecting parent and peer support (Meeus & Dekovic, 1995). The opinions of parents and friends overlap in most moral, educational, and career areas, although differences are found in more superficial areas (Hartup, 1983). And peer pressure that runs counter to parental beliefs is stronger in some areas than others. Adolescents asked to report real peer pressure (rather than to rate hypothetical incidents of peer pressure) report strong pressure to spend time with peers, conform to peer norms (in such areas as dress and language), and participate in peer-related activities (Brown, 1982; Brown, Clasen, & Eicher, 1986). All groups expect peers to devote time to them, which means spending less time with parents. Pressure from friends to use drugs or engage in sexual activity is lower than pressures in other areas, and many adolescents report that friends discourage these activities. Pressure to drink and be sexually active is stronger in the later grades than the early grades. Students in grades 7 to12 in two communities were asked about peer pressure; the respondents felt considerable pressure to become more involved with peers, but they reported much less pressure to become involved in misconduct, although such pressure was present (see Figure 6.5) (Clasen & Brown, 1985).

Girls generally encounter more peer pressure than do boys, especially in the areas of being socially active, dress and grooming, and having relationships with boys. Being socially active is the area of greatest pressure for males, with grooming far behind. Boys admit to experiencing more pressure to drink, engage in sexual activity, and take drugs (Brown, 1982).

Adolescents often do not feel overt peer pressure (de Bois-Reymond & Ravesloot, 1994). The pressure may come more from a desire to fit in and adhere to group norms, which is a subtle pressure, than from direct peer pressure (Brown, 1982). This subtler pressure, though, can be intense. The more an individual wants to be a member of a group, the harder it is to resist it. Adolescents who hold a lower position in the group, are marginal members, or are less certain of their standing are more likely to be influenced than those with higher standing. They may conform to keep their membership. Susceptibility to peer influence is negatively related to adolescents' social confidence; the more confident the teen, the less susceptible to peer influence he or she will be (Berndt, 1979).

Much conformity, then, is an attempt to remain in the good graces of friends or a clique. Adolescents want acceptance and often behave in ways they perceive their friends want them to act. However, they may perceive their friends as

Adolescents face considerable pressure to conform in outward ways, such as in dress and music preferences.

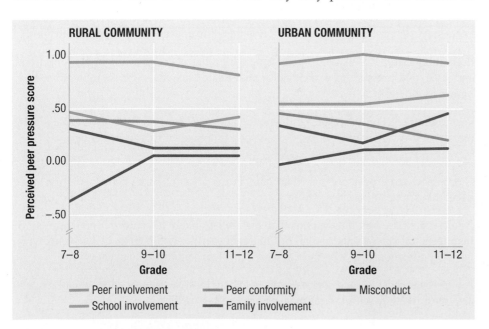

RURAL COMMUNITY   **URBAN COMMUNITY**

Perceived peer pressure score

— Peer involvement   — Peer conformity   — Misconduct
— School involvement   — Family involvement

Figure 6.5
Pressure to Conform from Different Sources
The greatest area of peer pressure is simply pressure to spend time with peers. Perceived peer pressure toward misconduct increased with advancing grades among rural participants, whereas increases in the urban sample were not significant. Perceived pressure toward peer conformity decreased across grades in the urban sample but not the rural sample.
Source: Clasen & Brown (1985).

engaging in undesirable behavior more often than they really do. Teens assume that they know their friends' attitudes, but often they do not, and they merely project their own views onto others. For example, adolescents assume that their friends' attitudes toward sex are similar to their own, when the actual similarity may be low (Wilcox & Udry, 1986). They also see themselves as agreeing more with their friends on issues such as smoking, alcohol and drug use, behavior in school, and academic achievement than they really do (Berndt, 1996).

Conformity to Peers: The Parental Dimension

Some adolescents are more oriented toward parents and others, toward peers. Most adolescents are able to maintain their balance between parents and peers and develop their own sense of autonomy—that is, they develop the ability to make their own decisions. Even with the increased susceptibility to peer influence, especially during early adolescence, most adolescents negotiate adolescence with a healthy interdependence with both parents and peers. A relatively few adolescents show such a dependence on peers that they are willing to break their parents' rules, neglect schoolwork, and even neglect development of their own talents in order to stay in the good graces of their peers. These adolescents exhibit lower academic performance and show more behavior problems (Fuligni et al., 2001). Autonomous youngsters come from homes that use authoritative methods of child rearing. Peer-oriented adolescents come from homes that are less nurturing and either very controlling or very permissive (Steinberg, 1996). Those who perceive their parents as neglecting or rejecting are also more influenced by their

---

AT A GLANCE 6.6 BEHAVIORAL AUTONOMY AND CONFORMITY

KEY POINT: Although peer pressure exists, adolescents are not slavishly devoted to following their peers in all behaviors.

SUPPORTING POINTS	EXPLANATION
Peer pressure may operate in a number of ways.	Peer pressure may be based on coercive power, reward power, referent power, expert power, or legitimate power. Most peer pressure operates through reward, referent, or expert power.
During early adolescence, young people become more autonomous from their parents but depend more on their peers.	Susceptibility to peer influences peaks at about age 14, but conformity to antisocial behavior peaks in the early part of middle adolescence. Late adolescents are less susceptible to peer influence.
Peer pressure need not be negative.	Peers may exert pressure to achieve or pressure not to engage in a dangerous behavior.
Peer pressure is stronger in some areas than others.	Peers report strong pressure to spend time with other peers, pressure in areas of dress and style, and pressure to participate in peer-related activities (for example, to attend parties or movies).
Peer pressure to enter into antisocial behavior is weaker than pressure in other areas.	Peer pressure certainly has some influence on antisocial behavior, but adolescents report more peer pressure in other areas, such as spending time with peers or dating.
Girls encounter more peer pressure than boys.	Girls report more peer pressure than boys in the areas of social activities, dress, and developing opposite-sex relationships.
An adolescent's degree of conformity is related to the child-rearing style of the parents.	Adolescents raised by authoritative parents are less likely to conform to peer pressure than teens raised by authoritarian or indulgent (permissive) parents. Adolescents who have good relationships with their parents show less conformity to peers.
Adolescents see parents and peers as being experts in different areas.	Adolescents consider age mates as more expert in styles, music, and school-related activities, and they see adults as more expert in other matters.

peers (Dishion, 1990). Adolescents who have a close and satisfying relationship with their parents are less influenced by friends (Steinberg & Silverberg, 1986).

Their relationship with parents affects the extent to which adolescents rely on their peers (Curtner-Smith & MacKinnon-Lewis, 1994). Peer influence on behavior and attitudes is magnified for adolescents who perceive their relationship with their parents as negative, nonsupportive, or uncaring (Savin-Williams & Berndt, 1990). Adolescent boys who report that their fathers do not monitor them are more susceptible to pressure to misbehave. Authoritarian parenting that involves very harsh punishments without any hint of caring, rather than simply greater monitoring and organization of the child's time, is also related to greater susceptibility to antisocial values and peer pressure. Perhaps parents who do not monitor their children and discipline harshly do not seem very approving, and adolescents look elsewhere for approval (Stouthamer-Loeber & Loeber, 1988).

Parents are often uneasy about the extent of their teens' peer group conformity. If parents would like their teenager to behave in one way and the wishes of peers differ, what the teen will do depends on the situation. Adolescents perceive peers and parents as competent guides in different areas (Brittain, 1963). They view their peer group as more knowledgeable in superficial and social areas, such as styles and feelings about school. Adolescents are more likely to conform to peers' opinions on day-to-day social matters of style, dress, music, and leisure activities, especially in junior high and early high school. When behavior reflects deeper values involving family, education, or financial affairs, adolescents report being closer to their parents, as long as the relationship is good. With age, adolescents simply report turning to those they see as experts for advice (Sebald, 1986, 1989; Wintre et al., 1988).

Parents have great influence in the more serious aspects of life. One study found that when a mother wanted her adolescent child to attend college but the adolescent's best friend had no plans, 50 percent of the adolescents went to college, and 50 percent reported no college plans. When the mother was opposed to college and the best friend was in favor of it, only 21 percent planned to attend college. The influence of the parent is greater than that of a best friend for educational plans. When both the mother and the best friend favored college, 83 percent of the adolescents had college plans, whereas only 8 percent had college plans when both were opposed (Kandel & Lesser, 1972).

It is a mistake to see adolescents as completely buffeted between parents and peers, without minds of their own. Adolescent decisions are often based on a reasoned sense of independence. Adolescents are able to sort alternatives into levels, assigning priority to various questions. Adolescents are not automatons; they often act on their own inclinations independent of friends, family, and peers (Sebald, 1986).

In summary, it is clear that peer pressure operates selectively in different areas and that some adolescents are more susceptible to it than others. Adolescents are more likely to conform in more neutral activities than they are to follow their peers into antisocial behaviors. A developmental trend toward less conformity with age is also found. Peer pressure is a factor in adolescent behavior, but it does not act alone to dictate behavior (Brown, Clasen, & Eicher, 1986). (For a review of this section, see At A Glance 6.6.)

PLACING PEERS IN PERSPECTIVE

Historically, many people believed that teenagers made up a group of individuals with a language and culture that pitted them against the larger culture. Many still perceive teen culture as promoting irresponsibility and being in constant opposition to adult society. According to this view, the media encourages this antiadult teen culture (see "The Media"), and at the heart of the culture is a peer group that demands and receives slavish conformity.

This concept of a dominant teen culture that is entirely antiadult and anti-establishment should be laid to rest. Most teens embrace conventional adult norms and career patterns. Popularity is important, but most adolescents do not purchase it by acting in antisocial ways. Peer pressure certainly exists, but teens do not mindlessly cave in and do anything their peers demand. Rather, teenagers pay attention to those they see as experts in different areas of life, and the extent of their conformity is based somewhat on their relationship with parents.

Differences between teen and adult culture are bound to exist because each cohort negotiates a different historical period. Each generation has its own music, dress, and preferred activities. Many adults remember their parents shaking their heads and criticizing the music they listened to when they were adolescents. Today's adolescent cohort is not the first, nor will it be the last, to bear the stigma of adult disapproval.

Another problem with the pervading negative view of adolescent culture is the idea that an all-powerful monolithic youth culture exists. This idea leads people to conclude that when parents and peers give conflicting advice, peers win consistently; that peers wean adolescents from adult values; and that teen

THEMES

THEME 1 **Adolescence is a time of choices, "firsts," and transitions.**	• Teenagers spend more time with their peers than do younger children. • Friendships with the other gender become common in adolescence, whereas they are almost absent during middle childhood. • Romantic relationships occur for the first time in adolescence. • Adolescents form cliques and crowds for the first time. • For the first time, adolescents see friends in terms of self-disclosure, intimacy, and commitment. • Adolescents are subjected to more pressure to conform, and they must make their own choices.
THEME 2 **Adolescence is shaped by context.**	• The peer group is an important social and educational context in adolescence. • Boy-girl relationships, whether romantic or based on friendship, form a context for development within adolescence. • The adolescent context includes cliques and crowds.
THEME 3 **Adolescence is influenced by group membership.**	• In adolescence, most friendships are found within one's group. • Male friendships tend to be based on similar interests, whereas female friendships emphasize emotional support. • The male and female roles differ in dating.
THEME 4 **The adolescent experience has changed over the past 50 years.**	• Psychologists and educators are more aware of the dangers of bullying today, realizing that a concerted effort by schools is necessary to reduce it. • Dating violence is now recognized as a major problem.
THEME 5 **Today's views of adolescence are becoming more balanced, with greater attention to its positive nature.**	• Rather than seeing teenagers as simply being reinforced by their peer group for conformity, psychologists now realize that teenagers also select friends who have similar attitudes. • Rather than viewing teenagers as conforming totally to the peer group, psychologists now realize that adolescents are more likely to follow the peer group in certain areas (such as style) than in other areas (such as morality). • Rather than viewing teenagers as slavishly conforming to the opinions of their peer group, psychologists now realize that adolescents make their own decisions. • Rather than viewing adolescent subculture as essentially antiauthority, psychologists now see it as more complex and far more accepting of adult values than was originally thought, although some antiauthority elements still exist.

values oppose those of their parents (Brown, 1990). No research supports these assumptions. As noted previously, when parents and peers conflict on what to do, teens do not always side with their peers. In areas such as college choice or career planning, adolescents rely on their own judgment or those adults they see as having more expertise. The generation gap is also vastly overrated; it is difficult to see how the basic values of most teens differ from those of their parents.

Then why, in the face of contrary evidence, does this negative view of adolescents still exist? Why do many journalists still see teen culture as an evil entity? First, newspapers and magazines tend to focus on a small, antisocial element of adolescents and thus make them seem to be the norm. Social scientists must also share some of the blame, because much more research focuses on negative aspects of behavior such as aggressive and antisocial behavior than on the positive side of adolescent behavior. Researchers may be simply mirroring society's interests and focusing on societal problems, but their emphasis leads the average citizen to believe that aggressive adolescents are more common than they really are.

As psychologists move away from seeing the youth culture, crowds, cliques, and adolescent interpersonal interactions as monolithic and entirely negative, a new picture that emerges is far more complex. Peer interaction becomes a dynamic context for adolescent development, one that responds to developmental changes. Psychologists and the general public today can more fully appreciate the nature of the peer group and the way it functions as a context for the personal growth and development of the adolescent (Brown, 1990).

CHAPTER SUMMARY AT A GLANCE

KEY TOPICS	KEY POINTS	KEY TERMS
The Peer Group	The nature of peer relationships changes in adolescence. (*At A Glance 6.1, p. 182*)	
Friends	Close friendships promote adolescent development, and the nature of friendship changes in adolescence. (*At A Glance 6.2, p. 189*)	*peer (p. 183)* *friendship (p. 183)*
Cliques and Crowds	Adolescents belong to cliques and crowds, which influence their attitudes and behaviors. (*At A Glance 6.3, p. 192*)	*clique (p. 189)* *crowd (p. 189)*
Popularity and Unpopularity	Popularity and unpopularity are determined by many factors. (*At A Glance 6.4, p. 199*)	*sociometric techniques (p. 192)* *popular adolescents (p. 192)* *controversial adolescents (p. 192)* *rejected adolescents (p. 192)* *neglected adolescents (p. 192)* *average adolescents (p. 192)* *bullying (p. 197)*
Romantic Relationships	Adolescents begin to form romantic relationships, which differ from other close relationships. (*At A Glance 6.5, p. 204*)	*script (p. 203)*
Behavioral Autonomy and Conformity	Although peer pressure exists, adolescents are not slavishly devoted to following their peers in all behaviors. (*At A Glance 6.6, p. 210*)	

Review questions for this chapter appear in the appendix.

7

THE SCHOOL EXPERIENCE

WHAT IS YOUR OPINION?

MIDDLE SCHOOL
• Transition to Middle School
  Perspective 1: Why the Change?
• The Wrong Fit?

HIGH SCHOOL
• Transition to High School
• Rating the Schools
• Achievement in High School
  FOCUS: "Of Course We Have Computers!"

ENHANCING THE SCHOOL EXPERIENCE
• Principles of Learner-Centered Education
• Motivation to Learn
• The Parental Role
• Teacher Expectations
• Tracking
• School Choices
  Perspective 2: A Community Divided
• The Transition to College

DROPPING OUT
  **Perspective 3: Standards
  for the Football Team**

**PLACING THE SCHOOL EXPERIENCE
IN PERSPECTIVE**
HAS YOUR OPINION CHANGED?
THEMES
CHAPTER SUMMARY AT A GLANCE

Think about what the lives of adolescents were like a hundred years ago. Most jobs required little training, and young people were routinely expected to leave school and help support their family. Their education consisted of little beyond basic reading and writing, some vocational training, and religious instruction. Young women were expected to marry and have their own families, as well as take care of their younger siblings. The idea that women would graduate from high school was relatively radical.

Almost every adolescent today, of course, attends high school, and most teens graduate. Academic credentials are more important than in the past—a fact acknowledged by parents, teachers, and adolescents alike. Most adolescents know that education leads to a brighter future.

The change from few adolescents attending high school to widespread high school attendance affects every area of an adolescent's life. The average adolescent's day revolves around school. Adolescents have a very long period of schooling that basically isolates them from adult society. They associate much more with other adolescents than with adults, and they do so in an atmosphere that encourages widespread social interaction. In fact, adolescents create their own culture partially based on this interaction. Widespread high school attendance also influences identity formation, for adolescents today have a longer period of exploration and experience a freer exchange of ideas. High school has become a major part of life for the vast majority of adolescents.

This chapter will examine the adolescent's experience in school. It begins with an analysis of the middle school and high school experiences. It continues with a discussion of achievement and then looks at factors that may influence and enhance the adolescent's school experience, including student motivation and attitudes, teacher practices, and parental involvement. Criticisms of the secondary school have led to suggestions for reform, such as the elimination of tracking (the practice of placing adolescents of similar ability in the same classes) and giving adolescents and their parents more choice of which school to attend. This chapter focuses on how each of these factors may affect the subjective experience of the adolescent. It concludes with a discussion of students who drop out of high school. Some students require special help to succeed in school because they have a learning disability, attention-deficit hyperactive disorder, or an emotional difficulty such as depression or anxiety. The nature of these disorders and special needs will be discussed in "Stress and Psychological, Physical, and Learning Problems."

MIDDLE SCHOOL

Most adolescents experience two important school-related transitions before the age of 18 years. The first transition is from elementary school to middle school or junior high school, and it occurs at varying ages. For example, some middle schools educate children in grades 6, 7, and 8; others, in grades 5, 6, 7, and 8; and still others, in grades 7, 8, and 9.

Transition to Middle School

One unmistakable sign that a child is growing up is the transition to middle school or junior high school. Traditionally, *junior high schools,* which were first established in 1909, enrolled students from seventh through ninth grades. *Middle schools,* which educate students from fifth or sixth grade through eighth

WHAT IS YOUR OPINION?

Please place the number best reflecting your opinion next to each of the following statements. We will return to this questionnaire at the end of the chapter so you can determine if your opinions have changed.

1 — Strongly Agree
2 — Moderately Agree
3 — No Opinion
4 — Moderately Disagree
5 — Strongly Disagree

_____ 1. Students would be better off attending a school with kindergarten through eighth grade and then switching to a high school rather than attending a middle school.

_____ 2. High schools are doing a good job of preparing students for college or the world of work.

_____ 3. Most teachers do not treat male and female students any differently in their classes.

_____ 4. A great deal of school reform is necessary if American schools are to be considered world class.

_____ 5. Most parents show considerable interest in how their adolescent children are doing in middle school and high school.

_____ 6. Most students work as hard as they can to master their schoolwork.

_____ 7. Success and failure in high school are due more to ability than to effort.

_____ 8. Tracking—placing students in classes with others of similar abilities—injures student self-esteem and should be eliminated.

_____ 9. Parents should be given a voucher (an amount of money to spend on their children's education) and be allowed to send their children to any public, private, or private religious school they choose.

_____ 10. Students who drop out of high school before the age of 18 should lose their driver's license.

The middle school and junior high school were designed to bridge the gap between the easier work of elementary school and the more complex work of high school.

grade, first made their appearance in 1950 (Manning & Buchner, 2000). These schools were originally designed to bridge the gap between the relatively easy curriculum of the elementary school and the much more demanding work of high school (Smith, 1987). Their advocates also cited a developmental basis: Early adolescence is a time of rapid physical, cognitive, and social changes. It is a transitional period in which students have different needs, which may be met best in a different school environment (Walker, Kozma, & Green, 1989). These student needs include understanding the physical and emotional changes they are undergoing, developing ways to encourage self-esteem and meaningful autonomy, and coming to accept themselves and adjust to their new station in life. Many psychologists see these years as critical, and they believe that the potential for increased risk taking in many areas—delinquency, sex, and drugs, for example—calls for a special environment dedicated to the needs of adolescent students (Manning & Allen, 1987). The emphasis began to shift from a focus on subject matter to an emphasis on meeting the developmental needs of students, including addressing young adolescents' personal and social problems and providing more counseling for children entering adolescence (Manning & Bucher, 2000).

Most middle schools differ substantially from elementary schools, not only in the type of work assigned but in structure as well. Middle schools provide a very different educational experience for young adolescents. Most elementary school students stay with one teacher most of the day, whereas most middle school students have different teachers for different subjects. Students usually travel from classroom to classroom, an arrangement that gives students more freedom. No longer does a student have to satisfy only one teacher; now the young teen has to satisfy five or six teachers. You probably remember most, if not all, of the names of your elementary school teachers but would be hard pressed to name all your middle school teachers without help. Students and teachers have much less personal contact in middle or junior high schools than in elementary school.

Middle schools also are larger. Usually, a number of elementary schools send their students to one or two middle schools. Many elementary school students know most of the children in their grade; they may have been promoted with their friends and stayed with the same group throughout their elementary school years. Now that arrangement changes. Many classmates in middle school are strangers, and many friends are no longer in the same class. Middle school alters the relatively secure social status of elementary school to one in which a young adolescent must make new friends. The older social networks may be torn asunder by lack of contact. Old friends from elementary school are also making new friends. The transition to middle school translates into a change in educational experience. Middle school students find themselves in a larger institution with many more strangers, are not as likely to have as close a relationship with their many teachers as they did with their one elementary school teacher, and must make new friendships.

In the critical transition from elementary to middle school, students must restructure their ways of doing things and adjust to a new environment (Yamamoto & Ishii, 1995). How do young teens adjust to this new educational experience in which so much changes? Most adolescents adjust well to the change from elementary school to middle school, but a minority of students experience problems. Girls are more vulnerable to problems than boys, perhaps because girls are experiencing multiple stresses at this time. For many girls, transition to middle school corresponds with many other developmental changes in the physical realm; this is not the case for boys, who mature somewhat later (Simmons et al., 1979). Most middle school students like going to the new school because that is where they meet their friends, and they enjoy what bigger schools offer, such as a wider range of activities. They appreciate being treated as more grown up (Nottelmann, 1987).

The major complaint of most middle and junior high students, even those who are adjusting well to their new surroundings, is that a sense of *anonymity* negatively affects their self-concept and self-esteem (Thornburg & Glider, 1984). They feel less attached to their school than they used to. This complaint is easy to understand. An elementary school teacher has perhaps twenty-five or so pupils and sees them most of the day. Within a few days, the teacher knows all their names. A middle school teacher, who teaches five classes of perhaps thirty students, has many more students to deal with and less time to give individual attention. The teacher may not know students' names or much about them for some time. Anonymity is not a subjective impression but a fact of life dictated by the structure of the school. Middle school students perceive a decline in the quality of school life. They do not believe their teachers are as warm and caring, and they perceive the school as more impersonal.

The most troublesome finding, though, is a decline in students' academic motivation, attitudes toward subject matter, and an increase in conduct problems (Alspaugh, 1998; Watt, 2000). Grades often decline (Alspaugh, 1998). A number of reasons have been advanced for this trend (Seidman et al., 1994). The social

More than anything else, middle school students complain about the feeling of anonymity that pervades the school.

PERSPECTIVE 1

WHY THE CHANGE?

SETTING THE SCENE: Janice has just entered junior high school. She was a good student in elementary school, but now her grades have declined, and she seems more interested in her social life than in her schoolwork. A teacher is contacting her parents because her work is poorly done.

PARENTS: *We don't know what to do. She doesn't seem interested in school and is barely passing her subjects. We know she can do better.*

TEACHER: *Her skill level in reading is fine, but she shows no interest in the work. Her homework is poorly done, and she does not study.*

JANICE: *School is boring. I'm not learning anything of importance. It seems meaningless. I don't cause any trouble. I have a lot of good friends, and I like seeing them in school.*

QUESTION: What, if anything, can Janice's parents and teachers do to improve her attitude toward school?

aspects of life become more important in early adolescence than they were previously. Perhaps students emphasize building social relationships more than studying. Middle school teachers grade lower and are stricter in their grading systems (Eccles, Midgley, et al., 1993); whereas elementary school teachers may factor effort into grades, middle school teachers are more likely to grade simply by averages on test grades. The structure of the middle school may also contribute to the decline in grades. Middle schools emphasize teacher control and discipline at a time when adolescents are striving for greater autonomy. They present few opportunities for student decision making. Teacher-student relationships are less positive and less personal, with little individual attention and more public evaluation. Students generally see their middle school teachers as less supportive than their elementary school teachers.

The importance of teacher support was demonstrated in a study of student attitudes toward mathematics before and after the transition to junior high school. Students who moved from elementary school math teachers perceived to be low in support to junior high school math teachers perceived to be high in support valued math more. Students who moved from math teachers perceived to be high in support to math teachers perceived to be low in support (the more common experience) experienced a sharp drop in how they viewed both the intrinsic value and the usefulness of math. These attitudes influenced achievement in mathematics (Midgley, Feldlaufer, & Eccles, 1989). One trait of supportive teachers is acting in a friendly and encouraging manner. However, students often find junior high school teachers to be less supportive than teachers in elementary school (Feldlaufer, Midgley, & Eccles, 1988).

The Wrong Fit?

The reduction in academic motivation and achievement between elementary and middle or junior high school may be due to the poor fit between the needs of the early adolescent and the educational experience provided (Eccles, Midgley, et al., 1993). Poor motivation may result from an environment that does not fit students' needs well. Imagine two trajectories: a developmental trajectory of early adolescent growth and a trajectory of environmental changes across the school years. When these trajectories match, positive outcomes occur; when they do not match, negative outcomes are the rule.

The middle school environment may not be responsive to the needs of early adolescents. For example, as noted earlier, middle school classrooms are characterized by more emphasis on teacher control and discipline, and fewer opportunities for student decision making. Students encounter this environment at a time when they want more autonomy and need more practice in decision making. Many middle school students note that they "can't" do something, such as make certain decisions, but "should" be able to do so—an observation that shows a mismatch between students and their environment. In addition, middle school has more ability grouping, public evaluation of one's work, competition, and other form of social comparison, which are likely to conflict with the growing self-consciousness of young adolescents.

Social interaction increases substantially in early adolescence, and students desire more autonomy. They want to explore new possibilities, so they may need more choices of learning activities. In addition, because students may be overwhelmed by the new need to satisfy many teachers, they must learn organizational skills. Furthermore, students in these years of physical, cognitive, and social changes may require health-related discussions that emphasize these changes. The school also must allow time for peer interactions within a framework of meaningful extracurricular activities. Minicourses that allow students to follow their interests are also useful. Encouraging students to study together and using cooperative learning techniques can also help students improve their social skills (Manning & Allen, 1987).

Two detailed reports from the Carnegie Corporation (1995, 1996) argued that middle schools are not meeting young people's needs. The reports note the importance of the early adolescent period, young adolescents' tendency toward experimentation, and the unprecedented choices and pressures in their world. Middle schools are potentially the most powerful force to help young people during these years. The reports suggest a number of changes, including dividing large middle-grade schools into smaller communities for learning, teaching a core academic program, the elimination of tracking by achievement level, fostering health and fitness, connecting the school with the community through service opportunities, and establishing partnerships with community organizations. They also advocate the use of cooperative learning strategies (where small groups of students learn together; see "Cognitive Development"), social and life skills training, and a curriculum that strengthens problem-solving abilities and higher-order thinking. Research shows that when these changes are made, teachers become more receptive to student ideas, and young adolescents experience a school environment that more closely matches their needs. The students perceive the school environment more positively, believe they have better relationships with teachers, and have higher achievement or achieve more (Erb, 2000).

Improved student achievement is important. Middle schools are often seen as overemphasizing social and emotional growth and not sufficiently emphasizing academic growth. In a study of 28 middle schools in 13 states, only one-third of the teachers agreed strongly that the school pushed students to do their best; 60 percent reported giving 1 hour or less of homework weekly, and only 35 percent said they consistently required students to revise their work to meet standards (Christie, 2001). Obviously, the mandate of the middle school is very difficult, and perhaps even conflicting. Critics view the decline in achievement in terms of the school's vague expectations and want stricter standards and more emphasis on achievement. Some argue that the middle school must both meet the developmental needs of students and have high academic standards (Manning & Bucher, 2000).

Students change schools when they are just entering early adolescence. It is fair to ask if making a change at a later time might improve student motivation and achievement. Evidence that age at transition can indeed make a difference is found in studies comparing achievement, motivation, self-esteem, and conduct of students who make the transition to secondary school in sixth grade and those who do so after eighth grade. Students transferring after eighth grade show fewer problems (Alspaugh, 1998). Achievement certainly declines when students transfer to high school, but the decline is greater when two changes are required. The dropout rate is also higher for students who attended a middle school rather than a school that had kindergarten through eighth grade. The decline in self-esteem is greater with the transition to middle school than with a transition made after eighth grade (Seidman et al., 1994). Some districts have begun to eliminate middle school, bringing back the kindergarten through eighth grade structure (Schouten, 2002), but most have not done so and probably never will. It is doubtful that the middle school idea will simply disappear. The developmental needs of these young adolescents cannot be ignored, but neither can the public's distress over the lack of academic growth.

A final explanation of some of the problems in middle school may lie in the fact that teaching early adolescents is not a recognized specialty in teacher training. A majority of middle school teachers were prepared to teach either elementary school or high school. Those trained as elementary school teachers may be unprepared to teach young adolescents and deal with the more complex academic content of the middle school. Those who trained to be high school teachers may be poorly prepared to teach the younger students. The junior high and middle

AT A GLANCE 7.1 MIDDLE SCHOOL

KEY POINT: The middle school/junior high school was created to bridge the gap between the easier work of elementary school and the more challenging academic work of high school, as well as to meet the developmental needs of young adolescents.

SUPPORTING POINTS	EXPLANATION
The structure of the junior high/middle school differs from the structure of the elementary school.	Middle school students have a different teacher for almost every subject and travel from class to class. Middle schools are also larger than elementary schools.
Most students adjust well to their transition to middle school, but some have difficulties.	Most students like their new school environment. The major complaint is anonymity; that is, students feel that teachers don't know who they are.
The transition to middle school often brings about a decline in student achievement and an increase in behavior problems.	The decline in achievement may be due to an increasing emphasis on social activities, stricter grading systems, or the impersonal nature of the middle school.
There may be a mismatch between the developmental needs of young adolescents and the middle school.	The teacher-controlled, more impersonal middle school may not be in keeping with the developmental needs of young adolescents for more autonomy and peer interaction.
Reports from the Carnegie Corporation suggested many reforms in middle school structure and function.	Reforms included smaller learning communities, the elimination of tracking, a core academic program, and connecting schools with the community.
Many have questioned the academic strength of the middle school.	Many teachers and parents do not believe that middle schools are challenging their students academically.

school ages are formative, and teacher training programs often do not cover them well. Some states now require coursework in early adolescent development and teaching methods, but teaching young adolescents should be recognized universally as a specialty. *(For a review of this section, see At A Glance 7.1.)*

HIGH SCHOOL

By the time students enter high school, the early adolescent period has drawn to a close. Their social world is more complicated, and the transition to high school means a transition to a still more diverse and complex world.

Transition to High School

The transition from middle school to high school has not been studied as extensively as the transition from elementary school to junior high school (Reyes, Gillock, & Kobus, 1994; Seidman et al., 1996). The shift is subtler. Although high schools are usually larger than middle schools, the structural differences between high school and middle school are not as great. Furthermore, by the end of eighth grade, many of the major physical changes in adolescence have already occurred. Yet any transition can be stressful, even a necessary one (no one claims that all twelve years of school should be spent in the same building). The freshman year in high school is a period of new experiences and opportunities, and a pattern of decline in grades, increasing failures, more absences, and decreased involvement in school activities is common (Barone, Aguirre-Deandreis, & Trickett, 1991). Students who did very well in junior high school benefit from attending the same high school as their eighth-grade classmates, whereas those who are struggling benefit from enrolling in a different high school (Schiller, 1999). Perhaps poorly achieving students get a new start in a school where they have no established reputation. For example, some students who had social difficulties in middle school blossom both academically and socially because of the greater diversity in most large high schools. Young adolescents who may have been alone in junior high can now find others who are more like them in high school (Kinney, 1993).

Just as in the transition to middle school, students entering high school find that their peer relationships change and the work is more demanding. There is a lack of support in high school; students see their high schools as less engaging and less user friendly. A study following students transferring to high school found that their grades had declined but their self-esteem was not significantly affected, and students felt more socially confident. Students perceived more academic hassles and less social support, and they were involved less often in school related functions. Daily hassles with peers declined and involvement with peers increased, perhaps because of a more mature attitude toward the interactions (Seidman et al., 1996). There is no evidence of an increase in psychological disorders or serious adjustment problems (Wallis & Barrett, 1998). The decline in grades following a transition seems to be a common theme (Barone et al., 1991). The more difficult the transition, the more it seems to adversely affect academic achievement. Although such transitions increase stress for most students, students gradually report becoming acclimated to their new school, which reduces their stress.

The transition to junior high is generally more difficult than the transition to high school. Whereas a relatively intensive transition program may be required to facilitate the transition to junior high or middle school, a less intensive orientation to high school is needed. After a period of uncertainty, most high school students adjust well to the changes. However, some do not, and the identification of students who performed much better in elementary school than junior high and those who performed better in junior high school than high school would enable school officials to help these students better adjust to the more rigorous work and different social environment of their new schools. Perhaps a small decline in achievement is the norm as new and more difficult standards are imposed, but larger declines should signal students who need help.

The decreasing involvement of many students in high school also needs a remedy. Students who are active in school and after-school activities feel a connection to their schools and are less likely to drop out. However, some students do not feel welcome, and high school activities do not always seem open to anyone but the "best." For example, an athlete may find it more difficult to make the high school team than the junior high school team, and a musician who was in the junior high orchestra may not make the high school orchestra. In addition, students often find that activities seem to be monopolized by older students. High schools thus should offer ways to involve students who will not make the basketball team or the orchestra, or those who do not feel welcome at meetings of the school newspaper staff. Otherwise, these students experience a disengagement at a time when what they need is greater involvement. Every transition creates both stress and opportunities. With some help, most students can adjust well to their new situations and make good use of the new and expanding opportunities that a larger school offers.

Many after-school activities, such as high school athletic teams and art or music activities, are increasingly limited to the most talented, leaving many students out. After-school programs are important, because participation in them encourages students to feel connected with the school.

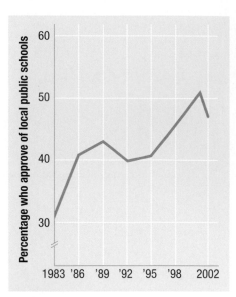

Figure 7.1
Overall Approval Ratings for Local Schools, 1983 to 2002
Since 1983, the public's attitude toward local schools has shown improvement. In 2001 the approval rating hit its highest level, and then showed a decline in 2002.
Source: Rose & Gallup (2002).

Rating the Schools

We live in an age of dissatisfaction with the nation's schools, at least judged by the media. Criticisms of schools and school achievement abounds. Public opinion surveys, however, show that people do not seem dissatisfied with their *local* schools. In fact, parents routinely rate the schools in their community as superior to the nation's schools. More than half of all parents give them an A or a B, whereas only 25 percent give such high grades to the nation's schools (Rose & Gallup, 2002). The public's rating of local schools is much higher than it was in 1983 when the surveys began (see Figure 7.1).

Another trend is greater dissatisfaction with secondary schools than with elementary schools. Most criticisms of education are aimed at secondary schools, especially high schools. For example, half of all elementary school students give their school an A or A– rating, but only a third of the secondary students do so. Parental ratings show a similar trend, with many more rating the elementary school positively than the high school. Many more elementary school students rate their teachers as A or A– than do secondary school students, and again this trend extends to parents (Rose, Gallup, & Elam, 1997).

A number of factors may contribute to these differences, including factors that may stem directly from the structural differences between elementary and secondary schools. Elementary school students are more likely to have a close relationship with their teachers than are high school students, as the younger children stay in one class with one teacher for most of the day and get to know their teachers well. Parents also understand their children's work in elementary school but have more difficulty understanding high school lessons. The general public can easily understand the clear mandate of the elementary school to teach the basics, whereas the mandate of the secondary school is more ambiguous (Bracey, 1996). High school work is also more challenging and abstract, which also may lead to less favorable comparisons.

Another poll of high school students found that 20 percent said they "hated school" or liked it "only a little." These students' high school experiences are decidedly negative. Forty-five percent feel a great deal of pressure to get good grades. One in five students reports grappling with five or more serious problems at a time. These and other data can be interpreted as showing that 80 percent of teens seem to be doing reasonably well, but the remaining 20 percent are floundering and need help (Riley, 1999).

Two-thirds of the high school students, however, assign their school a grade of B or better for giving them a good education. They give their schools high grades for providing access to technology (see "Focus: 'Of Course We Have Computers!'"), and a surprising 70 percent of high schoolers say they have a teacher to whom they feel close. An unexpected 77 percent of the students say they feel very safe going to high school, but this overall figure hides important demographic differences. More than 40 percent of African American students give their schools a C or lower when it comes to safety (an area that will be discussed in "Drug Use and Violence"). About 40 percent of all teens work just hard enough to get by in school, another finding that we will discuss more later in the text.

A recent survey of parents, employers, and college professors provides a more critical evaluation of high schools (Reality Check, 2000). About 75 percent of employers and college professors say that today's graduates have just "fair" or "poor" skills in grammar, spelling, and writing. However, they give schools credit for what they see as major improvements in students' knowledge of computers and their ability to use technology.

Perhaps the most interesting difference among people surveyed is that parents believe their children are better prepared for later study and work than do either teachers or employers. More than seven in ten parents believe their local high schools are doing a "good" or "excellent" job, and 65 percent say academic expectations are about right. Almost half of the parents strongly believe their children's school places a great deal of emphasis on academics and high grades.

They also give teachers generally high grades for dedication and effort, although about half believe teachers are not doing everything possible.

Although two-thirds of all high school parents say their child will have the skills to succeed on the job, just a third of employers agree. And whereas 61 percent of the parents of high school students are confident that their child will do well in college, only 46 percent of the college professors think so. Obviously, parents are more optimistic than college professors or employers are.

Achievement in High School

Complaints about students' educational attainment are not hard to find; just open up any newspaper or speak to any employer. The complaints are both of a general nature (high school students don't have the skills they should) and more specific (the achievement level of many minority students is disappointing).

According to the National Assessment of Educational Programs (a report card of sorts for U.S. schools), students in fourth grade are performing at higher levels than generations ago, and minority youth show substantial improvements. However, secondary school students are not doing any better today than they did 30 years ago.

It is popular to compare American students to students from other countries and to complain about the achievement level of American students. International comparisons show that fourth graders in the United States compare favorably in math and science, trailing only Korean and Japanese children; by eighth grade, however, they are in the middle of the pack, and by twelfth grade they fall even further behind (Peterson, 1999). However, upon closer inspection the situation becomes more complicated. First, there is great variability among U.S. states—as much as among countries (Bracey, 1998). Second, there is incredible variation within states. Of course, there is also variation within other countries, including Japan. Students from some U.S. school districts compare extremely well with their peers in Japan and other countries, whereas students from other U.S. school districts do not. Third, the scores of most countries are very close. To say that American students score fifth or twelfth on some measure often omits the fact that the differences between fifth and twelfth, or between second and third, are often very small.

Furthermore, there is some good news. Enrollments in advanced science and math courses have increased in the United States (West, 1994). The achievement gap between white and African American students in science, math, and reading has narrowed, as has the gender gap (Jacobson, 1997). Graduation rates are higher, and the percentage of high school students taking core academic subjects has increased substantially (Toch, Bennefield, & Bernstein, 1996). Scores on the SAT and ACT tests have improved somewhat, and high school work has become more rigorous.

Complaints about school achievement and calls for reform are far from new. In 1957, when the Russians launched the first satellite to orbit Earth, the idea that the United States was behind in science and math became popular and led to changes in the curriculum. After this reform movement had spent its energy, the pendulum swung back toward a greater emphasis on personal growth and understanding one's own needs. Then, in 1981, the National Commission on Excellence in Education publicized the results of 18 months of study in *A Nation at Risk*. The commission documented many problems in the educational system and recommended, among other things, stricter requirements for graduation, especially in English, math, science, foreign language, and social studies; a lengthening of the school year; and curriculum reform. This report, combined with test results showing that American high school students lagged behind students in other countries, such as China and Japan, spurred states to reform their public school systems. Students in other countries do spend more time in school and studying at home, and they are exposed to a more rigorous curriculum (Fuligni & Stevenson, 1995).

"Of course we have computers!" was the proud statement made by a junior high school principal as he showed parents around the newly wired and computerized classrooms. Down the hall, a teacher was busy having the two computers in her room removed to give her more space. She noted how impressed the parents were. "Did anyone ask how they were being used?" the teacher asked in a laughing manner. "They are being used very little." Pointing to another teacher's room, she noted that one of the computers was not working and that the teacher wasn't even bothering to put in a work order to have it fixed.

There is no doubt that technology is changing the face of our society and influencing students. Email, chat rooms, and searching the Web are no longer only for the technologically sophisticated. Most schools are connected to the Web. Local school districts are spending about $4 billion a year on computer technology, and schools are being pressured to computerize (Conte, 1998; Healy, 1999). Advocates of the use of technology argue persuasively that if students are to be prepared for the world of technology, they must have access to it and learn to use it. Evidence exists that computer assisted instruction can positively influence student achievement and contribute to the development of higher order thinking skills and problem solving abilities (Cradler et al., 2002). The public is also sold on the idea; most people believe that computers are very helpful in teaching high-tech skills, providing access to the latest information, making learning more fun, and increasing students' understanding of the world.

There are two aspects to computer use at school: computer literacy and the use of computers in the classroom. Computer literacy consists of the skills and knowledge that allow a person to function successfully in an information-based society (Upchurch & Lochhead, 1987). For example, many people argue that students should be able to access and use the Internet, understand how to use email, know something about software, and perhaps be able to use word-processing and spreadsheet programs. Some understanding of the ethics of computer use, the damage a hacker could do, and the right to privacy is also required (Zuckerman & Rodger, 2000).

The other side of computer use is how the technology is used in the classroom. The computer is viewed as a teaching and learning tool (Archer, 1998; Ohler, 2000). Computers traditionally have been used for drills, practice, and tutorials. After all, a computer can be programmed to ask questions and explain why an answer chosen by a student is wrong. The computer never loses patience and efficiently delivers drills and guides practice. It allows students to move at their own pace through material and to compete against themselves (Roth, 1999). Students who have difficulty with a concept can seek out the part of a computer program that focuses on this area. A student who was absent can catch up using such programs.

More and more often, though, the computer is seen as a tool to encourage students to think and develop new skills (Cradler et al., 2002; Norman, 1999). One computer program, for example, allows students to test velocity, a concept students understand easily but have difficulty quantifying. The program shows the up-and-down movement of an elevator alongside a graph showing its changing speed in floors per second. The program asks where the elevator would end up based on the graph, showing that a lower velocity does not mean that the elevator is going down but just that the speed is decreasing. Finally, it asks students to create their own graphs that make a second elevator wind up at the same floor at the same time, but varying the speed (Archer, 1998). Another computer program allows students who have collected water samples to understand how water quality is affected by increasing or decreasing levels of oxy-

Minority Group Youth and Achievement Differences in educational achievement between ethnic and racial groups in the United States show themselves early in elementary school and continue throughout secondary school (Stevenson, Chen, & Uhal, 1990). African Americans and Latinos are more likely to do poorly than Asian Americans and whites. Students from minority groups often begin elementary school with deficits in language skills, and many do not catch up or succeed. A greater proportion of children from minority groups are raised in poverty, a factor that often confounds ethnic or racial differences. Poverty is often accompanied by poor housing, greater exposure to violence, lower parental educational level, poor access to health care, and lack of family stability, and these factors in turn are related to low achievement (Ford & Harris, 1996). Along with these difficulties are language differences (Duran, 1989). A smaller proportion of Latinos attend college than African Americans, whites, or Asian Americans. Only 35 percent of all Latino students are in college preparatory programs, and Latino students are less likely than other minority students to be engaged in school activities (Lewis, 1998). There is substantial room for improvement (Bennefield, 1997).

gen in the water, temperature, light intensity, phosphate levels, and other substances (Manno et al., 1998). Evidence clearly shows that computerized material does help motivate students (Archer, 1998), but whether this improvement is short term or long term is currently not known.

Relatively few teachers use computers for the kind of instruction just described. They use them most often for drill and practice (Norman, 1999). Many technology advocates argue that the use of computers in the classroom is meager and unimaginative and that many high-tech schools have low-tech teaching (Cuban, 1999). A number of reasons explain this lack of progress. Foremost is the lack of teacher training and professional development. Only 20 percent of public school teachers say they feel very well prepared to integrate technology into the classroom. Although schools should allocate at least 30 percent of their technology funding to professional development, most schools use only 5 percent for this purpose (Norman, 1999).

Computers may look great in the back of the room, but most teachers do not know how to use them in class. In addition, having one or two computers in the classroom does not allow all students to use them. Teachers also may not have access to software that gives their students important practice in simulations, applications, and advanced thinking skills (Cuban, 1999).

Although the public and most professionals support the use of technology in schools, contrary voices are raised. Some claim that the headlong rush to use technology has not answered the simple question of where we are going (Ohler, 2000). Others argue that it takes 5 years of in-service training before teachers can fully integrate computers into their classroom lessons, and few districts are willing to spend the necessary money (Healy, 1999). Few schools have technology experts who can help with the continuous challenges of working with computers, including what to do when something doesn't run.

These detractors argue that computers are often glitzy frills, and the money could be better spent improving instruction, especially in the lower grades. For example, it is estimated that the cost of connecting all classrooms to the Internet could provide every child in the United States with an adequate preschool program (Healy, 1999). Other opponents ask whether the mere use of technology makes something educationally valid, pointing out that endless surfing of the Internet is not educational (Burniske, 1998). There is little evidence that mere access to the Web improves thinking skills or teaches problem solving.

Computers and the use of the Internet are hardly the dangerous things their detractors say they are, nor are they the potential savior of American education. What is important is not whether students use a computer or the Internet but how they use it. It is easy to confuse access to information with real knowledge, as well as to confuse the ability of students to download information with their ability to analyze the material (Conte, 1998).

Computerization and interest in the Web will continue to grow. The generation of students now entering adolescence will certainly be the most technologically sophisticated ever (Tapscott, 1998). Computers and the use of appropriate software can motivate these students and allow them to learn in new ways. Yet technology and computers are tools to achieve an end, not ends in themselves. Like all tools, they are more useful in some areas than others. Computers can help students approach material in ways that were not available even a generation ago. However, patient research, creative use of software, and tremendous expenditures for teacher training will be needed to teach students both how to use technology and how to understand how this technology affects society. Schools will need additional resources to integrate technology into the educational process at all levels.

Some students raised in poverty do achieve. Perhaps studying them is the key to helping others, given that it is so difficult to change socioeconomic status. Better academic success among lower- and working-class children is associated with parents' efforts to instill good study habits, as well as an emphasis on self-discipline (Clark, 1983). Parental education is also a factor; the better educated the parents, the better the students perform (Luster & McAdoo, 1994). Children from smaller families also achieve more, probably because they receive more attention. African American children from poverty backgrounds who achieve have a positive attitude toward school and do their homework. Their parents encourage them to study, communicate high hopes for their education, and speak optimistically about their future. Both maternal support and control are important. The combination of warmth, affection, and discipline improves achievement. Under conditions of low risk, maternal restrictive control correlates negatively with grades. However, within high-risk neighborhoods, somewhat greater restrictions and control are positively associated with higher grades (Gonzalez et al., 1996). These high parental expectations exist despite terrible living conditions.

Parents who try to instill good work habits and self-discipline find that their adolescent children do better in school.

Other researchers, although not denying that the home has a significant influence on academic achievement, claim that neighborhood and peer influences are crucial factors explaining minority group youth achievement, especially among African Americans (Dornbusch, Ritter, & Steinberg, 1991). Minority youth may not associate with peers who encourage achievement, and the dominant peer values may be too powerful to offset the positive influence of parental values (Steinberg, Dornbusch, & Brown, 1992). In other words, some African American peer groups discourage academic achievement, seeing it as acting "white" and as giving into a majority that will take their unique culture away (Fordham, 1991; Fordham & Ogbu, 1986). The evidence for this idea is contradictory. Where peer and neighborhood influences often work against achievement, parents must forge a good relationship with their adolescents, as well as provide the discipline necessary to overcome the negative peer and neighborhood effects. Some argue that this lack of peer encouragement to achieve in school is more a symptom of a problem than a cause, whereas others claim that although peer influence does not directly cause achievement problems, it makes it more difficult to close the gap in achievement between minority group members and the majority (Viadero, 2000).

Another difficulty is high mobility. Many students raised in poverty change residences a great deal and don't stay in their schools very long. Schools with high student turnover offer slower-paced instruction, probably because teachers must deal with students of many different educational backgrounds. Other possible causes for the differences in achievement among racial and ethnic groups include the quality of teaching; some argue that schools with high concentrations of minority and poor students are more likely to have less experienced teachers. Still another view focuses on the fact that students from minority groups lose more ground academically over the summer, and teacher expectations are lower for these students (Viadero, 2000). Others claim that the gap begins very early and is difficult to close because the schools are not set up to do so. About half the gap in school achievement between African Americans and whites is explained by learning differences that are present before students even begin elementary school. It is certainly possible that a combination of these reasons, and perhaps some unknown factors, contribute to the achievement gap. Some persuasively argue that the reforms that began to decrease the gap between African American and Latino students and their white peers have basically stopped, and thus the gap is no longer closing (Fashola & Slavin, 1998).

When African American students were asked what would enhance academic achievement, their answers included better academic preparation, active participation in class, positive peer influences, empowering students by teaching them self-management techniques, and receiving more encouragement and praise by teachers and parents (Tucker et al., 2000).

Despite this achievement gap, some improvements have occurred. More minority students are earning high school diplomas. The high school graduation gap among African Americans, Latinos, and whites has narrowed. Nearly 75 percent of all African Americans between the ages of 18 and 24 earned high school diplomas as of 1997, up from 68 percent in 1977. Some 62 percent of Latinos graduated, up from 55 percent in 1977. About 83 percent of all white students completed high school, about the same percentage as in 1977 (Blair, 2000).

The experience of minority group students living in poverty is certainly different from that of minority and nonminority students raised in a middle-class area. Exposure to violence and stress due to poverty, substandard schools, and starting first grade behind their peers may make school and learning more difficult. However, many minority students in these circumstances do succeed, and parental interest and child-rearing strategies that promote achievement form the basis for academic success.

The gap between graduation rates for whites and African Americans has narrowed substantially.

Gender and Achievement In elementary school, girls achieve at least as well as boys, and perhaps somewhat higher. Girls perform better on measures of reading, verbal fluency, spelling, and mathematical computation, whereas boys are superior in mathematical reasoning and problem solving that involves spatial analysis (Marshall & Smith, 1987). Of course, a great deal of overlap occurs, with some girls performing better than boys in math and some boys reading better than girls. Even in the first grade, before they have had much experience in school, boys believe they are more competent in math and science, whereas girls believe they are more competent in reading (Eccles, Wigfield, et al., 1993). Girls also spend more time in academic activities (Posner & Vandell, 1999). Females are less likely to repeat grades and show higher writing proficiency in elementary school (U.S. Department of Education, 1995a).

As children negotiate elementary school, boys remain confident in their abilities and often overestimate them, whereas girls show an increasing tendency to underestimate their academic competence (Cole et al., 1999). Girls have an advantage in elementary school: The atmosphere is feminine, with its high percentage of female teachers, its emphasis on obedience, and its focus on activities that require fine motor coordination. Boys and girls experience school in different ways, and both male and female teachers value the stereotyped feminine traits of obedience and passivity rather than aggressiveness and independence (Etaugh & Hughes, 1975). This may affect student achievement in secondary school, where the atmosphere changes. In middle school girls continue to outperform boys, but in high school boys improve considerably, and the gap between males and females closes rapidly (Henry, 1996).

Teachers may interact differently with boys and girls. A controversial study by the American Association of University Women (1992) found widespread discrimination by teachers, as well as in texts and tests. Teachers pay less attention to girls, and some tests remain biased against girls or stereotype or ignore women. Even though girls get better grades, they are still shortchanged. Teachers observed over a 3-year period called on boys more often than girls, offered boys more detailed and constructive criticism, and allowed boys to shout out answers but reprimanded girls for this practice (Sadker & Sadker, 1985). When students demand attention, teachers respond to boys with instructions and girls with nurturance (Beal, 1994). Instructors frequently tell girls that they are right or wrong and give them the correct answers. These differences are not deliberate, and even female teachers show these patterns (Kerr, 1991).

These analyses have almost become conventional wisdom and are found often in newspaper articles and television talk shows. Not everyone agrees with the conclusion that girls are shortchanged, though. Some authorities question the quality of some of the research reviewed, noting that some research findings run contrary to these assertions. Many other authorities argue that strides in educational achievement made by women are often disregarded (Schmidt, 1994).

A completely different view of gender differences in academic achievement recently has been offered (Bowman, 2000b). This view claims that schools discriminate against boys, not girls (Lewin, 1998). After all, there are more females in college than males, girls get better grades, they read at a higher level and write better, girls achieve higher class ranks, and they receive more school honors. They are more likely than boys to take Advanced Placement exams in English, social studies, and foreign languages. Boys are more likely to repeat grades, drop out, and be placed in special education classes for learning disabilities. Although there are some gaps—for example, in physics, which more boys study than girls—more girls take biology and chemistry (Chatterjee, 1999; Kleinfeld, 1999).

Some believe that the original report of the American Association of University Women increased the awareness of how girls were treated to the extent that meaningful progress has been made. A newer report by the same organization claims that girls have made real progress while boys have not, and it focuses attention on some groups that still lag behind, for example, Latino girls and African American boys (AAUW, 1998; Ginorio & Huston, 2000).

Although many believe that teachers discriminate against girls, recent research raises some doubts, as boys are more likely to repeat grades and drop out.

The area of most concern is advanced science and math. School personnel, including teachers, administrators, and guidance counselors, sometimes discourage girls from taking particular courses because they may not be "useful." This type of blatant sexism has been publicly scrutinized and criticized, as it should be. But such statements are probably less common than the subtle communication of expectations. Many schools and homes today do not actively restrict females but rather do not encourage them to take such courses (Sadker & Sadker, 1994). By the time students choose advanced courses in high school, a considerable gender difference is found. Girls take advanced biology, and boys take physics. Girls proceeding through high school are trying to balance their desires for career and family, and they perceive science and math as less and less relevant to their futures (see "Work and Career Development"). Once girls avoid high school math and some sciences, they close out some career options, or at least make them more difficult to attain (Murray, 1995a). Women have made great strides in the areas of computers and math, as well as in some areas of science. The lack of female participation in physics and engineering may have less to do with anything that occurs in the school than to female students' questions about combining certain occupations with family responsibilities. However, the fact that males fall behind females needs greater investigation and remediation. Perhaps the genders have different vulnerabilities, and educators should look less at gender discrimination and more at the school experiences of both male and female students to help them strive for excellence.

Pervasive Disengagement   Although many critics of education focus on the academic achievement difficulties of students from minority groups or examine the possible difficulties boys or girls have in specific areas, it is impossible to avoid the general complaints about low overall academic achievement in high school. A startling approach to explaining academic problems points to a teen culture that does not value academic achievement as the key problem. In group

One major research study found that many high school students were only going through the motions rather than being engaged in their schoolwork.

discussions with many students and parents, Steinberg, Brown, and Dornbusch (1996) found that roughly 40 percent of the students admitted they were just going through the motions in school. The researchers argue that improvements in curriculum and standards will not help much unless a change takes place in students' attitudes. Students must come to school interested in, and committed to, learning.

Disengagement is pervasive. Some students report deliberately hiding their abilities because of concerns about what friends might think. Few students believe their friends value getting good grades. Most said that they could bring home grades of C or worse without their parents getting upset, and many students said they do not do assigned homework. American students are much busier watching television, socializing, and working part-time than students in other countries, and they do not give academics equal attention.

Parents are also disengaged from the educational process. Many do not attend school functions such as open school week or parent-teacher conferences, and a quarter of all parents have no idea how their children are doing in school. Parenting style and involvement are related to academic achievement in secondary school, but parents become less involved (Paulson, 1994). Parental involvement does not mean tutoring students in advanced chemistry but rather giving encouragement, holding high expectations, showing interest in schoolwork, monitoring progress, and being involved in school functions. Adolescents who report parental demandingness, responsiveness, and involvement show high achievement (Dornbusch et al., 1987). Adolescents who perceive parents as having higher achievement values, being more interested in schoolwork, and being involved in school functions achieve higher grades. Of course, other factors, including peer relationships, ability, and motivation, are important as well.

Steinberg and colleagues argue for implementing more parenting education to draw parents into their children's schools, adopting a system of national academic standards and examinations, cutting back student work hours, and making it harder for students to merely go through the motions. Their analysis is sure to cause controversy (Viadero, 1996). Some do not believe that adolescents are any more disengaged than they were years ago and that Steinberg and colleagues have overgeneralized. Others argue that curriculum and school reforms are meaningful and more practical than trying to change home or peer group attitudes and behaviors. *(For a review of this section, see At A Glance 7.2.)*

AT A GLANCE 7.2 HIGH SCHOOL

KEY POINT: The achievement of high school students is a concern, and parents, college teachers, students, and employers all have different evaluations of the high school.

SUPPORTING POINTS	EXPLANATION
The transition to high school requires an adjustment by students.	Students report more academic hassles and less social support, but their self-esteem is not adversely affected. Some decline in grades also occurs.
Students are more dissatisfied with secondary schools than elementary schools.	Students and parents rate elementary schools and teachers much more positively than secondary schools and teachers.
American high school students do not seem to compare favorably with students in some other countries.	General statements often mask the fact that there are significant differences among schools, states, and communities in educational achievement.
The educational achievement levels of students from some minority groups is troubling.	The achievement of African Americans and Latinos is lower than that of whites and Asian Americans. Although the achievement gap has narrowed, it still exists. Poverty is a major reason for this gap.
Parents, peers, and the community influence school achievement.	Parents who are more involved are likely to encourage their children to succeed in school. Peers who are interested in doing well in school are a positive influence on a student's achievement.
Some studies indicate that schools discriminate against girls, but more recent studies do not agree.	Boys and girls may have different vulnerabilities and problems.
Some argue that both students and their parents are disengaged from school and schoolwork.	Many students and parents seem satisfied with marginally passing grades.

ENHANCING THE SCHOOL EXPERIENCE

If students and parents are disengaged from school and school achievement is not adequate, what can be done about these problems? Some psychologists and educators focus on how to enhance the student's experience in school and improve motivation; others focus on parental and peer influence. Another group calls for changes in school policies and school structure, whereas others want major changes in the options available for parents and students. Each of these areas influences students' school experiences and their ultimate achievement.

Principles of Learner-Centered Education

One suggestion for improving engagement in schoolwork and achievement is to adopt a learner-centered approach to education (Norman & Spohrer, 1996). In 1990, the American Psychological Association formed a task force to determine how 100 years of psychological research could contribute to the debate on the best ways to improve the educational process. The task force's report provided a framework for understanding the learning process and advanced fourteen principles of **learner-centered education** (see Table 7.1). Learner-centered education

learner-centered education An approach to education that focuses on the learner's experience and the learning process rather than on the teacher.

Table 7.1

Fourteen Learner-Centered Psychological Principles

Category	Principles
Cognitive and Metacognitive Factors	**Nature of the learning process.** The learning of complex subject matter is most effective when it is an intentional process of constructing meaning from information and experience.
	Goals of the learning process. The successful learner, over time and with support and instructional guidance, can create meaningful, coherent representations of knowledge.
	Construction of knowledge. The successful learner can link new information with existing knowledge in meaningful ways.
	Strategic thinking. The successful learner can create and use a repertoire of thinking and reasoning strategies to achieve complex learning goals.
	Thinking about thinking. Higher order strategies for selecting and monitoring mental operations facilitate creative and critical thinking.
	Context of learning. Learning is influenced by environmental factors, including culture, technology, and instructional practices.
Motivational and Affective Factors	**Motivational and emotional influences on learning.** What and how much is learned is influenced by the learner's motivation. Motivation to learn, in turn, is influenced by the individual's emotional states, beliefs, interests and goals, and habits of thinking.
	Intrinsic motivation to learn. The learner's creativity, higher order thinking, and natural curiosity all contribute to motivation to learn. Intrinsic motivation is stimulated by tasks of optimal novelty and difficulty, relevant to personal interests, and providing for personal choice and control.
	Effects of motivation on effort. Acquisition of complex knowledge and skills requires extended learner effort and guided practice. Without learners' motivation to learn, the willingness to exert this effort is unlikely without coercion.
Developmental and Social Factors	**Developmental influences on learning.** As individuals develop, there are different opportunities and constraints for learning. Learning is most effective when differential development within and across physical, intellectual, emotional, and social domains is taken into account.
	Social influences on learning. Learning is influenced by social interactions, interpersonal relations, and communication with others.
Individual Differences	**Individual differences in learning.** Learners have different strategies, approaches, and capabilities for learning that are a function of prior experience and heredity.
	Learning and diversity. Learning is most effective when differences in learners' linguistic, cultural, and social backgrounds are taken into account.
	Standards and assessment. Setting appropriately high and challenging standards and assessing the learner as well as learning progress—including diagnostic, process, and outcome assessment—are integral parts of the learning process.

Source: American Psychological Association (1997).

focuses on the learner's experience and the learning process rather than on the teacher (Hansen & Stephens, 2000). The effective learner is actively engaged in the learning process through the use of a variety of teaching methods, including problem solving, projects, and group discussion. Instruction takes into account student interests and developmental levels (Manning & Bucher, 2000). The goal is active exploration rather than passive listening. What and how much a student learns, according to these principles, are influenced by the learner's motivation, which is affected by his or her emotional state, beliefs, interests and goals, habits of thinking, and expectations for success.

Motivation to Learn

The term *motivation* derives from a Latin word meaning "to move." Because education is a participatory activity that requires active engagement on the student's part, motivation is a key determinant of achievement. The importance of motivation to the educational experience was well stated by Terrel Bell, former U.S. secretary of education: "There are three things to remember about education, the first is motivation. The second one is motivation. The third one is motivation" (Maehr & Meyer, 1997, p. 372). Motivation affects achievement because motivated students are more likely to pay attention and actively participate in class, as well as to study. Revising classroom practices and teaching methods may improve student motivation by changing the student's classroom experience. What goes on in the family, including family values about education and practices such as talking about school, also may motivate students in school.

Intrinsic and Extrinsic Motivation   Traditionally, motivation is divided into two types: intrinsic and extrinsic. Motivation is said to be **intrinsic motivation** when it emanates from within the person, as when an adolescent who is curious about the weather conducts an experiment at home. Motivation is said to be **extrinsic motivation** when it comes from outside an individual, as when a student does homework to achieve a good grade or to receive praise from others. A behavior may come from a combination of the two: a student may conduct an experiment both because he or she is interested in the work and because designing and conducting an experiment is required to complete a course.

Intrinsic motivation is related to many desirable educational outcomes. Students who show high levels of intrinsic motivation show higher levels of academic achievement and more self-confidence, have better perceptions of their academic competence, and experience less anxiety about their schoolwork (Gottfried, Fleming, & Gottfried, 2001). Intrinsic motivation is also linked to greater creativity (Koestner et al., 1984).

Intrinsic motivation can also be viewed as a subjective experience that occurs when people are truly engaged in an activity; they are absorbed in the experience, and time seems to stop (Csikszentmihalyi, 1988). Climbers, dancers, chess players, and athletes, among others, describe their self-chosen activities as producing a specific type of experience that Csikszentmihalyi labels *flow* (1988). Flow is characterized by complete immersion in the activity, being carried away by the activity, a narrowing of attention, a lack of self-consciousness, and a feeling of being in control of one's actions and environment. Flow is a state of being that occurs only when people can match opportunity with ability. The tasks must be challenging and the skills highly developed. Obviously, this exceptionally deep intrinsic motivation would not occur in every activity.

What happens to intrinsic motivation in adolescence? Intrinsic motivation shows its steepest decline in early adolescence and then regains some stability (Gottfried, Fleming, & Gottfried, 2001; Pekrun, 1993). The decline may be due to a greater emphasis on grades in secondary school, a more controlling school atmosphere at a time when students want more autonomy, and greater academic anxiety. This decline may also involve school-related factors such as less teacher support, but it also may parallel the emergence of social interests.

Extrinsic rewards, such as attention, praise, or awards, also can play a part in motivation. Extrinsic incentives are very useful when people are first learning a skill or are not very good at it (Bandura, 1986). For instance, a beginning piano student may not find it very enjoyable to practice scales; piano playing takes on intrinsic incentives only when the student can play an enjoyable composition. Until the feeling of satisfaction can take over, some reinforcement may be necessary. This reinforcement may be self-delivered; for example, after performing some activity you need to do, you allow yourself to engage in a more interesting activity.

Extrinsic motivation may also help students become involved in some activity in which they would normally not participate. Teachers may give additional credit for attending a special lecture or tackling a difficult problem, for example. A student originally may not have wanted to participate in an activity because of its reputation, the time or effort involved, or the lack of certainty for success. Teachers can encourage participation in new activities through such incentives as praise and additional credit. In addition, students may not find everything they need to learn very interesting, and extrinsic reinforcers may promote learning.

intrinsic motivation   Motivation that flows from within the individual.

extrinsic motivation   Motivation that comes from outside the individual, as when a student does work to get a reward from a parent or teacher.

Table 7.2

Attributions for Grades on a Science Test

Attribution	Example for High Grade	Example for Low Grade
Ability	I'm good in science.	Science is not my good subject. I'm no good at science.
Effort	I studied hard for the science exam, and it paid off.	I didn't study hard enough for the test.
Ability and effort	I'm good in science, and I studied hard.	I'm no good at science, and I didn't study hard enough.
Task ease/difficulty	The test was really easy.	The test was too difficult.
Luck	I just guessed right. I studied just the right material.	I was unlucky. I studied the wrong material for the test.

Attribution Theory: Why Did I Succeed or Fail?

Motivation is also affected by how people attribute their successes and failures, triumphs and disappointments. **Attribution theory** seeks to explain how people make sense of events by ascribing the causes of these events. According to the classic work of Bernard Weiner (1985, 1999; Weiner, Russell, & Lerman, 1979), causal attributions can be understood in terms of three dimensions: internal-external, stability-instability, and controllable-uncontrollable. For example, a high school student who did poorly on an exam could tell herself that it was due to internal factors, such as poor effort or lack of ability. Or she could attribute doing poorly to external factors by saying that the work was too difficult or she just had bad luck. This internal-external dimension leads to emotional reactions concerning achievement outcomes. A student who attributes success to ability or effort (internal factors) feels pride and has positive self-esteem. A student who attributes success to external factors, in contrast, gains little in self-esteem. A person who ascribes a failure to internal factors, such as lack of effort or lack of ability, experiences negative self-esteem. Attributing failure to external factors does not result in negative self-esteem.

How will this student attribute her good grade? If she attributes it to her hard work, chances are she will study hard for the next test.

Stability or *instability* is the second dimension of causal attribution. A student can attribute success or failure either to some factor that is almost always going to be there or to a temporary factor. Ability is a rather stable attribute, whereas effort and luck are unstable. The stability-instability dimension underlies expectations for future success or failure (Weiner et al., 1983). Students who ascribe their success to a stable factor will expect to succeed at the same task the next time it is presented. Students who attribute success to an unstable factor, such as luck or unusual help from the teacher, will have little or no expectation of later success. Failure ascribed to a stable cause, such as low ability, decreases the expectation of future success. Failure ascribed to an unstable cause, such as a temporary illness, bad luck, or too much environmental noise, should not affect expectations for later success.

The third dimension of causal attribution, *controllable* versus *uncontrollable*, relates to whether the student ascribes the success or failure to factors that are under the student's control or under someone else's control. A student can't control luck but can certainly control effort. If a student believes that failure was due to low ability, which is an uncontrollable factor, rather than to lack of effort, a controllable factor, he is more likely to give up. If he believes that effort is the problem, he may study harder for the next exam. This dimension influences interpersonal evaluation. Individuals anticipate more punishment from others when they attribute failure to personally controllable causes than to uncontrollable ones.

Perhaps most significant is whether a person attributes success or failure to effort or ability (see Table 7.2), as this significantly affects motivation. Effort is unstable, internal, and controllable, whereas ability is stable, internal, and

attribution theory An approach that seeks to explain how people make sense of events occurring both within and about the individual by ascribing the causes of these events.

uncontrollable. A student who attributes success to an internal stable dimension, such as ability, expects success in the future and will continue to strive (Fennema, 1987). These students believe they can and will attain success. Students who attribute their success to effort will continue to work hard. In contrast, a student who attributes success to an external cause, such as an easy-grading teacher or luck, will not be confident of success in the future.

Failure works differently. Students who attribute failure to lack of ability will have reduced future expectations for success because they believe they have little control over subsequent outcomes (Eccles, Wigfield, & Schiefele, 1998). Attribution of failure to a stable cause, such as lack of ability, leads students to believe that failure is inevitable. Adolescents may use a lack of ability as an excuse not to try. Students who attribute their poor performance to lack of effort, however, may try harder next time. Therefore, success leads to more success, depending on how one attributes the success. Failure may or may not lead to more failure, again depending on the attributions. Attributions, then, are critical to later performance (Weiner, 1979).

Adolescents differ in the way they attribute their successes and failures compared with younger children. Elementary school children see ability and effort as complementary; that is, smart people work harder and put more effort into their work. By ages 11 or 12, students understand the nature of ability and effort. People with less ability have to put more effort into their work just to catch on. People with high ability find the subject matter easier. In fact, having to try hard may be seen as a sign that one is less able. As students age, they are more and more likely to ascribe their achievement or lack of achievement to ability.

American teens are more likely to attribute grades to ability than Chinese or Japanese students (Stevenson, Chen, & Lee, 1993). The consequences can be substantial. If students believe that ability is so much more important, they are likely to put much less time into their schoolwork, especially in subjects that they find difficult.

Because effort is internal, unstable, and controllable, it is important that students ascribe their failures and successes largely to it; however, this attribution is counter to the prevailing thoughts of high school students (Covington, 1984, 2000). Unfortunately, adolescents see ability as more important than effort. Furthermore, adolescents see ability or lack of ability as reflecting on an individual's worth. High school students see people with ability as capable and people without ability as incompetent, and they avoid feeling incompetent or being seen by others as incompetent at almost any cost.

Goal Setting and Self-Evaluation One of the newer approaches to understanding why some students expend energy on their schoolwork and others do not is to view motivation as deeply influenced by the goals students set for themselves, whether these goals are to obtain a certain grade, build a robot, solve a challenging math problem, or perform competently in a theatrical play (Harackiewicz, Barron, & Elliot, 1998). The nature of these goals influences student efforts (Dweck, 1989; Urdan & Maehr, 1995). Their sense of self-efficacy will affect the goals they set, and meeting these goals, in turn, will affect their sense of self-efficacy. If students do not believe they can master the work, they either will not set goals or set very low goals. However, attaining a goal can sometimes lead them to adopt a higher one, as it increases their sense of self-efficacy (Bandura, 1982).

Many studies show that the type of achievement goal adopted by students influences how they work in class, which in turn influences the outcome (Harackiewicz et al., 1998). Dweck (1986; Dweck & Leggett, 1988) identified two primary types of goal orientations found in achievement settings: learning or mastery goals and performance or ego goals. Students adopt **mastery goals** or **learning goals** when they undertake challenging tasks for the sake of learning and to improve their competence. Students adopt **performance goals** or **ego goals** when they try to validate their superior ability or conceal their lack of competence. The goal of students with performance goals is to compare well with

mastery goals (learning goals) An orientation in which students take on challenging tasks for the sake of the desire to know or to improve competence.

performance goals (ego goals) An orientation in which students try to achieve in order to show their ability or conceal their lack of competence.

Self-efficacy is the belief that one can do something. These actors may have a high degree of self-efficacy in performing in front of people.

others or avoid looking incompetent. Students adopt performance or ego goals when they become overly conscious about how others are evaluating them (Bong, 2001). Recently, performance goals have been divided into performance-approach and performance-avoidance goals. Students adopt **performance-approach goals** when they seek to maximize grades and gain a better rating than their peers. They adopt **performance-avoidance goals** when they try to conceal their feelings of incompetence (Church, Elliot, & Gable, 2001; Elliot & Church, 1997; Elliot, McGregor, & Gable, 1999).

Students who adopt mastery goals engage in more self-regulatory learning and more self-monitoring of what they are learning. They are more likely to use organizing strategies, such as paraphrasing and summarizing, because they focus on understanding the material rather than just doing well on the next examination (Archer, 1994). They choose more challenging activities and are less afraid of making errors in public (Elliott & Dweck, 1988; Koestner & Zuckerman, 1994). Mastery goal orientation is related to the belief that effort is a key factor in achievement, and this belief keeps these students working.

Students with performance-approach goals desire good grades and will work for them, but they seek shortcuts and are not interested in improving their knowledge base or engaging in any work outside of what is required for an examination. Students with performance-avoidance goals often exhibit maladaptive behaviors, including self-defeating performance attributions ("I can't do it") and negative self-evaluations ("I'm stupid"). They try to protect themselves from any evaluation that would endanger their self-worth.

Each of these goals is associated with different approaches to studying and information processing. Students who adopt mastery goals put forth general effort and persistence. They more actively process material to be learned. These students actively challenge the truthfulness of the information and attempt to integrate new information with prior knowledge and experience. This process is called *deep processing*. Performance-approach goals are similar to mastery goals

performance-approach goals   An orientation in which students seek to maximize grades or compare more favorably with their peers.

performance-avoidance goals   An orientation in which students show a fear of failure, and attempt to conceal their feelings of incompetence often by protecting themselves from any evaluation that might endanger their self-worth.

in that they are grounded in the need to achieve. They positively relate to effort and persistence, but they are also related to *surface processing*. These students do what is required to receive high grades, but they are not really involved in the work. Performance-avoidance goals are grounded in the fear of failure and focus on possible negative outcomes (Elliot, 1997). Self-protective concerns are most important, and these students are not persistent.

Undergraduates in a psychology course (average age, about 20 years) were asked to complete questionnaires to assess achievement goal orientation for an upcoming exam. The questionnaire contained six items that reflected three achievement goal orientations. For example, "I desire to completely master the material presented in this section of the class" measured the mastery learning orientation. The performance-approach orientation was typified by items such as "I am striving to demonstrate my ability relative to others," and performance-avoidance goals were shown by items such as "I just want to avoid doing poorly on this exam." Participants indicated their response to each item on a scale from 1 ("not at all true") to 7 ("very true of me"). The responses were averaged. The researchers also measured deep or surface processing and disorganization (difficulty establishing or maintaining a structured approach to preparing for the exam). Mastery goals were positive predictors of deep processing, persistence, and effort; performance-approach goals were positive predictors of surface processing, persistence, and effort; and performance-avoidance goals predicted surface processing, disorganization, and poor performance on the next exam. It should come as no surprise that persistence and effort are positively related to exam performance and that disorganization is a negative predictor of grades. Notice that students who adopted mastery or performance-approach goals did well on the exam, but one group used deep processing and the other surface processing. Disorganization may be a major problem arising from performance-avoidance goals, as the threat of failure may interfere with developing an organized approach to studying (Elliot et al., 1999).

Motivation Reconsidered Evidence certainly shows that intrinsic motivation—attributing success to one's efforts, believing that one can succeed (self-efficacy), and adopting a mastery goal orientation—has positive consequences for learning. Figure 7.2 shows some of the classroom structures that support intrinsic, mastery-based learning goals. These structures involve the nature of the task, authority orientation, and the nature of evaluation or recognition used (Ames, 1992; Church et al., 2001).

THE NATURE OF THE TASK   Tasks that involve variety and diversity encourage student interest and a mastery orientation (Nicholls, 1984). When students perceive a meaningful reason for engaging in an activity, and when the presentation emphasizes personal relevance, students are more likely to be motivated (Brophy, 1987; Meece, 1991). Challenge, interest, and perceived control are task characteristics that support the development of intrinsic motivation.

AUTHORITY ORIENTATION   When those in authority give students some ability to choose and influence what is going on, they adopt more intrinsic motivation (deCharms, 1976). When teachers allow students some input in decision making, choices, and opportunities to develop responsibility, the students often adopt self-management and monitoring skills, along with mastery learning goals. Teacher control and student choice must balance, however. With too much teacher control, students feel they have few choices; too little teacher control, however, leads to anarchy in the classroom.

EVALUATION   Evaluation of students is more likely to lead to increased effort when it focuses on individual improvement, progress, or mastery, and when the evaluation is given in private. When mistakes are viewed as part of the learning process and students have opportunities to improve, their intrinsic motivation is higher, and more positive feelings toward schoolwork appear (Ames, 1992).

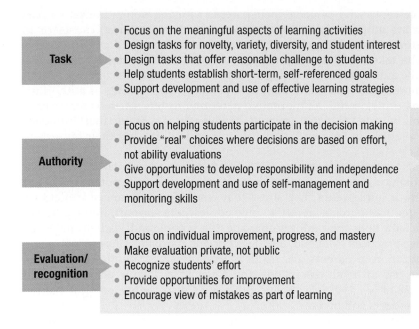

Figure 7.2

Classroom Structure and Instructional Strategies That Support Mastery Goals

The nature of the task, the authority orientation, and evaluation/recognition influence student motivation.

Source: Ames (1992).

Task
- Focus on the meaningful aspects of learning activities
- Design tasks for novelty, variety, diversity, and student interest
- Design tasks that offer reasonable challenge to students
- Help students establish short-term, self-referenced goals
- Support development and use of effective learning strategies

Authority
- Focus on helping students participate in the decision making
- Provide "real" choices where decisions are based on effort, not ability evaluations
- Give opportunities to develop responsibility and independence
- Support development and use of self-management and monitoring skills

Evaluation/ recognition
- Focus on individual improvement, progress, and mastery
- Make evaluation private, not public
- Recognize students' effort
- Provide opportunities for improvement
- Encourage view of mistakes as part of learning

- Focus on effort and learning
- High intrinsic interest in activity
- Attributions to effort
- Attributions to effort-based strategies
- Use of effective learning and other self-regulatory strategies
- Active engagement
- Positive affect on high-effort tasks
- Feelings of belongingness
- "Failure-tolerance"

Students in classrooms where grading is harsh and public and where teachers compare students are likely to adopt more performance-avoidance goals. Grades themselves may act as a positive or a negative factor in student motivation. Students who believe that effort may lead to better grades and that grades can be improved with effort may try harder, especially if grades reflect self-improvement rather than comparisons with others.

Motivation, then, is enhanced when teachers offer meaningful and interesting tasks; some shared authority; and fair, private evaluation that emphasizes self-improvement (Ames, 1992). When teachers focus on effort rather than ability and show students that they can achieve, the students become more engaged in their work (Ames, 1992; Elliott & Dweck, 1988). Classrooms differ greatly in the extent to which these features operate, but improvements in these areas may positively affect student motivation and learning.

The Parental Role

Parents have many choices as they create the home environment. In some homes the television constantly blares, parents rarely take their children to the library, and little conversation occurs about events in the world. In other homes television time is more restricted, parents introduce their children to reading at an early age, and intellectually stimulating conversations occur. Homes that provide cognitive stimulation encourage academic curiosity. One study analyzed the home environments of 8-year-olds to determine the amount of intellectual stimulation available. The researchers measured many components of the environment, including encouragement of hobbies, limitations on television viewing, use of the library, and talking about political and social problems. They obtained measurements of intrinsic motivation at ages 9, 10, and 13 years and found a relationship between measures of cognitive stimulation in the home and later intrinsic motivation of children in the late elementary school years and early adolescence (Gottfried, Fleming, & Gottfried, 1998). Intellectually stimulating experiences in the home predict greater intrinsic motivation in school, a greater enjoyment of learning, and valuing learning for its own sake.

Parenting style also influences adolescent achievement. Adolescents who perceive their parents as using the authoritative parenting style are more likely to attribute academic success to internal causes such as high ability and effort, whereas adolescents who perceive their parents as using nonauthoritative parenting styles are more likely to attribute achievement to external causes or to attribute failure to low ability, although as noted in "Families," cultural differences must be taken into account (Glasgow et al., 1997). Adolescents whose parents use the authoritative parenting style have higher self-perceptions of ability and are more self-reliant than youth who perceive their parents as authoritarian, indulgent, or neglectful. Authoritative parenting fosters self-reliance, a sense of responsibility, and a higher degree of self-efficacy, traits that influence adolescents to attribute their successes to effort and ability and their failures to lack of effort.

Many factors affect parenting skills, and as discussed earlier, Bronfenbrenner's ecological theory states that factors that affect parents potentially affect their children or adolescents. The stress that results from financial difficulties and poverty reduces parents' ability to give adolescents support, limits parental involvement with both their adolescents and the school, and leads to inconsistent parenting practices (McLoyd, 1998). Economic hardship causes depression and demoralization in parents; the result is less effective parenting practices—including the use of harsh discipline—and lowered academic achievement in school (Conger et al., 1992). Economic difficulties also reduce communication between adolescents and parents.

Parents need only perceive a sense of financial strain to be affected. The mere perception of financial strain can lead to negative parenting behaviors, which create poor parent-adolescent relationships and adversely affect parental involvement with school. Middle-class or even upper middle class parents who experience a sense of financial strain may show negative parenting behaviors, even though they do not live in poverty. Parents across the economic spectrum—including African Americans and European Americans in single-parent or two-parent families—are similarly affected (Gutman & Eccles, 1999).

Parents differ in their ability to help their children. Some parents who have not received much education themselves may not be able to help their children, even in elementary school. In junior high school, and to a greater extent in high school, much of what is taught in math and the sciences is relatively new; most parents can't help their children much, even if they studied the same subjects 20 years before. Parental involvement, though, does not have to involve tutoring, and in most studies it does not. Rather, parents can show they value education by participating in such school-related activities as a parents' organization, remaining in contact with teachers, and monitoring student progress. Much of the difference in achievement between children within the same racial/ethnic or socioeconomic group is explained by parenting practices in the home and involvement with the school (Duncan et al., 1998). For example, authoritative parenting practices that combine being demanding and yet responsive, having high expectations and aspirations, having frequent discussions about school, and participating in school events are related to student achievement (Eccles & Harold, 1993).

Research is mixed on the extent of minority group involvement in school activities, and as always, socioeconomic status confounds this variable. Some reports claim that minority group parents are less involved, whereas others argue that only minority group parents living in poverty are less involved. When socioeconomic status is taken out of the equation, only a few types of involvement show any differences, and minority group parents are actually more involved in a few areas. Lower socioeconomic status seems to reduce volunteering in school and participating in parent-teacher organizations and meetings, but it does not necessarily influence home involvement (Sui-Chu & Williams, 1996). This finding is reasonable, because having to work full-time limits the time a parent has to attend school functions but does not necessarily affect monitoring homework and discussing what is going on in school.

The research on parental involvement in school often fails to take an ecological view and consider cultural differences. Ignoring cultural differences leads to misunderstandings and incorrect generalizations. For example, many Latino parents emphasize correct behavior and maturity over cognitive development, and they may see their role in their children's education differently than do parents in other cultures. Parents of Asian American students, especially those from the Pacific Rim, often have a formal parent-child relationship that differs from the authoritative parenting that seems to lead to achievement in white middle-class homes. In an interesting comparison, Huntsinger and colleagues (2000) followed the interactions of Chinese American and European American parents and their young children, as well as the children's school achievement, over a 4-year period. Chinese American mothers take their responsibility as teachers very seriously. Although they may be less involved in the school itself, they structure their children's time and use more formal methods of instruction, such as teaching letters and numbers, compared with European American mothers. Chinese American mothers also expect their children to do more homework. The Chinese American children showed superior achievement in mathematics

Parental volunteering certainly shows an interest in a child's school. However, parents may show involvement in other ways as well.

and, by fourth grade, in vocabulary. Chinese American children also showed more positive attitudes toward reading and school in general. European American parents provided less active teaching and less structure, emphasizing social skills. Huntsinger and colleagues suggest that a reassessment of the more formal methods used by Chinese Americans, which some American educators and European American mothers consider less developmentally appropriate, might be useful (Huntsinger, Jose, & Larson, 1998).

High school students' perception of parental involvement is more important than parents' perceptions of their involvement for all groups. Students who know their parents are involved tend to succeed. But there are many roads to parental involvement. Volunteering to help in a school is a better predictor of success for white and middle-class students than for Asian American, African American, or Latino students, especially those who live in poverty. Parental involvement in a parent-teacher organization is a very significant predictor of school achievement, especially for African American and Latino students. Involvement in such organizations empowers parents. Student-reported discussions with parents is one of the best predictors of achievement, second only to parent-teacher organization involvement, for African Americans and Latinos. There is a strong relationship between such communication and achievement. In any case, parents' choice of involvement is a function of their culture, perceived skills and abilities, employment, and other demands on their time (Hoover-Dempsey & Sandler, 1995). It is also a function of how the school deals with parents; some parents feel intimidated and not welcome in schools.

Some authorities call for a parent-school partnership (Connors & Epstein, 1995). Research shows that regardless of income or parental education, students at all grade levels do better and have a more positive school attitude and higher aspirations if they have parents who are aware, knowledgeable, encouraging, and involved.

Teacher Expectations

The adolescent's experience in school depends on the organization of the school and what goes on in the classroom. Some of these classroom variables, such as teacher control, communication with students, and encouraging students to participate, were explored in the discussion of student motivation. Many other teacher-related factors influence both the student's experience in the classroom and academic achievement, but the expectations that teachers hold and communicate to their students have received the most attention.

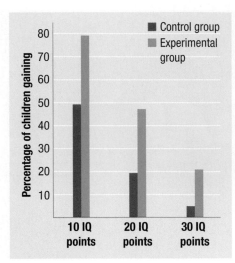

Figure 7.3

Percentage of First and Second Graders Gaining 10, 20, or 30 Total IQ Points

When researchers led teachers to believe that the children in the experimental group were "late bloomers" and therefore special, the teachers behaved differently toward them; the result was an increase in intelligence scores.

Source: Rosenthal & Jacobson (1968), Figure 7.2.

In 1968, Robert Rosenthal and Lenore Jacobson performed the most famous study on teacher expectations. They chose 20 percent of the children in an elementary school serving a lower-income community and then told the children's teachers that according to tests, these children were likely to bloom academically during the following year. They planted expectations in the teachers' minds as to the academic performance of the children. Their sample included 20 percent from each of three tracks—low, average, and high achievement. The results showed that within a year, the students labeled "late bloomers" showed higher academic achievement and greater gains in scores on IQ tests than those who were not so labeled (see Figure 7.3). The teachers also rated these students as being more interested, curious, and happy, and as having greater intellectual potential. When teachers rated children who were not labeled "late bloomers" but who nevertheless had gained substantially during the year, they did not give them as much credit or rate them as highly. This finding was especially true of children in the low track.

At the end of the second year, some differences favoring the group of "late bloomers" still existed, but most of the differences had decreased substantially. The results of this study have been explained by the **self-fulfilling prophecy**— the phenomenon that expectations increase the likelihood that a particular event will occur. If teachers expect students to do well, they are more likely to achieve. The self-fulfilling prophecy is also found in junior high and high school.

These expectations may be communicated verbally, as when a teacher compliments some students and not others. They also may be communicated nonverbally by showing approval with a smile or a nod. Teachers may communicate expectations by treating high- and low-achieving students in ways that unnecessarily discriminate between these groups of students. Teachers sometimes seat low-achieving students further away, pay less attention to them, call on these students less frequently, wait less time for them to answer questions, fail to ask them follow-up questions, and praise them less for giving the correct answers (Good, 1981). Such students are discouraged from participating in class and are less motivated to do their work. Instead, they play it safe and remain passive (Kaplan, 1990).

The self-fulfilling prophecy phenomenon is well documented. Observers could tell the differences between videotaped recordings of teachers speaking about or to students for whom they had either higher or lower expectations, despite the fact that the observers could not see or hear the students on the film clips. The observers judged that teachers had more positive expectations for the high achievers than the low achievers (Babad, 1993). Students also can detect teachers' expectations and are highly sensitive to their differential behaviors (Weinstein, 1989). Yet most teachers do not believe they show these behaviors, perhaps because they are not aware of such nonverbal behaviors as tone of voice, facial expression, body stance, and eye contact, which are frequently the channels they use to communicate with students. Expectations are most harmful when they are based on factors unrelated to achievement, such as student appearance, neatness, or dependency (Alvidrez & Weinstein, 1999). Research on the question of whether students' race affects teacher expectations has yielded mixed results, with some studies finding race a factor and others failing to find teacher expectations for ability affected by race (Jussim, Madon, & Chatman, 1994). Some teachers' expectations may be influenced by children's race or socioeconomic status, and this influence certainly may affect a student's experience in the classroom and subsequent academic achievement (Baron, Tom, & Cooper, 1985).

The fact that teacher expectations can affect student achievement, however, does not mean that expectations explain much about achievement or that inaccurate expectations are widespread. In fact, the proposition that severely inaccurate initial expectations substantially alter academic achievement of students is not supported by research (Cooper & Tom, 1984). Teacher expectations contribute to between 5 and 10 percent of the differences in academic achievement among students (Jussim & Eccles, 1992; Kuklinski & Weinstein, 2001). This percentage is

self-fulfilling prophecy The concept that a person's expectations concerning some event affect the probability of the event's occurrence.

significant, but the finding also means that low student achievement cannot be explained exclusively by teacher expectations. Teacher expectations may sustain, rather than set, an achievement level (Cooper, 1979). For example, if students are not expected to show interest but they do, teachers may not notice or respond appropriately because of previous expectations.

Most teacher expectations are accurate and based on valid information (Jussim, 1991; Smith et al., 1998). In fact, the main reason teacher expectations predict student achievement is because they are accurate, and self-fulfilling prophecy effects are small (Jussim & Eccles, 1992). Small differences, however, may be important.

Tracking

Of all the school practices that affect students, **tracking**—the placement of students in classes by ability level—both affects students the most and is the most controversial (Hallinan, 1996). Tracking is very common; it is practiced in about 80 percent of schools to some extent.

Advocates of tracking argue that it increases teacher productivity by making lesson planning more effective; teachers can gear their lessons to the ability of their students (Rogers, 1998). Consider a seventh-grade class in which some students are reading at a third-grade level and others, at a tenth-grade level. How can a teacher meet the needs of students with such different abilities? In addition, our society seems to have no objection to grouping in sports or music on the basis of talent, so why should academics be any different (Shanker, 1988)? Teachers usually prefer homogeneous grouping of students because they find it difficult to teach the same lesson to students of high, average, and low academic skills. Although some available methods, such as cooperative learning, allow students of various levels to work together, many teachers do not feel they are appropriate for every lesson.

Opponents of tracking claim that students who are placed in lower tracks receive inferior instruction and that tracking damages student self-esteem. Track assignments often tend to be fixed, especially in math, and students miss out on learning opportunities when the curriculum differs greatly between the tracks. Others claim that students from higher socioeconomic backgrounds are placed in higher tracks than students who come from poverty backgrounds, even if their abilities are equal (Roscigno & Ainsworth-Darnell, 1999). Tracking increases the inequalities between groups, because members of minority groups are more likely to be raised in poverty and placed in lower tracks. Tracking may result in segregation, as minority group youth are less likely than whites to be placed in advanced and challenging courses (Frazier, 1999). Opponents also argue that tracking does not enhance productivity in the classroom (Nyberg et al., 1997).

The track in which a student is placed does matter (Gamoran & Mare, 1989). For students of the same ability level, placement in the upper track increases achievement, and placement in the lower track reduces achievement (Hoffer, 1992). In addition, teachers may have different attitudes and show different behaviors toward students in different tracks. There is also evidence that lower-track classes tend to be assigned to less qualified teachers and receive less of their share of educational resources. The experience of students in the lower track is often poor; these classes generally have more students with conduct problems, teachers may not look forward to teaching these slower students, and students become aware that less is expected from them. Opponents of tracking see it as increasing the achievement differences between high and low students.

Research finds that tracking has a negative effect on the students in lower tracks, negligible effects on students in the middle or regular track, and positive effects on the achievement of students in the higher tracks (Brewer, Rees, & Argys, 1995). De-tracking, or switching to a system of heterogeneous grouping, might create both winners and losers. Students in the lower tracks might gain, but those in the upper tracks might lose. De-tracking might lead to an increase in test scores for students now in the lower tracks and a decrease in scores for those

tracking An educational practice in which students are grouped and taught in classes of homogeneous ability.

in above average classes (Fielder, Lange, & Winebrenner, 2002; Hoffer, 1992; Shields, 2002). It is only fair to say that although the research conclusions are relatively consistent, some educators argue that de-tracking would have little or no effect on the achievement of students in the upper tracks (Slavin, 1995).

School Choices

A relatively new approach to improving the educational experience of high school students suggests giving students and parents additional choices of which schools to attend. Students and parents who have meaningful options and choose among them may feel a greater dedication to the school. One option is the **magnet school,** which provides some choice by offering special courses of study. One magnet school, for example, may offer excellent computer applications courses. Another may offer comprehensive core studies combining English with history, or government with economics, and students may conduct research and produce multimedia presentations (Salpeter, 1999). Magnet schools are viewed as especially desirable, and students are proud to attend them and succeed in their special programs. More than half of all magnet schools use some form of admissions test, most frequently a standardized achievement test (Nathan, 1998). They can be exclusionary, because students must apply and be accepted. Some magnet schools require a particular average to stay in the school. Some require parents of incoming students to pledge their dedication to the more rigorous requirements of the school or to volunteer for particular programs (*U.S. News and World Report*, January 18, 1999). One criticism is that the use of entrance exams may lead to segregation and continue the inequalities commonly found in the educational system (Stokley, 1999).

Another innovation is the **charter school,** which is well described by its name. It is a school that receives a charter describing its mission and standards for success. The charter is a contract negotiated between organizers and sponsors (Vergari, 1999). The organizers may be teachers, parents, or other people from the public or private sectors. The sponsors may be local school boards; state school boards; or other public authorities, such as universities. The organizers manage the schools, and the sponsors monitor compliance with the charter, which may govern curriculum, performance measures, management, and financial plans.

The idea behind charter schools is to allow creativity to reign (Stewart, 2002). Each charter school has its own philosophy and differs from others. Some charters focus on civic education and others, on a back-to-basics, highly structured curriculum; still others offer a team-teaching, progressive curriculum. A few are structured to serve a special population, for example, students at risk (Bowman, 2000a). Accountability is built into the system, for a charter school that does not show success can be closed, although only a very small number are ever actually closed (Vergari, 1999). Charter schools tend to be smaller schools; some have longer school days, longer school years, and different after-school programs. There are no standard charter schools. Some state rules and regulations, along with some local teacher contract provisions, are waived in exchange for the promise of results. Charter schools are not allowed to use entrance testing for admissions; if more students want to attend than space allows, students are chosen by lottery.

Not everyone is enamored with charter schools (Farber, 1998). Their critics argue that mediocre standards have plagued the charter movement, that evaluations are not as positive as often claimed, and that precise, measurable goals are sometimes absent, which is strange for a movement that stresses accountability (Lin, 2001; Toch, 1998). Others claim that many charter schools set informal admissions standards, often finding ways around admitting students with disabilities or poor grades (Lewis, 1998; Manno et al., 1998). The charter movement has grown in the United States from 1 school in 1 state in 1992 to 2,000 schools in 38 states in 2002 (Bush, 2002), suggesting that the movement is thriving (Vergari, 1999). Only time will tell if it is working.

magnet schools Schools offering special course work, making them stand out. These schools often have specific entrance requirements.

charter schools Schools with a well-described mission statement describing standards for success. These schools may be organized by parents, teachers, or others from the public or private sector.

The most radical plan for structural change is the **voucher plan.** The idea is to give parents a voucher for tuition and allow them to place their children into any public or private school they want that will accept them. Voucher proponents believe that public schools would improve their operations in order to compete, and that the best schools would rise while the worst would be forced to close because no one would send their children to them (Bennefield, 1997). Its proponents claim the voucher plan would improve education as poorly functioning schools lose students to other schools. Proponents say the plan allows parents to decide which educational program is best for their children. Under the current system many adolescents, especially those in poverty, find themselves trapped in unresponsive schools, whereas high-income parents have choices. Vouchers would give more parents the freedom to choose (Mullen, 1999).

A number of questions surround the voucher program. For example, should all students receive vouchers, or only students whose schools are failing ("School Vouchers," 1999)? Should students who want to attend religious schools receive vouchers? Should private schools who value their independence be forced to release data on attendance, dropout rates, or suspension rates, because they are receiving public funds (Minor, 1998)?

Proponents of the voucher plan argue for choice and talk about the bright prospect of better education, whereas opponents argue that vouchers would have a negative impact on the public school system, diverting public funds to private institutions (Miner, 2000). Others argue that voucher programs have not yet demonstrated their effectiveness or that when they seem more effective it is due to the smaller classes these schools sometimes provide (Bracey, 2000; Shafer, 2001). Still others argue that, under the voucher plan, the best students would attend private school (at public expense), leaving the public schools with more poorly functioning students.

If choices become available, adolescents will have more input into which schools to attend than younger children will. Different educational experiences will become available as choices expand. Adolescents, together with their parents, may decide to attend a more artistically oriented school or one that devotes more time to core academics. Perhaps student engagement will increase as students and parents see more educational options open to them.

PERSPECTIVE 2

A COMMUNITY DIVIDED

SETTING THE SCENE: The community has been in a state of agitation for weeks. The firing of a gay teacher by a private school participating in the voucher program has polarized the community. Many parents and students have forced the school to participate in a public hearing.

SCHOOL ADMINISTRATOR: *We do not say that Mr. R. is a poor teacher. He is not a bad teacher, but his outspoken admission to his classes that he is gay runs counter to the policy of this private school. Again, we say private school. When you placed your children in this school, you agreed to abide by our philosophy. You, our students and their parents, knew where you were going, and you could have gone to any number of other schools that accept vouchers in our community.*

STUDENT: *Mr. R. is a good teacher who has broken no laws. He is an excellent individual who is active in charities and raising money for student projects. His lifestyle outside of class, which does not interfere with his duties and breaks no law, should not be a deciding factor on whether he should teach in the school. Gay men, in this state, are slowly winning many rights, and you are turning back the clock.*

QUESTION: If you were a high school student attending this school, how would you feel about the issue? Should private schools accepting public vouchers be allowed to continue such policies?

The Transition to College

For about half of all high school graduates, the school experience continues on to college. The transition from high school to college is gradual. Many adolescents adjust well and find better relationships with their parents (Aseltine & Gore, 1993). Perhaps the improvement occurs because contact is somewhat reduced, and many of the issues that affected the relationship earlier have been resolved.

Some students, though, find the transition to college very difficult. By the end of the first year of college, 27 percent of all entering students drop out, and only about 40 percent of all entering students graduate within 5 years (Perry et al., 2001). Some very bright high school students do poorly in their first year and consider dropping out. Why do students have difficulty with the transition to college? What can colleges do about it?

voucher plan A proposed plan which would give parents the right to send their children at public expense to any school they choose.

The answer to why so many entering students do not do well may lie in the differences between high school and college. High school students live at home with their parents and are more closely monitored by them. High school teachers have the responsibility to report absences and poor work to parents, who presumably will take some action. College professors, in contrast, do not contact parents when students are failing or not attending classes.

The college environment differs as well. Colleges are often much larger than high schools and the work more challenging. Many college students live in dorms away from home, and they must get used to living with other students whose habits may be less than ideal. One student, for example, complained that his roommate "never slept," was always making noise, and was generally messy. Students who attend college while living at home spend less time at home than they did in high school, and they have considerable freedom. College requires more self-discipline, because the work is more rigorous and distractions are numerous. Students encounter a large number of activities and no parents to monitor their study habits.

Entering college students sometimes experience a shock when they find their initial grades are lower than they were in high school. As one student said, "Frankly, I wasn't properly prepared for college. I didn't go into my freshman year with the right attitude. At age 18, I thought I had the world figured out; I thought I could ace my college classes like high school. I couldn't have been more off. I was failing three classes, and I didn't see the point of sticking around [the college]" (Whitbourne, 2002, p. 26). The shock of doing poorly may lead to reduced academic self-confidence. Other students may find themselves constantly behind in their classes and not able to catch up. Many students, especially African Americans and Latinos, may find they do not seem to fit in. Some experience prejudice. Others feel alone, a feeling shared by students of all cultural backgrounds faced with building a new social life among people they do not know (Weissman, Bulakowski, & Jumisko, 1998). Almost everyone in college is a stranger at first, whereas in the transition to high school most students knew others who progressed with them from junior high school. Some students find they made a faulty college choice, and their college turns out to be not what they expected. The monetary aspects should not be ignored. Many college dropouts cite a lack of money as a principal reason for leaving school, and this problem may be due to faulty planning.

Colleges and universities are doing something about these problems. The most common solutions are to offer not only a fuller orientation program before student registration but also to offer full courses (sometimes called *freshman survival courses*) covering study habits, managing time and money, note taking, pacing oneself in a course, other academic skills, and how things (especially registration) work at college (Whitbourne, 2002).

Successful students must balance work and socializing. Sometimes a study group can perform both a social and academic function. Study groups can help students academically, as well as help them develop new friendships. Colleges are offering social events specifically for freshmen to reduce the feeling of being alone and ease the social transition. A delicate balance is needed, however. Students who are always socializing may find they do not study enough. In contrast, those who cannot easily make new friends often retreat to their rooms or go to the library alone, and they may be overwhelmed by feelings of isolation and loneliness (Whitbourne, 2002). Many colleges are attacking these problems by improving their support services, especially their counseling services (Bergman, McClelland, & Demont, 1999).

Many factors influence persistence and success in college, but family support and faculty attention, patience, and support are prominent (Weissman et al., 1998). Parents who listen to their college students can help give them the emotional support to persevere despite the setbacks that so often occur at the beginning of college. Faculty members who are sensitive to the difficulties and self-doubts of first-year students and who give support and understanding can also help students persevere. *(For a review of this section, see At A Glance 7.3.)*

AT A GLANCE **7.3** ENHANCING THE SCHOOL EXPERIENCE

KEY POINT: Adolescents' school experiences depend on classroom practices, parental behavior, teacher skills, internal factors, and school practices, all of which continue to change.

SUPPORTING POINTS	EXPLANATION
Learner-centered education focuses on the needs, interests, and experiences of the learner.	Learner-centered education promotes the active engagement of the learner through projects, group activities, and group discussions.
Motivation is divided into intrinsic and extrinsic motivation.	Motivation is intrinsic when students work because of an inherent interest in their work. Motivation is extrinsic if it is based on rewards and punishments. Intrinsic motivation is related to better academic achievement, but intrinsic motivation declines through the early adolescent years.
Attribution theory seeks to explain how people ascribe the causes of their behavior.	Attributions may be ascribed as internal-external, stability-instability, and controllable-uncontrollable. Students who attribute their success to effort are more likely to work hard.
Student goals are divided into mastery goals, performance-approach goals, and performance-avoidance goals.	Mastery goals involve the desire to master the material or skill for its own sake. Performance-approach goals involve doing well in order to compare well with others, whereas performance-avoidance goals aim at protecting oneself from failure. Mastery goals encourage learning and self-regulation more than performance goals do.
Parental involvement can improve student achievement.	Parental involvement is related to better student achievement. Parents from different ethnic/racial groups may see their school responsibilities differently.
Teacher expectations can influence students positively or negatively.	Negative teacher expectations based on factors irrelevant to student achievement, such as appearance, race, or socioeconomic status, can influence achievement. Most teacher expectations, however, are based on relevant factors related to achievement.
Tracking, a practice that places students in classes of homogeneous ability, is controversial.	Some authorities claim that tracking is necessary to allow teachers to function effectively. Others argue that it injures student self-esteem and that students in the lower track receive an inferior education.
Some authorities advocate more options for adolescents and parents as a way to improve the educational experience.	Magnet schools offer special programs of interest. Charter schools have a mission statement that spells out details of their philosophy, which may differ substantially from the local public school. Voucher plans give parents the right to choose any public or private school for their children, which is then paid from public funds.
Some high school graduates have difficulty with their transition to college.	The college and high school environments are very different, with college being more demanding. College students must balance their social and academic spheres.

DROPPING OUT

Today, a majority of students graduate from high school. High school dropouts are more likely to live at or near the poverty level, to experience unemployment, and to depend on government support. The average annual income of dropouts is less than half the income of high school graduates. Half of all families on public assistance are headed by dropouts, and dropouts account for half the prison population (Educational Testing Service, 1995). Students from minority groups, who often live in poverty, have a higher dropout rate than middle-class youths (McNeal, 1997).

Dropping out of high school is considered almost shameful in American society. Some states severely chastise dropouts. For instance, one state revokes the driver's license of a minor who drops out of school, and other states may do so in the future. Some states cut welfare benefits if adolescents drop out (Toby, 1999). School districts with high dropout rates are severely criticized.

Some argue that not every student can or should get a high school diploma. Some students are internal dropouts (Toby, 1999); they become disruptive and disengaged, put little effort into their schoolwork, and even may have a negative effect on students who want to learn. And although there is no doubt that high school dropouts do not earn as much as graduates in general, dropping out need not mean permanent unemployability, and formal education is not the only path to responsible adulthood. One New Jersey governor dropped out of school at age 17, joined the U.S. Navy, understood that his lack of diploma was a problem and took a general equivalency diploma (GED) exam, and eventually completed college and even law school. Instead of trying to keep everyone in school, perhaps we ought to find better ways of allowing students to return to school when they are ready. Some argue that the crime rate would increase tremendously if more students dropped out, but the argument can be made that high delinquency rates actually precede, rather than follow, dropping out.

The idea that some students are so disengaged that they get little out of their education and perhaps hinder the educational experiences of others may be true to some extent. The idea of creating a useful system for allowing older students to return to their studies later is interesting, although it is difficult to create such a system. One problem is that most students who drop out, at least in the final 2 years of high school, have the ability to succeed and are not dropping out because they cannot do the work. Other difficulties may cause them to drop out, and they may require a different educational experience. A second problem is that dropout rates differ across social and ethnic groups. Many more students from minority groups, those from single-parent homes, and those living in poverty drop out now, and they would drop out in much greater numbers under a system that did not encourage attendance (Rumberger, 1995).

In the past, African Americans dropped out of school at a much higher rate than whites, but today the gap is narrowing substantially. The dropout rate for African Americans, however, is still higher than the white or Asian American dropout rates. Latinos have a very high dropout rate and spend less time in school than Asian Americans, whites, or African Americans (Aviles et al., 1999). Latinos experience the same difficulties as other minority groups who live in poverty, but they also may have poor English language skills, and their parents often have little schooling (DeBlassie & DeBlassie, 1996). Moreover, many more Latinos drop out before or in the early years of high school ("Hispanic Dropouts," 1993).

Some teens drop out of school early to work in relatively low skill occupations to help their families. Some authorities differentiate between teens who drop out and go into gainful employment and those who are idle. It is the idle youths who are most likely to become involved in problem behavior. Furthermore, cultural expectations may differ. Some traditional Latino families may not expect their daughters to complete high school but rather expect them to fulfill the valued roles as wives and mothers (Valdivieso & Nicolau, 1994).Teens from these backgrounds who drop out should not necessarily be seen as disaffected, although they are surely limiting their future. Being married young, living in a father-absent household, or living in poverty has negative consequences for the educational attainment of minority teens (Aviles et al., 1999).

Teens who are at risk for dropping out are characterized by consistent failure, grade-level placement below average, poor attendance, active antagonism to teachers, disinterest in school, low reading ability, unhappy family situations, and conduct problems in school (Brooks-Gunn, Guo, & Furstenberg, 1993;

Dropping out of high school is the culmination of a long process rather than a sudden event.

Horowitz, 1992). Many have been left back a grade. They often come from large families or have backgrounds of poverty, discord, and divorce (Zmiles & Lee, 1991). Dropouts often have friends who have also dropped out. When asked, dropouts often cite disliking school, poor grades, and disciplinary problems as the most important reasons for leaving school (Janosz et al., 1997; McNeal, 1997). The general picture of the potential dropout as low achieving, poorly motivated, hanging out with friends who are not doing well, and attending school on a spotty basis is fairly accurate.

African American and Latino students are more likely to have been held back, have more frequent changes of schools, and feel less control over their surroundings (Rumberger, 1987). Even controlling for other factors such as intelligence, teens from low socioeconomic areas are twice as likely to drop out than students from middle-class families. As is so often the case, socioeconomic status and minority status confound each other. Although some studies show that African Americans and Latinos are more likely to drop out of school, other studies find that once socioeconomic status is controlled, there is little or no difference between the groups (Janosz et al., 1997).

Most high school dropouts have average intelligence scores, so it is not the difficulty of the work that causes them to drop out. In fact, dropping out is best considered a process of disengagement from school rather than an event. Most factors that differentiate graduates from dropouts are present before the teens drop out. The students have low self-esteem, higher rates of delinquency, and higher rates of drug abuse before they stop attending school, so these factors are not consequences of dropping out.

Dropouts are less engaged in their schoolwork and are involved in fewer extracurricular activities (Mahoney & Cairns, 1997). In fact, the school dropout rate is much lower for at-risk students who participate in such activities as clubs, the school newspaper, the theater, or athletics. Early school failure sets the stage for negative attitudes toward school and feelings of rejection and alienation (Kaplan, Peck, & Kaplan, 1997). At-risk students associate with others who also share these feelings and attitudes (Battin-Pearson et al., 2000). Dropping out, then, is the culmination of a long process of failure, disengagement, poor adjustment, low aspirations, low intellectual stimulation, and poverty. This process begins in primary school with failure, behavior problems, and gradual disengagement

(Alexander, Entwisle, & Horsey, 1997). Students who fail to learn to read, are prone to problem behaviors, and have poor skills in early elementary school are more likely to drop out later (Vallerand, Fortier, & Guay, 1997). Dropouts have lower levels of motivation and perceive themselves as less competent. They perceive their teachers, parents, and school as not being supportive. For some, dropping out is a decision, but for others it is just another step that naturally follows from their school-related behavior (Brouilette, 1999).

Some factors influencing students to drop out may be regarded as pushing the student to drop out; other factors may pull the individual from the school (Jordan, Lara, & McPartland, 1996). Consider the adolescent whose family needs an extra paycheck. This need may pull the student from the school. Other factors, most often school related, push the adolescent out. Poor achievement, not getting along with teachers, and feeling incompetent may push students out of school. Some factors can be either push or pull factors, for example, the peer group. Adolescents at risk for dropping out often associate with others with similar difficulties (Ellenbogen & Chamberland, 1997). The development of an out-of-school friendship network with other dropouts may accelerate the disengagement process during middle adolescence and pull a student out of school. In contrast, students may be pushed out if they are afraid of physical violence by their peers in the schools. Although pull factors may be important for some dropouts, push factors are more important for the majority of dropouts (Jordan et al., 1996).

There are two models for explaining dropping out (Finn, 1989). The *frustration–self-esteem model* argues that continuous failure leads to low self-esteem and problem behaviors such as absenteeism, which finally culminate in dropping out. The *participation-identification model* argues that lack of participation in school activities leads to poor school performance and alienation from school, which lead to dropping out. There is probably truth in both models, and dropout prevention strategies might be based on either theoretical approach. For example, because dropouts have a long history of school failure, early intervention may be effective. Because many dropouts have little or no identification with their school, encouraging participation in extracurricular activities may forge a connection between student and school. Some believe that requirements that restrict students from participating in sports or social events because of misbehavior or poor achievement may encourage dropping out by not allowing students to become involved in school activities (Walters & Bowen, 1997). This viewpoint, however, is highly controversial.

Whatever model for dropping out they follow, schools must address both push and pull factors. For example, students who are pregnant require help to stay in school or home teaching at the end of their pregnancies. Students whose families require an extra paycheck may be eligible for different governmental programs and might benefit from help in researching them. Too often, schools do not pursue questioning or counseling of students who withdraw. One reason may be that many have not been attending anyhow, or the school views them as troublesome.

Many school districts, however, do recognize the need for bold new approaches to the dropout problem. Some school districts have instituted promising programs in which potential dropouts attend alternative schools or work-study programs and receive more attention and tutoring in basic academic skills. Alternative schools may help

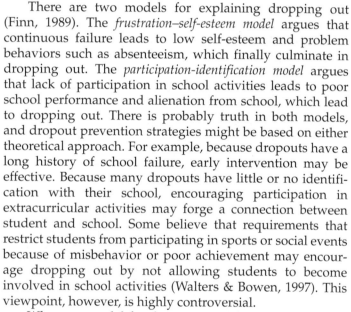

PERSPECTIVE 3

STANDARDS FOR THE FOOTBALL TEAM

SETTING THE SCENE: Your local high school has been criticized for poor academic standards. Students aren't reading well, and the atmosphere in the school does not seem conducive to learning. The school has decided to improve its standards. One of the suggestions is to require any student playing a varsity sport (or participating in certain other school activities) to have a particular grade average.

ADVOCATE: *Students who are failing, whose attendance is spotty, or who misbehave should not represent the school on a team or participate in other high-profile school-related activities. These students should understand that schools are places for academic work. Students should not be allowed to participate in a sport if they are not doing their schoolwork.*

DETRACTOR: *These rules would increase the dropout rate, because these activities are the only areas of engagement for many students. In addition, students might not be able to get athletic scholarships to college because they would not be allowed to show their skills.*

QUESTION: Think about how you would answer the following questions at a public hearing: Should there be academic requirements for participation in sports or to become a member of the senior yearbook committee? What consequences would such requirements have?

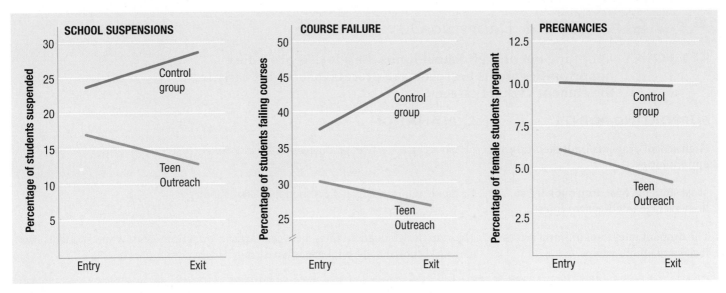

Figure 7.4

A Comparison of Program Entry to Program Exit Changes in Problem Behaviors Between Adolescents in the Teen Outreach Program and a Control Group

When a group of adolescents who participated in the Teen Outreach group was compared with a control group, the changes in school suspensions, percentage of teens failing courses, and number of teen pregnancies testified to the effectiveness of this program.

Source: Allen et al. (1997).

many students who find that conventional high school does not fulfill their needs. Many of these schools offer a better teacher-pupil ratio and a more personalized environment. They may offer more individualized instruction, work-study programs, and even part-time enrollment and evening courses so students can work during the day. Discipline problems are somewhat reduced because of the small size of the schools and lower teacher-student ratios. Random drug tests and checks for weapons are common, and a "one strike and you're out" policy often prevails. Some schools emphasize teaching students with behavior problems appropriate ways of dealing with anger (Duke & Griesdorn, 1999). Mentorship programs seem to help as well (Dondero, 1997). Mentors provide support in academic and social development and serve as role models, offering friendship and guidance.

One interesting program, Teen Outreach, consists of three elements: supervised community volunteer service, classroom-based discussions of these service experiences, and classroom-based discussions and activities related to important developmental tasks of adolescence (Allen et al., 1997). Participants in the Teen Outreach program volunteer in hospitals and nursing homes or for peer tutoring, and in class they discuss their experiences and challenges. They engage in group exercises and role playing, and guest speakers make presentations. Trained facilitators lead small-group discussions of values, life skills, handling close relationships, dealing with family stress, and other problems.

In one study, student volunteers were assigned to either the Teen Outreach program or a control situation. Those in the Teen Outreach program attended it in place of health or social studies classes, whereas students in the control group remained in their regular health or social studies classes. The results, shown in Figure 7.4, demonstrate the effectiveness of this program in reducing some of the causes of dropping out. The program does not concentrate on preventing misbehavior in school, school failure, or pregnancy, but rather focuses on enhancing participants' decision-making abilities, improving their interactions with others, helping adolescents handle their emotions, and providing teens with a meaningful experience helping others. Although this evaluation is valuable, some of the

AT A GLANCE 7.4 DROPPING OUT

KEY POINT: Dropping out of high school limits the adolescent's future opportunities and is best seen as a process that begins early in the student's school career.

SUPPORTING POINTS	EXPLANATION
High school dropouts limit their future opportunities.	Dropouts earn less than graduates and are more likely to live in poverty.
Most students who drop out have at least average intelligence scores.	Dropping out is usually not a response to lack of ability.
The dropout rate is not uniform across racial and ethnic groups.	The gap in graduation rates between African American and white students has narrowed substantially, but Latinos have a much higher dropout rate.
Certain patterns predict dropping out of high school.	Students who drop out are consistently failing; have poor attendance; show active antagonism to teachers and a disinterest in school; and have low reading ability, unhappy family situations, and conduct problems in school.
Dropping out is a process of disengagement from school.	Students who drop out are less engaged in school and school activities. They show a long history of failure, poor reading skills, low aspirations, and dislike of school.
Factors that lead to students dropping out may be categorized as push or pull factors.	Push factors involve finding schooling a negative experience, not getting along with teachers, and failure. Pull factors involve the need for money to support oneself or one's family, as well as greater reinforcements outside the school.
Dropout prevention programs can be successful.	Work-study programs, alternative educational opportunities, and mentorship programs can be successful in reducing the dropout rate.

differences between the treatment and control groups may have been due to the special attention received by participants in the special program. The researchers acknowledged this possibility but argued that giving a great deal of attention has not been found to be successful in changing these behaviors, and that control group students received substantial attention in their regular classes. Still, the addition of a control group consisting of students who receive additional attention through discussions of adolescent problems, perhaps in small groups, would be useful. *(For a review of this section, see At A Glance 7.4.)*

PLACING THE SCHOOL EXPERIENCE IN PERSPECTIVE

The adolescent's experience in secondary school depends on many factors, including the teacher's attitudes and practices; the student's prior experiences, ability, and achievement level; parental and peer attitudes; the policies of the school; and school structure. Although achievement in middle school and high school requires attention, it is difficult to know just what to do about it. Some authorities want to begin with the problem of student and parent disinterest and disengagement. As we have seen, psychologists have taken a long and detailed look at student motivation and suggested some changes in the class-room. Often, these psychologists see the goals of education as including more than achievement on standardized tests; they also emphasize personal responsi-bility, identification of a personal value system, and understanding the demo-cratic process. They consider personal growth and individual needs as impor-tant, and they place much less emphasis on standardized testing.

In contrast, a powerful reform movement today emphasizes student accountability through test scores. Almost all states have initiated reforms in response to what is seen by the public as poor academic achievement. These reforms often lead to a greater emphasis on monitoring student achievement and teaching the basics (Paul, 2002). Reforms are often test driven; that is, they use standardized tests as the basis for measuring accountability and showing whether or not the educational system is working. Other reforms involve strengthening the curriculum, improving student technological skills, strength-ening graduation requirements, and involving parents. This emphasis on content is seen as promoting higher standards, requiring more assessments, and provid-ing consequences for not achieving, such as not being admitted to desirable tech-nical programs or apprenticeships (Shanker, 1997).

A report by the Carnegie Corporation (1996) on restructuring high schools, called "Breaking Ranks," advocated some far-reaching structural changes. Many high school students feel that few people really know them; anonymity is a major problem, as it is in junior high school. The report suggests limiting high schools to six hundred students to help solve this problem. In addition, each stu-dent should have a personal adult advocate who meets regularly with the teenager and can serve as a liaison between the student and others in the school environment. Schools should emphasize more practical learning and issue a war-ranty guaranteeing that students can meet performance standards for entry-level jobs. The warranty would permit employers to return students lacking basic skills to high schools for additional training (Henry, 1996). All students should have individualized plans to guide their education. Schools should ask full-time teachers to teach no more than ninety students per day to foster individual atten-tion. Schools also should be required to develop a long-term plan for using com-puters and other technologies. The report also advocates teaching a core set of values, stressing that possession of weapons, drugs, and violence will not be tol-erated. Students should have a role in decision making within the school. Whether these structural changes are practical in the present environment is questionable, of course. School reform is not easy, and the process is often messy and inexact (Olson, 1998).

The psychological research on motivation emphasizes intrinsic motivation and goal setting. This approach is at odds with the more test-driven movement that emphasizes standards more than the learning experience, and external rewards and punishments more than motivating an intrinsic desire to learn. In fact, both approaches are rooted in a desire to improve learning, but their meth-ods differ. Those who emphasize making the high school experience more mean-ingful for students expect this method to lead to better achievement. Those who emphasize higher standards and test-driven assessment also want better achievement, but they emphasize structural changes in the schools, the use of incentives, consequences for failure, and higher standards. The public clamors for better achievement, and many students would like a better school experience. It remains to be seen whether the two movements can be fused so that students may both have a more meaningful experience in school and successfully meet higher standards.

THEMES

THEME 1 Adolescence is a time of choices, "firsts," and transitions.	• The transition to junior high school is a time of adaptation to a new set of rules and standards. • The transition to high school does not seem as difficult as the transition to junior high, but it still requires some adaptation. • The secondary school experience introduces students to a more complex and demanding environment.
THEME 2 Adolescence is shaped by context.	• The high school experience is a crucial factor in the adolescent's cognitive and social development. • The junior high/middle school is structured differently than the elementary school; it provides a context in which students meet more teachers and peers. • Junior high/middle schools are larger and less personal than elementary schools. • The family, peer group, and neighborhood influence adolescent achievement. • Classroom and school practices create an environment that either encourages or discourages student achievement. • Adolescents' educational experience may be affected by educational innovations such as magnet schools, charter schools, and the voucher plan.
THEME 3 Adolescence is influenced by group membership.	• Although most teens make a positive transition to junior high school, girls are more likely to have difficulty than boys. • Groups of friends are more likely to be separated in the transition to a larger school, and this change disrupts friendships and introduces the need to find new friends. • The achievement of African American and Latino high school students lags behind that of white and Asian American students. • The experience of a minority group student living in poverty certainly differs from that of a nonminority student raised in a middle-class area.
THEME 4 The adolescent experience has changed over the past 50 years.	• Many more adolescents attend and graduate from high school today. • More high school girls are taking advanced math and science courses than years ago.
THEME 5 Today's views of adolescence are becoming more balanced, with greater attention to its positive nature.	• People today have a greater understanding that many of the problems associated with minority group achievement in school are due to poverty. • Researchers today appreciate the fact that many students from minority groups do succeed in school, and they look to these students to answer their questions about why some students do and do not achieve. • More African American and Latino students are receiving high school diplomas than in the past, although their graduation rates are still lower than those of other groups. • Although girls were traditionally viewed as being discriminated against in the classroom, today the differences in teacher treatment of girls and boys seem to have declined.

CHAPTER SUMMARY AT A GLANCE

KEY TOPICS	KEY POINTS
Middle School	The middle school/junior high school was created to bridge the gap between the easier work of elementary school and the more challenging academic work of high school, as well as to meet the developmental needs of young adolescents. *(At A Glance 7.1, p. 220)*
High School	The achievement of high school students is a concern, and parents, college teachers, students, and employers all have different evaluations of the high school. *(At A Glance 7.2, p. 230)*
Enhancing the School Experience	Adolescents' school experiences depend on classroom practices, parental behavior, teacher skills, internal factors, and school practices, all of which continue to change. *(At a Glance 7.3, p. 245)*
Dropping Out	Dropping out of high school limits the adolescent's future opportunities and is best seen as a process that begins early in the student's school career. *(At A Glance 7.4, p. 250)*

KEY TERMS
learner-centered education (p. 230)
intrinsic motivation (p. 232)
extrinsic motivation (p. 232)
attribution theory (p. 233)
mastery (learning) goals (p. 234)
performance (ego) goals (p. 234)
performance-approach goals (p. 235)
performance-avoidance goals (p. 235)
self-fulfilling prophecy (p. 240)
tracking (p. 241)
magnet school (p. 242)
charter school (p. 242)
voucher plan (p. 243)

Review questions for this chapter appear in the appendix.

THE MEDIA

WHAT IS YOUR OPINION?

THE MEDIA AND THE TEEN
- The Teenager as Consumer
- Mechanisms of Influence
- The Cohort Effect and Teenage Culture

**THE COMPUTER REVOLUTION:
EMAIL AND THE INTERNET**
- Adolescents as Internet Users
- Uses of the Internet
- Dangers in Paradise
  Perspective 1: Does He Ever See the Daylight?

VIDEO GAMES
- Video Games and Gender
- You Missed One of the Monsters:
  Video Games and Aggression
- Video Games, Prosocial Behavior,
  and Social Skills
- The Overuse of Video Games
- Video Games and Adolescents:
  A Summary

MUSIC AND RADIO
- The Meaning of Music
- The Controversial Face of Music
  Perspective 2: Why the Obsession?
- Music Videos
  **FOCUS: Censorship, Warning Labels,
  and Rating Systems**

TELEVISION AND THE MOVIES
- Violence on Television and in the Movies
- Fantasy and Sex in the Media
- Stereotypes
- Television Talk Shows
- Advertising
- Western Influences on Other Societies
  Perspective 3: Legal Responsibility
- The Influence of Movies and Television:
  A Final Word

MAGAZINES

PLACING THE MEDIA IN PERSPECTIVE
HAS YOUR OPINION CHANGED?
THEMES
CHAPTER SUMMARY AT A GLANCE

Adolescents spend roughly 39 percent of their waking time watching television, listening to the radio and CDs, using the Internet and email, playing video games, or reading magazines (Merrill, 1999). This is more time than they devote to any other waking activity. Adolescents, on average, view 17 hours of television per week (Nielsen Media Research, 1998). Preteens and teenagers, ages 9 to 17 years, use the Internet on the average of 4 days a week and spend almost 2 hours on-line at a time (Roper Starch Worldwide, 1999). When 15- to 18-year-old adolescents in 26 countries rated their enjoyment of popular activities, watching television, listening to music, going to the movies, and talking on the telephone stood out as enjoyable to most teens. When participants in a national sample of children and adolescents were asked to choose which medium they would bring with them to a desert island, more children from 8 to 18 years old chose a computer with Internet access than any other medium (Rideout et al., 1999). People between the ages of 12 and 24 years make up 39 percent of all moviegoers (James, 2001), and adolescents spend a considerable amount of time listening to music.

Since 1997, the Annenberg Public Policy Center of the University of Pennsylvania has annually surveyed the extent of media use and perception of the media in the United States (Woodard & Gridina, 2000). The most recent survey drew a sample of more than 1,250 parents and about 600 children between the ages of 8 and 16 years through random telephone digit dialing around the United States. Of the families sampled, 68 percent had video game equipment, and the percentage increased to 78 percent for homes with teenagers. Seventy percent of all homes have computers, and 52 percent have access to the Internet. Computer ownership is related to family income, but it is growing among families with modest incomes. Children of all ages use each medium somewhat, but adolescents spend more time using the Internet, playing video games, talking on the telephone, reading magazines, and generally using the computer than do younger children. An interesting finding is that although parents may provide their children with the equipment to access the media, they still show great concern about their children's media use (see Figure 8.1).

Adolescents often find they are more comfortable with some forms of the media—for example, the Internet and email—than their parents are (Villani, 2001). This comfort with the media, which allows instantaneous communication and a feeling of belonging, is part of the adolescent subculture.

This chapter begins with a look at adolescents' relationship with the media, a relationship that differs substantially from the relationship their parents have with the media. It then explores each medium, beginning with the most recently developed, the computer and video games. A discussion of the influence of music (especially music with aggressive themes) and music videos follows. The chapter then turns to the influence of television and movies on adolescent attitudes and behaviors. The discussion wraps up with an investigation of the influence of magazines aimed at teenage audiences. The text uses an ecological approach, viewing the adolescent as enmeshed in many media contexts, being influenced by each context, and at the same time influencing each context. In considering each context, keep in mind that teenagers do not come to the Internet, video games, music videos, and the television as blank slates on which what they see or hear is automatically encoded and accepted. They come with attitudes, values, problems, and beliefs that influence not only what they will do, watch, or listen to but also what ideas they will accept.

WHAT IS YOUR OPINION?

Please place the number best reflecting your opinion next to each of the following statements. We will return to this questionnaire at the end of the chapter so you can determine if your opinions have changed.

1 — Strongly Agree
2 — Moderately Agree
3 — No Opinion
4 — Moderately Disagree
5 — Strongly Disagree

_____ 1. The influence of the media on adolescents is generally positive.

_____ 2. Email and chat rooms help teenagers improve their interpersonal and computer skills.

_____ 3. Overuse of video games, chat rooms, and the Internet can lead to emotional disturbances.

_____ 4. Families without computers and Internet access in their homes place their children at an academic disadvantage compared with children who have home access to computers with Internet access.

_____ 5. Playing violent video games increases the probability that an adolescent will be aggressive.

_____ 6. It is the government's responsibility to make certain that sexist, racist, and extremely violent video games, music lyrics, and music videos do not reach the eyes and ears of children and adolescents under 18 years of age.

_____ 7. Parents who do not know what television programs their adolescent children are watching, which websites they are visiting, and what music they are listening to are not doing an adequate job.

_____ 8. Violence on television, including violent music videos, contributes to violence in our society.

_____ 9. The portrayal of women as sexual objects in heavy metal and rap music and in some music videos contributes to violence against women.

_____ 10. All CDs and video games should have rating labels.

Figure 8.1

Percentage of Parents with Children Aged 2 to 17 Expressing at Least "Some" Concern About Medium

Parents express concern about the influence of the media on their children and adolescents.

Source: Woodard & Gridina (2000), Figure 3.2.

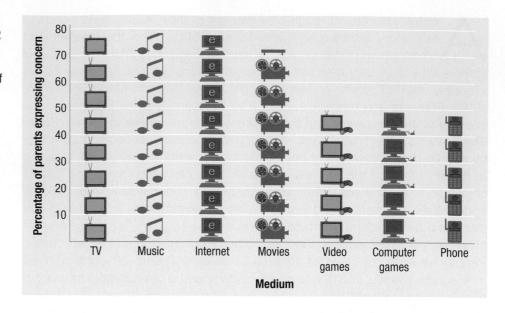

Exploring the effects of the media on adolescent attitudes and behavior requires special care. Keep in mind the following five precautions as you read the chapter:

1. *Much remains to be researched in the area of adolescents and the media.* The computer, the Internet, instant messaging, chat rooms, and email have come into being so recently, and their uses are expanding so rapidly, that research has just begun to unravel their influences on the lives of adolescents (Villani, 2001). Our knowledge of these media has many gaps. Some provocative research evidence exists, but research in this area is still in its infancy.

2. *Much of the research concerns undesirable effects of the media on adolescents.* It is natural for psychologists to research questions of special interest to the public. Unfortunately, many of these questions concern the possible negative influences of the media, and research interest is unbalanced. For example, many more studies concern the influence of television programs and movies on aggression than on prosocial (helpful) behavior.

3. *The research in some areas is heavily weighted toward children rather than adolescents.* Many more studies explore the effect of television violence on children than on adolescents. In contrast, research on the influence of music and magazines naturally focuses more on adolescents. This chapter will focus on studies that deal with adolescents. Remember, though, that childhood experiences are important factors in determining how adolescents act, as well as how they process and interpret information.

4. *The text will make few general statements about the effect of the media on adolescents.* Consider two teenage males playing a violent video game or listening to music with a hard beat and aggressive lyrics. One teen comes to the experience angry after having had a frustrating argument with his parents. The other adolescent is calmer, having had a pleasant dinner with his family. The content of the game or music selection may affect each adolescent differently. Many studies of the media emphasize the importance of the characteristics the viewer brings to the situation. General statements become much more difficult to make when the background, mood, and prior experiences of the viewer must be considered. What may be true for angry or depressed adolescents may not be true for other adolescents.

5. *Data concerning the media become old quickly.* The numbers of adolescents using the Internet, email, or chat rooms change rapidly. The data presented here are best seen in terms of a trend demonstrating the degree to which adolescents' use of a particular medium has increased or decreased.

THE MEDIA AND THE TEEN

The media differ from other aspects of the teen's environment in two distinct ways. First, teenagers have a great deal more control over their exposure to the media than to other parts of their environment. Adolescents choose which radio station they will listen to, whom to email, which movie to attend, and which video game to play. An adolescent who does not want to watch a television show can turn it off or tune in another show. This control does not extend to other components of the adolescent's environment, such as parents, teachers, siblings, and friends. Teens can certainly limit the time spent in their presence, but completely avoiding them is impossible.

Second, teenagers as a group have a tremendous influence on the media. The media are profit driven and must respond accurately and quickly to what teenagers are interested in. Media that do not respond appropriately will be tuned out and will not make a profit. Television networks that wish to tap this lucrative market must broadcast shows that teens will watch, radio stations must play music that an adolescent audience will listen to, and the movie industry must make films that adolescents will attend. In contrast, the interactions between teens and their parents, friends, siblings, and teachers are not chiefly motivated by financial considerations.

Psychologists today are very interested in the leisure activities of youth. Questions abound concerning the health consequences of the sedentary lifestyle involved in watching television, playing video games, and surfing the Internet. For instance, adolescent males who are heavy viewers of television (those who watch more than 4 hours per day) exercise less, drink more alcohol, and smoke more cigarettes than adolescent males who are moderate and light television viewers (Page et al., 1996). The finding that leisure pursuits tend to remain stable throughout life adds importance to the health issue (Scott & Willits, 1989). Participation in five types of leisure activities was sampled in 1947 and then in 1984, when the participants were in their 50s. Interests remained stable; the frequency with which participants engaged in each activity was similar 37 years later. Another follow-up study in 1992 found the same results (Scott & Willits, 1998).

Adolescents have much control over their exposure to the media. If they do not want to watch or listen to something, they can turn it off. The media must grab the attention of teens to have an influence.

The Teenager as Consumer

Why are the media so interested in the adolescent market? On the surface, teenagers would seem not to be a very important market, because few teens have full-time jobs. However, the teenage market is one of the most competitive and important consumer markets. One of the few societal roles open to teenagers is that of consumer, and teenagers are a potent force in the marketplace. Adolescents have a great deal of disposable income. Even though relatively few work full-time, many work part-time and receive allowances or gifts. They are free to spend their money on the goods and services they choose, because they have few necessary expenditures, such mortgages or heating bills. Teens spent $155 billion in the year 2000, $2 billion more than in 1999 (Paul, 2001). Teen spending has risen every year since it has been tracked beginning in 1953, despite eight recessions and declines in the number of teenagers at particular times (Klein, 1998). Teen spending is expected to continue to increase by about 4 percent per year (Stoneman, 1998). Adolescents spend approximately 34 percent of their money on clothing, 22 percent on entertainment, 22 percent on food, and 8.3 percent on personal care items (Day, 2000). This spending pattern has remained constant since the 1950s ("Teen spending," 1998).

Adolescents also spend a considerable amount of the family money. Because of structural changes in the family, such as two working parents and single-parent families, teens have assumed more responsibility for household shop-

Adolescents are an important consumer group. They have a great deal of disposable income that they can spend on goods and services that they want.

ping. An impressive 83 percent of all teens do at least some of their family's grocery shopping (Fischer & Meyer, 1996). They also provide their parents with much information about purchases. Some 56 percent of the girls polled by *Seventeen* magazine said they helped their parents buy their family computer (Brown, 1999).

Finally, teenagers are a trendsetting group. What teenagers wear or use may become popular with other cohorts, although perhaps tailored a bit differently. Television programs use actors who will appeal to the teenage audience, and what these celebrities wear is an important fashion clue to what teens may buy. Adolescents also tend to stay with products they are satisfied with and believe work for them. A solid reputation with teens or even younger children may form the basis for lifelong brand loyalty. Most teens already have their favorite brands, and their interest in change wanes rather than increases through the high school years. Teenagers stick with brands they are comfortable with, and brand names are important to both male and female teens, especially younger teens (Simpson, Douglas, & Schimmel, 1998).

Mechanisms of Influence

It is not enough to know that music videos, video games, or television influences teenagers. Psychologists must also understand how the media have these influences. The media influence teens in many ways. Many adolescents depend on the media for much of their information on health. Adolescents may watch a music video or a television program to see what the actors or recording artists are wearing or to keep abreast of current fashions. Television programs and movies may provide information about how to handle various interpersonal situations as well.

In addition, constant exposure to the media may cause people to develop attitudes and beliefs that are in agreement with those they see and hear in the media, a theory called **cultivation theory** (Gerbner et al., 1994). The media cultivate viewer attitudes about violence, sex roles, and marriage. Cultivation theory argues that media's constant bombardment of viewers with images and portrayals gradually causes them to adopt attitudes and expectations about the world that typically coincide with what is shown on television or in the movies.

cultivation theory A theory of media influence that postulates that constant exposure to a particular value, attitude, or opinion leads to viewers adopting that value, attitude, or opinion.

For example, cultivation theory would predict that if television and music videos showed that unprotected sex were glamorous, prevalent, risk-free, and a matter of recreation, frequent viewers would be more likely than light viewers to adopt this perspective (Ward & Rivadeneyra, 1999).

The media may also reinforce behaviors and attitudes (Liebert & Sprafkin, 1988). Teenagers watching a movie or listening to a CD may find evidence that their behaviors or attitudes are acceptable. One reason an aggressive adolescent may prefer violent programs is that the use of violence shown on the program validates and reinforces the adolescent's idea that violence is an acceptable and effective way to solve problems.

Another possible mechanism of effect for the media is **desensitization,** the process whereby continued exposure to a particular stimulus may reduce an individual's sensitivity to that stimulus. A steady diet of violence, for example, may lead to reduced sensitivity to violence (Liebert & Sprafkin, 1988). Individuals who watch a great deal of violence seem to lose empathy for victims and consider violence just "part of life." In contrast, the media may also sensitize people to certain issues. Individuals who see coverage of issues such as sexism, racism, child abuse, or the environment may become more sensitive to them.

The media also present viewers with models. People may model themselves after television personalities they see as powerful, beautiful, capable of getting things done, or trendsetters. Corporations often spend huge sums on advertising using attractive models to sell products to teens, obviously hoping that adolescents will buy these products to imitate the models (Villani, 2001).

Finally, the media may influence adolescent leisure activities through a *substitution effect.* Teens have only a certain amount of waking time available, and the time they take to go on the Internet, use a chat room, or play a video game has to come from somewhere. There is evidence that extensive use of the media has led to less exercise, as sitting in front of the computer or television substitutes for physical exercise (Page et al., 1996). Furthermore, chat rooms and email may substitute for face-to-face interpersonal interactions.

Research on media influence shows both short- and long-term effects. It is relatively easy to demonstrate the short-term effects of a particular music video on an audience. A psychologist may ask a group of adolescents to watch the video and then measure its effects by comparing attitudes before and after seeing the video. Another possibility is to randomly assign adolescents to an experimental or control group, have the experimental group view the program, and then compare the behavior of the two groups afterward.

Psychologists interested in the long-term effects of the media have a much more daunting task. Long-term experimental research using control groups and manipulating variables is very difficult to conduct, because researchers cannot control exposure to a particular medium over the long term. A researcher cannot take adolescents at age 13, randomly assign participants to groups that will be exposed to a medium (such as music videos) for a stated number of months or years, and measure the effects. Instead, a researcher may compare a group of adolescents who use a medium more often with a group that uses it less often. Such a comparison, although interesting, cannot demonstrate cause and effect. A group of adolescents may have been first attracted to a medium for many reasons, so the groups being compared are not equivalent. Most long-term studies use correlations in which heavy use of a medium is related to a particular behavior, such as eating habits or a sedentary lifestyle, but these correlations do not allow cause-and-effect statements. Therefore, it is more difficult to make statements about the long-term effects of media exposure than about its short-term effects.

Athletes and musicians are often models. They appear on television to sell various products, hoping people will follow their lead in using them.

desensitization The process whereby continued exposure to a particular stimulus, such as violence, may reduce an individual's sensitivity to the stimulus.

The Cohort Effect and Teenage Culture

Teenage culture today emphasizes technology. This is nothing new. Each generation is exposed to a new level of technology and often cannot understand how other generations could have gotten along without the latest technological wizardry. Furthermore, every generation acts as if the present level of technology has always been here and takes it for granted. After all, they have known nothing else. Almost every American home has at least one telephone, for example, and even the grandparents of today's teens take this technology for granted. Newer technologies, such as the computer and cellular phones, are now accepted as the norm by the younger generations, and few think about what life was like before them.

Consider the following television commercial. You see a middle-aged business executive (a baby boomer) telling a computer operator, "I need to be in Los Angeles by the 12th." The operator, who you do not see, strikes some keys. "I want an aisle seat." Again keys are struck. "And a vegetarian meal." Again, we hear the sound of keys. "And, I want to return on the 15th." For the final time, we hear keys. Then, slowly, the camera shows us the computer operator: a preteen who says, "You got it, Dad. Can I go out to play now?"

The generation gap is what differentiates the generations from each other and complicates communication. The present generation, born since 1977, is often called *generation Y*, the *Net generation*, or the *digital generation*. It might also be called the *lap generation*, according to the author of *Growing Up Digital*, Dan Tapscott (1998), because adolescents are lapping their elders in knowledge of computers and technology. They navigate the Internet with apparent ease and generally with much greater comfort than their parents (Subrahmanyam et al., 2001). Adolescents know more about computers and are catching on to new technologies much faster than adults.

For the first time in history, younger people are more comfortable, knowledgeable, and literate than their parents about an innovation central to society. Children and teens today are learning, communicating, working, and creating communities in a different way than their parents did. In a 1995 study on home computing called HomeNet, researchers introduced computers and the Internet into a number of families (Kraut et al., 1998). In most of these families, the heaviest user was a child. In fact, adolescents were more likely to help their parents with computer-related problems than parents were to help their children. Stories abound about children and teens programming new videocassette recorders for their confused parents. Two-thirds are more proficient than their parents, a situation that may lead to a new relationship (Tapscott, 1998).

Many adolescents are more comfortable with modern technology than are their parents.

AT A GLANCE 8.1 THE MEDIA AND THE TEEN

KEY POINT: Adolescents both are affected by, and influence, the media.

SUPPORTING POINTS	EXPLANATION
Adolescents have more control over their media experiences than they do over other aspects of their environment.	Adolescents can tune into a program or not, as they choose. Teenagers influence the content of the music, movies, and television shows produced.
There is fierce competition for the adolescent market.	Although few adolescents have full-time jobs, they have a great deal of disposable income with few fixed expenses.
Adolescent spending patterns have remained stable since the 1950s.	Adolescents spend most of their money on clothing, entertainment, food, and personal care items.
The media may influence adolescents in many ways.	The media may act as teacher, reinforce adolescents, show models, and encourage imitation. The media also may either sensitize or desensitize adolescents to particular behaviors. The time adolescents spend with the media may reduce the time they spend doing other things.
Computer technology is part of the teenage culture.	Adolescents are more comfortable with the new technologies than their parents are.
The use of technology fits in well with the values of this generation of adolescents.	This generation of adolescents may be defined in terms of accessibility, interactiveness, diversity, immediacy, and self-reliance.

The Net generation uses computers for communicating and even to form relationships. Chat groups are commonly populated by young people hungry for expression. Adolescents are accustomed to immediate contact with others. Cell phones and "real time" instant messaging on the computer, which allows users to identify a list of people and to be notified when they go on-line, keep teens in touch.

The present generation of teens and the forthcoming one can be described by the terms *accessibility, interactiveness, diversity, immediacy,* and *self-reli*ance (Tapscott, 1998). The combination of the technological revolution and societal changes is molding these generations. Technology gives rise to instant information and communication. The fact that so many teens are raised in single-parent families or families in which both parents work leads to an increase in self-reliance and independence. Technology, then, fits nicely into the lifestyle of most teenagers. *(For a review of this section, see At A Glance 8.1.)*

THE COMPUTER REVOLUTION: EMAIL AND THE INTERNET

Almost three-quarters of all adolescents use the Internet (NUA, 2001). This figure is amazing if you realize that 15 years ago, the Net and email were virtually unknown to the public. Teen computer use has increased at a fantastic rate as teens log on to chat rooms, surf for information, download photos, and read on-line magazines (Berman, 1999). They read about their favorite stars and chat about them, download music, and shop for purchases. Girls are more likely than boys to make purchases on-line. Although teens make up less than half the public reaching these e-commerce sites, the proportion of teens using e-commerce is greater than for any other age group (Cheng, 1999).

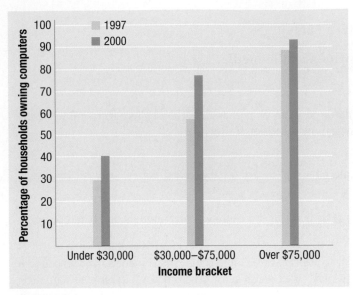

Figure 8.2
Percentage of Families (by Income) with Children Aged 2 to 17 Who Own a Computer, 1997–2000
Children and adolescents whose families have greater resources are more likely to have home access to a computer. Nevertheless, 40 percent of families with incomes under $30,000 own computers.

Source: Woodard & Gridina (2000), Figure 1.7.

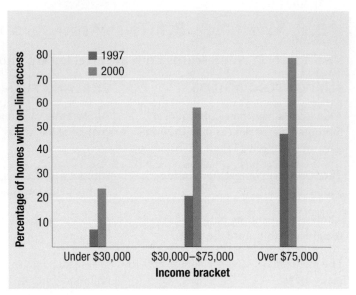

Figure 8.3
Percentage of Families (by Income) with Children Aged 2 to 17 Who Have On-line Access, 1997–2000
Children and adolescents whose families have more financial assets are more likely to have access to the Internet at home. However, 24 percent of all children and adolescents whose families make less than $30,000 have access to the Internet at home.

Source: Woodard & Gridina (2000), Figure 1.8.

Adolescents as Internet Users

About 6.87 million teens, or 35 percent of the total teen population, are considered active Internet users, meaning they logged on at least once a week during the past year and spent at least an hour per week on-line. Adolescents spend more time on-line than people of other age groups. They average 7.3 hours a week on-line, compared with an average of 5.4 hours for the general population (Day, 2000).

Adolescents from middle- and upper-income homes are more likely to have access to computers than adolescents who live in poverty (see Figure 8.2) (Woodard & Gridina, 2000). This difference in computer availability, referred to as the "**digital divide**," may have serious consequences, as experience with computers is such an important element of life today. Yet 40 percent of homes in which parents make less than $30,000 a year have a computer, and 24 percent of these families have access to the Internet at home (see Figure 8.3). Furthermore, the digital divide may be somewhat exaggerated because most adolescents have access to computers and the Internet at school (Borzekowski & Rickert, 2001).

There is little evidence of a gender divide in the use of computers, with the exception of computer game playing (Subrahmanyam et al., 2001). Males and females report an equal level of computer use and confidence in their computer skills. There are no statistically significant differences in male and female adolescent computer use for schoolwork. Boys surf the Net more, and girls use the computer more for communication; however, both males and females use the Internet for both purposes (Berman, 1999; Roberts et al., 1999).

The Gallup organization, in a national survey of adolescents in grades 7 through 12, found that about two-thirds of all teens feel confident with technology, and a majority say they usually can master electronic equipment and computer software on their own (Gallup Poll, 2000). Although boys have a slightly greater interest in computer science than girls, both believe a strong background is important. Levels of confidence and the belief that they can conquer new computer software on their own are similar for boys and girls.

digital divide A term used to describe the difference among people of different socioeconomic groups in their access to computers and other technology.

Uses of the Internet

The Internet is used for communication, information gathering, entertainment, and commerce. Email is an extremely popular form of communication. It is not only a way to stay in touch but also a medium through which one can communicate without worrying about how one looks or one's body language (Berman, 1999). Chat rooms allow teens to meet new people and converse with others on issues of mutual interest, whereas instant messaging informs teens in real time when friends are also on-line, increasing the probability that the adolescents will communicate with someone they already know.

Adolescent use of the Internet for information is also prominent. For example, many adolescents use the Internet to obtain health-related information. A study using an ethnically diverse sample (40 percent African American, 30 percent white, 10 percent Latino, and 20 percent other) of suburban tenth graders found that half had used the Internet to obtain health information, most commonly on sexually transmitted diseases, diet, fitness and exercise, and sexual behavior (Borzekowski & Rickert, 2001). About a third used the Internet to find information about birth control. Adolescents considered the Internet information to be highly valuable, trustworthy, and relevant. Teens see the Internet as a confidential and nonthreatening way to obtain information. This study did not evaluate the Internet sites used, so the actual truthfulness and reliability of the information is not known.

Adolescents also use computers for entertainment. Many teens play computer video games and download music. Others surf the Net, looking for interesting sites. They also use the Internet to find out where their favorite recording artists are performing and whether concert tickets are available.

Teens use the Internet to obtain information about products they are interested in purchasing (Brown, 1999). Many adolescents also purchase goods over the Internet. A recent survey found that 26 percent of all teens who use the Internet spend money on-line, but they make only a small fraction of their purchases on-line (Day, 2000). This percentage is expected to increase, however. In 2001, teens in the United States and Europe spent an estimated $1.3 billion shopping on the Internet, and that total is expected to increase to $10.6 billion by 2005 (NUA, 2001). Half of all children and adolescents have asked their parents to purchase products they have seen while surfing the Net. Many teens do not have

Some people are concerned that one consequence of the "digital divide"—the idea that adolescents living in poverty may not have access to the Internet and computer technology—might be fewer opportunities later in life. However, most adolescents have some access to the Web, often in school.

ready access to credit or debit cards, of course, but companies are prepared to help out in some novel ways. For instance, one retailer has a website that allows teens to choose their favorite clothing seen on television. The teens place the items on a gift list (a sort of registry), and individuals who want to buy them a gift simply choose from the list. Another website encourages parents to post an on-line allowance that teens can then use to shop for what they want (Brown, 1999). Some may laugh at this idea, but it is wise to remember that what seems outlandish today may become commonplace tomorrow.

Dangers in Paradise

The tremendous growth of the Internet and email has raised many questions. For instance, how will email, chat rooms, and instant messaging affect interpersonal relationships? How can children and adolescents be protected from the dangers of inappropriate personal relationships and website content? How does computer use affect an adolescent's thinking style? How can teens be taught to use computers appropriately as study aids? And what are the dangers of overuse of computers?

Computer Use and Social Relationships   Some argue that the Internet and email communication will lead to a greater number of interpersonal relationships as users email friends or make new friends on the Net. Others argue that these forms of communication may lead to a reduction in the number of friendships and level of intimacy. Psychologists often distinguish between strong ties and weak ties. *Strong ties* are associated with frequent contact, deep feelings of affection and obligation, and interaction for many purposes; *weak ties,* in contrast, are superficial and easily broken, marked by infrequent contact, and narrowly focused. On-line ties tend to be weak (Constant, Sproull, & Kiesler, 1996). People receive most of their social support from other people with whom they have a close relationship, so stronger ties are most important. These stronger ties are supported by physical proximity. Certainly, people can and do form on-line social relationships, but their depth is questionable.

The question of whether computer interactions will substitute for deep relationships was investigated in an interesting study by Kraut and colleagues (1998). Ninety-three families from diverse neighborhoods in Pittsburgh participating in the HomeNet study were given free computers, access to the Internet, software, and telephone lines in return for having their use monitored and answering questionnaires for 2 years. The research team recorded 66,383 Internet sessions during the first year. Participants used email during 48.9 percent of their Internet sessions, and it was certainly the most popular use for the computer (Gardyn, 2000). The researchers found a novelty effect, with some decline in the use of both the Internet and email over time; the effect was greater for the use of the Internet for informational purposes than for email. Perhaps the reason is that email is more reinforcing than Internet use, and users feel a social obligation to respond to messages.

The researchers also found that individuals who used the computer more frequently engaged in less social interaction, as measured by both communication within the family and the size of people's social groups. The participants, many of whom were teenagers, reported an increase in loneliness and mild depression (such as an inability to shake off the blues), perhaps due to a lack of face-to-face interactions.

As computer use expanded, so did feelings of isolation and unhappiness, regardless of race, age, gender, household income, or initial level of social interaction. Adolescents who used email and the Internet more reported greater isolation and loneliness. Perhaps adolescents were using the computer as an escape— a way of withdrawing from social contacts. The relatively shallow interactions, often with strangers, that are common on the Internet may not provide the same type of social support and communication as face-to-face interactions do (Bower, 1998; Kraut et al., 1998).

There are two ways to explain the overall findings of the study. First, perhaps the Internet replaced other activities, such as conversing at home. Because Internet use is similar to other passive, nonsocial activities such as watching television or listening to music, it further encourages a trend called the "**privatization of entertainment**," in which individuals experience modes of entertainment individually rather than as a social experience (Kraut et al., 1998, p. 1029). Such findings are common in research on people who watch a great deal of television (Putnam, 1995). Although the privatization of entertainment may be a part of the puzzle, it cannot be the entire answer, and the researchers reject it as a major explanation. Although surfing the Net may be essentially nonsocial, email and chat rooms are socially interactive. In addition, some, but not all, research indicates that using the Internet reduces the time spent watching television (Gardyn, 2000).

The second way to explain the study's findings, and the one favored by the researchers, uses the substitution argument: People are substituting weak ties for strong ties. Most Internet links are considered weak. A few participants in the study met new people on-line who became true friends, but most did not. After looking at the friendships made on-line, the researchers argue that it is less effective as a means of making new friends and conducting social interactions than face-to-face interactions. They caution, though, that extensive use of the Internet may not lead to a reduction in social interaction among those who are already isolated or who have particular problems.

Another study that monitored Internet use by high school students found a reduction in close relationships as use increased. Students who used the Internet for less than 1 hour a day were considered *low users,* those who used the Internet for 1 to 2 hours were categorized as *moderate users,* and *high users* were on the Internet for more than 2 hours a day. The researchers administered questionnaires concerning social relationships and measures of depression. Low users reported better relationships with their mothers and friends (Sanders et al., 2000). It is impossible to determine from this study whether adolescents with poorer relationships with parents and peers gravitate toward heavy use of the Internet or whether heavy use of the Internet leads to decreased social ties. In this study, the level of Internet use was not related to depression, but the researchers comment that this finding may be due to the very high initial depression scores for students in all three groups of the sample. We will look at adolescent depression in "Stress and Psychological, Physical, and Learning Problems."

Dangerous Liaisons In addition, how do we protect young adolescents from predators who may lurk in chat rooms, seemingly showing their interest and concern for an adolescent, and then luring the adolescent into a meeting with tragic results? Chat rooms offer an anonymous way of meeting new people, but they offer predators an avenue of attack as well. There is also the question of how to prevent young adolescents from visiting inappropriate sites.

The Internet is basically unregulated. Some sites may be inappropriate, especially for young teens; other sites may be offensive because of their racist, anti-Semitic, or pornographic content. An adolescent exploring the Internet can be trapped in such a site by a marketing technique that disables the "back" or "close" navigational options (National Institute on Media and the Family, 1998). In a recent survey, more than half of all adolescent Internet users admitted to visiting sites that contain pornography, offensive music lyrics, gambling, or messages of violence and hate (Ciolli, 1999). Whereas 58 percent of respondents claimed to visit these sites, those with poor grades reported doing so much more often. Seventy-eight percent of teens with a "C" average or less said they visited these sites; most had done so from the classroom or school library (79 percent); 67 percent, from their home; and 64 percent, from a friend's home. Another problem is giving confidential information, such as credit card or social security numbers, over the Internet that can then be used by others without one's permission. Many parents do not know what their children and adolescents are viewing or who they are contacting on the Web (Ciolli, 1999).

privatization of entertainment The trend toward individuals experiencing modes of entertainment individually rather than socially.

Styles of Thinking   Other questions that arise from the popularity of computer use are not as obvious. For instance, how will computer use affect an individual's thinking style? Most people engage in what psychologists call *linear thinking;* that is, they begin to read a story, finish it, and go on to something else. Teenagers using the Net today, however, are **multitasking;** that is, as they are on-line, they are also doing other things, such as watching television or visiting two sites at the same time. Eighty-six percent of teenage girls listen to the radio while they are using the computer (Pastore, 2000). Adolescents may be emailing a friend and looking something up at the same time. People surfing the Internet become used to reading short snatches of material rather than books and to doing two or three things at a time. They quickly switch from subject to subject and object of attention to object of attention. Might this lead to a lack of patience or to a different style of processing information? These questions remain to be answered.

The Internet and Homework: Currency, Relevancy, and Truthfulness   Almost all teens who have access to the Internet have used it for homework assignments, and 70 percent said their on-line research made them better students (Ciolli, 1999). Some studies do suggest that use of the computer can improve academic achievement (Subrahmanyam et al., 2001). A survey of junior and senior high school students with computers found that those who used them extensively reported better grades (Rocheleau, 1995).

Many teachers are not so certain, though. One librarian noted that students often come into her library with research assignments. When she directs them to different sources, they complain that they want to conduct a search on the Internet—not because their teachers required such a research tool but because they think the material found on the Net is automatically going to be more accurate and up to date. This is not true. Anyone can post something on the Internet, and some information found there is incorrect and out of date, as well as biased and incomplete. Websites may include the date of posting, but often not the date the material was written. In addition, Internet research is often fragmented and incomplete. The material is rarely subjected to critical comment and correction, and the qualifications of the authors are not included (Turow, 2001). The Internet can be a useful tool, but it can lead a student astray if not used correctly.

Overuse of the Internet   Another concern is the possible overuse of the Internet. About 5 million Americans have serious problems with the round-the-clock social opportunities, entertainment, and (to a much lesser extent) information available on the Web (Chang, 1998). Some people can become so involved with the Web that they use it for as many as 38 hours a week. Their favorite uses are chat rooms and interactive games. Searching for information and email seems to be less likely to lead to a preoccupation with the Web.

Some authorities use the terms *addiction* or *dependence* to describe a person's extreme preoccupation with the Internet. Although the term *internet dependence* is still ill defined and not well researched, addiction and dependence are characterized by symptoms such as preoccupation with a substance (or in this case, an activity); heavier or more frequent use than the person had intended; finding that one's day revolves around activities that allow more use; loss of interest in other social, occupational, or recreational activities; and disregard for physical and psycho-

PERSPECTIVE 1

DOES HE EVER SEE THE DAYLIGHT?

SETTING THE SCENE: Ned is a 16-year-old sophomore who is computer literate and enjoys using the Internet for everything. His parents were thrilled with his ability to use the computer to locate the best buys, communicate with others, and download items of interest. He participates in a number of chat rooms, all of which seem appropriate for his age. However, these computer activities are all he does. Ned does not go outside very much, has no interest in sports, and spends all his free time in front of the computer.

PARENTS: *We don't know what to do or even if there is a problem. Ned spends every free moment in a chat room and on the Net. He neglects everything else, although his grades are OK. We'd like to see him go out more and be with others. We think he may be too involved in computer stuff.*

NED: *I enjoy the Net. What's wrong with that? I spend a lot of time in chat rooms and emailing my friends. My grades are fine, and this is like a hobby. Like always, my parents are overreacting.*

QUESTION: Does Ned have a problem? If you were his parents, what would you do?

multitasking   Performing two tasks at the same time.

At a Glance 8.2 The Computer Revolution: Email and the Internet

KEY POINT: Computer technology is changing the adolescent experience.

SUPPORTING POINTS	EXPLANATION
The growth of Internet use by adolescents is striking.	Adolescents use the Internet to communicate, obtain information, entertain themselves, and buy goods.
Most adolescents have access to the Internet.	The digital divide, the greater access to the Internet for middle- and upper-class youth than lower-income youth, is a concern, but most students have access to the Internet in school.
Adolescents meet other adolescents on the Internet and create new but weak relationships.	Most of the ties formed on the Internet are "weak" ties, which are superficial, rather than "strong" ties, which are more intimate.
Heavy email and Internet use may influence the quality of social relationships.	People who use the computer more frequently engage in less social interaction. They may experience increased feelings of loneliness and declines in feelings of psychological well-being if they substitute computer use for person-to-person interaction.
The use of the Internet and email raises some important concerns.	Adolescents communicating with strangers over the Net do not have any information about the other individual, and some have been taken advantage of by pedophiles. Other adolescents have given privileged information to strangers. Adolescents may also visit pornographic sites or sites inciting racism. Internet sites may not provide accurate or current information.

logical consequences (Walters, 1996). Indeed, some people do feel irritable and out of control when not able to use the Net; spend increasing amounts of time and money on hardware and software; and neglect work, school, or family obligations (Gawel, 1999). Some authorities claim that these symptoms arising from computer use actually relate to a personality disorder (Young & Rogers, 1998). Individuals who are lonely, bored, depressed, or introverted, or who lack self-esteem or have a history of compulsive behaviors, are most at risk. Whether the behaviors of people who overuse computers are symptomatic of an actual disorder that someday will be recognized or reflect some personality disorder, some people do show symptoms that are similar to dependence (Chang, 1998). The extent of the problems caused by overuse of the computer remains to be seen (Yang, 2000). *(For a review of this section, see At A Glance 8.2.)*

VIDEO GAMES

"Pong," the first video game, was introduced in the 1970s. It was an innocuous, technologically unsophisticated game similar to table tennis. The next sensation was the 1980s Pac-Man, in which a yellow orb with a mouth raced around eating ghosts and goblins. Some commentators actually worried about the "violence" of this game.

The technology of video games has come a long way, and so has their violence. In fact, 80 percent of the most popular video games are violent, and 21 percent include violence against women (Dietz, 1998). These violent games offer no options for compromise or reaching any agreement with one's foes; violence is the only way out. Games showing violence against women reinforce negative stereotypes, presenting women as brainless victims (Funk & Buchman, 1996). Almost all teens have played video games at some time, and many continue to enjoy them throughout adolescence and into adulthood. Video games are big business. A total of 219 million computer and video games were sold in 2000, and it is predicted that people will spend 29 billion dollars on video games by 2005, an increase from the 9.4 billion spent in 2001 (Guitteau, 2002). On-line video games are becoming very popular as well. Adolescents play video games to fill in time, relieve boredom, and challenge themselves, as well as use them as social activities with friends (Arthur, 1993).

Some video games are simple "shoot-em-up" games in which a player saves the world from aliens; others require a great deal of thought as a player solves mysteries. Still others involve action/fantasy, such as testing skills as a race car driver. Video games can be used to help young children practice numbers and letters. Some video games have taught junior high, high school, and even college students certain concepts, for instance, the law of supply and demand in economics. Most video games played at home are not educational in the standard sense.

Video Games and Gender

Most families with children have video game equipment (see Figure 8.4). Boys play video games much more often than girls, and males regard the activity more highly than do females (Barnett et al., 1997; Griffiths, 1991). About two-thirds of all teenage girls play video games at least occasionally, but only 20 percent play in arcades; in contrast, 90 percent of boys play at home, and 50 percent of all boys play in arcades (Dorman, 1997; Funk, 1993). Many "shoot-em-up" or more violent adventure games focus on characters and interests that are stereotyped as masculine. Sitting by a console and firing at alien ships invading the galaxy doesn't appeal to girls as much as boys. Not only are boys more likely to play video games than girls; the group of heavy players consists almost exclusively of boys.

Although both males and females recognize challenge as an important characteristic of their favorite video games, males prefer games with more aggressive themes than do females. In a survey of undergraduate video game players, males reported that they played for competition and to master the games, whereas girls preferred less aggressive games that emphasized whimsical fantasy (Morlock, Yando, & Nigolean, 1985). Boys prefer games with sports themes, more violent games, and to a lesser extent action/fantasy; in contrast, girls clearly favor intellectual, creative, and action/fantasy games (Barnett et al., 1997). Gender stereotypes and socialization may explain these differences. Girls are not socialized to express aggression in public and are clearly less comfortable with it. Females are more likely than boys to agree that video games are bad for youngsters and that parents should monitor their children's video game playing (Funk & Buchman, 1996).

Figure 8.4
Percentage of Families with Children Aged 2 to 17 Who Own Video Game Equipment, by Child Age Group, 2000
Most adolescents have video games in their homes. The percentage of families with video game equipment increases with the age of the child.
Source: Woodard & Gridina (2000), Figure 1.4.

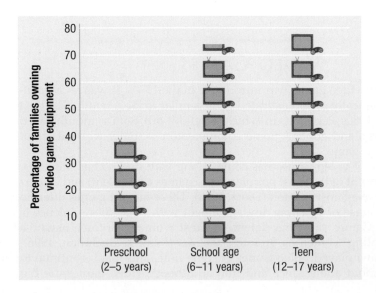

You Missed One of the Monsters: Video Games and Aggression

About half the parents surveyed have some concern about video games, which is somewhat lower than the percentage concerned about the content of television, music, the Internet, or movies (Woodard & Gridina, 2000). Psychologists also are troubled by the violent content of these games. The possible effects of video game violence became a headline issue when it was found that the teens who shot their classmates at Columbine High School in Littleton, Colorado, were avid fans of some very violent video games, including one that teaches killing so effectively that the U.S. military uses a version of it to train soldiers (Dickinson, 2000).

Violent video games often reward points for massive killing with gruesome results. In one of these games, a lone gunman confronts a variety of monsters. For each kill, he receives points and advances in the game. As he does so, the weapons become more powerful and the results gorier. Some games are simply simulations of murder (Hanson, 1999).

The research on the effects of violent video games on children and adolescents is not easy to summarize (Scott, 1995). Short-term studies with children show some evidence for imitation of aggression after playing video games (Silvern & Williamson, 1987). When 5- to 7-year-olds were randomly assigned to play a nonviolent or a violent video game and observed afterward during free play, both children who had played the violent game and the nonviolent game showed more of the behaviors they had seen in the game. Thus, playing a video game seems to encourage children to exhibit what they have seen and experienced in the game (Schutte et al., 1988). Some studies find a greater effect for girls than for boys, perhaps because the experience of playing some of these video games is relatively new to girls, and it brings their level of aggression up to the level of boys (Cooper & Mackie, 1986).

The results of studies with adolescents are more difficult to interpret. Some studies show a positive relationship between video game play and aggression among tenth- and eleventh-grade students, but other factors, such as the adolescents' background, are more important than the extent of video game playing (Dominick, 1984). Playing highly violent video games increased hostility among undergraduates in another study (Anderson & Ford, 1986). A more recent study

Many of the most popular video games involve aggression, and some are incredibly violent. Does playing these violent video games contribute to aggression in adolescents? Some psychologists think it does, but more evidence is needed.

measured aggressive personality traits, recent delinquent behavior, and game-playing habits in a group of college students. Students who reported playing more violent video games in the past engaged in more aggressive behavior and had lower grades in college (Anderson, 2000). A number of studies using correlations show a relationship between violent behavior and violent video game playing using a variety of measures of aggressive behaviors (Dickinson, 2000; Dominick, 1984; Fling et al., 1992; Lin & Lepper, 1987). These correlations, though, do not permit determinations of cause and effect.

Some short-term experimental studies also find a possible influence of violent video games. Undergraduates played or observed either violent virtual reality games or no games; those who played the violent games had the highest number of aggressive thoughts (Calvert & Tan, 1994). However, the study did not investigate emotional arousal. Perhaps playing these games simply increased emotional arousal, which made the participants more likely to think aggressively.

Other studies show no increase in violence for adolescents after video game playing (Scott, 1995; Winkel, Novak, & Hopson, 1987). When junior high school students from the Netherlands recorded their out-of-school activities in a diary and answered a questionnaire, no relationship was found between aggressive behavior and amount of time spent playing video games (Van Schie & Wiegman, 1997).

One possible explanation for the inconsistent findings is that the influence of violent video game playing may be *greatest* on individuals with particular personality traits. When male and female undergraduates were asked to play violent video games and their personality characteristics were measured, violent video game exposure and aggressive personality traits, both together and separately, were major determinants of aggression (Anderson, 2000). Perhaps people who are easily frustrated, angry, and impetuous are more likely to be influenced by violent games, or video game violence may have the greatest effect on individuals who already have a penchant for violence.

Another possible reason for the inconsistent results is that studies may not account for many important variables, such as excitement, difficulty level, or enjoyment. Rather than the violent content, it may be the excitement of the game or the frustration caused by the level of difficulty that contributes to aggression. In fact, when adolescents play video games, they are highly aroused as measured by heart rate and blood pressure, and they show greater arousal than when they are watching television (Kubey & Larson, 1990). Violent material is more exciting and arousing than nonviolent material, and arousal may be the culprit (Anderson & Dill, 2000).

One study tried to equalize these factors. Researchers randomly assigned undergraduates to play a highly violent or a nonviolent video game. The violent video game involved a "hero" who could choose from a variety of weapons, including knives, automatic weapons, and even a flame thrower, to kill Nazi guards, with the ultimate goal to kill Adolf Hitler. This game involved murders and extreme violence, including the groans and screams of the guards. The other, nonviolent game was an interactive adventure between an alien spaceship and humanoid aliens. The researchers used some deception, telling participants that they were taking part in a study investigating motor skills ability and learning. Each participant played either the adventure or the violent game for 15 minutes, and data on hostility and world view were then gathered. Both games produced the same physiological effects and were rated equal in difficulty, enjoyment, frustration, and speed, although males saw the violent game as more exciting.

Later, participants returned to the lab to play again, and this time they were asked to compete on a task. They were able to set a noise level that their opponent would hear if he or she lost and determine for how long the opponent would have to "suffer." Participants who played the aggressive video game—especially those who had been angered—delivered significantly longer noise blasts than those who played the nonviolent game. In addition, students who reported having played more violent video games over a period of years engaged in more violent behavior. Perhaps people who play these games identify with the hero, and the active participation adds to their feelings of hostility. Or perhaps the reinforcement for aggressive performance in the game transfers to real life, teaching adolescents to use aggressive solutions to problems.

Summarizing the influence of violent video games on adolescents is complicated by the fact that adolescents who spend a great deal of time playing these games also watch a great deal of violent television, and both relate to the frequency of aggressive behavior (Dominick, 1984; Van Schie & Wiegman, 1997). Some researchers reviewing the research on video games and aggression argue that experimental and nonexperimental studies with both males and females support the conclusion that violent video games increase aggressive behavior (Anderson & Bushman, 2001). Other researchers are not as certain (Scott, 1995). It may be fair to conclude that for some adolescents with particular personality characteristics, playing violent video games may encourage aggressive behavior. It is also possible that some children and adolescents with poorer family situations may be more affected. Several other social and psychological variables probably help determine the influence of such games, and more research is needed to clarify the relationships.

Video Games, Prosocial Behavior, and Social Skills

Although the effects of video game playing and aggression are hotly debated, the effect of playing video games on prosocial (helping) behaviors is well established. Teens who play violent video games are less likely to show prosocial behavior. One study, for example, found that individuals donated less money to a charitable cause after playing aggressive video games (Chambers & Ascione, 1987). Perhaps prosocial behavior declines because players observe aggressive and selfish models punishing others for misdeeds. Also, there isn't a great deal of goodwill in these games. Junior high schools students who spend a great deal of time playing video games are judged by classmates as significantly less prosocial (Van Schie & Wiegman, 1997).

Psychologists question the effects of video games on social skills, just as they do for Internet and email use. Playing a video game for hours by oneself can be seen as isolating, but many teens and younger children play these games with others. There is no relationship between playing video games and social alienation, social isolation, loneliness, or unpopularity, nor between video game playing and school performance (if the games are played at home) (Lin & Lepper, 1987; Van Schie & Wiegman, 1997). Video game playing is so common that all types of adolescents play them, and the mere playing of video games does not relate to personality or interpersonal problems (Phillips et al., 1995).

Researchers find very few differences between adolescents who play once or twice a month and those who play every day. They do not differ in frequency of serious conduct disorders, drinking, smoking, or alcohol use. There is no evidence that just playing video games is related to psychopathology, social deviance, or withdrawal (Gibb et al., 1983; Kastenbaum & Weinstein, 1985). When junior and high school students in an urban middle-class neighborhood were divided into high- and low-frequency game players, they all were basically healthy. There is no evidence that video game playing leads to adjustment disorders for the average player (Funk & Buchman, 1996). However, much less is known about the long-term effects of the 7 to 9 percent of all children and adolescents who play video games for more than 30 hours a week (Subrahmanyam et al., 2001).

The Overuse of Video Games

Some psychologists believe that video game playing can become similar to a compulsion (Griffiths & Hunt, 1998). Some very heavy users show a need to play the game, lack interest in other activities, associate mainly with others who play these games, and show physical and emotional withdrawal symptoms when attempting to stop the behavior (Griffiths, 1991). Very heavy users may stop going to the movies, use most of their money to buy new games, use the games as an escape, and sacrifice other activities to play these games (Egli & Meyers, 1984; McClure & Mears, 1984). Much of this evidence is based on case studies, though, with little experimental research on adolescents who play these games the most.

Many people who play video games—97 percent, in one study—thought it was possible to become "addicted" to games, and arcade games were considered more addicting, because they are more challenging and encourage players to spend more money (Arthur, 1993). A few adolescents may display a compulsive need to play video games, but the overwhelming majority certainly does not (Fisher, 1994).

Video Games and Adolescents: A Summary

Most adolescents do not play video games at the expense of their social interactions, school performance, or adjustment. However, the substantial evidence that video game players show less prosocial behavior deserves attention (Van Schie & Wiegman, 1997). In addition, although studies relating video game playing in adolescence to later aggression are difficult to interpret, the amount of recent evidence that these games could contribute to aggression is troubling. Some groups would like the government to take a more active role regulating video games, and the industry has responded by formulating its own rating system (Goldstein, 1993). Warnings appear on some of the more violent games, but parents know little about the games their children and adolescents are playing. In a

AT A GLANCE 8.3 VIDEO GAMES

KEY POINT: Playing video games is a common activity, but questions surround its possible link with aggressive behavior.

SUPPORTING POINTS	EXPLANATION
Video games are popular with children and adolescents.	Video games are more technologically sophisticated today compared with 20 years ago. Most adolescents play video games at least occasionally.
Video games are more popular with males than females.	Many popular video games are violent and emphasize masculine themes.
Some research studies find that playing violent video games makes adolescents more likely to behave aggressively, whereas other studies do not.	The influence of video games on adolescents depends on their personalities, and adolescents who have a penchant for violence are most likely to become violent.
Playing violent video games is related to less prosocial behavior.	Video games model very little prosocial behavior, and this characteristic may influence later prosocial behavior.
Adolescents who play video games do not seem to lack social skills or have significant mental disorders.	Research does not find video game players to be socially isolated or more prone to psychopathology.
Some heavy video game players may become so involved that they do little else with their spare time.	Very heavy users show a lack of interest in other activities, associate mainly with others who play these games, and exhibit physical and emotional withdrawal symptoms when attempting to stop the behavior. However, very few adolescents display these symptoms.

subgroup of individuals, violent video game playing may combine with violent tendencies and association with aggressive and alienated friends to encourage aggression. The early identification of this subgroup requires more study. *(For a review of this section, see At A Glance 8.3.)*

MUSIC AND RADIO

R adio is the forgotten medium, and people constantly underestimate its influence. Adolescents listen to a great deal of radio, mostly music. The typical teenager listens to 10 hours of radio a week. Whereas television reaches 86 percent of all teens and young adults daily, radio reaches 93 percent daily (Merrill, 1999). About 95 percent of American teens listen to FM radio, and FM radio means music, which is why radio and music are discussed in the same section of the chapter (Zollo, 1999).

The Meaning of Music

Music has a multifaceted meaning for adolescents. It is a channel for communication, for expressing sentiments, conflicts, values, attitudes, and emotions (Plopper & Ness, 1993; Wells & Hakanen, 1991). It is also a form of entertainment and a symbol for a generation, allowing teens to feel a bond with one another and membership in a cohort. Music is an important symbol in the adolescent's search for independence and autonomy. Shared enjoyment of music solidifies a group and allows a basis for friendship.

Females listen more to radio than do males (Carroll et al., 1993). Females use music for changing moods and to ease anxieties more than males do. Males use music to become more excited and seek more hard-driving, percussive music, whereas females are more likely to be attracted by ballads and love songs (Larson, Kubey, & Colletti, 1989). Teens consider musicians as heroes to a greater extent than even athletes.

The music world offers more choices than ever before. In the late 1960s, teens asked what they would like to listen to would choose rock or maybe soul. Today, music is more fragmented; it may be rap, alternative, metal, techno, house, punk, reggae, rhythm and blues, country, classic rock, jazz, or even swing. The preference for a certain type of music sometimes correlates with language, fashion, activities, and attitudes. African Americans often like rap and rhythm and blues, and whites may listen to classic rock and country. Latinos are the most diverse group, showing interest in many areas.

Some styles of music appeal to one ethnic group more than another. Music is certainly part of an individual's culture.

The Controversial Face of Music

Music has always been a source of controversy. Rock music has been criticized since it was first introduced by Bill Haley and His Comets in 1955 (Ballard & Coates, 1995), perhaps because many individuals felt it was based on defiance, rebellion, and expression of the anxieties of young people. Public concern about song lyrics is not new, and censorship of rock music began early in its history; early rock groups were often forced to alter their lyrics if they wanted to appear on television (Brown & Hendee, 1989a, 1989b). However, the concerns about swinging hips and mentioning the word *sex* seem quaint as music lyrics have

Elvis Presley's act was shocking to many viewers. Today, however, his songs and behavior would be considered tame.

become more violent and certainly more sexually explicit over the past three decades (Christenson & Roberts, 1998).

The question of why music has become more sexually explicit and violent is difficult to answer. Some argue that music merely reflects the nature of the social world in which many live. However, music has always had a rebellious side. Adolescents may see the more sexually explicit and violent music as something of their own, something that breaks the conventional bonds of restraint that have been imposed by parents raised on rock music (Brown & Hendee, 1989a, 1989b).

Another way of looking at the trend toward more violence and sexuality in music is to consider the nature of the antiestablishment counterculture. In the 1960s and 1970s, the Vietnam War took center stage, and the counterculture revolved around love, a rejection of violence, the search for peace and a certain degree of gentleness. The end of the war (and the draft) ushered in a period of aimlessness. The new counterculture that arose reflected a fascination with violence, death, and blatant sexuality; counterculture shifted from a preoccupation with love and optimism to evil and pessimism (Stack, Gundlach, & Reeves, 1994). Rap music may also represent a reaction to the lack of economic progress for youth from minority groups living in poverty (Ogbar, 1999). The violence that has surrounded some rap recording stars adds to the concern about its influence on youth (Reynolds, 1995). Although some rap songs may have positive content or deal with societal issues, others are violent and have lyrics that are degrading to women (Ballard & Coates, 1995).

Concern about how music might affect adolescents has led to a number of research studies, mostly on heavy metal and violent rap music. Heavy metal music is not easy to define. The National Academy of Recording Arts and Sciences may award a Grammy in the category, but it gives no formal definition of it. In general, heavy metal music has a loud and powerful style. It is differentiated from hard rock (a wider and more generic term) by its harsh, uncompromising, explicit lyrics that often glorify violence and fatalism and sometimes seem to accept violence against females (Singer, Levine, & Jou, 1993; Took & Weiss, 1994). Typically in heavy metal music, sexuality is seen as a symbol of male power, but nothing is said about commitment. Some say that the theme of chaos is what clearly distinguishes heavy metal from rock (Stack et al., 1994).

Rap music combines street language often concerning social and political issues, male boasting (if the singer is male), and sometimes comic lyrics carried over from blues, rhythm and blues, soul, and rock (Campbell, Martin, & Fabos, 2002). Rap music lyrics are sometimes angry and violent, and may advocate drug use, contain many obscenities, glamorize materialism, and show women as sexual objects (Kenon, 2000). Some heavy metal groups seem somewhat similar to some rap acts because of the violence and stereotypes in their music (Ogbar, 1999). Criticisms of rap focus on its potential to encourage violence toward others. Criticism of heavy metal music, in contrast, says that it will harm the listener by encouraging drug use and self-destructive behavior (Binder, 1993).

Heavy metal music declined in popularity in the 1990s, at least in the United States; by the end of the decade it made a comeback (Flick, 1999; Waldman, 1999), although it gets less publicity today. The most objectionable and violent rap music also is less common today. The research on these two forms of music, though, can be instructive in the quest to answer the controversial question of whether music can negatively influence behavior.

There are two possible ways in which any type of music may cause negative attitudes in listeners. First, music may have a direct effect; that is, adolescents who hear the music may be influenced to adopt the attitudes it reflects. Second, music may prime already existing attitudes. For instance, it may affect only adolescents who already espouse stereotypes and anger toward women, intensifying these feelings (Wester et al., 1997). Some claim that it is not the music itself that leads to problems but rather that some types of music with aggressive themes may attract people who are already alienated, and that angry individuals choose angry and violent music (Arnett, 1991a). In other words, the feelings of alienation precede the adoption of the music style.

Some researchers claim that music with violent themes is more likely to influence adolescents with poor family situations and those who are already troubled (Singer et al., 1993). Compared with nonfans, fans of sexually violent heavy metal music are more likely to see society as more callous, unforgiving, and deserving of the violent acts suggested by the songs (Hansen & Hansen, 1990a). Studies show that many heavy metal fans are troubled (King, 1988), and heavy metal music is more popular among antisocial teens than among the general population (Wass, Miller, & Redditt, 1991). Adolescents who prefer the explicitly violent or sexual types of rap are more likely to have below-average grades, behave poorly in school, and engage in more drug and alcohol use (Hall, 1998). One study divided adolescents into listeners of heavy metal, rap, and other styles of music. Adolescents who preferred rap or heavy metal music, as well as their parents, reported significantly more turmoil in their lives (Took & Weiss, 1994). Early poor academic achievement and family problems may draw these adolescents to these types of music.

Many people are concerned about the violent and sexually explicit song lyrics. Do these lyrics influence adolescents to take risks or act aggressively?

Clear evidence exists that heavy metal music, which glorifies sexual gratification and living for the moment, encourages risk taking. It could also be argued, however, that heavy metal music aggravates a tendency that is already present to reject or defy societal values and participate in reckless behavior. Adolescents (average age about 17 years) were asked to fill out a report on the number of times they had engaged in a variety of reckless activities over the past year. Respondents who noted their musical preference as heavy metal were more likely to have engaged in some types of reckless behavior (Arnett, 1991b). Boys who were heavy metal fans were more likely to have acted recklessly in the areas of driving, sexual behavior, and drug use. They were more likely to have driven while drunk, to have had sex with someone they knew casually, and to have used cocaine and other drugs. Girls who liked heavy metal music were more reckless as well; they had sex without using contraception more often and engaged in more marijuana use, shoplifting, and vandalism. Heavy metal fans also scored much higher on sensation seeking. Boys, especially, were less satisfied with their family relationships (Arnett, 1991b). Boys who liked heavy metal did not differ significantly in self-esteem from their peers who did not like such music, but girls who liked heavy metal music reported lower self-esteem.

Among boys, a liking for heavy metal may reflect higher sensation seeking and poorer satisfaction with their families. If this is true, the preference of these boys for

PERSPECTIVE 2

WHY THE OBSESSION?

SETTING THE SCENE: You are a good friend of Alexis, a 16-year-old who is relatively uncommunicative. Alexis has a difficult home life. His mother and father work very hard, but they seem too tired to pay much attention to him. He is one of six children. Alexis is an average student. Lately, he has become fascinated with some of the more violent heavy metal groups. He has hung their posters all over his walls, and some of the songs that he listens to over and over involve suicide or violence against others.

FRIEND: I'm concerned. Alexis seems to have an "obsession" with these groups, and some songs are scary. I don't know if he is suicidal or about to become violent. I don't know what to do.

ALEXIS: What I listen to is my business. How I feel is my business. I'll admit I am angry; that's all. I don't want to talk about it.

QUESTION: If you were Alexis's friend, would you be concerned? If you answered yes, what would you do?

heavy metal music would be a symptom of their underlying unhappiness with their families and their need for sensation rather than the cause of the problem. However, heavy metal music may encourage this behavior even if it does not directly cause it.

There is also a possible link between heavy metal music and depression and suicide (Scheel & Westefeld, 1999; Stack et al., 1994). In one study, high school students completed self-report questionnaires on preferred music type, the messages in the music, and were asked to provide information about suicide ideation, deliberate self-harm, depression, and delinquency (Martin, Clarke, & Pearce, 1993). The study found a significant relationship between preference for heavy metal and suicidal thoughts, deliberate self-harm, depression, and drug taking.

About a third (31 percent) of the males and two-thirds of the females preferring heavy metal music had suicidal thoughts in the previous 6 months, compared with 14 percent and 35 percent, respectively, of those who were not heavy metal fans. It is interesting to note that although most participants admitted that the music contained messages about drugs, violence, suicide, death, war, and devil worship, and contained few messages about love, happiness, and optimism, only about a third frequently agreed with the messages, and 14.6 percent never agreed with them.

Some research does not find a relationship between listening to heavy metal music and suicide (Lacourse, Claes, & Villeneuve, 2001). One study asked undergraduate students to listen to both heavy metal and rap music with different messages, including lyrics that dealt with killing or suicide or nonviolent lyrics. The study found no significant differences in depression, suicidal ideation, or anxiety (Ballard & Coates, 1995). It may not be that the lyrics cause suicide and aggression, but that adolescents who listen to these songs are already alienated, have family problems and school difficulties, and they may be teens who are at risk for suicidal behavior (Stack et al., 1994). In addition, many adolescents who listen to heavy metal music claim it reduces their anger, and heavy metal music may give adolescents a way of expressing their feelings (Arnett, 1991a). A number of adolescents who prefer heavy metal music say that it made them feel better after listening. Some, though, say they felt angrier or worse after listening to the music, and perhaps these teens are most negatively influenced by the music (Scheel & Westefeld, 1999).

Some researchers suggest that preference for heavy metal music should serve as a sign to look at the individual's social and emotional functioning (Scheel & Westefeld). Those who feel worse or angrier after listening to heavy metal may be a group at even greater vulnerability to suicidal thoughts and other problems. The source of the problem lies more in interpersonal and family characteristics than in the direct effects of the music, but a preference for such music may be a red flag signaling vulnerability to suicide.

A significant concern about both heavy metal and rap music is their denigration of women and acceptance of violence toward women. A constant diet of stereotyped portrayals and the antifemale bias may encourage an acceptance of violence against women; indeed, males exposed to violent rap music have a greater acceptance of violence against women, including dating violence, as well as lower academic goals (Johnson, Jackson, & Gatto 1995). Some experts argue that the case has been exaggerated, and some research denies that even violent rap music has any significant effect on adolescents. When college males with little experience with violent rap music were exposed to the music, the lyrics, both, or neither, no significant differences were found among any of the groups, with one exception (Wester et al., 1997). The participants exposed to the lyrics only, though, expressed greater adversarial sexual beliefs; that is, they viewed their relationships with women as a conflict between the genders.

Criticism of the research on the influence of music with aggressive themes points to the same problems found in investigations of the influence of other media, such as television and the movies. For example, many people watch violent movies and listen to violent music, but relatively few individuals are moved to action. It seems reasonable, then, that some background and personality factors make some teens more vulnerable than others to the message of this music. Some experts also criticize the research on aggressive music on the grounds that this music is not the only form of entertainment that is sexual or violent; television and movies are sexually explicit and violent as well. It is difficult to determine not only whether the media are partially responsible for the general level of aggression but also which medium is most influential (Di Saia, 1990). Defenders of rap music also argue that rap is overly criticized due to racial prejudice and stereotypes. They say that rap music is judged harshly because it is associated with African American recording artists and culture (Fried, 1999; Salem, 1993). Other defenders claim that rap music mirrors the serious urban problems in the lives of the young African American performers. They see rap as a protest for individuals left out of the mainstream and point out that it calls attention to social issues (Fried, 1999).

Nevertheless, the outcry against objectionable lyrics in music continues. Criticism of violent music cuts across racial and political boundaries (Fried, 1999). Major African American and white political leaders, liberal and conservative alike, have condemned violent forms of rap. Many African Americans object to rappers' portrayals that denigrate women (Delaney, 1995; Stapleton, 1998). Some female rappers objecting to these portrayals sing about self-reliance, independence, and self-respect (Reynolds, 1994).

Some social commentators, though, complain about the rough, explicit, unromantic type of sex sometimes shown in music, as well as the brutal violence. Commentator Allan Bloom, in his book *The Closing of the American Mind,* emphasized the importance of music but noted that young teens, whose concepts of sensuality are just emerging, are not nurtured into the beauty and meaning of sexuality by music. Rather, music bombards them with messages about sexual perversity and aggression at an age when they have immature concepts of love, caring, and commitment, which in turn undermines morality (Bloom, 1987). The problem of what to do about violent and offensive music lyrics, as well as violent video games, music videos, and websites, is difficult to solve (see "Focus: Censorship, Warning Labels, and Rating Systems").

Music Videos

The music video is a relatively new art form that began officially on August 1, 1981, with the launching of Music Television (MTV) (Sherman & Dominick, 1986). The medium is theoretically very powerful. The music presented in an elaborately produced video format acts as a running advertisement for the recording artist and the song, and having a music video boosts sales of the recording (Steinbach, 1997). Many people who have seen a music video find that hearing the song reminds them of the images on the video; a video format that illustrates the music lyrics magnifies their potential impact (Strasburger, 1995; Zillmann & Mundorf, 1987). Music videos are very popular. A survey of college students found that MTV was by far their favorite cable channel, with 39 percent calling it their top choice (Paul, 2001).

An analysis of more than five hundred videos found that many were violent and contained sexual themes (DuRant et al., 1997). About 15 percent of the videos contained portrayals of individuals engaging in interpersonal violence, and in 80 percent of these cases, the aggressor was an attractive role model (Rich et al., 1998). Many other rock music videos portray rebellion against parental and lawful society and the work ethic, along with drunkenness, promiscuity, the devaluation of women, and negative family situations (Hansen & Hansen, 1990b).

Music videos are constantly criticized for their stereotyped portrayal of men, women, and racial groups (Seidman, 1999; White, 2001). They feature males who are aggressive, and women are seen as accepting aggression. African American males are shown as the aggressor more often than their relative numbers in the population would merit, and white women are seen as victims most often (Rich et al., 1998). Music videos do not portray women in nontraditional roles; they cast them as sex objects and sometimes as mothers with very stereotyped per-

You are on a jury asked to decide the damages due to the family of the victim of a school shooting. Both the victim's and the perpetrator's parents blame the teen's violent behavior on his fascination with—or as his lawyer claims, the teen's compulsive playing of—an extremely violent video game. The lawyer demonstrates the video game, which is indeed gruesome and realistic, and asks you to hold the company licensing the video to blame. The video game company claims that it does not advocate violence—that the game is simply a game. The company further points out that it has sold more than 100,000 games, and only this teen claims the game caused him to become aggressive. Will you make the video game company pay damages?

Whenever a tragedy occurs and the perpetrators are described as compulsive game players, listeners of rap or heavy metal music, or consumers of violent television, the question of the media's influence is raised. Attempts to censor the media are not new, nor are warnings about the potential negative effects of the media on youth. Some groups in the 1960s fought to censor the lyrics of rock music. In the 1980s, the National Education Association and the National Parent-Teacher Association lobbied Congress to require warning labels on rock music considered offensive or inappropriate for adolescents. Even the American Academy of Pediatrics expresses concern about rock music's effect on young people (Committee on Communications, 1989). The American Academy of Child and Adolescent Psychiatry recommends psychiatric evaluations for troubled teens who show interest in, or preoccupation with, music with destructive themes, such as suicide (Alessi et al., 1992).

What, if anything, should be done about the levels of sex and violence in the media? There is little agreement on any action to be taken. A few people advocate censorship. Obscenity laws have been on the books for generations, and in 1990, a U.S. district court judge in Fort Lauderdale, Florida, found a rapper's album obscene (Jones, 1993). The sale of "adult" magazines is restricted, so why not restrict songs with similar content (Jipping, 1999)? In a free society, most individuals see the dangers of censorship. The standards are not uniform, and what was unacceptable to one generation is acceptable to another. In addition, who will choose the censors?

Some people advocate the use of warning labels. Since 1985, recording companies have affixed parental advisory labels to tapes and CDs that are judged offensive. This warning label, though, is not a rating system that keeps the recordings from the hands of children and young adolescents (Holland, 1994). Adolescents who want to hear songs can always find ways to do so. In addition, many labels are either missing or very small. Some people argue that video games ought to have warning labels as well, and many games do have warnings such as "realistic medium violence."

How effective are such warning labels? Two theories exist. The *"forbidden fruit" theory* argues that such labels make the products more attractive. When people's freedom is in some way restricted, they tend to fight back, to want to know why they cannot listen to the songs. In contrast, the *"tainted fruit" theory* suggests that these warnings do caution young adolescents and their parents, making the products less attractive.

Do labels make a CD a "forbidden fruit" or a "tainted fruit" for young adolescents (12 to 15 years of age)? There is not much research on the topic, but a fascinating study of 11- to 15-year-old adolescents sheds some light on the situation. Researchers assigned participants to one of two conditions: a label condition, in which the album cover was shown to some with a parental warning label, and the control group, in which the album cover had no label (Christenson, 1992). The music consisted of a hard rock album and a pop album, both by unfamiliar groups. Every participant listened to selections and rated them. Participants shown the albums with parental advisory labels rated both selections lower and less desirable than albums that did not have labels. The labels seemed to have a "tainted fruit" effect on the young adolescents.

When asked how teens like them would react to the presence of the advisory label on an album, 62 percent said it would make no difference, 22 percent said it would make them want it more, and 16 percent said they would want it less. This finding can be interpreted in two ways. First, most

sonality traits. Males are independent and unemotional, whereas females are dependent and passive (Seidman, 1999). The videos show women working only in blue-collar jobs, or as fashion models or prostitutes. Their clothing is skimpy and suggestive.

Research on the effects of music videos is more definite and less controversial than research on music alone. Individuals who view these sexually explicit videos have more positive views toward premarital sex (Calfin, Carroll, & Schmidt, 1993) and expressing aggression (Hansen & Hansen, 1990a). Adolescents were more likely to employ retaliatory violence when exposed to high-impact music videos with sexual imagery, violence, and antiestablishment themes (Rehman & Reilly, 1985). One study assigned a group of teens to view adolescents did not believe labeling would stop others from buying CDs. Second, they did not feel that most adolescents would find the labels a motivation to buy the albums, either. Most young adolescents said they shop for their music themselves, and they didn't think their parents cared much about what they listened to.

Many teens claim that they do not listen as much to the lyrics as critics believe, nor take them as seriously. They emphasize that lyrics count less in determining their music preferences than do the auditory characteristics of the music. Most adolescents admit to owning music with lyrics they do not agree with at all. They are simply not concerned about the lyrics. Warning labels probably will have little effect in either encouraging or dissuading young teens from listening to CDs with objectionable content.

In response to complaints by parents and politicians, several music retailers have refused to market recordings with obscene lyrics (Reynolds, 1995). Pressure from the African American community and its leaders has prompted some radio stations to stop airing the most controversial of the rap music (Delaney, 1995). The highly visible campaign against rap artists for offensive and socially irresponsible music is a visible battle in what some call the "culture wars," pitting critics against defenders of the media (Ogbar, 1999).

Some critics have also warned about children and adolescents finding inappropriate or dangerous websites. Filtering software is becoming more popular, but adolescents can find computers without such filters at their friends' houses or even the library (Ciolli, 1999; New York Libraries, 1999).

All this criticism misses the point, however. Parents claim to be concerned about media content; more than 70 percent show concern about the content of television, music, the Internet, and movies, whereas only 50 percent show any concern about video or computer games (Woodard & Gridina, 2000). Yet parents know little about what their children, and especially their adolescents, are listening to or viewing and even less about what their adolescents are accessing on the computer. Parents of youth involved in heavy metal music rarely object to the music (Arnett, 1991a). A survey of teens (seventh through twelfth graders) found that they generally go to chat rooms and websites alone (Holton, 2000). Parents do not know much about video games, either. In one survey, whereas 80 percent of the junior high students were familiar with a violent video game rated "mature," fewer than 5 percent of their parents had heard of it (Goldberg, 1998).

Recently manufactured televisions include a V-Chip, a device that allows parents to program out objectionable television shows. Parents can establish the level of violence they want to screen out (Carney, 1996), and a rating sent out electronically with the program activates the V-Chip. Yet most parents do not use the device, and its use with older teens may be questionable (Woodard & Gridina, 2000). Parents have the responsibility to know what their children are watching and listening to. Warning labels will not be effective if parents don't care about them or aren't aware of what their children are doing. Keeping track is admittedly much harder with the variety of media available today than it was years ago, when all parents had to worry about was television and the radio.

In the end, community outcry and parental action are necessary to counter the messages of the more objectionable lyrics. Artists have free speech, but the First Amendment guarantees only that government will not interfere with its exercise (with some very narrow exceptions). The First Amendment does not keep parents from interfering or communities from responding responsibly to their concerns.

The media's influence on teens is determined not only by the content and extent of exposure but also by the personality, motives, and background of the listeners. Adolescents who listen to music do not automatically emulate what they hear. However, pretending that the message makes no difference flies in the face of much research. In the end, panic and overreaction will have to give way to a better understanding of how the adolescent uses the media. Although governmental censorship is inappropriate, parents do have the right to censor. And artists have the freedom to communicate, but parents and community leaders have the responsibility to counter the messages they feel are inappropriate while understanding that they do not have to like everything an adolescent listens to or watches.

either a video with demeaning sexual content and violence or a video without such content. Males and females exposed to the demeaning video had a higher acceptance of interpersonal violence than research participants not exposed to this video (Johnson, 1999). In addition, after viewing violent videos, teens are likely to become more desensitized to violence. Junior and senior high school students report more favorable attitudes toward violence after watching an hour of violent music videos (Greeson & Williams, 1986). In fact, aggressive behavior is reduced after teens stop watching music video broadcasts (Waite, Hillbrand, & Foster, 1992).

One study of the short-term influence of music videos divided 11- to 16-year-old African American teens into a group that viewed a violent music video, a group that viewed a nonviolent video containing erotic representations, and a control group that did not view any video. After viewing, participants were asked to read two vignettes. The first story was about a dating couple, John and Susan. Susan meets an old male friend (Jerry) who gives her a big hug and a small kiss on the lips. When John hears about this, he goes to Susan, grabs and pushes her, and tells her never to kiss another boy. John then finds Jerry, hits him, and pushes him to the ground.

The other story concerns two friends, one who is in college and expects to go to law school and the other who has a "mysterious" job but a great car and nice clothes. The researchers then asked participants questions examining their attitudes toward violence, probability of similar violent behavior, and attitudes toward academics. The results, presented in Tables 8.1 and 8.2, show that participants who saw the violent music videos were more likely to accept the use of violence, especially against women, and reported a higher probability that they would engage in violence. Participants who saw the videos were also more likely to want to be like the materialistic young man with the "mysterious" job and were less confidant that the other young man would achieve his educational goals (Johnson, Jackson, & Gatto, 1995).

A relationship also exists between engaging in risky behaviors and watching music videos (Klein et al., 1993). Perhaps one reason for this correlation is that many music videos present a world that is harsh, violent, unforgiving, and sexual, and these media images reinforce teens' perceptions of their social environment as being that way. The main character in a video rarely suffers any adverse consequences, despite violence or criminal behavior. In fact, music videos present these individuals as glamorous (Brown & Hendee, 1989a, 1989b; Strasburger, 1990).

Some authorities question the health consequences of watching music videos. At least 10 percent of these videos depict tobacco use and 20 percent, drinking; almost 30 percent of the rap videos present smoking and 75 percent, drinking. Drinking and smoking are portrayed positively. A third of the alcohol use in music videos is accompanied by sexual behavior, linking alcohol and sexuality (Raloff, 1997). A correlation exists among high school girls between video watching and the drive to be very thin, probably because many of the women shown who are attractive to men are very thin (Tiggemann & Pickering, 1996).

Table 8.1

Mean Ratings of Attitudes Toward the Use of Violence and Probability of Similar Violence as a Function of Video Type

Adolescents who viewed the violent video were more likely to agree with the use of violence and more likely to say they might use violence.

	Video Type		
Ratings	Violent	Nonviolent	Control
Attitudes toward use of violence			
Hitting Jerry*	8.1	5.4	4.3
Pushing Jane*	4.5	3.0	1.6
Probability of similar violence			
Hitting Jerry*	7.2	5.5	4.0
Pushing Jane	4.4	3.5	2.8

Note: Higher values denote higher acceptability and probability of violence.
*Indicates statistical significance.
Source: Johnson, Jackson, & Gatto (1995).

Table 8.2

Mean Academic-Related Perceptions as a Function of Video Type

Adolescents who viewed the violent video were more likely to want to be like the flashy, materialistic young man with the "mysterious" job than like the aspiring lawyer.

	Video Type		
Perception Rating	Violent	Nonviolent	Control
Desire to be like*	4.7	5.0	8.1
Probability of success*	6.4	6.2	8.6

Note: Lower values denote a greater desire to be like the materialistic young man with the mysterious job. Higher values denote greater desire to be like Bobby (the aspiring lawyer) and greater subjective probability that Bobby will succeed.
*Indicates statistical significance.
Source: Johnson, Jackson, & Gatto (1995).

AT A GLANCE 8.4 MUSIC AND RADIO

KEY POINT: Music serves many important functions, but the public is concerned about its aggressive and sexual themes.

SUPPORTING POINTS	EXPLANATION
Music serves many purposes for adolescents.	Music is a channel for expressing feelings, conflicts, values, and attitudes. Music is also a form of entertainment and a symbol for a generation.
Males and females use music somewhat differently.	Females are more likely than males to use music to change moods and ease anxieties. Males are more likely to use music to obtain excitement.
Music may have a direct effect on adolescents or may encourage them to express attitudes they already hold.	A preference for heavy metal is related to increases in risk taking in adolescents. Adolescents who listen to the more violent forms of rap music are more likely to accept violence against women.
Some evidence correlates heavy metal music with adolescent suicide.	Some research suggests a relationship between heavy metal music and suicide, while other research casts some doubt. Heavy metal music may be a factor in suicide, but perhaps adolescents who are troubled are more likely to listen to heavy metal music.
The music video is a powerful medium.	Hearing music often reminds adolescents of the portrayals they have seen in music videos.
Research demonstrates a direct effect of music videos on adolescent attitudes.	Adolescents who watch music videos have more permissive sexual attitudes and more positive attitudes toward violence.

The evidence on the influence of music videos, then, is fairly strong. The combination of music and video seems to have a greater influence than either music or video alone. Of course, the purpose of such videos is to sell CDs and to entertain. In any case, the denigrating and stereotyped portrayal of women seems to be a constant theme running through some music offerings, video games, and music videos, and it requires attention. (*For a review of this section, see At A Glance 8.4.*)

TELEVISION AND THE MOVIES

Almost every family in the United States has at least one television, many families have more than one, and the television set is used frequently. Adolescents watch about 17 hours of television each week (Nielsen Media Research, 1998). Parents consistently underreport the number of hours their children watch television. This should be no surprise, because one-fourth of all American preschoolers, about half of all elementary school children, and 60 percent of all teenagers have a television set in their bedroom, making it more difficult for parents to know when their children are watching television (see Figure 8.5) (Woodard & Gridina, 2000). Favored programming includes movies, music videos, stand-up comedy, and sports, with movies the most popular (Walker, 1996).

Concerns about what children and adolescents watch on television and see in the movies are certainly not new. Many groups focus their criticisms on the aggression and sexuality portrayed on television and in the movies. The American Academy of Pediatrics (2001) has expressed concerns about the amount of time both children and adolescents spend viewing television and the content of what they view.

Figure 8.5

Percentage of Children Aged 2 to 17 with TV Sets in Bedroom, by Child Age Group, 2000

The majority of adolescents and almost half of elementary school students have a television set in their bedrooms. It is no surprise that parents do not know what their children are watching.

Source: Woodard & Gridina (2000), Figure 1.11.

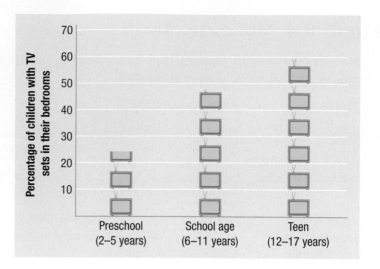

Violence on Television and in the Movies

Perhaps no psychological issue related to the media is discussed as often as the influence of television and movie violence on children and adolescents. Children and adolescents are exposed to a great deal of violence on television. The National Television Violence Study, in an examination of more than 10,000 hours of cable and noncable programming between 1994 and 1997, found that 61 percent of the shows depicted some kind of violence; 26 percent of the violence involved guns; 38 percent of the violence was committed by attractive perpetrators; more than 50 percent of the victims showed no apparent pain or suffering; 75 percent of all violent acts caused no remorse, criticism, or penalty; and 40 percent of the violence was accompanied by humor (Federman, 1997). A study of more than 700 high school students found that 75 percent reported exposure to violence at moderate to high rates. Of high schoolers studied, 10 percent sought counseling for such symptoms as nightmares, anxiety, being afraid to be alone, withdrawal, and even missing school, which they considered consequences of viewing violence (Joshi & Kaschak, 1998).

An overwhelming number of studies find a connection between violence on TV and aggressive behavior in real life (Hughes & Hasbrouck, 1996; Huston, Watkins, & Kunkel, 1989). Yet no authority claims that violent television is the only, or even the main, culprit causing children's and teen's aggression. Although numbers vary, some estimate that between 5 and 15 percent of all antisocial or illegal acts can be linked to exposure to violent television programming (Comstock & Paik, 1991; Graham, 1994). Other estimates are higher, attributing between 10 and 20 percent of the real-life violence to media violence, which is a significant contribution (Strasburger, 1993).

Television may influence aggressiveness in a number of ways (Liebert & Sprafkin, 1988). First, some people may directly imitate; they may simply copy what they see on television. Obviously, however, other factors are involved, as most people do not imitate such behavior. Second, televised violence disinhibits aggression. People have certain inhibitions against violence, and witnessing aggression may reduce them. Third, television violence may lead to antisocial attitudes, encouraging children and adolescents to hit first and talk later, as well as to accept violence as a way of dealing with problems. Last, people may become desensitized to violence on television and come to accept it as a normal and natural part of life; they may not show empathy for others or not take violence seriously (Coie & Dodge, 1998).

The short-term, immediate effects of televised violence are the easiest to document (Wood, Wong, & Chachere, 1991). If two groups of youths who are originally similar in aggressiveness are compared after one group sees a violent program and the other group does not, the first group will react more aggressively. This short-term effect is common, as we have seen, with children and teens who play violent video games (Griffiths, 1991).

A positive statistical relationship between aggression and television violence has been amply demonstrated (Comstock & Paik, 1991; Hughes & Hasbrouck, 1996). A review of the more than two hundred studies across age groups found a relationship between viewing television violence and aggressive behavior, regardless of age (Paik & Comstock, 1994). The effects on males were only slightly greater than the effects on females. Youth who are heavy viewers of television violence are more likely to respond with aggression to conflict situations. These studies that use correlations, however, do not demonstrate cause and effect. Perhaps viewing violence may lead to aggressiveness, but it is also possible that aggressive children and adolescents simply choose to watch more aggressive television (Eron et al., 1983). Indeed, aggressive youth are often heavy viewers of crime dramas and adventure shows, especially those with high levels of violence (Sprafkin, Watkins, & Gadow, 1990). These youth are also more likely to identify with the violent characters than are nonaggressive youth (Sprafkin, Gadow, & Abelman, 1992).

After years of research, the consensus among most of the research community is that violence on television does lead to aggressive behavior by both children and adolescents (American Academy of Pediatrics, 2001). Teenagers are attracted to the action and violence on television. As a group, they seek out more stimulation in their environment than do older people (Zuckerman, 1994), and they show greater interest in programs with highly stimulating content (Arnett, 1991a; Kremar & Greene, 1999). In addition, adolescents who are impulsive and nonconforming are attracted to violent films and horror films (Weaver, 1991).

The National Television Violence Study concluded that viewing violence is related to aggressive behavior and attitudes, desensitization to violence, and fear of being victimized. If the violence is perpetrated by an attractive person who uses weapons with humor, viewing the televised aggression is even more strongly associated with later aggression. The more graphic the violence, the greater the desensitization and the less empathy for the victim (Federman, 1997).

Fantasy and Sex in the Media

The average American adolescent views about 14,000 sexual references per year, yet only 165 of these references deal with birth control, self-control, abstinence, or the risk of pregnancy or sexually transmitted infections (American Academy of Pediatrics, 2001). Sexuality is a common theme in roughly a third of the content of prime-time shows popular with adolescents (Ward, 1995). Television shows often depict sexual relations as a competition in which men comment on women's bodies and being masculine means being sexual. Another common theme is that women are sexual objects and valued solely for their physical appearance (see Table 8.3). The third most common theme is the strong link between sex and masculinity. Regardless of what characters are doing, they talk sex. They rarely talk of love and commitment, however. These sexual themes have changed little over time (Chapin, 2000).

Research evidence links exposure to sexual material with adolescent attitudes and behavior. When adolescents were repeatedly exposed to fictional prime-time television programming with nonmarital sexual content, the adolescents rated sexual indiscretions as less morally wrong than those who saw less of the content (Bryant & Rockwell, 1994). In fact, a relationship exists between the amount of time spent viewing television generally and the adoption of sexual attitudes in line with the values shown on the programs (Ward & Rivadeneyra, 1999). Watching more hours of prime-time television is linked to a stronger endorsement of recreational sex, and viewing soap operas is linked to the acquisition of traditional gender-roles attitudes. These findings may be explained by *cultivation theory,* discussed earlier, in which constant exposure to a particular stimulus "cultivates" a particular attitude.

Table 8.3

Ranking of Common Themes About Sexuality in Prime-Time Television

Television shows popular with adolescents often depict relationships as a form of competition, show men valuing women almost solely on the basis of physical appearance, and portray sex as a defining act of masculinity.

Rank	Percentage of 875 TV Shows	Theme
2	11.5	Men value and select women based on their physical appearance.
3	9.6	Sex is a defining act of masculinity; to be male is to be sexual with women.
8	4.5	Men use a number of specific strategies to attract women.
10	3.3	Men will do unpleasant, rude, or deviant things to meet and bed women.
11	2.3	In sexual relations, men are the initiators and the aggressors.
	31.3	*Total for male sexual role*
3	9.6	Women are attracted to specific types of men.
9	3.7	Women know that looking good is important for attracting partners and for success in life.
11	2.3	There is a link between sex and women's virtue (i.e., good/bad girls).
14	1.8	Women are responsible for setting the sexual limits.
15	1.5	Women are the passive partners in sexual relations.
	18.9	*Total for female sexual role*
1	11.8	Sexual/romantic relations are a competition.
7	6.3	Sexual relations are an exciting amusement for people of all ages.
16	1.1	As objects or prizes, sexual activities serve various functions.
17	0.7	Love is the same as physical attraction.
	19.9	*Total for recreational orientation*
5	8.9	Maintaining a relationship is serious and often involves pain and conflict.
6	8.8	Openness and intimacy are keys to a successful relationship.
	17.7	*Total for relationship/marital orientation*
13	2.2	*Total for procreational orientation*
	9.5	Counterscripts
	0.6	Other

Source: Ward (1995).

Watching television programs and movies that so often involve the theme of sexuality may cause adolescents to believe that certain sexual behaviors are more common than they really are. In one study, researchers asked college students about their viewing habits and perceptions of real-world sexuality. They found that respondents who watched more soap operas believed that sexual activities outside of marriage were much more common than did respondents who did not watch such programs (Buerkel-Rothfuss & Strouse, 1989). It is interesting to note that soap operas portray sexual activity as occurring more often outside marriage than within it, and they show such activity every 9 minutes or so (Lowry & Towles, 1989). Adolescents believe more often than adults that the depiction of intimacy and sex on television is realistic (Harris, 1986).

Viewing sexual content may affect sexual behavior. A longitudinal study found that watching sex on television in early adolescence is related to early initiation of sexual intercourse in middle and late adolescence. Males who watch television apart from their families have a rate of intercourse three to six times higher than males who view it with their families (Peterson, Moore, & Furstenberg, 1991). Perhaps when television is viewed in a family context, parents can discuss the issues that are not being raised on the show. Alternatively, the results of these studies may indicate that teens who are sexually active are more attracted to shows in which freer sex is apparent. Adolescents believe that the constant theme of sexuality transmitted on television influences behavior. Survey data derived from teenagers indicate that 76 percent of teens believe one reason young people have sexual intercourse is because television shows and movies make it seem normal for adolescents to do so (Kunkel et al., 1999).

A related issue is the idealized, unrealistic view of sexuality on television and in the movies, as well as the unrealistic consequences of sexual activities. Consider what television programs and the movies show about single parenting. In real life, the consequences of single parenthood are often serious, including poor health, poverty, and stress. Yet television and the movies do not give that impression. These mothers are well off, they have a number of male friends who help out constantly, and they don't seem stressed about basic issues (Larson, 1996). They offer almost an ideal view of single mothers that does not square with the facts. Heavy viewers of television tend to believe that the real world is like the television world (Gerbner et al., 1994). A survey of three thousand high school seniors found that heavy television viewers hold views about marriage coinciding with how it is shown on television (Signorielli, 1991).

The possible negative consequences of viewing unrealistic sexual themes on television sometimes hide the fact that television and the movies can serve a positive function. Some dramatic television shows and movies do raise important issues concerning sexual issues, such as AIDS, teenage pregnancy, and rape. Over the past decade, some programs have become more responsible in showing methods to avoid unintended pregnancies and sexually transmitted infections, as well as in promoting more responsible sexual behavior. In addition, commercials advocating contraception and advertising condoms elicit very few viewer complaints and encourage greater sexual responsibility among teens who are sexually active (American Academy of Pediatrics, 2001).

Stereotypes

Most of the adolescent characters on television and in the movies are rich, and almost all are beautiful. (Even those who aren't beautiful could be if they only tried harder, we are told.) Parents are either bothersome, completely out of touch, or unimportant, and they exist mostly to give the teen money or the keys to the car. The peer group sets the standards and the rules (Rapping, 1993). No one has career problems and few have money problems, but relationships are always a problem. Everyone worthwhile wears what is in style and is in tremendous physical condition. One's appearance is what is important, and there are few adult models, little discussion of meaningful work or politics, and little evidence that relationships can be satisfying. The portrayal of adolescents is stereotyped as well.

For many years television and the movies included few, if any, members of minority groups, and they certainly stereotyped them (Gunter, 1998). Although no one could possibly say this stereotypical treatment has been eliminated, there has been a noticeable shift away from stereotyping some ethnic and racial minorities on television and in the movies. A conscious effort to include counter-stereotyped images that offer information that contradicts the prevailing stereotypes is apparent (Murphy, 1994). Certain types of television shows seem to include more minority group members. For example, situation comedies offer parts for people from many backgrounds. Action shows have been somewhat slower to present minority group members in higher-level positions, but changes are occurring (Gunter, 1998). No one is saying that the portrayals of minority group characters on television and in the movies should always be positive, of course; the part of the "bad guy" in the movies should be an equal opportunity position.

Television and its viewing public must be sensitive to how its programming depicts particular groups. The status of minority group members and the increasing number of minority group actors on television, though, certainly reflect the new reality in the United States, with its diverse population.

Television will probably always be criticized for its presentation of minority groups, but it is evolving in the right direction.

Television Talk Shows

Television talk shows often are singled out for special criticism. Talk shows certainly treat problems in a sensational manner. Four criticisms of talk shows are common: (1) talk shows give viewers a warped sense of reality, making dysfunctional relationships and bizarre behavior seem typical; (2) they desensitize viewers to human suffering by focusing on the sensational; (3) they trivialize social issues; and (4) they cause teens to have a negative attitude toward relationships.

Research, though, shows only one of these criticisms to be based on fact. Adolescents from grades 9 through 12 were surveyed about their attitudes toward particular behaviors, the extent to which these behaviors occurred, and the extent to which they watched talk shows.

Viewers of talk shows did think that many problems are much more common than they really are. Table 8.4 shows national figures on such issues as teenage runaways and wives and husbands cheating on each other, along with the figures suggested by teens who watch talk shows consistently, once in a while, rarely, or never. Notice that the more adolescents viewed talk shows, the higher their estimates of the behavior (Davis & Mares, 1998). Even nonviewers overestimated the prevalence of these problems, however. Furthermore, there was no support for the idea that these shows made viewers more negative about relationships or desensitized them to the other people's problems.

The sweeping condemnation of talk shows is not warranted by the evidence. Heavy viewers were not much more pessimistic than light viewers. Rather than trivialize the issues, these programs place issues, such as adolescent-parent communication and sexual irresponsibility, on the agenda. People watching these

---

Table 8.4

Talk Show Viewers' Estimates of the Frequency of Real-World Occurrences: A Comparison with Reality

Generally, adolescents overestimate how many teens run away or become pregnant, as well as the extent to which husbands and wives cheat in their marriages. Adolescents who watch television talk shows believe these things happen more frequently than adolescents who do not watch these shows. Perhaps one of the consequences of watching these shows is the belief that the problems shown on television are more common than they really are.

Occurrence in Real World	Actual Frequency	Every Day n = 35	Sometimes n = 94	Rarely n = 82	Never n = 71
Teens who run away from home each year[a]	8%	48.7%	33.3%	32.0%	24.0%
Teen girls who become pregnant before age 18[b]	4	55.1	42.0	39.8	30.0
Boys between 15 and 19 who have had sex[c]	60	79.7	72.3	69.4	59.5*
Girls between 15 and 19 who have had sex[c]	50	72.6	61.4	62.0	52.3*
Teens who bring guns to school each day[d]	<1	26.9	25.1	28.2	21.2
Husbands who cheat on their wives[e]	20	45.7	43.2	45.2	38.5
Wives who cheat on their husbands[e]	10	31.4	34.5	30.2	26.8

Note: Cells contain frequency estimates out of a possible 100%. With the exception of the two estimates marked by an asterisk, all estimates are significantly different from the real-world figure at $p < .05$.
[a]From Hull (1994); data from the National Network of Runaway and Youth Services. [b]Computed from figures from the Allen Guttmacher Institute (1994) and U.S. Bureau of the Census populations estimates. [c]From the Youth Risk Behavior Survey (1990). [d]From Fox and Pierce (1994). [e]From A. M. Greeley (1994); data from the 1991 General Social Survey.
Source: Davis & Mares (1998).

Although people criticize television talk shows for their outlandish themes and sometimes for the behavior of their guests, most of the time the audience actually is critical of the guests' ideas and behavior.

programs do not believe the participants are helpless and believe the problems can be solved (Davis & Mares, 1998). These shows must be seen as entertainment as well as a source of information.

Talk shows are sometimes criticized because people claim that they encourage antisocial or sexually inappropriate behavior. However, in most cases the audience and host disapprove of females dressing too provocatively, males cheating on their steadies, or drug-related activity. The shows do not desensitize people to the problems, either. Some people watch these shows because they can relate to the problems and characters on them, and the reactions of others may confirm their beliefs (Livingstone, 1994). Others watch talk shows because the guests are often unusual and entertaining. Some talk show hosts have allowed their shows to become stages for fighting and temper tantrums, whereas others try to approach social problems in an entertaining, yet serious, manner.

Advertising

Advertising pervades our world; it is found in print media, on the radio, and even on hamburger wrappers. Television advertising, because it combines auditory and visual properties, is especially influential, and it influences teens both directly and indirectly. As one 14-year-old watching commercials about acne and personal grooming noted, "I do think one thing commercials try to do is to make you feel self-conscious. They want you to worry about zits and clean pores, about your hair being shiny enough, about how muscular you are, and how much you weigh. They push at me, bring it up more in my mind" (Farrington, 1999, p. 6). This teen also noted that sometimes a commercial affected her directly, making her more likely to purchase an item. At other times the effect was indirect; for example, seeing a product in the store might remind her of a commercial.

Unlike this teen, though, many adolescents deny that advertising affects them. Indeed, as a group, teenagers are more likely than any other group to use the remote control to tune out a television commercial (Gonzales, 1988). Still, it is hard to believe that all of the twenty thousand ads that batter the average American each year can be tuned out (Shepherdson, 2000). As one 19-year-old girl noted, "I've never met a girl who was satisfied with her appearance, and I think that advertising has a lot to do with it" (Farrington, 1999, p. 8).

Some authorities blame advertising for teenagers' poor eating habits. They say that nutrition problems, such as the consumption of too many empty calories, too little consumption of fruits and vegetables, and too many high-fat meals, are partially due to advertising (Farrington, 1999). Although it is unfair to place all the blame on ads—after all, teenagers are often busy and are given less time to eat—the influence of advertising is substantial.

Western Influences on Other Societies

Western television and radio programming, movies, and music reach much of the world. During the Gulf War, people from all over the world tuned into their favorite news station, such as CNN or the BBC World Service, for up-to-the-minute reports. MTV is televised in countries all over the world (Walker, 1996). Thus, teens in many countries view similar programs with similar commercials for similar brands. Testimony to the global effects of television are the political changes in Europe. Many former totalitarian governments tried to keep Western television away from their youth, not because of their stated objection that it showed "decadent images" but because it raised expectations. Government officials feared that after seeing the goods available in the West and the freedom shown on television, their people no longer would be satisfied with what they had. In fact, some observers partially credit television for the removal of the Berlin Wall. As East Germans received Western-style programming, it became more difficult for their government to explain its inability to satisfy the needs of the population.

AT A GLANCE 8.5 TELEVISION AND THE MOVIES

KEY POINT: The content of television and movies influences adolescents, but the background and experiences of the viewer must be taken into account.

SUPPORTING POINTS	EXPLANATION
Viewing violence influences adolescent behavior.	Studies find that viewing violence leads to a greater propensity for aggression, a desensitization toward violence, and an acceptance of violence as a way to resolve disputes.
The cultivation effect may be partially responsible for adolescents' beliefs about relationships and sexuality.	Adolescents who constantly see and hear the message that extramarital sexuality is acceptable and all that matters is physical appearance are more likely to hold these beliefs.
Although stereotyping minority groups is a problem, television and the movies have made significant improvements in this area.	Some stereotyping does occur, but it is less common than years ago. More actors and actresses from minority group backgrounds are getting a chance to show their talents.
Talk shows are among the most criticized television shows.	Talk shows make dysfunctional relationships and bizarre behavior seem typical. However, they do not desensitize viewers to human suffering or trivialize social issues. Audiences condemn antisocial behavior.
A great deal of advertising is aimed at adolescents.	Adolescents are more likely than other age groups to tune out commercials, but some commercials, especially for food and personal grooming products, are effective at reaching them.
Western television and movies are now widely viewed throughout the world and affect traditional attitudes and behaviors.	Western cultural values shown in the media affect many young people in non-Western societies, an influence that some see as endangering their cultures.

The influence of global television on various cultures is a source of irritation to some. Western images pouring into a country modify the culture. The extent of media penetration in various countries differs. In most Western countries, almost every adolescent has access to television (although not necessarily cable television). In other countries, geographical location within the country and socioeconomic status may determine exposure to television and movies. Many adolescents exposed to Western transmissions for the first time show distinct changes in language, dress, and musical preference as they adopt what they see on the screen. Interviews with television viewers and nonviewers in India revealed distinct differences between the two groups (Varma, 2000). Viewers were significantly more likely to get drunk on occasion, be more particular about the way they dressed, and favor more sexual freedom than nonviewers. Even people who do not have television sets in their homes may be affected, because the content of Western programs is discussed, and changes in their peers' dress and music preferences are obvious. Prolonged exposure to television programs increases disapproval of traditional norms in Indian society, and the ideas of viewers and nonviewers differ.

Non-Western societies do change as they have wider exposure to Western media. Many individuals in more traditional societies resent the influence of Western media, as Western values (at least the values shown on television and in the movies) clash with their more traditional values. For example, the greater sexual freedom of adolescents, the reduced reverence for age, and changes in clothing style may foment disapproval from more traditional minded adults in a society, who may fear a threat to their culture.

PERSPECTIVE 3

LEGAL RESPONSIBILITY

SETTING THE SCENE: You are a juror sitting on the case of a 17-year-old who has been paralyzed performing an obviously very dangerous activity that was shown in a made-for-television movie. The teen and her family are suing the movie distributor and the television station. As you are shown the section of the movie dealing with the risky behavior, you note that the teen performed the same behavior in the same way.

PLAINTIFF'S ATTORNEY: *My client, influenced by the film she saw, performed the same act in the same way two nights later. If the film hadn't shown this behavior, my client would never have performed the act and would not now be paralyzed. Movie distributors must be held responsible for their offerings.*

DEFENSE ATTORNEY: *We are truly sorry for what has happened, but it is not right to blame us. More than 350,000 teens have watched this movie without imitating the stunt. Movies and television shows include car chases and murders, yet are they responsible for speeding on the highway or drive-by shootings? I say "no." Something else must have been going on in this young woman's mind that led to this obviously dangerous behavior. We are not responsible.*

QUESTION: Would you support the plaintiff or the defendant in this case? Why?

The Influence of Movies and Television: A Final Word

Television and movies are potent forces in Western societies and, increasingly, in many less developed countries. Televised violence influences children and teenagers, and the continuous repetition of particular ideas and attitudes may cause adolescents to adopt them. Advertising also is influential, despite the fact that teens are impatient and often tune them out. Enough ads get through to create a need or a demand for a product.

Adolescents, though, do not come to television or the movies ready to accept everything they see. As with other forms of media, the influence of television programs and the movies depends on the individual's background, needs, and attitudes. Some teenagers identify with the characters and situations more than others. Yet there is no question that television and the movies are, and will continue to be, a major force in the lives of adolescents in the United States and around the world. *(For a review of this section, see At A Glance 8.5.)*

MAGAZINES

Look around any public library, and you will find that the magazines aimed at teenagers are dog-eared from constant reading. Most teen magazines are aimed at girls, and companies often have a developmental concept; that is, they have some magazines targeted at young teens and others at late teens, and they continue to create magazines for early adults and beyond. Therefore, each magazine targets girls of a specific age (Weissman, 1993). Magazines aimed at teenage girls from minority groups are available, although the best-known teen magazines often include items of interest to these girls.

Magazines aimed at teenage boys are rare. Publications for boys generally cover special interests (computers, for example) or aim at both boys and girls (for example, music publications) (Willemsen, 1998). A growing number of "teen fan" magazines and newspapers carry little or no advertising and concentrate on entertainment and celebrity news (Evans et al., 1991).

The magazines aimed at teen girls contain advice on self-improvement, which often translates into fashion and beauty advice, as well as discussions of how to attract boys and get along with others (Evans et al., 1991; Garner, Sterk, & Adams, 1998). An analysis of both articles and advertisements shows that these magazines advance the idea that happiness and life satisfaction lie in looking your best, being popular, and attracting males through becoming beautiful. Articles with such titles as "How can I get guys to notice me?" "What can I do if my boyfriend likes my friend too much?" "What am I supposed to wear?" and "How far should I go?" reflect concerns that these magazines address.

The magazine articles offer definite answers to these questions. To be successful, you must know how to dress, be well groomed, and act appropriately in social situations. The articles do not advance the idea that a woman's personal achievement, education, public service, friendships, or long-lasting relationships are more important than outward appearances (Duffy & Gotcher, 1996). They emphasize the romantic, and much of the fiction found in the magazines further emphasizes these themes (Pierce, 1993). Most of the advice is fairly mainstream (Evans et al., 1991).

Advertisers find teen magazines a potent way of getting to the teenage market. Each of the most popular magazines, *YM, Teen, Seventeen,* and *Glamour,* can claim over 1.5 million in circulation. Their emphasis on fashion makes them a natural place to advertise. The magazines, in turn, make their profits largely

Many teenage girls read fashion magazines, which emphasize beauty and relationship problems. In turn, many girls report that they feel worse about themselves after looking at the thin models wearing the newest fashions than they did before they read the magazines.

through advertising sales. A problem could arise if advertisers pressure the magazines to avoid including explicit information about AIDS, abortion, and pregnancy because these controversial topics might hurt sales of products advertised.

Another problem is the fact that so many of the models pictured in these magazines have "perfect" figures, which may affect adolescent girls already focused on their bodies. One researcher found that 71 percent of her adolescent respondents stated that when they see models in clothing ads, they think about how badly they compare with these models (Richins, 1991). In fact, exposure to these magazines lowers self-perceptions of attractiveness. Another study found a relationship between adolescent girls reading beauty and fashion magazines and some unhealthy eating habits, such as taking diet pills (Thomsen, Weber, & Brown, 2002).

Not all girls who read teen magazines embrace or uncritically accept these beliefs, of course (Willemsen, 1998). One girl reported that she enjoyed a romantic story because the boys were so different—much nicer than the ones she knew in real life. She liked the story, but she did not confuse fantasy and reality or agree with the stereotypical opinions in the magazine (Frazer, 1987). In fact, girls may use these magazines for advice in specific areas, fully understanding that other areas, such as alternative lifestyles, future vocational plans, and issues such as AIDS and abortion, appear to be largely beyond their scope.

Critics often attack teen magazines for being traditional, emphasizing appearance over substance, and not dealing with the more difficult issues. Criticism of sexual content is often based on the titles of articles, which often actually exaggerate the sexual nature of the somewhat tamer articles. These magazines have to strike a balance in the advocacy or nonadvocacy of sexual intercourse. Many present useful information and answer questions that parents find difficult (Mellanby, 1996). The magazines often discuss relationship problems and developmental concerns that are the subject of conversation at the high school lunch table (Weissman, 1993).

It would be interesting to compare teen magazines aimed at females with those written for males, but few exist. There seems to be little interest in general magazines for boys, although small-circulation magazines may exist. When British adolescent males were asked if they wished there were a boys' magazine, most answered negatively, as if to read such a magazine would not be gender-appropriate behavior (Kehily, 1996, cited in Willemsen, 1998).

There is one general magazine meant for teen boys in the Netherlands that is similar to magazines meant for teenage girls. A comparison of magazines meant for teen girls and the magazine for adolescent boys found that fashion and beauty were the most important topics in magazines meant for girls, accounting for more than a quarter of all the pages, whereas in the magazine for boys the most important topics were celebrities and hobbies, occupying about a third of the pages. The boys' magazine had no fiction, whereas the fiction in the girls' magazines was basically romantic. The boys' magazine stressed where to go in various cities, cars, and motorcycles, and a special feature covered computer games, films, and the media.

The most interesting differences, though, were in the treatment of sexuality. The female magazines wrote about love, being in love, and how to be noticed by boys. These magazines mostly dealt with sex in answers to questions from readers. The boys' magazine treated sex as a prime topic when relationships were discussed, and it did not present love in an overwhelmingly positive way. How to break up with a girl was a prime topic of interest (Willemsen, 1998). Another difference was that the girls' magazines used many more emotion-filled words, and the magazine aimed at males used rougher language.

Two different value systems seem to be at work in the magazine for boys compared with those for girls. This finding is especially interesting in light of the fact that in the Netherlands, boys and girls have more or less the same opinions about dating, preferring a steady partner and attaching much importance to love

At a Glance 8.6 Magazines

KEY POINT: Magazines, especially those aimed at adolescent girls, are a major source of information about relationships, sexuality, and popular culture.

SUPPORTING POINTS	EXPLANATION
Most magazines that target adolescents are aimed at adolescent girls.	Some magazines, such as fan magazines, are aimed at both genders, but magazines with major circulations target teenage girls.
Magazines aimed at teenage girls emphasize appearance, style, how to attract boys, and relationships.	The emphasis on beauty found in teen magazines matches their advertising. Magazines portray success in terms of attracting boys and include little information about vocational development, personal worth, or longer-term friendships and relationships.
Most advice in teen magazines is mainstream.	Any advice these magazines give tends to be conservative. They include few controversial issues, such as abortion, AIDS, or pregnancy, because their coverage might affront some readers and thus reduce sales.
Some relatively new magazines aimed at female adolescents do not emphasize beauty and sexuality.	These alternative magazines may emphasize spirituality, volunteering, political activism, and self-improvement.

and affection within the relationship. Perhaps the finding can be partially explained by the way boys and girls greet articles about relationships (Kehily, 1996, cited in Willemsen, 1998). Girls take relationship problems and sexuality seriously, whereas boys react with cold detachment, perhaps because boys don't talk much about such things. Boys invest in a masculine identity based on concealment of problems and vulnerabilities, whereas girls find that these problems fit well with their greater and acceptably public discussion about relationships.

Today a number of alternative magazines are available for teenage girls. They include magazines that emphasize the role of religion and belief, political and social issues, multiculturalism, and improving self-esteem, as well as those that encourage girls to be agents of social change. These magazines do not emphasize style, makeup, or appearance, and some do not accept advertisements. As one managing editor wrote, "We got tired of magazines that advertised 7-foot-tall, 90-pound drug-addicted models. We wanted a magazine that promoted a positive view of womanhood" (Means, 1997). Each alternative magazine has a small circulation, and only time will tell whether there is sufficient interest to allow them to grow and prosper. *(For a review of this section, see At A Glance 8.6.)*

Placing the Media in Perspective

The influence of the media is widespread. The media provide an inexhaustible assortment of entertainment and information, as well as help create the environment that surrounds adolescents. The media may influence adolescents in many ways, some obvious and some not so obvious.

The public is concerned about the sexuality, violence, and portrayal of women in the media. Many commentators criticize media content, focusing on the need for the media to encourage tolerance, sexual responsibility, and prosocial activities such as volunteering within the community. Still other critics point to the dangers inherent in the media revolution and explosion. With both parents at work and single-parent families more common, are the media playing the part of guide to a greater extent than is desirable? Are the media encouraging antisocial behaviors? Are dangers lurking on the Web and in email correspondence with people one does not see? These important questions deserve attention.

Ample evidence exists that some adolescents are influenced negatively by movies, television programs, music videos, music on the radio and CDs, or websites. Yet for others, the possible negative influences are moderated by good family situations, friends who act in a prosocial manner, a positive relationship with adults, and religious values. Not everyone who watches violence on television becomes violent, and not everyone who listens to heavy metal or rap music or watches music videos imitates what is seen or heard. In any case, though, the media's portrayals of violence and sexuality, their denigration of women, and their imposition of impossible physical standards contribute to an atmosphere that emphasizes the superficial.

Defenders of the media note that they present views of sex and violence, as well as relationship issues, that interest teens, and that when teens no longer pay attention, these messages will change. However, the media not only reflect the interests of teens but also help create the atmosphere that surrounds them. It is patently unfair to blame societal problems on the media, but it is equally inappropriate to exonerate the media for the part they play by encouraging particular attitudes and behaviors.

Television, music, music videos, and video games have to entertain. As a student said after her own research determined that the portrayals of single mothers were much more glamorous than reality, "Who wants to see a harried, poverty-stricken woman who has no help, can't pay her bills, and is a stock clerk at a local store?" The student has a point; often reality just isn't entertaining. Yet someone has to point out that what television shows is not real life.

In the midst of these negative images and problems, we should not forget the positive influence of the media. Internet access opens up a new world to adolescents. They can use the Internet to obtain information on almost every subject and keep in touch with one another through email. Many volunteer groups use email to inform their members of what is going on. Music can and does help adolescents deal with their feelings, and television and the movies both entertain and raise important issues. It is unfortunate that these more positive contributions to the adolescent's development are less researched and disseminated than the negative aspects.

We can only hope that the media will balance their responsibilities to stockholders with their civic responsibilities. We can only hope that in our current love affair with the Net, we will not forget that most information is not available electronically and rediscover the need to read books. We can only hope that people will remember that email and instant messaging cannot replace face-to-face interactions. And we can only hope that in our passion for staying instantly and constantly in touch, we can also appreciate the importance of private time.

HAS YOUR OPINION CHANGED?

Please place the number best reflecting your opinion next to each of the following statements. Then compare your opinions now with those you held before reading the chapter.

1 — Strongly Agree
2 — Moderately Agree
3 — No Opinion
4 — Moderately Disagree
5 — Strongly Disagree

_____ 1. The influence of the media on adolescents is generally positive.

_____ 2. Email and chat rooms help teenagers improve their interpersonal and computer skills.

_____ 3. Overuse of video games, chat rooms, and the Internet can lead to emotional disturbances.

_____ 4. Families without computers and Internet access in their homes place their children at an academic disadvantage compared with children who have home access to computers with Internet access.

_____ 5. Playing violent video games increases the probability that an adolescent will be aggressive.

_____ 6. It is the government's responsibility to make certain that sexist, racist, and extremely violent video games, music lyrics, and music videos do not reach the eyes and ears of children and adolescents under 18 years of age.

_____ 7. Parents who do not know what television programs their adolescent children are watching, which websites they are visiting, and what music they are listening to are not doing an adequate job.

_____ 8. Violence on television, including violent music videos, contributes to violence in our society.

_____ 9. The portrayal of women as sexual objects in heavy metal and rap music and in some music videos contributes to violence against women.

_____ 10. All CDs and video games should have rating labels.

THEMES

THEME 1 **Adolescence is a time of choices, "firsts," and transitions.**	• The media give adolescents many choices for gathering information, communicating with others, and entertainment. • Adolescents have more money to spend than younger children, and parents give them more freedom to spend their money.
THEME 2 **Adolescence is shaped by context.**	• The media form an important part of the adolescent's environment. • The computer and Internet access have added a new level of communication, one that influences how adolescents spend their days.
THEME 3 **Adolescence is influenced by group membership.**	• Adolescents living in poverty are less likely to have a computer in the home and Internet access than adolescents of middle or upper socioeconomic status, but many have access in school. • Preference for different types of music is related to ethnicity and race.
THEME 4 **The adolescent experience has changed over the past 50 years.**	• The media play a much larger role in the daily lives of adolescents today compared with years ago, as the amount of time adolescents spend with the media has increased. • Adolescents today have many more media choices than in the past. • Adolescents have more money to spend on goods than they had years ago. • Adolescents have a greater influence on family purchases today, because working and single parents leave more of the shopping to their adolescent children. • For the first time in history, adolescents are much more conversant with modern technology than their parents. • Adolescents today are very likely to use the Internet rather than books as a primary source of information. • Song lyrics have become more violent and more sexually explicit over the years. • Violence on television and in the movies is more realistic and gruesome than in the past. • Although stereotyping of members of minority groups on television and in the movies still occurs, it is less common than years ago.
THEME 5 **Today's views of adolescence are becoming more balanced, with greater attention to its positive nature.**	• Compared with just a few years ago, there is a greater balance between the positive and negative aspects of computer and Internet use. • Adolescents are no longer seen as merely passive receivers of messages from the media; they are now seen as being active and bringing attitudes and characteristics to their media experiences.

CHAPTER SUMMARY AT A GLANCE

KEY TOPICS	KEY POINTS	
The Media and the Teen	Adolescents both are affected by, and influence, the media. *(At A Glance 8.1, p. 261)*	← **KEY TERMS** *cultivation theory (p. 258)* *desensitization (p. 259)*
The Computer Revolution: Email and the Internet	Computer technology is changing the adolescent experience. *(At A Glance 8.2, p. 267)*	← *digital divide (p. 262)* *privatization of entertainment (p. 265)* *multitasking (p. 266)*
Video Games	Playing video games is a common activity, but questions surround its possible link with aggressive behavior. *(At A Glance 8.3, p. 272)*	
Music and Radio	Music serves many important functions, but the public is concerned about its aggressive and sexual themes. *(At A Glance 8.4, p. 281)*	
Television and the Movies	The content of television and movies influences adolescents, but the background and experiences of the viewer must be taken into account. *(At A Glance 8.5, p. 288)*	
Magazines	Magazines, especially those aimed at adolescent girls, are a major source of information about relationships, sexuality, and popular culture. *(At A Glance 8.6, p. 292)*	

Review questions for this chapter appear in the appendix.

9

SELF-CONCEPT AND IDENTITY FORMATION

WHAT IS YOUR OPINION?

BASIC CONCEPTS RELATED TO THE SELF

SELF-CONCEPT IN ADOLESCENCE
- Developmental Changes in the Self-Concept
- Acting Phony: Which Is My Real Self?
- Is the Self-Concept Stable?
- The Real and Ideal Selves

SELF-ESTEEM IN ADOLESCENCE
- Trends in Self-Esteem
  Perspective 1: I Just Can't Do It
- Self-Esteem in Adolescents from Minority Groups
- Self-Esteem: Can There Be Too Much of a Good Thing?
- Self-Esteem, the Self-Concept, and Cognitive Development
- Improving Self-Esteem

IDENTITY
- Theories of Identity Formation
- Exploration and Commitment: Erikson on Identity
- The Four Identity Statuses
  Perspective 2: Just Puzzled
- Do Males and Females Take Different Paths to Identity Formation?
  FOCUS: Squeaky Wheels and Nails That Stick Out: The Self and Culture
- Concerns About Identity Status

GENDER ROLES
- Gender Stereotypes
- Sex Typing: A Developmental View
- Gender and Voice
- How Gender Roles Develop: A Focus on Process

ETHNIC/RACIAL IDENTITY
- The Process of Exploration
- Forming a Racial/Ethnic Identity
- Separation, Assimilation, Integration, and Marginality

PLACING THE SELF-CONCEPT AND IDENTITY FORMATION IN PERSPECTIVE

HAS YOUR OPINION CHANGED?

THEMES

CHAPTER SUMMARY AT A GLANCE

Describe myself? OK, here goes. I'm happy-go-lucky, friendly, and helpful, but sometimes I'm moody, anxious, and very serious. I would like to be nice to everyone, but some people just make me angry, and when I get angry I'm disappointed in myself. I'm pretty smart, but I don't want to appear too smart—you know, stuck-up. I'm really lively around my friends, but I'm quiet around my parents, even though we get along OK. I don't feel they know who I really am. Sometimes I try out new ways of acting, like being really cool and calm, but then I find it doesn't come easy. I'm really an emotional person.

I don't understand how I can be one way one minute—like being confident—and then be so anxious and doubtful the next. I don't want to act phony, to be one way with one person and another with someone else. It really bothers me. I sometimes don't know if I'm serious or goofy. Sometimes I think my friends think I'm totally weird. I don't want to care what anyone else thinks, but then I have to admit it bothers me if people think I'm acting stupidly. I sometimes wonder who I really am and what I will become (adapted from Harter, 1990, pp. 352–353).

Asked to describe themselves, most 15-year-olds, like the one quoted above, will offer a string of characteristics, many of them contradictory. Adolescents this age understand these contradictions and are bothered by them. They often experiment with different ways of acting and have a great interest—some might say a preoccupation—in how others see them. There is an evolving, unsettled quality to their descriptions of themselves, as if the self is a work in progress.

This chapter deals with the adolescent's inner experience. It begins with a discussion of the nature of the self, the self-concept, and self-esteem and then discusses the ways in which they change during the adolescent years. It then turns to adolescent identity formation as adolescents try to answer such questions as "Who am I?" and "Where am I going?" The chapter then investigates gender and racial/ethnic differences in identity and discusses how to help adolescents form solid personal identities.

BASIC CONCEPTS
RELATED TO THE SELF

Psychologists have been interested in the self, the self-concept, self-esteem, and identity of children and adolescents for many years. The **self** is the organizer of a person's subjective experience (Kaplan & Stein, 1984). The concept of self is a theoretical construct that implies some conscious understanding of one's own being (Marohn, 1997). The self contains a collection of feelings, attitudes, concepts, values, goals, and ideals that influence how we behave. The **self-concept** is the perception one has of oneself. It is a picture drawn in words that verbally describe the qualities that define the individual. It is most often measured by asking people to describe themselves, usually by giving a list of traits. **Self-esteem** refers to judgments that one places on the self-concept or various aspects of the self (Frey & Carlock, 1989; Emler, 2002). Although the self-concept is usually viewed in descriptive and nonjudgmental terms, self-esteem is self-evaluative (Scott et al., 1996). One problem with this definition of self-esteem is that it could make high self-esteem appear to be a self-centered and selfish trait. People with high self-esteem who like themselves and value their contributions might be seen as being uncaring toward others. Some definitions of self-esteem thus emphasize not only appreciating one's own worth and

self The organizer of a person's subjective experience, which implies some conscious understanding of one's own being.

self-concept The picture people have of themselves.

self-esteem A term that refers to judgments that one places on the self-concept or on various aspects of the self. Newer definitions suggest that self-esteem involves not only appreciating one's own worth and importance but also being accountable for oneself and acting responsibly toward others.

importance but also being accountable for oneself and acting responsibly toward others (California State Department of Education, 1990). Self-esteem is most often measured by asking people to rate favorably or unfavorably their list of traits, and an overall self-esteem measure may be found by looking at the relative balance between the two ratings. Sometimes self-esteem is measured by determining the difference between what individuals want to be and how they see themselves today.

When most people speak of an identity, they mean an individual's name, age, gender, profession, and other data that make the individual unique. In contrast, psychologists use the term **identity** to refer to the unique combination of personality characteristics and social style by which one defines oneself and is recognized by others (Grotevant, 1998). Sometimes *identity* is used to describe a person's subjective sense of coherence of personality that continues over time, as in a person's having a *sense of identity.*

Psychologists use the constructs of the self, self-concept, self-esteem, and identity because they are helpful in understanding an individual's behavior and development. Unfortunately, their definitions are often vague, and various authors use the terms differently. There is really no single accepted definition for *self* (Cross, 1997) or *identity.* Still, most people have an idea of what these terms mean, and their general meaning is not difficult to communicate.

Interest in the nature of the self and how it develops dates back to the beginnings of psychology. William James (1890, 1892/1961) identified two important aspects of the self: the "I" and the "me." The "I" is the knower, whereas the "me" is the total of all a person can call his or hers, including material characteristics, personality traits, and spiritual characteristics. The "me" is what most people mean when referring to the self-concept, whereas the "I" is actively responsible for constructing the "me." James believed that the self could be divided into three parts: the material self (knowledge of the physical self and possessions), the social self (your awareness of how others are seeing you), and the spiritual self (thoughts, feelings, and moral judgments). These parts could be placed in a hierarchy with the material self at the bottom, the social self in the middle, and the spiritual sense at the top. James argued that an individual could have many social selves, as people have many roles, and these selves could be in conflict. James's view of multiple selves and the possible conflict between selves remains popular in self theory (Grotevant, 1998).

The question of how the self was formed arose a bit later, and sociological theories took center stage. Most theories emphasized the social nature of the self. For example, Cooley (1902) and Mead (1934) viewed the self as constructed through verbal exchanges with others. People in the environment become a social mirror into which the individual looks, detects the opinions of others, and finally internalizes them to create a sense of self. Cooley called this self the *"looking-glass self."* Mead, in contrast, emphasized the idea of *reflected appraisals of the generalized other.* The self, then, is formed through social interaction and feedback; it is basically what others think of us, including our appearance, deeds, motivations, and character. The picture one has of oneself, the self-concept, is partially formed by these internalized reflected appraisals from others.

This theory does not imply that each comment from others initiates a distinct change in the self or the self-concept. That mechanism would make the self entirely too unsteady and changeable and would not mesh with people's subjective experiences, in which they perceive a more stable self. Mead argued that people take the view of the *generalized other* and are not truly affected by specific comments made by one individual on a given day. Today many behavioral scientists agree that feedback from others helps create the self, which is shaped through social interaction. Other people do not speak with only one voice, and our view of ourselves can include contrasts and contradictions (Harter, 1990).

Further developments in our understanding of the self come from cognitive and humanistic psychologists. The self can be viewed as a cognitive (intellectual) construct. If the individual constructs the self from the feedback received from

identity The sense of knowing who you are; the unique combination of personality characteristics and social style by which individuals define themselves and are recognized by others.

AT A GLANCE   9.1 BASIC CONCEPTS RELATED TO THE SELF

KEY POINT: Self-concept and self-esteem are important aspects of an adolescent's inner experience.

SUPPORTING POINTS	EXPLANATION
The self-concept is the perception one has of oneself.	The self-concept is an individual's verbal picture of the qualities that define him or her.
Self-esteem is the judgment that a person places on parts of the self.	Some definitions of *self-esteem* emphasize not only self-worth but also personal accountability and responsibility for what one does.
Identity is the unique combination of personality characteristics and social style by which one defines oneself and is recognized by others.	Identity, self-concept, and self-esteem are constructs that psychologists use to better understand development and behavior.
James believed that the self-concept could be divided into three parts: the material self, the social self, and the spiritual self.	James's idea that the self may be divided into different parts remains popular with psychologists.
The self is formed through social interaction with others.	Sociological theorists, such as Cooley and Mead, argued that the self evolves from the appraisals and feedback received from others.
Cognitive psychologists argue that the self is a cognitive construct and that the way information received from others is processed is important.	People actively create a self and search for feedback about themselves.
Humanistic psychologists argue that personal experience influences the formation of the self-concept.	People have many different experiences and actively evaluate their experiences, forming and sometimes changing their self-concept.

others, then not only the nature of the information but also the way it is processed are important. Cognitive psychologists argue that people create a theory about themselves and search out information that may confirm their theory. Thus, an individual might ignore some comments from others that are not in keeping with that person's conception of self and accept other comments that are in keeping.

Finally, humanistic psychologists emphasize the importance of personal experiences in the construction of the self. Consider a teenager who lists honesty and integrity as important aspects of the self and then cheats on a chemistry test. The teen must deal with the experience of cheating in some way. He might deny that he cheated ("I only checked my answers"), rationalize the cheating ("Everyone else was doing it"), or modify his self-image.

Although the self is unique—that is, each person has a unique blend of characteristics—it cannot stand on its own. On the one hand, an individual confronts forces that require communion—that is, building relationships and creating bonds with others. On the other hand, the individual also searches for a sense of uniqueness and separateness. Through *differentiation* the individual finds uniqueness, and through *socialization* the person forms and maintains bonds with others (Adams & Marshall, 1996). The individual must integrate both separateness/uniqueness and commonality with others. (*For a review of this section, see At A Glance 9.1.*)

SELF-CONCEPT IN ADOLESCENCE

Young children asked to describe themselves often offer descriptions of their physical selves ("I am tall") or behaviors ("I like baseball"). In middle childhood, a more psychologically based self appears, including some characteristics ("I am happy") and comparisons with others ("I am smarter than Jim"). A shift occurs in adolescence from these more concrete descriptions to a more abstract self-portrait (Damon & Hart, 1982). The adolescent self-concept includes a variety of personal and interpersonal traits that are complex and sometimes in opposition to each other ("I am friendly, obnoxious, tolerant, and popular"). Teenagers also describe emotions ("I am embarrassed" or "I am sad"), wishes, motives ("I am ambitious"), attitudes ("I am concerned about the earth"), and beliefs ("I can be vindictive"). A teen's self-concept might include ideas about what the individual wants to be or does not want to be.

Developmental Changes in the Self-Concept

One difference between adolescents' descriptions of self and the descriptions of younger children is that adolescents use many more categories for self-description than do younger children (Marsh & O'Neill, 1984). Their descriptions of self with parents, close friends, romantic partners, and classmates differ (Harter & Monsour, 1992). The teen may experience a "sarcastic" self with parents but a "comforting" self with friends. Adolescents become sensitive to the context and more aware that they see themselves differently across contexts—for example, self with father, self with mother, self with close friend, and self with romantic partner (Griffin, Chassin, & Young, 1981). This differentiation arises from the adolescent's increased awareness of social roles and emerging cognitive ability to use abstractions (see "Cognitive Development"). Adolescents may construct opposites, seeing themselves as "outgoing," "self-conscious," "angry," and "calming," but early adolescents are not aware of the contradictions, perhaps because these behaviors are separated by time (Fischer, 1980).

"How can I be so outgoing with some people and so inhibited with others?" Many teenagers, especially in middle adolescence, are bothered by the seeming contradictions in their behaviors and feelings.

Middle adolescents develop the cognitive skills necessary to engage in comparisons, and the conflicting descriptions (for example, being outgoing, yet introspective) are a source of distress. Furthermore, they are unable to integrate these contradictions into a coherent self-concept. The self-concept is unstable during this stage. Middle adolescents may engage in all-or-nothing thinking, changing from one extreme to the other. They may feel brilliant at one point and totally stupid at another. This period of flux is due to their increasing awareness of the contradictions in the self.

Psychoanalytic writer Peter Blos (1962) perceived adolescence to be a period of intense preoccupation with the self, with swings from grandiosity to self-devaluation. Individuals are preoccupied with what others think of them but are not certain of these appraisals, because feedback often varies from individual to individual and changes often. This feedback is likely to be contradictory, and feedback on a behavior may be both positive and negative. The adolescent must integrate these multiple attributes into a coherent and unified sense of self, creating internal consistency (Allport, 1961; Harter, 1990). This process can be difficult. Like the individual quoted at the beginning of the chapter, middle adolescents do not understand how they can be both depressed and cheerful, and they wonder who they really are.

In late adolescence, these opposites are integrated into a coherent whole, and adolescents understand that they can be both introverted and extroverted with different people and in different situations (Harter, 1988). By this time, adolescents typically understand that it is not only acceptable but actually desirable to show different sides of the self to different people. The number of such opposites peaks in middle adolescence (ninth grade) and then declines through eleventh grade (see Figure 9.1). This decline becomes even more substantial in twelfth grade (Harter & Monsour, 1992).

Figure 9.1

Developmental Differences in Adolescents' Perceptions of Opposing and Conflicting Self-Attributes

Notice the similarity in these graphs. The perception of opposing or conflicting characteristics increases from early to middle adolescence, when it peaks, and it declines later in adolescence as teens are able to integrate these opposites into their conceptions of self.

Source: Harter & Monsour (1992).

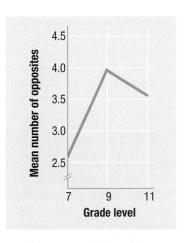

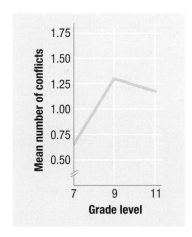

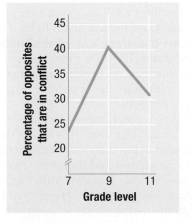

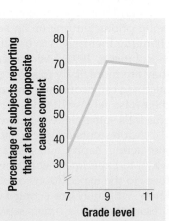

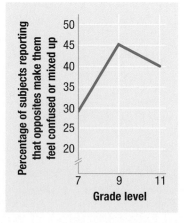

Middle adolescents are bothered by these inconsistencies more than younger or older adolescents. A young adolescent noting that he was nice to friends but not to others explained that it was no problem. "I guess I just think about one thing at a time and don't think about the other until the next day." When asked why opposing attributes did not bother her, one 13-year-old exclaimed, "That's a stupid question. I don't fight with myself!" (Harter, 1990, p. 358).

The comments of a middle adolescent girl (15 years old) differ significantly. She explained her behavior on a date by noting "I hate the fact that I get so nervous! I wish I wasn't so inhibited. The real me is talkative; I just want to be natural, but I can't" (Harter, 1990, p. 358). Another explained how he thought of himself as a happy person and wanted to be that way with everyone, but found he was unhappy around his family and it bothered him, because that was not the way he wanted to be. Older adolescents no longer experience such intense conflict. When asked about this, one older adolescent noted, "Sometimes, it's fun to be rowdy but at other times you just want to be in a quiet mood; you really need to do both with really good friends." Another explained that "You can be shy on a date, and then outgoing with friends because you are just different with different people; you can't always be the same person and probably shouldn't be" (Harter, 1990, p. 358).

A major reason for this integration is the development of the cognitive skills needed to integrate abstractions. The cognitive skills necessary to compare such abstractions emerge in middle adolescence, but the ability to integrate them into an abstract system (seeing oneself as both cheerful and depressed, and thus as moody) does not appear until late adolescence (Fischer, 1980). Many opposites can be represented as meaningful single abstractions. For example, an individual can integrate both extroversion and introversion by adopting the higher-order abstraction of flexibility across social situations. A person can be both smart and dumb if inconsistent academically, and both cheerful and depressed if moody (Harter, 1998). Another way to reduce the conflict is to adopt a philosophical stance that acting differently in different roles is functional and advantageous (Harter, 1990). Late adolescents often believe it would be undesirable to display the same characteristics in different contexts. Consistency within a role may be necessary, but consistency across roles is not. Thus, late adolescents do not see the formation of multiple selves as inconsistent but rather as a necessary and desirable type of discrimination between situations and roles (Vallacher, 1980).

Acting Phony: Which Is My Real Self?

Many adolescents, especially during the middle years, become concerned about which of the contradictions is their "real self" or "the real me" (Harter & Monsour, 1992). They are concerned about being phony and acting falsely—that is, acting in ways that do not reflect their true selves (Harter, 1998). Adolescents' descriptions of their true selves include stating their true opinions, expressing their true feelings, saying what they really think, and acting the way they want to act and not how someone else wants them to act. They describe false selves as being phony, putting on an act, expressing things they don't really believe in, or changing themselves to be what someone else wants them to be (Harter, Stocker, & Robinson, 1996). Adolescents admit that there are some situations in which they are more likely to show false behavior. They are more likely to display their false selves in romantic and dating situations and with classmates than to show their false selves with close friends, whereas the level of false behavior with parents falls somewhere in between (Harter, 1990).

Adolescents may act falsely to make a good impression on others (for example, acting happy and self-assured at an interview when they don't feel that way), to experiment with new roles and behaviors, and because they must conform to the expectations of others to be valued and accepted. Adolescents often know why they are acting falsely. Teens who perceive little support and great pressure to be like others report the greatest amount of false behavior, lower self-esteem, and more depressive symptoms. Adolescents who report acting falsely as a way of experimenting with different roles and behaviors report the least amount of false behavior. Those who report acting falsely to impress others show a moderate amount of false behavior (Harter et al., 1996).

Adolescents are especially distressed when they feel they cannot act or express their true feelings because important people in their lives do not accept them for whom they are. They believe parents will value and support them only if they express opinions that are similar to their parents' opinions. This belief causes adolescents to suppress their real selves. They perceive their parents' acceptance and support as dependent on their being what the parents want them to be, and teens do not see this conditional support as true support (Harter, Marold, & Whitesell, 1992).

Is the Self-Concept Stable?

If you asked 12-year-olds to describe their selves and then asked them again at 15 and 19 years, would you obtain reasonably similar or widely varying descriptions? Studies investigating this question report stability over the long term (Harter, 1998). People are quite resistant to change. They have a vested interest in maintaining their personal theories; they seek information that confirms their self-concept and reject feedback that disconfirms it (Swann, 1987).

Yet there is some evidence that people do modify their self-concept. The degree of modification depends, to some extent, on the part of the self-concept that is being challenged. The more central the characteristic is to the individual, the more resistant it is to change. The less central it is, the easier it is to change. For example, if being a kind person is a basic part of an individual's self-concept, then the person will greet any feedback to the contrary with disbelief or rationalize it away. If being a good athlete is not very important, the individual will accept messages about not being athletic more readily, and that part of the self-concept will be easier to change.

The Real and Ideal Selves

Describe the type of person you would like to be. Describe the kind of person you are now. The self-concept consists of perceptions of one's actual self, but people also create a picture of their ideal self, or what they want to be like and what they want to feel like. In the description at the beginning of the chapter, the 15-year-old was not comfortable with some of her feelings. She wanted to be a cheerful and friendly person all the time.

Improvements in cognitive functioning lead to a new awareness of the difference between the real self and the ideal self. With formal operations comes the ability to think about other possibilities. Teens realize they don't have to act or be what they are; there are many alternatives. They recognize the difference between what they are and what they would like to be, and they often come up short of their own expectations. The greatest disparity exists in physical appearance, which is related to self-esteem. Girls feel less secure about their appearance than boys (Simmons & Blyth, 1987). The differences between the ideal and actual self are larger in middle adolescence than in early or late adolescence (Strachen & Jones, 1982). The humanistic psychologist Carl Rogers argued that a large discrepancy between real and ideal selves in adulthood was a prime indicator of maladjustment. In fact, one of the goals of therapy, according to Rogers, is movement toward the ideal self.

There are other ways of looking at this disparity, though. The widening of the difference between the ideal self and the real self is somewhat typical of adolescence. With age, adolescents may take a more realistic and less positive view of themselves, which results in a greater difference between the real and ideal selves. Also, the ideal self may be not so much what the individual wants to be but rather

The area of greatest disparity between one's ideal self and real self is physical appearance.

At a Glance 9.2 Self-Concept in Adolescence

KEY POINT: The self-concept becomes more differentiated in adolescence, and by the end of adolescence the contradictory parts have been integrated into a coherent self-concept.

SUPPORTING POINTS	EXPLANATION
In adolescence, descriptions of the self change from being concrete to being more abstract.	The self-concept in early adolescence is defined in terms of personality characteristics, emotions, attitudes, and beliefs, some of which are in opposition to others.
The self-concept becomes more differentiated in adolescence.	Adolescents realize that they act differently when interacting with other people and playing different roles (for example, friend or child).
During middle adolescence, contradictions in the descriptions of self become a source of difficulty. During late adolescence, these contradictions are integrated into a coherent sense of self.	During middle adolescence, an awareness of the contradictions in the self leads to fear of appearing or acting phony. During late adolescence, teens can integrate these conflicting parts of their selves; they realize they can act one way with one person and another way with someone else.
The self-concept remains relatively stable during adolescence.	Individuals may modify their self-concepts to some extent. Aspects of the self that are not central to one's self-definition are easier to change.
The ideal self is the individual one would like to be.	The differences between the ideal self and the real self may cause disappointment. The discrepancy is greater in middle adolescence than in early adolescence (when the individual is less aware of it) and in late adolescence (when more integration has occurred).

an almost unobtainable dream. For instance, a teenager who is a good athlete may want to make the varsity squad but may dream of being a great basketball player. Which is the athlete's ideal self? In addition, not all discrepancy is bad. The discrepancy between the real and ideal selves may serve as a motivator to improve. People who think they are exactly what they want to be may become smug (Rosales & Zigler, 1989). Certainly people create goals for themselves that motivate them. *(For a review of this section, see At A Glance 9.2.)*

Self-Esteem
in Adolescence

Self-esteem, or the judgment that an individual places on parts of the self, is related to a number of significant outcomes in both children and adolescents. High self-esteem is related to academic success and to an internal locus of control—a feeling that one is basically in control of one's life (Chubb, Fertman, & Ross, 1997). Teens with high self-esteem are less preoccupied with peer approval and are less susceptible to peer pressure than those with low self-esteem (Thorne & Michaelieu, 1996). High self-esteem is also related to closer, more positive interpersonal relationships (Fullerton & Ursano, 1994). High self-esteem seems to buffer teens against stress and is associated with better coping (Rutter, 1987). People with high self-esteem make mistakes and sometimes fail, but they take these setbacks in stride and strive to learn from their disappointments (Brooks, 1994). Researchers have found a positive relationship between self-esteem and prosocial behavior (doing things for others) beginning in fourth grade (Eisenberg & Fabes, 1994).

Low self-esteem, in contrast, is associated with anxiety and depression (Francis, 1997; McGee, Williams, & Nada-Raja, 2001). When people with low self-esteem face difficult tasks, they may quit, avoid them, cheat, bully others, clown, or make excuses to escape the challenge (Davies & Brember, 1995).

Unfortunately, the relationship between self-esteem and outcomes is not really so simple. First, the relationship between high self-esteem and academic success is positive but relatively low, meaning that it involves other factors (Hansford & Hattie, 1982; Kohn, 1994). Second, when self-esteem is correlated with some positive outcome, we cannot make any statement about cause and effect. Even if some causative relationship exists, there is considerable doubt about the relationship's direction. For example, it may be that high self-esteem has a positive effect on achievement, but it is also possible that doing well in school leads to high self-esteem (Cross, 1997; Kahne, 1996). In fact, some evidence exists that academic performance influences self-esteem even when the effects of gender and race are taken to account (Filozof et al., 1998). Or both may be true: Self-esteem may influence academic performance, and success in academics may influence self-esteem (Davies & Brember, 1995).

Children and adolescents make evaluative judgments in many different areas. Just as the self-concept is multifaceted, so is self-esteem. Profiles of children in elementary school often find that they use such categories as scholastic competence, athletic competence, being liked by peers, physical appearance, and behavior, and children evaluate themselves differently across these domains (Harter, 1998). Even so, individuals possess a general sense of value and worth—an overall global self-esteem. This overall sense of self-esteem is based on how the person performs in domains he or she considers most important. High self-esteem results from performing adequately in areas considered important, and low self-esteem comes from poor performance in very important areas. Performing well in areas not considered very important does not appreciably aid one's overall sense of self-esteem, and doing poorly in these unimportant areas usually does not hurt very much. For example, if being a good mathematician and scientist is an important element of your self, then how you do in math and science classes will affect your self-esteem. If being a good musician is not an important part of your self, then your performance in music class will not have much effect on your self-esteem.

Both William James's ideas about multiple selves and the sociological concept of the self as a reflection of appraisals from others have currency in the study of self-esteem. The self comprises many parts or layers, and as just noted, an adolescent's self-esteem is directly influenced by how adequate the individual feels in the domains where success is important. The concept of reflection of appraisals is supported by evidence showing that adolescents' perceptions of the attitudes of significant others are closely related to global self-esteem (Harter, 1986). Adolescents who feel they are receiving support and positive regard from parents and peers are likely to have high self-esteem. The opinions of other students at school seem to be especially important. Although close friends are influential, adolescents consider the general feedback received from classmates most important. It may be that adolescents expect support and positive feedback from their close friends and parents and believe that classmates are more objective.

Self-esteem may be viewed in two ways. On the one hand, the opinions of others are very important; some argue that our self-concept and self-esteem are really reflections of the appraisals of others. On the other hand, psychologists emphasize the importance of our personal evaluation of aspects of ourselves, such as having a good academic self-concept because we do well in school. These psychologists argue that self-esteem will be affected greatly if the individual values the area of competence. Of course, the opinions of others and personal evaluation may both be important to self-esteem.

Which theoretical idea of self-esteem appeals to teens? In one study, adolescents were asked to endorse one of three orientations to self-esteem: (1) If others approve of me, then I will like myself; (2) If I like myself as a person, then others will like and approve of me; and (3) Neither one makes a difference (Harter et al., 1996). Individuals who agree with the first orientation reflect the importance of others' appraisals. Individuals who agree with the second orientation believe that their own evaluations of competencies influence how others view them, and individuals endorsing the third view do not agree with either of the two previous orientations. The researchers asked young adolescents in middle school to choose which orientation they agreed with and then to write an example of something that happened to them to make them feel that way. Table 9.1 shows some of the statements. The greatest number of adolescents endorsed the "no connection" idea, followed by the reflected appraisals orientation and finally the self-worth orientation. There were no gender differences. When the researchers asked teachers to rate how much each student was distracted from schoolwork because of a competing focus on peers, they rated the reflected appraisal group as significantly more distracted; this group also showed greater fluctuations in self-worth, had lower levels of self-esteem, and had a lower level of approval from others.

Adolescents who emphasize the importance of receiving approval from others were found to be likely to focus on negative evaluations, whereas those in the group in which self-worth precedes approval were more likely to report positive evaluations by others. Those who are always looking for others to tell them how to feel are more likely to seek out these appraisals, which often are not positive and lead to poorer self-esteem. Other problems that accompany the reflected appraisal perspective include being more preoccupied with peer approval and more vulnerable to changes in self-worth. Of course, this study focuses on ado-

---

Table 9.1

Examples of Adolescents' Open-Ended Descriptions for Each of Three Orientations to Self-Esteem

The following statements written by adolescents can be categorized under three different orientations to self-esteem.

Approval Precedes Self-Worth

When I meet new kids and they approve of me, then I look at myself and say, 'I'm not so bad,' and it makes me feel good."

"They made fun of my clothes. Then I felt stupid like I was an idiot and didn't like myself."

"When other kids make you feel left out you don't feel good about yourself."

"When people praise everything you do, then you start to really like yourself as a person."

"If other people don't like me as a person, then I wonder if I am a good person. I care about what people say about me."

Self-Worth Precedes Approval

"You have to appreciate yourself first, as a person. If you wait for other people to make you feel good, you could be waiting for a long time."

"In seventh grade I didn't like myself as a person, so I didn't have very many friends, but then in eighth grade, I felt confident about myself and then I found that I had many more friends."

"I just like myself, and then other people like me too."

"When I like the way I look, other kids say good and nice things about me."

"The way I figure it, if you can't like the person you are first, then how do you expect other people to like you?"

No Connection Between Approval and Self-Worth

"When a classmate cuts me down, I really don't care."

"I really don't care if someone doesn't like me because it's their problem."

"Well, somebody said I was stupid. Go ahead, let them think I'm stupid, who cares!"

"The popular people were mean to me, but I kept my head high and ignored it, because I like the way I am, it's me."

"If someone doesn't like me, they can't make me feel bad if I'm confident enough about myself. What they think doesn't matter."

Source: Harter, Stocker, & Robinson (1996), p. 293.

lescents' perception of their orientation. Furthermore, although the vast majority who claimed to be in one orientation wrote stories demonstrating these beliefs, it is reasonable to ask whether those who said they really don't care about what others think truly do not care. In any case, this study does indicate that there are certainly liabilities to believing that one's self-esteem is based on the evaluations of others.

Trends in Self-Esteem

Researchers have noted a number of interesting trends in self-esteem among adolescents (Chubb et al., 1997). Groups of teens followed for a relatively long period show moderate stability in self-esteem (O'Malley & Bachman, 1983). Adolescents with high self-esteem are likely to continue to show high self-esteem, and those with low self-esteem will probably continue to show low self-esteem (Alsaker & Olweus, 1992; Simmons & Blyth, 1987). When researchers followed individual teens when they were between 14 and 18 years and then from 18 to 23 years, individuals with relatively high or low self-esteem at age 14 tended to be the same at ages 18 and 23 (Block & Robins, 1993). Even so, the majority of participants showed some, but not a dramatic, change in self-esteem. Individuals who show improvements in self-esteem manifest greater competence in domains considered important and receive more social approval from others. Those whose self-esteem declines report a perception of reduced competence in valued domains and less social support. Those who show no changes or minimal changes in self-esteem show neither pattern (Harter, 1998). In one survey, about half the adolescents showed considerable stability, whereas the remaining participants were less stable (Demo & Savin-Williams, 1992).

Another trend is an increase in global self-esteem as teens move into middle and later adolescence, which reverses a trend toward lower self-esteem that starts in middle childhood (McCarthy & Hoge, 1982). During the early childhood period, children are relatively inaccurate in their judgments of their abilities. In fact, despite their failures, young children often continue to believe they have ability in an area and retain very high expectations and even unrealistic beliefs (Cole, 1991). This tendency results from a failure to differentiate the wish to be competent and the reality of how one is doing. Children in early childhood also are less sensitive to the evaluations of others and are less likely to meet with failure, probably because they are rarely compared with others. This characteristic is one reason why young children have exceptionally high self-esteem and a positive self-concept.

In elementary school, however, children's estimates of themselves become more realistic. Elementary school children become more aware of their successes and failures, and these outcomes affect their self-esteem. These children sometimes compare their abilities with those of others and find they do not compare well (Harter, 1993a, 1993b). This greater realism and accuracy in judging performance translate into a decline in self-esteem (Crain, 1996; Davies & Brember, 1995).

Self-esteem continues to decline in early adolescence (ages 11 to 13), as adolescents' self-evaluations become even less positive (Wigfield et al., 1991). Self-esteem reaches its low point between 12 and 13 years (Harter, 1990). This decline in self-esteem at the beginning of adolescence is found across socioeconomic groups and ethnic/racial groups, including blacks, Latinos, and whites (Seidman et al., 1994).

Why does this decline in self-esteem occur? The transition to middle or junior high school, with its greater social pressures, competition, stricter standards, less personal attention, and disruption in social networks results in a general lowering of self-esteem (Simmons, Rosenberg, & Rosenberg, 1973). In one study, 12-year-olds who began junior high school had lower self-esteem than their age peers who were still in elementary school. When the researchers measured the self-esteem of students beginning in sixth grade and continuing through seventh grade, they found that students' self-esteem fell right after the

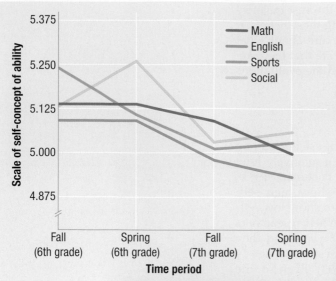

Figure 9.2
Changes in Young Adolescents' Self-Concepts of Ability for Different Activities
Young adolescents who change from sixth grade in an elementary school to seventh grade in a junior high or middle school show declines in feelings of competence in math, English, sports, and social interactions. Notice that feelings of competence in math and English seem not to improve, whereas student estimations of their ability in social interactions and athletics do improve somewhat.
Source: Wigfield et al. (1991), p. 558.

The transition to junior high school causes a general lowering of self-esteem, as students must make so many new adjustments.

transition to middle school (see Figure 9.2) (Wigfield et al., 1991). In sixth grade, the students were the oldest students in the school and had the most status. They also were accustomed to the elementary school routine. In seventh grade, in contrast, these students were the youngest in the school and had to adjust to a new environment, which may partially explain the decline in self-esteem in seventh grade (shown in Figure 9.2 as the fall of seventh grade). The students' self-esteem increased during the second part of seventh grade in some areas such as sports and social areas. Students making the transition to middle school showed a decline in their feelings of competence in English and math, with some rebound in social self-confidence. As the students made and cemented new relationships, their confidence rose somewhat but had not returned to the sixth-grade level. Some never regain their confidence (Simmons & Blyth, 1987). The reduction in self-esteem may also be partially due to the biological and cognitive changes associated with early adolescence (Leahy & Shirk, 1985). Young adolescents' perception of their physical competence is lower in seventh grade than in sixth grade; it improves somewhat in the later part of seventh grade, but it is still far below the sixth-grade mark.

A more detailed look at the students who gained and lost self-esteem during the transition to middle school shows that they matched the predictions of James's theory. Changes may occur in the domains considered important to the adolescent. Indeed, evaluations of physical appearance and social abilities become more important than at earlier ages, and both decline. However, students whose self-esteem increased during this transition showed increases in competence in domains that they now considered more important, such as the physical and social; those who showed a decline in self-esteem showed a decrease in competence in the areas they considered most important, as well as a lack of social support. Students who showed no changes or minimal changes in self-esteem showed minimal changes in these areas. Another possible reason for the decline in self-esteem is that with the transition to adolescence comes an expansion of social networks and many more judgments and comparisons, some of which are critical (Harter, 1990).

Global self-esteem and domain-specific evaluations gradually become more positive over the course of adolescence. Carefully conducted longitudinal studies reveal gradual improvements in self-esteem from the end of early adolescence through grade 12 (McCarthy & Hoge, 1982; O'Malley & Bachman, 1983). One possible reason for the gradual increase in self-esteem is that as adolescents negotiate this period, they become more sure of themselves and their relationships with others, as well as more comfortable with their newfound abilities and the challenges of the period.

Many psychologists believe that the greater personal autonomy and freedom that come with increasing age may also lead to the increase in self-esteem found in middle and late adolescence. Teenagers assert that with time, they have become more capable, mature, and personable, and they find some of their negative emotional, cognitive, and personality characteristics diminished (Hart, Fegley, & Brengelman, 1993). As people age, they also choose more of their own activities—perhaps the activities that are most important to them. They tend to choose activities in which they are more competent and that promote self-esteem, and they choose to interact with people who are more reinforcing (Harter, 1990).

A final trend in self-esteem is that males generally show higher self-esteem than females, especially after early adolescence (Knox et al., 1998; Quatman & Watson, 2001). Girls show a decline in self-esteem somewhat earlier than boys, perhaps because girls experience their pubertal transition earlier and show greater dissatisfaction in body image (Hoffmann, 2002). Furthermore, more girls than boys report low self-esteem during middle and late adolescence (Chubb et al., 1997). Some studies find that the self-esteem of boys increases, whereas the self-esteem of girls does not recover from the loss in the transition to junior high (Blyth, Simmons, & Carlton-Ford, 1983). Self-esteem in males increases from early adolescence to early adulthood, but many—although certainly not all—females fail to show such increases. The gender gap in self-esteem seems to widen with age between 14 and 23 years (Block & Robins, 1993). Those who make the earliest school transitions suffer the greatest losses in self-esteem and do not recover during the high school years (Brooks-Gunn & Petersen, 1983; Simmons & Blyth, 1987). Early-maturing girls fare the worst. Although most people agree with these research findings, they are open to another interpretation: It may be that boys tend to be somewhat more boastful and girls more modest in public statements about their self-esteem. Studies of self-esteem rely on

PERSPECTIVE 1

I Just Can't Do It

SETTING THE SCENE: Margaret is an eighth grader with a problem. For a number of years her teachers have commented on what they see as her poor self-image and poor self-esteem. Margaret puts herself down and gives up easily. She is basically a cheerful person, is a very good friend, and does not seem overly prone to depression. However, she focuses more on what she sees as her weaknesses than on her strengths. She is one of five children and has a good relationship with her parents.

ELENA (MARGARET'S BEST FRIEND): Margaret is so pretty and smart. She gets good grades, is artistic, and everyone likes her, but she never accepts a compliment. She doesn't seem to like herself. She believes that whatever she can do well is easy and unimportant, and she's always comparing herself with others, thinking others are prettier or smarter. I don't know what to do.

MARGARET: I'm OK, but Elena is prettier and has a better personality, and lots of the girls are smarter than I am. I don't think I'm anyone special. I'm just average in everything. I don't understand why people are concerned.

QUESTION: In your opinion, does Margaret have a problem? If you think she does and you were her friend, parent, or teacher, how would you deal with her "low" self-esteem?

individual ratings of self or public statements to interviewers, and girls may be raised to be somewhat less boastful. Even if this interpretation is partly true, most researchers believe the gender difference is real.

Boys have higher self-evaluations of their physical abilities, appearance, and math ability, whereas girls have higher self-evaluations of verbal and reading abilities, along with total school performance. The main reason for this disparity in self-esteem centers on body image. Physical appearance correlates highly with self-esteem for both genders. In early childhood and the early years of elementary school, both boys and girls evaluate their appearance positively. Then, beginning in fourth grade, a decline occurs for girls; it continues so that by the end of high school, girls' evaluations of their appearance are much lower than those of boys (Allgood-Merten, Lewinsohn, & Hops, 1990). A combination of factors may cause this disparity, as discussed in "Physical Development," but greater social emphasis on physical appearance and the media's focus on body image (especially trying to meet what is an impossible body image for females) may be two important factors.

The decline in global self-esteem in early adolescence is not as great as the decline in perceived self-esteem for appearance, so other factors must lift self-esteem somewhat. Self-esteem is particularly low for females who say they base their self-esteem on appearance, which males tend to assess more positively than do females (Thorne & Michaelieu, 1996). This difference may also result from varying messages about adequacy sent to males and females (Chubb et al., 1997). Perhaps society values the more stereotyped competencies of males and devalues the female emphasis on caring and helping.

In late adolescence, body image still strongly influences self-esteem (Mendel-son, Mendelson, & Andrews, 2000). Toward the end of college, or sometimes in the graduate school years, most students learn to value themselves and others using a measuring rod that has less to do with looks and more to do with character and achievement. Sixty percent of adolescents questioned reported that self-perceptions of their appearance affect their self-esteem, and the remaining 40 percent reported that self-esteem affects their view of how they look (Harter, 1993a, 1993b). Focusing on physical appearance causes difficulty for female teens whose appearance determines self-worth, and these adolescent females report more negative evaluations of their appearance, lower self-esteem, and more depression than people who do not consider appearance as central to their self-worth.

Self-esteem depends heavily on reassurance by others that the adolescent is worthwhile. Only when youths know and accept who they are, regardless of their looks and comparisons with others, will they attain an inner sense of worth that is no longer dependent on how they appear to others. They must reconstruct the ideal self in more realistic terms by taking account of their own strengths and weaknesses (Godenne, 1997).

Self-Esteem in Adolescents from Minority Groups

A belief persists among educators that the self-esteem of African Americans is lower than that of other groups, but this is simply not true. The self-esteem of African American youth is equal to or even greater than European Americans (Gray-Little & Hafdahl, 2000; Twenge & Crocker, 2002). When the self-esteem of African American, Latino, and Native American adolescents is measured, African Americans have the highest and Native Americans, the lowest (Filozof et al., 1998).

How can we explain the finding that, despite encounters with prejudice and achievement differences in school favoring the majority group, African American adolescents as a group do not show lower self-esteem? Perhaps other areas of functioning compensate for any school-related achievement problems. Indeed, there is a stronger correlation between school grades and self-esteem among European Americans than among African Americans (Cross, 1985). People tend to value areas in which they have had consistent success, and some African

Americans may base their self-esteem on other areas in which they have had success. This does not mean that an individual who has experienced considerble difficulty in academic areas is unaffected by these problems, only that other areas can sometimes compensate for difficulties in one particular area.

Another possibility is that the African American community may actively filter out destructive racist messages and offer positive feedback about other abilities. The processes underlying self-esteem formation among African American adolescents are no different from those among white adolescents. Self-esteem depends on the attitudes of parents, friends, and peers, as well as the adolescents' evaluations of their own experiences. This positive feedback from people so close to them may counter the effects of the more negative messages from other areas of the adolescent's environment.

Little research has been conducted on the self-esteem of Latinos and Native Americans, and more research is certainly needed. Latinos, especially those who have immigrated to the United States recently, may find that their ideals, beliefs, and culture are less valued here. These circumstances, along with difficulties in school, may cause problems in self-esteem. Native Americans' cultural attitudes and beliefs differ radically from those of mainstream America, which leads to lower evaluations from society.

Self-Esteem: Can There Be Too Much of a Good Thing?

Most psychologists agree that high self-esteem—that is, valuing, liking, and accepting oneself—is good. High levels of self-esteem are related to a host of positive behaviors, whereas low self-esteem is related to undesirable behaviors (Salmivalli, 2001). At one time, having an exaggerated, unrealistically high level of self-esteem was considered healthy and related to mental health. This view came from research showing that people who are depressed or have low self-esteem have more accurate perceptions of their selves than people who are not depressed. This finding led some to conclude that people who engage in self-enhancing positive illusions are better adjusted (Taylor & Brown, 1988). It did not matter if the positive self-esteem was based on any actions, ideas, or characteristics reflected in the person's actual behavior; just feeling good about oneself was considered important, even if the feeling was not based on anything real.

Within the past decade or so, though, psychologists have discovered negative effects of exaggerated or unstable high self-esteem (Colvin, Block, & Funder, 1995). In some situations, high self-esteem is related to defensiveness, egocentrism, and even violence (Schimel et al., 2000).

Self-Esteem and Aggression   One of the first challenges to the idea that the higher the self-esteem the better was based on the observation that many aggressive adolescents appear confident, and even arrogant, to the outside world and accept themselves and their behaviors (Baumeister, 1997). Aggressive children and adolescents often have idealized and inflated ratings of their own competence. After reviewing the literature, Baumeister and colleagues (1996) suggested that violence may result when overly positive views of the self are threatened by others. Some people with high self-esteem seem vulnerable to threats, and these threats lead to a violent defensive reaction.

Bushman and Baumeister (1998) clarified the issue. Undergraduate psychology students were told that researchers were studying how people react to positive and negative feedback. The participants were asked to write an essay on abortion, which was to be evaluated by another participant considered the "partner." All participants then saw what they thought was their partner's essay—either a pro-choice or a pro-life essay. Actually, there was only one version of each essay, but each participant was led to believe that his or her own partner had written it. The researchers then returned the essay that each participant had written with the researchers' comments, although they led the participants to believe these comments were from their partners. The comments were either wonderfully positive ("No suggestions, great essay") or terribly critical ("This is

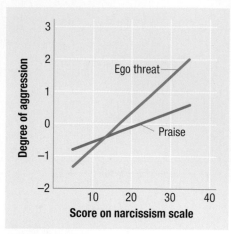

Figure 9.3

The Relationship Between Narcissism and Aggression for Participants Who Received Either a Positive or a Negative Evaluation
As their narcissism scores increased, participants showed increasing degrees of aggression both in the ego threat and praise conditions, but the larger increase was in the ego threat condition.

Source: Bushman & Baumeister (1998), p. 223.

one of the worst essays I have read"), based on nothing but a flip of the coin. Some participants received praise and some criticism. The partners then entered into a simple competition in which they had to press a button as fast as they could when shown a stimulus. The faster partner could administer to the loser a blast of noise between 60 decibels and 105 decibels (or no noise, if desired) and keep it on for as much or as little time as desired.

Undergraduates who scored high on the scale of **narcissism**—that is, extreme and grandiose self-love—and who received criticism (a threat to their self-esteem) showed significantly more aggressive behavior than participants scoring lower on the narcissism scale. Participants scoring high on the scale of narcissism were aggressive under both conditions—the threat (criticism) and the ego boost (positive evaluation)—but they were significantly more aggressive when they received the threat than the praise (see Figure 9.3). People with grandiose images of themselves have a considerable emotional investment in maintaining these images. Researchers argue that this "threatened egotism" is one cause of aggression. Low self-esteem was not related to aggression. Similarly, high self-esteem as measured on the standard measuring instrument, when defined simply as having a favorable opinion of oneself, was not related to aggression. (Scoring high on the narcissism scale, in contrast, involves passionately wanting to think well of oneself.) Some people can brush off criticism easily, and others view it as valid and well deserved; in neither of these cases will aggression result. However, people who are preoccupied with validating and maintaining a grandiose self-image find criticism upsetting and lash out at others.

This study and others may demonstrate the dangers of an inflated self-esteem that comes not from actual achievement but from teachers and parents continually telling children how great they are no matter what they do or say (Begley, 1998). These children then develop unrealistic opinions of themselves. When these children face an outside world that rejects this self-image, hostility, anger, and aggression may result. These adolescents become supersensitive to criticism and slights, and on some level they may suspect that their feelings of superiority are based on nothing.

Inflated self-esteem is certainly not the only influence on aggression, as we will see in "Drug Use and Violence." However, when the real world fails to deliver the praise that individuals with inflated self-esteem need, when rejection occurs (perhaps by a girlfriend or boyfriend), or when the person is taunted, an explosion may occur. Some people with unreasonably high self-esteem cannot tolerate frustration. When people with very high exaggerated self-esteem are criticized, their self-esteem is threatened, and their negative reactions may cause others to see them as antagonistic, rude, uncooperative, fake, unfriendly, and arrogant. Two other conditions contribute to these unsettling behavioral patterns: having unstable self-esteem and having self-esteem not connected to anything real.

Unstable Self-Esteem Unstable self-esteem—short-term fluctuations in global self-evaluation—is related to anger and interpersonal problems (Kernis et al., 1993). Adolescents with unstable self-esteem may be more insecure and sensitive to negative feedback. Their high self-esteem is fragile and easily threatened. People with a stable sense of self-esteem are not as threatened by negative feedback and are more secure.

The importance of stability in self-esteem was shown in a study using the experimental sampling method. Students carried beepers and were told that when they received a signal, they were to complete a quick self-feelings inventory. This measuring instrument consisted of twenty words denoting positive feelings, such as *confident* or *happy,* and negative feelings, such as *frustrated* or *unloved* (Kernis et al., 1993). Students with unstable high self-esteem, as measured by shifts in their feelings about themselves, were more likely to experience anger than students with stable high or low self-esteem. Kernis and colleagues attribute this to the existence of a positive, but fragile, self view. Anger served a protective function, allowing them to deny the threat.

narcissism Extreme, grandiose self-love.

Why is the self-esteem of some people so fragile? Fragile self-esteem may develop if self-esteem is not based on inner qualities or long-term achievements but rather on daily achievements and immediate feedback from others (Kernis, Grannemann, & Barclay, 1989; Schimel et al., 2000). People with fragile self-esteem must prove themselves every day. They are constantly challenged by comments or events that destabilize their self-esteem. They are so concerned about winning approval from others and living up to standards that they become defensive.

Baseless Inflated Self-Esteem   Self-esteem that does not seem to be based on anything may also lead to difficulties (Gresham et al., 2000). One study measured self-enhancement at 18 years by comparing self-descriptions of participants with descriptions obtained from peers and trained examiners (Colvin et al., 1995). Self-enhanced individuals—that is, those who viewed themselves much more highly than others did—were less popular.

Others described self-enhanced males as guileful, deceitful, distrustful, and having a rigid defense system. Self-enhanced females were seen as rigid, self-centered, and thin skinned. Self-enhanced individuals were deemed less well adjusted. They were also seen as more hostile and less likeable, especially when challenged on some aspect of their performance. This high self-esteem may be a defense against feelings of worthlessness or self-doubt. Individuals whose self-appraisals are more favorable than objective criteria would indicate may be vulnerable to threatening feedback (Baumeister, Smart, & Boden, 1996).

Causes of Inflated Self-Esteem   Why do some people develop an inflated sense of self-esteem? One hypothesis is that parents, perhaps because of their own insecurities, have an idealized image of how their children should be—that is, engaging and brilliant. When their children perform to these expectations, the parents give them warmth and love; when they fail to reach the expectations, the parents replace warmth and love with rejection and restrictions. The children realize that parental affection depends on social performance, and this realization produces feelings of self-doubt, insecurity, and anger that cannot be expressed, as it would lead to a loss of love from parents. The children thus avoid the self-doubt and manage their feelings by adopting a view of themselves that involves glory, success, power, or wisdom; they put on an act for everyone, often showing dominance of others, which leads to self-esteem. Grandiosity protects the self from doubt and depression (Raskin, Novacek, & Hogan, 1991). Indeed, people who score high on the scale of narcissism are often domineering.

High self-esteem may be considered healthy if it reflects an individual's actual acceptance of, and liking for, various aspects of the self. Unhealthy, or false, self-esteem involves high self-esteem that is inflated, that leads to beliefs in a person's overall superiority, or that is not based on any external verification. False self-esteem is held together by a defensive refusal to believe anything negative about oneself and is marked by a need for constant attention and self-enhancement (Salmivalli, 2001). This view of inflated self-esteem does not challenge the relationships between high self-esteem and positive outcomes or the findings that high self-esteem generally is preferable to low self-esteem. However, it does demonstrate that there is a group of adolescents and adults with high self-esteem that is grandiose, unstable, or not based on anything real who show emotional and behavioral problems.

Self-Esteem, the Self-Concept, and Cognitive Development

The changes in the adolescent's view of the self and developmental changes in self-esteem demonstrate that adolescents are taking a more mature view of the self. The adolescent's self-concept is more differentiated and more abstract than it was. Some aspects of life—for example, social and physical aspects—become more important. Accepting oneself is not common, at least until late adolescence.

It is no coincidence that a greater acceptance of self occurs at the same time that the contradictions in the self are integrated into a coherent sense of self, for developments in cognitive functioning may underlie both.

According to Jean Piaget, adolescents enter the stage of formal operations, during which they develop new cognitive abilities (see "Cognitive Development") (Inhelder & Piaget, 1958). The most important development involves the ability to understand and use abstractions. The change in self from concrete ("I am tall") to more abstract ("I am compassionate") results from this ability to form abstractions. In addition, understanding abstractions allows adolescents to think about philosophical ideas concerning the meaning of life and what one believes in. This ability allows for greater introspection into the self and, as we will shortly see, the development of a personal identity.

Another major cognitive change is the emergence of the ability to separate the real from the possible. Adolescents can think about other realities, which allows them to explore new ideas and roles. This ability also enables adolescents to differentiate their real self from their ideal self and perhaps take action to reduce the discrepancy. For example, an adolescent who feels selfish but whose ideal self includes giving to others may now volunteer at a homeless shelter. The ability to see other paths also enables adolescents to consider different possibilities for their future.

Adolescents can also think about their own thoughts; that is, they become more aware of their thought processes and of the origin and development of their ideas and behaviors. This leads to greater awareness of the self. Adolescents become more aware of the contradictions in their thoughts about themselves and their behavior, especially in middle adolescence. Eventually they integrate these contradictions, realizing that it is reasonable to act one way with friends and another with family. They privately study their thoughts about the self and evaluations of different aspects of the self.

Another formal operational skill is the ability to use hypothetical-deductive logic. This ability allows adolescents to think more logically and to critically analyze arguments to detect their strengths and weaknesses. Combined with other formal operational abilities, this more rational thought process allows more competent exploration of different identities. For example, adolescents who are more aware of their own thoughts and who are capable of analyzing experiences and opportunities will find identity exploration easier.

As adolescents become better able to use formal operational abilities, they rely more on rational reasoning than experiential reasoning. Experiential reasoning involves using "gut" feelings to guide one's understanding of events, whereas rational reasoning involves more logically thinking through an interpretation of events. One study gave adolescents various measures of critical thinking, reasoning style, and identity formation (Klaczynski, Fauth, & Swanger, 1998). For example, an item on the reasoning style questionnaire was "When it comes to trusting people, I can usually rely on my 'gut' feelings," which demonstrates experiential reasoning; another item stated, "I prefer my life to be filled with puzzles that I must solve," which is related to more rational reasoning. Adolescents who use rational processes showed greater progress in developing their identity.

The ability to use formal operations paves the way for adolescents to systematically evaluate their future goals to make certain they are compatible with their abilities, personality, and motivation. The ability to better integrate the complex feedback from others and from personal experiences encourages the development of a more realistic view of the self. Formal operational abilities are important for identity achievement, because future-oriented decisions, such as what college to apply to and what career meets their personal needs, require rational analysis and critical thinking. Adolescents who are further along in developing their identity are also more cognitively advanced in formal operational abilities (Boyes & Chandler, 1992).

Formal operational abilities develop gradually. As adolescents gain experience using these abilities, they can better evaluate the feedback from others and become somewhat less sensitive to moment-to-moment environmental changes. Late adolescents show greater understanding of what they want to be like, what they want to stand for, and what aspects of their self they value most. They are more likely to integrate the many aspects of their self into a coherent sense of who they are and where they are going.

Improving Self-Esteem

High self-esteem (although not exaggerated self-esteem) is related to many positive outcomes. The research finding that self-esteem declines in early adolescence and then increases (but perhaps never reaches the positive childhood level) leads to questions about how to improve self-esteem. Perhaps the best way to help foster self-esteem is to create an environment at home and at school that reinforces the probability of success and to attribute this success to the adolescent's efforts and motivation. As noted in "The School Experience," adolescents believe that ability is much more important to success than is effort. Showing how effort can allow an individual to succeed despite having average ability can certainly help.

Self-esteem is maximized when adolescents have a degree of choice, personal control, and responsibility as they develop a feeling that they are contributing to the home, school, and community (Brooks, 1994). They can find success in many areas. Few people are competent at everything, but every person has some areas of competence that can be reinforced.

Parental support that involves approval and acceptance is associated with higher self-esteem and a sense that one can be loved even while thinking differently from parents (Feiring & Taska, 1996). Unfortunately, however, as children mature into adolescence and proceed through the period, they perceive their parents' opinions of them as more negative than they really are (Oosterwegel & Oppenheimer, 1993). Adolescents often perceive an absence of positive feedback as a negative appraisal. Again, it is difficult to interpret the direction of effects here. Appraisals from others may lead to negative or positive self-evaluations, but self-evaluations may drive the perceptions of what others are saying. Adolescents' self-esteem may influence how they evaluate other people's statements. Those with low self-esteem may deny compliments that do not reflect their own evaluations of their behavior, or expect negative appraisals and consider even neutral appraisals as criticism.

Formal, often school-based, programs that aim to help students improve their self-esteem usually involve efforts to improve either their self-worth or self-efficacy and take two different approaches. One approach advocates helping teens feel better about themselves and who they are by giving them positive feedback about the abilities they have and making them feel that they are worthwhile people despite not always being successful. This approach, as reasonable as it sounds, has not had much success for a variety of reasons. First, many teens with low self-esteem perceive everything negatively and may not take compliments well. Second, many of their successes may be in areas they do not value as much as the areas they perceive as their weaknesses. Complimenting teens on doing well in math is fine, but if their lack of self-esteem is due to their inability to succeed interpersonally, the compliments will have little effect. Third, some people taking this approach often use effusive praise, which teens may view with suspicion, and praise about poor performance may interfere with skill building.

The second approach concentrates on giving teens the skills they require to succeed in areas they believe are important. Skill theorists argue that self-esteem is based on real achievements, as well as that teaching adolescents the skills to succeed and their subsequent success raise their self-esteem. These programs are based on teaching social and academic skills and have a cognitive basis. They are significantly more effective than what skill theorists often deride as the "feel good" approach (Hattie, 1992; Strein, 1988). Perhaps skill-based programs are targeting narrower areas and have goals that are better defined. However, their

AT A GLANCE   9.3 SELF-ESTEEM IN ADOLESCENCE

KEY POINT: High self-esteem is related to many positive outcomes, but high unstable self-esteem or self-esteem bordering on narcissism leads to negative outcomes.

SUPPORTING POINTS	EXPLANATION
High self-esteem is related to many positive outcomes, and low self-esteem is related to many negative outcomes.	High self-esteem is related to better interpersonal relations and better academic achievement. Low self-esteem is related to lack of persistence on tasks and poor academic performance.
Evidence points to moderate stability in self-esteem.	Adolescents who enter adolescence with higher self-esteem tend to stay that way. Some adolescents, though, show a decline or increase in self-esteem.
Developmental changes in self-esteem are commonly found.	Longitudinal studies of children, as a group, find a decrease in the absolute level of self-esteem during the transition to early adolescence. Self-esteem generally increases through middle and late adolescence.
Males generally show higher self-esteem than females after early adolescence.	Female adolescents base more of their self-esteem on their physical appearance and body image, and females are more critical of their body image than are males.
African American youth have self-esteem at least equal to that of adolescents from European backgrounds.	Minority youth may find some areas of self-esteem more important than do youth from European backgrounds. Parents of minority group children and adolescents may counter negative images of their group.
Recent studies find behavioral difficulties in people with inflated self-esteem.	People whose high self-esteem is unstable, who have narcissistic tendencies, or whose self-esteem is not based on their accomplishments or their real personality attributes tend to be seen as phony and shallow; they are also defensive, hostile, and aggressive.

success is also narrow; that is, raising academic self-esteem does not seem to raise self-esteem in any other areas. This, again, agrees with James's ideas about the multidimensionality of the self and self-esteem.

Perhaps both approaches may be necessary to raise self-esteem. To be successful, strategies must be directed toward areas of greatest importance to the individual. For example, teaching academic skills may be required, followed by positive feedback from significant others. Parents and siblings are often too critical in their evaluations, and as noted, their neutral evaluations are often interpreted as criticism. The evaluations of classmates are not under parental control, but it is hoped that changes in the adolescent's behavior and skills lead to improved feedback from classmates.

Attempts to improve self-esteem require consistency and time. An individual's low self-esteem was not created overnight, after all, and we should expect attempts to raise it to take considerable time and effort. *(For a review of this section, see At A Glance 9.3.)*

IDENTITY

Who am I? Where do I belong? Where am I going? These three questions typify the adolescents' search for a personal identity (Ruittenbeck, 1964). Erik Erikson (1950, 1968) saw the positive outcome of adolescence as the formation of a solid, personal **ego identity,** whereas the negative outcome of adolescence is an aimlessness known as **role confusion** (the state of not knowing who

ego identity   The sense of knowing who you are, which is the positive outcome of adolescence in Erikson's psychosocial theory.

role confusion   In psychosocial theory, the negative outcome of adolescence, which involves feelings of aimlessness and a failure to develop a personal identity.

one really is). An individual experiences a solid identity as a sense of psychosocial well-being, a feeling of being at home with one's own body, a sense of knowing where one is going, and a sense of confidence. Two central components of identity include finding a vocational identity and developing a personal ideology (that is, central values, spiritual beliefs, and a philosophy) (Erikson, 1950).

The self-concept is part of an identity, but identity is much more. The self-descriptions of adolescents reveal the self in terms of specific attributes, but identity encompasses the general roles teens will adopt within the society when they become adults. In adolescence, especially late adolescence, the self-portrait shifts to "a larger canvas where broad brush strokes are used to define occupational and gender identities and religious and political identities" (Harter, 1990, p. 376).

Many psychologists look at identity as a single, coherent entity—a global identity. Others view identity as having many parts, including a personal identity, religious identity, occupational identity, interpersonal identity, and racial/ethnic identity. An individual may be well along in forming one of these identities and not very far in developing another (Meeus & Dekovic, 1995). Most people agree on the principal areas of identity formation: career; religious/moral; political and philosophical; and adopting a set of social roles, including a gender role (Waterman, 1984).

Most identity domains allow the individual some control and choice. For instance, vocational choice, choice of a political or religious ideology, and ways of relating to others are largely under one's control. Some domains, such as gender, race, or ethnicity are assigned, but individuals develop a sense of personal meaning about these domains as well (Grotevant, 1998).

Identity formation involves choosing from conflicting alternatives. A person cannot be both a doctor and an engineer at the same time. An individual cannot be both a liberal and a conservative on the same issue or both a believer and a nonbeliever in a particular religious theology (Harter, 1990). As people make choices, they discard some ideas and roles. Identities help people maintain a sense of personal continuity over past, present, and future. The task of identity formation is broader than the formation of a coherent self, for identity formation also requires consolidating social roles into a coherent sense of identity, not merely listing attributes of the self. Identities must take the larger context into account. Having a sense of self precedes the establishment of an identity, and a solid sense of self is a necessary, but not a sufficient, condition for formulating an identity (Marcia, 1994).

The resolution of Erikson's earlier stages contributes to the development of a sense of identity in adolescence. The sense of trust developed in infancy allows for a faith in people. The sense of autonomy helps develop a feeling that one can make personal choices. A feeling of industry leads to a sense of competence about one's work and accomplishments (Shapiro & Kalogerakis, 1997).

Our identity provides a structure for understanding who we are. A person who identifies himself as a liberal labels himself in that way and identifies with liberal causes; a person who identifies herself as a conservative labels herself in that manner. An identity also provides meaning and direction through commitments, values, and goals. An individual who sees himself as a social worker has a different commitment and goals than a person who sees herself as an owner of a small business. An identity also allows for consistency, creating a harmony between values and behavior. For instance, an identity as a parent is accompanied by a number of important responsibilities and values, and it clearly adds to one's sense of commitment.

Individuals who see themselves as liberals or conservatives will identify with such causes, and this identification becomes part of their identities.

Once individuals have formed their identity in late adolescence, this identity may influence how they view themselves, how they process information, and how they behave (Marcia, 1994). For instance, a conservative political identity influences how the individual interprets issues, such as the cause of crime and what to do about it. Such an identity would also influence voting behavior.

Western societies recognize adolescence as the period of identity formation and as a time for searching for, and experimenting with, new identities. In more traditional societies, rites of passage confirm the change to a culturally pre-scribed identity (Marcia, 1994). Neither type of society is very supportive of identity crises in adulthood, as both expect individuals to accomplish much of their identity work during adolescence. Like the development of the self-concept, identity formation requires a balance between being unique and distinctive on the one hand and remaining connected with others on the other hand.

Theories of Identity Formation

Many theoretical perspectives offer a view of identity formation. Psychoanalytic thinkers argue that achieving an identity is part of the process by which a person resolves emotional conflicts with parents by breaking away from them. Identity, then, reflects the separation process and the need to become an individual (Blos, 1962). Many social psychologists believe that becoming self-aware motivates us to see ourselves as unique and to find new and individualistic ways of relating to others. Putting the two theories together, we might say that self-awareness, distress, discomfort, confronting the ideas of others, and resolving the resultant differences are the mechanisms for change. Identification with others and imitation can influence identity formation as well. Other psychologists emphasize the importance of cognitive changes that heighten self-awareness and lead to incongruent thoughts and feelings. Adolescents realize they are not their parents, yet they are not completely different. To achieve coherence and balance, both differentiation and integration are necessary (Adams & Marshall, 1996). Each of these approaches has something to offer, but the most influential have been Erikson's ideas that greatly expanded the psychoanalytic concepts about how people form an identity.

Exploration and Commitment: Erikson on Identity

Erikson (1958/1980, 1968) argued that the psychosocial crisis of adolescence is identity versus role confusion. The positive outcome of adolescence is the formation of a solid personal identity; the negative outcome is role confusion, the state of not knowing who one really is. Erikson (1968) looked at the process of identity in terms of two variables, crisis (now called *exploration*) and commitment. The term **crisis** refers to a turning point or significant moment in a person's life. A crisis occurs when an individual actively confronts an aspect of identity and explores. According to Erikson, exploration is the crux of adolescent transition. His use of the term *crisis* has been criticized as being too dramatic and connoting a serious problem, and the term is likely to be misunderstood. Today, therefore, the term **exploration** is most often used (Marcia, 1967; Meeus & Dekovic, 1995). The adolescent explores through questioning basic values, priorities, interpersonal styles, and habits. This exploration may occur in a gradual, intermittent fashion rather than in one sustained, intense period (Baumeister, 1991). Achieving an identity requires exploration, which one researcher called the "work" of adolescence (Grotevant, 1987).

During a period of exploration the individual is more in flux and experiences subjective discomfort, confusion, mood swings, and heightened physical complaints (Erikson, 1963, 1968; Kidwell et al., 1995). The person feels a loss of certainty and a disruption in psychological balance. For instance, a college student may have to choose a major when approaching the junior year. In the personal sphere, the student may have to decide whether to get more deeply involved with a romantic partner.

crisis (exploration) According to psychosocial theory, a time in which individuals actively face and question aspects of their own identities.

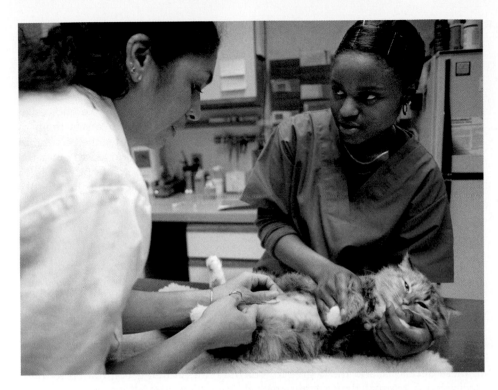

Exploration is one of the basic processes of identity formation, and vocational identity is very important.

Erikson coined the term *identity crisis,* a period of making decisions about important matters, in the early 1940s, and it quickly became popular. Identity crises are products of certain cultural environments and are neither universal nor innate (Baumeister, 1986). Western societies give people a great deal more choice than more traditional societies. In our society, actively confronting an aspect of an identity, such as occupational identity, means choices and alternatives—something that people in earlier times, as well as in some cultures today, may not have had.

The second variable Erikson emphasized in the process of identity is **commitment,** which relates to the presence or absence of a decision (Flum, 1994). An individual making a commitment follows a plan of action that reflects the decision. A person who investigates many vocational choices and decides on a particular career, for example, will follow the appropriate course of study. Making a decision to end a relationship or to become engaged leads to different behavioral paths.

When teens in the middle years of adolescence were tested and interviewed, impulsiveness, heightened physical complaints, and emotional turmoil were greatest in individuals who were currently exploring some aspect of their identities; this finding supports Erikson's idea that exploration is at the heart of the identity crisis (Kidwell et al., 1995). In contrast, high commitment scores did not produce these symptoms, because commitment leads to a sense of purpose and direction (Waterman, 1984). Some confusion appears to be typical of the exploration process.

Adolescents have a difficult course to chart. If they are to function as adults, they must be able to make their own decisions; they cannot simply be carbon copies of their parents. However, the attitudes and values they gained from their parents during childhood serve as anchors, providing security in a sea of change. Adolescents who totally abandon these values may become utterly confused. In addition, surrendering older ideals assumes all such ideals to be worthless, a conclusion that is difficult to support.

Why does the search for identity arise during adolescence? First, a prerequisite for an identity crisis is reaching a certain level of cognitive development in which the individual understands that many different paths are available and different realities exist. Preadolescent children rarely have identity crises, because they are not mentally sophisticated enough to examine their identities from multiple perspectives and contemplate different realities (Baumeister,

commitment In psychosocial theory, making a decision concerning some question involved in identity formation and following a plan of action reflecting that decision.

1991). A second reason is that the physical changes that occur during adolescence point out the transition from child to adult. As adolescents realize that they are no longer children, they are motivated to search for who they are and what they want to be. Third, adolescents become aware of the need to make choices in the areas of sexuality and vocation, and the pressure of time causes them to reexamine identity-related topics. Finally, cultural demands enter the picture. In Western society, the adolescent remains in school and is not forced to enter the adult world. However, our culture still requires adolescents to adopt new roles and make decisions, such as those regarding vocational choice, and the identity crisis may be a response to these cultural expectations (Baumeister, 1991).

The Four Identity Statuses

The most popular way of viewing identity development is in terms of where an individual is along the continuum of exploration and commitment. A prominent researcher in this field, James Marcia (1967, 1980), grouped adolescents into four categories, called *statuses,* according to their experiences with crises (exploration) and commitments (see Table 9.2). Researchers determine identity status in a semistructured interview in which they ask questions about decisions the individual may or may not have made, the process by which the individual arrived at these decisions, and the degree to which the individual is committed to these decisions. A manual that accompanies the questionnaire allows researchers to interpret the responses and determine the current identity status of the individual. The topics vary from culture to culture and time to time, but almost all topics cover the domains of vocational choice, religious and political beliefs, interpersonal values such as gender-role attitudes, and sexuality. Because identity status is related to specific attitudes and behaviors, a more detailed look at each status is useful.

Identity Foreclosure Identity foreclosure is a status that includes teens who have not experienced a crisis—that is, teens who have not explored alternatives—but have made commitments anyway. Their commitments may be seen as

---

Table 9.2

James Marcia's Four Identity Statuses

Identity Status	Description	Comments
Identity foreclosure	A person has made commitments, but without going through a meaningful period of exploration.	Adolescents in the foreclosed status are conventional and conforming. Often their commitment follows parental preferences. Making a premature choice reduces anxiety. It is a common status in high school.
Identity diffusion	A person has not meaningfully explored alternatives, shows no inclination to explore, and has not made any commitments.	Identity-diffused adolescents appear aloof, confused, and aimless. It is a common status in high school. Being in this status becomes a problem only when the individual continues through life without exploration or commitment.
Identity moratorium	An individual is in the process of exploring alternatives but has not made a commitment yet.	Adolescents in the moratorium status are preoccupied with identity questions and seem confused and apprehensive.
Identity achievement	An individual has explored alternatives and made commitments.	Identity achievers have the highest grade-point averages and are better adjusted than adolescents in the other statuses. Two kinds of achievers have been found; one kind does not change once identity has been achieved, and the other remains open to change.

premature. They identify very well—perhaps too well—with an older person, usually a parent. For example, some people go into their parents' business because they were always expected to. They were not permitted, or they did not permit themselves, to search for other alternatives. Or a woman may marry very early in life and not explore other possible choices or alternatives to early marriage. Identity-foreclosed people are very certain about their future plans and spend little time on self-examination (Flum, 1994). An individual may make an early commitment because it reduces the uncertainty and anxiety of the exploration process.

Identity Diffusion An individual who shows **identity diffusion** has made little progress in exploration, has not made any commitments, and is not in the process of forming any commitments. People described as diffused may have done some cursory, but little serious or in-depth, exploration. Identity-diffused people may actively seek noncommitment, avoiding demanding situations. They are unwilling or unable to make commitments (Valde, 1996). Some may be socially isolated, whereas others may move rapidly from partner to partner. The former avoid contact, and the latter seek out contact almost compulsively but are shallow. They may appear aimless, aloof, drifting, confused, and empty (Orlofsky, Marcia, & Lesser, 1973). They find it difficult to plan ahead or make firm decisions (Flum, 1994). They often show excessive dependence on others, especially peers, and do not believe they are in control. Their excessive conformity to group expectations means that they accomplish very little individual growth.

Identity Moratorium Adolescents who are experiencing a crisis but whose commitments are vague are considered to be in the **identity moratorium** status, a period of delay in which a person is not yet ready to make definite commitments (Erikson, 1968). Individuals in the moratorium status are exploring many possibilities, some of them radical, but their final commitments tend to be more conservative.

The moratorium status is not a happy one. Adolescents engaged in identity exploration show more self-doubts, apprehension, confusion, and conflict with parents and other authority figures (Kidwell et al., 1995). They are often found alone, thinking about and considering their options. Moratorium status may be linked to greater risk taking and a desire for new experiences, as exploration often involves a search for answers (Hernandez & DiClemente, 1992; Rotheram-Borus, 1989). Yet these teens are also likely to be rated higher in moral reasoning and are internally directed, even though they are more anxious (Marcia, 1980).

Erikson used the term *moratorium* to describe the social condition of youth in modern society, who are ready for adult life in many respects but have no clear place in the social structure and no long-term commitments or obligations. Erikson felt that this period would encourage identity crises, and this theory appears to be true. In fact, lower- and lower-middle income youth who are working full-time rather than going to college are less prone to these identity crises than are college youth, probably because they have a solid role and place in society (Morash, 1980). Of course, they may also have experienced their crises at an earlier age.

Identity moratorium is the least stable of all the statuses (Marcia et al., 1993; Waterman, 1982), but it may be necessary for a person to experience it. Only after a period of searching for answers can individuals make a commitment that is their own.

PERSPECTIVE 2

JUST PUZZLED

SETTING THE SCENE: Araz is a 15-year-old with a great many questions. He is confused about who he really is and what he wants to be in life. He always thought he would be a doctor, but his grades in biology are not the best. He always thought of himself as a good athlete, but he failed to make the high school team in baseball, his best sport. He does not understand who he is and sees himself as a mass of contradictions. He is unhappy and feels alone. He seems preoccupied, and his grades have slipped.

ARAZ: *I thought I knew who I was, but now I'm not sure. I find I'm very sensitive to criticism—too sensitive. Everyone else seems to know more than I do.*

ARAZ'S OLDER BROTHER BEN (21 YEARS OLD): *He's confused—well, who isn't. I was at his age. He's having a more difficult time than I had, though. Our parents asked me to speak with him, but I don't know how to help.*

QUESTION: If you were Araz's brother, what would you say to him if you tried to help?

---

identity foreclosure An identity status marked by a premature identity decision.

identity diffusion An identity status in which exploration is minimal and no commitments have been made.

identity moratorium An identity status in which a person is actively searching for an identity.

Identity Achievement   Individuals in the **identity achievement** status have made it. They have explored alternatives and made their commitments. Their independent personal identities are not carbon copies of their parents' identities, nor are they totally the opposite. Their identities include some of their parents' values and attitudes and omit others. These individuals are well adjusted (Bernard, 1981) and have good relationships with both peers and authority figures (Donovan, 1975). Identity achievers have higher grade-point averages than individuals in any of the other statuses (Cross & Allen, 1970), as well as better study habits (Waterman & Waterman, 1971).

Individuals in early or middle adolescence usually have not become identity achievers. The number of identity achievers increases with age, and the number of adolescents in the foreclosure, and especially diffusion, statuses declines (Allison & Schultz, 2001; Archer & Waterman, 1983). The years between ages 18 and 21 seem especially crucial for developing an identity. Before this time, the overwhelming number of adolescents are either foreclosed or diffused (Archer; 1982), and only very limited changes occur before or during the high school years (Meeus, 1996). Generally, older adolescents are more oriented toward, and concerned with, their future; and the older an adolescent, the more exploration is likely, and the greater the commitment is likely to be (Markstrom-Adams & Adams, 1995). Status changes are much more common at the end of the teen years and the beginning of the early adult years.

Identity status is not carved in stone. People may move from one group to another as they experience a crisis or make a new commitment. An unusual event might lead an individual back to a moratorium. For example, after spending a number of years preparing to become a newspaper reporter, one young woman found she could not find a job and had to search for an occupational identity all over again. After a divorce, a person may have to search anew for a personal or social identity, because the original identity is no longer viable.

One's identity status is linked to the depth of intimacy developed in early adulthood. The psychosocial crisis of early adulthood can be expressed as **intimacy versus isolation** (Erikson, 1968). Intimacy involves the development of very close personal relationships, whereas isolation involves a lack of commitment. Intimacy requires that two people share their identities without a complete merging of selves. People in the moratorium and achievement statuses experience deeper levels of intimacy than people in the other two statuses (Fitch & Adams, 1983; Orlofsky et al., 1973).

Although the basic relationship between identity and intimacy is correct, it may be somewhat different for males and females. Some women can deal successfully with intimacy issues prior to identity, but very few men can (Bartle-Haring & Strimple, 1996; Schiedel & Marcia, 1985). Men may not be able to achieve intimacy unless they have already made substantial progress on the identity front, but that relationship does not necessarily apply to all women. Perhaps women are raised to view relationships as more important and are more likely to consider relationships as part of their identities than are men.

The descriptions of identity diffusion and identity foreclosure do not seem very flattering. Individuals in these statuses seem less mature and less developed. Neither status involves much, if any, exploration. However, people in these statuses are not suffering from mental illness. Identity diffusion becomes a problem only when a person leaves adolescence without making any tentative steps toward commitments. A period of confusion often precedes the establishment of a firm identity (Erikson, 1950). In fact, there may be two different types of diffusion—one that is a permanent status and one that is a temporary state (Flum, 1994). High school students who are diffused can easily defend their status. A teen who tells a romantic partner that he or she is not ready for a commitment or an adolescent who does not want to make a premature career decision and keeps all options open may well be showing an awareness of true feelings that reflects an unreadiness to make commitments. In addition, such statuses temporarily may serve important purposes. The identity-diffused status allows teens to go about their business without becoming paralyzed with indeci-

identity achievement   An identity status in which a person has developed a solid personal identity.

intimacy versus isolation   The sixth psychosocial stage, occurring during young adulthood, in which the positive outcome is the development of deep interpersonal relationships and the negative outcome is a flight from close relationships.

sion until they are ready to explore. The identity-foreclosed individual may not be able to tolerate the anxiety and disorganization required during the exploration period at that time; the status becomes a way of delaying exploration. However, if an individual remains in these statuses, the lack of exploration can be troublesome.

Do Males and Females Take Different Paths to Identity Formation?

Erikson (1968) believed that the identities of males and females differed. The identities of males mainly focused on such factors as vocational identity and personal identity, whereas females were more likely to tie their identities to interpersonal relationships.

Thirty-five years ago many psychologists agreed, suggesting that females place more emphasis on *interpersonal identity,* whereas males emphasize *intrapersonal identity* (Douvan & Adelson, 1966). Males and females may approach identity formation from different perspectives. Traditionally, males tended to focus on intrapersonal factors, such as vocational identity and separateness, and women were more likely to tie their identities to interpersonal relationships (Schiedel & Marcia, 1985). Relational identities are stronger, more important, and developed at a higher level than occupational identity for most women, but not for men (Meeus & Dekovic, 1995; Waterman, 1993). Historically, identity formation in males reflected the cultural expectations of autonomy and separateness, whereas female identity formation stressed connectedness to others and intimate relationships (Bernard, 1981; Gilligan, 1982).

Carol Gilligan, whose ideas will be more fully developed in "Moral Development, Values, and Religion," argues that Erikson's theory views identity development as a process of increasing separation and individualization. Gilligan suggests that females follow a different course—one that emphasizes the importance of relationships and being connected to others. This tendency may reflect different socialization processes, as girls may be raised to share, be more sensitive to the needs of others, and see themselves in relation to others. Male identity formation may indeed involve separateness and independence. The female self and identity are organized in the context of important relationships. Females appear to spend more time integrating identity and intimacy than males and to have a greater need to do so (Lacombe & Gay, 1998).

This idea sensitized psychologists to the possible differences in identity development between males and females, and it has received some support. However, in today's society, in which most women are employed outside the

At one time, women had little choice. They were expected to marry, have children, and stay at home to take care of them. Today women have many more alternatives, and the decision-making process is more difficult.

"The squeaky wheel gets the grease." "The nail that sticks out gets hammered down." Which of these sayings reflects life in the United States? As you read this chapter, it may occur to you that the concepts of the self, self-concept, self-esteem, and identity seem somewhat egocentric and egotistical. Individuals, it seems, must learn to think for themselves, to make their own decisions, to evaluate parts of their own selves positively, and to build a personal identity. We are preoccupied with separateness and uniqueness; the individual is king (Guisinger & Blatt, 1993).

Not all societies view the self-concept, self-esteem, and identity this way. One of the most important ways of categorizing cultures is to look at how they stand on the individualism-collectivism dimension. No culture completely ignores the individual, and no culture completely ignores the group. However, cultures differ widely on this critical dimension (Brislin, 2000).

In individualistic cultures, people work toward their own goals, and each person is seen as developing an individual identity. Dependency is not considered a positive attribute. The advice "Stand on your own two feet" and "Learn to blow your own horn, because no one will do it for you" characterizes individualistic societies. The task of parents is to prepare their adolescent children to leave home, have separate identities, and lead successful and independent lives.

Many cultures in Africa, Asia, and Latin America are less concerned with the self as a completely separate construct and see the self as developing and being actualized only in relation to others as part of a group. The self becomes whole through a connection with others and by assuming social obligations. For example, when asked to describe the self, Indian youth often use behavioral acts that involve others, such as "I bring cakes to my family on festival days," whereas Americans are more likely to use general terms such as "I am friendly" (Shweder & Miller, 1991). In many Asian Pacific Rim cultures, the self and identity are meaningful only when they are attached to others. People in these cultures elevate qualities such as obedience and living in harmony with others but do not talk about personal accomplishments and abilities. In these cultures, which are sometimes called *sociocentric,* the self is characterized by interdependence with others rather than independence from others. Such cultures define the self-concept by how people fit in.

This interdependence requires that individuals see their behavior as being determined by what they believe are the thoughts, feelings, and actions of others in the group. People in sociocentric cultures are motivated to find ways to fit in and to fulfill their obligations to others. Identity involves being a member of the group. Members of collectivist groups asked to complete statements such as "I am . . ." are more likely to offer membership in a group than are people from Western countries (Bochner & Hesketh, 1994). Among many African groups, being sensitive to others is crucial, and seeing others in the group as an extension of oneself is common. In China, people tend to act primarily in accordance with the expectations of the family and kin group, rather than according to internal wishes (Haviland, 2003). This orientation places a premium on self-effacement, humility, deference, and the avoidance of disturbing others. Maintaining harmony in the group is most important. Japanese people often show a constant concern for belongingness, reliance, dependency, empathy, and occupying their proper place (Lebra, 1976). The Japanese nightmare is exclusion—that is, failing at the goal of connecting to others—which is in contrast to the American nightmare of failing to separate from others, remaining dependent, and not standing up for what one believes (Markus & Kitayama, 1991).

People in many non-Western countries make no distinction between personal and collective goals, or if they do make a distinction, they deliberately subordinate individual goals to the goals of the group (Triandis, 1989). Individuals

home and want both a career and family, most studies find that females attempt to integrate both interpersonal and intrapersonal issues, whereas males relate mostly to intrapersonal issues (Lytle & Romig, 1997). A woman's identity requires balancing separation and connectedness, and this balance may become a significant issue for her. Many women today find their period of exploration marked by consideration of both family and career possibilities, whereas men still appear to emphasize the intrapersonal sphere (Kroger, 1997; Lytle, Bakken, & Romig, 1997).

Women accurately perceive their new role as both worker and family caregiver. Men, however, may not yet see their dual responsibility in these balanced terms, which may have far-reaching consequences later in adulthood. Women often find themselves with two full-time jobs—one at their place of employment and another at home—but men do not. Conflicts may arise between what Hochschild (1989) describes as "faster-changing women and slower-changing in such societies are more concerned about the effects of their actions on members of their group, are more willing to share resources, obey their group's authority figures, are willing to fight for the integrity of their group, and cooperate with group members. Relationships, rather than being means for realizing individual goals, often are ends in and of themselves.

The primary concerns of parents in these sociocentric cultures are obedience, reliability, and proper behavior, whereas the primary concerns of parents in individualistic cultures are self-reliance, independence, and creativity (Triandis, 1989). Non-Western child-rearing patterns lead to greater conformity, obedience, and reliability and are associated with rewards for conformity to one's group, leading to an internalization of these goals.

In Eastern cultures, the self does not merge with others, nor do people always have to be in the company of others to do what is expected of them. They internalize the views and expectations of their group. Individuals need a high degree of self-control to adjust themselves to the interpersonal needs of others. Being part of the group means that one does not emphasize personal triumphs as a way of improving self-esteem; self-assertion is viewed as immature. When second-, third-, and fifth-grade Japanese students were asked how their classmates and they themselves would evaluate two hypothetical classmates—one who commented on his own superior athletic performance and another who did not—they perceived the modest peer as a better athlete than the boastful child (Yoshida, Kojo, & Kaku, 1982). They viewed self-enhancement and self-promotion as immature, and this feeling increased with age. The children perceived the personality of the modest individual much more positively and respected the child more (Bond, Leung, & Wan, 1982).

This comparison between individualistic and sociocentric cultures is a bit too simplistic, though. First, it is obvious that some aspect of the self must be individual in all cultures. For example, all individuals see themselves as physically distinct and having certain physical traits. Some experiences, such as one's dreams, surely belong to a separate self, and some needs are also individualistic. After all, a statement such as "I am thirsty" has the same meaning all over the world.

Second, in many sociocentric or collectivist cultures, obligation and interdependence are directed only at an in-group, not the entire society. The in-group may be the extended family or people at work, but individuals who are not in the in-group and strangers clearly may have little influence on the behavior of others.

Third, although dividing cultures into individualistic and sociocentric is conceptually reasonable, few cultures are either one or the other. A more accurate view would feature a continuum with elements of both kinds of cultures.

Fourth, individuals vary in the extent to which they are representative of their culture. For example, people from non-Western societies who have traveled extensively in the West may understand the differences and perhaps even adopt some ideas of individual autonomy.

Finally, within each culture exist a number of subcultures that may modify the individualistic or sociocentric orientation of the society. For example, many Latinos in the United States are raised with a family oriented ideal and may retain it, but the orientation may be modified through acculturation.

The meaning of the self and one's identity can be understood only by looking at the context. A culture in which individualism is king produces people who are independent and competitive and whose behavior is governed by what they perceive as their own needs. People whose culture is more collective would be more sensitive to the needs of others, be more likely to subjugate their needs to the group's needs, and see relationships with others as important in themselves rather than as a means to an individualistic end. The self and one's identity are viable topics for universal study; however, their meanings may differ among cultures, and people may derive self-esteem either from fitting in and meeting group expectations and goals or from individual achievement. Western and non-Western conceptions of the self and identity differ substantially, and as always, culture defines the meaning and significance of particular behaviors.

men" (p. 11). Women may expect more equal sharing of the homemaking and child-rearing chores, whereas men, who do not see their role or identity as changing that much, may not. The differing expectations may lead to dissatisfaction and interpersonal problems. The task of identity exploration may be more complex for females than males, as women attempt to establish their identities in a greater number of domains and often must balance confusing options.

Although the vocational and family domains may differ in importance, it is wrong to assume that the basic processes of identity formation differ between males and females. In fact, males and females make about equal use of the identity statuses (Archer, 1991). Both males and females show increasing frequencies of moratorium and achievement status and decreasing frequencies of diffusion and foreclosure statuses with age (Kroger, 1997). They show relatively few differences in identity structure, content, or developmental process. Adolescent men and women alike must explore, and no gender differences appear in their statuses in the domains of vocational choice, religious beliefs, or political ideology. Women, though, are more likely to be found in the identity achievement or moratorium statuses and less likely to be in the foreclosed or diffused statuses regarding family priorities and sexuality. Males are more likely to be foreclosed or diffused in these areas (Archer, 1991; Harter, 1990). Although the salience of the family/work priorities and sexuality domains may differ and women may be further along than men in them, the similarities outweigh the differences.

Concerns About Identity Status

Marcia's view of identity status is a useful way of looking at identity, but it has its critics. First, according to this view, once a person has reached identity achievement status, the search for identity ends. In reality, though, many people continue the search. The identity achievement status may be split between individuals who are inflexible and closed and those who continue their search even though they have made commitments. For example, someone who has considered political philosophies and made a commitment may be considered an achiever, but what if no further development takes place? The individual would be considered an achiever, but closed to new exploration. Other achievers may be open to new experiences. People who remain open score higher in sensitivity, realism, spontaneity, and self-acceptance (Valde, 1996).

Second, the concept of identity status appears more relevant to Western than Eastern societies (see "Focus: Squeaky Wheels and Nails That Stick Out: The Self and Culture"). The concept views individuals as searching for their own individual identity, as distinct from others, and as achieving autonomy and emancipation from parents. It sees exploration as relatively unrestricted. Some Eastern societies, however, communicate a set of values, expect conformity to those values, and hold responsibility to one's family and community of origin above all else.

Third, the concept of identity status lacks a process orientation. Identity status concepts have been more useful in noting individual differences than in

At a Glance 9.4 Identity

KEY POINT: Developing a coherent identity is one of the primary developmental tasks of adolescence.

SUPPORTING POINTS	EXPLANATION
Erikson argued that adolescents need to form a solid sense of identity.	The positive outcome of the psychosocial stage of adolescence is ego identity, whereas the negative outcome is role confusion.
Erikson argued that identity formation is defined by the processes of crisis (now called *exploration*) and commitment.	Identity formation requires the adolescent to explore new ideas and roles. *Commitment* refers to making an identity decision and following it through. During crises, adolescents often experience anxiety and confusion.
Adolescents may be in one of four identity statuses.	The identity foreclosure status includes individuals who have not yet experienced a crisis, yet have made commitments. People in the identity diffusion status have done little or no exploration, have made no commitments, and avoid commitments. Individuals in the identity moratorium stage are experiencing a crisis but have not yet made commitments, and those in the identity achievement status have experienced a crisis and made commitments. Adolescents in the identity achievement status have the best grades and rate higher on a number of indexes of adjustment.
Researchers have found gender differences in identity.	Females tend to center on their interpersonal identities more than males, and males focus on their intrapersonal identities more than females. Studies indicate that females try to integrate both the interpersonal and intrapersonal aspects of their identity.

tracing developmental patterns (Grotevant, 1998). The process by which an individual travels from status to status remains largely unexplained. *(For a review of this section, see At A Glance 9.4.)*

GENDER ROLES

One of the most important aspects of identity is developing a sense of what it means to be a male or a female in one's society. The term **sex typing** is used to describe the process by which an individual acquires values and behaviors considered more appropriate for one gender or the other in the particular culture. Such sex-typed behavior regulates shows of emotional expression, behavior while dissecting a frog, or behavior at a dance. Girls learn that crying is acceptable when they are sad; boys learn to hold their sadness in. Many of these behaviors and personality traits are stereotyped. **Gender roles** involve expectations regarding the proper behavior, attitudes, and activities of males and females within a particular culture.

Gender Stereotypes

Consider the list of personality traits in Figure 9.4, and try the exercise. Gender stereotypes are alive and well today (Lueptow, Garovich-Szabo, & Lueptow, 2001). However there may be some evidence that more traits are considered equally representative of males and females alike. In addition, psychologists today are somewhat more realistic in their treatment of sex typing and stereotypes. Instead of determining whether particular behaviors are seen as masculine or feminine, psychologists now ask whether these behaviors or traits are more likely to be found in one gender or the other (as was the case in Figure 9.4) (Stangor & Lange, 1994). This new approach is certainly overdue. People are more likely to describe males as competitive and aggressive and females as warm and nurturant, but most females have some traits that would be considered more masculine,

Psychologists, today, are less likely to ask whether a particular trait is found only in one gender, but rather whether the trait is found more often in one gender than the other. This girl may be described as patient, helpful, and caring, descriptions that may also apply to many males. Some traits, however, such as being gentle and nurturant, are rarely used to describe males.

Figure 9.4
Gender Stereotypes

In this exercise, next to each item, please note an "M" if you believe most people associate the characteristic with males more than females, and an "F" if you believe that most people associate the characteristic with females more than males. Use an equal sign (=) to indicate that you think most people think of it as about equal. See if your choices compare with those of other students in your class.

____ friendly	____ compassionate	____ changeable
____ powerful	____ passive	____ aggressive
____ kind	____ funny	____ neat
____ strong	____ imaginative	____ loud
____ emotional	____ polite	____ talkative
____ talkative	____ gentle	____ show-off
____ meticulous (careful about doing things)	____ ambitious	____ helpful
	____ open	

sex typing The process by which an individual acquires attitudes, values, and behaviors viewed as appropriate for one gender or another in a particular culture.

gender roles Behaviors expected of people in a given society on the basis of whether an individual is male or female.

and most males have some traits that are more typical of females (Feingold, 1994).

These traits are not opposites. An individual may be assertive and kind, as well as self-assured and warm. Years ago, the term **androgyny** was coined to refer to possessing characteristics that are representative of both males and females. These characteristics often were considered the "best." The use of rigid gender stereotypes was seen as limiting, and some research did show advantages to people who held more flexible ideas about roles (Spence, Helmreich, & Stapp, 1975). However, other studies found no differences between androgynous and masculine individuals (Ruble, 1988), or found that the advantages may be due to the fact that masculine traits are simply more valued than feminine ones. More important, although the concept of androgyny may be an improvement over traditional gender stereotypes, it still perpetuates gender-related stereotypical characteristics. Perhaps we ought to transcend all traditional stereotypes (Doyle, 1985). Androgyny then becomes a transitional concept rather than the ideal alternative to traditional stereotypes.

Even though most men and women do not conform fully to cultural stereotypes, these expectations still serve as a standard against which people judge themselves and others. Men are generally considered high in agency—that is, getting things done for oneself—and are described in such terms as *aggressive, competitive,* and *self-confident.* Women are still described in terms of communion, or a concern for relationships with others; terms such as *gentle* and *nurturant* are stereotypically feminine (Costa, Terracciano, & McCrae, 2001; Kite, 1996). The same stereotypes are found among college students and the general public, regardless of age, gender, or socioeconomic status (Street, Kromrey, & Kimmel, 1995).

Sex Typing: A Developmental View

Children know that they are boys or girls at about age 2 (Ruble & Martin, 1998). By 3 or 4 years, most children can accurately apply gender-stereotyped labels to toys, activities, household tasks, and even adult occupations (Turner & Gervai,

Gender differences in play appear rather early in life.

androgyny   Possessing some characteristics considered typical of males and others considered typical of females.

1995). Knowledge of gender stereotypes grows rapidly between 3 and 5 years, reaching a high level of awareness by kindergarten (Martin & Little, 1990). Consistent gender differences in preferred toys and play activities are found: Boys play more with toy vehicles and blocks, whereas girls engage in more artistic activities, play with dolls, and dress up (Huston, 1983). Gender differences in personality are less pronounced at this age and show themselves somewhat later.

During the elementary school years, gender stereotypes persist but become much less rigid. Children become aware of exceptions and are more flexible (Signorella, Bigler, & Liben, 1993). Girls are much more flexible than boys throughout this period. In fact, from about 8 through 11 years, girls are strong, self-confident, and somewhat outspoken. They are not afraid to say what they think or play the games they want to, and they give little thought to what is appropriate for their gender (Basow & Rubin, 1999; Brown & Gilligan, 1992).

This flexibility does not continue, however, and early adolescents become more rigid in their stereotypic beliefs. When researchers surveyed flexibility in gender stereotypes in students from fourth through eleventh grades, flexibility increased through the first year of junior high school and then declined. Over the remaining years of junior high school and through eleventh grade, flexibility continued to decline (Alfieri, Ruble, & Higgins, 1996). After that, in late adolescence, flexibility increased. Females remain more flexible than males, which is a common finding in other cultures as well (Gibbons, Stiles, & Shkodriani, 1991).

The reasons for the increase in gender stereotypes with age include an increasing self-consciousness combined with the physical changes that occur, as well as an increased focus on one's sexuality and gender. As children enter puberty, they focus their attention on their sexual selves and their attractiveness to others. Teens become concerned about how they are supposed to act and are often evaluated on the basis of whether they behave in "gender-appropriate" ways.

Gender stereotyping increases in early adolescence, as adolescents want to fit in and live up to stereotypical standards.

Parents, peers, and the media expect teens to consider what it is to be a male or a female, and they especially push adolescent girls to become more interested in their appearance and social relationships (Evans et al., 1991). Society emphasizes appearance and popularity due to appearance but not achievement and being oneself. It asks females in particular to change, which may make them more anxious about themselves as they try to live up to a difficult societal standard of thinness, sexuality, and nurturance that may not mesh with how they see themselves. Some argue that this anxiety and confusion shows itself in the increased rate of depression, lower self-esteem, and greater dissatisfaction with body image found in adolescent females (Basow & Rubin, 1999; Hill & Lynch, 1983). Boys, too, are told that their looks are important and pressured to look their best, according to the cultural standards of the group, and pressures on males to show a particular body type seem to be increasing. Adding to the problem is the fact that early adolescents are more self-conscious than either older or younger people, and girls are more self-conscious than boys, especially in the area of appearance (Adler, Kless, & Adler, 1992).

These societal demands to change make teens uncertain of who they are. One way to deal with these issues is to try to blend in by conforming to others and doing what everyone else is doing (Beal, 1994). Teens who are unsure of themselves may turn to the security of the familiar and adopt traditional gender roles (Brown, Clasen, & Eicher, 1986). Safety means fitting in, and teens who do not live up to the stereotypes may be teased and rejected. Early adolescents, in one study, were less tolerant than elementary school children of people who deviated from the stereotypes. They said, for example, that they would not want to go to a school that allowed boys to wear nail polish or girls to wear a crew cut,

When asked to describe the "ideal" man or woman, teenage females envision the "chivalrous football player" stereotype, whereas males envision the "smiling sunbather."

even though all the students understood that these choices are personal (see Beal, 1994).

Gender stereotypes can be very restrictive. Young teen girls describe the ideal man as kind, honest, fun loving, smiling, and a person who would bring flowers; researchers call this description the "chivalrous football player" stereotype. Teenage boys describe the ideal woman as good looking, sexy, and spending hours running and having fun rather than studying—what researchers call the "smiling sunbather" stereotype (Stiles, Gibbons, & Schnellmann, 1987).

These stereotypes may influence teenage behavior in many ways. Some teens may feel they have to act in a way that is counter to how they feel in order to be accepted by the group. Teens who refuse to do so, or who find that their attempts meet with failure, may be ostracized and feel alone and unwanted. In addition, female adolescents in particular may find that stereotyped gender traits interfere with their lifestyle choices; they may find it more difficult to fulfill their own talents or pursue fields such as physical sciences or engineering. Similarly, male students who find that their interests lie in areas such as elementary school teaching or nursing may find that adopting these stereotypes may cause difficulties (Brooks-Gunn & Reiter, 1990). As long as stereotypes serve as standards against which people are measured both physically and behaviorally, they are limiting forces.

Gender and Voice

Gilligan (1982; Gilligan, Lyons, & Hammer, 1989), whose extensive and controversial writings on gender role and behavior have led to much fruitful discussion and research, argued that girls are more likely to believe they cannot voice their true feelings and show their real self because they are taught to identify with the cultural role of the polite, quiet, nurturant person. Women are taught not to express their opinions assertively, thereby leading to a suppression of self. Gilligan (1993; Gilligan, Brown, & Rogers, 1990) argued that adolescent women face a dilemma. They have been raised to value human relationships and to define themselves in terms of their relationships with others. Part of this is the ethic of caring, which encourages women to be more sensitive to the needs and desires of others than their own. If they begin to allow their own desires and goals to show and begin to become self-sufficient, they label themselves, and risk being labeled by others, as selfish. Yet a selfless giving to others may not allow them to realize their own desires. Thus, they face a conflict based on concerns of inclusion and exclusion. *Inclusion* involves being connected with, and giving to, others and is a value for women. *Exclusion* involves being centered on oneself and one's own desires and needs. Gilligan (1988) noted that *selfishness* connotes the exclusion of others and *selflessness,* the exclusion of self. Women may believe that their need to become more autonomous means that they must ignore their need for connectedness (Lytle & Romig, 1997).

Women often solve this dilemma by silencing their special and distinctive voice rather than offering opinions, and thus they lose confidence in themselves. This pattern may continue through adulthood. Young women, then, must find an answer to the dilemma of inclusion and exclusion. Indeed, conflict over opposing roles and self-descriptions diminishes significantly for boys, but not for girls. Girls may be more concerned with creating harmony across multiple relationships and roles and may find the contradictions difficult to integrate: How can someone continue to bring harmony to a group and compete as well? Boys view their roles as more independent of one another and have less need to harmonize roles and beliefs across situations (Harter, 1990).

This view is controversial for a number of reasons. Women's roles have changed, and women today may solve the dilemma by becoming assertive rather than being quiet. In addition, dramatic individual differences rather than gender differences may explain differing willingness to voice opinions (Harter et al., 1996). The most important variables determining the willingness to voice one's opinions, feelings, and needs is not gender but rather perceived support and gender orientation. The higher the level of support for speaking out and being oneself, the more adolescents of both genders will be able to voice their true convictions without fear of being ridiculed or losing love (Harter et al., 1998) (see Figure 9.5). In addition, women who combine both masculine and feminine traits (androgyny), rather than scoring very high only on femininity, are more likely to voice their opinions. Finally, expressing oneself is often situational, and even individuals who may not voice their opinions in a group or in school may do so with parents or close friends.

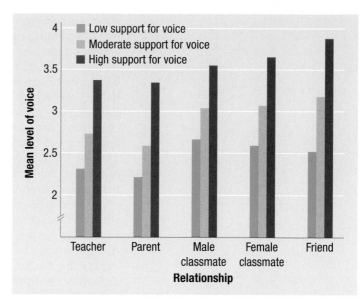

Figure 9.5

Level of Voice as a Function of Support for Voice
When adolescents receive support from different people in their environment, they are more willing to voice their opinions.
Source: Harter et al. (1998), p. 898.

How Gender Roles Develop: A Focus on Process

Just how does an individual develop a sense of what it means to be a male or a female? Psychologists argue that these roles are culturally determined. Some people simply explain the formation of gender-role conceptions by referring to parental models, the media, or peers, but to date simple explanations have not been successful. Recently, though, two changes in how psychologists look at gender role have been introduced. First, although childhood certainly prepares individuals for their gender roles, these roles are refined and sometimes changed in adolescence and throughout adulthood. Second, looking at one agent of socialization (such as parents) or one process (such as imitation or reinforcement) is insufficient. Many agents of socialization influence one's conception of role, and more than one psychological process is responsible for it.

The Learning Theory Approach   The most obvious reason males and females act differently is that they learn to do so. Parents actively channel their children into play with gender-stereotyped toys, especially by buying them for their children (Eisenberg et al., 1985). The same parents who say it would not bother them if their son played with dolls are apt to provide him with only footballs, baseball gloves, and trucks and to encourage him to play with them. Parents view girls as more fragile and play with sons more roughly. Throughout childhood, boys are sex typed more rigidly than girls and are discouraged from engaging in "gender-inappropriate" behavior more than girls (Langlois & Downs, 1980). Boys also receive more encouragement for gross motor activities and more freedom from supervision, whereas girls receive more affectionate behavior and more immediate help when they request it (Ruble & Martin, 1998).

When differences are found, fathers are more likely than mothers to treat sons and daughters differently (Lytton & Romney, 1991). A father is more likely to criticize his son when he sees him playing with dolls than he is to criticize his daughter when he observes her beating up a doll. This finding could be a clue in explaining the finding that girls are more flexible in their sex typing than boys; girls may be allowed more freedom to explore their stereotyped masculine characteristics and interests than boys are encouraged to explore their stereotyped feminine characteristics and interests. Another possibility is that society respects and values stereotyped male characteristics more than stereotyped female characteristics, so parents are more lenient in allowing their daughters to take on some stereotyped competencies of males than they are in allowing their sons to develop characteristics usually attributed more to females.

The situation is really more complicated than this, however. Child-rearing methods are not so fundamentally different that they directly explain the later differences in stereotypes and gender-role perceptions. For example, there are no significant differences between parents of boys and girls in such child-rearing variables as warmth, encouragement of dependence, restrictiveness, encouragement of achievement, or verbal interaction (Lytton & Romney, 1991). Although parents do encourage sex-typed activities and some gender-stereotyped characteristics, the differences in parental treatment are few and the similarities in treatment more than what would probably be expected. The question is not whether parents treat sons and daughters differently but rather whether the differences are strong and important enough to explain later sex-typed behavior patterns.

Boys are sex typed more strictly than girls. Girls are not criticized as much for taking on some stereotyped competencies of males, but boys are not encouraged to take on the stereotyped competencies of females.

Another problem with using child-rearing strategies as a guide for understanding later gender-role stereotypes and behaviors is that this approach ignores other societal agents and individual differences. For example, peers may reinforce adolescents for particular behaviors, and the way the media portrays gender roles is another factor.

Role Models   Children and adolescents are affected by the role models they see around them. As they observe their parents, other adults, and their peers, they learn much about gender roles. A girl who looks up to her mother and respects her, and also sees her mother valued in the labor market, may learn that women can combine a family and a career. In fact, mothers who participate more in traditionally male household chores and child-care tasks have children who are less typical in their gender activity preferences (Serbin, Powlishta, & Gulko, 1993).

Children are also exposed to models in the outside world—for example, peers, teachers, and characters in books and on television. Males are overrepresented on most television programs and are shown as problem solvers, whereas females follow their lead (Ruble & Martin, 1998).

The Cognitive View   What is absent from the previously discussed views of role formation is the cognitive component. After all, people judge what is appropriate for each gender, with some people being more flexible than others. According to **gender schema theory,** once children understand that they are boys or girls (at about age 2), they begin to develop a body of knowledge about what boys and girls do, called a *gender schema.* They glean this network of gender-related information from their experiences in the environment that influence perception and behavior. This body of knowledge helps people organize and interpret information and influences their preferences and activities (Bem, 1981, 1993; Martin & Halverson, 1981). The gender schema acts as a lens through which children and adolescents perceive and think. Consider a girl with a doll. She knows that dolls are for girls and that she is a girl; therefore, dolls are for her. The girl will then explore the doll, ask questions, and obtain information about it. What if the same girl is offered a truck? She may think that trucks are for boys, and because she is a girl, she'll decide that trucks are not for her. Avoidance results, and the girl will not actively gather further information (Martin, 1995). In fact, children will play with a less attractive toy that is considered "gender appropriate" than a more attractive one that is neutral but labeled for the other gender (Martin, Eisenbud, & Ross, 1995).

As children acquire society's gender schema, they learn which characteristics are related to their own gender and which are not. Bem (1981) notes that part of the gender schema for boys is strength, whereas nurturance is part of the schema for girls. The strong-weak dimension appears to be absent from the female gender schema, and the nurturant dimension is almost absent from the male gender schema. Children apply the same schema to themselves and attend more thoroughly to the possible dimensions of personality and behavior that are applicable to their own gender.

One of the strengths of gender schema theory is that it explains why people maintain their gender stereotypes even when confronted with contrary information. Once children learn their own schema, such knowledge biases the way they process information. Children remember information that best fits their gender schema and may even change information that is inconsistent with their beliefs (Welsh-Ross & Schmidt, 1996). For example, a child who believes that boys are soldiers and is told of a heroic female soldier may later change the gender of the soldier when retelling the story. People use many techniques to keep their gender stereotypes and gender schema intact. They may not pay attention to a story about a female or male who violates their gender schema or may simply label it as an exception. For example, a teen may see an excellent female science student and label her an exception to the rule. Boys may even deny the femininity of a female athlete or the masculinity of a male dancer.

gender schema theory   A theory of gender-role acquisition in which a person develops a body of knowledge about the behaviors of each gender that helps organize and interpret information and guide behavior.

Gender roles and sex typing are also based on one's particular culture and subculture. For example, African American women are twice as likely to describe themselves as androgynous (both strongly active and nurturant) than are European American women, perhaps because they had to develop these qualities in the face of prejudice and adverse economic situations (Binion, 1990). In the Latino culture, expectations for females are often based on *marianismo,* which respects self-sacrifice and nurturance, and expectations for men are rooted in *machismo,* which honors courage and protection. Latino women may seem submissive and dependent as a result of such traditional beliefs (Vasquez-Nuttall, Romero-Garcia, & De Leon, 1987). Asian American women are often expected to be passive, and sometimes subservient as well. Yet these culturally based expectations often change through acculturation, sometimes leading to conflicts within a family as more traditionally oriented parents face more acculturated adolescent children.

Biological Contributions   The complex nature of sex typing and the acquisition of gender roles is further complicated by the physiological differences between males and females that may contribute to personality characteristics and behaviors. No one seriously entertains the idea that we can explain social roles solely in terms of biological differences; there is no single theory of gender roles based on biological factors. The question is simply the degree to which physiological differences may directly influence personality and behavior and indirectly affect the adoption of particular roles. For example, could males be more aggressive because of the greater amount of testosterone in their systems? Some researchers do link testosterone to aggressive behavior in males (Buchanan, Eccles, & Becker, 1992b; Ruble & Martin, 1998). Of course, not all males are aggressive, and some females are aggressive. The hormonal factor may explain only a tendency—one that interacts with learning to determine the behavior. Other experts point to maturational differences as a possible cause for gender differences in behavior. Still others note that differences in strength and other biological factors may directly or indirectly influence behavior and roles. For example, parents monitor teenage girls more closely and allow them less freedom because they are afraid their daughters will face sexual assault or unwanted pregnancy. Thus, many parents allow their 13-year-old sons to walk home a few blocks at night from a friend's house, but not their daughters.

The role of biological differences in sex typing and the acquisition of gender roles is still largely unknown, and these differences can be understood only in the context of a particular society. And even if one accepts the idea that males are more likely to be aggressive than females because of hormonal reasons, for example, there are still many nonaggressive males, and learning seems to be a more important factor. Furthermore, there is a danger that biological explanations may cause people to assign unequal roles to males and females. In the case of gender roles and behavior, biology is not destiny.

The formation of one's gender role is complicated. Most psychologists believe that we need increased flexibility in gender roles so people can develop their talents and feel free to be who they are. It may be necessary to counter the stereotyped masculine and feminine roles and sex-typed behaviors shown in the media and to educate people who merely accept these roles. Teenagers must understand that they are worthwhile, valuable people even if they do not measure up, or do not want to measure up, to the stereotyped physical and behavioral stereotypes set by society. People often comment on the physical appearance of a female reporter or an athlete, as if these qualities were more important than their talents in their fields. We also hear comments about the lack of masculinity of a male who shows nurturant traits or enters a stereotypic female occupation. Teens hearing these comments may not show who they really are in order to simply fit in.

It may be useful to try to forestall this flight into stereotyped beliefs right before it occurs in junior high school (Basow & Rubin, 1999). Discussing with adolescents the roles and expectations shown in the media and in their own

AT A GLANCE 9.5 GENDER ROLES

KEY POINT: The meaning of what it is to be a male or a female is an important element of an individual's global identity, and many factors influence its development.

SUPPORTING POINTS	EXPLANATION
Sex typing and gender roles are important concepts for understanding how males and females behave.	*Sex typing* refers to the process by which an individual acquires values and behaviors considered more appropriate for one gender or the other. Gender roles involve expectations regarding the proper behavior, attitudes, and activities of males and females within a particular culture.
Early adolescents are more rigid in their stereotypes and less tolerant of deviation from them.	Holding rigid stereotypes and behaving in a stereotypical manner allow early adolescents a measure of security. Early adolescents often are not tolerant of others' defiance of gender stereotypes.
Gilligan argued that females are taught not to voice their points of view and to identify with the stereotyped passive view of being a female. They suppress their unique "voice."	Studies demonstrate that not gender but gender orientation and support lead to individuals voicing their true feelings and opinions. Women who have both masculine and feminine traits are more likely to voice their own opinions.
Males and females learn to act differently.	Boys and girls are reinforced for different behaviors. Boys are more likely to be punished for adopting behaviors or attitudes that are stereotypically female.
Males and females are affected by the role models they see around them.	Males and females have different role models, and these models may influence how they act.
The most prominent cognitive theory of gender-role formation is gender schema theory.	Once children develop an understanding of being boys or girls, they develop a body of knowledge about what boys or girls do. A child's gender schema biases his or her information processing. A boy realizes that footballs are for him; a girl realizes that dolls are for her.
Gender role is determined by one's culture.	The cultures of various groups, including African Americans, Latinos, and Asian Americans, have an ideal image of how males and females should act.
The extent to which physiological differences between males and females contributes to sex typing and gender roles is controversial.	Physiological factors, such as hormone differences, may contribute to differences in behavior (for example, aggression). However, no psychologist today argues that biological factors are primary in the formation of gender roles.

groups may help. Teenagers must be allowed to express themselves unfettered by gender stereotypes. But while countering gender stereotypes, we should avoid demanding that every female be competitive and every male nurturant. We should allow adolescents to develop their abilities and personality traits in an atmosphere of acceptance, not determine which traits they should show. (*For a review of this section, see At A Glance 9.5.*)

ETHNIC/RACIAL IDENTITY

Identity development is a complex task for all youth, but it is particularly complicated for adolescents in ethnic and racial minority groups (Spencer & Markstrom-Adams, 1990). Often, these adolescents must come to terms with rejection and hostility at the same time that they are trying to accept themselves (Burnette, 1995). They also must reject the stereotypes common in the outside world.

The Process of Exploration

Adolescents from some minority groups find their exploration blocked or made more difficult by societal and familial factors; indeed, black adolescents are more likely to be found in the foreclosed identity status than whites (Hauser & Kasendorf, 1983). African Americans face restrictions in occupational choice because of poverty and discrimination, and this limitation may preclude a moratorium status (Grotevant & Cooper, 1985, 1986). Sometimes a lack of models inhibits exploration. For Native Americans raised on reservations and many Latino youth, social roles and ideologies are more clearly defined, and exploration is not always encouraged (Spencer, 1991). Asian American adolescents often face parental pressure for academic excellence but may not necessarily be allowed opportunities to explore their options fully (Nogata, 1989). The cultural emphasis on obedience, family responsibility, and obligations may not allow for the type of exploration typical of most other groups in Western societies.

This foreclosure often depends on socioeconomic status. People living in poverty may lack the resources to allow them to consider what they want to do or be. A lack of role models and certain neighborhood experiences limit, rather than encourage, exploration. For example, an adolescent who is very interested in art may not believe she can obtain the needed training or succeed because her family is so poor. Instead, the talented adolescent may realize she has to earn a living quickly.

Forming a Racial/Ethnic Identity

All adolescents must develop vocational and gender identities. An adolescent from a minority group, however, must also develop an ethnic/racial identity, which takes on increased importance and meaning as the teen negotiates adolescence. Adolescents become more aware of the relationship of their ethnic group to the majority group (Phinney, Cantu, & Kurtz, 1997). Achieving a satisfying ethnic identity is related to self-confidence, a sense of purpose in life, and self-esteem (Martinez & Dukes, 1997), although it certainly is not the only, or even the most important, predictor of self-esteem (Bagley & Copeland, 1994; Phinney

Poverty and discrimination restrict exploration and choice, making identity formation more difficult.

& Alipuria, 1990). Exploration of ethnic issues is significantly greater among minority group college students than among those in the majority group (Phinney et al., 1997).

One basic approach to understanding the development of ethnic identity uses Erikson's and Marcia's work (Phinney, 1989, 1993) and views the process in terms of identity statuses. Many minority youth begin by internalizing the views held by the majority group. This is similar to identity foreclosure in that people may take on the values to which they have been exposed without questioning them. Erikson (1968) assumed that minority youth would accept the negative self-images projected onto them by society and be prone to developing a negative identity. However, studies do not support this idea, and positive self-attitudes are common (Spence & Markstrom-Adams, 1990). Other processes must be at work, perhaps in the community or at home, to counter negative messages from outside sources.

Minority group youth who have not yet faced issues of ethnicity may give little thought to them. This tendency might be considered diffusion, but little research has been conducted in this area. Phinney sees these two statuses—identity foreclosure and identity diffusion—as constituting a general first stage in the formation of an ethnic identity.

An ensuing period of exploration or moratorium involves experimentation, inquiry, and an attempt to clarify personal implications of ethnicity (Phinney & Tarver, 1988). The search process takes various paths, including reading books, taking courses, having discussions, and becoming politically involved. This period is hypothesized to be the second stage of identity formation.

The final stage in attaining an ethnic identity is identity achievement, during which the individual resolves questions and makes commitments. People feel confident and better about who they are by accepting themselves as members of a minority group.

Minority group youth often find themselves in two cultures: a dominant culture that sometimes does not give full credit to their group's contributions and a culture shaped by their ethnicity or race. Living in two cultures can be difficult. Cultural values may conflict. One culture may value individual achievement and the other, more group-oriented achievement. One culture may value school achievement and the other see it as "selling out" and requiring a surrendering of group identity (Fordham, 1988).

Separation, Assimilation, Integration, and Marginality

People from ethnic and racial minorities have four different choices when dealing with the majority culture and society. They can undergo *separation* from the dominant group and emphasize their unique values and culture, having little or no interaction with the dominant culture. Another choice is *assimilation,* in which the minority group members choose identification with the dominant society and cut all ties to their own group. *Integration,* a third option, involves identifying with, and involvement in, both the dominant culture and the minority culture, whereas *marginality* is a lack of involvement in either the minority or the majority culture. Minority group members who can be classified as *integrated* show better psychological adjustment and have higher self-esteem than those choosing the other options (Phinney, Chavira, & Williamson, 1992).

Minority group members who opt for full assimilation may find that they are rejecting their own minority group culture, a step that may pose problems of nonacceptance in both the majority and minority cultures. Separation—complete absorption in one's own culture—poses problems as well. It assumes that all the ideals and beliefs of the majority group are less valuable and that there is nothing to be learned from its culture and experiences. A rejection of the dominant culture makes participation in society difficult. The bicultural alternative, in which people see themselves as existing in both the dominant culture and their own culture, is one answer (Miller, 1999). Individuals choosing this alternative respect both cultures and can behave appropriately in different culturally defined situations.

People can achieve a sense of belonging to two cultures without sacrificing a sense of cultural/ethnic identity (LaFramboise, Coleman, & Gerton, 1993). They need not choose between the two cultures or assume that one culture is superior to the other. They may use one language when interacting with people from the majority group and another when speaking to someone in their own ethnic group.

When researchers administered questionnaires measuring values and attitudes of Lakota children, the younger children provided cultural answers matching the views of their minority society (Plas & Bellet, 1983). However, the older children maintained their preference for Native American values of community and style of relating to others but adopted the majority value toward school achievement. Differences in world views and value conflicts are real, but people can develop both solid ethnic identities and bicultural competence. In fact, bicultural Native American students are better adjusted in college, particularly in the academic and cultural domains, than their non-bicultural counterparts (LaFramboise et al., 1993).

Most descriptions of identity formation among minority group youth emphasize the growing group identification that occurs in adolescence, leading to an acceptance of subculturally approved values and attitudes, and perhaps a rejection of mainstream values. The task in late adolescence is to integrate the two sets of values.

McWhorter (2000) stirred up controversy by arguing that African Americans may be limiting their opportunities when they react to historical and present-day racism with separatism (the belief that African Americans must reject anything from another culture), victimization, and anti-intellectualism (rejecting knowledge for the sake of knowledge). McWhorter finds these characteristics in middle- and upper-income African Americans, as well as those with lower incomes, and he claims that they prevent African Americans from succeeding by creating a fatalistic attitude and limiting their participation in mainstream culture. Such an argument was sure to garner considerable criticism. Painting a community with such a wide brush risks overgeneralization and takes the spotlight off social problems and external factors, such as poverty and racism, that place barriers in the way of achievement (Burdman, 2001). If minority group

AT A GLANCE 9.6 ETHNIC/RACIAL IDENTITY

KEY POINT: Achieving a meaningful ethnic/racial identity is difficult, as it requires a balance between identifying with a group and living in a world created by the majority group.

SUPPORTING POINTS	EXPLANATION
Achieving an ethnic identity may be considered in terms of identity statuses.	Many adolescents from minority groups first may be foreclosed as they take on the view of the predominant group. Some adolescents are in the diffused status because they have not faced identity issues. They then enter a period of moratorium or exploration, leading to identity achievement.
Adolescents from minority groups have four alternatives when dealing with the majority group.	Adolescents may separate and have little to do with the majority group. They may assimilate completely into the dominant culture. They may integrate, maintaining their identity yet living in the majority culture. They also may choose marginality, or nonparticipation in either culture. Individuals who are integrated show the best adjustment.

adolescents are to succeed in mainstream society, as well as develop a meaningful ethnic/racial identity, they must be able to exist in two worlds—that is, be biculturally competent. Although the task may not be easy, it is both possible and desirable. *(For a review of this section, see At A Glance 9.6.)*

PLACING THE SELF-CONCEPT AND IDENTITY FORMATION IN PERSPECTIVE

Most parents and teachers have no difficulty accepting a teen's identity, as long as it fits neatly into what is acceptable to them. It seems that parents want their children to be who they want to be only as long as who their children want to be is who their parents want them to be! Yet adolescents are members of a different cohort. They cannot be carbon copies of the people around them, and at least in our society, they must make individual decisions. However, pretending that one's identity is completely divorced from others in the environment, including parents, leads to a sense of being alone and adrift without any connection with others. As noted earlier, individuality and connectedness must balance.

Parents and teachers can help adolescents in their search for a coherent identity by improving their communication with teenagers. Sometimes, an adolescent's attempts to communicate with parents are met by an attitude best described as "You may consider only the options I deem the best." This stance may inhibit communication and exploration. Adults also may suggest ways to overcome barriers. A teen living in poverty with excellent credentials, for example, might never consider the field of medicine because of perceived barriers, and adults could discuss ways of overcoming these barriers.

Parents and teachers may also support adolescents' search for identity by encouraging them to think about who they are and what they want to be. Discussing moral, religious, and social issues, showing both sides of various political and moral dilemmas, and encouraging adolescents to become involved in community activities that have meaning to them all can help a teen's search. Adults can also remind teens that consideration of the consequences of one's actions is part of the exploration process. For example, adolescents who want to show an identity by dressing in an outlandish manner must realize that this action has consequences in the way people see them. Adolescents who adopt a social identity as a leader must realize that sometimes others may disagree and that consequences may arise if their leadership is perceived as bossy.

Parental emotional support is also important as it is related to the attainment of the identity achievement status (Sartor & Youniss, 2002). Parents who show care, attention, and understanding encourage their adolescents to explore. Adolescents need to know that they are valued and loved even if they follow a path that differs from the one a parent or teacher may have followed. Although adolescents may consider many paths that seem radical, their final commitments tend to be less so. Many of the radical youth from the 1960s, a time of revolution in the United Sates, grew up to take their place in helping occupations. Exploration is much easier and more effective if it takes place in an atmosphere of acceptance and warmth, with parents and teachers helping adolescents understand the nature of the choices available and the consequences of each choice.

Developing a positive sense of who one is, where one is going, and where one belongs is an important developmental task in adolescence. Developing a healthy self-esteem is difficult in a world that is often critical. Adolescence is the first time people must ask themselves what type of person they are and want to be, what they stand for, what type of lifestyle they want in the future, and what values they should adopt. Adolescents make these decisions in a society that offers much less structure and many more alternatives than ever before. It is easy

HAS YOUR OPINION CHANGED?

Please place the number best reflecting your opinion next to each of the following statements. Then compare your opinions now with those you held before reading the chapter.

1 — Strongly Agree
2 — Moderately Agree
3 — No Opinion
4 — Moderately Disagree
5 — Strongly Disagree

_____ 1. People who have a high sense of self-esteem are selfish and conceited.

_____ 2. People see themselves essentially as a reflection of how others view them.

_____ 3. People who act one way with one individual and a different way with another do not really know who they are.

_____ 4. People should always act in a way that reflects their true feelings and desires, rather than reflecting how others feel they should act.

_____ 5. Promoting self-esteem is an important responsibility of teachers and parents.

_____ 6. If parents can't say anything positive to their teens, they should say nothing at all.

_____ 7. Parents should not criticize their teenage children's dress and grooming, as they reflect part of a teenager's self.

_____ 8. Women have a more difficult time forming a personal identity than men.

_____ 9. Parents should give their children maximum freedom to explore new identities.

_____ 10. To develop a healthy personal identity, minority youth must develop a strong ethnic/racial identity.

for adolescents to become impatient with themselves and for others to be impatient with them. It is more difficult to answer these questions today than it was years ago, but with the help and encouragement of others, adolescents can find their way in the faster-paced, less structured world they face.

THEMES

THEME 1 **Adolescence is a time of choices, "firsts," and transitions.**	• The self-concept becomes more differentiated and complex in adolescence. • Adolescents must form a clear, coherent identity. • Adolescents develop a more complex conception of gender roles.
THEME 2 **Adolescence is shaped by context.**	• An individual's self-concept is partially formed through evaluative feedback from others in the environment. • Identity formation differs greatly in Western nations, where adolescents are given a great deal of individual choice, and more traditional societies, where less choice and more guidance is offered. • An individual's gender role is influenced by the total environmental context, including parents, peers, heroes, and the media.
THEME 3 **Adolescence is influenced by group membership.**	• Males show higher self-esteem than females after early adolescence. • The global self-esteem of African American youth is at least as high as that of adolescents from European backgrounds. • Women seem to emphasize both the interpersonal and intrapersonal aspects of identity, whereas males emphasize largely the intrapersonal. • Adolescents who belong to minority groups face a complicated process of forming an ethnic/gender identity that will allow them to identify with their group and function effectively in society.
THEME 4 **The adolescent experience has changed over the past 50 years.**	• It is probably more difficult for adolescents to formulate a coherent identity today, because society is changing at a faster pace than ever before. • Women, especially, may find developing a coherent identity more difficult today because of the role changes that have occurred so quickly. • Adolescents have many more alternatives today than they had years ago.
THEME 5 **Today's views of adolescence are becoming more balanced, with greater attention to its positive nature.**	• Rather than viewing minority group adolescents as having poor self-esteem, psychologists today realize that many adolescents from minority group backgrounds have good self-esteem. • Rather than believing that the higher the level of self-esteem the better, psychologists are now aware that unstable high self-esteem, grandiose self-esteem, and self-esteem that is not based on anything real can lead to major difficulties. • Rather than believing that adolescent females base their identities on interpersonal factors alone, psychologists now believe that females base their identities on both interpersonal and intrapersonal factors. • Rather than seeing particular behaviors as masculine or feminine, psychologists now note that some behaviors or traits are more likely to be found in one gender or the other. • Rather than arguing that women suppress their opinions to seem feminine, modern researchers argue that females will feel confident in expressing themselves when they receive encouragement from their parents. • Rather than viewing gender role as dependent solely on early learning, psychologists now argue that many complex processes are involved in developing a gender role, as well as that the development continues past childhood through adolescence.

CHAPTER SUMMARY AT A GLANCE

KEY TOPICS	KEY POINTS	
Basic Concepts Related to the Self	Self-concept and self-esteem are important aspects of an adolescent's inner experience. (*At A Glance 9.1, p. 299*)	← **KEY TERMS** *self (p. 297)* *self-concept (p. 297)* *self-esteem (p. 297)* *identity (p. 298)*
Self-Concept in Adolescence	The self-concept becomes more differentiated in adolescence, and by the end of adolescence the contradictory parts have been integrated into a coherent self-concept. (*At A Glance 9.2, p. 304*)	
Self-Esteem in Adolescence	High self-esteem is related to many positive outcomes, but high unstable self-esteem or self-esteem bordering on narcissism leads to negative outcomes. (*At A Glance 9.3, p. 316*)	← *narcissism (p. 312)*
Identity	Developing a coherent identity is one of the primary developmental tasks of adolescence. (*At A Glance 9.4, p. 326*)	← *ego identity (p. 316)* *role confusion (p. 316)* *crisis, exploration (p. 318)* *commitment (p. 319)* *identity foreclosure (p. 321)* *identity diffusion (p. 321)* *identity moratorium (p. 321)* *identity achievement (p. 322)* *intimacy versus isolation (p. 322)*
Gender Roles	The meaning of what it is to be a male or a female is an important element of an individual's global identity, and many factors influence its development. (*At A Glance 9.5, p. 335*)	← *sex typing (p. 327)* *gender roles (p. 327)* *androgyny (p. 328)* *gender schema theory (p. 333)*
Ethnic/Racial Identity	Achieving a meaningful ethnic/racial identity is difficult, as it requires a balance between identifying with a group and living in a world created by the majority group. (*At A Glance 9.6, p. 338*)	

Review questions for this chapter appear in the appendix.

10

LOVE AND SEX

WHAT IS YOUR OPINION?

PHYSICAL DEVELOPMENT AND SEXUALITY
- Physical Changes and Adolescent Sexuality
- Masturbation

DATING, LOVE, AND SEX
- Dating
  Perspective 1: Dating Kevin
- Love
- The Link Between Love and Sex

SEXUAL ATTITUDES AND BEHAVIOR
- The Revolution in Sexual Attitudes
- The Evolution of Adolescent Sexual Behavior
  Perspective 2: Love, Sex, and Commitment
- Motives for Intercourse
- Contraceptive Use
- Sexual Orientation: Homosexual Behavior

SEX EDUCATION
- Sex Education at Home
- Sex Education in the Schools
  Perspective 3: What Did You Find?
  FOCUS: Do Parents Have the Right to Know That Their Daughter Is Seeking an Abortion?
- Sexually Transmitted Infections
- Teenage Pregnancy
- Forced Sexual Behavior
- Sexual Harassment

PLACING ADOLESCENT SEXUALITY IN PERSPECTIVE

HAS YOUR OPINION CHANGED?

THEMES

CHAPTER SUMMARY AT A GLANCE

Do you remember your first romantic relationship? Do you remember feeling unsure of yourself, not knowing exactly what to say or what to do? The importance of romance, love, and sexuality is reflected in the movies and on television. The media depict high school as no more than a place for adolescents to meet one another. They urge boys and girls to try to look as alluring as possible so as to attract others. They portray success as having one or more boyfriends or girlfriends. Movies and television shows depict boys as chasing after sex with little else on their minds, whereas girls seem to resist until finally they are swept off their feet.

Certainly, the physical changes of adolescence, which are discussed in "Physical Development," directly lead to a significant increase in sexual interest, arousal, and sexual behavior. Adolescents who must adjust to the sexual nature of life face four problems (Muuss, 1982). First, they must adjust to their own changing bodies and see themselves as sexually adult males and females. Second, they must understand physiological and psychological gender differences and learn to establish new love relationships. Third, they must incorporate their newly matured sex drives into their personalities, a task that requires them to redefine sexuality in relation to social values and demands. Fourth, they must reconcile the conflict between their own sex drive and society's rules. Adolescents receive many conflicting and confusing messages about sexuality. Some sources tell them to remain abstinent until they are emotionally ready for sex; others counsel abstinence until marriage but being informed about contraception and disease prevention. Still others permit having sex but advocate using precautions to protect against disease and unwanted pregnancy (Blinn-Pike, Berger, & Rea-Holloway, 2000).

We begin our investigation of adolescent love and sex by examining the nature of early sexual experience. Then we examine the relationship between love and sex. Many aspects of the environment influence adolescent sexuality, so we look at the complex environmental factors that shape adolescent sexual attitudes and expression. We then examine the changes in sexual attitudes and behaviors that some have called a revolution, and we analyze contraceptive use. Last, we will look at sex education in the home and the school, sexually transmitted infections, teenage pregnancy, forced sexual behavior, and sexual harassment.

WHAT IS YOUR OPINION?

Please place the number best reflecting your opinion next to each of the following statements. We will return to this questionnaire at the end of the chapter so you can determine if your opinions have changed.

1 — Strongly Agree
2 — Moderately Agree
3 — No Opinion
4 — Moderately Disagree
5 — Strongly Disagree

_____ 1. The concept of love cannot be adequately defined.

_____ 2. People should never marry unless they are in love.

_____ 3. Early adolescents are too young to know what love really is.

_____ 4. It is acceptable for parents to have an earlier curfew for their daughters than for their sons.

_____ 5. It is acceptable for 16-year-olds who are in love to engage in sexual intercourse.

_____ 6. There has been a revolution in sexual behavior.

_____ 7. Males and females want different things in a relationship.

_____ 8. Schools should freely offer condoms to their students.

_____ 9. Sex education is solely the responsibility of parents.

_____ 10. The only real difference between homosexuals and heterosexuals is their sexual orientation.

PHYSICAL DEVELOPMENT AND SEXUALITY

The rapid pubertal development during early adolescence is significantly related to the initiation of sexual activity (Katchadourian, 1990). In fact, there is a clear relationship between physiological development and sexual activities. Biological influences operate both directly and indirectly.

Physical Changes and Adolescent Sexuality

Puberty involves a substantial increase in testosterone levels in boys and is clearly related to increases in sexual activity, regardless of the development of any secondary sex characteristics (Udry et al., 1985). A link between increases in testosterone levels in girls (primarily adrenal androgens) and sexual interest, but not necessarily sexual behavior, is also found (Dyk, 1993). This finding may indicate that social forces, such as greater social taboos against female sexuality, may restrain the sexual behavior of girls.

Puberty also involves the maturation of secondary sex characteristics. Indirectly, breast development in females and physical changes in males may make teenagers more attractive to others and more likely to engage in sexual conduct. Hormones, such as estrogen in women and testosterone in men, are important causes of these physical changes.

Although physical maturation certainly sets in motion a series of important changes, it only sets the stage for an increase in sexual activity. The effects of these changes depend on the individual's culture, upbringing, religious convictions, personality, and peer relations. Sexual attitudes and behavior can be understood only within a larger interpersonal and social context (DeLamater & Friedrich, 2002).

Masturbation

Masturbation, or self-stimulation of the genitals, is a common sexual activity. In an Australian high school study, 58.5 percent of the males and 42.7 percent of the females reported masturbating at some time (Smith, Rosenthal, & Reichler, 1996). In a study of college students in the United States, 73 percent of the males and 34.3 percent of the females said they had masturbated during the past year (Leitenberg, Detzer, & Srebnik, 1993). In any group studied, a much higher percentage of males than females report masturbating.

Masturbation is not related to any other sexual behavior. The later sexual behavior of men or women who masturbated during preadolescence or early adolescence does not differ from the behavior of those who did not (Leitenberg et al., 1993). That is, masturbation is not related to whether teens experience intercourse at an early age, the frequency of intercourse reported, or the number of sexual partners. Furthermore, individuals who do and do not masturbate do not differ in general sexual satisfaction in relationships, sexual difficulties, or sexual arousal. In other words, masturbation has no effect on later sexual behavior.

Despite the fact that masturbation is common, social and religious taboos remain, and teens often feel guilty about this behavior (Lo Presto, Sherman, & Sherman, 1985). Those who think it is wrong, harmful, or sinful are more likely to experience guilt and anxiety. The more educated are less likely to believe myths about masturbation or experience guilt. *(For a review of this section, see At A Glance 10.1.)*

AT A GLANCE 10.1 PHYSICAL DEVELOPMENT AND SEXUALITY

KEY POINT: Physical changes lead to an increased sex drive during adolescence.

SUPPORTING POINTS	EXPLANATION
Physical development is related to sexual interest and activity.	The increase in hormone levels during adolescence directly influences sexual interest and activity. The maturation of the body increases sexual attraction.
Physical development sets the stage for sexual behavior, but it does not determine the type of sexual behavior an adolescent displays.	Sexual behavior is affected by cultural practices; an individual's family, friends, and beliefs; and numerous other environmental factors.
Masturbation is a common sexual activity for adolescents.	Males masturbate more than females. Masturbation does not relate to later sexual satisfaction or dissatisfaction, or to the frequency or timing of later interpersonal sexual experiences.

DATING, LOVE, AND SEX

Adolescence is the time of one's first true romance.

Much sexual behavior occurs within a dating relationship. The chapter titled "Peers" discussed dating as a vehicle for exploring one's roles and interpersonal relationship. Here we will look at the role of dating in sexual behavior.

Dating

By age 15, most teens have had some experience dating and have engaged in some sexual experimentation, although a minority of them have experienced sexual intercourse. In romantic relationships they may further develop social skills involving intimacy and communication that they learn and maintain in same-gender relationships. At least in early adolescence, teens spend much of their time in mixed groups, allowing easier, though less intimate, interaction. You may remember being part of such a group of teen boys and girls in junior high school and even in the first year or so of high school. It is within such a group that dating often begins.

Dating has many functions, one of which is a venue in which adolescents practice and experiment with romantic relationships and sexuality (Feiring, 1996). When teenagers from sixth grade and eleventh grade, as well as college students, were asked about their reasons for dating and concerns about who they should date, early and middle adolescents held a more egocentric orientation and tended toward immediate gratification. Recreation, intimacy, and status were the most important factors, in order of importance. Late adolescents concentrated more on reciprocity in dating relationships, and they rated intimacy and companionship as more important than learning, experiencing, and the reactions of their peers to the romantic relationships. Late adolescents showed more interdependence and a greater orientation to the future (Roscoe, Diana, & Brooks, 1987).

Of course, two people dating may have different motivations. For example, a young man whose primary goal is recreation may ask out a young woman who considers status very important. Perhaps this sort of mismatch is one reason why most dating relationships are short-lived. Certainly, not all dating relationships progress past the level of recreation, status seeking, and situational convenience. Dating partners may move slowly or quickly to sexual intimacy. Dating is fraught with anxiety, and disappointment and rejection are quite common (Greenberg et al., 1989).

Dating relationships are not just friendships. Romantic relationships, as noted in "Peers," involve fascination and sexual attraction, qualities not indicative of friendships (Furman & Wehner, 1994). Romantic relationships require the integration of affiliation (wanting to be with others), attachment, caregiving, and sexuality. These relationships do not substitute for same-gender friendships, but they offer both intimacy and support.

Teens are dating at an earlier age today than in the past. In 1924, girls started to date at the age of 16 years, whereas today they begin at about 13 years (Thornton, 1990). Adolescents from single-parent families begin to date earlier than those from intact families (Coleman, Ganong, & Ellis, 1985). Formal dating has declined somewhat, and informal meetings have become more common. Girls

PERSPECTIVE 1

DATING KEVIN

SETTING THE SCENE: Deena is a physically mature 14-year-old girl who looks somewhat older. Her parents allow her to date boys, but the boy she is now seeing, Kevin, seems rough. He is doing poorly in school and gets in some minor trouble.

DEENA: *It's the most embarrassing thing. I understand my parents' concerns, but Kevin is a nice guy, and my friends think he's great. We like each other, and I see no reason why I shouldn't date him. I'm willing to live by a curfew. I should be able to date anyone I want.*

PARENTS: *We don't want to be too intrusive into her social life, but Kevin is unacceptable. He is not the sort of boy we want Deena dating. We feel she is too young to date just anyone she wants, and she should listen to us.*

QUESTION: What would you do if you were Deena's parents? If you were Deena, how would you deal with this situation?

complain more about their parents' rules concerning dating than do boys, probably because parents are stricter with girls. Because girls tend to date somewhat older boys, they experience increased pressure for sexual activity, which often causes parents to become stricter and more protective (de Gaston, Weed, & Jensen, 1996).

Dating relationships end, and breakups are rarely easy. However, these relationships are an important part of adolescence and help adolescents develop the types of skills they will require in long-term romantic relationships in adulthood.

Love

In Western society, interpersonal sexuality is connected with love and romance. Americans are raised on romantic love. Movies and television programs show a great deal of romantic love—most of it outside of marriage—and much poetry is written about it. Even young children are exposed to romance through stories about Cinderella, Sleeping Beauty, or The Little Mermaid. In movies based on these tales and others like *Pretty Woman,* as well as in many television shows, the female lead seeks romance and is often swept off her feet by the romantic male lead. Love must be differentiated from sexuality and friendship, yet romantic love certainly involves both.

What Is Love?   Over the years, psychologists have tried, with varying degrees of success, to define the nature of love (Aron & Westbay, 1996). Sternberg (1986) views love as a dynamic quality of relationships composed of three elements: intimacy, passion, and commitment. **Intimacy** is the emotional attachment that two people experience, requiring open communication and self-disclosure. Intimacy involves promoting the partner's welfare, feeling happy with the partner, holding the partner in high respect, being able to count on the partner, and giving and receiving emotional support and understanding

How would you define love? According to Robert Sternberg love involves intimacy, passion, and commitment.

intimacy   The emotional attachment experienced in a romantic relationship, requiring open communication and self-disclosure.

Table 10.1

Different Kinds of Love

Different types of love are defined by specific combinations of intimacy, passion, and commitment. Most loving relationships fit between categories, because the various components of love are expressed not discretely but along continua.

	Component		
Kind of Love	*Intimacy*	*Passion*	*Commitment*
Nonlove	−	−	−
Liking	+	−	−
Infatuated love	−	+	−
Empty love	−	−	+
Romantic love	+	+	−
Companionate love	+	−	+
Fatuous love	−	+	+
Consummate love	+	+	+

Note: + = component present; − = component absent.
Source: Adapted from Sternberg (1986), p. 123.

(Sternberg & Grajek, 1984). **Passion** refers to the romantic and physical aspects of the relationship. **Commitment** is the desire to maintain the relationship and a willingness to stay with the relationship, to work things out and overcome problems, and to devote oneself to the relationship. The strongest predictor of satisfaction and endurance within a relationship is commitment (Whiteley, 1993).

Not all romantic relationships contain these three components in equal parts. **Romantic love** involves intimacy and passion alone, but no commitment; **companionate love** involves intimacy and commitment but lacks passion; and **fatuous love** contains passion and commitment but has no intimacy. Only **consummate love** contains intimacy, commitment, and passion (see Table 10.1).

Two of these types of love, romantic love and companionate love, have been extensively studied. Romantic love is basically erotic. There is a strong need for the presence of the loved one and for physical contact. It is characterized by the belief that there is only one true love and by idealization of the loved one. Realistic or companionate love characterizes people who have been in a relationship for an extended period. The passion is less intense, and the relationship evolves into a steady concern for the other individual. Passionate moments do occur, but they are not as intense (Schultz, 1984). Normally, adolescents who feel they are in love are characterized more by the romantic than the companionate type.

Romantic love is not unique to our culture. The idea that people fall in love is found in some form in most societies, even societies in which parents traditionally arrange marriages. An analysis of songs and folklore in 166 different cultures found evidence of romantic love in 147 of them (Jankowiak & Fischer, 1992). The absence in the remaining cultures may have been due to the methods used in the study. However, some non-Western cultures may not share the Western idealization of love. Western culture is centered on the self, independence, and emotional expression. This orientation is a natural outgrowth of what was described as broad socialization practices in "The World of Adolescence." Broad socialization practices emphasize freedom, independence, and the importance of fulfilling one's potential.

Some more traditionally oriented Eastern societies view love differently. Chinese society is centered on obligation to others. According to anthropologist Francis Hsu (1985), an American asks, "How does my heart feel?" whereas a Chinese individual asks, "What will other people say?" (p. 50). Western culture concentrates on romance and passion, and in such relationships we expect to find intimacy. In Chinese society, parents and kin are often the sources of intimacy, and people remain tied to their families throughout life. In fact, love itself may have a negative connotation.

Young people in North America, Italy, and China were interviewed about their emotional experiences (Shaver, Wu, & Schwartz, 1991). They agreed on the meaning of joy, happiness, anger, sadness, and many other emotions, as well as on whether these emotions were experienced positively or negatively. However, they did not agree on love. Both North Americans and Italians equated love with happiness, but Chinese students associated it with sadness, probably because the English word *love* translates into "a passionate but illicit relationship" in Chinese. Its meaning is closer to "infatuation."

Some cultures engage in the custom of arranged marriages. These marriages are still common in India, some Muslim countries, and sub-Saharan Africa. However, today the two prospective partners usually have the right to agree or disagree to marry.

Too often, the discussion of differences between Eastern and Western views centers on absolutes. Because of technological advances in communication, Western influences are common in non-Western cultures, and they often modify traditional views of love. For example, when researchers asked young people in Eastern and Western countries if they would marry someone they did not love but who had all the qualities they wanted in a mate, almost all college students in Western cultures said no (Levine et al., 1995). Students in Australia, Brazil, Hong Kong, and Mexico answered similarly, as those societies are more devel-

passion The romantic and physical aspects of a romantic relationship.

commitment The desire to maintain a relationship and overcome the obstacles to maintaining it.

romantic love Love that contains passion and intimacy but no commitment and that is basically erotic.

companionate love A mature love that contains intimacy and commitment but no passion.

fatuous love Passionate, committed love without intimacy.

consummate love Love that contains intimacy, commitment, and passion.

Figure 10.1

Would You Marry Someone You Didn't Love?
When adolescents from many countries were asked "if a man (woman) had all the other qualities you desired, would you marry this person if you were not in love with him (her)?" most respondents from Western countries or nations most influenced by Western culture said "no." Respondents from some other countries, such as India and Pakistan, answered quite differently.

Source: Adapted from Levine et al. (1995).

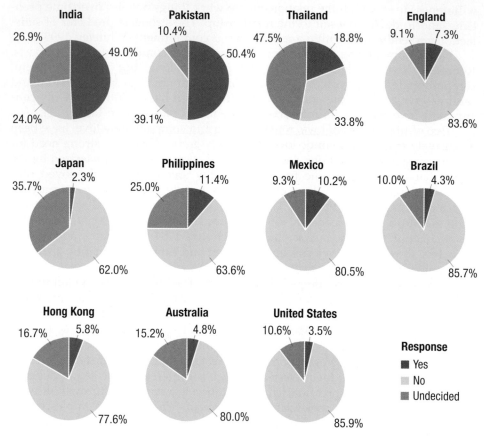

Responses to Question: "If a man (woman) had all the other qualities you desired, would you marry this person if you were not in love with him (her)?"

oped and westernized. However, about half the students surveyed in India and Pakistan said yes, they would marry someone they did not love but who had all the other qualities (see Figure 10.1). Of course, these college students may not be representative of the general population, but it is fair to say that around the world most young people consider love a prerequisite for marriage. Exceptions might be found in some Eastern, collectivist, or poorer countries (Hatfield & Rapson, 1996).

Styles of Love   Another approach to describing love looks at what John Lee called *styles of love* (Lee, 1974a, 1974b). Love styles refer to how people define or approach love. A romantic partner's approach to love guides behavior within the relationship, deeply affecting the experience of the other individual in the relationship. For example, some people are more possessive in their relationships than others, and some treat love as a game. Lee described six different styles of love:

- *Eros*   Love is very important to the erotic lover, and this person's love has a strongly physical component. Erotic love develops quickly, and early sexual activity is the rule. The erotic lover is not especially jealous or possessive, and although emotions are intense, this lover is not likely to undergo much self-sacrifice in the effort to obtain love.

- *Ludus*   The ludic lover sees love as a game played for fun. This individual avoids deep relationships and may juggle a number of partners at the same time. Just the right degree of emotionality is maintained so that personal commitment never becomes too demanding. To maintain this level, the ludic lover may encourage a partner to see other people. The ludic lover is also more likely to use verbal coercion to obtain sex.

- *Storge* The storge sees love as a slow, steady climb toward commitment. Neither intense emotions nor sexual encounters are central to the relationship. Instead of seeking the roller-coaster ups and downs of a passionate relationship, the storgic lover approaches love as a relationship mostly based on sharing activities and interests.

- *Mania* The manic lover contrasts with the storge. This individual is obsessed with his or her partner, jealous and possessive, and filled with anxiety that something will happen to ruin the relationship. Such jealousies and insecurities make achieving intimacy difficult.

- *Pragma* The pragmatic lover is more calculating than those with the other styles. The pragmatic lover knows what he or she wants and "shops" to find a partner with the desired interests and goals. The relationship that ensues is not a highly passionate or intense one; rather, it is one that fits into a well-defined pattern.

- *Agape* Agapic love is pure, patient, kind, altruistic, and compassionate. Love is given without any conditions and may involve more self-sacrifice than any of the other styles. Agapic love is not intensely emotional, but rather more spiritual. If a sexual relationship exists, it is more an act of intimate communication than of sensual pleasure. Lee found no examples of pure agapic love in his research but did find some aspects of agape in a number of relationships.

These six styles of love should be seen as ideal types; very few people fit exactly one or another of these descriptions. Some combinations of styles seem more incompatible than others. For example, a storge and an erotic lover might find it difficult to build a satisfying relationship.

Lee's six styles of love yield a useful picture of how people approach love and perhaps widen our ideas of what love may mean to various people. These styles of love may be related to the dimensions of intimacy, passion, and commitment described earlier. The eros and agape styles of love are positively related to high levels of intimacy in a relationship (Levy & Davis, 1988). The ludic style of loving, in contrast, is negatively related to intimacy and commitment.

Two Views of Intimacy Interpersonal sexuality often revolves around romantic relationships and the development of intimacy. At least two views of intimacy exist to explain some of the developmental changes in romantic relationships that occur during adolescence. Both views deal with the question of how intimate relationships develop.

One theorist, Harry Stack Sullivan (Perry & Gawel, 1953), noting the increase in sexuality that occurs in adolescence, argued that romantic relationships arise from the closer preadolescent relationships with members of the same gender. The capacity for this intimacy comes from a preadolescent "chumship" stage, in which friendships with people of the same gender become deeper, paving the way for these heterosexual relationships. (The chapter titled "Peers" discusses the development of these closer relationships with friends.) Through these close relationships, preadolescents learn sensitivity to others and caring, which paves the way for adolescent romantic and sexual relationships. Romantic relationships contain many of the characteristics of close friendships, such as intimacy, understanding, and companionship. This interpersonal view considers romantic relationships as developing from the lessons learned in close friendships.

The second theory, called *attachment theory* (see "Families"), sees an individual's loving relationships as developing from early relationships with the parents. Because of the physical changes that occur in puberty, adolescents shift their attachment from parental figures to a boyfriend or girlfriend. According to the theory, romantic relationships integrate attachment and caregiving with sexuality and are deeply influenced by the nature of early relationships with caregivers (Hazan & Shaver, 1990).

If the attachment theory is to have any validity, the nature of one's early relationship with the caregiver must influence behavior in a romantic relationship in some way. Some research does link one's early relationships with the mother to later relationships with romantic partners. The central idea is that the nature of these early relationships forms a working model that includes expectations for the behavior of others, how one acts, and ways of regulating one's emotions that act as guides for future relationships (Bartholomew & Horowitz, 1991; Collins & Read, 1990).

As noted in "Families," attachment patterns in very young children are often categorized as secure attachment, anxious/avoidant attachment, and anxious/ambivalent attachment. Young children who are classified as securely attached have the most satisfying relationship with their caregivers and use their mothers as a source of comfort and security. Children showing anxious/avoidant attachment do not use their mothers as a base for exploring the environment and do not find much comfort in their relationship with their mother when frightened. Children classified as showing anxious/ambivalent attachment show a great deal of anxiety; they have an intense, yet unsatisfying, relationship with their caregiver, and the caregiver's inconsistent behaviors lead to anxiety about the true nature of the relationship.

Psychologists have developed a structured questionnaire that can measure attachment category in late adolescents or adults by asking specific questions about what participants remember about their early relationship with their parents. The categories are similar to the ones found when testing young children, and placement in one of these classifications relates to the nature of the individual's romantic relationships.

In one study, researchers asked people about their early memories of their parent-child relationships, as well as which of three descriptions best described their most important romantic relationship (see Table 10.2) (Hazan & Shaver, 1987). More than half the participants described their relationship with their parents as affectionate, caring, happy, and accepting. Others described relationships that were less positive. For example, individuals categorized as anxious/avoidant described their mothers as cold and rejecting, whereas those classified

---

Table 10.2

Descriptions of Relationship with Romantic Partner and Types of Adult Attachment

Participants were asked which of the three descriptions best fit their most important romantic relationship. Previously, they had been asked about their early relationship with their parents. Participants with secure attachments to their parents also described secure relationships with their romantic partners. Individuals with anxious/avoidant or anxious/ambivalent relationships with their parents were more likely to describe anxious relationships with their romantic partners.

Type of Adult Attachment	Description of Relationship with Romantic Partner
Secure (56%)	I find it relatively easy to get close to others and am comfortable depending on them and having them depend on me. I don't often worry about being abandoned or about someone getting too close to me.
Anxious/avoidant (25%)	I am somewhat uncomfortable being close to others; I find it difficult to trust them completely, difficult to allow myself to depend on them. I am nervous when anyone gets too close, and often, love partners want me to be more intimate than I feel comfortable being.
Anxious/ambivalent (19%)	I find that others are reluctant to get as close as I would like. I often worry that my partner doesn't love me or won't stay with me. I want to merge completely with the other person, and this desire sometimes scares people away.

Source: Adapted from Hazan & Shaver (1987), p. 515.

as anxious/ambivalent saw their fathers as unfair and unsupportive and reported a lack of independence.

Participants placed in each attachment category characterized their romantic relationships differently. Participants classified as secure described their love experiences as happy, friendly, and trusting and were able to accept and support their partner. People characterized as avoidant showed a fear of intimacy and a desire for independence. They were mistrustful and wanted distance, finding it difficult to engage in self-disclosure (Cooper, Shaver, & Collins, 1998; Feeney & Noller, 1991). Anxious/ambivalent participants experienced love as an obsession, a desire for complete union, and a roller coaster of emotional highs and lows; they showed tremendous jealousy. Anxious/ambivalent participants often noted how easy it is to fall in love but how hard it is to find true love, were dependent, required complete commitment, and worried about being abandoned.

Studies linking early childhood relationships to later relationships are interesting but should be interpreted cautiously. The correlations obtained are often positive but not very strong. In addition, the relationship between attachment category and the nature of the relationship declines in adulthood as people rework their models of relationships. For example, 25 percent of the participants in one study reported a change in romantic attachment style, probably because they were in a relationship that disconfirmed their model. Their changes often moved toward a more secure model (Hazan & Hutt, 1990, cited in Kirkpatrick & Davis, 1994).

Which of these two models—the interpersonal or the attachment model—fits teenage romantic relationships? It is possible that both early experiences and relationships with peers are important. Perhaps early experiences with parents influence relationships with peers, which carries over to romantic relationships. Finally, perhaps one model better fits early romantic relationships and the other, later romantic relationships (Furman & Wehner, 1994). Mature attachments to others do not emerge during intense relationships that are short-lived, and because these relationships are most common in early and middle adolescence, the interpersonal theory fits better here. Late adolescence and early adulthood usher in longer-lasting, more stable and committed relationships in which attachment and caregiving emerge as prime components. The attachment theory may help explain these relationships.

The Link Between Love and Sex

Beginning in the 1960s and continuing through the 1970s and 1980s, the percentage of teens engaging in sexual intercourse increased significantly (Singh & Darroch, 1999). This increase reflected a liberalization of attitudes regarding premarital sex that led to a dating code in which sexual activity is considered acceptable within an affectionate/loving/caring relationship even outside marriage. Sex is viewed, especially by females, as an expression of love and intimacy, but sexual intercourse need not take place only within marriage (McCabe & Cummins, 1998). Although the trend of more teens experiencing intercourse has leveled off and even declined in recent years, the link between love and sex continues to increase, and the link was stronger in the 1990s than in the 1970s (Schmidt et al., 1994).

The relationship between affection, love, and sex continues to evolve. Most teenagers today accept the view of sex as a part of a loving relationship. This sexual ethic, often described as "permissiveness with affection," continues to develop and change. The ethic of acceptable sex within a loving, affectionate relationship continues, but love and affection now involve much less commitment for the future (Feldman, Turner, & Araujo, 1999). This ethic allows adolescents to indulge in sexual behavior earlier in the relationship and at an earlier age. A 15-year-old teen's social immaturity makes commitment difficult. Being in love makes sexuality much more acceptable, but this love and affection need not lead to long-term commitment. *(For a review of this section, see At A Glance 10.2.)*

AT A GLANCE **10.2** DATING, LOVE, AND SEX

KEY POINT: Love may be defined in many ways, and its relationship to sexuality is determined by many social and personal factors.

SUPPORTING POINTS	EXPLANATION
American adolescents are raised on a diet of love, romance, and sex.	Western culture, and especially the media, relates love and romance to sex. Many fairy tales involve romance.
Sternberg defines love in terms of intimacy, passion, and commitment.	*Intimacy* involves attachment and self-disclosure. *Passion* describes the physical aspect of the relationship, and *commitment* is the desire to maintain the relationship despite difficulties and barriers.
Lee suggested that six different styles of love exist.	Lee's six styles of love include erotic, storgic, ludic, manic, pragmatic, and agapic love. People with each style of love look at love differently and behave differently.
There are two approaches to explaining the development of intimate relationships.	Sullivan sees love as growing out of the intimacy and caring found in earlier same-sex friendships. Attachment theory sees later intimate relationships as arising from the early relationship with parents, which forms a model for later relationships.
The relationship between love and sex has changed significantly in the last 40 years.	In the 1960s, adolescents began to believe that sex within a loving, caring relationship, and not necessarily within marriage, was acceptable. Today intercourse within a loving, caring relationship is acceptable, and many individuals require less commitment.

SEXUAL ATTITUDES AND BEHAVIOR

No one doubts that sexual attitudes have changed, that the changes are continuing, and that a greater percentage of teens are engaging in sexual intercourse than in the past. The nature of these changes in attitudes and behavior, however, is often misunderstood.

The Revolution in Sexual Attitudes

The traditional attitude concerning sexuality reflects a double standard. Males have been permitted sexual freedom, whereas females have been denied it. Males have been encouraged to experiment, yet sanctions against female sexuality traditionally have been substantial. The sexual needs of males have been recognized, but the same needs in females have been denied, even within marriage. To some extent this double standard has declined, although it still influences the way parents bring up their children (Bingham & Crockett, 1996). Parents often give their sons more freedom than their daughters and react differently to the sexual behavior of their sons and daughters.

Generally, attitudes have changed in the direction of greater acceptance of sexual behavior before marriage and a live-and-let-live orientation to sex. Sexual behavior is considered more a matter of personal choice than the business of society (Chilman, 1983). Adolescents' attitudes toward sexuality are likely to be more permissive than their parents' attitudes. These variations may be due partly to cohort differences (different generations see things differently) and partly to the different roles and responsibilities of parents and teenagers. Parents often underestimate the sexual activity of their adolescent teens, perhaps because they do not want to think about it. Teens underestimate their mothers' level of disapproval for such behavior (Jaccard & Dittus, 2000), especially when the parents and children communicate poorly.

The revolution in attitudes has been greater for females than for males, probably because women had more conservative attitudes to start with. Yet the idea that sex itself is looked on casually, or that the attitudes of males and females are identical, is false. Males have more liberal attitudes toward sexuality than females, and females are more likely to view sex as part of a loving relationship (De Gaston et al., 1996; Knox, Sturdivat, & Zusman, 2001; Wilson & Medora, 1990). Females are also more likely to believe that people having sex should always use some method of birth control and that a person should not be pressured into having sex (Carver, Kittleson, & Lacey, 1990). More women are committed to abstinence, somewhat less permissive in their views, and more likely to see sexual activity as a barrier to future goal attainment (Harvey & Spigner, 1995).

Both males and females become more permissive as the relationship gets more serious. And both believe that more sexual intimacy is proper when an individual is in love or engaged than when dating without affection or even when dating with affection but without love (Roche, 1986). However, males and females show differences in what sexual behavior they believe is appropriate at the beginning stages of dating, with males being more permissive than females. In the later stages of dating—which include dating only one person, being in love, and engagement—the differences narrow substantially.

Males, then, expect sexual intimacy earlier in a relationship, whereas females tie sexual intimacy to love. This tendency was nicely demonstrated in a study that asked adolescent males and females whether they believed a particular behavior was appropriate during a given stage of dating, whether they engaged in such behavior, and what they believed others did (see Table 10.3). In the early stages of a relationship (dating with no particular affection, dating with affection but not love, and dating and being in love but still dating others), what males

Do adolescent boys and girls view sexual expression differently? Research shows that females see sexuality as an expression of love and intimacy, while males often do not.

Table 10.3

When Is It Acceptable to Engage in Particular Sexual Behaviors?

College students were asked at what stage of a relationship certain sexual behaviors were appropriate, if they had engaged in the behaviors, and what percentage of others they believed engaged in the behaviors. The results show that males believe it is acceptable to engage in a variety of sexual behaviors earlier in a relationship than do females.

Behavior	Gender	Stage 1: Dating with No Particular Affection			Stage 2: Dating with Affection but Not Love			Stage 3: Dating and Being in Love			Stage 4: Dating One Person Only and Being in Love			Stage 5: Being Engaged		
		PRO	BEH	OTH	PRO	BEH	OTH	PRO	BEH	OTH	PRO	BEH	OTH	PRO	BEH	OTH
Light petting	Males	7%	37%	38%	41%	58%	61%	69%	74%	91%	87%	91%	94%	93%	100%	97%
	Females	1%	8%	22%	13%	21%	50%	50%	57%	88%	81%	85%	96%	93%	95%	99%
Heavy petting	Males	6%	32%	29%	32%	50%	49%	54%	69%	83%	77%	82%	91%	90%	81%	96%
	Females	0%	6%	15%	5%	14%	40%	31%	38%	76%	69%	76%	92%	83%	90%	98%
Intercourse	Males	3%	23%	10%	17%	33%	29%	44%	60%	72%	69%	80%	83%	76%	69%	96%
	Females	0%	2%	10%	1%	7%	18%	15%	16%	58%	52%	59%	84%	67%	75%	96%
	n males	71	65	69	71	66	70	70	62	69	71	56	70	71	16	69
	n females	197	192	197	197	189	195	196	172	195	196	168	195	196	77	195

Note: PRO refers to the percentage of adolescents believing the behavior is proper; BEH shows the percentage of participants who engage in the behavior; and OTH indicates the participants' estimate of how many college students engage in the behavior.

Source: Adapted from Roche & Ramsbey (1993), Table 1, p. 70.

and females believe are appropriate differs, with boys being more liberal than girls. As the relationship progresses to dating only one person, being in love, and becoming engaged, the differences narrow substantially and disappear in many areas (Roche & Ramsbey, 1993). Many more males actually engaged in behavior they did not think proper or appropriate than did females. For example, during stage 1 (dating with no particular affection), 32 percent of the males engaged in heavy petting, whereas only 6 percent thought it proper; in contrast, none of the girls thought it proper at that stage, and only 6 percent engaged in the behavior. It seems that when given the opportunity, males will engage in sexual behavior even if they do not think it is theoretically appropriate to do so.

An analysis of studies on gender differences in sexuality found relatively large gender differences in the incidence of masturbation (males report higher rates) and attitudes toward casual premarital sex (males are more permissive) (Oliver & Hyde, 1993). The analysis found small to moderate differences in attitudes toward premarital sex when the couple was engaged or committed (males are a bit more permissive), the frequency of sexual intercourse (males report a higher frequency), anxiety and guilt (females report more), age of first intercourse (males are somewhat younger), and number of partners (males report more). Males, then, appear more permissive. These differences have narrowed over time, though.

The Evolution of Adolescent Sexual Behavior

American men and women are more likely than ever to have intercourse by age 18 years. By the end of the teen years, more than half are sexually active (Alan Guttmacher Institute [AGI], 2002; Stryker, 1997). About 76 percent of the young women and 80 percent of the young men in the United States have had sexual intercourse by age 20. Males typically begin having sex earlier than females, even though the gender gap is closing, and males typically report higher levels of sexual activity at earlier ages (Moore et al., 1995). The age of first sexual intercourse has declined over the past 25 years as well, and American adolescents are engaging in sexual intercourse at younger ages (Cooksey, Rindfuss, & Guilkey, 1996).

African American males are more likely to report younger ages for first intercourse than white, Latino, or Asian American males (Sonenstein, Pleck, & Ku, 1991). In one study of Los Angeles adolescents, African American males reported experiencing their first sexual intercourse at a median age of 15, white males at 16.6 years, Latino males at 16.5 years, and Asian American males at 18.1 years (Upchurch et al., 1998). African American males, as a group, then, engage in their first intercourse significantly earlier than males of other groups. The differences among females of various groups are somewhat smaller. White and African American females report beginning to engage in sexual intercourse at about the same median age (about 16.6 and 16.3 years), and Latino females at 17.3 years. The sample did not contain enough Asian American females to estimate the age of first intercourse, but other studies show it is later than the other groups (Okazaki, 2002).

The trend toward more teenagers having sex does not show a continuous increase over time, however. The proportion of adolescents having sexual intercourse increased during the 1980s but stabilized late in the decade and began to decline in the 1990s (Singh & Darroch, 1999). The results of a recent survey of adolescent sexual behavior for grades 9 to 12 show the changes from 1991 through 1999. In 1991, 57.4 percent of the high school males and 50.8 percent of the high school females surveyed had experienced sexual inter-

PERSPECTIVE 2

LOVE, SEX, AND COMMITMENT

SETTING THE SCENE: Carlos and Lattie, both juniors in high school, have been going out for more than a year. Lattie has set clear limits on the extent of their sexual activities, but Carlos clearly is not happy with them.

CARLOS: *We've been going out for quite a while, and we're in love. I don't know why we can't make love. It's natural.*

LATTIE: *It's not like I don't want to, but I know that after next year we'll go our separate ways when we go to college. I don't think we'll marry, although you never know. He thinks I don't really love him because we haven't had sex. I know many of my friends do it. Maybe I have a hang-up about it. I guess it's always difficult the first time.*

QUESTION: If you were Lattie, would you agree to have sex with Carlos?

course, whereas in 1999, the figures stood at 52.2 percent and 47.7 percent, respectively. A greater proportion of teenagers in 1999 were abstaining from sexual intercourse than in 1991 (Centers for Disease Control and Prevention [CDC], 2000b). An 11 percent decline in the percentage of sexually active teens was noted between 1991 and 1997, but the percentage of high school males having had sexual intercourse increased somewhat between 1997 and 1999. The rate for females between 1997 and 1999 has stayed the same (see Figure 10.2). In addition, fewer sexually active teens reported multiple partners (CDC, 1998b).

These figures underestimate the extent of adolescent sexual behavior. The percentage of adolescents engaging in oral sex has increased (Remez, 2000), but many teens do not consider it as sex (American Health Consultants, 2001; Peterson, 2000b). These teens are also unaware of the fact that sexually transmitted infections (STIs, also called *sexually transmitted diseases*, or *STDs*) can be contracted through oral sex. Most studies of teenage sexuality do not include oral sex and therefore may not show the full extent of adolescent sexual behavior.

Various reasons are given for the increase in sexual intercourse rates from the middle of the 20th century through the 1980s. The dramatic liberalization of attitudes is certainly one reason. Although behavior does not always follow attitudes, changes in attitudes pave the way for behavioral changes. The women's movement also contributed by challenging the double standard and the traditional role expectations for women. The increased availability of contraceptive devices also may have contributed somewhat.

Motives for Intercourse

At first glance, the question of why teens engage in sexual intercourse seems simple enough to answer: because they want to. Physiological changes increase sexual attraction, sexual interest, and sexual behavior. However, some teenagers begin having sexual intercourse earlier than others, and some abstain altogether. Affection for the partner is a primary reason for first intercourse among about half the women and a quarter of the men (Michael et al., 1994). The earlier that adolescents begin to date and the earlier they limit themselves to one partner, the earlier they have sex (Thornton, 1990). However, many personal and environmental factors influence the decision to engage in sexual intercourse, which shows the extent to which the adolescents' total environment influences their behavior.

Personal Values Personal values affect both males' and females' decisions to engage in sexual intercourse (Rotheram-Borus & Koopman, 1991). For example, deep religious beliefs are related to a reduced likelihood of engaging in sexual intercourse. Participation in religious activities shows the same relation to abstaining from intercourse (Werner-Wilson, 1998). Sexual behavior is also influenced by the attitude that it may hinder one's future plans because of an unwanted pregnancy, and teens who are more career oriented are more likely to abstain from intercourse (Keith et al., 1991). Personal views of the appropriateness of sex at different stages of a relationship also influence sexual behavior. Adolescents who view sexuality as acceptable only in a serious relationship are less likely to have sex at the early stage of a relationship.

Peer and Partner Pressure Some adolescents admit that peer pressure and pressure from their dating partner are important reasons for engaging in sexual intercourse. For example, more than three-quarters of the virgins in one national sample noted that they had few, if any, friends who had engaged in sexual intercourse, whereas only a bit more than one-quarter of the nonvirgins said so (Coles & Stokes, 1985). Sometimes, friends place subtle or not-so-subtle pressure on others to have sex.

The same trend is found for romantic partners; about a quarter of adolescent women sampled in one major study said they had intercourse only to please

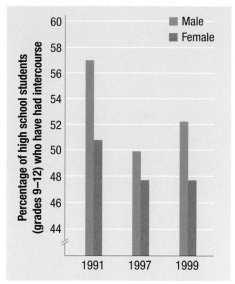

Figure 10.2
Percentage of High School Students Who Report Ever Having Had Sexual Intercourse
These percentages combine the answers from high school students in grades 9 through 12.

Source: Centers for Disease Control and Prevention (1998b, 2000a).

their partners, and 8 percent of the men said the same (Michael et al., 1994). The fact that pressure may be involved is shown in an interesting study that asked adolescents to report when they had first engaged in sexual intercourse and the age at which they felt it was best to do so. Of the sexually experienced adolescents in junior and senior high school, 83 percent said the best age for sexual intercourse was older than the age at which they first experienced it (Zabin et al., 1984). This finding may explain why so many teens express disappointment at their first intercourse experience. In one study, 67 percent of the males, but only 28 percent of the females, were psychologically satisfied with their first sexual experience (Darling & Davidson, 1986). In fact, fewer girls find sexual activities including intercourse "really satisfying sexually" or "fun" than males (Schmidt et al., 1994), and many factors may be at work. Perhaps young teenage boys concentrate more on their own pleasure than their partners'. Perhaps teenage girls experience more guilt and anxiety about the experience. In addition, boys and girls may have different perspectives on the meaning of their first sexual experiences.

Family Influence   Family variables are also related to the decision to have intercourse. When a diverse sample of 26,000 junior high and high school students was studied, lower rates of sexual activity across all age groups and both genders were found for adolescents from dual-parent families and families with higher incomes. Lower rates were also found (again, across age groups and genders) for adolescents who showed better school performance, were more religious, and felt that an adult or parent cared about them and had high expectations for them (Lammers et al., 2000).

Higher rates and early sexual intercourse are related to early puberty, poverty, violence in the home, marital disruption, lack of family connectedness, lack of parental monitoring, lack of religious affiliation, sexual abuse, poor school performance, and low educational aspirations. Higher rates of sexual activity are also related to extremes in parental discipline and control. When parental discipline and control are either very harsh or very lax, more sexual activity is found in the teens (Miller et al., 1986).

Parental influence can also be indirect. A study of seventh-grade females found that parental distance is related to depressive symptoms in females, which are positively associated with permissive sexual attitudes and having friends who engage in intercourse (Whitbeck, Conger, & Kao, 1993). Adolescents who perceive parental, and especially maternal, disapproval of sexual intercourse and those who feel highly connected to their mothers initiate sexual intercourse later than adolescents who are not close to their mothers (Reiff, 2001a). Having a cohesive family life and a good relationship with parents is related to a delay in the age of first intercourse.

Perhaps some adolescents engaging in sexual intercourse at an early age are trying to compensate for their poor relationships at home. In fact, major differences are found between individuals who begin to have sex in their early teens and those who become sexually active at age 17 or older. The teens involved in early sexual intercourse are less likely to use contraception regularly; are more prone to become involved in drug use; and are more likely to show poor school achievement, delinquency, behavioral problems, depression, and poor family relationships (Tubman, Windle, & Windle, 1996). This troubled behavior may indicate poor impulse control and may be related to sensation seeking and risk taking. Teenagers engaging in sexual intercourse at an early age have comparatively poorer communication with their parents (Casper, 1990) and are less well monitored (Meschke & Silbereisen, 1997). The poor quality of family relationships, an impulsive nature, and school problems may lead a teen to seek affection through sex. Sexual intercourse may also be a form of rebellion. Teens, then, may use sex to ease feelings of loneliness, gain affection, confirm their masculinity or femininity, or vent anger (White & DeBlassie, 1992). Girls who engaged in early sex are more likely to date males who are much older, who have experienced family breakups, and who are involved in antisocial behavior themselves

Table 10.4

Factors Associated with Early and Late Initiation of Sexual Intercourse Among Adolescents

The American Academy of Pediatrics reported these results after reviewing the studies on adolescent sexual behavior.

Factors Associated with Sexual Intercourse During Early Adolescent Years	Factors Associated with a Delay in the Initiation of Sexual Intercourse
Early pubertal development	Living with both parents
History of sexual abuse	Stable family environment
Poverty	Regular attendance at places of worship
Lack of attentive and nurturing parents	Increased family income
Cultural and familial patterns of early sexual experience	
Lack of school or career goals	
Poor school performance	
Dropping out of school	

Source: American Academy of Pediatrics, Committee on Adolescence (1999).

(Pawlby, Mills, & Quinton, 1997). Table 10.4 shows some of the factors associated with early and later initiation of sexual intercourse (American Academy of Pediatrics, 1999).

These conditions often are present before adolescence. Poor family relationships and other difficulties may set the stage for unprotected sexual behavior and later developmental problems. The problems experienced by adolescents engaging in sex at an early age, then, are not so much the result of the timing of intercourse as they are a part of a general pattern of poor development and familial relationships that appear before adolescence and continue into this period (Bingham & Crockett, 1996).

The Media   Anyone who watches television, music videos, or movies can testify to the tremendous exposure to sexuality that most children and adolescents have. A review of the literature on adolescents and sex in the media found that adolescents view 143 incidents of sexual behavior on network television at prime time each week, much of it between unmarried partners (Grube & Grube, 2000). About 60 percent of all music videos contain sexual content. As noted in "The Media," sex is presented in a casual and certainly positive light, with little exploration of love, commitment, or the need to take precautions against STIs or pregnancy.

Children 11 or 12 years old are not as likely to understand the suggestive material of what they see in the media as older adolescents are, but they do learn the rules and rituals of sexual conduct. Preadolescents and early adolescents learn that looking right and attracting the other gender are the most important aspects of teen life. No one argues that the media are the prime motivator for adolescents, and especially early adolescents, to have intercourse, but they remain an important part of the adolescents' environment.

Adolescents base their decision to have sex, then, on more than just biological urges. Personal and peer factors, family characteristics, and the media influence this decision as well.

Children and adolescents are constantly bombarded by sexuality on television, in the movies, and even on billboards.

Contraceptive Use

Contraceptives are more available today than in the past. There was a time when contraceptives, such as condoms, weren't displayed in drugstores. A teenager (or for that matter, an adult) would have to gingerly ask a clerk (often a young female) for a box of condoms, which the store kept hidden from sight. Discussions of contraception in sex education classes used to be considered dangerous, as they might encourage students to experiment sexually. However, there is absolutely no evidence that refusing to provide contraception to an adolescent results in abstinence or the postponement of sexual activities (American Academy of Pediatrics, 1999). In fact, just the opposite seems to be true; that is, adolescents who perceive obstacles to obtaining contraception are less likely to use them but are more likely to engage in sexual behavior leading to unwanted pregnancies and STIs (Guttmacher et al., 1997). Discussions of contraception may not be as detailed as they should be, but there is no doubt that times have changed and that more information about contraceptive alternatives and the alternatives themselves are available.

In 1985, 45 percent of adolescent girls aged 15 to 19 were sexually active, and just over half used a contraceptive method during their first intercourse. By 1995, 51 percent of the girls this age were sexually active, but more than three-quarters used some contraceptive method at first intercourse (Hogan, Sun, & Cornwell, 2000). This change shows a shift toward earlier, but more planned, sexual activity. The number of sexually active teens using contraceptives increased 24 percent between 1991 and 1997 (CDC, 1998b). However, teens use condoms inconsistently (CDC, 1992, 1998b), and most sexually active teens admit they have had sex at least once without having used any form of birth control (Morton et al., 1996). When first becoming sexually active, girls often rely on male contraceptive methods.

One way of measuring contraceptive use is to ask teens whether they used some method the last time they had sexual intercourse. The percentage of 15- to 19-year-olds responding yes to this question increased from 57 percent in 1988 to 67 percent in 1995 and remained at this level through 1999 (CDC, 2000b; Sonenstein et al., 1998). The proportion reporting contraception use the last time they had intercourse rose from 66 to 74 percent among African Americans and

Condoms are readily available and more teenagers are using contraception at their first intercourse than in the past. However, one in four teens who are sexually active admit to not using any contraception at least once during the previous year.

from 54 to 67 percent among whites. The 1995 respondents used condoms during 69 percent of their acts of intercourse in the previous year, compared with 56 percent for the 1988 respondents. About a quarter of the sexually active white females responded in 1999 that they used the birth control pill, whereas the totals for African American and Latino American females were 11.9 and 6.2 percent, respectively (CDC, 2000b). Nevertheless, more than one in four respondents reported having had unprotected sex in the previous year (Althaus, 1999). Contraceptive trends are encouraging, but the inconsistency of contraceptive use remains a challenge (American Academy of Pediatrics, 1999). The increased use of contraceptives may be due to better sex education, concern about acquired immune deficiency syndrome (AIDS), and a subtle change in attitudes. For example, more male teens currently believe that their partner would appreciate their willingness to use condoms, and fewer teens today find condom use embarrassing compared with a sample of teenagers in 1988 (Murphy & Boggess, 1998).

One reason for the inconsistent use of contraceptives is ignorance. Although adolescents know something about contraception, they often believe myths or downright inaccuracies (Padilla & Baird, 1991). Older teens know more than younger teens. The public often confuses increases in sexual activity with increases in sexual knowledge, but the two don't always go hand in hand (Morrison, 1985). Many teens simply do not believe that a pregnancy could occur from their first intercourse and cannot identify the time during the menstrual cycle when the greatest risk of pregnancy exists. Adolescents given a test of general sexual knowledge answer about half the questions correctly, and teens who are sexually active show no greater knowledge than those not sexually active (Carver et al., 1990; Leland & Barth, 1992). Younger teens, especially, may not have basic information about contraception or simply may not understand the consequences of their actions (Handler, 1990).

However, lack of knowledge is not the only reason for the inconsistent use of contraceptives by teens. Many sexually active teenagers, when asked why they don't use contraceptives, point out that they are not having sex frequently. Their attitude seems to be that they aren't having sex often enough to use contraception—an incredible cognition. Others claim that condom use interferes with the enjoyment of sex (Coles & Stokes, 1985). They may see applying a condom as disrupting the experience. Other teens do not realize that they are welcome at family planning clinics and believe they need to be a certain age or have their parents' consent to go to clinics (Brooks-Gunn & Furstenberg, 1989). Educational efforts can counter all these misconceptions.

Lack of consistent contraceptive use is related to other risky behaviors (Brown, DiClemente, & Park, 1992). For example, over half of sexually active college students report having had intercourse when drunk or high, and half these adolescents did not use any method of birth control on those occasions (Leland & Barth, 1992). About a quarter of all high school students claim they used alcohol or drugs the last time they had sexual intercourse (CDC, 2000b). Using alcohol is correlated with having sexual relations without any contraception (Gordon, Carey, & Carey, 1997). For females especially, both drinking alcohol and spending time with peers who drink are linked with not using contraception (Kowaleski-Jones & Mott, 1998). Other teens simply do not believe they (or their partners) will become pregnant, a form of the personal fable ("It can't happen to me because I'm different") discussed in "Cognitive Development."

The failure by young teens to use contraceptives also may be due to immaturity. Some young adolescents may not be mature enough to admit they are in a sexual relationship. Oral contraception requires both planning and an admission of being in such a relationship. The teen rationalizes the first sexual encounter as a moment of passion, and the young couple depends on the male's use of a condom. Often adolescents would rather believe they were carried away by the moment. Many teenagers find that preplanned sex is unromantic and would rather believe that it "just happened" than to plan for it. They also experience less guilt if they tell themselves that the sexual intercourse just happened than if they admit to themselves that they are in a sexual relationship. Most methods of birth control, however, require users to acknowledge that they are sexually active and to view the situation realistically (Pestrak & Martin, 1985).

The nature of the relationship also affects contraceptive use (Bibace, 1999). Couples with superior communication tend to be more likely to discuss intimate subjects, one of which is contraception. One study of university students measured levels of intimacy among dating couples who were sexually active and compared them with consistency of contraceptive use. Couples who showed higher levels of social, emotional, and intellectual intimacy were more likely to use contraceptives consistently. After all, intimacy involves affectionate concern for the partner's safety and growth. Couples experiencing lower levels of intimacy in their relationship may be less likely to talk about contraception because they lack the comfort that intimacy brings—comfort that allows discussion of sexual issues. Many college students admit not feeling comfortable discussing their contraceptive use with a partner (Brafford & Beck, 1991).

Familial and social factors also influence the use of contraception. Teens who have poor family relationships or say their communication with parents is poor are less likely to use contraception consistently (Beaty, 1999; Brooks-Gunn & Furstenberg, 1989). Teens living in families with good general communication are more likely to use contraception, probably because their sexuality is less likely to be a response to a familial deficit.

Sexual Orientation: Homosexual Behavior

A number of adolescents direct their sexual activities toward people of the same gender. The term **gay** is now used to describe both males and females whose primary sexual orientation is toward members of the same sex. The term **lesbian** is used to describe women whose sexual orientation is to other women. **Bisexual** describes sexual behavior directed toward members of both the same and the opposite sex. Homosexuality does not define an individual's gender role, personality, attitudes toward life, or physical appearance, but only the person's sexual orientation.

Between 3 and 10 percent of all men define themselves as gay, and between 1 and 3 percent of all women define themselves as lesbian (Fay et al., 1989; Strong & DeVault, 1995). The number of people who have engaged in homosexual behavior, often as teenagers, is much greater, but when such behavior occurs only once or twice it does not necessarily mean that the person is gay (Rice, 1989). Despite this contact, most individuals become exclusively heterosexual.

The origins of homosexuality are controversial. It may have a genetic component (Bailey & Pillard, 1995; Hershberger, 1997; Savin-Williams, 1988). For example, when one identical twin is homosexual, more than 50 percent of the time the other twin is also homosexual. The percentage is reduced to less than 20 percent for fraternal twins or other siblings (Bailey & Pillard, 1991; Whitman, Diamond, & Martin, 1993). Because the rate of agreement between the twins is not nearly perfect, other causative factors must be considered. Possibilities include some early experience or a chemical or other hormonal event that causes changes in the structure and organization of the brain (Berenbaum & Snyder, 1995).

Social factors also have been advanced as at least part of the cause of homosexuality. Pillard (1990; Pillard & Weinrich, 1986) found that gay males perceived their fathers as more distant during childhood than did either a sample of heterosexual controls or the gay men's own heterosexual brothers The gay men also reported a greater closeness to their mothers. These circumstances might lead to a lack of identification with the father. Unfortunately, the studies did not include the reason for the distance from the father. A similar argument is made for lesbians, who as a group perceive their mothers as cold and distant (Bell, Weinberg, & Hammersmith, 1981). These patterns do not hold for all gay men or lesbians,

gay A term used to describe both males and females whose primary sexual orientation is toward members of the same sex.

lesbian A term used to describe women whose sexual orientation is to other women.

bisexual A term that describes sexual behavior directed toward members of both the same and the opposite sex.

There are many myths about homosexuality. Homosexuality is not a mental disorder; nor is there any one personality pattern among gays.

though, and no one pattern fits all cases. The patterns may be important only if certain genetic or biological predispositions exist.

Gay men are often stereotyped as effeminate and lesbians, as masculine. Like all stereotypes, they are exaggerated. However, gay men and lesbians are somewhat more likely, though, than heterosexuals to report extensive behavior more stereotypical of the other gender (Friedman & Downey, 1994). Gay male children who are effeminate experience themselves as both different and effeminate (Bailey & Zucker, 1995). They report feeling more sensitive than their peers during childhood, crying more easily, having more female playmates, and preferring stereotyped female toys (Isay, 1990). Some evidence of more masculine play among lesbian children exists as well, for example, preferring rough-and-tumble play and not liking to wear dresses (Bailey & Zucker, 1995). No one knows whether genetic factors, hormones, prenatal factors, or early experience causes this behavior. Most gay men, though, are *not* effeminate, so this pattern certainly does not fit every gay man. In addition, not all highly effeminate boys turn out to be gay; many are exclusively heterosexual. And many studies that follow effeminate boys ignore the fact that many gay men report the same masculine play as heterosexuals, so perhaps there may be a number of paths to homosexuality.

Obviously, many pieces are missing from our attempt to explain the origins of homosexuality. The findings of genetic and biological differences, though, support the feelings of many homosexuals who claim that sexual orientation is not a choice as such. It is fair to say that sexual orientation is probably shaped by a complex interaction of social and biological influences (Paul, 1993).

For adolescents whose primary orientation is toward members of the same sex, the teenage years may be difficult. Most are confused about their sexual feelings, and half try to deny them (Newman & Muzzonigro, 1993). These teenagers may reject their sexual orientation, hide it from their family, and find it very difficult to cope with their feelings. They may fear family rejection (Townsend et al., 1997) or the rejection and ridicule of their peers (Waldner-Haugrud & Magruder, 1996).

Coming out—that is, publicly acknowledging that one is gay—is often difficult and may create a crisis in the family (Holtzen & Agresti, 1990). The initial disclosure of a child's gay or lesbian orientation is traumatic for most parents and may interfere with their relationship (Robinson, Walters, & Skeen, 1989). Parental reactions to being told that their child is gay vary. About half of all parents respond with disbelief, denial, or negative comments suggesting that it is only a phase (Robinson et al., 1989). Some parents don't discuss the issue, hoping it will disappear (Cohen & Savin-Williams, 1996). Most parents do eventually arrive at a tolerance or acceptance of their child's sexual orientation (Savin-Williams & Dube, 1998) and become supportive over time.

Generally, the better the relationship before the disclosure, the better the relationship afterward. Parental reaction is important, because acceptance is related to a sense of well-being in these adolescents (Floyd et al., 1999). Parents influence the self-esteem and adjustment of their gay children. Their self-acceptance and self-esteem are higher when their parents accept them, especially those who find their parents' opinions most important. Although mothers are generally closer and more supportive than fathers, relationships with both parents are important indicators of personal adjustment.

Adolescents usually experience homosexual feelings years before identifying themselves as gay. The average gay male does not identify himself as gay until age 19 or 21 years (Strong & DeVault, 1995). Various stage theories describe the process of coming out (Beaty, 1999). Often, the first phase in acquiring a homosexual identity involves awareness of one's own feelings and recognition of emotional and physical desires. Fears of discovery and confusion mark this stage. In fact, this confusion is often greatest during early adolescence (Troiden, 1989). In the second phase, the individual acknowledges these feelings. The third phase involves a self-definition of being gay. Defining oneself as gay is difficult, for it is frowned upon by society. In addition, families must deal with this acknowledgment. Some gay men and lesbians may go through two additional phases. One phase involves entrance into a gay subculture, including acquiring gay friends and frequenting gay bars and clubs. The final phase involves entrance into a gay or lesbian love affair, and most gay individuals experience at least one long-term relationship (Strong & DeVault, 1995). Not all gays publicly acknowledge their sexual orientation, though. Some acknowledge their own feelings but may not wish to publicly identify with the gay subculture.

Expressing one's homosexual identity may be very difficult. Violence and prejudice against gay men and lesbians may make a gay teen think twice about coming out. Individuals suspected of being homosexual often face harassment (Gelman, 1993; Muñoz-Plaza, Quinn, & Rounds, 2002). A recent survey of high school students in Massachusetts found that students who identified themselves as gay males, lesbians, or bisexuals were seven times more likely than other students to have skipped school because they felt unsafe. A 1997 study in Vermont found that gay students were threatened or injured with a weapon in school three times more often than straight teens (Ireland, 2000). Ninety-two percent of all gay men and lesbians report being subjected to verbal abuse and threats, often from members of their own families, and 24 percent have been physically attacked because of their sexual orientation (Herek, 1989; Herek et al., 1996). Others fear the possible loss of friends at school, and more religious youth often must deal with the fact that their churches view homosexuality negatively (Waldner-Haugrud & Magruder, 1996). A national survey of white, black, and Latino adolescents concerning their attitudes toward homosexuality and homosexuals showed the extent of the prejudice, and ethnicity was not a factor. The majority (59 percent) of respondents disagreed either "a lot" or "a little" with the statement "I could be friends with a gay person" (Marsiglio, 1993a).

Many people may believe myths about homosexuality. For instance, some people believe that gay men and lesbians can be readily recognized and that they show a particular behavior pattern. In truth, most gay men and lesbians cannot be identified simply by looking at them and watching their behavior (Greenberg et al., 1989). Some people also believe that all gay men are effeminate, whereas the actual percentage is only about 15 percent (Voeller, 1980). Gay men who do show effeminate behavior tend to stand out, but the great majority of gay men who do not show this behavior go unnoticed. In addition, people sometimes confuse sexual orientation with gender identity. Contrary to many people's opinions, gay men and lesbians are comfortable with their gender and do not want to change (Comer, 1995). There is also no identifiable homosexual personality, nor are people who engage in homosexuality more prone to psychopathology.

Finally, some people consider homosexuality itself to be some sort of mental illness rather than a sexual orientation. The American Psychiatric Association does not consider homosexuality a mental disorder (American Psychiatric Association, 2000). Any psychological difficulties homosexuals have are either unrelated to their sexual orientation or caused by the continuing lack of acceptance on the part of some members of society. Their difficulties do not arise from the homosexual orientation itself (see Davison & Neale, 2003).

Despite the harassment and the public's acceptance of myths about homosexuality, society is actually more tolerant of homosexuality today than it was 30 or 40 years ago (Beaty, 1999). The continuing rejection and violence against homosexuals, though, show that society must make a good deal of progress before it accepts homosexuals as citizens with full rights and responsibilities. *(For a review of this section, see At A Glance 10.3.)*

AT A GLANCE 10.3 SEXUAL ATTITUDES AND BEHAVIOR

KEY POINT: Sexual attitudes and the extent of sexual behavior, such as the age of first intercourse, frequency of intercourse, and extent of contraceptive use, are determined by many personal and social factors.

SUPPORTING POINTS	EXPLANATION
Adolescents view sexual behavior more as a matter of personal choice.	Adolescents are tolerant of differences in sexual behavior among others. They generally are more permissive than their parents.
Females are more likely to view sexual intercourse as acceptable only in a loving relationship.	Females are more likely to link sexual intercourse with a loving relationship and to see sexual behavior as a barrier to achieving their goals. Females are less permissive than males in their views on the subject.
Males believe sexual intercourse is appropriate earlier in a relationship than do females.	In the early stages of a relationship, males have a more permissive attitude toward sexuality than females. The differences narrow as relationships become deeper.
Teenagers are more likely to have premarital sex today than generations ago.	More than half of all males and females have engaged in sexual intercourse by age 18. Recent figures show stability in this percentage rather than a continued increase. The age of first intercourse also has declined.
Many factors influence an individual's sexual behavior.	Personal values, especially religious values, influence the decision to have sexual intercourse. Peer pressure and partner pressure also can influence sexual behavior.
More adolescents are using contraceptives than in the recent past.	More teens are using contraceptives at their first intercourse and with greater frequency thereafter. However, many adolescents still use contraceptives inconsistently.
The term *gay* describes both males and females who engage exclusively in homosexual relationships. The term *lesbian* refers to females who engage exclusively in homosexual relationships. The term *bisexual* relates to people who have both heterosexual and homosexual relationships.	There appears to be a genetic basis for homosexuality, but other factors also must be involved. Family factors, including a lack of identification with the father and a closeness to the mother, may be involved for gay men.. Lesbians tend to see their mothers as cold and distant. These family factors may be important only if genetic or particular physiological factors are present.
Homosexual adolescents often have difficulties adjusting to their sexual orientation because of society's lack of acceptance.	Many gay men and lesbians report rejection and harassment. Most parents eventually accept their child's sexual orientation, and family acceptance improves the quality of the adolescent's life.

SEX EDUCATION

People generally agree that the family should be the basic transmitter of education about sexuality. However, most parents also believe the school has a part to play. Sex education efforts focus not only on educating the adolescent about sex and contraception but also on reducing the incidence of STIs, the rate of teenage pregnancy, forcible sexual behavior, and sexual harassment.

Sex Education at Home

Although teens cite their parents as the most important source of information on sex, pregnancy, and contraception, only a third discuss contraception with their parents. Sexually active teens who discuss contraception are about twice as likely to use contraceptives as those who don't (Pick & Palos, 1995; Stone & Ingham, 2002). When a great deal of communication occurs, teens are also more likely to share the sexual values of their parents. Generally, both adolescent males and females are more likely to discuss sexual topics with their mothers than their fathers (Wyatt, 1989). Fathers and daughters especially are not comfortable talking about sex (Dilorio, Kelley, & Hockenberry-Eaton, 1993). However, discussions with friends about sex increase with age in adolescence.

Parents frequently find it difficult to talk with their children about these sensitive topics, and communication about sex is often incomplete or even nonexistent. Parents also must be careful not to give mixed messages to their teens (Jaccard, Dittus, & Gordon, 1986). Discussions of sexuality are often dominated by explanations of birth control and safer sex, or simply instructions not to have sex (Dittus & Jaccard, 2000). Parents often omit the moral, ethical, familial, and social reasons for not having sex, leaving teens with the idea that their engaging in sexual activity is acceptable as long as they don't get pregnant or contract an STI. Discussions of sexuality within the family should include morals and values, as well as information on birth control and safer sex. It is also important that parents listen to the opinions and beliefs of their adolescent children.

Sex Education in the Schools

Most state education departments either strongly recommend or mandate sex education and AIDS education (Haffner, 1992; Kirby, 2002). As many as 80 percent of all parents favor sex education in the schools, although the minority of parents who oppose it are often very vocal (Barron, 1987). In fact, although 8 of 10 adults believe teenagers should be given a strong message that they should abstain from sex until they are out of high school, 6 in 10 believe that sexually active young people should have access to birth control, and only 2 in 10 object to that idea (Princeton Survey, 1997).

What should sex education classes include? Other than in offering students the basic biological information on sex, opinions differ. Recently, a greater emphasis has been placed on promoting abstinence (Landry, Kaeser, & Richards, 1999). However, comprehensive sex education programs involve not only teaching abstinence but also giving information about contraception and STI prevention and informing students about available community clinics (Kreinen, 2002). Comprehensive sex education programs also frequently discuss values, choices, and communication with partners. Unfortunately, few sex education programs address abstinence as one option in a broader sex education program that also includes discussions of contraception. Many require that teaching abstinence be the only option and either prohibit discussions of contraception or highlight its ineffectiveness in preventing pregnancy and STIs.

Perhaps the most controversial aspect of sex education programs is the proposal to give out condoms in the schools. Some parents are concerned that condom availability or explicit sex education will encourage sexual activity, but this is not so (Stryker, 1997). Studies of AIDS prevention programs that included the promotion and distribution of condoms do not find an increase in sexual activity among adolescents (Kirby, 2002; Sellers et al., 1994). In one important study, packets consisting of condoms, an instruction sheet, and a card warning that condoms are not completely effective in preventing AIDS but abstinence is were available at a Los Angeles County high school. A year later, no significant increases in the percentage of males or females having intercourse occurred, but a significant increase in condom use by sexually active individuals was reported (Schuster et al., 1998). Even the most comprehensive sex education programs do not lead to sexual experimentation (Kirby, 1994, 2002).

How effective are sex education programs? Impressive evidence exists that comprehensive programs delay sexual intercourse (Global Programme on AIDS, 1997; Kirby, 1997). The issue of whether abstinence-only programs are effective in controversial, with some arguing that they can be (Toups & Holmes, 2002) and others stating that they are not (Kirby, 1997, 2002). Experimental studies are lacking in this area. And if current figures showing that the majority of teens ages 18 to 19 years are sexually active are correct, we must question whether abstinence-only programs are sufficient. Certainly, one of the central ideas behind any sex education program is to encourage young teens to delay the age of first sexual intercourse, and individuals who abstain should be supported (Landry et al., 1999). Abstinence may be promoted, but so must contraception for those who decide to follow a different path.

Some sex education programs have been successful, whereas others have failed to achieve their goals (Firestone, 1994). For example, a large national representative survey found that the likelihood that a teenager will use some contraceptive method at first intercourse increases by about one-third following instruction about birth control (Mauldon & Luker, 1996). Generally, programs

PERSPECTIVE 3

WHAT DID YOU FIND?

SETTING THE SCENE: Lakeeta and Arthur are parents of a 15-year-old son, Adam. As Lakeeta was putting the laundry away, she found an opened pack of condoms in Adam's drawer.

LAKEETA: *I don't know what to do. I'm shocked, but I'm more concerned than anything else. Adam isn't very mature, and I think he's too young to be having sex. He'll make a mistake and get a girl pregnant.*

ARTHUR: *Lakeeta told me about her discovery. She's annoyed because I don't think it's anything too important. Adam is taking precautions, which is good. I don't know what Lakeeta wants me to do. I told her I'd talk with Adam, but honestly, I don't know what to say.*

QUESTION: If you were Lakeeta or Arthur, what would you do? If you found birth control pills or condoms in your teenage daughter's drawer, would you react any differently?

Most people are in favor of sex education. The question is what to cover in the course.

Nancy is a 16-year-old girl who discovers she is pregnant. She has been having sex with her 17-year-old boyfriend for about 6 months. They thought they had taken sufficient contraceptive precaution, but obviously they were mistaken. After talking it over with her boyfriend, Nancy decides to seek an abortion. Should she be forced by law to inform her parents that she is contemplating an abortion?

In a landmark 1992 case, *Planned Parenthood v. Casey,* the Supreme Court of the United States held that states may require minors seeking abortions to obtain parental consent as long as a procedure allowing a minor to bypass parental notification laws in certain cases is in place (Bach, 1999). Most states have laws requiring parental notification for abortion (Planned Parenthood, 2001). Some state laws require only parental notification, whereas others require parental consent (Tomal, 2000). Some states require notification of one parent, and others require notification of both parents. Some states allow notification of grandparents as an alternative to parents, or even notification of a sibling who is at least 25 years old. Some states allow a physician to waive notification if the doctor thinks it is not in the best interest of the minor (perhaps because of evidence that notification could lead to abuse or the doctor's belief that the teenager is mature enough to make her own decision) (Planned Parenthood, 2001).

State laws are routinely tested for their constitutionality. For example, the New Jersey Supreme Court struck down a parental notification bill in 2000 even though it included a judicial bypass procedure (Lovell, 2000). The court's majority argued that the practical difficulties involved in going to court, getting a lawyer, obtaining transportation, taking time off from school, and maintaining anonymity were onerous and only delayed the abortion, making it more dangerous. The majority argued that the law violated the rights of the minor. The justices who voted to sustain the law argued that it protected the interests of both minors and parents, as well as fostered family integrity. They also argued that the judicial bypass procedure was not an undue burden. When these justices measured the law against the right of parents to be informed of the significant health issues in their children's lives, they saw it as sustainable.

Parental notification laws do not really affect the majority of pregnant teenagers, for most girls voluntarily inform their parents when they seek an abortion. A study of unmarried minors having abortions in states without parental notification and consent laws found that 61 percent reported that at least one of their parents knew about their abortions (Henshaw & Kost, 1992). About a third of the teens who did not tell their parents had histories of violence in their families, feared violence, or were afraid of being thrown out of their homes.

Advocates of parental notification and consent legislation, often called *parental involvement legislation,* use a number of arguments to bolster their view. They state, for example, that parents are responsible for their children and have a right to know when their minor children are going to make an important medical decision. Advocates also argue that parental notification allows parents to provide their children with emotional support (Harris, 1997). Adolescents do not have much experience in making important decisions, and parents can help their teenagers consider their alternatives. Finally, advocates note that parents have a right to decide what medical services their minor children receive and that any routine overriding of parental authority threatens the parents' right to raise their children in the way they think best. One medical provider noted that he could not remove a splinter from the finger of a minor without a parent's consent, but that without parental notification laws a minor could receive an abortion without the family's knowing.

Opponents of laws regarding mandatory parental involvement argue that we do not live in an ideal world, and many adolescents do not feel they can tell their parents about an abortion (Planned Parenthood, 1999). Teens who do not wish to notify their parents often have a very good

emphasizing delay are more effective with younger adolescents. Among older adolescents, comprehensive sex education programs significantly increase the percentage of sexually active adolescents who consistently use contraceptives (Frost & Forrest, 1995).

Many unsuccessful sex education programs spend too much time on safe, noncontroversial topics, such as simple biological information, and little time on contraception and disease prevention. Their discussions of risk taking are far too general (Alan Guttmacher Institute, 1989). Sex education also frequently comes too late, after students have already begun having intercourse (Rodriguez & Moore, 1995). Some programs fail to focus clearly on preventing unprotected sex. They may try to use a nonbiased, nonjudgmental model, encouraging students simply to make their own decisions (Kirby, 1994). Studies show that this approach is not as effective, probably because spontaneous, unprotected sex is often considered romantic and produces short-term, immediate pleasure, whereas waiting or using contraception involves long-range considerations.

Seeking an Abortion?

reason. In addition, being forced to notify parents or to receive their consent often causes a delay in seeking medical care; and because earlier abortions are safer, delaying an abortion increases the physical and emotional risk to the teenager (Raab, 1998).

Individuals opposed to parental notification also argue that states have routinely allowed minor adolescents to consent to their own medical care in critical areas, such as treatment for STIs and drug or alcohol addiction, when confidential care is deemed a public health necessity (Donovan, 1998b). Many states allow minors to consent to contraceptive services, and a majority of states allow pregnant minors to obtain prenatal care and delivery services without parental consent.

Two pieces of legislation have been introduced into Congress to further limit access to abortions. One, the Child Custody Protection Act, makes it a federal crime for a nonparent to take a pregnant minor across state lines to obtain an abortion for the purpose of avoiding laws requiring parental involvement in their home states. Another, the Putting Parents First Act (PPFA), would require minors to get parental consent for abortion referrals or contraceptives obtained at any facility receiving federal funds, and it would reverse many years of public policy (Katz, 1999).

People who passionately believe in a woman's right to choose whether to have an abortion argue against almost any limitation on abortion rights. People who passionately believe that abortion is wrong and should be illegal argue for just about anything that limits abortion rights. However, many people in between consider bypass procedures to be a feature that would protect the pregnant teen who has reason to believe she would suffer negative consequences from parental notification. However, what seems reasonable in theory may not work in practice.

Bypass procedures have proved to be both erratic and problematic. Some states deny very few petitions. For example, in Massachusetts only 13 of 15,000 waivers were denied, and of the denied petitions, 11 were reversed on appeal, meaning that only 2 minors were denied their request for an abortion without parental notification (Lovell, 2000). In other states the situation is very different, and teens have more trouble obtaining exemptions. Even within states, courts function very differently. Some counties almost routinely grant abortion petitions, whereas other counties routinely reject them (Bach, 1999). Another problem is the requirement in some states that both parents must be notified. Many teens do not live with both parents, and they may have little or no contact with their noncustodial parent or fear involving that parent.

On the other side is the question of whether an occasional horrific story about a teenage girl beaten by her father because he was notified of her impending abortion is sufficient to certify that parents generally should not be informed. There will always be some parents who act improperly, but that fact does not mean that the vast majority of parents who can and will provide emotional support and guidance should not be involved.

The issue of parental notification seems to pit parental rights against the minor's right of self-determination. Parents are told that they are responsible for their children, the argument goes, but without legislation they may not participate in an important decision made by their minor daughter. However, it can be argued that a teenage girl faced with an unwanted pregnancy who does not want to tell her parents should not be forced to do so. It is unfortunate that judicial bypass seems so erratic and problematic that it does not solve the problem in a practical way.

We are faced with the same questions that have been raised over and over. Should adolescents have the same rights as adults? If not, what rationale should be used to determine which rights minors should have and which rights they should not have? Both questions are difficult to answer, and balancing parental rights and responsibilities with adolescent rights and responsibilities remains difficult.

Ineffective programs also often center on lectures; an adult offers biological information or warnings without dealing with the pressures to have sex that are so common in teenage life.

The provision of comprehensive sex education raises the question of parental consent and parents' right to know. Some people want a federal law allowing parents to object to their children's receiving contraception or explicit information on AIDS. This attitude is part of the parental rights movement, which seeks to give parents a larger say in their children's education and health (Donovan, 1998a, 1998b; Gavora, 1997). Advocates argue that parents should have the right to know when their children are receiving contraceptive devices or explicit information about sex, which may be contrary to the values of the home. Although parents who feel excluded may deserve some sympathy, such a requirement for parental notification or approval would have devastating consequences for teens who would not visit clinics to receive contraceptive or prenatal help because they were afraid their parents would find out. One study found that half the teens under 18 years of age who use clinic services for contraception and testing for sexually transmitted infections would discontinue if parents were notified (Reddy, Fleming, & Swain, 2002). Many states now allow teens to receive such help in a confidential manner because of society's overriding need to reduce the transmission of STIs and teen pregnancy. Federal policy also has emphasized confidentiality for many years. Advocates of the parental rights movement also claim that parents have a right to know if their adolescent daughters intend to have an abortion (see "Focus: Do Parents Have the Right to Know That Their Daughter Is Seeking an Abortion?").

Successful school-based sex education programs share a number of elements. Effective programs focus on reducing sexual risk-taking behaviors that lead to STIs or pregnancy. They may recommend abstinence but also talk about contraception and tell students how to obtain contraceptive devices. They all emphasize goal setting, teach resistance skills (that is, how to say no to sex), and most important, teach teens how to negotiate and communicate within relationships (Ku, Sonenstein, & Pleck, 1993). Comprehensive sex education programs also explore the context for, and meaning of, sex. They emphasize values and choices (Stryker, 1997). It is also important to dispel the myth that almost everyone has sex by the age of 15 or so, a prominent belief that leads to pressure to have early sex. Effective sex education programs are not value free. They reinforce values and group norms against unprotected sex and are tailored to the experience and needs of the students (Kirby, 1994).

One thing is certain about sex education programs: They will continue to be controversial in some circles. Although research has yielded some answers to the difficult questions of which programs are effective and which do not work, many communities still use programs that are ineffective. Communities armed with knowledge of what works and what does not should insist that their sex education programs be based on the research on effectiveness rather than on habit or wishful thinking.

Sexually Transmitted Infections

A **sexually transmitted infection (STI),** also known as a *sexually transmitted disease (STD),* is a disease contracted primarily through sexual contact. This sexual activity need not be vaginal intercourse; for example, STIs may be communicated through oral sex. Some diseases such as AIDS, caused by the human immunodeficiency virus (HIV), can be transmitted in other ways, such as through infected needles or from mother to fetus (Dickover et al., 1996).

One in six sexually experienced teens has had an STI (Sellers et al., 1994), and more than 3 million teens a year contract them (Grimley & Lee, 1997). Teenagers account for a quarter of all people diagnosed with STIs, and almost two-thirds of all reported cases occur among people less than 25 years of age (Little, 2000).

There are many types of STIs. Some, such as chlamydia, gonorrhea, and syphilis, are caused by bacteria; others, such as genital warts, genital herpes, and AIDS, are caused by viruses.

Chlamydia   About 3 million new cases of **chlamydia** occur in the United States each year (Family Practice News, 2001). Chlamydia is caused by the *Chlamydia trachomatis* bacterium. Many people with chlamydia do not show any symptoms and therefore do not know they have the infection (Marr, 1998). About 80 percent of women with chlamydia do not realize it until complications arise (Little, 2000). Sometimes, inflammation of the cervix may occur early in the infection, but again the woman may not notice it. Other symptoms in the early stages include vaginal bleeding between menstrual periods, painful urination, and lower abdominal pain. Men are more likely to have early symptoms, such as inflammation of the urethra, a feeling of having to urinate frequently, and discharge from the penis.

sexually transmitted infection (STI)   A disease that is contracted primarily through sexual contact.

chlamydia   A sexually transmitted infection caused by the *Chlamydia trachomatis* bacterium, which can be treated successfully with antibiotics.

If untreated, chlamydia can spread through the reproductive organs, causing infections and sterility. The infection can spread to the lining of the uterus, the fallopian tubes, and the ovaries, resulting in pelvic inflammatory disease (PID), a bacterial inflammation of the pelvic organs that increases the chances of infertility and chronic pelvic pain (Marr, 1998). The treatment for PID is antibiotics. Chlamydia in pregnant women may cause miscarriage and low birth weight, and infants of mothers with chlamydia may develop conjunctivitis and pneumonia (Schachter, 1989). Men may have inflammation of the vessels that carry sperm from the testes to the urethra. Chlamydia can be successfully treated with antibiotics such as tetracycline and erythromycin (Little, 2000).

Gonorrhea Gonorrhea is caused by the bacterium *Neisseria gonorrhoeae*, and is almost always spread through activity that involves direct contact with mucous membranes through vaginal, anal, or oral intercourse (Little, 2000). The cervix is the most common site of infection in females, and the urethra in males. Gonorrhea is not easy to detect because symptoms can be very weak and easily ignored. Only about 20 percent of women with the infection experience noticeable symptoms until more serious complications develop, but even an asymptomatic condition is still infectious. The most common signs are inflammation of the cervix and a discharge in women (Little, 2000). Gonorrhea is a common cause of PID. Fetuses exposed to gonorrhea can be premature and have damaged eyesight; to prevent blindness, the standard hospital treatment is to place a protective solution in an infant's eyes at birth in case the mother has gonorrhea. Gonorrhea is easier to detect in men, as symptoms appear 80 percent of the time; they include a burning sensation during urination, a discharge from the penis, and soreness and swelling at the opening of the urethra (Little, 2000). Gonorrhea can be treated with antibiotics.

Syphilis Syphilis is an infection caused by the bacterium *Treponema pallidum* and is transmitted through direct contact with a lesion or sore of a sexual partner, including lesions on the mucous membranes lining the genitals, the mouth, and the anus (Little, 2000). The initial symptoms include a painless bump, or chancre, at the bacteria's point of entry. Multiple bumps or chancres may appear, most often on the genitals but possibly on the lips, tongue, or elsewhere. Because they are painless, these chancres may go unnoticed and will vanish in 3 to 6 weeks without treatment (Marr, 1998). The infection then proceeds to the second stage, in which a skin rash and lesions appear, along with symptoms similar to the flu. When these symptoms finally disappear, the infection enters a latent phase in which no new symptoms occur. This stage may last 20 to 40 years; the last stage then occurs, in which serious damage to the internal organs and brain results in an inability to walk, loss of bladder control, blindness, insanity, and death. Syphilis can cause multiple birth defects in infants, but pregnant mothers who receive prompt treatment can minimize the danger. Syphilis can be cured through the use of antibiotics at all stages, but the damage to bodily organs is permanent (Little, 2000).

Genital Warts About 1 million new cases of **genital warts** occur in the United States each year, making it the most common STI caused by a virus. Actually, a group of viruses called the *human papillomavirus (HPV)* is responsible for genital warts. The viruses are most often transmitted through sexual intercourse. More than 70 strains of HPV have been identified (McIlhaney, 1997). Even when too small to see, the warts are highly contagious. In men, genital warts are found on the tip or shaft of the penis, the scrotum, or the anus; in women, they develop on the lips of the vagina, within the vagina, in the urethra, on the cervix, or around the anus. They are usually painless, although they can itch. Warts in the urethra can cause painful urination (Little, 2000).

Genital warts have a characteristic appearance that an experienced health care provider can recognize. Medical treatment involves removal of the warts

gonorrhea A sexually transmitted infection caused by the bacterium *Neisseria gonorrhoeae* that can be treated successfully with antibiotics.

syphilis A sexually transmitted infection caused by the bacterium *Treponema pallidum* and with three distinct phases.

genital warts The most common sexually transmitted infection caused by a virus.

(Marr, 1998). Some strains of the virus can play a role in the development of cervical, vaginal, or vulvar cancer in women, as well as penile cancer in men (Little, 2000). The percentage of people with HPV who develop these cancers is very small, considering the fact that HPV is quite common in the population (Marr, 1998).

Herpes Simplex   Herpes refers to a number of related viruses. **Herpes simplex type 1 (HSV-1)** often originates in the mouth and can be recognized as cold sores on the lips. **Herpes simplex type 2 (HSV-2),** called genital herpes, produces lesions in the genital areas. The type 1 and type 2 viruses are similar, and either type can infect the genitals or mouth (Little, 2000; McCammon, Knox, & Schacht, 1993). Genital herpes is very common; about 45 million people in the United States over the age of 15 have genitals herpes type 2. The virus can be spread when it is active, causing an outbreak of sores. If the outbreak is mild and the sores small and relatively painless, an individual may spread the virus without realizing it. However, it can be spread at other times as well. A person with herpes simplex can spread the virus between outbreaks, as cells of the virus are sometimes shed or discarded even when an infection has subsided (Curran, 1998). In fact, many people become infected with herpes simplex when they have intercourse with someone who is unaware at the time that they are infectious (McIlhaney, 1997).

The symptoms of herpes infection include recurrent fluid-filled blisters that appear anywhere on genital skin. These blisters rupture, leaving painful ulcers that heal in about 12 days (American College Health Association, 2001). The symptoms can be subtler sometimes, and many people who have genital herpes may be unaware that they have been infected, either because they have no symptoms or they don't recognize the symptoms as those of herpes (Marr, 1998). However, 80 percent of people with herpes will have some symptoms sometime in their lives.

After infection with the herpes simplex virus, whether or not symptoms occur, the virus travels from the skin to nerve endings that supply that area of skin that was infected. It then migrates along nerve endings to the nerve root body near the spinal cord, where the virus remains in an inactive stage until the next outbreak (Marr, 1998). In fact, the Greek word for *herpes* means "to creep," referring to the way the virus moves along nerves. No one knows for certain what triggers another outbreak. Stress, illness, injury, and fatigue increase the chances of a recurrence. These recurring outbreaks are usually not as severe as the first attack.

A fetus can contract herpes simplex while passing through the birth canal, a problem that is prevented by performing a cesarean section (that is, delivering the fetus surgically, through the mother's abdomen). Infants infected with the herpes virus face many medical problems.

At this time, no cure for herpes simplex exists, but antiviral agents such as acyclovir and other medications can limit the severity of the symptoms. A diagnosis of herpes is often frightening, and although most people manage the infection well, it can negatively influence relationships with others. Today, researchers are seeking a vaccine to prevent herpes simplex and antiviral drugs that will destroy the virus in its latent stage.

Acquired Immune Deficiency Syndrome (AIDS)   **Acquired immune deficiency syndrome,** or **AIDS,** is a fatal infection that affects the immunological system, leading to an inability to fight infection. It is caused by the human immunodeficiency virus, or HIV. The virus infects cells with a particular protein, the CD4 protein, on the surface. One cell type, called CD4 lymphocytes or T helper cells, plays an important part in fighting off infection.

Some people infected with HIV do not have any initial symptoms, but between 30 and 70 percent develop a flulike illness lasting 1 or 2 weeks. After infection, a significant amount of the virus is found in the body, and the number of CD4 cells declines. The body then seems to regain control and suppresses the

herpes simplex type 1   A viral infection that can cause blistering, typically of the lips and mouth, but it may infect the genitals.

herpes simplex type 2:   A viral infection that may cause blistering, typically of the genitals, but may also infect the lips, mouth, and eyes.

acquired immune deficiency syndrome (AIDS) A fatal disease caused by the human immunodeficiency virus, or HIV, which affects the immunological system and leads to an inability to fight infection.

virus for 10 years or so. The virus can be transmitted to others regardless of the stage of infection, however (Marr, 1998). Antibodies to the infection develop, but people may notice lymph node enlargement. Eventually, the virus reappears, making the infected person very vulnerable to other infections and malignancies. At this point, the person has AIDS. The disease is defined in an HIV-positive person as a syndrome comprising various clinical conditions, a decline in CD4 cells to a count below 200 (a healthy person has a count of more than 500), or both (Marr, 1998). It is when the CD4 count drops that infected persons are more vulnerable to infections and cancer.

AIDS is the sixth leading cause of death among persons aged 15 to 24 years (National Center for Health Statistics, 1997). About 20 percent of all HIV-positive adults contracted the virus in adolescence (Brown et al., 1996). As of June 2000, approximately 300,000 Americans were reported as living with AIDS, and between 800,000 and 900,000 are infected with HIV (CDC, 2000c). African Americans and Latinos are disproportionately represented among the infected in the United States; although they make up somewhat more than 20 percent of the population, they represent 35 and 18 percent, respectively, of all AIDS patients (Marr, 1998). Worldwide, 36.1 million adults are living with HIV/AIDS. It is estimated that one-third of all individuals who are infected do not know it. The long incubation period for the HIV infection, which averages 11 years, means that many people infected as teens will get AIDS in their 20s or 30s (Sellers et al., 1994).

The most common way individuals spread the infection is through sexual contact. HIV is also spread through the shared use of infected needles by drug users. AIDS prevention is vital in adolescence, because the behaviors of some teens put them at risk for acquiring the virus. Many youths with HIV infection continue to engage in risky behaviors even after the infection has been diagnosed (Diamond & Buskin, 2000). Adolescents are more than twice as likely as adults to continue to engage in risky behaviors, such as unsafe sex with anonymous partners or sharing needles. AIDS also can be transmitted prenatally or at birth, but in many cases women with HIV infection can be given medications that help prevent transmission of the virus to their fetuses (Wade et al., 1998), and the rate of mother-fetus HIV transmission has declined substantially in the United States.

There have been many advances in the treatment of HIV infection, although no cure is yet available. A number of antiviral drugs prolong the period between HIV infection and the appearance of AIDS. These medications also delay death from AIDS (Marr, 1998).

While medical treatment is becoming more effective in lengthening life, the psychological aspects of the infection must be considered. People who are HIV positive or have AIDS are often shunned and treated as outcasts. Some of this treatment is due to misinformation about HIV. There is a social stigma to all STIs, but especially to HIV infection. It is hoped that with better understanding of the infection, individuals with HIV will be accorded their rights.

Preventing the Spread of Sexually Transmitted Infections

Adolescents are the highest risk group for nearly all STIs (Rosenthal et al., 1997). Teens are especially at risk because they often have multiple partners and are less likely to take action to prevent STIs, such as using condoms (Biro & Rosenthal, 1992; Grimley & Lee, 1997). Generally, boys engage in more high-risk sexual activities than do girls (Leland & Barth, 1992). Girls report having fewer sexual partners and question their partners about high-risk sexual behaviors more often, although evidence shows that lying about one's sexual history is very common (Leland & Barth, 1992). Failure to disclose having previous sexual partners, not using condoms, and failure to disclose testing positive for HIV or other STIs occurs quite often among both men and women (Desiderato & Crawford, 1995; Kalichman, Kelly, & Rompa, 1997).

One important variable influencing the use of safer sexual practices in the United States is perception of vulnerability (Campbell, Peplau, & DeBro, 1992).

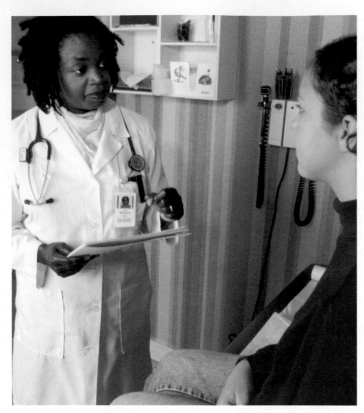

Clinics offer many services, including testing for sexually transmitted infections, which, if left untreated, can have serious consequences.

People are more likely to use condoms if they feel vulnerable to infection or to becoming pregnant (Bryan, Aiken, & West, 1997). Logic would dictate that unprotected sex could lead to these consequences, but situational variables are crucial. An adolescent may say he will use a condom, but the emotional nature of the moment may influence his actual behavior. Perceptions of risk and vulnerability vary with the emotional content of the situation. For example, if a male knows that a very appealing female has had a number of partners and did not consistently use condoms, he certainly cannot conclude that there is little risk of infection transmission. Yet many reach that illogical conclusion because they are motivated to use irrelevant information—for example, that the partner is an honor student—to reduce their perception of risk (Blanton & Gerrard, 1997). When people are motivated to find a way around their perception of risk, they rationalize and find one. Educational programs need to take motivation and justification into account if they are to help teens reduce their chances of pregnancy and contracting STIs.

Combatting STIs involves three levels. The first level involves research to develop new treatments and vaccines to prevent the infections from taking hold. The second level is educating people about how to reduce the risk of contracting STIs. For example, people can reduce their chances of contracting HIV by taking some precautions. Because AIDS is spread most often through sexual contact, it is recommended that people refrain from engaging in sexual practices that might cut or tear the skin, as well as avoid sexual activity with people who engage in activities that place them at greater risk for contracting the virus, such as intravenous drug users. The correct use of condoms is highly recommended as well (Curran, 1998; Stein, 1995). The third level in combatting STIs involves educational programs that eliminate the stigma of contracting an STI and educate people to appreciate the experience of others with STIs.

Teenage Pregnancy

About 10 percent of American teenage girls between ages 15 and 19 become pregnant each year, adding up to nearly 1 million pregnancies a year. One in five 14-year-old girls becomes pregnant before reaching the age of 18 (Henshaw, 1994). Between 1960 and 1992, the number of births to unmarried women aged 15 to 19 increased by a factor of 4, and the birthrate tripled for this group (Bachrach et al., 2000). The increase in teenage pregnancy and births is often ascribed to greater social acceptability of teenage sexuality and even of births outside marriage, the earlier age at which teens become sexually active, the decline in early marriage, and a decline in feelings of community (a feeling of alienation from the community and family). The rates of pregnancy and childbirth are higher for some minority groups in the United States. African American and Latino teens are more likely to live in poverty, which is a strong indicator of early sexual activity and pregnancy.

Progress in preventing teenage pregnancy has been made, however. The birthrate for female teens has declined 25 percent from 1991 through 2001, to the lowest rate in the 60 years that the data on teen births have been recorded. The teen birthrate has declined among white, African American, Native American, and Asian American adolescents. For example, the birthrate for African American teenagers (15–19 years) has declined 37 percent since 1991

("Preventing teenage pregnancy," 2002; "U.S. teen birth rate falls," 2002). The birthrate among young teens (15–17 years) has declined 26 percent since 1991.

Although research has not yet been able to pinpoint the exact reason for the decline, proponents of different strategies are quick to claim credit (Moore & Sugland, 1999). The increase in abstinence is one contributing factor, and the rates of adolescent sexual activity have leveled; the increase in contraceptive use and the provision of better sex education to counter the spread of AIDS deserve credit as well (CDC, 2001).

The teen birthrate in the United States, though, is still high. Many other countries have seen much greater declines (Singh & Darroch, 2000). Even with the decline, the United States has one of the highest teenage birthrates of all developed countries. Although the U.S. teenage birthrate was about twice as high in the 1950s and 1960s as it is today, the majority of teen births today, unlike then, occur outside of marriage (U.S. Census Bureau, 2001). The proportion of births to adolescents who are unmarried continues to rise, from 14 percent in 1940, 15 percent in 1960, 67 percent in 1990, to 79 percent in 2000 (CDC, 2001). If a teenager today is giving birth, the chances are overwhelming that she is unmarried.

Many teenagers who become pregnant are at risk for a second pregnancy within the next 3 years. Between 30 and 35 percent of adolescent mothers have a repeat pregnancy within 1 year of the birth of their first child, and 40 to 50 percent have another pregnancy within 2 years. In 1996, 22 percent of all births to 15- to 19-year-olds were repeat births (Coard, Nitz, & Felice, 2000). Women who are poor or very young are most likely to become pregnant again. More than half the teenage mothers say they did not use any form of contraception at last intercourse despite stating that they wanted no more children at that time (Maynard & Rangarajan, 1994). There has been some progress in this area, and these rates are dropping (Smith, 1999). However, the need for contraceptive services is obvious.

Experience itself, then, is not as good a teacher as many people think. A full 58 percent of urban adolescents who received negative pregnancy test results at a clinic became pregnant within 18 months (Zabin et al., 1996). Presumably, these teenage girls had believed there was a good chance they were pregnant and found out they were not. Yet this experience did not seem to change their behavior, as more than half did become pregnant quite soon. These teenage girls constitute a population at risk for pregnancy who can be helped, because they have some contact with clinics. The use of home pregnancy tests is common, and teenagers using them, in contrast, may not have contact with a clinic until they are pregnant (Shew et al., 2000). Some of these girls may not be using the test properly, and getting services to them is more difficult.

Not all teenage girls are at equal risk for becoming pregnant. Poverty is the greatest risk factor (Santelli et al., 2000). Poverty is associated with less opportunity, poorer education, family instability, and living in areas in which hopelessness flourishes and in which the age of first intercourse is younger. The younger the age of first intercourse, the lower the probability that the teen will use contraception. In addition, beginning to engage in intercourse at a very early age is related to familial difficulties and personal problems, which may lead to a less responsible attitude toward risk taking (Miller, 2002).

Most psychologists treat teen pregnancy as a personal decision—a failure of rational choice and planning on the part of the teenager. However, it can be viewed as a response to the very limited opportunities a teenage girl sees open to her. Teenagers who become pregnant often do not have a very hopeful view of their future. Teenage girls who have goals and are hopeful about attaining them are much less likely to become pregnant and bear children. Some teens become pregnant on purpose to elicit a commitment from a partner or to fill an emotional void. Some feel that having a child is a way of becoming an adult, by producing someone they can love and care for (Stevens-Simon, Kelly, & Singer,

1998), and some do not mind the idea of being a parent (Coard et al., 2000). They may view parenting as a role that is respected and may receive attention while they are pregnant.

Teenage Mothers and Their Children   Virtually all studies investigating adolescent pregnancy comment negatively on the outcome (Trad, 1999), although a different interpretation of the evidence has recently been put forth and will be discussed later. Pregnancy is a prominent reason for female students to drop out of school. Although about 7 in 10 pregnant girls eventually complete high school, they are far less likely than their peers to go on to college (AGI, 1994). Bearing a child before the age of 20 significantly reduces schooling by about 3 years among females in all ethnic and racial groups (Klepinger, Lundberg, & Plotnick, 1995). The direct consequence of this lack of education is that teens who have children report lower incomes, hold lower-prestige jobs, and are much more likely to live in poverty than teens who are not mothers (Weissberg & Greenberg, 1998). Teenage mothers also express less satisfaction with their jobs in their 20s, and one-half of all teen mothers require public financial support within a year of the child's birth ("Face up to sex education," 1993; Grogger & Bronars, 1993). Working teen mothers earn about half as much as mothers who give birth in their 20s (National Research Council, 1993). Having a child may also preclude teens from establishing their own identity, and they may remain dependent on their parents because they require extensive help (Trad, 1999).

Teen mothers also face increased medical risks. Physical problems are more common among teenagers who are pregnant, perhaps because of biological immaturity, inadequate prenatal care, or drug use. Pregnancy complications are four to five times higher for adolescent mothers (Eure, Lindsay, & Graves, 2002; Stoudemire, 1998). These teems are also less likely to receive early prenatal care (Wiemann et al., 1997). Adolescents who initiate late prenatal care are younger and less educated.

As a group, teenage mothers are not ready for their role. Teenage parents are impatient and insensitive. They lack empathy (Baranowski, Schilmoeller, & Higgins, 1990). They are more physical and less verbal than adult mothers (Garcia-Coll, Hoffman, & Oh, 1987). In addition, they are not as responsive or involved, show fewer positive emotions toward their children, and create less

Young mothers face many challenges and risks. Some do well, but as a group, they are not ready for their role as parents.

stimulating home environments (Karraker & Evans, 1996). When adolescent mothers are compared with older mothers while feeding their babies, the adolescent mothers are less expressive, show fewer positive attitudes, and vocalize less to their infants than the older mothers. Adolescent mothers show less patience and less inventiveness during play (Culp et al., 1991).

Children born to teenagers are also at greater risk of prematurity, birth complications, and infant mortality (Fraser, Brockert, & Ward, 1995; Goldenberg & Klerman, 1995). These risks may result from inadequate prenatal care. However, even when prenatal care is adequate, these children are at greater risk than the children of women in their 20s.

The risk continues. Most children of teen mothers will live in single-parent families and are much more likely to live in poverty. They are more likely to experience physical, emotional, and intellectual problems in their preschool years because of poor nutrition, poor health, family instability, and especially, inadequate parenting (Furstenberg, Brooks-Gunn, & Chase-Lansdale, 1989). They are more aggressive and impulsive as preschoolers than children of older mothers. They are more likely to be abused. The problems continue through middle childhood as well; they are at a greater risk for poor academic achievement and maladjustment (Dubow & Luster, 1990). Of course, individual differences are significant. This evidence should not be used to argue that every child of a teenage mother suffers greatly. Some adolescent parents, especially if they receive help, do a good job. The stresses and difficulties, however, make the task much more difficult.

A Different Look at Teenage Pregnancy and Parenthood Some research disputes the universally negative outcomes traditionally associated with adolescent parenthood. A 17-year follow-up of African American adolescents found that not all the parents and their children experienced negative outcomes (Furstenberg, Brooks-Gunn, & Morgan, 1987). More than two-thirds of all the adolescent mothers completed high school, and most had regular employment and did not depend on the government for income. Their offspring did display more difficulties in school and more behavioral problems at home than did the offspring of older mothers, though. Family factors associated with better outcomes included a grandmother's help in providing for the child during the early years, family support that allowed the mother to finish school, and playful interactions between the father and child (Cooley & Unger, 1991). The mere presence of the father did not improve outcome, however.

Studies of African American teenage mothers find that many had extensive child-care experience in their own homes and believe that their extended family will help them (Geronimus, 1992, 1996). The same is true for some low-income Latino adolescents. If the extended family is supportive rather than adversarial, many of these parents can do well. However, if families simply take over the child-care responsibilities, the mother's skills do not improve. The outcome for teenage mothers and their children thus is more variable than previously thought.

Some studies focus on the differences between "successful" adolescent mothers and those who are less successful. One study, which followed adolescent mothers for as long as 20 years, defined long-term success as high school completion and employment or support by a spouse (Horwitz et al., 1991). Women who had actively participated in a program for pregnant adolescents, remained in school with no second pregnancies, achieved a sense of control over their lives, and were less socially isolated were more effective parents.

The problems young mothers experience are often attributed to their having a child early in life. The assumption is that they would have led much more desirable lives if they had delayed parenting. However, early childbearing may not be the cause of the problems these adolescents experience. When adolescents who bear children and those who do not are matched for socioeconomic and background variables, the picture is not as clear; some studies dispute the assumption that early childbearing is the cause of the problems (Hoffman,

Foster, & Furstenberg, 1993). In comparisons of sister pairs in which one sister gave birth before age 20 and one did not, little difference is found in economic, educational, and social life (Corcoran & Kunz, 1997).

In addition, some, but not the majority, of these adolescents see becoming a mother as redirecting their lives and providing a sense of purpose for them (Arenson, 1994). Becoming a young mother certainly does not allow a teen to escape her problems, but the problems often were present before she became pregnant. Some teen mothers, with the help of their families, may become motivated to return to school to build a better life, thus becoming more responsible.

The teen mother is also seen as creating tremendous public costs. Yet some studies suggest that although teen mothers earn less initially, they earn more over their lifetimes than teens with similar backgrounds and later childbearing (Hotz, McElroy, & Sanders, 1997). Many teen mothers rely on welfare for a short period, but most eventually work. Many continue their education well into their 20s, and some attend college.

The idea that teen mothers are children raising children and are condemned to lives of poverty because of their early childbearing is no longer completely tenable. Neither is it entirely true that they are an economic drain on society. A relational view might be more appropriate; this perspective sees the adolescent mother in a particular environment and recognizes how her perception of her future prospects, which reflects the environment around her, may be the root cause of the problem (Coley & Chase-Landsdale, 1998). This view reminds us not to stereotype all teenage mothers as incompetent and to look at those adolescent mothers who have succeeded.

The relational view also leads us to look at ways to reduce the hopelessness, isolation, and lack of expectation for success that are at the root causes of teenage pregnancy. Many young, poor teenage mothers did not see many available alternatives. This analysis meshes nicely with research showing that teenagers with solid goals and hope for the future are more likely to protect themselves from pregnancy. To be successful, a program to reduce teenage pregnancy must change the girls' attitudes.

The Father   Most people picture the fathers of infants born to teenage mothers as teenagers who are confused and immature, not adequately able to care for the mothers or children. Few people realize that the fathers of the majority of children born to teen mothers are 20 years of age or older. Between 30 and 50 percent of these children have a father younger than 20 years at their birth (Roye & Balk, 1996). That fact explains why there are fewer adolescent fathers than adolescent mothers. Very little research is available on how these early adult fathers deal with the situation, but we do know that they tend to live in poverty (East & Felice, 1996). Much more research is needed on both adolescent and early adult males who father children with adolescent females.

About 7 percent of all teenage males become fathers, and most of them do not live with their children (Marsiglio, 1987; Pirog-Good, 1995). Many teen fathers refuse to believe they are fathers, perhaps out of ignorance, disbelief, or refusal to accept the obligations of fatherhood (Furstenberg et al., 1989). Most teenage fathers are poorly educated and face an uphill climb to succeed in the world of work (Hardy & Duggan, 1988; Winstanley, Meyers, & Florsheim, 2002). Most did not intend to become fathers, but a survey of men aged 15 to 19 found that some disadvantaged young men may view paternity as a source of self-esteem. They are more likely than advantaged young males to say that fathering a child would make them feel like a real man and that they would be pleased, or at least not upset, by an unplanned pregnancy (Marsiglio, 1993b). Teenage fathers are also more likely to have academic problems and be pessimistic about the future.

Teenage fathers face many concerns. Those who accept responsibility worry about supporting a new family, finishing school, and developing a relationship with their in-laws. They often feel alienated (Elster & Panzarine, 1983). The amount of contact teen fathers have with the mother and child differs greatly.

Some have extensive contact, some very little, and some none at all. Many have some contact with the baby, but often it is not extensive and does not continue. The degree of contact depends on the continuing nature of their relationship with the mother.

Teenage fathers suffer both educationally and occupationally. Economic changes around the world increase the need for training and education. Adolescent fathers fare worse educationally than their peers who delay parenting until their 20s or longer. Teen fathers are more likely to come from single-parent, impoverished homes with more siblings but less stability (Pirog-Good, 1995). They are also more likely to be involved with drugs and delinquency at younger ages.

Many teen fathers enter the labor market early and, because they are more committed to work, immediately make more money than their peers. By their mid to late 20s, however, they are more likely to be unemployed or to earn less income when they are employed. The early earnings advantage quickly disappears, and teen fathers earn much less than teenagers who delay parenting, as their poor education and training hold them back. These fathers are less likely to reach their desired educational level or to complete their education. Although teenage fathers generally do not earn much money, they do earn at least as much as dropouts who did not father children. They can provide some, but certainly not much, financial support (Toledo-Dreves, Zabin, & Emerson, 1995).

The Extended Family   Many parents are shocked to learn that their unwed daughter is pregnant (Furstenberg, 1976). When the decision to have the child is made, anger and disappointment gradually changes to acceptance, and mother and daughter may grow closer. The quality of the relationship between the pregnant teen and her parents during the pregnancy determines what will happen after the birth. A young mother whose bond is close is less likely to marry and more likely to stay with her parents, who provide some help in raising the child (Furstenberg, 1981).

In fact, most young mothers will stay with their infants if their parents agree to help out. Young mothers who receive parental help, especially until the child goes to school, are in a better economic position than those who leave home to live on their own. Grandmothers provide much of the child care in these situations. Young mothers who return to school are better off years later, although problems do exist, and the benefits should not be overstated. As the child matures, family relationships may deteriorate, partly because the child's mother remains subordinate to her parents because she is dependent on them.

The adolescent mother's teenage siblings also may be affected. They may be required to help out, and their share of their family's resources may be reduced. Because older sisters often serve as role models, younger sisters of childbearing adolescents are at risk of bearing children themselves as adolescents. Compared with young teens whose older sisters did not bear children, they are more accepting toward nonmarital adolescent childbearing. They consider the best age for events such as having children or getting married to be younger than the age given by the average individual. They are more pessimistic about school and more likely to be involved in early sexual relationships (East, 1996; East & Jacobson, 2001). These differences exist even when such variables as age, family size, educational level of the family, income and welfare status, mother-daughter communication, and other family experiences are taken into consideration.

Programs to Prevent Adolescent Pregnancy   Everyone in the family is affected when a teenage girl becomes a mother, and everyone needs help. Programs to improve the interactions between teenage parents and their children are often quite successful (Murray, 1995b). They significantly lower the child abuse rate. One interesting program sends child development specialists to homes on a weekly basis for 2 years. It offers child-care services within the community, allowing mothers to receive job training or formal education and prepare for a better life. The program also teaches young parents parenting

Some grandparents find themselves taking care of their grandchildren on a regular basis so that the child's mother may finish school or take a job.

techniques and helps them understand the difference between harsh and firm parenting. After participation, these parents have more realistic expectations for their children. Other programs involve fathers as well. These programs are cost-effective because they lead to less delinquency, abuse, and unemployment.

Special programs that emphasize family planning help pregnant teens develop competence in parenting, and enable them to finish school can make a difference both to the mother and the young child. Teens who attend and complete programs are more likely to graduate, use contraception regularly, have better employment prospects, and achieve better outcomes years later (Horwitz et al., 1991; Rabin, Seltzer, & Pollack, 1991). These young mothers must progress on their own developmental journeys and cope with the typical emotional upheavals that accompany pregnancy and the adjustment to parenting. They also must achieve a sense of control over their own lives.

Reducing the teenage pregnancy rate is an important goal of many sex education programs. In general, however, sex education and abstinence-based programs have not been especially successful in reducing pregnancy rates among teens (Nitz, 1999). The students sometimes show short-term changes in attitude, but long-term behavior does not seem to change for adolescent girls at risk for pregnancy. Programs that emphasize communication, self-esteem, and future plans are more successful. For example, some organizations, such as Girls, Inc., provide female teens with a combination of assertiveness training, health services, communication skills, counseling, and information about sexuality, and these efforts reduce the incidence of teen pregnancy (USDHHS, 1998).

Community-based programs incorporating elements of ecological theory and that extend beyond pregnancy prevention to enhance adolescents' life options hold great promise and have been successful (Kirby, 2002). The Teen Outreach program includes discussions on decision making, parenting, family relationships, communication skills, life options, and values. Results show reduced pregnancy rates. Another program, the Teen Pregnancy Prevention Program (Carrera & Dempsey, 1988), provides comprehensive services including a recreational program, education regarding family life, physical and mental health services, a job club, and mentoring. The program contains a performing arts component in which adolescents participate in music, dance, and drama. Evaluations show that participants are more likely to complete school and attend college and are less likely to become pregnant (Philliber, 1994).

Any program aiming at reducing teenage pregnancy must go beyond giving information and even discussing contraception; it must also help young teens living in poverty to see more alternatives and a brighter future (Cassell, 2002). In other words, to be successful, these programs must deal with the motivation to avoid pregnancy in addition to giving information about, and access to, contraception.

Forced Sexual Behavior

Sexual assault is a general term that includes situations in which sexual contact with or without penetration occurs because of physical force or psychological coercion (American Academy of Pediatrics, 2001). **Rape** is defined as forced sexual intercourse that occurs because of physical force or psychological coercion. Rape involves vaginal, anal, or oral penetration by the offender. The terms **acquaintance rape** and **date rape** are applied to situations in which the assailant and victim know each other.

Adolescents have the highest rate of rape and other sexual assaults of any age group (Rennison, 1998). Female victims exceed male victims by a ratio of 13.5 to 1.6. Although the great majority of sexual assaults involve female victims, males also report unwanted sexual contact (Struckman-Johnson & Struckman-Johnson, 1994). Between two-thirds and three-quarters of all adolescent rapes and sexual assaults are perpetrated by people the victims know (Quint, 1999). Adolescent and adult victims of sexual assault differ in some ways. Adolescent female victims are more likely to delay seeking medical care after the assault and

sexual assault A general term that includes situations in which sexual contact with or without penetration occurs because of physical force or psychological coercion.

rape Forced sexual intercourse that occurs because of physical force or psychological coercion.

acquaintance rape (date rape) Rape in which the assailant and victim know each other.

are less likely to press charges. In addition, adolescent rape victims as well as their assailants are more likely to have used alcohol or drugs prior to the rape than are adult female victims (Muram et al., 1995; Seifert, 1999). About 50 percent of the victims, the perpetrators, or both were using alcohol prior to the sexual assault (Abbey et al., 2001). Some drugs, referred to as *date rape drugs* (see "Drug Use and Violence") produce sleepiness, decreased anxiety, muscular relaxation, and profound sedation, and they may also cause amnesia (Schwartz & Weaver, 1998).

Attitudes toward acquaintance rape need to be changed, as studies show misconception and ignorance. In a study of high school students, more than half believed that some girls encourage rape just by the way they dress (Kershner, 1996). Researchers asked high school seniors to read a vignette describing an obvious date rape. They showed some adolescents a photograph of the victim dressed in provocative dress and others, a photo of the victim conservatively dressed; the rest of the participants did not see any photographs. About a third of the adolescents shown the provocative picture believed the girl was partially responsible and the boy was justified, or they denied that the girl in the vignette was even raped (Cassidy & Hurrell, 1995). The study found no gender differences, but other studies show that males assign more blame to the victims than women (White & Kurpius, 2002). Obviously, both males and females need rape education.

One of the reasons for the relatively high incidence of sexual coercion is the existence of rape-tolerant attitudes and misunderstandings about rape. Some people do not understand that acquaintance rape is rape, or they blame the victim if she is wearing revealing clothing or is intoxicated. Some people do not consider the perpetrators of acquaintance rape as really responsible for their actions if they were intoxicated at the time (Johnson, Kuck, & Schander, 1997). Males hold more tolerant attitudes toward sexual coercion than females (Ching & Burke, 1999), but the magnitude of the differences is often not great (Hannon et al., 2000).

Women often fail to report acquaintance rape because it does not fit the classic stereotype of the stranger who attacks without warning (Pino & Meier, 1999). There is still a stigma to rape, especially acquaintance rape, and the charges are often difficult to prove.

Immediate reactions to rape may involve disbelief, anxiety, and guilt (American Academy of Pediatrics, 2001). The psychological consequences of sexual assault can be severe. Rape during childhood or adolescence is associated with many negative consequences, including feelings of not being in control of one's life, depression, and drug use, as well as a host of other psychological problems (Miller, Monson, & Norton, 1995; Nagy, DiClemente, & Adcock, 1995). The victim may develop **posttraumatic stress disorder,** a psychological disorder involving recurring symptoms of numbing, reexperiencing the trauma, and hyperarousal following a traumatic event (American Psychiatric Association, 2000).

Victims of sexual assault require medical care and counseling (Kaplan & Holmes, 1999; Rose, 1998). They need a sensitive approach and assurance that the assault was not their fault. Woman can take steps to reduce the possibility of date rape—for example, by communicating limits, being assertive, not placing themselves in vulnerable situations, not accepting pressure, and avoiding excessive use of alcohol and other drugs (American College Health Association, 1986). Men should be advised to accept a woman's decision (no means no), improve communication, and avoid alcohol and other drugs. There is a movement to introduce antirape education in high schools, and many colleges have initiated programs aimed at reducing acquaintance rape.

Sexual Harassment

In recent years the public has become more aware of **sexual harassment,** defined as unwelcome conduct of a sexual nature (U.S. Department of Education, 2001b). Sexual harassment can include unwelcome sexual advances; requests for sexual

posttraumatic stress disorder A psychological disorder that may occur after a traumatic event and includes such symptoms as numbing, reexperiencing the trauma, and hyperarousal.

sexual harassment Unwelcome conduct of a sexual nature.

AT A GLANCE   **10.4**   SEX EDUCATION

KEY POINT: Comprehensive sex education, which may include information about sex, advocate sexual abstinence, offer information about contraception, and discuss values, can be effective in preventing teenage pregnancy, reducing the transmission of sexually transmitted infections, and making people more aware of the problems of date rape and sexual harassment.

SUPPORTING POINTS	EXPLANATION
Parents are the most important providers of sex education for their children.	Many parents do not speak extensively with their children on topics such as contraception or sexual values. Mothers communicate more than fathers.
Effective and ineffective sex education programs differ extensively.	Effective sex education programs talk about abstinence but offer information about contraception. They take a stand against unprotected sex. The most effective programs also deal with communication and values.
Sexually transmitted infections (STIs) are common in adolescents and young adults.	Chlamydia, gonorrhea, and syphilis are caused by bacteria, whereas genital warts, herpes simplex, and AIDS are caused by viruses. Adolescents are more likely to engage in unsafe sexual practices than older people.
The number of teenage pregnancies increased from the 1960s through the 1980s, and it then began to decline in the 1990s.	The decline in teenage pregnancy and births may be due to an increase in abstinence, a leveling off of teen sexual activity, increased use of contraception, and better sex education.
Studies emphasize the negative effects of early childbearing on the mother's future.	Teenage mothers are less likely to finish school and more likely to find themselves in low-paying jobs. Physical risks to themselves and their infants are more common. Many teenage mothers lack parenting skills.
Some research disputes the traditional view that relates teenage parenting to negative outcomes.	Some studies show that if family support is present, some teenage parents can do well. In addition, teenage pregnancy is not always the cause of the teen's lack of achievement; instead, it may be a symptom of the hopelessness and lack of opportunity in the teen's environment.
Teenage fathers may not be ready for their roles.	The children of a teenage girl are more likely to be fathered by a man in his 20s than by a teenage boy. Adolescent fathers are often not present and have poor economic prospects.
Forced sexual behavior and sexual harassment are now receiving considerable attention.	Education about rape, especially acquaintance rape, is greatly needed to prevent it. Victims of rape need both medical and psychological counseling. To reduce sexual harassment, schools and workplaces must increase awareness of what it is and how they will handle complaints about it.

quid pro quo sexual harassment   A type of sexual harassment that involves the use of benefits or consequences for sexual favors, including bribery or threats of being fired at work or failed in class.

hostile environment sexual harassment   A type of sexual harassment that involves the creation of a hostile and offensive climate at work or in school through some offensive sexual action that interferes with the victim's ability to function in the environment.

favors; and other verbal, nonverbal, or physical conduct of a sexual nature. Sexual harassment is divided into two categories (Hartmus & Niblock, 2000). **Quid pro quo sexual harassment** involves the use of benefits or consequences for sexual favors and includes bribery, threats, or even physical force. **Hostile environment sexual harassment** involves creating a hostile and offensive climate through some sexual action that interferes with the victim's ability to function in the environment (Equal Employment Opportunity Commission, 1989). Both males and females can be the victims of sexual harassment.

Sexual harassment is widespread. A survey of adolescents in grades 8 through 11 found that 83 percent of the girls and 79 percent of the boys had experienced sexual harassment (American Association of University Women, 2001).

One in four students said they had experienced it "often." Seventy-six percent had experienced nonphysical harassment, including sexual taunting, rumors, jokes, gestures, or graffiti, and 58 percent reported experiencing physical harassment often or occasionally. Between 25 and 30 percent of undergraduate students are sexually harassed in a given year (Hippensteele & Pearson, 1999). Between 42 and 50 percent of women and 15 percent of men will experience sexual harassment at work during their working lives (Charney & Russell, 1994).

People most often do not report sexual harassment. Fewer than 5 percent of the sexual harassment cases on college campuses is ever reported to a university official (Hippensteele & Pearson, 1999). Victims often fear retaliation (Fitzgerald & Shulliman, 1993), and because sexual harassment often takes place without witnesses, it can be difficult to corroborate.

Sexual harassment can have serious consequences for the victim. It blocks the individual's opportunities by making the atmosphere hostile and preventing the person from functioning in the environment (Sev'er, 1999). Some victims miss time from work or school and report anxiety, depression, reduced feelings of well-being, tension, insomnia, and reduced productivity (Hippensteele & Pearson, 1999).

It is important for schools and employers to have a well-publicized policy against sexual harassment and clear ways of handling complaints. The American Council on Education's sexual harassment guidelines (1992) identify five elements of an effective college campus sexual harassment program: (1) a basic definition of sexual harassment; (2) a strong policy clearly stating that sexual harassment will not be tolerated; (3) effective channels for communicating the policy to everyone; (4) educational programs to recognize and discourage sexual harassment; and (5) an accessible, effective, and timely grievance procedure. (For a review of this section, see At A Glance 10.4.)

PLACING ADOLESCENT SEXUALITY IN PERSPECTIVE

Sexuality cannot be divorced from the familial, cultural, community, and societal environment that surrounds the teenager. Societal changes over the past 40 years have led to a liberalization of attitudes. The ethic of sex as acceptable within a caring, loving relationship is undergoing a change, and commitment may no longer play as significant a part as it once did. Yet despite this liberalization, rates of sexual intercourse lately has shown stability or some decline, and the percentage of younger teens abstaining from engaging in sexual relations has increased somewhat. These findings may be due to sex education, fear of AIDS, or a possible attitudinal change in which sex is no longer seen as a quick fix for filling an emotional void. More of those teens who are sexually active are using contraception, which is one reason why teenage pregnancies have declined in the past decade. Many teens use contraception inconsistently, however, and teenage pregnancy remains a major problem.

Sexuality is a natural part of adolescence. Sexual expression should develop gradually, be personally and physically pleasurable, be characterized by concern for the other individual, and be marked by a willingness to take responsibility and act responsibly. However, engaging in sexual intercourse at an early age, forced or coerced sex, engaging in sexual intercourse as a way to compensate for some personal or familial deficit, or engaging in irresponsible sexual behavior can lead to feelings of guilt, anxiety, and anger, as well as to pregnancy and STIs. The context in which the adolescent develops an awareness of sexuality, a meaning for sexual expression, and an understanding of sexual responsibility makes all the difference. This fact underscores the role of parents, the school, and the community at large in helping teenagers adjust to developmental changes in sexuality.

Please place the number best reflecting your opinion next to each of the following statements. Then compare your opinions now with those you held before reading the chapter.

1 — Strongly Agree
2 — Moderately Agree
3 — No Opinion
4 — Moderately Disagree
5 — Strongly Disagree

_____ 1. The concept of love cannot be adequately defined.

_____ 2. People should never marry unless they are in love.

_____ 3. Early adolescents are too young to know what love really is.

_____ 4. It is acceptable for parents to have an earlier curfew for their daughters than for their sons.

_____ 5. It is acceptable for 16-year-olds who are in love to engage in sexual intercourse.

_____ 6. There has been a revolution in sexual behavior.

_____ 7. Males and females want different things in a relationship.

_____ 8. Schools should freely offer condoms to their students.

_____ 9. Sex education is solely the responsibility of parents.

_____ 10. The only real difference between homosexuals and heterosexuals is their sexual orientation.

THEMES

THEME 1 Adolescence is a time of choices, "firsts," and transitions.	• Adolescence is often the time of an individual's first romantic relationship. • Adolescence is often the time of an individual's first mature sexual experience. • An adolescent's concept of love changes from one based mostly on passion to one that includes intimacy and commitment. • Adolescents must choose the extent to which they wish to engage in various sexual activities. • Adolescents must choose whether they will use contraception when they become sexually active.
THEME 2 Adolescence is shaped by context.	• Parents, peers, the media, religious values, and cultural values all help shape the adolescent's sexual attitudes and behaviors. • Adolescents with close relationships with their parents are less likely to engage in intercourse early in adolescence. • The peer group and friends can influence sexual behavior, and a subtle or not so subtle pressure to have sex may influence an adolescent. • The media portray adolescent sex in a positive way and thus influence adolescent attitudes and behavior. • Adolescents are more likely to use contraception when they become sexually active if they have a good family life and have received comprehensive sex education.
THEME 3 Adolescence is influenced by group membership.	• Most cultures have the concept of romantic love. • In Western society the concept of love is centered on the self and emotional expression, whereas some Eastern societies see love in terms of obligations. • Females have more conservative attitudes toward sex than do males. • Group differences exist in the age of first sexual experience.
THEME 4 The adolescent experience has changed over the past 50 years.	• Attitudes toward sex have become more liberal. • The attitude that sex within a loving, committed relationship is acceptable even outside of marriage has emerged. • A recent attitudinal change is the acceptance of sex within an affectionate relationship even without commitment. • Rates of premarital sex have increased markedly but have remained relatively stable in the past 10 years. • Teenagers date at a younger age than they did 50 years ago. • The rates of contraception use have increased. • An adolescent today is more likely to have had some sex education.
THEME 5 Today's views of adolescence are becoming more balanced, with greater attention to its positive nature.	• The sexual behavior of adolescents is no longer viewed as being most strongly affected by physiological causes; today the many environmental influences on sexual behavior are appreciated. • Rather than viewing discussions of contraception as encouraging sexual activity, most members of the public, as well as professionals, realize that such discussion is necessary and does not encourage sex. • Rather than viewing homosexuality as a mental illness, modern psychologists view it as a different sexual orientation and appreciate the problems homosexuals encounter because of societal rejection. • Teenage mothers are no longer automatically assumed to be incompetent and unsuccessful; a more modern view accepts the greater challenges these mothers face but appreciates the fact that some young mothers are successful.

CHAPTER SUMMARY AT A GLANCE

KEY TOPICS	KEY POINTS
Physical Development and Sexuality	Physical changes lead to an increased sex drive during adolescence. (*At A Glance 10.1, p. 344*)
Dating, Love, and Sex	Love may be defined in many ways, and its relationship to sexuality is determined by many social and personal factors. (*At A Glance 10.2, p. 352*)
Sexual Attitudes and Behavior	Sexual attitudes and the extent of sexual behavior, such as the age of first intercourse, frequency of intercourse, and extent of contraceptive use, are determined by many personal and social factors. (*At A Glance 10.3, p. 363*)
Sex Education	Comprehensive sex education, which may include information about sex, advocate sexual abstinence, offer information about contraception, and discuss values, can be effective in preventing teenage pregnancy, reducing the transmission of sexually transmitted infections, and making people more aware of the problems of date rape and sexual harassment. (*At A Glance 10.4, p. 380*)

← **KEY TERMS**
intimacy (p. 346)
passion (p. 347)
commitment (p. 347)
romantic love (p. 347)
companionate love (p. 347)
fatuous love (p. 347)
consummate love (p. 347)

← *gay (p. 360)*
lesbian (p. 360)
bisexual (p. 360)

← *sexually transmitted infection (STI) (p. 368)*
chlamydia (p. 368)
gonorrhea (p. 369)
syphilis (p. 369)
genital warts (p. 369)
herpes simplex type 1 (p. 370)
herpes simplex type 2 (p. 370)
acquired immune deficiency syndrome (AIDS) (p. 370)
sexual assault (p. 378)
rape (p. 378)
acquaintance rape (date rape) (p. 378)
posttraumatic stress disorder (p. 379)
sexual harassment (p. 379)
quid pro quo sexual harassment (p. 380)
hostile environment sexual harassment (p. 380)

Review questions for this chapter appear in the appendix.

11

MORAL DEVELOPMENT, VALUES, AND RELIGION

WHAT IS YOUR OPINION?

APPROACHES TO MORAL DEVELOPMENT
- Piaget's Theory of Moral Reasoning
- Kohlberg's Theory of Moral Reasoning
- Moral Behavior
- Morality and Emotion
- Morality and Culture
- Putting It All Together

THE SPIRITUAL DIMENSION
- Stages of Religious Development
- Adolescents and Religion
  Perspective 1: My Beliefs Have Changed
- Religious Values and Behavior
  FOCUS: Cults

PROSOCIAL AND ALTRUISTIC BEHAVIOR
- Activism and Volunteering
- Prosocial Behavior and Gender
- The Emergence of the Moral Adolescent

MORAL EDUCATION
- Values Clarification
- Kohlberg's Approach to Moral Education
- The Teaching Approach
  Perspective 2: How Do We Do It?
- Home and Community Involvement
- Problems with Moral Education

PLACING MORAL DEVELOPMENT IN PERSPECTIVE

HAS YOUR OPINION CHANGED?

THEMES

CHAPTER SUMMARY AT A GLANCE

Do you believe there is more cheating today than years ago? Do you believe that moral and ethical behavior have declined lately? If you answered yes to these questions, you are not alone. More than half of all adults in a national survey believed that "kids are failing to learn such values as honesty, respect and responsibility" and that "fewer families are teaching religion/values" (Public Agenda, 1998).

The public is concerned about the morals and values of adolescents. People read about rampant cheating in schools and lack of concern for others, and they wonder what is wrong. The Josephson Institute of Ethics reported that in its recent survey of twenty thousand American middle and high school students, 76 percent confessed to lying to their teachers within the past year, and 63 percent said they had cheated on at least one test in the last year. The percentage of high school students who admit to cheating or lying has increased sharply since the last survey in the mid-1990s (Thatcher, 1999). Adolescents often rationalize that an assignment or test is meaningless, cite pressure to succeed, or argue that sports or other activities prevent them from doing their work (Sohn, 2001). Another study of high-achieving high school students found that half didn't believe cheating was necessarily wrong (Kleiner & Lord, 1999).

In Piper, Kansas, a high school teacher discovered that one-fifth of her class had plagiarized their biology project from the Internet (Bellamy, 2002). With the support of the principal and superintendent, she gave each of these students a grade of 0 for the project. Parents loudly complained, and the school board ordered the teacher to give the students partial credit and decrease the project's contribution to the final grade from 50 to 30 percent. The teacher resigned.

Many people are demanding that schools do more to instill teenagers with values. This interest in morals and values is certainly not new, but the feeling that something is definitely wrong is more pervasive in our society today. Perhaps we should also focus attention on the morals and ethics of the adults in the community, who serve as models. One poll found that one in four adults believes cheating is necessary to get ahead (Kleiner & Lord, 1999).

Yet there is another side to the coin. Society gives adolescents little credit for the good works they perform. Newspaper headlines across the country trumpet adolescent crime and cheating, but the media rarely cover stories of adolescents helping others and sharing. In a poll of 12- to 17-year-olds, 61 percent said they did some volunteer work, 45 percent said they tried to stop someone from using drugs or alcohol, 43 percent said they cared for someone who was very sick, and 36 percent said they worked on a community service project (NEA, 1994).

Adolescence is a period of questioning. The examination of one's beliefs, morals, and ethics is an important task in the development of a coherent identity (Erikson, 1958). The belief systems of teenagers are in a state of flux as their developing cognitive abilities and new experiences motivate them to alter and reformulate their childhood values.

This chapter explores the nature of adolescent moral values and behavior. It begins with an overview of the most prominent theories of moral development, emphasizing the research on adolescence. It then turns to a discussion of religious beliefs and practices; religious and spiritual beliefs often play a part in moral behavior. Because so much of the research on morality involves such behaviors as cheating, lying, and violence, the text devotes a section to

WHAT IS YOUR OPINION?

Please place the number best reflecting your opinion next to each of the following statements. We will return to this questionnaire at the end of the chapter so you can determine if your opinions have changed.

1 — Strongly Agree
2 — Moderately Agree
3 — No Opinion
4 — Moderately Disagree
5 — Strongly Disagree

_____ 1. Today's adolescents are not as moral or ethical as adolescents were 50 years ago.

_____ 2. Adolescents found to have plagiarized from the Internet should receive a 0 for the paper or project.

_____ 3. When adolescents cheat, steal, or lie, it is mainly because they have not learned the proper values at home.

_____ 4. Men and women generally reason differently about moral issues.

_____ 5. People can learn to act more morally.

_____ 6. If people felt more empathy for others, they would act in a kinder and more considerate manner.

_____ 7. Teenagers who come to doubt the teachings of their own religion are basically going through a normal phase of questioning, and others should read nothing more serious into this rejection or criticism of their religious heritage.

_____ 8. Cults use brainwashing in their recruitment practices and pose a psychological danger to their members.

_____ 9. Schools have the responsibility to instill moral values in their students.

Which picture do you think will get into the newspaper? Often, the good works of adolescents are not publicized but their negative behavior is trumpeted across the headlines.

prosocial and altruistic behavior, which are much more common than many people believe. The chapter concludes with a discussion of moral education, how to promote positive moral decision making, and the role various environmental influences play in determining moral behavior.

APPROACHES TO MORAL DEVELOPMENT

Just how does a person develop a sense of right and wrong? Psychologists of various schools of thought approach the question from different perspectives. One major approach looks at *moral reasoning*, or how an individual faced with a problem reasons about what to do. Consider a high school junior taking a chemistry midterm who has the opportunity to cheat from a neighbor's paper. Psychologists studying moral reasoning are interested in how the adolescent decides what to do in this situation. They are less interested in what the decision is than in the reasoning behind it.

The second approach to studying the development of morality emphasizes the importance of studying the behavior itself, such as cheating, stealing, lying, helping others, sharing, or returning an item to its owner. This approach does not emphasize the reasoning that may lead to a behavior but instead looks at the environmental factors that influence the behavior itself.

Still another approach to moral development emphasizes the importance of the individual's emotional state and ability to experience **empathy**—that is, to understand what another person or group of people is experiencing at the time, as well as to understand their needs and feelings. This approach does not necessarily stand alone, but any comprehensive understanding of moral development must include the emotional component.

empathy The ability to understand what another person or group of people is experiencing.

Piaget's Theory of Moral Reasoning

Introduce a 5-year-old and a 13-year-old to a new card game that requires fifteen cards to play. A few days later, after they have learned the game, announce that you are playing a shortened version of the game. The 13-year-old will accept the change, but the 5-year-old may balk at it.

Give both a 5-year-old and a 13-year old this scenario: "John broke one dish trying to sneak a cookie from the jar, and Barry broke three dishes trying to help his mother clean up the table. Who did worse?" The 5-year-old will choose Barry because he broke three dishes; the 13-year-old will choose John because he was stealing, whereas Barry accidentally broke the dishes.

Prominent cognitive developmental psychologist Jean Piaget (1932) viewed morality in terms of how children develop a sense of justice. He argued that children's understanding of rules follows a general sequence. In the first stage, **moral realism,** preschoolers and children in the early years of elementary school consider rules firm, rigid, and created by all-powerful authority figures. They follow rules rigidly. One parent of a 6-year-old told me that his child refused to do his first-grade homework when he came home from school because his teacher had told him that it was to be done that *night* for homework. The letter of the rule or law, not its spirit, is important. Young children become upset if rules are changed. They also see values and morality in absolute terms. They fail to take intention into account when judging right and wrong. The greater the damage, the more "evil" the individual's deed.

At about 7 or 8 years, children reach an intermediate stage. They become somewhat more flexible and sometimes will take intention into account. They begin to look at what is fair, rather than simply accepting what the authority figure says.

The stage of **moral relativism** emerges at about 11 or 12 years and continues into adolescence. Adolescents are more flexible and understand that rules can change. They take extenuating circumstances into account and can weigh many factors before deciding on a course of action. Children develop this more sophisticated view of morality and values through social interaction and cognitive growth (Piaget, 1932). Notice that by the time children reach adolescence, they understand intention well, become more flexible in deciding what is right and wrong, and can consider other people's points of view.

Piaget's theory is valuable, but narrowly constructed. It shows how people perceive rules and understand intention, but it does not deal with how people reason about complex moral issues, such as whether to return an item to its owner. Lawrence Kohlberg advanced the most complete and controversial theory of moral reasoning.

Kohlberg's Theory of Moral Reasoning

Kohlberg (1969, 1976) presented moral dilemmas to many people of various ages. The most famous moral dilemma involves the case of Heinz, whose wife suffers from cancer. There is a drug that might cure her, but the only dose is owned by a pharmacist who wants a great deal of money for it. Heinz doesn't have the money. The question is, Should he steal it? After carefully evaluating many participants' responses to dilemmas such as the case of Heinz, Kohlberg proposed a three-level, six-stage model that describes the development of moral reasoning. Kohlberg believes the stages are sequential and universal (that is, found in every culture). Each stage requires more sophisticated reasoning skills than the stage that precedes it. In addition, moral reasoning progresses from externalized standards (for example, doing something because someone will reward you or because you follow the rules) to internalized standards (for example, helping others because you believe it is the right thing to do).

To better understand these levels and stages, consider the following dilemma that is probably within your experience. You are stopped at a traffic light in the middle of the country. It is late at night, but you don't feel threatened.

moral realism The Piagetian stage of moral reasoning during which justice is authority based and intention is not taken into account.

moral relativism The Piagetian stage of moral reasoning during which people weigh the intentions of others before judging their actions as right or wrong.

The light is not broken, for it changed as you approached it. You are tired. After stopping for the red light and checking that it is safe, would you go through the red light? Remember that your stage or level of moral reasoning is determined not by your behavior or decision itself ("I'd proceed once I stopped and checked that it was safe" or "I wouldn't go through the light") but by your reasoning itself ("I would/wouldn't go through the red light because . . .").

Level 1: Preconventional Moral Reasoning People reasoning at level 1, the level of **preconventional moral reasoning,** make their decisions on the basis of reward and punishment. That is, they want to satisfy their own needs and avoid punishment. In the case just mentioned, a person might go through the light after stopping and checking for traffic because she was tired and wanted to get home. Notice that the motivation is to satisfy her own needs. In contrast, a person might remain at the light until it changed if he feared that a police car was hiding in the bushes and the law enforcement officer was just waiting for someone to go through the light to give the driver an expensive ticket. Here, the motivation is to avoid punishment.

STAGE 1: PUNISHMENT AND OBEDIENCE ORIENTATION A person in stage 1 avoids breaking rules because it might lead to punishment. Individuals in this stage show a complete deference to rules and take only their own interests into account.

STAGE 2: INSTRUMENTAL-RELATIVIST ORIENTATION In stage 2, the moral action is one that satisfies the individual's own needs and, sometimes, the needs of others. The only reason to help others is because then they will owe you something in the future. An acceptable deal and a sense of fairness involve a kind of "You scratch my back, and I'll scratch yours" attitude.

Level 2: Conventional Moral Reasoning Conformity is the central feature of level 2, **conventional moral reasoning.** People conform to the expectations of others and to society's rules. They feel it is important to do the "right" thing, defined as the behavior expected by their parents and other authority figures. People reasoning at this level often believe that people should conform to the law generally, and the fear of punishment is not necessary to promote "good" behavior. The driver at this stage may decide to go through the light because other people would do the same, or decide not to because it would be against the rules.

STAGE 3: INTERPERSONAL CONCORDANCE OR "GOOD BOY/NICE GIRL" STAGE Living up to the expectations of others and being "good" are important considerations in stage 3. The emphasis is on gaining the approval of others through performing socially acceptable behaviors.

STAGE 4: LAW-AND-ORDER ORIENTATION Individuals in stage 4 look toward authority and the need to maintain the social order. They believe that people must do their duty and show respect for duly constituted authority. People in this stage often reason, "What if everyone did this? The consequences would be. . . ."

preconventional moral reasoning The first level of moral reasoning in Kohlberg's theory, in which people reason on the basis of avoiding punishment and receiving rewards.

conventional moral reasoning The second level of moral reasoning in Kohlberg's theory, in which moral reasoning is based on conformity to rules and law.

postconventional moral reasoning The third level of moral reasoning in Kohlberg's theory, in which moral reasoning is based on self-accepted, abstract ethical principles.

Level 3: Postconventional Moral Reasoning People reasoning at level 3, **postconventional moral reasoning,** have internalized values that do not depend on group membership. They weigh the ethics of various viewpoints and create abstract guidelines that direct their behavior (Kohlberg & Kramer, 1969). Postconventional moral reasoning does not appear before Piaget's formal operational stage (see "Cognitive Development"), because formal operational reasoning is necessary for postconventional reasoning. Postconventional moral reasoning involves using an internalized set of abstract values that guide behavior. Younger children do not have the cognitive ability to formulate such values.

According to Kohlberg, the level and stage of moral reasoning that an individual is in is defined by the reasoning behind an action. Psychologists studying moral reasoning would ask this individual why she shoplifted or why she refrained from doing so.

The simple red light situation does not lend itself to postconventional reasoning, but say a passenger in the car is late for an important airline flight. Let's make the situation even more of a dilemma by suggesting that if the driver receives one more ticket, he will have his driver's license suspended, receive a hefty fine, and find that his insurance premiums increase substantially. Now a decision to go through the light involves balancing the value of helping another against self-interest (Thompson, 1995). People reasoning at the postconventional level differentiate themselves from the rules and expectations of others and think in terms of self-chosen principles (Ward, 1991).

STAGE 5: SOCIAL CONTRACT: LEGALISTIC ORIENTATION   Individuals in stage 5 define moral behavior in terms of individual rights and the consensus of society. What is right is a matter of personal values, but the emphasis is on the legal point of view. Such reasoning might include referring to the Bill of Rights.

STAGE 6: UNIVERSAL ETHICAL PRINCIPLE ORIENTATION   People in the highest stage define moral behavior as a decision of conscience in accordance with self-chosen ethical principles that are logical, universal, and consistent (Turiel, 1998). They desire that others understand these higher values and often, but not always, are willing to suffer sanctions from others for holding these beliefs.

At What Stage of Moral Development Do Teens Reason?

Kohlberg's theory of moral reasoning is not an age/stage theory in the conventional sense. It does not say that a 9-year-old must reason at a higher level than a 7-year-old or that a teenager will reason at a higher level than a preteen. However, as noted, an individual reasoning at the highest level (level 3, stages 5 and 6) must have the ability to reason at Piaget's stage of formal operations. Formal operational abilities—for example, being able to understand abstractions, consider many alternatives, and use deductive logic—are necessary, but not sufficient, to allow an adolescent to reason at the higher stages of moral reasoning. In fact, most adolescents and adults do not develop beyond stage 4 (Shaver & Strong, 1976).

The adolescent's moral reasoning does not fall neatly into a single stage (Kohlberg, 1969). At times, adolescents operate on a higher level, but at other times they operate on a lower one (Holstein, 1976). Kohlberg argues that people's moral reasoning can be placed mostly in one stage but that they often operate in the surrounding stages as well. For example, a teen may reason mostly at stage 4 but also reason on some issues at stages 3 or 5. According to Kohlberg, this situation explains some of the variability in moral reasoning that is commonly found in life.

The consistency of moral reasoning across situations is controversial, and the research is mixed. Some studies find moral reasoning scores consistent across both real-life and hypothetical dilemmas (Walker, deVries, & Trevethan, 1987). Other studies do not find this consistency. For example, one study gave older and younger adolescents a series of moral dilemmas, one of which involved notification of past partners that one has a sexually transmitted disease. The level of moral reasoning of the participants depended on the content of the dilemmas themselves, suggesting that moral reasoning is not consistent across different types of dilemmas (Jadack et al., 1995). Research evidence points to a greater amount of variability than Kohlberg suggested (Hoffman, 1988; Wark & Krebs, 1996). That is, a person might reason at stage 5 for one subject and at stages 1 or 2 for another. It seems that when people develop the ability to reason at a higher level, they retain the ability and willingness to reason at lower stages as well (Carpendale & Krebs, 1995).

It should not surprise anyone, then, that adolescents (as well as adults) show considerable variability in reasoning and inconsistency in behavior. Sometimes, this inconsistency is due to the possible consequences of a particular behavior. It is relatively easy to reason at a very high stage when there is nothing personal to lose, but it is much harder to do so when the consequences of such reasoning are significant. For example, it is easy to argue that people should drive their cars less and accept higher gas taxes to encourage conservation if you don't drive much or are wealthy. It is much more difficult to argue this case if you must drive frequently and are financially strapped.

Is Moral Reasoning Related to Moral Behavior?   Would an adolescent reasoning at stage 5 act differently than one reasoning at stage 2? Although followers of Kohlberg would remind us that this is a theory of moral reasoning, not moral behavior, it is a fair question to ask. Most studies find a relationship between moral reasoning and moral behavior (Blasi, 1980; Kohlberg, 1987), but the strength of that relationship varies from area to area and issue to issue. Adolescents reasoning at higher levels are generally more altruistic—that is, they are more likely to do things for others without any contemplation of a reward—probably because they are motivated by more abstract values (Ma, 1989). However, the correlation is modest.

Support exists for the idea that people who reason at higher moral stages are more honest, but only relatively weak associations are found between progressing to higher levels of moral reasoning and whether someone will cheat or yield to temptation if the personal consequences are considerable (Maccoby, 1980). For example, college students cheat less as the level of their moral reasoning increases, and students reasoning at lower levels certainly do cheat more. However, students reasoning at high levels also cheat if the temptation becomes strong (Malinowski & Smith, 1985). An inverse relationship exists between higher levels of moral reasoning and reported risk taking. Adolescents who reason at higher levels of moral reasoning are less likely to take risks, such as having sexual relations without using a condom (Hubbs-Tait & Garmon, 1995). There is some support, then, for the idea that higher moral reasoning leads to more moral behavior, but the relationship is far from perfect.

Do Males and Females Reason Differently About Moral Issues?
Kohlberg's theory strongly emphasizes justice and individual rights (Thompson, 1995). Individuals with higher moral reasoning use abstract reasoning and base

their stands on abstract moral principles they have internalized. Such reasoning seemingly has little to do with interpersonal relationships, caring, or the human context of the dilemma.

Carol Gilligan (1982) argued that women have a different orientation to moral questions than do men. Women see moral issues in terms of how actions and decisions affect interpersonal relationships, whereas men are more likely to stress individual rights and abstract principles. Gilligan suggested that females speak with a caring voice and males speak with a voice of justice (Gilligan & Attanucci, 1988; Gilligan, Lyons, & Hanmer, 1989). When asked to discuss certain moral dilemmas, females more often than males explain their reasoning by mentioning the importance of caring about others, relationships, and relieving the burdens of others (Lyons, 1988). Males more frequently explain their choices using reasons of fairness, the Golden Rule, and abstract principles.

Gilligan suggested an alternative stage sequence for the development of moral reasoning by females. The first step is an initial selfishness, which soon changes into a style of reasoning composed of giving and caring primarily for others and finally proceeds to integrating concern for the needs of self and others. Gilligan emphasizes the importance of attachments, allowing for both self-sacrifice and self-promotion, and she views connections with others as most important (Gump, Baker, & Roll, 2000).

The differences in moral reasoning are rooted in the varying experiences of boys and girls throughout childhood. Boys are taught to be independent, assertive, achievement oriented, and individualistic, as well as to attach great importance to law. This description seems like Kohlberg's stage 4 perspective. Girls, in contrast, are raised to be more concerned with the needs of others, to care for other people, and to be more concerned about interpersonal relationships (Hotelling & Forrest, 1985). They are encouraged to be more oriented toward connectedness, care, sensitivity, and responsibility to others rather than toward abstract principles of justice (Muuss, 1982). Women may see moral problems as conflicts between what they want and the needs of others; they may base their decisions on how they will affect relationships with others and a desire not to hurt others (Ward, 1991). This emphasis on care reads more like Kohlberg's stage 3 perspective. Gilligan notes, though, that neither reasoning is superior but rather just different, and the differences need to be respected. She also argues that Kohlberg's emphasis on justice overlooks a morality of care for others, which is a principle consideration of women (Turiel, 1998).

Do males and females really reason differently on moral issues? Some studies do support Gilligan's ideas. When researchers gave students in grades 6, 8, 10, and 12 word pairs consisting of "caring words" and "justice words," such as *patience* versus *determination,* and asked them to circle the word in each pair that was more important, they found significant gender differences (see Table 11.1). In almost all cases, females chose the caring item over the justice item (Badger, Craft, & Jensen, 1998). Other studies show a gender-related preference for different styles of reasoning among university students in Asian countries as well (Stimpson, Jensen, & Neff, 1991). These gender differences do not become any more consistent as teens progress through adolescence; that is, these orientations are in place by sixth grade and then maintained. A larger percentage of females are characterized by a value orientation that

Table 11.1

Percentage of Males and Females Choosing the Caring Item or the Justice Item

When researchers asked adolescents which of two qualities—one that represented caring and one that represented justice—was more important, they found significant gender differences. Females were more likely to choose the caring item (first item in the pair) over the justice item (second item in the pair).

Pairs	Male (%)	Female (%)
Intuition versus *logic*	41	44
Compromise versus *power*	53	79
Kindness versus *character*	53	66
Forgiveness versus *consistency*	65	84
Children versus *freedom*	27	44
Feelings versus *facts*	69	84
People inside versus *people do*	72	82
Mercy versus *justice*	31	26
Enjoy people versus *enjoy work*	74	83
Patience versus *determination*	29	55
Getting along versus *achievement*	57	65
Friends versus *success*	63	75
Cooperative versus *competitive*	50	77
Helping versus *being in charge*	61	80

Source: Adapted from Badger, Craft, & Jensen (1998), Table 1, p. 593.

emphasizes kindness, getting along with others, cooperation, and helpfulness (Hill & Lynch, 1983).

The majority of studies, however, either fail to find consistent gender differences or find that the differences are minimal (Friedman, Robinson, & Friedman, 1987; Galotti, 1989; Walker, 1984, 1991). One fascinating study examined the moral reasoning of thirty people with genital herpes and twenty-nine people without any sexually transmitted infection (STI) (Conley, Jadack, & Hyde, 1997). The researchers determined each participant's level and stage of moral reasoning through answers to a variety of moral dilemmas, some of which involved STIs. They found no gender differences. For example, females were no more likely than men to use a care orientation.

It is interesting to note that participants with genital herpes reasoned at higher stages on the dilemmas involving STIs than participants who did not have an STI. Perhaps people with herpes have faced some of these moral issues in their personal lives, and experience with ethical problems in a particular domain may be important in moral reasoning. Similarly, gender differences in reasoning style may appear when using dilemmas in which males and females have different personal experiences. An analysis of studies on whether males and females reason differently found very small differences in the direction Gilligan claims, however, and the researchers conclude that the available studies do not lend strong support to the idea that females reason predominantly in a caring manner and males mostly by a justice orientation (Jaffee & Hyde, 2000).

In fact, few people reason exclusively using a care or justice orientation; most people use both. Research results basically call into question Gilligan's thesis that men and women reason differently about moral dilemmas. Although some dilemmas may show a tendency or trend, the pattern is not clear-cut. Even though consistent gender differences have not been found, though, Gilligan's contribution to the field is secure. Her outlook broadens the view that the moral person integrates concepts of abstract justice and concern for others (Muuss, 1988).

Criticisms of Kohlberg's Theory Kohlberg's theory offers a valuable framework for understanding moral development, but serious criticisms have surfaced. One criticism focuses on Kohlberg's interest in moral reasoning, noting that it is related to moral behavior only modestly. Although Kohlberg was interested in both behavior and reasoning, he believed that the best way to understand behavior was to understand moral reasoning (Turiel, 1990). However, the discrepancy between reasoning and action is a problem. For whatever reason, people sometimes act in ways they think are theoretically best, and sometimes they do not (Chandler & Boyes, 1982).

Another problem is that it is theoretically possible to reason at any of Kohlberg's levels and stages and still find a rationale to cheat, steal, or lie; the theory needs more predictability. Kohlberg's theory also assumes that a person should reason fairly consistently in different situations, but as noted earlier, this consistency does not always exist (Carpendale & Krebs, 1995).

Kohlberg's theory would be stronger if he had depended more on the actual life experiences of people and less on verbal responses to hypothetical situations (Vitz, 1990). We know a great deal about hypothetical dilemmas but very little about real-life moral judgments (Wark & Krebs, 1996). Real-life dilemmas are different from those Kohlberg presented, and they may be more important than hypothetical dilemmas in distinguishing among people (Wygant, 1997).

Finally, Kohlberg argued that the earliest stages of moral reasoning are not based on any universal ideals but rather are situational. However, research shows that children as young as 3 or 4 years understand that such actions as hurting others and stealing are universally wrong. Other behaviors, such as violating a dress code, are based on social convention and are subject to change (Wainryb, 1993).

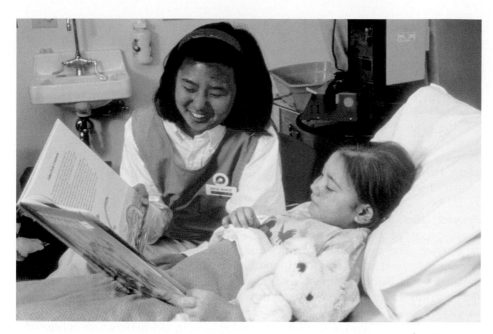

Another approach to moral development is to consider the behavior itself rather than the reasoning behind the behavior.

Moral Behavior

An equally impressive approach to understanding moral development emphasizes studying the behavior itself instead of the moral reasoning behind the action. This approach directly investigates sharing, helping, giving, lying, cheating, or stealing. Moral behavior is often explained in terms of the situation, the adolescent's background, and the reinforcers present in the environment. This framework adopted from the **behavioral perspective** assumes that moral behaviors are learned in the same way as any other behaviors. Operant conditioning explains some behaviors. Parents and peers may influence behaviors by reinforcing desired actions (Ward, 1991); for example, people who are reinforced for giving and sharing are more likely to give and share.

Social learning theory, which emphasizes the importance of observation learning, is also helpful in understanding moral behavior. If adolescents see their parents helping out at the local homeless shelter, they are more likely to volunteer for community work themselves. Of course, people do not imitate everything they see. They are more likely to imitate others they see as powerful and respected and those who get things done. Such factors as the character of the model, the consequences of the behavior, and the person's own characteristics and goals affect whether or not the individual shows the modeled behavior.

Social learning theory also uses cognitive processes to explain moral behavior. People may perceive situations differently and thus make different behavioral choices. Consider the following scenario. You are sitting in the school auditorium when another student tries to climb over your feet to get into his seat and spills soda on you. How would you react? Probably, your reaction would depend on how you interpreted his action. If you thought it was an accident, you might react one way; if you thought he did it on purpose, you might react differently. In fact, people who are considered aggressive usually interpret accidental behaviors as purposeful and react aggressively; nonaggressive people interpret such behaviors as accidental and do not react with violence (Hudley & Graham, 1993). People who are not aggressive tend to give others the benefit of the doubt. Another factor affecting moral behavior is competence to deal with a particular situation (Mussen & Eisenberg-Berg, 1977). A person who feels competent may act one way; a person who is bewildered may act in a totally different manner.

behavioral perspective   An approach to explaining behavior that studies observable behavior and examines the environmental stimuli that shape behavior.

social learning theory   An approach to explaining behavior that combines the principles of learning theory and cognitive processes, such as thoughts and expectations, and emphasizes the importance of observation learning.

Morality and Emotion

Both the moral reasoning and moral behavior approaches seem somewhat cold. Neither approach includes an emotional component (Matsuba & Walker, 1998). When someone needs help, however, we often experience an emotion of empathy—the ability to understand and vicariously experience what another person is going through—and we are moved to help. We read about families who have lost their homes to a flood, and our emotional reactions motivate us to donate money to help them. We see some injustice and we experience anger, motivating us to act in some way. Emotional reactions can also prevent us from doing something. Perhaps we are thinking about doing something that is against our moral code and feel guilty even considering such a course of action.

Freud and Morality   Sigmund Freud's view of morality is based on the development of the **superego,** which consists of two parts, the ego ideal and the conscience. The **ego ideal** involves the individual's standards of perfection, which are formed when children identify and internalize the ideals and values of the adults who surround them. Individuals who maintain these standards experience pride. The conscience causes individuals to experience guilt when misbehaving or considering a misbehavior (Eidelberg, 1968; Freud, 1933/1961).

According to Freud, the main concept explaining moral behavior is **identification.** Children identify with their parents and internalize values and standards. Even when parents are not present, the adolescent acts in a way that would make parents proud and experiences guilt when acting bad. The emotions of pride and guilt become important internal forces that regulate behavior. Even the anticipation of these emotions may motivate an individual.

Most psychologists agree that identification takes place, but teenagers' values are hardly carbon copies of their parents' values. Although some similarity may exist, the idea of total identification is unacceptable; adolescents cannot maintain their parents' complete moral structure. After all, adolescents and parents belong to different cohorts—different realities. Adolescents will use what they learn from their parents, but they must change it to keep up with their new experiences. Freudian theory sees the adolescent's moral structure as developing from anxiety over conflicts between an ideal moral code found in the superego and the adolescent's perceived reality. The adolescent attempts to balance reality and the superego. The most important conflict is between the adolescent's desire to establish new emotional relationships away from parents and the desire to retain the dependencies of childhood. Moral development during adolescence, then, may be seen as a struggle to establish new standards of behavior or social norms that modify or replace parental standards (Ward, 1991).

Empathy   Guilt and pride are not the only emotions that influence moral behavior. Empathy is also important. Imagine seeing your friend upset because he has just failed an important test. You took the same course with the same tough teacher last term and know that your friend has had a difficult year. You understand what he is experiencing—that is, you empathize with him—and you go over to him and offer emotional support.

Martin Hoffman (1983, 1991) argues that empathy develops with age. Infants, in the first stage, empathize with others by feeling the distress that another infant shows and crying when other infants cry. At 1 year or so, children show an egocentric empathy, understanding that other people are physically distinct entities, but they cannot distinguish their own internal states from those of others. For example, a child may ask his mother to help another crying child whose mother is also present (Turiel, 1998).

In the third stage, children are able to empathize with a larger range of feelings than just distress. The elementary school child is better able to take the perspective of another child. The ability to empathize with other people improves during middle childhood as children become less egocentric. This characteristic explains the finding that older children are more empathic than younger children.

superego   In Freudian theory, the portion of the mind in which the conscience, as well as standards of conduct internalized from parental teaching, are found.

ego ideal   An individual's positive and desirable standards of behavior.

identification   The process by which children take on the characteristics of another person, most often a parent.

The fourth stage, which involves showing empathy for another person's condition in life, emerges at about 10 to 12 years and continues to develop throughout adolescence. Older children become more aware that they have a different history than other children. They experience empathy not only in particular situations but also for more general life circumstances, such as for the poor or the oppressed. Empathy for general concerns, then, may continue to develop throughout adolescence.

Theoretically, adolescents should experience more empathy for others than younger preteens. However, many studies fail to find a consistent increase in empathy with age past the preteen age group (Francis & Pearson, 1987). An improvement in teenagers' cognitive skills, especially in perspective taking, may make empathy more likely while another factor—perhaps teenagers' more complex attributions as to why an individual is experiencing distress—may have the opposite effect, decreasing the likelihood for empathy. For example, a teenager may believe that a person who is upset because she failed a test may be partially responsible for the situation because she hadn't read the material.

One of Hoffman's (1991) main contributions is the integration of affect (emotion) and cognition. The quality of our empathy is shaped by the attributions we make about the causes of the victim's distress. When the cause is beyond the victim's control (such as an illness, accident, or loss), our empathic feeling is transformed into sympathy or compassion. If someone else caused the tragedy, our sympathetic distress may become anger toward that person. However, we experience less empathy if we believe the people themselves are responsible for their present situation.

Hoffman's (1983) focus on emotion brings another element into the moral development picture. Although there is no doubt that emotion plays some role, the extent of its contribution is still controversial. Some points are well established. Adolescents have the ability to empathize not only with a person in a specific situation (for example, an unfortunate victim of a flood) but also with the general situation in which a group of people find themselves (for example, people who have not had many opportunities to succeed in society). Adolescents can empathize not only with the individual's aversive emotions (anger, anxiety, and outrage) but also with positive emotions (joy and admiration). Emotions may activate an individual; feeling empathy may encourage someone to help out at a food kitchen for people who are homeless. Empathy and anticipatory guilt may motivate helping behavior, but they depend on the individual's level of cognitive development. Emotions, then, are a part of the puzzle that is moral behavior; but like moral reasoning, they cannot stand alone.

Due to cognitive improvements, adolescents should show more empathy, but this is not always the case. Adolescents also make attributions about the cause of the distress and will show much more empathy if they feel the cause of the person's problem is beyond the person's control.

Morality and Culture

Moral reasoning, learning, cognitive advancement, and the ability to experience empathy are all important aspects of morality. Yet these elements are influenced by the culture in which an adolescent lives. People from various cultures may interpret moral dilemmas differently and choose different ways to solve them. Adolescents from the United States grow up with a rights-based morality because they learn early on about the Bill of Rights, whereas people from India are raised more on a duty-based morality (Shweder, Mahapatra, & Miller, 1987). American adolescents often base their moral reasoning on the individual rights of others, whereas Indian adolescents often look at how their actions might affect others to whom they have a responsibility. Interviews in China find that community, filial piety, and the ideal of social harmony are more important than individual justice in Chinese society (Wygant, 1997).

Stories that illustrated moral dilemmas were given to sixth graders and college students in India and the United States (for example, a robber contracts a mysterious deadly disease). Some of the stories included statements such as "What goes around comes around," which emphasize what is called *immanent justice,* or the idea that people are naturally punished for their misdeeds. Indian society emphasizes this concept, and Indian students were more likely to agree that the robber became ill because he was bad. Furthermore, immanent justice beliefs increased in frequency with age in India. Indian college students applied such beliefs more than five times as often as U.S. college students.

Cultures may emphasize one value above another. A study of cheating in English colleges and universities found rates and patterns similar to those found in the United States (Newstead, Franklyn-Stokes, & Armstead, 1996). However, a study of cheating among Australian students found much less cheating than in the United States or England (Davis et al., 1994). The reasons are uncertain, but Australian students may be less tolerant of cheating because of a cultural emphasis on fair play (Waugh et al., 1985). The central point here is that culture is an important variable in moral decision making and behavior. Some cultures respect sacrifice for the group more than individual achievement and thus may approve or disapprove of a particular moral value or behavior over another.

Putting It All Together

Just how do teenagers convert environmental information into a moral action sequence? The process involves a number of factors, including reasoning, empathy, and learning. James Rest (1983) suggests a four-stages sequence by which information leads to action (see Table 11.2). Adolescents and children differ at each stage.

In the first stage, a person must be sensitive enough to notice and evaluate a situation in terms of moral questions. This sensitivity may involve the ability to see the world from other people's points of view and to empathize with them. As previously discussed, both perspective taking and empathy may improve in adolescence.

Table 11.2

James Rest's Four-Stage Model of Moral Behavior

James Rest argues that moral behavior can be explained in terms of four stages. People must first understand that there is a moral dilemma and then use their reasoning abilities to comprehend the situation. They then take environmental factors into account and finally decide whether they are competent to implement their plan of action.

Stage	Question	Developmental Consideration
Stage 1: Sensitivity	1. Does the person perceive the situation as a moral dilemma?	Perspective taking and empathy improve in adolescence.
	2. Does the person feel empathy for the individual who needs help?	
	3. Can the person take the perspective of the other individual?	
Stage 2: Reasoning	What type of moral reasoning does the person show?	Adolescents have the ability to reason at Kohlberg's higher stages of moral reasoning. Adolescents are better at using deductive logic.
Stage 3: Environmental influences	1. What is the personal cost? 2. Are any competing values involved?	Adolescents are more likely to use multiple aspects of the environment and to do a cost-benefit analysis.
Stage 4: Practical considerations	Is the person competent to handle this situation?	Adolescents have more practical experience and are generally more competent than younger children.

Source: Adapted from Rest (1983).

In the second stage, the adolescent attempts to reason the problem out, which is where Kohlberg's moral reasoning theory fits in. Adolescents have the ability to reason at higher stages of moral reasoning than younger children.

In the third stage, the individual takes environmental influences into consideration, such as the personal cost of the decision to help ("I would like to help this person out, but if I am late for work again, I might be fired"). Personal cost is an important aspect of a decision, and one that other formulations do not adequately consider. Environmentally sound behavior is sometimes a function of the personal costs involved and the awareness of these costs, and there are clearly competing motives and values. In a study of environmental understanding, ado-

AT A GLANCE 11.1 APPROACHES TO MORAL DEVELOPMENT

KEY POINT: Moral development can be investigated by researching moral reasoning or moral behavior itself, but the emotional component cannot be ignored.

SUPPORTING POINTS	EXPLANATION
Jean Piaget investigated how children develop a sense of fairness and justice.	Children younger than 7 years are in the stage of moral realism and depend on authority figures to tell them right from wrong. Children of this age cannot take intention into account. Children between 7 and 10 years show less reliance on adults and sometimes can take intention into account. After age 10, children enter the stage of moral relativism, in which they realize that rules can change and regularly take intention into account.
Lawrence Kohlberg argued that people's development of moral reasoning can be seen in terms of three levels and six stages.	People reasoning at the preconventional level base their decisions on obtaining rewards and avoiding punishment. People reasoning at the conventional level base their decisions on conformity and obeying the rules. People reasoning at the postconventional level base their reasoning on their own self-accepted principles. There is a relationship between higher moral reasoning and more moral behavior, but it is far from perfect.
Carol Gilligan argued that women reason differently than men.	Gilligan argued that women reason about moral questions using an ethic of caring and promoting interpersonal harmony. Men tend to use concepts of abstract justice when reasoning about moral issues. Research shows that men and women actually use both approaches to moral reasoning.
Some psychologists emphasize the importance of studying moral behavior itself.	Some psychologists study a particular behavior, such as helping others, rather than the reasoning behind the action. Such factors as the individual's background, the characteristics of the situation, and available reinforcement and models influence moral behavior.
Moral behavior is also determined by emotional factors.	People who experience empathy—that is, an emotional feeling of understanding of another person's plight—are more likely to help. Sigmund Freud argued that children and adolescents identified with their parents and thereby internalized their moral values.
Culture is an important factor in determining moral reasoning and moral behavior.	Although some values are widespread, cultures may value one behavior over another.
James Rest suggests that information is converted to moral action in a four-stage sequence.	First, a person must be aware that a moral issue is involved. Second, the person attempts to figure out the situation through reason. Third, the person takes into account environmental factors, such as the personal costs. Fourth, the person considers practical difficulties.

lescents were well aware that they were making a cost-benefit analysis, and they sometimes decided against doing something because it was too costly from a personal point of view. In a discussion with adolescents about the destructive effects of mass tourist skiing on the environment, one teen pointed out that he believed he would be willing to collect aluminum cans to help the environment, because it does not take much effort, but then he would not give up or curtail skiing, because he loved skiing and the personal cost was simply too great for him (Nevers, Gebhard, & Billmann-Mahecha, 1997). Some younger children admitted that they would not be willing to eat less meat to improve the conditions of farm animals, indicting that they had performed a cost-benefit analysis; however, they were not aware that they had done so.

In the fourth stage, the individual considers the practical difficulties in implementing the plan of action. A person may want to help her best friend, who has a problem in math class, but she may be unsure of the material herself. Adolescents have more experience than younger children and are generally more competent, and these characteristics may explain the greater instrumental (practical) help they provide (Bailey & Piercy, 1997).

By its very nature, then, moral behavior is complicated by the many factors that influence it. Cognitive advances, prior learning, and emotional factors combine to motivate or fail to motivate moral behaviors. *(For a review of this section, see At A Glance 11.1.)*

THE SPIRITUAL DIMENSION

Any discussion of values and moral behavior must take the adolescent's religious beliefs into account. Until recently, psychologists have been less than enthusiastic about researching this variable (Gorsuch, 1988), even though Erikson emphasized the importance of religion in the formation of a coherent identity (Erikson, 1963, 1968). Religious belief and practice are difficult to study. Religion contains a set of beliefs and involves some participation in observances, prayer, and ritual. It also has an emotional component. People who differ widely on these variables may still call themselves religious. Some people claim to be deeply spiritual even though they do not belong to a particular religious group and do not participate in the practices of an organized religion. Others may attend religious services and consider themselves religious but not really be influenced by their religion's moral teachings. Some people attend religious services more out of social obligation. Individuals may believe in some of the teachings of their religion and reject others, or even not be aware of how religious beliefs are affecting them. Measuring religiosity is difficult, and the measuring devices differ widely. Some studies measure religiosity in terms of religious beliefs; others, by religious feelings; and still others, by participation in religious practices.

Stages of Religious Development

James Fowler (1981, 1991, 1996) argues that the development of religious belief is closely related to the development of moral reasoning. His six stages of religious belief are based on the theories of Piaget, Kohlberg, and Erikson, as well as his own interviews with people ranging from preschoolers to the elderly. Fowler characterizes faith as the process underlying the formation of beliefs, values, and a view of the meaning underlying life, either within or outside an established religion. Following are his six stages of religious belief:

- *Stage 1: Intuitive-projective faith.* Preschoolers pick up bits and pieces from what they see and hear around them. They use their imaginations and try to understand good and evil. Their descriptions of God are very concrete; they often see God as big and with human features. When asked about God, one 4-year-old said that "he lives in the sky with Casper" (Kantrowitz, 1998).

- *Stage 2: Mythic-literal faith.* Later in childhood, as children enter Piaget's stage of concrete operations (see "Cognitive Development"), their ideas about God become more coherent but are still concrete. They take religious rules literally and see God as a parental figure, who at the same time rewards people for doing good and punishes them for doing bad things. Older children may see God as a powerful physical entity.

- *Stage 3: Synthetic-conventional faith.* As they enter Piaget's stage of formal operations, adolescents become capable of more abstract thought and no longer view God in concrete terms. Individuals' religious beliefs become part of their identity. Yet according to Fowler, adolescents basically conform to what they have been taught, and most have not looked into alternative beliefs. Most adolescents and adults do not develop past this stage.

- *Stage 4: Individuative-reflective faith.* In late adolescence and early adulthood, individuals begin to seriously question the nature of their religious beliefs and build a system of beliefs that is unique to them. They accept some traditional religious values and modify or reject other values. Not everyone proceeds to this stage. To do so, individuals need formal operational abilities, such as the ability to use abstractions, apply hypothetical-deductive logic, and be able to reflect on their own beliefs. Some event may force an evaluation of religious issues, such as attending college and being exposed to many different beliefs.

- *Stage 5: Conjunctive faith.* People in middle age develop a belief system that allows them to make sense of inconsistencies in the world, such as why some good people must suffer. Their world-view becomes more complex. Not many people go on to this stage.

- *Stage 6: Universalizing faith.* In the final stage, which very few people reach, individuals transcend specific dogma, achieve a sense of unity with all other human beings, and seek to help unite people. This is an ideal stage that in some ways is similar to Kohlberg's final stage, universal ethical principle orientation.

Because of their improving cognitive abilities, adolescents are more likely to perceive God in a more abstract manner. Adolescents are also more likely to question various aspects of their religion and reject or modify these beliefs. Adolescence is a time of developing one's identity and part of that identity is religious.

Adolescents and Religion

Religious beliefs are important to many adolescents. Most adolescents believe in the existence of God. In one poll, 95 percent said they believed in God, and 74 percent said they pray at least occasionally (Donahue & Benson, 1995a). In another poll, 76 percent of the adolescents, aged 13 to 17, said they believe in a personal God, and 48 percent had attended church in the previous week (Gallup & Bezilla, 1992). Still another study found that less than a third of all adolescents attended organized religious services at least once a week (Johnston, Bachman, & O'Malley, 1995). A little more than half of all adolescents claim that their religion or faith is very important to them (Bachman et al., 1993; Benson, 1993; Brightman, 1994).

Generally, females are more religious than males—a finding that holds for children, adolescents, young adults, and older adults (Donelson, 1999)—although the differences reported are sometimes small. African Americans are more religious than white Americans (Donahue & Benson, 1995a, 1995b; USD-HHS, 1996).

Religious values and practices are important for many adolescents, but certainly not all. Furthermore, evidence clearly indicates a decline in religious convictions, and cross-sectional studies comparing people of different ages show a significant decline in religious observance throughout adolescence. In an extensive study of mostly Christian adolescents in midwestern U.S. communities, 54 percent of the sixth-grade students, but only 46 percent of the twelfth graders, claimed that their religion was "important" or "very important" to them (Donahue & Benson, 1995b). In this study, 51 percent of the sixth graders, but only 34 percent of the twelfth graders, said they attended church once or more per week. By the end of adolescence, teenagers are less involved in religious activities than they were as younger teens (Benson, Donahue, & Erickson, 1989).

Adolescents become less reliant on rituals or visible observations of religious activity and more concerned with their own internal beliefs and principles (Wurthnow & Gluck, 1973). Some researchers claim that when religious beliefs are measured, especially in a longitudinal format, there is some decline in middle adolescence and frequently some increase in late adolescence (Francis & Pearson, 1987; Kotesky, Walker, & Johnson, 1990). However, the late adolescent's religious commitment is somewhat different from the commitment found among children and younger adolescents, as it is based on a more personalized commitment.

This decline in religious identification should come as no surprise. If adolescence is a time of questioning, then questioning and some rejection of religious beliefs should be expected. Also, organized religion may represent a type of authority, and some questioning of, or even rebellion against, authority occurs during adolescence. Many adolescents are bothered by the religious "hypocrisy" they see around them; they notice that some religious people say the right things but do not act according to those principles. Others believe that people would be better off and more tolerant if they weren't divided into groups. In addition, their religious experience may not match what they desired or expected.

Some researchers see the period of doubting that occurs in adolescence as necessary for a person' attainment of religious potential (Donohue & Benson, 1995a, 1995b). Younger children often hold religious beliefs based on conventional or authoritarian ideals and think in terms of "This is right, and that is wrong." The late adolescent's religious beliefs, in contrast, may be internalized from his or her own chosen beliefs. Their values are more intrinsic to them, and they are more committed to the beliefs, because they have doubted, experienced, and matured. They do not view questioning of religion beliefs as rebellion against all religion, and perhaps some disillusionment is part of the developmental process by which one gains a mature sense of spirituality (Hill, 1986). The search for values and beliefs can be seen in terms of the general search for a personal identity (see "Self-Concept and Identity Formation"). In this view, conformity to the religious beliefs that were taught in childhood gives way to questioning that may result in an internalized religious ideology (Fowler, 1976, 1981). It is often thought that highly religious individuals merely conform to parental or societal views, but often high religiosity is found in people who have experienced a period of doubt and exploration (De Haan & Schulenberg, 1997).

P E R S P E C T I V E   1

MY BELIEFS HAVE CHANGED

SETTING THE SCENE: Eli is a sophomore in high school. Although he is doing fairly well in school, most of his friends are not especially motivated. Eli's parents do not like his friends, who seem rough and aggressive, although none has been in serious trouble.

ELI: *My parents demand that I go to church every Sunday. I did it when I was young, but I do not want to do it now that I'm 15. I don't want to join any of their youth activities, either. I respect my parents' beliefs, but they don't respect the fact that I just don't believe the way they do. I don't think I should be forced to go to church if I don't want to. My friends don't have to go.*

ELI'S MOTHER: *I know that Eli's friends don't seem to go to either church or youth group, but I would like him to try attending some church activities. If he would go, he would meet new people and perhaps realize how beautiful his religious heritage is. I don't expect him to go every week, but I think it's important for him to have some religious identity.*

ELI'S FATHER: *I don't feel as strongly as my wife does about it, but I think it is one of those things that we can do as a family together. We have three younger children. Eli's our eldest, and I don't think he's setting a good example. When he asks us to do things, we try to accommodate him. Why is this so different? It won't hurt him to go.*

QUESTION: Should Eli's parents "force" him or encourage him to attend church? Why or why not?

Although a decline in religiosity is the most frequently found pattern in adolescence, a minority of adolescents find that their religious experiences and beliefs intensify and deepen. Many adolescents are searching for a spiritual/religious experience, and teenagers may even become caught up in cults (see "Focus: Cults"). Others may flirt with complete nonbelief. Most, though, experience a decline, but not a complete loss, of religious experience and belief (Wulff, 1997).

Religious Values and Behavior

Religious values can influence behavior and attitudes. People who are religious are less likely to engage in premarital sex, use drugs, or become involved in delinquent behavior (Donahue & Benson, 1995a, 1995b). One major study found 50 percent lower rates of substance abuse and violence among religiously involved teenagers than among noninvolved teens (Eklin & Roehlkepartain, 1992). In a random sample of more than ten thousand adolescents, family religiosity was found to be correlated with significantly less illicit drug use (Bahr et al., 1998). In addition, religiosity is linked to less sexual risk taking behavior (Brewster et al., 1998).

There is also a modest correlation between measures of caring (such as concern for the poor), helping behavior, and religiosity (Benson, Williams, & Johnson, 1987). Religious youths are more likely to be involved in service projects, perhaps because many religious education programs emphasize service (Dean & Yost, 1991). Adolescents who view religion as a meaningful part of their lives are also less likely to be depressed (Neeleman et al., 1998; Wright, Frost, & Wisecarver, 1997).

Religious beliefs and practices, then, do influence behavior, but they are one influence among many. The influence of religion is more salient for some people than others, but it would be a mistake to ignore religion as an important part of the moral perspective of many teens. *(For a review of this section, see At A Glance 11.2.)*

Most adolescents believe in God and a little more than half claim that their religion is very important to them. Still, adolescence is a time of questioning, and religious beliefs are often questioned.

AT A GLANCE 11.2 THE SPIRITUAL DIMENSION

KEY POINT: Religion and spirituality are factors that may influence adolescent behavior.

SUPPORTING POINTS	EXPLANATION
James Fowler describes the development of religious belief.	Adolescents begin to perceive God in a more abstract manner and late in adolescence may question religion, accepting some aspects of their religion and rejecting others. In later adolescence and early adulthood, people may create a unique system of beliefs.
Religious beliefs are important to some adolescents.	Most adolescents say they believe in God, and about half say their religion is important to them.
Many adolescents experience a decline in religious conviction and belief.	Adolescence is a time of questioning, and these questions often focus on religious convictions. This questioning may be seen as part of the identity formation process.
Religious values can influence behavior.	People who subscribe to religious values are more likely to be involved in community service, less likely to be depressed, and less likely to use drugs.

When you hear the word *cult,* what goes through your mind? Many people think of a group of mindless automatons listening to a leader and saying or doing everything the leader suggests. Others think of shocking mass suicides. Indeed, the mass suicide of the followers of Jim Jones in Guyana in 1978 and the suicide of the Heaven's Gate believers in San Diego in 1997 cannot but make one think that cults are dangerous. Satanic cults often involve violence and the desecration of cemeteries. Other cults do not engage in such behaviors, but many psychologists are concerned about the psychological consequences of cult membership on adolescents.

Sometimes people apply the term *cult* to any religious group they dislike. This is an unfortunate use of a useful term. However, differentiating a cult from a sect sometimes is not easy. A sect is an offshoot of a church that shares mainstream values, but in a more idealistic sense that sets the offshoot against the more powerful church. A cult, in contrast, lies outside the prevailing religious-cultural tradition. It represents dissent but is more deviant in its beliefs (Spilka, 1991a). Cults also may be defined in terms of their communal atmosphere and rejection of dominant societal values. They often reject questioning, requiring unbridled acceptance of their doctrine as explained and expounded upon by a strong leader. The cult calls for a totally new and unique lifestyle under the direction of a charismatic leader (Eshleman & Cashion, 1983). Cult members consider this leader a special being—a kind of prophet or interpreter with unusual powers or insight—and the leader rules with an iron hand. Doubters are often considered misguided, and they are either disciplined or expelled. Religious cults often separate the individual from the family and, sometimes, from all but the most regimented contact with the outside world. A cult offers a total belief system with no grounds for interpretation or disputation. It condemns any sense of individuality, and a pattern of insulation, isolation, and sometimes paranoia and contempt for the outside world prevails (Elshtain, 1997). Another pervasive characteristic of cults is

their demand that members contribute money or raise money for the cause (Lingeman & Sorel, 1997). Members often see the cult as a new family, and emotional support is forthcoming as the individual surrenders everything to the will of the cult (Sellers, 1998).

Cults use various methods to recruit and keep their members. Cults are very proficient at finding potential converts by identifying individuals who are adrift or isolated. The conversion procedure differs among groups, but frequently the first step is giving affection and understanding. Then the cult isolates the neophyte from nonmembers and introduces all sorts of rituals and disciplines, many of which reduce the individual's physical and emotional resistance and increase commitment. The cults asks first for small commitments ("Stay one more hour") and then for larger and larger commitments until the completion of the final conversion. Cult members carry out all these conversion activities under the watchful eye of a leader or surrogate with the support of the group. Finally, when individuals move into the cult home, they are increasingly isolated, both physically and psychologically, from family and older values, and the cult controls the flow of information.

A distinguishing characteristic of cults is their tendency to cut members off from family in order to establish new values and standards requiring total dependence on the cult itself (Hunter, 1998). Sometimes cults maintain discipline through fear or abusive treatment (isolation or badgering) and at other times through the threat of expulsion from the community, upon which the member has grown totally dependent. Few cult members have been forced to stay through the use of physical force. It is usually not needed. The cult member becomes dependent on the cult for both physical and psychological support, and group pressure can be a powerful force encouraging the convert to stay. Guilt and fear are the primary reasons people remain in cults even after they show a desire to leave them.

Cults are most successful in recruiting older adolescents (19 to 23 years of age) who may be unable to make long-

PROSOCIAL AND ALTRUISTIC BEHAVIOR

The media tend to cover teenage violence, cheating, and crime but rarely discuss adolescents who help others (Chou, 1998). Literally hundreds, if not thousands, of studies have been conducted on adolescent violence, crime, and unsavory conduct, but research on adolescent helping behaviors is scarce (Eisenberg et al., 1995; Hart & Fegley, 1995). **Prosocial behavior** is defined as any behavior that helps another individual. **Altruistic behavior** is a special form of prosocial behavior that involves helping others with no anticipation of a reward. A person returning someone's lost wallet in hopes of earning a reward is show-

prosocial behavior   Any behavior that helps another individual.

altruistic behavior   Voluntary, intentional behavior that benefits another individual and is not motivated by the expectation of external rewards or the avoidance of external punishments.

term commitments and may feel adrift in a complex world (Wright & Piper, 1986). In fact, cults seem to have a special fascination for adolescents. The vulnerability of adolescents to cults may be due to the in-between nature of the stage (Doress & Porter, 1978). Adolescence is a transitional period between absolute acceptance of parental values learned in childhood and emergence of individual values. Religious cults try to fill the gap or void between the two periods of life. Adolescents may join cults to achieve an instant family, spiritual rebirth, security, adventure, structure, or escape from their problems. Cult adherents value spiritual experience, particularly unconventional experience (Spilka, 1991a). They reject the success- and achievement-oriented values of society, seeking spiritual alternatives, communal life, and love.

Adolescents may be searching for meaning and purpose in life and for an identity of their own, and cults try provide them (Albrecht, Thomas, & Chadwick, 1980). The cult gives each individual an identity; no more thinking or searching is required. Cults supply easy answers to most of the questions of late adolescents, who can then end their search. Cult members are often taught to repeat answers over and over until they become a way of thinking, blocking out contrary thoughts (Conway & Siegelman, 1978).

The personality profile of an adolescent susceptible to cult overtures includes confusion; alienation from family; weak cultural, religious, and community ties; and feelings of powerlessness in an out-of-control world (Hunter, 1998). Although some adolescents who join cults have severe psychological problems at the time of their initiation, most are simply a bit depressed, alienated, and isolated from their families. Most converts are relatively normal and sometimes are engaging in a type of experimentation (Kilbourne & Richardson, 1985).

Cults have strict, well-defined rules—often better defined than the members' family rules. They also require radical behavior changes, sometimes including loss of identity, creation of a new identity, and further estrangement from the family. The cult is almost always stricter than the environment in which the individual was raised. Cult members often come from families who are not religious and may be searching to satisfy spiritual needs, feeling adrift without any beliefs. Cults provide a highly structured sense of belonging and an escape from the doubts of everyday life (Rudin, 1990). Sometimes they take adolescents who have been involved in drugs and crime and counter such behavior with a particular style of living (Spilka, 1991a). These cult members have already rejected society's dominant values and do so again in the cult, but often at the other extreme. Some cults offer members a new personality, a new name, and the promise of beginning again. Other cult members, especially males, may come from abusive families, and the cult gives them a sense of power (Belitz & Schacht, 1992).

People who drop out of cults often need help readjusting to the world. Adolescents still face the problems they had before entering cult life. They also have become used to regimentation and extreme support, and leaving the controlled environment may lead to aimlessness and loneliness. Many former cult members require extra emotional support (Walsh & Bor, 1996). In addition, some former cult members must learn how to think for themselves, a skill they did not develop or use extensively in cult life.

There is no doubt that cult members pay a price for giving up their individuality. As Walsh and Bor state in their study of cult life, the cult "provides solutions to a broad section of life's dilemmas and emotional problems, it offers a well focused social identity and unites people around shared understandings. However, it does seem to do this at a cost to the individual, appearing to encourage over reliance, conformity and suggestibility, resulting in dependency and harmful levels of guilt with an accompanying destructive repression of anger" (1996, p. 57). Personal growth and development require continuous questioning, meeting new challenges, sometimes failing and sometimes succeeding, and learning from these experiences. Unfortunately, many cult members stop questioning, have regimented lives in which they rarely encounter new experiences, and find their personal and emotional growth stunted as they suspend their critical faculties and completely submit to the will of the group.

ing prosocial behavior; a person who returns someone's lost wallet with no hope of a reward, perhaps anonymously, is showing altruistic behavior.

Most of the available research on helping behavior deals with younger children. There is a rapid increase in prosocial and altruistic behaviors in middle childhood, probably because of the increase in the ability to take someone else's viewpoint and the reduction in egocentrism. Age is certainly related to altruistic behavior (Chou, 1998).

The research on moral reasoning, empathy, and cognitive development discussed in this chapter and in "Cognitive Development" leads us to expect differences between younger children and adolescents in helping, comforting, and sharing. As children mature, they become more aware of the emotional states of others and can empathize more with them. Moral reasoning becomes more sophisticated during adolescence as well. These advancements in moral reasoning and empathy may lead to more prosocial behavior, and a relationship does exist between scores of tests on empathy and sympathy on the one hand and prosocial behavior on the other (Estrada, 1987, as cited in Eisenberg, 1990). More advanced moral reasoning is modestly related to moral action, including honesty, altruistic behavior, resistance to temptation, and nondelinquency (Perry & McIntire, 1995; Snary, 1985). In other words, cognitive advancements that may lead to better moral reasoning and increased empathy should also lead to more prosocial and altruistic behavior (Bar-Tal, Korenfeld, & Raviv, 1985; Eisenberg, 1991).

Indeed, older children and adolescents show more prosocial behavior compared with preschoolers and children in the early years of middle childhood (Eisenberg, 1991). However, only some studies show an increase in prosocial behavior, such as helping others, from middle childhood through adolescence (Berndt, 1985; Chou, 1998). This finding is surprising. Why wouldn't strong increases be found in prosocial behavior between late middle childhood and adolescence?

The answer may be found partly in the conditions or situations under which the adolescents and preteens are being tested. If higher levels of role-taking skills or age-related knowledge or skills are involved, adolescents are more likely than preteens to show prosocial behavior (Eisenberg, 1991). For example, when someone is bleeding, adolescents are more likely to understand the situation and use their knowledge to help the person. If helping behaviors involve simply complying with a request—for example, a request from a friend to pick up papers that have dropped from a notebook—there is little reason to expect differences between adolescents and preteens. In other words, a higher quality and a greater quantity of prosocial and altruistic behaviors are found in adolescents compared with preteens only when those behaviors require the advanced cognitive skills that adolescents acquire. When these skills are not required, few differences in prosocial behavior are found between adolescents and younger children.

Adolescents and younger children, though, differ in their motivation to help. Adolescents are more likely to cite personal values than are younger children. As adolescents continue to develop, the differences in motivation for prosocial and altruistic acts become even more pronounced. Between early and very late adolescence, individuals increasingly devalue prosocial behaviors that are performed for a reward, for praise, or to avoid criticism or punishment (Peterson & Gelfand, 1984). Late adolescents show a much greater appreciation for, and more highly value, prosocial or altruistic acts based on personal values or empathy. When early and late adolescents are asked for their reasons to assist others, older adolescents are more likely to cite altruistic reasons and reasons related to personal beliefs than are younger adolescents (Bar-Tal & Nissim, 1984).

Children and adolescents also choose not to help for different reasons. Younger children often base their lack of helpfulness on their lack of competence ("I don't know what to do"), whereas adolescents who decide not to help are more likely to do so because they anticipate disapproval from the recipient or the possibility of embarrassing the other person (Midlarsky, Hannah, & Corley, 1995). Adolescents are much more aware of the internal states, privacy needs, and rights of the other individual, and they sometimes are reluctant to interfere if their help may not be wanted or would be intrusive. Even studies that do not find that the quantity of helpfulness increases during adolescence do find that when adolescents help, their motives differ from those of younger children, and they are more proficient and effective.

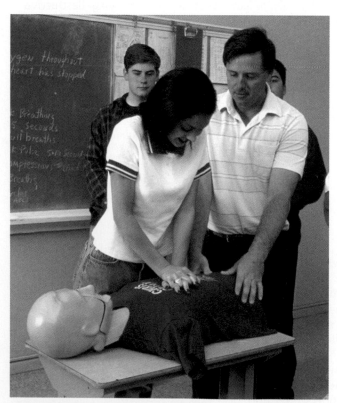

If a situation occurs in which age-related knowledge or skills are required, adolescents are more helpful than younger children.

Summarizing the research on developmental trends in prosocial behavior is difficult because of the scarcity of research and the fact that adolescents are more sensitive to the context of a situation. Improvements in perspective taking, moral reasoning, cognitive abilities, and helping skills give adolescents a greater ability to help. If the helping situation requires these advanced skills, adolescents are more likely to help than younger children. If the situation is very simple, there is little reason to expect more helping behavior. Adolescents, though, are more likely to base their helping on altruistic values. Adolescents who reason at higher levels are more empathic, have better perspective-taking skills, and are more likely to show prosocial behaviors when these skills are needed. At the same time, adolescents are more sensitive to the context and personal cost of helping, which limits when they will help others.

Activism and Volunteering

Many say that today's generation of youth is less idealistic and more apathetic than previous generations. The legendary political activism of the youth of the 1960s is sometimes used as a benchmark. That generation was unusually politically active, and it is difficult to make a case that youth today are as interested in politics and world issues as the youth of that generation. However, when today's youth are compared with youth of 1980s on political activism, the differences are not as startling.

Political activism is not the only way of showing idealism, of course, and today's youth need not apologize to anyone on that score. Today's youth volunteer at very high rates, but these volunteers rarely receive press coverage. The noisy demonstrations of the 1960s concerning national issues such as civil rights were newsworthy; in contrast, the volunteers of the early 2000s who are helping to better their communities are rarely shown on the 6 o'clock news.

Neighborhood activism has replaced political activism for many youth. Over half of all people between the ages of 18 and 24 volunteer for service in their communities and neighborhoods (Moseley, 1999). Many teens feel they can make a greater difference acting closer to home, building housing for poor people, working in a shelter for homeless people, helping the elderly, and tutoring younger children in their own communities (Moseley, 1995). Some high schools introduce adolescents to community needs by requiring some community service as a prerequisite for graduation.

Prosocial Behavior and Gender

Imagine that you are a researcher who has chosen a large, representative group of male and female adolescents. Would you predict any gender differences in cheating, empathy, or helping others? Gilligan argued that females are socialized into a pattern of care and concern for others and that they are encouraged to be more emotionally sensitive to others. Men are raised to be more individualistic and less communicative, at least emotionally. Based on differences in socialization, gender differences in moral behavior might be expected. Yet the evidence for these gender differences is hardly clear.

How much would you be able to predict about a student's prosocial behavior or resisting the temptation to indulge in behavior that society frowns upon based on the student's gender alone? Probably very little. Research demonstrates that gender differences in moral behavior exist, although typically they are relatively small. A review of the literature on cheating found that males have a more positive attitude toward cheating and report having cheated to a slightly greater degree than women (Baldwin et al., 1996). Differences in cheating are smaller in traditionally male dominated courses, such as economics (McCabe & Trevino, 1997). Perhaps women taking these courses adopt the male role norm of competitiveness. Indeed, a correlation between pressure for success, competition, and cheating exists (Whitley, 1998).

Studies show that cheating has increased in the past decade. Do males or females cheat more? It depends on the situation and the type of cheating being studied.

Some students cheat by copying examination answers; others, by copying homework; and still others, by plagiarizing term papers. Students do not see these activities as equally unethical. They perceive copying on exams as much worse than copying homework and plagiarizing (Newstead et al., 1996). It is interesting to note that whereas males generally cheat more than females when all cheating is lumped together, this is not the case when different types of cheating are separated. A survey of university students found that plagiarizing was the only area in which males cheated more than females; it found no differences on copying answers during exams (Thorpe, Pittenger, & Reed, 1999). In addition, most of the gender differences in cheating are found in self-report studies rather than through direct observation. Women report experiencing more shame and guilt over cheating than men, so females may be more motivated not to admit their cheating.

Do men or women show more prosocial behavior motivated by empathy? Again, clear-cut differences are simply not found (Karniol et al., 1998). Despite socialization differences in males versus females, most studies do not show clear differences in empathic behavior (Lennon & Eisenberg, 1987). Both males and females who are emotionally expressive and sensitive to the plight of others show increased empathy, which often leads to helping others. The results of studies of gender differences in altruism are mixed. Some studies show girls as more altruistic (Ma, 1989), whereas others find either no differences or even differences favoring males (Chou, 1998).

Factors other than gender are more important in prosocial development. Males and females who are more sensitive to the needs and feelings of others will help more. In addition, people's personal experiences influence their moral reasoning and moral behavior. Situational factors, such as the personal cost of the moral behavior, also enter the picture, as do cultural factors. Finally, stable individual differences are found in prosocial behavior (Eisenberg et al., 2002). Early adult self-reports of helping behavior are related to mothers' reports of their children's helping behavior in adolescence and friends' reports of empathy at 10 and 12 years. Some evidence for a relationship between prosocial behavior in the preschool period and prosocial dispositions in early adulthood exists as well. Individual differences in prosocial behavior seem to arise in childhood and continue into adulthood. The important point is that knowing someone's gender does not tell you much about his or her moral reasoning or behavior.

The Emergence of the Moral Adolescent

Some children and adolescents clearly show more helpful behavior than others. Some can delay gratification and are more successful at resisting temptation than others. Are such qualities as honesty and helpfulness characteristics of an individual, or are they completely situational? These questions were the subject of some of the earliest research in the field of moral development. Hartshorne and May (1928) tested thousands of children on a number of tasks. They concluded that children's behavior varied with the situation. A child could be honest in one situation and not in another. One who cheated on an athletics test might or might not cheat on an arithmetic test (Cairns, 1979). This situational view prevailed for decades, but later research using statistical tests not available to Hartshorne and May found a carryover of honesty from one situation to another, although it is not very strong (Burton, 1963). Some people, then, are more honest than others, but few people are honest in every situation. Research shows that stable individual differences in level of prosocial responding exist, despite some situational differences (Eisenberg, 1991). Helping seems to be a general predisposition, and helping within the family is related to helping outside the family (Midlarsky et al., 1995). To explain individual differences in prosocial behavior and moral development generally, we must look at the many influences on children and adolescents (see Figure 11.1).

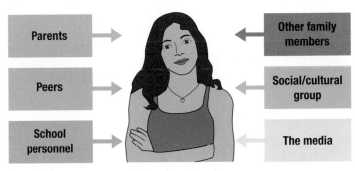

Figure 11.1
Influences That Promote Prosocial Behavior in Adolescents
Many individuals and groups influence adolescents' prosocial and moral development.

The first place to look for the explanation is the home. Parents want to transmit their value system to their children. For this transmission to occur, children and adolescents must accurately perceive the beliefs and then, often in adolescence, decide to adopt them as their own (Grusec & Goodnow, 1994). An adolescent's perception of parental beliefs is more important than a parent's actual beliefs (Okagaki & Bevis, 1999). The clearer the message sent in an age-appropriate manner by parents to their children, the greater the chance that the children and adolescents will share these values. In addition, when parental behavior and verbal statements match, children are more likely to clearly understand parental values. When a parent says, "Don't drink," but comes home drunk frequently, children receive a mixed message. Mothers and fathers who differ significantly on values often send mixed messages. Clearly verbalizing and acting on values, though, is not sufficient. Adolescents are more likely to adopt parental values under certain situations. For example, when parents have a warm relationship with their children, the children are more likely to internalize parental values.

Parents can encourage their children to act more ethically. They influence their adolescent children through the type of home they create and the type of discipline they use (Boyes & Allen, 1993). Each family has its own moral climate—that is, the atmosphere in which children and adolescents gain their experience. Adolescents are more likely to show empathy if their parents show nurturance, are responsive, and accept their children's feelings, as well as if fathers are more positively involved in the child rearing (Koestner, Franz, & Weinberger, 1990). Perhaps an involved father is a greater role model or creates a greater feeling of cohesion in the family.

Family cohesion (perceptions of the closeness and concern family members have for one another) is related to adolescents' empathic concern for others (Eisenberg et al., 1991). Family cohesion provides a sense of stability and connectedness from which adolescents can safely explore their world and expand their horizons. Cohesive families offer an emotionally solid foundation from which adolescents can be concerned about not only themselves but also others. Youths who have had a family experience of concern, encouragement, and praise show more concern for others (Eisenberg, 1992; Henry, Sager, & Plunkett, 1996). When parents elicit their teens' opinions, ask clarifying questions, and paraphrase and check their understanding of how their teenage children feel about issues, the adolescents are more likely to show a higher level of moral reasoning and awareness of their behavior.

Particular child-rearing styles that remain consistent throughout adolescence influence prosocial behavior (Boyes & Allen, 1993). Authoritative parents, who are both responsive and demanding, grant their children and adolescents an appropriate amount of autonomy and thus create an atmosphere that supports the growth of prosocial moral reasoning and behavior. Authoritative parents are more likely to raise children whose values are somewhat similar to their own, whereas parents who are permissive or authoritarian tend to have children whose values differ more substantially from their own.

Parents who use supportive parenting, reason with their adolescent children, and aren't overly punitive encourage prosocial behavior in their children (Eisenberg et al., 1991). Parents who also focus their children's attention on others rather than on themselves and who provide positive models have children who are more giving and altruistic. However, just because parents donate a great deal of time to community affairs does not always mean that their children will follow their example. The adolescent's perception is crucial. If adolescents resent the fact that their mother and father are always out in the community and seem to have no time for them, we would not expect imitation to take place. In contrast, if the relationship between parents and their children is good, adolescents may demonstrate similar behaviors.

Peers, who share similar everyday experiences, also influence the emergence of mature moral behavior. Both Piaget (1932/1977) and Kohlberg (1969) specifically argued that peers have a great impact on moral development. In fact, they argued that peers have a greater impact than parents. As peers discuss issues, one individual may show a slightly higher level of moral reasoning and cause

AT A GLANCE 11.3 PROSOCIAL AND ALTRUISTIC BEHAVIOR

KEY POINT: Development during adolescence allows for increases in prosocial and altruistic behavior, but other factors determine whether an individual acts on that potential.

SUPPORTING POINTS	EXPLANATION
Developmental advances during adolescence increase the potential for prosocial and altruistic behavior.	Expanded role-taking skills and improved cognitive abilities allow adolescents to show more altruism.
Some, but not all, studies show an increase in prosocial and altruistic behavior between preteens and adolescents.	When prosocial and altruistic behavior requires advanced role-taking skills or more knowledge, differences between preteens and adolescents are found.
Gender differences in moral behavior sometimes are found, but these differences are often inconsistent and slight.	Males admit to cheating more, but direct observations do not document this trend. Evidence does not show consistent gender differences in empathic behavior. Studies of gender differences in altruistic behavior are mixed.
Some people are more likely to help than others.	Parental factors that lead to parent-adolescent agreement on values and greater prosocial behavior include a match between verbally stated parental values and parents' actions, actively listening to adolescents, the presence of a cohesive family structure, and an authoritative parenting style. Friends who are more prosocial may have an impact on others. Some cultures emphasize helping others more than other cultures.

the other to reconsider his or her reasoning. When a sample of girls discussed dilemmas with either a peer or her mother, those in peer discussions showed evidence of higher moral reasoning than girls in the mother-child dyads (Kruger, 1992; Kruger & Tomasello, 1986). However, research generally finds that both peer and parent contexts are important contributors to moral development (Walker, Hennig, & Krettenauer, 2000).

Culture is another factor determining prosocial behavior. Cultures in which children live in extended families or have more responsibilities, as well as those that have simpler social structures, are more likely to show greater amounts of prosocial behavior (Eisenberg & Mussen, 1989). Cultures that emphasize obligation to the community, trust, and cooperation rather than individualism and self-reliance are more likely to produce people who are prosocial, but also more conforming (Stevenson, 1991). *(For a review of this section, see At A Glance 11.3.)*

MORAL EDUCATION

Interest in moral education is surging (Damon & Gregory, 1997). A surprising 71 percent of all Americans believe it is more important to teach values than academic subjects in school, and respect for others tops the list of values (Wagner, 1996).

Values Clarification

Years ago, schools offered values clarification courses, which encouraged children and adolescents to develop and define their own values without adult interference. It was thought inappropriate to try to foist values on teenagers. Instead, these programs challenge students to discover their own values (Raths, Harmin, & Simon, 1966). Teachers offer a number of anecdotes, situations, and other activities aimed at getting students to freely adopt and clarify their own values, but the teachers do not force their own values onto students.

Values clarification courses use many techniques. For example, teachers may ask students to make choices and identify their priorities or preferences in an exercise called *rank ordering*. In *values voting*, the teacher offers the students a series of questions by asking, "How many of you. . . . ?" Students respond with hand signals showing whether they are in favor of or against the idea in the question, and to what extent. In the *spread-of-opinion activity*, the teacher draws a line on the blackboard and identifies an issue, labeling each extreme position and asking students to place their initials on the line to indicate where they stand on the issue. In a *values inventory*, students take stock of their beliefs and become aware of their preferences in activities. The students view a list of items on a particular topic—perhaps what they might like to do in life or which people are important to them—and analyze their responses, finally drawing conclusions from the inventories (Read, Simon, & Goodman, 1977).

The values clarification approach did not work as well as hoped, and it has fallen from favor. It placed too much emphasis on process and focused too little attention on the end product (Ryan, 1981). There was no right or wrong (Bauer, 1987). What if a student comes to the conclusion that racism or sexism is an appropriate value? The neutrality required by teachers is troublesome. Teachers give students no information relating to what our culture has discovered about moral and ethical questions (Ryan, 1986); the values clarification approach assumes that all values are equally false, equally true, and equally useful. Most authorities claim that simply fostering values through self-discovery is inappropriate and that students cannot be allowed to simply find their own values without input from adults. Such a hands-off approach runs the risk of children's developing antisocial or prejudiced values without correction by adults. Thus, such an open-ended format is rarely practiced today (Herbert, 1996).

Kohlberg's Approach to Moral Education

Another approach to moral education uses Kohlberg's dilemmas in an attempt to improve moral reasoning. Students play the roles of different characters within the dilemmas. Teachers offer a dilemma to the class in the form of a story. The students then determine how the situation should be resolved, giving reasons for their solutions, which they share in group discussion. A great many age-appropriate dilemmas are available (see Table 11.3).

Remember that Kohlberg is interested in improving moral reasoning, not necessarily in teaching children and adolescents what is right or wrong. According to Kohlberg, students reasoning at lower stages will be influenced by the reasoning of students at higher stages, causing cognitive conflict that eventually leads to improvements in moral reasoning. The teacher probes, explains, and suggests. Although there is a preferred type of reasoning, there is not necessarily a preferred answer. Kohlberg was not morally neutral and argued that there are

Table 11.3

Moral Dilemmas That Can Be Presented to Students for Discussion

Situation	Moral Dilemma
You want to sell your old car. It has a transmission problem. A 19-year-old student loves the car and is ready to make an offer.	Do you inform the potential buyer of the transmission problem?
Your best friend has been going out with her boyfriend for quite some time. At a restaurant you see your friend's boyfriend with another girl, hugging her and acting as if they were a couple.	Do you tell your friend what you saw?
Your boss comes into work with a new dress that she thinks is wonderful. She asks you what you think. You think the dress is awful—so bad, in fact, that she could be laughed at by others.	Do you give your boss your honest opinion about the dress?
You are buying groceries at the local market. The cashier, who is very rushed, gives you a 10-dollar bill instead of a 1-dollar bill in your change.	Do you tell the cashier and give back the money?
Your younger brother, who is a little wild, was supposed to be in by 11:00. He tells your parents, who were visiting friends at the time, that he was in by 11:00. You saw him come home at 1:00. Your parents trust you and your brother.	Do you volunteer this information to your parents? If your parents ask you, do you tell them the truth?
Your friend is active in a worthy charity and asks you if you could spend a few hours helping him out. You really don't want to do it because you'd rather spend your Sunday out with your friends having fun.	Do you help your friend out? Do you tell him the truth? Do you lie, telling him that you will be visiting your grandmother?
The person you really would like to go out with is in your history class. The teacher announces that it is time for one of five surprise tests she will be giving during the semester. The person you like tells you that he or she didn't have time to read the material and asks you to leave your answers uncovered for the person to "check."	Do you allow the individual to cheat from your paper?
You witness a fight between your friend and another person you don't like very much. You know your friend will get into trouble for fighting. You were there and were the only witness. A teacher, who knows you were there, asks you if you saw your friend fighting.	Do you lie to the teacher?
As you open your car door in the grocery store parking lot, it hits the car beside you and causes a very noticeable dent. You also realize that the car belongs to your neighbor. You look around and realize that no one saw you do it	Do you tell your neighbor?
The person you have been going out with for a month gives you a very expensive birthday gift, which you know took quite a bit out of the individual's weekly paycheck. You do not feel very strongly toward this person; he or she is just someone you are going out with at the moment.	Do you accept the gift?

Moral education has become a popular topic today. How much responsibility does the school have in fostering moral values?

universal moral principles that ought to be held, including respect for the individual and tolerance. These principles arise not from lecture but through rational argument and thoughtful decisions about values that may be in conflict (Power & Kohlberg, 1987). Some evidence indicates that exposing young adolescents to higher-level reasoning about moral issues can lead to improved moral reasoning (Grier & Firestone, 1998).

Kohlberg also argued for transforming schools into *just communities,* which involves establishing democratic structures and student participation in making and enforcing rules and policies (Oser, 1996). These schools discuss and deal with realistic issues that arise, and student responsibility increases (Kohlberg, 1981). Kohlberg argued that schools should provide students with opportunities to examine many school values that are implied but rarely stated, such as competition and achievement at all costs, and to relate them to basic values of justice and caring. Some schools that have adopted participatory democratic practices give students a real voice and have decided to mandate restitution for victims of theft, to voluntarily switch classes to achieve greater racial integration, and to enforce no-cutting rules by accepting responsibility to help students get to class (Kohlberg & Lickona, 1987; Power & Kohlberg, 1987). These schools encourage teachers to be more democratic and explain the reasons behind rules. There are limits to student participation, of course, but students need to feel they have some power to submit grievances and get things done—a feeling few students have in today's schools.

Criticisms of Kohlberg's attempts at moral education through dilemmas center around the highly verbal nature of the approach. It does not seem to lead to action (Ryan, 1986). In addition, because the relationship between moral reasoning and moral behavior is positive but low, the use of dilemmas may not be especially effective in moral education. It is also not clear whether such programs lead to the values that Kohlberg himself valued so greatly, including social justice, tolerance, and integrity. Finally, although the just community is an interesting idea, whether schools can easily be transformed into more democratic institutions is questionable.

The Teaching Approach

A teaching-oriented approach to moral education has replaced the more open ended approaches (Bauer, 1987). This change may be a response to students who seem to be morally adrift, as well as an answer to arguments that schools have the responsibility to instill particular moral values in their students rather than permit them to figure out values on their own.

But whose values should be taught? On the surface, it would seem easy to agree on the type of values to be transmitted. Problems abound, however, especially in priorities (Wagner, 1996). Two sets of values, espoused by two different philosophical approaches, vie for public support. *Character education* emphasizes such values as self-discipline, patriotism, respect for authority, obedience, perseverance, and courage. These values are often perceived as conservative virtues and are sometimes religious (although they are not associated with any particular religion). On the other side are *citizenship values,* which include altruism, concern for democratic values, civility, tolerance, respect for the environment, compassion, and self-esteem. An argument today rages over which values adolescents should be taught. People who emphasize more traditional values

PERSPECTIVE 2

HOW DO WE DO IT?

SETTING THE SCENE: The principal of a high school has asked teachers and administrators to formulate a plan for moral education.

TEACHER 1: *We can't tell students what to believe or what values they should have. They must form their own values. They have to find themselves by being asked to consider the many issues that surround them. We also should be constructing a school environment in which the children experience democracy, sharing, and caring.*

TEACHER 2: *That's nonsense. We should be instilling these values in our students through a code of conduct that stresses individual responsibility, honor, and self-discipline. The students should be reading stories and novels about people who show these traits, and discussions in all classes should focus on these values.*

TEACHER 3: *I know this will not sound right, but I don't think the schools can do much to help instill values in students. That occurs in the home. No matter how you look at it, students are a product of their home and peer environment. The schools can teach reading, writing, arithmetic, and computer skills, but they can't do what parents have failed to do over the years. It's unrealistic to expect them to.*

QUESTION: If you were a teacher or an administrator involved in such deliberations, what would you say?

often claim the breakdown in society is due in some measure to the loss of these values, as well as to indulgent parenting, and they advocate a return to firmness, character training, and respect of, and deference to, authority. People who favor citizenship values point out that traditional values are often "preachy," and they consider them more divisive than citizenship values (Wagner, 1996).

Some authorities argue that instilling any set of values is an active endeavor. Moral education involves the five *E*s: example (the use of history and literature to teach values), explanation, exhortation (encouragement), environment (changing the environment to reflect these values), and experience (placing values into action) (Ryan, 1986). All programs must have an action component, and placing values into action is a key to moral education. This goal can be accomplished in many ways, including helping elderly people, collecting and distributing food at shelters, and providing special holiday gifts for homeless and needy children (Spaide, 1995). However, adolescents may verbalize values without really internalizing them unless teachers provide opportunities to put the values into practice. Some people maintain that the action component in moral education often is nothing more than a required set of behaviors to graduate, which students perform without any feeling or commitment. Even so, schools need activity-based programs to supplement programs aimed at attitude change to encourage students to live their ideals and practice what they preach.

The teaching approach has gained popularity, but important criticisms also have surfaced. Students see hypocrisy in teaching values that society may not actually practice. Adolescents may tell teachers what they want to hear but never think about their own values. Like approaches based on moral reasoning, the teaching approach may be criticized as being too verbal unless teachers make a concerted effort to include situations in which students can put their values into practice.

Home and Community Involvement

Today, people are turning to the schools to teach moral values, but some authorities argue that the schools cannot successfully fulfill this role (Zern, 1997). Students do not see the school as a very caring place (Bosworth, 1995), perhaps because of its emphasis on achievement, competitive activities, and teacher-centered rules. The teens' community must be involved in moral education.

AT A GLANCE 11.4 MORAL EDUCATION

KEY POINT: Although the home is the primary place for instilling values, most people believe the school has a part to play in the development of moral behavior.

SUPPORTING POINTS	EXPLANATION
Values clarification courses encourage adolescents to discover their own values.	Adults guide adolescents through exercises and questioning to consider their own values, but the adults do not actively try to instill their values in adolescents.
Lawrence Kohlberg's approach to moral education involved presenting moral dilemmas to students and allowing for discussion about them.	Kohlberg argued that students would develop higher-level reasoning about moral dilemmas if faced with reasoning that was at a level a little higher than the adolescent's original reasoning. Kohlberg also wanted to create just communities in schools, which would foster democratic values.
The teaching approach attempts to actively instill values in young people.	The teaching approach identifies values, discusses these values with young people, and includes an action component.
Home and community involvement are recognized as important, encouraging moral behavior.	Some community groups actively encourage safer driving, less drug taking, and developing a sense of community pride, all of which may lead to more moral behavior.

One method, the Youth Charter approach, requires responsible adults in the community to come together and clarify the community's expectations, standards, problems, and solutions. They then involve young people in discussions and implementation of a community action plan. A Youth Charter is a consensus of clear expectations that the important people in a young person's life share and communicate to the adolescent in many ways. Different communities may have different problems; for example, a rash of cheating incidents in one community led to discussions and an action plan. Successful Youth Charters have transformed the moral atmosphere of their communities. A 12-year study of American youth concluded that the best predictor of adolescent social conduct was the extent to which people and institutions in the adolescent's life shared and communicated a set of common standards for behavior (Ianni, 1989). When messages clash, confusion reigns. The Youth Charter movement hopes to clarify behavioral expectations for adolescents.

Problems with Moral Education

One problem with moral education programs is that very few controlled studies of their effectiveness exist (Emler, 1996). Some programs may influence some young people, but not others. In addition, there is a striking lack of coordination among programs. Sex education programs do one thing, drug education programs another, driver's education (safe driving) programs a third, and conflict resolution programs a fourth. These programs seem to lack a coherent moral approach that might help students develop values they could generalize from one situation to another, such as honesty, caring, fairness, and respect for themselves (Wynne & Ryan, 1992). Many programs are crisis oriented and focus almost exclusively on preventing antisocial or destructive behaviors (Oser, 1996). Perhaps it is time to turn our attention to encouraging prosocial behaviors as well (Nisan, 1996). In fact, positive behaviors can become an important part of an individual's identity and self-concept, whereas the avoidance of negative behaviors rarely is (Hart & Fegley, 1995). For example, helping children with disabilities in the community is more likely to be part of one's identity than the fact that one does not steal.

Almost everyone is in favor of moral education, and the public demands it. Yet effective programs must be multifaceted, allowing for questioning and rational discussion, along with encouragement of positive moral action. They must also present a clear message about what is expected from people in the community. At the same time, the effectiveness of such programs must be constantly evaluated and modifications made when needed.

Whether or not it is a major emphasis, the schools and community do communicate values, and these values sometimes conflict. For example, a society that operates according to the philosophy of "get whatever you can anyway you can" sends a strong signal to its youth. If teens are not held accountable for their behavior, they soon learn that there are no consequences. Moral education programs, then, must promote a well-defined group of values that everyone in the community can put into action so that adolescents receive the message that these values have a purpose and are an integral part of the fabric of both the school and the community. *(For a review of this section, see At A Glance 11.4.)*

PLACING MORAL DEVELOPMENT IN PERSPECTIVE

As a society, we focus more on moral development, reasoning, and behavior today than in the recent past. Perhaps this increasing interest stems from the high-profile cases of adolescents committing crimes or concerns about the stability of the family. Whatever the reason, the goal of promoting moral development is not only to help adolescents refrain from injurious or antisocial behav-

Please place the number best reflecting your opinion next to each of the following statements. Then compare your opinions now with those you held before reading the chapter.

1 — Strongly Agree
2 — Moderately Agree
3 — No Opinion
4 — Moderately Disagree
5 — Strongly Disagree

_____ 1. Today's adolescents are not as moral or ethical as adolescents were 50 years ago.

_____ 2. Adolescents found to have plagiarized from the Internet should receive a 0 for the paper or project.

_____ 3. When adolescents cheat, steal, or lie, it is mainly because they have not learned the proper values at home.

_____ 4. Men and women generally reason differently about moral issues.

_____ 5. People can learn to act more morally.

_____ 6. If people felt more empathy for others, they would act in a kinder and more considerate manner.

_____ 7. Teenagers who come to doubt the teachings of their own religion are basically going through a normal phase of questioning, and others should read nothing more serious into this rejection or criticism of their religious heritage.

_____ 8. Cults use brainwashing in their recruitment practices and pose a psychological danger to their members.

_____ 9. Schools have the responsibility to instill moral values in their students.

iors but also to actively encourage teenagers to develop positive values and engage in prosocial and altruistic behaviors. Perhaps we can begin by publicizing the good works performed by adolescents rather than solely focusing on aggressive and antisocial behaviors.

We cannot pretend that the schools alone can foster moral development. The home, which has the major responsibility in this area, as well as the community, must become involved. In the end, adolescents are enmeshed in many environments, and the morals and values they learn are partially products of these envi-

THEMES

THEME 1 Adolescence is a time of choices, "firsts," and transitions.	• Adolescents face many more moral choices. • Adolescents develop new cognitive abilities that allow them to reason about moral issues on a higher level. • Adolescents are capable of experiencing empathy, not only toward another individual but also for the general condition of a group. • Adolescence is a time of questioning religious beliefs and practices.
THEME 2 Adolescence is shaped by context.	• Adolescent moral codes are shaped by family influences, as well as by peer, neighborhood, and cultural considerations. • Adolescents are more likely to internalize parental values if parents create an atmosphere of acceptance, good communication, and warmth. • Religious experiences can influence adolescents' behavior.
THEME 3 Adolescence is influenced by group membership.	• Carol Gilligan argues that males approach moral reasoning from a point of view emphasizing justice and individual rights, whereas women approach moral dilemmas using a more interpersonally sensitive and caring perspective. • People in different cultures may perceive moral questions and their alternatives for moral action differently. • Women tend to be more religious than men. • African-Americans are more religious than white Americans. • Cohesive families in which parents use authoritative parenting are more likely to have teenage children who act morally.
THEME 4 The adolescent experience has changed over the past 50 years.	• Adolescents today face more temptations than did adolescents 50 years ago. • Adolescents are less likely to be politically active than they were in the past, but they are more likely to be active in their communities. • More adults today believe that the schools should actively promote morals and values than in the past.
THEME 5 Today's views of adolescence are becoming more balanced, with greater attention to its positive nature.	• Although psychologists focus their research in the areas of cheating, stealing, and lying, they are beginning to show a greater appreciation for the extensive amount of adolescent prosocial behavior. • Although today's generation is much less politically active than the generation of the 1960s, many psychologists now realize that political activism is not the only way to show community interest and that many adolescents do devote time to community needs.

ronments. As the psychologist Haim Ginott said, "Character traits cannot be taught directly; no one can teach loyalty by lectures, courage by correspondence, or manhood by mail. Character education requires presence that demonstrates and contact that communicates. A teenager learns what he lives and becomes what he experiences" (1969, p. 243). It will take a concerted effort on the part of everyone involved to change these experiences and help teenagers create and maintain a set of morals and values that will serve them not only during adolescence but into adulthood as well.

CHAPTER SUMMARY AT A GLANCE

KEY TOPICS	KEY POINTS	KEY TERMS
Approaches to Moral Development	Moral development can be investigated by researching moral reasoning or moral behavior itself, but the emotional component cannot be ignored. (*At A Glance 11.1, p. 397*)	*empathy (p. 386)* *moral realism (p. 387)* *moral relativism (p. 387)* *preconventional moral reasoning (p. 388)* *conventional moral reasoning (p. 388)* *postconventional moral reasoning (p. 388)* *behavioral perspective (p. 393)* *social learning theory (p. 393)* *superego (p. 394)* *ego ideal (p. 394)* *identification (p. 394)*
The Spiritual Dimension	Religion and spirituality are factors that may influence adolescent behavior. (*At A Glance 11.2, p. 401*)	
Prosocial and Altruistic Behavior	Development during adolescence allows for increases in prosocial and altruistic behavior, but other factors determine whether an individual acts on that potential. (*At A Glance 11.3, p. 408*)	*prosocial behavior (p. 402)* *altruistic behavior (p. 402)*
Moral Education	Although the home is the primary place for instilling values, most people believe the school has a part to play in the development of moral behavior. (*At A Glance 11.4, p. 412*)	

Review questions for this chapter appear in the appendix.

WORK AND CAREER DEVELOPMENT

WHAT IS YOUR OPINION?

WORKING ON THE CLOCK
- Adolescents Consider the World of Work
- The World of Work Today
- The Adolescent with a Job

VOCATIONAL CHOICE
- The Life-Span, Life-Space Approach to Careers
- Holland's Typology
- Career Choice
  Perspective 1: Hamlet on the Edge

GENDER AND CAREER CHOICE
- Women's Career Choices
- Men and Career Choice

MINORITY GROUP MEMBERSHIP AND CAREER CHOICE
- Explaining the Trends
- Career Choice Among African Americans and Latinos
- Career Choice Among Asian Americans
- Career Choice Among Native Americans
- A Plan of Action

THE FORGOTTEN 42 PERCENT
- The Transition Between School and Work
  Perspective 2: I Don't Know What to Do
- Employers and High School Graduates
  FOCUS: Career and Technical Education: Salvation or Trap?
- Apprenticeship
- Youth Unemployment

PLACING VOCATIONAL CHOICE IN PERSPECTIVE

HAS YOUR OPINION CHANGED?

THEMES

CHAPTER SUMMARY AT A GLANCE

Let's assume that a person begins full-time employment at age 22 and retires at age 65. Let's further grant that the individual works 40 hours per week for 48 weeks a year (allowing for holidays, vacation, and sick leave). This typical individual would spend an impressive total of 82,560 hours at work during adulthood. The average person who works full-time throughout adulthood spends more hours at work than engaged in any other activity except sleep!

Although children think about what they want to be as they grow up, it is in the later years of adolescence and the first years of early adulthood that they make meaningful decisions about vocational choice. Adolescents recognize the importance of vocational decisions, for their choice of career will greatly affect their lifestyle and satisfaction with life.

This chapter looks at vocational development and decision making in adolescence. It begins by investigating changes in the world of work and the nature of the adolescent's experience working in part-time jobs. It then outlines two major theoretical approaches to vocational choice and looks at the factors that influence adolescents to choose one career over another. It continues by discussing how gender and minority group membership influence vocational choice. So much is written about vocational choice among college students that it is easy to forget the 42 percent of all adolescents who do not go on to college, and the last section of the chapter is devoted to these often-forgotten adolescents.

WORKING ON THE CLOCK

It is difficult to overestimate the importance of work. Type of work determines an individual's financial status. A physician makes more money than a file clerk; an accountant, more than a bank teller. Financial resources influence where one lives, the types of vacations one can take, the types of entertainment one may enjoy, and the ability to provide for one's family in the future. People naturally associate employment with money, but there is much more to a job than the financial considerations (see Figure 12.1). A job can be a significant source of personal satisfaction and accomplishment. It may satisfy personal needs, such as the need to help others. It is also a focal point for social relationships, as people form friendships at work. Given that work is a significant part of an adult's life, it is not surprising that satisfaction with one's job is related to general happiness, and that vocational success is related to self-esteem (Marshall, 1983).

Adolescents Consider the World of Work

Erik Erikson (1963, 1968) argued that the psychosocial crisis of adolescence could be understood in terms of *identity versus role confusion* (see "Self-Concept and Identity Formation"). Vocational identity is a part of overall identity. College students who choose occupations that reflect their measured abilities and interests show more successful resolution of Erikson's first six stages, including identity formation in adolescence (Munley, 1977). Psychologists readily acknowledge that career exploration and decision making are basic developmental tasks central to adolescence (Wallace-Broscious, Serafica, & Osipow, 1994). The importance of vocational choice increases with age, so it is not surprising that older adolescents are more concerned about their vocational future than are younger adolescents (Farmer et al., 1995).

People earn their living through their work, but work is also a place for developing friendships.

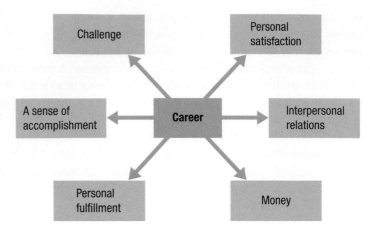

Figure 12.1
A Career Means Money and More

How do adolescents feel about their future in the world of work? In one survey, more than two-thirds strongly agreed that they should be optimistic about their chances of having a good job (Mogelonsky, 1998). Many adolescents surveyed had some work experience, and more than one-third worked 18 hours per week. Teens are also well aware of the need for social skills in the workplace; more than half surveyed felt it is "extremely important" to get along well with other people and be part of a team. Almost half of all respondents rated computer skills as "extremely important." About a third believed that women are likely to face sexual harassment on the job, but about a third also believed that the **glass ceiling** will disappear.

What do adolescents want in a job? They seem to want everything! When adolescents were asked to rate factors such as interest in work, opportunity to influence decisions on the job, ability to help others, interpersonal relationships on the job, extrinsic rewards such as salary, and opportunity for free time and leisure, they rated almost all of them as "very important" (Marini et al., 1996). A particular job cannot offer all of these features, and with age people become more realistic (Johnson, 2002). Historically, females emphasized the greater importance of intrinsic factors (satisfaction), altruism (doing things for others), and social interactions on the job, whereas males were more interested in extrinsic rewards, such as salary. Today, women are just as interested in extrinsic job rewards, though differences in desire for satisfaction, altruism, and social interactions remain between males and females (Johnson, 2002; Marini et al., 1996).

The World of Work Today

At one time, a worker may have thought that he or she would work for one company for a lifetime, the firm would offer security, and the employee would respond with loyalty. Workers no longer think like this, as the workplace of the early 2000s differs significantly from the workplace of 50 years ago in many ways.

First, the basic industrial pattern in the United States and other Western nations has changed; the number of people working in service-related industries has increased greatly, whereas manufacturing has declined (Barringer, 1990; U.S. Bureau of Labor Statistics, 1999). Older manufacturing industries, which traditionally offered fairly good pay, have been closed as overseas competition has increased (Personick, 1990).

Second, jobs today require more education and skills. The workplace is changing faster than ever. The growth of new industries, such as biotech and computer-related businesses, requires workers to have more technical skills.

glass ceiling Artificial barriers, based on attitudinal or organizational bias, that prevent women and minorities from advancing within their organization and reaching their full potential.

Today's work force is a multicultural one, making it even more important to understand other people's traditions and beliefs and respect them.

Third, there is more insecurity in the workplace. Only 55 percent of all workers in one study believed that their companies provided job security, a decline from earlier studies (Reinemer, 1995). The tremendous economic expansion in the 1990s made workers more optimistic about their vocational futures, but when the economy faltered, layoffs became common.

Fourth, the growth of temporary, part-time, and contract workers has changed the vocational landscape. The "temping" of America is causing alarm, as many workers are not offered benefits such as health insurance. The ability to save on benefits is one reason companies have increased their use of temps and contract workers.

Fifth, the world of work is more diverse and multicultural today (Evans & Larrabee, 2002). The fastest-growing groups in the labor force are Asian Americans and Latinos. The participation rate of women in the labor force is also expected to increase in the early part of the 21st century (U.S. Bureau of Labor Statistics, 1999). A growing number of women are entering fields that were almost totally composed of men in the past. In addition, the percentage of adolescents belonging to minority groups is increasing. Respect and tolerance for differences in customs and culture will be even more important in the future.

Sixth, although the 9-to-5 office workday will not be consigned to the history books, alternative working arrangements will flourish in the future. *Telecommuting*—that is, working from home on a computer—flexible work hours, and a host of other structural changes are now becoming more popular with both workers and employers.

The Adolescent with a Job

Almost all adolescents today attend high school and have limited experience with the vocational world. Most adolescents do not start full-time, year-round work until early adulthood. Yet an estimated three-quarters of all teens will be employed sometime during their high school years (Bachman & Schulenberg, 1993). Nearly 90 percent of high school juniors and seniors who work do so at least part of the school year (Manning, 1990). High school students are twice as likely to be working part-time as they were in 1950 (Singh, 1998). Indeed, part-time work is now the norm for teens in the middle years of adolescence (Skorikov & Vondracek, 1997).

This high rate of teenage employment is a distinctly American phenomenon and is not found in any other Western society (Greenberger & Steinberg, 1986). Many U.S. retail and service companies need entry-level, part-time workers. These jobs pay minimum wage or slightly above (Carr, Wright, & Brody, 1996). Such jobs are easy to find, and teens are in great demand.

Thirty years ago, this entrance into the world of work was greeted with approval. It was almost universally believed that work gives teenagers a greater understanding of the job market, builds a sense of responsibility, and develops both self-esteem and a good work ethic (Meyer, 1987). Teenagers who work learn the value of a dollar as they spend the money they earn on personal items (Shanahan et al., 1996). Work encourages teens to think about their occupational goals and perhaps learn some skills that may help them in the future. In fact, both teenage boys and teenage girls show better psychological adjustment when they perceive their jobs as providing such important skills (Mortimer et al., 1992a, 1992b). At the least, adolescent workers learn how to fill out an application, meet a supervisor's expectations, and get along with the public and coworkers (Mortimer et al., 1996).

Employment may also spur at-risk students to continue their education. Students who work fewer than 20 hours per week have a lower high school dropout rate, perhaps because both employers and teachers reward the same personality traits that promote achievement (D'Amico, 1984). People who favor early employment experience, then, see it as a character-building exercise that fosters responsibility, feelings of usefulness, self-confidence, and the appreciation of the value of work, as well as leading to the development of higher occupational aspirations and positive work values.

Public attitudes toward teenage employment are very favorable (Mihalic & Elliott, 1997). In fact, federal education and labor policies encourage work experience on the grounds that it facilitates career exploration and helps adolescents develop the skills needed in the job market later on (Stone & Mortimer, 1998).

Research studies conducted throughout the 1980s, however, challenged this positive view of adolescent employment. Most jobs open to teens provide no training in useful skills and little opportunity for growth or challenge (Greenberger & Steinberg, 1986). Even governmental programs designed to give work experience to teenagers from minority groups often do not teach work skills the teens will need later in the workplace (Foster, 1995). Most high school seniors work in jobs they describe as not being acceptable for their future, and they work only for the money (Bachman & Schulenberg, 1993). After all, most work is in unchallenging, low-paying, entry-level jobs in sales, service, or manual labor (Skorikov & Vondracek, 1997). These jobs are unrelated to real career exploration and have little effect on career choice or development. Some work-study jobs do teach important job-related skills and thus are an exception. Most teens, though, do not believe they learn much from their work.

Furthermore, most (but not all) research studies find that working has a negative effect on achievement and conduct in school, including lower grades, less time spent on homework, and an increase in behavioral problems (Cooper et al., 1999; Hansen & Jarvis, 2000; Mihalic & Elliott, 1997). Even after controlling for socioeconomic status, gender, and previous achievement, employment is nega-

Most people think that adolescents who work gain a great deal of useful experience. However, studies show that if an adolescent works more than 20 hours a week, work can interfere with academic achievement and social development.

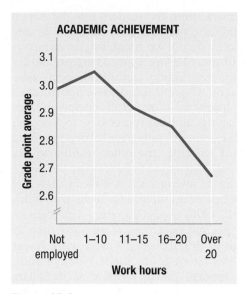
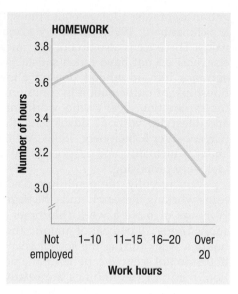
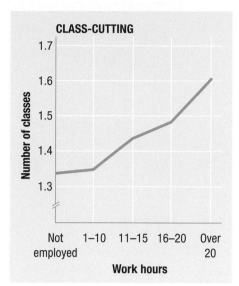

Figure 12.2
Adolescent Employment and School Achievement
This figure shows the relationship between hours of work per week and grade-point average, time spent on homework, and class cutting. As adolescents spend more hours at work, their grade-point averages decline, they spend less time on homework, and they cut more classes.
Source: Steinberg & Dornbusch (1992), p. 308.

tively related to achievement in major subjects such as English, math, science, and social studies (Singh, 1998; Singh & Ozturk, 2000). These finding are the most serious challenge to the value of employment for teenagers.

Adolescents who work more hours show poorer achievement, do less homework, and cut more classes (Steinberg & Dornbusch, 1992) (see Figure 12.2). Certainly, the nature of the job is important, for rewarding and complex jobs may encourage school achievement (Mortimer, Shanahan, & Ryu, 1993). However, few jobs can be described in this manner. Critics of teenage employment argue that the negative effects on achievement outweigh the gains (Carr et al., 1996; Steele, 1991).

These negative school outcomes may result from work-related activities replacing homework, reading, and other academic activities. Students with low academic achievement are more likely to work longer hours than students with high academic achievement (Singh, 1998). The greater the number of hours worked during the school week, the larger the negative effect. Teenagers who work more than 20 hours have lower grades and show poorer school achievement than nonworkers or teens who work fewer hours (Steinberg et al., 1982). These students also show less involvement in both extracurricular activities and school (Steinberg, Fegley, & Dornbusch, 1993). Teens who work long hours are also more likely to show adjustment problems, smoke, use alcohol immoderately, use other drugs, and be delinquent (Steinberg, Fegley, & Dornbusch, 1993; Steinberg et al., 1982). They also face an increased risk for pregnancy and sexually transmitted infections (Valois & Dunham, 1998).

Some argue that working during the school year is a deterrent to criminal activity and substance abuse, but there is no support for this assertion (Steinberg & Dornbusch, 1992). Others argue, however, that adolescents who work may be exposed to older teens and adults who introduce them to risk taking (Safyer, Hawkins, & Colan, 1995). Parents may consider adolescents who work long hours as more mature and consequently monitor them poorly (Steinberg et al., 1993). Other detractors claim that working many hours may interfere with the process of forming an identity. Work may take up the time necessary to explore different ideas, and students may have difficulty juggling home, schoolwork, and extracurricular activities.

The relationship between working long hours and these negative consequences is explained by the concept of **pseudomaturity,** or the premature

pseudomaturity The premature entrance into adulthood, which involves individuals taking on adult roles before they are ready.

entrance into the adult role and the withdrawal from the student role (Bachman & Schulenberg, 1993). Adolescents may take on an adult role before they are ready. These teens also do not get much sleep, do not eat breakfast, do not exercise, and do not have much satisfaction in their leisure time. Their premature entrance into adulthood doesn't allow for after-school activities, social relationships, or participation in community activities, and it reduces opportunities for exploration. Teens who work many hours take on adult responsibilities and lifestyles without developing the coping abilities necessary to succeed (Greenberger & Steinberg, 1986). Although teens with jobs may learn something about punctuality and responsibility about working, the other results do not look very promising.

Very recently, the pendulum has begun to swing back a little in views of teens working. Research finds the negative outcomes mostly for teens who work 20 hours or more a week (Mortimer et al., 1996). Approximately 3 percent of sophomores, 10 percent of juniors, and 19 percent of seniors work more than 20 hours a week during the school year (Ruhm, 1995). Students who work fewer hours do not seem to experience the problems (Stone & Mortimer, 1998). In addition, many of the findings are relatively modest (Masi, Morath, & McLellan, 1997). Although most students work in jobs that are not related to their later careers, some jobs do offer valuable experience, such as work in construction, coaching, sports, helping children after school, and caring for the elderly. The quality of the work is important. Also, it is not appropriate to paint all teen workers with a broad brush. Adolescents who work to save money for college may be quite different from those who spend their money on luxuries.

Also, if students had more time, would they actually spend it on homework or school pursuits? Perhaps they would spend it watching television (Smith, 1992). Finally, poor grades and alcohol-related problems may actually precede working rather than result from it (Steinberg et al., 1993). Not being interested in school and school-related programs may lead to working longer hours. Indeed, many students who work long hours were doing poorly in school before they started to work.

In the end, individuals on both sides of the issue have valid points. Although many students who are doing poorly at school work extra hours, taking a job for more than 20 hours a week further disengages a student from school and is related to increased rates of delinquency and drug use. Leaving employment after having worked long hours leads to improvements in school perform-

At a Glance 12.1 Working on the Clock

KEY POINT: The world of work has become more competitive, requires more skills, and is more multicultural.

SUPPORTING POINTS	EXPLANATION
The type of work individuals do influences many aspects of life.	Individuals' jobs influence where they live and their spending habits. Jobs are a source of personal satisfaction and social interaction.
Erik Erikson emphasized the importance of vocational choice.	Vocational choice is an important part of an individual's identity.
The world of work has changed.	More service-oriented jobs and fewer manufacturing jobs exist today than in the past. Workers need more education and training. The changing job scene is multicultural and features more flexible work hours.
Many teenagers work part-time during the school year and vacations.	Adolescents who work may develop characteristics such as punctuality and responsibility, but working more than 20 hours per week is associated with poorer grades and more adjustment problems. Adolescents who work fewer hours, however, do not experience the negative effects.

ance but does not reverse the other negative effects (Steinberg et al., 1993). Perhaps the students have established relationships with friends who are engaged in harmful activities. Most psychologists conclude that working more than 20 hours a week adversely affects adolescents. However, even teens who work less than 20 hours a week have to be monitored to ensure that their lives allow adequate time for schoolwork, social interaction, after-school activities, and community involvement, which are so necessary for personal growth and development during the adolescent years. *(For a review of this section, see At A Glance 12.1.)*

VOCATIONAL CHOICE

What should I be? is a question that becomes more salient as teens proceed through the adolescent years and prepare themselves to enter adult life (Skorikov & Vondracek, 1997). But what leads a person to choose to become a teacher or an auto mechanic? Personal characteristics, abilities, and interests certainly enter the equation. The adolescent who wants to work outside in a natural environment would probably not choose to be a financial planner, and a teen who cannot pass chemistry would not become a chemical engineer. Someone with two left feet would not decide to become a dancer. Although academic ability and achievement are certainly related to career choice, most careers include individuals with a wide span of intelligence levels. For example, accountants are generally more intelligent (as measured on standardized intelligence tests) than miners, but some miners are brighter than some accountants (Cronbach, 1970). Although general relationships hold, the correlation between intelligence and vocational choice should not be overemphasized.

The Life-Span, Life-Space Approach to Careers

A vocational choice doesn't just happen. An individual doesn't just wake up one morning, look in the mirror, and say, "I'll be a computer programmer." According to Donald Super, vocational choice is an expression of the self as it develops and individuals find out more about themselves (Super, Savickas, & Super, 1996). Vocational choice is a developmental process. The development of an individual's understanding of the world of work begins in childhood as children observe people working, identify with working adults, and have contact with people in various jobs (Zunker, 1998).

Super (1972) identified five stages of vocational development. During each stage, particular behaviors and attitudes develop through activities called *vocational developmental tasks*. Although the tasks can occur at different ages, they are most commonly found during a typical age range. During the *growth stage* (birth through 14 or 15 years), the child's attitudes, needs, and aptitudes are developed. Children begin thinking about their vocational futures as they observe the occupations around them and imagine themselves working in them (Super, 1953). Yet their level of self-awareness and knowledge of occupational choice is low. An analysis of the occupational knowledge of third-, sixth-, ninth-, and twelfth-grade students found that it increased with age (Walls, 2000).

During the *exploratory stage* (ages 15 through 24), individuals narrow their choices and make tentative choices, but they do not necessarily finalize them. Often, teens know more about what they do not want than what they do want. The *establishment stage*, which takes place during early adulthood, is characterized by trial and stabilization. Middle age, the *maintenance stage*, is followed by a *stage of disengagement*, in which individuals reduce their work loads, focus more on interests outside of work, and ultimately retire. Recent studies suggest that people are making occupational choices at later ages; most adolescents and many people in their early 20s are not making definite choices (Wallace-Broscious et al., 1994). The self-concept influences each stage of career development as it seeks expression through matching its needs with the requirements of the occupation (Super, 1984). Many factors influence career choice, including the individual's characteristics (needs, values, and interests) and the resources of the family and school.

One of Super's most interesting concepts is **vocational maturity,** the readiness of individuals to cope with the developmental tasks of vocational choice appropriate to their life stages (Drummond & Ryan, 1995). In a classic study of ninth-grade boys, Super found that most had not reached the appropriate level of understanding of the world of work to make adequate career decisions (Super & Overstreet, 1960). Students showed little ability to plan or accept responsibility for their plans, and they were not aware of various aspects of vocational life, even in high school. However, the boys who were more vocationally mature were more successful as young adults. Adults may improve the vocational maturity of teens by helping them learn about occupations and develop planning skills. Super's theory emphasizes the developmental nature of occupational choice.

Holland's Typology

Beyond doubt, the most influential theory of career choice was formed by John Holland (1985, 1992, 1997). Holland suggested that personality characteristics are the most important factor in career choice. Personality includes interests, values, needs, skills, beliefs, attitudes, and learning styles. The most important part of personality, as far as vocational choice is concerned, is interests.

Holland introduced the hexagon model (see Figure 12.3) for understanding the relationship between interests/personality and occupational choice. Most people's interests can be categorized as one of six types: realistic, investigative, artistic, social, enterprising, or conventional (see Table 12.1 for a description of each type). For example, realistic individuals enjoy making things with their hands, are practical, and are conservative. Carpenters and truck drivers have these characteristics. The model puts the more similar personality structures adjacent to each other and places the structures that are most different the farthest from each other. For example, enterprising and social orientations are

Figure 12.3
Holland's Six Occupational Categories
John Holland argued that there are six occupational categories, which can be visualized in terms of a hexagon. The adjacent categories are considered to have more in common than the categories that are opposite.

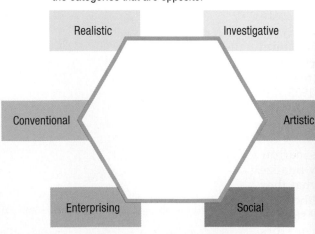

Holland argued that there are six types of work environments. This carpenter would fall into the realistic category.

vocational maturity   The ability to cope with the developmental tasks related to vocational choice at each stage of life.

Table 12.1

Holland's Model of Personality Types and Occupational Environments

John Holland described six different types of interests (themes), which match different occupational environments. An individual's personality can be described in terms of characteristics and interests that fit into these categories. According to Holland, a good match between an individual's personality and interests on the one hand and particular occupational environments on the other hand should lead to greater career satisfaction.

Personal Style	Theme	Occupational Environment
May lack social skills; prefers concrete work over abstract work; may seem frank, materialistic, and inflexible; usually has mechanical abilities	Realistic	Skilled trade, such as plumber, electrician, and machine operator; technical, such as airplane mechanic, photographer, draftsperson, and some service occupations
Is very task oriented; is interested in math and science; may be described as independent, analytical, and intellectual; may be reserved; defers leadership to others	Investigative	Scientific, such as chemist, physicist, and mathematician; technical, such as laboratory technician, computer programmer, and electronics worker
Prefers self-expression through the arts; may be described as imaginative, introspective, and independent; values aesthetics and creation of art forms	Artistic	Artistic, such as sculptor, artist, and designer; musical, such as music teacher, orchestra leader, and musician; literary, such as editor, writer, and critic
Prefers social interaction and has good communication skills; is concerned with social problems and is community-service oriented; has interest in educational activities	Social	Educational, such as teacher, educational administrator, and college professor; social welfare, such as social worker, sociologist, rehabilitation counselor, and professional nurse
Prefers leadership roles; may be described as domineering, ambitious, and persuasive; makes good use of verbal skills	Enterprising	Managerial, such as personnel, production, and sales manager; sales, such as life insurance salesperson, realtor, and car salesperson
May be described as practical, well controlled, sociable, and rather conservative; prefers structured tasks such as systematizing and manipulation of data and word processing	Conventional	Office and clerical, such as timekeeper, file clerk, teller, accountant, keypunch operator, secretary, bookkeeper, receptionist, and credit manager

Source: Zunker (1998), p. 54.

closer together than social and realistic or conventional and artistic (Holland, 1994). Notice that the realistic interest type appears opposite the social type because they do not have much in common, whereas the realistic and investigative types appear next to each other, showing that they share certain qualities (Day, Rounds, & Swaney, 1998).

Six types of occupational environments match Holland's six personality types. People search for environments that allow them to exercise their skills and abilities and to express their attitudes and values. This does not mean that a person is wholly investigative or wholly realistic. Instead, according to Holland's perspective, personality is a pie with six slices; some are larger than others, but one predominates (Reardon et al., 2000). Certain environments are dominated by people with certain personalities. A successful individual in a selling environment, for example, must possess certain characteristics, so people with similar personalities will be found there. Artistic environments are dominated by people with artistic interests. The people within each occupational environment create their own environment.

According to Holland (1992), people are attracted to their careers by their personalities, and career choice is an expression and extension of personality. A socially oriented individual prefers to work in an environment allowing interaction with others of similar bent. People seek out environments where they are most comfortable, respected, valued, and rewarded. Artistic people value creativity and independence, and they are often found together. Finally, a person's vocational satisfaction results from interaction between personality and environmental factors. A realistic person who ends up in a social environment may be unhappy and stressed, and try to change careers. People's interests and competencies create a personal disposition that leads them to think, perceive, and act in a particular way and to seek out environments in which they feel comfortable (Holland, 1985). Vocational choice is an expression of personality.

To successfully choose an occupation, then, individuals must understand their own interests and personality characteristics on the one hand and the requirements for the job on the other. A number of measuring instruments, such as the Self-Directed Search (SDS), have been developed to help people identify their interests or personality types (Holland, 1994). Individuals who complete the Self-Directed Search receive a three-letter summary describing their personality structure. For instance, a code of IAS would indicate that I (investigative) is most prominent, A (artistic) somewhat less, and finally S (social) third. High school students are relatively stable in their scores over a 3-year period (Mullis, Mullis, & Gerwels, 1998). Holland also developed an occupational finder and dictionary that codes occupations the same way. Individuals seek the type of environment that matches their personality structure.

One of the basic assumptions of Holland's theory is that a good fit between the person and the environment will lead to higher levels of well-being, satisfaction, stability, and achievement (Gati, Garty, & Fassa, 1996). Much research shows a positive relationship between personality-based career choice and satisfaction and achievement (Mullis & Mullis, 1997). However, some researchers question the strength of the relationship (Luzzo & MacGregor, 2001).

Holland's main concepts have been successfully applied to women and members of various minority groups, including African Americans, Latinos, Asian Americans, and Native Americans (Day & Rounds, 2000; Hansen, Scullard, & Haviland, 2000). Some gender differences are found, however. Males generally have a higher mean score on the realistic theme and females on the social, artistic, and conventional themes (Mullis et al., 1998). Differences among cultural groups also exist (Brown, 1995). Asian Americans often show higher interest in the investigative area, which reflects interest in scientific occupations. African Americans are more likely to score either highest or second highest on occupations indicating a social orientation (Miller, Springer, & Wells, 1988). Cultural variables emphasizing the importance of human relationships may be partly responsible for these patterns, because more people from certain groups choose vocations in a particular area. However, it may be that interests follow rather than lead. In other words, perhaps feeling that you can succeed in an occupation, called *occupational self-efficacy,* may contribute to choosing that work (Betz & Hackett, 1996). If a group has had a history of success in one area but not in another, it would tend to have role models in that area, who in turn might sway the interests of others in the group. Holland's theory seems applicable to people from minority groups, but factors other than matching interests and job characteristics may be required for people from minority groups to be successful. For example, their occupational success may depend on their ability to transcend or deal effectively with discrimination and stereotypes, as well as on how successfully they can be bicultural (that is, function effectively both as a member of society and as a member of a particular group) (Brown, 1995; Edwards & Polite, 1992). The experience of racial and ethnic discrimination not only restricts an individual's range and types of opportunities but also shapes perceptions of various occupations and one's self-concept. Holland argued that ageism, classism, racism, and sexism restrict career options and that these and other non–interest/personality factors may block people from pursuing occupational choices that might be reflected in their interests and personalities. Indeed, the profiles of African American workers show less congruence with their personality/interests than the profiles of white workers because of the barriers that exist (Greenlee, Damarin, & Walsh, 1988).

If matching personality and occupational requirements is as important as Holland suggests, then reasoned occupational choice will be largely a function of self-knowledge and occupational knowledge. Holland's theory leads to the solid, practical advice to match one's personality/interest structure to that required for the job (Gati et al., 1996). This approach is certainly challenging and useful.

Career Choice

Vocational choice is most often viewed as a process of matching one's needs, interests, and abilities to the requirements, characteristics, and opportunities of each work environment. Understanding oneself and the world of work is a developmental process in which individuals become more aware of their own personality, their interests, and the requirements for particular vocations over time. Career choice is perceived as a cognitive or intellectual process of deliberating and seeking information. Making a "good" choice is defined as finding a good fit between one's abilities and needs and what the workplace requires and can offer.

Such an exceptionally rational approach, however, must admit to the role of cohort effects, family needs, chance factors, subjective individual experiences, and emotional factors. The cohort effect comes into play as some professions become more in demand than others at different times. The prospect of finding a job may be more important than interest if family pressures are great. An individual may be very interested in becoming an artist, for example, but be discouraged by the lack of a stable income. Finally, chance factors enter into the picture. Some people find themselves at the right time and in the right place. I know of a teacher who was having a difficult time finding a full-time position. During his interview, one of the teachers in the school fell ill, and they asked him if he would fill in for the day. He did so well that they hired him for the next full-time position. So although weighing individual and job-related factors in a rational manner is important, other factors should not be forgotten.

If occupational choice were solely a matter of matching the individual's needs, priorities, and abilities to the requirements of a career, each individual would enter a satisfying career that met his or her needs, and little more would have to be said. But this is not the case, for three reasons. First, people may be unaware of their needs or characteristics, or they may not understand what each occupation requires and offers. Second, as noted previously, other factors may enter the picture, for example, chance opportunities. People also have emotional reactions to various occupations, being emotionally attracted to, or repelled by, certain careers. Third and most important are the perceived or actual barriers that prevent an individual from entering an occupation of interest (Evans & Larrabee, 2002).

Some barriers are personal, for example, poor performance in school. A person may want to become a doctor but find his C average in science an impediment. Other barriers are environmental, making an ideal choice more difficult. For example, a single mother of two young children with few resources may find the very long training period required to enter a particular field a financial hardship. An adolescent who wants to be an actor may find his family unwilling to finance education in a field that is perceived as difficult and lacking opportunity.

Some personal barriers are difficult to overcome. No one would argue that an individual who has little ability in the sciences should become a research chemist, for example. Others may run up against barriers based on lack of knowledge, such as an individual with excellent grades who believes that she can't continue her education because she cannot afford postsecondary education and has little idea of available financial aid. Various groups in society experience what psychologists call the *ability-attainment gap*; that is, despite measured ability, they do not seem to choose or successfully enter a particular field. Psychologists have been searching for reasons for the ability-attainment gap in the occupational choices of women and minority group youth for quite a while (McWhirter, 1997). The term *barrier* refers to the beliefs or situations that prevent people from a particular group from choosing certain occupations for which they have shown ability. *(For a review of this section, see At A Glance 12.2.)*

PERSPECTIVE 1

HAMLET ON THE EDGE

SETTING THE SCENE: Dina wants to be an actress. She has always loved the theater and been involved in school plays. She is graduating high school and wants to major in theater, but her parents do not want her to do so.

DINA: *All I ever wanted to be was an actress. I want a chance. I've done well in high school, but I'm not interested in anything else. Why can't my parents understand that?*

DINA'S MOTHER: *Acting is a nice avocation, but entering a field where the unemployment rate is over 90 percent or more is impractical. I hate to say this, but although Dina is good, she never received anything close to a big role in any school play. And the schools that she wants to go to cost a great deal of money, and we don't believe that spending so much money in that area is a good idea. We're not rich people, and sending her to these schools will make things financially difficult. She will receive some money, but not much. We think majoring in theater is a mistake.*

QUESTION: If you were Dina, what would you do? If you were her parents, how would you deal with the situation?

At a Glance 12.2 Vocational Choice

KEY POINT: An adolescent's vocational choice is influenced by such factors as personal interests, personality, cultural forces, and familial factors.

SUPPORTING POINTS	EXPLANATION
Vocational choice is a developmental process.	Donald Super argued that people proceed through a series of stages. Adolescents are negotiating the exploratory period (ages 15 to 24 years), in which they narrow alternatives and make tentative choices.
Vocational maturity is the readiness to take on the age-appropriate challenges of vocational development.	Research indicates that young adolescents do not have the vocational maturity required to make job-related commitments.
John Holland offered the most influential theory of vocational development.	Holland argued that personality characteristics, including interests, values, needs, and attitudes, are the most important factor in career choice. Six types of personality styles—realistic, investigative, artistic, social, enterprising, or conventional—fit different occupations, and people who enter occupations that fit their personalities are more satisfied.
Other factors besides personality may be important in vocational choice.	Socioeconomic status, job demand, parental reinforcement, and chance factors may influence vocational choice.
Barriers sometimes prevent people from entering the occupations they would like to pursue.	Barriers include poor grades and the need to immediately support a family. Some barriers, such as inadequate information about careers and ways to finance education, can be removed.

Gender and Career Choice

How many men consider early childhood education as a career choice? How many women see engineering as a viable career option? Relatively few make these choices. Despite the progress Western societies have made in opening up to women what were once almost completely male dominated occupations, gender remains a factor in the occupational choice of adolescents.

Women's Career Choices

Most adolescent girls realize their future involves employment (McCracken & Weitzman, 1997). By 2005, women will make about 48 percent of the labor force in the United States. The occupational standing of women has improved steadily. Although in 2001, women earned about 76 percent as much as men did, this figure was a significant improvement over the 1979 figure of 63 percent (U.S. Department of Labor, 1999, 2001). In some ways, however, women have done better than males. Earnings for female college graduates increased much faster than earnings for college-educated males. In 2000, 45.3 percent of full-time workers in executive, administrative, and managerial occupations were women, a rise from the 32.4 percent in 1983 (U.S. Census Bureau, 2001). As these figures show, the occupational segregation of women has largely diminished. Although women are still overrepresented in certain fields (such as clerical and service positions) and in some professional fields (such as elementary school teachers and librarians), more women are entering nontraditional fields. (A *nontraditional field* is one in which the overwhelming majority—more than two-thirds—of the

Figure 12.4
The Percentage of Women in Certain Professional Fields
From 1983 to 2000, the percentages of females in various professions have increased significantly. Women make up 51.1 percent of the population and approximately 46 percent of the work force today.
Source: U.S. Census Bureau (2001).

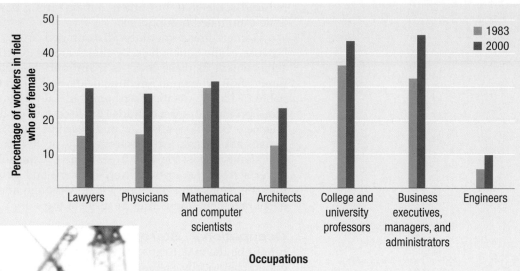

Although women have made excellent progress entering what were once male-dominated occupations, some fields such as engineering have shown less progress.

workers are of the other gender [Hayes, 1986].) Women are making substantial, though uneven, progress. The percentage of women who are doctors, lawyers, and business executives has increased substantially, although females make up less than half of the people in these occupations (see Figure 12.4).

This improvement is less substantial in the scientific and technical fields. The number of women working in the biological sciences has increased significantly, but the increases for women in math, engineering, and the physical sciences are not as great as would be expected, given the increase in the number of women attending college and pursuing careers (Nauta, Epperson, & Kahn, 1998). Although women are equally or more likely to graduate from college than men, they remain underrepresented in math and science careers (Stumpf & Stanley, 1996). The difference cannot be due to any possible gender differences in ability. Indeed, gender differences in math- and science-related career choice exist even among men and women who do not differ in actual or perceived competence in math and science (American Association of University Women, 1992).

Historically, woman have selected from a narrow range of female-dominated occupations, so considerable efforts have been made to identify and understand personality and background factors that may restrict or encourage women's range of career options (Tokar & Jome, 1998). Why do female career choices still show a traditional bent?

Encouragement to Enter Male-Dominated Occupations The difficulties experienced by women entering male-dominated occupations are usually ascribed to lack of encouragement, stereotypes, background factors, interest patterns, and the need to redefine gender roles. Some of these difficulties have been reduced somewhat, but others remain strong barriers to women entering some male-dominated occupations.

Women are sometimes discouraged from pursuing a particular career because of the beliefs held by their parents, teachers, and even some peers that achievement in these areas is inappropriate. Television programs and movies rarely show women in scientific fields, and when they do, the women seem incapable of having a satisfying family life along with their careers. Parents sometimes propagate sexist attitudes by discouraging daughters from achieving in the sciences. School counselors and teachers are often blamed for discouraging female adolescents from entering the professions, but adolescents themselves often have a sexist view of career choices. Counselors of both genders often have fewer stereotypes in their view of work and gender roles than do the females they are counseling (Hawley, 1982). Although adolescent females certainly need encouragement, there must be more to the story.

Occupational Stereotypes   The existence of occupational stereotypes cannot be the major cause of the traditional tendencies in female career choices, either. Historically, stereotyping in occupations was considered a major problem (Stockard & McGee, 1990). And studies find that children from 5 to 13 years old are strongly gender typed with respect to job choices, with girls less rigid than boys (Henderson, Hesketh, & Tuffin, 1988). Although occupational stereotyping still exists, fewer occupations are now seen as stereotyped, and there are no differences for some occupations (for example, artist, doctor, and judge). Vocational stereotyping also declines with age but does not completely disappear. Some stereotyping remains even at 16 years of age, especially for males, but again, this tendency is declining (Miller & Budd, 1999). This finding does not mean that typically male-dominated occupations, such as engineer and architect, are no longer stereotyped. The stereotypes remain, but to a lesser degree than in the past. The reduction in stereotyping is much greater for male-dominated than female-dominated occupations. Stereotypes in some female-dominated occupations, such as registered nurse, have declined somewhat, whereas they have changed only slightly in others, such as flight attendant, dietitian, and elementary school teacher (White, Kruczek, & Brown, 1989). Stereotyping, then, may still be an issue to some extent, but it is declining and does not seem to be the main difficulty.

Background Factors and Vocational Choice   Background factors are important in women's vocational choice. Early research found that mothers' employment status affected their daughters. Daughters who chose to enter male-dominated careers were more likely to have mothers who were employed outside the home than daughters who chose more traditionally female-dominated occupations. But later research showed that it was really the mothers' attitudes toward employment, their role, and their employment satisfaction that were associated with their daughters' attitudes, not merely the fact that the mothers were employed (Lerne, 1994; Piotrkowski & Stark, 1987). Mothers who are generally satisfied with their gender role and employment communicate this to their daughters, which affects the daughters' vocational choice (Steele & Barling, 1996).

An Emphasis on Interpersonal Goals   Another possible explanation of why women do not enter technical fields in great numbers is that they may place a stronger emphasis on the personal and social elements of different career roles than on personal achievement (Kerr & Maresh, 1994). Women generally rank interpersonal work goals as more important than do men (Morgan, Isaac, & Sansone, 2001). Compared with men, women place more value on helping people at work or enjoying positive relationships with coworkers (Eccles, 1994; Rowe & Snizek, 1995).

According to Holland's theory, the I and R codes are prominent in 94 percent of all science, math, and technology occupations, and the S code is not very prominent (Gottfredson & Holland, 1989). Yet gender differences are found between the R and S codes, with men obtaining higher scores on realistic codes and women on social codes (Holland, 1994). These findings are difficult to interpret, however. For example, perhaps these differences reflect the fact that women have little opportunity to see other women in occupations described in the realistic and investigative areas (Betz & Hackett, 1983).

Many women with interpersonal goals do not believe that jobs in the scientific area offer interpersonal satisfaction, and they do not believe that some scientific careers hold much promise for them (Morgan et al., 2001). Women show more interest in education, social services, and medicine, as they perceive these career fields as better able to meet their needs.

The Issue of Balance   In the past, it was popular to divide women into those who were oriented toward home and family and those who were career oriented—in other words, women who were traditionally minded and women who were not. These divisions are no longer useful (O'Brien & Fassinger, 1993). There is absolutely no evidence that the trend for women to enter occupations that were previously dominated by males is associated with plans for nontraditional lives. Society has changed and now offers more role models for females in executive positions and a greater acceptance of them. In short, attitudes are more liberal than in the past (Rainey & Borders, 1997). Most women want a balance between families and careers, and many realize that they must plan and struggle to obtain it (McCracken & Weitzman, 1997).

A study of Canadian high school students demonstrates this point well (Looker & McGee, 2000). Both males and females stated a desire to enter the world of work and to combine a family and work. Young women and men shared similar vocational expectations for success, and women believed that they could enter any field, including high-status professional and managerial jobs. Yet many women still opted for the more traditional female clerical, sales, and service positions. Women fully expected to have the primary responsibility for child care, especially when the children were young, and this expectation affected their career choices.

A prominent reason women may not be entering the physical sciences may involve the desire to combine a family and a career; many women do not believe it can be done in careers involving the physical sciences. It is the belief that family and career cannot be combined, rather than traditional gender beliefs, that often affects career plans (O'Connell, Betz, & Kurth, 1989). For example, one gifted female student told me that she would love to go into the computer software field but felt that if she took off 3 years or more from the job to raise her children when they were young, she would return without adequate knowledge and skills, because the field changes so quickly. Thus, it is not so much the view that science and math careers are the province of males (Lightbody & Durndell, 1996), but the question of balance that seems to be troublesome in the career choices of many intelligent women. Female college students who value their future homemaking roles are less likely to major in science (Ware & Lee, 1988).

Men are socialized to accept the role of breadwinner, but women have developed a dual role as mother and worker, which they often perceive as limiting their career choices. It is relatively common for a girl in the later years of adolescence to consider how she can raise a family and continue in a career at the same time. This balancing act is rarely, if ever, a factor in the career choices of adolescent males, according to counselors.

A look at gifted boys and girls sheds further light on how gender influences the career choices of adolescents. Gifted boys and girls have similar educational and career aspirations in elementary school, and they are quite high. However, girls tend to lower their aspirations in high school and college even when they continue to excel academically (Kerr & Maresh, 1994). Gifted boys are more likely to aspire to the most advanced doctoral-level programs (Leung, Conoley, & Schel, 1994). Gifted female students are more likely to experience confusion in planning their careers, and they sometimes see their giftedness as creating confusion in their life planning. Gifted and talented boys have a higher level of vocational identity than the girls and are more likely to have a clear, stable picture of their career talents and interests. This difference is related to the conflict many girls experience in considering the possibility of balancing multiple roles, such as career and family (Leung, 1998). The conflict may cause some gifted girls to compromise their career goals and give up rewarding and demanding career options that they see as inconsistent with the multiple roles they seek. A larger number of gifted girls are undecided about careers than boys, and their educational and career choices are often not as congruent with their abilities.

Women often lower their career aspirations as they begin to perceive barriers. Female college students with superior math and science ability often perceived the number of years required for training for higher-prestige occupations as an impediment (Farmer et al., 1998). The issue of balance was critical. Women viewed these science and technology occupations as requiring a high level of commitment in terms of willingness to travel, relocate, and work evenings and weekends, which was not compatible with parenting. Many of these women had entered other occupations such as nursing, seeing these careers as useful in getting employment anywhere they chose to live, flexible, and fitting well into the need to balance work and family. Some women, who were not pregnant or even married at the time, even mentioned that would fit in with the single mother or divorced lifestyle.

Research shows that female students perceive role models as especially important for women who are pursuing nontraditional careers. These role models may demonstrate how they handle the **role conflict,** which occurs when a person believes that the demands required by work and family roles are incompatible or difficult to combine (Nauta et al., 1998).

Women experience both internal and external barriers in deciding to enter vocations in the fields of math and the physical sciences. External barriers include sexism, discrimination, and lack of role models. Internal barriers include fear of being considered too bright and falling back on very traditional societal roles (Delisle, 1992). These traditional barriers have been eroded, and the key to

People can have high career aspirations to succeed in a traditional career option, such as elementary education. This principal has reached a very high position in a traditional field.

role conflict A state in which performance of one role makes it difficult to meet the requirements of another role.

further progress may not be to convince women that they can be successful with technology but instead to demonstrate that they can have a career in nontraditional fields without giving up their desire for a family.

This tidy analysis is not without its detractors, however. Some critics argue that this view fails to differentiate between traditional career orientation and having high aspirations. For example, a study of early adolescent girls found their occupational aspirations clearly traditional, but they also had a strong desire to advance to leadership positions within their chosen careers (Rainey & Borders, 1997). The authors suggest that women can have a traditional career orientation while exhibiting high aspirations, and they can be nontraditional in orientation while exhibiting minimal aspirations.

Others argue that the disparity in numbers of males and females in some occupations may be a function of interest. As noted earlier, women are more interested in the professions that can be placed under the social category described by Holland. This social orientation may be caused by differences in childhood experiences; parents may emphasize nurturance with girls and not boys. Another background factor may be the different games boys and girls play in childhood. Researchers asked men and women entering male-dominated engineering and technical scientific fields about their childhood games, toys, and activities and found that individuals of both genders were more likely to have played with masculine or neutral toys than with stereotyped feminine toys (Cooper & Robinson, 1989). Realistic activities and interests (in terms of Holland's categories) may be spurred by fixing things, repairing cars, and operating tools.

Although concern about vocational choice and artificial barriers to achievement is valid, adults and peers should not force on teenagers some politically correct view of how men and women should live. Too often, older stereotypes are merely replaced by newer ones. For instance, one female student felt guilty because she wanted to pursue a career in elementary school teaching. Her counselor, teachers, and friends, who believed she could "do better," did not approve of her decision. Women should be encouraged to enter their field of choice unencumbered by artificial barriers.

Men and Career Choice

Because men historically have been expected to make career choices and become the main breadwinner in the family, changes in trends related to men's careers have come about more slowly. Men have traditionally been expected to go out and obtain what is necessary for family survival. Men perceive career success in terms of achievement, status, power, and control (Reardon et al., 2000). However, these attitudes may need to be reexamined, and some changes are appearing. Most men marry, and many women contribute to the family income. This situation requires increased willingness on the part of men to participate in child care and homemaking activities, and a more flexible perception of role is required (Kaplan, 2000).

Many of the stereotypes that surround men's vocational choices operate in their favor (Skovholt & Morgan, 1981). For example, our society gives positive ratings to personal characteristics such as strength and determination. It sees men's job choices, such as engineer and electrician, in an equally positive light. In addition, society approves of rewards such as power, money, and status. For men, occupational success often means high self-esteem. Success in life is often measured by success in vocational pursuits. These advantages explain why men are less willing than women to explore nontraditional life and career patterns (Hawley & Even, 1982). Because they generally choose high-status positions, men experience less urgency to question their lifestyles.

However, two negative factors are becoming evident. First, not all men are going to succeed, and vocational failure often leads to self-esteem problems in men. Basing self-esteem on job success can lead to problems, including violence in the family, deterioration of health, and stress. Second, even if males succeed,

Gender stereotyping of occupations has been reduced for females entering male-dominated occupations but the male entering female-dominated occupations is still rare. Why?

their lives may become narrowly focused. In many cases, they do not develop the kinds of relationships with their families they might have liked.

Furthermore, unlike women, men have been less willing to move into non-traditional occupations, and this further limits their alternatives (Reardon et al., 2000). Some of the most segregated occupations are dominated by women, including nursing, elementary school teaching, and office work. Men are often discouraged from entering female-dominated careers, which are often perceived as being lower in status and salary (Chusmir, 1990). Men who enter stereotypic

AT A GLANCE 12.3 GENDER AND CAREER CHOICE

KEY POINT: Gender remains an influence on vocational choice.

SUPPORTING POINTS	EXPLANATION
Most adolescent girls believe they will be gainfully employed.	About half the work force is made up of females. Most teenage girls believe their futures will include family and work.
More women are entering nontraditional fields.	More women today are entering such fields as law, medicine, and management.
Some technical fields remain male dominated.	Women may not enter some fields because of lack of encouragement and gender stereotypes. Some women do not believe it is possible to combine a technical career and a family.
Gender stereotyping of occupations still exists.	Gender stereotyping of occupations is less prevalent than it was a few decades ago. The reduction is greater for male-dominated than female-dominated vocations.
Females may enter more socially oriented, helping professions because of their upbringing.	Female's greater interest in socially oriented vocations may be due to their early socialization, which emphasizes the importance of relationships, or to a lack of models in some technical areas.
Most women who enter male-dominated fields are not planning to lead nontraditional lives.	Society's view of women's roles has changed, and most women who enter male-dominated fields of study want a career and a family.
Many factors in vocational choice operate in favor of men.	Society sees the stereotypic male characteristics of strength and competitiveness as positive. It also views stereotypic male careers as having high status. However, men with aptitudes for stereotypic female occupations may feel constrained from entering them.

female fields receive little support and may be ridiculed for engaging in what others see as gender-inappropriate behavior. They also may adhere less to gender-role stereotypes, however; indeed, men in such jobs are more flexible in their views of masculinity (Jome & Tokar, 1998).

Thus, the advantage the male status provides is a two-edged sword. Attitude changes are needed to allow men to widen the scope of their occupational choices to include some traditionally female-dominated occupations and to balance their family and leisure activities with their work. In addition, female-dominated occupations must open up to men who have the talents to succeed in them. *(For a review of this section, see At A Glance 12.3.)*

MINORITY GROUP MEMBERSHIP AND CAREER CHOICE

The proportion of African Americans and Latinos in white-collar professional jobs has increased over the past 20 years (see Figure 12.5). The progress has been slow, however. In addition, African Americans and Latinos are especially underrepresented in the technology careers, and today 60 percent of all jobs in the United States require technical skills. There are many unfilled positions in the computer industry, and the field is expected to generate more than 1 million new openings by 2006 (Jacoby, 1999).

Explaining the Trends

One difficulty in examining the reasons for the slow progress of minority group members in entering many professions is the confounding of minority group status and poverty. African Americans, Latinos, Native Americans, and some groups of Asian Americans are more likely to live in poverty than whites, which makes interpretation of studies of vocational choice more difficult. Suppose you researched the perceived barriers to occupational choice of white and African American adolescents and found some differences. Unless the socioeconomic

Figure 12.5

Percentages of African Americans and Latinos in Various Professions
The proportion of professionals who are African American or Latino has generally increased. For reference, African Americans made up 12.8 percent of the U.S. population, and Latinos, 11.8 percent.

Source: U.S. Census Bureau (2001).

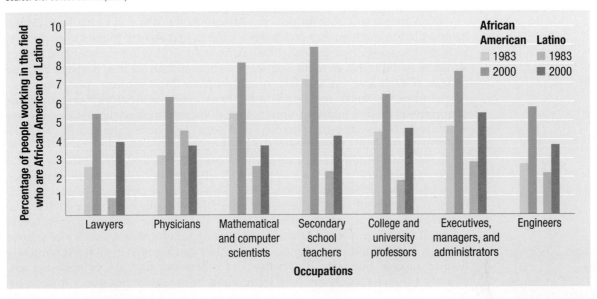

Minority group members have made progress entering the professions but the progress has been somewhat slow.

status of the two groups was similar, you could not be certain whether your findings were due to the different perceptions of African Americans and whites or to the differing economic resources available to the groups (Arbona, 1990; McWhirter, 1997). Differences attributed to ethnicity actually may reflect differences in socioeconomic status. Research often finds that African Americans and whites have equal aspirations but that lower socioeconomic status lowers aspirations (Rojewski & Yang, 1997).

It is easy to explain differences between adolescents in different socioeconomic groups. Adolescents raised in poverty often are exposed to fewer high-achieving role models, which causes them to aspire to a narrow and stereotyped range of occupations (Mitchell & Krumboltz, 1996). The educational background of children and adolescents raised in poverty, as well as their families' lack of resources, leads them to perceive fewer opportunities (Hotchkiss & Borow, 1996). Adolescents raised in poverty also are less aware of the various occupations open to them.

Many poor adolescents do not perceive themselves as having choices. African American males living in poverty may see themselves as having no real career exploration period. They may take a job in their teens but then have a succession of unrelated jobs for 50 years, with no discernable career path. Many Latino youth living in poverty have poor English language skills; English language proficiency is directly related to socioeconomic status and level of education (Arbona, 1995). Middle-class and college-educated Mexican Americans and Anglos are similar in their attitudes toward work, as well as in characteristics related to achievement and progression to white-collar professional occupations. Latino and non-Latino white college graduates have similar career strategies and expectations, as well as decision-making skills and strategies (Hackett et al., 1992; Bores-Rangel et al., 1990). However, lower-income Latino youth, who often have English language difficulties, show less understanding of what is needed to succeed in higher-status occupations and do not believe they can succeed in them.

Adolescents from middle-class families believe they can influence their own futures; that is, they have an **internal locus of control.** This is not true of poorer adolescents, who often have an **external locus of control** and see themselves as being at the mercy of the system, the outside world, or luck. They are more fatalistic in their outlook. This tendency is unfortunate, because having an internal locus of control is related to making career decisions based on choice (Hartman, Fiqua, & Blum, 1985). An internal locus of control is essential for exploration and career planning.

Even after accounting for poverty, African Americans and Latinos are underrepresented in mathematics and science careers and among majors in these subjects at colleges (Gainor & Lent, 1998). African American high school and college students enroll in fewer math and science courses than whites, perhaps because of lack of early interest and lack of exposure to these subjects, poor academic preparation, or fewer role models in these areas. Self-efficacy and outcome expectations predict interest in math; that is, interest in math activities increases as students believe they can succeed and perceive that engaging in such activities will produce positive outcomes (Lent, Lopez, & Bieschke, 1991).

Judgments of self-efficacy result from past experiences, observations of others, verbal persuasion, and one's physiological state (see "The Scientific Approach to Adolescence") (Bandura, 1986, 1997). Two of these influences—past experiences and observations of others—are especially important to career choice. Past experiences of success in similar situations increase self-efficacy, whereas repeated failures lower it. Many minority group youth have no history of success with the system, and they may not believe they can succeed or that studying will lead to success. Similarly, observations of others can increase or decrease self-efficacy. Positive models can help individuals believe that they, too, can succeed.

internal locus of control   The belief that one is in control of one's own life.

external locus of control   The belief that others or luck is in control of one's life.

However, relatively few role models are available for minority group adolescents in many professions, which may negatively affect self-efficacy.

Even though career aspirations do not seem to differ much between ethnic minority and white youth, minority youth have lower expectations concerning their ability to reach their career goals (Arbona, 1990; Arbona & Novy, 1991). In other words, adolescents from minority groups aspire to high-level careers but do not believe they can attain them. They perceive fewer career choices and opportunities and see successful jobs as more difficult to attain. These perceptions have a negative impact on occupational choices and motivation.

Career Choice Among African Americans and Latinos

A number of barriers impede the progress of African Americans and Latino adolescents into highly paid professions (Constantine et al., 1998). Impediments for African American and Latino adolescents in particular include a lack of self-efficacy regarding occupational choice, lack of information about jobs, and poorer preparation for careers. Poverty, fewer role models in particular occupational areas, exposure to crime, and racial and ethnic bias are also significant barriers. Some argue that the problem goes beyond these barriers. For example, some African Americans perceive certain fields, including the sciences and math, as being what "white people do," and success in these fields may raise questions about group membership, either consciously or unconsciously (Jacoby, 1999). Summer programs for minority group youth attempt to address the lack of role models and have strengthened interest and acceptability of goals in the sciences. Career paths may be blocked early, however. Academic tracking may impede career choice, and African American and Latino teens are less likely than white or Asian students to be placed in college preparatory courses, regardless of test scores (Oakes & Guiton, 1994).

Any discussion of barriers must include the experience of minority group women. Parents of adolescent Latino females often do not give their daughters a great deal of support to continue their education and enter prestigious fields, either because their culture does not encourage such achievement or because they are living in poverty. In fact, Latinos are more likely to note financial barri-

Career choice assumes an open field in which capable adolescents can make a choice and follow it through. Unfortunately, poverty reduces vocational choice and many adolescents living in poverty do not believe they have much of a choice.

ers, whereas African Americans say ethnicity is a barrier (Luzzo, 1993). Many Latinos drop out of school early. Some have received little education in their country of origin and find the adaptation to U.S. culture difficult.

Minority groups, though, are not monolithic entities. Various subgroups of Latinos have different histories. Their immigration patterns differ, as some groups immigrated earlier. The two largest groups, Mexicans and Puerto Ricans, immigrated mostly for economic reasons; Cubans, for political reasons; and people from Central and South America, for both reasons. Mexican and Puerto Rican immigrants are more likely to live in poverty than Cuban immigrants. Among Latinos, Mexican Americans have the lowest high school and college completion rate, and Mexican American women are less likely to graduate from college than their male counterparts and are overrepresented in low-paying occupations (Flores & O'Brien, 2002).

The amount of time Latinos have been in the United States and their level of adaptation to the culture are important variables in their career choices. *Acculturation* is the process by which individuals' contact with a different culture affects their original cultural values and behaviors. In the United States, people who are more acculturated have more liberal gender-role attitudes, which may lead to a greater variety in vocational choices but also more conflict at home (McWhirter, Hackett, & Bandalos, 1998).

Males and females from the same minority groups may see the world differently. For example, when Mexican Americans were tested on a measure of perceived barriers, female respondents were more likely to anticipate sex discrimination and less likely to anticipate ethnic discrimination than their male counterparts. Females were more likely than males to agree that if they did not go to college, it would be because of lack of interest or a belief that it would not help their future. Thus, enhancing the perceived value and relevance of college for Latino females might help increase their numbers in higher education.

Career Choice Among Asian Americans

As noted in "The World of Adolescence," people categorized as *Asian Americans* come from many different cultures. The term does not differentiate people from the Pacific Rim (Japanese, Chinese, and Koreans) from individuals from Pakistan and India, making generalizations very difficult. Asians, especially people from the Pacific Rim, are often depicted in the media as working in laboratories, on scientific teams as engineers, or as mathematicians but as being less successful in sales (Leong & Hayes, 1990). Indeed, Asian Americans are much more likely to be found in these technical occupations than their overall numbers would predict. Many, but not all, Asian groups have fared well relative to other minority groups; some groups have been more successful than others. For example, Japanese, Chinese, and Koreans have achieved higher levels of entrance into the professions than Vietnamese or Cambodians. And discrimination remains a problem in any case (Leong & Serafica, 1995).

Evidence shows that Asian Americans take more interest in scientific fields compared with other groups. In fact, studies find that Asian Americans are more interested in the physical sciences, technical fields, and business fields and less interested in the social sciences and areas requiring extensive linguistic skills (Leong & Serifica, 1995). Asian Americans are more than five times as likely to work in medicine and the physical sciences, three times more likely to be astronomers and engineers, and twice as likely to be accountants; however, they are less than half as likely to be lawyers, judges, or general administrators (Hsia, 1988). Asian Americans are very concerned about their career possibilities. Many groups, including Chinese, Filipinos, Koreans, and Japanese, are much more likely to present counselors with career problems than personal problems (Tracey, Leong, & Glidden, 1986).

As previously discussed, role models or the lack of role models for success in various fields may affect vocational choice. Asian Americans have many role models for success in science and technical fields and fewer in sales and social sciences (Leong & Gim-Chung, 1995). Self-efficacy is also a factor (Bandura, 1997; Lent et al., 1991). Asian Americans show greater confidence for success in scientific fields than other occupations.

Some investigators suggest that Asian American parents have a greater input into their children's occupational choice than parents in other groups. Asian parents want their children to enter occupations that are stable and have good career ladders—characteristics of careers in the sciences. In fact, there is some evidence that Asian Americans interested in artistic careers choose medicine or engineering instead because of pressure or guidance from their families (Leong & Serafica, 1995). Asian American teens perceive more parental pressure in career choice than do white teens. Asian American cultures place high values on collectivism, interdependence, deference to authority and older people, family, and conformity with social norms. These values, in turn, affect career-related behaviors (Leong, 1991). Young Asian Americans choose careers that both satisfy their own interests and are acceptable to their parents. They sometimes see career choice not only as providing for their own families but also for helping siblings and fulfilling responsibilities to parents (Leong & Chou, 1994).

Again, acculturation is an important factor in the career choice of Asian Americans. Asian Americans who are most acculturated tend to choose less stereotyped and less traditional occupations. More acculturated Asian Americans feel a greater degree of self-efficacy in other fields and may be more likely to follow individualized desires. Less acculturated Asian Americans, in contrast, may be more susceptible to stereotyping and choose careers based more on family desires than on their own needs (Leong & Chou, 1994; Tang, Fouad, & Smith, 1999).

Western society views career choice in terms of an individual's rights and highly respects the goal of self-actualization. Asian Americans and some other groups, in contrast, may see achievement as a family-oriented exercise, in which an individual's decision reflects on and affects the whole family. Modern America places a high value on individuality, whereas more traditional societies do not. An understanding of these cultural prescriptions helps elucidate the pressures on Asian American adolescents, especially male adolescents, who may want to enter less traditionally acceptable fields. More acculturated Asian American teens may find themselves in conflict with their family's expectations. Indeed, this conflict represents their constant need to balance two cultures—that of mainstream America and the more traditional culture.

Career Choice Among Native Americans

Very little research on the career choices of Native Americans has been conducted. As a group, however, they have the highest rate of unemployment and the lowest levels of education in the United States (Juntunen et al., 2001; Koegel et al., 1995). About a third of all Native Americans live below the poverty level, compared with approximately 13 percent of individuals nationwide. Native Americans often experience barriers, such as discrimination, and they face more challenges due to cultural differences from mainstream society than any other minority group. The cultural foundations of Native American life include connectedness, balance, and responsibility to a larger community. The supportive family and community system that is part of many Native American tribal cultures, together with a less competitive atmosphere, makes it even more difficult for Native Americans to succeed in mainstream society. The emphasis on community instead of the individual makes vocational planning more difficult (Juntunen et al., 2001). Native Americans, especially individuals living on reservations, find the cultural differences daunting. Yet to succeed in high-status occupations, Native Americans must receive extensive education, mostly outside the community. They must deal with institutions that have a different cultural orientation. In addition, Native Americans may not receive parental encouragement to follow a career path requiring extensive contact and education in mainstream society (Garrett & Garrett, 1994).

Some Native Americans may not see career choice as a key to individual success, and many individuals take jobs the tribal community deems necessary instead of seeking personally rewarding or interesting work. Native Americans describe success in dual terms; successful individuals are not only able to support themselves and their children but also able to contribute to Native Americans in general and their tribe in particular (Juntunen et al., 2001). The value of contributing to the larger community is an inherent part of one's career. Thus, successful vocational counseling among Native Americans must take cultural factors into account (Neumann et al., 2000). For example, successful career counselors may demonstrate how higher education may help the tribe and improve its economic situation.

Although most everyone agrees that barriers exist for many minority group students, some experts call for a greater understanding of other factors that may cause people from certain groups to follow particular career paths. This idea has particular application to Native Americans. It may be unrealistic or inappropriate to believe that the percentage of people entering various occupations should always mirror their percentages in society.

A Plan of Action

Adolescents from some minority groups face special challenges in vocational choice, and a number of areas must be addressed if these youth are to have vocational choice. First, some beliefs must be changed. For example, the majority group and some minorities who have achieved success view education as a gateway to higher-paying jobs. But the African American community and some groups in the Latino community have had a history of discrimination and lack of opportunity, which may restrict their youth's outlook on jobs. African American and Latino youth often believe that the labor market will not offer them rewards equal to the effort they may put in and the educational credentials they may attain. They may respond to the belief that educational effort may not pay off with a lack of motivation (Ogbu, 1978, 1981, 1992). To change perceptions, companies must open up job opportunities for minority group members so they can see for themselves the value of schooling. Role models in the community, including business and professional people, must demonstrate that success is possible. Unfortunately, in many poverty-stricken communities, individuals who succeed move out, so these role models may not be at hand.

Second, schools in poverty areas must receive the resources needed to carry out their missions. Students must be given an opportunity to learn in schools that are safe, secure, and environmentally conducive to learning.

Third, because occupational knowledge influences choice, minority group youth need education about different types of occupations; they know less than majority youth at present (Drummond & Ryan, 1995). Racial and ethnic minority youth are more likely than whites to want occupational information, need assistance with career planning, and perceive job discrimination (Brown, Minor, & Jepsen, 1991). In fact, African Americans are three times as likely as whites to express a need for career development assistance (Wilson & Brown, 1992).

If vocational choice is indeed to be a true choice, then youth need access to information about jobs and careers: What do I need to become a teacher? Where can I learn to fly an airplane? How can I become an engineer if I don't have much money? How much does a nurse make? A career decision requires not only knowledge of one's own needs and desires but also a knowledge of what is available in the job market, what types of training each career requires, and what each career offers. This information allows the individual to consider many alternatives and weigh them carefully.

The most common way teens learn about the world of work is by observing others working and by hearing about jobs from friends and relatives. However, youth from poverty backgrounds may not observe many people in skilled jobs or hear about technical professions from relatives as frequently as middle-class adolescents do.

Another source of information is television. Generally, television overrepresents professional and law enforcement jobs, including doctors, judges, entertainers, police officers, and private investigators, while underrepresenting jobs such as teachers, clerical and secretarial workers, sales workers, and other blue-collar workers. Television shows feature relatively few bank tellers, shopkeepers, or factory workers. They often show white men in higher-status occupational roles than women or members of minority groups (Signorielli, 1993). However, television is now portraying more women in nontraditional occupational roles.

Television also sensationalizes jobs. The TV lawyer is always involved in an incredibly interesting and complex case; the police officer catches the criminal who was responsible for sixteen bank robberies. Many early adolescents learn about occupations from television, and the work they say they would like to do in the future is related to the kinds of jobs they see on this medium (Wroblewski & Huston, 1987).

Another concern is that television does not present work as very difficult or time-consuming; also, except for individuals in law and medicine, it rarely shows people actually working. Many programs show workers taking long vacations, making a great deal of money, and being home most of the time. Viewing a great deal of television is related to wanting a job with status and respect and to believing that actual work in the chosen occupation is easy. Of course, the purpose of most shows on television is to entertain; presenting information is a distinctly secondary aim, if it exists at all. However, the influence of the media should not be taken lightly. Preadolescents and early adolescents glean a great deal of occupational information from television, and changes in occupational stereotyping can have a positive influence. Counterstereotyped portrayals of women as lawyers, police officers, and detectives have an impact on young girls (Wroblewski & Huston, 1987).

Adolescents certainly need to be exposed to different careers and receive information about their future trends and educational needs. Workers might visit schools, or students might spend a day with someone in a particular field.

AT A GLANCE 12.4 MINORITY GROUP MEMBERSHIP AND CAREER CHOICE

KEY POINT: Members of minority groups have made progress in entering professions, but barriers still remain.

SUPPORTING POINTS	EXPLANATION
More African Americans and Latinos have entered high-status occupations in the past 20 years than in the past.	Overall progress has been slow and uneven for African Americans and Latinos in gaining access to high-status occupations. Many minority group youth are raised in poverty; children and adolescents often face difficult barriers in their quest for a better life.
Middle-class children and adolescents have a greater sense that they can shape their future.	Middle-class children and adolescents are more likely to have an internal locus of control. Children and adolescents raised in poverty are more likely to have an external locus of control.
Children and adolescents raised in poverty often face difficult barriers in their quest for a better life.	Many children and adolescents raised in poverty do not have role models in the professions, attend poorer schools, and do not believe they have the opportunity to obtain the education necessary to enter higher-status fields.
Adolescents from some ethnic minority groups have more doubts about reaching their goals. Adolescents from minority group backgrounds need greater access to vocational guidance.	Adolescents from minority groups believe they face more barriers to get where they want to be, and they know less about vocations. They need help dealing with a bureaucracy and more opportunities to relate to people working in higher-status jobs.

Written material can be helpful (Miller & Cunningham, 1992), but educators must constantly screen it to ensure that it is current and factual.

Finally, it should be noted that barriers in themselves do not necessarily prevent adolescents from making choices. Indeed, almost everyone has to overcome some barrier. Even a teen's realistic perception of multiple barriers might not prevent a good match between interests and occupational choice if the teen has high self-efficacy expectations for overcoming barriers. Indeed, the influence of perceived barriers on postsecondary educational aspirations, achievement, and attainment is mediated by self-efficacy. Many teens who perceive financial, family, or discrimination barriers believe they can succeed, and they do overcome the hurdles. Thus, providing solid career paths though education, financial information, and job-related instruction may help students both see that they can succeed and do so. *(For a review of this section, see At A Glance 12.4.)*

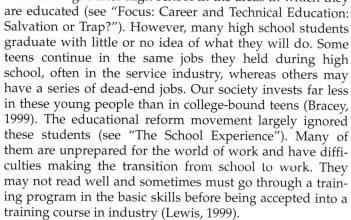

THE FORGOTTEN 42 PERCENT

Not everyone goes to college. In fact, approximately 42 percent of all U.S. high school graduates do not go on for further education, at least not directly from high school (Bracey, 1999). Some of these youth attend vocational education programs (often called *career and technical education programs*) in high school and begin their careers right after high school in the areas in which they are educated (see "Focus: Career and Technical Education: Salvation or Trap?"). However, many high school students graduate with little or no idea of what they will do. Some teens continue in the same jobs they held during high school, often in the service industry, whereas others may have a series of dead-end jobs. Our society invests far less in these young people than in college-bound teens (Bracey, 1999). The educational reform movement largely ignored these students (see "The School Experience"). Many of them are unprepared for the world of work and have difficulties making the transition from school to work. They may not read well and sometimes must go through a training program in the basic skills before being accepted into a training course in industry (Lewis, 1999).

Most research on adolescents and vocational choice emphasizes the college experience. This focus is natural, because most higher-paying, upper-level careers involve some education after high school. Newspapers emphasize the idea that education "pays" as they trumpet the salaries of people with advanced education. At the same time, students who do not go to college are too often ignored. They are often neglected in high school and usually receive fewer services.

The Transition Between School and Work

The transition between school and work is an important step in the lives of late teens and early adults, and it can be difficult. School is so very predictable and secure: One term follows the next, and the student follows a prearranged schedule with limited choices. After a teen has spent many years in school, however, the rules change.

Many teens just out of high school have difficulty getting jobs, and their rates of unemployment are high. Many

PERSPECTIVE 2

I Don't Know What to Do

SETTING THE SCENE: Perry is a junior in high school with average ability and a 74 percent average overall. He gets into a little trouble in high school but nothing major, and he tunes out most of his classes. He does next to no homework—just enough to get by.

PERRY: *I find high school boring. I don't read well, and I don't enjoy English or math. In fact, I don't think there is a subject I really like. I will graduate next year, and I don't know what I should do. I like to work with my hands, but I don't know what I can do. Most of my friends are in the same boat, and we just figure something will come along. Even if I found something I wanted to do, my family doesn't have any money.*

SHANDRA (PERRY'S GIRLFRIEND): *We've been going out for about a year now. I told Perry to go to the guidance counselor, but he doesn't want to. He said the counselor is busy with college applications and recommendations. Perry works part-time in a card store and will probably continue after he graduates, but there's no future there. I'm going on to a community college for nursing. I think Perry would be good at something like computer repair, but he doesn't know how to get into a field like that.*

QUESTION: If Perry asked you for advice, what would you tell him?

high school graduates who are not planning to go to college seem to be floundering, often in dead-end jobs (Grant Commission, 1988).

Few school districts in the United States have any meaningful programs available to assist high school graduates in moving from school to work. Counseling efforts focus primarily on encouraging teens to continue their education in college and obtain a degree. Most high school graduates who do not go on are left to sink or swim without any career advice, career counseling, or job placement assistance (Glover & Marshall, 1993; Marshall, 1997). The Commission on Skills in the American Workforce (1990) noted that for these students, no curriculum meets their needs, no employment services and few guidance services are offered, and there is no reward for hard work at school. This situation is especially injurious to poor and minority students, who have fewer family resources. But these problems are not confined to poor or minority group youth. A number of studies show that the United States lags behind other developed nations in preparing students for a successful posteducation transition to careers (McWhirter, Rasheed, & Crothers, 2000).

To remedy this problem, Congress passed the School-to-Work Opportunities Act in 1994, which noted the lack of both a coherent system of transition and a link between students' education and employable skills. The act offers funds for a variety of programs that link student education and employers. Some of these programs claim success in raising achievement, reducing dropout rates, and boosting employment rates after high school, but few experimental studies exist that would allow cause and effect statements to be made (Guest, 2000).

Not everyone sees this early floundering as a problem, either. Some people argue that many high school graduates do not want commitments (Osterman, 1980). They often see jobs after high school as temporary and functional, offering a living for people with fewer responsibilities who are not ready for a more permanent bond with an employer. Many teens experience a gap of several years between leaving school and settling down, and no relationship exists between the first and later jobs. There is little evidence to show that not going directly on to postsecondary education leads to serious economic difficulties later on. Some of these teens will seek out additional training when they are ready.

Employers and High School Graduates

Employers often complain that high school graduates lack basic academic skills, including reading, writing, and math skills (Rosenbaum, 1996). Some reform groups advocate giving employers the opportunity to return these students to

Employers often complain that high school graduates lack the skills necessary for work. However, others suggest that employers are part of the problem as they do not emphasize the importance of high school achievement and are not willing to offer sufficient job training.

No one has ever argued that everyone ought to go to college, but few argue that it is easy to be successful without some training or skills. For students who do not wish to go on to college, many schools advocate vocational programs, which now are called *career and technical education* ("Beyond the 'V' Word," 2002). These programs aim at providing a closer link between education and the workplace. They feature training and often involve cooperative programs with employers, so students receive realistic training and experience. Many vocational programs require some academic work—for example, in English—but they are not meant as academic paths to college. Unfortunately, vocational education is too often considered a second-class education for individuals who cannot succeed in academia.

Advocates for vocational education argue that students in career and technical education have solid goals and are more likely to find employment after graduating. They receive training in their field and earn more than graduates without any training. They are more motivated, because they must apply to, and be accepted into, the programs and learn what is necessary in the field they choose. Students in vocational education programs are less likely to drop out and more likely to graduate (Lewis, Hearn, & Zilbert, 1993).

Vocational programs, though, have been sharply criticized. Critics commonly raise three points. First, some argue that vocational education is a dumping ground for students who have conduct problems or are unmotivated. Research refutes this criticism, however. Studies by the National Assessment of Vocational Education find that students in these programs are highly motivated and do not have conduct problems (Wirt et al., 1989). Technical education is not for students who can't succeed in the mainstream programs but rather for individuals who want to focus in a certain area ("Beyond the 'V' Word," 2002). In addition, although conventional wisdom may be that minority students are commonly placed into these programs, this is not so. Low-income students and some minority group students do not have adequate opportunity for entry into the more desirable programs. Schools with the highest poverty rates and lowest academic achievement are much less likely to offer their students the more varied and best vocational education programs. Furthermore, many vocational programs are selective; that is, more students want admission than the programs can accommodate.

The second criticism is that career and technical education programs require students to make premature career decisions and preclude college admission. This idea is especially problematic today, as people seem to be making career decisions somewhat later in life. Could an individual who decides to enter a high school vocational program in child care be making a decision too early? This question is difficult to answer.

Relatively few adolescents in these programs follow a high school program that will easily allow for college admis-

school for extra training in these basic areas at the school district's expense. However, employers may be partly at fault. Relatively few employers ask students about their grades or seek transcripts from high school. The few employers who do ask for this information may find it difficult to obtain in a timely fashion. Most high school graduates who do not go on to college are hired on the basis of a simple interview or a recommendation. The selection process does not reward a student's effort, and employers see a high school diploma as more indicative of perseverance than achievement (Bishop, 1989). Students who believe that high school education has relevance to their future success are more strongly motivated and work harder in school. When students who do not want to go on to college see high school graduates with worse grades getting the same jobs they want, they often doubt the value of achieving good grades. The strongest motivator for these students is the desire to get a better job (Rosenbaum, 1996).

Other reform groups argue that employers do not want to do the required training. American firms spend much less on training than do Japanese or German firms, and perhaps U.S. employers are asking schools to do their work for them (Lynch, 1993). Many American employers do not hire young high school graduates for training programs leading to career ladders, and they avoid hiring youth for all but entry-level positions (Grant Commission, 1988). Instead, they open up opportunities only to potential employees in their early 20s or older, possibly because they believe that younger graduates are less devoted to work or are less reliable.

sion, but the percentage who do is growing. In 1990, only 19 percent of all technical students followed a college preparatory curriculum, defined as at least 4 years of English and 3 years each of math and science. By 1998, 45 percent were taking these classes ("Beyond the 'V' Word," 2002). Even so, fewer than 5 percent of all vocational students ever go on to earn a 4-year degree (U.S. Department of Education, 1998). However, perhaps it is not that vocational programs prevent students from going to college but that the students decide not to go to college before entering a vocational program. Recently, more students from vocational programs have elected to go on to community college, depending on the program. Although relatively few high school graduates from agricultural, home economics, or trade programs attend community college, a substantial proportion of students in marketing and sales (25.7 percent), business (20.6 percent), and health (22.2 percent) do (Rosenbaum, 1996).

The third and most important criticism of career and technical education is the question of whether they teach valuable skills. Some argue that vocational programs often prepare students for low-skill jobs, and this criticism is true for some programs. Most studies, though, find that individuals who continue in the field benefit from vocational courses. They are more likely to find jobs, and their pay is higher (Kang & Bishop, 1989). However, vocational education students do better only if they enter their field of training (National Assessment of Vocational Education, 1994; Wirt et al., 1989). About half of the students find jobs

related to their training, and these graduates earn somewhat higher salaries. Assistance in finding an appropriate job is obviously crucial, but links between schools and employers are often informal and tenuous. Furthermore, students whose training matches the needs of the industry do well, and individuals whose training does not earn much less (Wirt et al., 1989). Some critics points out that the advantages of career and technical education may relate only to specific fields, such as cosmetology, and that the majority of high school vocational programs have no significant positive effects on earnings (Kantor, 1994).

Career and technical education, then, merits close examination. The programs must teach marketable skills and provide placement help. Educators must strengthen their course programs and make them more rigorous to keep up with changes in the workplace, including the extensive use of technology ("Beyond the 'V' Word," 2002). Some critics advocate a "new vocationalism," which emphasizes applying problem-solving and reading skills rather than teaching job-specific skills. Others want a blend of academic and vocational education that can take many forms, such as business English (Lewis, 1999).

Technical and career programs serve an important function, but schools must be vigilant in ensuring that they teach employable skills and use up-to-date equipment. Vocational programs may not be the answer for everyone, but they are an answer for some, and an alternative whose value ought to be recognized.

Apprenticeship

Work entry difficulties may be pervasive in the United States, but they are not inevitable, as the experience of other countries shows. Virtually all Japanese high school graduates who do not attend college start working right after high school graduation, whereas only half of all American noncollege graduates obtain jobs by graduation, and most of these adolescents simply continue in the same job they had in high school. Many do not have jobs until 3 or 6 months later, and most work in dead-end jobs with little opportunity for advancement. Japanese graduates are more likely to obtain jobs that offer training and opportunity for advancement. American graduates also have a higher turnover rate at work than do Japanese youth.

Other countries, especially in Europe, have been able to better integrate school and work (Lewis et al., 1998). The best-known system is in Germany, a country widely known for its training provided in apprenticeship (Rieble-Aubourg, 2000). German students who want apprenticeships receive help though the German Federal Employment Office, which collects information on students' grades and other matters, evaluates the students, and recommends appropriate apprenticeships. The program thus forges a link between grades and work. Large counseling and guidance systems acquaint these teens with the options available and help them make their decisions. Students go on plant tours, job shadow (spend time with workers who are doing a particular job), and spend 2 weeks in a selected apprenticeship on a tryout basis. The German apprenticeship program is as much a socialization process as a training program. Teens spend most of their day in an adult environment, learning about their jobs and developing a work ethic. German youth compete for these apprenticeships, so academic standards are high.

Under the German apprenticeship system, beginning at age 16, teens spend 3 or 4 days a week in an industrial, nationally approved program of occupational instruction and the rest of the time in school. Because apprenticeship programs involve two learning tracks, the job and the school, the German system is known as the **dual system** (Glover & Marshall, 1993). This program lasts for 3 years. German companies actively recruit the highest-achieving youth. Participants usually spend a day or a day and a half each week attending a school where they receive instruction in academic areas such as German, social studies, math, and science. This school also introduces them to knowledge related to their occupations and essential skills in drafting or accounting. During their working time, apprentices perform productive tasks and are paid, but they also receive instruction and the opportunity to gain proficiency in a large range of new skills specified for each occupation. Employers absorb the cost of training received at work, and the government pays for the schooling. Apprentices who pass the qualifying examination administered at the completion of their training are certified as skilled workers and are thereby entitled to compensation established for their occupation.

Competition is fierce for some apprenticeships in Germany, such as those in administration or chemical laboratory technology, because they are in fields with better career ladders. Training in small firms is generally less prestigious. Students with the best school records obtain the most desirable apprenticeships. In the United States, in contrast, there is little connection between hard work in school and the job after graduation, and little contact exists between schools and employers.

Criticisms of the apprenticeship system have surfaced (Kantor, 1994). The training received in small firms is not as good as the training in larger firms. In addition, the dual system requires a commitment to a field very early and does not easily allow for a change of careers (Osterman, 1995). Teen unemployment is

Other countries, such as Germany, have a much better developed apprenticeship program than exists in the United States. In addition, their companies do far more training.

dual system A system of apprenticeship that combines on-the-job training and course work in high school.

low in Germany because of this system, but unemployment among early adults is relatively high as some workers leave their fields. Thus, the system may defer the difficulties but not eliminate them.

The Japanese system works differently. The largest Japanese firms actively recruit not only the best university graduates but also the best high school graduates. This system gives students an incentive to work hard and puts power in the hands of teachers, whose recommendations carry weight. After hiring graduates, Japanese firms put them into company training programs and jobs. Evaluations of foremen and supervisors include how well they instruct young workers, and supervision and teaching are integral parts of their jobs (Glover & Marshall, 1993). In Japan, work entry is smooth because of formal links between schools and employers. Schools consider it part of their job to help students get positions in industry. Whereas American high schools help only 8 percent of work-bound students find jobs, Japanese high schools help over 75 percent. The Japanese system fosters direct interaction between schools and employers; the schools don't just offer advice but also provide access to jobs (Rosenbaum & Kariya, 1989, 1991). The linkages offer employers information about students' skills and work habits, and the importance of teacher recommendations gives teachers increased authority over work-bound students.

Apprenticeship programs are rare in the United States, and no one can tell whether the German or Japanese system could be transferred to the United States without structural changes. Employers in the United States are not used to taking on this added responsibility, and schools have rarely considered job placement a prime responsibility. Instead of borrowing the German or Japanese system, some suggest more modest changes for U.S. education. For example, high school students could be prepared for postsecondary technical education in a 2-year vocational program or community college, a system called *tech-prep* (Parnell, 1985).

The tech-prep solution uses secondary vocational institutions and community colleges (which serve both academic and vocational needs) as intermediaries between school and work. Students chose careers from offerings of postsecondary institutions, and courses in the last 2 years of high school align with the requirements for these vocational programs. Students transfer easily to their chosen programs. Tech-prep offers both an academic and a vocational curriculum that is coherent and unified. The formal agreement between high schools and community colleges allows better cooperation between them. It provides students with advanced skills and a purpose during this important transitional period. Students completing the sequence receive a high school diploma and then a 2-year associate's degree or a certificate. Tech-prep programs are flexible and can include on-site work training and work experience, and they can be combined with formal apprenticeships. A significant advantage is their use of the community college, a popular American institution that has developed into a very valuable and flexible institution.

However, tech-prep has at least two serious limitations. First, the system requires that students make a dedicated choice of occupation very early in life, but adolescents today are actually making these choices somewhat later. Second, questions concerning tracking, minority group participation, and whether these programs teach currently needed, up-to-date skills leading to future employability remain.

Apprenticeships are not well established in the United States, but cooperative programs are. About a tenth of all students enrolled in vocational education programs participate in cooperative education. This system differs from apprenticeship because it is more school based, the training ends with high school, and work stations often are specially designed to be training stations rather than permanent jobs. Cooperative programs combine school learning and work experience (often on-the-job training related to students' career goals). Juniors and seniors in high school are allowed to work in their jobs as they attend school (Lewis et al., 1998). Employers are often satisfied with teens in these programs, as most take their opportunities seriously.

German apprenticeship programs and U.S. cooperative programs are similar in providing youth an opportunity to learn skills at both school and work. To be effective, any system, whether a modified apprenticeship or a tech-prep program, must offer valuable training leading to a career path. Employers must not see it as a source of cheap labor. It must offer challenging training, and students should learn many different skills, perhaps through job rotation. In addition, the academic parts of the program should relate to the work area. Access to the most desirable programs must be fair, and the programs must be constantly monitored and updated to account for changes in the world of work.

Obviously, the future of noncollege youth will improve only through radical changes. What is necessary is a commitment among the schools, employers, and the government, which will not be easy to achieve. It remains to be seen whether a social commitment to the noncollege-bound youth, who make up almost half the high school graduates, will be forthcoming. The need is great, and the opportunity to create a meaningful system is present. The question is whether society is willing to accept the challenge.

Youth Unemployment

Unemployment remains a serious problem among teens, and youth unemployment is higher than unemployment for people of other age groups. The problem is even greater among minority teens, whose unemployment rate is approximately 30 percent higher than that of whites (Lewis, 1999). The unemployment rates of African American youth are double the rates of similarly educated white youth (Kantor, 1994). Long-term unemployment has an adverse effect on future wages and can negatively affect a youth's self-concept and self-esteem.

Brief periods of unemployment are not unusual. It is common for teens and early adults to switch jobs or be unemployed for a relatively short period. Even 2 years after graduation from high school, a period of unemployment does not seem to depress or lower an individual's self-esteem. In one study, those who

AT A GLANCE 12.5 THE FORGOTTEN 42 PERCENT

KEY POINT: A little less than half of all high school graduates do not go on directly to further education right after high school, and these adolescents often do not receive the services they need.

SUPPORTING POINTS	EXPLANATION
The 42 percent of all high school graduates who do not go on to college are often forgotten.	Few students not bound for college receive sufficient services, despite evidence that they may have difficulty with the transition to the world of work.
Apprenticeship programs hold promise for students who do not want to go on to college.	Other countries, such as Japan and Germany, have special programs that help students who will not be going on to college. In the United States, community colleges offer technical programs. Cooperative programs, which combine school and work experience, are often successful.
Career and technical education in high school is a controversial alternative to college.	Some career and technical education programs prepare their students for desirable careers. Some authorities, however, are concerned that students opting for vocational programs at a young age may be closing out other vocational options.
Youth unemployment is higher than the unemployment rates for other age groups.	Minority youth unemployment is higher than white youth unemployment. Younger workers are more likely to be laid off, but they are more likely than older workers to find jobs quickly and at better pay than are older workers.

were employed showed a greater sense of psychological well-being than those who were not employed, but those with periods of unemployment even 2 years after graduating from high school did not show the negative psychological effects that might have been predicted (Winefield & Tiggemann, 1990). However, those who were not employed in a stable position in the third year after leaving school showed a marked deterioration in psychological well-being. The authors suggest that not having stable employment after longer periods of time may be especially damaging for adolescents. Being stuck in dead-end jobs is more common than experiencing long-term unemployment, especially during a sustained period of economic growth. Unemployment becomes a more serious problem for everyone when the economy slumps.

Young workers, though, are more commonly laid off than older workers because of seniority provisions; because they were the last hired, they are the first to be laid off. However, younger workers who are laid off have a better chance of finding a job that pays better and are out of work for less time than older workers (Kossen, 1983). This situation results from the fact that there are fewer available jobs the further up the corporate ladder a person climbs. *(For a review of this section, see At A Glance 12.5.)*

PLACING VOCATIONAL CHOICE IN PERSPECTIVE

"If I only knew what I wanted to be, I would do so much better in school." This is a familiar refrain of students who truly are confused about their vocational future. Because a vocational identity is a large part of a person's total identity, such feelings are understandable. Students are well aware of the importance of vocational decisions, and they often look for direction. Yet individuals who make premature career decisions may ignore alternatives or lack openness to new ideas. Many people do not really know what they want to be until their 20s.

We usually think of vocational choice in terms of the college-bound student. Not as obvious, and often forgotten, are the needs of the almost half of all high school graduates who will not go on to college, at least not immediately after high school. These students receive very little help and are asked to sink or swim in the world of work. Their need for more transitional services is obvious, and many such programs may be needed to help students of different ability levels.

The idea of matching an individual's needs to the opportunities and requirements of a career is certainly reasonable. Adolescents must know themselves and their needs, as well as understand what the world of work offers. They should be able to obtain such information not only through reading materials and discussion but also through industry tours, interviews with workers in the field, or spending a few days with someone who does the work. In fact, a poll of employed Americans found that 72 percent of all respondents would try to obtain more information about career options than they had when entering their careers (Hoyt & Lester, 1995). Even greater efforts in career education are needed to break down the internal and external barriers that remain for many members of minority groups and some women. These barriers can be overcome, but models and relevant information are crucial.

The decision to enter a particular career is one of the most personal and meaningful decisions an individual will make. With sufficient help and guidance, adolescents and early adults may make these decisions based on their needs, interests, and abilities and unfettered by artificial barriers and stereotypes.

Please place the number best reflecting your opinion next to each of the following statements. Then compare your opinions now with those you held before reading the chapter.

1 — Strongly Agree
2 — Moderately Agree
3 — No Opinion
4 — Moderately Disagree
5 — Strongly Disagree

_____ 1. Teenagers who work as well as attend high school are more responsible, are more punctual, and have a better understanding of the value of a dollar than teens who do not work.

_____ 2. It is more difficult to choose a vocation today than 50 years ago.

_____ 3. It is better to delay making an occupational choice until at least the junior year of college.

_____ 4. Chance and luck (being at the right place at the right time) are important factors in determining which career a person enters.

_____ 5. Women and men have an equal chance of occupational success.

_____ 6. It is possible for a woman to simultaneously have a full-time career in the sciences and raise a family.

_____ 7. Discrimination is still a significant barrier to the occupational success of people from minority groups.

_____ 8. Vocational choice is an individual's decision, and parents and other family members should have little or no input into a teen's choice.

_____ 9. Vocational educational programs (now called *career and technical education*) in high school force students to make career decisions too early.

_____ 10. Schools have a responsibility to teach students work-related competencies such as punctuality, the value of a job, and how to get along with supervisors.

THEMES

THEME 1 **Adolescence is a time of choices, "firsts," and transitions.**	• Adolescence is the first time an individual seriously considers vocational choice. • Adolescence is the time of first employment. • The transition for many adolescents from high school to work is difficult.
THEME 2 **Adolescence is shaped by context.**	• Adolescents who have role models in high-status occupations are more likely to enter high-status occupations. • Adolescents' vocational choices are influenced by family background and available resources. • Adolescents raised in poverty perceive themselves as having fewer vocational choices. • In the United States, adolescents who are going directly from high school to employment receive far fewer services than adolescents in other industrialized countries.
THEME 3 **Adolescence is influenced by group membership.**	• Despite progress, women are underrepresented in professions involving physics, chemistry, and mathematics. • Women are more likely than men to limit their choices to careers they believe will allow them to combine their perceived role as primary caregiver of children and their occupational pursuits. • Although progress has been made, many members of minority groups still face both external and internal barriers to career choice. • African American adolescents have less of a history of success with the system and may not believe they will be able to reach their goals. • Latinos may be limited in their vocational choices by poor educational opportunities, linguistic problems, and difficulties adopting to a new culture. • Asian Americans have been successful in scientific occupations, but they are less likely to see themselves as successful in other areas. • Native American culture often clashes with mainstream culture, narrowing vocational choices.
THEME 4 **The adolescent experience has changed over the past 50 years.**	• Adolescents must prepare for a world of work that has changed markedly over the past 50 years as work becomes more competitive and less secure and requires greater education. • More adolescents today work in part-time jobs while in school than years ago. • Individuals are making occupational choices at later ages today than in the past. • Most adolescent women now realize that their future includes employment. • Gender stereotyping of occupations is significantly less prevalent today than 50 years ago, especially in male-dominated occupations.
THEME 5 **Today's views of adolescence are becoming more balanced, with greater attention to its positive nature.**	• Society takes a more balanced approach toward adolescent employment today; it warns against teens' working too many hours but also takes into account the positive aspects of working. • Adolescents were assumed to be pessimistic about their vocational futures, but studies show that they are really quite optimistic.

CHAPTER SUMMARY AT A GLANCE

KEY TOPICS	KEY POINTS	KEY TERMS
Working on the Clock	The world of work has become more competitive, requires more skills, and is more multicultural. *(At A Glance 12.1, p. 422)*	*glass ceiling (p. 418)* *pseudomaturity (p. 421)*
Vocational Choice	An adolescent's vocational choice is influenced by such factors as personal interests, personality, cultural forces, and familial factors. *(At A Glance 12.2, p. 428)*	*vocational maturity (p. 424)*
Gender and Career Choice	Gender remains an influence on vocational choice. *(At A Glance 12.3, p. 434)*	*role conflict (p. 432)*
Minority Group Membership and Career Choice	Members of minority groups have made progress in entering professions, but barriers still remain. *(At A Glance 12.4, p. 441)*	*internal locus of control (p. 436)* *external locus of control (p. 436)*
The Forgotten 42 Percent	A little less than half of all high school graduates do not go on directly to further education right after high school, and these adolescents often do not receive the services they need. *(At A Glance 12.5, p. 448)*	*dual system (p. 446)*

Review questions for this chapter appear in the appendix.

13

STRESS AND PSYCHOLOGICAL, PHYSICAL, AND LEARNING PROBLEMS

WHAT IS YOUR OPINION?

STRESS
* Is Adolescence a Particularly Stressful Period of Life?
* Why Be Concerned About Stress?
* Gender, Minority Status, and Stress
* The Nature of Stressors
  Perspective 1: With a Little Help from a Friend
* Stress-Resilient Adolescents
* A Model for Stress Resilience
* Long-Term Outcomes for Stress-Resilient Adolescents
* Coping with Stress

INTERNALIZING BEHAVIORS AND DISORDERS
* Shyness
* Social Phobia
* Depression in Adolescence
  Perspective 2: I Won't Go
* Suicide

EATING DISORDERS
* Anorexia Nervosa
  Perspective 3: I'm Not Starving Myself
* Bulimia
* Treatment Options

COPING WITH CHRONIC ILLNESS
  FOCUS: Young Americans with Disabilities

LEARNING DISABILITIES
* What Is a Learning Disability?
* The Social and Emotional Functioning of Adolescents with Learning Disabilities
* Secondary and Postsecondary Education

ATTENTION-DEFICIT/HYPERACTIVITY DISORDER
* Symptoms of ADHD
* Life with ADHD
  Perspective 4: On Medication
* Treatment of ADHD

PLACING ADOLESCENTS WITH SPECIAL NEEDS IN PERSPECTIVE
HAS YOUR OPINION CHANGED?
THEMES
CHAPTER SUMMARY AT A GLANCE

Most adolescents are happy and healthy. They cope well with the stresses of adolescence. Some adolescents, however, must face additional challenges because they have difficulty coping with stress, have a psychological disorder, or have a disability. Some conditions, such as eating disorders and depression, usually first appear during adolescence (although the seeds of these difficulties may be present at an earlier age). Other conditions, such as a physical illness or disability, may occur during adolescence or earlier in childhood. Still others, such as a learning disability or attention-deficit/hyperactivity disorder (ADHD), are most often diagnosed in elementary school, but they take on an added or different meaning in adolescence.

Interest in the psychological problems experienced by adolescents has increased. Recent research on anxiety, depression, and eating disorders has led to a better understanding of the troubled adolescent. Our improved understanding of the nature of stress and how it affects the adolescent's emotional and physical states has led to a greater appreciation of the role stress plays in life.

This chapter begins with a discussion of stress, because stress is an important influence on the mental and physical health of adolescents. The discussion then turns to anxiety and depression. It continues with a discussion of the most puzzling, though perhaps most well publicized, of all disorders seen in adolescents: eating disorders. Some adolescents must cope with a chronic disorder, such as asthma or diabetes, and the discussion of the challenges they face can sensitize us to the challenges encountered by all adolescents who feel they are "different." The last portion of the chapter discusses learning disabilities (LD) and ADHD. These topics are usually discussed in terms of how they affect school performance, an area on which a good deal of research has focused. However, these conditions also influence life outside of school, in such important areas as interpersonal relationships, vocational choice, and emotional adjustment.

STRESS

Everyone knows what the term *stress* means, but defining the concept remains difficult. For our purposes, **stress** is an unpleasant state of arousal that occurs when people perceive that an event or condition threatens their ability to effectively and comfortably cope with the situation (Lazarus & Folkman, 1984; Smith & Carlson, 1997). The sources of stress, or **stressors,** may include normative life events, such as the transition from elementary school to junior high, or events that are unique to the individual, such as dealing with the divorce of parents during adolescence. Sources of stress include both daily stressors, such as dealing with a teacher an adolescent does not like, and specific events in life, such as the death of a friend.

Some adolescents find it harder to cope with the challenges of adolescence than others. We all know two adolescents exposed to virtually the same stressors over the school year. One copes well, whereas the other shows somatic (bodily) symptoms and tremendous anxiety. Why does this difference occur? First, it is the *perception* of the stressor, not the stressor itself, that matters. Notice that the definition of stress emphasizes the subjective nature of stress by including interpretation (the word *perceive),* or what psychologists call *cognitive appraisal.*

Second, the ability to cope with a stressor is important in differentiating one person from another. Most people experience some stress when they give a speech in front of the class. Some people, perhaps because they have had more

stress An unpleasant state of arousal that occurs when people perceive that an event or condition threatens their ability to effectively and comfortably cope with a situation.
stressor A source of stress.

Adolescence is a period of considerable stress because many changes in life occur.

experience or have received some coaching, cope better with the stressor. In addition, as we negotiate the years, we look at the world differently. Failing to receive an invitation to a party may not be as devastating as we age. However, experience and maturation may not always lead to effective coping mechanisms. Some people continue to use the same psychological coping mechanisms (such as blaming others, giving up, or withdrawing) when faced with stressors and never change. Experience with a stressor does not necessarily lead to better ways of coping with it.

Is Adolescence a Particularly Stressful Period of Life?

Adolescence is indeed a more stressful time of life than early or middle childhood. The number of changes that require the individual to adapt is one reason these years are stressful. Adolescence, as we have seen so often, is a time of "firsts." In addition, the self-consciousness that is often at high levels in adolescence adds to the stress. Adolescents continually judge themselves in terms of their interpersonal competence and evaluate how others are seeing them, which results in stress. The period is also stressful because of increasing expectations to act in a more adult manner. Some argue that early adolescence is an incredibly stressful time because so many of the events—for example, physical changes and transitions to different schools—are not under the individual's control.

When researchers ask both children and adolescents what events are most stressful, the respondents most often report daily hassles with parents and teachers and ordinary transitions, such as school changes (Burnett & Fanshawe, 1997; Compas, 1987b). They also often include school-related stressors, such as exams and grades (Puskar, Lamb, & Bartolovic, 1993). Interpersonal stressors and time-related stressors (feeling rushed) are important as well. Young people view family problems, including parental divorce, parental conflict, parental health problems, and general conflict with parents, as very stressful (Forehand, Biggar, & Kotchick, 1998).

The pioneer in the psychology of adolescence, G. Stanley Hall, viewed adolescence as a period of storm and stress, and more stress does indeed occur.

Conflict with parents, mood disruptions (more ups and downs), and risky behaviors often lead to stress because of both their consequences and the potential for conflict with others (Arnett, 1999). However, as noted, individual differences among adolescents in these areas are significant, and it is wrong to see storm and stress as inevitable. Nor is it truly universal, as stress levels are much lower among adolescents in traditional cultures, probably because their societies value obligation to family and interdependence rather than individualism and independence (Schlegel & Barry, 1991).

Uncertainties about the future also add to the general stress of adolescence. Teens are fully aware of the many decisions they face involving their vocational, educational, familial, and social futures, and wondering if their decisions are sound adds to the stress. Still another reason adolescence is so stressful is because teens emphasize the interpersonal aspects of life, which in turn become much more complicated.

Why Be Concerned About Stress?

We should be concerned about stress for several reasons. First, stress is linked to psychological and social problems, such as substance abuse, depression, anxiety disorders, and other emotional and adjustment problems (Herman-Stahl & Petersen, 1996; McAndrew et al., 1998). A consistent, though moderate, relationship is found between stress and psychological and behavioral problems (Compas, 1987b). Unhealthy reactions to stress can take many forms, such as school maladjustment, poor motivation, verbal and physical aggression, defiance, anxiety, and depression (Printz, Shermis, & Webb, 1999).

Second, a positive relationship exists between physical stress and illness, including headaches, stomach pain, and other symptoms (Natvig et al., 1999). People who experience a large number of stressful life events in a short period are more susceptible to disease, especially infectious diseases (Cohen & Williamson, 1991). Because some people experiencing a great deal of stress do not become ill, however, other factors must be involved as well. Even so, psychologists argue that stress is positively correlated with reported illnesses (Baldwin, Harris, & Chambliss, 1997).

This relationship has many explanations. Stress places a hardship on the body, perhaps directly leading to illness. The body's systems are forced to work harder in times of stress. In addition, the body's reaction to stress disrupts the immune system and makes it less responsive to fighting disease. Stress may also indirectly lead to problems by altering an individual's behavior. People experiencing a great deal of stress may not sleep well or may change their eating habits. They may not take very good care of themselves.

Gender, Minority Status, and Stress

Are males or females more affected by stressors? Most studies find that females are more likely than men to report negative life events that cause them stress (Groer, Thomas, & Shoffner, 1992). Females report significantly more physical symptoms related to stress than males (Baldwin et al., 1997). Women seem more vulnerable to changes in their social networks, and their reactions to stressful events, especially events that involve their social interactions, are more intense (Kessler & McLeod, 1984).

The interpretation of these data, though, is problematic. Are females really more vulnerable to stress, or are they just more willing to admit it? Differences in reported stress may partially reflect socialization differences; men are raised not to admit illness, to deal with a stressor stoically, and not to react publicly, whereas women are permitted to express themselves. Some adolescent males believe that admitting being bothered by stressful events is a sign of weakness.

Reporting bias thus may be a factor, but gender differences in stress do seem real (Almeida & Kessler, 1998). Women may experience more stress because two

One reason females seem more affected by stressors than males is because females are more likely to ruminate, that is, focus on their negative emotions, than men.

important areas that cause it, interpersonal relations and physical appearance, concern females more than males. Males are often socialized to deal with issues directly and to get their needs fulfilled by acting on them. Women, in contrast, are often socialized to balance their needs against the needs of others and to think more about others' needs than their own. Females may encounter more stress than males if they consider interpersonal relations as more important, for we cannot control others' feelings and behaviors as readily as our own. Women, then, have less control than men over important areas of their lives (Nolen-Hoeksema, Larson, & Grayson, 1999). Women also often assume roles that require them to support others, be more empathic, and show concern for others in ways that may increase stress. When stress occurs within the family, daughters may be expected to provide more support than sons. In an examination of adolescents whose parent had been diagnosed as having cancer, girls reported more stressful events, mainly because their family responsibilities had increased (Grant & Compas, 1995).

Women are also more likely to use **rumination,** a style of coping in which individuals concentrate on negative emotions and focus on their own symptoms. Rumination prolongs the distress (Nolen-Hoeksema, 1991, 2000). Women tend to ruminate more than men as early as early adolescence, and the trend continues throughout adulthood (Nolen-Hoeksema & Girgus, 1994).

African American adolescents (and adults) report more frequent negative life events and more stress in their daily lives than adolescents and adults of European background (Jung & Khalsa, 1989), but this finding is not consistent (Baldwin et al., 1997). African Americans and Latinos more often live in poverty and are exposed to violence and discrimination, which may explain these findings (Barrera, Li, & Chassin, 1995).

The Nature of Stressors

Sometimes, stressors are measured in particular major life events that may affect adolescents, such as the death of someone close or being rejected for college admission. The occurrence of many stressful life events in a short time is a predictor of psychological distress and physical problems, regardless of an individual's nationality or ethnic background (McAndrew et al., 1998).

Another way of looking at stress is to investigate the daily hassles an individual experiences. Homework, quarrels with friends, and the hundred daily stressors that haunt adolescents may be even more related to physical and emotional difficulties than are negative life events (Dumont & Provost, 1999). Although the common finding is that daily hassles are more predictive of emotional and physical problems than particularly difficult major life events, major life events often predict daily hassles anyway (Printz et al., 1999). Parental divorce or a parent's sudden and difficult illness certainly changes an adolescent's daily routine and stress level.

The most important variable in the experience of stress is the individual's perception, and different cultures consider stressors to have different intensities (Zheng & Lin, 1994). Researchers asked college and university students in the United States, Germany, India, and South Africa to rate thirty-two life events according to how stressful each was and to assign a rank of 1 to the most stressful and so on; the results showed strong cultural agreement on the relative

rumination A style of coping in which an individual concentrates on negative emotions and focuses on symptoms.

Daily hassles are more related to physical and emotional problems than are major life events.

stressfulness of both major and minor life events. Of course, because all the respondents were university students with much in common, this consensus might be expected. It may simply show that the concerns of university students transcend the usual cultural and national borders. For example, the students considered events such as taking two exams the same day or starting the first semester very stressful. However, the study also found some differences among the students. Adolescents from India found parental problems more stressful than did the other groups. Americans and Germans perceived pregnancy as more stressful. Germans ranked academic problems, such as failing a course or getting low grades, as less stressful than the other groups; South Africans perceived these events as quite stressful. Germans and Indians perceived problems in drugs, friendships, and romantic breakups as more stressful than Americans or South Africans did, although adolescents from these cultures also rated them as stressful (McAndrew et al., 1998). More research is needed on the influence culture might have in the perception of stressors and the experience of stress.

Stress-Resilient Adolescents

Have you known adolescents who still seem to be healthy, well-functioning individuals despite having experienced incredible amounts of stress? You may have marveled at their ability to deal with the stressors. In fact, these adolescents may be the norm rather than the exception (Masten, 2001). Despite many problems and challenges, most adolescents develop into independent, well-functioning adults (Herrenkohl, Herrenkohl, & Egolf, 1994).

Many psychologists have studied why some children and adolescents seem to be more deeply affected by stress than others. Researchers are tremendously interested in risk factors that contribute to stress-related problems and protective mechanisms that buffer the individual from the negative effects of stress (Haggerty et al., 1994).

PERSPECTIVE 1

WITH A LITTLE HELP FROM A FRIEND

SETTING THE SCENE: Jasper is an eighth grader with one younger sibling. A friendly, extroverted individual, Jasper has become quiet and withdrawn, often daydreaming in class. Jasper's grandmother is dying of cancer, and she is living with the family. His mother tries to attend to her needs. Jasper's father was involved in an accident at work and is having a difficult time adjusting to a disability. Jasper's mother has recently taken a job for 30 hours a week to help pay the bills.

MOTHER AT A PARENT-TEACHER CONFERENCE: *I know things aren't easy for Jasper at home. I'm busy and emotional, and my husband and my mother are going through difficult times. I try to pay attention to the kids, but I am exhausted.*

ANDRE (JASPER'S BEST FRIEND): *I'm worried about Jasper. He's not the same. It's as if he's given up. He never wants to talk anymore or do anything. I'd like to help, but I don't know what to do.*

QUESTION: What suggestions would you give Jasper's parents and best friend?

Adolescents who do well despite experiencing significant stressors are called **stress-resistant adolescents,** or more recently, **stress-resilient adolescents** (Rutter, 1985; Wyman et al., 1999). Stress-resilient children and adolescents seem to bounce back, despite pressures that seem too much for almost anyone. Psychologists have noted a number of differences between teens who are resilient and those who are not.

Temperament and Personality   Stress-resilient teens have easy temperaments. They are more flexible, adaptable, and easygoing. Teens with these qualities are more likely to cope well with stress than teens with a difficult temperament, who are more stubborn and contrary (Wertlieb et al., 1987). The more adaptable youth are more likely to receive positive responses from others, which reduce stress (Rutter, 1985). These adolescents are also optimistic and view their futures positively (Herman-Stahl & Petersen, 1996).

Social Orientation and Social Support   Resilient adolescents show a strong social orientation (Werner, 1993). They have good social skills, which may help them gain social support and positive reinforcement (Neher & Short, 1998). They are especially good at creating satisfying relationships with adults, sometimes finding adults who act almost as surrogate parents and models, and this social support helps moderate the effects of stress.

Research suggests that perceived social support is related to better adjustment to stressors (Prinz et al., 1999). However, some studies show that peer support reduces stress, whereas other research does not show such benefits. Connections with peers and activities that are socially beneficial and are reinforced by peers can be protective (Smith & Carlson, 1997). However, some at-risk teens may withdraw from their peers or interact with others in an aggressive or hostile manner. If peers reinforce aggressive behavior then this will not lead to better adjustment to stressors.

Hobbies and Activities   Resilient individuals often spend time outside their strife-ridden homes. They often use hobbies and outside interests as a refuge. They are active in after-school clubs and activities.

Family Relationships   Often the family is a source of stress. However, a good relationship with an adult is the greatest buffer or protective device for adolescents. A good relationship with even one parent may buffer an adolescent from the effects of stress. In fact, research shows that support from families is even more vital for healthy functioning than support from friends. Perhaps peers serve as a primary coping resource when an adolescent's family is nonsupportive (Printz et al., 1999).

Internal Locus of Control   Adolescents with an internal locus of control—that is, a belief that they are in control of at least part of their lives—are more resilient. They have not given up. A study of inner-city ninth graders showed the importance of locus of control (Luthar, 1991). Adolescents who were externally oriented showed declines in self-initiated, assertive behavior as stress levels increased, whereas teens with an internal locus of control did not.

Coping Style   Adolescents adjust more positively if they use active coping that involves attempts to act on or modify stressors by seeking information, altering the source of stress, or looking at the stress in a different way and placing it into perspective (Printz et al., 1999; Weist et al., 1995). Teens who use avoidant strategies such as denial have worse outcomes (Herman-Stahl & Petersen, 1996).

Self-Esteem   Stress-resilient adolescents have high self-esteem. They like themselves and have a sense of self-efficacy, that is, they see themselves as being

stress-resilient (stress-resistant) adolescents
Adolescents who do well despite experiencing significant stressors.

able to accomplish various tasks. They derive their self-esteem from schoolwork, hobbies, and experiences outside the home (Werner, 1993).

Helping Others   Some adolescents who have experienced considerable stress find meaning in life by helping others, most often younger siblings. This behavior, called *required helpfulness,* seems to help improve morale and coping skills and provides a sense of purpose for these teens (Werner & Smith, 1982).

Self-Regulation   Stress-resilient children and adolescents have the ability to control their behavior, attention, and emotions (Masten & Coatsworth, 1998). Good regulation of one's emotions and behavioral control are linked to popularity and prosocial behavior, whereas difficulties in self-control and self-regulation are related to academic problems and antisocial behavior.

Intelligence and Cognitive Skills   Better cognitive skills and higher intelligence positively correlate with academic achievement. Success in school, in turn, may both reduce one source of stress and improve an individual's self-esteem. Adolescents who have better cognitive skills also are better at solving problems, thereby reducing stress. Therefore, students with better cognitive skills often both experience less stress in some areas and more effectively deal with the stress they do experience.

A Model for Stress Resilience

Resilience may seem to be simply a group of personality traits, but this view may oversimplify the real situation. Warm, nurturant relationships with others enable adolescents to develop and maintain skills that help them deal with stress, according to Ann Masten (2001; Masten & Coatsworth, 1998). Studies quite consistently describe the qualities of the child and environment that are associated with better outcomes despite considerable stress. Major predictors of resilience are caring relationships with adults, most often parents; good intellectual and cognitive functioning, which relate to good self-regulation; and motivation to learn and master the environment. In fact, the same assets relate to competence in children and adolescents under typical circumstances. For example, a close, affectionate bond with parents is linked to better outcomes in both people who are at risk and individuals who are not under excessive stress. Parenting has a protective function both physically and emotionally. Effective parenting involves monitoring children, giving support and warmth, and maintaining reasonable discipline. This type of parenting helps children develop and maintain their

According to Ann Masten, a noted researcher in the area of resilience, good family relationships allow adolescents to retain the resources needed to cope with stress.

problem-solving skills, which are then present and available in the face of threat. Good intellectual skills, which relate to better school achievement, and competent verbal skills allow adolescents to express themselves better and communicate with others, and better problem-solving abilities allow adolescents to cope more effectively with stress.

Masten notes that resilient children and adolescents do not have any mysterious qualities, but rather they have obtained and retained important resources that protect them and enable them to cope better with stress. Competency develops in the midst of adversity when fundamental social and cognitive abilities that generally foster competence are available. Poor results ensue only if these elements, which include the parent-child relationship and intellectual skills, are severely hampered or damaged, or if the adversity exceeds the ability to cope.

Resilience, then, is a common phenomenon arising from typical adaptive processes. The true threats to development are the ones that place the caregiver-child relationship and intellectual skills in jeopardy. Masten does admit that in specific instances, extraordinary talents or good fortune can play a key role in resilience, but normal processes account for most children and adolescents who are resilient.

Long-Term Outcomes for Stress-Resilient Adolescents

The research on stress-resilient children and adolescents is impressive, but what is the long-term outcome for such adolescents? Four outcomes are possible: (1) no noticeable effect of stress; (2) a short-term effect but no long-term effect; (3) a delayed effect, meaning that there is no short-term effect of the stress, but there is a long-term effect; and (4) both short-term and long-term effects. When researchers followed adolescents between 11 and 15 years of age (average age, 13 years) for 6 years, they found a relationship between cumulative risk factors in the family during adolescence and achievement problems and a delayed effect for anxiety problems and depression (see Figure 13.1). As the number of stressors increased, so did vulnerability to internalizing and externalizing problems later on. In each case a change from three to four stressors led to a significant increase in problems 6 years later. An increase from three to four risk factors related to a significant decrease in academic achievement during adolescence, and academic achievement problems continued. Researchers suggest that some adolescents may initially seem to handle stress well, but their resources may be eventually stretched and finally depleted (Forehand et al., 1998).

Of course, many researchers find that multiple stressors have a more immediate effect on youth (Smith & Carlson, 1997). Single risk factors rarely determine later outcomes. However, as the stressors add up, adolescents appear to become less resilient. Some research indicates that experiencing four or more simultaneous stressors is associated with a tenfold increase in disorders compared with experiencing none of the risk factors or situations that reflect them (Rutter, 1978). Many home-based stressors, such as divorce, cascade into multiple stressors, making it more difficult for the adolescent to deal with the problems. For example, parents' divorce may lead to attending a different school if the family moves, adjusting to fewer resources, getting less attention, and facing increased demands for helping at home. Table 13.1 shows some warning signs of stress-related problems.

Table 13.1

Warning Signs of Stress-Related Problems

There are many signs that a person may be adversely affected by stress. The following signs may indicate that positive action is required to better cope with stress.

Category	Sign
Physical signs	Headaches
	Upset stomach
	Muscle tightness in neck or back
	Constant fatigue
Behavioral changes	Quick tears
	Feelings of depression or fear
	Confusion
	Talking too fast or too slowly
	A sudden turn to reckless behavior
	Irritability
	More frequent accidents or errors
	Nervous habits
Changes in daily habits	Sleeping too much or too little
	Nightmares
	Decreased ability to work or concentrate
	Changes in eating habits

Source: Adapted from Farrington (1996).

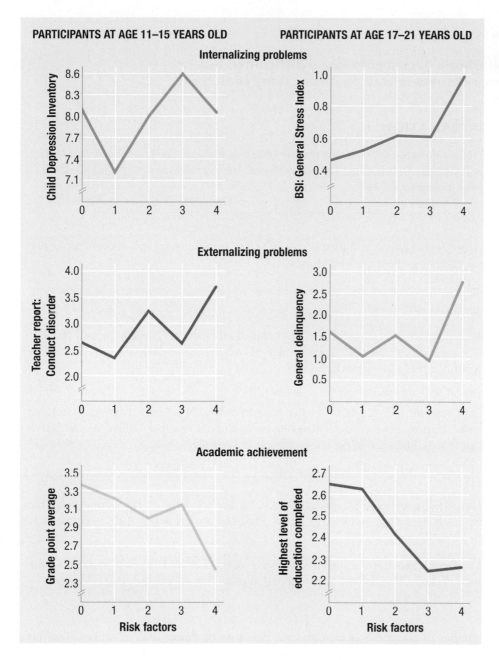

PARTICIPANTS AT AGE 11–15 YEARS OLD

PARTICIPANTS AT AGE 17–21 YEARS OLD

Internalizing problems

Externalizing problems

Academic achievement

Figure 13.1

The Relationship Between Number of Family Risk Factors and Three Areas of Psychosocial Adjustment During Adolescence

Researchers measured five stressors in a sample of adolescents 11 to 15 years old: (1) parental marital status, (2) parental depressive mood, (3) maternal physical health problems, (4) maternal depressive mood, and (5) mother-adolescent relationship problems. They determined measures of depression, conduct disorders (from a checklist administered to teachers), and academic progress. They again tested the same adolescents 6 years later. For the internalizing and externalizing measures, higher values mean greater problems. For the measures of academic achievement, lower values indicate less progress. The researchers found a delayed action effect for internalizing and externalizing problems as a number of stressors increased and evidence for immediate (as well as long-term) academic problems with an increase in the number of stressors.

Source: Adapted from Forehand, Biggar, & Kotchick (1998), p. 124.

Coping with Stress

The effects of stress on an adolescent may be reduced in three ways: (1) alter the adolescent's exposure to the stressor; (2) alter the meaning of the experience to the teen, that is, help the adolescent see it in a different way; or (3) help the adolescent develop better coping skills. It is difficult to alter the adolescent's exposure to a stressor. Adolescents are more aware of, and more sensitive to, their environments than younger children. However, parents may be able to ease the pressure on adolescents by not fighting in front of them or helping them organize their time. Because multiple stressors seem to be most destructive, allowing time for adolescents to adjust to a stress, such as parental divorce, is desirable.

It is more practical to teach adolescents to perceive a stressor in a different way and develop better ways of dealing with stressors. For example, adults might teach teens to view their difficulty mastering a subject as a challenge rather than a catastrophe or personal failure. An adolescent may feel overwhelmed by the

At a Glance 13.1 Stress

KEY POINT: Stress is a major contributor to many emotional difficulties, but despite the prevalence of stress-related problems, many adolescents cope well with stress.

SUPPORTING POINTS	EXPLANATION
Stress is an unpleasant state of arousal that occurs when people perceive that an event or condition threatens their ability to effectively and comfortably cope with the situation.	Situations or events that cause stress are known as *stressors*. The same stressor may affect two adolescents differently. The perception of stress is most important, and adolescents differ in their coping skills.
Adolescence is a particularly stressful period.	Many life changes occur during adolescence, and transitions to new schools and greater expectations increase the level of stress.
High stress levels are related to many negative outcomes.	High levels of stress are related to illness, school maladjustment, poor motivation, anxiety, and depression.
Females and members of minority groups report more stress than males and adolescents from European backgrounds.	Women report more stressors, with the areas of interpersonal functioning and physical appearance most stressful. Poverty may also cause the increased stress that some minority group adolescents face.
Stress-resilient, or stress-resistant, individuals meet their developmental challenges well and do not show psychopathology despite significant stress.	Stress-resilient individuals have easy temperaments, have good social skills, receive social support, have good relationships with parents or other adults, use an active coping style, and show better self-regulation and cognitive skills.
Stress resilience is a normal expression of the average individual's ability to cope with stress.	Ann Masten argues that adolescents are resilient as long as the normal adaptive processes are not compromised by lack of adult care or poor intellectual development.
Adolescents can learn to deal more effectively with stress.	Adolescents can learn to perceive stressors differently and develop more adequate planning skills. Exercise and social support also can help reduce the effects of stress.

number of assignments due and the pressure of doing well in school. Teaching planning skills may help in this case. Adolescents can be taught to use active coping strategies, such as seeking out information. They can also learn to look at events from a different perspective, to seek support when necessary, and to differentiate between what they can change and what they cannot. Many adolescents do not get enough exercise or sleep, and a change in daily routine may help allow for more exercise and adequate rest and sleep (see "Physical Development" for more information about sleep and exercise needs during adolescence). Some people also find that spiritual and religious beliefs are helpful in times of stress.

Two types of coping have been isolated (Lazarus & Folkman, 1984). **Problem-directed coping** involves confronting a problem directly, whereas **emotion-focused coping** aims to reduce the discomfort associated with the stress. For example, if the stress is based on making a decision about which college to attend, a problem-directed strategy is possible. An adolescent may collect information in various ways and visit colleges. However, when individuals can do little to change the stressful situation, they may counter the stress with activities that make them feel better but do not change the stressor. For example, adolescents cannot change the fact that their parents are not getting along. They may counter the stress by talking out their feelings, learning to relax, or even focusing

problem-directed coping Strategies of coping with stress that involve actively confronting the problem in an effort to solve it.

emotion-focused coping Strategies of coping with stress that focus on reducing the discomfort associated with stress.

on other activities. They can actively seek out satisfying relationships and engage in meaningful and enjoyable activities. Finding healthy ways of actively coping with stressors helps adolescents become more capable of handling the increased stress of adolescence and ready to tackle the stresses of adulthood. *(For a review of this section, see At A Glance 13.1.)*

INTERNALIZING BEHAVIORS AND DISORDERS

We have seen how stress relates to physical and emotional problems and that some people cope better with stress than others. It may be difficult to know when a problem reaches the point at which it is clinically significant. Everyone is anxious or sad at some time, but when do such difficulties become severe enough to merit a diagnosis? When does the feeling of sadness become a disorder called *depression?* A **disorder** is defined as a clinically significant behavioral or psychological group of symptoms that is associated with distress (painful symptoms), disability, or an important loss of freedom (American Psychiatric Association, 2000). The term **disability** refers to an impairment in one or more important areas of functioning. Some disabilities may affect the individual's ability to learn and others, the individual's physical abilities.

The most common way to categorize disorders is to use a system devised by the American Psychiatric Association and found in the *Diagnostic and Statistical Manual of Mental Disorders,* 4th edition, text revision *(DSM-IV-TR).* The system divides disorders into types based on their defining features, and a person must show certain behaviors to be diagnosed with the disorder. For example, an individual with anorexia nervosa, an eating disorder in which individuals literally starve themselves, would have to meet four criteria to receive this diagnosis. *DSM* acknowledges the part stress plays in illness, and the manual includes a diagnostic category titled "Psychological Factors Affecting Medical Condition."

Not every psychologist agrees with the *categorical approach,* in which a person either has the disorder or does not. Another way to look at problems is to use a *dimensional approach,* which sees the difference between people with and without a disorder in terms of the severity or intensity of the symptoms rather than the kind of symptoms shown. Depression provides a good example. Under a categorical system, a teenager must satisfy certain criteria to receive the diagnosis of major depression. Under a dimensional approach, depressive symptoms would be rated on a continuum from 1 (very little) to 10 (extreme). A dimensional system can use a cutoff or threshold, if desired, to determine who does or does not have a significant problem (for example, a cutoff of 7 or more on the scale). A dimensional system is especially useful when investigating disorders with no absolute boundaries, such as disorders involving anxiety and depression. The dimensional approach allows people to receive help even if their symptoms fall below the threshold level for a categorical system. For example, a person who satisfies three of the four criteria might not be considered to have the disorder under a categorical system.

The categorical system also has advantages. Categorical labels are familiar, and some disorders cannot easily be seen in terms of a continuum. Although this chapter uses a categorical approach, it recognizes that some adolescents may show symptoms that do not completely satisfy the *DSM* criteria and may still require counseling. For example, an individual adversely affected by anxiety may not meet the *DSM* criteria for an anxiety disorder but still require help.

Psychologists often categorize conditions that involve aggression and acting out as **externalizing disorders;** these conditions will be discussed in "Drug Use and Violence." People also experience **internalizing disorders,** such as disorders involving anxiety and depression. These disorders are directed inward. Whereas externalizing disorders result from undercontrolled behavior, internalizing dis-

disorder A clinically significant behavioral or psychological group of symptoms that is associated with distress (painful symptoms), disability, or an important loss of freedom.

disability An impairment in one or more important areas of functioning.

externalizing disorders Disorders in which problems such as fighting, disobedience, and destructiveness seem directed at others.

internalizing disorders Disorders, such as anxiety, depression, and withdrawal, that have their greatest effect on the individual rather than on others in the environment.

orders are associated with overcontrolled behavior. Such disorders are often far less obvious to the casual observer, but they present major challenges for the adolescent (Reynolds, 1992).

Everyone feels anxious at one time or another. Psychologists define **anxiety** as an unpleasant emotional state of apprehension, fear, and/or worry and that is accompanied by an increase in physiological arousal. Asking someone out or getting ready to take a big test are both anxiety-provoking situations. Most people have some fears; not everyone likes spiders or heights, for example. However, for some adolescents, anxiety can become more than a transient problem. These adolescents may suffer from phobias (irrational fears), panic attacks, or other forms of anxiety that affect their daily lives. Generally, studies find that girls report more fears and a greater intensity of fear than boys (King et al., 1989). Of course, gender-role expectations may confound the results; boys may think it is not "manly" to admit to such fears.

Sometimes anxiety involves meeting new people and participating in new activities, which can add to the stress of everyday life and make interpersonal relationships more difficult. The following discussion focuses on two such problems, shyness and social phobia.

Shyness

Shyness itself is *not* considered a disorder. It is not mentioned in the *DSM* at all. Yet shyness is bothersome for the more than 40 percent of the public who claim they are sometimes shy (Carducci, 2000). Shyness is the tendency to avoid others, as well as uneasiness and stress when socializing. Shy people often do not make eye contact, retreat when spoken to, and speak very softly. People are shy for many reasons. Many prefer to do things by themselves, lack self-confidence or social skills, and feel at risk for being embarrassed.

The fact that 40 percent of all people claim they are sometimes shy always surprises readers; it seems inflated. However, there are two types of shyness. Only about 15 to 20 percent of all individuals claiming to be shy are *publicly shy;* that is, they fit the stereotype of ill-at-ease people who avoid social events, stumble over words, and express their shyness behaviorally. The rest are *privately shy;* in other words, they behave in the usual fashion but feel shyness in a pounding heart and sweating when meeting people, and they chide themselves for being inept. They often evaluate whether the person they are talking to really likes them after all (Carducci & Zimbardo, 1995). Many have learned to hide their shyness and even become extroverts, such as politicians, entertainers, and teachers. They have learned to act outgoing. What unites shy people of both types is acute self-consciousness.

Shyness is not considered an emotional disorder. However, many shy people are bothered by their social anxiety.

anxiety An unpleasant emotional state of apprehension, fear, and/or worry that is accompanied by an increase in physiological arousal.

Shy people often react to fears of being evaluated. Many people have these fears to some extent, but shy people often have greater fears of appearing inadequate, being embarrassed, or being ridiculed. They are excessively self-conscious; they constantly evaluate themselves negatively and are preoccupied with what others think of them (Carducci & Zimbardo, 1995; Henderson & Zimbardo, 1998). Shy adolescents often make unrealistic social comparisons. In a room filled with people, for example, they compare themselves with the adolescent who is the life of the party (Carducci, 2000). This tendency causes them to appraise themselves even more negatively.

Shy individuals also show a distortion in thinking, as they blame themselves whenever an encounter does not go well. They are more likely to accept negative feedback about themselves (Shepperd, Arkin, & Slaughter, 1995). They may freeze up in conversation. Some shy people simply lack social skills, for example, not knowing how to enter into a conversation when two people they know are conversing in the schoolyard.

Shyness increases in formal settings and with unfamiliar people. Shy individuals are not overconcerned with their own thoughts but rather are more aware of themselves as a social object of evaluation. They often are very concerned about how others see them and what others think about them, and they worry about saying the wrong thing. They see themselves as feeling different from others, whereas people who are not shy assume others feel the same way in the same situation (Zimbardo, 1977). Shy people tend to consider their social anxiety a personality trait, and it may become part of their self-concept. In other words, shy people believe their anxiety is coming from their personality—from themselves—whereas people who are not shy believe their anxiety is situationally based. Shy persons often do not have high self-esteem, because they give themselves no credit and never believe failure was due to circumstances. Shyness, then, is a personal problem arising from characteristics such as self-consciousness, low self-esteem, and anticipation of rejection (Carducci, 2000).

Is being shy really a problem? Shyness is a personality trait and should not be "pathologized," that is, treated like an emotional disorder. Yet children and adolescents who are shy recognize their shyness as a difficulty. Most studies show that children and adolescents would rather not be shy (Carducci, 2000). Shy adolescents do not see shyness as a desirable personality trait.

Some psychologists argue that shyness can be more serious than previously thought. Shy people have lower self-esteem, are lonelier, and are more likely to be depressed (Paulhus & Morgan, 1997). They have more difficulty making new friends (Carducci & Zimbardo, 1995). Shy adolescents do not participate as much in sports, probably because they feel uncomfortable in groups, and interacting in social situations causes anxiety (Page & Zarco, 2001). Shy girls often form a few close relationships with other girls, but shy boys may engage in risky behavior to garner attention. If they have difficulty talking to someone they may become frustrated and angry, and their rejection by others may result in alienation (Gard, 2000). They may also turn to alcohol or drugs as a way to ease their social anxieties. Shy men marry later, have less stable marriages, and delay settling into a career (Caspi, Elder, & Bem, 1988). Others tend to rate them as less intelligent, even though they certainly are not (Paulhus & Morgan, 1997).

Although adolescents may feel imprisoned by their shyness, there is nothing clinically wrong with being shy. However, because adolescents often do not see shyness as a desirable trait, they may seek or accept help. For example, shy adolescents may be helped by social skills training and then reinforced in their efforts to begin a conversation with other students or attend a public function.

Social Phobia

A relatively small number of teens suffer from a persistent and intense fear of being in a social situation, called **social phobia.** They are withdrawn and anxious. They feel utterly alone and solitary, refusing invitations to attend parties because of their social fears (*Harvard Mental Health Letter,* 1998).

social phobia A classification of emotional disorder in which an individual experiences persistent and intense anxiety during social situations that prevents the individual from functioning effectively in the environment.

The characteristic that distinguishes a social phobia from shyness is the degree of impairment (Walsh, 2002). Shy teens, like adolescents with social phobia, may experience anxiety in social situations, but they do not become so distressed that their academic, interpersonal, or occupational functions are severely impaired. People with social phobia show the same concerns as people who are very shy, but the intensity, extreme reactions, and irrationality of their reactions set them apart. Adolescents with social phobia may completely avoid eating in public places and avoid public situations at all cost. Teenagers considered shy do not show as intense a reaction.

About 1 percent of all adolescents experience tremendous and persistent anxiety in situations where they are exposed to unfamiliar people or are being evaluated by others (Kashani & Orvaschel, 1990). This social anxiety occurs in peer settings, not just with unfamiliar adults. They may fear public speaking because of a concern that others will notice their trembling hands or experience extreme anxiety when conversing with others because they are afraid they will appear foolish or say the wrong thing (American Psychiatric Association, 2000). Often, they experience physical symptoms such as palpitations and sweating in feared social situations (Beidel & Randall, 1994). Anticipatory anxiety also may occur in advance of the social situation. This condition interferes with the formation of interpersonal relationships and academic progress. Adolescents with social phobias may avoid the feared situations or force themselves to endure them, but with great anxiety (Wicks-Nelson & Israel, 2000).

The characteristics of social phobia in adolescence are not always clear, because social anxiety is common at that age. Some experts argue that to earn the diagnosis, the condition's severity must be intense, and the anxiety must interfere significantly with the individual's life (D.B. Clark et al., 1994). Individuals with social phobia often meet the criteria for other anxiety disorders and may also experience depression. Some authorities argue that it may be underdiagnosed in adolescents. Adults with social phobia often say that the onset was in their mid-teens, often emerging out of childhood shyness, and others report an even earlier onset.

The cause of social phobia is still not well established. A poor social experience may cause anxiety, which then may lead the teen to avoid social situations and not to develop social skills. The avoidance continues and is enhanced as adolescence progresses and self-awareness increases. Another possibility is that these children and adolescents may not have the social skills necessary to interact successfully with others. In addition, a genetic involvement may make some children and adolescents more vulnerable to social phobia than others.

Depression in Adolescence

Everyone is unhappy at times. The adolescent who does not make the basketball team, breaks up with a romantic partner, says something silly and becomes angry at herself, or fails a test that he should have passed experiences sadness and disappointment. **Depression** is not just a feeling of sadness, though. It involves cognitive, motivational, and physical symptoms as well (see Table 13.2). The most common emotional symptom is a mood of unhappiness and dejection, as well as an inability to find any pleasure in activities. Motivational symptoms include withdrawal from interpersonal relationships, a lack of initiative, and sometimes, suicidal thoughts. The physical symptoms involve chronic fatigue and loss of energy. Sleep disorders and somatic complaints, such as headaches and stomachaches, are common. Cognitive symptoms include hopelessness and a negative attitude toward oneself and the future. Depressed people evaluate situations negatively and engage in self-blame.

Depression is the most common diagnosis for adolescents referred to mental health clinics. Depressed adolescents show impaired functioning in their relationships with others and their school performance (Birmaher et al., 1996). Adolescent depression is a significant predictor of adult depression. Adolescents with a major depressive disorder are 2.2 times more likely to experience a

depression A disorder marked by sadness, despair, low self-esteem, and loss of interest in usually satisfying activities.

Depression is a significant problem among adolescents and is the most common diagnosis for adolescents referred to mental health clinics.

Table 13.2

Symptoms of Depression

Most people understand that sadness is a prime symptom of depression, but depression has cognitive, motivational, and physical symptoms as well as emotional symptoms.

Type of Symptom	Example
Emotional	Feelings of dejection[a], sadness, loneliness, agitation, unhappiness
	Feelings of worthlessness or inappropriate guilt; a lack of interest or pleasure in activities
Cognitive	Hopelessness; helplessness; a negative attitude toward oneself, the world, and one's future
	Blaming oneself for everything
Motivational	Withdrawal from interpersonal relationships, significant changes in appetite, a lack of initiative, suicidal thoughts
Physical	Chronic fatigue, loss of energy, sleep problems (including insomnia or sleeping too much), somatic complaints

[a] In children and adolescents, the mood may be irritable.

depressive episode in early adulthood than adolescents who do not have a major depressive disorder (Weissman et al., 1999).

Depressed adolescents often have poor self-esteem and a poor sense of self-efficacy (Brage & Meredith, 1994; Fleming, Boyle, & Offord, 1993). Depression occurs along with a number of other difficulties, such as conduct disorders, eating disorders, substance abuse disorders, and very commonly, anxiety disorders (Angold, Costello, & Erkanli, 1999). Between 40 and 70 percent of depressed adolescents have some additional emotional disorder (Birmaher et al., 1996).

The *DSM*'s diagnostic category of **major depressive disorder** (also called a *major depressive episode)* refers to a group of symptoms, one of which must be depressed mood (or irritability, in adolescents) or diminished interest or pleasure in almost all activities for at least 2 weeks. Other possible symptoms include significant weight loss or weight gain, insomnia or sleeping too much, agitation, fatigue, feelings of worthlessness or guilt, diminished ability to think or concentrate, and recurrent thoughts of death. Major depressive disorder can be a recurrent problem; often people have bouts of such depression throughout the years (Birmaher et al., 1996). Another category, **dysthymic disorder,** involves longer bouts with depressive mood. The individual shows a depressed mood for most of the day, for more days than not, and for at least 1 year in children and adolescents (2 years in adults). Again, the mood can be irritable instead of depressed in children and adolescents. Other symptoms are similar to those of major depressive disorder. Whereas major depressive disorder involves depression that is severe and brief, people with dysthymic disorder show milder, but more prolonged, depression.

The classification of children and adolescents with depression is similar to the adult description, with a few differences. Adolescents show more sleep and appetite disorders, delusions, suicidal thoughts and attempts, and impairment of functioning than younger children. Also, children and adolescents with depression are more irritable than adults with the condition (American Academy of Child and Adolescent Psychiatry, 1998).

Prevalence of Depression in Adolescence Depression is very uncommon in preschool children, in whom its incidence is about 1 percent, according to most studies. Estimates rise to about 2 percent or even 3 percent in

major depressive disorder A form of depression typified by a distinct period of at least 2 weeks of moderate to severe symptoms.

dysthymic disorder A category of depression that involves mild, prolonged depression.

middle childhood (Cohen et al., 1993). In adolescence, the percentages climb to rates similar to adult rates: between 4 and 8 percent, if both major depression and dysthymic disorder are combined (Cooper & Goodyer, 1993). The incidence markedly increases between the ages of 13 and 15 years, reaches a peak around 17 to 18 years, and then stabilizes at the adult rate (Marcotte, 1996). This increase with age may be due to physiological changes, increased social and academic demands, greater exposure to negative events, and cognitive changes in thinking that occur during adolescence (American Academy of Child and Adolescent Psychiatry, 1998).

The rates of depression in adolescence are much higher if individuals who have depressed mood but who do not meet the stringent requirements for being clinically depressed are added to people who fall under this category. When depression is defined somewhat less clinically, in terms of symptoms such as painful emotion and negative mood and thoughts, as many as 40 percent of 14- to 15-year-olds report depression and dysphoria (McFarlane et al., 1994); some estimates are as high as 65 percent (Varley, 2002). Approximately a third of the adolescent population not receiving any professional services for depression can be considered mildly to severely depressed (Hammond & Romney, 1995). Although depression is found in every economic class, it is more common among the poor (Roberts, Roberts, & Chen, 1997). African Americans have a higher rate of depression than whites, and Mexican Americans have a higher rate than African Americans. The reason may be partly cultural; the belief in fate that is part of the Mexican culture may lead to increased depression rates. The culture stresses external control, and this focus may impair coping abilities.

Depression is increasing in our society. There is evidence that each successive generation since 1940 is at greater risk for depressive disorders and that these disorders are being recognized at younger ages. To date, no one knows why (American Academy of Child and Adolescent Psychiatry, 1998). Some argue that changes in our society are partly to blame, because there is less permanence. Adolescents are facing greater challenges, and families are somewhat more scattered and less capable of giving support.

What Causes Depression?   Depression has many causes, and an individual may be depressed for more than one reason. One of the problems in describing the causes of depression is that it is difficult to know whether some of the factors are causes or simply correlates (that is, factors that occur along with depression). Does a particular thinking pattern cause depression, or is it a symptom of depression? Many of the theoretical approaches described in "The Scientific Approach to Adolescence" contribute to our understanding of depression.

SEPARATION AND LOSS   A common reason for depression is separation or loss. It is natural for adolescents to begin and end romantic relationships. Separation from family and loved ones is also more common in adolescence than earlier. Psychoanalytically oriented psychologists consider separation and loss as important factors in depression (Rendleman & Walkup, 1997). Often separation and loss lead to aggressive and hostile feelings toward the lost object, and individuals may turn their anger against themselves, causing depression. An adolescent may begin by blaming a poor grade on the teacher or blaming unpopularity on a peer and then slowly change to believe that these problems are due to poor test preparation or some of their own behaviors; the adolescent turns the anger on the self and becomes depressed. Loneliness, which is relatively common in adolescence, is also related to feelings of depression (Brage & Meredith, 1994).

BEHAVIORAL PERSPECTIVE   Behaviorists argue that a lack of positive reinforcement and the absence of pleasant events cause depression (Lewinsohn, 1974). Depressed individuals do not receive positive reinforcement from others and receive more criticism. An absence of pleasant events may set in motion a downward spiral. The fewer events someone enjoys, the more depressed the individual may feel and the less likely to take the initiative to engage in other activities

(Lewinsohn & Graf, 1973). Alternatively, the adolescent's poor interpersonal skills may lead to a loss of reinforcement from parents and peers. Unpopular and rejected adolescents are often at risk for depression.

NOTHING EVER TURNS OUT WELL: COGNITIVE EXPLANATIONS Cognitive explanations for depression emphasize the importance of adolescent thought patterns (Garber & Hilsman, 1992). This approach has become more popular over the past 30 years.

LEARNED HELPLESSNESS: I CAN'T DO ANYTHING, SO WHY TRY? **Learned helplessness** is the belief that no action can help, so the individual might as well give up trying to make anything better (Seligman, 1974). When people believe it doesn't matter how or whether they respond to a situation, they may stop trying. Students show learned helplessness when they quit studying because they don't believe they can pass a course, or they believe it makes no difference whether they go somewhere or not because they won't make any friends or meet anyone they like. "I can't succeed with _____ no matter what I do, so I might as well just do nothing (or watch television)" is a common line of thinking for individuals showing learned helplessness. They see no relationship between what they do and the consequences of their actions. If they later have an opportunity to exercise control, they behave as if they were helpless. One of the frustrating things about this pattern of thinking is that a course of action that would help or even solve the individual's problem is often obvious to an outsider, but not to the depressed individual. Symptoms of depression are commonly found in people who give up and who believe there is nothing they can do.

Why do some people give up while others forge ahead and are more active? *Attributional style* seems to be an important key (Alloy, Lipman, & Abramson, 1992; Seligman & Peterson, 1986). When something happens, an individual attributes a cause to that event. Say a teen applies for an internship and is rejected. He may attribute the rejection to himself and his poor interview or to the fact that someone may have had better qualifications. He may say that he is always rejected or believe that this sort of rejection happens to everyone once in a while. He may generalize the rejection to other activities or believe it is isolated and occurred in this one area. People just don't shrug their shoulders in response to an event; they go through a complex cognitive process to understand what caused it.

Psychologists identify three different types of attributions (see Figure 13.2). First, attribution can either be *internal* or *external*. That is, individuals can place blame for a situation on either themselves (internal attribution) or others (external attribution). Internal attribution is more likely than external attribution to lead to depression. Adolescents are more likely to be upset if they fail math despite their best efforts, but they probably can deal with the failure better if everyone else is having difficulty in the class, the teacher is not good, and the work is very hard.

Attribution may also be either *global* or *specific*. Individuals may construe a problem as either broadly or narrowly related to their efforts. Global attributions are more likely than narrow attributions to relate to depression. For instance, a teen is more likely to feel depressed if she sees a failure as evidence that she can't do anything right. A specific attribution, such as "I'm just not great in art, but I'm good at other things," is less damaging to self-esteem and less likely to lead to depression.

Figure 13.2
Attributions That May Lead to Depression
Attributing a failure or other negative happening to internal, global, and stable factors is more likely to lead to depression.

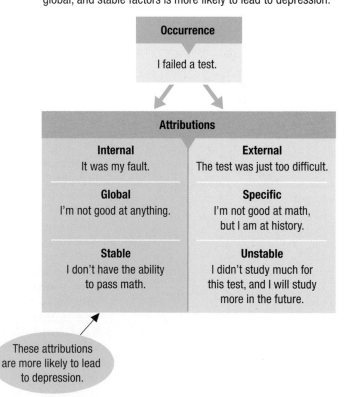

learned helplessness The learned inability to overcome obstacles, which involves the belief that one cannot do anything to improve one's lot and leads to depression.

Third, attributions may be *stable* or *unstable*. A teen may attribute poor performance to ability (a stable attribute) or to not sleeping last night because of concern over a friend's problem (an unstable, changing attribution). Attributing a failure to a stable cause is more likely to lead to depression.

The attributions people make influence whether they experience depression (Abramson, Seligman, & Teasdale, 1978; Jacobson et al., 1996). Adolescents with depression are likely to make more internal, stable, and global attributions for negative events and more external, unstable, specific attributions for positive events than are nondepressed teens (Gladstone & Kaslow, 1995).

BECK'S THEORY OF DEPRESSION   Another way of looking at the thought patterns of depressed adolescents emphasizes the way they look at the world. Aaron Beck (1970; Sacco & Beck, 1995) uses the concepts of schema, cognitive errors and distortions, and the negative cognitive triad to explain the thought processes of depressed people. The negative cognitive triad is the depressed adolescent's negative view of the self, the world, and the future.

A schema, as used here, is an organized representation of past experiences and knowledge that guides the processing of new information (Garber & Hilsman, 1992). Depressed people interpret events as negative—in a way that supports their view that they are inadequate. Suppose an adolescent girl with a vulnerability in the domain of physical attractiveness and body satisfaction faces a negative event, such as a classmate criticizing her weight or hairstyle. If she has a pessimistic orientation, she may attribute these comments to stable and global causes ("I will always be heavy and not pretty") and infer that negative consequences will follow ("I will never go to the prom or get married"). Her interpretation may lead to a negative self-concept ("I am worthless") (Hankin & Abramson, 2001).

Depressed people also show distortions in thinking, including self-defeating, pessimistic attitudes and thought patterns. They do not accept compliments. When shown proof that they are good students, good friends, good workers, or good athletes, depressed individuals will note an isolated criticism from a teacher, parent, or friend in the past. Instead of seeing the positive, depressed adolescents concentrate on the negative aspects of life, overgeneralizing from one less-than-perfect situation to all others (Beck, 1967). They often anticipate negative outcomes, exaggerate them, and assume that other events will also be negative—a form of overgeneralization. They take responsibility for these negative events and say they are to blame (a tendency called *personalizing*).

Depressed adolescents tend to see mildly negative events as catastrophes ("It is horrible that I didn't have a date on Saturday night"), and they show low frustration tolerance ("I can't stand some things in school"). They also make absolute demands on themselves ("I should be liked by everyone"), and sometimes on others ("My family should give me 100 percent support in what I want to do"). They tend to evaluate themselves on the basis of a specific behavior, believing that a person who makes mistakes is a bad person (Demaria, Kassinove, & Dill, 1989).

Depressed people often distort reality; they devalue themselves and their accomplishments, see the environment in negative terms, and fail to see any positive events. They make unrealistic demands on themselves. Depression is related to low self-esteem, high self-criticism, significant cognitive distortion, and a feeling of lacking control over negative events. Individuals who are exposed to stressful events and have negative styles of interpreting and coping with stress are at high risk of developing depressive symptoms.

Negative schemata (the plural of schema) and distortions and errors in thinking maintain what Beck calls the negative cognitive triad—that is, the depressed person's negative view of the self, the world, and the future. Negative thoughts about oneself (I'm not good at anything), a pessimistic view of the world (No one cares about me), and negative views of the future (nothing good will ever happen to me; there is little hope for the future) set the stage for depression.

This adolescent is being given a number of positive comments, but if the teen has a negative outlook on life she will remember the one negative comment among the many positive ones and feel somewhat sad after the evaluation.

At this point, psychologists are not certain how children and adolescents develop these negative thought patterns. Perhaps these ways of thinking are modeled in the environment. Perhaps experiences of criticism and rejection that appear uncontrollable may lead to the development of such cognitive distortions (Birmaher et al., 1996).

FAMILY DIFFICULTIES   Family difficulties also may set the stage for depression. For example, depressed adults' reports of their own childhood often involve rejection by parents, neglect, or overcontrol. Studies of children and adolescents find a generally negative quality to childhood interactions with adults (Hammen, 1991). Perhaps these negative interactions cause the child or adolescent to feel unloved or insecure. Parents of depressed children and adolescents may also be depressed or have other psychiatric or medical illnesses that reduce their effectiveness as parents. Early adverse experiences, such as parental death or separation, set the stage for an increase in depressive risk (American Academy of Child and Adolescent Psychiatry, 1998).

It would be wrong to automatically blame family interactions for depression, however. Parenting problems may arise from parental interactions with a depressed or irritable child; it is difficult to determine cause and effect. In addition, negative parental interactions may lead to many other problems besides depression. It may be best to say that they set the stage for the development of depressive thoughts and feelings. And positive parent-child relationships buffer the adolescent from depression (Wong & Wiest, 1999).

BIOLOGICAL EXPLANATIONS   Some evidence exists for moderate genetic influence in major depression, although the evidence is not entirely clear (Plomin et al., 1997; Rutter et al., 1999). Many people do not understand that genetic factors may increase the risk of depression somewhat but do not cause depression in the way that genetic factors influence hair color, eye color, or even height. Rather, genetic factors moderately increase the risk of depression. So far, researchers have found no particular gene that is strongly linked to depression. Studies show that environmental factors are important as well. Individuals with high genetic risk appear to be more sensitive to the effects of adverse environments than people with low risk (Birmaher et al., 1996).

Genetic factors influence behavior through physiology. Some evidence indicates that neurotransmitters (chemical substances that allow the transmission of electrical impulses between neurons) are involved. The neurotransmitters serotonin and norepinephrine appear to be most important (Garrett, 2003). Many of the medications that help people with depression increase the activity of these neurotransmitters, especially serotonin. Unfortunately, demonstrating whether neurotransmitter activity levels cause or are the effect of depression is difficult. Although psychologists know that neurotransmitters are involved, they do not fully understand their role in depression. One problem is that one depressed person might show different neurotransmitter abnormalities than another depressed person, and mood seems to be caused by a combination of neurotransmitters (Kalat, 2001).

In fact, depression in children and adolescents is even more confusing. Very little research on the physiological factors influencing depression has been conducted on children and adolescents. It is known that they can differ significantly in their reactions to medication and physiological functioning compared with adults. Researchers have found both similarities and differences in biological aspects of depression between children and adolescents on the one hand and adults on the other hand (Rendleman & Walkup, 1997).

Gender Differences in Depression One of the most startling research findings in adolescent depression is the sharp gender difference. Most studies find either no gender differences for depression in middle childhood or find that boys are perhaps a bit more likely to be depressed (Marcotte, Alain, & Gosselin, 1999). Beginning in adolescence, though, at least twice as many females as males are depressed (Hankin & Abramson, 2001; Marcotte et al., 2002). This finding applies to minority groups as well (Roberts et al., 1997). The discrepancy appears at 14 to 15 years of age and remains throughout adulthood.

The cause of this gender difference is controversial. Generally, explanations for different rates of depression among males and females look at gender differences in factors relating to vulnerability to depression and negative life events. Teenage girls report more negative events than boys (Davies & Windle, 1997). Girls report more negative interpersonal events, especially peer-related events, whereas boys report more negative school events (Rudolph & Hammen, 1999).

Teenage girls are also more likely to experience negative evaluations in the physical realm, which creates a vulnerability to depression. The interpersonal realm may be more important to girls than to boys; that is, girls are socialized to consider relationships as more important than are boys (Cyranowski et al., 2000). Interpersonal relationships are common sources of stress to all teenagers, and especially teenage girls, who are more likely to define themselves in terms of their success or failure in such relationships. Loneliness is another important determinant of depression, and female adolescents are lonelier than male adolescents (Brage & Meredith, 1994). Furthermore, teenage girls are more likely to be critical of themselves than teenage boys in the physical realm.

Many other factors may explain gender differences in depression. Adolescents may fall back on gender-stereotyped ways, which may cause more difficulties for some females. Males are traditionally more agentic or efficacious (seen as getting things for themselves). Indeed, female adolescents who score somewhat higher on masculinity scales reflecting a sense of efficacy and control report lower levels of depression, especially if they come from families in which parents exhibit egalitarian marital roles (Marcotte et al., 1999; Obeidallah, McHale, & Silbereisen, 1996). Women generally have lower expectations than men regarding their ability to control important events. Compared with men, women are also more dependent on others for self-worth (Nolen-Hoeksema & Girgus, 1994).

Teenage girls also show more self-criticism and depressive styles of thinking, including preoccupation about feelings of competence and loss of self-esteem (Hankin & Abramson, 2001; Marcotte et al., 1999). In addition, they are more likely than males to engage in rumination, or to focus on their selves and their negative feelings (Nolen-Hoeksema, 1991; Nolen-Hoeksema, Larson, & Grayson, 1999). Self-focused criticism, in turn, may increase or maintain a depressed mood and generate less effective solutions to problems (Lyubomirsky & Nolen-

Hoeksema, 1995). Ruminators also believe they do not have adequate social support, perhaps because they continue to think and mull over their distress long after friends and peers believe they should stop (Nolen-Hoeksema & Davis, 1999).

Some researchers suggest that biological factors are important in depression and that genetic factors in depression are more salient in females (Silberg, 1999). Thus, females might be more vulnerable to depression generally due to genetic factors.

Treatment for Depression The most successful psychotherapy for depression is **cognitive-behavioral therapy (CBT)** (Marcotte, 1997). Cognitive-behavioral therapy offers a combination of cognitive therapy, which changes self-defeating or irrational thoughts, and behavior therapy, which changes behavior itself. Cognitive-behavioral therapy for depression is based on the ideas that adolescents have cognitive distortions in how they view themselves, the world, and the future and that these distortions contribute to depression. The therapy teaches adolescents to identify and counter these distorted thinking patterns (American Academy of Child and Adolescent Psychiatry, 1998).

One program based on CBT is the Coping with Depression Course, an intervention addressing areas that involve discomfort and anxiety, irrational and negative thoughts, poor social skills, and a low rate of pleasant activities (Lewinsohn et al., 1990). It consists of fourteen 2-hour sessions conducted over 7 weeks. Various studies show that CBT can be effective, with a recovery rate of 65 to 85 percent for clinically depressed patients who undergo CBT (Clarke et al., 1992; Cuijpers, 1998). Another promising type of therapy, interpersonal therapy, concentrates on solving problems in such areas as grief, role disputes, role transitions, and family problems (Mellin & Beamish, 2002).

Similar results are obtained with adults. An impressive National Institute of Mental Health study compared a therapy based on Beck's work (treating negative cognitions), interpersonal therapy, and medication (Elkin, 1995; Elkin et al., 1985). This study, called the Treatment of Depression Collaborative Research Program, found that all three therapies achieved improvement in overall functioning; none was superior to the others over the long term, though medication worked the fastest. The American Psychiatric Association (2000) issued guidelines recommending that medication be used first to treat severe depression. Adults who received interpersonal therapy showed improvements in social functioning more than individuals given medication or CBT, and the adults offered CBT showed a greater reduction in dysfunctional attitudes. The interpretation of this study is controversial, with some psychologists claiming that the differences in short-term benefits for medication were misinterpreted and others agreeing with the interpretations (Jacobson & Hollon, 1996; Klein, 1996). In addition, new antidepressants available today are more effective and have fewer adverse effects than the one used in the study.

The use of antidepressants with adolescents has increased significantly in the past 10 years (Zito et al., 2002). Health care providers often combine psychotherapy and medication to treat depression (Varley, 2002). The use of antidepressant medications with children and adolescents is controversial, however, and few well-designed studies compare placebo and antidepressant use in the treatment of major depressive disorders in this group (Ambronsini, 2000; Geller et al., 1999). Studies using older antidepressants did not show much improvement, but studies with newer antidepressants, including Prozac (fluoxetine), are more encouraging, although their results are still inconsistent (Fishbein, 1997).

PERSPECTIVE 2

I WON'T GO

SETTING THE SCENE: It doesn't take a clinical psychologist to see that Mary is depressed. She shows all the signs of depression, and everyone is aware of her problem.

SISTER: *My parents want Mary to go for therapy. They've asked me to suggest it to her, which I did. Mary refused. I think she needs help, too, but I don't know what to do, since she refuses.*

MARY: *I once spoke to someone about my problems, but she didn't help. I don't need to see a "shrink," because I'm not crazy. I just have some problems. If people would just leave me alone, I'd be OK.*

QUESTION: What, if anything, can be done if Mary refuses to go for help despite the fact that everyone believes it is necessary?

cognitive-behavioral therapy (CBT) A therapy that combines cognitive therapy, which seeks to change self-defeating and irrational thoughts, and behavior therapy, which aims at changing behavior itself.

Therapy for depression can often be successful.

Some open clinical trials that were not controlled showed good response to medication, but there is a lack of controlled research on the subject (Katic & Steingard, 2001). In one impressive controlled study, 96 children and adolescents with major depression were randomly divided into two groups; one group received Prozac and the other, a placebo. Neither the participants nor the researchers knew what the participants were receiving. Prozac was superior to the placebo for participants with severe, persistent depression, although complete remission of symptoms was rare (Emslie et al., 1997). Antidepressants, then, may be useful for some depressed adolescents (American Academy of Child and Adolescent Psychiatry, 1998). However, more research is needed to determine which adolescents may be helped, as well as the medication's long-term effectiveness and effects.

Suicide

Suicide is the third leading cause of death among people between the ages of 15 and 24 years, after accidents and homicide (Centers for Disease Control and Prevention, 2001). Males complete suicide four times as often as females, but females try three times more often than males. The difference is probably due to the more lethal methods of suicide (often firearms) used by males (Zametkin, Alter, & Yemini, 2001). Between 7 and 8 percent of high school students attempt suicide each year, and approximately 10 to 13 percent of junior high and high school students show moderate to severe levels of suicidal thoughts (Mazza, 1997). African Americans currently have a lower rate of suicide than whites, but the suicide rate of African American adolescents and young adults has been rising. Latinos have a higher suicide rate than whites, and Native Americans have the highest suicide rate (American Academy of Child and Adolescent Psychiatry, 2001).

People who commit suicide may show a number of underlying problems. Depression plays an important part in many suicides (de Man, 1999). It is estimated that more than half of the individuals who attempt suicide are depressed and despondent at the time (Hendriksson et al., 1993), and the rate of suicide among depressed people is much higher than among nondepressed people (Angst, Angst, & Stassen, 1999). However, some people who are not depressed make suicidal attempts, and other psychiatric conditions may be involved (Sanchez, 2001). Factors that appear in psychological autopsies (analyses of why suicides occur after they have already taken place) include drug and alcohol use, prior suicide attempts, depression, antisocial or aggressive behavior, psychopathology, and family history of suicidal behavior (Mazza, 1997; Sheras, 2001). Mental illness and suicidal behavior often coexist (Huffman, 2002). Most adolescents who commit suicide (more than 90 percent) have some psychiatric disorder at the time of their death, and more than half had experienced the disorder for at least 2 years (American Academy of Child and Adolescent Psychiatry, 2001).

Most adolescents who attempt suicide have experienced many stressful events in childhood, with a marked increase in stress in the year preceding the attempt. The best predictor is a previous suicide attempt, and about 40 percent of all suicide victims have tried before (Zametkin et al., 2001). A suicide attempt often is precipitated by a psychosocial stressor, such as a loss, rejection, humiliating experience, arrest, perceived or actual family rejection, firing from work, or romantic conflict.

Whenever a suicide occurs, people in the community start looking for answers and clues to its cause. Indeed, in a majority of cases, clues are found. Research finds that some clues do predict the possibility of suicide, but unfortunately people do not always pay attention to them. For instance, many believe that people who talk about suicide never actually do it. But this idea is not true. People who talk about suicide are actually *more* likely to attempt it (Marttunen et al., 1998). Other warning signs include giving treasured items away and talking about "ending it." A previous attempt at suicide is also a warning that the individual might make a future attempt if the predisposing factors are not controlled or adequately dealt with (see Table 13.3 for potential warning signs of adolescent suicide) (Stevens, 2001). However, suicide, especially in adolescent males, may be a relatively impulsive act that occurs shortly after a precipitating event, such as a loss or humiliation (Marttunen et al., 1998).

Some schools offer classes that teach students to recognize the warning signs of suicide and introduce them to the community resources available for help. Some authorities are concerned about the possible negative effect such programs might have on already troubled students and doubt their effectiveness (Mazza, 1997), whereas other experts argue the programs can be helpful (Nelson, 1987).

Table 13.3

Warning Signs and Risk Factors in Adolescent Suicide

It is important to recognize the warning signs and risk factors in suicide. The following are some of the behavioral warning signs, verbal warning signs, and personal and environmental factors that indicate an individual needs to receive immediate help.

Behavioral Warning Signs	Verbal Warning Signs	Stressful Life Events, Past History, and Environmental Factors
Depression	"I'm going to kill myself."	Changes in close relationships (becoming more isolated)
Change in appetite or weight	"I want to die."	
Change in school performance	"I can't stand living anymore."	History of suicide in the family
Helplessness/hopelessness	"I don't want to be a burden anymore."	Previous suicide attempt
Loss of energy	"I've had it; I don't want to bother anyone with my troubles anymore."	Ready access to firearms
Loss of interest in once-pleasurable activities		Recent disappointment (a breakup or failure)
	"My family would be better off without me."	Recent loss (death of a loved one)
Giving away cherished possessions	"I've had enough: I am ending it all."	Serious illness or a belief that one is seriously ill
Morbid ideation		
Substance abuse		
Withdrawal/isolation		

Source: Adapted from King (2001).

AT A GLANCE 13.2 INTERNALIZING BEHAVIORS AND DISORDERS

KEY POINT: Anxiety and depression have many causes, and their effects can be found both inside and outside of school.

SUPPORTING POINTS	EXPLANATION
Psychologists distinguish between internalizing and externalizing behavior disorders.	Internalizing behavior disorders usually involve anxiety, depression, or both and reflect a "turning inward," whereas externalizing disorders, which often involve aggression, reflect a "turning outward."
Many adolescents claim to be shy.	People who are shy experience considerable anxiety when meeting new people. Shyness is not a pathological condition. Social skills training may help shy individuals.
Social phobia is a clinically significant anxiety about social situations.	People with social phobia experience great anxiety when meeting new people, causing them to avoid social situations.
Depression is the most common psychological malady found in adolescents.	Depression involves emotional, physical, cognitive, and motivational symptoms.
There are many theories on the causes of depression.	Psychoanalytic theorists believe depression may be due to separation or loss. Behavioral approaches emphasize the lack of positive events. Cognitive theories emphasize various ways of thinking that contribute to depression. Genetic and physiological contributions to depression also exist.
Female adolescents show much higher rates of depression than male adolescents.	Female adolescents report more negative life events, perceive events more negatively, and concentrate on them more than males.
Depression can be treated successfully.	Cognitive-behavioral therapy is often successful in treating depression. Although modern antidepressants may be useful, more controlled studies are needed.
Many risk factors are found among youth who try to take their own lives.	A sense of helplessness and hopelessness pervades the individual. Risk factors include drug and alcohol use, prior suicide attempts, depression, antisocial or aggressive behavior, psychopathology, and a family history of suicidal behavior.

One effective way of preventing suicide is to identify individuals at risk. School and mental health professionals should be aware of the warning signs (King, 2001). In addition, self-report questionnaires or interviews can screen adolescents for suicide risk by asking them about suicidal thoughts, depression, substance use, and self-destructive behavior (Fritz, 2001). Indeed, there is evidence that teenagers in middle to late adolescence, the group most at risk for suicide, will directly reveal this information if asked (American Academy of Child and Adolescent Psychiatry, 2001). Immediate action then can be taken to help these adolescents. *(For a review of this section, see At A Glance 13.2.)*

EATING DISORDERS

Eating disorders are possibly the most publicized psychological problems experienced by adolescents. Until recently, major eating disorders, such as anorexia nervosa and bulimia, were considered rare, but the number of reported cases has increased substantially. This trend may reflect an actual increase in eating disorders or simply greater awareness of them and better reporting. Revelations of anorexic and bulimic behavior by Karen Carpenter and Princess

Diana have led to increased public interest and news coverage of eating disorders (Wicks-Nelson & Israel, 2000).

An estimated 10 percent of American high school and college students have an eating disorder. The most serious eating disorders are **anorexia nervosa** (self-starvation) and **bulimia** (a disorder in which the individual binges and then purges). The incidence of anorexia among females is approximately 0.5 percent and of bulimia, between 1.0 and 3.0 percent, whereas the incidence rate among males is about one-tenth that of females (American Psychiatric Association, 2000). Subclinical problems are much more prevalent, with many adolescent girls exhibiting less extreme, but still unhealthy, eating behaviors (Graber et al., 1994).

Anorexia Nervosa

Anorexia nervosa is a disorder marked by self-imposed starvation. It involves an abnormal fear of becoming obese, a disturbance of body image, significant weight loss, and a refusal to maintain even a minimal normal body weight. Between 2 and 6 percent of all anorexics die because of medical problems caused by the starvation (Neumarker, 1997; Nielsen et al., 1998). Approximately 96 percent of all anorexics are female, and the onset is most often during the teen years.

Anorexics are obsessed with food, weight loss, and dieting, and they are physically active. Their physical activity may be a socially accepted activity, such as participation in sports, or it may be unusual, such as running up and down the driveway until exhausted (Wenar, 1994). Once they achieve significant weight loss, anorexics do not stop but continue until they are too thin to be physically healthy. Losing weight becomes an obsession, and they fear they will lose control if they eat a normal diet. Controlling their weight becomes their passion. They undergo changes in their physiology, thinking, and personality. They misperceive their weight, believing they are fat or about to become so. In fact, they often complain about feeling bloated after eating very small amounts of food. Their condition becomes serious as their body begins to waste away. Menstruation ceases, they become ill and anemic, they cannot sleep, they suffer from low blood pressure, and their metabolism rate decreases. In most cases, they also have depression.

The cause of anorexia is a mystery. There is evidence for a genetic predisposition (DeAngelis, 2002; Vink et al., 2001). Studies find a much higher concordance rate—that is, the rate of agreement between twins on a particular characteristic—in identical than fraternal twins (Kendler et al., 1991).

One theory of what causes anorexia emphasizes the effects on girls of our society's view of the glamorous female as very thin (Nagel & Jones, 1992). An analysis of articles in a magazine aimed at female teens found that the models became thinner and the hips narrower over the years, and the primary reason given for eating a good diet was to look attractive, not to be healthy (Guillen & Barr, 1994). Yet females often find themselves surrounded by calorie-rich foods at social functions. The theory postulates that anorexics are unable to integrate these contradictory messages and develop a fear of losing control and of eating too much and gaining weight. There must be more to this mechanism, though, because only a minority of females exposed to such media messages develop these eating disorders (Cauffman & Steinberg, 1996).

It is popular to emphasize the possible contribution of family problems for people with anorexia. Anorexics often come from educated, success-oriented, middle-class families that are quite weight conscious. They also tend to come

PERSPECTIVE 3

I'M NOT STARVING MYSELF

SETTING THE SCENE: Teresa is a 15-year-old high school sophomore who is maturing early. Most of her friends are older.

TERESA: *It's not like I starve myself. I eat fine, but my parents are always complaining about what I eat and how much I eat. I limit my fat intake. Is that bad? Yeah, I skip breakfast, and sometimes lunch when I'm busy, but so what? I feel fine, and I want to fit into the same bathing suit I was in last year. I don't throw up or anything. I don't like them constantly on my back about it.*

PARENTS: *We don't want Teresa to eat everything on her plate or anything like that. We don't want her to eat piles of ice cream, either. We are just concerned because she is constantly trying to lose weight and diet. We don't remember when she last ate a good meal. She's eating less and less, and we're worried. Can you blame us?*

QUESTION: If you were Teresa's parents, would you be concerned? If so, what would you do?

anorexia nervosa   A condition of self-imposed starvation found most often among adolescent females.

bulimia   An eating disorder marked by episodic binge eating and purging.

Some argue that our cultural concept of beauty in terms of being thin is one reason that many young girls have eating disorders.

from rigid, overprotective families where conflicts are avoided and people are overinvolved with each other. This environment interferes with the formation of a personal identity (Minuchin, 1985). Other psychologists, though, point out that the families of anorexics vary considerably in enmeshment, overprotectiveness, rigidity, and conflict resolution (Dare et al., 1994). Furthermore, assessments conducted before and after treatment for anorexia found that family functioning clearly improved after treatment that did not involve the family, perhaps showing that eating disorders may have caused the family problems rather than family problems causing anorexia (Woodside et al., 1995).

Two types of anorexia have been reported. In the *restricting type,* the person relies on strict dieting, whereas the individual with the *bulimic type* alternates between extreme dieting and binge eating followed by purging. Both types are characterized by great loss of weight. Restricters tend to be more conforming, reliable, socially insecure, obsessive, and inflexible in their thinking. Bulimic types, in contrast, are more extroverted and sociable but somewhat less stable; they have more problems with impulse control and are more likely to become substance abusers (Wenar, 1994).

Bulimia

Bulimia involves recurrent episodes of overeating followed by a number of different behaviors intended to control weight and body shape, including vomiting and the misuse of laxatives. Bulimics maintain relatively normal weights, and their fluctuations in body weight are rarely extreme enough to be life threatening. However, their behavior is abnormal, and purging can cause serious physical problems. They display a characteristic set of disturbed attitudes concerning body shape and weight, sometimes referred to as a *morbid fear of fatness* (Fairburn et al., 1991). The overwhelming majority of bulimics are women. The average age of onset for bulimia in clinical samples is 18 to 19 years of age. Binge eating precedes the onset of purging by about a year or two (Stice et al., 1998). One difference between bulimia and the bulimic type of anorexia is in weight loss. Individuals with bulimia maintain a relatively normal weight but show abnormal behaviors, whereas people with the bulimic type of anorexia have a severe weight loss.

Bulimics binge secretly. They stop eating when they experience stomach pain, require sleep, are interrupted by someone, or induce their own vomiting. Just as with anorexics, bulimic teens are obsessed with their body image. Bulimics are perfectionists and high achievers, and they fear losing control. They often believe that others are watching them, and they are constantly worried about how others perceive them. Bulimics are likely to have histories of mood swings, are more extroverted than anorexics, become easily frustrated and bored, and may abuse drugs (Fahy & Eisler, 1993). They are very concerned about pleasing men and being attractive, whereas anorexics do not care about attracting others or engaging in sexual activities.

Bulimics have an all-or-none way of thinking, believing that if they eat a small portion of a forbidden food they will lose control completely. They often jump from one eating fad to another. They make lists of forbidden foods and begin by denying themselves these foods. Later, they break down and binge. They have unreasonably high goals and may believe that if they gain any weight at all they will be fat, or that if they can't stick to a diet they are failures (Muuss, 1986). These attitudes toward eating often appear early, and disordered eating behaviors are relatively stable across time.

Treatment Options

A combination of therapies can be successful in treating anorexia and bulimia. About half of all anorexics recover, but the other half continue to have eating difficulties and psychological problems such as depression, social phobia, and recurrent bouts of self-imposed starvation (Wenar, 1994). Depression and other coexisting problems such as anxiety disorders require separate treatment.

The first priority in treating anorexia is to restore a reasonable weight, which sometimes requires hospitalization. In severe cases, intravenous feeding is necessary. Family therapy that focuses on the relationships among family members and behavior modification to reinforce proper eating also may be required (Muuss, 1985). Cognitive-behavioral therapy is also used to alter faulty cognitions and self-damaging behaviors. A treatment for anorexia that recently has been suggested as effective involves enlisting parental involvement as parents encourage the patient to eat and then gradually return control to the anorexic adolescent. An early session may involve a family picnic in front of the therapist to observe the quality of the meal and find ways to improve food consumption. This treatment philosophy sees the family not as the cause of the problem but as part of the solution as the family searches for ways to help the anorexic family member (DeAngelis, 2002; Eisler et al., 2000).

Treatment for bulimia also requires therapy, along with antidepressant medications. The goal of the psychotherapy is to change the patient's eating behaviors and cognitive distortions, such as low self-esteem and perfectionist thinking. The first stage of treatment attempts to control eating behaviors using behavioral strategies such as self-monitoring of what is eaten and prescribing a pattern of regular food intake; at the same time, patients receive information about body weight, dieting, and the adverse effects of vomiting. The second stage involves cognitive restructuring, in which thought patterns are altered. The final therapeutic stage is the establishment of a maintenance program. The initial success rate for CBT in bulimia is close to 80 percent (Garner, Fairburn, & Davis, 1987). Recent studies have found that both CBT and interpersonal therapy, which helps bulimics with their relationships with others, can be successful (Agras et al., 2000).

AT A GLANCE 13.3 EATING DISORDERS

KEY POINT: Eating disorders, such as anorexia nervosa (self-starvation) and bulimia (bingeing and purging), are serious problems that require therapeutic attention.

SUPPORTING POINTS	EXPLANATION
Adolescents with anorexia nervosa literally starve themselves and can die from the disorder.	Anorexics refuse to maintain a normal body weight. They are obsessed with food, are afraid of gaining any weight, and misperceive their weight, believing they need to lose weight when they are dangerously thin.
Genetic and environmental factors may cause anorexia.	Both genetic vulnerability and environmental factors may contribute to anorexia.
Bulimics overeat and then purge their systems, either through vomiting or taking laxatives.	Although bulimics often maintain a relatively normal body weight, their behaviors can cause serious medical problems.
Bulimics have a characteristic set of attitudes.	Bulimics show a morbid fear of fatness. They are perfectionistic and fear losing control.
Treatment for eating disorders can be successful.	Anorexics may require hospitalization, as the first step is to stabilize their weight. Cognitive-behavioral therapy and new treatment that enlists the family's help can be successful in treating individuals with anorexia. Both cognitive-behavioral and interpersonal therapy may be helpful in treating bulimia.

Therapy for both anorexics and bulimics challenges misconceptions and attitudes about eating and weight control (Wilson & Fairburn, 1993). It is important to change the way these adolescents think—for example, to alter their belief that weight determines their value as a person, or to improve the low self-esteem and temper the perfectionism of bulimics. Longer-term therapy focuses on body image and interpersonal problems, making anorexics more aware of underlying difficulties with autonomy and helping them find other ways to assert their independence (Bruch, 1986). *(For a review of this section, see At A Glance 13.3.)*

COPING WITH CHRONIC ILLNESS

Most adolescents give scant attention to their physical health, which they take for granted. However, some adolescents have to deal with chronic illness or physical disability. A **chronic illness,** or **chronic condition,** is a continuous or recurring illness or a condition of long duration that has long-term consequences. An **acute illness,** in contrast, has a sudden onset, runs its course, and usually results in a complete recovery. Approximately 10 percent of all adolescents in the United States have a chronic illness or condition (Blum, 1992). The most common chronic condition in adolescents is asthma, followed by sensory disorders (visual or auditory impairment) and nervous system disorders. Other chronic conditions or diseases include infection with HIV, diabetes mellitus, lupus erythematosus, cystic fibrosis, anorexia nervosa, spina bifida, and heart disease. African American and Latino youths are more likely than whites to have some chronic diseases, possibly the continuation of difficulties experienced in childhood due to higher rates of poverty.

Adolescence is a time of gaining autonomy and independence. It is a time of social change. Imagine having an illness that makes you feel and look different and does not allow you to develop the autonomy and independence you desire. Early adolescents who have a chronic disease are at an increased risk for depression because they feel they are different from their peers at a time when fitting in is important; however, the majority are not depressed (Bennett, 1994). Adolescents often feel that everyone is watching and evaluating them (see "Cognitive Development"), and this is even more so for teens with chronic diseases. Teens with chronic disabilities or diseases may also feel isolated from others (Boice, 1998). They may believe they are alone and that no one else is experiencing these problems. This perception can be countered through participation in groups with other adolescents who have similar conditions.

Adolescents with chronic disorders often have difficulty in school, most commonly because of absences (Thies, 1999). These absences may occur once or twice a week, or the teen may be absent for a week or more at a time. The teen may fall behind and not be able to catch up, even with tutoring. These absences, combined with the greater amount of time spent alone, may also adversely effect the development of social relationships at school (Wicks-Nelson & Israel, 2000).

The unpredictability of the disorder may also weigh heavily on the teenager. Adolescents with chronic disorders may be doing well when suddenly the illness flares up. They develop an external locus of control, believing they have little control of their situation. The uncertain long-term outcome makes the future an even greater concern than is usual in adolescence.

Many teens with chronic diseases have activity limitations. In some ways, these daily physical limitations may cause more frustration and psychological adjustment problems than other aspects of the disease (Midence, 1994). Individuals with the greatest impairment in day-to-day living are most likely to experience psychological and social problems.

chronic illness (chronic condition) A continuous or recurring illness or a condition of long duration that has long-term consequences.

acute illness An illness with a sudden onset that runs its course and usually results in a complete recovery.

These challenges may result in tension and problems in the family if teens actively refuse to properly care for themselves. Parents may overprotect them, which may send a signal of incompetence to the teen and others. Adolescents with chronic illness naturally experience much more anxiety about their health. Their desire to fit in and the bothersome limitations of their daily health regimens may lead to behaviors that are not in their long-term best interest. Many teens with health problems must confront their disease each day in their regular medical regimens, which may include medication, medical monitoring, and various other strategies. These necessary treatments, even when efficiently performed, sometimes interrupt the teens' plans. Some medications may influence behavior; for example, some medications for seizure disorders may cause adverse effects such as slower response time (Dodrill & Matthews, 1992). Noncompliance with medical regimens is a greater problem among adolescents than younger children, because parents have less responsibility to monitor and even perform the medical routines (Tebbi et al., 1988). Adolescents may let their medical regimens slip. They may even fake their monitoring—for example, reporting the wrong blood sugar levels if they have diabetes—in order to participate in a particular social event or to deny their problem. Complicated programs of medical intervention often require lifestyle changes that are particularly difficult for adolescents. In some cases, counseling may be needed.

Despite these possible problems, most adolescents with chronic diseases or disabilities do well. They find ways to cope with any limitations, and advancements in medical science may bring their conditions under greater control. Still, many of these adolescents are concerned about their future educational and job possibilities. Many do not need any special help, whereas others may require changes in the environment or rules. For example, a student with excessive absences because of medical problems must find a way to stay current in class. This problem has become much easier to solve with the advent of class websites and email. The situation has further improved because of laws such as the Individual with Disabilities Education Act, which mandates that students with chronic illnesses and other disabilities, including physical and sensory disabilities, be given a free and appropriate education and offers protection from discrimination (see "Focus: Young Americans with Disabilities"). *(For a review of this section, see At A Glance 13.4.)*

AT A GLANCE **13.4** COPING WITH CHRONIC ILLNESS

KEY POINT: Adolescents with chronic illnesses must cope with additional difficulties that may influence their ability to deal successfully with the challenges of adolescence.

SUPPORTING POINTS	EXPLANATION
Adolescents with chronic illnesses or disabilities experience a number of problems.	Adolescents with illnesses or disabilities may be more isolated than their peers, experience more anxiety about the future, and find that their medication affects their behavior. Their increased absences from school may lead to academic problems, and their activities may be limited.
Most adolescents with chronic diseases or disabilities find ways to cope with their special challenges and do well.	Some adolescents require additional help. Laws mandate that adjustment be made in both schools and places of business to allow people with disabilities to actively participate.

FOCUS Young Americans with Disabilities

Approximately 10.6 percent of all children and adolescents have a disability (U.S. Department of Education, 2001a), including learning disabilities, communication disorders, mental retardation, behavior disorders, visual or auditory impairments, or physical disabilities. In the history of people with disabilities, both in education and in the workplace, discrimination and limited opportunity abound. As late as the middle 1970s, about 1 million students with disabilities weren't even attending school (*NEA Today*, 1999).

This situation has changed considerably. The most important law mandating educational services for students is the Individuals with Disabilities Education Act (IDEA), formerly called the Education for All Handicapped Children Act (Public Law 94–142). This complicated law was first passed in 1975 and has been updated periodically. It requires school districts to actively identify children and adolescents with disabilities; to provide them with a free, appropriate public education; to use due process; and to evaluate students in a nondiscriminatory manner (Kaplan, 1996). It also requires that each student be given an Individualized Education Program (IEP), a written document stating the educational goals for the student and the means for accomplishing them (Gable et al., 2000). The 1997 revision places a greater emphasis on measurable annual goals, regular progress reports to parents, and the requirement of student participation in standardized testing (Huefner, 2000). The movement toward accountability has now embraced special education services (Shriner, 2000).

The 1997 revision also mandates a definite transition plan, a coordinated set of activities that help students move from high school to activities after high school (Grigal et al., 1997). Finally, the IDEA requires students with disabilities to be placed in the *least restrictive environment*, which is usually defined as the regular classroom. In fact, a movement called *full inclusion* advocates that children and adolescents with disabilities receive their education solely in a regular classroom where the teacher and other specialists are responsible for providing for their special needs. Although there is no legal mandate that every child be placed in regular classrooms all day, a school district must make a good faith attempt to offer support services in the regular classroom. Students with special needs are to be placed in whatever environment is developmentally appropriate and least restrictive (Boyd & Parish, 1996).

The situation changes somewhat after high school. Colleges do not have the responsibility of identifying students with disabilities. Rather, the responsibility falls on the student to provide evidence of the disability. Upon receiving documentation, the college has the responsibility to provide adequate services (American Speech-Language-Hearing Association, 2000).

More students with disabilities attend college today than ever before. More than 9 percent of all entering college freshmen have a recognized disability, compared with only 2.6 percent in 1978 (Thomas, 2000). Colleges differ greatly in the services they provide for students with disabilities, but many will provide excellent services if students document their disabilities. The basic law protecting students in college is Section 504 of the Rehabilitation Act of 1973, which guarantees equal access to programs and facilities for

LEARNING DISABILITIES

Some children and adolescents face difficulties learning basic skills, such as reading. Place yourself in the position of an adolescent who has difficulty reading and does not process information as well as his or her peers. Consider how you would feel if school were constantly frustrating at a time when you were most sensitive to how others react to you. Consider, too, how this situation might affect your daily life.

Individuals who have **learning disabilities** do not learn well despite attending class and having the same teachers as their peers. More children and adolescents with disabilities are diagnosed as having a learning disability than any other disability (U.S. Department of Education, 2001a).

What Is a Learning Disability?

Children and adolescents with learning disabilities show significant difficulties acquiring and using listening, speaking, reading, writing, or reasoning skills or mathematics. They do not achieve up to their age and ability in some basic skill

people with disabilities. The law requires all federally funded programs and activities to provide reasonable accommodations to people with disabilities, and this provision extends to postsecondary education and institutions.

Legal changes also protect people with disabilities in their quest for employment. The Americans with Disabilities Act (ADA), signed into law in 1990, extends basic civil rights protection already given to members of minority groups and women to people with disabilities (Price & Gerber, 2001). The ADA guarantees equal opportunity for individuals with disabilities in employment, public accommodation, transportation, state and local government, and telecommunications (National Rehabilitation Information Center, 1993). The law prohibits firms from discrimination in the hiring or promotion of workers with physical or mental impairments.

It also requires restaurants, stores, and other public accommodations to widen doorways and provide ramps for people in wheelchairs, and it mandates that inner-city buses be accessible to individuals with disabilities. Businesses must make new buildings and grounds conform to strict codes for access. Renovated or new hotels, retail stores, and restaurants must become accessible and existing barriers be removed if "readily achievable" (Berko, 1992).

The ADA requires employers to provide "reasonable accommodations" in both the application process and employment (Friedland, 1999). These reasonable accommodations might require both making existing employment facilities readily accessible to disabled employees and job restructuring. For example, an individual with a learning disability might not be able to pass a written test for a job and thus might require a verbal presentation. This change would be expected as long as the job did not require a great deal of reading. Other possible accommodations involve providing raised letters on elevator control panels or a computer interface for verbalizing what is written on the screen so that an individual with a visual disability could work (Kaplan, 1996). The accommodations might involve changes in the use of technology, for example, providing a telecommunications device that would allow a person with an auditory impairment to use the telephone (McCrone, 1994). Reasonable accommodations in the jobs themselves might require restructuring jobs, modifying work schedules, purchasing equipment, or changing training procedures. A worker with a learning disability might require one-on-one training to master a new computer program, and employers must provide this instruction (Hatch & Hall, 2000). The law also notes that these accommodations should not place an "undue burden" on the employer. Unfortunately, the language of the law is vague, and phrases such as "reasonable accommodations" and "undue burden" will require interpretation by the courts.

Most people with disabilities would like to work, and the ADA is opening up new opportunities by requiring changes in the workplace. People with disabilities themselves require better education and job training, along with instruction in job-finding skills. At the same time, the nondisabled population must change its attitudes toward people with disabilities and better understand the nature of the various disabilities. With legal advances, attitudinal changes, and better job training and education, more Americans with disabilities will take their place as equals in the workplace.

(Van den Broeck, 2002). The problem is not the result of sensory disabilities, such as blindness or deafness; mental retardation; emotional disturbance; or environmental, cultural, or economic disadvantage (Gaskill & Brantley, 1996).

Although by definition, a learning disability can occur in a child of any intelligence level, the overwhelming majority of children and adolescents with a learning disability have average intelligence. The incidence of learning disabilities is in the range of 2 to 5 percent of the general population. Boys are identified with learning disabilities about three to five times as often as girls (Wicks-Nelson & Israel, 2000). Perhaps teachers are more likely to notice boys with learning disabilities because their frustrations show themselves in acting-out behavior, whereas girls with learning problems may not react the same way.

Children and adolescents with learning disabilities are a heterogeneous group. Learning disabilities may affect people's ability to interpret what they see or hear, or to link information from different parts of the brain. These limitations show themselves as specific difficulties with spoken or written language, coordination, self-control, or attention. The most obvious difficulty is a problem reading; the term **dyslexia** describes a learning disorder characterized by severe reading impairment. The causes of learning disabilities are still controversial, but disturbances in brain structure and function may make it more difficult to bring

dyslexia A learning disorder characterized by severe reading impairment.

together information from different parts of the brain and thus be at the root of the problem (Neuwirth, 1993; Rourke & Del Dotto, 2001).

People with learning disabilities may show problems in perception, motor skills, communication, and memory strategies. They often do not use memory or learning strategies such as rehearsal appropriately, show poor organizational skills, and have short-term memory problems (Swanson, 1994).

Psychologists believe that a primary feature of a learning disability is a deficit in *phonological awareness* (Serniclaes et al., 2001; Wagner, Torgeson, & Rashotte, 1994). Phonological awareness involves a number of skills—for example, understanding that words can be divided into sounds such as *d, o, g* for *dog* or possessing such skills as being able to blend sounds such as *tr* in *trend* or to recognize the beginning sound of a word. The inability to blend, segment, rhyme, and manipulate sounds causes students to have problems recognizing words (O'Connor, Jenkins, & Slocum, 1995). Because of these phonological problems, students with learning disabilities have trouble abstracting and transferring. For example, when students with learning disabilities are taught to read *dine* and *pink,* they are not better able to identify *fine* and *link* (Lovett et al., 1994). Students with learning disabilities can be directly taught these phonological skills, however, and when they are integrated with reading instruction, the students make significant progress (Hatcher, Hulme, & Ellis, 1994).

Children and adolescents with learning disabilities experience more difficulty in school achievement. Educators most often use two approaches to help these students. Direct instruction targets academic problems and, for example, teaches children how to sound out words. Another approach is to teach children learning strategies, such as how to approach a task, how to monitor progress, and how to organize (Butler, 1995; Swanson, 2001).

The Social and Emotional Functioning of Adolescents with Learning Disabilities

Learning disabilities may influence a wide range of behaviors inside and outside school. The academic difficulties are obvious, as students with learning disabilities have more difficulty learning to read and mastering academic skills. But learning disabilities may directly or indirectly influence many other behaviors.

The social interactions of children and adolescents with learning disabilities are frequently difficult (Tur-Kaspa & Bryan, 1995). These individuals are more likely than others without learning disabilities to be rejected or ignored by peers and to have difficulty making and keeping friends (Gresham & Elliott, 1989; McIntosh, Vaughn, & Zaragoza, 1991). Others may reject and ignore them because of various behavioral patterns they show. The children who are rejected are more likely to show aggressive and disruptive behaviors, whereas those who are neglected are more likely to be withdrawn and socially isolated. They are generally not as popular with their classmates (Stone & La Greca, 1990).

Students with learning disabilities often show social skills deficits (Haager & Vaughn, 1995). They have difficulty interpreting social cues, show poor ability to adjust their communication to what is being said, and have difficulty responding to the thoughts and feelings of others (Conte & Andrews, 1993). These social skills problems may be due to many causes. Some individuals show more inappropriate behavior than their peers without learning disabilities, whereas others may have problems in social perception and may not read social situations well (Holder & Kirkpatrick, 1991; Toro et al., 1990). For example, a smirk and a smile may appear similar but have different meanings, and youth with learning disabilities may interpret facial expressions less accurately (Axelrod, 1982). Their language-related problems might also lead to social problems as they may not stay on topic or miss the point of jokes.

Not all children and adolescents with learning disabilities have social problems. Some show good social skills. Social skills development usually shows continuity. Adolescents with good social skills continue to function well; some even compensate for perceived deficiencies in other areas by using their social skills. Individuals who have had difficulty in social areas continue to experience hardship. They continue to adapt slowly and overreact, and they become less able to understand subtle communication and less accurate in interpreting social interactions and emotions. These students may become isolated. Some turn to music, cars, or athletics, whereas others use food or drugs as a method of escape. Parents of younger children with learning disabilities can actively organize their children's social lives—for example, inviting other children to the home—but adolescents must do so on their own.

Adolescents with learning disabilities are also at risk for emotional difficulties. For example, they are more likely to experience depression (Maag & Behrens, 1989) and disorders related to anxiety and sleep (Dollinger, Horn, & Boarini, 1988). The anxiety is related to making mistakes, being teased, getting poor grades, and being criticized. Adolescents with learning disabilities are frequently overwhelmed and disorganized, and they often have a fear of failure. They are less able to use active coping mechanisms, such as seeking information about a problem or a stressor, and they are highly pessimistic about academic matters. Sometimes they feel they are letting their parents down. They are very angry at themselves and engage in self-criticism.

When researchers compare adolescents with and without learning disabilities, those with learning disabilities score lower on some aspects of self-concept, but not others (Montgomery, 1994; Raviv & Stone, 1991). They show no appreciable differences in global self-concept; in fact, adolescents with learning disabilities show about the same reaction to the transition to junior high school as students without learning disabilities (Forgan & Vaughn, 2000). They show some decline in academic achievement and some anxiety, but their reactions are no greater than the reactions of youth without learning disabilities. Their academic self-concept is lower, though (Chapman, 1988; Kistner et al., 1987). Perhaps the reason global self-concept is similar is that adolescents with learning disabilities may emphasize strengths in nonacademic areas and compensate for their academic problems (for example, by participating in school activities, sports, and extracurricular activities) (Silverman & Zigmond, 1983). Other investigators suggest that the key factor in global self-concept is locus of control. Adolescents with learning disabilities who have an internal locus of control for academic success have an average global self-concept (Hagborg, 1996). These students take control of their learning. Thus, not every adolescent with learning disabilities has a low academic self-concept.

Secondary and Postsecondary Education

The focus of programs designed to help adolescents with learning disabilities changes as students enter secondary school. Although they may continue to teach basic skills, secondary schools place a greater emphasis on planning and organization and on teaching students to summarize, ask questions, and solve problems (Smith, 1988). There are many ways to help students organize. For example, helping them break down a task into small parts and making lists can be helpful. Adolescents with learning disabilities may work on organizational skills by being required to make a video, run a dance, or operate a school store. Often, these students have not been given much responsibility in these areas because of their planning and organizational weaknesses. Adolescents are taught how to compensate for their problems and use active coping strategies, because success in adulthood often requires these skills.

Both academic and occupational attainment for late adolescents and early adults with learning disabilities generally are disappointing; they usually have lower academic performance and less developed career development (Rojewski, 1999). Remember that most of these teens have at least average intelligence. One significant problem found in junior and senior high school learning disabilities students is attendance, which is often very poor (Lovitt, 1989). More students with learning disabilities fail regular courses because of their attendance problems than for any other reason. Poor motivation seems to be a key. Adolescents with learning disabilities are less likely to graduate high school, and more than a quarter do not get a high school diploma. High educational aspirations and successful completion of an academic or college preparatory course predict enrollment in postsecondary education, regardless of disability status. Many students with learning disabilities can succeed, however, if educators are willing to make changes in the educational environment. Computers can help these adolescents write and check spelling. Reading tests aloud and allowing students to respond orally may help. Many students with learning disabilities do better if given more time. It may also help to administer test items from least to most difficult, provide larger margins to help guide the eye while reading, and place answer bubbles next to multiple-choice questions to avoid the need for answer sheets. Reading-comprehension passages can be set off within shaded boxes from other test items and signs used to indicate continuation of material or the end. Sometimes it helps to present only a few sections of a test at a time. These changes are relatively easy and do not adversely affect the validity of an exam. They ensure that the students' knowledge is still being examined while also giving students the best chance of showing what they know.

Vocational preparation is also necessary, especially preparation in social skills. Adolescents with learning disabilities may need more help preparing for job interviews, completing forms, and writing follow-up letters after interviews. Some high schools offer work-study options, which may be appropriate for students with severe learning disabilities. These programs are designed to teach students vocational and personal decision-making skills.

It is estimated that 1.3 percent of all college students have learning disabilities, making it the most common disability on the college campus (Skinner, 1998). Of all college freshmen with disabilities, more than 35 percent say they have learning disabilities (Thomas, 2000). The number of college students with learning disabilities has increased substantially, as many more now follow college preparatory courses. Good transition plans, such as one-on-one help from guidance counselors familiar with colleges that welcome such students, can help,

Most adolescents with learning disabilities are diagnosed in elementary school where they receive instruction in basic skills. In secondary school the emphasis changes to planning, organization, and finding ways to compensate for the learning disability.

AT A GLANCE 13.5 LEARNING DISABILITIES

KEY POINT: The most common disability among teenagers is learning disabilities, which can affect many areas of an adolescent's life.

SUPPORTING POINTS	EXPLANATION
Children and adolescents with learning disabilities have difficulty learning in the classroom.	Students with learning disabilities show significant difficulties acquiring and using listening, speaking, reading, writing, or reasoning skills or mathematics.
Children and adolescents with learning disabilities often have difficulty reading.	Many children and adolescents with learning disabilities have phonological problems (that is, problems with the sounds of the letters and putting together these sounds).
Children and adolescents with learning disabilities can learn and succeed.	Direct instruction can be very useful, as can teaching children and adolescents with learning disabilities specific learning strategies and skills, such as how to approach an assignment and how to monitor their progress.
Children and adolescents with learning disabilities often experience problems other than academic difficulties.	People with learning disabilities often experience social problems and are at increased risk for depression and anxiety. However, many cope well with their learning difficulties.
The educational focus changes as children with learning disabilities reach secondary school.	Although some instruction in basic skills may continue, the focus changes to teaching planning and organization skills and strategies that help students with learning disabilities deal more effectively with people.
Some college students have learning disabilities, and changes in the learning and testing environment may help them succeed.	Modifications in testing procedures (being given a test orally), being allowed to tape classes, and obtaining help in organizing and planning projects may enable the adolescent with a learning disability to succeed.

as can the availability of educational technologies that allow students to compensate for their weaknesses (by taping classes, for example) (Shaw, McGuire, & Brinckerhoff, 1994). College students with learning disabilities are more resilient and more achievement oriented than similar students without learning disabilities (Hall, Spruill, & Webster, 2002). Of particular importance is training in academic survival skills. Many students require help in budgeting time and money, long-range planning, and organizing their work.

With assistance, many students with learning disabilities can succeed in college (American Speech-Language-Hearing Association, 2000). A college degree offers a better chance for advancement, and individuals who succeed in college have a much better chance of entering professional and managerial careers (Greenbaum, Graham, & Scales, 1995). Unfortunately, many students with learning disabilities find their college professors less prepared to accommodate their needs than their teachers in elementary and secondary school (Thomas, 2000).

Adolescents with learning disabilities may not outgrow their problems, but they can be very successful nonetheless. Their success lies in developing coping strategies that allow them to meet the challenges of the world. Successful adults are aware of their strengths and weaknesses, capitalize on their strengths, and find ways of coping with their weaknesses. For example, a bank manager noted that he depends on a computer a great deal, and a sheriff with poor spelling keeps two dictionaries in the car. Most adults with learning disabilities adjust to the complex demands of the work environment, but they admit that some problems remain. Many take control of their own lives and adapt well to the environment (Gerber, Ginsberg, & Reiff, 1992). *(For a review of this section, see At A Glance 13.5.)*

Attention-Deficit/ Hyperactivity Disorder

Attention-deficit/hyperactivity disorder (ADHD) is a disorder that involves such symptoms as hyperactivity, inattentiveness, and impulsiveness to such an extent that they cause difficulties in academic and social relationships (Burcham & Carlson, 1995). Individuals with ADHD must exhibit these symptoms in at least two different settings—for example, the school and the home, or the school and the workplace. These symptoms have their onset before age 7 but may continue in full or part form into adolescence and adulthood. There are three types of ADHD, each of which emphasizes different symptoms. One type emphasizes inattention, and the second type focuses on hyperactivity and impulsiveness. The third type, a combined type, is characterized by inattention, hyperactivity, and impulsiveness (American Psychiatric Association, 2000). Between 3 and 5 percent of all children have ADHD, although some experts claim a somewhat lower incidence (American Psychiatric Association, 2000). Boys are much more likely than girls to be diagnosed as having ADHD (Barabasz & Barabasz, 1996). Approximately 30 percent of all children with ADHD have a learning disability (Seidman et al., 2001).

Symptoms of ADHD

Students with ADHD are impulsive, easily distracted, and inattentive, and they show a great deal of inappropriate behavior (Barkley, 1990, 1998). They have difficulties controlling their behavior (Anastopoulos & Shaffer, 2001). In fact, ADHD is most often characterized as a problem in behavioral inhibition. Children and adolescents with ADHD experience difficulty regulating their behavior in response to the environment. They have more problems with executive functions, such as planning and organization; complex problem solving; and response inhibition (Seidman et al., 2001). They have difficulty in school, and their relationships with their teachers are often strained. It is estimated that between 35 and 70 percent show oppositional defiant disorder, which involves frequent conflict with others, and between 30 and 50 percent develop conduct disorder, which involves aggression and often criminal behavior (Johnston & Ohan, 1999). Individuals with ADHD and oppositional defiant disorder or conduct disorder show higher levels of aggression, lying, cheating, and stealing (Barkley, 1998). The combination of ADHD with other disruptive behaviors is much more significantly related to negative outcomes than a diagnosis of ADHD without these other problems.

Some children and adolescents with ADHD are considered aggressive and annoying and are not well accepted by their peers. Their parents see them as less compliant and less responsive to their questions, and parents report many more conduct problems than they do for their other children who do not have ADHD (Tarver-Behring, Barkley, & Karlsson, 1985). Children with ADHD have social problems; others often see them as bothersome, socially awkward, disruptive, talkative, loud, and aggressive (Wicks-Nelson & Israel, 2000).

The cause of ADHD is still largely a mystery, and many biological explanations have been advanced. The disorder appears to arise because of difficulties in the functioning of specific parts of the brain—especially the frontal lobes—that play a major part in performing executive functions, such as planning, implementing goal-oriented strategies, and controlling impulses (Aman, Roberts, & Pennington, 1998). Studies show reduced blood flow to the prefrontal regions, as well as to the pathways connecting these regions to the limbic system, which plays a significant part in emotion (see Anastopoulos & Shaffer, 2001). Evidence for some genetic involvement also exists (Plomin et al., 1997).

attention-deficit/hyperactivity disorder (ADHD)
A diagnostic classification in the *DSM-IV* system involving a number of symptoms, including inattention, impulsivity, and hyperactivity.

Life with ADHD

Symptoms of ADHD often decrease in severity as a child moves into adolescence, and approximately 30 percent of children diagnosed with ADHD no longer meet the American Psychiatric Association's diagnostic criteria when they are adolescents (Barkley et al., 1990). These individuals experience fewer problems as adolescents and young adults (Klein & Mannuzza, 1991).

Most adolescents, however, continue to meet the criteria for ADHD, and they experience significant problems. They show more antisocial behavior and have a greater risk of being involved in delinquent activities (Hechtman, Weiss, & Perlman, 1984; Mannuzza et al., 1989). They also have poorer academic outcomes than their peers and are more likely to drop out (Biederman, 1991). They complete less schooling as well, averaging about 2.2 years less (Mannuza et al., 1993; Weiss et al., 1985). They are much less likely to attend college or graduate school. They are more likely to have problems in family relations, especially conflicts (Barkley, Grodzinsky, & DePaul, 1992). They also have fewer friends (Taylor et al., 1996).

The situation improves in early adulthood, however, when individuals with ADHD do not differ in living and family arrangements (for example, in percentage married, divorced, living alone, or living with others) from individuals who do not have ADHD (Mannuzza et al., 1993). They do move around more than others, however, which explains why many follow-up studies of adolescents with ADHD have attrition rates as high as one-third (Hansen, Weiss, & Last, 1999).

A study that compared adolescents with ADHD with adolescents without ADHD at age 20 found that the ADHD group had overcome many of the difficulties they had experienced in childhood and adolescence. Significant improvements occurred in the educational and occupational areas. However, they continued to experience and report more psychological difficulties and to seek out mental health services at a significantly higher rate than control group participants. They reported more trouble with the law during adolescence, and the males were more likely to have fathered children, perhaps because they were more impulsive and did not consider the consequences of their actions (Hansen et al., 1999). The arrest rate is much lower in adulthood than in adolescence, but individuals with hyperactivity and conduct problems in adolescence continue to have more difficulties with the law (Satterfield & Schell, 1997). The relationship between childhood hyperactivity and adult trouble with the law is mediated by the presence of childhood conduct problems and serious antisocial behavior in adolescence. Hyperactivity without antisocial behavior does not indicate an increased risk for serious antisocial behavior later in life.

The evidence indicates that some children with ADHD may not continue to meet the criteria for the disorder in adolescence, and these adolescents do not seem much different from their peers without ADHD. Adolescents with ADHD who do not show antisocial behavior may experience some difficulties, but they seem to work through them. Many adolescents with ADHD obtain a high school equivalency diploma, and substantial improvements in educational and occupational achievement are common. Others, especially individuals with a history of antisocial behavior, continue to need extensive help and have poorer outcomes. The evidence showing that adolescents with ADHD can improve with time and can achieve means that adolescents with ADHD should be encouraged to strive toward their educational and occupational goals (Hansen et al., 1999).

PERSPECTIVE 4

ON MEDICATION

SETTING THE SCENE: Dean is a 13-year-old who has been diagnosed as having attention-deficit/hyperactivity disorder. He took medication for a while when he was younger. Although his symptoms have diminished, Dean still is impulsive and engages in behaviors that annoy others. He is also inattentive.

TEACHER: *I just told Dean's parents what he is like at school. They see it at home. They would like to believe that he is so much better that he doesn't need any more treatment, but he is impossible in the classroom. He can't seem to concentrate. I can't suggest medication. It isn't my place, but I think they know how I feel.*

PARENTS: *We're not especially happy about putting Dean back on medication, and to tell you the truth, he doesn't want it, either. The medication helped when he was younger, but he's better now. I think the teacher just has to learn to deal with him better.*

QUESTION: If you were Dean's parents, would you place him on medication?

Treatment of ADHD

The most common treatment for ADHD is the use of stimulant medications, most often methylphenidate hydrochloride (Ritalin), to reduce the symptoms of the disorder (Elia, Ambrosini, & Rapoport, 1999). Children and adolescents with ADHD who receive such medication become calmer and more attentive (Forness & Kavale, 1988), and the number of aversive and disruptive acts declines (National Institutes of Health [NIH], 2000). One reason this treatment works is that Ritalin increases the activity of dopamine in the person's brain; dopamine is a neurotransmitter that inhibits the firing of other neurons (Joekler, 1998; Kalat, 2001). Attention increases because of a decrease in activity in many brain areas, thereby reducing background noise and narrowing attention to one stimulus and away from competing stimuli (Mattay et al., 1996). Approximately 70 to 75 percent of individuals with ADHD receiving medication show increased attention, reduced impulsiveness, and lower activity levels. In turn, parents and teachers interact more positively when students with ADHD show less disruptive and impulsive behavior.

The evidence on the medication's effect on academic performance is more equivocal due to methodological problems involved in such research. Some studies report that approximately 60 percent of the students given medication show cognitive improvements; therefore, as many as 40 percent do not (NIH, 2000; Swanson et al., 1991). Any improvement would be due to the increased attention to lessons that students could pay. Many students who do not show improvement may be behind their classmates and need special help to catch up. A clear answer, though, is not possible at present. Some, but not all, evidence indicates that the individuals' social status improves as disruptive behavior decreases, but peer appraisals of these students still are not as positive as for children who do not have ADHD (Whalen et al., 1989).

The use of medication is widely criticized because the medication treats only the symptoms, not the underlying cause, and it may produce adverse effects such as insomnia and decreased appetite (Elia et al., 1999). In addition, although

AT A GLANCE 13.6 ATTENTION-DEFICIT/HYPERACTIVITY DISORDER

KEY POINT: Adolescents with attention-deficit/hyperactivity disorder (ADHD) may be inattentive, impulsive, distractible, and hyperactive, characteristics that lead to personal, interpersonal, and academic problems.

SUPPORTING POINTS	EXPLANATION
There are three types of attention-deficit/hyperactivity disorder (ADHD).	One type of ADHD emphasizes inattention; a second type focuses on hyperactivity and impulsiveness; and a third type includes inattention, hyperactivity, and impulsiveness.
Children and adolescents with ADHD experience many difficulties.	Many children and adolescents with ADHD exhibit aggression and problems with self-control. They are not popular with their peers.
The cause of ADHD is controversial.	Most psychologists believe that the cause of ADHD can be found in brain functioning.
Both medication and environmental changes are used to treat ADHD.	The use of medication, such as Ritalin, often relieves symptoms. Providing structure and academic tutoring also may help.
Many adolescents with ADHD can succeed as adults, although they do have more problems.	Adolescents, especially those with ADHD without aggression, can make reasonably good adjustments, although they still show some problems. Individuals with ADHD and antisocial behavior are more likely to continue to have more serious difficulties with the law.

medication is effective in reducing the symptoms in the short run, it may not be effective in the long run unless accompanied by teaching substitute behaviors to aggression and antisocial behaviors (Weiss, 1990). Others have criticized the overuse of drugs. The overall benefits may not be long lasting and may disappear when the medication is halted (Hinshaw & Erhardt, 1993).

No one claims that the use of medication will improve intelligence or even schoolwork, but only that it reduces the symptoms of ADHD. The use of medication may not always be the treatment of choice, and it should be part of a complete treatment approach. Often, medication is combined with psychological treatments that involve manipulating the environment and using reinforcers. For example, providing structure and solid routines and using positive reinforcers can be helpful (Walden & Thompson, 1981). Reinforcing on-task behavior may be effective as well (Abramowitz & O'Leary, 1991). Sometimes, parents can be taught to use behavioral strategies, such as positive reinforcement. Counseling to help parents understand the disorder also can improve family functioning (Anastopoulos et al., 1993). Finally, some form of tutoring may bring a student who is behind to the proper level, and practice in social skills also may be necessary. *(For a review of this section, see At A Glance 13.6.)*

PLACING ADOLESCENTS WITH SPECIAL NEEDS IN PERSPECTIVE

There is no doubt that adolescents with stress-related problems, emotional difficulties, disabilities, and chronic conditions or illnesses have a more difficult road to travel. The difficulties and challenges of dealing with a disability are magnified in adolescence, when individuals desire to fit in and be like everyone else. Adolescents cannot easily be forced or coerced into treatment, and they may find it difficult to face the idea that they need help.

It is easy to focus on the increased risk for social and vocational problems in adulthood that exists among adolescents with disabilities or disorders, which is a real problem that must be addressed. Yet many adolescents who receive help do succeed and enter adulthood with the skills, attitudes, motivation, and understanding they need to be successful in interpersonal relationships and reach their occupational goals. Just as it is inappropriate to avoid stating the risks and problems, it is equally wrong to forget the majority who succeed and create a meaningful life for themselves despite the greater challenges they must face.

THEMES

THEME 1 Adolescence is a time of choices, "firsts," and transitions.	• Adolescence may more stressful than childhood because of the number of changes and transitions that occur. • Adolescents must make choices regarding their willingness to face their problems at a time when they desire to fit in and not feel different from others. • Adolescents with disabilities must cope with additional challenges to the ones typically associated with adolescence.
THEME 2 Adolescence is shaped by context.	• The social support available in the environment can be a prime mediator of the effects of stress. • Some stressors are perceived as more stressful in one culture than another. • Some ways of thinking that result in anxiety or depression may be learned from the family.
THEME 3 Adolescence is influenced by group membership.	• Females report more incidents of stress than males. • African Americans and members of other minority groups report more stress than whites. • African Americans and members of some other minority groups are more likely to have a chronic disease, because they are more likely to live in poverty. • Females are more likely to have anorexia nervosa and bulimia than males. • Females have much higher rates of depression than males. • Latinos have higher suicide rates than whites, who have higher suicide rates than African Americans. • Native Americans have the highest suicide rate. • Males are more likely than females to have a learning disability or attention-deficit/hyperactivity disorder.
THEME 4 The adolescent experience has changed over the past 50 years.	• There is more help available today for children and adolescents with disabilities than there was years ago. • Depression and eating disorders are more common today in adolescents than they were years ago.
THEME 5 Today's views of adolescence are becoming more balanced, with greater attention to its positive nature.	• Rather than believing that children with problems will "grow out of them," psychologists today realize that many children may continue to experience these problems, perhaps in different ways, in adolescence. • Rather than seeing children and adolescents who are stress resilient as exceptions, psychologists now understand that they are typical.

CHAPTER SUMMARY AT A GLANCE

KEY TOPICS	KEY POINTS	KEY TERMS
Stress	Stress is a major contributor to many emotional difficulties, but despite the prevalence of stress-related problems, many adolescents cope well with stress. *(At A Glance 13.1, p. 462)*	*stress (p. 453)* *stressor (p. 453)* *rumination (p. 456)* *stress-resilient (stress-resistant)* *adolescents (p. 458)* *problem-directed coping (p. 462)* *emotion-focused coping (p. 462)*
Internalizing Behaviors and Disorders	Anxiety and depression have many causes, and their effects can be found both inside and outside of school. *(At A Glance 13.2, p. 476)*	*disorder (p. 463)* *disability (p. 463)* *externalizing disorders (p. 463)* *internalizing disorders (p. 463)* *anxiety (p. 464)* *social phobia (p. 465)* *depression (p. 466)* *major depressive disorder (p. 467)* *dysthymic disorder (p. 467)* *learned helplessness (p. 469)* *cognitive-behavioral therapy* *(CBT) (p. 473)*
Eating Disorders	Eating disorders, such as anorexia nervosa (self-starvation) and bulimia (bingeing and purging), are serious problems that require therapeutic attention. *(At A Glance 13.3, p. 479)*	*anorexia nervosa (p. 477)* *bulimia (p. 477)*
Coping with Illness	Adolescents with chronic illnesses must cope with additional difficulties that may influence their ability to successfully deal with the challenges of adolescence. *(At A Glance 13.4, p. 481)*	*chronic illness (chronic condition)* *(p. 480)* *acute illness (p. 480)*
Learning Disabilities	The most common disability among teenagers is learning disabilities, which can affect many areas of an adolescent's life. *(At A Glance 13.5, p. 487)*	*learning disabilities (p. 482)* *dyslexia (p. 483)*
Attention-Deficit/Hyperactivity Disorder	Adolescents with attention-deficit/hyperactivity disorder (ADHD) may be inattentive, impulsive, distractible, and hyperactive, characteristics that lead to personal, interpersonal, and academic problems. *(At A Glance 13.6, p. 490)*	*attention-deficit/hyperactivity disorder* *(ADHD) (p. 488)*

Review questions for this chapter appear in the appendix.

14

DRUG USE AND VIOLENCE

WHAT IS YOUR OPINION?

DRUG USE
- The Extent of Drug Use in the United States
- Appreciating the Dangers of Drugs

TOBACCO AND ALCOHOL
- Cigarette Smoking
- Alcohol
- The Gateway Drug Effect Theory

OTHER DRUGS
- Marijuana
  Perspective 1: Sibling Action
- Cocaine and Crack
- Heroin
- Methamphetamine
- The Club Drugs

PREDICTORS OF DRUG USE AND DRUG ABUSE
- Individual Characteristics
- Family Relations
- Peers
- Protective Factors Against Drug Use
- Drug Education
  Perspective 2: Answer the Question!

VIOLENCE AND DELINQUENCY
- Types of Violence
- Is Aggression a Stable Trait?
- The Causes of Violence
  FOCUS: Gangs
- Predicting Violence
- Protective Factors Against Violence
- Can Violence Be Curbed?
  Perspective 3: The Witness
- Lost Boys
- The Link Between Drug Use and Violence

PLACING DRUG USE AND VIOLENCE IN PERSPECTIVE
HAS YOUR OPINION CHANGED?
THEMES
CHAPTER SUMMARY AT A GLANCE

When adolescents between the ages of 12 and 17 were asked about the most important problems facing people their age, they chose the problems of drugs and violent crime (Center on Addiction and Substance Abuse, 1995). These two problems are often associated with adolescents, yet it is wrong to see them as "teenage problems." Most teenagers do not abuse drugs, nor are they violent. However, stories of teenage drug abuse and violence prominently appear in the newspapers and are graphically depicted on television. Every unfortunate example simply validates the prejudice that many people have against adolescents.

This chapter will investigate the nature of drug use and violence. It begins with a look at the trends for drug use in the United States. It then investigates tobacco and alcohol, the most commonly used drugs, along with other drugs, including marijuana, cocaine, heroin, and club drugs (such as ecstasy). The discussion covers both factors that predict drug abuse and factors that protect against drug abuse. The second part of the chapter looks at the problem of violence and delinquency, including the types of violence, factors that cause violence, and factors that reduce the probability of violence. This chapter also examines some of the misconceptions about drug use and violence.

DRUG USE

A **drug** is defined as any substance that alters psychological functioning. For our purposes, **drug abuse** is the use of a drug to the extent that it causes difficulty in meeting normative daily challenges. Most people identify drug abuse with addiction, because the term *addiction* is so often used. However, the American Psychiatric Association's almost universally used classification of mental disorders, *The Diagnostic and Statistical Manual of Mental Disorders,* 4th edition, text revision *(DSM-IV-TR),* never uses the term *addiction* when describing the features of various "substance-related disorders." It uses the term **substance dependence,** which describes a cluster of cognitive, behavioral, and physical symptoms indicating that the individual continues to use a substance despite significant substance-related problems (American Psychiatric Association, 2000). The term **tolerance** refers to the need for a greatly increased amount of a substance to achieve either intoxication or a desired effect, or to a significantly diminished effect with the continued use of the same amount of the substance. The extent to which tolerance develops varies greatly across substances.

Most people are aware of the symptoms that occur when, for example, a habitual user of heroin ceases its use. These symptoms describe **withdrawal,** the physical, psychological, and cognitive symptoms that occur when concentrations of a drug in the body decline in an individual who has maintained prolonged, heavy use of a drug. Dramatic physical symptoms do not always accompany withdrawal from a dangerous drug. In fact, many drugs that cause dependence do not have very severe withdrawal symptoms (Leshner, 1999). Crack is very addictive, but it produces fewer physical withdrawal symptoms than does alcohol or heroin. The essence of dependence, then, is the compulsive drug seeking and drug use even in the face of negative health and social consequences, not the extent to which a drug causes withdrawal symptoms. This compulsive substance use often involves taking larger amounts over a longer period than was originally intended. The individual may express a desire to cut down or quit and may have unsuccessfully tried to do so many times. The user spends a great deal of time obtaining the drug, using it, and recovering from its use and effects. The person's daily activities may revolve around the substance use, and it may substitute for other activities. Despite understanding its effects, the person continues to take the drug and often craves it.

drug Any substance that alters psychological functioning.

drug abuse The use of a drug to the extent that it causes difficulty in meeting normative daily challenges.

substance dependence A cluster of cognitive, behavioral, and physical symptoms indicating that the individual continues to use a substance despite significant substance-related problems.

tolerance The need for a greatly increased amount of a substance to achieve either intoxication or a desired effect; a significantly diminished effect with the continued use of the same amount of the substance.

withdrawal The physical, psychological, and cognitive symptoms that occur when concentrations of a drug in the body decline in an individual who has maintained its prolonged, heavy use.

The Extent of Drug Use in the United States

The Monitoring the Future Study began in the middle 1970s using a representative sample of high school students across the United States in an ongoing project sponsored by the National Institute on Drug Abuse. Students respond to the same questions in this ongoing survey, allowing a detailed analysis of long-term trends.

Figure 14.1 compares the results of this survey for 2001 and some earlier years (Johnston, O'Malley, & Bachman, 2002). The use of illegal drugs significantly increased for eighth, tenth, and twelfth graders from the early 1990s through the mid-1990s. Despite this increase, the level of drug use remains well below the peak level during the late 1970s. There is evidence for some decline in drug use for eighth graders, but comparatively little change for tenth and twelfth graders, especially since 1998. About a fifth of all eighth graders and a little more than 40 percent of all twelfth graders have experimented with illegal drugs.

Two additional conclusions of the study stand out. First, a trend exists for adolescents to become involved in drugs at an earlier age. Substance use has increased substantially for the youngest teens, those in sixth through ninth grades (Johnston et al., 2002). In fact, the transition from ages 12 to 13 appears to be a critical turning point for young people. A dramatic change in their exposure to drugs occurs, and they report greater distance from parents. According to a survey of youth aged 12 to 17, a 13-year-old is about three times more likely than a 12-year-old to know someone who uses cocaine or heroin, to be able to buy marijuana and other drugs, and to know someone who sells drugs. A 13-year-old is also nearly three times more likely not to report a student he or she sees using drugs ("Surveys call attention," 1998). Second, the percentage of adolescents who appreciate the dangers of drugs has declined greatly. Since the early 1990s, fewer students understand the consequences of drug use (Johnston et al., 2002). This lack of knowledge leads to an increase in peer tolerance for drug taking and eventually to increased use.

Figure 14.1
Trends in the Annual Use of Drugs for Eighth, Tenth, and Twelfth Graders

This graph shows the use of drugs other than tobacco and alcohol by eighth, tenth, and twelfth graders. Drug use increased in the early 1990s, began to decline somewhat in the late 1990s, and was stable in 2000 and 2001.

Source: Johnston, O'Malley, & Bachman (2002).

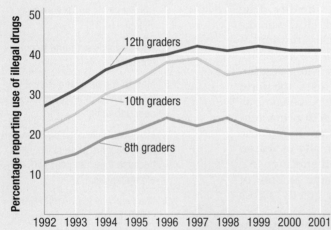

One trend from a recent nationwide survey on drug use is that adolescent drug use starts at an earlier age than it did a generation ago.

Appreciating the Dangers of Drugs

Warnings about the dangers of drug use are certainly not new. In the 1920s, society blamed "demon rum" for all its ills and tried to prohibit alcohol. In the 1930s and 1940s, youth were warned against "Killer Weed," as marijuana was called. In the 1970s, warnings about hippies frying their brains on LSD and suffering flashbacks were broadcast to youth, and the popular "dope fiend" characterization on television depicted the dangers of heroin (Luce & Merrell, 1995). Although some of these campaigns use obvious exaggeration, objective scientific research leads to the clear message that drug use can be harmful.

A positive relationship exists between beliefs in the dangers of drug use and refraining from drug use (Johnston et al., 2002). That is, adolescents who believe that drugs are dangerous are less likely to use these drugs. As teen perceptions of danger from drugs declined in the early 1990s, drug use increased. Perceived risks then increased in the late 1990s, leading to a decline in drug use.

Unfortunately, many adolescents still do not believe that drugs are very harmful. Table 14.1 shows how teens reacted to the statement "How much do you think people risk harming themselves (physically or in other ways), if they . . . ?" Notice that the percentage of teens who think these behaviors are harmful generally declined since 1991 for most, but not all, substances (Johnston et al., 2002). Only a little more than half the eighth graders believe that smoking one or more packs of cigarettes is harmful, whereas only about 65 percent of the 10th graders do, along with 73 percent or so of the twelfth graders.

Even older adolescents misperceive the damage done by smoking cigarettes. When researchers asked undergraduates to estimate how many deaths occur annually in the United States due to tobacco use, cocaine use, or homicide, 96 percent of the freshmen and 89 percent of the seniors overestimated the number

Table 14.1

Trends In Harmfulness as Perceived by Eighth, Tenth, and Twelfth Graders

Researchers asked participants in eighth, tenth, and twelfth grades the following question: "How much do you think people risk harming themselves (physically or in other ways), if they . . . ?"

Behavior	Grade	Percentage Saying "Great Risk"		
		1991	*1996*	*2001*
Smoke marijuana occasionally	8th	57.9	44.3	46.3
	10th	48.6	32.8	31.2
	12th	40.6	25.9	23.5
Try LSD once or twice	8th	*	36.5	31.6
	10th	*	45.1	41.3
	12th	46.6	36.2	33.2
Try crack once or twice	8th	62.8	51.0	48.6
	10th	70.4	60.9	57.1
	12th	60.6	56.0	49.4
Try cocaine powder once or twice	8th	55.5	45.2	43.9
	10th	59.1	53.6	50.6
	12th	59.4	54.2	50.7
Take one or two drinks nearly every day	8th	31.8	28.6	30.0
	10th	36.1	31.2	31.5
	12th	32.7	25.1	23.4
Smoke one or more packs of cigarettes every day	8th	51.6	50.4	57.1
	10th	60.3	57.9	64.7
	12th	69.4	68.2	73.3

*Data not available.
Source: Johnston, O'Malley, & Bachman (2002).

AT A GLANCE 14.1 DRUG USE

KEY POINT: Drug use, drug abuse, and drug dependence are major problems among adolescents.

SUPPORTING POINTS	EXPLANATION
The term *drug* refers to any substance that alters psychological functioning.	*Drug abuse* is the use of a drug to the extent that it causes difficulty in meeting normative daily challenges. *Drug dependence* describes a cluster of symptoms indicating that the individual continues to use a substance despite significant substance-related problems.
Drug taking is common among American teens.	More than half of U.S. high school seniors say they have experimented with an illegal drug. Drug taking increased in the early 1990s but generally declined in the late 1990s and early 2000s.
The more harmful adolescents believe drugs are, the lower their rate of drug use.	Fewer adolescents believed drugs were harmful in the early 1990s, which correlated with the increase in drug use at the time. In the late 1990s drugs were seen as more dangerous, and their use declined.

of deaths from cocaine and by homicide, while significantly underestimating the smoking-related deaths (Giacopassi & Vandiver, 1999). These university students believed that deaths from cocaine and homicide were more common than tobacco-related deaths. In fact, tobacco is the drug leading to the greatest number of potential deaths—between 400,000 and 430,000 deaths annually for direct users and between 40,000 and 67,000 deaths for individuals exposed to tobacco (passive smoking, or breathing in the smoke) (Houston & Kaufman, 2000; Thun, Apicella, & Henley, 2000). It is no wonder that reducing the rate of teenage smoking is difficult. Some authorities believe that public attention almost totally focuses on the use of illicit drugs even though drugs that are legal (for adults, at least), such as alcohol and tobacco, cause more deaths and more harm to society than other drugs (Bogenschneider et al., 1998). *(For a review of this section, see At A Glance 14.1.)*

TOBACCO AND ALCOHOL

The two drugs most commonly used by adolescents are tobacco and alcohol (Bruner & Fishman, 1998). The legal age for using alcohol is 21, and the legal age for purchasing cigarettes is 18 years. According to younger and older teens, both drugs are readily available (Johnston et al., 2002).

Cigarette Smoking

Cigarette smoking is considered the greatest preventable cause of diseases and mortality in the United States (Johnston et al., 2002). Despite all the studies linking smoking to cancer, heart disease, and so many other health-related concerns, smoking remains a national problem. Every day in the United States, six thousand youth try cigarettes, and three thousand become daily cigarette smokers (Centers for Disease Control and Prevention, 1998a). The percentage of twelfth graders who smoked cigarettes within the past month reached a peak in 1976, at 39 percent. A significant reduction then occurred until 1992, when the incidence of smoking increased substantially. Smoking peaked in 1996 for eighth and tenth graders and in 1997 for twelfth graders; a significant reduction then occurred, and

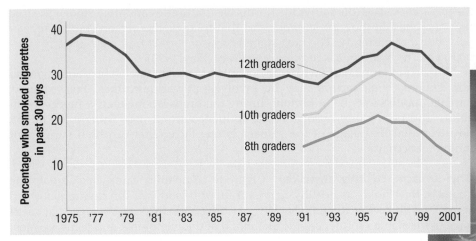

Figure 14.2
Cigarette Smoking Among Eighth, Tenth, and Twelfth Graders
Cigarette smoking declined steadily from 1976 to the early 1990s, when it began to increase; it now shows some decline.
Source: Johnston, O'Malley, & Bachman (2002).

Cigarette smoking has declined among American youth, but is still a major health problem.

the decline continues (see Figure 14.2). In 2001, 12.2 percent of eighth graders, 21.3 percent of the tenth graders, and 29.5 percent of twelfth graders used cigarettes within the last month (Johnston et al., 2002).

Fewer African American teens smoke than Caucasian teens, but in early adulthood the pattern changes, and about the same percentage of African Americans and whites smoke. African Americans begin smoking somewhat later (Robinson & Klesges, 1997), for reasons that are not entirely clear. African American teens view smoking somewhat less favorably than do white adolescents. However, recent data show that the rate for smoking, especially among male African Americans, has doubled since 1991 (Robinson et al., 1997; Yates, 2002). Native Americans have the highest rates of smoking (Preboth, 2001).

Patterns of Cigarette Smoking Most drug use follows a predictable pattern, with increases in adolescence and declines in young adulthood. Adolescents increase their use of alcohol, marijuana, and sometimes other illicit drugs when they leave home to attend college. This drug use declines when they assume adult responsibilities. Becoming engaged, marrying, or having children are all associated with substantial reductions in alcohol and illicit drug use.

Cigarette smoking does not follow this pattern, however (Bachman, Johnston, & O'Malley, 1998). People frequently smoke more cigarettes after high school, and the quantity smoked shows a small decline after age 25 or so (Chassin, Presson, et al., 1996). The stability of smoking may reflect the addictive nature of nicotine, lack of legal sanctions for its use, and compatibility between cigarette smoking and adult roles (Chassin et al., 2000).

Most adolescent smokers say they will quit in a few years, but many do not. A little less than half of all adolescents who just try cigarettes become regular smokers. The time from first use of cigarettes to regular consumption is quite variable, with an average of several years. One student told her classmates that she had believed she could always quit, and after about a year of smoking she tried, only to find that she could not quit. Years later, now in her early 20s, she has a history of trying to stop and then returning to the habit. The student could not pick out the day or month in which she became hooked, but she remembered telling people during her first year or so of smoking that she could always quit.

Becoming a smoker involves a stagelike progression from being initially receptive to the idea of smoking to actually being dependent on nicotine. During the *preparation stage,* the individual forms basic attitudes and may smoke the first few cigarettes. In the *experimental period* that follows, the person smokes repeatedly, but inconsistently. The next stage is *regular use across a wide range of situations,* and the final stage is *nicotine dependence* (Flay, 1993).

We do not understand why some people proceed to later stages and some do not. Different risk factors may be involved at various times. For example, parental models may be important during the preparation stage, whereas availability and peer group influence may influence actual use. There is no doubt, however, that the image of the smoker is one factor that can both support or inhibit tobacco use.

The Image of the Smoker   Cigarette companies carefully cultivate the image of the smoker as healthy, fit, beautiful or handsome, fun loving, sexy, and sometimes throwing off the shackles of conventionality. The image that teens have of the smoker influences the likelihood of their smoking, and teens are most likely to smoke when the image of the smoker is relatively attractive (Dinh et al., 1995; Gibbons & Gerrard, 1995). Most smokers in the younger teen years choose a brand that is heavily advertised, especially near their schools (Sun et al., 1998).

The media often show cigarette smoking in a positive context. Music videos and movies show many performers smoking (DuRant et al., 1997). The media portray women using tobacco products to control their emotions, show power or sex appeal, enhance their body image, control weight, or comfort themselves. Men are shown using tobacco to reinforce their masculine identity and to depict power and prestige. The prevalence of smoking in movies is higher than it is in the general public for people between 18 and 44 years. The depiction of smoking in films, however, reinforces the idea that it is an acceptable, normative behavior in society (Escamilla, Cradock, & Kawachi, 2000).

What would happen if adolescents were asked to rate the same person appearing as both a smoker and a nonsmoker? One study asked adolescents to rate people just that way. Two groups of teens watched a 10-minute video segment in which the female lead speaks with a friend, walks out of the room, and reads a book until a male friend arrives and they talk. Half the group saw a female who smoked as the lead, and the other half saw the same female in the same situation, but this time she did not smoke (Jones & Carroll, 1998). Adolescents viewed the female who smoked as more outgoing, more sophisticated, not as easily manipulated, and less emotional about breaking up with a boyfriend compared with the nonsmoking female. The adolescents did not see the smoker as more popular or more certain of herself, however, and they did not think people would admire her more or find her more attractive. Participants perceived the smoker as less healthy, less desirable as a friend, tougher, and more interested in the opposite sex.

The closer the stereotyped perceived image of the smoker is to a teen's desired self-image, the more likely the teen is to report intentions to begin smoking. Young adolescents who think that smokers are "with it" and who want others to see them in the same way are more likely to smoke (Norman & Tedeschi, 1989). And as children develop into teenagers, their opinions of smokers improve. Fifth graders see smokers as unhealthy, as trying to act "cool," and as older. They perceive nonsmokers as healthy, smart, and nice. The positive perceptions of nonsmokers and the negative perceptions of smokers stand out, with one exception: Fifth graders consider smokers more daring. Approximately 10 percent of fifth graders perceive smokers positively, and these preteens are the most likely to smoke. Fifth graders who perceive smokers as healthy, cool, and good at sports are more likely to be smoking in ninth grade (Dinh et al., 1995).

Both the positive and negative aspects of smoking come through clearly to seventh graders. They describe smokers as dirty and less healthy, but also as exciting and glamorous. They describe nonsmokers as healthy and conforming. Seventh graders associate smokers, rather than nonsmokers, with positive terms like *mature, glamorous,* and *exciting,* showing a change from fifth grade. For girls, the perception of smokers as leaders is a powerful predictor of later smoking. Adolescents may begin to smoke to project an image that is consistent with what they believe are desirable characteristics, such as confidence, maturity, and independence—the same images they see in tobacco ads. The trend toward more positive social images of cigarette smoking continues between seventh and eighth grade (Botvin, Botvin, & Baker, 1983).

Two possible mechanisms account for the relationship between teenage smoking behavior and intentions to smoke on the one hand and similarity between the self and one's stereotype of smokers on the other hand. First, *self-consistency* motivation suggests that people smoke because their self-image matches their image of the smoker. *Self-enhancement* motivation indicates that if people value their image of the smoker more than their present self-image, they may elect to improve their image by smoking. At present, more evidence exists for self-consistency than self-enhancement (Aloise-Young & Hennigan, 1996). In other words, adolescents may smoke in part because their image of the smoker corresponds to their own image. When researchers measured self-consistency for three traits, the difference between the self and smoker became less between grades 5 and 8.

Cigarette advertising and promotion effectively encourage smoking. Either attending to the advertising or becoming involved in a promotion, such as receiving a free sports bag with a cigarette logo, predicts a progression to smoking (Biener & Siegel, 2000). Obviously, just looking at an ad or ordering a sports bag does not cause a person to become a smoker. Rather, these promotions and images are particularly attractive to adolescents, who may find their identity in the image of the smoker that tobacco companies have so carefully crafted. The Multistate Tobacco Settlement of claims against tobacco companies places restrictions on cigarette advertising and some forms of promotion, but it does not eliminate cigarette advertising altogether.

Alcohol

Adolescents have a fundamentally different experience with alcohol than with any other drug. Whereas the majority of American children do not grow up with parents who smoke (some 53 percent of U.S. homes are smoke-free), alcohol use is a different story (Pirkle et al., 1996). Most children and adolescents are aware that their parents occasionally have a drink, be it a beer, a glass of wine, or a mixed drink. Parents often drink alcohol in front of their children, and everyone knows where it is kept. In addition, whereas parents who are smokers tend to tell their children not to smoke, this is not the case with parents who drink alcohol. Teens see toasts on television and at weddings, they are well aware of the availability of alcohol at parties, and movies and television programs often show drinking. Whereas restaurants and even baseball parks often restrict cigarette smoking, our society often encourages drinking. Indeed, beer companies sponsor many sporting events. Of course, parents often do not know that their teenage children are using alcohol. Less than one-third of all parents in one survey were aware of their adolescents' regular drinking (Bogenschneider et al., 1998). Parents who were aware were more concerned about their teenage children's drinking and were more likely to discuss the topic with them.

Alcohol is the most frequently used drug in adolescence (Johnston et al., 2002). Adolescents are experimenting with alcohol earlier than in the past; the age of first

One of the differences between alcohol and other drugs is that adolescents often see their parents drink at least occasionally and are well aware of the use of alcohol at celebrations.

initiation is now about 12 years. Alcohol use has remained fairly stable over the past few years, but its level remains very high. In 2001, the percentages of eighth, tenth, and twelfth graders who admitted using alcohol in the past month were 22, 39, and 50 percent, respectively (Johnston et al., 2002). Binge drinking is also common, especially among older adolescents. It is measured by the number of occasions during the prior 2 weeks in which the person had five or more drinks in a row. On college campuses, drinking, and especially binge drinking, has become alarming (O'Neal, 1998; Temple, 1998). A study of more than 14,000 students at 4-year colleges found that 6 percent met the criteria for alcohol dependence, and 31 percent met the clinical criteria for alcohol abuse (Knight et al., 2002).

Although people tend not to consider alcohol use a serious problem, the facts prove otherwise. Alcohol causes at least 200,000 deaths per year, according to estimates, compared with about 8,000 deaths for all completely illegal drugs; its use also leads to a tremendous amount of injury, job absence, and familial disruption (Gahlinger, 2002). In fact, death in a motor vehicle accident, of which about half involve alcohol, is the single greatest cause of death in adolescence (Brody et al., 1998). Higher minimum drinking ages, stricter laws, and increased educational efforts have had some effect, as the number of alcohol-related automobile accidents involving young people has declined significantly (United States Department of Transportation, 2000). Alcohol use is related to other risky behaviors, such as delinquency, unprotected sexual activity, poor school performance, and dropping out of school (Hawkins, Catalano, & Miller, 1992). The relationship between alcohol use and aggression is well established (Giancola, 2002; Preboth, 2002). Alcohol is a depressant that acts as a disinhibitor, increasing risk taking and negatively affecting judgment.

Many teens see people drinking all around them and thus perceive warnings from adults as hypocritical. Male adolescents drink more and start using alcohol at an earlier age than female adolescents do, and older adolescents drink more than younger adolescents (Parker & Calhoun, 2000). Early drinking is most likely to lead to dependence and to persist into adulthood. About 40 percent of all youth who begin drinking at age 14 or younger develop alcohol dependence sometime in their lives (Grant & Dawson, 1997).

Caucasians consume more alcohol than African Americans or Asians. Significant differences exist within cultures and subcultures. For example, the rates of heavy drinking are higher among Mexican American and Puerto Rican men than among Cuban American men (Clark & Tam, 1998). Alcohol is a significant problem among many Native Americans, and tribes differ in their consumption patterns and tolerance for alcohol. The Navajo view social drinking as acceptable, whereas the Hopi consider drinking irresponsible (Mail & Johnson, 1993).

The Gateway Drug Effect Theory

Does smoking cigarettes and consuming alcohol predict a progression to marijuana use and then a further escalation to the use of other illicit drugs? This question has been asked for many years. The *gateway drug effect* theory states that individuals progress from one drug to another. It does not say that the progression is inevitable or even common, however.

Research strongly supports the gateway drug effect theory in this narrow context. Students who smoke one or more packs of cigarettes per day are three times more likely to use alcohol and ten to thirty times more likely to use illicit drugs than are students who do not smoke tobacco (Torabi, Bailey, & Majd-Jabbari, 1993). Evidence clearly shows that adolescents first use at least one drug that is legal for adults—either alcohol or tobacco—before using marijuana and then may progress to the use of illicit drugs (Kandel, Yamaguchi, & Chen, 1992). Adolescents are unlikely to experiment with marijuana without prior use of these "legal" drugs. The progression from tobacco and alcohol use to later use of illicit drugs is common among drug abusers, and marijuana is usually the first illicit drug used. For someone who has ever smoked tobacco or consumed alcohol, the risk of moving to marijuana is 65 times higher than for a person who never smoked or drank. The risk of moving on to cocaine is 104 times higher for individuals who smoked marijuana at least once than for people who did not (Leshner, 1999).

This narrow interpretation of the gateway theory does indeed have merit, but the broader version involving inevitability of progression does not. Most drug users do not progress from one drug to another, and the progression is not insidious or universal. Most drug users set limits on which drugs they will use and avoid certain drugs altogether (Venturelli, 2000). Many youths stop at a particular stage and do not progress further. The narrow version of the theory would argue that one drug facilitates the use of the next, but does not cause the use or make it inevitable. Entry into a particular stage is a common and perhaps even necessary prerequisite for entry into the next stage, although it is not the only factor.

The narrow version of the gateway drug effect theory may be applicable for several reasons. First, as individuals begin smoking and drinking, they learn to use tobacco and alcohol to change mood, experience a high, or deal with a problem through avoidance or escape. Their first illicit drug use often satisfies the same needs, and users are likely to have friends who use drugs and thus may influence them to try new ones. Other factors, though, must be present to propel individuals to use other, "harder" drugs. Unfortunately, our knowledge about what makes people stop drug use or continue on to harder drugs is incomplete. (For a review of this section, see At A Glance 14.2.)

AT A GLANCE 14.2 TOBACCO AND ALCOHOL

KEY POINT: Many people do not appreciate the dangers of tobacco and alcohol, two drugs commonly used by adolescents.

SUPPORTING POINTS	EXPLANATION
Tobacco use among adolescents increased during the early and middle 1990s and then began to decline.	Between 1996 and 2001, 30-day tobacco use declined significantly. Still, almost a third of all high school seniors use cigarettes.
The pattern for cigarette smoking differs from other drugs.	Cigarette smoking does not show the decline in usage during early adulthood that occurs with other drug use.
Teens are most likely to smoke cigarettes when the image of the smoker matches the image they would like to project.	Tobacco companies show the smoker as healthy, beautiful, fun loving, sexy, and throwing off the shackles of conformity.
Alcohol, which is the most used drug in adolescence, is related to many physical and social problems.	Many adolescents die each year from accidents caused by driving while intoxicated. Alcohol also may negatively affect social relationships and promote risky behaviors.
The gateway drug effect theory states that tobacco and alcohol are "gateway drugs" that lead to the use of illicit drugs.	The gateway theory is correct in that users of illicit drugs almost always have used alcohol, tobacco, or both. However, the progression to other drugs is not inevitable; many users stop at the use of particular drugs, not progressing to other drug use.

OTHER DRUGS

The use of cigarettes by adolescents before the age of 18 and the use of alcohol before 21 years are illegal in most states, but adults may legally use these substances. The use of many drugs, such as marijuana and cocaine, is not legally permitted for adolescents or adults.

Marijuana

Marijuana is the most commonly used illegal drug for both adolescents and adults. Annual marijuana use reached a peak of 51 percent among twelfth graders in 1979, after which a long decline occurred, until use reached 22 percent in 1992. The 1990s saw an increase in marijuana use, as with so many other drugs. Annual incidence rates peaked in the late 1990s, and a relatively small decline followed (see Figure 14.3).

The psychoactive ingredient in marijuana is delta-9-tetrahydrocannabinol (delta-9-THC), one of the sixty chemicals found in the resin of cannabis (the dried flowering tops of some species of hemp plants). Specific brain receptors, mostly in the cerebellum, basal ganglia, and hippocampus, are sensitive to THC (Herkenham et al., 1991a, 1991b). The THC in marijuana binds to these receptors, which are involved in pain, emotion, memory, and motor control (Musty, Reggio, & Consroe, 1995). The hippocampus is involved in laying down new memories, which explains why marijuana interferes with memory. The delta-9-THC content in marijuana has increased, and today's marijuana is about twice as powerful as it was 20 or 30 years ago.

Many adolescents do not believe marijuana use is harmful (Brook, Balka, & Whiteman, 1999), and its consequences are controversial. However, it is universally accepted that marijuana slows reaction time and impairs attention and coordination (Gahlinger, 2002). Driving under the influence of marijuana, like driving under the influence of alcohol, is a serious problem today. The drug adversely affects coordination, tracking, and reaction time and thus detracts from driving ability.

Figure 14.3

Marijuana: Trends in Annual Use and Perceived Risk Among Eighth, Tenth, and Twelfth Graders

Marijuana use increased in the early 1990s after a long period of decline and recently has shown a plateau or modest decline (A); in contrast, perception of risk has increased and decreased over the years (B). Perception of risk and use are inversely related; that is, as perception of risk increases, use usually begins to decline.

Source: Johnston, O'Malley, & Bachman (2002).

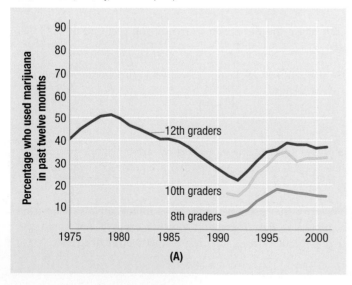

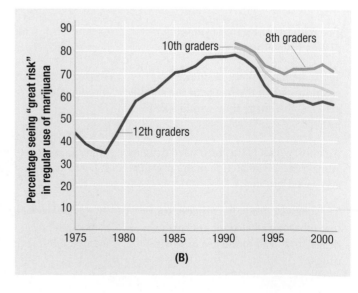

Another established danger is the link between marijuana use and lung diseases, probably even cancer (Sussman et al., 1996). One joint (marijuana cigarette) is equal to about five cigarettes in terms of the amount of carbon monoxide intake, to four cigarettes in terms of the amount of tar, and to ten cigarettes in terms of the amount of microscopic damage to cells lining the airways (Grinspoon & Bakalar, 1997).

Some marijuana users believe the drug has no lasting effects. This idea is not true, as shown by a study of college students who were marijuana users but had not smoked for most of a month before testing. Heavy users still performed worse on measures of attention and general learning (Painter, 1996). Laboratory studies show that marijuana use interferes with a wide range of cognitive functions, including reading comprehension and short-term memory. However, the extension of these findings raises considerable controversy. The *amotivational syndrome* is a group of symptoms, including poor motivation, that has been advanced to explain the behavior patterns of heavy marijuana users. There is some evidence that people who chronically smoke marijuana show a pattern of poor achievement and motivation, but whether marijuana use is the cause of this pattern of behavior or merely an effect of it is still debated (Shedler & Block, 1990). Many other correlations have been found between marijuana use and negative consequence; for example, an increase in marijuana use is associated with a decline in the likelihood of educational achievement, an increase in deviance, and an increase in risk-taking behaviors (see Brook et al., 1999). Because these correlations do not demonstrate cause and effect, however, interpretation is difficult.

Can marijuana use lead to dependence? Some evidence supports the existence of dependence with heavy use of marijuana. Some high school students show a pattern of marijuana abuse that affects their lives adversely. They report becoming physically dependent; developing a tolerance; and showing flulike symptoms, restlessness, and irritability when trying to stop smoking (Kouri, Pope, & Lukas, 1999). Long-term, chronic marijuana users report increases in anxiety, irritability, and physical tension after abstaining from use (Kouri & Pope, 2000). An estimated 4 to 5 percent of the American public may become dependent on marijuana at some time in their lives (American

PERSPECTIVE 1

SIBLING ACTION

SETTING THE SCENE: You and your younger brother, who is 16 years old, are alone in the house. You smell an unusual odor coming from his room, and when you enter you find him smoking marijuana.

BROTHER: *It's no big deal. I've been smoking cigarettes on and off since I was 13. A couple of my friends gave me a joint a couple of months ago, and now I smoke once in a while.*

QUESTION: What would you say to your brother? Would you inform your parents?

The amount of delta-9-THC, the psychoactive ingredient in marijuana, is much higher than it was a generation ago. Marijuana slows reaction time and impairs coordination.

Psychiatric Association, 2000; Ray & Ksir, 1993). The problem of marijuana dependence is growing, probably because of the increasing amounts of THC in marijuana today.

Adult users who have been unable to quit often seek treatment (Stephens, Roffman, & Simpson, 1993). They report being unable to stop, feeling bad about using marijuana, and feeling that they are procrastinating and not achieving goals. They also describe a loss of self-confidence, memory problems, irritability, and nausea while trying to stop using the drug (Stephens, Roffman, & Simpson, 1993). Approximately 40 percent of the adults who seek treatment specifically for marijuana use do not use any other drug (Sussman et al., 1996). Little is known about regular teenage users who try to stop. It is known that only 15 percent of adolescent daily users stop using the drug 5 years after high school graduation, and over half remain users in adulthood. Most teens do not use marijuana on a daily basis, and the majority of marijuana users remain light users. Heavy users often show emotional difficulties, a characteristic that distinguishes heavy from light marijuana users (Kandel & Chen, 2000).

Marijuana, then, is not the harmless drug it is sometimes made out to be, nor is it the mad Killer Weed of the 1930s and 1940s. Some people advocate implementing the same guidelines for marijuana use as are now applied to alcohol or nicotine use (Sidney et al., 1997), whereas others argue that the drug should remain illegal.

Cocaine and Crack

Cocaine is a stimulant, affecting the central nervous system and producing feelings of euphoria. Physiological effects include extreme changes in blood pressure, increases in heart and respiration rates, insomnia, nausea, tremors, and convulsions. Cocaine use can lead to paranoid behavior, and dependence is very common. Cocaine's effects are caused by increasing levels of neurotransmitters, such as norepinephrine, serotonin, and dopamine, within the brain. Cocaine use leads to euphoric highs and very depressive lows, and increases in frequency and dose are common, in part to avoid the lows. Crack is a highly purified form of cocaine that produces a quick high and wears off quickly.

The use of cocaine and crack is related to violence because of both the energizing effect of the drug and the violent drug dealing that surrounds it. The need to finance the drug habit is one reason for violent offenses and property crimes in areas with high levels of cocaine addiction. Cocaine use can lead to a number of health problems, and two thousand fatalities a year are linked to its use.

Heroin

The use of heroin, an opiate derivative, leads to substance dependence. Heroin produces feelings of euphoria that suppress worries and even awareness of needs. Drugs like heroin and opium bind to receptor sites in the brain that are responsible for reductions in pain, changes in mood, and pleasure (Reisine, 1995). Dangers in heroin use are well known. Overdoses can be fatal, and the use of the drug takes over one's life. Withdrawal is difficult, and the cravings are great.

The annual incidence of heroin use among twelfth graders is 0.9 percent. Some evidence shows that its use is on the rise, and most users are not getting the treatment they require (Office of National Drug Control Policy, 2001).

Methamphetamine

Methamphetamine is a class of amphetamines, or stimulants. Amphetamine use increases blood pressure and can cause nausea, vomiting, fatal heart arrhythmias, and even stroke. Users report fatigue, depression, confusion, nightmares, irritability, and aggression. A user rapidly develops tolerance for the drug, and progression to greater levels of use is a serious problem (Adams, 2001). Use of the drug may even lead to a condition known as *amphetamine psychosis,* in which users experience paranoid delusions, feel threatened, and can become violent. A potent form that is smoked, known as *ice,* causes swift dependence and leads to compulsive abuse. The annual incidence of methamphetamine use for eighth, tenth, and twelfth graders is 2.8, 3.7, and 3.9 percent, respectively (Johnston et al., 2002).

Although a relationship between perceived risk and methamphetamine use can be found, it is less predictive than for other drugs. Perhaps this relatively weak relationship can be explained by the fact that some people take methamphetamine for weight reduction or to stay awake, uses not found for other drugs. Physicians no longer prescribe methamphetamine for weight loss, as use of the drug commonly results in dependence and health problems. Furthermore, methamphetamine actually causes the body to increase its use of resources rather than supplying any energy. Disapproval rates for methamphetamine are relatively high; between 70 and 87 percent of all high school seniors disapprove of its use.

The Club Drugs

Recently, the so-called club drugs have received much publicity. These drugs form a very broad category and include LSD, ketamine, flunitrazepam (Rohypnol), gamma hydroxybutyrate (GHB), and 3,4-methylenedioxymethamphetamine (MDMA, or ecstasy). They are called *club drugs* because they are most often used in nightclubs and all-night parties (raves) (Wood & Synovitz, 2001). Rohypnol and GHB have sometimes been labeled "date rape" drugs because they induce amnesia and have been used in connection with rapes or seduction by both dates and acquaintances. These drugs cause the victim to fall into a helpless, comatose state (Gahlinger, 2002). Ketamine, another club drug, induces bizarre thoughts and hallucinations. The Monitoring the Future Survey found an annual use of 1.6 percent by high school seniors for GHB and 2.5 percent for ketamine (Johnston et al., 2002).

Ecstasy (MDMA) is really a form of methamphetamine used for its hallucinogenic properties. It has a combination of stimulant and hallucinogenic effects, including elevated mood and altered perceptions (Gahlinger, 2002). Its use rose from 1995 through 2001; annual use for eighth, tenth, and twelfth graders is 3.5, 6.2, and 8.2 percent, respectively (Johnston et al., 2002). Although the increase in use continues, the rate of increase may be slowing.

Recently, so-called "club drugs" such as ecstasy have been brought to the public's attention. A growing body of evidence points to their danger.

At a Glance **14.3** Other Drugs

KEY POINT: Adolescent use of marijuana, methamphetamine, cocaine, heroin, and ecstasy is a serious problem.

SUPPORTING POINTS	EXPLANATION
Marijuana is the most commonly used illegal drug.	Marijuana is more potent today than it was in the 1960s and 1970s. Marijuana adversely affects coordination, tracking, and reaction time. It detracts from driving ability.
Cocaine is a stimulant drug often discussed in the media.	The use of cocaine and crack is linked with violence, not only because of the energizing aspects of the drug but also because of its link with a violent subculture.
Methamphetamine is a class of amphetamines, which are stimulants.	Methamphetamine can cause dangerous increases in heart rate and blood pressure, and dependence ensues.
Club drugs, such as Rohypnol and ecstasy, have recently become major concerns.	Rohypnol is sometimes called a date rape drug, because it induces amnesia. Ecstasy is toxic to neurons, and its use can cause a dangerous spiking of body temperature, leading to death.

Many adolescents are not familiar with the dangers of ecstasy, although they are now well researched (Dennis & Ballard, 2002). A growing body of evidence indicates that even in small doses, MDMA can result in acute toxic reactions (Wood & Synovitz, 2001). Ecstasy can destroy neurons and impair brain function (Lurie, 2002; Morris, 1998). It can lead to long-lasting behavioral effects, including memory loss and mood changes ("Study: Ecstasy," 2001). Deaths are linked to MDMA, because it causes drastic increases in core body temperature, which can contribute to kidney failure, hemorrhage, and liver damage (Boot, McGregor, & Hall, 2000). The drug induces tolerance very rapidly, and its adverse effects include muscular aches, abdominal pain, sweating, rapid heart rate, tremors, exhaustion, depression, and suicidal feelings (Gahlinger, 2002).

Other drugs may be abused as well. Hallucinogens are numerous, and abuse of prescription drugs has become a problem. People take other drugs, such as anabolic steroids (see "Physical Development"), to enhance performance, although the long-term consequences can be severe. *(For a review of this section, see At A Glance 14.3.)*

Predictors of Drug Use and Drug Abuse

If we could predict who is most likely to become a drug abuser, we could commit our resources more effectively. We do know that the factors predictive of drug use and abuse can be broadly placed in three categories: individual characteristics, family (parent-child) factors, and peer group influence.

Individual Characteristics

Although no single personality pattern is predictive of drug abuse, some characteristics do stand out. A pattern of ego undercontrol and antisocial behavior at young ages predicts drug abuse (Shedler & Block, 1990; Sher, Bartholow, & Wood, 2000). Ego undercontrol involves being unable to delay gratification, reacting quickly, being very emotionally expressive, showing rapidly shifting moods, overreacting to minor frustrations, and being easily irritated. Drug abusers have poor impulse control and high anxiety levels in interpersonal relationships. They tend to have a low frustration tolerance and to be chronically angry, depressed, and bored (Segal & Stewart, 1996). A predictive pattern for later drug use in girls includes a lack of ego resilience involving an inability to initiate activities, be energetic or self-reliant, trust their own judgment, and recover after a stressful experience.

Heavier drug users are more likely to have low self-esteem, to equate drug use with entertainment, and to have weaker family ties, whereas nonusers of alcohol and other drugs equate them with negative consequences while showing higher self-esteem and stronger family ties. Light to moderate users fall somewhere in the middle (DeAngelis, 1994). The use of other drugs, such as marijuana, often follows this pattern, in which heavy users differ from light users and nonusers. For example, regular heavy users of marijuana are much more rebellious and angry, show a lack of responsibility, and score high on measures of sensation seeking (Brook et al., 1981). They see themselves as inadequate, have friends who smoke marijuana heavily, often come from turbulent homes filled with discord, and show an inability to conform to rules.

The research linking personality characteristics to the risk of drug use often points to the role of sensation seeking (Donohew et al., 1999), a personality trait describing preferences for novel, unusual, or risky situations. Individuals with a high need for sensation begin using drugs earlier and are more likely than low sensation seekers to become regular drug users. The risk and illegality associated with substance use are a source of stimulation for high sensation seekers.

Exposure to violence is another factor related to drug use. Children and adolescents who are physically or sexually assaulted or who witness violence in the family and neighborhood are at a greater risk for substance abuse and dependence (Kilpatrick et al., 2000). Substance use may be an attempt to cope with the stress produced by the aggression or to escape from the situation. Adolescents may use drugs to reduce their negative emotions (Kilpatrick et al., 1997).

Biological Factors in Drug Use Could biological factors and the genes that underlie them make it more likely for one person to take drugs than another? Could biological factors make it more likely that one person will become more dependent on a drug than another? The answers to these questions are complicated but appear to be yes.

Drugs influence specific parts of the brain and particular neurotransmitters. For example, nicotine, as well as some other drugs, affects the neurotransmitter dopamine; nicotine stimulates dopamine production, and increases in dopamine levels lead to feelings of satisfaction. The reinforcing properties of nicotine are due in part to activation of dopamine in the limbic system, which is the brain's pleasure and reward system. Many different addictive drugs (for example, cocaine) share this action. Cigarette smoke also contains substances that inhibit the brain from breaking down the neurotransmitter. Genetic factors could underlie the workings of this system, and recent studies find evidence for a genetic basis for dopamine levels and the action of the neurotransmitter that may make some people more responsive to particular drugs (Cloninger, Adolfsson, & Svrakic, 1996; Lerman et al., 1999; Pomerleau & Kardia, 1999).

Evidence for genetic involvement in smoking is well established (Heath & Madden, 1995). There is no "smoker's gene," but people with a particular genetic makeup may show differences in the dopamine system that make them more responsive to nicotine (or other drugs). They may be more likely to desire sensation and novelty. Dopamine plays a role in novelty-seeking personality traits and the need for external stimulation. For example, an artificial decrease in dopamine levels also decreases novelty seeking and exploration, and an artificial increase in dopamine levels increases both novelty seeking and exploration. Differences in novelty seeking and responsiveness related to dopamine levels, then, may influence the risk of smoking, because smokers express a greater need for stimulation and novelty than nonsmokers (Sobol et al., 1999).

Genetic factors for alcoholism also exist (Plomin et al., 1997). Studies show that when one identical twin has alcoholism, the other twin is more likely to have alcoholism than is the case with fraternal twins (McGue, 1993). Because identical twins have identical genes, whereas fraternal twins share an average of half their genes, this finding is evidence for genetic involvement.

Many studies conclude that there is a genetic predisposition to alcoholism (Schuckit et al., 1996). People with alcoholism metabolize alcohol differently than individuals who are not alcoholics and build up tolerance more easily (Schuckit, 1987). One study compared the sons of fathers with alcoholism with sons of fathers who did not have the disease. At the time of the study, none of the children had alcoholism. Even with the same level of alcohol in their systems, the sons of fathers with alcoholism reported being less intoxicated than the sons of fathers without alcoholism (Schuckit, 1986).

There is a danger in designating individual personality characteristics as influencing drug use. Personality differences and the genetic differences underlying them may make an individual more likely to use drugs, but they do not cause the individual to take drugs, continue to take them, or become a drug abuser. We must guard against overinterpreting this material to make it more important than it is or believing that someone is "fated" to become a drug user, which no one is.

Many people fail to understand that what might be inherited would not be a gene for having alcoholism or being a smoker but rather a predisposition—a greater tendency to use drugs because of personality differences or differences in the way people react to drugs. Genetic mechanisms may underlie personality traits related to the use of drugs (for example, sensation seeking) and influence the effect of a particular drug on the individual. No one is genetically fated to become a drug user, however.

Family Relations

Adolescents who describe their family lives as troubled and who are alienated from family at the age of 7 years are more frequent users and abusers of drugs in adolescence (Shedler & Block, 1990). Marital discord also is related to substance abuse, as are physical and sexual abuse (Mayes, 1995).

Certain types of parenting seem to predispose adolescents to abuse drugs. When parents are described as cold, forbidding, or neglectful, their children are more likely to be aggressive and to take drugs (Stein, Newcomb, & Bentler, 1993). Problem drinkers and illicit drug users often describe experiencing inconsistent parenting, a lack of family cohesiveness, and more conflict. They often perceive their parents as showing less warmth and as being rejecting (Barnow et al., 2002). Parents who abuse drugs also show poorer parenting strategies, which may predispose their children to the use of drugs.

Parenting style is often viewed in terms of two dimensions: *demandingness* and *responsiveness* (sometimes called *supportingness*). The responsiveness construct involves such behaviors as praising, encouraging, and giving physical affection—showing that the adolescent is loved. The demanding or control dimension is somewhat more difficult to define and ranges from coercive parental control involving threats and yelling to explanations of why the adolescent should change behavior. The demandingness construct also involves enforcing rules and actively monitoring adolescents, knowing where they are and with whom they are associating, and being aware of what they are doing (see "Families"). Evidence clearly shows that support is related to positive outcomes and less drug use (as well as less violence). The relationship between control and drug use is much more complicated. Too much control and rigidity or too much laxness leads to problems (Peterson & Rollins, 1987). One factor in the control dimension related to drug use is level of parental monitoring. Higher levels of parental monitoring are associated with lower instances of alcohol and illicit drug use, as well as less school misconduct (Barnes & Farrell, 1992).

Parental support and active monitoring are strong predictors of lower rates of alcohol and other drug use. When parents are supportive, adolescents are less oriented toward their peers and less likely to choose friends who are drug users

(Barnes & Windle, 1987). Closeness with parents discourages drug use, both directly by removing risk factors that promote it and indirectly through an impact on choice of friends (Kandel & Andrews, 1987). Low parental monitoring increases the likelihood of drug use by increasing the probability that adolescents are spending time with drug-using peers (Dishion & Loeber, 1985). Youth who are not well monitored often believe their parents don't care what they do. The combination of lack of support and poor monitoring often predicts drug use (Hawkins et al., 1992).

The situation is really somewhat more complicated. An adolescent's personality may influence the child-rearing strategies the parents use. For example, a child's aggressiveness may cause parents to resort to inconsistent and inappropriate discipline, which may then lead to poor family relationships, which encourage drug use (Stice & Barrera, 1995). In addition, poor and inconsistent parenting practices may cause children to react in a way that isolates them from others and adds tension and conflict to the family situation.

Parental drug use also influences adolescents, both directly and indirectly (Chassin, Curran, et al., 1996). When parents use drugs, they are modeling the behavior. For example, children whose parents smoke are three times more likely to smoke by age 15 (Males, 1997a). In addition, continued drug use by parents makes their admonishments not to use drugs sound hollow. Parental drug use leads to less effective discipline practices and indirectly to a greater risk of drug abuse by the adolescents (Tarter et al., 1993). Excessive parental drinking may lead to impaired parental control. In fact, parental drug use is associated with poor monitoring of adolescents' activities and with adolescents' membership in drug-using peer groups (Dishion, Patterson, & Reid, 1988). Parental drug use, such as alcoholism, is also associated with increased environmental stress and negative emotions, which may lead adolescents to use drugs as a way to escape or regulate these negative feelings.

Peers

Explaining her adolescent child's use of marijuana and alcohol at an early age, one parent remarked that "he fell in with a bad crowd" and left it at that. Most parents believe that peer pressure is the primary reason teens use drugs, and indeed, two-thirds of the adolescents cite peer pressure as one reason for their

Peer pressure may be one reason for drug use, but research also shows that drug users often choose other users as friends.

drug use. Evidence is very clear that adolescents who use drugs are often found in groups with others who do the same. In fact, of all the variables found to be related to adolescent substance use, having friends who use drugs is the strongest predictor (Curran, Stice, & Chassin, 1997; Fergusson, Horwood, & Lynskey, 1995).

Peer pressure is certainly a factor in drug use, but despite the availability of alcohol, tobacco, and marijuana, many teenagers do not smoke or drink excessively. Peer pressure is a force, but it does not operate in a vacuum. As noted earlier, the quality of the relationship with parents mediates peer influence (Chassin et al., 1993). The better the relationship, the less likely that peer influence for use of drugs will be effective. In addition, the overwhelming majority of teenagers say they use alcohol and other drugs for the high or to forget their problems rather than to be part of the group (Boeck & Lynn, 1995). This evidence leads some researchers to believe that the role of peer pressure in initiating drug use has been overestimated (Morojele & Brook, 2001).

Rather than being seduced by a desire to fit in and socialized into drug use, adolescents who are prone to use drugs may actively choose drug users as friends. Adolescents with certain personality characteristics and family backgrounds may choose to be around other adolescents with the same characteristics and backgrounds. They may select friends who are at risk for drug use or who already use drugs. These adolescents may have similar interests or outlooks on life and then both model and reinforce drug use (Swain et al., 1989). Whether selection or socialization is more important is still controversial; perhaps both are equally important (Curran et al., 1997; Fisher & Bauman, 1988).

Protective Factors Against Drug Use

Not all adolescents, even the ones at risk, will become drug abusers. A number of protective factors mediate between risk and outcome. Four environmental and social factors that appear to guard against substance use are a positive, supportive relationship with parents, involvement in community-based activities, a positive school climate and achievement, and relationships with positively influencing peers. Some family interaction patterns—for example, patterns based on support, less conflict, and warm parent-child bonds—are associated with less adolescent drug abuse (Brook, Nomura, & Cohen, 1989). Warm family relations provide a buffer against the use of drugs, perhaps by reducing the need for escape and providing models and lessons in how to deal with stress (Stephenson, Henry, & Robinson, 1996; Zhang, Welte, & Wieczorek, 1999). These families combine warmth and interest with adequate parental supervision and discussions about family rules on dating, curfews, and chores (Jessor et al., 1995).

A positive attitude toward school and health, placing personal value on academic achievement, and understanding the health consequences of drug use also predict less drug taking. One way to combat drug abuse is to reduce risk factors and increase factors that seem to buffer children against drug abuse.

Drug Education

Almost everyone is in favor of drug education, and millions of dollars are spent on it yearly. Unfortunately, drug education programs have not been as effective as both professionals and the public would like, and many promising programs are inadequately evaluated (Gorman, 1997; Szalavitz, 2002). It is known that programs that rely on scare tactics or moral exhortations about how good people don't use drugs are not successful. Strategies that simply give information about drugs or try to enhance character also are doomed to fail (Donaldson et al., 1995). One reason for their ineffectiveness is that these programs cannot remove the social problems that may lead to drug abuse or harmful adult models (Males, 1997b). An adolescent may abuse drugs to get immediate pleasure, experiment, or rebel. These reasons are easy to understand and are reasonable targets for drug education efforts. However, individuals may also use drugs to escape from the harsh realities of life, such as failure, rejection, and family problems. These reasons are much more difficult to remedy. To be effective, drug education programs must help students find alternative ways of dealing with their problems, and some new programs are doing just that.

Twenty years ago, teens knew more about drugs than adolescents know today. Drugs were always in the news years ago, and parents of that generation were more likely to talk to their children about the dangers of drug abuse. The phenomenon of one generation knowing so much more about a particular subject than the younger generation is called **generational forgetting** (Johnston, Bachman, & O'Malley, 1995). At the same time that teens are hearing less about the consequences of drug taking, they are receiving more encouragement for using drugs. The lyrics of many popular songs display prodrug sentiments and have drug-related themes. Thus, adolescents today hear fewer cautions and more reassurance and encouragement about drug use.

Drug prevention should start early, because studies show that children are starting to use drugs at a younger age. Parents should play a significant role in any drug abuse prevention program. Some television ads emphasize the need for parents to talk with their children about drugs. Adolescents whose parents communicate with them about drugs and are involved in community and school activities are half as likely to use illegal drugs (Manning, 1994).

Most people admit that teens need factual information about the dangers of drug taking, but accurate information is only one aspect of drug education. Most modern drug education programs go beyond telling students to "just say no" or why they should say no; they teach adolescents how to say no. Modern programs aim to build drug resistance skills and improve the adolescent's involve-

One thing we have learned from the increase in drug use in the early 1990s after years of decline is that drug education must be a continuing priority.

generational forgetting The phenomenon in which the older generation knows more about a particular subject than the younger generation.

ment in community and school, because drug-taking youth are often alienated from family, community, and society in general (Murray, 1995c). Some of these approaches have raised hopes and may be somewhat effective (Bangert-Drowns, 1988; Lipsey & Wilson, 1993).

Teaching refusal skills helps most in situations where there is direct pressure to use drugs, which are not as common as most adults believe. Successful programs address the subtle and situational pressure to use drugs that comes from peers, siblings, friends, and the media. Adolescence is a time of experimentation, seeking independence, identity formation, and separation from adults. It is also a time of trying to fit into a group. The decision to drink sometimes depends on the ability to resist the situational social pressure that is common, especially in early adolescence. Adolescents who are educated to cope with both high pressure and more subtle pressure develop social skills to refuse drugs without experiencing negative social consequences, such as losing friends or being stereotyped. For example, resistance training includes lessons covering types of social pressure, including friendly teasing, threats, tricks, dares, lies, and silent pressure; techniques to say no; assertiveness and refusal practice; and reports of personal resistance experiences. The development of refusal skills is the main goal of resistance skills training (Donaldson et al., 1995).

Merely teaching refusal skills, however, does not predict reduced drug use. Two distinct reasons account for this finding. First, refusal skills are effective only for individuals who believe that drinking or drug use is inappropriate. If an adolescent thinks it's acceptable to drink or use marijuana, refusal skills are superfluous. Second, adolescents often overestimate the percentage of teens who use drugs. This overestimation, which makes them think that most others are using drugs, adds a subtle pressure to take drugs or makes them reason that if so many are doing so, it must be all right. Older adolescents on college campuses often overestimate the number of their peers who drink heavily. When students learn the real figures, their perceptions realign with the facts, and they reduce their alcohol consumption (DeAngelis, 1994). The same is true for cigarette smoking (Robinson & Klesges, 1997).

Unfortunately, teaching refusal skills without giving the facts about the amount of drug use often exacerbates the tendency to overestimate the percentage of teens taking particular drugs. As students focus on resistance skills, they may become more sensitive to drugs in their environment and overestimate the percentage of peers who use them. Besides teaching refusal skills and talking about the acceptability of drug use, then, correcting misconceptions about the percentage of users is also important. One major study of more than ten thousand teens found that resistance skills training combined with education about the true numbers delayed the onset of alcohol use when adolescents believed drinking was not acceptable (Donaldson et al., 1995). When adolescents felt it was acceptable to use alcohol, the educational program did not lead to any decline in alcohol use.

One parental factor discussed earlier that constantly arises in studies of teen drug use is lack of parental monitoring (Richardson et al., 1989). Poorly monitored children are at a greater risk for drug taking (Chilcoat, Dishion, & Anthony, 1995). Although it may not be possible to reconstitute poorly functioning families or change the parents' personality or other characteristics, parents may learn to better supervise and monitor their younger adolescent children.

Another aspect of drug prevention is reducing cigarette advertising, as well as making tobacco and alcohol less available to underage adolescents. The Multistate Tobacco Settlement, noted earlier, has allowed many states to formulate tobacco prevention programs. One program, the Florida Pilot Program on Tobacco Control, attempts to

PERSPECTIVE 2

ANSWER THE QUESTION!

SETTING THE SCENE: You have been asked to speak to a group of young adolescents about the dangers of drugs, beginning with tobacco and alcohol and continuing through marijuana and cocaine. The group seems comfortable with you and freely asks questions.

YOUNG ADOLESCENT: *I know a lot of people who smoke marijuana, and they seem fine to me. I don't think it's dangerous. And smoking tobacco isn't so bad, either. My grandmother is 83, and she smokes. Why are you trying to scare us? And don't you ever have a drink? What's wrong with that?*

QUESTION: How would you answer this adolescent's questions?

change attitudes about tobacco, empowering youth to lead community action against smoking, reducing the availability of cigarettes and reducing exposure to second-hand smoke. The slogan used for the program is Our Brand Is Truth, Their Brand Is Lies.

Over a 2-year period, cigarette smoking among program participants declined by 40 percent among middle school students and by 18 percent among high school students. The number of cigarettes smoked by tobacco users declined. The percentage of students defined as committed nonsmokers increased significantly in both middle and high school. These students were less likely to buy into the allure of the image portrayed by the tobacco industry, and they believed that smokers were manipulated solely for the profits of the tobacco companies.

Psychosocial prevention strategies that target social influences, in combination with education in general personal and social skills, also can be effective (Botvin et al., 2001). One successful program teaches anxiety management, communication skills, understanding and resisting advertising, and assertiveness. It also teaches specific skills related to drug use, such as resistance skills, along with the consequences of drug use. This program succeeded in reducing drinking among middle school and young high school students.

No single drug prevention program will work for everyone. Some adolescents, such as homeless or runaway teens who have used drugs, need special help (Edmonds, 1995). Drug treatment is also needed, and these programs reduce crime in the community. In fact, for every $1 spent on treatment, the public saves $7 in criminal justice and health costs (Office of National Drug Control Policy, 1996). *(For a review of this section, see At A Glance 14.4.)*

AT A GLANCE   14.4 PREDICTORS OF DRUG USE AND DRUG ABUSE

KEY POINT: Such factors as personality characteristics, biological factors, family, and peer influences affect adolescent drug use.

SUPPORTING POINTS	EXPLANATION
Particular personality characteristics are related to drug use.	A pattern of ego undercontrol or antisocial behavior is related to drug use. Heavy drug users are more rebellious and unable to delay gratification. Drug users show a higher need for sensation seeking.
Biological factors may contribute to drug abuse and dependence.	Drugs influence the action of neurotransmitters in the brain, and genetic factors may underlie the production of these substances. Some people may be more genetically responsive to the action of certain drugs.
Negative family situations are related to drug use and abuse.	Drug abusers are more likely to experience serious family difficulties. Parental drug use is related to adolescent drug use.
Parenting style is related to drug use.	Adolescents whose parents are described as either very punishing or very lax are more likely to use drugs.
Friends' use of drugs is related to an adolescent's use of drugs.	Having friends who use drugs is a factor predicting drug use. Adolescents who use drugs may select others who do so as friends, and these friends then may reinforce one another for using drugs.
Some factors buffer an adolescent against drug use.	A warm, supportive family serves as a buffer against drug use. Having a positive attitude toward the future, valuing academic achievement, and understanding the risks of drug use also may act as buffers.
Drug education programs vary in their success.	Successful drug education programs not only give information but also help teenagers build drug resistance skills and community involvement.

VIOLENCE AND DELINQUENCY

M any Americans believe that violent crime is soaring and that today's teenagers are more violent than they were years ago. The media abound with articles showing youth in handcuffs being arrested for violent crimes, superpredators (young, violent criminals without any feelings of guilt for the victim), and seemingly senseless shootings at schools. The public has a heightened awareness of teen violence. Many people were shocked by the homicides in Littleton, Colorado; Paducah, Kentucky; Jonesboro, Arkansas; and Conyers, Georgia (Evans & Rey, 2001). Yet, the annual incidence of violent deaths among students is actually a very low 0.068 per 100,000 (Anderson et al., 2001). More common are assaults and threats, which newspapers rarely cover.

Violence in schools, however, is a significant concern. Almost half of all adolescents believe their schools are becoming more violent, 10 percent are afraid of being shot or hurt by classmates carrying weapons, and 20 percent fear going to restrooms (Safe Schools, 2002). Adolescents between the ages of 12 and 19 years remain at the highest risk for victimization by violent crime.

A study of over 15,000 middle and high school students found that more than 27 percent of the middle school students and 31 percent of the high school students surveyed think it is sometimes all right for people to hit or threaten an individual who makes them very angry. An astonishing 70 percent of the middle school students and 66 percent of the high school students physically struck another person in the last 12 months because they were angry. Eleven percent of the middle school students and 14 percent of the high school students took a weapon to school in the past 12 months. About a quarter of the middle school students and almost half the high school students reported that they could get a gun if they wanted to. Finally, more than a third of all secondary school students do not feel safe in school (Josephson Institute of Ethics, 2001). Even young children 7 to 10 years old fear violence and death. Male students are almost twice as likely as female students to have been in a fight (46 versus 26 percent), and African American and Latino adolescents have higher rates of fighting than Caucasians (43 and 41 percent versus 34 percent) (Kann et al., 1998).

The shocking events in Littleton, Colorado, and in other areas have led to many questions concerning adolescent violence.

At the same time, it is important not to paint adolescents with a broad stroke. Teenagers are not uniquely violent or crime prone, and adolescents have good reason to object to this stereotype (Males, 1997b). Many adults see teenage crime as constantly on the rise, but this perception is not accurate. Adolescent violence has decreased markedly in the United States. Figure 14.4 shows juvenile arrest rates for violent crimes; the rate increased in the early 1990s and then declined significantly in the last half of the 1990s (Office of Juvenile Justice, 2001).

Some interesting gender differences in criminality exist. Arrest statistics, victim reports, and self-reports all show that males are much more likely to engage in criminal and delinquent acts than females (Siegel & Senna, 2000). The *Uniform Crime Reports,* published by the Federal Bureau of Investigation, shows that male adolescents are six times more likely to be arrested for violent crimes and about three times more likely to be arrested for property crimes than females (Federal Bureau of Investigation, 2001).

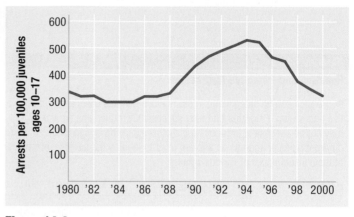

Figure 14.4
Juvenile Arrests, 1980 to 2000
The juvenile Violent Crime Index arrest rate in 2000 was at its lowest level since 1985—41 percent below the peak year of 1994.
Source: Adapted from Snyder (2002).

The *rate* of arrest for female adolescents has grown much faster than for male delinquents, however. Between 1988 and 1997, the number of arrests of males for all crimes increased about 28 percent, and the number of arrests of females increased about 60 percent. The change in number of arrests for violent crimes shows this trend even more clearly: Arrests for violent crimes between 1988 and 1997 increased 42 percent for males but 100 percent for females. Between 1996 and 2000, arrests for all crimes decreased 6.4 percent for males and only 0.2 percent for females. Arrests for male violent crimes fell 13.4 percent, whereas female violent crime arrests actually rose 2.1 percent (Federal Bureau of Investigation, 2001). About one in ten females reported at least one physical fight in school in the past year, and much of the violence is perpetrated against other females (Bower, 2002).

The factors underlying this trend toward increased female criminality and violence are uncertain. Some argue that in the past, female social roles simply did not allow women the opportunity to commit crimes, and women were raised to be more socially responsible, less violent, and to emphasize the needs of others. With changing and more equal roles, it is argued, comes a narrowing of the differences in criminality (Austin, 1993). Although fewer females than males commit crimes, especially violent crimes, females who do commit crimes show the same factors of family dysfunction, educational failure, and even personality characteristics as their male counterparts (Bjerregaard & Smith, 1993).

Not everyone agrees with the idea that role changes are the cause, however, as the major increases in female arrests are in the drug- and alcohol-related areas (Murphy & Cleeton, 2000). Even taking this fact into consideration, there has been some increase in female criminality in general and violent crime in particular (Matlin, 2000). Furthermore, crime statistics show that the rate for females is still significantly lower than that for males, and a cause-and-effect relationship cannot be inferred between social changes and the increase in female rates of criminality.

Types of Violence

Psychologists categorize aggression in a number of ways. **Proactive aggression** is goal directed and deliberate, and it occurs without provocation. Some proactive aggression involves taking something from a victim (instrumental); another type allows the perpetrator to gain dominance through bullying (see Table 14.2). **Reactive aggression** occurs in response to a provocation or a threat and is seen as defensive, at least by the perpetrator of the violence (Smithmyer, Hubbard, & Simons, 2000). The threat does not have to seem real to an outsider, as long as it

proactive aggression Aggression that is goal directed, is deliberate, and occurs without provocation.

reactive aggression Aggression that occurs in response to a provocation or threat and that is perceived as defensive.

There are a number of ways to categorize aggression. The aim of proactive aggression is to gain dominance or to take something from another person. The aim of reactive aggression is to defend oneself against a threat, whether it be real or imagined.

Table 14.2

Reactive and Proactive Aggression

Aggression can be categorized in many ways—in this case, as reactive or proactive aggression. Programs that may successfully reduce one type of aggression may not be successful in reducing the other type. These vignettes demonstrate different types of aggression and are used to identify the adolescent's perception of the consequences of various actions.

Context	Vignette
Reactive	One day in the cafeteria, you're waiting in line when a student cuts right in front of you. You tell her she can't cut, but she just laughs and says, "What 'cha gonna do about it?" What if you shoved her as hard as you could?
Proactive-instrumental	One day your T-shirt shrinks in the wash, and now it's too small for you to wear. Another student is smaller than you and has a really big T-shirt. What if you told him you'd beat him up if he didn't trade with you?
Proactive-bullying	A new student gets on some people's nerves because he acts really stupid. Some of the other students have a plan to get the teacher out of the room so they can jump the new student in the classroom. What if you helped them jump the new student?

Source: Smithmyer, Hubbard, & Simons (2000), p. 89.

appears real to the aggressor. Obviously, some adolescents show both types of aggression.

A study of 13- to 18-year-olds incarcerated in a maximum security correctional facility for delinquent boys clearly showed the difference between proactive and reactive aggression. The teens who showed proactive aggression expected positive outcomes from their aggressive behavior, regardless of whether the aim of their action was to achieve dominance or take something they wanted. Reactive aggression, in contrast, was not related to outcome expectations. The teens viewed reactive aggression as a defensive reaction to a perceived threat or as retaliation for a past aggressive act.

The difference is important. Consider a program trying to reduce aggression in a high school. If the problem is one of reactive aggression, it will respond to interventions designed to better understand the intent behind particular actions, but emphasizing the consequences will have no effect (Hudley & Graham, 1993). The consequences of aggression have little meaning for teenagers who are retaliating or seeing themselves as acting in self-defense. If the problem is proactive aggression, a successful program might teach adolescents to anticipate the consequences of their aggression and to think through the situation (Spivack & Shure, 1982).

Not all aggression involves physical violence. Some aggression, often called **relational aggression,** is aimed at hurting others' social position and may include spreading vicious rumors. Many people do not see this as aggression, for people are more interested in **predatory violence,** which refers to violent behaviors such as mugging, robbery, and assault that are part of a criminal or antisocial behavior pattern.

relational aggression   Aggression that is aimed at hurting someone's social position.

predatory violence   Violent behavior, such as assault, mugging, and robbery, that forms a part of a criminal or antisocial behavior pattern.

Aggression is a definite problem. The behavior itself causes pain to others, as well as having consequences for the perpetrator. Psychologists use the term *externalizing disorders* to describe disorders of undercontrol, in which the individual shows acting out, aggression, noncompliance, and oppositional behavior. The term *internalizing disorders* refers to a group of disorders that involve overcontrolled behavior and include anxiety and depression (see the chapter "Stress and Psychological, Physical, and Learning Problems").

The American Psychiatric Association's *DSM-IV-TR* recognizes aggressiveness as a prominent symptom in a number of psychological disorders. Individuals with one such disorder, **conduct disorder,** react violently and violate both the basic rights of others and basic social norms. Aggression, cruelty to animals, damaging property, lying, and stealing are symptomatic. The diagnosis of conduct disorder denotes an intensity and frequency that goes beyond pranks and an occasional fight. Another disorder, **oppositional defiant disorder,** includes children and adolescents who are defiant, disobedient, spiteful, and hostile toward authority figures but whose behavior is not physically aggressive.

Aggression, though, even if it does not reach the intensity sufficient for a diagnosis of conduct disorder, is seen all too often in society. Children and adolescents see violence in football and wrestling, which society condones, and much violence on the television screen and in the movies is perpetrated by "good guys" punishing "bad guys" (see "The Media"). Indeed, self-defense is often an accepted response. Children must learn to tell the difference between more acceptable and less acceptable forms of aggression, and this education depends largely on their parents.

Is Aggression a Stable Trait?

Aggressiveness is a stable characteristic. An early history of fighting and anger predicts later aggression and other antisocial behavior (Lewin, Davis, & Hops, 1999). In one sample of boys, nearly half the 6-year-olds who were rated aggressive by their teachers were arrested for violent crimes by age 33, compared with one-third of their nonaggressive peers (Hawkins et al., 2000). One-half the boys guilty of a delinquent offense between the ages of 10 and 16 were convicted of a violent crime by the age of 24, compared with only 8 percent of the juveniles who were not violent between those ages (Farrington, 1995a, 1995b).

These relationships are far from perfect, however, indicating that some people continue to show violent behavior, whereas others desist. Some aggressive adolescents show a very early onset of violence, some show an onset in middle childhood, and others even begin to be aggressive in adolescence (Loeber & Stouthamer-Loeber, 1998). Generally, the earlier the onset of violence (and delinquent behavior), the more serious and chronic the problem (Farrington, 1991; Tolan & Thomas, 1995). In addition, correlations show only that the rank ordering of individuals on the basis of their aggressiveness at an earlier time is similar to the order at a later time. For example, a child may be rated as highly aggressive relative to others in the group at age 6 and rated the same way again at a later time. This rating does not tell us anything about the severity of the aggression or even the frequency of the aggression. In fact, many children considered aggressive reduce their gross amount of fighting and aggression over time.

Two conclusions stand out. First, researchers find a positive relationship between early aggression and later aggression. Second, some adolescents who were rated aggressive as younger children or even some adolescents who committed an aggressive act during adolescence do not become violent offenders in adulthood. The relationship between early aggression and later antisocial behavior is positive, but far from perfect. Individuals can change. Perhaps some adolescents desist when they better understand the possible consequences of aggression, have nonviolent relationships, succeed in school, or receive counseling.

Aggressiveness in relation to others the same age may be a stable characteristic because of its causes. A child will change aggressive behavior only

conduct disorder   A disorder in which the individual shows violence and behaviors that violate the rights of others and basic social norms.

oppositional defiant disorder   A disorder marked by high levels of disobedience, and defiant and hostile behavior that does not involve repetitive aggression against others.

if the reasons for it change or the child receives some help for the behavior. Indeed, improvements in a child's life sometimes do occur. Unfortunately, the factors that contribute to aggressive behavior continue to operate in the lives of some children, and they may receive little help to overcome their aggressive behavior.

The Causes of Violence

The most modern view depicts violence and delinquency as a developmental problem that may begin very early in life (Henry et al., 1996). Risk factors can be categorized as individual (including personality, biological, and cognitive factors), family, peer, and community factors. These factors interact, often making it difficult to separate one from the other. The greater the number and importance of risk factors in a child's life, the greater the risk for violence (Hawkins et al., 2000). In fact, the percentage of youth convicted for violent crimes increases from only 3 percent for youth with no risk factors to 31 percent for youth with four risk factors (Farrington, 1997).

Individual Factors: Personality The personality profiles of aggressive and delinquent adolescents differ from their nonaggressive and nondelinquent peers. Aggressive and delinquent adolescents are often described as impulsive, resentful, socially assertive, defiant, suspicious, and lacking in self-control (Farrington, 1988). They often feel inadequate and see themselves as lazy or bad. When adolescents who committed violent crimes were compared with their peers who were convicted of nonviolent crimes (such as theft, burglary, or vandalism), the violent teens showed a lack of control and of self-regulation (Henry et al., 1996). The explosive, impulsive response in childhood may result in temper tantrums or aggression, whereas in adolescence it may result in violent behavior. This undercontrolled behavior may also cause parents, peers, and teachers to react negatively.

Impulsiveness, hyperactivity, concentration problems, restlessness, and risk taking are all correlated with aggression and delinquency (Browning & Loeber, 1999). Impulsive adolescents who live in poverty witness more violence, which encourages them to react violently to everyday challenges. Aggressive adolescents also have a low threshold for the expression of negative emotions such as fear, anxiety, and anger, and they react to these circumstances with aggression.

Individual Factors: Biological Few topics are as controversial as the possible biological bases for aggression. The existence of any biological or genetic component to aggression might be misinterpreted, as genetic influence often is, to mean that people are fated to become aggressive. Actually, it means nothing of the sort. A genetic and biological influence would explain why some people were more likely to become aggressive or might react more strongly to threats in the environment, but environmental factors would still be most important.

Some evidence exists for a role of genetics in aggression (Tellegen et al., 1988), but it is far from consistent. Animal research shows that deactivating particular genes can increase aggression (Plomin et al., 1997). A part of the brain, the amygdala, appears to be involved in aggression, and a reduction in neural activity may lead to less aggression. Brain research indicates that aggression can also result from damage to various parts of the brain. For example, particular damage to the prefrontal cortex leads to a general loss of inhibitions and sometimes violent behavior (Giancola, 1995). Perhaps these research results linking neurological factors with aggressive behavior explain why aggressive behavior is often found in people with deficits in verbal ability and executive functions, such as sustaining attention, reasoning, goal formation, planning, and awareness, which are related to early onset of conduct disorder (Moffitt, 1993). Evidence shows that people with a lower level of the neurotransmitter serotonin are more prone to aggressive behavior (Coccaro et al., 1996). For example, a study of children and adolescents with conduct disorder found that low levels of serotonin predicted higher levels of aggression 2 years later (Kruesi et al., 1992). This evidence indicates that some obvious or subtle differences in brain structure and functioning may be related to antisocial and aggressive behavior (Johnson, 1996).

Evidence also exists that testosterone, a male sex hormone, plays a role in aggression (Banks & Dabbs, 1996). Because males have more testosterone in their systems than do females, they should have a greater predisposition to become aggressive; this prediction does seem to fit reality. Of course, some women are aggressive as well. Although biochemical factors may be involved, they do not explain all the variations, and most of the differences are due to learning.

It would be wrong to conclude that psychologists have reached any consensus concerning the degree to which genetic factors contribute to aggression. Twin studies of aggression have been inconclusive and show mixed results (Christiansen, 1977; Plomin et al., 1997; Yoshikawa, 1994). Research on adopted children does not show much genetic involvement for violent crime, either. On any characteristic with a strong genetic basis, adopted children should resemble their biological parents more than their adopted parents. A study of adopted children in Denmark whose biological parents had criminal records found no significant genetic involvement for violent crime; it is interesting to note, though, that the study found some genetic involvement for property crimes (Mednick, Gabrielli, & Hutchings, 1984). An analysis of a number of studies linking criminality and genetics found a weak relationship, especially in well-conducted, more recent studies (Walters, 1992). If a relationship does exist, genetic factors may influence personality characteristics at some level, which may be a risk factor in aggression.

Individual Factors: Cognitive Cognitive factors are of great interest today. When youth believe that aggression will get them what they want and that it is acceptable, they will be more aggressive (Hawkins et al., 2000). Generally, aggressive youth expect fewer negative consequences and more positive outcomes for their aggressive behavior. Aggressive adolescents argue that their victims deserve the violence, and they do not empathize with their victims' suffering (Slaby & Guerra, 1988). Aggressive children and teens analyze social situations differently than nonaggressive children and adolescents (Fraser, 1996). Boys in both middle childhood and adolescence hold more favorable views toward the use of aggression than girls do (Huesmann & Guerra, 1997). However, although boys commit more violent acts than girls, both boys and girls who hold such attitudes commit more acts of aggression.

Aggressive behavior may be seen in terms of a stagelike decision-making process, and differences between aggressive and nonaggressive people exist at every stage. First, individuals *encode* and *interpret* elements of the social situation. Children who are aggressive attribute more aggressiveness to others, seeing peer behavior as more provocative and hostile than it really is and then retaliating (Crick & Dodge, 1994, 1996). This attitude stems from aggressive children's view of the world as a more hostile place, sometimes due to a history of being harshly punished (Egan, Monson, & Perry, 1998). If children are asked to imagine that someone spills water on them during lunchtime and are given no additional information, aggressive children are much more likely to believe it was done on purpose than are nonaggressive children (Hudley & Graham, 1993). The next step involves *clarification of goals.* A child's goals in a social situation may include avoiding embarrassment, being first in line, or showing strength. Aggressive children may want to get even with a peer or avoid the feeling of failure. The step that follows is the *construction of one or more response possibilities,* which relates to the number of behavioral alternatives generated and their content. Aggressive children often do not understand that other alternatives are available in a social situation. The individual then *decides* which response to use by evaluating the possibilities (if there is more than one). Aggressive children evaluate their actions positively, as they expect positive outcomes from their own aggressiveness. Finally, the individual *enacts* the behavior.

Family Processes and Relationships Children who are rejected by their parents, who grow up in conflict-filled homes, or who are not properly supervised are at a great risk of being aggressive (Wright & Wright, 1995). Aggressive adolescents are often raised in families that do not set clear expectations for their children's behavior; monitor them poorly; and use very lax, very severe, or inconsistent discipline (Hawkins et al., 2000).

Boys with very punitive parents often report the most violence (Siegel & Senna, 2000). Boys with very permissive parents report the second highest level of violence. Boys whose parents sometimes punish them and sometimes ignore the same problem behaviors are more likely to show aggression (Wells & Rankin, 1991). Their parents yell, threaten, and nag but do not follow through and are unable to deal with family problems (Wilson & Hernstein, 1985). This inconsistency frustrates children and adolescents and does not send a clear message. The very strict authoritarian style of parenting; poor parental supervision; very harsh discipline; and a cruel, passive, or neglectful attitude predicts later violence (Farrington, 1989).

Aggressive children and adolescents often come families characterized by rigidity, lack of cohesion, little positive communication, rejection, and indifference. Indeed, many delinquents come from neglectful homes. These children are often alienated from their parents and do not internalize their moral rules.

Children who are physically abused or neglected or who witness domestic abuse are more likely to show serious aggression (Holden & Ritchie, 1991; Mason, 1993; Smith & Shornberry, 1995). Witnessing or experiencing abuse teaches children to solve their problems using violence, prevents them from experiencing empathy for others, and reduces their ability to deal with stress (Siegel & Senna, 2000). In fact, violent youth often report higher levels of exposure to violence and victimization than others (Flannery, Singer, & Wester, 2001).

A major study of delinquent males found that poor supervision was the most common variable increasing the risk of delinquency, by a factor of 2.6 for older adolescents. A little less than a quarter of all youth crime occurs between 2 P.M. and 6 P.M. on schooldays. In fact, one in five violent crimes among juveniles occurs right after school hours (Snyder, Sickmund, & Poe-Yamagata, 1996). Many adolescents are left unmonitored after school, and many parents do not know where their teenagers are. Researchers surveyed sixth- and seventh-grade students on how they typically spent their after-school time; the extent of their aggressive behavior, substance abuse, and susceptibility to peer pressure; and their parental monitoring (Flannery, Williams, & Vazsonyi, 1999). Adolescents who spent after-school time with peers without parental presence reported the lowest levels of overall parental monitoring. In other words, not only were there no adults around but also parents were less likely to know where their teens

One factor that always shows itself in studies of delinquents is the lack of parental monitoring.

were. Both boys and girls who spent time with peers and without adult supervision were more likely to report higher levels of delinquency, aggression, substance use, and susceptibility to peer pressure compared with adolescents with a parent at home after school.

Often, no parents are home because they both work. Working parents can still monitor their adolescents, however, by calling them at home, requiring their adolescent children to keep in contact with them, and knowing the adolescent's plans for the next day. Although long-distance monitoring is more difficult, it is not impossible.

Peer Factors As in the case with drug use, it is not easy to determine whether selectivity or socialization is the key to understanding peer influence in aggression. Do adolescents who associate with aggressive peers receive reinforcement for such behaviors and imitate what they see; in other words, are they socialized into aggression? Or do aggressive teens simply choose friends with the same characteristics?

Both mechanisms seem to operate. Aggressive friends both model and reinforce aggression. They more readily accept aggressiveness and consider it the norm. At the same time, aggressive adolescents often select friends who show the same bent. This tendency is important because when peers disapprove of violence, adolescents are less likely to be violent (Elliott, 1994). Aggressive children and adolescents, in contrast, seek out peers with the same characteristics and then reinforce each other for their aggressive behavior. Peer factors are crucial in understanding how aggression and problematic peer relations add to the risk of becoming aggressive. Researchers who followed girls and boys in grades 6, 8, and 10 found that boys who were both rejected by peers and aggressive committed many more serious acts of delinquency. For girls, only aggression predicts more serious delinquency.

These gender differences should not be surprising. Aggression is far from acceptable in most female peer groups, and it is natural for this group characteristic to be related to later aggression. Aggression stands out and runs contrary to what females find acceptable. For boys, aggressiveness must be combined with rejection to predict later aggression. Not all aggressiveness in boys is antisocial, nor are all aggressive boys rejected. Some boys use aggressive behavior selectively and do not go so far as to become unpopular. Boys who are both aggressive and rejected often use aggression as their response to almost every behavior; in their case, being aggressive and rejected means lacking social skills and possibly not understanding the dynamics of the situation (Kaplan, 2000). These boys then interact with others who are aggressive and rejected; in fact, by age 10 or 12, children who are chronically rejected often form, or become initiated into, deviant peer cliques that are fertile training grounds for delinquent activities (Miller-Johnson et al., 1999). Aggressive boys who are rejected by peers show the highest rate of aggressive behavior compared with boys who are either aggressive or rejected, but not both (Bierman & Wargo, 1995; Coie et al., 1995). Rejected, aggressive boys display many problem behaviors, including poor attention, hyperactivity, verbal aggression, and lower levels of prosocial behavior (Bierman, Smoot, & Aumiller, 1993). They see the world as hostile and have difficulty handling their emotions and modulating behavioral responses. They often overestimate their own social competence and are not aware of how others view them (Zabriski & Coie, 1996).

Community Factors Many adolescents witness violence in their homes and communities, and living in a violent neighborhood doubles the risk for violence (Browning & Loeber, 1999). Their communities may be wracked not only by acts of individual violence but also by violence perpetrated by teens in gangs, which is intensifying (see "Focus: Gangs"). Poverty is related to involvement in violence, probably because poverty often predicts living in a neighborhood characterized by violence, unstable structures, and greater gang activity (Hawkins et al., 2000).

They may wear special colors, be involved in violent initiations, band together to violently protect their turf from other gangs, and terrorize neighborhoods. Gangs are a major source of violence both in and out of school. In 1999, 26,000 gangs with a membership of about 840,500 members existed (Surgeon General, 2001).

The composition of gangs fluctuates substantially over the years. In the early 20th century, youth gangs were predominantly Irish, Jewish, and Italian (Sante, 1991), but today they are more likely to be African American and Latino (Curry, Ball, & Decker, 1996). In one major study, 31 percent of adolescents claiming to be gang members were African American; 25 percent, Latino; 25 percent, Caucasian; 5 percent, Asian American; and 15 percent, "others" (Esbensen & Osgood, 1997). Most gang members are male.

Historically, gangs took root in urban areas, especially where poverty flourished. Today, although urban youth gangs are still prominent, gang activity has grown in rural counties, small cities and towns, and the suburbs (Howell, 1998). The average age of a youth gang member is about 17 to 18 years (Curry & Decker, 1998). The typical age range is from 12 to 24 years (Bjerregaard & Smith, 1993).

Youth gangs are responsible for a great deal of the crime and violence in the community (Battin et al., 1998). They commit violent offenses at a rate several times higher than do nongang adolescents (Howell, 1998). Years ago, gangs considered schools as neutral territory, but recently gang activity in schools has increased. Schools with gang activity report more violence, gun possession, and drug sales (Howell & Lynch, 2000), and their students are much more likely to report fear of being a crime victim (Burnett & Walz, 1994). Some gang violence is related to drug sales, but gangs also use violence to settle disputes, define their turf, and protect their honor. Of the nearly 1,000 homicides in Chicago between 1987 and 1994 committed by gangs, three-quarters were between gangs, 11 percent were within a gang, and 14 percent involved nongang victims (Block et al., 1996). Gang members use violence to demonstrate their toughness and gain status. The willingness to use violence is a key characteristic distinguishing youth gangs from other adolescent peer groups (Sanchez-Jankowski, 1991). Many gang members have access to guns, which is why gang violence has turned deadly (Sheley & Wright, 1993).

Adolescents offer many reasons for joining gangs. Some gangs provide a family-like relationship that appeals to adolescents who are isolated, drifting between a native and adopted culture, and feeling somewhat alienated from both (Vigil & Long, 1990). Gang membership enhances prestige and status, provides a social agenda and excitement, and offers a chance to make money through illegal activities. Social, economic, and cultural forces may push people to join gangs (Decker & van Winkle, 1996). Some individuals

The general attitude of society toward violence is another influence. Our society seems to have a love-hate relationship with violence. Society condemns violence, but heroes in our movies and television frequently use it. The media often portray violence, and violence on television, in movies, in video games, and in song lyrics may both directly and indirectly influence aggressiveness, as was discussed in "The Media." Children and teens may directly imitate what they see, especially if they are frustrated or angry at the time. They may directly learn that violence is an acceptable approach to meeting needs or settling a conflict. Media portrayals may indirectly encourage violence by creating an atmosphere in which violence is considered a natural, typical, and frequent response to stress, social conflict, and frustration.

Predicting Violence

Risk factors for violence often occur together. Risk factors are also cumulative, and many longitudinal studies find that the greater the number, the more likely the teen will show aggressive behavior and delinquency (Catalano & Hawkins, 1995). When researchers followed thousands of seventh-grade students through twelfth grade, they found that predictors of violence among high school seniors were early deviant behavior, poor grades, weak elementary school bonds, and middle school environments that promoted drug use. Adolescents who acted out by stealing or getting into trouble for major infractions were more likely to use violence 5 years later. Thus, programs aimed at reducing violence should include efforts to prevent or reduce troublesome school behavior, as well as to improve academic performance beginning in elementary school (Ellickson & McGuigan, 2000). Reducing drug use in middle schools will also help, so programs that are even join to gain protection from the violence perpetrated by other gangs. These teens feel marginalized; they feel they do not belong in school or in their communities, and they may have family problems. They find their sense of identity in gang membership (Vigil & Long, 1990).

Long-term studies find that the most important community risk factor for gang membership is growing up in neighborhoods with low social integration and attachment. Family characteristics include poverty, parental absence, low parental attachment to the adolescent, and little parental supervision. Three school-related characteristics are very significant: low expectations for success in school by both parents and adolescents, low student commitment to school, and low attachment to teachers. Peers naturally have a substantial impact, and associating with delinquent friends and unsupervised hanging around are a potent combination leading to gang membership. Individual risk factors include low self-esteem, numerous negative life events, depressive symptoms, easy access to drugs, and favorable views of drug use. The greater the number of risk factors operating, the greater the chances a person will join a gang.

A number of programs attempt to reduce gang violence (Burch & Kane, 1999). Some involve the use of outreach workers and other professionals to provide services and opportunities for community-based activities. Outreach workers encourage youth to attend schools, obtain job training, seek regular employment, and use social services.

Preventing adolescents from joining gangs is a cost-effective long-term strategy (Howell, 1998). The Gang Resistance Education and Training (GREAT) Program, which is directed at 3rd and 4th graders and 7th and 8th graders, has obtained positive results (Esbensen & Osgood, 1997; Humphrey & Baker, 1994). The middle school program consists of eight lessons promoting cultural sensitivity, improving conflict resolution, meeting basic needs without joining a gang, and establishing short- and long-term goals. In a summer program, the youth participate in numerous recreational and community projects, including food programs and painting over graffiti. Students completing the program report lower levels of gang affiliation and delinquency, including drug use, minor offenses, and both property crimes and crimes against persons. Other effective programs, such as the Comprehensive Community Wide Gang Prevention, Intervention and Suppression program, mobilize the community and outreach workers to provide social outlets, better monitoring of gang activities, and social interventions (Spergel et al., 1994; Thornberry & Burch, 1997).

Progress has been made in identifying the major risk factors involved in joining gangs, although reducing these factors is not easy. Some successful programs combine social intervention, rehabilitation, and suppression, but few have been rigorously evaluated. Combating gang violence and delinquency, which have a tremendous effect on everyone within the community, requires the cooperation of police, social workers, and members of the community.

successful in preventing or reducing drug use may yield an extra bonus of reducing violence.

When researchers followed a sample of children between 8 and 14 years of age through age 27, they found that the risk of aggressiveness increased for individuals who showed early rule-breaking behavior, such as disobeying teachers (as early as age 8); little prosocial behavior; smoking and drinking by age 14; and poor school achievement (Hamalainen & Pulkkinen, 1996). Aggressiveness at age 8 predicted later violence (as measured by arrests) only when other risk factors were present. Women who were aggressive engaged in much less prosocial behavior and more bullying. They often teased others, especially smaller and weaker peers. Both male and female criminals had more conduct problems and lower school success (Hamalainen & Pulkkinen, 1995).

The best predictors of violence may change with age. Between the ages of 6 and 11, the strongest predictor is being involved in delinquent behavior, even if it is not violent. Very early substance use is also a powerful predictor of violence. The best predictor of aggressive behavior for 12- to 14-year-olds is a lack of social ties and an involvement with antisocial peers (Lipsey & Derzon, 1998).

Protective Factors Against Violence

The factors that increase the risk of children and adolescents becoming aggressive are well known, but they must not be overstated. Not all children who grow up in violent homes become violent adults (Wright & Wright, 1995). Along with risk factors, protective factors also function. These factors either reduce the impact of the risk factors or change how the adolescent reacts to them. Many delinquency prevention programs aim to enhance the protective factors.

Personal characteristics such as warmth, flexibility, and being socially oriented are related to less delinquency and aggression (Hawkins et al., 2000). Families marked by support, affection, and supervision are less likely to produce aggressive teens. Peers who do not accept violence also serve as checks, as do community programs that promote a sense of inclusion and school activities that enhance social and academic competence.

Can Violence Be Curbed?

The issue of curbing violence has been approached from two directions: punishment and prevention. The public naturally fears violence, and its first response often is to advocate harsh punishment. Americans seem to be more interested in punishing violence than in preventing it (Braaten, 1999). Although violence prevention programs have proliferated, few have been rigorously evaluated (Tolan & Guerra, 1994). Psychologists have learned that violence has many causes and no simple solutions.

Some effective programs do exist, but none prevents all violence. Some prevention programs attempt to improve family relationships and begin in the first 5 years. Programs that prevent abuse, improve parenting abilities, and reduce violence in the family are sometimes successful. These programs promote family cohesion and improve the way parents discipline. Delinquents usually have negative interpersonal relationships with others, including family members, often because of their social behavior and the reactions others have to them. Some programs try to reduce these negative interactions by teaching better ways to interact (Reiff, 2001b).

Early childhood education also can make an impact. In fact, well-designed and intensive preschool programs prevent aggression, although exactly how they do so is unknown. Perhaps the better-prepared youngsters do better in school, which reduces their frustration. Programs that prevent academic failure and promote social competence also prevent delinquency. Children whose social and intellectual development is nurtured when they are as young as 3 or 4 years grow up with a greater sense of social competence and later commit fewer criminal acts (High/Scope Educational Research Foundation, 1993).

Programs emphasizing conflict resolution and social skills training also look promising (Lawton, 1994). To be useful, though, they must be a long-term and consistent part of education. Students today need such skills desperately. A Louis Harris poll found that more than half the teenagers surveyed said it was almost impossible to back off from a confrontation (Rubin, 1995). Many violent incidents in middle and high school escalate from trivial events (Lockwood, 1997). With the increasingly violent reaction of some students, yesterday's couple of punches may be a shootout today. In New York City, the Resolving Conflict Creatively program aims at reducing violence and promoting cooperation by offering students a special curriculum dealing with resolving conflicts and peer mediation. Evaluations have been positive, with teachers and administrators reporting less physical violence in the classroom (Bilchik, 1995).

Some programs promote community attachment through community work combined with parenting programs. Structured programs that focus on social skills and alternatives to gang membership provide a safe haven in the community for youngsters. They teach social skills and goal setting, improve communication, nurture interests, and recognize good work (Carnegie Council, 1994). Evidence shows that community youth programs promote constructive behavior, reduce high-risk behavior, and help reduce feelings of isolation and alienation. Unfortunately, few American communities have such programs.

Violence prevention programs can take many forms. Some try to change family interaction patterns, others emphasize social skills training or conflict resolution.

Other programs try to alter some of the cognitions of aggressive and violent youth by teaching them to interpret social situations differently and improve social skills (Guerra & Slaby, 1990). Social skills training must address many domains of functioning, including the social, behavioral, cognitive, interpersonal, and emotional. Adolescents need to practice these skills, especially skills in the areas of self-control, coping with anger, regulating emotions, and solving social problems (Miller-Johnson et al., 1999). Mentoring programs are a promising approach to preventing delinquency and drug use. They address the need for positive adult one-on-one contact and building positive relationships (Grossman & Garry, 1997).

Violence is not a behavior that suddenly appears out of nowhere. It arises over the years and is encouraged or discouraged by a great many different factors. The best approach would involve psychologists who could alter the community and family factors that cause violence to arise in the first place, called *primary prevention,* and improving parenting skills and early childhood programs also may help. Unfortunately, by the time a child enters adolescence, many risk factors have been operating for years.

Secondary prevention activities aim at early identification of children with violence potential to prevent serious problems from arising in adolescents who are at risk. These programs show promise. For example, tutoring students so they will have more success in school and working with parents to better monitor their children may reduce factors that encourage aggression. Although completely changing a family's dynamics is not possible, parents can learn how to monitor their young teens better and make some changes in the home.

Finally, aggressive adolescents need treatment. Programs that help adolescents who already show violence, called *tertiary prevention* programs, may prevent the violence from getting worse (Guetzloe, 1999). Alternative schools offering programs emphasizing different ways of handling anger, the negative consequences of aggression, and coping with aggressive impulses can be successful.

PERSPECTIVE 3

THE WITNESS

SETTING THE SCENE: You attend a rough high school, which has been wracked by violence. At this point, you have not been the victim of much of it, as you mind your own business and are careful about where you go and with whom you associate. The other day you witnessed two boys robbing another boy of his wallet and beating him. The boys have a history of violence. The injured boy reported the theft to the school authorities, who called in the police. The two aggressors deny the charge, and the police are looking for a witness who the victim thought saw the crime. You have the choice to come forward or not. You told two of your closest friends what you saw.

FRIEND 1: *Don't do anything, or you'll be beaten up. These guys are rough. Play dumb. It's not your problem.*

FRIEND 2: *If you don't come forward, these guys will get away with it. How would you like it if you were the victim and were waiting for someone to come forward?*

QUESTION: If you were the witness, what would you do?

Lost Boys

A number of new perspectives on youth violence have appeared in the wake of the shocking school shootings of the late 1990s. One of the most interesting approaches to adolescent violence is found in James Garbarino's books on violent boys, such as *Lost Boys: Why Our Sons Turn Violent and How We Can Save Them* (1999) and *Raising Children in a Socially Toxic Environment* (1995). Garbarino interviewed teenage boys who had used deadly violence. Garbarino offered an interesting analogy to explain violence: Consider a person with healthy lungs living in a dirty, polluted city. The person may never notice the air pollution problem. However, if the person has asthma—that is, the individual is vulnerable to the toxic atmosphere—the person begins to choke (Garbarino, 1998). Similarly, whereas some children can live in a violent, hateful atmosphere in peace, children who end up violent are like psychological asthmatics. They are vulnerable and react to the toxic atmosphere with violence.

A child develops vulnerability because of poor parenting practices, abuse or neglect, drug use by parents, and other factors that lead to early trauma. A socially poisonous atmosphere includes violent neighborhoods, violent television imagery and video games that portray aggression as a solution to problems, little adult supervision, and access to guns. These violent boys develop a moral view that violence is an acceptable strategy to counter a challenge, perceived injustice, or slight. They have been traumatized as children, have been exposed to multiple risk factors, and lack the protective factors discussed earlier. Garbarino believes that inside almost every violent teenager is an untreated, traumatized child (1999, p. 28). These boys learn that they cannot trust adults, so they must fend for themselves. They are disconnected and very angry. The boys use guns to replace adults as a form of protection. They see their violence as morally justified and as a response to wrongs by others, even if their reasoning often escapes us.

Some parents are surprised at their children's explosive and violent behavior. One of Garbarino's most interesting insights is that many boys lead what is best described as secret lives. Their parents are not aware of their alienated friends, their violent fantasies, the extent of their unhappiness, the video games they are playing, and the sites they are visiting on the Internet. Adolescents show different selves to their family, friends, and teachers. When Garbarino and colleagues conducted a survey at a major university, many students reported committing crimes, drinking, taking drugs, and having sex without their parents ever knowing (Garbarino & Bedard, 2001).

Garbarino's solution to the problem of violence is to promote protective factors and remediate risk factors. Adolescents require supportive adults and predictable routines. They need anchors to socially connect them to their communi-

AT A GLANCE 14.5 VIOLENCE AND DELINQUENCY

KEY POINT: Psychologists have made major strides in understanding the causes of violence and ways of preventing it.

SUPPORTING POINTS	EXPLANATION
Arrests of adolescents for crime have declined rapidly since 1994. Still, aggression is a major concern.	Many adolescents are victims of crime, and assault and threats are major problems. Many adolescents fear for their safety.
Aggression is a symptom in many psychological disorders.	*Externalizing disorders* are behavioral disorders of undercontrol that involve violence. An individual with *conduct disorder* violates the basic rights of others.
Investigations of violence and delinquency must take personality into account.	Aggressive adolescents and delinquents, as a group, show less empathy, are more egocentric, and have poor impulse control compared with nondelinquent teenagers.
Cognitive factors are related to aggression.	Belief in the efficacy of aggression is related to aggressive behavior. Cognitive differences that differentiate aggressive from nonaggressive people are found at every stage of the decision-making process.
Family relationships and child-rearing variables relate to aggression.	Lack of parental monitoring, conflict within the family, rejection and indifference, inconsistent discipline, and discipline that is either too lax or too strict correlate with aggressive behavior in children and adolescents.
Aggressive adolescents are often found with other aggressive adolescents.	Aggressive adolescents choose friends who are also aggressive, and these adolescents reinforce one another for aggressive behavior.
Violence in the community affects adolescents.	Adolescents growing up in violent communities are not only likely to observe violence but also to be victims of violence.
Some factors serve as buffers against violence.	Warm, cohesive families, peers who do not accept violence, and communities that promote inclusion and a sense of community can reduce the probability of violence.
Some programs successfully prevent violence.	Programs that promote family cohesion, comprehensive early childhood programs that lead to early success in school, and conflict resolution programs may help prevent violence. Programs that help connect adolescents to the community reduce violence as well.

ties and spiritual help that gives their lives meaning. Programs that promote positive parenting skills, early intervention programs, and helping angry young children to manage their anger are all necessary.

The Link Between Drug Use and Violence

Drug use and violence are related problems. Certainly not all people who use, or even abuse, drugs are violent, and not all violent people use drugs. However, positive correlations exist between the two. Individuals who abuse drugs are more likely to engage in other illegal activities, as well as in violent behaviors, than individuals who do not (Dawkins, 1997; Friedman et al., 1996). Drug use is related even more strongly to property crimes and vandalism. Research on juvenile offenders finds that about one-half report using alcohol, other drugs, or both just prior to perpetrating their crimes (White & Hansell, 1998). Among the drugs most associated with violence are cocaine and crack, amphetamines, and alcohol. Other drugs, such as PCP, hallucinogens, and inhalants/solvents, also are related to violent acts (Friedman et al., 1996).

A number of possible reasons may account for this relationship. One possibility is a direct link between the properties of the drug and aggression (White & Hansell, 1998). For example, abusing certain substances, such as alcohol, may encourage violent behavior by reducing the inhibitions that normally would restrain the individual from acting on violent impulses. Second, teens often must negotiate a violent environment to use drugs. Crack use, for example, is related to violence not only because of the workings of the drug but also because of the systemic violence connected with the illicit market for this drug. In addition, violent individuals may be attracted to drug selling rather than drug selling initially causing individuals to become violent (van Kammen & Loeber, 1994). Drug users may interact with other drug users who are violent and be exposed to a greater subculture of violence than people who do not use drugs.

Another possible reason for the relationship between violence and drug use is that similar factors underlie both. Many predictors of violent behaviors are also predictors of other problems, such as substance abuse, delinquency, dropping out of school, and even teenage pregnancy (Hawkins et al., 1992). For example, some personality characteristics, such as hostility, and other family and peer risk factors may predict both violent behavior and substance use.

Even though violence and drug use may be correlated, however, the fact that the correlation is moderate shows that one cannot always be used to predict the other. In addition, many teens may use a drug only experimentally or occasionally. The greater the use of drugs, the higher the correlation between drug use and violence. Although drug abuse and violence have been discussed separately, they may share some roots (U.S. Department of Justice, 1997). *(For a review of this section, see At A Glance 14.5.)*

PLACING DRUG USE AND VIOLENCE IN PERSPECTIVE

The problems of drug abuse and violence haunt society. Many of the same individual, familial, peer, and community factors underlie both, although certainly each problem has unique aspects. Some experts argue that drug abuse is a personal issue, because it injures the individual, whereas violence is an interpersonal issue, because it involves injury to another person. This view is narrow, however. Drug abuse negatively affects not only the abuser but also the entire family and community. Violence not only injures the target but also causes the perpetrator to be isolated and rejected by others.

Although drug abuse and violence affect everyone in society, they have special meaning for adolescents. Adolescents are more likely to be both the perpetrators and the victims of violence than people of other ages. They are more likely to experiment with drugs than younger children or older adults. Most adolescents, though, are neither drug abusers nor especially violent. Yet violence and drug use affect every adolescent's environment, so their prevention, as well as the treatment of individuals who are aggressive or abuse drugs, must be a high priority.

The problems of drug abuse and violence did not arise overnight, and we will not solve them easily. There are many paths to drug use and violence, so dif-

THEMES

THEME 1 **Adolescence is a time of choices, "firsts," and transitions.**	• Adolescents must make important choices in the area of drug use. • Adolescents often must deal with violence in their schools and neighborhoods. • Adolescents must decide how they will react to provocation and interpersonal challenges.
THEME 2 **Adolescence is shaped by context.**	• Adolescents who live in homes marked by conflict, violence, or drug use are more likely to use drugs. • Having a positive family situation and good relationships with adults leads to less drug taking. • Having friends who use drugs is related to drug use. • Aggressive children and adolescents often experience harsh, very lax, or inconsistent parental discipline and are surrounded by aggressive models and thus learn that aggression is an acceptable way to solve problems. • Consistently witnessing aggression in the community may encourage aggressive behavior in adolescents.
THEME 3 **Adolescence is influenced by group membership.**	• Males generally drink alcohol more often and consume more than females. • Cultural factors influence how much alcohol an individual consumes. • Many members of minority groups live in poverty and in neighborhoods where violence is common, situations that influence their outlook on life.
THEME 4 **The adolescent experience has changed over the past 50 years.**	• Adolescents today are introduced to drugs at an earlier age, and drug use begins earlier. • Today's adolescents hear less about the dangers of drugs than adolescents heard in the 1980s. • Adolescents are more fearful and concerned with violence than they were years ago.
THEME 5 **Today's views of adolescence are becoming more balanced, with greater attention to its positive nature.**	• In the past, psychologists viewed drug use and abuse as a simple process or event, but they now appreciate the complex interaction of factors that encourage or inhibit it. • Rather than only appreciating the risk factors encouraging drug use, psychologists now also identify the individual, family, peer, and neighborhood factors that reduce the risk that adolescents will abuse drugs. • Psychologists no longer accept the idea that peer pressure is the major cause of drug use; they now understand that adolescents may actively select friends who use drugs, and the friends then reinforce one another's drug use. • Rather than emphasizing scare tactics or giving information about drugs, modern drug education programs emphasize dealing with problems without drugs and resisting subtle, situational pressures to use them. • Whereas psychologists once concentrated on the risk factors for aggression, they now focus on individual, family, peer, and neighborhood factors that reduce the risk that adolescents will act aggressively.

ferent programs are required to eliminate them. As noted earlier, a program that teaches adolescents to think through the consequences of violence may help teens who perpetrate proactive violence. In contrast, teaching teens to process social situations differently (for example, teaching that not every stare is a provocation and that some things do happen by accident) may help adolescents who show reactive violence. Programs that counter the image of the smoker and emphasize the immediate consequences of smoking (such as shortness of breath and smelling bad) may reduce smoking, and a different type of program may be required to deal with binge drinking.

The challenge of reducing violence and drug abuse is ongoing, and efforts must continue as well. Parents, psychologists, educators, and religious and political leaders all have a stake in the success of these programs. However, programs that appear to be successful must be continued. The success in reducing drug abuse in the 1980s led to a complacency and a lack of continuity that showed itself in the resurgence of drug use in the early and middle 1990s. There is room for many different approaches. Success will lead to better communities and healthier adolescents ready to take on the responsibilities of adulthood.

CHAPTER SUMMARY AT A GLANCE

KEY TOPICS	KEY POINTS	
Drug Use	Drug use, drug abuse, and drug dependence are major problems among adolescents. *(At A Glance 14.1, p. 498)*	← **KEY TERMS** *drug (p. 495)* *drug abuse (p. 495)* *substance dependence (p. 495)* *tolerance (p. 495)* *withdrawal (p. 495)*
Tobacco and Alcohol	Many people do not appreciate the dangers of tobacco and alcohol, two drugs commonly used by adolescents. *(At A Glance 14.2, p. 503)*	
Other Drugs	Adolescent use of marijuana, methamphetamine, cocaine, heroin, and ecstasy is a serious problem. *(At A Glance 14.3, p. 508)*	
Predictors of Drug Use and Drug Abuse	Such factors as personality characteristics, biological factors, family, and peer influences affect adolescent drug use. *(At A Glance 14.4, p. 515)*	← *generational forgetting (p. 513)*
Violence and Delinquency	Psychologists have made major strides in understanding the causes of violence and ways of preventing it. *(At A Glance 14.5, p. 528)*	← *proactive aggression (p. 517)* *reactive aggression (p. 517)* *relational aggression (p. 518)* *predatory violence (p. 518)* *conduct disorder (p. 519)* *oppositional defiant disorder (p. 519)*

Review questions for this chapter appear in the appendix.

EPILOGUE

SOCIETIES ARE BECOMING MORE PLURALISTIC

TECHNOLOGY DIFFERENTIATES GENERATIONS

GENDER ROLES CONTINUE TO EVOLVE

FAMILY STRUCTURES ARE MORE VARIED AND FLUID

ADOLESCENTS MUST COMPETE IN A GLOBAL MARKETPLACE

ACHIEVING BALANCE

We have come to the end of this text, but not to the end of the study of adolescence. The scientific study of the adolescent experience is ongoing, as we can see from the advances in theoretical perspectives and research that have improved our current understanding of adolescence. Throughout the text, we have explored many constants of the adolescent experience, including such challenges as forming a personal identity and achieving emotional and behavioral autonomy. We also have considered many of the challenges of being an adolescent, which have changed over time and over generations.

Let's take a moment to look forward, to consider what the future may bring in the realm of adolescence. To be sure, looking into the future is a slippery task. About the best we can do is look at the emerging trends and consider what new challenges and opportunities they may provide for adolescents in the future. The world of tomorrow's adolescents will be quite different from the one their parents knew, just as their parents' world differed from that of their grandparents. Each generation must face a new environment and new challenges.

Five areas of change in Western culture will no doubt test the adaptive power of adolescents today and in the future. These areas of change are grounded in several of the themes emphasized throughout the book.

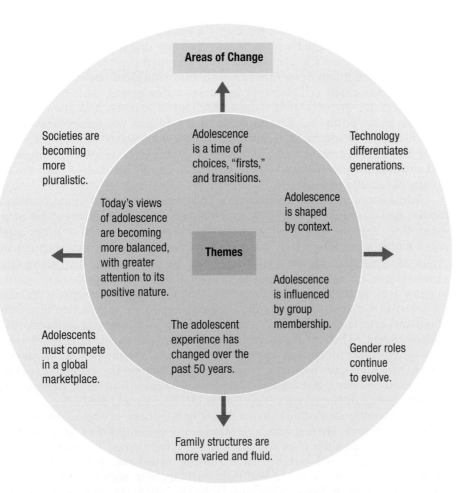

SOCIETIES ARE BECOMING MORE PLURALISTIC

The population of the United States, as well as most other Western countries, is more diverse than ever before. Whites will make up a smaller and smaller percentage of the total population of the United States as the first half of the 21st century progresses. Many of today's schools and workplaces are composed of people from many different groups, with cultures and traditions that must be respected. Tomorrow's schools and workplaces will be even more diverse. Social and business interactions among people of different groups will increase, and adolescents from both the majority and minority groups must be prepared to enter this multicultural world with increased understanding and acceptance of other people's ideas and traditions. As we appreciate our differences, however, we must always remember our many similarities in desires, hopes, and values.

TECHNOLOGY DIFFERENTIATES GENERATIONS

Technologies, including advances in telecommunications, have changed and will continue to change the world in which adolescents live. Technological sophistication differentiates generations, and with the faster development of technology today, the gulf between generations becomes wider. We may laugh at the comedian's jokes about the family who would not let their adolescent child attend a faraway college because he was the only one in the family who knew how to program the VCR, but we recognize our own experiences in the comedy. Adolescents are much more familiar with, and confident about, new technologies. They take email, cell phones, computers, video games, cable television, and the Internet for granted, as if these technological marvels had always existed. Whereas many adults have to think about where and when they want to alter their lifestyles to use these technologies, most adolescents simply incorporate them into their emerging lifestyle. Many of these technologies allow immediate and constant information and entertainment, a significant change from the technology of just 20 years ago.

Adolescents today are confronted with specialization and immediacy in the media. Radio and cable television stations may present only one type of programming, be it all sports, news, or music. Television, as well as other media, will become more interactive. For example, home audiences may express their opinions by simply pushing a button. We see the beginning of interactive television today, as audiences of some shows can either vote or express their opinions in some way, perhaps through the show's Internet site. For people with access, the Internet is always available, allowing the immediate satisfaction of informational and entertainment needs. Cell phones keep us in constant contact with the outside world, whether at school or walking on the street. Email and instant messaging allow for almost instant communication with people all over the world. Much of this technology emerged just before the current generation reached adolescence, but adolescents already wonder how their parents could possibly have functioned effectively before cell phones and the Net.

We generally don't think about how the telephone changed society in the early 20th century; we just accept it. Succeeding generations of adolescents will continue to adapt their lives to whatever new technology is available. In fact, adolescents today, and certainly in the future, will have to be technologically sophisticated to make a living and fully participate in society. Technology may affect adolescents in both subtle and not-so-subtle ways. For example, in the future people may be able to vote in elections from their homes by computer, which may encourage more young people to vote. More colleges may offer courses over the Internet, making higher education accessible to a wider range of people.

Adolescents also will have to deal with questions that arise from these technological innovations. How will being in constant contact affect privacy needs? How can adolescents protect themselves from predators and swindlers on the Internet? How can adolescents learn to discriminate accurate and current information on the Net from incorrect and dated or irrelevant information? Furthermore, each new technology raises different ethical issues—for example, the problem of plagiarism and the Internet—and requires us to extend our time-honored values to new situations. Parents and teachers can help children and adolescents deal with the moral and ethical concerns raised by technology, but ultimately, adolescents must deal with these issues themselves.

GENDER ROLES CONTINUE TO EVOLVE

The third change that will confront the next generation of adolescents is evolving gender roles. Most female adolescents in Western cultures plan for a future that includes marriage, children, and a career, although many will leave full-time employment for varying amounts of time when their children are young. Women today and in the future will continue to seek a balance between home and career. As women's roles have changed, so has the demand for men's roles to change. Split-shift families, in which one parent works during the day and the other at night, are becoming more common, requiring that fathers take over more of the child-care responsibilities. Although a 50–50 split in child care is rare—mothers still do the lion's share of the child care—there is pressure on men to change their perception of their roles. I often ask my female students how they would feel if they came home from work and found their two children having a loud argument, the dishes still unwashed in the sink, and their husband looking up from the newspaper and saying, "What's for dinner?" Their responses are, to say the least, disapproving.

With today's changing gender roles, dating is less formal; sexual attitudes and, to a somewhat lesser extent, sexual behavior are more liberal. In the midst of this change, women ask themselves how they can have the best of both worlds. How can a woman enjoy her femininity and social life and prepare for a future in which she will be competing with men? Men must ask themselves how they wish to integrate their family responsibilities and leisure activities with the traditional emphasis on a career.

Certainly, women will continue to enter what were once male-dominated fields, but will men begin to enter fields that are presently dominated by women? It is difficult to predict how the greater equality between the sexes will influence their future relationship. We still have a long way to go in developing gender roles that meet the needs of all members of the modern family.

FAMILY STRUCTURES ARE MORE VARIED AND FLUID

The fourth change is in the family itself. The family is the most important influence in the adolescent's life, just as it has been in past generations. The family is the basis of attachment, care, guidance, and comfort and support in times of need. These qualities continue to be as important today as ever. However, our concept of family is quite different today, and adolescents understand this fact. Many families are composed of single parents, stepfamilies, and gay parents. Often in two-parent families, both parents work full-time. Many fewer adolescents today experience what is often referred to as the *traditional family*, a family with an employed father and a mother who is a full-time homemaker. With these expanding family structures come different challenges.

The experiences of adolescents in these varying families—for example, a stepfamily versus a single-parent family—differ. Although family structure is important, we have come to understand that how a family functions is more important than its structure. Some families in each structure will function more effectively than others and better meet the needs of its members.

The family will continue to evolve, as will the parent-adolescent relationship. Because both parents or the single parent work full-time in so many families, children and adolescents are more on their own, and families emphasize independence training. Yet we know that monitoring is very important. The family in the future will have to balance independence with monitoring, as well as find ways to offer adolescents the help and emotional support they require in a more hurried lifestyle.

ADOLESCENTS MUST COMPETE IN A GLOBAL MARKETPLACE

The fifth change in the lives of adolescents is that the world is more competitive, and thus more expertise and skills are expected of people entering the work force. Many vocations require cutting-edge technological skills. At the same time, people skills will likely grow in importance. Adolescents entering the work force will need to combine technological knowledge with the ability to deal effectively with people. Other competitive challenges for adolescents will appear in the academic sphere. More pressure for accountability exists, and demands on adolescents to perform in school will increase.

ACHIEVING BALANCE

Meeting the challenges created by the five changes discussed above requires a gradual process of growth and adaptation, which often goes unappreciated. As late adolescents and early adults go through their days, they may not realize how they have changed and developed. They act as if they have always been comfortable at school and at work, as well as in interacting with the other gender. They take for granted the emotional and behavioral autonomy that they have gained. It is easy not to appreciate how much we have changed over the years. Consider your own situation. If you compare a photo of yourself when you were 12 or 13 years old with a current photo, you become aware of the physical changes that occurred throughout your adolescence. If you think back to your first romantic relationship and consider the relationship you now have or have recently had with another romantic partner, the two relationships will differ greatly. Think of your experience with your family and friends when you were in middle or high school, including the nature of conflict, and compare it with your relationships today. Perhaps, after considering these changes, you will gain a new appreciation of the gradual nature of developmental progress. One paradox, though, is that although change occurs, adolescents still see themselves as being the same person they were the year before and the year before that. Some elements of the self seem to be continuous.

Adolescents must adapt to the challenges these changes bring, and this adaptation has already begun. Most of today's teenagers have never wound a watch, dialed a telephone, or used a manual typewriter, but many have no difficulty downloading music from the Internet or setting their cell phones to receive voice, data, and video material. It is interesting that this generation of adolescents is more independent and more entrepreneurial. They are more optimistic, embrace environmentalism, and are technologically sophisticated. They have an I-can-do-it-myself attitude (Woodyard, 1998).

We have looked at some predictable challenges, but life always includes unexpected events and changes—for example, the terrorist attacks of September

11, 2001. Just as generations of adolescents struggled with the Cold War and its implications, this generation and perhaps future generations will struggle with the ramifications of terrorist activity. Increased security, vigilance, uncertainty about future terrorist attacks, and feelings of vulnerability are now constantly with us.

In the midst of all this change, how can we understand the nature of adolescence? The key to appreciating the period of adolescence may lie in the individual's need to achieve a sense of balance. The adolescent must seek a balance between the new and the old, between individuality and being part of a group, between achieving one's own needs and being sensitive to the needs of others, between idealism and pragmatism. The adolescent needs to integrate the past with the present, and the past and the present with his or her perceived needs for the future. Family, school, religious institutions, and community resources can offer guidance in this quest for balance, but all adolescents must finally achieve this balance on their own. Most adolescents succeed, but achieving balance does not occur quickly or without tribulations.

Indeed, psychologists who study adolescence have begun to appreciate the success many adolescents have in coping with these challenges and eventually finding this balance. The fifth theme of this text emphasizes the strides psychologists have made in understanding that the problems of adolescence are frequently balanced by the opportunities and other positive features of this time of life. Instead of adopting a crisis mentality and focusing only on the negative aspects of adolescence, modern psychologists also look at the positive coping mechanisms adolescents use and just how they achieve autonomy within the framework of the family, the peer group, and the total environment. This perspective does not ignore the problems that often follow adolescents, but it also no longer views them as inevitable and severe. Instead, today's perspective gives more attention to individuals who successfully master the challenges of adolescence.

The research conducted by psychologists can help parents, teachers, medical personnel, and counselors to better understand the dynamics of this important period of life. Research into the adolescent experience and the challenges that adolescents face can enable parents and professionals to help adolescents achieve a sense of balance. Adolescence is not a smooth transitional period, for the developmental tasks are complicated, and multiple paths to adulthood exist. However, with support and understanding, adolescents can emerge as individuals ready to take on adult responsibilities, and perhaps they can make the world a little better place for the generation that will follow them.

Appendix: Review Questions

Chapter 1 The World of Adolescence

Review 1.1: Adolescence: A Frame of Reference

Level 1

1. _____ refers to the physical changes that occur as the individual develops the ability to reproduce.
   A. Puberty
   B. Adolescence
   C. Autonomy
   D. Individualization

2. One reason why obtaining a driver's license or graduating from high school is **not** considered a rite of passage in U.S. society similar to those in less technological societies is that these events
   A. do not signal a change of status.
   B. lack a moral, spiritual, or philosophical dimension.
   C. do not involve enough people.
   D. are considered important by teens but not by adults.

3. Which term does not correctly reflect broad socialization practices?
   A. individualism
   B. choice
   C. self-expression
   D. obedience

4. Adolescents being raised in cultures using narrow socialization practices tend to be
   A. more obedient.
   B. more conforming.
   C. more group oriented.
   D. described by all of the above.

Level 2

1. Write a list of criteria you would use to declare someone an adult. Do you consider yourself to be an adolescent or an adult?

2. Bjornsen's study of "the blessing" (a parent's acknowledgment of the child's changed status) is an interesting view of the attainment of adult status. How would you answer the following two questions?
   a. Was there a time when your parent did something or said something to you that meant that you were "all grown up" or had reached maturity?
   b. Was there a time when you wanted your parent to do something or say something to you that meant that you were "all grown up" or had reached maturity?

Review 1.2: Modern Views of Adolescence

Level 1

1. The most important change in the lives of teenagers in the 20th century was
   A. the advent of better medical care.
   B. the invention of television.
   C. the expansion of schooling.
   D. greater emphasis on part-time work.

2. The turning point for teenagers in the 20th century was
   A. World War II.
   B. the Great Depression.
   C. World War I.
   D. the civil rights movement of the 1960s.

3. Which of the following statements about the public's attitudes toward adolescents is correct?
   A. Most adults have a balanced view of teen behavior.
   B. Most adults hold a somewhat negative view of adolescents.
   C. Adults generally believe that teens are too busy with organized activities to develop a sense of community.
   D. Adults generally believe teenagers are hard working, but confused, individuals.

4. An adult with a negative view of teens
   A. will dismiss a courageous act by a teen as an exception.
   B. will pay more attention to an antisocial act performed by a teen than a prosocial act.
   C. takes examples and generalizes.
   D. is characterized by all of the above.

5. The best conclusion concerning the legal status of adolescents is that
   A. adolescents are basically treated as adults.
   B. adolescents are basically treated as children.
   C. adolescents do not have even the rights accorded to children.
   D. the legal status of adolescents is confused.

6. In which of the following legal areas has there been the greatest change in the past 20 years?
   A. the age at which one can marry
   B. the age at which one can make a binding contract
   C. the age at which one can be tried as an adult for a serious crime
   D. the age at which one can practice free speech

Level 2

1. Why do adults generally have a negative view of adolescents?

2. How can you explain the fact that most adolescents are happy and optimistic, while many adults hold rather negative opinions of teenagers?

3. Evaluate the following statement: It is more difficult to be an adolescent today than it was 50 years ago.

4. A recent legal case concerned a high school student who was not allowed to wear an accepted religious symbol because it looked like one that is used by some gangs in the neighborhood. The school board said that its actions were a way of keeping gang influences out of the school, whereas the teen argued that they interfered with his right to free speech and religious expression. Everyone admitted that the teen did not belong to a gang. In your opinion, does a school board have the right to ban these symbols? Does it have the right to ban gang-related clothing?

5. A 15-year-old is tried and convicted for a brutal murder of a shopkeeper he was robbing at the time. The state has the death penalty. During the penalty phase of the trial, the assistant district attorney argues that the teen knew what he was doing and should receive the same penalty as an older person. The defense attorney argues that the teen is young and is the victim of an alcoholic mother and an abusive father and claims that a person so young should not be given the ultimate penalty. You are a member of the jury. How would you vote, and why?

Review 1.3: Themes of Adolescence

Level 1

1. Which of the following is an important change in the nature of the peer group during the adolescent years?
   A. The peer group becomes more important to the teen.
   B. There is greater intimacy between friends than during the elementary school years.
   C. Adolescents are more likely to spend time with groups of peers in cliques or crowds.
   D. All of the above are important changes in the nature of the peer group during the adolescent years.

2. Which statement concerning the experiences of teens from many minority groups is correct?
   A. Adolescents from many minority groups are more likely to be raised in poverty.
   B. African American adolescents are more likely than white adolescents to be raised in a permissive atmosphere.
   C. Native American adolescents are most often taught the importance of becoming individuals capable of standing firm against pressures to conform.
   D. All of the above are correct.

3. The effect of growing up in a particular generation is called the _____ effect.
   A. longitudinal
   B. historical
   C. cohort
   D. group membership

4. One important consequence of the increase in single parents, two-parent working families, and self-care is
   A. an increasing emphasis on independence training.
   B. greater amounts of child abuse.
   C. a lack of emphasis on academic values.
   D. a feeling of no longer being loved or needed.

5. One change in the high school today compared with the high school 30 years ago is that
   A. high schools graduate a lower percentage of students.
   B. requirements for graduation are stricter.
   C. teachers are less likely to be well educated.
   D. fewer teens are graduating.

6. Today, which minority group is the largest in the United States?
   A. Latinos
   B. African Americans
   C. Native Americans
   D. Asian Americans

Level 2

1. How could the cohort effect cause a misunderstanding between parents and their adolescent children?

2. What effects will the increasing number of teens belonging to minority groups have on the schools, advertising, business, and American culture?

Answers to Multiple Choice Questions

Review 1.1: 1. A, 2. B, 3. D, 4. D
Review 1.2: 1. C, 2. B, 3. B, 4. D, 5. D, 6. C
Review 1.3: 1. D, 2. A, 3. C, 4. A, 5. B, 6. A

CHAPTER 2 THE SCIENTIFIC APPROACH TO ADOLESCENCE

Review 2.1: Theoretical Approaches to Adolescence

Level 1

1. A theory is like a
   A. framework.
   B. jacket that fits too tightly.
   C. loose-fitting pair of jeans.
   D. feedback loop.

2. A good theory
   A. is supported by expert testimonials.
   B. is useful in understanding and predicting behavior.
   C. introduces many new concepts and terms that describe behavior and development.
   D. can be used in a narrow, rather than wide, context.

3. Which of the following is part of the criteria for judging a theory as "good"?
   A. It is inclusive.
   B. It leads to testable hypotheses.
   C. It presents as few new terms as possible.
   D. All of the above.

Level 2

1. How would you determine if a specific theory is "good" or "useful"?

2. How would you respond to the following complaint? "We don't need theories. All we need is the answer to practical questions."

Review 2.2: Perspectives on Adolescence

Level 1

1. Which statement concerning G. Stanley Hall is correct?
   A. Hall was the leading pioneer in adolescent research.
   B. Hall emphasized the importance of the physical changes in adolescence.
   C. Hall believed that adolescence was a time of storm and stress.
   D. All of the above are correct.

2. Sigmund Freud argued that an adolescent's personality results from
   A. experiences that have been repressed.
   B. conditioning.
   C. what the individual observes and imitates.
   D. sibling rivalry.

3. According to Anna Freud,
   A. adolescents want to be as much like their parents as possible.
   B. an adolescent's striving for emotional autonomy is not easy.
   C. adolescents need to identify with peers to achieve autonomy.
   D. all of the above are true.

4. Peter Blos argued that _____ and _____ were important to adolescent development.
   A. cognitive development, conformity
   B. dependence on peers, dependence on parents
   C. de-idealization of parents, individuation
   D. interdependence with others, feelings of high self-esteem

5. According to Erik Erikson, the psychosocial crisis of adolescence is
   A. intimacy versus isolation.
   B. industry versus inferiority.
   C. trust versus mistrust.
   D. identity versus role confusion.

6. Adolescents can develop their own moral and value system based on their own ideas because they have gained the ability to
   A. take the perspective of other people.
   B. understand and use abstractions.
   C. separate from their parents.
   D. work cooperatively with others.

7. "You act the way you do because you have been reinforced for doing so." Such a statement would most probably be made by a
   A. follower of Jean Piaget.
   B. behaviorist.
   C. follower of Sigmund Freud.
   D. follower of Erik Erikson.

8. Social learning theorists emphasize the importance of
   A. operant conditioning.
   B. observation learning.
   C. feelings of being part of a group.
   D. the self-concept.

9. Kathy believes that she can get in A in art history, but Lena does not. According to Albert Bandura, they differ in
   A. self-efficacy.
   B. their ego ideal.
   C. sources of reinforcement.
   D. personality characteristics.

10. The ecological system emphasizes the importance of understanding
    A. the complex way natural events influence human behavior.
    B. the way in which people are influenced by the entire environmental context in which they live.
    C. how people cope with the family problems they encounter.
    D. the way in which people influence others in their daily interactions.

11. According to Urie Bronfenbrenner, parents' experience at work might influence their teenager. This example demonstrates the
    A. microsystem.
    B. mesosystem.
    C. macrosystem.
    D. exosystem.

Level 2

1. Compare and contrast the basic ideas on adolescent development advanced by the psychoanalytic school, Erik Erikson, the behaviorists, social learning theorists, and ecological theory.

2. How would the concept of self-efficacy work if someone were deciding whether to take a course in calculus?

3. One of the most interesting ideas proposed by Urie Bronfenbrenner is the macrosystem—that is, the idea that the political, cultural, and economic system that one lives under affects development. In what ways would the political, cultural, and economic system influence an adolescent's development in a Western culture, such as the United States or Canada?

4. The influence of the media on adolescent behavior is a source of controversy. How would you explain the fact that so many people watch sexually explicit and violent videos, whereas only a small handful of people directly imitate them? What personality dimensions, in your opinion, differentiate people who directly imitate from those who do not? Should recordings with "objectionable" lyrics come with a warning sticker? Should there be a minimum age for buying particular recordings?

Review 2.3: Research Methods

Level 1

1. Dr. Chin measures the amount of time that groups of 14-, 16-, and 18-year-olds sleep on a school night. He is conducting _____ research.
   A. correlational
   B. cross-sectional
   C. longitudinal
   D. case study

2. In contrast to cross-sectional studies, longitudinal studies
   A. cannot show stability or change within a group.
   B. follow one sample over an extended period of time.
   C. are useful in researching childhood, but not adolescence.
   D. are cheaper and easier to conduct.

3. One difference between case studies and other methods of research is that case studies
   A. can reveal cause and effect.
   B. emphasize the individual, not the group.
   C. do not use observation.
   D. use correlational, not experimental, methods.

4. Dr. Simons obtains a sample of college students by having a computer choose participants at random, and then she contacts them. She believes she can generalize her results to the entire college because her sample is _____ of the population.
   A. conditional
   B. representative
   C. instructive
   D. a subgroup

5. There is a positive correlation between intelligence scores and academic achievement. Which of the following would be true?
   A. High scores on one factor are related to high scores on the other factor.
   B. Low scores on one factor are related to high scores on the other factor.
   C. High scores on one factor cause low scores on the other factor.
   D. High scores on one factor are unrelated to what scores appear on the other.

6. Dr. Rastogi is conducting research on the influence of parents on adolescents' relationship with their friends. In this study, the dependent variable is
   A. parental influence.
   B. the researcher.
   C. a measure of their relationship with friends.
   D. the number of friends an adolescent has.

Level 2

1. Design five questions you would include in a questionnaire concerning adolescent students' attitudes toward their high schools.

2. A researcher wants to find out how adolescents feel about their future. He attends a meeting of the honor society at a junior high school and, after receiving parental permission, finds that every one of the 120 students wants to participate. They all fill out the questionnaire, and the researcher finds that the students basically feel positive about their future. He concludes that junior high school students are basically optimistic about the future. Is his conclusion warranted? Why or why not?

3. Design an experiment to determine the effect of competition on the self-esteem of adolescents.

4. Explain why only experimental research can show cause and effect.

Review 2.4: Ethical Standards and Dilemmas

Level 1

1. A cardinal rule of ethical research is that
   A. research results for an important study supersede the rights of the participant in a study.
   B. participants must not be harmed in the research.
   C. participants must complete the study once they agree to participate in it.
   D. participants may never be paid for their involvement in the study.

2. Participation in a study must be voluntary, and potential participants must be told of any significant factors that might affect their decision to become involved in the study. This is called
   A. informed consent.
   B. voluntary involvement.
   C. reciprocal agreement.
   D. adequate warning.

3. Adolescents below the age of 18 years
   A. are not legally allowed to participate in a research study.
   B. require parental permission as well as their own willingness to become involved in the study.
   C. must have their parents physically present in order to participate in the study.
   D. may participate without parental permission if they are considered to be mature enough by the researcher.

4. In psychological research, deceiving participants as to the true purpose of the study, even if approved by institutional review boards
   A. can never be done.
   B. can only be done with the participant's expressed consent.
   C. can be used if it is absolutely necessary, but participants may never be deceived about any potential risks.
   D. may be done only if the study is conducted outside the college campus.

5. A parent of a 15-year-old who participated in a study on parenting style (with parental permission) would like to know how her child answered certain questions. The researcher

   A. will tell the parent that only if both parents give the researcher permission will the information be given.
   B. will ask the reason for the parent's desire, and if it seems reasonable will release the information.
   C. will cite confidentiality and not release the information.
   D. probably will release the information to a third party who will then make the final decision.

Level 2

1. You are on the review board looking at the ethics of a study that requires deception. Participants will be asked to write a story about people—labeled Asian, African American, Native American, and Caucasian—in different situations. Participants will be told that the study is investigating attitudes toward various occupations, when in reality the study is looking at racial and ethnic stereotypes. Is such deception acceptable? Why or why not?

2. One major question is whether active parental consent, in which parents must sign a consent form, should ever be replaced by passive consent, in which parents are informed of the study but as long as they do not object, participation is determined by the adolescent. Should passive consent be sufficient for participation in a study, or should active consent continue to be the standard? If you believe passive consent is sufficient, at what age should it be allowed?

Answers to Multiple Choice Questions

Review 2.1: 1. A, 2. B, 3. D
Review 2.2: 1. D, 2. A, 3. B, 4. C, 5. D, 6. B, 7. B, 8. B, 9. A, 10. B, 11. D
Review 2.3: 1. B, 2. B, 3. B, 4. B, 5. A, 6. C
Review 2.4: 1. B, 2. A, 3. B, 4. C, 5. C

CHAPTER 3 PHYSICAL DEVELOPMENT

Review 3.1: Pubertal Changes

Level 1

1. A physiological change in the testes that allows for more mature sexual functioning would be considered a
   A. primary sex characteristic.
   B. secondary sex characteristic.
   C. initializing sex characteristic.
   D. maturational gender characteristic.

2. Which statement concerning a teen's growth spurt is correct?
   A. Boys experience their growth spurt before girls.
   B. The rate of growth during a teen's growth spurt is greater than at any time since infancy.
   C. Each teen grows at the same rate.
   D. All of the above are correct.

3. You take a poll of young girls who have just begun to menstruate. Of the following statements, which would you consider the most unusual or atypical according to the research evidence on menstruation?
   A. I felt I wanted privacy.
   B. I experienced some bothersome symptoms.
   C. It was mildly stressful.
   D. It was quite traumatic.

4. Young adolescents show greater emotional reactions than early adults. From a neurological standpoint, the reason may be that
   A. the brain of a young adolescent does not have any myelin sheathing.
   B. the amygdala of young adolescents is not yet present.
   C. the prefrontal cortex is still developing.
   D. the early adolescent's motor cortex does not function properly.

Level 2

1. Some research shows that girls still consider menstruation a sign of weakness, embarrassment, or shame. Why do such attitudes arise?

2. How could your own early education about puberty have been improved?

Review 3.2: The Biological Bases for Behavior and Development

Level 1

1. Which of the following is *not* one of the principal structures responsible for puberty?
   A. hypothalamus
   B. pituitary gland
   C. gonads
   D. pancreas

2. The adrenal glands produce hormones that are partially responsible for
   A. increased emotional control.
   B. early sexual attraction.
   C. feelings of depression, anxiety, and fear.
   D. all of the above.

3. You read that higher testosterone levels are related to increased aggression. To be more accurate, higher levels of testosterone are related to aggression when
   A. the child is in a resting state.
   B. the aggression leads to social dominance.
   C. aggression gets the individual the desired toy or object.
   D. all of the above are true.

4. Which of the following concerning genetic influence on development is *correct*?
   A. Genetic factors are more important during early childhood than during adolescence.
   B. If genetic factors underlie a particular trait, environmental factors cannot influence it.
   C. If a person possesses a gene for a particular trait, the individual must show the trait.
   D. None of the above are correct.

5. Which term describes the degree of agreement between twins on a particular trait?
   A. similarity rating
   B. concerned rate
   C. concordance rate
   D. inheritance rate

6. Twin studies that attempt to discover whether a particular characteristic has a genetic component are based upon the idea that
   A. twins are not affected by the environment.
   B. a significant difference in the rate of agreement on a particular characteristic between identical and fraternal twins demonstrates genetic influence.

C. identical twins are more intelligent than fraternal twins.
D. the variation between identical twins on any characteristic is greater than the variation between fraternal twins.

7. How could genetic factors influence personality and social behavior?
   A. There are genes for friendliness and happiness.
   B. Genetic factors influence physiological functioning, which may influence social behavior and personality.
   C. Genes influence the number of neurons a person has, and this influences personality.
   D. Genetic factors cannot influence personality or social behavior.

8. The fact that attractive teenagers garner greater approval than nonattractive adolescents would show which type of genotype/environmental interaction?
   A. active
   B. passive
   C. evocative
   D. educational

9. People with high intelligence scores are more likely to choose particular activities than people with lower intelligence scores. This tendency shows which type of genotype/environmental interaction?
   A. active
   B. passive
   C. evocative
   D. educational

10. Rather than an individual's temperament influencing his or her adjustment, many psychologists believe that it is the _____ that influences adjustment.
    A. individual's subjective reaction to his or her temperament
    B. fit between the individual's temperament and the demands of the situation
    C. individual's level of intelligence
    D. level of hormones in the bloodstream

11. An individual's hobbies and unique experiences are _____ influences.
    A. shared environmental
    B. shared genetic
    C. nonshared environmental
    D. nonshared genetic

Level 2

1. You read about a study that finds that aggression is related to the level of a particular hormone. The author of the study argues that this finding demonstrates that high levels of this hormone cause aggression. Discuss two other possible conclusions from the data. (Hint: Consider the meaning of a correlation.)

2. What is the advantage of measuring temperament in terms of activity level, sociability, and emotionality rather than as easy, slow to warm up, and difficult?

3. How would you explain to parents why their two adolescent sons are so different from each other?

Review 3.3: The Interplay of Physical Development and Experience

Level 1

1. The secular trend is shown by which of the following situations?
   A. The average boy is taller than the average girl.
   B. Each generation in a particular country seems to be getting taller since medical care and nutrition have improved.
   C. Each girl matures at her own rate.
   D. All of the above are examples of the secular trend.

2. Which of the following factors influences the timing of puberty?
   A. stress
   B. genetic endowment
   C. intense exercise
   D. all of the above

3. Based on the research, you would expect an early-maturing boy, compared with a later-maturing boy, to show all the following characteristics except
   A. higher self-esteem.
   B. greater popularity.
   C. greater satisfaction with his physical appearance.
   D. a higher degree of restlessness.

4. A psychologist is giving a speech about the research evidence showing that early-maturing girls are more likely to be drawn into early dating and sex and to have more difficulties in school. To be correct, though, the psychologist should add that
   A. this is true only for girls from suburban and rural areas.
   B. many of the difficulties experienced by these girls can be seen before puberty, and puberty is just another stressor for them.
   C. it is the way parents deal with their daughters' early puberty that causes these tendencies, and the blame lies in parents' unfair restrictions of their daughter's activities.
   D. this was truer in the 1980s than in the 1990s and early 2000s.

Level 2

1. If the secular trend toward earlier maturation continues, what effect would it have on children's social interaction and family relationships?

2. Female gymnasts who engage in very strenuous and intensive exercise delay puberty, thereby maintaining a prepubescent body longer. These young girls are some-what more agile and lighter than their peers. Should these young girls be allowed to compete with older teenage girls and early adults in international competitions?

Review 3.4: The Health of Today's Teenagers

Level 1

1. Which of the following statements about the health of today's adolescents is correct?
   A. Most teens rate their health positively.
   B. Teens from minority groups, such as African American teens, are less likely to rate their health as "excellent."
   C. Many teen health problems stem from the teens' own behavior.
   D. All of the above are correct.

2. You are taking a poll of teenage girls' perceptions of their own weight. Most of your sample of 15-year-old girls have weights that are within the normal range. If you were to ask the girls with such weights about how they perceived themselves,
   A. most would be pleased that they were within the normal range and would see themselves as normal.
   B. most would believe they were too fat and would want to be thinner.
   C. most would believe they were too thin and underdeveloped.
   D. you would not find any particular pattern.

3. The best predictor of eating problems in teenage girls is
   A. subjective perception of weight.
   B. objective differences between actual and ideal weight.
   C. feelings of being unloved.
   D. lack of athletic ability.

4. Obese teens
   A. often experience social problems.
   B. always have low self-esteem.
   C. were probably thin as children.
   D. can be described by all of the above.

5. Most studies concerning adolescents and exercise find that
   A. adolescents become more active as they progress through that stage of life.
   B. this generation of adolescents is more physically fit than any generation in the past.
   C. girls are less active than boys.
   D. all of the above occur.

6. Which statement concerning teenagers and sleep is incorrect?
   A. Most teenagers sleep less than they did when they were in elementary school.
   B. Most teenagers do not get enough sleep.
   C. Teenagers today get less sleep than their grandparents did.
   D. Teenagers do not need as much sleep as preadolescents.

Level 2

1. How does the doctor-patient relationship change in adolescence?

2. Research shows that even if teenagers are at risk for developing heart disease or cancer later, they do not change their behavior now. Why do you think this is so?

3. Why is discontent with weight so prevalent among teenage girls, even those who are not overweight? What can be done about it?

4. Some critics point to the very thin models who appear in women's magazines as the source of teenage girls' body dissatisfaction. Others disagree, claiming that the influence of these models is not that great. In your opinion, what influence do models in these magazines have on teenage girls' body dissatisfaction?

5. If your 10-year-old daughter showed a fear of becoming heavy, went on a diet, and refused to eat any cake or cookies, how would you react? What, if anything, would you do?

6. Many blame the reduction in physical activity in adolescence on the nature of the school physical education program. In your opinion, is this position defendable? How do you rate the physical education program in your junior and senior high school? What changes, if any, would you make?

Answers to Multiple Choice Questions

Review 3.1: 1. A, 2. B, 3. D, 4. C
Review 3.2: 1. D, 2. B, 3. B, 4. D, 5. C, 6. B, 7. B, 8. C, 9. A, 10. B, 11. C
Review 3.3: 1. B, 2. D, 3. D, 4. B
Review 3.4: 1. D, 2. B, 3. A, 4. A, 5. C, 6. D

CHAPTER 4 COGNITIVE DEVELOPMENT

Review 4.1: Developmental Approaches

Level 1

1. Piaget used the _____ method, which required both observation and questioning techniques.
   A. statistical
   B. behavioral
   C. clinical
   D. broad

2. After learning about mammals, Phil sees a kangaroo and looks for a new classification of animals for the kangaroo, which he finds is called a *marsupial.* This demonstrates Piaget's idea of
   A. assimilation.
   B. accommodation.
   C. interpretation.
   D. means-end analysis.

3. Piaget's mechanism for explaining change is the concept of
   A. assimilation.
   B. object permanence.
   C. equilibration.
   D. object analysis.

4. Children in the _____ stage understand that an 8-ounce cup and an 8-ounce glass hold the same amount of water.
   A. sensorimotor
   B. preoperational
   C. concrete operational
   D. masking

5. A teenager argues that the way his parents run their home is not the only way and that there are many other alternatives. This argument shows the teen's ability to
   A. separate the real from the possible.
   B. understand the nature of the adult world.
   C. work through problems in a scientific manner.
   D. engage in inductive reasoning.

6. Adolescents can understand contrary-to-fact arguments and reason scientifically because they have formed the ability to
   A. use inductive reasoning.
   B. use hypothetical-deductive logic.
   C. participate in the decision-making process.
   D. use empathy in their problem solving.

7. The most significant advance during adolescence, according to Piaget, is the adolescent's ability to
   A. use inductive reasoning.
   B. interact in a less egocentric manner.
   C. understand problems requiring a knowledge of conservation.
   D. understand and use abstractions.

8. Research concerning the universality of formal operational reasoning shows that it
   A. exists to the same extent in every society.
   B. is found only in the United States and Western Europe.
   C. is not universal.
   D. can be found in elementary school children to about the same extent as in teens.

9. The existence of postformal operational thought is based on the idea that
   A. little cognitive change occurs after age 15.
   B. formality in thought is more important than informality in thought.
   C. a different mode of thought occurs in late adolescence and early adulthood.
   D. informality in thought is more important than formality in thought.

10. To understand behavior and development, you must appreciate the cultural, historical, and social context that influences the individual. This is in keeping with _____ theory.
    A. Freud's
    B. behavioral
    C. Piaget's
    D. Vygotsky's

11. The sociocultural orientation to cognitive development stresses
    A. personal discovery.
    B. people with more expertise teaching people with less expertise.
    C. equilibration.
    D. reinforcement and punishment.

12. A teacher gives students a great deal of help solving a problem and then, as they become better at it, gradually reduces his involvement. This is an example of
    A. reciprocal inhibition.
    B. programmed learning.
    C. scaffolding.
    D. launching.

13. Your friend tells you that she is in a special reading program in which she is being taught how to summarize, generate questions, clarify, and predict. You surmise that her program is using
    A. cooperative learning.
    B. peer tutoring.
    C. reciprocal teaching.
    D. rehabilitative teaching.

Level 2

1. How does the ability to see alternative realities contribute to idealism?

2. How would the ability to use abstractions lead to the development of an adolescent's own system of values and morals?

3. How would a young adult's thought processes differ from those of an adolescent reasoning at the formal operational level?

4. You are going to attend a conference in which one professor will argue Piaget's point of view and another will argue Vygotsky's ideas. How do you think these professors will deal with the importance of formal teaching and personal discovery?

Review 4.2: Information Processing

Level 1

1. The major difference between children's and adolescents' cognitive abilities lies in their processing capacity, familiarity with content, and processing speed. This view is similar to a view suggested by
    A. Sigmund Freud.
    B. Jean Piaget.
    C. information-processing specialists.
    D. Lev Vygotsky.

2. Despite the radio blaring from a car outside the classroom and the student talking to her friend, you can still attend to what your professor is saying, an ability called
    A. attention span.
    B. selective attention.
    C. mnemonics.
    D. suggestive attention.

3. A group of elementary school children, teenagers, middle-age people, and older people are being tested for their speed of information processing. According to prior research, which group should be the fastest?
    A. older adults
    B. middle-age adults
    C. adolescents
    D. elementary school children

4. Adolescents already know the multiplication table so well that it takes very little effort to retrieve the right answer, whereas younger children who are just learning it must use much of their processing capacity to obtain the right answer. The adolescents' advantage is due to
    A. automaticity.
    B. reciprocal training.
    C. baseline coordination.
    D. buttressing.

5. Jerry is trying to understand how to use his new cell phone, which has many special features. He knows that he must read everything very slowly because he isn't particularly knowledgeable about the technology and that he must ask himself questions about the material to make sure that he understands it. Jerry's approach illustrates the concept of
    A. disinhibitory learning.
    B. primary learning.
    C. metacognition.
    D. demand memory.

6. Compared with teenagers, younger children
    A. underestimate what they know.
    B. overestimate what they know.
    C. are just about as accurate about what they know.
    D. cannot answer questions about what they know.

7. Lakeesha spends at least an hour each night studying for her high school chemistry class. She spends even more time if she does not easily understand the material. She makes goals for herself and rewards herself when she meets them. Psychologists would describe her as
    A. having a high fear of failure.
    B. a self-regulated learner.
    C. a cooperative learner.
    D. a disinhibited learner.

8. Three important aspects of self-regulation are
   A. setting goals, choosing strategies, and monitoring progress.
   B. helping others achieve their goals, looking for rewards, and taking pride in success.
   C. doing exactly what the teacher says, reading slowly for meaning, and taking pride in successes.
   D. reducing social activities, creating priorities, and refusing to acknowledge failure.

Level 2

1. How do information-processing psychologists and Piagetian psychologists differ in their areas of interest?

2. In what ways would adolescents have an advantage over younger children in solving problems?

Review 4.3: Approaches to Intelligence

Level 1

1. There is _____ between scores on standardized intelligence tests and achievement in school.
   A. a positive correlation
   B. a negative correlation
   C. an inverse correlation
   D. no correlation

2. If a 12-year-old taking an intelligence test has the mental abilities of a 14-year-old, what would his intelligence quotient be?
   A. approximately 116
   B. about 135
   C. 100
   D. about 88

3. If Larry's intelligence scores at 8 years, 12 years, and 16 years follow the most common pattern, you will find
   A. stability.
   B. a significant improvement.
   C. a slight reduction.
   D. a significant reduction.

4. Your professor argues that people who score high on standardized intelligence tests usually do well in most academic areas. The professor is arguing for
   A. the *g* concept of intelligence.
   B. the *s* concept of intelligence.
   C. intelligence with a capital *I*.
   D. intelligence with a small *i*.

5. Which of the following is not one of Gardner's types of intelligence?
   A. interpersonal
   B. intrapersonal
   C. linguistic
   D. persuasive

6. According to Sternberg, an individual with interpersonal skills and the ability to solve everyday problems has what is called _____ intelligence.
   A. analytic
   B. cultural
   C. practical
   D. creative

7. Which of the following would not be a component of emotional intelligence?
   A. social skills
   B. reading social situations well
   C. delaying gratification
   D. mathematical skills

Level 2

1. How can adolescents score the same on intelligence tests as they did when they were children even though they now know more?

2. Gardner argues that there are many types of intelligence. Write down each type of intelligence and next to it the name of a public figure who you believe is high in this intelligence.

3. What would the practical implications be if schools decided that all of Gardner's types of intelligence were equally important?

4. In your opinion, do people with high standardized intelligence scores lack emotional intelligence? What evidence do you have for your opinion?

5. Evaluate the arguments made for and against the proposition that intelligence tests are unfair to students from some minority groups.

6. In your opinion, should standardized intelligence tests be used in schools? If so, under what circumstances? If you would not use standardized intelligence tests, is there anything that you would recommend in their place?

Review 4.4: Using Cognitive Abilities

Level 1

1. Which of the following is a reason why psychologists argue that the ability to think critically increases in adolescence?
   A. Speed of processing increases during adolescence.
   B. Adolescents have a superior knowledge base compared with younger children.
   C. Adolescents understand that a number of different alternative solutions exist.
   D. All of the above add to the superiority of adolescents on critical thinking tasks.

2. Critical thinking involves all the following except
   A. refusing to believe anything said on television.
   B. analyzing the credentials of a communicator.
   C. looking for possible biases.
   D. analyzing the logic of an argument.

3. Which criterion for creativity is difficult to determine when looking at art or music?
   A. novelty
   B. appropriateness
   C. commercial value
   D. individual satisfaction

4. Creativity is often defined in terms of _____ thinking.
   A. convergent
   B. divergent
   C. group
   D. beneficial

5. Older and younger teens are asked what decisions they would make in various situations. You would expect the younger teens to
   A. overlook possible negative consequences to their actions.
   B. process the information very slowly.
   C. refuse to participate because they do not have the power to make these decisions.
   D. base their information on multiple sources of information rather than any one experience or case.

Level 2

1. Why is creativity only weakly related to scores on standardized intelligence tests?

2. At what age do you believe people should be able to make the following decisions?
   _____ a. have access to any reading material they want
   _____ b. be able to drop out of school
   _____ c. make medical decisions on their own
   _____ d. receive contraceptives without their parents' permission
   _____ e. be responsible as an adult for a criminal act
   _____ f. drive a vehicle with no restrictions
   _____ g. marry without parental permission
   _____ h. be employed without any restrictions
   _____ i. enter into a legal and binding contract
   _____ j. buy cigarettes
   _____ k. buy alcoholic beverages
   What is your reasoning behind the age you have given? Have a few of your friends, and perhaps your parents, do the same, and compare your answers.

Review 4.5: Social Cognition

Level 1

1. Your professor is investigating the influence that cognitive variables have on social behavior, which is called
   A. behavioral psychology.
   B. social cognition.
   C. individual psychology.
   D. psychomotor individuation.

2. One major improvement in the ability of adolescents to take the perspective of others is the ability to
   A. take the perspective of a third party, such as a teacher or a parent.
   B. understand that a friend can have a different view of an issue.
   C. appreciate the fact that a friend can have other friends.
   D. understand that other people can evaluate their actions and motives.

3. The inability to differentiate between what one is thinking and what others are thinking is called adolescent
   A. conservation.
   B. idealism.
   C. egocentrism.
   D. involvement.

4. Richard believes that everyone is looking at him as he walks through the classroom door. This is known as the
   A. personal fable.
   B. zone of proximal development.
   C. imaginary audience.
   D. personal filter.

5. Gina believes that she is the only person to have loved so deeply, given so much, and then been treated so badly. This belief is called the
   A. personal fable.
   B. alter ego.
   C. ego filter.
   D. zone of proximal development.

Level 2

1. What limits, if any, would you place upon the free speech of adolescents in schools? For example, should adolescents be allowed to give speeches promoting drug use, racism, or sexism?

Answers to Multiple Choice Questions

Review 4.1: 1. C, 2. B, 3. C, 4. C, 5. A, 6. B, 7. D, 8. C, 9. C, 10. D, 11. B, 12. C, 13. C
Review 4.2: 1. C, 2. B, 3. C, 4. A, 5. C, 6. B, 7. B, 8. A
Review 4.3: 1. A, 2. A, 3. A, 4. A, 5. D, 6. C, 7. D
Review 4.4: 1. D, 2. A, 3. B, 4. B, 5. A
Review 4.5: 1. B, 2. A, 3. C, 4, C, 5. A

CHAPTER 5 FAMILIES

Review 5.1: The Adolescent-Parent Relationship

Level 1

1. The popular view of adolescent-parent conflict was modified because it
   A. did not allow for adolescents' showing their true feelings toward their parents.
   B. was not supported by research.
   C. had no theoretical basis.
   D. was true only for late adolescents, not for early or middle adolescents.

2. According to the most current view, the adolescent-parent relationship is
   A. filled with conflict and stress.
   B. stress-free and forgiving.
   C. a renegotiation of power.
   D. equal in power from early adolescence through late adolescence.

3. As adolescents progress through early to middle adolescence, they still show difficulties
   A. seeing their parents as people.
   B. not idealizing their parents.
   C. spending holidays with their parents.
   D. believing they should be different from their parents.

4. Children who show _____ attachment develop better interpersonal relationships.
   A. directive
   B. secure
   C. elementary
   D. definitive

5. Which of the following statements concerning attachment is correct?
   A. Attachment theory has a great deal of relevance to infants but not to adolescents.
   B. The nature of attachment to parents cannot change in childhood.
   C. Attachment is a useful concept when speaking of adolescent relationships.
   D. Few adolescents show attachments to parents, as they reduce their contact with parents and redirect their attachments to other adults.

6. Adolescents rate the ideal family as _____ in cohesion and as having _____ power differences between parent and child.
   A. low, low
   B. moderate, moderate
   C. high, moderate
   D. high, high

Level 2

1. How would one's expectations for the adolescent-parent relationship change if the relationship was seen in terms of transformation rather than conflict?

2. Why do teenagers have difficulty seeing their parents as people and accepting their parents' strengths, weaknesses, and foibles?

3. Explain why adolescents, even when they are independent, still do not see their relationship with their parents as completely symmetrical and equal.

4. On a graph, roughly sketch how you would expect the qualities of nurturance, intimacy, and control to change over time between adolescents and their parents and between adolescents and their peers.

Review 5.2: Parenting Styles

Level 1

1. A parent who expects obedience without question and shows little responsiveness typifies the _____ style of parenting.
   A. authoritarian
   B. authoritative
   C. permissive
   D. neglectful

2. A parent using the _____ style of parenting allows a great deal of discussion, wants a good relationship with the child, but does not demand much of the child.
   A. authoritarian
   B. authoritative
   C. permissive
   D. neglectful

3. Generally, adolescents raised by parents who use the _____ parenting style are more self-reliant, self-controlled, contented, and independent.
   A. authoritarian
   B. authoritative
   C. neglectful
   D. permissive

4. A researcher finds that parents from Asia demand unquestioned obedience, yet show responsiveness through their interest in their children and the closeness of the family. Such a pattern is called
   A. antidemocratic.
   B. indulgent.
   C. independent.
   D. traditional.

5. African American and Latino parents often show a higher degree of _____ than white European parents.
   A. supportiveness
   B. demandingness
   C. personal communication
   D. communicational effectiveness

Level 2

1. Why does authoritative parenting generally lead to desirable outcomes?

2. Why would some African American, Asian American, and Latino parents effectively use a different parenting style or variant of parenting style compared with European American parents?

Review 5.3: Communication and Conflict

Level 1

1. Which term best describes communication between parents and their adolescent children?
   A. mutuality
   B. infrequent
   C. directive
   D. nonexistent

2. Parents tend to _____ the differences between themselves and their adolescent children, and teenagers tend to _____ these differences.
   A. underestimate, underestimate
   B. overestimate, underestimate
   C. underestimate, overestimate
   D. overestimate, overestimate

3. Most conflicts between parents and their adolescent children center around
   A. sexual behavior.
   B. moral and political issues.
   C. everyday activities.
   D. goals for the future.

4. Conflict between parents and their adolescent children may be somewhat greater in Western countries than in other cultures because Western cultures
   A. encourage individuality.
   B. punish children more actively for misbehavior.
   C. do not value conformity at all.
   D. are more oriented toward tradition.

5. Which of the followings statements about conflict between adolescents and their parents is correct?
   A. Some adolescent conflict is found in most cultures.
   B. Most non-Western cultures report a greater amount of adolescent-parent conflict than parents in Western cultures.
   C. In non-Western cultures, the kind of conflict that is typical for Western teens occurs at an earlier age.
   D. In non-Western cultures, the kind of conflict that is typical with Western teens occurs during early adulthood.

6. If you were conducting a study of how adolescents perceive communication with their parents and your findings agreed with previous studies in the field, you would expect which of the following results?
   A. Teenagers perceive communication with their mother as better than communication with their father.
   B. Adolescents perceive their father as more distant than they mother.
   C. Teenagers see more openness in communication with friends than with parents.
   D. You would expect to find all of the above.

Level 2

1. Some research shows that parents do not actively discuss their values with their adolescent children. Why do you think this might be so?

2. Why do teenagers commonly believe they are ready for freedoms that their parents feel they are too young to experience?

3. How is or was conflict settled in your home? What was the nature of the most common and most continuing source of conflict? Will you settle conflicts with your own adolescent children differently? If so, how?

Review 5.4: Other Family Relationships

Level 1

1. Which statement concerning sibling relationships is correct?
   A. Siblings can provide emotional support to the adolescent.
   B. Adolescents are more satisfied with their sibling relationships than their parental relationship.
   C. Sibling relationships become more intense with age.
   D. All of the above are correct.

2. Sibling relationships differ from friendships because of
   A. the high level of positive emotion shown.
   B. the lack of contact.
   C. the relatively high level of conflict.
   D. all of the above.

3. Research shows that three changes occur in sibling relationships during adolescence. Which of the following *is not* one of these changes?
   A. Sibling relationships become less based on power.
   B. Older siblings become less nurturant.
   C. The intensity of the relationships diminishes.
   D. Conflict increases during adolescence.

4. If you studied and compared children and adolescents raised by grandparents and children from intact families, you would most likely find similarities in many areas but a difference in
   A. behavioral disturbances.
   B. health.
   C. academic achievement.
   D. all of the above.

Level 2

1. If you had grown up with more or fewer siblings, how would it have affected your life?

2. What are the arguments for and against the idea that parents' rules should be the same for each child? Under what circumstances, if any, would you treat two adolescent children differently?

Review 5.5: The Changing American Family

Level 1

1. Which of the following statements about "only children" is correct?
   A. Only children show better achievement in school.
   B. Only children are more likely to show serious personality disturbances.
   C. Only children have poor social skills.
   D. Only children have more arguments with their parents than do children with siblings.

2. Tadeusz claims that maternal employment leads to more antisocial behavior in adolescents. Malini believes that maternal employment leads to more personality disturbances. Joseph argues that maternal employment does not lead to antisocial or personality problems in children or adolescents, and Paul argues that mothers who work are less concerned with their adolescents' behavior and achievement. Only _____ is correct.
   A. Tadeusz
   B. Malini
   C. Joseph
   D. Paul

3. One key factor that determines whether adolescents will get into trouble is
   A. maternal employment status.
   B. the number of siblings in the home.
   C. parental monitoring.
   D. temperament.

4. After a divorce, the custodial parent becomes _____ controlling, whereas the noncustodial parent becomes _____ permissive.
   A. more, more
   B. more, less
   C. less, more
   D. less, less

5. Adolescents whose parents divorce during adolescence are more likely to
   A. question the value of a relationship.
   B. question the stability and permanence of relationships.
   C. choose mates who are unemployed.
   D. work harder in school to forget their home problems.

6. Which of the following statements concerning adolescents and stepfamilies is correct?
   A. Adolescents often have a particularly easy time adjusting to the stepfamily.
   B. Daughters have a harder time than sons adjusting to a stepfather.
   C. The research on the influence of a stepfamily on adolescents is totally positive.
   D. All of the above are correct.

Level 2

1. Based on your readings, what advice would you give to divorcing parents who have two teenage children, who are 12 and 15 years old?

2. Critique the following statement: Children and adolescents develop best when they live in an intact two-parent family.

Answers to Multiple Choice Questions

Review 5.1: 1. B, 2. C, 3. A, 4. B, 5. C, 6. C
Review 5.2: 1. A, 2. C, 3. B, 4. D, 5. B
Review 5.3: 1. C, 2. C, 3. C, 4. A, 5. A, 6. D
Review 5.4: 1. A, 2. C, 3. D, 4. C
Review 5.5: 1. A, 2. C, 3. C, 4. A, 5. B, 6. B

CHAPTER 6 PEERS

Review 6.1: The Peer Group

Level 1

1. Which of the following statements about time spent with peers and parents during adolescence is correct?
   A. American teens spend more time with their peers than teens from other countries, such as Japan.
   B. The amount of time adolescents spend with other teens increases, but so does the amount of time teens spend with their parents.
   C. Most of the increase in the amount of time adolescents spend with peers occurs during late adolescence.
   D. All of the above are correct.

2. For adolescents, the best predictor of adult adjustment is
   A. academic achievement.
   B. getting along with peers.
   C. having an interest in something outside the home.
   D. not conforming to peer influence.

3. A psychologist being interviewed on television claims that puberty causes conflict with parents, and therefore teens turn to their peers for support and help. This psychologist probably identifies with which school of psychological thought?
   A. behaviorism
   B. cognitive psychology
   C. psychoanalytic school
   D. humanistic school

4. Harry Stack Sullivan emphasized the importance of _____ to the later development of intimate relationships.
   A. biological maturity
   B. close friendships
   C. parent-teen conflict
   D. membership in a clique

Level 2

1. Why does the peer group take on increasing importance in adolescence?

2. Contrast the nature of the peer group in adolescence and in childhood on the basis of importance, intimacy, grouping, and membership in groups.

Review 6.2: Friends

Level 1

1. According to teens, their most enjoyable activity is
   A. spending time with friends.
   B. listening to music.
   C. spending time on their hobbies.
   D. sleeping.

2. Based on the research on friendship, you would expect an adolescent compared to an elementary school child to emphasize which of the following?
   A. enjoying each other's company
   B. intimacy
   C. psychological traits such as honesty
   D. positive interpersonal interactions

3. Which of the following areas shows the least similarity between friends?
   A. school-related attitudes
   B. personality
   C. school achievement
   D. behaviors such as smoking, drug use, and religious practices

4. Which statement concerning conflicts between teens and friends and teens and parents is correct?
   A. Conflicts between teens and friends are more likely to end with no winner or loser.
   B. Conflicts between friends are more likely to be settled through negotiation.
   C. Adolescents have a greater fear that a friendship will be destroyed due to a conflict than a family relationship.
   D. All of the above are correct.

Level 2

1. Contrast the meaning of friendship in childhood with its meaning in adolescence by writing two sentences about a friend—one that would be spoken by a 7-year-old and one by a 15-year-old.

2. Mature friendships involve a balance of individuality and relatedness. Name three ways in which you would be able to determine whether a friendship met this criterion.

3. Psychologists have argued whether people with similar attitudes choose each other as friends or whether friends reinforce each other for particular behaviors (socialization influence). Evaluate each viewpoint. In your opinion, how does each of the two factors operate?

4. In both adolescent and adult friendships, female friendships are more intimate and supportive, whereas male friendships are based more on similarity of interests. Why is this so?

Review 6.3: Cliques and Crowds

Level 1

1. Teens are often members of small groups of friends called _____.
   A. cliques
   B. crowds
   C. generals
   D. associates

2. You are questioning students in sixth through twelfth grades about their membership in a crowd in school. Based on previous studies, you would expect the students' perception of the importance of crowd membership to
   A. increase with age.
   B. decline with age.
   C. show no particular pattern.
   D. decline with age for males and increase with age for females.

3. One reason why it is very difficult for a teen to change crowds is that the teen already has a
   A. reputation.
   B. feeling of alienation from society.
   C. sense of identity.
   D. sense of worth.

Level 2

1. The names for crowds vary in different schools, but "preppies," "druggies," "nerds," "jocks," and "burnouts" are common. Briefly list the personality, dress, and interests of people belonging to these crowds. In your opinion, do people choose the crowd to which they belong, or are people assigned to a crowd? How would someone change crowds?

2. List all the benefits and drawbacks of a clique and a crowd. In your opinion, are cliques and crowds mainly a positive or a negative factor in adolescence?

Review 6.4: Popularity and Unpopularity

Level 1

1. Which is a factor in popularity?
   A. athletic ability
   B. social dominance
   C. being very attractive
   D. all of the above

2. Studies of cheerleaders clearly show that there is a difference between
   A. grades and athletic abilities.
   B. being popular and being well liked.
   C. being helped and being helpful.
   D. being socially dominant and being behaviorally dominant.

3. According to research, a pattern that leads to active rejection involves
   A. irritability and inattentiveness.
   B. being overly helpful and being unemotional.
   C. talking too much and being nonathletic.
   D. getting good grades and having a good relationship with one's parents.

4. Two tough 14-year-olds threaten each other and finally get into a fight. The one who started it still would not be considered a bully because
   A. bullying cannot occur after age 12.
   B. the adolescents were of equal strength.
   C. there is no real way to determine who started the fight.
   D. this type of situation is too common to be considered bullying.

Level 2

1. Why is being popular so important for adolescents?

2. You are the principal of a middle school. Recently, two boys have been robbed and one beaten up by a couple of bullies in the school. After speaking to a number of students, you find that bullying is common in the school. How would you deal with the situation?

Review 6.5: Romantic Relationships

Level 1

1. You are questioning a number of late adolescents about the amount of emotional support they receive from their friendships and romantic relationships. If your results agree with prior research, the participants in your study will say they receive
   A. more support from friends.
   B. more support from romantic partners.
   C. about the same amount of support from both friends and romantic partners.
   D. almost no support from either friends or romantic partners.

2. When asked about what they liked about their romantic partners, teenage boys are more likely to mention _____ and teenage girls, _____.
   A. physical attractiveness, support
   B. helpfulness, emotional closeness
   C. sexual activity, mutual interests
   D. similar interests, similar personality traits

3. At least in the United States, the most common ways for romantic partners to deal with disagreements are
   A. seeking distraction and attacking.
   B. seeking distraction and getting help from others.
   C. avoidance and compromise.
   D. withdrawing and attacking.

Level 2

1. How would you determine if your son or daughter was ready to date?

2. Studies show that dating behaviors are well understood and relatively structured. Boys do certain things; girls do others. Why have these conventions developed? Are they changing?

3. Teens usually believe that dating is their own business, but parents disagree. What influence on their middle adolescent children, if any, should parents have in various aspects of dating?

4. Why do some women in abusive dating relationships continue to see their partners?

5. Some argue that people who witness their parents' physical aggression against each other should realize the consequences and not do the same. Although many individuals do learn not to abuse their dating partners, being exposed to spousal violence or being physically abused is related to dating violence. Why is this the case?

Review 6.6: Behavioral Autonomy and Conformity

Level 1

1. Of the following bases of power, which is least likely to explain conformity?
   A. referent power
   B. expert power
   C. coercive power
   D. reward power

2. You are testing a group of 14-, 17-, 19-, and 22-year-olds on their susceptibility to peer influence to dress in a certain way. Based on past research evidence, you would probably find the _____-year-olds most conforming.
   A. 14
   B. 17
   C. 19
   D. 22

3. Adolescents seem more conforming than adults because
   A. their conformity always leads to social problems.
   B. they see fewer situations negatively.
   C. few understand the concept of emotional autonomy.
   D. most are followers, not leaders.

4. In which area are teens most likely to experience direct peer pressure?
   A. smoking
   B. spending time with peers
   C. talking back to parents
   D. helping others

5. Parents who use the _____ parenting style are more likely to have teens who are less susceptible to peer influence.
   A. authoritarian
   B. authoritative
   C. permissive
   D. rejecting

Level 2

1. How would the five bases for power influence a teen's decision to say he likes a particular recording artist when he actually does not?

2. Think of a time when you conformed to something because of direct or indirect peer pressure and consider another time when you did not. Why did you conform in the first instance and not in the second situation?

3. People often characterize the teen culture as antiestablishment, anti-adult, and pleasure seeking. What, if anything, differentiates teen culture from the mainstream culture? To what extent do you believe this anti-adult view matches today's teen culture?

Answers to Multiple Choice Questions

Review 6.1: 1. A, 2. B, 3. C, 4. B
Review 6.2: 1. A, 2. B, 3. B, 4. D
Review 6.3: 1. A, 2. B, 3. A
Review 6.4: 1. D, 2. B, 3. A, 4. B
Review 6.5: 1. C, 2. A, 3. C
Review 6.6: 1. C, 2. A, 3. B, 4. B, 5. B

CHAPTER 7 THE SCHOOL EXPERIENCE

Review 7.1: Middle School

Level 1

1. Which of the following is *not* a difference between elementary and secondary schools?
   A. Secondary schools tend to be larger than elementary schools.
   B. Students experience more freedom in secondary schools.
   C. Students have to satisfy more teachers than they did in elementary school.
   D. Students have more personal contact with their teachers than they did in elementary school.

2. Girls are more vulnerable to transition problems in middle or junior high school because they
   A. are physically weaker.
   B. are experiencing many rapid physical changes.
   C. have fewer close friends.
   D. begin secondary school with poorer cognitive skills.

3. The largest general complaint about junior high or middle schools, even from students who are relatively well adjusted, is that
   A. the work is just too hard.
   B. teachers do not truly understand their students.
   C. students feel that teachers don't know who they are.
   D. students are not liked in the school.

4. The most common trend in grades seen after the transition to middle school is
   A. an improvement.
   B. a decline.
   C. staying about the same as in elementary school.
   D. an improvement for girls and a decline for boys.

5. Which of the following was not advocated by the Carnegie Reports?
   A. teaching a core academic curriculum
   B. creating small learning communities
   C. a greater use of cooperative learning strategies
   D. changing the structure of the school so that students have only one teacher all day

6. You read that the decline in achievement is greater for students who experience two transitions, one to junior high and then another to high school, compared with students who transfer only once (from eighth grade to high school). According to research, this information is
   A. correct.
   B. incorrect.
   C. correct for males but incorrect for females.
   D. correct for females but incorrect for males.

7. One important problem for middle school teachers is that they
   A. do not like their subject matter.
   B. often are not specially trained to deal with young adolescents.
   C. are overwhelmingly male and do not understand the problems of female adolescents.
   D. expect too much from their students academically.

Level 2

1. How do the structural changes between elementary and junior high school explain some of the transitional difficulties students experience?

2. Analyze Eccles's claims that the fit between junior high school and the needs of the students is poor. If you agree with Eccles's ideas, what do you think can be done to change the situation?

3. What are the advantages and disadvantages of replacing the current structure of elementary school, middle school, and high school with a structure of one school for kindergarten through eighth grade and then high school?

Review 7.2: High School

Level 1

1. The transition to high school is not marked by
   A. more absenteeism.
   B. lower grades.
   C. greater participation in school activities.
   D. more failures in courses.

2. One pattern found in the research concerning the transition to high school is
   A. more academic hassles but fewer daily hassles with peers.
   B. fewer academic hassles and fewer daily hassles with peers.
   C. more academic hassles and more daily hassles with peers.
   D. fewer academic hassles and more daily hassles with peers.

3. You are conducting a poll concerning how students feel about their elementary school and high school. If your findings agree with most polls, you will find
   A. the high school being rated higher than the elementary school.
   B. the elementary school being rated higher than the high school.
   C. both being rated equally high.
   D. the elementary school being rated higher by males than females, but the high school being rated equally high by both boys and girls.

4. One area in which parents, college professors, and employers give the schools great credit is
   A. writing skills.
   B. advanced reading skills.
   C. mathematical skills.
   D. computer literacy skills.

5. Comparing whites, blacks, Asian Americans, and Latinos, the group with the lowest percentage in college preparatory classes is
   A. whites.
   B. blacks.
   C. Latinos.
   D. Asian Americans.

6. Which of the following is a factor correlated with children in poverty doing well in school?
   A. parental encouragement
   B. good study habits
   C. coming from smaller families
   D. all of the above

7. If you researched the achievement of male and female high school students, you would probably find that
   A. female students are at risk for doing poorly in English and foreign language.
   B. female students get better grades than males but are found more often in special education classes.
   C. male students drop out more and do more poorly than girls.
   D. male students rate their educational experiences as "superior" or "good" more often than females.

Level 2

1. Why are researchers much more interested in the transition to junior high school than the transition to high school?

2. "All transitions cause some problems." Why would anyone make this statement? Do you believe it is true?

3. Rate the following aspects of your education from 1 (poor) to 5 (excellent). Consider elementary school, junior high or middle school, and high school.
   ___ Teachers ___ Social interactions
   ___ Amount learned ___ Academic hassles
   ___ Welcoming atmosphere ___ Feeling of closeness
   ___ Feeling of belonging   to a teacher
   ___ Involvement in extra- ___ Emotional support
     curricular activities
   Using your own ratings, how would you evaluate your total school experience?

4. There is much debate as to whether schools discriminate against males or females. In what ways might schools be seen as discriminating against males? In what ways might they be seen as discriminating against females? In your opinion, does schooling favor either gender?

5. Some researchers argue that many students are disengaged from school and do only enough to get by. According to your experience, do you agree with the disengagement theory? If you do, what can be done about the problem of disengagement?

Review 7.3: Enhancing the School Experience

Level 1

1. Which of the following statements about learner-centered education is incorrect?
   A. Learner-centered education considers the learner to be active in seeking out answers to problems.
   B. Learner-centered education is concerned with the needs and interests of the student.
   C. Learner-centered education believes that students are recipients of knowledge that is given by teachers through lectures.
   D. Learner-centered education emphasizes the importance of the learner's experience.

2. Jana works on a physics experiment because she finds it an interesting challenge. Her motivation can be said to be
   A. intrinsic.
   B. extrinsic.
   C. primary.
   D. secondary.

3. Psychologists find that some experiences are so compelling that time almost seems to stand still, and nothing else seems to exist but the challenge. This phenomenon is known as
   A. goal compulsion.
   B. total regard.
   C. the flow.
   D. creative obsession.

4. According to attribution theory, effort is
   A. stable, internal, and controllable.
   B. unstable, external, and uncontrollable.
   C. stable, external, and controllable.
   D. unstable, internal, and controllable.

5. Which statement concerning attributions of success and failure in high school is correct?
   A. High school students are more likely to attribute successes and failures to effort than they were in elementary school.
   B. High school students are more likely to attribute successes and failures to ability than they were in elementary school.
   C. High school students are less likely to make attributions than they were in elementary school.
   D. High school students are more likely to attribute their failures to lack of ability and their successes to luck.

6. Mark works hard in class to get the best grades he can. Mark's goals can be considered
   A. mastery goals.
   B. performance-avoidance goals.
   C. performance-approach goals.
   D. individualized goals.

7. Mastery goals are best described in terms of
   A. working to improve one's knowledge base and better understand the material for one's own sake.
   B. working hard to succeed so others will be proud.
   C. working hard to avoid punishment.
   D. the belief that one can exceed even the teacher's expectations.

8. What conclusion can be reached about parental involvement in their adolescent children's schooling?
   A. Adolescents' perception of parental interest is important.
   B. There are many ways for parents to show their interest in their adolescent child's schooling.
   C. Parental discussions of school-related issues can show interest.
   D. All of the above are correct.

9. "If you expect more from students, they will do better in school." This quotation uses the concept of _____ to explain achievement.
   A. internal locus of control
   B. the self-fulfilling prophesy
   C. generational chauvinism
   D. the secular trend

10. Studies show that if tracking is eliminated,
    A. average students improve, but weak students do not.
    B. weak students improve, and gifted students do not gain as much as if they were in homogeneous classes.
    C. average students' achievement declines, but gifted students' achievement increases.
    D. the achievement of poorer-, average-, and higher-achieving students improves.

11. A _____ school is a public school that offers very desirable coursework and is allowed to use entrance examinations.
    A. charter
    B. magnet
    C. format
    D. candidate

12. Which of the following statements about charter schools is false?
    A. Charter schools are allowed to use entrance testing to determine who will be admitted.
    B. Charter schools may be closed if they do not show results.
    C. Charter schools may be sponsored by a group of teachers or parents.
    D. Charter schools are permitted to waive certain aspects of the state's educational law and teachers' contracts.

Level 2

1. Why is intrinsic motivation considered so important in education?

2. How does the attribution of academic success or failure to effort or ability affect student achievement?

3. Consider the type of goals you have for your studies. How would you categorize your goals in your various classes? How does the adoption of a particular goal affect your studying and learning practices?

4. If you had the power to change high school classes so they might be more motivating to students, how would you change the curriculum, the methods used by teachers, and the structure of the classroom?

5. Why would student perception of parental interest and involvement be more highly correlated with achievement than the actual amount of parental involvement and parental perception of involvement? How would student perceptions lead to improved student achievement?

6. Both magnet and charter schools attract adolescents whose parents, especially mothers, have better educational credentials. Why would this characteristic underlie choosing these schools? What are the implications of better-educated parents placing their adolescent children in magnet and charter schools?

7. Some opponents of the voucher program argue that it would be extended to include everyone and would severely injure the public schools. Would voucher programs severely injure public education? Why or why not?

8. How would an adolescent's experience in high school differ if the voucher program were available in the community?

Review 7.4: Dropping Out

Level 1

1. You hear a television commentator argue that not everyone needs a high school diploma and that schools should stop trying to retain students who do not want to be in school. Which of the following counterarguments is the most sound?

A. Most dropouts are actually very intelligent, creative students who do not fit into the school.
B. Most dropouts have at least average intelligence scores and can succeed.
C. Keeping students in school allows more time for job creation in poor neighborhoods.
D. Most dropouts have actually succeeded in school at an earlier age and only recently have started having difficulties.

2. High school students at risk for dropping out often
A. show poor achievement.
B. show little attachment to school.
C. have been left back in school.
D. may be characterized by each of these.

3. Which of the following is a "pull" factor explaining why students drop out?
A. the need for a paycheck at home
B. fear of violence in the school
C. not feeling an attachment to the school
D. not being able to read

4. Alternative schools for potential dropouts offer all of the following except
A. lower pupil-teacher ratios.
B. more work-study programs.
C. more individualized attention.
D. a somewhat greater tolerance for aggression and drug use.

Level 2

1. If you know anyone who has dropped out of high school or seriously thought about doing so, discuss why the individual wanted to do so and what could have been done to prevent him or her from dropping out.

2. What changes in the high school could improve the dropout rate?

Answers to Multiple Choice Questions

Review 7.1: 1. D, 2. B, 3. C, 4. B, 5. D, 6. A, 7. B
Review 7.2: 1. C, 2. A, 3. B, 4. D, 5. C, 6. D, 7. C
Review 7.3: 1. C, 2. A, 3. C, 4. D, 5. B, 6. C, 7. A, 8. D, 9. B, 10. B, 11. B, 12. A
Review 7.4: 1. B, 2. D, 3. A, 4. D.

Chapter 8 The Media

Review 8.1: The Media and the Teen

Level 1

1. Which of the following statements is incorrect?
   A. Teens spend more time in contact with the media than in any other waking activity.
   B. Teens rate their experiences with the media as generally negative.
   C. Adolescents spend more time using the Internet and playing videogames than younger children.
   D. Teens are more comfortable with technology than their parents are.

2. Which of the following is a major difference between a teen's relationship with the media and his or her relationship with parents, teachers, and others in the environment?
   A. The teen's relationship with the media is fraught with more negative emotions.
   B. The teen's relationship with the media is more satisfying than relationships with people, because adolescents see the media as their constant "friend."
   C. Teens have more control over their exposure to the media.
   D. Adolescents see the media as guiding and teaching them more than they see parents, teachers, and other people doing so.

3. Adolescents who watch a great deal of television
   A. drink alcohol less, are less active, and smoke more.
   B. drink alcohol more, are less active, and smoke more.
   C. drink alcohol more, are less active, and smoke less.
   D. drink alcohol less, are less active, and smoke less.

4. Why do advertisers consider the teenage market so important?
   A. Teenagers have a great deal more income than adults.
   B. Teenagers are willing to pay more for goods than adults.
   C. Teenagers have a great deal of disposable income.
   D. Teenagers buy gifts for their parents, which makes them an important market.

5. Which of the following statements concerning teen spending is incorrect?
   A. Teen spending tops $100 billion annually.
   B. Teen spending has increased and decreased over the years, depending on the economic situation.
   C. Teen spending is expected to increase in the future.
   D. Teens spend more on clothing than on any other item.

6. Which theory notes that constant and prolonged exposure to the media causes teenagers to adopt the attitudes shown in the media?
   A. Freudian theory
   B. social foundation theory
   C. cultivation theory
   D. tangential theory

7. A psychologist discovers that a group of teens who play very violent video games show less empathy to victims of violent crime than another group that does not play such games. Most probably, the psychologist will use _____ theory to explain her findings.
   A. cultivation
   B. insinuation
   C. desensitization
   D. Eriksonian

8. Which of the following statements best differentiates the current generation of teens and the upcoming generation of teens from their elders?
   A. Teens are more comfortable with family disputes.
   B. Teens are less comfortable with cultural differences.
   C. Teens are more comfortable with technology.
   D. Teens are less comfortable with school.

9. The term _____ *generation* is used to signify the fact that the present generation is far ahead of the older generation in their understanding of technology.
   A. *lap*
   B. *gap*
   C. *propositional*
   D. *tech*

10. Which phrase best reflects the current generation of teens?
    A. Look before you leap.
    B. I can do it, myself.
    C. If it works, don't fix it.
    D. You do not have to seek; it will find you.

11. Which of the following adjectives describes generation Y?
    A. interactive
    B. diverse
    C. self-reliant
    D. all of the above

Level 2

1. "The media have taken over parenting responsibilities as moral guides and teachers," one television commentator says. Evaluate the statement. Do you agree or disagree, and why?

2. How does the profit motive influence the relationship between teenagers and the media?

3. How would you explain the fact that interests, hobbies, and lifestyles tend to remain stable from adolescence through adulthood?

4. Why do teens tune out advertising to a greater extent than other groups?

5. Keep a log showing how much of the day you are in contact with the media.

6. In what ways would teenagers born in 1985 differ from their parents born in 1953?

7. What are the consequences of the fact that teenagers know more about computers and technology than their parents? Will this situation change their relationship?

Review 8.2: The Computer Revolution: Email and the Internet

Level 1

1. Which of the following statements concerning the Internet is correct?
   A. Most teens feel comfortable with new technology.
   B. Most teens are positively disposed toward Internet use.
   C. About three quarters of all adolescents use the Internet.
   D. All of the above are correct.

2. What is meant by the *digital divide?*
   A. Males and females do not feel the same way toward computers.
   B. American adolescents living in poverty are less likely to have a computer at home.
   C. A few adolescents are computer experts, and the rest do not seem to care much about computerization.
   D. Many students are unable to do math problems on paper once they begin to use computers and calculators.

3. Which of the following statements is correct?
   A. Middle class and upper income adolescents are more likely to have access to the Internet at home than are adolescents from lower income families.
   B. Males and females report an equal level of computer use.
   C. Adolescents consider Internet information highly valuable and trustworthy.
   D. All of the above are correct.

4. Joshua's relationship with Karen is marked by frequent contact in many areas, affection, and a feeling of obligation. These characteristics describe _____ ties.
   A. strong
   B. weak
   C. moderate
   D. implicit

5. Most of the relationships on the Web may be categorized as
   A. strong ties.
   B. implicit ties.
   C. inadequate ties.
   D. weak ties.

6. In one major study, heavy use of email and the Net led to
   A. increasing numbers of close friends and better social interactions.
   B. more feelings of mild depression and less psychological well-being.
   C. less anxiety and a greater feeling of confidence.
   D. greater social support and a feeling of confidence in one's abilities.

7. The fact that teens using the Internet are often switching from one subject to another leads to which of the following questions?
   A. Will adolescents lack patience?
   B. Will adolescents understand how important it is to find out things for themselves?
   C. Will adolescents understand that they still need to be taught?
   D. Will adolescents believe that communication from peers is more accurate than communication from parents?

Level 2

1. In what ways has the computer changed your life? Have the changes been essentially positive or negative?

2. Explain the results of the study that related computer use with loneliness, mild depression, and fewer face-to-face close relationships.

Review 8.3: Video Games

Level 1

1. Approximately what percentage of the most popular video games are violent?
   A. 20
   B. 30
   C. 50
   D. 80

2. Which statement about video games is correct?
   A. Boys play them more often than girls.
   B. Most girls have never played a video game.
   C. The market for video games is relatively small.
   D. All of these statements are correct.

3. The relationship between video game playing and aggression in adolescence is best described as
   A. mostly negative, and the influence is insignificant.
   B. consistently positive, and the influence is significant.
   C. inconsistent, with many positive studies and some negative ones.
   D. neutral, with no study showing any influence.

4. Which of the following is the major factor in determining the influence of violent video games on teenagers' aggression?
   A. personality
   B. enjoyment of sports
   C. perceived similarity with the characters in the game
   D. the amount of time spent reading

5. Teens who play a great many violent video games also
   A. tend to be bullies.
   B. watch more violent television.
   C. go to work at an earlier age.
   D. do not show much interest in sports.

6. Studies are unanimous in finding that playing violent video games is related to
   A. feelings of loneliness.
   B. less prosocial behavior.
   C. less social competence.
   D. excessive anxiety.

7. Studies of the relationship of video game playing with psychological disorders and social skills show that
   A. individuals who play most often suffer from moderate psychological disorders, but no social skills deficits.
   B. individuals who play less often actually suffer more psychological disorders than those who play most often.
   C. individuals who play most often show no greater incidence of psychological disorders but do show poorer social skills.
   D. video game playing is not related to psychological disorders or poor social skills.

Level 2

1. The results of the research on video games differ depending on whether the individuals play at an arcade or at home. Why would this be the case?

2. Your friend notes that some teens who have committed horribly violent crimes had a fascination with gory video games, and he claims that this is evidence enough that these games are dangerous. Analyze your friend's conclusions.

3. Walk into a store that sells computer video games, read the descriptions, and see if there are any warning labels. Note how many could be described as violent, adventure/fantasy, or mysteries.

4. How could we identify which young adolescents would be affected by playing violent video games and which would not?

Review 8.4: Music and Radio

Level 1

1. Which of the following statements concerning teenagers' listening habits is true?
   A. Males use music to change moods more than females do.
   B. Radio reaches more teens daily than television does.
   C. Males listen to the radio more than females do.
   D. Males are actually more attracted to love songs and romantic ballads than females.

2. Individuals who believe that heavy metal music does not have an unduly negative influence often claim that
   A. the lyrics are not really violent.
   B. the lyrics are not particularly sexual.
   C. the negative consequences are caused by the listener's problems before listening, not the music.
   D. only people below the age of 13 are negatively affected.

3. Heavy metal music probably has the most influence on teens
   A. who are older but poorly educated.
   B. with poor family relationships and who are already troubled.
   C. who have never been in a close interpersonal relationship with another teen.
   D. who are extraverted and work at blue-collar jobs.

4. Research has found that fans of heavy metal music are more likely to
   A. also like rap and rhythm and blues music.
   B. take risks.
   C. work longer hours than fans of other types of music.
   D. have close relationships with their siblings.

5. When asked about the negative messages in heavy metal music, most fans of the genre claim that
   A. these messages reflect their innermost feelings.
   B. they do not understand the lyrics.
   C. they do not agree with the sentiments in the songs.
   D. these lyrics are actually prosocial and not violent.

6. One concern for both heavy metal and some types of rap music is
   A. that music may interfere with schoolwork.
   B. their treatment of women.
   C. their emphasis on the need to be happy.
   D. that listening to these types of music may take valuable time away from interpersonal relationships.

7. Which of the following is an explanation for the bitter, violent lyrics of heavy metal and some types of rap music?
   A. The music represents an antiestablishment counter-culture.
   B. The lyrics reflect the feelings of frustration of individuals who live in poverty.
   C. The lyrics mirror the increasing amount of violence in the culture.
   D. All of the above.

8. Defenders of rap argue that
   A. its effect is not as great as people think.
   B. Some people who criticize it may be biased against African Americans or their art forms.
   C. its lyrics are a symptom of a problem, not the cause of the problem.
   D. all of the above are true.

9. Evidence shows that the influence of music videos is
   A. less than that of the music played alone.
   B. about the same as radio or television advertisements.
   C. greater than for music or videos shown separately.
   D. about the same as music played alone.

Level 2

1. Music serves many purposes. It can communicate meaning, be a means of relaxation, help express emotions, and symbolize membership in a generation. Briefly describe three pieces of music that have had a significant meaning to you, and explain why they are significant.

2. Why have the lyrics and antics of performers become more sexually explicit and violent over the past 15 years?

3. Some social commentators argue that the antifemale lyrics of rap music (as well as some heavy metal music) contribute to violence against women. Is this connection reasonable? How could we design a study to investigate the possible connection?

4. Watch an hour of music videos each day for a week, and keep track of the themes of the songs, placing them into categories. What conclusions can you reach about the themes of these songs?

Review 8.5: Television and the Movies

Level 1

1. The fairest way to summarize the many studies linking viewing aggression on television to aggressive behavior is that
   A. viewing television violence is the most important cause of children's and teenagers' aggressive behavior.
   B. viewing television violence increases the likelihood of violent behavior.
   C. there are relatively few studies on the matter.
   D. the studies find that watching violent television actually decreases anger and aggression in teens.

2. Some teens are attracted to violent television because
   A. they are seeking stimulation.
   B. they are trying to encounter others like themselves.
   C. it reduces their anxiety level.
   D. of all of the above.

3. Many television programs meant for teens involve
   A. exploring the world of nature.
   B. relationship problems.
   C. artistic themes.
   D. realistic depictions of family life.

4. On television, and especially in soap operas, single mothers are shown as
   A. being constantly under stress.
   B. having a great deal of help from male friends and being wealthy.
   C. being in poor health and pitiable.
   D. mastering the situation despite the many problems they face.

5. Research shows that people who watch television talk shows on a regular basis
   A. are less sensitive to people's problems.
   B. think that many behaviors, such as running away from home, are more common than they really are.
   C. believe that relationships just don't work out.
   D. are described by all of the above.

6. One reason why teenagers are a difficult group for advertisers to reach is that they
   A. do not watch much television.
   B. are not brand conscious.
   C. tend to tune out commercials more than people of other age groups.
   D. believe that commercials are dangerous and refuse to be influenced.

Level 2

1. Evaluate the following statement: The lack of reality in television's depiction of single mothers, sexuality, and earning a living has no influence on how teenagers see the world.

2. Ask people who watch television talk shows why they do so. Then ask them how common they think the behaviors shown in Table 8.4 are, and compare their estimates to those given in the table. Why do people usually overestimate the prevalence of such behaviors?

Review 8.6: Magazines

Level 1

1. Magazines meant for young women usually do not emphasize
   A. beauty and fashion.
   B. relationships with boys.
   C. public service and future careers.
   D. getting along with others.

2. The criticisms of magazines aimed at young women are countered by the fact that
   A. the circulations of these magazines are low, and few young women read them.
   B. their advice on relationship problems tends to be radical.
   C. most readers accept these magazines as informing them of only a part of life and realize there is more to life than fashion.
   D. older teens stop reading these magazines, as they no longer need their help and advice.

Level 2

1. Why are there no general magazines aimed at teenage boys?

2. Magazines targeted at teenage girls are very popular, but they have been soundly criticized for their emphasis on fashion, beauty, and popularity. In your opinion, are these criticisms deserved? Why or why not?

Answers to Multiple Choice Questions

Review 8.1: 1. B, 2. C, 3. B, 4. C, 5. B, 6. C, 7. C, 8. C, 9. A, 10. B, 11. D
Review 8.2: 1. D, 2. B, 3. D, 4. A, 5. D, 6. B, 7. A
Review 8.3: 1. D, 2. A, 3. C, 4. A, 5. B, 6. B, 7. D
Review 8.4: 1. B, 2. C, 3. B, 4. B, 5. C, 6. B, 7. D, 8. D, 9. C
Review 8.5: 1. B, 2. A, 3. B, 4. B, 5. B, 6. C
Review 8.6: 1. C, 2. C

CHAPTER 9 SELF-CONCEPT AND IDENTITY FORMATION

Review 9.1: Basic Concepts Related to the Self

Level 1

1. A psychologist is asking a 13-year-old to describe himself in terms of his traits and characteristics. Most likely the researcher is trying to measure the teen's
   A. temperament.
   B. self-concept.
   C. emotional intelligence.
   D. formal operational reasoning abilities.

2. Self-concept is essentially _____, whereas self-esteem is _____.
   A. unmeasurable, measurable
   B. personal, public
   C. descriptive, judgmental
   D. public, personal

3. Perhaps William James's greatest contribution to self theory is the idea that
   A. culture contributes to the formation of self.
   B. people have multiple selves.
   C. the self cannot be measured accurately.
   D. the self is always changing.

4. Sociological theories, such as those expounded by Cooley and Mead, view the self as formed through
   A. an individual's construction of his or her experience.
   B. appraisals from others.
   C. understanding the cultural requirements of the situation.
   D. unconscious conflicts with parents.

5. In addition to appraisals of others, another important factor influencing the self-concept is the individual's
   A. evaluations of his or her experience.
   B. ability to reinforce himself or herself.
   C. feelings of ambivalence toward others.
   D. ability to integrate the physical self and the social self.

Level 2

1. Assume that sociological theory is correct, and the self is a group of "reflected appraisals." Choose one of your own characteristics, and consider how it may have developed.

2. What implications would the idea that people form their self-concepts out of appraisals have for parents and teachers?

Review 9.2: Self-Concept in Adolescence

Level 1

1. A change from _____ to _____ occurs in the self-concept as children mature into adolescents.
   A. healthy, unhealthy
   B. general, specific
   C. concrete, abstract
   D. antisocial, prosocial

2. Which of the following describes early adolescents?
   A. They are aware of the contradictions in their self but cannot do anything about them.
   B. They are unaware of the contradictions in their self.
   C. They are very bothered by the contradictions in their self and integrate them well.
   D. They see contradictions in their self as a sign of maturity.

3. During _____, contradictions in the self are integrated.
   A. early adolescence
   B. middle adolescence
   C. late adolescence
   D. late middle childhood

4. Which teenager would show the greatest amount of false behavior?
   A. a teen experimenting with new roles
   B. a teen trying to act happy when feeling sad at a party
   C. a teen having a long talk with a friend
   D. a teen with little support and under pressure to act like others

5. Sheila defines herself in terms of being a kind person. Her friends now tell her that she has been very unkind to one of the girls in her group. How will this feedback affect Sheila's self-concept?
   A. Sheila will now see herself as unkind.
   B. It will change her self-concept so that being kind will no longer be a central idea.
   C. Sheila probably will rationalize her behavior, and the feedback will not have any effect on her self-concept.
   D. Sheila will become depressed and overly friendly with the girl she wronged.

6. Julio would like to be smart, entertaining, unemotional, and proud. This might be seen as
   A. his realistic self.
   B. his ideal self.
   C. his honored self.
   D. the self one ought to be.

Level 2

1. Create three sentences, one each for an early, middle, and late adolescent who is describing the traits of being cheerful and moody.

2. Adolescents do not like support that is conditional on their acting in a particular manner. Is the idea of giving unconditional support realistic? Under what circumstances would you not give unconditional support to your friends?

3. Write down six adjectives that describe the type of person you would like to be. Now rate how descriptive they are of you today on a scale from 1 (very descriptive) to 5 (not very descriptive). Do you find the idea of becoming closer to your ideal self a motivator? Why or why not?

Review 9.3: Self-Esteem in Adolescence

Level 1

1. A study finds a positive relationship between self-esteem and academic achievement, and your friend says that it demonstrates that having high self-esteem causes high grades. What is wrong with your friend's conclusion?
   A. The relationship between self-esteem and grades is inverse, not positive.
   B. This correlation does not demonstrate causation.
   C. Academic achievement cannot be accurately measured.
   D. Few adolescents have high self-esteem, so the relationship does not have much meaning.

2. Kelly does not think that being a good athlete is important, but she performs well on tests of fitness—probably better than most of the girls in her school. How will this situation influence her self-esteem?
   A. Her overall self-esteem should gain greatly from the experience.

B. This experience will have a negligible influence on her self-esteem.
   C. Her self-esteem will probably increase immediately following the athletic tests and decline thereafter.
   D. This experience will improve her academic self-esteem but not her overall self-esteem.

3. Why is feedback from classmates so important in the teen years?
   A. Teens receive much less feedback from their peers but parents fill the void.
   B. Teens expect social support from friends, but see their classmates as more objective.
   C. Teens do not care what their classmates think about their behavior.
   D. Teens see classmates as friends, and no differences between classmates and close friends exist for teenagers.

4. Based on research in the field, you would expect a teen who agrees with which of the following statements to have the lowest self-esteem and to be less focused on schoolwork?
   A. People like me for who I am.
   B. My opinion of myself is based on others' opinions of me.
   C. People will like me for what I do.
   D. I cannot be anything but myself.

5. You are following groups of teenagers with high and low self-esteem for an extended period of time. Based on past research, you would expect to find
   A. instability and substantial changes in most adolescents' self-esteem.
   B. moderate stability, but some evidence for change.
   C. almost total stability.
   D. an increase in self-esteem throughout adolescence, followed by a drop at the end of adolescence.

6. You are following many teenagers through adolescence to measure their self-esteem. You find that some of the teens have shown improvements in their self-esteem. Based on research in the field, you would look for what types of experiences in these teens?
   A. a period of great stress, which they handled well
   B. accomplishments in areas they consider important
   C. improving relationships with their parents
   D. increases in their appreciation of the feelings of others

7. Which domain increases in importance during early adolescence?
   A. physical
   B. cognitive
   C. religious
   D. intuitive

8. Which of the following is not a reason for the improvement in self-esteem in middle and later adolescence?
   A. greater autonomy
   B. greater feelings of competence
   C. receiving fewer comparisons with others
   D. a reduction in perceived negative traits

9. Which statement about the self-esteem of males and females is correct?
   A. Males tend to have higher self-esteem than females.
   B. The chief reason for the disparity between males and females is their different evaluations of their physical appearance.
   C. More females than males report low self-esteem.
   D. All of the above are correct.

10. Which of the following statements describes the self-esteem of European American and African American adolescents?
    A. European American adolescents have the higher self-esteem.
    B. African Americans adolescents have higher academic self-esteem, but no other self-esteem differences are found.
    C. European American teens have higher self-esteem in middle adolescence, but not in later adolescence.
    D. Global self-esteem is not lower in African Americans.

11. John has very high self-esteem; he believes he is among the best students and feels that he should be the center of attention. He reacts very defensively and often angrily to anyone who disagrees with him or any teacher who corrects him. John's behavior may be due to
    A. narcissistic tendencies.
    B. a feeling that he lives among enemies.
    C. an inability to create a meaningful environment for himself.
    D. a lack of cognitive skills.

Level 2

1. Why would people with high or low self-esteem tend to stay that way? What forces might help create stability in self-esteem?

2. You are at a meeting of professionals. One teacher says that the decline in self-esteem during middle childhood and into early adolescence should not occur and is a cause for concern. Do you agree or disagree with this statement? Why?

3. What can middle and junior high schools do to reduce their contribution to the decrease in self-confidence and self-esteem that occurs with the transition to secondary school?

4. You are giving a lecture on improving self-esteem among early and middle adolescents. List five ideas you think might help improve self-esteem, and justify them.

5. Why do adolescents consider their parents' evaluations as being more negative than they really are?

6. Why is it so difficult to raise the self-esteem of teenagers?

Review 9.4: Identity

Level 1

1. According to _____, the formation of a sense of ego identity is the positive outcome of the adolescent years.
   A. Freud
   B. Skinner
   C. Erikson
   D. Rogers

2. A teen looking at vocational options is asking questions about the education necessary and the lifestyles attached to the jobs. The process of _____ explains this scenario.
   A. revocation
   B. evocation
   C. exploration
   D. announcement

3. A teacher states that adolescents in the process of considering some aspect of their identities tend to be confused and show discomfort. According to research, this statement
   A. really does not describe reality and is a myth.
   B. describes a situation that too often leads to mental disturbances.
   C. is true.
   D. is true for males but not for females.

4. Ari considered his political beliefs and, after careful consideration, decided what he believes. He chooses a candidate to campaign for and devotes his energies to supporting certain political policies. His behavior illustrates
   A. pronouncement.
   B. commitment.
   C. avocation.
   D. predicting.

5. Lattie's parents suggest that she study to be a nurse and she agrees, not considering any other occupations. Lattie is in the identity status called
   A. achievement.
   B. moratorium.
   C. diffusion.
   D. foreclosure.

6. Most 15-year-olds are found in which two identity statuses?
   A. moratorium and commitment
   B. primary and secondary
   C. moratorium and achievement
   D. diffusion and foreclosure

7. A radio commentator claims that there is a positive relationship between identity and intimacy. Although this statement is true, the relationship is stronger for
   A. males than females.
   B. females than males.
   C. early adolescents than late adolescents.
   D. late adolescents than early adolescents.

8. Concerning gender differences in identity formation, Erikson
   A. believed males concentrate on vocational and personal areas and females on interpersonal areas.
   B. considered males more people-oriented than females.
   C. considered females well ahead of males.
   D. did not comment on the differences.

9. Traditionally, males were seen as defining themselves through their _____ and females, through their _____.
   A. relationships with others, individuality
   B. inclusion, exclusion
   C. vocations, relationships with others
   D. thought processes, emotional processes

10. The most current view of male-female differences in identity formation argues that females
    A. emphasize only their interpersonal needs and do not concern themselves with vocational needs.
    B. emphasize only their intrapersonal needs and suppress their interpersonal needs.
    C. have to balance their intrapersonal and interpersonal needs.
    D. focus on their educational identities instead of their personal identities.

11. Identity achievement is the final status, one commentator claims. To be more exact,
    A. there is another status that follows, although most individuals do not get to it.
    B. identity achievement is the final status in Eastern, but not Western, societies.
    C. there may be two identity achievement statuses, one of which involves continuing exploration.
    D. there may be three identity achievement statuses, one of which is basically antisocial.

12. One concern about the concept of identity statuses is that
    A. the concept lacks a process orientation.
    B. the concept of statuses does not seem to come from any theoretical perspective.
    C. they are too complicated to understand and thus are not useful.
    D. they do not predict any behavior.

Level 2

1. Does finding an identity necessarily mean moving away from the values and aspirations of parents? Why or why not?

2. Consider one aspect of your identity that you believe is well thought out. Give at least one way in which you show commitment. How did you explore your options?

3. James Marcia described an identity status in which an individual made premature commitments. Why would an individual make commitments before ever conducting any exploration?

4. Why is there a positive relationship between identity formation and the attainment of intimacy?

5. Evaluate the idea that males define themselves mostly in terms of separateness and females, in terms of their relations with others.

6. You are running a PTA meeting on the topic of identity formation. Some parents ask how they can help their children with their identity exploration. Other parents are uncomfortable with the idea of exploration, fearing that their children will make inappropriate or poor choices. What can parents do to help their teenage children with their exploration process? How would you deal with the parents' discomfort concerning inappropriate choices?

Review 9.5: Gender Roles

Level 1

1. The concept of androgyny involves
   A. males acting like females and females acting like males.
   B. feelings of confusion concerning gender roles.
   C. combining characteristics typical of males and others typical of females.
   D. feelings of sexual prowess.

2. The difficulty with the concept of androgyny is that it
   A. cannot be accurately measured.
   B. can itself be considered a type of stereotyping.
   C. describes individuals who are high in femininity and low in masculinity, making it unfair for males.
   D. cannot be defined accurately.

3. Which of the following statements about early adolescents' views of gender stereotypes is correct?
   A. Early adolescents show considerable flexibility concerning what behaviors are acceptable for males and females.
   B. Early adolescents become somewhat less flexible concerning what behaviors are acceptable for males and females.
   C. Early adolescents are so unstable that gender stereotypes cannot be accurately measured.
   D. No studies to date have investigated the flexibility of gender stereotypes in early adolescents.

4. You are testing a large group of male and female participants from elementary school through middle adolescence on flexibility of gender stereotypes. If your results agree with other research in the field, you would expect to find
   A. the male participants more flexible than the female participants.
   B. the female participants more flexible than the male participants.
   C. male and female participants equally flexible.
   D. the male elementary school students and the female adolescents to be the most flexible.

5. The pressure to conform to a difficult societal concept of being female or male in adolescence leads to
   A. schizophrenia.
   B. sexual confusion.
   C. the adoption of traditional roles and stereotypes.
   D. all of the above.

6. Manuelita is playing with trucks, and her brother, Robert, is playing with a doll. Which of the following is true?
   A. Their parents are unlikely to comment on the activities of either child.
   B. Their parents will criticize both children about their play.
   C. Their father is likely to criticize Robert, but not Manuelita.
   D. Their mother is more likely to criticize Manuelita, but not Robert.

Level 2

1. Television programs often receive criticism for emphasizing gender-related stereotypes. Spend one evening watching situation comedies, and note the traditional or nontraditional personality profiles or interests they portray.

2. Some authorities argue that early-adolescent girls have major difficulties integrating the impossible image of the beautiful, sexy woman with great interpersonal skills on the one hand with physical reality and their desires to fulfill their individual promise on the other hand, and that these difficulties lead to depression and anxiety. In your opinion, do females have a more difficult time than males in developing a gender role? Are females subject to greater conflict between what they want and what society says they should be like?

3. You are the parent of a boy and a girl. Can you think of any situations in which you would treat them differently because of their gender? Would any personality characteristics or behaviors of your son bother you if you saw them in your daughter? Would any personality characteristics or behaviors of your daughter bother you if you noticed them in your son?

4. Ask your friends to do the gender stereotype exercise in Figure 9.4. Feel free to add any other descriptive adjectives you feel are appropriate. After giving the test to a number of people, see if any patterns arise.

Review 9.6: Ethnic/Racial Identity

Level 1

1. More African Americans are in the foreclosed status than whites because of
   A. family and gender-role considerations.
   B. feelings of guilt and disappointment over their financial status.
   C. poverty and discrimination.
   D. lack of high school education and gender-role considerations.

2. Some ethnic groups—for example, some Latinos and Native Americans—do not show as much exploration as other groups because
   A. their culture does not encourage it.
   B. they must care for a number of people in their family.
   C. they do not aspire to professional occupations.
   D. few believe that such exploration will lead to a reasoned commitment.

3. Teenagers who are involved in neither the minority nor the majority culture are considered
   A. marginalized.
   B. assimilated.
   C. accommodated.
   D. internalized.

4. Minority group youth who can participate in both the minority and majority cultures and have the best adjustment are in the _____ category.
   A. fulfilled
   B. integrated
   C. actualized
   D. infused

Level 2

1. What personal characteristics do you believe an individual needs to be biculturally competent?

2. Why do psychologists today feel that it is important to have a competent racial/ethnic identity?

Answers to Multiple Choice Questions

Review 9.1: 1. B, 2. C, 3. B, 4. B, 5. A
Review 9.2: 1. C, 2. B, 3. C, 4. D, 5. C, 6. B
Review 9.3: 1. B, 2. B, 3. B, 4. B, 5. B, 6. B, 7. A, 8. C, 9. D, 10. D, 11. A
Review 9.4: 1. C, 2. C, 3. C, 4. B, 5. D, 6. D, 7. A, 8. A, 9. C, 10. C, 11. C, 12. A
Review 9.5: 1. C, 2. B, 3. B, 4. B, 5. C, 6. C
Review 9.6: 1. C, 2. A, 3. A, 4. B

CHAPTER 10 LOVE AND SEX

Review 10.1: Physical Development and Sexuality

Level 1

1. Which of the following is related to increases in sexual arousal during adolescence?
   A. increases in sex hormones
   B. increases in testosterone
   C. improvements in mental abilities
   D. increases in heart and lung capacity

2. Which of the following statements about masturbation is correct?
   A. Females report masturbating more often than males.
   B. More males than females report masturbating.
   C. In many non-Western countries, more females than males report engaging in masturbation.
   D. Social factors encourage masturbation in females but not in males.

3. Research shows which of the following concerning the effects of masturbation on later sexual behavior?
   A. Males and females who masturbate during preadolescence are more sexually active later in adulthood.
   B. Early masturbation in both males and females decreases the sex drive later in adolescence, but not in adulthood.
   C. Early masturbation in males leads to an increase in the sex drive later in adolescence, but early masturbation in females does not.
   D. Masturbation does not influence later sexual behavior.

Level 2

1. Why do hormone increases seem to lead to greater sexual activity in males but only to greater sexual interest in females?

2. Why do prohibitions and myths about masturbation still exist, despite our greater understanding of sexuality today?

Review 10.2: Dating, Love, and Sex

Level 1

1. If you were comparing younger and older teens on their views of dating, which of the following statement would you expect from younger teens?
   A. We share our problems and concerns.
   B. My partner's welfare is just as important to me as my own.
   C. Everyone thinks I'm lucky because my partner is so popular.
   D. We have a future together.

2. Which of the following concerning dating is correct?
   A. Older teens are more likely to emphasize the status in dating someone than younger teens.
   B. Most teens do not date until 17 years of age.
   C. Dating relationships help develop social skills.
   D. All of these are correct.

3. The three dimensions that appear most often in studies of the nature of love are
   A. possessiveness, intimacy, and involvedness.
   B. shared experiences, joy, and commitment.
   C. passion, caring, and friendship.
   D. passion, intimacy, and commitment.

4. The strongest predictor of longevity and satisfaction in a relationship is
   A. passion.
   B. sharing.
   C. support.
   D. commitment.

5. Two people who have been in love for many years may find they have less passion than they once did, but still have intimacy and commitment. This type of relationship may illustrate _____ love.
   A. fatuous
   B. companionate
   C. true
   D. romantic

6. In a study of men and women from many different countries, the overwhelming majority
   A. felt that love was necessary for marriage.
   B. felt that love was not as important in a marriage as getting along and having the same goals.
   C. of men believed that love was necessary in a marriage, but the majority of women felt that being able to support a family was more important.
   D. of women believed that love was necessary in a marriage, but the majority of men felt that getting along and sexual intimacy were more important.

7. Which of the following arguments would be made by an attachment theorist trying to describe how attachment theory explains later interpersonal relationships?
   A. Adolescents become attached to many people, and the better their relationship is with their parents in adolescence, the more difficult their relationships with their romantic partners.
   B. Later interpersonal relationships with romantic partners depend on an adolescent's identification with the same-sexed parent.
   C. A child's early relationship with parents is a model for later relationships.
   D. Attachment theorists do not believe that early relationships with parents have any influence on later relationships with romantic partners.

8. Which is the best description of the change of attitude toward sexuality that began the 1960s and continues today?
   A. Sex is unacceptable except in marriage.
   B. Sex is acceptable during a loving relationship.
   C. Sex is acceptable anytime two consenting partners feel it is.
   D. Sex is unacceptable until age 17.

9. The relationship between love and sex continues to develop, and the most recent change is that
   A. many teens believe that love and sex can and should be separated.
   B. sexuality outside of marriage is acceptable only with a great deal of commitment.
   C. sexuality outside of marriage is acceptable in a loving relationship, but commitment is not required.
   D. many teens believe that sexuality is a normal and natural part of any relationship, even a casual one.

Level 2

1. How does a person know that he or she is in love? Compare your answer to that of a friend. How are your answers similar or different?

2. Can you love someone who is not good for you? If so, how could you differentiate "healthy love" from "unhealthy love"?

3. Which one of Lee's styles of love seems to best describe you and your dating partners?

Review 10.3: Sexual Attitudes and Behavior

Level 1

1. Which of the following best describes the sexual attitudes of most young people?
   A. I can do anything I like.
   B. Live and let live.
   C. I must experiment and learn, no matter what the costs.
   D. Honesty is the best policy.

2. Male and female attitudes toward the appropriateness of sex show the greatest difference
   A. at the beginning of a relationship.
   B. when a couple is dating steadily but without commitment.
   C. when a couple is engaged.
   D. when the two people are not engaged but are talking about a commitment.

3. An analysis of studies of sexual attitudes and behaviors found only two major differences, although a number of lesser ones exist. Which of the following are the two major differences?
   A. Women fall in love more often than men, and men are more likely to link sex with a relationship.
   B. Men masturbate more frequently and hold more permissive views of sexuality.

C. Women consider sex as less important in a relationship and believe that marriage ought to precede sexual intercourse.
D. Men do not see any relationship between sex and commitment, and women are more likely to experience guilt over their sexual behavior.

4. Which statement about the sexual behavior of teenage boys and girls is correct?
   A. More than half of all male and female teens have engaged in sexual intercourse by age 20.
   B. Boys report an earlier age for their first sexual experience than do girls.
   C. American teenagers today report an earlier age of first intercourse than they did a generation ago.
   D. All of the above are correct.

5. Your friend says that the proportion of teens having sex continues to increase steadily. According to recent reports, your friend's statement is
   A. correct.
   B. correct for males but incorrect for females.
   C. correct for females but incorrect for males.
   D. incorrect, as the percentage has been relatively stable over the past 10 years.

6. Which of the following statements concerning the use of contraception by teens is correct?
   A. The percentage has increased markedly since 1985.
   B. The percentage has declined somewhat since 1985.
   C. The percentage has stayed about the same since 1985.
   D. No figures are currently available.

7. The results of tests of the sexual knowledge of teenagers show that
   A. teens know very little about sex.
   B. the average teen answers about 90 percent of the questions correctly.
   C. teens who are sexually active know approximately the same amount about sex as teens who are not sexually active.
   D. boys are much more knowledgeable than girls about sex.

8. Not using contraception is related to
   A. other forms of risk taking.
   B. a woman's not believing she can become pregnant.
   C. denying that one is in a sexual relationship.
   D. all of the above.

9. Which of the following statements concerning homosexuality is correct?
   A. There is some evidence for a genetic basis.
   B. Most gay men are not effeminate.
   C. A great deal of prejudice against gays still exists.
   D. All of the above are correct.

Level 2

1. Research shows that sexually active students often claim that they engaged in sexual intercourse at an earlier age than they think is best. How would you explain this finding?

2. The text suggested that males and females may have a different perspective on sex. In your opinion and based on your experiences, do you believe that males and females look at sex differently? If so, describe the differences.

3. Why is there so much harassment and violence against homosexuals in our society?

Review 10.4: Sex Education

Level 1

1. Surveys of how people feel about sex education in the schools show that
   A. most people believe the schools should be active in sex education.
   B. most adults believe that abstinence should be stressed.
   C. most people believe the schools should offer contraceptives to students who want them.
   D. all of the above.

2. Which statement about sex education is correct?
   A. Most American students receive a comprehensive sex education program in school.
   B. There is an increasing trend toward emphasizing abstinence in sex education programs.
   C. Most high schools now give out contraceptives to sexually active teenagers.
   D. Few parents want students to learn about contraception in sex education classes.

3. When condoms are distributed in high schools,
   A. the rate of sexual intercourse increases.
   B. teens who otherwise would not be sexually active begin having intercourse.
   C. there is no increase in the percentage of teens having intercourse.
   D. declines in academic performance occur.

4. Which STI is a bacteria infection?
   A. gonorrhea.
   B. genital warts.
   C. herpes simplex.
   D. AIDS.

5. Which of the following STI's name means to "creep" because the virus moves along nerves?
   A. syphilis
   B. herpes simplex
   C. chlamydia
   D. gonorrhea

6. Which of the following statements about AIDS is correct?
   A. The term *AIDS* is synonymous with *HIV positive*.
   B. New treatments can cure AIDS if it is discovered early.
   C. AIDS occurs mostly in adolescence.
   D. AIDS is a disease that reduces the body's ability to fight off disease.

7. Which of the following statements about STIs is correct?
   A. An STI may be contracted through oral sex.
   B. Many STIs can be cured.
   C. Some STIs are caused by viruses, whereas others are caused by bacteria.
   D. All of the above are correct.

8. One significant variable determining whether American teens will engage in safer sexual conduct that will prevent the spread of STIs is
   A. asking partners whether they ever had an STI.
   B. a feeling of vulnerability.
   C. feeling confident in one's sexuality.
   D. being medically certain of one's health status.

9. In the 1990s the pregnancy rate among teenage girls
   A. increased marginally.
   B. increased substantially.
   C. decreased.
   D. stayed the same.

10. Your friend says that teenagers will learn through experience what they should and should not do sexually. Based on the research, you would answer that this
   A. does not seem to be the case, as teenage mothers often have repeat pregnancies.
   B. does seem to be the case, as teenagers who believe they are pregnant and find out that they are not are less likely to become pregnant.
   C. does seem to be the case for most teens will carefully listen to advice given by experts and change their behavior.
   D. does not seem to be the case, because teens don't seem to care about the consequences of sexual behavior.

11. The best conclusion about teenage mothers and their children is that
   A. most mothers are doing an excellent job, and certainly as good a job as older mothers.
   B. the mothers are generally very poor, but their children do as well as other children in two-parent families.
   C. many teenage mothers do not seem to have the requisite child-rearing skills, and their children are at risk for a variety of problems.
   D. teenage mothers seem to be doing well, but their children are at risk for a number of personality problems related to mental illness.

12. Which one of the following statements is not included in a reinterpretation of the traditional status of teen mothers?
    A. Some teenage mothers are successful.
    B. The problems of teenage mothers may be based on their poor environments and lack of plans for the future rather than on having had a child early.
    C. Children of teenage mothers actually experience fewer problems than children of mothers in their 20s.
    D. Most teenage mothers become self-supporting with time.

13. One objection to the emphasis on the role of teenage boys who are fathers is that
    A. they do better than most people think at providing for their children.
    B. the majority of children of teenage mothers are fathered by men in their 20s.
    C. most have extensive contact with their families and do their best.
    D. these young fathers should not be held to the same standard as other fathers.

Level 2

1. Research shows that condom distribution in high schools does not increase the percentage of teens engaging in sex. How would you explain this finding?

2. In your opinion, what can be done to further reduce the teenage pregnancy rate?

3. Your 17-year-old friend tells you that she is pregnant. The father is a 19-year-old college student. Your friend does not know what to do. What advice would you give her?

Answers to Multiple Choice Questions

Review 10.1: 1. B, 2. B, 3. D
Review 10.2: 1. C, 2. C, 3. D, 4. D, 5. B, 6. A, 7. C, 8. B, 9. C
Review 10.3: 1. B, 2. A, 3. B, 4. D, 5. D, 6. A, 7. C, 8. D, 9. D
Review 10.4: 1. D, 2. B, 3. C, 4. A, 5. B, 6. D, 7. D, 8. B, 9. C, 10. A, 11. C, 12. C, 13. B

CHAPTER 11 MORAL DEVELOPMENT, VALUES, AND RELIGION

Review 11.1: Approaches to Moral Development

Level 1

1. If Jill is reasoning at Jean Piaget's stage of moral relativism, we would expect her to
   A. take intention into account.
   B. be flexible in her interpretation of the rules.
   C. be willing to change rules if they do not match the situation.
   D. do all of the above.

2. Which reasoning would you most expect from a person reasoning at Lawrence Kohlberg's level 1?
   A. I disobeyed because I truly believed the rule was wrong.
   B. I disobeyed because it was fun.
   C. I disobeyed because everyone else was doing it.
   D. I disobeyed because my parents would not want me to do it.

3. Which term best describes a person's reasoning at Kohlberg's level 2?
   A. individualistic
   B. reward and punishment
   C. conformity
   D. internalized

4. To reason at Kohlberg's highest level, a person must be capable of reasoning at Piaget's stage of
   A. formal operations.
   B. postformal operations.
   C. dimensional reasoning.
   D. advanced social reasoning.

5. According to Carol Gilligan, women base their moral reasoning more on _____, whereas men base it on _____.
   A. moral principles, moral actions
   B. abstract principles, caring and sharing
   C. caring, abstract principles
   D. helping others, helping only those they know

6. Janet's friends admire her for helping at the community center, and they communicate this admiration to her. She volunteers quite often. Janet's behavior is explained by _____.
   A. reinforcement
   B. cognitive sophistication
   C. Erik Erikson's theory of personality
   D. modeling

7. Sigmund Freud emphasized the importance of _____ in forming a moral code.
   A. reinforcement
   B. modeling
   C. ego involvement
   D. identification

8. Psychologists like Martin Hoffman argue that the emotion called _____ is vital to understanding moral behavior.
   A. empathy
   B. ego functioning
   C. reinforcement
   D. modeling

Level 2

1. Why do the media offer so little coverage of the good works of adolescents and so much coverage of adolescent cheating and aggressive behavior?

2. How would you explain the fact that teenagers (as well as adults) will reason at a very high level for one issue and at a basic, very low level for another issue? How would you explain the fact that a very famous person you admire, whose reasoning and deeds show tremendously advanced moral reasoning in the public domain, is found to have had a number of extramarital affairs?

3. Make up your own moral dilemma, and ask some of your friends to explain their reasoning.

4. How would a behaviorist explain the finding that some people are clearly more honest than others?

5. Using James Rest's four-stage theory, explain how a person might decide to help or not to help a friend study for a test when he or she has other important things to do.

Review 11.2: The Spiritual Dimension

Level 1

1. Which of the following statements about religion in adolescence is correct?
   A. Cross-sectional studies show that religious practice declines in adolescence.
   B. Most adolescents believe in God.
   C. Women are somewhat more religious than men.
   D. All of the above are correct.

2. Which of the following is not a common characteristic of cults?
   A. Cults are led by a strong, inflexible leader.
   B. Cults encourage members to have contact with their families and childhood friends.
   C. Cults discourage their members from questioning their philosophy.
   D. Cults provide a great deal of support for their members.

3. Adolescents who have strong religious beliefs and participate in religious observances are
   A. less likely to use illicit drugs.
   B. more likely to volunteer to help their community.
   C. less likely to be violent toward others.
   D. described by all of the above.

Level 2

1. If a religious institution interested in helping adolescents in the community asked you how it should approach adolescents who were questioning and sometimes rejecting their religious values, what advice would you give?

2. How have your religious values changed since early adolescence?

3. College students' attitudes have changed substantially in the past 30 years. It seems that teens have become somewhat more politically neutral, more socially liberal, more economically conservative, and more cynical about government. In your opinion, what has caused these changes?

4. Bearing in mind that religious freedom is an important right, should government become involved in countering the influence of cults?

Review 11.3: Prosocial and Altruistic Behavior

Level 1

1. Prosocial behavior includes
   A. only helpful behavior that is rewarded.
   B. only helpful behavior that is not rewarded.
   C. interpersonal relationships of all kinds.
   D. any behavior that helps others.

2. Which of the following is the best example of altruistic behavior?
   A. Alexis helps George with his homework because he figures that someday he may need help, and George will help him.
   B. Juan helps Tina with the household chores because their mother told him to do so.
   C. Angel finds a wallet and returns it anonymously.
   D. All of the above are examples of altruistic behavior.

3. The major difference between preteens and teenagers in helping behavior lies in
   A. the decrease in altruistic behavior found in adolescents.
   B. the motives that underlie their behavior.
   C. the size of the gap between what they think they should do and what they actually do.
   D. the amount of self-satisfaction they receive if they do the "right" thing.

4. The relationship between advancements in moral reasoning and prosocial behavior is
   A. very strong.
   B. strong.
   C. modest.
   D. nonexistent.

5. Adolescents will show greater amounts of prosocial behavior than younger children if
   A. the helping behavior requires more complex skills or sophisticated perspective-taking skills.
   B. the teens are angry or depressed.
   C. their parents or teachers ask the teens directly to help.
   D. there is some reward for the behavior.

6. Which of the following statements concerning adolescent moral behavior and their families is correct?
   A. Parents who use an authoritarian style of parenting usually have children who identify with their values and show a great deal of prosocial behavior.
   B. Adolescents who feel that their families are close are more likely to show prosocial behavior.
   C. Prosocial behavior is stable across cultures, and no culture emphasizes prosocial behavior more than any other.
   D. All of the above are correct.

Level 2

1. If a man helped out in a hospital and volunteered to work at a shelter because he believed he would be rewarded by God later in life, would you consider the behavior altruistic or just prosocial?

2. Why would parents who use an authoritative style of parenting be more likely to have children who identify with their values?

Review 11.4: Moral Education

Level 1

1. In the _____ approach, students are encouraged to define their own values without input from adults.
   A. values clarification
   B. full communication
   C. intensive moral teaching
   D. turntable

2. Kohlberg argued that we should transform the schools into _____, which would allow students to deal with realistic issues in school.
   A. elevated communities
   B. just communities
   C. independent entities
   D. valued communities

3. Community leaders and then adolescents establish a dialogue about community problems and standards; action plans emerge, creating what is called

A. a caring world plan.
B. a Youth Challenge.
C. a Youth Charter.
D. an Imminent Justice Review.

4. The variable that most accurately predicts adolescent social conduct is
   A. the adolescents' feeling that they are capable of succeeding in school.
   B. a set of clear, agreed-upon standards communicated to adolescents by all the people and institutions in the teens' environment.
   C. whether there is a school-based program aimed at improving moral reasoning.
   D. parental involvement in the adolescents' school experiences.

Level 2

1. If you were an administrator who was interested in starting a moral education program, how would you rank the following values in order of importance?
   ___ self-discipline   ___ volunteering
   ___ tolerance   ___ patriotism
   ___ perseverance   ___ respect for authority
   ___ individual responsi-   ___ obedience
       bility   ___ altruism
   ___ compassion   ___ self-esteem
   ___ respect for the envi-   ___ courage
       ronment   ___ hard work (diligence)
   ___ community responsi-   ___ caring for others
       bility   ___ sharing
   ___ honesty   ___ political involvement
   ___ truthfulness

2. How would you design a program to discourage cheating in high school?

Answers to Multiple Choice Questions

Review 11.1: 1. D, 2. B, 3. C, 4. A, 5. C, 6. A, 7. D, 8. A
Review 11.2: 1. D, 2. B, 3. D
Review 11.3: 1. D, 2. C, 3. B, 4. C, 5. A, 6. B
Review 11.4: 1. A, 2. B, 3. C, 4. B

CHAPTER 12 WORK AND CAREER DEVELOPMENT

Review 12.1: Working on the Clock

Level 1

1. Which of the following statements about work is correct?
   A. Adults spend more time at work than engaged in any other activity, with the exception of sleep.
   B. Work is an important aspect of personal satisfaction.
   C. Vocational success is related to self-esteem.
   D. All of the above are correct.

2. The idea that one's vocation is an integral part of one's identity was advanced by
   A. Albert Ellis.
   B. Erik Erikson.
   C. Lawrence Peter.
   D. B. F. Skinner.

3. Most teenagers
   A. are optimistic about getting a good job.
   B. believe that an individual cannot get ahead in the world of work and act ethically at the same time.
   C. believe there is less opportunity for them than there was for their parents.
   D. argue that education is not as important as their parents think.

4. Which of the following *is not* a change from the past in the world of work?
   A. The number of temporary jobs have increased.
   B. Jobs generally require more reading and computer skills.
   C. Manufacturing jobs have increased significantly in the United States.
   D. Employees are offered more flexibility in work schedules.

5. The percentage of high school students working has _____ over the past 50 years.
   A. increased significantly
   B. declined significantly
   C. declined modestly
   D. stayed about the same

6. Public attitudes today toward teenagers' working can be described as
   A. unfavorable.
   B. very favorable.
   C. neutral.
   D. favorable for males but not for females.

7. Studies show that teenagers who work more than 20 hours per week are less likely to
   A. drink alcohol immoderately or smoke cigarettes.
   B. be high achievers in high school.
   C. cut classes.
   D. have a romantic relationship.

8. The term that psychologists use to describe teenagers taking on adult roles prematurely is
   A. premature maturation.
   B. pseudomaturity.
   C. the Henderson Effect.
   D. artificial latency.

Level 2

1. The workplace of the 2000s is multicultural. What are some of the consequences of this change? What changes must employers and employees make to prosper in a multicultural workplace?

2. After reviewing the research in the text, what is your opinion about the benefits and drawbacks of teenagers working during the high school years?

3. The finding that working more than 20 hours per week is related to some negative outcomes is perhaps the most important negative finding of studies on teenage employment. This finding is based on correlations. In your opinion, does working many hours lead to poor achievement? Does poor achievement lead to working many hours? Or does a third factor—perhaps some personality characteristic—underlie both working many hours and doing poorly in school?

Review 12.2: Vocational Choice

Level 1

1. Donald Super saw vocational choice as
   A. a developmental process.
   B. the consequence of deep-seated, often unconscious needs.
   C. a consequence of a person's interaction with parents.
   D. a chance occurrence that involves little planning.

2. An individual who chooses an occupation in which personal needs and characteristics match those required for the job would be expected to experience
   A. boredom and a lack of challenge.
   B. feelings of personal satisfaction.
   C. achievement, but a lack of stability.
   D. excessive pride and complacency.

3. Which of the following statements about Holland's theory is incorrect?
   A. Generally, females score higher on the social theme than males.
   B. Generally, males score higher on the realistic theme than females
   C. All ethnic and racial groups score the same on Holland's occupational themes.
   D. Holland's theory has been applied to both majority and minority group youth.

4. Successful career choice, as implied by Holland's theory, is basically a(n)
   A. social process.
   B. cognitive (intellectual) process.
   C. emotional process.
   D. process of elimination.

Level 2

1. Look at Table 12.1. Although this approach certainly is not very scientific, which of these descriptions of personal styles matches your need structure?

2. Many theories see vocational choice as a matching of an individual's needs (however defined) and the requirements of a particular job. In your opinion, is this way of looking at career choice satisfactory? What other factors may be involved?

Review 12.3: Gender and Career Choice

Level 1

1. In which occupation would you expect to find the smallest percentage of women?
   A. lawyers
   B. doctors
   C. managers of retail stores
   D. physicists

2. Which of the following statements concerning occupational stereotyping is false?
   A. Occupational stereotyping still exists.
   B. Stereotyping of male-dominated occupations has increased, whereas the stereotyping of female-dominated occupations has been reduced.
   C. As they proceed through adolescence, teens are less likely to stereotype occupations.
   D. In general, the stereotyping of occupations by adolescents has declined somewhat.

3. Most women who enter male-dominated occupations
   A. show no desire for a family.
   B. want to balance a family and a career.
   C. have been discouraged by counselors from doing so.
   D. do not believe they will succeed but want to try anyway.

4. One difficulty with viewing traditional career orientations negatively and nontraditional ones positively is that it
   A. has reduced the number of women looking at traditional careers and caused a labor shortage in these areas.
   B. confuses high aspirations with nontraditional careers and ignores individuals who have high aspirations and want to enter traditional careers.
   C. differentiates between traditional and nontraditional occupations, categories that no longer have much meaning.
   D. looks at women's career choices from a male perspective.

Level 2

1. Why do women consider the need to balance family and work when making career decisions, but few men think about this problem?

2. *Role conflict* is defined as the conflict that occurs when the demands of two or more roles are incompatible or difficult to combine. Is role conflict between work and family inevitable? How can it be reduced?

3. What difficulties might face men who want to enter traditionally female occupations?

4. Consider this scenario: You are looking for child care. You visit a daycare facility and are surprised to find that the director and most, but not all, of the personnel are male. How would you feel about leaving your child in such a facility. Why?

Review 12.4: Minority Group Membership and Career Choice

Level 1

1. A friend talks about the difficulty members of many minority groups have entering the professions and shows you percentages that are quite low. One problem in the interpretation of these figures is that

   A. they are produced by the government and are not reliable.
   B. minority group status and socioeconomic status may be confounded
   C. they do not show the personal experience of people in these jobs.
   D. these statistics are not available to the general public.

2. Middle-class youth are more likely to have a(n) _____ locus of control, whereas youth raised in poverty are more likely to have a(n) _____ locus of control.
   A. primary, secondary
   B. secondary, primary
   C. external, internal
   D. internal, external

3. Minority group and white youth differ significantly in their
   A. career aspirations.
   B. feelings that they can attain their career goals.
   C. desire to get ahead on the job.
   D. estimation of the importance of financial rewards.

4. The idea that Asian youth, especially youth from the Pacific Rim, have more interest in careers in the technical and scientific areas and choose these fields more often is
   A. a stereotype not based on any statistical evidence.
   B. correct, based on the statistics.
   C. half correct, as these youth show more interest the sciences but are actually less likely than whites to choose careers in this field.
   D. half correct, as these youth show less interest in the sciences in school but are more likely than whites to choose occupations in these fields.

5. Which group is more likely to experience parental pressure to enter a particular occupation?
   A. African Americans
   B. Latinos
   C. whites
   D. Asian Americans

6. Which statement concerning television and careers is correct?
   A. Television overemphasizes the interest level of jobs.
   B. Television focuses on people in prestigious occupations such as judges and successful businesspeople rather than on the salaried individuals in most jobs.
   C. Television does not present work as difficult and time-consuming.
   D. All of the above are correct.

Level 2

1. Self-efficacy is the belief that one can succeed at a task. Name five careers in which you believe you could definitely succeed and five in which you have major doubts. For each of these careers, list one or two reasons why you feel the way you do.

2. According to research, acculturation leads many Latino women to have higher career aspirations and more liberal ideas about gender roles, but it also may increase family conflict. Why would this be so?

Review 12.5: The Forgotten 42 Percent

Level 1

1. Employers complain that recent high school graduates
   A. lack academic skills.
   B. are unwilling to go through the interview process.
   C. believe that jobs should be mostly "fun."
   D. want to make executive level salaries when the are first starting to work.

2. Employers hiring recent high school graduates may be faulted because they
   A. hire young graduates for training programs for which the workers are not yet ready.
   B. do not look at the graduates' high school grades.
   C. are not willing to understand the problems of young graduates.
   D. want more to say in structuring high school students' programs.

3. The German system, which helps youth develop skills needed in the workplace, is a type of
   A. apprenticeship.
   B. mentor program.
   C. modified academic program.
   D. school-based cooperative program.

4. One of the advantages of the German and Japanese systems over the conventional American system is that
   A. youth not bound for college are motivated to do well because their performance will lead to a better job.
   B. the systems make discrimination impossible.
   C. German and Japanese students who take a nonacademic track can enter college more easily than American high school graduates.
   D. parents have a greater say in their child's education.

5. Which of the following is a criticism of high school career and technical education programs?
   A. They may teach out-of-date skills.
   B. They reduce the ability for students to go to college.
   C. They force students to make choices too early.
   D. All of the above.

6. Which of the following concerning adolescent unemployment is correct?
   A. The unemployment rate for African American youth is higher than for white youth.
   B. Teens who are laid off find new jobs more easily and more often at a higher salary than older workers who are laid off.
   C. Younger workers are more likely to be laid off than older workers.
   D. All of the above are correct.

Level 2

1. Why do schools show so little interest in students who are not college bound?

2. How would you answer the criticism that high school vocational programs require students to make their vocational choices too early?

3. Contrast the advantages and disadvantages of high school career and technical education.

4. What, if any, is the school's responsibility to produce graduates with a positive work ethic who value work and understand the importance of punctuality and responsibility?

5. Would the German model of apprenticeship work in the United States? Why or why not?

Answers to Multiple Choice Questions

Review 12.1: 1. D, 2. B, 3. A, 4. C, 5. A, 6. B, 7. B, 8. B
Review 12.2: 1. A, 2. B, 3. C, 4. B
Review 12.3: 1. D, 2. B, 3. B, 4. B
Review 12.4: 1. B, 2. D, 3. B, 4. B, 5. D, 6. D
Review 12.5: 1. A, 2. B, 3. A, 4. A, 5. D, 6. D

CHAPTER 13 STRESS AND PSYCHOLOGICAL, PHYSICAL, AND LEARNING PROBLEMS

Review 13.1: Stress

Level 1

1. People who argue that adolescence is a particularly stressful time of life base their arguments on
   A. the future uncertainties of adolescence.
   B. the adolescents' exposure to many new situations.
   C. the many physical and social changes that occur in adolescence.
   D. all of the above.

2. Lucy has been under a great deal of pressure and is experiencing prolonged and intense stress. If we investigated changes in her immune system, we would probably find
   A. indications of a decline in efficiency.
   B. no important changes.
   C. indications of an increase in immune system functioning.
   D. an equal number of changes showing an increase and a decrease in efficiency.

3. The correlation between stress on the one hand and psychological and medical problems on the other hand is best described as
   A. almost perfect.
   B. inverse.
   C. moderately positive.
   D. nonexistent.

4. The most important moderator between stress and its consequences is the
   A. perception of the stressor.
   B. amount of time the stressor is present.
   C. time the stressor occurs.
   D. area of the individual's life that is affected.

5. Which of the following characteristics does not differentiate stress-resilient adolescents from adolescents who are deeply affected by stress?
   A. Stress-resilient adolescents are more likely to be found alone, thinking about their problems.
   B. Stress-resilient adolescents find adults who can help them.
   C. Stress-resilient adolescents use more active coping styles, such as asking for information and seeking out answers to problems.
   D. Stress-resilient adolescents often help others.

6. According to research in the area of stress and adjustment
   A. the number of stressors have no effect on the adolescent's ability to adjust.
   B. a single stressor is generally worse than multiple stressors.
   C. female adolescents adjust better to multiple stressors, whereas male adolescents adjust better to a single stressor.
   D. adolescents find it harder to adjust to multiple stressors than single stressors.

Level 2

1. Why is interpretation an important part of the definition of *stress?*

2. Some people argue that adolescence is more stressful today than 40 years ago. How would you research this issue?

3. Why is there not a perfect relationship between the level of stress experienced and the possibility of illness or psychological problems?

4. Why do some studies show teenage girls as more affected by stressful events than teenage boys?

5. Some studies find a delayed effect for stress in adolescence. What are the implications of these studies for programs attempting to foster mental health?

6. Individuals can approach stress in three ways: (1) alter their exposure to stress, (2) take a different perspective, or (3) develop active coping skills. Consider one stressor (for example, the divorce of parents or the breakup of a relationship), and discuss how two or all three of these approaches might help.

Review 13.2: Internalizing Behaviors and Disorders

Level 1

1. Internalization disorders do not include
   A. aggression.
   B. withdrawal.
   C. depression.
   D. anxiety.

2. Emily feels very self-conscious and uneasy with others, but despite the anxiety she forces herself to seem calm and competent. Her friends are surprised that she describes herself as shy. Emily's personality may be an example of
   A. unconscious shyness.
   B. public shyness.
   C. private shyness.
   D. innate shyness.

3. All shy people share
   A. excessive self-consciousness.
   B. feelings of academic incompetence.
   C. feelings of constant danger.
   D. intense anger.

4. A shy individual engages in a conversation that does not go very well. The shy person will probably
   A. just believe that it was unfortunate and go on to the next interaction.
   B. blame the other individual.
   C. blame himself or herself.
   D. take it out on others in the environment.

5. We would expect an individual with a social phobia to
   A. experience high levels of anxiety when interacting with unfamiliar people.
   B. withdraw from contact with others when possible.
   C. avoid social situations.
   D. do all of the above.

6. The most common emotional component of depression is
   A. learned helplessness.
   B. lack of motivation.
   C. sleep disturbances.
   D. unhappiness.

7. Teenagers are most often referred for therapy because of
   A. anxiety.
   B. attention deficit.
   C. depression.
   D. chronic fatigue syndrome.

8. An individual who has prolonged bouts of depressive mood lasting at least a year probably has
   A. dysthymic disorder.
   B. ADHD.
   C. bipolar disorder.
   D. seasonal affective disorder.

9. According to some psychoanalytically oriented psychologists, depression is due to
   A. anger turned inward.
   B. separation.
   C. loss.
   D. all of the above.

10. Adolescents who believe there is nothing they can do to improve their situation may experience
    A. social anxieties.
    B. learned helplessness.
    C. learned helpfulness.
    D. attention-deficit hyperactivity disorder.

11. According to Aaron Beck's theory of depression, you would expect depressed adolescents to
    A. show perseverance.
    B. feel that everyone is persecuting them.
    C. be pessimistic about everything.
    D. feel they are always right.

12. The biological explanation of depression centers on
    A. heart and respiratory problems.
    B. enzyme deficiencies.
    C. neurotransmitter levels.
    D. oxygen consumption in the brain.

13. Which of these statements concerning suicide is true?
    A. People who talk about suicide are more likely to try it.
    B. People who have made a previous suicide attempt and failed are not likely to try again.
    C. Suicide is not related to hopelessness or depression, as was once thought.
    D. All of these are true.

Level 2

1. In your opinion, is shyness a psychological problem?

2. What reasons could underlie the fact that the incidence of depression has increased in every generation since World War II?

3. Three types of attributions are important in understanding learned helplessness: internal- external, global-specific, and stable-unstable. Consider an adolescent's attributions for poor performance in math ("I'm not doing well in math at all") on these three dimensions. Name the internal, external, global, specific, stable, and unstable attributions.

4. One of the most robust research findings is that adolescent girls have depression more commonly than adolescent boys, a situation that does not exist in childhood. In your opinion, what factors are responsible for the increased rates of depression in teenage girls?

Review 13.3: Eating Disorders

Level 1

1. Which of the following is not true of teens with anorexia nervosa?
   A. They often misperceive their weight, believing they are fat or about to become fat.
   B. They most often come from poor, disadvantaged families.
   C. Almost all diagnosed cases of anorexia nervosa are female.
   D. They are often physically active.

2. Many individuals blame eating disorders in women on our society's emphasis on the thin image of beauty. This factor may be contribute to the problem, but
   A. many anorexics and bulimics don't really want to be thin.
   B. it does not explain why some women become anorexic while others exposed to the same stereotypes do not.
   C. it does not explain why men are less affected.
   D. it has never been demonstrated that such forces have any effect on female adolescents.

3. Most teenage girls with bulimia
   A. do not injure their physical health, but rather their psychological health.
   B. show massive weight losses.
   C. show no interest in men.
   D. binge secretly.

4. After the initial challenge of restoring weight, therapy for people with anorexia nervosa and bulimia focuses on
   A. emotional control.
   B. cognitive factors.
   C. improving peer popularity.
   D. working closely with teachers.

Level 2

1. The number of reported cases of eating disorders is increasing. In your opinion, is the increase in reported cases simply due to more public awareness, or does it show an actual increase in the incidence of such disorders? If the latter is the case, why is the incidence of anorexia nervosa and bulimia increasing?

2. Some critics point to the very thin models that appear in women's magazines as the source of teenage girls' body dissatisfaction. Others disagree, claiming that the influence of these models is not that great. In your opinion, what influence do models in these magazines have on teenage girls' body dissatisfaction?

Review 13.4: Coping with Chronic Illness

Level 1

1. You read that acute diseases, such as diabetes, are long, lingering affairs. This statement is
   A. basically true.
   B. wrong, because diabetes is not a long, lingering disease.
   C. wrong, because diabetes is not an acute disease.
   D. wrong, because diabetes is an acute disease only in childhood, not adolescence.

2. The most common chronic disorder in adolescence is
   A. diabetes.
   B. a heart condition.
   C. asthma.
   D. cancer.

3. The most common school-related problem for adolescents with chronic diseases is
   A. below-average intelligence.
   B. lack of social skills.
   C. frequent absences from school.
   D. feelings of vulnerability to depression.

4. Which of the following is not one of the major difficulties of adolescents with chronic health problems?
   A. They may feel different from their peers.
   B. They may develop an internal locus of control, believing that they are in total control of their lives.
   C. They may spend more time alone.
   D. They are more uncertain about their future than other adolescents.

5. Which of the followings statements about keeping to a medical regimen is correct?
   A. Adolescents are more likely to follow their medical regimens than are adults or younger children.
   B. There are no age differences in keeping to a medical regimen.
   C. Adolescents are less likely to follow their medical regimens than are younger children.
   D. Few adolescents will even acknowledge that they have any health problems, so no research is available on this topic.

Level 2

1. Why do adolescents with chronic disorders often feel isolated from their peers?

2. Why are the problems of adolescents with chronic illnesses somewhat greater than the problems of children with the same illnesses?

Review 13.5: Learning Disabilities

Level 1

1. _____ is defined as a group of disorders marked by significant difficulties in acquiring and using listening, speaking, reading, writing, reasoning, or math skills.
   A. ADHD
   B. Learning disabilities
   C. Mental retardation
   D. Emotional disorder

2. Which of the following statements concerning learning disabilities is incorrect?
   A. Children with learning disabilities often have difficulty with reading.
   B. The learning problems of children and adolescents who have learning disabilities may result from mental retardation or emotional disturbances.
   C. Students with learning disabilities show academic problems.
   D. Students with learning disabilities often experience social problems.

3. What probably causes the greatest difficulty in reading for children and adolescents with learning disabilities?
   A. difficulty understanding one's emotions
   B. difficulty understanding that each word has an abstract meaning
   C. problems with phonological awareness
   D. frustration

4. Compared to adolescents without learning disabilities, adolescents with learning disabilities are more likely to
   A. have a fear of failure.
   B. experience depression and anxiety disorders.
   C. be pessimistic about academic matters.
   D. be described by all of the above.

5. Adolescents with learning disabilities are more likely to show
   A. lower global self-concepts.
   B. lower academic self-concepts.
   C. more transitional problems between elementary and junior high school.
   D. all of the above characteristics.

6. In the later years of high school, adolescents with learning disabilities require an emphasis on
   A. "curing" the problem.
   B. learning to compensate for and cope with any difficulties.
   C. learning to relax and enjoy life.
   D. using abstract reasoning skills.

Level 2

1. Why are teenagers with learning disabilities more likely to have an external locus of control and believe in fate? How do they develop these beliefs?

2. Why is the school attendance of adolescents with learning disabilities so poor?

3. In your opinion, should a high school–age student with learning disabilities who cannot pass one area on the minimum competency test be denied a diploma for that reason alone?

Review 13.6: Attention-Deficit/Hyperactivity Disorder

Level 1

1. Attention-deficit/hyperactivity disorder
   A. is not a valid diagnosis and should not be used.
   B. is more commonly found in girls than boys.
   C. may include such behavior patterns as inattentiveness and impulsiveness.
   D. is basically synonymous with learning disabilities.

2. Which of the following is not a type of attention-deficit/hyperactivity disorder?
   A. ADHD in which hyperactivity/impulsiveness is the primary symptom
   B. ADHD in which a learning disability is present
   C. ADHD in which attentional problems are the primary symptom
   D. ADHD in which hyperactivity/impulsivity and attentional problems occur

3. Children with ADHD
   A. often are popular with their peers because they are natural leaders.
   B. often are involved in misconduct.
   C. often are introverted and shy.
   D. most often have intelligence scores in the upper 10 percent of all children their age.

4. The difficulties experienced by children with ADHD have been localized in the
   A. frontal lobes of the brain.
   B. hypothalamus.
   C. thyroid gland.
   D. parasympathetic nervous system.

5. Which pattern is most common for children with ADHD as they mature into adolescence?
   A. Some individuals no longer fit the diagnostic definition for ADHD, and the symptoms lessen for most others.
   B. Almost all individuals continue to fit the diagnostic category of ADHD, and the symptoms become more severe.
   C. Almost all individuals continue to fit the diagnostic category of ADHD, and the symptoms stay the same.
   D. Almost none of the individuals fit the diagnostic category of ADHD, and those who do meet the diagnostic criteria show very few symptoms.

6. Studies show that in early adulthood, adolescents who had ADHD show
   A. improvement.
   B. a continuation of all the symptoms.
   C. greater impulsiveness and hyperactivity but fewer problems with attention.
   D. regression and greater problems.

7. Hyperactive children and adolescents are often treated with
   A. hallucinogens.
   B. depressants.
   C. stimulants.
   D. sedatives.

8. The evidence concerning drug treatment for ADHD shows that
   A. medication cures the ailment most of the time and almost always improves the child's attention span.
   B. drug treatment is often effective in reducing the symptoms, but it does not cure the disorder.
   C. medication is of little use.
   D. drug treatment usually increases the severity of the disorder over the long term.

9. Any improvement in academics attributed to medication is probably due to
   A. an increase in the intelligence score.
   B. greater and more sustained attention.
   C. greater interpersonal skills.
   D. all of the above.

Level 2

1. Why do adolescents with ADHD tend to get in trouble with the law more often? Why does this trend decline in early adulthood?

2. Your 12-year-old is unable to concentrate and is impulsive. The doctor and your child's teacher suggest you use medication to control the symptoms. What would be the advantages and disadvantages of doing so?

Answers to Multiple Choice Questions

Review 13.1: 1. D, 2. A, 3. C, 4. A, 5. A, 6. D
Review 13.2: 1. A, 2. C, 3. A, 4. C, 5. D, 6. D, 7. C, 8. A, 9. D, 10. B, 11. C, 12. C, 13. A
Review 13.3: 1. B, 2. B, 3. D, 4. B
Review 13.4: 1. C, 2. C, 3. C, 4. B, 5. C
Review 13.5: 1. B, 2. B, 3. C, 4. D, 5. B, 6. B
Review 13.6: 1. C, 2. B, 3. B, 4. A, 5. A, 6. A, 7. C, 8. B, 9. B

CHAPTER 14 DRUG USE AND VIOLENCE

Review 14.1: Drug Use

Level 1

1. What two problems do youth consider to be the most important ones facing people their age?
   A. drugs and violent crime
   B. AIDS and unequal opportunity
   C. poor education and drug use
   D. crime and bad government

2. The need to take more of a drug to receive the same effect is called
   A. withdrawal.
   B. tolerance.
   C. drug abuse.
   D. drug misuse.

3. Which term is not found in the American Psychiatric Association's *Diagnostic and Statistical Manual of Mental Disorders?*
   A. substance dependence
   B. withdrawal
   C. addiction
   D. tolerance

4. Which of the following is the essence of drug dependence?
   A. prominent physical withdrawal symptoms
   B. cognitive, behavioral, and physical symptoms showing continual use of a substance despite significant substance-related problems
   C. the more efficient way the body uses the drug
   D. the desire to get others involved in drug use

5. Which of the following best describes adolescents' use patterns for illegal drugs since 1990?
   A. An increase occurred in the early 1990s, followed by a decline or a plateau depending on the grade of the adolescent followed.
   B. Beginning in the early 1990s, a decrease occurred for all grades, which continued throughout the 1990s.
   C. An increase occurred for all grades beginning in the early 1990s, with a greater rate of increased use in the later 1990s.
   D. There was stability at all ages throughout the 1990s.

6. Adolescents underestimate the number of deaths from which of the following drugs?
   A. cocaine
   B. tobacco
   C. LSD
   D. speed

Level 2

1. When does drug use become drug abuse?

2. What led to the increase in drug use in the early 1990s and the change in the late 1990s and early 2000s?

3. Why is the change from being 12 years old to being 13 years old so crucial for drug use? Why do changes in attitudes appear to take place at this time?

4. Why is drug experimentation occurring at earlier ages than ever before?

5. Why do undergraduates underestimate the amount of danger from tobacco?

Review 14.2: Tobacco and Alcohol

Level 1

1. The most preventable cause of disease and mortality in the United States is
   A. heroin use.
   B. cigarette smoking.
   C. alcohol use.
   D. cocaine use.

2. Individuals often decrease their drug use
   A. in late adolescence.
   B. when they assume adult responsibilities.
   C. at age 15.
   D. in middle age.

3. Which statement concerning the image of the smoker is correct?
   A. Teenagers are well aware of how cigarette companies try to manipulate images to encourage them to smoke, and these attempts do not affect them.
   B. The image of the smoker portrayed in advertisements affects teenage boys, but not teenage girls.
   C. The image of the smoker portrayed in advertising affects teenage girls, but not teenage boys.
   D. Teenagers who view smokers as attractive are likely to smoke.

4. Which term does not belong with the image of the smoker as viewed by teenagers?
   A. sophisticated
   B. tougher
   C. healthy
   D. more outgoing

5. One major difference between teens' experience with alcohol compared with tobacco and marijuana is that teens
   A. are more aware of the dangers of alcohol.
   B. are likely to see their parents use alcohol at one time or another.
   C. do not think alcohol is dangerous, whereas they think tobacco and marijuana can cause health problems.
   D. do not believe that alcohol negatively affects youth, only older people.

6. _____ is the drug most frequently used by adolescents.
   A. Cocaine
   B. Tobacco
   C. Marijuana
   D. Alcohol

7. The number of fatal alcohol-related motor vehicle accidents involving adolescents
   A. increased during the 1990s.
   B. has declined.
   C. has stayed about steady.
   D. decreased until 1996, after which the trend shows an increase.

8. Which of the following statements correctly reflects the research on the subject of whether the use of certain drugs acts as a gateway to the use of other drugs?
   A. There is an inevitable progression from tobacco and alcohol use to the use of marijuana and other illicit drugs.
   B. People who use drugs like cocaine have progressed from the use of tobacco and alcohol to marijuana but the progression is not inevitable.
   C. Drugs are the gateway by which troubled people escape their problems.
   D. Drugs open the gateway for other troubling influences on adolescents.

Level 2

1. With all the health warnings about cigarette smoking, why does it continue to be a major problem among adolescents?

2. It is surprising that parents often do not know that their adolescent children are using alcohol on a regular basis. Why are parents seemingly ignorant of their adolescent children's use of this drug?

3. Why are some people able to limit their drug use while others seem unable to do so and progress to harder drugs and greater frequency of use?

Review 14.3: Other Drugs

Level 1

1. If governmental institutions, schools, and families looked at the lessons to be learned in the use patterns of marijuana and other illicit drugs, they would
   A. work toward limited legalization of these drugs.
   B. enforce all laws strictly and increase the legal sanctions on the sale and use of these drugs.
   C. continue education efforts even when the use of these drugs declines.
   D. separate drug users from the general student population, giving the users alternative schooling.

2. Which of the following is not a consequence of marijuana use?
   A. slower reaction time
   B. poorer attention

C. poorer coordination
D. increases in immune response

3. A type of drug that speeds up the body's use of its resources and can lead to many health problems is
   A. heroin.
   B. methamphetamine.
   C. barbiturates.
   D. antipsychotic medication.

4. A drug that induces amnesia and has been linked to rapes is
   A. amphetamines.
   B. LSD.
   C. Rohypnol.
   D. heroin.

Level 2

1. Give the arguments for and against the legalization of marijuana. If marijuana is legalized, at what age should its use be permitted?

2. Why is it so difficult to demonstrate whether chronic, heavy marijuana use causes the amotivational syndrome or whether such use is the result of something else (for example, personal problems or personality characteristics)?

3. Why has ecstasy become such a problem on college campuses?

Review 14.4: Predictors of Drug Use and Drug Abuse

Level 1

1. Which of the following personality characteristics is not predictive of drug use?
   A. early aggression
   B. impulsiveness
   C. low self-esteem
   D. slow information processing

2. Nicotine and some other drugs act principally on the neurotransmitter
   A. GABA.
   B. acetylcholine.
   C. glutamate.
   D. dopamine.

3. One personality characteristic linked to dopamine is
   A. sensation seeking.
   B. helpfulness.
   C. warmth.
   D. withdrawal.

4. Which of the following parenting patterns is not related to adolescent drug abuse?
   A. cold and distant parenting
   B. neglectful parenting
   C. inconsistent parenting
   D. overprotective parenting

5. Why is parental demandingness a difficult concept to define?
   A. It is so rarely practiced by parents that it does not show up often.
   B. It ranges from active monitoring to yelling.
   C. It does not seem to be important in the teen-parent relationship.
   D. Psychologists would rather emphasize the support function of parents than the demandingness function.

6. The one area of parental demandingness that appears to be closely related to less risk of drug use is
   A. the use of corporal punishment.
   B. helping to choose the adolescent's friends.
   C. discussing poor behavior with the teen.
   D. active monitoring.

7. When parents are supportive,
   A. their adolescents are less likely to take drugs.
   B. their adolescents are less likely to choose friends who take drugs.
   C. their adolescents are less peer oriented.
   D. all of the above occur.

8. The strongest variable relating to adolescent drug use is
   A. parental nonsupport.
   B. having friends who use drugs.
   C. being impulsive.
   D. being aggressive.

9. One major reason why drug education programs have not been as effective as desired is that they
   A. begin too early in the child's education, when the child is not ready for the information.
   B. cannot combat the societal problems that plague teens.
   C. are targeted too much at students who are going to drop out of school or run away.
   D. give false information and do not answer student questions.

10. Modern, promising drug education programs emphasize
    A. using autobiographies to underscore the horrible nature of drug abuse.
    B. a multimedia approach in which respected teen models speak with teens.
    C. learning refusal skills and improving personal skills such as communication.
    D. peer mediation for drug use.

Level 2

1. How would having a bad family environment add to an adolescent's risk of drug abuse?

2. How would you redesign drug education programs to make them more effective?

Review 14.5: Violence and Delinquency

Level 1

1. The statistics on violent crime show
   A. a continuing increase in violent crime for both adolescents and adults.
   B. that a plateau has been reached, but the levels remain the highest in history.
   C. a decline in violent crime for adolescents.
   D. a decline in violence among adults, but a significant increase among teens.

2. One boy throws a classmate against the wall to show who is really in control. Psychologists would label this violent behavior
   A. proactive aggression.
   B. reactive aggression.
   C. psychotic aggression.
   D. neurotic aggression.

3. Jason thinks that Kyoung is going to beat him up, so he turns on Kyoung first. This type of aggression would be labeled
   A. proactive.
   B. reactive.
   C. psychotic.
   D. neurotic.

4. Concerning the relationship between early aggressive behavior and later violence,
   A. studies find no relationship.
   B. studies often find a negative relationship, with nonaggressive children becoming more aggressive in adolescence and aggressive children becoming less aggressive in adolescence.
   C. studies find a positive relationship between the two.
   D. no research exists.

5. Which characteristic does not belong in a description of aggressive adolescents?
   A. impulsive
   B. empathic
   C. resentful
   D. defiant

6. Aggressive adolescents often believe that
   A. their victims deserved the attack.
   B. aggression has few consequences.
   C. aggression is necessary to get what they want.
   D. all of the above are true.

7. Which statement concerning peer and aggression is incorrect?
   A. Aggressive children and adolescents often choose other aggressive peers as friends.
   B. Aggressive children and adolescents are often reinforced for aggression by their peers.
   C. Boys who are both rejected by peers and aggressive commit more delinquent acts.
   D. Most aggressive adolescents underestimate their popularity and social competence.

8. Which of the following personal characteristics is considered a buffer to aggression?
   A. sensitivity to the environment
   B. supportive and affectionate relationships with the family
   C. wanting to be alone
   D. inflexibility

9. Which of the following shows evidence of successfully decreasing violence in youth.
   A. extensive early childhood programs
   B. programs that promote community attachment
   C. programs that involve conflict resolution and improve social skills
   D. all of the above

10. Drug use and violence are
    A. positively correlated.
    B. negatively correlated.
    C. inversely correlated.
    D. unrelated.

Level 2

1. Why does the perception that violence is out of control and increasing exist despite the recent impressive reductions in violent crime?

2. Two young teens, one with a long history of aggression and the other without such a history, are involved in similar incidents: Another teen, who is looking the wrong way, accidentally bumps into each of them in the hallway at school. Using the cognitive approach, describe how each of the two teens would react at each stage of the process.

3. If you were asked to reduce the violence in a high school, what type of program would you institute?

4. Why would belonging to a gang be related to higher crime rates?

Answers to Multiple Choice Questions

Review 14.1: 1. A, 2. B, 3. C, 4. B, 5. A, 6. B
Review 14.2: 1. B, 2. B, 3. D, 4. C, 5. B, 6. D, 7. B, 8. B
Review 14.3: 1. C, 2. D, 3. B, 4. C
Review 14.4: 1. D, 2. D, 3. A, 4. D, 5. B, 6. D, 7. D, 8. B, 9. B, 10. C
Review 14.5: 1. C, 2. A, 3. B, 4. C, 5. B, 6. D, 7. D, 8. B, 9. D, 10. A

GLOSSARY

accommodation The process by which an individual alters existing schemata to fit new information (p. 96).

acquaintance rape (date rape) Rape in which the assailant and victim know each other (p. 378).

acquired immune deficiency syndrome (AIDS) A fatal disease caused by the human immunodeficiency virus, or HIV, which affects the immunological system and leads to an inability to fight infection (p. 370).

acute illness An illness with a sudden onset that runs its course and usually results in a complete recovery (p. 480).

adolescence The transitional stage between childhood and adulthood (p. 1).

adolescent egocentrism The adolescent failure to differentiate between what one is thinking and what others are considering (p. 131).

altruistic behavior Voluntary, intentional behavior that benefits another individual and is not motivated by the expectation of external rewards or the avoidance of external punishments (p. 402).

androgyny Possessing some characteristics considered typical of males and others considered typical of females (p. 327).

anorexia nervosa A condition of self-imposed starvation found most often among adolescent females (p. 477).

anxiety An unpleasant emotional state of apprehension, fear, and/or worry that is accompanied by an increase in physiological arousal (p. 464).

asceticism A defense mechanism, often used by adolescents according to Ann Freud, in which people use excessive self-denial and pleasure-avoiding tactics to deal with emotionally difficult impulses (p. 31).

assimilation The process by which information is altered to fit into one's already existing schemata (p. 96).

attachment An emotional tie that binds people together over space and time (p. 140).

attention-deficit/hyperactivity disorder (ADHD) A diagnostic classification in the *DSM-IV* system involving a number of symptoms, including inattention, impulsivity, and hyperactivity (p. 488).

attention span The time during which an individual can focus psychological resources on a particular stimulus or task (p. 110).

attribution theory An approach that seeks to explain how people make sense of events occurring both within and about the individual by ascribing the causes of these events (p. 233).

authoritarian parenting A style of parenting in which parents rigidly control their children's behavior by establishing rules and valuing obedience while discouraging questioning (p. 145).

authoritative parenting A style of parenting in which parents establish limits but allow open communication and some freedom for children to make their own decisions (p. 146).

average adolescents (sociometry) Adolescents who are generally accepted, but receive few extreme ratings from other adolescents (p. 192).

behavioral autonomy Acting in a manner that shows control of one's impulses and accepting responsibility for one's behaviors (p. 3).

behavioral perspective An approach to explaining behavior that studies observable behavior and examines the environmental stimuli that shape behavior (p. 393).

behaviorists Psychologists who focus on observable behavior and explain behavior in terms of the processes of learning, emphasizing the importance of the environment in determining behavior (p. 36).

bisexual A term that describes sexual behavior directed toward members of both the same and the opposite sex (p. 360).

broad socialization Child-rearing procedures and societal beliefs that encourage individual choice and freedom rather than conformity to traditional values (p. 4).

bulimia An eating disorder marked by episodic binge eating and purging (p. 477).

bullying Repeated, intentionally harmful actions by a more powerful child or group against another child (p. 197).

case study A method of research in which one person's progress is followed for a period of time (p. 46).

cerebral cortex The outer surface of the cerebrum, responsible for sensory and motor functions as well as higher mental processes (p. 66).

charter schools Schools with a well described mission statement describing standards for success. These schools may be organized by parents, teachers, or others from the public or private sector (p. 242).

chlamydia A sexually transmitted infection caused by the *Chlamydia trachomatis* bacterium, which can be treated successfully with antibiotics (p. 368).

chronic illness (chronic condition) A continuous or recurring illness or a condition of long duration that has long-term consequences (p. 480).

clique Small group of people who interact very frequently and develop close relationships with one another (p. 189).

cognitive-behavioral therapy (CBT) A therapy that combines cognitive therapy, which seeks to change self-defeating and irrational thoughts, and behavior therapy, which aims at changing behavior itself (p. 473).

cohort effect The effect of growing up in a particular generation (p. 20).

combinational logic The ability to produce all possible alternatives to answer a question (p. 99).

commitment In psychosocial theory, making a decision concerning some question involved in identity formation and following a plan of action reflecting that decision (p. 319). The desire to maintain a relationship and overcome the obstacles to maintaining it (p. 347).

companionate love A mature love that contains intimacy and commitment but no passion (p. 347).

concordance rate The degree of similarity between twins on a particular characteristic (p. 72).

conduct disorder A disorder in which the individual shows violence and behaviors that violate the rights of others and basic social norms (p. 519).

consummate love Love that contains intimacy, commitment, and passion (p. 347).

controversial adolescents (sociometry) Adolescents who receive many very favorable and very unfavorable ratings from other adolescents (p. 192).

conventional moral reasoning The second level of moral reasoning in Kohlberg's theory, in which moral reasoning is based on conformity to rules and law (p. 388).

convergent thinking A type of thinking in which people solve problems by integrating information in a logical manner and arriving at a single answer (p. 125).

cooperative learning Learning strategies that require students to work together to achieve some common goal (p. 106).

correlation A term denoting the statistical relationship between two variables (p. 48).

creativity Novel behavior that is appropriate to solve the problem at hand (p. 125).

crisis (exploration) According to psychosocial theory, a time in which individuals actively face and question aspects of their own identities (p. 318).

critical thinking Reasonable and reflective thinking concerning what to do or believe (p. 123).

cross-sectional design A research design in which people at different ages are studied to obtain information about changes in some variable (p. 43).

crowd A large group of teens who are tied together by interests and often can be recognized by dress, behavior, or both. Members of crowds may or may not have substantial interaction with one another (p. 189).

cultivation theory A theory of media influence that postulates that constant exposure to a particular value, attitude, or opinion leads to viewers adopting that value, attitude, or opinion (p. 258).

defense mechanism An automatic and unconscious strategy that reduces or eliminates feelings of anxiety or emotional conflict (p. 30).

demandingness The extent to which parents set firm rules and expect responsible behavior from their children (p. 145).

dependent variable The factor in a study that will be measured by the researcher (p. 48).

depression A disorder marked by sadness, despair, low self-esteem, and loss of interest in usually satisfying activities (p. 466).

desensitization The process whereby continued exposure to a particular stimulus, such as violence, may reduce an individual's awareness of the stimulus (p. 259).

developmental tasks Challenges that arise at specific ages, the successful completion of which leads to positive outcomes (p. 34).

digital divide A term used to describe the difference among people of different socioeconomic groups in their access to computers and other technology (p. 262).

disability An impairment in one or more important areas of functioning (p. 463).

disorder A clinically significant behavioral or psychological group of symptoms that is associated with distress (painful symptoms), disability, or an important loss of freedom (p. 463).

divergent thinking A type of thinking marked by the ability to see new relationships between things that are still appropriate to the situation (p. 126).

dizygotic twins Twins resulting from the fertilization of two eggs by two different sperm and whose genetic composition is no more similar than any other pair of siblings (p. 72).

drug Any substance that alters psychological functioning (p. 495).

drug abuse The use of a drug to the extent that it causes difficulty in meeting normative daily challenges (p. 495).

dual system A system of apprenticeship that combines on-the-job training and course work in high school (p. 446).

dyslexia A learning disorder characterized by severe reading impairment (p. 483).

dysthymic disorder A category of depression that involves mild, prolonged depression (p. 467).

ego ideal An individual's positive and desirable standards of behavior (p. 394).

ego identity The sense of knowing who you are, which is the positive outcome of adolescence in Erikson's psychosocial theory (p. 316).

elaborative rehearsal A memory strategy that involves attending to the meaning of information or relating information to what is already known (p. 111).

emotional autonomy The development of special, intimate relationships with others outside the family (p. 3).

emotion-focused coping Strategies of coping with stress that focus on reducing the discomfort associated with stress (p. 462).

empathy The ability to understand what another person or group of people is experiencing (p. 386).

equilibration The process by which people seek a balance between what they know and what they are experiencing (p. 96).

experimental study A research strategy using controls that allows the researcher to discover cause-and-effect relationships (p. 48).

externalizing disorders Disorders in which problems such as fighting, disobedience, and destructiveness seem directed at others (p. 463).

external locus of control The belief that others or luck is in control of one's life (p. 436).

extrinsic motivation Motivation that comes from outside the individual, as when a student does work to get a reward from a parent or teacher (p. 232).

fatuous love Passionate, committed love without intimacy (p. 347).

friendship A positive, reciprocal relationship between two people (p. 183).

gay A term used to describe both males and females whose primary sexual orientation is toward members of the same sex (p. 360).

gender roles Behaviors expected of people in a given society on the basis of whether an individual is male or female (p. 326).

gender schema theory A theory of gender-role acquisition in which a person develops a body of knowledge about the behaviors of each gender that helps organize and interpret information and guide behavior (p. 333).

generational forgetting The phenomenon in which the older generation knows more about a particular subject than the younger generation (p. 513).

generation gap The differences in attitudes among various generations (p. 151).

genital warts The most common sexually transmitted infection caused by a virus (p. 369).

glass ceiling Artificial barriers, based on attitudinal or organizational bias, that prevent women and minorities from advancing within their organization and reaching their full potential (p. 418).

gonorrhea A sexually transmitted infection caused by the bacterium *Neisseria gonorrhoeae* that can be treated successfully with antibiotics *(p. 369)*.

goodness-of-fit model A way of analyzing how adolescents with different temperaments adapt to their surroundings; the model states that an adolescent adapts best when there is a match between the individual's temperament and the demands of the social environment *(p. 76)*.

heritability The proportion of the measured differences among people in a given population on a particular characteristic that is due to genetic factors *(p. 72)*.

herpes simplex type 1 A viral infection that can cause blistering, typically of the lips and mouth, but it may infect the genitals *(p. 370)*.

herpes simplex type 2 A viral infection that may cause blistering, typically of the genitals, but may also infect the lips, mouth, and eyes *(p. 370)*.

hormones Chemical substances secreted by one organ that control the function of another organ *(p. 68)*.

hostile environment sexual harassment A type of sexual harassment that involves the creation of a hostile and offensive climate at work or in school through some offensive sexual action that interferes with the victim's ability to function in the environment *(p. 380)*.

hypothetical-deductive logic The ability to form a hypothesis, scientifically test it, and draw conclusions using deductive logic *(p. 98)*.

identification The process by which children take on the characteristics of another person, most often a parent *(p. 394)*.

identity The sense of knowing who you are; the unique combination of personality characteristics and social style by which individuals define themselves and are recognized by others *(p. 298)*.

identity achievement An identity status in which a person has developed a solid personal identity *(p. 322)*.

identity diffusion An identity status in which exploration is minimal and no commitments have been made *(p. 321)*.

identity foreclosure An identity status marked by a premature identity decision *(p. 321)*.

identity moratorium An identity status in which a person is actively searching for an identity *(p. 321)*.

imaginary audience A term used to describe adolescents' belief that they are the focus of attention and are being evaluated by everyone *(p. 132)*.

independent variable The factor in a study that will be manipulated by the researcher *(p. 48)*.

information-processing theory An approach to understanding cognition that delves deeply into the way information is taken in, processed, and then acted upon *(p. 109)*.

intellectualism A defense mechanism, often used by adolescents according to Ann Freud, in which people take a detached, abstract attitude toward an area of emotional difficulty *(p. 31)*

internalizing disorders Disorders, such as anxiety, depression, and withdrawal, that have their greatest effect on the individual rather than on others in the environment *(p. 463)*.

internal locus of control The belief that one is in control of one's own life *(p. 463)*.

intimacy The emotional attachment experienced in a romantic relationship, requiring open communication and self-disclosure *(p. 346)*.

intimacy versus isolation The sixth psychosocial stage, occurring during young adulthood, in which the positive outcome is the development of deep interpersonal relationships and the negative outcome is a flight from close relationships *(p. 322)*.

intrinsic motivation Motivation that flows from within the individual *(p. 232)*.

learned helplessness The learned inability to overcome obstacles, which involves the belief that one cannot do anything to improve one's lot and leads to depression *(p. 469)*.

learner-centered education An approach to education that focuses on the learner's experience and the learning process rather than on the teacher *(p. 230)*.

learning disabilities A group of disorders marked by significant difficulties in acquiring and using listening, speaking, reading, writing, or reasoning skills or mathematics *(p. 482)*.

lesbian A term used to describe women whose sexual orientation is to other women *(p. 360)*.

longitudinal design A research design in which participants are followed over an extended period to note developmental changes in some variable *(p. 44)*.

magnet schools School offering special course work, making them stand out. These schools often have specific entrance requirements *(p. 242)*.

maintenance rehearsal A memory strategy consisting of simple repetition of information *(p. 111)*.

major depressive disorder A form of depression typified by a distinct period of at least 2 weeks of moderate to severe symptoms *(p. 467)*.

mastery (learning) goals An orientation in which students take on challenging tasks for the sake of the desire to know or to improve competence *(p. 234)*.

menarche The first menstrual cycle *(p. 63)*.

metacognition The conscious monitoring and regulation of the way people approach and solve a problem or challenge *(p. 110)*.

monozygotic twins Twins who develop from one fertilized egg and have an identical genetic structure *(p. 72)*.

moral realism The Piagetian stage of moral reasoning during which justice is authority based and intention is not taken into account *(p. 387)*.

moral relativism The Piagetian stage of moral reasoning during which people weigh the intentions of others before judging their actions as right or wrong *(p. 387)*.

multitasking Performing two tasks at the same time *(p. 266)*.

narcissism Extreme, grandiose self-love *(p. 312)*.

narrow socialization Child-rearing procedures and societal beliefs that encourage conformity to traditional values and family loyalties and de-emphasize individualism *(p. 4)*.

neglected adolescents (sociometry) Adolescents who receive few favorable or unfavorable ratings from other adolescents *(p. 192)*.

nonshared environmental influences Environmental factors that are unique to the individual *(p. 77)*.

operant conditioning The learning process in which behavior is governed by its consequences *(p. 36)*.

operation An internalized action that is part of the individual's cognitive structure *(p. 96)*.

operational definition A definition that describes a behavior or a concept in a way that it can be measured *(p. 46)*.

oppositional defiant disorder   A disorder marked by high levels of disobedience, and defiant and hostile behavior that does not involve repetitive aggression against others *(p. 519)*.

passion   The romantic and physical aspects of a romantic relationship *(p. 347)*.

peer   Anyone of similar status *(p. 183)*.

performance-approach goals   An orientation in which students seek to maximize grades or compare more favorably with their peers *(p. 235)*.

performance-avoidance goals   An orientation in which students show a fear of failure, and attempt to conceal their feelings of incompetence often by protecting themselves from any evaluation that might endanger their self-worth *(p. 235)*.

performance (ego) goals   An orientation in which students try to achieve in order to show their ability or conceal their lack of competence *(p. 234)*.

permissive (indulgent) parenting   A style of parenting marked by open communication and a lack of parental demand for good behavior *(p. 145)*.

personal fable   Adolescents' belief that their experiences are unique and original *(p. 132)*.

popular adolescents (sociometry)   Adolescents who receive many very favorable ratings from other adolescents and very few unfavorable ratings *(p. 192)*.

postconventional moral reasoning   The third level of moral reasoning in Kohlberg's theory, in which moral reasoning is based on self-accepted, abstract ethical principles *(p. 388)*.

postformal operational reasoning   Any qualitatively different reasoning style that goes beyond formal operational reasoning and develops during late adolescence and early adulthood *(p. 101)*.

posttraumatic stress disorder   A psychological disorder that may occur after a traumatic event and includes such symptoms as numbing, reexperiencing the trauma, and hyperarousal *(p. 379)*.

preconventional moral reasoning   The first level of moral reasoning in Kohlberg's theory, in which people reason on the basis of avoiding punishment and receiving rewards *(p. 388)*.

predatory violence   Violent behavior, such as assault, mugging, and robbery, that forms a part of a criminal or antisocial behavior pattern *(p. 518)*.

prefrontal cortex   The part of the frontal lobes of the cortex responsible for executive decision making and planning *(p. 65)*.

primary sex characteristics   Body changes directly associated with sexual reproduction *(p. 61)*.

privatization of entertainment   The trend toward individuals experiencing modes of entertainment individually rather than socially *(p. 265)*.

proactive aggression   Aggression that is goal directed, is deliberate, and occurs without provocation *(p. 517)*.

problem-directed coping   Strategies of coping with stress that involve actively confronting the problem in an effort to solve it *(p. 462)*.

prosocial behavior   Any behavior that helps another individual *(p. 402)*.

pseudomaturity   The premature entrance into adulthood, which involves individuals taking on adult roles before they are ready *(p. 421)*.

psychometric approach   The approach to intelligence emphasizing mental testing using standardized intelligence tests *(p. 115)*.

puberty   Physical changes involved in sexual maturation, as well as other body changes that occur during the early adolescent years *(p. 1)*.

quasi-experimental study   A research design used when sufficient control over the variables under study is lacking. Because of the lack of control, definitive statements about cause and effect cannot be made *(p. 49)*.

quid pro quo sexual harassment   A type of sexual harassment that involves the use of benefits or consequences for sexual favors, including bribery or threats of being fired at work or failed in class *(p. 380)*.

rape   Forced sexual intercourse that occurs because of physical force or psychological coercion *(p. 378)*.

reactive aggression   Aggression that occurs in response to a provocation or threat and that is perceived as defensive *(p. 517)*.

reciprocal interaction   The idea that the individual is influenced by others and at the same time may influence others *(p. 11)*.

rehearsal   Rehearsal involves reviewing or repeating information to retain it in memory *(p. 111)*.

reinforcer   Any event that increases the likelihood that a behavior that preceded it will recur *(p. 36)*.

rejected adolescents (sociometry)   Adolescents who receive many very unfavorable ratings from other adolescents and few favorable ratings *(p. 192)*.

rejecting/neglecting parenting   A style of parenting in which uninvolved parents neither show warmth nor demand age-appropriate, responsible behavior from their children *(p. 146)*.

relational aggression   Aggression that is aimed at hurting someone's social position *(p. 518)*.

relativistic reasoning   Reasoning that involves an appreciation of the fact that knowledge depends on the individual's subjective experiences and perspective *(p. 102)*.

responsiveness   The extent to which parents express warmth, consider the needs of their child, and use a reasoning approach to discipline *(p. 145)*.

rite of passage   A ceremony or ritual that marks an individual's transition from one status to another *(p. 1)*.

role conflict   A state in which performance of one role makes it difficult to meet the requirements of another role *(p. 432)*.

role confusion   In psychosocial theory, the negative outcome of adolescence, which involves feelings of aimlessness and a failure to develop a personal identity *(p. 316)*.

romantic love   Love that contains passion and intimacy but no commitment and that is basically erotic *(p. 347)*.

rumination   A style of coping in which an individual concentrates on negative emotions and focuses on symptoms *(p. 456)*.

scaffolding   A temporary educational aid used to help students learn material. Once students are proficient, the scaffolding is slowly dismantled *(p. 105)*.

schema   A method of dealing with the world that can be generalized to many situations *(p. 96)*.

script   A structure that describes an appropriate sequence of events in a particular situation *(p. 202)*.

secondary sex characteristics   Physical changes that distinguish males from females but are not associated with sexual reproduction *(p. 61)*.

secular trend   The trend toward earlier maturation today, compared with past generations *(p. 78)*.

selection bias   The assignment of initially nonequivalent participants to the groups being compared *(p. 50)*.

selective attention   The ability to concentrate on one stimulus and ignore extraneous stimuli *(p. 110)*.

self The organizer of a person's subjective experience, which implies some conscious understanding of one's own being (p. 297).

self-concept The picture people have of themselves (p. 297).

self-efficacy The belief about what one can and cannot do in a particular situation (p. 37).

self-esteem A term that refers to judgments that one places on the self-concept or on various aspects of the self. Newer definitions suggest that self-esteem involves not only appreciating one's own worth and importance but also being accountable for oneself and acting responsibly toward others (p. 297).

self-fulfilling prophecy The concept that a person's expectations concerning some event affect the probability of the event's occurrence (p. 50, 240).

self-regulated learners Students who are self-motivated, actively select educational goals, choose ways of meeting challenges, monitor their progress, and change strategies when appropriate (p. 110).

sequential designs Research designs that combine elements of both cross-sectional and longitudinal research designs (p. 45).

sex typing The process by which an individual acquires attitudes, values, and behaviors viewed as appropriate for one gender or another in a particular culture (p. 326).

sexual assault A general term that includes situations in which sexual contact with or without penetration occurs because of physical force or psychological coercion (p. 378).

sexual harassment Unwelcome conduct of a sexual nature (p. 379).

sexually transmitted infection (STI) A disease that is contracted primarily through sexual contact (p. 368).

shared environmental influences Environmental factors, such as socioeconomic status or parental child-rearing styles, that are shared by siblings (p. 77).

sleeper effect A delayed increase in the persuasive impact of a noncredible source (p. 51).

social cognition The ways in which people perceive, interpret, and use information about themselves and others to make sense out of their social world (p. 129).

socialization The process by which new members of a society are instilled with the fundamental elements of their culture (p. 4).

social learning theory An approach to explaining behavior that combines the principles of learning theory and cognitive processes, such as thoughts and expectations, and emphasizes the importance of observation learning (p. 393).

social phobia A classification of emotional disorder in which an individual experiences persistent and intense anxiety during social situations that prevents the individual from functioning effectively in the environment (p. 465).

sociometric techniques A group of techniques used to measure friendship status and popularity (p. 192).

stage of formal operations Jean Piaget's last stage of cognitive development, in which a person develops the ability to deal with abstractions in a scientific manner (p. 97).

stereotype threat The threat of confirming as a characteristic of oneself a negative stereotype of one's group (p. 119).

stress An unpleasant state of arousal that occurs when people perceive that an event or condition threatens their ability to effectively and comfortably cope with a situation (p. 453).

stressor A source of stress (p. 453).

stress-resilient (stress-resistant) adolescents Adolescents who do well despite experiencing significant stressors (p. 458).

substance dependence A cluster of cognitive, behavioral, and physical symptoms indicating that the individual continues to use a substance despite significant substance-related problems (p. 495).

superego In Freudian theory, the portion of the mind in which the conscience, as well as standards of conduct internalized from parental teaching, are found (p. 394).

survey A method of study in which data are collected from a number of people through written questionnaires or oral interviews (p. 47).

syphilis A sexually transmitted infection caused by the bacterium *Treponema pallidum* and with three distinct phases (p. 369).

temperament An individual's style of responding to the environment (p. 75).

theory A systematic statement of underlying principles that explain a particular phenomenon (p. 27).

theory of multiple intelligences A conception of intelligence advanced by Howard Gardner, who argues that there are ten different types of intelligence (p. 120).

tolerance The need for a greatly increased amount of a substance to achieve either intoxication or a desired effect; a significantly diminished effect with the continued use of the same amount of the substance (p. 495).

tracking An educational practice in which students are grouped and taught in classes of homogeneous ability (p. 241).

triarchic theory of intelligence A theory of intelligence postulating three types of intelligence: analytic, creative, and practical (p. 121).

vocational maturity The ability to cope with the developmental tasks related to vocational choice at each stage of life (p. 424).

voucher plan A proposed plan which would give parents the right to send their children at public expense to any school they choose (p. 243).

withdrawal The physical, psychological, and cognitive symptoms that occur when concentrations of a drug in the body decline in an individual who has maintained its prolonged, heavy use (p. 495).

zone of proximal development The difference between a person's actual developmental level as determined by independent problem solving and the higher level of potential development as determined by problem solving under adult guidance or in cooperation with more capable peers (p. 104).

CREDITS

"Level of voice among female and male high school students: Relational context, support, and gender orientation," *Developmental Psychology, 34,* 1998, p. 898. Copyright © 1998 by the American Psychological Association. Reprinted with permission.

Table 10.1, p. 346: From R.J. Sternberg, "A triangular theory of love," *Psychological Review, 93,* 1986, p. 123. Copyright © 1986 by the American Psychological Association. Reprinted with permission. **Figure 10.1, p. 348:** From R. Levine, S. Sato, T. Hashimoto, & J. Verma, "Love and marriage in eleven cultures," *Journal of Cross-Cultural Psychology, 26,* pp. 554–571, copyright © 1995 by Sage Publications, Inc. Reprinted by permission of Sage Publications, Inc. **Table 10.2, p. 350:** Adapted from C. Hazan & P.R. Shaver, "Romantic love conceptualized as an attachment process," *Journal of Personality and Social Psychology, 52,* 1987, p. 515. Copyright © 1987 by the American Psychological Association. Adapted with permission. **Table 10.4, p. 357:** Used with permission of the American Academy of Pediatrics, from "Adolescent Pregnancy— Current Trends and Issues, 1998," *Pediatrics,* February 1999, pp. 103, 516–520. Copyright © 1999 by the American Academy of Pediatrics.

Table 11.1, p. 391: Adapted from K. Badger, R.S. Craft, & L. Jensen, "Age and gender differences in value orientation among American adolescents," *Adolescence, 33,* 1998, p. 593 (Table 1). Reprinted by permission of Libra Publishing Company.

Figure 12.2, p. 421: From L. Steinberg & S. Dornbush, "Negative correlates of part-time employment during adolescence: Replication and elaboration," *Developmental Psychology, 27,* 1992, p. 308. Copyright © 1991 by the American Psychological Association. Reprinted with permission. **Table 12.1, p. 425:** From *Career Counseling, Applied Concepts of Life Planning,* 5th edition by Zunker, © 1998. Reprinted with permission of Wadsworth, a division of Thomson Learning: www.thomsonrights.com Fax 800 730-2215.

Table 13.1, p. 460: Adapted from J. Farrington, "Stress and what you can do about it," *Current Health, 22,* 1996, pp. 6–13. Reprinted by permission of Weekly Reader Corporation. **Figure 13.1, p. 461:** Adapted from R. Forehand, H. Biggar, & B.A. Kotchick, "Cumulative risk across family stressors: Short- and long-term effects for adolescents," *Journal of Abnormal Child Psychology, 26,* 1998, pp. 119–129. Reprinted by permission of Kluwer Academic/Plenum Publishers. **Table 13.3, p. 475:** Adapted from K.A. King, "Developing a comprehensive school suicide prevention program," *Journal of School Health, 7,* 2001, pp. 132–136.

Table 14.2, p. 518: From C.M. Smithmyer, J.A. Hubbard, and R.F. Simons, "Proactive and reactive aggression in delinquent adolescents: Relations to aggression outcome expectancies," *Journal of Clinical Child Psychology, 29,* 2000, p. 89. Reprinted by permission of Lawrence Erlbaum Associates.

REFERENCES

Abbey, A., Zawacki, T., Buck, P. O., Clinton, A. M., & McAuslan, P. (2001). Alcohol and sexual assault. *Alcohol Research & Health, 25,* 43–52.

Abramovitch, R., Corter, C., Pepler, D. J., & Stanhope, L. (1986). Sibling and peer interaction: A final follow-up and a comparison. *Child Development, 57,* 217–229.

Abramovitch, R., Freedman, J. L., Thoden, K., & Nikolich, C. (1991). Children's capacity to consent to participation in psychological research: Empirical findings. *Child Development, 62,* 1100–1109.

Abramson, S. Y., Seligman, M. E. P., & Teasdale, J. D. (1978). Learned helplessness in humans: A critique. *Journal of Abnormal Psychology, 87,* 49–74.

Abromowitz, A. J., & O'Leary, G. (1991). Behavioral interventions for the classroom: Implications for students with ADHD. *School Psychology Review, 20,* 220–234.

Achenbach, T. M., & Edelbrock, C. S. (1981). Behavioral problems and competencies reported by parents of normal and disturbed children aged four through sixteen. *Society for Research in Child Development Monograph, 46*(Serial No. 188).

Acock, A. C., & Demo, D. H. (1994). *Family diversity and well-being.* Thousand Oaks, CA: Sage.

Adamczyk-Robinette, S. L., Fletcher, A. C., & Wright, K. (2002). Understanding the authoritative parenting-early adolescent tobacco use link: The mediating role of peer-tobacco use. *Journal of Youth and Adolescence, 31,* 311–319.

Adams, G. R., & Marshall, S. K. (1996). A developmental social psychology of identity: Understanding the person-in-context. *Journal of Adolescence, 19,* 429–442.

Adams, K. C. (2001, May 7). Psychostimulant abuse in youth. *Alcoholism & Drug Abuse Weekly, 13,* p. 5.

Adelson, J. (1996, January). Up with feelings. *Commentary, 101,* 59–61.

Adeyanju, M. (1989). Adolescent health status, behaviors and cardiovascular disease. *Adolescence, 25,* 155–169.

Adler, J. (1999, May 10). The truth about high school. *Newsday,* 56–57.

Adler, P. A., Kless, S. J., & Adler, P. (1992). Socialization to gender roles: Popularity among elementary school boys and girls. *Sociology of Education, 65,* 169–187.

Agras, W. S., Walsh, T., Fairburn, C. G., Wilson, G. T., & Kraemer, H. C. (2000). A multicenter comparison of cognitive-behavioral therapy and interpersonal psychotherapy for bulimia nervosa. *Archives of General Psychiatry, 57,* 459–466.

Ainsworth, M. D. S. (1974). The development of infant-mother attachment. In B. Caldwell & H. Riciutti (Eds.), *Review of child development* (Vol. 3). Chicago: University of Chicago Press.

Alan Guttmacher Institute. (1989). *Risk and responsibility: Teaching sex education in America's schools today.* New York: Author.

Alan Guttmacher Institute. (1994). *Sex and America's teenagers.* New York: Author.

Alan Guttmacher Institute. (2002). In their own right: Addressing the sexual and reproductive health needs of American men. New York: Author.

Albrecht, S. L., Thomas, D. L., & Chadwick, B. A. (1980). *Social psychology.* Englewood Cliffs: NJ: Prentice Hall.

Alessandri, S. M., & Wozniak, R. H. (1989). Perception of the family environment and intrafamilial agreement in belief concerning the adolescent. *Journal of Early Adolescence, 9,* 67–81.

Alessi, N., Huang, M., James, P., Ying, J., & Chowhan, N. (1992). The influence of music and rock videos. *Facts for families* (No. 40). American Academy of Child and Adolescent Psychiatry, Facts for Families Index.

Alexander, C. S., Youth, Y. J., Ensminger, M., Johnson, K. E., Smith, B., & Dolan, L. J. (1990). A measure of risk taking for young adolescents: Reliability and validity assessments. *Journal of Youth And Adolescence, 19,* 559–569.

Alexander, K. L., Entwisle, D. R., & Horsey, C. S. (1997). From first grade forward: Early foundations of high school dropout. *Sociology of Education, 70,* 87–107.

Alfieri, T., Ruble, D. N., & Higgins, E. T. (1996). Gender stereotypes during adolescence: Developmental changes and the transition to junior high school. *Developmental Psychology, 32,* 1129–1137.

Allen, B. P. (1994). *Personality theories.* Boston: Allyn & Bacon.

Allen, J. P., Moore, C., Kuperminc, G., & Bell, K. (1998). Attachment and adolescent psychosocial functioning. *Child Development, 69,* 1406–1419.

Allen, J. P., Philliber, S., Herrling, S., & Kuperminc, G. P. (1997). Preventing teen pregnancy and academic failure: Experimental evaluation of a developmentally based approach. *Child Development, 64,* 729–742.

Allen, R. P. (1992). Social factors associated with the amount of school week sleep lag for seniors in an early starting suburban high school. *Sleep Research, 21,* 114.

Allgood-Merten, B., Lewinsohn, P. M., & Hops, R. (1990). Sex differences and adolescent depression. *Journal of Abnormal Psychology, 99,* 55–63.

Allison, B. N., & Schultz, J. B. (2001). Interpersonal identity formation during early adolescence. *Adolescence, 36,* 509–524.

Alloy, L. B., Lipman, A. J., & Abramson, L. Y. (1992). Attributional style as a vulnerability factor for depression: Validation by past history of mood disorders. *Cognitive Theory and Research, 16,* 391–407.

Allport, G. W. (1961). *Pattern and growth in personality.* New York: Rinehart & Winston.

Almeida, D. M., & Galambos, N. L. (1991). Examining father involvement and the quality of father-adolescent relations. *Journal of Research on Adolescence, 1,* 155–172.

Almeida, D. M., & Kessler, R. C. (1998). Everyday stressors and gender differences in daily distress. *Journal of Personality and Social Psychology, 75,* 670–680.

Aloise-Young, P. A., & Hennigan, K. M. (1996). Self-image, the smoker stereotype and cigarette smoking: Developmental patterns from fifth through eighth grade. *Journal of Adolescence, 19,* 163–177.

Alsaker, F. D. (1992). Pubertal timing, overweight, and psychological adjustment. *Journal of Early Adolescence, 12,* 396–419.

Alsaker, F. D., & Olweus, D. (1992). Stability of global self-evaluations in early adolescence: A cohort longitudinal study. *Journal of Research on Adolescence, 2,* 123–145.

Alspaugh, J. W. (1998, September/October). Achievement loss associated with the transition to middle school and high school. *Journal of Educational Research, 92,* 20–26.

Althaus, F. (1999). After a teenage daughter has become pregnant or given birth, mothers monitor all their children less closely. *Family Planning Perspectives, 31,* 317–324.

Alvidrez, J., & Weinstein, R. S. (1999). Early teacher perceptions and later student academic achievement. *Journal of Educational Psychology, 91,* 731–746.

Aman, C. J., Roberts, R. J., Jr., & Pennington, B. F. (1998). A neuropsychological examination of the underlying deficit in attention deficit hyperactivity disorder: Frontal lobe versus right parietal lobe theories. *Developmental Psychology, 34,* 956–970.

Amato, P. R., & Keith, B. (1991). Parental divorce and the well-being of children. *Psychological Bulletin, 110,* 26–46.

Amato, P. R., & Partridge, S. (1987). Women and divorce with dependent children: Maternal, personal, family, and social well being. *Family Relations, 36,* 316–320.

Ambrosini, P. J. (2000). A review of pharmacotherapy of major depression in children and adolescents. *Psychiatric Services, 51,* 627–633.

American Academy of Child and Adolescent Psychiatry. (1998). Summary of the practice parameters for the adolescent and treatment of children and adolescents with depressive disorders. *Journal of the American Academy of Child and Adolescent Psychiatry, 37,* 1223–1239.

American Academy of Child and Adolescent Psychiatry. (2000). Summary of the practice parameters for the assessment and treatment of children and adolescents with suicidal behavior. *Journal of the American Academy of Child and Adolescent Psychiatry, 40,* 495–504.

American Academy of Pediatrics. (2001). *Sexuality, contraception, and the media, 107,* 191–198.

American Academy of Pediatrics. (2001, June). Care of the adolescent sexual assault victim. *Pediatrics, 107,* 1476–1487.

American Academy of Pediatrics, Committee on Adolescence. (1999). Adolescent pregnancy—Current trends and issues: 1998. *Pediatrics, 103,* 516–520.

American Association of University Women. (1992). *How schools shortchange girls: A study of major findings of girls and education.* Washington, DC: Author.

American Association of University Women. (1998). *Gender gaps: Where schools still fail our children.* Washington, DC: Author.

American Association of University Women. (2001). *Hostile hallways: Bullying, teasing, and sexual harassment in school.* Washington, DC: Author.

American Athletic Union. (1989). *Physical fitness trends in American youth.* Washington DC: Author.

American College Health Association. (1986). *Acquaintance rape: Is dating dangerous?* Rockville, MD: Author.

American College Health Association. (2001). *Sexually transmitted diseases: What everyone should know.* Baltimore, MD: Author.

American Council on Education. (1992). *Sexual harassment on campus: A policy and program of deterrence.* Washington, DC: Author.

American Health Consultants. (2001, May). Oral sex: Tell teens it's not without risk. *Contraceptive Technology Update, 22,* 55.

American Psychiatric Association. (2000). *Diagnostic and statistical manual of mental disorders* (4th ed., text rev.). Washington, DC: Author.

American Psychological Association. (1982). *Ethical principles in the conduct of research with human participants.* Washington, DC: Author.

American Psychological Association. (2002). Ethical principles of psychologists and code of conduct. Retrieved February 19, 2003, from http://www.apa.org/ethics/code2002.html

American Psychological Association. (1997, November). *Learner-centered psychological principles.* Retrieved July 3, 2002, from http://www.apa.org/ed/lcp.html

American Speech-Language-Hearing Association. (2000, April 25). Learning disabilities: Issues in higher education. *ASHA Leader, 5,* 32–45.

Ames, C. (1992). Classrooms: Goals, structures, and student motivation. *Journal of Educational Psychology, 84,* 261–271.

Anastopoulos, A. D., & Shaffer, S. D. (2001). Attention-deficit/hyperactivity disorder (pp. 470–495). In C. E. Walker & M. C. Roberts (Eds.), *Handbook of clinical child psychology* (3rd ed.). New York: Wiley.

Anastopoulos, A. D., Shelton, T., DuPaul, G. J., & Guevremont, D. C. (1993). Parent training for attention deficit hyperactivity disorder: Its impact on parent functioning. *Journal of Abnormal Child Psychology, 20,* 503–520.

Anderson, C. A. (2000). Playing video games and aggression. *Journal of Personality and Social Psychology, 78,* 772–790.

Anderson, C. A., & Bushman, B. J. (2001). Effects of violent video games on aggressive behavior, aggressive cognition, aggressive affect, physiological arousal, and prosocial behavior: A meta-analysis. *Psychological Science, 12,* 353–363.

Anderson, C. A., & Dill, K. E. (2000). Video games and aggressive thoughts, feelings, and behavior in the laboratory and in life. *Journal of Personality and Social Psychology, 78,* 772–790.

Anderson, C. A., & Ford, C. M. (1986). Affect of the game player: Short-term effects of highly and mildly aggressive video games. *Personality and Social Psychology Bulletin, 12,* 390–402.

Anderson, E. R., Hetherington, E. M., Reiss, D., & Howe, G. (1994). Parents' nonshared treatment of siblings and the development of social competence during adolescence. *Journal of Family Psychology, 8,* 303–320.

Anderson, M., Kaufman, J., Simon, T. R., Barrios, L., Paulozzi, L., Ryan, G., et al. (2001, December 5). School-associated violent deaths in the United States, 1994–1999. *Journal of the American Medical Association, 286,* 1695–1702.

Anderson, M. L., & Taylor, H. F. (2002). *Sociology: Understanding a diverse society* (2nd ed.) Belmont, CA: Wadsworth.

Andersson, T., & Magnusson, D. (1990). Biological maturation in adolescence and the development of drinking habits and alcohol abuse among young males: A prospective longitudinal study. *Journal of Youth and Adolescence, 19,* 33–42.

Andrade, M. M., Bendito-Silva, A. A., Domenice, S., Arnhold, I. J. P., & Menna-Barreto, L. (1993). Sleep characteristics of adolescents: A longitudinal study. *Journal of Adolescent Health, 14,* 401–406.

Angold, A., Costello, E. J., & Erkanli, A. (1999). Comorbidity. *Journal of Child Psychology and Psychiatry and Allied Disciplines, 40,* 57–87.

Angst, J., Angst, F., & Stassen, H. H. (1999). Suicide risk in patients with major depressive disorder. *Journal of Clinical Psychiatry, 60,* 57–62.

Apfel, N. H., & Seitz, V. (1991). Four models of adolescent mother-grandmother relationships in black-inner-city families. *Family Relations, 40,* 421–431.

Arbona, C. (1990). Career counseling research and Hispanics: A review of the literature. *The Counseling Psychologist, 18,* 303–323.

Arbona, C. (1995). Theory and research on racial and ethnic minorities: Hispanic Americans. In F. T. L. Leong (Ed.), *Career development and vocational behavior of racial and ethnic minorities* (pp. 37–66). Mahwah, NJ: Erlbaum.

Arbona, C., & Novy, D. M. (1991). Career aspirations and expectations of Black, Mexican American, and white students. *The Career Development Quarterly, 39,* 231–239.

Archer, J. (1994). Achievement goals as a measure of motivation in university students. *Contemporary Educational Psychology, 19,* 430–436.

Archer, J. (1998, November 4). N.Y.C. voucher students post modest gains. *Education Week,* p. 3.

Archer, S. L. (1982). The lower boundaries of identity development. *Child Development, 53,* 1555–1556.

Archer, S. L. (1991). Gender differences in identity development. In M. Lerner (Ed.), *Encyclopedia of adolescence* (pp. 522–524). New York: Wiley.

Archer, S. L., & Waterman, A. S. (1983). Identity in early adolescence: A developmental perspective. *Journal of Early Adolescence, 3,* 203–214.

Arenson, J. D. (1994). Strengths and self-perceptions of parenting in adolescent mothers. *Journal of Pediatric Nursing, 9,* 251–257.

Arias, I., & Johnson, P. (1989). Evaluations of physical aggression among intimate dyads. *Journal of Interpersonal Violence, 4,* 298–307.

Arias, I., Samios, M., & O'Leary, K. D. (1987). Prevalence and correlates of physical aggression during courtship. *Journal of Interpersonal Violence, 2,* 82–90.

Armistead, L., Wierson, M., & Forehand, R. (1990). Adolescents and maternal employment: Is it harmful for a young adolescent to have an employed mother? *Journal of Early Adolescence, 10,* 260–278.

Arnett, J. (1991a). Adolescents and heavy metal music: From the mouths of metalheads. *Youth and Society, 23,* 76–98.

Arnett, J. (1991b). Heavy metal music and reckless behavior among adolescents. *Journal of Youth and Adolescence, 20,* 573–592.

Arnett, J. J. (1995a). Adolescents' uses of media for self-socialization. *Journal of Youth and Adolescence, 24,* 519–523.

Arnett, J. J. (1995b). Broad and narrow socialization: The family in the context of a multidimensional theory. *Journal of Marriage and the Family, 57,* 617–628.

Arnett, J. J. (1999). Adolescent storm and stress, reconsidered. *American Psychologist, 54,* 317–326.

Arnett, J. J., & Taber, S. (1994). Adolescence terminable and interminable: When does adolescence end? *Journal of Youth and Adolescence, 23,* 517–536.

Aro, H., & Taipale, V. (1987). The impact of timing of puberty on psychosomatic symptoms among fourteen-to-sixteen-year-old Finnish girls. *Child Development, 58,* 261–268.

Aron, A., & Westbay, L. (1996). Dimensions of the prototype of love. *Journal of Personality and Social Psychology, 70,* 535–551.

Arthur, C. (1993, December 4). How kids cope with video games. *New Scientist, 140,* 5.

Aseltine, R. H. (1995). A reconsideration of parental and peer influences on adolescent deviance. *Journal of Health and Social Behavior, 36,* 103–121.

Aseltine, R. H., & Gore, S. (1993). Mental health and social adaptation following the transition from high school. *Journal of Research on Adolescence, 3,* 247–270.

Astone, N. M., & McLanahan, S. S. (1991). Family structure, parental practices, and high school completion. *American Sociological Review, 56*, 309–320.

Attie, I., & Brooks-Gunn, J. (1989). The development of eating problems in adolescent girls: A longitudinal study. *Developmental Psychology, 25*, 70–79.

Austin, R. L. (1993). Recent trends in official male and female rates: The convergence controversy. *Journal of Criminal Justice, 21*, 447–466.

Aviles, R. M. D., Guerrero, M. P., Howarth, H. B., & Thomas, G. (1999). Perceptions of Chicano/Latino students who have dropped out of school. *Journal of Counseling and Development, 77*, 465–477.

Axelrod, L. (1982). Social perception in learning disabled adolescents. *Journal of Learning Disabilities, 15*, 610–613.

Babad, E. (1993). Pygmalian 25 years after: Interpersonal expectation in the classroom. In P. D. Blanck (Ed). *Interpersonal expectations* (pp. 125–144). Cambridge, England: Cambridge University Press.

Bach, A. (1999, October 11). No choice for teens. *The Nation, 269*, p. 7–12.

Bachman, J. G., Johnston, L. D., & O'Malley, P. M. (1993). *Monitoring the future: Questionnaire responses from the nation's high school seniors, 1992.* Ann Arbor: Survey Research Center, Institute for Social Research, The University of Michigan.

Bachman, J. G., Johnston, L. D., & O'Malley, P. M. (1998). Explaining recent increases in students' marijuana use: Impacts of perceived risks and disapproval, 1976 through 1996. *American Journal of Public Health, 88*, 887–892.

Bachman, J. G., & Schulenberg, J. (1993). How part-time work intensity relates to drug use, problem behavior, time use, and satisfaction among high school seniors: Are these consequences or merely correlates? *Developmental Psychology, 29*, 223–235.

Bachrach, C. A., Ventura, S. J., Newcommer, S. F., & Mosher, W. D. (1997). Why have births among unmarried teens increased? In D. J. Besharov, F. H. Stewart, K. N. Gardiner, & M. L. Parker (Eds.), *Sexuality and American social policy.* Menlo Park, CA: Henry J. Kaiser Family Foundation.

Baddeley, A. D. (1986). *Working memory.* Oxford: Clarendon Press.

Badger, K., Craft, R. S., & Jensen, L. (1998). Age and gender differences in value orientation among American adolescents. *Adolescence, 33*, 591–596.

Bagga, A., & Kulkarni, S. (2000). Age at menarche and secular trend in Maharashtrian (Indian) girls. *Acta Biologica Szegediensis, 44*, 53–587.

Bagley, C. A., & Copeland, E. J. (1994). African and African American graduate students' racial identity and personal problem-solving strategies. *Journal of Counseling and Development, 73*, 157–173.

Bahr, S. J., Maughan, S. L., Marcos, A. C., & Li, B. (1998). Family, religiosity, and the risk of adolescent drug use. *Journal of Marriage and the Family, 60*, 979–992.

Bailey, C. E., & Piercy, F. P. (1997). Enhancing ethical decision making in sexuality and AIDS education. *Adolescence, 32*, 989–998.

Bailey, J. M., & Pillard, R. C. (1995). Genetics and human sexual orientation. *Annual Review of Sex Research, 6*, 126–150.

Bailey, J. M., & Zucker, K. J. (1995). Childhood sex-typed behavior and sexual orientation: A conceptual analysis and quantitative review. *Developmental Psychology, 31*, 43–55.

Baird, A. A., Gruber, S. A., Fein, D. A., Maas, L. C., Seingard, R. J., Renshaw, P. F., et al. (1999). Functional magnetic resonance imaging of facial affect recognition in children and adolescents. *Journal of the American Academy of Child and Adolescent Psychiatry, 38*, 195–199.

Baker, L. A., & Daniels, D. (1990). Nonshared environmental influences and personality differences in adult twins. *Journal of Personality and Social Psychology, 58*, 103–110.

Baldwin, D. C., Daugherty, S. R., Rowley, B. D., & Schwarz, M. R. (1996). Cheating in medical school: A survey of second-year students in 31 schools. *Academic Medicine, 71*, 267–273.

Baldwin, D. R., Harris, S. M., & Chambliss, L. N. (1997). Stress and illness in adolescence: Issues of race and gender. *Adolescence, 32*, 839–854.

Ballantine, J. (2001). Raising competent kids: The authoritative parenting style. *Childhood Education, 78*, 46–49.

Ballard, M. E., & Coates, S. (1995). The immediate effects of homicidal, suicidal, and nonviolent heavy metal and rap songs on the moods of college students. *Youth & Society, 27*, 148–168.

Baltes, P. B., Lindenberger, U., & Staudinger, U. M. (1998). Life-span theory in developmental psychology. In W. Damon (Ed.) & R. M. Lerner (Vol. Ed.), *Handbook of child psychology* (5th ed., Vol. 1, pp. 1029–1143). New York: Wiley.

Bandura, A. (1982). Self-efficacy mechanism in human agency. *American Psychologist, 37*, 122–147.

Bandura, A. (1986). *Social foundations of thought and action: A social cognitive theory.* Englewood Cliffs, NJ: Prentice Hall.

Bandura, A. (1994). *Self-efficacy: The exercise of control.* New York: Freeman.

Bangert-Drowns, R. L. (1988). The effects of school-based substance use education: A meta-analysis. *Journal of Drug Education, 18*, 243–264.

Banks, T., & Dabbs, J. M. (1996). Salivary testosterone and cortisol in a delinquent and violent urban subculture. *The Journal of Social Psychology, 136*, 49–57.

Barabasz, M., & Barabasz, A. (1996). Attention deficit disorder: Diagnosis, etiology and treatment. *Child Study Journal, 26*, 1–14.

Baranowski, M. D., Schilmoeller, G. L., & Higgins, B. S. (1990). Parenting attitudes of adolescent and older mothers. *Adolescence, 25*, 781–789.

Barber, B. K. (1994a). Cultural, family, and personal contexts of adolescent-parent conflict. *Journal of Marriage and the Family, 56*, 375–386.

Barber, B. K. (1994b). Support and advice from married and divorced fathers: Linkages to adolescent adjustment. *Family Relations, 43*, 433–438.

Barenboim, C. (1981). The development person perception in childhood and adolescence: From behavioral comparisons to psychological constructs to psychological constructions. *Child Development, 52*, 129–144.

Barkley, R. A. (1990). *Attention deficit hyperactivity disorder.* New York: Guilford.

Barkley, R. A. (1998). *Attention-deficit hyperactivity disorder: A handbook for diagnosis and treatment* (2nd ed.). New York: Guilford Press.

Barkley, R. A., Fischer, M., Edelbrock, C. S., & Smallish, L. (1990). The adolescent outcome of hyperactive children diagnosed by research criteria I: An 8-year prospective follow-up study. *Journal of the American Academy of Child and Adolescent Psychiatry, 29*, 546–557.

Barkley, R. A., Grodzinsky, G., & DePaul, G. J. (1992). Frontal lobe function in attention deficit disorder with and without hyperactivity: A review and research report. *Journal of Abnormal Child Psychology, 20*, 164–188.

Barnes, G. M., & Farrell, M. P. (1992). Parental support and control as predictors of adolescent drinking, delinquency, and related behaviors. *Journal of Marriage and the Family, 54*, 763–776.

Barnes, G. M., Reifman, A. S., Farrell, M. P., & Dintcheff, B. A. (2000). The effects of parenting on the development of adolescent alcohol misuse: A six-wave latent growth model. *Journal of Marriage and the Family, 62*, 175–187.

Barnes, G. M., & Windle, M. (1987). Family factors in adolescent alcohol and drug abuse. *Pediatrician: International Journal of Child and Adolescent Health, 14*, 13–18.

Barnes, H. L., & Olson, D. H. (1985). Adolescent-parent communication and the circumplex model. *Child Development, 56*, 438–447.

Barnett, M. A., Vitaglione, G. D., Harper, K. G., Quackenbush, S. W., Steadman, L. A., & Valdez, B. S. (1997). Late adolescents' experiences with and attitudes towards video games. *Journal of Applied Social Psychology, 27*, 1319–1335.

Barnow, S., Schuckit, M. A., Lucht, M., Ulrich, J., & Freyberger, H. J. (2002). The importance of a positive family history of alcoholism, parental rejection and emotional warmth, behavioral problems, and peer substance use for alcohol problems in teenagers: A path analysis. *Journal of Studies on Alcohol, 63*, 305, 316.

Baron, R. M., Tom, D. Y. H., & Cooper, H. M. (1985). Social class, race, and teacher expectations. In J. B. Dusek (Ed.), *Teacher expectancies* (pp. 251–270). Hillsdale, NJ: Erlbaum.

Barone, C., Aguirre-Deandreis, A. L., & Trickett, E. J. (1991). Means-end-problem-solving skills, life-stress and social support as mediators of adjustment in the normative transition to high school. *American Journal of Community Psychology, 19*, 207–225.

Barr, S. I. (1994). Associations of social and demographic variables with calcium intakes of high school students. *Journal of the American Dietetic Association, 94*, 260–266, 269.

Barrera, M., Jr., Chassin, L., & Rogosch, F. (1993). Effects of social support and conflict on adolescent children of alcoholic and nonalcoholic fathers. *Journal of Personality and Social Psychology, 64*, 602–612.

Barrera, M., Li, S. A., & Chassin, L. (1995). Effects of parental alcoholism and life stress on Hispanic and non-Hispanic Caucasian adolescents: A prospective study. *American Journal of Community Psychology, 23,* 479–508.

Barrett, M. E., Simpson, D. D., & Lehman, W. E. (1988). Behavioral changes of adolescents in drug abuse intervention programs. *Journal of Clinical Psychology, 44,* 461–473.

Barringer, F. (1990, September 2). What America did after the war: A tale told by the census. *The New York Times,* pp. 1–5.

Barron, J. (1987, November 8). Sex education programs that work in public schools. *New York Times,* Section 12, pp. 16–19.

Bar-Tal, D., Korenfeld, D., & Raviv, A. (1985). Relationships between the development of helping behavior and the development of cognition, social perspective, and moral judgment. *Genetic, Social, and General Psychology Monographs, 11,* 23–40.

Bar-Tal, D., & Nissim, R. (1984). Helping behavior and moral judgment among adolescents. *British Journal of Developmental Psychology, 2,* 329–336.

Bartholomew, K., & Horowitz, L. (1991). Attachment styles among young adults: A test of a four-category model. *Journal of Personality and Social Psychology, 61,* 226–244.

Bartle-Haring, S., & Strimple, R. E. (1996). Association of identity and intimacy: An exploration of gender and sex-role orientation. *Psychological Reports, 79,* 1255–1265.

Basow, S. A., & Rubin, L. R. (1999). Gender influences on adolescent development. In N. G. Johnson, M. C. Roberts, & J. Worell (Eds.), *Beyond appearance* (pp. 25–52). Washington, DC: American Psychological Association.

Battin, S. R., Hill, K. G., Abbott, R. D., Catalano, R. F., & Hawkins, J. D. (1998). The contribution of gang membership to delinquency beyond delinquent friends. *Criminology, 36,* 93–115.

Battin-Pearson, S., Newcomb, M. D., Abbott, R. D., Hill, K. G., Catalano, R. F., & Hawkins, J. D. (2000). Predictors of early high school dropout: A test of five theories. *Journal of Educational Psychology, 92,* 568–582.

Bauer, G. (1987, March). Teaching morality in the classroom. *Education Digest,* 2–5.

Bauer, U. E., Johnson, T. M., Hopkins, R. S., & Brooks, R. G. (2000, August 9). Changes in youth cigarette use and intentions following implementation of a tobacco control program: Findings from the Florida Control Program. *Journal of the American Medical Association, 284,* 723–728.

Baumeister, R. F. (1986). *Identity: Cultural change and the struggle for self.* New York: Oxford University Press.

Baumeister, R. (1991). *Meaning of life.* New York: Guilford Press.

Baumeister, R. F. (1997). Esteem threat, self-regulatory breakdown, and emotional distress as factors in self-defeating behaviors. *Review of General Psychology, 1,* 145–174.

Baumeister, R., Smart, L., & Boden, J. M. (1996). Relation of threatened egotism to violence and aggression: The dark side of high self-esteem. *Psychological Review, 103,* 5–33.

Baumrind, D. (1967). Child care practices anteceding three patterns of preschool behavior. *Genetic Psychology Monographs, 75,* 43–88.

Baumrind, D. (1978). Parental disciplinary patterns and social competence in children. *Youth and Society, 9,* 239–276.

Baumrind, D. (1980). New directions in socialization research. *American Psychologist, 35,* 639–652.

Baumrind, D. (1984). Reciprocal rights and responsibilities in parent-child relations. In J. Slife & B. D. Slife (Eds.), *Taking sides in controversial issues* (pp. 237–244). Guilford, CT: Dushkin.

Baumrind, D. (1985). Research using intentional deception: Ethical issues revisited. *American Psychologist, 40*(2), 165–174.

Baumrind, D. (1989). Rearing competent children. In W. Damon (Ed.), *Child development today and tomorrow* (pp. 349–378). San Francisco: Jossey-Bass.

Baumrind, D. (1991a). Parenting styles and adolescent development. In R. M. Lerner, A. C. Petersen, & J. Brooks-Gunn (Eds.), *Encyclopedia of adolescence* (pp. 746–758). New York: Garland.

Baumrind, D. (1991b). The influence of parenting style on adolescent competence and substance use. *Journal of Early Adolescence, 11,* 56–95.

Baumrind, D. (1993). The average expectable environment is not good enough: A response to Scarr. *Child Development, 64,* 1299–1318.

Beal, C. R. (1994). *Boys and girls: The development of gender roles.* New York: McGraw-Hill.

Beaty, L. A. (1999). Identity development of homosexual youth and parental and familial influences on the coming out process. *Adolescence, 135,* 597–602.

Beck, A. (1967). *Depression: Clinical, experimental and theoretical aspects.* New York: Harper & Row.

Beck, A. T. (1970). *Depression: Causes and treatment.* Philadelphia: University of Pennsylvania Press.

Begley, S. (1998, July 13). You're OK, I'm terrific, "self-esteem" backfires. *Newsweek, 132,* 60.

Beidel, D. C., & Randall, J. (1994). Social phobia. In T. H. Ollendick, N. J. King, & W. Yule (Eds.), *International handbook of phobic and anxiety disorders in children and adolescents* (pp. 111–130). New York: Plenum.

Belitz, J., & Schacht, A. (1992). Satanism as a response to abuse: The dynamics and treatment of satanic involvement in male youths. *Adolescence, 27,* 855–872.

Bell, A., Weinberg, M., & Hammersmith, S. (1981). *Sexual preference: In development in men and women.* Bloomington, IN: Indiana University Press.

Bell, R. Z. (1968). A reinterpretation of the direction of effects in socialization. *Psychological Review, 75,* 81–95.

Bellamy, C. (2002, February 7). Teacher quits after board overrules plagiarism punishment. *The Journal News,* 4A.

Belsky, J., Steinberg, L., & Draper, P. (1991). Childhood experience, interpersonal development, and reproductive strategy: An evolutionary theory of socialization. *Child Development, 62,* 647–670.

Bem, S. L. (1981). Gender schema theory: A cognitive account of sex typing. *Psychological Review, 88,* 354–364.

Bem, S. L. (1993). *The lenses of gender: Transforming the debate on sexual inequality.* New Haven, CT: Yale University Press.

Bennefield, R. (1997, October). Black America and the great debate over school reform. *Crisis, 104,* 27–32.

Bennett, D. S. (1994). Depression among children with chronic medical problems: A meta-analysis. *Journal of Pediatric Psychology, 19,* 149–169.

Benson, P. L. (1993). *The troubled journey: A portrait of 6th–12th grade youth.* Minneapolis, MN: Search Institute.

Benson, P., Donahue, M., & Erickson, J. (1989). Adolescence and religion: Review of the literature from 1970–1986. *Research in the Social Scientific Study of Religion, 1,* 153–181.

Benson, P. L., Sharma, A. R., & Roehlkepartain, E. C. (1994). *Growing up adopted.* Minneapolis, MN: Search Institute.

Benson, P. L., Williams, D., & Johnson, A. (1987). *The quicksilver years: The hopes and fears of early adolescence.* San Francisco: Harper & Row.

Berenbaum, S. A. & Snyder, E. (1995). Early hormonal influences on childhood sex-typed activity and playmate preferences: Implications for the development of sexual orientation. *Developmental Psychology, 31,* 31–42.

Berg, F. (1992, July/August). Harmful weight loss practices are widespread among adolescents. *HWJ Obesity and Health, 6,* 69–72.

Berger, E. P. (1995). *Parents as partners in education* (4th ed.). Upper Saddle River, NJ: Prentice Hall.

Bergman, B., McClelland, S., & Demont, J. (1999, November 15). First-year confidential: In a competitive market, universities are trying to smooth the transition for newcomers. *Maclean's,* pp. 85–91.

Berko, E. G. (1992). *The Americans with Disabilities Act of 1990.* Albany: Advocate for the Disabled.

Berman, M. (1999, May 31). Teen angles. *Brandweek, 40,* 24.

Bernard, H. S. (1981). Identity formation during late adolescence: A review of some empirical findings. *Adolescence, 16,* 349–358.

Berndt, T. (1979). Developmental changes in conformity to peers and parents. *Developmental Psychology, 15,* 606–616.

Berndt, T. J. (1985). Prosocial behavior between friends and middle childhood and early adolescence. *Journal of Early Adolescence, 5,* 307–317.

Berndt, T. (1987). The distinctive features of conversations between friends: Theories, research, and implications for sociomoral development. In W. M. Kurtines & J. L. Gewirtz (Eds.), *Moral development through social interaction* (pp. 281–300). New York: Wiley.

Berndt, T. (1996). Transitions in friendship and friends' influence. In J. A. Graber, J. Brooks-Gunn, & A. C. Petersen (Eds.), *Transitions through adolescence: Interpersonal domains and contexts* (pp. 57–84). Hillsdale, NJ: Erlbaum.

Berndt, T. J., Hawkins, J. A., & Hoyle, S. G. (1986). Changes in friendship during a school year: effects on children's and adolescents' impressions of friendship and sharing with friends. *Child Development, 57,* 1284–1297.

Berndt, T. J., & Keefe, K. (1995). Friend's influence on adolescents' adjustment to school. *Child Development, 66,* 1312–1329.

Berndt, T. J., & Perry, T. B. (1990). Distinctive features and effects of early adolescent friendships. In R. Montemayor, G. R. Adams, & T. P. Gulotta (Eds.), *From childhood to adolescence: A transitional period?* (pp. 269–287). Newbury Park, CA: Sage.

Berndt, T. J., & Savin-Williams, R. C. (1993). Variations in friendships and peer-group relationships in adolescence. In P. Tolan & B. Cohler (Eds.), *Handbook of clinical research and practice with adolescents* (pp. 203–219). New York: Wiley.

Bethke, T., & De Joy, D. M. (1993). An experimental study of factors influencing the acceptability of dating violence. *Journal of Interpersonal Violence, 8,* 36–51.

Betz, N., & Hackett, G. (1983). The relationship of mathematics self-efficacy expectations to the selection of science-based college majors. *Journal of Vocational Behavior, 23,* 329–345.

Betz, N., & Hackett, G. (1996). Applications of self-efficacy theory to understanding career choice behavior. *Journal of Social and Clinical Psychology, 4,* 279–289.

Beyer, B. K. (1985, April). Critical thinking: What is it? *Social Education, 49,* 276.

Beyer, B. (1998, May/June). Improving student thinking. *The Clearing House, 71,* 262–268.

Beyth-Marom, R., Austin, L., Fischoff, B., Palmgren, C., & Jacobs-Quadrel, M. (1993). Perceived consequences of risky behaviors: Adults and adolescents. *Developmental Psychology, 29,* 549–563.

Bezilla, R. (Ed.). (1993). *America's youth in the 1990s.* Princeton, NJ: The George H. Gallup International Institute.

Bibace, R. (1999). Dating couples and their relationships: Intimacy and contraceptive use. *Adolescence, 34,* 1–8.

Bidgood, B. A., & Cameron, G. (1992). Meal/snack missing and dietary adequacy of primary school children. *Journal of the Canadian Dietary Association, 53,* 164–168.

Biederman, J. (1991). Attention deficit hyperactivity disorder (ADHD). *American Journal of Clinical Psychiatry, 3,* 9–22.

Biener, L., & Siegel, M. (2000). Tobacco marketing and adolescent smoking: More support for a causal inference. *American Journal of Public Health, 90,* 407–411.

Bierman, K. L., & Furman, W. (1984). The effects of social skills training and peer involvement on the social adjustment of preadolescents. *Child Development, 55,* 151–162.

Bierman, K. L., Smoot, D. L., & Aumiller, K. (1993). Characteristics of aggressive-rejected, aggressive (nonrejected), and rejected (nonaggressive) boys. *Child Development, 64,* 139–151.

Bierman, K. L., & Wargo, J. B. (1995). Predicting the longitudinal course associated with aggressive-rejected, aggressive (non-rejected), and rejected (nonaggressive) status. *Development and Psychopathology, 7,* 669–683.

Bigner, J. J. (1994). *Parent-child relations: An introduction to parenting* (4th ed.). New York: Macmillan.

Bilchik, S. (1995). *Delinquency prevention works.* Washington, DC: Office of Juvenile Justice and Delinquency Prevention, U.S. Justice Department.

Binder, A. (1993). Constructing racial rhetoric: Media depiction of harm in heavy metal and rap music. *American Sociological Review, 58,* 753–768.

Bingham, C. R., & Crockett, L. J. (1996). Longitudinal adjustment patterns of boys and girls experiencing early, middle and late sexual intercourse. *Developmental Psychology, 32,* 647–658.

Binion, V. J. (1990). Psychological androgyny: A Black female perspective. *Sex Roles, 22,* 487–507.

Birmaher, B., Ryan, N. D., Williamson, D. E., Brent, D. A., Kaufman, J., Dahl, R. E., et al. (1996). Childhood and adolescent depression: A review of the past 10 years. *Journal of the American Academy of Child and Adolescent Psychiatry, 35,* 1427–1440.

Biro, F. M., & Rosenthal, S. L. (1992). Psychological sequelae of sexually transmitted diseases in adolescents. *Obstetric Clinics of North America, 19,* 109–218.

Bishop, J. (1989, January/February). Why the apathy in American high schools? *Educational Researcher, 18,* 6–10.

Bishop, J. A., & Inbertdizen, H. M. (1995). Peer acceptance and friendship: An investigation of their relation to self-esteem. *Journal of Early Adolescence, 15,* 476–489.

Bjerregaard, B., & Smith, C. (1993). Gender differences in gang participation, delinquency, and substance use. *Journal of Quantitative Criminology, 9,* 329–355.

Bjorklund, D. F. (1995). *Children's thinking: Developmental function and individual differences.* Pacific Grove, CA: Brooks/Cole.

Bjornsen, C. A. (2000). The blessing as a rite of passage in adolescence. *Adolescence, 35,* 357–363.

Blair, J. (2000, February 16). Minorities post gains in higher education, but still trail whites. *Education Week,* p. 6.

Blake, J. (1989). Family size and achievement. Berkeley, CA: University of California Press.

Blanton, H., & Gerrard, M. (1997). Effect of sexual motivation on men's risk perception for sexually transmitted disease: There must be 50 ways to justify a lover. *Health Psychology, 16,* 374–379.

Blasi, A. (1980). Bridging moral cognition and moral action: A critical review of the literature. *Psychological Bulletin, 88,* 1–45.

Blinn-Pike, L. (1999). Why abstinent adolescents report they have not had sex: Understanding sexually resilient youth. *Family Relations, 48,* 295–302.

Blinn-Pike, L., Berger, T., & Rea-Holloway, M. (2000). Conducting sexuality research in schools: Lessons learned. *Family Planning Perspectives, 32,* 246–266.

Block, C. R., Christakos, A., Jacob, A., & Przbylski, R. (1996). *Street gangs and crime: Patterns and trends in Chicago* [Research bulletin]. Chicago: Illinois Criminal Justice Information Authority.

Block, J. H., Block, J., & Gjerde, P. F. (1986). The personality of children prior to divorce: A prospective study. *Child Development, 57,* 827–840.

Block, J., & Robins, R. W. (1993). A longitudinal study of consistency and change in self-esteem from early adolescence to early adulthood. *Child Development, 64,* 909–923.

Bloom, A. (1987). *The closing of the American mind.* New York: Simon & Schuster.

Blos, P. (1962). On adolescence: A psychoanalytic interpretation. In P. Blos (Ed.), *Phases of adolescence* (pp. 52–87). New York: Free Press.

Blos, P. (1967). The second individuation process of adolescence. *Psychoanalytic Study of The Child, 22,* 162–186.

Blos, P. (1979). *The adolescent passage.* New York: Macmillan.

Blum, R. W. (1992). Chronic illness and disability in adolescence. *Journal of Adolescent Health, 13,* 364–368.

Blyth, D. A., & Foster-Clark, F. S. (1987). Gender differences in perceived intimacy with different members of adolescents' social networks. *Sex Roles, 17,* 689–718.

Blyth, D., Hill, J., & Thiel, K. (1982). Early adolescents' significant others: Grade and gender differences in perceived relationships with familial and nonfamilial adults and young people. *Journal of Youth and Adolescence, 11,* 425–450.

Blyth, D. A., Simmons, R. G., & Carlton-Ford, S. (1983). The adjustment of early adolescents to school transitions. *Journal of Early Adolescence, 3,* 105–120.

Bochner, S., & Hesketh, B. (1994). Power distance, individualism/collectivism, and job-related attitudes in a culturally diverse work group. *Journal of Cross-Cultural Psychology, 25,* 233–247.

Boeck, S., & Lynn, G. (1995, December 27). Why teens choose to use. *USA Today,* p. 1A.

Bogenschneider, K., Wu, M. Y., Rafaelli, M., & Tsay, J. C. (1998). "Other teens drink, but not my kid": Does parental awareness of adolescent alcohol use protect adolescents from risky consequences. *Journal of Marriage and the Family, 60,* 356–373.

Boice, M. M. (1998). Chronic illness in adolescence. *Adolescence, 33,* 927–938.

Bond, M., Leung, K. & Wan, K. C. (1982). The social impact of self-effacing attributions. The Chinese case. *Journal of Social Psychology, 118,* 157–166.

Bong, M. (2001). Between- and within-domain relations of academic motivation among middle and high school students: Self-efficacy, task-value, and achievement goals. *Educational Psychology, 93,* 23–34.

Bookwala, J., Frieze, I. H., Smith, C., & Ryan, K. (1992). Predictors of dating violence: A multivariate analysis. *Violence and Victims, 7,* 297–311.

Boot, B. P., McGregor, I. S., & Hall, W. (2000, May 20). MDMA (Ecstasy) neurotoxicity: Assessing and communicating risks. *The Lancet, 355,* 1818–1822.

Bores-Rangel, E., Church, T., Szendre, D., & Reeves, C. (1990). Self-efficacy in relation to occupational consideration and academic performance in high school equivalency students. *Journal of Counseling Psychology, 37,* 407–418.

Borzekowski, D. L. G., & Rickert, V. I. (2001). Adolescents, the Internet, and the issues of access and content. *Journal of Applied Developmental Psychology, 22,* 49–59.

Bosworth, K. (1995, May). Caring for others and being cared for. *Phi Delta Kappan,* 686–693.

Botvin, E. M., Botvin, G. J., & Baker, E. (1983). Developmental changes in attitude toward cigarette smokers during early adolescence. *Psychological Reports, 53,* 547–553.

Botvin, G. J., Griffin, K. W., Diaz, T., & Ifill-Williams, M. (2001). Preventing binge drinking during early adolescence: One and two year follow-up of a school based preventive intervention. *Psychology of Addictive Behaviors, 15,* 360–365.

Bouchard, T. J., Lykken, D. T., McGue, M., Segal, N. L., & Tellegen, A. (1990). Sources of psychological differences: The Minnesota study of twins reared apart. *Science, 250,* 223–228.

Bower, A. (2002). The gentler sex? *Time, 159,* p. 58+. Retrieved December 24, 2002, from http://www.time.com/time/2002/wdrinking/behavior.html

Bower, B. (1998, September 12). Social disconnections on-line. *Science News, 154,* 168.

Bowlby, J. (1969). *Attachment and loss.* New York: Basic Books.

Bowman, D. H. (2000a, May 3). Charters, vouchers earning mixed report card. *Education Week,* pp. 1, 28.

Bowman, D. H. (2000b, May 3). Federal study finds gains in gender equity. *Education Week,* pp. 1, 18.

Boyd, D. A., & Parish, T. S. (1996). An examination of the educational and legal ramifications of "full inclusion" within our nation's public schools. *Education, 116,* 478–481.

Boyes, M., & Allen, S. (1993). Styles of parent-child interaction and moral reasoning in adolescence. *Merrill-Palmer Quarterly, 39,* 551–570.

Boyes, M. C., & Chandler, M. (1992). Cognitive development, epistemological doubt, and identity formation during adolescence. *Journal of Youth and Adolescence, 2,* 277–304.

Braaten, S. (1999). Youth violence and aggression: "Why?" Or, should we be asking, "Why not?" *Preventing School Failure, 44,* 32–37.

Bracey, G. W. (1996). 75 years of elementary education. *Principal, 75,* 17–21.

Bracey, G. W. (1998). Test scores of nations and states. *Phi Delta Kappan, 80,* 347–351.

Bracey, G. W. (1999, May). The forgotten 42%. *Phi Delta Kappan, 80,* 711–712.

Bracey, G. W. (2000, December). Research—Small classes 1, Vouchers 0. *Phi Delta Kappan, 82,* 331–334.

Brafford, L. J., & Beck, K. H. (1991). Development and validation of a condom self-efficacy scale for college students. *Journal of American College Health, 39,* 219–225.

Brage, D., & Meredith, W. (1994). A causal model of adolescent depression. *The Journal of Psychology, 128,* 455–468.

Bray, J. H. (1988). Children's development during early remarriage. In E. M. Hetherington & J. D. Arasteh (Eds.), *Impact of divorce, single parenting and stepparenting on children* (pp. 279–298). Hillsdale, NJ: Erlbaum.

Bray, J. H., & Berger, S. H. (1993). Developmental issues in stepfamilies research project: Family relationships and parent-child interactions. *Journal of Family Psychology, 7,* 1–17.

Brehm, S. S., & Kassin, S. M. (1996). *Social psychology* (3rd ed.). Boston: Houghton Mifflin.

Breslin, E., Riggs, D., O'Leary, D., & Arias, I. (1990). Expected and actual consequences of dating aggression. *Journal of Interpersonal Violence, 5,* 247–258.

Brewer, D. J., Rees, D. I., & Argys, L. M. (1995). The reform without cost: A reply to our critics. *Phi Delta Kappan, 77,* 442–445.

Brewster, K. L., Cooksey, E. C., Guilkey, D. K., & Rindfuss, R. R. (1998). The changing impact of religion on the sexual and contraceptive behavior of adolescent women in the United States. *Journal of Marriage and the Family, 60,* 493–504.

Brightman, J. (1994, November). What smells like teen spirit? *American Demographics,* 10–11.

Brislin, R. (2000). *Understanding culture's influence on behavior* (2nd ed.). Fort Worth, TX: Harcourt College Publishers.

Brittain, C. V. (1963). Adolescent choices and parent-peer cross-pressures. *American Sociological Review, 28,* 385–391.

Broadbear, J. T., & Keyser, B. B. (2000). An approach to teaching for critical thinking in health education. *Journal of School Health, 70,* 322–330.

Brody, G. H., Flor, D. L., Hollett-Wright, N., & McCoy, J. K. (1998). Children's development of alcohol use norms: Contributions of parent and sibling norms, children's temperaments, and parent-child discussions. *Journal of Family Psychology, 12,* 209–219.

Brody, G. H., Moore, K., & Glei, D. (1994). Family processes during adolescence as predictors of parent-young adult attitude similarity. *Family Relations, 43,* 369–373.

Brody, G. H., Zolinda, S., MacKinnon, C. E., & MacKinnon, R. (1985). Role relationships and behavior between preschool-aged and school-aged siblings. *Developmental Psychology, 21,* 124–129.

Broman, S. H., Nichols, P. I., & Kennedy, W. A. (1975). *Preschool IQ: Prenatal and early developmental correlates.* Hillsdale, NJ: Erlbaum.

Bronfenbrenner, U. (1979). *The ecology of human development.* Cambridge: Harvard University Press.

Bronfenbrenner, U. (1986). Ecology of the family as a context for human development: Research perspectives. *Developmental Psychology, 22,* 723–743.

Bronfenbrenner, U. (1989). Ecological systems theory. In R. Vasta (Ed.), *Annals of child development* (Vol. 6, pp. 187–250). Greenwich, CT: JAI Press.

Bronfenbrenner, U., & Crouter, A. C. (1982). *Work and family through time and space.* In S. Kamerman & C. D. Hayes (Eds.), *Children in a changing world* (pp. 39–83). Washington DC: National Academy Press.

Bronfenbrenner, U., & Crouter, A. C. (1983). The evolution of environmental models in developmental research. In P. H. Mussen (Ed.), *Handbook of child psychology* (4th ed., pp. 357–415). New York: Wiley.

Bronfenbrenner, U., & Morris, P. A. (1998). The ecology of developmental processes. In W. Damon (Ed.) & R. M. Lerner (Vol. Ed.), *Handbook of child psychology* (5th ed., Vol. 1, pp. 993–1028). New York: Wiley.

Bronstein, P., Stoll, M., Caluson, J. A., Abrams, C. L., & Briones, M. (1994). Fathering after separation or divorce: Factors predicting children's adjustment. *Family Relations, 43,* 460–473.

Brook, J. S., Balka, E. B., & Whiteman, M. (1999). The risks for late adolescence of early adolescent marijuana use. *American Journal of Public Health, 89,* 1549–1554.

Brook, J. S., Nomura, C., & Cohen, P. (1989). Prenatal, perinatal, and early childhood risk factors and drug involvement in adolescence. *Genetic, Social and General Psychology Monographs, 115,* 221–241.

Brook, J. S., Whiteman, M., Brook, D. W., & Gordon, A. S. (1981). Parental determinants of male adolescent marijuana use. *Developmental Psychology, 17,* 841–847.

Brook, J. S., Whiteman, M., & Gordon, A. S. (1983). Stages of drug use in adolescence: Personality, peer, and family correlates. *Developmental Psychology, 19,* 269–277.

Brooks, R. B. (1994). Children at risk: Fostering resilience and hope. *American Journal of Orthopsychiatry, 64,* 545–553.

Brooks-Gunn, J. (1988). Antecedents and consequences of variations in girls' maturational timing. *Journal of Adolescent Health, 9,* 365–373.

Brooks-Gunn, J. (1991). Maturational timing variations in adolescent girls. In R. M. Lerner, A. C. Petersen, & J. Brooks-Gunn (Eds.), *Encyclopedia of adolescence* (pp. 609–613). New York: Wiley.

Brooks-Gunn, J., & Furstenberg, F. F. (1989). Adolescent sexual behavior. *American Psychologist, 44,* 249–257.

Brooks-Gunn, J., Guo, G., & Furstenberg, F., Jr. (1993). Who drops out and who continues beyond high school? A 20 year follow-up of Black urban youth. *Journal of Research on Adolescence, 3,* 271–294.

Brooks-Gunn, J., Klebanov, P. K., & Duncan, G. J. (1996). Ethnic differences in children's intelligence test scores: Role of economic deprivation, home environment, and maternal characteristics. *Child Development, 67,* 396–409.

Brooks-Gunn, J., Newman, D. L., Holderness, C., & Warren, M. P. (1994). The experience of breast development and girls' stories about the purchase of a bra. *Journal of Youth and Adolescence, 23,* 539–565.

Brooks-Gunn, J., & Petersen, A. C. (1983). *Girls at puberty: Biological and psychological perspectives.* New York: Plenum.

Brooks-Gunn, J., & Petersen, A. C. (1984). Problems in studying and defining pubertal events. *Journal of Youth and Adolescence, 13,* 181–196.

Brooks-Gunn, J., & Reiter, E. O. (1990). The role of pubertal processes. In S. S. Feldman & G. R. Elliott (Eds.), *At the threshold: The developing adolescent* (pp. 16–53). Cambridge: Harvard University Press.

Brooks-Gunn, J., & Warren, M. P. (1988). Mother-daughter differences in menarcheal age in adolescent dancers and nondancers. *Annals of Human Biology, 15,* 35–43.

Brooks-Gunn, J., & Warren, M. P. (1989). Biological contributions to affective expression in young adolescent girls. *Child Development, 60,* 372–385.

Brophy, J. (1983). Conceptualizing student motivation. *Educational Psychologist, 18,* 200–215.

Brophy, J. E. (1987). Synthesis of research on strategies for motivating students to learn. *Educational Leadership, 44,* 40–48.

Brouilette, L. (1999). Behind the statistics: Urban dropouts and the GED. *Phi Delta Kappan, 81,* 313–315.

Brown, B. B. (1982). The extent and effects of peer pressure among high school students: A retrospective analysis. *Journal of Youth and Adolescence, 11,* 121–133.

Brown, B. B. (1989). The role of peer groups in adolescents' adjustment to secondary school. In T. J. Berndt & G. W. Ladd (Eds.), *Peer relationships in child development* (pp. 188–215). New York: Wiley.

Brown, B. B. (1990). Peer groups and peer cultures. In S. S. Feldman & G. R. Elliott (Eds.), *At the threshold: The developing adolescent* (pp. 171–196). Cambridge: Harvard University Press.

Brown, B. B., Clasen, D. R., & Eicher, S. A. (1986). Perceptions of peer pressure, peer conformity dispositions, and self-reported behavior among adolescents. *Developmental Psychology, 22,* 521–530.

Brown, B. B., & Lohr, M. J. (1986). Peer group affiliation and adolescent self-esteem: An integration of ego identity and symbolic interaction theories. *Journal of Personality and Social Psychology, 52,* 47–55.

Brown, B. R., Baranowski, M. D., Kulig, J. W., & Stephenson, J. N. (1996). Searching for the Magic Johnson effect: AIDS, adolescence, and celebrity disclosure. *Adolescence, 31,* 253–265.

Brown, D., Minor, C. W., & Jepsen, D. A. (1991). The opinions of minorities about preparing for work: Report of the second NCDA national survey. *The Career Development Quarterly, 44,* 341–353.

Brown, E. (1999, April 12). The future of Net shopping? Your teens. *Fortune, 139,* 152.

Brown, E. F., & Hendee, W. R. (1989a). Adolescents and their music. *Journal of the American Medical Association, 262,* 1659–1663.

Brown, E. F., & Hendee, W. R. (1989b). In reply. *Journal of the American Medical Association, 263,* 814.

Brown, J. E. (2002). *Nutrition through the life cycle.* Belmont, CA: Wadsworth.

Brown, L. K., DiClemente, R. J., & Park, T. (1992). Predictors of condom use in sexually active adolescents. *Journal of Adolescent Health, 13,* 651–657.

Brown, L. M., & Gilligan, C. (1992). *Meeting at the crossroads: Women's psychology and girls' development.* Cambridge: Harvard University Press.

Brown, M. T. (1995). The career development of African Americans: Theoretical and empirical issues in F. T. L. Leong (Ed.), *Career development and vocational behavior of racial and ethnic minorities* (pp. 7–36). Mahwah, NJ: Erlbaum.

Browning, K., & Loeber, R. (1999, February). *Highlights of findings from the Pittsburgh Youth Study* [OJJDP Fact Sheet]. Washington, DC: U.S. Department of Justice.

Bruch, M. (1986). Anorexia nervosa: The therapeutic task. In K. D. Brownell & J. P. Forey (Eds.), *Handbook of eating disorders: Physiology, psychology and treatment of obesity, anorexia, and bulimia* (pp. 328–332). New York: Basic Books.

Bruner, A. B., & Fishman, M. (1998, August 19). Adolescents and illicit drug use. *Journal of the American Medical Association, 280,* 597–603.

Bryan, A. D., Aiken, L. S., & West, S. G. (1997). Young women's condom use: The influence of acceptance of sexuality, control over sexual encounter, and perceived susceptibility to common STDs. *Health Psychology, 16,* 468–479.

Bryant, J., & Rockwell, S. C. (1994). Effects of massive exposure to sexually oriented prime-time television programming on adolescents' moral judgment. In D. Zillmann, J. Bryant, & A. C. Huston (Eds.), *Media, children, and the family: Social scientific, psychodynamic, and clinical perspectives* (pp. 183–195). Hillsdale, NJ: Erlbaum.

Buchanan, C. M., Eccles, J. S., & Becker, J. B. (1992a). Are adolescents the victims of raging hormones?: Evidence for activational effects of hormones on moods and behavior at adolescence. *Psychological Bulletin, 111,* 62–107.

Buchanan, C. M., Eccles, J. S., & Becker, J. (1992b). Changes in hormones, moods, and behavior in adolescence. *Psychological Bulletin, 111,* 62–107.

Buerkel-Rothfuss, N., & Mayes, S. (1981). Soap opera viewing: the cultivation effect. *Journal of Communication, 31,* 108–115.

Buhrmester, D. (1992). The developmental courses of sibling and peer relationships. In F. Boer & J. Dunn (Eds.), *Children's sibling relationships: Developmental and clinical issues* (pp. 19–40). Hillsdale, NJ: Erlbaum.

Buhrmester, D., & Furman, W. (1987). The development of companionship and intimacy. *Child Development, 58,* 1101–1113.

Buhrmester, D., & Furman, W. (1990). Perceptions of sibling relationships during middle childhood and adolescence. *Child Development, 61,* 1387–1398.

Buis, J. M., & Thompson, D. N. (1989). Imaginary audience and personal fable: A brief review. *Adolescence, 24,* 773–781.

Bukowski, W. B., Hoza, B., & Boivin, M. (1994). Measuring friendship quality during pre and early adolescence: The development and psychometric properties of the friendship qualities scale. *Journal of Social Personal Relationships, 11,* 471–484.

Bukowski, W. B., & Kramer, T. L. (1986). Judgments of the features of friendship among early adolescent boys and girls. *Journal of Early Adolescence, 6,* 331–338.

Bulcroft, R. A., Carmody, D. C., & Bulcroft, K. A. (1998). Family structure and patterns of independence giving to adolescents. *Journal of Family Issues, 19,* 404–435.

Bullock, J. R. (2002). Bullying among children. *Childhood Education, 78,* 130–134.

Burch, J., & Kane, C. (1999). *Implementing the OJJDP comprehensive gang model* [OJJDP Fact Sheet, No. 112]. Washington, DC: U.S. Department of Justice.

Burcham, B., & Carlson, L. (1995, March). Attention deficit hyperactivity disorder. *Education Digest,* 42–44.

Burdman, P. (2001, May 10). Voice of dissent. *Black Issues in Higher Education, 18,* 28–34.

Burnett, G., & Walz, G. (1994). *Gangs in schools.* ERIC: Clearinghouse on Urban Education (EDO-UD-94-5).

Burnett, P. C., & Fanshawe, J. P. (1997). Measuring school-related stressors in adolescents. *Journal of Youth and Adolescence, 26,* 415–429.

Burnette, E. (1995, June). Black males retrieve a noble heritage. *APA Monitor, 1,* 32.

Burniske, R. W. (1998, December). Think critically about classroom technology. *Education Digest, 64,* 65–62.

Burton, L. M. (1992). Black grandparents rearing grandchildren of drug-addicted parents: Stressors, outcomes, and social service needs. *The Gerontologist, 32,* 744–751.

Burton, R. V. (1963). Generality of honesty reconsidered. *Psychological Review, 70,* 481–499.

Bush, G. W. (2002, May 2). *Proclamation 7552. National Charter School Week, 2002.* Retrieved December 26, 2002, from http://www.pacrim.org/FedReg1.pdf

Bush, P. J., Weinfurt, K. P., & Iannotti, R. J. (1994). Families versus peers: Developmental influences on drug use from grade 4–5 to grade 7–8. *Journal of Applied Developmental Psychology, 15,* 437–456.

Bushman, B. J., & Baumeister, R. F. (1998). Threatened egotism, narcissism, self-esteem, and direct and displaced aggression: Does self-love or self-hate lead to violence? *Journal of Personality and Social Psychology, 75,* 219–229.

Buss, A. H., & Plomin, R. (1984). *Temperament: Early developing personality traits.* Hillsdale, NJ: Erlbaum.

Butler, D. L. (1995). Promoting strategic learning by postsecondary students with learning disabilities. *Journal of Learning Disabilities, 28,* 170–190.

Butler, D. L. (1998). The strategic content learning approach to promoting self-regulated learning: A report of three studies. *Journal of Educational Psychology, 90,* 682–697.

Byrnes, J. P. (1988). Formal operations: A systematic reformulation. *Developmental Review, 8,* 1–22.

Cairns, R. B. (1979). *Social development: The origins and plasticity of behavior.* San Francisco: Freeman.

Cairns, R. B. (1998). The making of developmental psychology. In W. Damon (Ed.-in-Chief) & R. M. Lerner (Vol. Ed.), *Handbook of child psychology* (5th ed., Vol. 1, pp. 25–106). New York: Wiley.

Cairns, R. B., Cairns, B. D., Neckerman, H. J., Gest, S., & GariepPy, J. l. (1988). Peer networks and social behavior: Peer support or peer rejection? *Developmental Psychology, 24,* 815–823.

Calfin, M. S., Carroll, J. L., & Schmidt, J. (1993). Viewing music-videotapes before taking a test of premarital attitudes. *Psychological Reports, 72,* 485–481.

Calfras, K., & Taylor, W. (1994). Effects of physical activity on psychological variables in adolescents. *Pediatric Exercise Science, 4,* 406–423.

California State Department of Education. (1990). *Toward a state of esteem: The final report of the task force to promote self-esteem and personal social responsibility.* Sacramento, CA: Author.

Calvert, S. L., & Tan, S. L. (1994). Impact of virtual reality on young adults' physiological arousal and aggressive thoughts. *Journal of Applied Developmental Psychology, 15,* 125–139.

Camarena, P. M., Sargiani, P. A. & Peterson, A. C. (1990). Gender specific pathways to intimacy in early adolescence. *Journal of Youth and Adolescence, 19,* 19–32.

Campbell, R., Martin, C. R., & Fabos, B. (2002). *Media and culture: An introduction to mass communication.* New York: Bedford/St. Martin.

Campbell, S. M., Peplau, L. A., & DeBro, S. C. (1992). Women, men and condoms: Attitudes and experience of heterosexual college students. *Psychology of Women Quarterly, 16,* 273–288.

Carducci, B. J. (2000, January). Shyness: The new solution. *Psychology Today, 33,* 38–44.

Carducci, B. J., & Zimbardo, P. G. (1995, November/December). Are you shy? *Psychology Today,* 34–41.

Carnegie Corporation of New York. (1996). *Breaking ranks.* New York: Author.

Carnegie Corporation on Adolescent Development. (1995). *Great transitions: Preparing adolescents for the new century.* Washington, DC: Author.

Carnegie Council on Adolescent Development. (1994). *A matter of time: Risk and opportunity in the out-of-school hours.* New York: Author.

Carnegie Council on Adolescent Development. (1995). *Great transitions: Preparing adolescents for the new century.* Washington, DC: Author.

Carney, D. (1996, March 2). Members eye new efforts to police the airways. *Congressional Quarterly Weekly Report, 54,* 553–555.

Carpendale, J. I. M., & Krebs, D. L. (1995). Variations in level of moral judgment as a function of type of dilemma and moral choice. *Journal of Personality, 63,* 289–313.

Carr, R. V., Wright, J. D., & Brody, C. J. (1996). Effects of high school work experience a decade later: Evidence from National Longitudinal Survey. *Sociology of Education, 69,* 66–81.

Carrera, M. A., & Dempsey, P. (1988, January/February). Restructuring public policy priorities on teen pregnancy: A holistic approach to teen development and teen services. *SIECUS Report,* pp. 6–9.

Carroll, R. L., Silbergleid, M. I., Beachum, C. M., Perry, S. D., Pluscht, P. J., & Pescatore, M. J. (1993). Meanings of radio to teenagers in a niche-programming era. *Journal of Broadcasting and Electronic Media, 37,* 159–176.

Carruth, B., & Goldberg, D. (1990). Nutritional issues of adolescents. *Journal of Early Adolescence, 10,* 122–140.

Carskadon, M. A. (1990). Patterns of sleep and sleepiness in adolescents. *Pediatrician, 17,* 5–12.

Carskadon, M. A., Harvey, K., & Duke, P. (1980). Pubertal changes in daytime sleepiness. *Sleep, 2,* 453–460.

Carskadon, M. A., & Mancuso, J. (1988). Daytime sleepiness in high school adolescents: Influence of curfew. *Sleep Research, 17,* 75.

Carskadon, M. A., Viera, C., & Acebo, C. (1993). Associations between puberty and delayed phase preference. *Sleep, 16,* 258–262.

Carver, V. C., Kittleson, M. J., & Lacey, E. P. (1990). Adolescent pregnancy: A reason to examine gender knowledge in sexual knowledge, attitudes and behavior. *Health Values, 14,* 24–29.

Case, R. (1998). The development of conceptual structures. In W. Damon (Ed.), D. Kuhn, & R. S. Siegler (Vol. Eds.), *Handbook of child psychology* (5th ed., Vol. 2, pp. 745–801). New York: Wiley.

Casey-Cannon, S., Hayward, C., & Gowen, K. (2001). Middle-school girls' reports of peer victimization: Concerns, consequences, and implications. *Professional School Counseling, 5,* 138–148.

Cash, T. F., & Henry, P. E. (1995). Women's body images: The results of a national survey in the USA. *Sex Roles, 33,* 19–28.

Cash, T. F., & Hicks, K. L. (1990). Being fat versus thinking fat: Relationships with body image, eating behaviors, and well being. *Cognitive Therapy and Research, 14,* 327–341.

Cash, T. F., Winstead, B. A., & Janda, L. H. (1986). The great American shape-up: Body image survey report. *Psychology Today, 20,* 30–37.

Casper, L. M. (1990). Does family interaction prevent adolescent pregnancy? *Family Planning Perspectives, 22,* 109–114.

Caspi, A., Elder, G. H., Jr., & Bem, D. J. (1988). Moving away from the world: Life-course patterns of shy children. *Developmental Psychology, 24,* 824–831.

Caspi, A., Lynam, D., Moffitt, T. E., & Silva, P. A. (1993). Unraveling girls' delinquency: Biological, dispositional, and contextual contributions to adolescent misbehavior. *Developmental Psychology, 29,* 19–30.

Caspi, A., & Moffitt, T. E. (1991). Individual differences are accentuated during periods of social change: The sample case of girls at puberty. *Journal of Personality and Social Psychology, 61,* 157–168.

Cassell, C. (2002). Let it shine: Promoting school success, life aspirations to prevent school-age parenthood. *SIECUS Report, 30,* 7–13.

Cassidy, L., & Hurrell, R. M. (1995). The influence of victim's attire on adolescent's judgments of date rape. *Adolescence, 30,* 319–323.

Catalano, R. F., & Hawkins, J. D. (1995). *Risk focused prevention: Using the social development strategy.* Seattle, WA: Developmental Research and Programs.

Catania, A. C. (1998). *Learning* (4th ed.). Upper Saddle River, NJ: Prentice Hall.

Cauffman, E., & Steinberg, L. (1996). Interactive effects of menarcheal status and dating on dieting and disordered eating among adolescent girls. *Developmental Psychology, 32,* 631–635.

Caya, M. L., & Liem, J. H. (1998). The role of sibling support in high-conflict families. *American Journal of Orthopsychiatry, 68,* 327–333.

Center on Addiction and Substance Use. (1995, August 2). A matter of opinion. *Education Week,* p. 4.

Centers for Disease Control. (1991). Dieting and purging behavior in black and white high school students. *JADA, 92,* 306–312.

Centers for Disease Control and Prevention. (1992). Selected behaviors that increase risk for HIV infection among high school students—United States, 1990. *Morbidity and Mortality Weekly Report, 41,* 237–240.

Centers for Disease Control and Prevention. (1995, March 24). CDC surveillance summaries. *Morbidity and Mortality Weekly Report, 44,* 289–291.

Centers for Disease Control and Prevention. (1998a). Incidence and initiation of cigarette smoking-United States, 1965–1996, *Morbidity and Mortality Weekly Report, 47,* 837–840.

Centers for Disease Control and Prevention. (1998b). Trends in sexual risk behaviors among high school students—United States, 1991–1997. *Morbidity and Mortality Weekly Report, 47,* 749–752.

Centers for Disease Control and Prevention. (2000a, June 8). CDC growth charts. *Advance Data,* No. 314.

Centers for Disease Control and Prevention. (2000b, June 9). *Youth Risk Behavior Surveillance—United States.* Retrieved July 31, 2002, from http://www.cdc.gov/mmwr/preview/mmwrhtml/ss4905a1.htm

Centers for Disease Control and Prevention. (2000c, December). World AIDS Day. *Morbidity and Mortality Weekly Report, 49,* 1–24.

Centers for Disease Control and Prevention. (2001, July 24). The Global HIV and AIDS Epidemic, 2001. *Morbidity and Mortality Weekly Report, 50,* 434–439.

Chadwick, B. A., & Heaton, T. B. (1996). *Statistical handbook on adolescents in America.* Phoenix, AZ: Oryx.

Chambers, J. H., & Ascione, F. R. (1987). The effects of prosocial and aggressive video games on children's donating and helping. *Journal of Genetic Psychology, 148*, 499–505.

Chand, I. P., Crider, D. M., & Willets, F. K. (1975). Parent-youth disagreement as perceived by youth: A longitudinal study. *Youth and Society, 6*, 365–375.

Chandler, M., & Boyes, M. (1982). Social-cognitive development. In B. B. Wolman (Ed.), *Handbook of developmental psychology* (pp. 387–400). Englewood Cliffs, NJ: Prentice-Hall.

Chang, M. (1998, March/April). Trapped in the web. *Psychology Today,* 66–70.

Chao, R. K. (1994). Beyond parental control and authoritarian parenting style: Understanding Chinese parenting through the cultural notion of training. *Child Development, 65*, 1111–1119.

Chao, R. K. (2001). Extending research on the consequences of parenting style to Americans and European Americans. *Child Development, 72*, 1832–1844.

Chapin, J. R. (2000). Adolescent sex and mass media: A developmental approach. *Adolescence, 35*, 799–811.

Chapman, J. W. (1988). Cognitive motivational characteristics and academic achievement of learning disabled children: A longitudinal study. *Journal of Educational Psychology, 80*, 357–365.

Charney, D. A., & Russell, R. C. (1994). An overview of sexual harassment. *American Journal of Psychiatry, 42*, 155–162.

Chassin, L., Curran, P. J., Hussong, A. M., & Colder, C. R. (1996). The relation of parent alcoholism to adolescent substance use: A longitudinal follow-up study. *Journal of Abnormal Psychology, 105*, 70–80.

Chassin, L., Pillow, D., Curran, P., Molina, B., & Barrera, M. (1993). Relation of parental alcoholism to early adolescent substance use: A test of three mediating mechanisms. *Journal of Abnormal Psychology, 102*, 3–19.

Chassin, L., Presson, C. C., Montello, D., Sherman, S. J., & McGrew, J. (1986). Changes in peer and parent influence during adolescence: Longitudinal versus cross-sectional perspectives on smoking initiation. *Developmental Psychology, 22*, 327–334.

Chassin, L., Presson, C. C., Rose, J. S., & Sherman, S. J. (1996). The natural history of cigarette smoking from adolescence to adulthood: Demographic predictors of continuity and change. *Health Psychology, 15*, 478–484.

Chassin, L., Presson, C. C., Sherman, S. J., & Pitts, S. C. (2000). The natural history of cigarette smoking from adolescence to adulthood in a Midwestern community sample: Multiple trajectories and their psychosocial correlates. *Health Psychology, 19*, 223–231.

Chatterjee, C. (1999, September/October). Boys against girls. *Psychology Today,* p. 15.

Chen, X., Liu, M., & Li, D. (2000). Parental warmth, control, and indulgence and their relations to adjustment in Chinese children: A longitudinal study. *Journal of Family Psychology, 14*, 401–419.

Chen, X., Rubin, K. H., & Li, Z. (1995). Social functioning and adjustment in Chinese children: A longitudinal study. *Developmental Psychology, 31*, 531–539.

Cheng, K. (1999, October 11). *Mediaweek, 9*, 100.

Chess, S., & Thomas, A. (1984). *Origin and evolution of behavior disorders: From infancy to early adult life.* New York: Brunner/Mazel.

Chilcoat, H. D., Dishion, T. J., & Anthony, J. C. (1995). Parent monitoring and the incidence of drug sampling in urban elementary school children. *American Journal of Epidemiology, 141*, 25–30.

Children's Defense Fund. (1998). *The state of America's children.* Boston: Beacon Press.

Childress, A. C., Brewerton, T. D., Hodges, E. L., & Jarrell, M. P. (1993). The Kids' Eating Disorders Survey (KEDS): A study of middle school students. *Journal of the American Academy of Child and Adolescent Psychiatry, 32*, 843–850.

Chilman, C. S. (1983). *Adolescent sexuality in a changing American society* (2nd ed.). New York: Wiley.

Ching, C. L., & Burke, S. (1999). An assessment of college students' attitudes and empathy toward rape. *College Student Journal, 33*, 573–600.

Chiras, S. (1993). *Biology: The web of life.* St. Paul, MN: West.

Choi, C. Y., & Kane, P. (1999, October 9). China's one child family policy. *British Medical Journal, 319*, 992–995.

Chou, K. L. (1998). Effects of age, gender, and participation in volunteer activities on the altruistic behavior of Chinese adolescents. *The Journal of Genetic Psychology, 159*, 195–202.

Christensen, L. (1988). Deception in psychological research: When is its use justified? *Personality and Social Psychology Bulletin, 14*, 664–675.

Christenson, P. (1992). The effects of parental advisory labels on adolescent music preferences. *Journal of Communication, 42*, 106–114.

Christenson, P. G., & Roberts, D. F. (1998). *It's not only rock & roll: Popular music in the lives of adolescents.* Cresskill, NJ: Hampton Press.

Christiansen, K. O. (1977). A preliminary study of criminality among twins. In S. A. Mednick & K. O. Christiansen (Eds.), *Biosocial bases of criminal behavior* (pp. 89–108). New York : Gardner.

Christie, K. (2001). The middle level: More than treading water. *Phi Delta Kappan, 82*, 649–655.

Chubb, N. H., Fertman, C., & Ross, J. L. (1997). Adolescent self-esteem and locus of control: A longitudinal study of gender and age differences. *Adolescence, 32*, 113–130.

Church, M. A., Elliot, A. J., & Gable, S. L. (2001). Perceptions of classroom environment, achievement goals, and achievement outcomes. *Journal of Educational Psychology, 93*, 43–54.

Chusmir, L. H. (1990). Men who make nontraditional career choices. *Journal of Counseling and Development, 69*, 11–16.

Cicchetti, D., & Toth, S. L. (1998). Perspective on research and practice in developmental psychopathology. In W. Damon (Ed.), I. E. Sigel, & A. Renninger (Vol. Eds.), *Handbook of child psychology* (5th ed., Vol. 4, pp. 479–585). New York: Wiley.

Cillessen, A. H. N., Van Ijzendoorn, H. W., van Lieshout, C. F. M., & Hartup, W. W. (1992). Heterogeneity among peer rejected boys: Substyles and stabilities. *Child Development, 63*, 893–905.

Ciolli, R. (1999, September 7). Teens' unseemly web visits. *Newsday,* A17.

Cipriani, D. C. (1996). Stability and change in personality across the life span: Behavioral genetic versus evolutionary approaches. *Genetic, Social, and General Psychology Monographs, 122*, 57–74.

Clark, C. L., & Tam, T. (1998). Alcohol consumption among racial/ethnic minorities. *Alcohol Health & Research World, 22*, 233–241.

Clark, D. B., Smith, M. G., Neighbors, B. D., Skerlec, L. M., & Randall, J. (1994). Anxiety disorders in adolescence: Characteristics, prevalence, and comorbidities. *Clinical Psychology Review, 14*, 113–137.

Clark, M. L., Beckett, J., Wells, M., & Dungee-Anderson, D. (1994). Courtship violence among African American college students. *Journal of Black Psychology, 20*, 264–281.

Clark, R. M. (1983). *Family life and school achievement: Why poor Black children succeed in school.* Chicago: University of Chicago Press.

Clarke, G., Hops, H., Lewinsohn, P. M., Andrews, J., Seeley, J. R., & Williams, J. (1992). Cognitive-behavioral group treatment of adolescent depression: Prediction of outcome. *Behavior Therapy, 23*, 341–354.

Clarkin, A. J. (1997). Altered relations with peers: Peer-group affiliation, friendships, first love. In J. D. Noshpitz (Ed.), L. T. Flaherty, & R.M. Sarles (Vol. Eds.), *Handbook of child and adolescent psychiatry* (pp. 113–124). New York: Wiley.

Clasen, D. R., & Brown, B. B. (1985). The multidimensionality of peer pressure in adolescence. *Journal of Youth and Adolescence, 14*, 451–468.

Clingempeel, W. G., & Segal, S. (1986). Stepparent-stepchild relationships and the psychological adjustment of children in stepmother and stepfather families. *Child Development, 57*, 474–484.

Cloninger, C. R., Adolfsson, R., & Svrakic, N. M. (1996). Mapping genes for human personality. *Nature Genetics, 12*, 3–4.

Coard, S. I., Nitz, K., & Felice, M. E. (2000). Repeat pregnancy among urban adolescents: Sociodemographic, family, and health factors. *Adolescence, 35*, 193–201.

Coccaro, E. F., Kavoussi, R. J., Sheline, Y. I., Lish, J. D., & Csernansky, J. G. (1996). Impulsive aggression in personality disorder correlates with tritiated paroxetine binding in the platelet. *Archives of General Psychiatry, 53*, 531–536.

Coffey, P., Leitenberg, H., Henning, K., Bennett, R. T., & Jankowski, M. K. (1996). Dating violence: The association between methods of coping and women's psychological adjustment. *Violence and Victims, 11*, 227–242.

Cohen, K. M., & Savin-Williams, R. C. (1996). Developmental perspectives on coming out to self and others. In R. C. Savin-Williams & K. M. Cohen (Eds.), *The lives of lesbians, gays, and bisexuals: Children to adult* (pp. 113–151). Fort Worth, TX: Harcourt Brace.

Cohen, P., Cohen, J., Kasen, S., Velez, C. N., Hartmark, C., Johnson, J., et al. (1993) An epidemiological study of disorders in late childhood and adolescence. 1. Age- and gender-specific prevalence. *Journal of Child Psychology and Psychiatry and Allied Disciplines, 34,* 851–867.

Cohen, S., & Williamson, G. (1991). Stress and infectious disease. *Psychological Bulletin, 109,* 5–24.

Cohn, L., Adler, N., & Irwin, C. (1987). Body-figure preferences in male and female adolescents. *Journal of Abnormal Psychology, 96,* 275–279.

Coie, J. D. (1990). Toward a theory of peer rejection. In S. R. Asher & J. D. Coie (Eds.), *Peer rejection in childhood* (pp. 365–402). New York: Cambridge University Press.

Coie, J. D., & Dodge, K. A. (1998). Aggression and antisocial behavior. In W. Damon (Ed.) & N. Eisenberg (Vol. Ed.), *Handbook of child psychology* (Vol. 3, pp. 779– 862). New York: Wiley.

Coie, J. D., & Lenox, K. F. (1994). The development of antisocial individuals. In D. Fowles, P. Sutker, & S. Goodman (Eds.), *Psychopathology and antisocial personality: A developmental perspective* (pp. 45–72). New York: Springer.

Coie, J. D., Terry, R., Lenox, K., Lochman, J., & Hyman, C. (1995). Childhood peer rejection and aggression as predictors of stable patterns of adolescent disorder. *Development and Psychopathology, 7,* 697–713.

Cole, D. A. (1991). Change in self-perceived competence as a function of peer and teacher evaluation. *Developmental Psychology, 27,* 682–688.

Cole, D. A., Martin, J. M., Peeke, L. A., Seroczynski, A. D., & Fier, J. (1999). Children's over-and underestimation of academic competence: A longitudinal study of gender differences, depression and anxiety. *Child Development, 70,* 459–473.

Coleman, J. S. (1961). *The adolescent society.* New York: Free Press.

Coleman, M., Ganong, L. H., & Ellis, P. (1985). Family structure and dating behavior of adolescents. *Adolescence, 20,* 537–543.

Coles, R., & Stokes, G. (1985). *Sex and the American teenager.* New York: Harper & Row.

Coley, R. L. (1998). Children's socialization experiences and functioning in single-mother households: The importance of fathers and other men. *Child Development, 69,* 219–230.

Coley, R. L., & Chase-Lansdale, P. L. (1998). Adolescent pregnancy and parenthood: Recent evidence and future direction. *American Psychologist, 53,* 152–166.

Colin, V. L. (1996). *Human attachment.* New York: McGraw Hill.

Collins, N. L., & Read, S. J. (1990). Adult attachment, working models, and relationship quality in dating couples. *Journal of Personality and Social Psychology, 58,* 644–663.

Collins, W. A. (1990). Parent-child relationships in the transition to adolescence: Continuity and change in interaction, affect and cognition. In R. Montemayor, G. Adams, & T. Gulotta (Eds.), *Advances in adolescent development: Vol. 2. From childhood to adolescence: A transitional period?* (pp. 85–106). Beverly Hills, CA: Sage.

Collins, W. A., & Laursen, B. (1992). Conflict and relationships during adolescence. In C. U. Schantz & W. W. Hartup (Eds.), *Conflict in child and adolescent development* (pp. 216–241). Cambridge, MA: Cambridge University Press.

Collins, W. A., Laursen, B., Mortenson, N., & Ferriera, M. (1997). Conflict processes and transitions in parent and peer relationships: Implications for autonomy and regulation. *Journal of Adolescent Research, 12,* 178–198.

Collins, W. A., & Repinski, J. (1994). Relationships during adolescence: Continuity and change in interpersonal perspective. In R. Montemayor, G. R. Adams, & T. P. Gullotta (Eds.), *Personal relationships during adolescence* (pp. 7–36). Thousand Oaks, CA: Sage.

Colvin, C. R., Block, J., & Funder, D. C. (1995). Overly positive self-evaluations and its negative implications for mental health. *Journal of Personality and Social Psychology, 68,* 1152–1162.

Comer, R. J. (1995). *Abnormal psychology* (2nd ed.). New York: Freeman.

Commission on Skills in the American Workforce. (1990). *America's choice: High skills or low wages!* Rochester, NY: National Center on Education and the Economy.

Committee on Communications, American Academy of Pediatrics. (1989). The impact of rock lyrics and music videos on children and youth. *Pediatrics, 83,* 314–315.

Compas, B. E. (1987a). Coping with stress during childhood and adolescence. *Psychological Bulletin, 101,* 393–403.

Compas, B. E. (1987b). Stress and life events during childhood and adolescence. *Clinical Psychology Review, 7,* 275–302.

Comstock, G., & Paik, H. (1991). *Television and the American child.* San Diego, CA: Academic Press.

Conger, R. D., Conger, K. J., Elder, G. H., Lorenz, F. O., Simons, R. L., & Whitbeck, L. B. (1992). A family process model of economic hardship and adjustment of early adolescent boys. *Child Development, 63,* 526–541.

Conley, T. D., Jadack, R. A., & Hyde, J. S. (1997). Moral dilemmas, moral reasoning, and genital herpes. *The Journal of Sex Research, 34,* 256–267.

Connors, L. J., & Epstein, J. L. (1995). Parent and school partnerships. In M. H. Bornstein (Ed.), *Handbook of parenting* (Vol. 4, pp. 437–458). Mahwah, NJ: Erlbaum.

Constant, D., Sproull, L., & Kiesler, S. (1996). The kindness of strangers: On the usefulness of weak ties for technical advice. *Organization Science, 7,* 119–135.

Constantine, M. G., Erickson, C. D., Banks, R. W., & Timberlake, T. L. (1998). Challenges to the career development of urban racial and ethnic minority youth: Implications for vocational intervention. *Journal of Multicultural Counseling and Development, 26,* 83–95.

Constantino, J. N., Grosz, D., Saenger, P., Chandler, D. W., Nandi, R., & Earls, F. J. (1993). Testosterone and aggression in children. *Journal of the American Academy of Child and Adolescent Psychiatry, 32,* 1217–1222.

Conte, C. (1998). Technology in schools: Hip or hype? *Education Digest, 63,* 28–33.

Conte, R., & Andrews, J. (1993). Social skills in the context of learning disability definitions: A reply to Gresham and Elliott and directions for the future. *Journal of Learning Disabilities, 26,* 146–153.

Conway, F., & Siegelman, J. (1978). *Snapping: America's epidemic of sudden personality change.* Philadelphia: Lippincott.

Coogan, J. C., Bhalla, S. K., Sefa-Dedeh, A., & Rothblum, E. D. (1996). A comparison study of United States and African students on perceptions of obesity and thinness. *Journal of Cross-Cultural Psychology, 27,* 98–113.

Cooksey, E., Rindfuss, R., & Guilkey, D. (1996). The initiation of adolescent sexual and contraceptive behavior during changing times. *Journal of Health and Social Behavior, 37,* 59–74.

Cooley, C. H. (1902). *Human nature and the social order.* New York: Scribner.

Cooley, M. L., & Unger, D. C. (1991). The role of family support in determining developmental outcomes in children of teen mothers. *Child Psychiatry and Human Development, 21,* 217–234.

Cooney, T. M., & Smyer, M. A. (1991). Divorce (parental) during late adolescence. In R. M. Lerner, A. C. Petersen, & J. Brooks-Gunn (Eds.), *Encyclopedia of adolescence* (pp. 244–249). New York: Garland.

Cooney, T. M., Smyer, M. A., Hagestad, G. O., & Klock, R. (1986). Parental divorce in young adulthood: Some preliminary findings. *American Journal of Orthopsychiatry, 56,* 470– 477.

Cooper, C. R. (1988). Commentary: The role of conflict in adolescent-parent relationships. In M. R. Gunnar & W. A. Collins (Eds.), *21st Minnesota symposium on child psychology* (pp. 181–187). Hillsdale, NJ: Erlbaum.

Cooper, H. (1979). Pygmalion grows up: A model for teacher expectations, communication, and performance influence. *Review of Educational Research, 49,* 389–410.

Cooper, H. M., & Tom, D. Y. H. (1984). Teacher expectation research: A review with implications for classroom instruction. *Elementary School Journal, 85,* 77–89.

Cooper, H., Valentine, J. C., Nye, B., & Lindsay, J. J. (1999). Relationships between five after-school activities and academic achievement. *Journal of Educational Psychology, 91,* 369–378.

Cooper, J., & Mackie, D. (1986). Video games and aggression in children. *Journal of Applied Social Psychology, 16,* 726–744.

Cooper, M. L., Shaver, P. R., & Collins, R. (1998). Attachment styles, emotional regulation, and adjustment in adolescence. *Journal of Personality and Social Psychology, 74,* 1380–1397.

Cooper, P. J., & Goodyer, I. M. (1993). A community study of depression in adolescent girls: I and II. *British Journal of Psychiatry, 163,* 369–374, 379–380.

Cooper, S., & Robinson, D. (1989). Childhood play activities of women and men entering engineering and science careers. *School Counselor, 36,* 338–342.

Corcoran, M. E., & Kunz, J. P. (1997, June 1). Do unmarried births among African- American teens lead to adult poetry? *Social Service Review, 71,* 275–289.

Costa, P. T., Terracciano, A., & McCrae, R. R. (2001). Gender differences in personality traits across cultures: Robust and surprising findings. *Journal of Personality and Social Psychology, 81,* 322–331.

Coughlin, C., & Vuchinich, S. (1996). Family experience in preadolescence and the development of male delinquency. *Journal of Marriage and the Family, 58,* 491–502.

Covington, M. V. (1984). The self-worth theory of achievement motivation: Findings and applications. *Elementary School Journal, 85,* 5–20.

Covington, M. V. (2000). Goal theory, motivation, and school achievement: An integrative review. *Annual Review of Psychology, 51,* 171–200.

Cowan, G., Drinkard, J., & MacGavin, L., (1984). The effects of target, age, and gender on use of power strategies. *Journal of Personality and Social Psychology, 47,* 1391–1398.

Cowan, P. A., Powell, D., & Cowan, C. P. (1998). Parenting interventions: A family systems perspective. In W. Damon (Ed.), I. E. Sigel, & K. A. Renninger (Vol. Eds.), *Handbook of child psychology* (5th ed., Vol. 4, pp. 3–72). New York: Wiley.

Cox, F. D. (1990). *Human intimacy: Marriage, the family and its meaning.* St. Paul, MN: West.

CQ Researcher. (1997, September 26). Why physical activity drops in adolescence. *CQ Researcher, 7,* 852–854.

Cradler, J., McNabb, M., Freeman, M., & Burchett, R. (2002). How does technology influence student learning? *Learning & Leading with Technology, 29,* 46–51.

Crain, R. M. (1996). The influences of age, race, and gender on child and adolescent multidimensional self-concept. In B. A. Bracken (Ed.), *Handbook of self-concept* (pp. 395–420). New York: Wiley.

Crain, W. (1992). *Theories of development: Concepts and applications* (2nd ed.). Englewood Cliffs, NJ: Prentice Hall.

Crain, W. (2000). *Theories of development: Concepts and applications* (4th ed.). Upper Saddle River, NJ: Prentice Hall.

Cravatta, M. (1997, August). Online adolescents. *American Demographics, 27.*

Crick, N. R., & Bigbee, M. A. (1998). Relational and overt forms of peer victimization: A multi-informant approach. *Journal of Consulting and Clinical Psychology, 66,* 337–347.

Crick, N. R., & Dodge, K. A. (1994). A review and reformulation of social information- processing mechanisms in children's social adjustment. *Psychological Bulletin, 115,* 74–101.

Crick, N. R., & Dodge, K. A. (1996). Social information-processing mechanisms in reactive and proactive aggression. *Child Development, 67,* 993–1002.

Cronbach, L. J. (1970). *Essentials of psychological testing* (3rd edition). New York: Harper & Row.

Cropley, A. J. (1999). Creativity and cognition: Producing effective novelty. *Roeper Review, 21,* 253–267.

Crosbie-Burnett, M., & Giles-Sims, J. (1994). Adolescent adjustment to stepparenting styles. *Family Relations, 43,* 394–399.

Cross, B. (1997). Self-esteem and curriculum: Perspectives from urban teachers. *Journal of Curriculum and Supervision, 13,* 70–92.

Cross, H. J., & Allen, J. G. (1970). Ego identity status, adjustment and academic achievement. *Journal of Counseling and Clinical Psychology, 34,* 288.

Cross, W. (1985). Black identity: Rediscovery of the distinction between personal identity and reference group orientation. In M. B. Spencer, G. C. Brookings, & W. R. Allen (Eds.), *Beginnings: The social and affective development of black children* (pp. 155–171). Hillsdale, NJ: Erlbaum.

Crouter, A. C., MacDermid, S. M., McHale, S. M., & Perry-Jenkins, M. (1990). Parental monitoring and perceptions of children's school performance and conduct in dual- and single-earner families. *Developmental Psychology, 26,* 649–657.

Crowell, A. (1996, August). Minor restrictions: The challenge of juvenile curfews. *Public Management,* 4–12.

Csikszentmihalyi, M. (1988). The flow experience and its significance for human psychology. In M. Csikszentmihalyi & I. S. Csikszentmihalyi (Eds.), *Optimal experience* (pp. 15–31). New York: Cambridge University Press.

Csikszentmihalyi, M., & Epstein, R. (1999, July). A creative dialog. *Psychology Today,* pp. 58–60.

Csikszentmihalyi, M., & Larson, R. (1984). *Being adolescent: Conflict and growth in the teenage years.* New York: Basic Books.

Cuban, L. (1999). High-tech schools, low-tech teaching. *Education Digest, 64,* 53–54.

Cuijpers, P. (1998). A psychoeducational approach to the treatment of depression: a meta-analysis of Lewinsohn's "coping with depression course." *Behavior Therapy, 29,* 52–65.

Culp, R. E., Culp, A. M., Osofsky, J. D., & Osofsky, H. (1991). Adolescent and older mothers' interaction with their six-month-old infants. *Journal of Adolescence, 14,* 195–200.

Cummings, M. R. (1995). *Human heredity: Principles and issues* (3rd ed.). St. Paul, MN: West.

Curran, C. P. (1998). *Sexually transmitted diseases.* Springfield, NJ: Enslow Publishers, Inc.

Curran, P. J., Stice, E., & Chassin, L. (1997). The relation between adolescent alcohol use and peer alcohol use: A longitudinal random coefficients model. *Journal of Counseling and Clinical Psychology, 65,* 130–140.

Curry, G. D., Ball, R. A., & Decker, S. H. (1996). *Estimating the national scope of gang crime from law enforcement data: Research in brief* [NCJ 161317]. Washington, DC: U.S. Department of Justice, Office of Justice Programs, National Institute of Justice.

Curry, G. D., & Decker, S. H. (1998). *Confronting gangs: Crime and community.* Los Angeles, CA: Roxbury.

Curtner-Smith, M. E. (2000). Mechanisms by which family processes contribute to school-age boy's bullying. *Child Study Journal, 30,* 169–175.

Curtner-Smith, M. E., & MacKinnon-Lewis, C. E. (1994). Family process effects on adolescent males' susceptibility to antisocial peer pressure. *Family Relations, 43,* 462–468.

Cutler, G. B., Jr. (1991). Adrenarche. In R. M. Lerner, A. C. Petersen, & J. Brooks-Gunn (Eds.), *Encyclopedia of adolescence* (pp. 14–17). New York Wiley.

Cyranowski, J. M., Frank, E., Young, E., & Shear, K (2000). Adolescent onset of the gender difference in lifetime rates of major depression: A theoretical model. *Archives of General Psychiatry, 57,* 21–27.

D'Amico, R. (1984). Does employment during high school impair academic progress? *Sociology of Education, 57,* 152–164.

Dahl, R. E. (2001). Affect regulation, brain development, and behavioral/emotional health in adolescence. *CNS Spectrum,* 60–72.

Damon, W., & Gregory, A. (1997). The Youth Charter: Towards the formation of adolescent moral identity. *Journal of Moral Education, 26,* 117–130.

Damon, W., & Hart, D. (1982). The development of self-understanding from infancy through adolescence. *Child Development, 53,* 841–864.

Dare, C., LeGrange, D., Eisler, I., & Rutherford, J. (1994). Redefining the psychosomatic family: Family process of 26 eating disordered families. *International Journal of Eating Disorders, 16,* 211–226.

Darling, C. A., & Davidson, J. K. (1986). Coitally active university students: Sexual behaviors, concerns, and challenges. *Adolescence, 21,* 403–419.

Dasen, P., & Heron, A. (1981). Cross-cultural tests of Piaget's theory. In H. C. Triandis & A. Heron (Eds.), *Handbook of cross-cultural psychology* (Vol. 4, pp. 295–343). Boston: Allyn & Bacon.

Dasgupta, S. D. (1998). Gender roles and cultural continuity in the Asian Indian immigrant community in the U.S. *Sex Roles, 38,* 95–117.

Davies, J., & Brember, L. (1995). Change in self-esteem between year 2 and year 6: A longitudinal study. *Educational Psychology, 15,* 171–181.

Davies, P. T., & Windle, M. (1997). Gender-specific pathways between maternal depressive symptoms, family discord, and adolescent adjustment. *Developmental Psychology, 33,* 657–668.

Davis, C., Fox, J., Brewer, H., & Ratusny, D. (1996). Motivations to exercise as a function of personality characteristics, age, and gender. *Personality and Individual Differences, 19,* 165–174.

Davis, S., & Mares, M. L. (1998). Effects of talk show viewing on adolescents. *Journal of Communication, 48,* 69–86.

Davis, S. F., Noble, L. M., Zak, E. N., & Dreyer, K. K. (1994). A comparison of cheating and learning/grade orientation in American and Australian college students. *College Student Journal, 28,* 353–356.

Davison, G. C., & Neale, J. M. (2003). *Abnormal psychology* (9th ed.). New York: Wiley.

Dawkins, M. P. (1997). Drug use and violent crime among adolescents. *Adolescence, 32,* 395–405.

Day, J. (2000, February 18). One year ago: Teen online spending increases. *E-Commerce Times.* Retrieved July 18, 2002, from http://www.Ecommercetimes.com/news/articles2000/000218-tc.shtml

Day, S. X., & Rounds, J. (2000). Universality of vocational interest structure among racial and ethnic minorities. *American Psychologist, 53,* 728–736.

Day, S. X., Rounds, J., & Swaney, K. (1998). The structure of vocational interests for diverse racial-ethnic groups. *Psychological Science, 9,* 40–44.

Dean, K. C., & Yost, P. R. (1991, February). *Synthesis of the research on, and a descriptive overview of Protestant, Catholic, & Jewish religious youth programs in the United States.* New York: Carnegie Council on Adolescent Development.

DeAngelis, T. (1994, December). Perceptions influence student drinking. *APA Magazine,* p. 35.

DeAngelis, T. (2002). A genetic link to anorexia. *APA Monitor, 33,* 34–36.

Deater-Deckard, K., Dodge, K. A., Bates, J. E., & Petit, G. S. (1996). Physical discipline among African American and European American mothers: Links to children's externalizing behaviors. *Developmental Psychology, 32,* 1063–1072.

DeBlassie, A. M., & DeBlassie, R. R. (1996). Education of Hispanic youth: A cultural lag. *Adolescence, 31,* 205–215.

de Bois-Reymond, M., & Ravelsloot, J. (1994). The role of parents and peers in the sexual and relational socialization of adolescents. In F. Nestmann & K. Hurrelmann (Eds.), *Social networks and social support in childhood and adolescents* (pp. 217–239). New York: de Gruyter.

deCharms, R. (1976). *Enhancing motivation: Change in the classroom.* New York: Irvington.

Decker, S. H., & Van Winkle, B. (1996). *Life in the gang: family, friends and violence.* New York: Cambridge University Press.

De Gaston, J. F., Weed, S., & Jensen, L. (1996). Understanding gender differences in adolescent sexuality. *Adolescence, 31,* 217–231.

De Haan, L., & Schulenberg, J. (1997). The covariation of religion and politics during the transition to young adulthood: Challenging global identity assumptions. *Journal of Adolescence, 20,* 537–552.

Dekovic, M., Noom, M. J., & Meeus, W. (1997). Expectations regarding development during adolescence: Parental and adolescent perceptions. *Journal of Youth and Adolescence, 26,* 253–273.

DeLamater, J., & Friedrich, W. N. (2002). Human sexual development. *The Journal of Sex Research, 39,* 10–15.

Delaney, C. H. (1995). Rites of passage in adolescence. *Adolescence, 30,* 891–898.

Delaney, P. (1995, January). Gangsta rappers vs. the mainstream black community. *USA Today Magazine, 123,* 68–70.

Delgado-Gaitan, C., & Trueba, H. T. (1985). Ethnographic study of participant structures in task completion: Reinterpretation of "handicaps" in Mexican children. *Learning Disabilities Quarterly, 8,* 67–75.

Delisle, J. R. (1992). *Guiding the social and emotional development of gifted children.* New York: Longman.

de Man, A. E. (1999). Correlates of suicide ideation in high school students: the importance of depression. *Journal of General Psychology, 160,* 104–114.

Demaria, T. P., Kassinove, H., & Dill, C. A. (1989). Psychometric properties of the Survey of Personal beliefs: A rational-emotive measure of irrational thinking. *Journal of Personality Assessment, 52,* 329–341.

Demo, D. H. (1997, Spring). Family type and adolescent adjustment. *Stepfamilies, 17,* 13–14.

Demo, D. H., & Acock, A. C. (1996). Family structure, family process, and adolescent well-being. *Journal of Research on Adolescence, 6,* 457–488.

Demo, D. H., & Savin-Williams, R. C. (1992). Self-concept stability and change during adolescence. In R. P. Lipka & T. M. Brinthaupt (Eds.), *Self-perspectives across the life span* (pp. 116–150). Albany: State University of New York Press.

Dennis, D., & Ballard, M. (2002, April/May). Ecstasy: It's the rave. *High School Journal, 85,* 64–71.

Desiderato, L. L., & Crawford, H. J. (1995). Risky sexual behavior in college students: Relationships between number of sexual partners, disclosure of previous risky behavior, and alcohol use. *Journal of Youth and Adolescence, 24,* 55–68.

Di Saia, J. (1990, February 9). Adolescents and their music: Paganini, satanists, and insider trading. *Journal of the American Medical Association, 263,* 812–814.

Diamond, C., & Buskin, S. (2000). Continued risky behavior in HIV-infected youth. *American Journal of Public Health, 90,* 115–117.

Dickinson, A. (2000, May 8). Video playground: New studies link violent video games to violent behavior. *Time, 155,* 100.

Dickover, R. E., Garratty, E. M., Herman, S. A., Sim, M. S., Plaeger, S., Boyer, P. J., et al. (1996, February 28). Identification of levels of maternal HIV-1 RNA associated with risk of perinatal transmission. *Journal of the American Medical Association, 275,* 599–605.

Diener, E., Sandvik, E., & Larsen, R. (1985). Age had sex effects for emotional intensity. *Developmental Psychology, 21,* 542–546.

Dietz, T. L. (1998). An examination of violence and gender role portrayals in video games: Implications for gender socialization and aggressive behavior. *Sex Roles, 38,* 425–442.

Dilorio, C., Kelley, M., & Hockenberry-Eaton, M. (1993). Communication about sexual issues: Mothers, fathers, and friends. *Journal of Adolescent Health, 24,* 181–189.

Dinh, K. T., Sarason, I. G., Peterson, A. V., & Onstad, L. E. (1995). Children's perceptions of smokers and nonsmokers: A longitudinal study. *Health Psychology, 14,* 32–40.

Dishion, T. J. (1990). The family ecology of boys' peer relations in middle childhood. *Child Development, 61,* 874–892.

Dishion, T. J., & Loeber, R. (1985). Adolescent marijuana and alcohol use: The role of parents and peers revisited. *American Journal of Drug and Alcohol Abuse, 11,* 11–25.

Dishion, T. J., & McMahon, R. J. (1998). Parental monitoring and the prevention of child and adolescent problem behavior. *Clinical Child and Family Psychology Review, 1,* 61–75.

Dishion, T. J., Patterson, G. R., & Reid, J. R. (1988). Parent and peer factors associated with drug sampling in early adolescence: Implications for treatment. In E. R. Rahdert & J. Grabowski (Eds.), *Adolescent drug abuse: Analyses of treatment research* (pp. 69–93). [NIDA Research Monograph No 77, DHHS Publication No. ADM88-1523]. Rockville, MD: National Institute on Drug Abuse.

Dittus, P., & Jaccard, J. (2000). Adolescents' perceptions of maternal disapproval of sex: Relationship to sexual outcomes. *Journal of Adolescent Health, 26,* 268–278.

Dobash, R. P., Dobash, R. E., Wilson, M., & Daly, M. (1992). The myth of sexual symmetry in marital violence. *Social Problems, 39,* 71–91.

Dodge, K. A. (1980). Social cognition and children's aggressive behavior. *Child Development, 51,* 162–170.

Dodrill, C. B., & Matthews, C. G. (1992). The role of neuropsychology in the assessment and treatment of persons with epilepsy. *American Psychologist, 47,* 1139–1142.

Dolan, C. V., & Molenaar, C. M. (1995). A note on the scope of developmental behavior genetics. *International Journal of Behavioral Development, 18,* 749–760.

Dolcini, M. M., Cohn, L. D., Adler, N. E., Millstein, S. G., Irwin, C. E., Kegeles, S. M., & Stone, G. C. (1989). Adolescent egocentrism and feelings of invulnerability: Are they related? *Journal of Early Adolescence, 9,* 409–418.

Dollinger, S. J., Horn, J. L., & Boarini, D. (1988). Disturbed sleep and worries among learning disabled adolescents. *American Journal of Orthopsychiatry, 58,* 428–434.

Dominick, J. R. (1984). Video games, television violence, and aggression in teenagers. *Journal of Communication, 34,* 136–147.

Donahue, M. J., & Benson, P. L. (1995a). Religion and adolescents. *Journal of Social Issues, 51,* 161–175.

Donahue, M. J., & Benson, P. L. (1995b). Religion and the well-being of adolescents, *Journal of Social Issues, 51,* 145–160.

Donaldson, S. I., Graham, J. W., Piccinin, A. M., & Hansen, W. B. (1995). Resistance-skills training and onset of alcohol use: Evidence for beneficial and potentially harmful effects in public schools and in private Catholic schools. *Health Psychology, 14,* 291–300.

Dondero, G. M. (1997, Winter). Mentors: Beacons of hope. *Adolescence, 32,* 881–887.

Donelson, E. (1999). Psychology of religion and adolescents in the United States: Past to present. *Journal of Adolescence, 22,* 187–204.

Dong, Q., Weisfeld, G., Boardway, R. H., & Shen, J. (1996). Correlates of social status among Chinese adolescents. *Journal of Cross-Cultural Psychology, 27,* 476–493.

Donohew, R. L., Hoyle, R. H., Clayton, R. R., Skinner, W. F., Colon, S. E., & Rice, R. E. (1999). Sensation seeking and drug use by adolescents and their friends: Models for marijuana and alcohol. *Journal of Studies on Alcoholism, 60,* 622–631.

Donovan, J. M. (1975). Identity status and interpersonal style. *Journal of Youth and Adolescence, 4,* 37–55.

Donovan, P. (1998a). The Colorado parental rights amendment: How and why it failed. *Family Planning Perspectives, 29,* 187–191.

Donovan, P. (1998b). Teenagers' right to consent to reproductive health care. *Issues in Brief.* Washington, DC: Alan Guttmacher Institute.

Doress, I., & Porter, J. N. (1978). Kids in cults. *Society, 15,* 69–71.

Dorman, S. M. (1997). Video and computer games: Effect on children and implications for health education. *Journal of School Health, 67,* 133–139.

Dornbusch, S. M., Ritter, P. L., Leiderman, P. H., Roberts, D. F., & Fraleigh, M. J. (1987). The relation of parenting style to adolescent performance. *Child Development, 58,* 1244–1257.

Dornbusch, S., Ritter, P., Leiderman, P., Roberts, D., & Fraleigh, M. (1987). The relation of parenting style to adolescent school performance. *Child Development, 58,* 1244–1257.

Dornbusch, S., Ritter, P. L., & Steinberg, L. (1991). Community influences on the relation of family statuses to adolescent school performance: Differences between African American and non-Hispanic whites. *American Journal of Education, 99,* 543–547.

Douvan, E., & Adelson, J. (1966). *The adolescent experience.* New York: Jossey-Bass.

Dowdy, B. B., & Kliewer, W. (1998). Dating, parent-adolescent conflict, and behavioral autonomy. *Journal of Youth and Adolescence, 27,* 473–492.

Doyle, J. A. (1985). *Sex and gender.* Dubuque, IA: Brown.

Drummond, R. J., & Ryan, C. W. (1995). *Career counseling: A developmental approach.* Englewood Cliffs, NJ: Merrill.

DuBois, D. L., Felner, R. D., Brand, S., Adan, A. M., & Evans, E. G. (1992). A prospective study of life-stress, social support, and adaptation in early adolescence. *Child Development, 63,* 542–557.

Dubow, E. F., & Luster, T. (1990). Adjustment of children born to teenage mothers: The contribution of risk and protective factors. *Journal of Marriage and the Family, 52,* 393–404.

Dubow, E. F., Tisak, J., Causey, D., Huyshko, A., & Reid, G. (1991). A two-year longitudinal study of stressful life events, social support, and social problems-solving skills: Contributions to children's behavioral and academic adjustment. *Child Development, 62,* 583–599.

Duckworth, E. (1964). Piaget rediscovered. In R. E. Ripple & V. N. Rockcastle (Ed.), *Piaget rediscovered: A report of the conference on cognitive skills and curriculum development.* Ithaca, NY: Cornell University, School of Education.

Duffy, M., & Gotcher, M. J. (1996). Crucial advice on how to get the guy: The rhetorical vision of power and seduction in the teen magazine YM. *Journal of Communication Inquiry, 20,* 32–48.

Dufresne, A., & Kobasigawa, A. (1989). Children's spontaneous allocation of study time: Differential and sufficient aspects. *Journal of Experimental Child Psychology, 47,* 274–296.

Duke, D. L., & Griesdorn, J. (1999, November/December). Considerations in the design of alternative schools. *The Clearing House, 73,* 89–92.

Duke-Duncan, P. (1991). Body image. In R. M. Lerner, A. C. Petersen, & J. Brooks-Gunn (Eds.), *Encyclopedia of adolescence* (pp. 90–94). New York Wiley.

Dumont, M., & Provost, M. A. (1999). Resilience in adolescents: Protective role of social support, coping strategies, self-esteem, and social activities on experience of stress and depression. *Journal of Youth and Adolescence, 28,* 343–361.

Duncan, O. D., Featherman, D. L., Brooks-Gunn, J., & Smith, J. R. (1998). How much does childhood poverty affect the life chances of children? *American Sociological Review, 63,* 406–423.

Duncan, P. D., Ritter, P. L., Dornbusch, S. M., Gross, R. T., & Carlsmith, J. M. (1985). The effects of pubertal timing on body image, school behavior, and deviance. *Journal of Youth and Adolescence, 14,* 227–235.

Dunkle, M. E. (1993). The development of students' understanding of equal access. *Journal of Law and Education, 2,* 283–300.

Dunlop, R., & Burns, A. (2001). Parent-child relations and adolescent self-image following divorce. *Journal of Youth and Adolescence, 30,* 117–132.

Dunn, H., & Plomin, R. (1990). *Separate lives: Why siblings are so different.* New York: Basic Books.

Dunn, J., & Kendrick, C. (1982). Siblings: Love, envy and understanding. Cambridge: Harvard University Press.

Dunphy, D. C. (1963). The social structure of urban adolescent peer groups. *Sociometry, 26,* 230–246.

Duran, R. P. (1989). Assessment and instruction of at-risk Hispanic students. *Exceptional Children, 56,* 154–159.

DuRant, R. H., Rich, M., Emans, S. J., Rome, E. S., Allred, E., & Woods, E. R. (1997). Violence and weapon carrying in music videos: A content analysis. *Archives of Pediatric and Adolescent Medicine, 151,* 443–448.

DuRant, R. H., Rome, E. S., Rich, M., Allred, E., Emans, S. J., & Woods, E. R. (1997). Tobacco and alcohol use behaviors portrayed in music videos: A content analysis. *American Journal of Public Health, 87,* 1131–1135.

Durkin, K. (1995). *Developmental social psychology.* Oxford: Blackwell.

Dweck, C. S. (1986). Motivational processes affecting learning. *American Psychologist, 41,* 1040–1048.

Dweck, C. S. (1989). Motivation. In A. Lesgold & R. Glaser (Eds.), *Foundations for a psychology of education* (pp. 87–136). Hillsdale, NJ: Erlbaum.

Dweck, C. S., & Leggett, E. L. (1988). A social-cognitive approach to motivation and personality. *Psychological Review, 95,* 245–273.

Dyk, P. H. (1993). Physiology and gender issues. In T. P. Gullotta, G. R. Adams, & R. Montemayor (Eds.), *Adolescent sexuality* (pp. 30–56). Newbury Park, CA: Sage.

East, P. L. (1996). The younger sisters of childbearing adolescents: Their attitudes, expectations, and behaviors. *Child Development, 67,* 267–282.

East, P. L., & Felice, M. E. (1996). Pregnancy risk among the younger sisters of pregnant and childbearing adolescents. *Journal of Developmental and Behavioral Pediatrics, 13,* 128– 136.

East, P. L., & Jacobson, L. J. (2001). The younger siblings of teenage mothers: A follow- up of their pregnancy risk. *Developmental Psychology, 37,* 254–264.

East, P. L., & Rook, K. S. (1992). Compensatory patterns of support among children's peer relationships: A test using school friends, nonschool friends, and siblings. *Developmental Psychology, 28,* 163–172.

Eccles, J. S. (1994). Understanding women's educational and occupational choices. *Psychology of Women Quarterly, 18,* 585–609.

Eccles, J. S., & Harold, R. D. (1993). Parent-school involvement during the early adolescent years. *Teachers College Record, 94,* 568–587.

Eccles, J. S., Midgley, C., Wigfield, A., Buchanan, C. M., Reuman, D., Flanagan, C., & MacIver, D. (1993). Development during adolescence: The impact of stage-environment fit on young adolescents' experiences in schools and in families. *American Psychologist, 48,* 90–101.

Eccles, J. S., Wigfield, A., Harold, R. D., & Blumenfeld, P. (1993). Age and gender differences in children's self and task perceptions during elementary school. *Child Development, 64,* 830–847.

Eccles, J. S., Wigfield, A., & Schiefele, U. (1998). Motivation to succeed. In W. Damon (Ed.) & N. Eisenberg (Vol. Ed.), *Handbook of child psychology* (5th ed., Vol. 3, pp. 1017–1095). New York: Wiley.

Eder, D. (1985). The cycle of popularity: Interpersonal relations among female adolescents. *Sociology of Education, 58,* 154–165.

Eder, D., & Kinney, D. A. (1995). The effect of middle school extracurricular activities on adolescents' popularity and peer status. *Youth and Society, 26,* 298–324.

Edmonds, P. (1995, November 29). They're lost in the system and out on their own. *USA Today,* p. A6.

Edmondson, B. (1997, February). Asian Americans in 2001. *American Demographics,* 8–9.

Educational Testing Service. (1995). *Dreams deferred: High school dropouts in the United States.* Princeton, NJ: Author.

Edwards, A., & Polite, C. (1992). *Children of the dream: The psychology of Black success.* New York: Bantam.

Egan, S. K., Monson, T. C., & Perry, D. G. (1998). Social-cognitive influences on change in aggression over time. *Developmental Psychology, 34,* 996–1006.

Egli, E. A., & Meyers, L. S. (1984). The role of video game playing in adolescent life: Is there a reason to be concerned? *Bulletin of the Psychonomic Society, 22,* 309–312.

Eidelberg, L. (Ed.). (1968). *The encyclopedia of psychoanalysis.* New York: The Free Press.

Eisele, J., Hertsgaard, D., & Light, H. K. (1986). Factors related to eating disorders in young adolescent girls. *Adolescence, 21,* 283–290.

Eisenberg, N. (1986). *Altruistic emotion, cognition and behavior.* Hillsdale, NJ: Erlbaum.

Eisenberg, N. (1990). Prosocial development in early and mid-adolescence. In R. Montemayor, G. R. Adams, & P. T. Gulotta (Eds.), *From childhood to adolescence: A transitional period?* (pp. 240–268). Newbury Park, CA: Sage.

Eisenberg, N. (1991). Prosocial development in adolescence. In M. Lerner (Ed.), *Handbook of adolescence* (pp. 845–855). New York: Wiley.

Eisenberg, N. (1992). *The caring child.* Cambridge: Harvard University Press.

Eisenberg, N., Carlo, G., Murphy, B., & Van Court, P. (1995). Prosocial development in late adolescence: A longitudinal study. *Child Development, 66,* 1179–1197.

Eisenberg, N., & Fabes, R. A. (1994). Mothers' reactions to children's negative emotions: Relations to children's temperament and anger behavior. *Merrill-Palmer Quarterly, 40,* 138–156.

Eisenberg, N., & Harris, J. D. (1984). Social competence: A developmental perspective. *School Psychology Review, 13,* 267–277.

Eisenberg, N., Miller, P. A., Shell, R., McNalley, S., & Shea, C. (1991). Prosocial development in adolescence: A longitudinal study. *Developmental Psychology, 27,* 849–857.

Eisenberg, N., & Mussen, P. H. (1989). *The roots of prosocial behavior in children.* New York: Cambridge University Press.

Eisenberg, N., Wolchik, S. A., Hernandez, R., & Pasternack, J. F. (1985). Parental socialization of young children's play: A short-term longitudinal study. *Child Development, 56,* 1506–1513.

Eisenberger, R., & Cameron, J. (1998). Reward, intrinsic interest, and creativity: New findings. *American Psychologist, 53,* 676–678.

Eisler, I., Dare, C., Hodes, M., Russell, G., Dodge, E., & Le Grange, E. (2001). Family therapy for adolescent anorexia nervosa: The results of a controlled comparison of two family interventions. *Journal of Child Psychology and Psychiatry, 41,* 726–736.

Eklin, C. H., & Roehlkepartain, E. C. (1992, February). The faith factor: What role can churches play in at-risk prevention? *Source Newsletter, 8,* 1.

Elder, G. H., Jr. (1974). *Children of the great depression.* Chicago: University of Chicago Press.

Elder, G. H., Jr. (1980). Adolescence in historical perspective. In J. Adelson (Ed.), *The handbook of adolescent psychology* (pp. 3–46). New York: Wiley.

Elia, J., Ambrosini, P. J., & Rapoport, J. L. (1999). Treatment of attention-deficit hyperactivity disorder. *New England Journal of Medicine, 340,* 780–788.

Elias, M. (1994, November 8). Fewer teens exercise their workout option. *USA Today,* 1D.

Elias, M. (1997a, August 11). Kids tend to take after oft-divorced parents. *USA Today,* 1D.

Elias, M. (1997b, April 1). Violence grows in teen relationships: Girls face more assaults than boys. *USA Today,* D1.

Elias, M. (1998, July/August). Mom-daughter generation gap shrinks. *USA Today,* 8D.

Elkin, I. (1995). Treatment of Depression Collaborative Research Program: Where we began and where we are. In A. E. Bergin & S. L. Garfield (Eds.), *Handbook of psychotherapy and behavior change* (4th ed., pp. 114–139). New York: Wiley.

Elkin, I., Parloff, M. B., Hadley, S. W., & Autry, J. H. (1985). NIMH Treatment of Depression Collaborative Research Program. *Archives of General Psychiatry, 42,* 305–316.

Elkind, D. (1967). Egocentrism in adolescence. *Child Development, 38,* 1025–1034.

Elkind, D. (1985). Egocentrism redux. *Developmental Review, 5,* 218–226.

Ellenbogen, S., & Chamberland, C. (1997). The peer relations of dropouts: A comparative study of at-risk and not at-risk youths. *Journal of Adolescence, 20,* 355–367.

Ellickson, P. L., & McGuigan, K. A. (2000). Early predictors of adolescent violence. *American Journal of Public Health, 90,* 566–572.

Elliot, A. J. (1997). Integrating the "classic" and "contemporary" approaches to achievement motivation: A hierarchical model of approach and avoidance achievement motivation. In M. Maehr (Ed.), *Advances in motivation and achievement* (Vol. 10, pp. 243–279). Greenwich, CT: JAI Press.

Elliot, A., & Church, M. (1997). A hierarchical model of approach and avoidance-achievement motivation. *Journal of Personality and Social Psychology, 72,* 218–232.

Elliot, A. J., McGregor, H. A., & Gable, S. L. (1999). Achievement goals, study strategies, and exam performance: A mediational analysis. *Journal of Educational Psychology, 91,* 549–563.

Elliott, D. S. (1994). Serious violent offenders: Onset, developmental course, and termination. The American Society of Criminology, 1993, presidential address. *Criminology, 32,* 1–21.

Elliott, E. S., & Dweck, C. S. (1988). Goals: An approach to motivation and achievement. *Journal of Personality and Social Psychology, 54,* 5–12.

Elliott, L. (1996, July/August). Things adolescent adoptees wish they knew about their birthparents but often are afraid to ask. *Adoptive Families, 29,* 21–24.

Ellis, B. J., & Garber, J. (2000). Psychosocial antecedents of variation in girl's pubertal timing: Maternal depression, stepfather presence, and marital and family stress. *Child Development, 71,* 485–501.

Elshtain, J. B. (1997, May 5). Heaven can wait. *New Republic, 216,* 23–24.

Elster, A. B., & Panzarine, S. (1983). Teenage father: Stresses during gestation and early fatherhood. *Clinical Pediatrics, 22,* 700–703.

Emery, R. E. (1982). Interparental conflict and the children of discord and divorce. *Psychological Bulletin, 92,* 310–330.

Emery, R. E. (1988). *Marriage, divorce, and children's adjustment.* Newbury Park, CA: Sage Publications.

Emery, R., & Forehand, R. (1994). Parental divorce and children's well-being: A focus on resiliency. In R. J. Haggerty, N. Garmezy, M. Rutter, & L. R. Sherrod (Eds.), *Stress, coping and development: Risk and resilience in children* (pp. 64–99). Cambridge, England: Cambridge Press.

Emler, N. (1996). How can we decide whether moral education works? *Journal of Moral Education, 25,* 117–126.

Emler, N. (2002). The costs and causes of low self-esteem. *Young Studies Australia, 21,* 45–49.

Emmons, L. (1996). The relationship of dieting to weight in adolescents. *Adolescence, 31,* 167–179.

Emslie, G. J., Rush, A. J., Weiberg, W. A., Kowatch, R. A., Hughes C. W., Carmody, T., & Rintelmann, J. (1997). A double-blind randomized placebo-controlled trial of fluoxetine in depressed children and adolescents. *Archives of General Psychiatry, 54,* 1031–1037.

Engels, R. C. M. E., Finkenauer, C., Meeus, W., & Dekovi, M. (2001). Parental attachment and adolescents' emotional adjustment: The associations with social skills and relational competence. *Journal of Counseling Psychology, 48,* 428–439.

England, E. M., & Petro, K. D. (1998). Middle school students' perceptions of peer groups: Relative judgments about group characteristics. *Journal of Early Adolescence, 18,* 349–373.

Ennett, S., & Bauman, K. (1994). The contribution of influence and selection to adolescent peer group homogeneity: The cause of adolescent cigarette smoking. *Journal of Personality and Social Psychology, 67,* 653–663.

Ennett, S. T., & Bauman K. E. (1996). Adolescent social networks: School, demographic, and longitudinal considerations. *Journal of Adolescent Research, 11,* 194–215.

Ensign, J., Scherman, A., & Clark, J. J. (1998). The relationship of family structure and conflict to levels of intimacy and parental attachment in college students. *Adolescence, 33,* 575–582.

Epstein, J. L. (1983a). Examining theories of adolescent friendships. In J. L. Epstein & N. Karweit (Eds.), *Friends in school: Patterns of selection and influences in secondary schools.* New York: Academic Press.

Epstein, J. L. (1983b). The influence of friends on achievement and affective outcomes. In J. L. Epstein & N. Karweit (Eds.), *Friends in school:*

Patterns of selection and influence in secondary schools (pp. 177–200). New York: Academic Press.

Epstein, L. H. (1987). Behavioral treatment of childhood obesity. *Psychological Bulletin, 101,* 331–342.

Epstein, L. H., Kilanowski, C. K., Consalvi, A. R., & Paluch, R. A. (1999). Reinforcing value of physical activity as a determinant of child activity level. *Health Psychology, 18,* 599–603.

Equal Employment Opportunity Commission. (1989). *Guidelines on discrimination because of sex.* 29 CFR 1604 11(a).

Erb, T. O. (2000). Do middle school reforms really make a difference? *The Clearing House, 73,* 194–201.

Erikson, E. H. (1950). *Childhood and society.* New York: Norton.

Erikson, E. H. (1958). *Young man Luther: A study of psychoanalysis and history.* New York: Norton.

Erikson, E. H. (1963). *Childhood and society* (2nd ed.). New York: Norton.

Erikson, E. H. (1968). *Identity: Youth and crisis.* New York: Norton.

Erikson, E. H. (1980). The problem of ego identity. *Identity and the life cycle* (pp. 108–131). New York: Norton. (Original work published 1958)

Eron, L. D. (1998, April). What becomes of aggressive schoolchildren. *Harvard Mental Health Letter, 14,* p. 8.

Eron, L. D., Huesmann, L. R., Brice, P., Fischer, P., & Mermelstein, R. (1983). Age trends in the development of aggression, sex typing, and related television habits. *Developmental Psychology, 19,* 71–78.

Eron, L. D., Huessmann, L. R., Dubow, E., Romanoff, R., & Yarmel, P. (1987). Aggression and its correlates over 22 years. In D. Crowell, I. Evans, & D. O'Donnell (Eds.), *Childhood aggression and violence* (pp. 249–262). New York: Plenum.

Esbensen, F., & Osgood, D. W. (1997). *National evaluation of G.R.E.A.T.: Research in brief* [NCJ167264]. Washington, DC: U.S. Department of Justice, Office of Justice Programs, National Institute of Justice.

Escamilla, G., Cradock, A. L., & Kawachi, I. (2000). Women and smoking in Hollywood movies: A content analysis. *American Journal of Public Health, 90,* 412–414.

Eshel, Y., & Kurman, J. (1994). Availability, similarity, and gender as determinants of adolescent peer acceptance. *Journal of Applied Social Psychology, 24,* 1944–1964.

Eshleman, J. R., & Cashion, B. G. (1983). *Sociology: An introduction.* Boston: Little Brown.

Etaugh, C., & Hughes, V. (1975). Teachers' evaluations of sex-typed behaviors in children: The role of teacher sex and school setting. *Developmental Psychology, 11,* 394–395.

Eure, C. R., Lindsay, M. K., & Graves, W. L. (2002). Risk of adverse pregnancy outcomes in young adolescent parturients in an inner-city hospital. American *Journal of Obstetrics and Gynecology, 186,* 918–921.

Evans, E. D., Rutberg, J., Sather, C., & Turner, C. (1991). Content analysis of contemporary teen magazines for adolescent females. *Youth and Society, 23,* 99–120.

Evans, G. D., & Rey, J. (2001). In the echoes of gunfire: Practicing psychologists' responses to school violence. *Professional Psychology: Research and Practice, 32,* 157–164.

Evans, K. M., & Larrabee, M. J. (2002). Teaching the multicultural competencies and revised career counseling competencies simultaneously. *Journal of Multicultural Counseling and Development, 30,* 21–40.

Evans, M. D. R., Kelley, J., & Wanner, R. A. (2001). Educational attainment of the children of divorce: Australia, 1940–1990. *Journal of Sociology, 37,* 275–300.).

Eveleth, P. B., & Tanner, J. M. (1990). *Worldwide variation in human growth* (2nd ed.). New York: Cambridge University Press.

Face up to sex education. (1993, June 8). *USA Today,* p. A12.

Fagot, B. I. (1995). Parenting boys and girls. In M. H. Bornstein (Ed.), *Handbook of parenting* (Vol. 1, pp. 163–183). Mahwah, NJ: Erlbaum.

Fahy, T. A., & Eisler, I. (1993). Impulsivity and eating disorders. *British Journal of Psychiatry, 162,* 193–197.

Fairburn, C. G., Jones, R., Pevel, R. C., Carr, S. J., Solomon, R. A., O'Connor, M. E., et al. (1991). Three psychological treatments for bulimia nervosa. *Archives of General Psychiatry, 48,* 463–469.

Falbo, T., & Polit, D. (1986). Quantitative review of the only child literature: Research evidence and theory development. *Psychological Bulletin, 100,* 176–190.

Falbo, T., & Poston, D. L., Jr. (1993). The academic, personality and physical outcomes of only children in China. *Child Development, 64,* 18–35.

Farber, P. (1998, July/August). Boston Renaissance Charter School. *The American Prospect, 39,* 48–61.

Farmer, H., Rotella, S., Anderson, C., & Wardrop, J. (1998). Gender differences in science, math, and technology careers: Prestige level and Holland Interest Type. *Journal of Vocational Behavior, 53,* 73–96.

Farmer, H. S., Wardrop, J. L., Anderson, M. Z., & Risinger, R. (1995). Women's career choices: Focus on science, math and technology careers. *Journal of Counseling Psychology, 42,* 155–170.

Farrington, D. (1988). Psychobiological factors in the explanation and reduction of delinquency. *Today's Delinquent, 7,* 37–51.

Farrington, D. P. (1989). Early predictors of adolescent aggression and adult violence. *Violence and Victims, 4,* 79–100.

Farrington, D. P. (1991). Childhood aggression and adult violence: Early precursors and later-life outcomes. In D. J. Pepler & K. H. Rubin (Eds.), *The development and treatment of childhood aggression* (pp. 5–29). Hillsdale, NJ: Erlbaum.

Farrington, D. P. (1995a). The development of offending and antisocial behaviour from childhood: Key findings from the Cambridge study in delinquent development. *Journal of Child Psychology and Psychiatry, 36,* 1–36.

Farrington, D. P. (1995b). Key issues in the integration of motivational and opportunity-reducing crime prevention strategies. In P. O. H. Wikstrom, R. V. Clarke, & J. McCord (Eds.), *Integrating crime prevention strategies: Propensity and opportunity* (pp. 333–357). Stockholm, Sweden: National Council for Crime Prevention.

Farrington, D. P. (1997). Early prediction of violent and nonviolent youthful offending. *European Journal on Criminal Policy and Research, 5,* 51–66.

Farrington, J. (1996). Stress and what you can do about it. *Current Health, 22,* 6–13.

Farrington, J. (1999, April). Are ads making you sick? *Current Health, 25,* 6–12.

Fashola, O. S., & Slavin, R. E. (1998). Schoolwide reform models: What works? *Phi Delta Kappan, 79,* 370–379.

Fay, R., Turner, C., Klassen, A., & Gagnon, J. (1989, January 20). Prevalence and patterns of same-gender sexual contact among men. *Science, 243,* pp. 338–348.

Federal Bureau of Investigation. (2001). *Uniform crime reports.* Washington, DC: Author.

Federman, J. (Ed.). (1997). *National television violence study: Vol. 2. Executive summary.* Santa Barbara: The Regents of the University of California.

Feeney, J. A., & Noller, P. (1991). Attachment style and verbal descriptions of romantic partners. *Journal of Social and Personal Relationships, 8,* 187–215.

Feingold, A. (1994). Gender differences in personality: A meta-analysis. *Psychological Bulletin, 116,* 429–456.

Feiring, C. (1996). Concepts of romance in 15-year-old adolescents. *Journal of Research on Adolescence, 6,* 181–200.

Feiring, C., Deblinger, E., Hoch-Espada, A., & Haworth T. (2002). Romantic relationship aggression and attitudes in high school students: The role of ender, grade, and attachment and emotional styles. *Journal of Youth and Adolescence, 31,* 373–386.

Feiring, C., & Lewis, M. (1993). Do mothers know their teenagers' friends? Implications for individuation in early adolescence. *Journal of Youth and Adolescence, 22,* 337–354.

Feiring, C., & Taska, L. S. (1996). Family self-concept: Ideas on its meaning. In B. Bracken (Ed.), *Handbook of self-concept* (pp. 317–373). New York: Wiley.

Feldlaufer, H., Midgley, C., & Eccles, J. (1988). Student, teacher, and observer perceptions of the classroom before and after the transition to junior high school. *Journal of Early Adolescence, 8,* 133–156.

Feldman, S., & Gehring, T. (1988). Changing perceptions of family cohesion and power across adolescence. *Child Development, 59,* 1034–1045.

Feldman, S. S., & Gowen, L. K. (1998). Conflict negotiation tactics in romantic relationships in high school students. *Journal of Youth and Adolescence, 27,* 691–717.

Feldman, S. S., & Quatman, T. (1988). Factors influencing age expectations for adolescent autonomy: A study of early adolescents and parents. *Journal of Early Adolescence, 8,* 325–343.

Feldman, S. S., Rubenstein, J. L., & Rubin, C. (1988). Depressive affect and restraint in early adolescence: Relationships with family structure, family process, and friendship supports. *Journal of Early Adolescence, 8,* 279–286.

Feldman, S. S., Turner, R. A., & Araujo, K. (1999). Interpersonal context as an influence on sexual timetables of youths: Gender and ethnic effects. *Journal of Research on Adolescence, 9,* 25–52.

Fennema, E. (1987). Sex-related differences in education: Myths, realities, and interventions. In V. Richardson-Koehler (Eds.), *Educators' handbook* (pp. 329–347). White Plains, NY: Longman.

Fergusson, D. M., Horwood, L. J., & Lynskey, M. T. (1995). The prevalence and risk factors associated with abusive or hazardous alcohol consumption in 16 year olds. *Addiction, 90,* 935–946.

Ferrari, M., & Sternberg, R. J. (1998). The development of mental abilities and styles. In W. Damon (Ed.), D. Kuhn, & R. S. Siegler (Vol. Eds.), *Handbook of child psychology* (5th ed., Vol. 2, pp. 899–947). New York: Wiley.

Fiedler, E. D., Lange, R. E., & Winebrenner, S. (2002, Spring). In search of reality: Unraveling the myths about tracking, ability grouping and the gifted. *Roeper Review, 24,* 108– 112.

Field, T., Lang, C., Yando, R., & Bendell, D. (1995). Adolescents' intimacy with parents and friends. *Adolescence, 30,* 133–141.

Filozof, M., Albertin, H. K., Jones, C. R., Steme, S. S., Myers, L., & McDermott, R. J. (1998). Relationship of adolescent self-esteem to selected academic variables. *Journal of School Health, 68,* 68–73.

Fine, M. A., & Kurdek, L. A. (1992). The adjustment of adolescents in stepfather and stepmother families. *Journal of Marriage and the Family, 54,* 725–736.

Finn, J. D. (1989). Withdrawing from school. *Review of Educational Research, 59,* 117–142.

Firestone, W. A. (1994). The content and context of sexuality education: An exploratory study in one state. *Family Planning Perspectives, 26,* 125–131.

Fischer, D., & Meyer, M. (1996, July 1). Let the good times roll: A surge in teenage spending is helping to keep the economy in gear. *U. S. News & World Report, 12,* 51–53.

Fischer, J. L., Sollie, D. L., & Morrow, K. B. (1986). Social networks in male and female adolescents. *Journal of Adolescent Research, 6,* 1–14.

Fischer, K. W. (1980). A theory of cognitive development: The control of construction of hierarchies of skills. *Psychological Review, 87,* 477–531.

Fishbein, W. (1997). But is it ethical to withhold treatment to which some children respond? *The Brown University Child and Adolescent Behavior Letter, 13,* 1–4.

Fisher, C. B., & Lerner, R. M. (1994). Foundations of applied developmental psychology. In C. B. Fisher & R. M. Lerner (Eds.), *Applied developmental psychology* (pp. 3–23). New York: McGraw-Hill.

Fisher, C. B., & Tryon, W. W. (1988). Ethical issues in the research and practice of applied developmental psychology. *Journal of Applied Developmental Psychology, 9,* 27–39.

Fisher, L. A., & Bauman, K. E. (1988). Influence and selection in the friend-adolescent relationship. *Journal of Applied Social Psychology, 18,* 289–314.

Fisher, S. (1994). Identifying video game addiction in children and adolescents. *Addictive Behaviors, 19,* 545–554.

Fitch, S. A., & Adams, G. R. (1983). Egoidentity and intimacy: Replication and extension. *Developmental Psychology, 19,* 839–845.

Fitzgerald, L. F., & Shulliman, S. L. (1993). Sexual harassment: A research analysis and agenda for the 1990s. *Journal of Vocational Behavior, 42,* 5–27.

Flannery, D. J., Singer, M. I., & Wester, K. (2001). Violence exposure, psychological trauma, and suicide risk in a community sample of dangerously violent adolescents. *Journal of the American Academy of Child and Adolescent Psychiatry, 40,* 435–447.

Flannery, D. J., Torquati, J. C., & Lindemeier, L. A. (1994) The method and meaning of emotional expression and experience during adolescence. *Journal of Adolescent Research, 9,* 8–27.

Flannery, D. J., Williams, L. L., & Vazsonyi, A. T. (1999). Who are they with and what are they doing? Delinquent behavior, substance abuse, and early adolescents' after-school time. *American Journal of Orthopsychiatry, 69,* 247–253.

Flavell, J. H., & Miller, P. H. (1998). Social cognition. In W. Damon (Ed.), D. Kuhn, & R. S. Siegler (Vol. Eds.), *Handbook of child psychology* (5th ed., Vol. 2, pp. 851–899). New York: Wiley.

Flavell, J. H., Miller, P. H., & Miller, S. A. (2002). *Cognitive development* (3rd ed.). Upper Saddle River, NJ: Prentice-Hall.

Flay, B. R. (1993). Youth tobacco use: Risks, patterns, and control. In J. Slade & C. T. Orleans (Eds.), *Nicotine addiction: Principles and management* (pp. 36–384). New York: Oxford University Press.

Fleith, D. (2000, April). Teacher and student perceptions of creativity in the classroom environment. *Roeper Review, 22,* 148–154.

Fleming, J., Boyle, M., & Offord, D. R. (1993). The outcome of adolescent depression in the Ontario Child health Study follow-up. *Journal of American Academy of Child and Adolescent Psychiatry, 32,* 28–33.

Fletcher, A. C., Darling, N. E., Steinberg, L., & Dornbusch, S. M. (1995). The company they keep: Relation of adolescents' adjustment and behavior to their friends' perceptions of authoritative parenting in the social network. *Developmental Psychology, 31,* 300–310.

Flick, L. (1999, June 5). It's back, big-time: Metal returns for a match with the mainstream. *Billboard, 11,* 4–10.

Fling, S., Smith, L., Rodriguez, T., Thornton, D., Atkins, E., & Nixon, K. (1992). Videogames, aggression, and self-esteem: A survey. *Social Behavior and Personality, 20,* 39–45.

Flores, L. Y., & O'Brien, K. M. (2002). The career development of Mexican American adolescent women: A test of social cognitive career theory. *Journal of Counseling Psychology, 49,* 14–27.

Floyd, F. J., Stein, T. S., Harter, K. S. M., Allison, A., & Nye, C. L. (1999). Gay, lesbian, and bisexual youths: Separation-individuation, parental attitudes, identity consolidation, and well-being. *Journal of Youth and Adolescence, 28,* 719–739.

Flum, H. (1994). Styles of identity formation in early and middle adolescence. *Genetic, Social and General Psychology Monographs, 120,* 435–467.

Ford, D., & Harris, J. J., III. (1996). Perceptions and attitudes of black students toward school achievement and other educational variables. *Child Development, 67,* 1141–1152.

Fordham, S. (1988). Racelessness as a factor in Black students' school success: Pragmatic strategy or pyrrhic victory. *Harvard Educational Review, 58,* 54–84.

Fordham, S. (1991). Peer-proofing academic competition among Black adolescents: "Acting white" Black American style. In C. E. Sleeter (Ed.), *Empowerment through multicultural education* (pp. 69–94). Albany: State University of New York Press.

Fordham, S., & Ogbu, U. (1986). Black students' school success: Coping with the burden of "acting white." *Urban Review, 18,* 176–206.

Forehand, R., Armistead, L., & David, C. (1997). Is adolescent adjustment following parental divorce a function of predivorce adjustment? *Journal of Abnormal Child Psychology, 25,* 157–164.

Forehand, R., Biggar, H., & Kotchick, B. A. (1998). Cumulative risk across family stressors: Short-and-long-term effects for adolescents. *Journal of Abnormal Child Psychology, 26,* 119–129.

Forehand, R., & Nousiainen, S. (1993). Maternal and paternal parenting: Critical dimensions in adolescent functioning. *Journal of Family Psychology, 7,* 213–221.

Forgan, J. W., & Vaughn, S. (2000). Adolescents with and without LD make the transition to middle school. *Journal of Learning Disabilities, 33,* 33–43.

Forgatch, M. S., Patterson, G. R., & Skinner, M. L. (1988). A mediational model for the effect of divorce on antisocial behavior in boys. In E. M. Hetherington & J. D. Arasteh (Eds.), *Impact of divorce, single parenting, and stepparenting on children* (pp. 135–155). Hillsdale, NJ: Erlbaum.

Forness, S. R., & Kavale, K. A. (1988). Psychopharmacological treatment: A note on classroom effects. *Journal of Learning Disabilities, 21,* 144–147.

Foshee, V., Bauman, K., Arriaga, X., Helms, R., Koch, G., & Linder, G. (1998). An evaluation of safe dates: An adolescent dating violence prevention program. *American Journal of Public Health, 88,* 45–53.

Foshee, V., Linder, G., Bauman, K., Langwick, S., Arriaga, X., Heath, J., McMahon, P., & Bangdiwala, S. (1996). The safe dates project: Theoretical basis, evaluation design, and selected baseline findings. *American Journal of Preventive Medicine, 12,* 39–47.

Foster, E. M. (1995). Why teens do not benefit from work experience programs: Evidence from brother comparisons. *Journal of Policy Analysis and Management, 14,* 393–414.

Foster, G. D., Wadden, T. A., & Vogt, R. A. (1997). Body image in obese women before, during, and after weight loss treatment. *Health Psychology, 16*, 226–229.

Fouad, N. A. (1995). Career behavior of Hispanics: Assessment and career intervention. In F. T. Leong (Ed.), *Career development and vocational behavior of racial and ethnic minorities* (pp. 165–191). Mahwah, NJ: Erlbaum.

Fowler, J. W. (1976). Stages in faith: The structural-developmental approach. In T. Hennessey (Ed.), *Values and moral development* (pp. 173–210). New York: Paulist Press.

Fowler, J. W. (1981). *Stages of faith: The psychology of human development and the quest for meaning.* San Francisco, CA: Harper & Row.

Fowler, J. W. (1991). The vocation of faith developmental theory. In J. W. Fowler, K. E. Nipkow & F. Schweitzer (Eds.), *Stage of faith and religious development: Implications for church, education, and society.* New York: Crossroad.

Fowler, J. W. (1996). *Faithful change.* Nashville, TN: Abingdon Press.

Francis, L. J. (1997). Coopersmith's model of self-esteem: Bias toward the stable extravert? *Journal of Social Psychology, 137*, 139–143.

Francis, L. J., & Pearson, P. R. (1987). Empathic development during adolescence: Religiosity, the missing ink? *Personality of Individual Differences, 8*, 145–148.

Franzoi, S. L., Davis, M. H., & Vasquez-Suson, K. A. (1994). Two social worlds: Social correlates and stability of adolescent status groups. *Journal of Personality and Social Psychology, 67*, 462–473.

Fraser, A. M., Brockert, J. E., & Ward, R. H. (1995). Association of young maternal age with adverse reproductive outcomes. *New England Journal of Medicine, 332*, 113–117.

Fraser, M. W. (1996). Cognitive problem solving and aggressive behavior among children. *Families in Society, 77*, 19–32.

Frazer, W. (1987). Teenage girls reading Jackie. *Media, Culture and Society, 9*, 407–425.

Frazier, H. (1999, January 21). Rising up against tracking. *Black Issues in Higher Education, 15*, 24.

Freedland, J., & Dwyer, J. (1991). Nutrition in adolescent girls. In R. M. Lerner, A. C. Petersen, & J. Brooks-Gunn (Eds.), *Encyclopedia of adolescence* (pp. 714–723). New York: Wiley.

Freedman, D. S., Khan, L. K., Serdula, M. K., Srinivasan, S. R., & Berenson, G. S. (2000). Secular trends in height among children during 2 decades. *Archives of Pediatrics and Adolescent Medicine, 154*, 15–22.

Freeman, M. (1997, February/March). Electronic media and how kids (don't) think. *Reading Today, 14*, 8–9.

French, D. C., Conrad, J., & Turner, T. M. (1995). Adjustment of antisocial rejected adolescents. *Development and Psychopathology, 7*, 857–874.

French, S. A., Perry, C. L., Leon, G. R., & Fulerson, J. A. (1995). Dieting behaviors and weight change history in female adolescents. *Health Psychology, 14*, 548–555.

Freud, A. (1946). *The ego and the mechanisms of defense.* New York: International Universities Press. (Original work published 1936)

Freud, A. (1958). Adolescence. *Psychoanalytic Study of the Child, 13*, 255–278.

Freud, A. (1963). The concept of developmental lines. *Psychoanalytic Study of the Child, 18*, 245–265.

Freud, S. (1933). *New introductory lectures on psychoanalysis.* New York: Norton.

Freud, S. (1949). *An outline of psychoanalysis.* New York: Norton. (Original work published 1940)

Freud, S. (1953). Three essays on the theory of sexuality. In J. Strachey (Ed.), *The standard edition of the complete psychological works of Sigmund Freud* (Vol. 7, pp. 125–254). London: Hogarth Press. (Original work published 1905)

Freud, S. (1961). *New introductory lectures on psychoanalysis.* New York: Norton. (Original work published 1933)

Freud, S. (1961). *The ego and the id.* New York: Norton. (Original work published 1923)

Freud, S. (1962). *Three essays on the theory of sexuality* (J. Strachey, Trans.). New York: Basic Books. (Original work published 1905)

Frey, D., & Carlock, C. J. (1989). *Enhancing self esteem.* Muncie, IN: Accelerated Development.

Fried, C. B. (1999). Who's afraid of rap: Differential reactions to music lyrics. *Journal of Applied Social Psychology, 29*, 705–721.

Friedland, M. T. (1999). Not disabled enough: The ADA's "major life activity" definition of disability. *Stanford Law Review, 52*, 171–205.

Friedman, A. S., Kramer, S., Kreisher, C., & Granick, S. (1996). The relationship of substance abuse to illegal and violent behavior, in a community sample of young adult African American men and women (gender differences). *Journal of Substance Abuse, 8*, 379–402.

Friedman, M. A., & Brownell, K. D. (1995). Psychological correlates of obesity: Moving the next research generation. *Psychological Bulletin, 117*, 3–20.

Friedman, R. C., & Downey, J. I. (1994). Homosexuality. *New England Journal of Medicine, 331*, 923–930.

Friedman, W. J., Robinson, A. B., & Friedman, B. L. (1987). Sex differences in moral judgments? A test of Gilligan's theory. *Psychology of Women Quarterly, 11*, 37–46.

Fritsch, E. J., Caeti, T. J., & Taylor, R. W. (1999). Gang suppression through saturation patrol, aggressive curfew, and truancy enforcement: A quasi-experimental test of the Dallas anti-gang initiative. *Crime & Delinquency, 45*, 122–140.

Fritz, G. K. (2001). Prevention of child and adolescent suicide. *The Brown University Child and Adolescent Behavior Letter, 17*, 8–10.

Frost, J. J., & Forrest, J. D. (1995). Understanding the impact of effective teenage pregnancy prevention programs. *Family Planning Perspectives, 27*, 188–195.

Fry, A. F., & Hale, S. (1996). Processing speed, working memory, and fluid intelligence: Evidence for a developmental cascade. *Psychological Science, 7*, 237–242.

Fuligni, A. J. (1998). Authority, autonomy, and adolescent-parent conflict and cohesion: A study of adolescents from Mexican, Chinese, Filipino, and European backgrounds. *Developmental Psychology, 34*, 782–792.

Fuligni, A. J., & Eccles, J. S. (1993). Perceived parent-child relationships and early adolescents' orientation toward peers. *Developmental Psychology, 29*, 622–632.

Fuligni, A. J., Eccles, J. S., Barber, B., & Clements, P. (2001). Early adolescent peer orientation and adjustment during high school. *Developmental Psychology, 37*, 28–36.

Fuligni, A. J., & Stevenson, H. W. (1995). Time use and mathematics achievement among American, Chinese, and Japanese high school students. *Child Development, 66*, 830–842.

Fuligni, A. J., Tseng, V., & Lam, M. (1999). Attitudes toward family obligations among American adolescents with Asian, Latin American, and European backgrounds. *Child Development, 70*, 1030–1044.

Fuller-Thompson, E., & Minkler, M. (2000). African American grandparents raising grandchildren: A national profile of demographic and health characteristics. *Health and Social Work, 25*, 109–115.

Fullerton, C. S., & Ursano, R. J. (1994). Preadolescent peer friendships: A critical contribution to adult social relatedness. *Journal of Youth and Adolescence, 23*, 43–63.

Funk, J. B., & Buchman, D. D. (1996). Playing violent video and computer games and adolescent self-concept. *Journal of Communication, 46*, 19–33.

Funk, J. R. (1993). Reevaluating the impact of video games. *Clinical Pediatrics, 32*, 86–90.

Furby, L., & Beyth-Marom, R. (1992). Risk-taking in adolescence: A decision-making perspective. *Developmental Review, 12*, 1–44.

Furman, W. (1995). Parenting siblings. In M. H. Bornstein (Ed.), *Handbook of parenting* (Vol. 1, pp. 143–162). Mahwah, NJ: Erlbaum.

Furman, W., & Buhrmester, D. (1985). Children's perceptions of the personal relationships in their social networks. *Developmental Psychology, 21*, 1016–1024.

Furman, W., & Buhrmester, D. (1992). Age and sex differences in perceptions of networks of personal relationships. *Child Development, 63*, 103–115.

Furman, W., & Wehner, E. A. (1994). Romantic views: Toward a theory of adolescent romantic relationships. In R. Montemayor, G. R. Adams, & T. P. Gullotta (Eds.), *Advances in adolescent development: Vol. 3. Relationships in adolescence* (pp. 168–195). Beverly Hills, CA: Sage.

Furnham, A., Titman, P., & Sleeman, E. (1994). Perception of female body shapes as a function of exercise. *Journal of Social Behavior and Personality, 9*, 335–352.

Furstenberg, F. F. (1976). The social consequences of teenage parenthood. *Family Planning Perspectives, 8*, 148–164.

Furstenberg, F. F. (1981). Implicating the family: Teenage parenthood and kinship involvements. In T. Ooms (Ed.), *Teenage pregnancy in a family context: Implications for policy* (pp. 131–165). Philadelphia: Temple University Press.

Furstenberg, F. F. (1987). The new extended family: The experience of parents and children after remarriage. In K. Pasley & M. Ihinger-Tallman (Eds.), *Remarriage and stepparenting* (pp. 42–61). London: Guilford Press.

Furstenberg, F. F., Brooks-Gunn, J., & Chase-Lansdale, L. (1989). Teenaged pregnancy and childbearing. *American Psychologist, 44,* 313–320.

Furstenberg, F. F., Brooks-Gunn, J., & Morgan, S. P. (1987). *Adolescent mothers in later life.* Cambridge: Cambridge University Press.

Gable, R. A., Hendrickson, J. M., Tonelson, S. W., & Van Acker, R. (2000). Changing disciplinary and instructional practices in middle school to address IDEA. *The Clearing House, 73,* 205–209.

Gaddis, A., & Brooks-Gunn, J. (1985). The male experience of pubertal change. *Journal of Youth and Adolescence, 14,* 61–69.

Gadzella, B. M., & Penland, E. (1995). Is creativity related to scores on critical thinking? *Psychological Reports, 77,* 817–818.

Gahlinger, P. M. (2002). *Illegal drugs/(2001).* Salt Lake City: Sagebrush Press.

Gainor, K. A., & Lent, R. W. (1998). Social cognitive expectations and racial identity attitudes in predicting the math choice intentions of black college students. *Journal of Counseling Psychology, 45,* 403–413.

Galambos, N. L., Almeida, D. M., & Petersen, A. C. (1990). Masculinity, femininity, and sex role attitudes in early adolescence: Exploring gender intensification. *Child Development, 61,* 1905–1914.

Gallup, G. H., & Bezilla, R. (1992). *The religious life of young Americans.* Princeton, NJ: Gallup International University.

Gallup News Service. (2000, November 10). *Adults and teenagers.* Princeton, NJ: Author.

Gallup Poll/Executive Summary (2000). *U. S. teens and technology.* Retrieved July 17, 2002, from http://www.nsf.gov/od/lpa/nstw/teenov.htm

Galotti, K. M. (1989). Gender differences in self-reported moral reasoning: A review and new evidence. *Journal of Youth and Adolescence, 18,* 475–487.

Galotti, K. M., & Kozberg, S. F., (1996). Adolescents' experience of a life-framing decision. *Journal of Youth and Adolescence, 25,* 3–17.

Gamoran, A., & Mare, R. (1989). Secondary school tracking and educational inequality: Compensation, reinforcement, or neutrality? *American Journal of Sociology, 94,* 1146–1183.

Garbarino, J. (1995). *Raising children in a socially toxic environment.* San Francisco: Jossey-Bass.

Garbarino, J. (1998, April 13). Asking the question why? *People Weekly, 49,* p. 107.

Garbarino, J. (1999). *Lost boys: Why our sons turn violent and how we can save them.* New York: Free Press.

Garbarino, J. & Bedard, C. (2001). *Parents under siege: Why you are the solution.* New York: Free Press.

Garbarino, J., Dubrow, N., Kostelny, K., & Pardo, C. (1996). *Children in danger: Coping with the consequences of community violence.* San Francisco: Jossey-Bass.

Garber, J., & Hilsman, R. (1992). Cognition, stress, and depression in children and adolescents. *Child Adolescent Psychiatric Clinics of North American, 1,* 129–167.

Garcia-Coll, C., Hoffman, J., & Oh, W. (1987). The social ecology of early parenting of Caucasian adolescent mothers. *Child Development, 58,* 955–964.

Garcia-Coll, C. T., Meyer, E. C., & Brillon, L. (1995). Ethnic and minority parenting. In M. H. Bornstein (Ed.), *Handbook of parenting* (Vol. 2, pp. 189–209). Mahwah, NJ: Erlbaum.

Gard, C. (2000). How to overcome shyness. *Current Health, 27,* 28.

Gardner, H. (1983). *Frames of mind.* New York: Basic Books.

Gardner, H. (1987). Beyond the IQ: Education and human development. *Harvard Educational Review, 57,* 187–193.

Gardner, H. (1993). *Multiple intelligences: The theory in practice.* New York: Basic Books.

Gardner, H. (1998). Are there additional intelligences? The cases for naturalistic, spiritual, and existential intelligences. In J. Kane (Ed.), *Edu-*

cation, information, and transformation (pp. 111–131). Englewood Cliffs, NJ: Prentice Hall.

Gardner, H. (1999). *Intelligence reframed.* New York: Basic Books.

Gardyn, R. (2000, April). You can't download a hug. *American Demographics, 22,* 12–15.

Gargiulo, J., Attie, I., Brooks-Gunn, J., & Warren, M. P. (1987). Girls' dating behavior as a function of social context and maturation. *Developmental Psychology, 23,* 730–737.

Garner, A., Sterk, H. M., & Adams, S. (1998). Narrative analysis of sexual etiquette in teenage magazines. *Journal of Communication, 48,* 59–78.

Garner, D. M., Fairburn, C. G., & Davis, R. (1987). Cognitive, behavioral treatment for bulimia nervosa: A criminal appraisal. *Behavioral Medicine, 11,* 398–431.

Garrett, B. (2003). *Brain and behavior.* Belmont, CA: Wadsworth.

Garrett, J. T., & Garrett, M. W. (1994). The path of good medicine: Understanding and counseling Native American Indians. *Journal of Multicultural Counseling and Development, 22,* 134–144.

Gaskill, F. W., & Brantley, J. C. (1996). Changes in ability and achievement scores over time: Implications for children classified as learning disabled. *Journal of Psychoeducational Assessment, 14,* 220–228.

Gati, I., Garty, Y., & Fassa, N. (1996). Using career-related aspects to assess person-environment fit. *Journal of Counseling Psychology, 43,* 196–206.

Gavin, L. A., & Furman, W. (1989). Age differences in adolescents' perceptions of their peer groups. *Developmental Psychology, 25,* 827–834.

Gavora, J. (1997, March/April). Courts cast pall over parental-rights bill. *Policy Review, 82,* 12–14.

Gawel, R. (1999). Web addiction. *Electronic Design, 47,* 32.

Ge, X., Conger, R. D., & Elder, G. H. (1996). Coming of age too early: Pubertal influences on girls' vulnerability to psychological distress. *Child Development, 67,* 3386–3400.

Geller, B., Reising, D., Leonard, H. L., Riddle, M. A., & Walsh, B. T. (1999). Critical review of tricyclic antidepressant use in children and adolescents. *Journal of the American Academy of Child and Adolescent Psychiatry, 38,* 513–516.

Gelman, D. (1993, November 8). Tune in come out. *Newsweek,* pp. 70–71.

Gerber, P. J., Ginsberg, R., & Reiff, H. B. (1992). Identifying alterable patterns in employment success for highly successful adults with learning disabilities. *Journal of Learning Disabilities, 25,* 475–487.

Gerbner, G., Grossman, L., Morgan, M., & Signorielli, N. (1994). Growing up with television: The cultivation perspective. In J. Bryant & D. Zillman (Eds.), *Media effects: Advances in theory and research.* Hillsdale, NJ: Erlbaum.

Geronimus, A. (1992). The weathering hypothesis and the health of African American women and infants: Evidence and speculation. *Ethnicity and Disease, 2,* 207–221.

Geronimus, A. T. (1996, August 12). Mothers of invention. *Nation, 263,* 6–8.

Giacopassi, D., & Vandiver, M. (1999). University students' perceptions of tobacco, cocaine, and homicide fatalities. *American Journal of Drug and Alcohol Abuse, 25,* 163–179.

Giancola, P. R. (1995). Evidence for dorsolateral and orbital prefrontal cortical involvement in the expression of aggressive behavior. *Aggressive Behavior, 21,* 431–451.

Giancola, P. R. (2002). Alcohol-related aggression during the college years, theories, risk factors and policy implications. *Journal of Studies on Alcohol, 63,* 129–140.

Gibb, G. D., Bailey, J. R., Lambirth, T. T., & Wilson, W. P. (1983). Personality differences between high and low electronic video game users. *Journal of Psychology, 114,* 159–165.

Gibbons, F. X., & Gerrard, M. (1995). Predicting young adults' health risk behavior. *Journal of Personality and Social Psychology, 69,* 505–517.

Gibbons, J. L., Stiles, D. A., & Shkodriani, G. M. (1991). Adolescents' attitudes toward family and gender roles: An international comparison. *Sex Roles, 25,* 625–643.

Gil, V. E., & Anderson, A. F. (1999, November). Case study of rape in contemporary China. *Journal of Interpersonal Violence, 14,* 1151–1172.

Gilbert, J. (1985). Mass culture and the fear of delinquency in the 1950s. *Journal of Early Adolescence, 5,* 505–516.

Gilligan, C. (1982). *In a different voice.* Cambridge: Harvard University Press.

Gilligan, C. (1988). Exit-voice dilemmas in adolescent development. In C. Gilligan, J. V. Ward, J. M. Taylor, & B. Badige (Eds.), *Mapping the moral domain*. Cambridge: Harvard University Press.

Gilligan, C. (1993). Joining the resistance: Psychology, politics, girls, and women. In L. Weis & M. Fine (Eds.), *Beyond silenced voices: Class, race and gender in United States schools* (pp. 143–168). Albany, State University of New York Press.

Gilligan, C., & Attanucci, J. (1988). Two moral orientations: Gender differences and similarities. *Merrill-Palmer Quarterly, 34*, 223–244.

Gilligan, C., Brown, L. M., & Rogers, A. G. (1990). Psyche embedded: A place for body, relationships, and culture in personality theory. In A. I. Rabin, R. A. Zucker, R. A. Emmons, & S. Frank (Eds.), *Studying persons and lives* (pp. 86–147). New York: Springer.

Gilligan, C., Lyons, N. P., & Hanmer, T. J. (Eds.). (1989). *Making connections: The relational worlds of adolescent girls at Emma Willard School*. Cambridge: Harvard University Press.

Ginorio, A., & Huston, M. (2000). *¡Sí, se puede! Yes, we can: Latinas in school*. Washington, DC: American Association of University Women.

Ginott, H. G. (1969). *Between parent and teenager*. New York: Macmillan.

Giordano, P. C., Cernkovich, S. A., Groat, H. T., Pugh, M. D., & Swinford, S. P. (1998). The quality of adolescent friendships. Long term effects? *Journal of Health and Social Behavior, 39*, 55–72.

Gladstone, T. R. G., & Kaslow, N. J. (1995). Depression and attributions in children and adolescents: A meta-analytic review. *Journal of Abnormal Child Psychology, 23*, 597–606.

Glasgow, K. L., Dornbusch, S. M., Troyer, L., Steinberg, L., & Ritter, P. L. (1997). Parenting styles, adolescents' attributions, and educational outcomes in nine heterogeneous high schools. *Child Development, 68*, 507–529.

Global Programme on AIDS. (1997). *Effects of sex education on young people's sexual behavior*. Geneva: World Health Organization, 1993.

Glover, R. W., & Marshall, R. (1993). Improving the school-to-work transition of American workers. In R. Takanishi (Ed.), *Adolescence in the 1990s* (pp. 130–152). New York: Columbia University, Teachers College Press.

Godenne, G. D. (1997). The college years: A final phase of adolescent development. In L. T. Flaherty & R. M. Searles (Eds.), *Handbook of child and adolescent psychiatry* (Vol. 3, pp. 431–438). New York: Wiley.

Goldberg, C. (1998, December 15). Children and violent video games: A warning. *New York Times, 148*, A16.

Goldenberg, R. L., & Klerman, L. V. (1995). Adolescent pregnancy—Another look. *New England Journal of Medicine, 332*, 1161–1162.

Goldsmith, H. H., Buss, K. A., & Lemery, K. S. (1997). Toddler and childhood temperament: Expanded content, stronger genetic evidence, new evidence for the importance of the environment. *Developmental Psychology, 33*, 891–905.

Goldstein, A. P., & Pentz, M. A. (1984). Psychological skill training and the aggressive adolescent. *School Psychology Review, 13*, 311–323.

Goldstein, S. (1993, December 18). Ratings for video game violence debates: VSDA proposes voluntary industry system. *Billboard, 105*, 6–8.

Goleman, D. (1995). *Emotional intelligence: Why it can matter more than IQ*. New York: Bantam.

Golish, T. D. (2000). Is openness always better?: Exploring the role of topic avoidance, satisfaction, and parenting styles of stepparents. *Communication Quarterly, 48*, 137–159.

Golub, S. (1983). *Periods: From menarche to menopause*. Newbury Park, CA: Sage.

Gonzales, N. A., Cauce, A. M., Friedman, R. J., & Mason, C. A. (1996). Family, peer, and neighborhood influences on academic achievement among African-American adolescents: One-year prospective effects. *American Journal of Community Psychology, 24*, 365–387.

Gonzalez, J., Field, T., Yando, R., Gonzalez, K., Lasko, D., & Bendell, D. (1994). Adolescents' perception of their risk-taking behavior. *Adolescence, 79*, 701–710.

Gonzalez, M. (1988, March). Teens tune out TV. *American Demographics, 10*, 20.

Good, T. (1981). Teacher expectations and student perceptions: A decade of research. *Educational Leadership, 38*, 415–421.

Goodman, G. S., Emery, R. E., & Haugaard, J. J. (1998). Developmental psychology and law: Divorce, child maltreatment, foster care, and adoption. In W. Damon (Ed.), I. E. Sigel & K. A. Renninger (Vol. Eds.), *Handbook of child psychology* (5th ed., pp. 775–874). New York: Wiley.

Goodnow, J. J. (1988). Parents' ideas, actions, and feelings: Models and methods from developmental and social psychology. *Child Development, 59*, 286–320.

Goodnow, J. J., & Burns, A. (1988). *Home and school: Child's eye view*. Sydney: Allen & Unwin.

Gordon, C. M., Carey, M. P., & Carey, K. B. (1997). Effects of a drinking event on behavioral skills and condom attitudes in men: Implications for HIV risk from a controlled experiment. *Health Psychology, 16*, 490–495.

Gorman, D. M. (1997, February). The failure of drug education. *The Public Interest, 129*, 50–61.

Gorsuch, R. A. (1988). The psychology of religion. In M. K. Rosenzweig & L. W. Porter (Eds.), *Annual review of psychology* (Vol. 39, pp. 201–223). Palo Alto, CA: Annual Reviews Inc.

Gottfredson, G. D., & Holland, J. L. (1989). *Dictionary of Holland occupational codes*. Odessa, FL: Psychological Assessment Resources.

Gottfried, A. E., Bathurst, K., & Gottfried, A. W. (1994). Role of maternal and dual-earner employment status in children's development: A longitudinal study from infancy through early adolescence. In A. E. Gottfried & A. W. Gottfried (Eds.), *Redefining families: Implications for children's development* (pp. 55–97). New York: Plenum.

Gottfried, A. E., Fleming, J. S., & Gottfried, A. W. (1998). Role of cognitively stimulating home environment in children's academic intrinsic motivation: A longitudinal study. *Child Development, 69*, 1448–1460.

Gottfried, A. E., Fleming, J. S., & Gottfried, A. W. (2001). Continuity of academic intrinsic motivation from childhood through late adolescence: A longitudinal study. *Journal of Educational Psychology, 93*, 3–13.

Gottfried, A. E., Gottfried, A. W., & Bathurst, K. (1995). Maternal and dual-earner employment status and parenting. In M. H. Bornstein (Ed.), *Handbook of parenting* (Vol. 2, pp. 139–160). New York: Wiley.

Gottman, J., & Mettetal, G. (1986). Speculation about social and affective development: Friendship and acquaintanceship through adolescence. In J. M. Gottman & J. G. Parker (Eds.), *Conversations with friends: Speculations on affective development* (pp. 192–240). Cambridge: Cambridge University Press.

Graber, J. A., Brooks-Gunn, J., Paikoff, R. L., & Warren, M. P. (1994). Prediction of eating problems: An 8-year study of adolescent girls. *Developmental Psychology, 30*, 823–834.

Graber, J. A., Brooks-Gunn, J., & Warren, M. P. (1995). The antecedents of menarcheal age: Heredity, family environments, and stressful life events. *Child Development, 66*, 346–359.

Graber, J. A., Lewinsohn, P. M., Seeley, J. R., & Brooks-Gunn, J. (1997). Is psychopathology associated with the timing of pubertal development? *Journal of the American Academy of Child and Adolescent Psychiatry, 36*, 1768–1777.

Graber, J. A., Petersen, A. C., & Brooks-Gunn, J. (1996). Pubertal processes: Methods, measures, and models. In J. A. Graber, J. Brooks-Gunn, & A. C. Petersen (Eds.), *Transitions through adolescence: Interpersonal domains and context* (pp. 23–54). Mahwah, NJ: Erlbaum.

Grace, N. C., Kelley, M. L., & McCain, A. P. (1993). Attribution processes in mother-adolescent conflict. *Journal of Abnormal Child Psychology, 21*, 199–212.

Graham, J. (1994, January 28). TV executives lash out at violence study. *USA Today*, D1.

Graham, J. W., Beller, A. H., & Hernandez, P. M. (1994). The effects of child support on educational attainment. In I. Garfinkel, S. S. McLanahan, & P. K. Robins (Eds.), *Child support and child well-being* (pp. 317–354). Washington, DC: The Urban Institute Press.

Grandparents who care. (1995, September 18). *U.S. News and World Report*, p. 41.

Grant, B. F., & Dawson, L. D. (1997). Age of onset of alcohol use and its association with DSM-IV alcohol abuse and dependence: Results from the National Longitudinal Alcohol Epidemiologic Survey. *Journal of Substance Abuse, 9*, 103–110.

Grant, K. E., & Compas, B. E. (1995). Stress and anxious-depressed symptoms among adolescents: Searching for mechanisms. *Journal of Consulting and Clinical Psychology, 63*, 1015–1012.

Grant Commission (William T. Grant Foundation Commission on Work Family and Citizenship). (1988). *The forgotten half: Non-college youth in America*. Washington, DC: William T. Grant Foundation.

Gray, W., & Hudson, L. (1984). Formal operations and the imaginary audience. *Developmental Psychology, 20,* 610–627.

Gray-Little, B., & Haldahl, A. (2000). Factors influencing racial comparisons of self-esteem. A quantitative review. *Psychological Bulletin, 126,* 26–54.

Green, R. (1987). *The "sissy boy" syndrome and the development of homosexuality.* New Haven, CT: Yale University Press.

Green, S. (2001). Systematic vs. individualistic approaches to bullying. *Journal of the American Medical Association, 286,* 787.

Greenbaum, B., Graham, S., & Scales, W. (1995). Adults with learning disabilities: Educational and social experiences during college. *Exceptional Children, 61,* 460–472.

Greenberg, J. S., Bruess, C. E., Mullen, K. D., & Sands, D. W. (1989). *Sexuality: Insights and issues.* Dubuque, IA: Brown.

Greenberger, E. (1984). Defining psychosocial maturity in adolescence. In P. Karoly & J. J. Steffen (Eds.), *Adolescent behavior disorders: Foundation and contemporary concerns* (rev. ed., p. 3039). Lexington, MA: D.C. Heath.

Greenberger, E., & Steinberg, L. D. (1986). *When teenagers work.* New York: Basic Books.

Greenfield, P. M. (1997). You can't take it with you: Why ability assessments don't cross cultures. *American Psychologist, 52,* 1115–1124.

Greenlee, S. P., Damarin, F. L., & Walsh, W. B. (1988). Congruence and differentiation among Black and White males in two non-college-degreed occupations. *Journal of Vocational Behavior, 32,* 298–306.

Greeson, L. E., & Williams, R. A. (1986). Social implications of music videos for youth: An analysis of the contents and effects of MTV. *Youth and Society, 18,* 177–189.

Gregory, R. J. (2000). *Psychological testing* (3rd ed.). Needham Heights, MA: Allyn & Bacon.

Gresham, F. M., & Elliott, S. N. (1989). Social skills deficits as a primary learning disability. *Journal of Learning Disabilities, 22,* 120–124.

Gresham, F. M., Lane, K. L., MacMillan, D. L., Bocian, K. M., & Ward, S. L. (2000). Effects of positive and negative illusory biases. *Journal of School Psychology, 38,* 151–175.

Grier, L. K., & Firestone, I. J. (1998). The effects of an intervention to advance moral reasoning and efficacy. *Child Study Journal, 28,* 267–280.

Griffin, N., Chassin, L., & Young, R. D. (1981). Measurement of global self-concept versus multiple role-specific self-concepts in adolescents. *Adolescence, 16,* 49–56.

Griffiths, M. D. (1991). Amusement machine playing in childhood and adolescence: A comparative analysis of video games and fruit machines. *Journal of Adolescence, 14,* 53–73.

Griffiths, M. D., & Hunt, N. (1998). Dependence on computer games by adolescents. *Psychological Reports, 82,* 475–480.

Grigal, M., Test, D. W., Beattie, J., & Wood, W. M. (1997). An evaluation of transition components of individualized education programs. *Exceptional Children, 63,* 357–373.

Grigorenko, E. L. (2000). Heritability and intelligence. In R. J. Sternberg (Ed.), *Handbook of intelligence* (pp. 53–91). Cambridge, England: Cambridge University Press.

Grimley, D. M., & Lee, P. A. (1997). Condom and other contraceptive use among a random sample of female adolescents: A snapshot in time. *Adolescence, 32,* 771–779.

Grinspoon, L., & Bakalar, J. B. (1997). Marijuana. In J. H. Lowinson, P. Ruiz, R. B. Millman, & J. G. Longrod (Eds.), *Substance abuse: A comprehensive textbook* (3rd ed., pp. 199–206). Baltimore, MD: Williams & Wilkins.

Groer, M. W., Thomas, S. P., & Shoffner, D. (1992). Adolescent stress and coping: A longitudinal study. *Research in Nursing and Health, 15,* 209–217.

Grogger, J., & Bronars, S. (1993). The socioeconomic consequences of teenage childbearing: Findings from a natural experiment. *Family Planning Perspectives, 25,* 156–161.

Grossman, J. B., & Garry, E. M. (1997). *Mentoring: A proven delinquency prevention strategy* [NCJ 164834]. Washington, DC: NCJRS.

Grotevant, H. D. (1987). Toward a process model of identity formation. *Journal of Adolescent Research, 2,* 203–222.

Grotevant, H. D. (1998). Adolescent development in family contexts. In W. Damon (Ed.) & N. Eisenberg (Vol. Ed.), *Handbook of child psychology* (5th ed., pp. 1097–1140). New York: Wiley.

Grotevant, H. D., & Cooper, C. R. (1985). Patterns of interaction in family relationships and the development of identity exploration in adolescence. *Child Development, 56,* 415–428.

Grotevant, H. D., & Cooper, C. R. (1986). Individuation in family relationships. *Human Development, 29,* 82–100.

Grube, E., & Grube, J. W. (2000). Adolescent sexuality and the media: A review of current knowledge and implications. *The Western Journal of Medicine, 172,* 210–214.

Grusec, J. E., & Goodnow, J. J. (1994). Impact of parental discipline methods on the child's internalization of values: A reconceptualization of current points of view. *Developmental Psychology, 30,* 4–19.

Guerra, N. G., & Slaby, R. (1990). Cognitive mediators of aggression in adolescent offenders: 2. Intervention. *Developmental Psychology, 26,* 269–277.

Guest, C. L. (2000). School-to-work program. *Education, 120,* 614–624.

Guetzloe, E. (1999). Violence in children and adolescents: A threat to public health and safety: A paradigm of prevention. *Preventing School Failure, 44,* 21–24.

Guilford, J. (1967). *The nature of human intelligence.* New York: McGraw Hill.

Guillen, E. O., & Barr, S. L. (1994). Nutrition, dieting, and fitness messages in a magazine for adolescent women, 1970–1990. *Journal of Adolescent Health, 15,* 464–472.

Guisinger, S., & Blatt, S. J. (1993). Individuality and relatedness: Evolution of a fundamental dialectic. *American Psychologist, 49,* 104–111.

Guitteau, J. (2002, May). Gaming gets serious. *American Demographics, 24,* 39–43.

Gump, L. S., Baker, R. C., & Roll, S. (2000). The moral justification scale: Reliability and validity of a new measure of care and justice orientation. *Adolescence, 137,* 67–76.

Gundry, L. K., & Kickul, J. R. (1996). Flights of imagination: Fostering creativity through experiential learning. *Simulation and Gaming, 27,* 334–349.

Gunter, B. (1998). Ethnicity and involvement in violence on television. *Journal of Black Studies, 28,* 683–704.

Gutman, L. M., & Eccles, J. S. (1999). Financial strain, parenting behaviors, and adolescents' achievement: Testing model equivalence between African American and European American single- and two-parent families. *Child Development, 70,* 1464–1476.

Guttmacher, S., Lieberman, L., Ward, D., Freudenberg, M., Radosh, A., & Jarlais, D. (1997). Condom availability in New York City schools: Relationship to condom use and sexual behavior. *American Journal of Public Health, 87,* 1427–1433.

Gwartney-Gibbs, P. A., Stockard, J., & Brohmer, S. (1987). Learning courtship violence: The influence of parents, peers and personal experiences. *Family Relations, 36,* 276–282.

Haager, D., & Vaughn, S. (1995). Parent, teacher, peer, and self-reports of the social competence of students with learning disabilities. *Journal of Learning Disabilities, 28,* 205–215.

Hackett, G., Betz, N. E., Casa, J. M., & Rucha-Singh, I. A. (1992). Gender, ethnicity, and social cognitive factors predicting the academic achievement of students in engineering. *Journal of Counseling Psychology, 39,* 527–538.

Haffner, D. W. (1992). 1998 report card on the stats: Sexual rights in America. *SIECUS Report, 20,* 1–7.

Hagborg, W. J. (1996). Self-concept and middle school students with learning disabilities: A comparison of scholastic competence subgroups. *Learning Disability Quarterly, 19,* 117–126.

Haggerty, R. J., Sherrod, L. R., Garmezy, N., & Rutter, M. (1994). *Stress, coping and development: Risk and resilience in children.* Cambridge, England: Cambridge University Press.

Hall, C. W., Spruill, K. L., & Webster, R. E. (2002). Motivational and attitudinal factors in college students with and without learning disabilities. *Learning Disabilities Quarterly, 25,* 79–87.

Hall, G. S. (1904). *Adolescence: Its psychology and its relations to physiology, anthropology, sociology, sex, crime, religion, and education* (Vols. 1 & 2). New York: Appleton.

Hall, P. D. (1998). The relationship between types of rap music and memory in African American children. *Journal of Black Studies, 28,* 802–815.

Hallinan, M. T. (1996). Track mobility in secondary school. *Social Forces, 74,* 983–1002.

Halpern, C. T., Oslak, S. G., Young, M. L., Martin, S. L., & Kupper, L. L. (2001). Partner violence among adolescents in opposite-sex romantic relationships: Findings from the National Longitudinal Study of Adolescent Health. *The American Journal of Public Health, 91,* 1679–1685.

Halpern, D. F. (1998). Teaching critical thinking for transfer across domains. *American Psychologist, 53,* 449–455.

Hamachek, D. E. (1988). Evaluating self-concept and ego development within Erikson's psychosocial framework: A formulation. *Journal of Counseling and Development, 66,* 354–360.

Hamalainen, M., & Pulkkinen, L. (1995). Aggressive and non-prosocial behavior as precursors of criminality. *Studies on Crime and Crime Prevention, 4,* 6–21.

Hamalainen, M., & Pulkkinen, L. (1996). Problem behavior as a precursor of male criminality. *Development and Psychopathology, 8,* 443–455.

Hamilton, C. E. (2000). Continuity and discontinuity of attachment from infancy through adolescence. *Child Development, 71,* 690–694.

Hamm, J. V. (2000). Do birds of a feather flock together? The variable bases for African American, Asian American, and European American adolescents' selection of similar friends. *Developmental Psychology, 36,* 209–219.

Hammen, C. (1991). *Depression runs in families: The social context of risk and resilience in children of depressed mothers.* New York: Springer-Verlag.

Hammond, W. A., & Romney, D. M. (1995). Cognitive factors contributing to adolescent depression. *Journal of Youth and Adolescence, 24,* 667–684.

Handler, A. (1990). The correlates of the initiation of sexual intercourse among young urban Black females. *Journal of Youth and Adolescence, 19,* 159–170.

Hankin, B. L., & Abramson, L. Y. (2001). Development of gender differences in depression: An elaborated cognitive vulnerability-transactional stress theory. *Psychological Bulletin, 127,* 773–796.

Hannon, R., Hall, D. S., Nash, H., Formati, J., & Hopson, T. (2000, September). Judgments regarding sexual aggression as a function of sex of aggressor and victim. *Sex Roles: A Journal of Research,* 311–325.

Hansell, S. (1985). Adolescent friendship networks and distress in school. *Social Forces, 63,* 698–715.

Hansen, C. H., & Hansen, R. D. (1990a). The influence of sex and violence on the appeal of rock music videos. *Communication Research, 17,* 212–234.

Hansen, C. H., & Hansen, R. D. (1990b). Rock music videos and antisocial behavior. *Basic and Applied Psychology, 11,* 357–369.

Hansen, C., Weiss, D., & Last, C. G. (1999). ADHD boys in young adulthood: Psychosocial adjustment. *Journal of the American Academy of Child and Adolescent Psychiatry, 38,* 165–171.

Hansen, D. M., & Jarvis, P. A. (2000). Adolescent employment and psychosocial outcomes: A comparison of two employment contexts. *Youth and Society, 31,* 417–436.

Hansen, E. J., & Stephens, J. A. (2000, September). The ethics of learner-centered education. *Change, 32,* 40–45.

Hansen, J. C., Scullard, M. G., & Haviland, M. G. (2000). The interest structure of Native American college students. *Journal of Career Assessment, 8,* 159–165.

Hansford, B. C., & Hattie, J. A. (1982). The relationship between self and achievement/performance measures. *Review of Educational Research, 52,* 135–153.

Hanson, G. M. B. (1999, June 28). The violent world of video games. *Insight on the News, 15,* 14.

Hanson, T. L., McLanahan, S. S., & Thomson, E. (1996). Double jeopardy: Parental conflict and stepfamily outcomes for children. *Journal of Marriage and the Family, 58,* 141–155.

Harackiewicz, J. M., Barron, K. E., & Elliot, A. J. (1998). Rethinking achievement goals: When are they adaptive for college students and why? *Educational Psychology, 33,* 1–21.

Hardy, J., & Duggan, A. (1988). Teenage fathers and the fathers of infants of urban, teenage mothers. *American Journal of Public Health, 78,* 919–922.

Hardy, J. B., Welcher, D. W., Mellits, E. D., & Kagan, J. (1976). Pitfalls in the measurement of intelligence: Are standardized tests valid for measuring the intellectual potential of urban children? *Journal of Psychology, 94,* 43–51.

Harris, J. C. (1995). *Developmental neuropsychiatry* (Vol. 1). New York: Oxford University Press.

Harris, L. (1986). *American teens speak: Sex, myths, TV and birth control.* New York: Planned Parenthood.

Harris, Y. R. (1997). Adolescent abortion. *Society, 34,* 20–22.

Harrison, A. O., Wilson, M. N., Pine, C. J., Chan, S. Q., & Buriel, R. (1990). Family ecologies of ethnic minority children. *Child Development, 61,* 347–362.

Hart, D., & Fegley, S. (1995). Prosocial behavior and caring in adolescence: Relations to self-understanding and social judgment. *Child Development, 66,* 1346–1359.

Hart, D., Fegley, S., & Brengelman, D. (1993). Perceptions of past, present and future selves among children and adolescents. *British Journal of Developmental Psychology, 11,* 265–282.

Hart, E. R., & Speece, D. L. (1998). Reciprocal teaching goes to college: Effects of postsecondary students at risk for academic failure. *Journal of Educational Psychology, 90,* 670–681.

Harter, S. (1986). Cognitive-developmental processes in the integration of concepts about emotional and the self. *Social Cognition, 4,* 119–151.

Harter, S. (1990). Self and identity development. In S. S. Feldman & G. R. Elliott (Eds.), *At the threshold: The developing adolescent* (pp. 352–388). Cambridge: Harvard University Press.

Harter, S. (1993a). Causes and consequences of low self-esteem in children and adolescents. In R. F. Baumeister (Ed.), *Self-esteem: The puzzle of low self-regard* (pp. 87–116). New York: Allyn & Bacon.

Harter, S. (1993b). Visions of self: Beyond the me in the mirror. In J. Jacobs (Ed.), *Developmental perspectives on the self* (pp. 99–144). Lincoln: University of Nebraska Press.

Harter, S. (1998). The development of self-representations. In W. Damon & N. Eisenberg (Eds.), *Handbook of child psychology* (5th ed., Vol. 3, pp. 553–617). New York: Wiley.

Harter, S., Marold, D. B., & Whitesell, N. R. (1992). A model of psychosocial risk factors leading to suicidal ideation in young adolescents. *Development and Psychopathology, 4,* 167–188.

Harter, S., & Monsour, A. (1992). Developmental analysis of conflict caused by opposing attributes in the adolescent self-portrait. *Developmental Psychology, 28,* 251–260.

Harter, S., Stocker, C., & Robinson, N. (1996). The perceived directionality of the link between approval and self-worth: The liability of a looking glass self orientation among young adolescents. *Journal of Research on Adolescence, 6,* 285–308.

Harter, S., Waters, P. L., Whitesell, N. R., & Kastelic, D. (1998). Level of voice among female and male high school students: Relational context, support, and gender orientation. *Developmental Psychology, 34,* 892–901.

Hartman, B. W., Fiqua, D. R., & Blum, C. R. (1985). A path analytic model of career indecision. *Vocational Guidance Quarterly, 31,* 101–108.

Hartmus, D. M., & Niblock, S. B. (2000). Elements of a good sexual harassment policy. *The Public Manager, 29,* 50–61.

Hartshorne, H., & May, M. A. (1928). *Studies in the nature of character* (Vol. 1). New York: Macmillan.

Hartup, W. W. (1983). Peer relations. In P. H. Mussen (Ed.), *Handbook of child psychology: Vol. 4. Socialization, personality and social development* (4th ed., pp. 152–233). New York: Wiley.

Hartup, W. W. (1993). Adolescents and their friends. In B. Laursen (Ed.), *Close friendships in adolescence: New directions for child development* (pp. 3–22). San Francisco: Jossey-Bass.

Hartup, W. W. (1995). The three faces of friendship. *Journal of Social and Personal Relationships, 12,* 569–574.

Harvard Mental Health Letter. (1998, November). Forum: What are the adult consequences of childhood shyness? *Harvard Mental Health Letter, 15,* 5.

Harvey, S. M., & Spigner, C. (1995). Factors associated with sexual behavior among adolescents: A multivariate analysis. *Adolescence, 30,* 253–264.

Harwood, R. L. (1992). The influence of culturally derived values on Anglo and Puerto Rican mothers' perceptions of attachment behavior. *Child Development, 63,* 822–828.

Hassan, S. (1988). *Combating cult mind control.* Wellingborough: The Aquarian Press.

Hatch, D. D., & Hall, J. E. (2000, February). ADA requires disability-specific accommodations. *Workforce, 79,* 92–96.

Hatcher, P. J., Hulme, C., & Ellis, A. W. (1994). Ameliorating early reading failure by integrating the teaching of reading and phonological skills: The phonological linkage hypothesis. *Child Development, 65,* 41–57.

Hatfield, E., & Rapson, R. L. (1996). *Love and sex: A cross-cultural perspective.* Boston: Allyn & Bacon.

Hattie, J. (1992). *Self-concept.* Hillsdale, NJ: Erlbaum.

Hauser, S. T., & Kasendorf, E. (1983). *Black and white identity formation.* Malabar, FL: Robert E. Krieger.

Havighurst, R. J. (1972). *Developmental tasks and education* (3rd ed.). New York: David McKay.

Haviland, W. A. (2003). *Cultural anthropology* (10th ed.). Belmont, CA: Wadsworth.

Hawkins, J. D., Catalano, R. F., & Miller, J. Y. (1992). Risk and protective factors for alcohol and other drug problems in adolescence and early adulthood: Implications for substance use prevention. *Psychological Bulletin, 112,* 64–105.

Hawkins, J. D., Herrenkohl, T. I., Farrington, D. P., Brewer, L., Catalano, R. F., Hrachi, T. W., & Cothern, L. (2000, April). Predictors of youth violence. *Juvenile Justice Bulletin.* Washington, DC: U.S. Department of Justice. Retrieved December 24, 2002, from http://www.ncjrs.org/html/ojjdp/jjbul2000_04_5/contents.html

Hawley, P., & Even, B. (1982). Work and sex-role attitudes in relation to education and other characteristics. *Vocational Guidance Quarterly, 31,* 101–109.

Hayes, D. S., Gershman, E. S., & Halteman, W. (1996). Enmity in males at four developmental levels: Cognitive bases for disliking peers. *The Journal of Genetic Psychology, 157,* 153–160.

Hayes, R. (1986). Men's decisions to enter or avoid nontraditional occupations. *Career Development Quarterly, 34,* 89–101.

Haynie, D. L., Nansel, T., Eitel, P., Crump, A., Saylor, K., & Yu, K. (2001). Bullies, victims, and bully/victims: Distinct groups of youth at risk. *Journal of Early Adolescence, 21,* 29–50.

Haywood, C., Killen, J. D., Wilson, D. M., Hammer, L. D., Litt, I. F., Kraemer, H. C., et al. (1997). Psychiatric risk associated with early puberty in adolescent girls. *Journal of the American Academy of Child and Adolescent Psychiatry, 36,* 255–262.

Hazan, C., & Shaver, P. R. (1987). Romantic love conceptualized as an attachment process. *Journal of Personality and Social Psychology, 52,* 511–524.

Hazan, C., & Shaver, P. R. (1990). Love and work: An attachment-theoretical perspective. *Journal of Personality and Social Psychology, 59,* 270–280.

Hazan, C., & Zeifman, D. (1994). Sex and the psychological tether. In K. Bartholomew & D. Pearlman (Eds.), *Attachment processes in adulthood* (pp. 17–52). London: Jessica Kingsley Publishers.

Healy, J. M. (1999). Why slow down the rush toward school computers? *Education Digest, 65,* 32–37.

Heath, A. C., & Madden, P. F. (1995). Genetic influences on smoking behavior. In J. R. Turner, L. R. Cardon, & J. K. Hewitt (Eds.), *Behavior genetic approaches behavioral medicine* (pp. 45–66). New York: Plenum.

Hechtman, L., Weiss, G., & Perlman, T. (1984). Hyperactives as young adults: Past and current substance abuse and antisocial behavior. *American Journal of Orthopsychiatry, 54,* 415–425.

Heinrich, R., Corbine, J., & Thomas, K. (1990). Counseling Native Americans. *Journal of Counseling and Development, 69,* 128–132.

Helwig, C. C. (1997). The role of agent and social context in judgments of freedom of speech and religion. *Child Development, 68,* 484–495.

Hemmens, C., & Bennett, K. (1999). Juvenile curfews and the courts: Judicial responses to a not-so-new crime control strategy. *Crime and Delinquency, 45,* 99–122.

Hempelman, K. A. (1994). *Teen legal rights: A guide for the '90s.* Westport, CT: Greenwood Press.

Henderson, L., & Zimbardo, P. G. (1998). Shyness. *Encyclopedia of mental health* (Vol. 3, pp. 497–509). San Diego: Academic Press.

Henderson, S., Hesketh, B., & Tuffin, K. (1988). A test of Gottfredson's circumscription. *Journal of Vocational Behavior, 32,* 37–48.

Hendriksson, M. M., Aro, H. M., Marttunen, M. J., Heikkinen, M. E., Isometsa, E. T., Kuoppsalmi, K. I., & Lonnqvist, J. K. (1993). Mental disorders and comorbidity in suicide. *American Journal of Psychiatry, 150,* 935–940.

Hendry, J. (1999). *Other people's worlds.* New York: New York University Press.

Henry, B., Caspi, A., Mofitt, T., & Silva, P. (1996). Temperamental and familial predictors of violent and nonviolent criminal convictions. *Developmental Psychology, 32,* 614–623.

Henry, C. S., Sager, D. W., & Plunkett, S. W. (1996). Adolescents' perceptions of family system characteristics, parent-adolescent dyadic behaviors, adolescent qualities, and adolescent empathy. *Family Relations, 45,* 283–292.

Henry, T. (1996, February 22). Principals urge broad changes in high schools. *USA Today,* p. D1.

Henshaw, S. K. (1994). *U.S. teenage pregnancy statistics.* New York: Alan Guttmacher Institute.

Henshaw, S., & Kost, K. (1992). Parental involvement in minors' abortion decisions. *Family Planning Perspectives, 30,* 263–270, 287.

Herbert, W. (with Daniel, M.). (1996, June 3). The moral child. *U. S. News and World Report,* 52–59.

Herek, G. M. (1989). Hate crimes against lesbians and gay men: Issues for research and policy. *American Psychologist, 44,* 948–955.

Herek, G. M., Gillis, R., Kogan, J. C., & Glunt, E. K. (1996). Hate crime victimization among lesbian, gay, and bisexual adults. *Journal of Interpersonal Violence, 12,* 195–212.

Herkenham, M., Lynn, A. B., de Costa, B. R., & Richfield, E. K. (1991a). Cannabinoid receptor localization in brain: Relationship to motor and reward systems. *Annals of the New York Academy of Sciences, 654,* 19–32.

Herkenham, M., Lynn, A. B., de Costa, B. R., & Richfield, E. K. (1991b). Neuronal localization of cannabinoid receptors in the basal ganglia of the rat. *Brain Research, 547,* 267–274.

Herman, M. A., & McHale, S. M. (1993). Coping with parental negativity: Links with parental warmth and child adjustment. *Journal of Applied Developmental Psychology, 14,* 121–136.

Herman-Giddens, M. E., Slora, E. J., Wasserman, R. C., Bourdony, C. J., Bhapkar, M. V., Koch, G. G., & Hasemeier, C. M. (1997). Secondary sexual characteristics and menses in young girls seen in office practice: A study from the pediatric research in office settings networks. *Pediatrics, 99,* 505–512.

Herman-Stahl, M., & Petersen, A. C. (1996). The protective role of coping and social resources for depressive symptoms among young adolescents. *Journal of Youth and Adolescence, 25,* 733–754.

Hernandez, D. J. (1997). Child development and the social demography of childhood. *Child Development, 68,* 149–170.

Hernandez, J. T., & DiClemente, R. J. (1992). Self control and ego identity development as predictors of unprotected sex in late adolescent males. *Journal of Adolescence, 15,* 437–447.

Heron, A., & Kroeger, E. (1981). Introduction to developmental psychology. In H. C. Triandis & A. Heron (Eds.), *Handbook of cross-cultural psychology* (Vol. 4, pp. 1–17). Boston: Allyn & Bacon.

Herrenkohl, E. C., Herrenkohl, R. C., & Egolf, B. (1994). Resilient early school age children from maltreating homes: Outcome in late adolescence. *American Journal of Orthopsychiatry, 64,* 301–309.

Hershberger, S. L. (1997). A twin registry study of male and female sexual orientation. *Journal of Sex Research, 34,* 212–223.

Hertzler, A. A., & Frary, R. B. (1989). Food behavior of college students. *Adolescence, 24,* 349–355.

Hesse-Biber, S., Clayton-Matthews, A., & Doney, J. (1987). The differential importance of weight and body image among college men and women. *Genetic, Social and General Psychology Monographs, 113,* 509–528.

Hetherington, E. M. (1993). An overview of the Virginia longitudinal study of divorce and remarriage with a focus on early adolescence. *Journal of Family Psychology, 7,* 39–56.

Hetherington, E. M. (2002, April 8). Marriage and divorce American style: A destructive marriage is not a happy family. *The American Prospect, 13,* 62–64.

Hetherington, E. M., & Anderson, E. R. (1987). The effects of divorce and remarriage on early adolescents and their families. In M. D. Levine & E. R. McAnarney (Eds.), *Early adolescent transitions* (pp. 49–67). Lexington, MA: D.C. Heath.

Hetherington, E. M., Anderson, E. R., & Stanley-Hagan, M. S. (1991). Divorce: Effects on adolescents. In R. M. Lerner, A. C. Petersen, & J.

Brooks-Gunn (Eds.), *Encyclopedia of adolescence* (pp. 237–243). New York: Garland.

Hetherington, E. M., Arnett, J. D., & Hollier, E. A. (1988). Adjustment of parents and children to remarriage. In S. A. Wolchik & P. Karoly (Eds.), *Children of divorce: Empirical perspectives on adjustment* (pp. 34–59). New York: Gardner Press.

Hetherington, E. M., & Clingempeel, W. G. (1992). Coping with marital transitions: A family systems perspective. *Monographs of the Society for Research in Child Development, 57*(2–3, Serial no. 227), 1–242.

Hetherington, E. M., Cox, M., & Cox, R. (1982). Effects of divorce on parents and children. In M. Lamb (Ed.), *Nontraditional families: Parenting and child development* (Vol. 3, pp. 141–232). Chicago: University of Chicago Press.

Hetherington, E. M., Hagan, M. S., & Anderson, E. R. (1989). Marital transitions: A child's perspective. *American Psychologist, 44,* 303–313.

Hetherington, E. M., & Kelly, J. (2002). *For better or for worse: Divorce reconsidered.* New York: Norton.

Hetherington, E. M., & Stanley-Hagan, M. M. (1995). Parenting in divorced and remarried families. In M. H. Bornstein (Ed.), *Handbook of parenting* (Vol. 3, pp. 233–254). Mahwah, NJ: Erlbaum.

Hickson, L., Blackman, L. S., & Reis, E. M. (1995). *Mental retardation: Foundations of educational programming.* Boston: Allyn & Bacon.

Higgins, E. T. (1987). Self-discrepancy: A theory relating self and affect. *Psychological Review, 94,* 319–340.

Higginson, J. G. (1998). Competitive parenting: The culture of teen mothers. *Journal of Marriage and the Family, 60,* 135–150.

High/Scope Educational Research Foundation. (1993). *Significant benefits: The High/Scope Perry Preschool study through age 27.* Ypsilanti, MI: High/Scope Educational Research Foundation.

Higher standards: Magnet schools. (1999, January 18). *U. S. News and World Report, 126,* 52–54.

Hill, C. I. (1986). A developmental perspective on adolescent "rebellion" in the church. *Journal of Psychology and Theology, 14,* 306–318.

Hill, J. P. (1987). Research on adolescents and their families: Past and prospect. In C. E. Irwin (Ed.), *Adolescent social behavior and health* (pp. 15–32). San Francisco: Jossey Bass.

Hill, J. P., & Holmbeck, G. N. (1987). Familial adaptation to biological change during adolescence. In R. M. Lerner & T. T. Foch (Eds.), *Biological-psychosocial interactions in early adolescence* (pp. 207–233). Hillsdale, NJ: Erlbaum.

Hill, J. P., & Lynch, M. E. (1983). The intensification of gender-related role expectations during early adolescence. In J. Brooks-Gunn & A. C. Petersen (Eds.), *Girls at puberty: Biological and psychological perspectives* (pp. 201–230). New York: Plenum.

Hilton, N. Z., Harris, G. T., Rice, M. E., Krans, T. S., & Lavigne, S. E. (1998). Antiviolence education in high school. *Journal of Interpersonal Violence, 13,* 726–743.

Himaki, W. C., Arkowitz, H., Hinton, R., & Perl, J. (1980). Minimal dating and its relationship to other social problems and general adjustment. *Behavior Therapy, 11,* 345–352.

Hines, A. M. (1997). Divorce-related transitions, adolescent development, and the role of the parent-child relationship: A review of the literature. *Journal of Marriage and the Family, 59,* 375–388.

Hinshaw, S. P., & Erhardt, D. (1993). Behavioral treatment. In V. B. Van Halsselt & M. Hensen (Ed.), *Handbook of behavior therapy and pharmacology for children: A comparative analysis* (pp. 233–250). Boston: Allyn & Bacon.

Hippensteele, S., & Pearson, T. C. (1999, January/February). Responding effectively to sexual harassment. *Change, 31,* 48–54.

Hispanic dropouts. (1993, November 3). *Education Week,* p. 3.

Hochschild, A. (1989). *The second shift.* New York: Viking.

Hodgson, L. G. (1992). Adults, grandchildren and their grandparents: The enduring bond. *International Journal of Aging and Human Development, 34,* 209–225.

Hoffer, T. B. (1992). Middle school ability grouping and student achievement in science and mathematics. *Educational Evaluation and Policy Analysis, 14,* 205–227.

Hoffman, M. L. (1983). Affective and cognitive processes in moral internalization: An information processing approach. In E. T. Higgins, D. Ruble, & W. Hartup (Eds.), *Social cognition and social development: A socio-cultural perspective* (pp. 236–274). New York: Cambridge University Press.

Hoffman, M. L. (1988). Moral development. In M. Lamb & M. Bornstein (Eds.), *Developmental psychology: An advanced textbook* (2nd ed., pp. 497–548). Hillsdale, NJ: Erlbaum.

Hoffman, M. L. (1991). Commentary. *Human Development, 34,* 105–110.

Hoffman, S. D., Foster, E. M., & Furstenberg, F. F., Jr. (1993). Reevaluating the costs of teenage childbearing. *Demography, 30,* 1–13.

Hoffmann, J. P. (2002). The dynamics of self-esteem: A growth-curve analysis. *Journal of Youth and Adolescence, 31,* 101–114.

Hogan, D. P., Sun, R., & Cornwell, G. T. (2000). Sexual and fertility behaviors of American females aged 15–19 years: 1985, 1990 and 1995. *American Journal of Public Health, 90,* 1421–1425.

Hogue, A., & Steinberg, L. (1995). Homophily of internalized distress in adolescent peer groups. *Developmental Psychology, 31,* 897–906.

Holden, G. W., & Ritchie, K. L. (1991). Linking extreme marital discord, child rearing, and child behavior problems: Evidence from battered women. *Child Development, 62,* 311–327.

Holder, H. B., & Kirkpatrick, S. W. (1991). Interpretation of emotion from facial expressions in children with and without learning disabilities. *Journal of Learning Disabilities, 24,* 170–177.

Holland, B. (1994, March 5). Senate hearing examines gangsta lyrics: Possibility raised of movie-style rating system. *Billboard, 106,* 10–12.

Holland, J. L. (1985). *Making vocational choices: A theory of vocational personalities and work environments* (2nd ed.). Englewood Cliffs, NJ: Prentice Hall.

Holland, J. L. (1992). *Making vocational choices* (2nd ed.). Odessa, FL: Psychological Assessment Resources, Inc.

Holland, J. L. (1994). *Self-directed search.* Odessa, FL: Psychological Assessment Resources, Inc.

Holland, J. L. (1997). *Making vocational choices: A theory of vocational personalities and work environments* (3rd ed.). Odessa, FL: Psychological Assessment Resources, Inc.

Hollander, D. (2002). The perils of parental notification. *Perspectives on Sexual and Reproductive Health, 34,* 225.

Holmbeck, G. N., & Hill, J. P. (1988). Storm and stress beliefs about adolescence: Prevalence, self-reported antecedents, and effects of an undergraduate course. *Journal of Youth and Adolescence, 17,* 285–306.

Holmbeck, G. N., & Hill, J. P. (1991). Conflictive engagement, positive affect, and menarche in families with seventh-grade girls. *Child Development, 62,* 1030–1048.

Holmbeck, G. N., & O'Donnell, K. (1991). Discrepancies between perceptions of decision-making and behavioral autonomy. In R. L. Paikoff (Ed.), *Shared views in the family during adolescence: New directions for child development* (No. 51, pp. 51–69). San Francisco: Jossey-Bass.

Holmbeck, G. N., Paikoff, R. L., & Brooks-Gunn, J. (1995). Parenting adolescents. In M. H. Bornstein (Ed.), *Handbook of parenting* (Vol. 1, 91–118). Mahwah, NJ: Erlbaum.

Holmes, D. S. (1976a). Debriefing after psychological experiments: I. Effectiveness of post-deception dehoaxing. *American Psychologist, 31,* 858–868.

Holmes, D. S. (1976b). Debriefing after psychological experiments: II. Effectiveness of post-experimental desensitization. *American Psychologist, 31,* 868–876.

Holstein, C. B. (1976). Irreversible, stepwise sequence in the development of moral judgment: A longitudinal study of males and females. *Child Development, 47,* 51–61.

Holton, L. (2000, April). The surfer in the family. *American Demographics, 22,* 34–36.

Holtzen, D. W., & Agresti, A. A. (1990). Parental responses to gay and lesbian children. *Journal of Social and Clinical Psychology, 9,* 390–399.

Hoover, J. H., Oliver, R., & Hazier, R. J. (1992). Bullying: Perceptions of adolescent victims in the Midwestern USA. *School Psychology International, 13,* 5–16.

Hoover-Dempsey, K., & Sandler, H. M. (1995). Parental involvement in children's education: Why does it make a difference? *Teachers College Record, 97,* 310–331.

Horowitz, T. R. (1992). Dropout-Mertonian or reproductive scheme? *Adolescence, 27,* 451–459.

Horwitz, S. M., Klerman, L., Kuo, H. S., & Jekel, J. (1991). School age mothers: Predictors of long-term educational and economic outcomes. *Pediatrics, 87,* 862–868.

Hotchkiss, L., & Borow, H. (1996). Sociological perspectives on work and career development. In D. Brown & L. Brooks (Eds.), *Career choice and development* (3rd ed., pp. 281–334). San Francisco: Jossey-Bass.

Hottelling, K., & Forrest, L. (1985, November). Gilligan's theory of sex-role development: A perspective for counseling. *Journal of Counseling and Development, 64,* 183–186.

Hotz, V. J., McElroy, S. W., & Sanders, S. G. (1997). The costs and consequences of teenage childbearing for mothers. In R. A. Maynard (Ed.), *Kids having kids: Economic costs and social consequences of teenage pregnancy* (pp. 55–94). Washington, DC: Urban Institute Press.

Houston, T., & Kaufman, N. J. (2000, August 9). Tobacco control in the 21st century. *Journal of the American Medical Association, 284,* 752–753.

Howell, J. C. (1998, August). Youth gangs: An overview. *OJJDP Juvenile Justice Bulletin* (pp. 1–19). Washington, DC: U.S. Department of Justice.

Howell, J. C., & Lynch, J. P. (2000, August). *Youth gangs in school.* Washington, DC: OJJDP.

Hoyt, K. B., & Lester, J. N. (1995). *The NCDA Gallup survey* (Rep. No. L-1847). Columbus, OH: National Career Development Association.

Hsia, J. (1988). *Asian Americans in higher education and at work.* Hillsdale, NJ: Erlbaum.

Hsu, F. L. K. (1985). The self in cross-cultural perspective. In A. J. Marsella, G. DeVos, & F. L. K. Hsu (Eds.), *Culture and self: Asian and Western perspectives* (pp. 24–55). London, England: Tavistock.

Hubbs-Tait, L., & Garmon, L. C. (1995). The relationship of moral reasoning and AIDS knowledge to risky sexual behavior. *Adolescence, 30,* 549–564.

Huddy, D. C., Nieman, D. C., & Johnson, R. L. (1993). Relationship between body image and percent body fat among college male varsity athletes and nonathletes. *Perceptual and Motor Skills, 77,* 851–857.

Hudley, C., & Graham, S. (1993). An attributional intervention to reduce peer-directed aggression among African-American boys. *Child Development, 64,* 124–138.

Hudson, L., & Gray, W. (1986). Formal operations, the imaginary audience, and the personal fable. *Adolescence, 21,* 751–765.

Huefner, D. S. (2000). The risks and opportunities of the IEP requirements under IDEA '97. *Journal of Special Education, 33,* 195–214.

Huesmann, R. L., & Guerra, N. G. (1997). Children's normative beliefs about aggression and aggressive behavior. *Journal of Personality and Social Psychology, 72,* 408–419.

Huffman, G. B. (2002). Review of interventions in adolescent suicide. *American Family Physician, 65,* 1931–1933.

Hughes, J. N., & Hasbrouck, J. E. (1996). Television violence: Implications for violence prevention. *School Psychology Review, 25,* 134–151.

Humphrey, K. R., & Baker, P. R. (1994, September). The GREAT Program: Gang Resistance Education and Training. *FBI Law Enforcement Bulletin,* 1–4.

Hunter, E. (1998). Adolescent attraction to cults. *Adolescence, 33,* 709–715.

Hunter, F. T. (1984). Socializing procedures in parent-child and friendship relations during adolescence. *Developmental Psychology, 20,* 1092–1100.

Hunter, F. T. (1985). Adolescents' perception of discussions with parents and friends. *Developmental Psychology, 21,* 433–440.

Hunter, F. T., & Youniss, J. (1982). Changes in functions of three relations during adolescence. *Developmental Psychology, 18,* 806–812.

Huntsinger, C. S., Jose, P. E., & Larson, S. L. (1998). Do parent practices to encourage academic competence influence the social adjustment of young European American and Chinese American children? *Developmental Psychology, 34,* 747–756.

Huntsinger, C. S., Jose, P. E., Larson, S. L., Krieg, D. B., & Shaligram, C. (2000). Mathematics, vocabulary, and reading development in Chinese American and European American children over the primary school years. *Journal of Educational Psychology, 92,* 745–760.

Huston, A. C. (1983). Sex-typing. In E. M. Hetherington (Ed.), *Handbook of child psychology* (4th ed., Vol. 4, pp. 387–469). New York: Wiley.

Huston, A. C., Watkins, B. A., & Kunkel, D. (1989). Public policy and children's television. *American Psychologist, 44,* 424–433.

Huttunen, A., Salmivalli, C., & Lagerspetz, K. M. (1996). Friendship networks and bullying in schools. *Academic Science, 794,* 355–359.

Hymel, S. (1986). Interpretations of peer behavior: Affective bias in childhood and adolescence. *Child Development, 57,* 431–445.

Ianni, F. (1989). *The search for structure: A report on American youth today.* New York: Free Press.

Iheanacho, S. L. (1988). Minority self-concept: A research review. *Journal of Instructional Psychology, 15,* 3–11.

Ihinger-Tallman, M., & Pasley, K. (1987). *Remarriage.* Beverly Hills, CA: Sage.

Inhelder, B., & Piaget, J. (1958). *The growth of logical thinking from childhood to adolescence.* New York: Basic.

Ireland, D. (2000, January 31). Gay teens fight back. *The Nation, 270,* pp. 21–24.

Isay, R. A. (1990). Psychoanalytic theory and the therapy of gay men. In D. P. McWhirter, S. A. Sanders, & J. M. Reinish (Eds.), *Homosexuality/heterosexuality: Concepts of sexual orientation* (pp. 283–303). New York: Oxford University Press.

ITAR/TASS News Agency. (2001, January 11). *Poll shows many Russians prefer one child families.* Moscow: Author.

Jaccard, J., & Dittus, P. J. (2000). Adolescent perceptions of maternal approval of birth control and sexual risk behavior. *American Journal of Public Health, 90,* 1426–1430.

Jaccard, J., Dittus, P., & Gordon, V. (1996). Maternal correlates of adolescent sexual behavior. *Family Planning Perspectives, 28,* 159–165.

Jackson, C., & Foshee, V. A. (1998). Violence-related behaviors of adolescents: Relations with responsive and demanding parents. *Journal of Adolescent Research, 13,* 343–359.

Jackson, S., Bijstra, J., Oostra, L., & Bosma, H. (1998). Adolescents' perceptions of communication with parents relative to specific aspects of relationships with parents and personal development. *Journal of Adolescence, 21,* 305–322.

Jacobson, L. (1997, September 3). Long-term achievement study shows gains, losses. *Education Week,* p. 12.

Jacobson, N. S., Dobson, K. S., Truax, P. A., Addis, M. E., Koerner, K., Gollan, J. K., et al. (1996). A component analysis of cognitive-behavioral treatment for depression. *Journal of Consulting and Clinical Psychology, 64,* 295–304.

Jacobson, N. S., & Hollon, S. D. (1996). Cognitive-behavior therapy versus pharmacotherapy. Now that the jury's returned its verdict, it's time to present the rest of the evidence. *Journal of Consulting and Clinical Psychology, 64,* 74–80.

Jacoby, T. (1999, March 29). Color blind. *The New Republic, 220,* 23–28.

Jadack, R. A., Hyde, J. S., Moore, C. F., & Keller, M. L. (1995). Moral reasoning about sexually transmitted diseases. *Child Development, 66,* 167–177.

Jaffee, S., & Hyde, J. S. (2000). Gender differences in moral orientation: A meta-analysis. *Psychological Bulletin, 126,* 703–721.

James, C. (2001). *Addressing the issues: Industry addresses by the MAAA's Jack Valenti and NATO's John Fithian point to a bright future after a dark year.* Retrieved July 18, 2002, from http://www.boxoff.com/shows/showest/2001/valenti_fithian.html

James, W. (1890). *The principles of psychology.* New York: Holt.

James, W. (1961). *Psychology: The briefer course.* New York: Harper & Row. (Original work published 1892)

James, W. H., West, C., Deters, K. E., & Armijo, E. (2000). Youth dating violence. *Adolescence, 35,* 455–465.

Jani, S. (1997). Changing relationships with parents. In J. D. Noshpitz (Ed.-in-Chief) & L. T. Fraherty & R. M. Sarles (Vol. Eds.). *Handbook of child and adolescent psychiatry* (Vol. 3, pp. 87–96). New York: Wiley.

Jankowiak, W. R., & Fischer, E. F. (1992). A cross-cultural perspective on romantic love. *Ethnology, 31,* 149–155.

Janosz, M., LeBlanc, M., Boulerice, B., & Tremblay, R. E. (1997). Disentangling the weight of school dropout predictors: A test on two longitudinal samples. *Journal of Youth and Adolescence, 26,* 733–762.

Jencks, C., & Phillips, M. (1998). *The Black-White test score gap.* Washington, DC: Brookings Institution Press.

Jenkins, J. (1992). Sibling relationships in disharmonious homes: Potential difficulties and protective effects. In F. Boer & J. Dunn (Eds.), *Children's sibling relationships: Developmental and clinical issues* (pp. 125–138). Hillsdale, NJ: Erlbaum.

Jenkins, J. M., Smith, M. A., & Graham, P. J. (1989). Coping with parental quarrels. *Journal of the American Academy of Child and Adolescent Psychiatry, 28,* 182–289.

Jessor, R., van Den Bos, J., Vanderryn, J., Costa, F. M., & Turbin, M. S. (1995). Protective factors in adolescent problem behavior: Moderator effects and developmental change. *Developmental Psychology, 31,* 923–933.

Jiao, S., Ji, G., & Jing, Q. (1986). Comparative study of behavioral qualities of only children and sibling children. *Child Development, 57,* 357–361.

Jipping, T. L. (1999, July). Diagnosing the cultural virus. *World and I, 14,* 80–84.

Joekler, N. (1998, August 26). Dopamine defect and ADHD. *Journal of the American Medical Association, 280,* 687.

Johnson, B. E., Kuck, D. L., & Schander, P. R. (1997, June). Rape myth acceptance and sociodemographic characteristics: A multidimensional analysis. *Sex Roles, 36,* 693–708.

Johnson, H. C. (1996). Violence and biology: A review of the literature. *Families in Society, 77,* 3–18.

Johnson, J. D., Adams, M. S., Ashburn, L., & Reed, W. (1995). Differential gender effects of exposure to rap music on African American adolescents' acceptance of teen dating violence. *Sex Roles, 33,* 597–606.

Johnson, J., Jackson, L. A., & Gatto, L. (1995). Violent attitudes and deferred academic aspirations: Deleterious effects of exposure to rap music. *Basic and Applied Psychology, 16,* 27–41.

Johnson, M. K. (2002). Social origins, adolescent experiences, and work value trajectories during the transition to adulthood. *Social Forces, 80,* 1307–1341.

Johnson, M. P. (1995). Patriarchal terrorism and common couple violence: Two forms of violence against women. *Journal of Marriage and the Family, 57,* 283–294.

Johnston, C., & Ohan, J. L. (1999). Externalizing disorders. In W. K. Silverman & T. H. Ollendick (Eds.), *Developmental issues in the clinical treatment of children.* Boston: Allyn & Bacon.

Johnston, L. D., O'Malley, P. M., & Bachman, J. (2002). *Monitoring the future: National results of adolescent drug use: Overview of key findings, 2001* [NIH Publication No. 02–5105]. Bethesda, MD: National Institute on Drug Abuse.

Johnston, L., Bachman, J., & O'Malley, P. (1995). *Monitoring the future: National High School Seniors Survey.* Ann Arbor: University of Michigan, Survey Research Center.

Johnston, S. G., & Thomas, A. M. (1996). Divorce versus intact parental marriage and perceived risk and dyadic trust in present heterosexual relationships. *Psychological Reports, 78,* 387–390.

Joiner, G. W., & Kashubeck, S. (1996). Acculturation, body image, self-esteem and eating disorder symptomatology in adolescent Mexican-American women. *Psychology of Women Quarterly, 20,* 419–435.

Jome, L. M., & Tokar, D. M. (1998). Dimensions of masculinity and major choice traditionality. *Journal of Vocational Behavior, 52,* 120–134.

Jonah, B. A. (1986). Accident risk and risk-taking behavior among young drivers. *Accident Analysis and Prevention, 18,* 255–271.

Jones, B., & Carroll, M. (1998). The effect of a video character's smoking status on young females' perceptions of social characteristics. *Adolescence, 33,* 657–667.

Jones, J. T. (1993, November 3). Art or anarchy? Gunplay spurs debate. *USA Today,* 1D.

Jordan, W. J., Lara, J., & McPartland, J. M. (1996). Exploring the causes of early dropout among race-ethnic and gender groups. *Youth and Society, 28,* 67–94.

Jory, B., Rainbolt, E., Karns, J. T., Freeborn, A., & Greer, C. V. (1996). Communication patterns and alliances between parents and adolescents during a structured problem–solving task. *Journal of Adolescence, 19,* 139–146.

Josephson Institute of Ethics. (2001, April 2). *2000 report card: The ethics of American youth: Violence and substance abuse: Data and commentary.* Marina del Rey, CA: Author.

Joshi, P., & Kaschak, D. G. (1998). Exposure to violence and trauma: Questionnaire for adolescents. *International Review of Psychiatry, 10,* 208–218.

Jung, J., & Khalsa, H. K. (1989). The relationship of daily hassles, social support, and coping to depression in black and white students. *Journal of General Psychology, 116,* 407–417.

Juntunen, C. L., Barraclogh, D. J., Broneck, C. L., Weibel, G. A., Winrow, S. A., & Morin, P. M. (2001). American Indian perspectives on the career journey. *Journal of Counseling Psychology, 48,* 274–285.

Jussim, L. (1991). Social perception and social reality: A reflection-construction model. *Psychological Review, 98,* 54–73.

Jussim, L., & Eccles, J. S. (1992). Teacher expectations: Construction and reflection of student achievement. *Journal of Personality and Social Psychology, 63,* 947–961.

Jussim, L., Madon, S., & Chatman, C. (1994). Teacher expectations and student achievement: Self fulfilling prophecies, biases, and accuracy. In L. Health, R. S. Tindale, J. Edwards, E. J. Posavac, F. B. Bryant, E. Henderson-King, Y. Suarez-Bakazar, & J. Meyers (Eds.), *Applications of heuristics and biases to social issues* (pp. 303–334). New York: Plenum.

Juvonen, J., Nishina, A., & Graham, S. (2000). Peer harassment, psychological adjustment, and school functioning in early adolescence. *Journal of Educational Psychology, 92,* 349–359.

Kagan, J., Arcus, D., Snidman, N. (1993). The idea of temperament: Where do we go from here? In R. Plomin & G. E. McClearn (Eds.), *Nature nurture* (pp. 197–210). Washington, DC: American Psychological Association.

Kahlbaugh, P., & Haviland, J. M. (1991). Formal operational thinking and identity. In R. M. Lerner, A. C. Petersen, & J. Brooks-Gunn (Eds.), *Encyclopedia of adolescence* (pp. 369–372). New York: Garland.

Kahne, J. (1996, Spring). The politics of self-esteem. *American Educational Research Journal, 35,* 3–22.

Kail, R. (1991). Developmental change in speed of processing during childhood and adolescence. *Psychological Bulletin, 109,* 490–501.

Kalat, J. W. (1998). *Biological psychology* (6th ed.). Pacific Grove, CA: Brooks/Cole.

Kalat, J. W. (2001). *Biological psychology* (7th ed.). Belmont, CA: Wadsworth.

Kalichman, S. C., Kelly, J. A., & Rompa, D., (1997). Continued high-risk sex among HIV seropositive gay and bisexual men seeking HIV prevention services. *Health Psychology, 16,* 369–373.

Kandel, D. B. (1978a). Homophily, selection, and socialization in adolescent friendships. *American Journal of Sociology, 84,* 427–436.

Kandel, D. B. (1978b). Similarity in real life adolescent friendship pairs. *Journal of Personality and Social Psychology, 36,* 306–312.

Kandel, D. B., & Andrews, K. (1987). Processes of adolescent socialization by parents and peers. *The International Journal of Addictions, 22,* 319–342.

Kandel, D. B., & Chen, K. (2000). Types of marijuana users by longitudinal course. *Journal of Studies on Alcoholism. 61,* 367–380.

Kandel, D., & Lesser, G. S. (1972). *Youth in two worlds.* San Francisco: Jossey-Bass.

Kandel, D. B., Yamaguchi, K., & Chen, K. (1992). Stages of progression in drug involvement from adolescence to adulthood: Further evidence for the gateway theory. *Journal of Studies on Alcohol, 53,* 447–457.

Kang, S., & Bishop, J. (1989). Vocational and academic education in high school: Complements or substitutes? *Economics of Education Review, 8,* 133–148.

Kann, L., Kinchen, S. A., Williams, B. I., Ross, J. G., Lowry, R., Hill, C. V., et al. (1998). Youth risk behavior surveillance: United States, 1997. *Morbidity and Mortality Weekly Report, 47*(SS-3), 1–89.

Kantor, H. (1994). Managing the transition from school to work: The false promise of youth apprenticeship. *Teachers College Record, 95,* 442–461.

Kantrowitz, B. (1990, Summer/Fall). The push for sex education. *Newsweek,* p. 52.

Kantrowitz, B. (1998, December 7). *Newsweek,* pp. 62–65.

Kantrowitz, B., & Wingert, P. (1999, May 10). How well do you know your kid? *Newsday,* 36–40.

Kaplan, D. S., Peck, B. M., & Kaplan, H. B. (1997). Decomposing the academic failure-dropout relationship: A longitudinal analysis. *The Journal of Educational Research, 90,* 331–342.

Kaplan, D., & Holmes, M. M. (1999, April 30). Clinical management of rape in adolescent girls. *Patient Care, 33,* 42–53.

Kaplan, P. S. (1990). *Educational psychology for tomorrow's teacher.* St. Paul, MN: West.

Kaplan, P. S. (1996). *Pathways for exceptional children.* St. Paul, MN: West.

Kaplan, P. S. (1998). *The human odyssey* (3rd ed.). Pacific Grove, CA: Brooks/Cole.

Kaplan, P. S. (2000). *A child's odyssey* (3d ed.). Belmont, CA: Wadsworth.

Kaplan, P., & Stein, J. (1984). *Psychology of adjustment*. Belmont, CA: Wadsworth.

Karniol, R., Gabay, R., Ochion, Y., & Harari, Y. (1998). Is gender or gender-role orientation a better predictor of empathy in adolescence? *Sex Roles, 39,* 245–259.

Karraker, K. H., & Evans, S. L. (1996). Adolescent mothers' knowledge of child development and expectations for their own infants. *Journal of Youth and Adolescence, 25,* 651–666.

Kashani, J. H., & Orvaschel, H. (1990). A community study of anxiety in children and adolescents. *American Journal of Psychiatry, 147,* 313–318.

Kastenbaum, G. I., & Weinstein, L. (1985). Personality, psychopathology, and developmental issues in male adolescent video game use. *Journal of the American Academy of Child Psychiatry, 24,* 329–333.

Katchadourian, H. (1977). *The biology of adolescence*. San Francisco: Freeman.

Katchadourian, H. (1990). Sexuality. In S. S. Feldman & G. R. Elliott (Eds.), *At the threshold: The developing adolescent* (pp. 330–352). Cambridge, MA: Harvard University Press.

Katic, A., & Steingard, R. J. (2001). Pharmacotherapy. In C. E. Walker & M. C. Roberts (Eds.), *Handbook of clinical child psychology* (3rd ed., pp. 928–954). New York: Wiley.

Katz, J., Kuffel, S. W., & Coblentz, A. (2002). Are there gender differences in sustaining dating violence? An examination of frequency, severity, and relationship satisfaction. *Journal of Family Violence, 17,* 247–272.

Katz, K. D. (1999). The pregnant child's right to self-determination. *Albany Law Review, 62,* 1119–1139.

Katz, L. F., & Gottman, J. M. (1993). Patterns of marital conflict predict children's internalizing and externalizing behaviors. *Developmental Psychology, 29,* 940–950.

Kaufmann, K. (1987). Parental separation and divorce during the college years: Gender differences in response of young adults. In R. M. Lerner, A. C. Petersen, & J. Brooks-Gunn (Eds.), *Encyclopedia of adolescence* (pp. 397–399). New York: Garland.

Keating, D. P. (1990). Structuralism, deconstruction, reconstruction: The limits of reasoning. In W. F. Overton (Ed.), *Reasoning, necessity, and logic: Developmental perspectives* (pp. 299–319). Hillsdale, NJ: Erlbaum.

Keating, D. P. (1991). Adolescent cognition. In R. M. Lerner, A. C. Petersen, & J. Brooks-Gunn (Eds.), *Encyclopedia of adolescence* (pp. 119–129). New York: Garland.

Keith, J. B., McCreary, C., Collins, K., Smith, C. P., & Bernstein, I. (1991). Sexual activity and contraceptive use among low-income urban Black adolescent females. *Adolescence, 26,* 769–785.

Kelly, J. B., & Wallerstein, J. S. (1976). The effects of parental divorce: Experiences of the child in early latency. *American Journal of Orthopsychiatry, 46,* 20–33.

Kelly, M. L., Sanchez-Huckles, J., & Walker, R. R. (1993). Correlates of disciplinary practices in working-to-middle class African-American mothers. *Merrill-Palmer Quarterly, 39,* 252–264.

Kempton, T., Armistead, L., Wierson, M., & Forehand, R. (1991). Presence of a sibling as a potential buffer following parental divorce: An examination of young adolescents. *Journal of Clinical Child Psychology, 20,* 434–438.

Kendler, K. S., MacLean, C., Neale, M., Kessler, R., Heath, A., & Eaves, L. (1991). The genetic epidemiology of bulimia nervosa. *American Journal of Psychiatry, 148,* 1627–1637.

Kenon, M. (2000, April 1). A community at the cross roads. *Billboard, 112,* 36.

Kernis, M. H., Cornell, D. P., Sun, C. R., Berry, A., & Harlow, T. (1993). There's more to self-esteem than whether its high or low: The importance of stability of self-esteem. *Journal of Personality and Social Psychology, 65,* 1190–1204.

Kernis, M. H., Grannemann, B. D., & Barclay, L. C. (1989). Stability and level of self-esteem as predictors of anger arousal and hostility. *Journal of Personality and Social Psychology, 56,* 1013–1022.

Kerns, K. A., Klepac, L., & Cole, A. K. (1996). Peer relationships and preadolescents' perceptions of security of child-mother relationship. *Developmental Psychology, 32,* 457–466.

Kerr, B. (1991). Educating gifted girls. In N. Colangelo & G. A. Davis (Eds.), *Handbook of gifted education* (pp. 402–416). Needham Heights, MA: Allyn & Bacon.

Kerr, B., & Maresh, S. E. (1994). Career counseling for gifted women. In W. B. Walsh & S. O. Osipow (Eds.), *Career counseling for women* (pp. 43–85). Hillsdale, NJ: Erlbaum.

Kerr, M., & Stattin, H. (2000). What parents know, how they know it, and several forms of adolescent adjustment: Further support for a reinterpretation of monitoring. *Developmental Psychology, 36,* 366–380.

Kershner, R. (1996). Adolescent attitudes about rape. *Adolescence, 31,* 29–33.

Kessler, R. C., & McLeod, J. D. (1984). Sex differences in vulnerability to undesirable life events. *American Sociological Review, 49,* 620–631.

Kidwell, J. S., Dunham, R. M., Bacho, R. A., Pastorino, E., & Portes, P. R. (1995). Adolescent identity exploration: A test of Erikson's theory of transitional crisis. *Adolescence, 30,* 785–793.

Killen, J. D., Hayward, C., Wilson, D. M., Taylor, C. B., Hammer, L. D., Litt, I., et al. (1994). Factors associated with eating disorder symptoms in a community sample of 6th and 7th grade girls. *International Journal of Eating Disorders, 16,* 227–238.

Kilpatrick, D. G., Acierno, R., Resnick, H. S., Saunders, B. E., & Best, C. L. (1997). A 2-year longitudinal analysis of the relationships between violent assault and substance use in women. *Journal of Consulting and Clinical Psychology, 65,* 834–847.

Kilpatrick, D. G., Acierno, R., Saunders, B., Resnick, H. S., Best, C. L., & Schnurr, P. P. (2000). Risk factors for adolescent substance abuse and dependence data from a national sample. *Journal of Consulting and Clinical Psychology, 68,* 19–30.

Kim, K. J., Conger, R. D., Lorenz, F. O., & Elder, G. H. (2001). Parent-adolescent reciprocity in negative affect and its relation to early adult social development. *Developmental Psychology, 37,* 775–790.

King, K. A. (2001). Developing a comprehensive school suicide prevention program. *Journal of School Health, 7,* 132–136.

King, N. J., Ollier, K., Iacuone, R., Schuster, S., Bays, K., Gullone, E., & Ollendick, T. H. (1989). Fears of children and adolescents: A cross-sectional Australian study using the Revised-Fear Survey schedule for children. *Journal of Child Psychology and Psychiatry, 30,* 775–784.

King, N. M. P., & Churchill, L. R. (2000, July). Ethical principles guiding research on child and adolescent subjects. *Journal of Interpersonal Violence, 15,* 710–725.

King, P. (1988). Heavy metal music and drug abuse in adolescents. *Drug Abuse, 83,* 295–304.

King, V., & Elder, G. H. (1995). American children view their grandparents: Linked lives across three rural generations. *Journal of Marriage and the Family, 57,* 165–178.

Kinnaird, K. L., & Gerrard, M. (1986). Premarital sexual behavior and attitudes toward marriage and divorce among young women as a function of their mothers' marital status. *Journal of Marriage and the Family, 48,* 757–765.

Kinney, D. A. (1993). From nerds to normals: The recovery of identity among adolescents from middle school to high school. *Sociology of Education, 66,* 21–40.

Kirby, D. (1994). School-based programs to reduce sexual risk behaviors: A review of effectiveness. *Public Health Reports, 109,* 339–360.

Kirby, D. (1997). *No easy answers: Research findings on programs to reduce teen pregnancy*. Washington, DC: National Campaign to Prevent Teen Pregnancy.

Kirby, D. (2002). The impact of schools and school programs upon adolescent sexual behavior. *The Journal of Sex Research, 39,* 27–34.

Kirkpatrick, L. A., & Davis, K. E. (1994). Attachment style, gender, and relationship stability: A longitudinal analysis. *Journal of Personality and Social Psychology, 66,* 502–512.

Kistner, J., Haskett, M., White, K., & Robbins, F. (1987). Perceived competence and self-worth of LD and normally achieving students. *Learning Disabilities Quarterly, 10,* 37–44.

Kite, M. E. (1996). Age, gender, and occupational label: A test of social role theory. *Psychology of Women Quarterly, 20,* 361–374.

Kivett, V. R. (1993). Racial comparisons of the grandmother role: Implications for strengthening the family support system of older black women. *Family Relations, 42,* 165–172.

Klaczynski, P. A., Fauth, J. M., & Swanger, A. (1998). Adolescent identity: Rational vs. experiential processing, formal operations, and critical thinking beliefs. *Journal of Youth and Adolescence, 27,* 185–207.

Klaczynski, P. A., & Gordon, D. H. (1996). Everyday statistical reasoning during adolescence and young adulthood: Motivational, general ability, and developmental influences. *Child Development, 67,* 2873–2892.

Klaczynski, P. A., & Narasimham, G. (1998). Development of scientific reasoning biases: Cognitive versus ego-protective explanations. *Developmental Psychology, 34,* 175–187.

Klein, A. G., & Zehms, D. (1996, September). Self-concept and gifted girls: A cross-sectional study of intellectually gifted females in grades. *Roeper Review, 19,* 30–35.

Klein, D. F. (1996). Preventing hung juries about therapy studies. *Journal of Consulting and Clinical Psychology, 64,* 81–87.

Klein, J. D., Brown, J. D., Childers, K. W., Olivera, J., Porter, C., & Dykers, C. (1993). Adolescents' risky behavior and mass media use. *Pediatrics, 92,* 24–31.

Klein, M. (1998, February). Teen green. *American Demographics, 22,* p. 56.

Klein, R. G., & Mannuzza, S. (1991). Long-term outcome of hyperactive children: A review. *Journal of American Academy Child and Adolescent Psychiatry, 30,* 383–387.

Kleiner, C., & Lord, C. (1999, November 22). The cheating game. *U. S. News & World Report,* pp. 55–58.

Kleinfeld, J. (1999, Winter). Student performance: Males versus females. *Public Interest,* 3–21.

Klepinger, D. H., Lundberg, S., & Plotnick, R. D. (1995). Adolescent fertility and the educational attainment of young women. *Family Planning Perspectives, 27,* 23–28.

Knight, J. R., Wechsler, H., Kou, M., Seibering, M., Weitzman, E. R., & Schuckit, M. A. (2002). Alcohol abuse and dependence among U.S. College students. *Journal of Studies on Alcoholism, 63,* 263–271.

Knox, D., Custis, L. L., & Zusman, M. E. (2000). Abuse in dating relationships among college students. *College Student Journal, 34,* 505–513.

Knox, D., Sturdivant, L., & Zusman, M. E. (2001). College student attitudes toward sexual intimacy. *College Student Journal, 35,* 241–250.

Knox, M., Funk, J., Elliott, R., & Bush, E. G. (1998). Adolescents' possible selves and their relationship to global self-esteem. *Sex Roles, 39,* 61–81.

Koegel, H. M., Donin, I., Ponterotto, J. G., & Spitz, S. (1995). Multicultural career development: A methodological critique of 8 years of research in three leading career journals. *Journal of Employment Counseling, 32,* 50–63.

Koestner, R., Franz, C., & Weinberger, J. (1990). The family origins of empathic concern: A 26-year-longitudinal study. *Journal of Personality and Social Psychology, 58,* 709–717.

Koestner, R., Ryan, R. M., Bernieri, F., & Holt, K. (1984). Setting limits on children's behavior: The differential effects of controlling versus informational styles on intrinsic motivation and creativity. *Journal of Personality, 52,* 233–248.

Koestner, R., & Zuckerman, M. (1994). Causality orientations, failure, and achievement. *Journal of Personality, 62,* 321–345.

Koff, E., & Rierdan, J. (1991). Menarche and body image. In R. M. Lerner, A. C. Petersen, & J. Brooks-Gunn (Eds.), *Encyclopedia of adolescence* (pp. 631–636). New York: Wiley.

Koff, E., & Rierdan, J. (1993). Advanced pubertal development and eating disturbance in early adolescent girls. *Journal of Adolescent Health, 14,* 433–439.

Koff, E., & Rierdan, J. (1995). Preparing girls for menstruation: Recommendations from adolescent girls. *Adolescence, 30,* 795–811.

Kohlberg, L. (1969). Stage and sequence: The cognitive-developmental approach to socialization. In D. A. Goslin (Eds.), *Handbook of socialization theory and research.* Chicago: Rand-McNally.

Kohlberg, L. (1976). Moral stages and moralization: The cognitive-developmental approach. In T. Lickona (Ed.), *Moral development and behavior* (pp. 31–53). New York: Holt, Rinehart & Winston.

Kohlberg, L. (1981). *Essays on moral development: The philosophy of moral development* (Vol. 1). San Francisco: Harper & Row.

Kohlberg, L. (1987). The development of moral judgment and moral education. In L. Kohlberg (Ed.), *Child development and childhood education: A cognitive-developmental view* (pp. 259–329). New York: Longman.

Kohlberg, L., & Kramer, R. (1969). Continuities and discontinuities in childhood and adult moral development. *Human Development, 12,* 83–120.

Kohlberg, L., & Lickona, T. (1987). Moral discussion and the class meeting. In R. DeVries (with L. Kohlberg) (Ed.), *Programs of early education* (pp. 143–188). New York: Longman.

Kohn, A. (1994, December). The truth about self-esteem. *Phi Delta Kappan,* 272–285.

Kopp, C., & Krakow, J. B. (1982). *Child development in the social context.* Boston: Addison-Wesley.

Kossen, S. (1983). *The human side of organizations* (3rd ed.). New York: Harper & Row.

Kotesky, R. L., Walker, J. S., & Johnson, A. W. (1990). Measurement of identity from adolescence to adulthood: Cultural, community, religious, and family factors. *Journal of Psychology and Theology, 18,* 54–65.

Kouri, E. M., & Pope, H. G. (2000). Abstinence symptoms during withdrawal from chronic marijuana use. *Experimental and Clinical Psychopharmacology, 8,* 483–492.

Kouri, E. M., Pope, H. G., & Lukas S. E. (1999). Changes in aggressive behavior during withdrawal from long-term marijuana use. *Psychopharmacology, 143,* 302–308.

Kowal, A., & Kramer, L. (1997). Children's understanding of parental differential treatment. *Child Development, 68,* 113–126.

Kowaleski-Jones, L., & Mott, F. L. (1998). Sex, contraception and childbearing among high-risk youth: Do different factors influence males and females? *Family Planning Perspectives, 30,* 163–169.

Kraut, R., Patterson, M., Landmark, V., Kiesler, S., Mukopadhyay, T., & Scherlis, W. (1998). Internet paradox: A social technology that reduces social involvement and psychological well-being? *American Psychologist, 53,* 1017–1032.

Krcmar, M., & Greene, K. (1999). Predicting exposure to and uses of television violence. *Journal of Communication, 49*(3), 24–45.

Kreinen, T. (2002). Two ways to promote sexuality education. *SIECUS Report, 30,* 3.

Kreitler, S., & Kreitler, H. (1987). Conceptions and processes of planning: The developmental perspective. In S. L. Frieman, E. K. Scholnick, & R. R. Cocking (Eds.), *Blueprints for thinking* (pp. 205–272). Cambridge, England: Cambridge University Press.

Kroger, J. (1997). Gender and identity: The intersection of structure, content, and context. *Sex Roles, 36,* 747–770.

Kruesi, M. J., Hibbs, E. D., Zahn, T. P., Keysor, C. S. Hamburger, S. D., Bartko, J. J., & Rapoport, J. L. (1992). A 2-year prospective follow-up study of children and adolescents with disruptive behavior disorders. *Archives of General Psychiatry, 49,* 429–435.

Kruger, A. C. (1992). The effect of peer and adult-child transactive discussions on moral reasoning. *Merrill-Palmer Quarterly, 38,* 191–213.

Kruger, A. C., & Tomasello, M. 91986). Transactive discussions with peers and adults. *Developmental Psychology, 22,* 681–685.

Krunstal, F. (1996, January/February). All those questions. *Adoptive Families, 29,* 50.

Ku, L. C., Sonenstein, F. L., & Pleck, J. H. (1993). Factors affecting first intercourse among young men. *Public Health Reports, 108,* 680–694.

Kubey, R., & Larson, R. (1990). The use and experience of the new video media among children and young adolescents. *Communication Research, 17,* 107–130.

Kubiszyn, T., & Borich, C. (1987). *Educational testing and measurement* (2nd ed.). Glenview, IL: Scott, Foresman.

Kuhn, D. (1999). A developmental model of critical thinking. *Educational Researcher, 28,* 16–25.

Kuhn, D., Amsel, E., & O'Loughlin, M. (1988). *The development of scientific thinking skills.* Orlando: Academic Press.

Kuhn, D., Ho, V., & Adams, C. (1979). Formal reasoning among pre and late adolescents. *Child Development, 50,* 1149–1152.

Kuklinski, M. R., & Weinstein, R. S. (2001). Classroom and developmental differences in a path model of teacher expectancy effects. *Child Development, 72,* 1554–1578.

Kunda, Z. (1990). The case for motivated reasoning. *Psychological Bulletin, 108,* 480–496.

Kunkel, D., Cope, K. M., Farinola, W. M., Biely, E., Rollin, E. (1999). *Sex on TV: A biennial report to the Henry J. Kaiser Family Foundation.* Menlo Park, CA: Henry J. Kaiser Family Foundation.

Kurdek, L. A., & Fine, M. A. (1993). The relation between family structure and young adolescents' appraisals of family climate and parenting behavior. *Journal of Family Issues, 14,* 279–290.

Kurdek, L. A., & Fine, M. A. (1995). Mothers, fathers, stepfathers, and siblings as providers of supervision, acceptance, and autonomy to young adolescents. *Journal of Family Psychology, 9,* 95–99.

Kurdek, L., & Sinclair, R. (1988). Relation of eighth graders' family structure, gender, and family environment with academic performance and school behavior. *Journal of Educational Psychology, 80,* 90–94.

Labouvie-Vief, G. (1980). Beyond formal operations: Uses and limits of pure logic in life-span development. *Human Development, 23,* 141–161.

Labouvie-Vief, G. (1984). Logic and self-regulation from youth to maturity: A model. In M. L. Commons, F. A. Richards, & C. Armon (Eds.), *Beyond formal operations* (pp. 158–181). New York: Praeger.

Lacombe, A. C., & Gay, J. (1998). The role of gender in adolescent identity and intimacy decisions. *Journal of Youth and Adolescence, 27,* 795–803.

Lacourse, E., Claes, M., & Villeneuve, M. (2001, June). Heavy metal music and adolescent suicidal risk. *Journal of Youth and Adolescence, 30,* 321–335.

LaFramboise, T., Coleman, H. L. K., & Gerton, J. (1993). Psychological impact of biculturalism: Evidence and theory. *Psychological Bulletin, 114,* 395–412.

Lam, C. M. (1997). A cultural perspective on the study of Chinese adolescent development. *Child and Adolescent Social Work Journal, 14,* 95–113.

Lamborn, S. D., Mounts, N. S., Steinberg, L., & Dornbusch, S. M. (1991). Patterns of competence and adjustment among adolescents from authoritative, authoritarian, indulgent and neglected families. *Child Development, 62,* 1049–1065.

Lammers, C., Ireland, M. I., Resnick, M., & Blum, R. (2000). Influence on adolescents' decision to postpone onset of sexual intercourse: A survival analysis of virginity among youths aged 13 to 18 years. *Journal of Adolescent Health, 26,* 42–48.

Landau, M. (2000, April 21). Deciphering the adolescent brain. *Focus: News from Harvard, Medical, Dental & Public Health Schools.* Retrieved December 30, 2002, from http://focus.hms.harvard.edu/2000/Apr21_2000/psychiatry.html

Landry, D. J., Kaeser, L., & Richards, C. L. (1999). Abstinence promotion and the provision of information about contraception in public school district sexuality education policies. *Family Planning Perspectives, 31,* 280–186.

Lane, E. (1995, April 11). Teen surveys vs. parental consent. *Newsday,* p. B29.

Langley, J., Martin, J., & Nada-Raja, S., (1997). Physical assault among 21-year-olds by partners. *Journal of Interpersonal Violence, 12,* 675–684.

Langlois, J. H., & Downs, A. C. (1980). Mothers, fathers, and peers as socialization agents of sex-typed play behavior in young children. *Child Development, 51,* 1237–1247.

Laosa, L. M. (1996). Intelligence testing and social policy. *Journal of Applied Developmental Psychology, 17,* 153–173.

Lapsley, D. K. (1990). Continuity and discontinuity in adolescent social cognitive development. In R. Montemayor, G. R. Adams, & T. P. Gullotta (Eds.), *From childhood to adolescence* (pp. 183–205). New York: Sage.

Lapsley, D. K. (1991). Egocentrism theory and the "new look" at the imaginary audience and personal fable in adolescence. In R. M. Lerner, A. C. Petersen, & J. Brooks-Gunn (Eds.), *Encyclopedia of adolescence* (pp. 281–286). New York: Garland.

Larson, D. (1990/1991). Unplanned parenthood. *Modern Maturity,* 32–36.

Larson, M. S. (1996). Sex roles and soap operas: What adolescents learn about single motherhood. *Sex Roles, 35,* 97–110.

Larson, R. (1991). Moodiness. In R. M. Lerner, A. C. Petersen, & J. Brooks-Gunn (Eds.), *Encyclopedia of adolescence* (pp. 658–662). New York: Wiley.

Larson, R. W. (2000). Toward a psychology of positive youth development. *American Psychologist, 55,* 170–183.

Larson, R., Csikszentmihalyi, M., & Graef, R. (1980). Mood variability and the psychosocial adjustment of adolescents. *Journal of Youth and Adolescence, 9,* 469–490.

Larson, R., Kubey, R., & Colletti, J. (1989). Changing channels: Early adolescent media choices and shifting investments in family and friends. *Journal of Youth and Adolescence, 18,* 583–599.

Larson, R., & Lampman-Petraitis, C. (1989). Daily emotional states as reported by children and adolescents. *Child Development, 60,* 1250–1260.

Larson, R., Raffaelli, M., Richards, M., Ham, M., & Jewell, L. (1990). The ecology of depression in early adolescence: A profile of daily psychological states and activities. *Journal of Abnormal Psychology, 99,* 92–102.

Larson, R., & Richards, M. (1991). Daily companionship in late childhood and early adolescence: Changing developmental contexts. *Child Development, 62,* 284–300.

Larson, R. W., Richards, M. H., Moneta, G., Holmbeck, G., & Duckett, E. (1996). Changes in adolescents' daily interactions with their families from ages 10 to 18: Disengagement and transformation. *Developmental Psychology, 32,* 744–754.

Larson, R. W., & Verma, S. (1999). How children and adolescents spend time across the world: Work, play, and developmental opportunities. *Psychological Bulletin, 125,* 701–736.

Lauresen, B., & Collins, W. A. (1994). Interpersonal conflict during adolescence. *Psychological Bulletin, 115,* 197–209.

Laursen, B. (1993). Conflict management among close peers. In B. Laursen (Ed.), *Close friendships in adolescence: New directions for child development* (pp. 39–54). San Francisco: Jossey-Bass.

Laursen, B. (1995). Conflict and social interaction in adolescent relationships. *Journal of Research in Adolescence, 5,* 55–70.

Lavery, B., Siegel, A. W., Cousins, J., & Rubovits, D. S. (1993). Adolescent risk-taking: An analysis of problem behaviors in problem children. *Journal of Experimental Child Psychology, 55,* 277–294.

Lawton, M. (1994, November 9). Violence-prevention curricula: What works best? *Education Week,* pp. 1, 10.

Lazarus, R. S., & Folkman, S. (1984). *Stress, appraisal and coping.* New York: Springer.

Leadbeater, B. (1991). Relativistic thinking in adolescence. In R. M. Lerner, A. C. Petersen, & J. Brooks-Gunn (Eds.), *Encyclopedia of adolescence* (pp. 921–925). New York: Garland.

Leahy, R. L., & Shirk, S. R. (1985). Social cognition and the development of the self. In R. L. Leahy (Ed.), *The development of the self* (pp. 123–150). New York: Plenum.

Leahy, T. H., & Harris, R. J. (1997). *Learning and cognition* (4th ed.). Upper Saddle River, NJ: Prentice Hall.

Leary, M. R. (1995). *Behavioral research methods* (2nd ed.). Pacific Grove, CA: Brooks-Cole.

LeBlanc, R. S., Muise, J. G., & Blanchard, L. (1992). Backward masking in children and adolescents: Sensory transmission, accrual rate and asymptotic performance. *Journal of Experimental Child Psychology, 53,* 105–114.

Lebra, T. (1976). *Japanese patterns or behavior.* Honolulu, HI: University of Hawaii Press.

Lee, J. A. (1974a). *Colours of love.* Toronto: New Press.

Lee, J. A. (1974b, October). The styles of loving. *Psychology Today,* 44–51.

Leff, S. (1999). Bullied children are picked on for their vulnerability. *British Medical Journal, 318,* 1076.

Leitenberg, H., Detzer, M. J., & Srebnik, D. (1993). Gender differences in masturbation and the relation of masturbation experience in preadolescence and/or early adolescence to sexual behavior and sexual adjustment in young adulthood. *Archives of Sexual Behavior, 22,* 87–98.

Leiter, R. A. (1997). *National survey of state laws* (2nd ed.). Detroit, MI: Gale.

Leland, N. L., & Barth, R. P. (1992). Gender differences in knowledge, intentions, and behaviors concerning pregnancy and sexually transmitted disease prevention among adolescents. *Journal of Adolescent Health, 13,* 589–599.

Lennon, R., & Eisenberg, N. (1987). Gender and age differences in empathy and sympathy. In N. Eisenberg & J. Strayer (Eds.), *Empathy and its development.* Cambridge: Cambridge University Press.

Lent, R., Lopez, F. G., & Bieschke, K. J. (1991). Mathematics self-efficacy: Sources and relation to science based career choice. *Journal of Counseling Psychology, 38,* 424–430.

Leong, F. T. L. (1991). Career development attributes and occupational values of Asian American and white American college students. *The Career Development Quarterly, 39,* 221–230.

Leong, F. T. L., & Chou, E. L. (1994). The role of ethnic identity and acculturation in the vocational behavior of Asian Americans: An integrative review. *Journal of Vocational Behavior, 44*, 155–172.

Leong, F. T. L., & Gim-Chung, R. H. (1995). Career assessment and intervention for Asian Americans. In F. T. L. Leong (Ed), *Career development and vocational behavior of racial and ethnic minorities* (pp. 193–226). Hillsdale, NJ: Erlbaum.

Leong, F. T. L., & Hayes, T. J. (1990). Occupational stereotyping of Asian Americans. *The Career Development Quarterly, 39*, 143–154.

Leong, F. T. L., & Serafica, F. C. (1995). Career development of Asian Americans: A research area in need of a good theory. In F. T. L. Leong (Ed.), *Career development and vocational behavior of racial and ethnic minorities* (pp. 67–103). Hillsdale, NJ: Erlbaum.

Lerman, C., Caporaso, N. E., Audrain, J., Main, D., Bowman, E. D., Lockshin, B., et al. (1999). Evidence suggesting the role of specific genetic factors in cigarette smoking. *Health Psychology, 18*, 14–20.

Lerner, J. V. (1994). *Working women and their families.* Beverly Hills, CA: Sage.

Lerner, J. V., & Abrams, L. A. (1994). Developmental correlates of maternal employment influences on children. In C. B. Fisher & R. M. Lerner (Ed.), *Applied developmental psychology* (pp. 174–192). New York: McGraw Hill.

Lerner, J. V., & Galambos, N. L. (1986). Child development and family change: The influences of maternal employment on infants and toddlers. In L. P. Lipsitt & C. Rovee-Collier (Eds.), *Advances in infancy research* (Vol. 4, pp. 39–86). Hillsdale, NJ: Erlbaum.

Lerner, J. V., & Hess, L. E. (1991). Maternal employment influences on adolescent development. In R. M. Lerner, A. C. Petersen, & J. Brooks-Gunn (Eds.), *Encyclopedia of adolescence* (pp. 602–608). New York: Garland.

Lerner, R. M., Karson, M., Meisels, M., & Knapp, J. R. (1975). Actual and perceived attitudes of late adolescents and their parents: The phenomenon of the generation gap. *Journal of Genetic Psychology, 126*, 195–207.

Leshner, A. L. (1999, October). Addiction is a brain disease—and it matters. *National Institute of Justice Journal, 237*, 2–6.

Lesko, N. (1996). Denaturalizing adolescence. *Youth and Society, 28*, 139–161.

Leung, S. A. (1998). Vocational identity and career choice congruence of gifted and talented high school students. *Counseling Psychology Quarterly, 11*, 325–336.

Leung, S. A., Conoley, C. W., & Schel, M. J. (1994). The career and educational aspirations of gifted high school students: A retrospective study. *Journal of Counseling Development, 72*, 298–303.

Levine, E., & Guthrie, J. F. (1997). Nutrient intakes and eating patterns of teenagers. *Family Economics and Nutrition Review, 10*, 23–31.

Levine, R., Sato, S., Hashimoto, T., & Verma, J. (1995). Love and marriage in eleven cultures. *Journal of Cross-Cultural Psychology, 26*, 554–571.

Levy, C. J. (1999, February, 9). Leaders in Albany back new adoption and foster care rules. *New York Times*, B6.

Levy, M. B., & Davis, K. E. (1988). Lovestyles and attachment styles compared: Their relations to each other and to various relationship characteristics. *Journal of Social and Personal Relationships, 5*, 439–471.

Lewin, L. M., Davis, B., & Hops, H. (1999). Childhood social predictors of adolescent antisocial behavior: Gender differences in predictive accuracy and efficacy. *Journal of Abnormal Child Psychology, 27*, 277–292.

Lewin, T. (1998, December 12). How boys lost out to girl power. *The New York Times*, pp. 23–24.

Lewinsohn, P. M. (1974). A behavioral approach to depression. In R. J. Friedman & M. M. Katz (Eds.), *The psychology of depression: Contemporary theory and research* (pp. 157–178). Washington, DC: Winston-Wiley.

Lewinsohn, P. M., Clarke, G. N., Hops, H., & Andrews, J. (1990). Cognitive-behavioral treatment for depressed adolescents. *Behavior Therapy, 21*, 385–401.

Lewinsohn, P. M., & Graf, M. (1973). Pleasant events, activities, and depression. *Journal of Consulting and Clinical Psychology, 41*, 261–268.

Lewinsohn, P. M., Hops, H., Roberts, R. E., Seeley, J. R., & Andrews, J. A. (1993). Adolescent psychopathology: 1. Prevalence and incidence of depression and other DSM-III-R disorders in high school students. *Journal of Abnormal Psychology, 102*, 133–144.

Lewis, A. C. (1998). Growing Hispanic enrollments: Challenge and opportunity. *Phi Delta Kappan, 79*, 3–4.

Lewis, A. C. (1999). Time to remember the "forgotten half." *Phi Delta Kappan, 80*, 643–644.

Lewis, C. C. (1981). How adolescents approach decisions: Changes over grades seven to twelve and policy implications. *Child Development, 52*, 538–544.

Lewis, D. R., Hearn, J. C., & Zilbert, E. E. (1993). Efficiency and equity effects of vocationally focused postsecondary education. *Sociology of Education, 66*, 188–205.

Lewis, R. G., & Ho, M. K. (1979). Social work with Native Americans. *Social Work, 20*, 379–392.

Lewis, T., Stone, J., Shipley, W., & Madzar, S. (1998). The transition from school to work: An examination of the literature. *Youth and Society, 29*, 259–292.

Liebert, R. M., & Sprafkin, J. (1988). *The early window: Effects of television on children and youth* (3rd ed.). New York: Pergamon.

Lieu, T. A., Newacheck, P. W., & McManus, M. A. (1993). Race, ethnicity, and access to ambulatory care among US adolescents. *American Journal of Public Health, 83*, 960–965.

Light, D., Keller, S., & Calhoun, C. (1994). *Sociology* (8th ed.). New York: Knopf.

Lightbody, P., & Durndell, A. (1996). The masculine image of careers in science and technology: Fact or fiction? *British Journal of Educational Psychology, 66*, 429–433.

Lin, C. C., & Fu, V. R. (1990). A comparison of child-rearing practices among Chinese, immigrant Chinese, and Caucasian-American parents. *Child Development, 61*, 429–433.

Lin, Q. (2001). An evaluation of charter school effectiveness. *Education, 122*, 166–177.

Lin, S., & Lepper, M. R. (1987). Correlates of children's usage of video games and computers. *Journal of Applied Social Psychology, 17*, 72–93.

Lindauer, P., & Petrie, G. (1997). A review of cooperative learning: An alternative to everyday instructional strategies. *Journal of Instructional Psychology, 24*, 183–188.

Lindeman, M., Harakka, T., & Keltikangas-Jarvinen, L. (1997). Age and gender differences in adolescents' reactions to conflict situations: Aggression, prosociality, and withdrawal. *Journal of Youth and Adolescence, 26*, 339–351.

Lingeman, R., & Sorel, E. (1997, April 21). Heavengate. *The Nation*, p. 56.

Lipsey, M. W., & Derzon, J. H. (1998). Predictors of violent or serious delinquency in adolescence and early adulthood. In R. Loeber & D. P. Farrington (Eds.), *Serious and violent juvenile offenders: Risk factors and successful interventions* (pp. 86–105). Thousand Oaks, CA: Sage.

Lipsey, M. W., & Wilson, D. B. (1993). The efficacy of psychological, educational, and behavioral treatment: Confirmation from meta-analysis. *American Psychologist, 48*, 1181–1209.

Little, M. (2000). *Sexually transmitted diseases.* Philadelphia: Chelsea House.

Livesley, W. J., & Bromley, D. C. (1973). *Person perception in childhood and adolescence.* London: Wiley.

Livingstone, S. (1994). *Talk on television: Audience participation and public debate.* London: Routledge.

Lockwood, D. (1997). *Violence among middle school and high school students: Analytic and implications for prevention* [NCJ 166363]. Washington, DC: NCJRS.

Loeber, R., & Stouthamer-Loeber, M. (1998). Development of juvenile aggression and violence: Some common misconceptions and controversies. *American Psychologist, 53*, 242–259.

Loehlin, J. C. (1992). *Genes and environment in personality development.* Newbury Park, CA: Sage.

Looker, E. D., & Magee, P. A. (2000). Gender and work: The occupational expectations of young women and men in the 1990s. *Gender Issues, 18*, 74–82.

LoPresto, C. T., Sherman, M. F., & Sherman, N. C. (1985). The effects of a masturbation seminar on high school males' attitudes, false beliefs, guilt, and behavior. *The Journal of Sex Research, 21*, 142–156.

Lovell, S. (2000, August 21). Court strikes parental notification law, saying it violates state equal protection. *New Jersey Law Journal, 161*, 5–7.

Lovett, M. W., Borden, S. L., DeLuca, T., Lacerenza, L., Benson, N. J., & Brackstone, D. (1994). Treating the core deficits of developmental dyslexia: Evidence of transfer of learning after phonologically and strategy based reading training programs. *Developmental Psychology, 30*, 805–822.

Lovitt, T. C. (1989). *Introduction to learning disabilities*. Boston: Allyn & Bacon.

Lowry, D., & Towles, D. (1989). Soap opera portrayals of sex, contraception, and sexually transmitted diseases. *Journal of Communication, 39*, 76–83.

Luce, T., & Merrell, J. (1995). Perceived dangerousness of recreational drugs. *Drug Education, 25*, 297–306.

Lueptow, L. B., Garovich-Szabo, L., & Lueptow, M. B. (2001). Social change and the persistence of sex typing: 1974–1997. *Social Forces, 80*, 1–21.

Lurie, S. J. (2002, February 6). What should the public be told about the risks of ecstasy? *Journal of the American Medical Association, 287*, 585.

Luster, T., & McAdoo, H. P. (1994). Factors related to the achievement and adjustment of young African American children. *Child Development, 65*, 1080–1094.

Luthar, S. S. (1991). Vulnerability and resilience: A study of high-risk adolescents. *Child Development, 62*, 600–616.

Luzzo, D. A. (1993). Ethnic differences in college students' perceptions of barriers to career development. *Journal of Multicultural Counseling and Development, 21*, 227–236.

Luzzo, D. A., & MacGregor, M. W. (2001). Practice and research in career counseling and development 2000. *Career Development Quarterly, 50*, 98–140.

Lynch, L. M. (1993). Entry-level jobs: First rung on the employment ladder or economic dead end? *Journal of Labor Research, 14*, 249–263.

Lyons, N. P. (1988). Two perspectives: On self, relationships, and morality. In C. Gilligan, J. V. Ward, & J. M. Taylor (Eds.), *Mapping the moral domain* (pp. 21–48). Cambridge: Harvard University Press.

Lytle, L. J., Bakken, L., & Romig, C. (1997). Adolescent female identity development. *Sex Roles, 37*, 175–185.

Lytton, H., & Romney, D. M. (1991). Parents' differential socialization of boys and girls: A meta-analysis. *Psychological Bulletin, 109*, 267–296.

Lyubomirsky, S., & Nolen-Hoeksema, S. (1995). Effects of self-focused rumination on negative thinking and interpersonal problem solving. *Journal of Personality and Social Psychology, 69*, 176–190.

Ma, H. K. (1989). Moral orientation and moral judgement in adolescents in Hong Kong, mainland China, and England. *Journal of Cross-Cultural Psychology, 20*, 152–177.

Maag, J. W., & Behrens, J. T. (1989). Depression and cognitive self-statements of learning disabled and seriously emotionally disturbed adolescents. *Journal of Special Education, 23*, 17–27.

Maccoby, E. E. (1980). *Social development: Psychological growth and the parent-child relationship*. New York: Harcourt, Grace, Jovanovich.

Maccoby, E. E., & Martin, J. A. (1983). Socialization in the context of the family: Parent-child interaction. In P. H. Mussen (Ed.). *Handbook of child development* (4th ed., Vol. 4, pp. 1–103). New York: Wiley.

MacEwen, K. E., & Barling, J. (1991). Effects of maternal employment on children's behavior via mood, cognitive difficulties, and parenting behavior. *Journal of Marriage and the Family, 53*, 635–644.

Maehr, M. L., & Meyer, H. A. (1997). Understanding motivation and schooling: Where we've been, where we are, and where we need to go. *Educational Psychology Review, 9*, 371–409.

Magnusson, D. (1988). *Individual development from an interactional perspective: A longitudinal study*. Hillsdale, NJ: Erlbaum.

Mahoney, J. L., & Cairns, R. B. (1997). Do extracurricular activities protect against early school dropout? *Developmental Psychology, 33*, 241–253.

Mail, P. D., & Johnson, S. (1993). Boozing, sniffing, and taking: An overview of the past, present and future of substance use by American Indians. *American Indian and Alaska Native Mental Health Research, 5*, 1–33.

Makepeace, J. M. (1986). Gender differences in courtship violence victimization. *Family Relations, 35*, 383–388.

Males, M. A. (1997b). Stop blaming kids and TV. *The Progressive, 61*, 25–28.

Males, M. A. (1997a, December). Debunking 10 myths about teens. *Education Digest*, 48–50.

Malik, S., Sorensen, S. B., & Aneshensel, C. S. (1997). Community and dating violence among adolescents: Perpetration and victimization. *Journal of Adolescent Health, 21*, 291–302.

Malina, R. M., Bouchard, C., & Beunen, G. (1988). Human growth: Selected aspects of current research on well-nourished children. *Annual Review of Anthropology, 17*, 187–219.

Malinowski, C. I., & Smith, C. P. (1985). Moral reasoning and moral conduct: An investigation prompted by Kohlberg's theory. *Journal of Personality and Social Psychology, 49*, 1016–1027.

Manber, R., Pardee, R. E., Bootzin, R. R., Kuo, T., Rider, A. M., Rider, S. P., & Bergstrom, L. (1995). Changing sleep patterns in adolescence. *Sleep Research, 24*, 106.

Manis, F. R., Keating, D. P., & Morrison, F. J. (1980). Developmental differences in the allocation of processing capacity. *Journal of Experimental Child Psychology, 29*, 156–169.

Manning, A. (1994, October 21). Trouble follows armed students. *USA Today*, D1.

Manning, L., & Bucher, K. T. (2000). Middle schools should be both learner-centered and subject-centered. *Childhood Education, 77*, 41–45.

Manning, M. L., & Allen, M. G. (1987). Social development in early adolescence. *Childhood Education, 18*, 172–176.

Manning, W. (1990). Parenting employed teenagers. *Youth and Society, 22*, 184–200.

Manno, B. V., Finn, C. E., Jr., Bierlein, L. A., & Vanourek, G. (1998). How charter schools are different: Lessons and implications from a National Study. *Phi Delta Kappan, 79*, 489–498.

Mannuzza, S., Klein, R. G., Bessler, A., Malloy, P., & LaPadula, M. (1993). Adult outcome of hyperactive boys. *Archives of General Psychiatry, 50*, 565–576.

Mannuzza, S., Klein, R. G., Bonagura, N., Malloy, P., Giampino, T. L., & Addalli, K. A. (1991). Hyperactive boys almost grown up. *Archives of General Psychiatry, 48*, 77–83.

Mannuzza, S., Klein, R. G., Konig, P. H., & Giampino, T. L. (1989). Hyperactive boys almost grown up. IV: Criminality and its relationship to psychiatric status. *Archives of General Psychiatry, 46*, 1073–1079.

Manzo, A. V. (1998, May/June). Teaching for creative outcomes: Why we don't, and how we all can. *The Clearing House, 71*, 287–291.

Marcia, J. (1967). Ego identity status: Relationship to change in self esteem, "general adjustment," and authoritarianism. *Journal of Personality, 35*, 118–133.

Marcia, J. E. (1980). Identity in adolescence. In J. Adelson (Ed.), *Handbook of adolescent psychology* (pp. 159–187). New York: Wiley.

Marcia, J. E. (1994). The empirical study of ego identity. In H. A. Bosma, T. L. G. Graafsma, H. D. Grotevant, & D. J. de Levita (Eds.), *Identity and development: An interdisciplinary approach* (pp. 67–79). Thousand Oaks, CA: Sage.

Marcia, J. E., Waterman, A. S., Matteson, D. R., Archer, S. L., & Orlofsky, J. L. (1993). *Ego identity: A handbook for psychosocial research*. New York: Springer-Verlag.

Marcotte, D. (1996). Irrational beliefs and depression in adolescence. *Adolescence, 31*, 935–954.

Marcotte, D. (1997). Treating depression in adolescence: A review of the effectiveness of cognitive-behavioral treatments. *Journal of Youth and Adolescence, 26*, 273–284.

Marcotte, D., Alain, M., & Gosselin, M. J. (1999). Gender differences in adolescent depression: Gender-typed characteristics or problem-solving skills deficits. *Sex Roles, 41*, 31–41.

Marcotte, D., Fortin, L, Potvin, P., & Papillon, M. (2002). Gender differences in depressive symptoms during adolescence: Role of gender-typed characteristics, self-esteem, body image, stressful life events, and pubertal status. *Journal of Emotional and Behavioral Disorders, 10*, 29–43.

Marini, M. M., Fan, P.-L., Finley, E., & Betz, A. M. (1996). Gender and job values. *Sociology of Education, 69*, 49–65.

Markovits, H. & Vachon, R. (1989). Reasoning with contrary-to-fact propositions. *Journal of Experimental Child Psychology, 47*, 398–412.

Markstrom-Adams, C., & Adams, G. R. (1995). Gender, ethnic group, and grade differences in psychosocial functioning during middle adolescence. *Journal of Youth and Adolescence, 24*, 397–417.

Markus, H., & Kitayama, S. (1991). Culture and the self: Implications for cognition, emotion, and motivation. *Psychological Review, 98*, 224–253.

Marohn, R. C. (1997). The self in adolescence. In L. T. Flaherty & R. M. Searles (Eds.), *Handbook of child and adolescent psychiatry* (Vol. 3, pp. 139–147). New York: Wiley.

Marr, L. (1998). *Sexually transmitted diseases*. Baltimore, MD: Johns Hopkins Press.

Marsh, H. W., & O'Neill, R. (1984). Self-description questionnaire III (SDQ III): The construct validity of multidimensional self-concept ratings by late adolescents. *Journal of Educational Measurement, 21*, 153–174.

Marshall, J. (1983). Reducing the effects of work oriented values on the lives of male American workers. *Vocational and Guidance Journal, 32*, 109–115.

Marshall, R. (1997). School-to-work processes in the United States. In R. Takanishi & D. A. Hamburg (Eds.), *Preparing adolescents for the twenty-first century: Challenges facing Europe and the United States* (pp. 195–226). Cambridge, England: Cambridge University Press.

Marshall, S. P., & Smith, J. D. (1987). Sex differences in learning mathematics: A longitudinal study with item and error analysis. *Journal of Educational Psychology, 79*, 372–381.

Marsiglio, W. (1987). Adolescent fathers in the United States: Their initial living arrangements, marital experiences and educational outcomes. *Family Planning Perspectives, 19*, 240–251.

Marsiglio, W. (1993a). Adolescent male's orientation toward paternity and contraception. *Family Planning Perspectives, 25*, 22–31.

Marsiglio, W. (1993b). Attitudes toward homosexual activity and gays as friends: A national survey of heterosexual 15-to-19 year old males. *Journal of Sex Research, 30*, 12–17.

Martin, C. L., Eisenbud, L, & Ross, H. (1995). Children's gender-based reasoning about toys. *Child Development, 66*, 1453–1471.

Martin, C. L., & Halverson, C. F. (1981). A schematic processing model of sex-typing and stereotyping in children. *Child Development, 52*, 1119–1132.

Martin, C. L., & Little, J. K. (1990). The relation of gender understanding to children's sex-typed preferences and gender stereotypes. *Child Development, 61*, 1427–1439.

Martin, G., Clarke, M., & Pearce, C. (1993). Adolescent suicide: Music preference as an indicator of vulnerability. *Journal of the American Academy of Child and Adolescent Psychiatry, 32*, 530–536.

Martin, S. (1995, October). Practitioners may misunderstand bland families. *APA Monitor, 36*.

Martinez, R. O., & Dukes, R. L. (1997). The effects of ethnic identity, ethnicity, and gender on adolescent well-being. *Journal of Youth and Adolescence, 26*, 503–516.

Marttunen, M. J., Henriksson, M. M., Isometsa, E. T., Helkkinene, M. E., Aro, H. M., & Lonnqvist, J. K. (1998). Completed suicide among adolescents with no diagnosable psychiatric disorders. *Adolescence, 26*, 669–681.

Masi, F. A., Morath, R. A., & McLellan, J. A. (1997). Dimensions of adolescent employment. *The Career Development Quarterly, 45*, 351–368.

Mason, J. O. (1993). The dimensions of epidemic of violence. *Public Health Reports, 108*, 1–4.

Masten, A. S. (2001). Ordinary magic: Resilient processes in development. *American Psychologist, 56*, 227–238.

Masten, A. S., & Coatsworth, J. D. (1998). The development of competence in favorable and unfavorable environments: Lessons from research on successful children. *American Psychologist, 53*, 205–220.

Matlin, M. W. (2000). *The psychology of women* (4th ed.). Orlando, FL: Harcourt.

Matsuba, M. K., & Walker, L. J. (1998). Moral reasoning in the context of ego functioning. *Merrill-Palmer Quarterly, 44*, 464–480.

Matsueda, R. L., & Heimer, K. (1987). Race, family structure, and delinquency: A test of differential association and social control theories. *American Sociological Review, 52*, 826–840.

Mattay, V. S., Berman, K. F., Ostrem, J. L., Esposito, G., Van Horn, J. D., Bigelow, L. B., & Weinberger, D. R. (1996). Dextroamphetamine enhances "neural network-specific" physiological signals: A positron-emission tomography rCBF study. *Journal of Neuroscience, 15*, 4816–4822.

Matthews, S. H., & Sprey, J. (1985). Adolescents' relationships with grandparents: An empirical contribution to conceptual clarification. *Journal of Gerontology, 44*, S36–44.

Mauldon, J., & Luker, K. (1996). The effects of contraceptive education on method use at first intercourse. *Family Planning Perspectives, 28*, 19–24, 41.

Mayer, J. E., & Ligman, J. D. (1989). Personality characteristics of adolescent marijuana users. *Adolescence, 24*, 967–975.

Mayes, L. C. (1995). Substance abuse and parenting. In M. H. Bornstein (Ed.), *Handbook of parenting* (Vol. 4, pp. 101–125). Mahwah, NJ: Erlbaum.

Maynard, R., & Rangarajan, A. (1994). Contraceptive use and repeat pregnancies among welfare-dependent teenage mothers. *Family Planning Perspectives, 26*, 198–205.

Mazza, J. J. (1997). School-based suicide prevention programs: Are they effective? *School Psychology Review, 26*, 382–397.

McAdoo, H. P. (1991). Family values and outcomes for children. *Journal of Negro Education, 60*, 361–365.

McAndrew, F. T., Akande, A., Turner, S., & Sharma, Y. (1998). A cross-cultural ranking of stressful life events in Germany, India, South Africa, and the United States. *Journal of Cross-Cultural Psychology, 29*, 717–728.

McCabe, D. L., & Trevino, L. K. (1997). Individual and contextual academic dishonesty: A multi-campus investigation. *Research in Higher Education, 38*, 279–291.

McCabe, M. P., & Cummins, R. A. (1998). Sexuality and quality of life among young people. *Adolescence, 33*, 762–773.

McCall, R. B., Applebaum, M. L., & Hogarty, P. S. (1973). Developmental changes in mental performance. *Monographs of the Society for Research in Child Development, 38*(Serial No. 150).

McCammon, S., Knox, D., & Schacht, C. (1993). *Choices in sexuality*. Minneapolis, MN: West.

McCarthy, J., & Hoge, D. (1982). Analysis of age effects in longitudinal studies of adolescent self-esteem. *Developmental Psychology, 18*, 372–379.

McClintock, M. K., & Herdt, G. (1996). Rethinking puberty: The development of sexual attraction. *Psychological Science, 5*, 178–183.

McClure, R. F., & Mears, F. G. (1984). Video game playing and psychopathology. *Psychological Reports, 55*, 271–276.

McCracken, R. S., & Weitzman, L. M. (1997). Relationship of personal agency, problem- solving appraisal, and traditionality of career choice to women's attitudes towards multiple role planning. *Journal of Counseling Psychology, 40*, 149–159.

McCrone, W. P. (1994). A two-year report card on Title I of the Americans with Disabilities Act: Implications for rehabilitation. *Counseling with deaf people. Journal of Rehabilitation of the Deaf, 28*, 1–20.

McElhaney, K. B., & Allen, J. P. (2001). Autonomy and adolescent social functioning: The moderating effects of risk. *Child Development, 72*, 220–235.

McFarlane, A. H., Bellissimo, A., Normal, G. R., & Lange, P. (1994). Adolescent depression in a school-based community sample: Preliminary findings on contributing social factors. *Journal of Youth and Adolescence, 23*, 601–621.

McGee, R., Williams, S., & Nada-Raja, S. (2001). Low self-esteem and hopelessness in childhood and suicidal ideation in early adulthood. *Journal of Abnormal Child Psychology, 29*, 281–292.

McGue, M. (1993). From proteins to cognitions: The behavioral genetics of alcoholism. In R. Plomin & G. E. McLearn (Eds.), *Nature, nurture, and psychology* (pp. 245–269). Washington DC: APA.

McIlhaney, J. S. (1997). *Sex: What you don't know can kill you*. Grand Rapids, MI: Baker Books.

McIntosh, R., Vaughn, S., & Zaragoza, N. (1991). A review of social interventions for students with learning disabilities. *Journal of Learning Disabilities, 24*, 451–457.

McLanahan, S. S., & Booth, K. (1991). Mother-only families: Problems, prospects, and politics. In A. Booth (Ed.), *Contemporary families: Looking forward, looking back*. Minneapolis, MN: National Council on Family Relations.

McLeod, J. M., Atkin, C. K., & Chaffee, S. H. (1972). Adolescents, parents, and television use: Adolescent self-report measures from Maryland and Wisconsin samples. In G. A. Comstock & E. A. Rubinstein (Eds.), *Television and social behavior: Vol. 3. Television and adolescent aggressiveness* (pp. 173–238). Washington, DC: U.S. Government Printing Office.

McLoyd, V. C. (1998). Socioeconomic disadvantage and child development. *American Psychologist, 53*, 185–204.

McNamara, M. S. (1998, May/June). Separating from family. *Adoptive Families, 31*, 35–38.

McNeal, R. B. (1997, March). High school dropouts: A closer examination of school effects. *Social Science Quarterly, 78,* 209–223.

McWhirter, E. H. (1997). Perceived barriers to education and career: Ethnic and gender differences. *Journal of Vocational Behavior, 50,* 124–140.

McWhirter, E. H., Hackett, G., & Bandalos, D. L. (1998). A causal model of the educational plans and career expectations of Mexican American high school students. *Journal of Counseling Psychology, 45,* 166–181.

McWhirter, E. H., Rasheed, S., & Crothers, M. (2000). The effects of high school career education on social-cognitive variables. *Journal of Counseling Psychology, 47,* 330–341.

McWhorter, J. F. (2000). *Losing the race: Self-sabotage in Black America.* New York: The Free Press.

Mead, G. H. (1934). *Mind, self, and society.* Chicago: University of Chicago Press.

Mead, M. (1928). *Coming of age in Samoa.* New York: William Morrow.

Means, S. (1997, October 20). Alternative magazines promote "positive view" of womanhood. *Insight on the News, 13,* 41.

Mednick, S. A., Gabrielli, W. F., & Hutchings, B. (1984). Genetic factors in criminal behavior: Evidence from an adoption cohort. *Science, 224,* 891–893.

Meece, J. L. (1991). The classroom context and students' motivational goals. In M. Maehr & P. Pintrich (Eds.), *Advances in motivation and achievement* (pp. 261–286). Greenwich, CT: Jai.

Meeus, W. (1996). Studies on identity development in adolescence: An overview of research and some new data. *Journal of Youth And Adolescence, 25,* 569–598.

Meeus, W., & Dekovic, M. (1995). Identity development, parental, and peer support in adolescence: Results of a national Dutch study. *Adolescence, 30,* 931–944.

Megan, Z. (1994). Good parents: Comparative studies of adolescents' perceptions. *Current Psychology, 13,* 172–184.

Mellanby, A. (1996). Teen-zine sex is not all it seems. *British Medical Journal, 312,* 451–452.

Mellin, E. A., & Beamish, P. M. (2002). Interpersonal theory and adolescents with depression: Clinical update. *Journal of Mental Health Counseling, 24,* 110–126.

Mellin, L. M., Irwin, C. E., & Scully, S. (1992). Prevalence of disordered eating in girls: A survey of middle-class children. *Journal of the American Dietetic Association, 92,* 851–853.

Melton, G. B. (1991). Rights of adolescents. In R. M. Lerner, A. C. Petersen, & J. Brooks-Gunn (Eds.), *Encyclopedia of adolescence* (pp. 930–933). New York: Wiley.

Mendelson, B. K., & White, D. R. (1985). Development of self-body in overweight youngsters. *Developmental Psychology, 21,* 90–97.

Mendelson, B. K., White, D. R., & Mendelson, M. J. (1996). Self-esteem and body esteem: Effects of gender, age, and weight. *Journal of Applied Developmental Psychology, 17,* 321–346.

Mendelson, M. J., Mendelson, B. K., & Andrews, J. (2000). Self-esteem, body esteem, and body-mass in late adolescence. *Journal of Applied Developmental Psychology, 21,* 249–266.

Menesini, E., Melan, E., & Pignatti, B. (2000). Interactional styles of bullies and victims observed in a competitive and a cooperative setting. *Journal of Genetic Psychology, 161,* 261–272.

Merrell, K. W., & Gimpel, G. A. (1998). *Social skills of children and adolescents.* Mahwah, NJ: Erlbaum.

Merrill, S. A. (1999). Roselawn: A community regaining its youth. *The Clearing House, 73,* 101–110.

Meschke, L. L., & Silbereisen, R. K. (1997). The influence of puberty, family processes, and leisure activities on the timing of first sexual experience. *Journal of Adolescence, 20,* 403–418.

Meyer, K. A. (1987). The work commitment of adolescents: Progressive attachment to the work force. *Career Development, 36,* 140–147.

Michael, R. T., Gagnon, J. H., Laumann, E. O., & Kolata, G. (1994). *Sex in America: A definitive survey.* Boston: Little Brown.

Midence, K. (1994). The effects of chronic illness on children and their families: An overview. *Genetic, Social and General Psychology Monographs, 120,* 309–326.

Midgley, C., Feldlaufer, H., & Eccles, J. S. (1989). Student/teacher relations and attitudes towards mathematics before and after the transition to junior high school. *Child Development, 60,* 981–992.

Midlarsky, E., Hannah, M. E., & Corley, R. (1995). Assessing adolescents' prosocial behavior: The Family Helping Inventory. *Adolescence, 30,* 141–155.

Mihalic, S. W., & Elliott, D. (1997). Short and long term consequences of adolescent work. *Youth and Society, 28,* 464–498.

Mildrum, N. K. (2000, April). Creativity workshops in the regular classroom. *Roeper Review, 22,* 162–169.

Miller, B. C. (2002). Family influences on adolescent sexual and contraceptive behavior. *The Journal of Sex Research, 39,* 22–27.

Miller, B. C., Christopherson, C. R., & King, P. K. (1993). Sexual behavior in adolescence. In T. P. Gulotta, G. R. Adams, & R. Montemayor (Eds.), *Adolescent sexuality* (pp. 57–76). Newbury Park, CA: Sage.

Miller, B. C., McCoy, J. K., & Olson, T. D. (1986). Dating age and stages as correlates of adolescent sexual attitudes and behavior. *Journal of Adolescent Research, 1,* 361–371.

Miller, B. C., Monson, B. H., & Norton, M. C. (1995). The effects of forced sexual intercourse on white female adolescents. *Child Abuse and Neglect, 19,* 1289–1301.

Miller, D. B. (1999). Racial socialization and racial identity: Can they promote resiliency for African American adolescents? *Adolescence, 32,* 493–501.

Miller, J. G., & Bersoff, D. M. (1992). Culture and moral judgment: How are conflicts between justice and interpersonal responsibilities resolved? *Journal of Personality and Social Psychology, 62,* 541–554.

Miller, L., & Budd, J. (1999). The development of occupational sex-role stereotypes, occupational preferences and academic subject preferences in children at ages 8, 12 and 16. *Educational Psychology, 19,* 17–36.

Miller, M. J., Springer, T., & Wells, D. (1988). Which occupational environments do Black youths prefer? Extending Holland's typology. *School Counselor, 36,* 103–106.

Miller, P. H. (1993). *Theories of developmental psychology* (3rd ed.). New York: Freeman.

Miller, R. B., & Bengtson, V. L. (1991). Grandparent-grandchild relations. In R. M. Lerner, A. C. Petersen, & J. Brooks-Gunn (Eds.), *Encyclopedia of adolescence* (pp. 334–339). New York: Garland.

Miller, S. A. (1998). *Developmental research methods* (2nd ed.). Upper Saddle River, NJ: Prentice Hall.

Miller, S. (2003, January). Hispanics replace African Americans as largest U.S. minority group. Washington, DC: U.S. Department of State, International Information Program. (usinfo.state.gov)

Miller, S., & Cunningham, B. (1992). A guided look experience program for minority students. *Journal of College Student Development, 33,* 373–374.

Miller-Johnson, S., Coie, J. D., Maumary-Gremaud, A., Lochman, J., & Terry, R. (1999). Relationship between childhood peer rejection and aggression and adolescent delinquency severity and type among African American youth. *Journal of Emotional and Behavioral Disorders, 7,* 137–146.

Millstein, S. G., Petersen, A. C., & Nightingale, E. O. (Eds.). (1993). *Promoting the health of adolescents: New directions for the twenty-first century.* New York: Oxford University Press.

Minkel, W. (2000). No, it's not all true. *School Library Journal, 46,* 33–41.

Minor, B. (1998, November 30). Do students in voucher programs outperform students in public schools? *Nation, 267,* 4–6.

Minor, B. (2000, June 5). No one really knows how children in Milwaukee's voucher schools are faring. *The Nation, 270,* 233.

Minuchin, P. (1985). Families and individual development: Provocations from the field of family therapy. *Child Development 56,* 289–302.

Mirel, J. E. (1991). Adolescence in twentieth-century America. In R. M. Lerner, A. C. Petersen, & J. Brooks-Gunn (Eds.), *Encyclopedia of adolescence* (pp. 1153–1167). New York: Wiley.

Mirel, J. E., & Angus, D. L. (1985). Youth, work, and schooling in the Great Depression. *Journal of Early Adolescence, 9,* 489–504.

Mirel, J. E., & Angus, D. L. (1986). The rising tide of custodialism: Enrollment increases and curriculum reform in Detroit, 1928–1940. *Issues in Education, 4,* 101–120.

Mitchell, L. K., & Krumboltz, J. D. (1996). Krumboltz' learning theory of career choice and counseling. In D. Brown & L. Brooks (Eds.), *Career choice and development* (3rd ed., pp. 233–280). San Francisco: Jossey-Bass.

Moffitt, T. E. (1993). Adolescence-limited and life-course-persistent anti-social behavior: A developmental taxonomy. *Psychological Review, 100,* 674–701.

Moffitt, T. E., Belsky, J., & Silva, P. A. (1992). Childhood experience and the onset of menarche: A test of a sociobiological model. *Child Development, 63,* 47–58.

Moffitt, T., Caspi, A., Harkness, A., & Silva, P. (1993). The natural history of change in intellectual performance: Who changes? How much? Is it meaningful? *Journal of Child Psychology and Psychiatry, 34,* 455–506.

Mogelonsky, M. (1998, June). Teens' working dreams. *American Demographics,* pp. 14–17.

Mok, T. A. (1999). Asian American dating: Important factors in partner choice. *Cultural Diversity and Ethnic Minority Psychology, 5,* 103–117.

Monahan, S. C., Buchanan, C. M., Maccoby, E. E., & Dornbusch, S. M. (1993). Sibling differences in divorced families. *Child Development, 64,* 152–168.

Montemayor, R. (1982). The relationship between adolescent-parent conflict and the amount of time adolescents spend alone and with parents and peers. *Child Development, 53,* 1512–1519.

Montemayor, R. (1986). Family variation in storm and stress. *Journal of Adolescent Research, 1,* 15–31.

Montgomery, M. S. (1994). Self-concept and children with learning disabilities: Observer-child concordance across six context-dependent domains. *Journal of Learning Disabilities, 27,* 254–262.

Montgomery, R. L., Haemmerlie, F. M., & Zoellner, S. (1996). The "imaginary audience," self-handicapping, and drinking patterns among college students. *Psychological Reports, 79,* 783–787.

Moore, K. A. (1992). *National commission on children: 1990 survey of parents and children.* Los Altos, CA: Sociometrics Corporation, American Family Data Archive.

Moore, K. A., Miller, B. C., Sugland, B. W., Morrison, D. R., Glei, D. A., & Blumenthal, C. (1995). *Beginning too soon: Adolescent sexual behavior, pregnancy, and parenthood.* Washington, DC: Child Trends, Inc.

Moore, K. A., & Sugland, B. W. (1999). Placing together the puzzle of teenage childbearing. *Policy & Practice of Public Human Services, 57,* 36–43.

Moore, S. M. (1995). Girls' understanding and social constructions of menarche. *Journal of Adolescence, 18,* 87–104.

Moore, S. M., Gullone, E., & Kostanski, M. (1997). An examination of adolescent risk-taking using a story completion task. *Journal of Adolescence, 20,* 369–379.

Morash, M. A. (1980). Working class membership and the adolescent identity crisis. *Adolescence, 15,* 313–320.

Morgan, C., Isaac, J. D., & Sansone, C. (2001, March). The role of interest in understanding the career choices of female and male college students. *Sex Roles,* 295–304.

Morgan, R. L., Whorton, J. E., & Gunsalus, C. (2000). A comparison of short term and long term retention: Lecture combined with discussion versus cooperative learning. *Journal of Instructional Psychology, 27,* 53–61.

Morlock, H., Yando, T., & Nigolean, K, (1985). Motivation of video game players. *Psychological Reports, 57,* 247–250.

Morojele, N. K., & Brook, J. S. (2001). Adolescent precursors of intensity of marijuana and other illicit drug use among adult initiators. *Journal of Genetic Psychology, 162,* 430–451.

Morris, K. (1998, December 12). Ecstasy users face consequences of neurotoxicity. *The Lancet, 352,* 1913.

Morris, T., & Summers, T. (1995). *Sport psychology.* New York: Wiley.

Morrison, D. M. (1985). Adolescent contraceptive behavior: A review. *Psychological Bulletin, 98,* 538–568.

Morrow, R. D. (1987, November). Cultural differences—Be aware! *Academic Therapy, 23,* 143–149.

Mortimer, J. T., Finch, M. D., Ryu, S., Shanahan, M. J., & Call, K. T. (1996). The effects of work intensity on adolescent mental health, achievement, and behavioral adjustment: New evidence from a prospective study. *Child Development, 67,* 1243–1261.

Mortimer, J. T., Finch, M., Shanahan, M., & Ryu, S. (1992a). Adolescent work history and behavioral adjustment. *Journal of Research on Adolescence,* 59–80.

Mortimer, J. T., Finch, M., Shanahan, M., & Ryu, S. (1992b). Work experience, mental health, and behavioral adjustment. *Journal of Research on Adolescence, 2,* 25–57.

Mortimer, J. T., Shanahan, M. J., & Ryu, S. (1993). The effects of adolescent employment on school-related orientation and behavior. In R. K. Silbereisen & E. Todt (Eds.), *Adolescence in context* (pp. 304–326). New York: Springer-Verlag.

Morton, M., Nelson, L., Walsh, C., Zimmerman, S., & Coe, R. M. (1996). Evaluation of a HIV/AIDS education program for adolescents. *Journal of Community Health, 21,* 23–36.

Moseley, M. (1999, April 4). Young Americans volunteer but don't vote. *Campaigns & Elections, 20,* 35.

Moshman, D. (1993). Adolescent reasoning and adolescent rights. *Human Development, 36,* 27–40.

Moshman, D. (1998). Cognitive development beyond childhood. In W. Damon (Ed.), D. Kuhn & R. S. Siegler (Vol. Eds.), *Handbook of child psychology* (5th ed., Vol. 2, pp. 947–979). New York: Wiley.

Moshman, D., & Franks, B. A. (1986). Development of the concept of inferential validity. *Child Development, 57,* 153–165.

Mounts, N., & Steinberg, L. D. (1995). An ecological analysis of peer influence on adolescent grade point average and drug use. *Developmental Psychology, 31,* 915–922.

Mullen, J. (1999). School vouchers: An intractable dilemma. *Human Rights: Journal of the Section of Individual Rights and Responsibilities, 26,* 16–19.

Mullis, A. K., & Mullis, R. L. (1997). Vocational interests of adolescents: Relationships between self-esteem and locus of control. *Psychological Reports, 81,* 1363–1371.

Mullis, R. L., Mullis, A. K., & Gerwels, D. (1998). Stability of vocational interests among high school students. *Adolescence, 33,* 699–708.

Munley, P. H. (1977). Erikson's theory of psychosocial development and career development. *Journal of Vocational Behavior, 10,* 261–269.

Munoz, K. A., Krebs-Smith, S. M., Ballard-Barbash, R., & Cleveland, L. E. (1998, May). Food intakes of U.S. children and adolescents compared with recommendations. *Pediatrics, 191,* 952–953.

Muñoz-Plaza, C., Quinn, S. C., & Rounds, K. A. (2002). Lesbian, gay, bisexual and transgender students: Perceived social support in the high school environment. *High School Journal, 85,* 52–64.

Muram, D., Hostetler, B. R., Jones, C. E., & Speck, P. M. (1995). Adolescent victims of sexual assault. *Journal of Adolescent Health, 17,* 372–375.

Murphy, J. J., & Boggess, S. (1998). Increased condom use among teenage males, 1988–1995: The role of attitudes. *Family Planning Perspectives, 30,* 276–309.

Murphy, P. A., & Cleeton, E. C. (2000). *In the best interest of the child: Good mothers, behaving badly and the law.* Philadelphia: Temple University Press.

Murphy, S. T. (1994). The impact of factual versus fictional media portrayals on cultural stereotypes. *Annals of the American Academy of Political & Social Science, 560,* 165–179.

Murray, B. (1995a). Gender gap in math scores is closing. *APA Monitor,* p. 43.

Murray, B. (1995b). Key skill for teen parents: Having realistic expectations. *APA Monitor,* 51.

Murray, B. (1995c, November). Programs go beyond "just saying no." *APA Monitor,* p. 41.

Murray, B. (1996, April). Students stretch beyond the "three R's." *APA Monitor,* p. 46.

Mussen, P. H., & Eisenberg-Berg, N. (1977). *Roots of caring, sharing and helping.* San Francisco: Freeman.

Must, A., Jacques, P. F., Dallal, G. E., Bajema, C. J., & Dietz, W. H. (1992). Long-term morbidity and morality of overweight adolescents. *The New England Journal of Medicine, 327,* 1350–1355.

Musty, R. E., Reggio, P., & Consroe, P. (1995). A review of recent advances in cannabinoid research and the 1994 international symposium on cannabis and the cannabinoids. *Life Sciences, 56,* 1933–1940.

Muuss, R. E. (1982). *Theories of adolescence* (4th ed.). New York: Random House.

Muuss, R. E. (1985). Adolescent eating disorder: Anorexia nervosa. *Adolescence, 21,* 525–536.

Muuss, R. E. (1986). Adolescent eating disorder: Bulimia. *Adolescence, 21,* 257–167.

Muuss, R. E. (1988). Carol Gilligan's theory of sex differences in the development of moral reasoning during adolescence. *Adolescence, 23,* 235–243.

Myers, R. S., & Roth, D. L. (1997). Perceived benefits of and barriers to exercise and stage of exercise adoption in young adults. *Health Psychology, 16*, 277–283.

Nagel, K. L., & Jones, K. H. (1992). Sociological factors in the development of eating disorders. *Adolescence, 27*, 107–113.

Nagy, S., DiClemente, R., & Adcock, A. G. (1995). Adverse factors associated with forced sex among southern adolescent girls. *Pediatrics, 96*, 944–946.

Nalin, J. (2001, April 2). Juvenile law—curfews—municipalities. *New Jersey Law Journal, 164*, 61.

Nansel, T. R., Overpeck, M., Pilla, R. S., Ruan, W. J., Simons-Morton, B., & Scheidt, P. (2001). Bullying behaviors among U.S. youth: Prevalence and association with psychosocial adjustment. *Journal of the American Medical Association, 285*, 2094–2100.

Nansel, T. R., Simons-Morton, B., & Scheidt, P. (2001). In Reply, *Journal of the American Medical Association, 286*, p. 788.

Nathan, J. (1998). Heat and light in the Charter School movement. *Phi Delta Kappan, 79*, 499–505.

National Academy of Sciences. (2001). *BOCYF Current Activities: New research on brain development during the adolescent years.* Retrieved December 30, 2002, from http://www.bocyf.org/Brain_Develoment.html

National Academy of Sports Medicine (NASP). (1992). National Academy of Sports Medicine policy statement and position paper: Anabolic androgenic steroids, growth hormones, stimulants, ergogenics, and drug use in sports. In B. Goldman & R. Klatz (Eds.), *Death in the locker room II: Drugs and sports* (pp. 328–373). Chicago: Chicago Elite.

National Assessment of Vocational Education. (1994). *Interim report to Congress.* Washington, DC: U.S. Department of Education, Office of Educational Research and Improvement.

National Center for Health Statistics. (1997). *Healthy people 2000 review.* Hyattsville, MD: Public Health Service.

National Center for Health Statistics. (2002). *Preventing teenage pregnancy.* Retrieved December 26, 2002, from http://www.hhs.gov/news/press/2002pres/teenpreg.html

National Commission on Excellence in Education. (1981). *A nation at risk.* Washington, DC: U.S. Department of Education.

National Institute on Media and the Family. (1998, September 1). *Violent and sexually explicit Web sites hold "surfers" hostage.* Minneapolis, MN: Author.

National Institutes of Health. (2000). Consensus development conference statement: Diagnosis and treatment of attention-deficit/hyperactivity disorder (ADHD). *Journal of the American Academy of Child and Adolescent Psychiatry, 39*, 182–201.

National Rehabilitation Information Center. (1993, August 15). *The Americans with Disabilities Act (ADA). A NARIC Resource guide.* Lanham, MD: Author.

National Research Council. (1993). *Losing generations: Adolescents in high risk settings.* Washington, DC: National Academy Press.

Natvig, G. K., Albrektsen, G., Anderssen, N., & Qvarnstrom, U. (1999). School-related stress and psychosomatic symptoms among school adolescents. *Journal of School Health, 69*, 362–371.

Nauta, M. M., Epperson, D. L., & Kahn, J. H. (1998). A multiple-groups analysis of predictors of higher level career aspirations among women in mathematics, science, and engineering majors. *Journal of Counseling Psychology, 45*, 483–496.

Nazarro, J. N. (Ed.). (1981). *Culturally diverse exceptional children.* Reston, VA: Council for Exceptional Children.

NEA. (1994, May). Teen angels: Data bank. *NEA Today,* p. 18.

NEA Today. (2002, April), Beyond the "V" word: Vocational education has a new name and a new strategy for educating students. *NEA Today, 20*, 8–12.

Neeleman, J., Wessely, S., & Wadsworth, M. (1998, January 10). Predictors of suicide, accidental death, and premature natural death in a general-population birth cohort. *The Lancet, 351*, 93–98.

Neher, L. S., & Short, J. L. (1998). Risk and protective factors for children's substance use and antisocial behavior following parental divorce. *American Journal of Orthopsychiatry, 68*, 154–161.

Neimark, E. D. (1975). Intellectual development during adolescence. In F. D. Horowitz (Ed.), *Review of child development research* (Vol. 4, pp. 541–594). Chicago: University of Chicago Press.

Neimark, E. D. (1982). Adolescent thought: Transition to formal operations. In B. B. Wolman (Ed.), *Handbook of human development* (pp. 486–503). Englewood Cliffs, NJ: Prentice Hall.

Neisser, U., Boodoo, G., Bouchard, T. L., Jr., Boykin, A. W., Brody, N., Ceci, S. J., et al. (1996). Intelligence: Knowns and unknowns. *American Psychologist, 51*, 77–101.

Nelson, F. L. (1987). Evaluations of a youth suicide school program. *Adolescence, 22*, 813–825.

Nelson, W. L., Hughes, H. M., Handal, P., Katz, B., & Searight, H. R. (1993). The relationship of family structure and family conflict to adjustment in young adult college students. *Adolescence, 28*, 29–40.

Neufeld, J., McNamara, J. R., & Ertl, M. (1999). Incidence and prevalence of dating partner abuse and its relationship to dating practices. *Journal of Interpersonal Violence, 14*, 125–138.

Neumann, H., McCormick, R. M., Amundson, N. E., & McLean, H. B. (2000). Vocational counseling in Canada. *Canadian Journal of Counseling, 34*, 172–185.

Neumarker, K. J. (1997). Mortality and sudden death in anorexia nervosa. *International Journal of Eating Disorders, 21*, 205–212.

Neumark-Sztainer, D., Story, M., Perry, C., & Casey, M. A. (1999). Factors influencing food choices of adolescents: Findings from focus-group discussions with adolescents. *Journal of the American Dietetic Association, 99*, 929–935.

Neuwirth, S. (1993). *Learning disabilities* (No. 359–181/90240). Washington, DC: U.S. Government Printing Office.

Nevers, P., Gebhard, U., & Billmann-Mahecha, E. (1997). Patterns of reasoning exhibited by children and adolescents in response to moral dilemmas involving plants, animals, and ecosystems. *Journal of Moral Education, 26*, 169–186.

New York State Libraries. (1999). *Kids and the Internet.* Retrieved July 18, 2002, from http://www.nysl.nysed.gov/library/pub/parqa.htm

Newcomb, A. F., & Bagwell, C. L. (1996). Developmental significance of friendship. In W. M. Bukowski, A. F., Newcomb, & W. W. Hartup (Eds.), *The company they keep: Friendship in childhood and adolescence* (pp. 289–321). New York: Cambridge University Press.

Newcomb, A. F., Bukowski, W. M., & Pattee, L. (1993). Children's peer relations: A meta-analytic review of popular, rejected, neglected, controversial and average sociometric status. *Psychological Bulletin, 113*, 99–128.

Newman, B. S., & Muzzonigro, P. G. (1993). The effects of traditional family values on the coming out process of gay male adolescents. *Adolescence, 28*, 213–216.

Newman, D. L., Caspi, A., Moffitt, T. E., & Silva, P. A. (1997). Antecedents of adult interpersonal functioning: Effects of individual differences in age 3 temperament. *Developmental Psychology, 33*, 206–217.

Newman, P. R., & Newman, B. M. (1976). Early adolescence and its conflict: Group identity vs. alienation. *Adolescence, 10*, 127–136.

Newstead, S. E., Franklyn-Stokes, A., & Armstead, P. (1996). Individual differences in student cheating. *Journal of Educational Psychology, 88*, 229–241.

Nicholls, J. G. (1984). Achievement motivation: Conceptions of ability, subjective experience, task choice, and performance. *Psychological Review, 91*, 328–346.

Nicklas, T. A., Bao, W., Webber, L. S., & Berenson, G. S. (1993). Breakfast consumption affects adequacy of total daily intake in children. *Journal of the American Dietetic Association, 93*, 886–891.

Nielsen Media Research. (1998). *1998 report on television.* New York: Author.

Nielsen, S., Moller-Madsen, S., Isager, T., Jorgensen, J., Pagsberg, K., & Theander, S. (1998). Standardized mortality in eating disorders. A quantitative summary of previously published and new evidence. *Journal of Psychosomatic Research, 14*, 413–434.

Nigg, J. T., & Goldsmith, H. H. (1994). Genetics of personality disorders: Perspectives from personality and psychopathology research. *Psychological Bulletin, 115*, 346–380.

Nisan, M. (1996). Personal identity and education for the desirable. *Journal of Moral Education, 25*, 75–83.

Nisbett, R. E. (1998). Race, genetics, and IQ. In C. Jencks & M. Phillips (Eds.), *The black-white test score gap* (pp. 86–102). Washington, DC: Brookings Institute Press.

Nitz, K. (1999). Adolescent pregnancy prevention: A review of interventions and programs. *Child Psychology Review, 19*, 457–471.

Nitz, K., & Lerner, J. V. (1991). Temperament during adolescence. In R. M. Lerner, A. C. Petersen, & J. Brooks-Gunn (Eds.), *Encyclopedia of adolescence* (pp. 1127–1130). New York: Wiley.

Nogata, D. K. (1989). Japanese American children and adolescence. In J. T. Gibs & L. N. Huang (Eds.), *Children of color* (pp. 67–114). San Francisco: Jossey-Bass.

Nolen-Hoeksema, S. (1991). Responses to depression and their effects on the duration of depressive episodes. *Journal of Abnormal Psychology, 100*, 569–582.

Nolen-Hoeksema, S. (2000). The role of rumination in depressive disorders and mixed anxiety/depressive symptoms. *Journal of Abnormal Psychology, 109*, 504–511.

Nolen-Hoeksema, S., & Davis, C. G. (1999). "Thanks for sharing that": Ruminators and their social support networks. *Journal of Personality and Social Psychology, 77*, 801–804.

Nolen-Hoeksema, S., & Girgus, J. S. (1994). The emergence of gender differences in depression during adolescence. *Psychological Bulletin, 115*, 424–443.

Nolen-Hoeksema, S., Larson, J., & Grayson, C. (1999). Explaining the gender difference in depressive symptoms. *Journal of Personality and Social Psychology, 77*, 1061–1072.

Noller, P., & Callan, V. J. (1986). Adolescent and parent perceptions of family cohesion and adaptability. *Journal of Adolescence, 9*, 97–106.

Norman, D. A., & Spohrer, J. C. (1996). Learner-centered education. *Communications of the ACM, 39*, 24–28.

Norman, M. M. (1999). The human side of school technology. *American School Board Journal, 186*, 16–20.

Norman, N. M., & Tedeschi, J. T. (1989). Self-presentation, reasoned action, and adolescents' decisions to smoke cigarettes. *Journal of Applied Social Psychology, 19*, 543–559.

Norris, S., & Ennis, R. (1989). *Evaluating critical thinking*. Pacific Grove, CA: Critical Thinking Press and Software.

Nottelmann, E. D. (1987). Competence and self-esteem during transitions from childhood to adolescence. *Developmental Psychology, 23*, 441–451.

Nottlemann, E. D., Susman, E. J., Blue, J. H., Inoff-Germain, G., Dorn, L. D., Loriaux, D. L., et al. (1987). Gonadal and adrenal hormone correlates of adjustment in early adolescence. In R. M. Lerner & T. T. Foch (Eds.), *Biological-psychosocial interactions in early adolescence*. Hillsdale, NJ: Erlbaum.

Nua.com. (2001). *Online Internet surveys: Teenagers.* Retrieved July 18, 2002, from http://www.nua.com/surveys

Nyberg, K. L., McMillin, J. D., O'Neill-Rood, N., & Florence, J. M. (1997, September). Ethnic differences in academic retracking: A four-year longitudinal study. *The Journal of Educational Research, 91*, 33–41.

Oakes, J., & Guiton, G. (1994). Matchmaking: The dynamics of high school tracking decision. *American Education Research Journal, 32*, 3–34.

Obeidallah, D. A., McHale, S. M., & Silbereisen, R. K. (1996). Gender role socialization and adolescents' reports of depression: Why some girls and not others? *Journal of Youth and Adolescence, 25*, 775–786.

O'Brien, K. M., & Fassinger, R. E. (1993). A causal model of the career orientation and career choice of adolescent women. *Journal of Counseling Psychology, 40*, 456–469.

O'Connell, L., Betz, M., & Kurth, S. (1989). Plans for balancing work and family life: Do women pursuing nontraditional and traditional occupations differ? *Sex Roles, 20*, 35–45.

O'Connor, R. E., Jenkins, J. R., & Slocum, T. A. (1995). Transfer among phonological tasks in kindergarten: Essential instructional content. *Journal of Educational Psychology, 87*, 202–217.

Offer, D., & Schonert-Reichl, K. A. (1992). Debunking the myths of adolescence: Findings from recent research. *Journal of the American Academy of Child and Adolescent Psychiatry, 31*, 1003–1014.

Office of Juvenile Justice. (2002). *Juvenile arrest rates for violent crime index offenses, 1980–2000.* Retrieved December 24, 2002, from http://ojjdp.ncjrs.org/ojstatbb/asp/JAR_Display.asp?ID=qa2201012002

Office of National Drug Control Policy. (1996). *President Clinton's accomplishment in the fight against drugs in defense of our children and our families.* Washington, DC: Author.

Office of National Drug Control Policy. (2001, January 28). Heroin addiction is rising amid too little treatment. *Medical Letter on the CDC and FDA*, p. 5.

Ogbar, J. O. G. (1999). Slouching toward Bork. *Journal of Black Studies, 30*, 164–184.

Ogbu, J. U. (1978). *Minority education and caste.* New York: Academic Press.

Ogbu, J. U. (1981). Origins of human competence: A cultural-ecological perspective. *Child Development, 52*, 5–14.

Ogbu, J. U. (1992). Understanding cultural diversity and learning. *Educational Researcher, 21*, 5–14.

Ohler, J. (2000). Taking the future back from technology. *Education Digest, 65*, 8–14.

Okagaki, L., & Bevis, C. (1999). Transmission of religious values: Relations between parents' and daughters' beliefs. *Journal of Genetic Psychology, 160*, 303–318.

Okazaki, S. (2002, February). Influences on culture on Asian Americans' sexuality. *The Journal of Sex Research, 39*, 34–42.

O'Keefe, M. (1997). Predictors of dating violence among high school students. *Journal of Interpersonal Violence, 12*, 546–569.

Oliver, M. B., & Hyde, J. S. (1993). Gender differences in sexuality: A meta-analysis. *Psychological Bulletin, 114*, 29–51.

Ollendick, T. H., Greene, R. W., Francis, G., & Baum, C. G. (1991). Sociometric status: Its stability and reliability among neglected, rejected and popular children. *Journal of Child Psychology and Psychiatry, 32*, 525–534.

Ollendick, T. H., Weist, M. D., Borden, M. G., & Greene, R. W. (1992). Sociometric status and academic, behavioral, and psychological adjustment: A five-year longitudinal study. *Journal of Consulting and Clinical Psychology, 60*, 80–87.

Olson, L. (1998, April 1). Study: Schoolwide reform not easy. *Education Week*, pp. 1, 17.

Olszewski-Kubilius, P. (2000). The transition from childhood giftedness to adult creative productivity: Psychological characteristics and social supports. *Roeper Review, 23*, 65–70.

Olweus, D. (1986). Aggression and hormones: Behavior relationships with testosterone and adrenaline. In D. Olweus, J. Block, & M. Radke-Yarrow (Eds.), *Development of antisocial and prosocial behavior: Research, theory, and issues* (pp. 51–72). Orlando, FL: Academic Press.

Olweus, D. (1991). Bully/victim problems among school children: Basic problems and effects of a school based intervention program. In K. Rubin & D. Pepler (Eds.), *The development and treatment of childhood aggression* (pp. 411–448). Mahwah, NJ: Erlbaum.

Olweus, D. (1992). Bullying among schoolchildren: Intervention and prevention. In R. D. Peters, R. J. McMahon, & V. L. Quinsey (Eds.), *Aggression and violence throughout the life span* (pp. 100–125). London, England: Sage Publications.

Olweus, D. (1993). *Bullying at school: What we know and what we can do.* Oxford, England: Blackwell Publishers.

Olweus, D. (1994a). Annotation: Bulling at school: Basic facts and effective school based intervention program. *Journal of Child Psychology and Psychiatry, 35*, 1171–1190.

Olweus, D. (1994b). Bullying at school: Long-term outcomes for the victims an affective school-based intervention program. In L. R. Huesmann (Ed.), *Aggressive behavior: Current perspectives* (pp. 97–130). New York: Plenum.

Olweus, D., Mattsson, A., Schalling, D., & Low, H. (1980). Testosterone, aggression, physical and personality dimensions in normal adolescent males. *Psychosomatic Medicine, 42*, 253–269.

Olweus, D., Mattsson, A., Schalling, D., & Low, H. (1988). Circulating testosterone levels and aggression in adolescent males: A casual analysis. *Psychosomatic Medicine, 3*, 261–272.

O'Malley, P. M., & Bachman, J. G. (1983). Self-esteem: Change and stability between ages 13 and 23. *Developmental Psychology, 19*, 257–268.

O'Neal, G. (1998, March 30). Colleges run bars to battle binges. *USA Today*, D4.

O'Neil, D. M., & Sepielli, P. (1985). *Education in the United States, 1940–1983.* Washington, DC: Government Printing Office.

Oosterwegel, A., & Oppenheimer, L. (1993). *The self-system: Developmental changes between and within self-concepts.* Hillsdale, NJ: Erlbaum.

Orlofsky, J. L., Marcia, J. E., & Lesser, T. M. (1973). Ego identity status and the intimacy versus isolation crisis of young adulthood. *Journal of Personality and Social Psychology, 27*, 211–219.

Orr, D., & Ingersoll, G. (1995). The contribution of level of cognitive complexity and pubertal timing to behavioral risk in young adolescents. *Pediatrics, 95,* 528–533.

Oser, F. (1996). Learning from negative morality. *Journal of Moral Education, 25,* 67–74.

Oshman, H. P., & Manosevitz, M. (1976). Father absence: Effects of stepfathers upon psychosocial development in males. *Developmental Psychology, 12,* 477–480.

Osterman, P. (1980). *Getting started: The youth labor market.* Cambridge: MIT Press.

Osterman, P. (1995). The youth labor market: Skill deficiencies and public policy. In S. Zedeck (Ed.), *The changing nature of work* (pp. 223–251). San Francisco: Jossey-Bass.

Overton, W. F. (1991). Reasoning in the adolescent. In R. M. Lerner, A. C. Petersen, & J. Brooks-Gunn (Eds.), *Encyclopedia of adolescence* (pp. 912–916). New York: Garland.

Overton, W. F., & Byrnes, J. P. (1991). Cognitive development. In R. M. Lerner, A. C. Petersen, & J. Brooks-Gunn (Eds.), *Encyclopedia of adolescence* (pp. 151–156). New York: Garland.

Pace, B. (2001). Bullying. *Journal of the American Medical Association, 285,* 156.

Pachter, L. M., & Harwood, R. L. (1996). Culture and child behavior and psychosocial development. *Development and Behavioral Pediatrics, 17,* 191–198.

Padilla, A. M., & Baird, T. L. (1991). Mexican-American adolescent sexuality and sexual knowledge: An exploratory study. *Hispanic Journal of Behavioral Sciences, 13,* 95–104.

Page, R. M., Hammermeister, J., Scanlan, A., & Allen, O. (1996). Psychosocial and health-related characteristics of adolescent television viewers. *Child Study Journal, 26,* 319–331.

Page, R. M., & Zarco, E. P. (2001). Shyness, physical activity, and sports team participation among Philippine high school students. *Child Study Journal, 31,* 193–215.

Paik, H., & Comstock, G. (1994). The effects of television violence on antisocial behavior. *Communication Research, 21,* 516–546.

Paikoff, R. L., & Brooks-Gunn, J. (1991). Do parent-child relationships change during puberty? *Psychological Bulletin, 110,* 47–66.

Paikoff, R. L., Brooks-Gunn, J., & Warren, M. P. (1991a). Effects of girls' hormonal status on depressive and aggressive symptoms over the course of one year. *Journal of Youth and Adolescence, 20,* 191–215.

Painter, K. (1996, February 21). Heavy marijuana use may impair learning. *USA Today,* p. D1.

Palincsar, A. S. (1986). The role of dialogue in providing scaffolded instruction. *Educational Psychologist, 21,* 73–98.

Palincsar, A. S., & Brown, A. L. (1984). The reciprocal teaching of comprehension: Fostering comprehension-monitoring activities. *Cognition and Instruction, 1,* 117–175.

Palmonari, A., Pobeni, J. L., & Kirchler, E. (1989). Peer groups and evolution of the self-system in adolescence. *European Journal of Psychology of Education, 4,* 3–15.

Parish, T. S. (1991). Ratings of self and parents by youth: Are they affected by family status, gender and birth order? *Adolescence, 26,* 105–113.

Park, S. Y., Belsky, J., Putnam, S., & Crnic, K. (1997). Infant emotionality, parenting, and 3-year inhibition: Exploring stability and lawful discontinuity in a male sample. *Developmental Psychology, 33,* 218–227.

Parke, R. D. (1995). Fathers and families. In M. H. Bornstein (Ed.), *Handbook of parenting* (Vol. 3, pp. 27–63). Mahwah, NJ: Erlbaum.

Parke, R. D., & Buriel, R. (1998). Socialization in the family: Ethnic and ecological perspectives. In W. Damon (Ed.) & N. Eisenberg (Vol. Ed.), *A Handbook of child psychology* (Vol. 3, pp. 463–552). New York: Wiley.

Parker, J. G., & Asher, S. R. (1987). Peer relations and later personal adjustment: Are low-accepted children "at risk?" *Psychological Bulletin, 102,* 357–389.

Parker, J. G., & Gottman, J. M. (1989). Social and emotional development in a relational context: Friendship interaction from early childhood to adolescence. In T. J. Berndt & G. W. Ladd (Eds.), *Peer relationships in child development.* New York: Wiley.

Parker, K. D., & Calhoun, T. (2000). Variables associated with adolescent alcohol use: A multiethnic comparison. *Journal of Social Psychology, 140,* 51–63.

Parkhurst, J. T., & Asher, S. R. (1992). Peer rejection in middle school: Subgroup differences in behavior, loneliness and interpersonal concerns. *Developmental Psychology, 28,* 231–241.

Parkhurst, J. T., & Hopmeyer, A. (1998). Sociometric popularity and peer-perceived popularity: Two distinct dimensions of peer status. *Journal of Early Adolescence, 18,* 125–144.

Parks, P. S. M., & Read, M. H. (1997). Adolescent male athletes: Body image, diet, and exercise. *Adolescence, 32,* 593–603.

Parnell, D. (1985). *The neglected majority.* Washington DC: Community College Press.

Pastore, M. (2000, June 8). 40 percent of America's kids online. *Cyberatlas.* Retrieved July 18, 2002, from http://cyberatlas.internet.com/big_picture/demographics/article/0,,5901_390941,00.html

Pattatucci, A. M., & Hamer, D. H. (1995). Development and familiarity of sexual orientation in females. *Behavior Genetics, 25,* 407–420.

Patterson, G. R., Reid, J. B., & Dishion, T. J. (1992). *Antisocial boys.* Eugene, OR: Castalia Press.

Paul, J. (1993). Childhood cross-gender behavior and adult homosexuality: The resurgence of biological models of sexuality. *Journal of Homosexuality, 24,* 41–54.

Paul, P. (2001, September). Getting inside Gen Y. *American Demographics, 23,* 42–49.

Paul, P. (2002, June). Raising our standards. *American Demographics, 24,* 12.

Paulhus, D. L., & Morgan, K. L. (1997). Perceptions of intelligence in leaderless groups: The dynamic effects of shyness and acquaintance. *Journal of Personality and Social Psychology, 33,* 581–591.

Paulson, S. E. (1994). Relations of parenting style and parental involvement with ninth-grade students' achievement. *Journal of Early Adolescence, 14,* 250–267.

Paulson, S. E. (1996). Maternal employment and adolescent achievement revisited. *Family Relations, 45,* 201–208.

Paulson, S. E., Marchant, G. J., & Rothlisberg, B. A. (1998). Early adolescents' perceptions of patterns of parenting, teaching, and school atmosphere. *Journal of Early Adolescence, 18,* 5–26.

Paulson, S. E., & Sputa, C. L. (1996). Patterns of parenting during adolescence: Perceptions of adolescents and parents. *Adolescence, 31,* 369–381.

Pawlby, S., Mills, A., & Quinton, D. (1997). Vulnerable adolescent girls: Opposite-sex relationships. *Journal of Child Psychology and Psychiatry, 38,* 909–920.

Pawlby, S. J., Mills, A., Taylor, A., & Quinton, D. (1997). Adolescent friendships mediating childhood adversity and adult outcome. *Journal of Adolescence, 20,* 633–644.

Pekrun, R. (1993). Facets of adolescents' academic motivation: A longitudinal expectancy-value approach. In M. Maehr & P. Pintrich (Eds.), *Advances in motivation and achievement* (Vol. 8, pp. 139–189). Greenwich, CT: JAI Press.

Pellegrini, A. D., Bartini, M., & Brooks, F. (1999). School bullies, victims, and aggressive victims: Factors relating to group affiliation and victimization in early adolescence. *Journal of Early Adolescence, 91,* 216–224.

Perry, C. M., & McIntire, W. G. (1995). Modes of moral judgment among early adolescents. *Adolescence, 30,* 707–715.

Perry, D. G., Kusel, S. J., & Perry, L. C. (1988). Victims of peer aggression. *Developmental Psychology, 24,* 807–814.

Perry, H. S., & Gawel, M. L. (Eds.). (1953). *The collected works of Harry Stack Sullivan: Vol. 1. The interpersonal theory of psychiatry.* New York: Norton.

Perry, R. P., Hladyj, S., Pekrun, R. H., & Pelletier, S. T. (2001). Academic control and action control in the achievement of college students: A longitudinal field study. *Journal of Educational Psychology, 93,* 776–789.

Perry, W. B. (1981). Cognitive and ethical growth: The making of meaning. In A. Chickering (Ed.), *The modern American college* (pp. 76–117). San Francisco: Jossey-Bass.

Personick, V. A. (1990). Industry output and employment: A slower trend for the nineties. In *Outlook 2000* (Bulletin 2352, pp. 24–40). Washington, DC: Bureau of Labor Statistics.

Peskin, H. (1973). Influence of the developmental schedule of puberty on learning and ego functioning. *Journal of Youth and Adolescence, 14,* 191–206.

Pestrak, V. A., & Martin, D. (1985). Cognitive development and aspects of adolescent sexuality. *Adolescence, 20,* 981–987.

Petersen, A. C. (1991). History of research on adolescence. In R. M. Lerner, A. C. Petersen, & J. Brooks-Gunn (Eds.), *Encyclopedia of adolescence* (pp. 499–503). New York: Wiley.

Peterson, G. W., & Rollins, B. (1987). Parent-child socialization. In M. B. Sussman & S. K. Steinmetz (Eds.), *Handbook of marriage and the family* (pp. 471–507). New York: Plenum.

Peterson, J., Moore, K., & Furstenberg, F. (1991). Television viewing and early initiation of sexual intercourse: Is there a link? *Journal of Homosexuality, 21,* 92–118.

Peterson, K. L., & Roscoe, B. (1991). Imaginary audience behavior in older adolescent females. *Adolescence, 26,* 195–200.

Peterson, K. S. (1997, July 14). Split decision on how divorce affects kids. *USA Today,* p. D6.

Peterson, K. S. (2000, November 16). Sex: not sex: For many teens, oral doesn't count. *USA Today,* pp. 1D and 2D.

Peterson, L., & Gelfand, D. M. (1984). Causal attributions of helping as a function of age and incentives. *Child Development, 55,* 504–511.

Peterson, P. E. (1999, October 4). A liberal case for vouchers. *New Republic, 221,* 29–31.

Petrill, S. A., Luo, D., Thompson, L. A., & Detterman, D. K. (1996). The independent prediction of general intelligence by elementary cognitive tasks: Genetic and environmental influences. *Behavior Genetics, 26,* 135–147.

Phares, V., & Renk, K. (1998). Perceptions of parents: A measure of adolescents' feelings about their parents. *Journal of Marriage and the Family, 60,* 646–660.

Philliber, S. (1994). *Carrera/Dempsey replications programs: 1993–1994 summary of client characteristics and outcomes.* Accord, NY: Philliber Research Associates.

Phillips, C. A., Rolls, S., Rouse, A., & Griffiths, M. (1995). Home video game playing in schoolchildren: A study of incidence and patterns of play. *Journal of Adolescence, 18,* 687–601.

Phinney, J. S. (1989). Stages of ethnic identity development in minority group adolescents. *Journal of Early Adolescence, 9,* 34–49.

Phinney, J. S. (1993). A three-stage model of ethnic identity development in adolescence. In M. E. Bernal & G. P. Knight (Eds.), *Ethnic identity: Formation and transmission among Hispanics and other minorities* (pp. 611–680). New York Press: Albany.

Phinney, J. S., & Alipuria, L. L. (1990). Ethnic identity in college students from four ethnic groups. *Journal of Adolescence, 13,* 171–183.

Phinney, J. S., Cantu, C. L., & Kurtz, D. A. (1997). Ethnic and American identity as predictors of self-esteem among African American, Latino, and white adolescents. *Journal of Youth and Adolescence, 26,* 165–186.

Phinney, J. S., Chavira, V., & Williamson, L. (1992). Acculturation attitudes and self-esteem among high-school and college students. *Youth and Society, 23,* 299–312.

Phinney, J. S., & Tarver, S. (1988). Ethnic identity search and commitment in black and white eighth graders. *Journal of Early Adolescence, 8,* 265–277.

Piaget, J. (1969). *The child's conception of the world.* Totowa, NJ: Littlefield & Adams.

Piaget, J. (1970). *Genetic epistemology.* New York: Columbia University Press.

Piaget, J. (1972). Intellectual evolution from adolescence to adulthood. *Human Development, 15,* 1–12.

Piaget, J. (1977). *The moral judgment of the child.* London: Routledge & Kegan Paul. (Original work published 1932)

Piaget, J., & Inhelder, B. (1969). *The psychology of the child.* New York: Basic Books.

Piaget, J., & Inhelder, B. (1975). *The origin of the idea of chance in children.* New York: Norton. (Original work published 1951)

Pick, S., & Palos, P. A. (1995). Impact of the family on the sex lives of adolescents. *Adolescence, 119,* 667–674.

Pierce, K. (1993). Socialization of teenage girls through teen-magazine fiction: The making of a new woman or an old lady. *Sex Roles, 29,* 59–68.

Pike, A., & Plomin, R. (1996). Importance of nonshared environmental factors for childhood and adolescent psychology. *Journal of the American Academy of child and Adolescent Psychiatry, 35,* 560–570.

Pillard, R. C. (1990). The Kinsey Scale: Is it familial? In D. P. McWhirter, S. A. Sanders, & J. M. Reinisch (Eds.), *Homosexuality/heterosexuality: Concepts of sexual orientation* (pp. 88–100). New York: Oxford University Press.

Pillard, R. C., & Weinrich, J. D. (1986). Evidence of familial nature of male homosexuality. *Archives of Sexual Behavior, 43,* 808–812.

Pino, R. W., & Meier, R. F. (1999, June). Gender differences in rape reporting. *Sex Roles: A Journal of Research, 40,* 979–986.

Pintrich, P. R., & De Groot, E. V. (1990). Motivational and self-regulated learning components of classroom academic performance. *Journal of Educational Psychology, 82,* 33–40.

Pintrich, P. R., & Schrauben, B. (1992). Students' motivational beliefs and their cognitive engagement in classroom academic skills. In D. H. Schunk & J. L. Meece (Eds.), *Student perceptions in the classroom* (pp. 149–183). Hillsdale, NJ: Erlbaum.

Piotrkowski, C. C., & Stark, E. (1987). Children and adolescents look at their parents' jobs. In J. J. Leko (Ed.), *How children and adolescents view the world of work* (pp. 3–19). San Francisco: Jossey-Bass.

Piper, B. (1998, May/June). Comment. *Adoptive Families, 31,* 35–38.

Pirkle, J. L., Flegal, K. M., Bernert, J. T., Brody, D. J., Etzel, R. A., & Maurer, R. (1996). Exposure of the U.S. population to environmental tobacco smoke: The Third National Health and Nutrition Examination Survey, 1988 to 1991. *Journal of the American Medical Association, 275,* 1233–1240.

Pirog-Good, M. (1995). The family background and attitudes of teen fathers. *Youth and Society, 26,* 351–376.

Planned Parenthood Federation of America, Inc. (1999). *Fact sheet: Teenagers, abortion, and government intrusion laws.* Retrieved August 1, 2002, from http://www.plannedparenthood.org/library/abortion/laws.html

Planned Parenthood Federation of America, Inc. (2001, July 31). *Laws requiring parental consent or notification for minors' abortions.* Retrieved August 1, 2002 from http://www.plannedparenthood.org/library/abortion/statelaws.html

Plas, J. M., & Bellet, W. (1983). Assessment of the value-attitude orientations of American Indian children. *Journal of School Psychology, 21,* 57–64.

Plomin, R. (1991). Genetic change. In R. M. Lerner, A. C. Petersen, & J. Brooks-Gunn (Eds.), *Encyclopedia of adolescence* (pp. 400–402). New York: Wiley.

Plomin, R. (1994). The Emanuel Miller Memorial Lecture, 1993: Genetic research and identification of environmental influences. *Journal of Child Psychology and Psychiatry, 35,* 817–834.

Plomin, R. S., & Daniels, D. (1987). Why are children in the same family so different from each other? *Behavioral and Brain Sciences, 10,* 1–16.

Plomin, R., & Petrill, S. (1997). Genetics and intelligence: What's new? *Intelligence, 24,* 53–78.

Plomin, R., DeFries, J. C., & McClearn, G. E., & Rutter, M. (1997). *Behavioral genetics: A primer* (3rd ed.). New York: Freeman.

Plopper, B. L., & Ness, M. E. (1993). Death as portrayed to adolescents through top 40 rock and roll music. *Adolescence, 28,* 793–808.

Polit, D. F., & Falbo, T. (1987). Only children and personality development: A quantitative review. *Journal of Marriage and the Family, 49,* 309–325.

Pomerleau, O. F., & Kardia, S. L. R. (1999). Introduction to the featured section: Genetic research on smoking. *Health Psychology, 18,* 3–6.

Pope, A. W., & Bierman, K. L. (1999). Predicting adolescent peer problems and antisocial activities: The relative roles of aggression and dysregulation. *Developmental Psychology, 35,* 335–346.

Portes, P. R., Haas, R., & Brown, J. H. (1991). Predicting children's adjustment to divorce. *Journal of Divorce, 15,* 87–103.

Portes, P. R., Howell, S. C., Brown, J. H., Eichenberger, S., & Mas, C. A. (1992). Family functions and children's postdivorce adjustment. *American Journal of Orthopsychiatry, 62,* 613–617.

Posner, J. K., & Vandell, D. L. (1999). After-school activities and the development of low-income urban children: A longitudinal study. *Developmental Psychology, 35,* 868–879.

Potvin, L., Gauvin, L., & Nguyen, N. (1997). Prevalence of stages of change for physical activity in rural, suburban, and inner-city communities. *Journal of Community Health, 22,* 1–13.

Power, C., & Kohlberg, L. (1987, May). Using a hidden curriculum for moral education. *Education Digest,* pp. 10–13.

Preboth, M. (2001, June 1). Rates of cigarette smoking in the United States. *American Family Physician, 63,* 2284.

Preboth, M. (2002, June 15). NIAAA report on prevention of college drinking. *American Family Physician, 65,* 2596.

Price, L. A., & Gerber, P. J. (2001). At second glance: Employers and employees with learning disabilities in the Americans with Disabilities Act era. *Journal of Learning Disabilities, 34,* 202–214.

Princeton Survey Research Associates. (1997, May 2). *Nationwide survey conducted for the Association of Reproductive Health Professionals and National Campaign to Prevent Teen Pregnancy.* Princeton, NJ: Author.

Printz, B. L., Shermis, M. D., & Webb, P. M. (1999). Stress-buffering factors related to adolescent coping: A path analysis. *Adolescence, 34,* 715–731.

Pritchard, M. E., King, S. L., & Czajka-Narins, M. (1997). Adolescent body mass indices and self-perception. *Adolescence, 128,* 863–879.

Psychosocial attributes and life experiences of disadvantaged minority mothers: Age and ethnic variations. *Child Development, 61,* 566–580.

Public Agenda. (1997). *Kids these days: What Americans really think about the next generation.* New York: Author.

Puskar, K. R., Lamb, J. M., & Bartolovic, M. (1993). Examining the common stressors and coping methods of rural adolescents. *American Journal of Primary Health Care, 18,* 50– 53.

Putnam, R. (1995, January). Bowling alone: America's declining social capital. *Journal of Democracy, 6,* 65–78.

Pychova, I. (1995). Creativity program for young adults. In M. W. Katzko & F. J. Monks (Eds.), *Nurturing talent, individual needs and social ability* (pp. 217–233). Assen, The Netherlands: van Gorcum.

Quadrel, M., Fischoff, B., & Davis, W. (1993). Adolescent (in)vulnerability. *American Psychologist, 48,* 102–116.

Quatman, T., Sampson, K., Robinson, C., & Watson, C. M. (2001). Academic, motivation, and emotional correlates of adolescent dating. *Genetic, Social and General Psychology Monographs, 127*(2), 211–219.

Quatman, T., & Watson, C. M. (2001). Gender differences in adolescent self-esteem: An exploration of domains. *Journal of Genetic Psychology, 162,* 95–118.

Quint, E. H. (1999). Gynecological health care for adolescents with developmental disabilities. *Adolescent Medicine, 10,* 221–229.

Raab, M. (1998, July/August). Birthrates among teenagers are unaffected when states require parental involvement in their abortion decisions. *Family Planning Perspectives, 30,* 197.

Rabin, J., Seltzer, V., & Pollack, S. (1991). The long-term benefits of a comprehensive teenage pregnancy program. *Clinical Pediatrics, 20,* 305–309.

Rainey, L. M., & Borders, D. (1997). Influential factors in career orientation and career aspiration of early adolescent girls. *Journal of Counseling Psychology, 44,* 160–172.

Raloff, J. (1997). And music videos their image. *Science News, 152,* 111.

Rapping, E. (1993, February). The year of the young. *The Progressive, 57,* 36–39.

Raskin, R., Novacek, J., & Hogan, R. (1991). Narcissistic self-esteem management. *Journal of Personality and Social Psychology, 60,* 911–918.

Raths, L. E., Harmin, M., & Simon, S. B. (1966). *Values and teaching.* Columbus, OH: Charles Merrill.

Rathunde, K. (1997). Parent-adolescent interaction and optimal experience. *Journal of Youth and Adolescence, 26,* 669–689.

Rathus, S. A., Nevid, J. S., & Fichner-Rathus, L. (2000). *Human sexuality* (4th ed.). Boston: Allyn & Bacon.

Raviv, D., & Stone, C. A. (1991). Individual differences in the self-image of adolescents with learning disabilities: The roles of severity, time of diagnosis, and parental perceptions. *Journal of Learning Disabilities, 24,* 602–607.

Ray, O., & Ksir, C. (1993). *Drugs, society, and human behavior.* St. Louis: Mosby.

Ray, W. J. (1997). *Methods: Toward a science of behavior and experience* (5th ed.). Pacific Grove, CA: Brooks-Cole.

Read, D. A., Simon, S. B., & Goodman, J. B. (1977). *Health education: The search for values.* Englewood Cliffs, NJ: Prentice Hall.

Reardon, R. C., Lenz, J. G., Sampson, J. P., & Peterson, G. W. (2000). *Career development and planning: A comprehensive approach.* Belmont, CA: Wadsworth.

Reddy, D. M., Fleming, R., & Swain, C. (2002). Effect of mandatory parental notification on adolescent girls' use of sexual health care services. *Journal of the American Medical Association, 288,* 710–715.

Reese-Weber, M. (2000). Middle and late adolescents' conflict resolution skills with siblings: Associations with interparental and adolescent-parent conflict resolution. *Journal of Youth and Adolescence, 29,* 697–726.

Rehman, S. N., & Reilly, S. S. (1985). Music videos: A new dimension of televised violence. *Pennsylvania Speech Communication Annual, 41,* 61–64.

Reid, M., Ramey, S. L., & Burchinal, M. (1990). Dialogues with children about their families. *New Directions for Child Development, 48,* 5–27.

Reiff, M. I. (2001a). Maternal expectations, mother-child connectedness, and adolescent sexual debut. *Journal of Developmental and Behavioral Pediatrics, 22,* 79.

Reiff, M. I. (2001b, April). Reducing adolescents' aggressive and hostile behaviors. *Journal of Developmental and Behavioral Pediatrics, 22,* 148–164.

Reinemer, M. (1995). Work happy. *American Demographics, 45,* 26–31.

Reisine, T. (1995). Opiate receptors. *Neuropharmacology, 34,* 463–472.

Reisman, J. R., & Shorr, S. I. (1978). Friendship claims and expectations among children and adults. *Child Development, 49,* 913–916.

Reiss, D. (1993). Genes and the environment: Siblings and synthesis. In R. Plomin & G. E. McClearn (Eds.), *Nature, nurture, and psychology* (pp. 417–433). Washington, DC: American Psychological Association.

Remez, L. (2000). Oral sex among adolescents: Is it sex or is it abstinence? *Family Planning Perspectives, 32,* 298–310.

Rendleman, R., & Walkup, J. T. (1997). Mood disorders in adolescents. In J. D. Noshpitz (Ed. in Chief), L. T. Flaherty, & R. M. Sarles (Eds.), *Handbook of child and adolescent psychiatry* (Vol. 3, pp. 305–328). New York: Wiley.

Rennison, C. M. (1998). *Criminal victimization 1998: Changes 1997–1998 with trends 1993–1998.* Washington, DC: Bureau of Justice Statistics, 1999. Retrieved August 1, 2002 from http://www.ojp.usdoj.gov/bjs/abstract/cv98.htm

Rest, J. (1983). Morality. In P. H. Mussen (Ed.), *Handbook of child psychology: Cognitive development* (Vol. 3, 4th ed., pp. 556–630). New York: Wiley.

Retschitzki, J. (1989). Evidence of formal thinking in baoule awele players. In D. M. Keats, D. Munro, & L. Mann (Eds.), *Heterogeneity in cross-cultural psychology* (pp. 234–243). Amsterdam: Swets & Zeitlinger.

Reyes, O., Gillock, K., & Kobus, K. (1994). A longitudinal study of school adjustment in urban, minority adolescents: Effects of a high school transition program. *American Journal of Community Psychology, 22,* 341–369.

Reynolds, J. R. (1994, March 26). Women rap for dignity: Defiant voices fight misogny. *Billboard, 106,* 1–3.

Reynolds, J. R. (1995, February 25). Shocking lyrics earn '90s R&B monstrous popularity, backlash. *Billboard, 107,* 26.

Reynolds, W. M. (1992). Depression in children and adolescents. In W. M. Reynolds (Ed.), *Internalizing disorders in children and adolescents* (pp. 149–253). New York: Wiley.

Rice, M. L. (1989). *Human sexuality.* Dubuque, IA: Brown.

Rich, M., Woods, E. R., Goodman, E., Emans, J. & DuRant, R. (1998, April). Aggressors or victims: Gender and race in music video violence. *Pediatrics, 101,* 669–675.

Richards, M. H., Casper, R. C., & Larson, R. (1990). Weight and eating concerns among pre-and young adolescent boys and girls. *Journal of Adolescent Health Care, 11,* 203–209.

Richards, M., Crowe, P., Larson, R., & Swarr, A. (1998). Developmental patterns and gender differences in the experience of peer companionship during adolescence. *Child Development, 69,* 154–163.

Richardson, J. L., Dwyer, K., McGuigan, K., Hansen, W. B., Dent, C. W., Johnson, C. A., et al. (1989). Substance abuse among eighth-grade students who take care of themselves after school. *Pediatrics, 84,* 556–566.

Richardson, R. A., Galambos, N. L., Schulenberg, J. E., & Petersen, A. C. (1984). Young adolescents' perceptions of the family environment. *Journal of Early Adolescence, 6,* 131–153.

Richardson, S., & McCabe, M. P. (2001). Parental divorce during adolescence and adjustment in early adulthood. *Adolescence, 36,* 467–490.

Richins, M. (1991). Social comparison and the idealized images in advertising. *Journal of Consumer Research, 18,* 71–83.

Rideout, V. J., Foehr, U. G., Roberts, D. F., & Brodie, M. (1999). *Executive summary: Kids and the media at the new millennium.* Menlo Park, CA: Henry J. Kaiser Family Foundation.

Rieble-Aubourg, S. (2000). Institutional arrangements of Germany's vocational education system: What are the policy implications for the U.S.? *International Journal of Comparative Sociology, 37,* 174–191.

Rigby, K., & Bagshaw, D. (2001). What hurts? The reported consequences of negative interactions with peers among Australian adolescent school children. *Children Australia, 26,* 36–41.

Riggs, D. S., & O'Leary, K. D. (1989). A theoretical model of courts and aggression. In M. A. Pirog-Good (Ed.), *Violence in dating relationships* (pp. 53–71). New York: Praeger.

Riley, R. W. (1999, July). High school students: Values and expectations. *Presidents and Prime Ministers, 8,* 21.

Robbins, T., & Anthony, D. (1978, May/June). New religions, families and brainwashing. *Society, 15,* 150–168.

Roberts, D. F., Foehr, U. G., Rideout, V. J., Brodie, M. (1999). *Kids and media at the new millennium: A comprehensive national analysis of children's media use.* Menlo Park, CA: Henry J. Kaiser Family Foundation.

Roberts, R. E., Roberts, C. R., & Chen, Y. R. (1997). Ethnocultural differences in prevalence of adolescent depression. *American Journal of Community Psychology, 25,* 95–111.

Robinson, B. E., Walters, L. H., & Skeen, P. (1989). Response of parents to learning that their child is homosexual and concern over AIDS: A national study. *Journal of Homosexuality, 18,* 59–80.

Robinson, L. A., & Klesges, R. C. (1997). Ethnic and gender differences in risk factors for smoking onset. *Health Psychology, 16,* 499–505.

Robinson, L. A., Klesges, R. C., Zbikowski, S. M., & Glaser, R. (1997). Predictors of risk for different stages of adolescent smokers. *Journal of Consulting and Clinical Psychology, 65,* 653–662.

Roche, J. P. (1986). Premarital sex: Attitudes and behavior by dating stage. *Adolescence, 21,* 107–121.

Roche, J. P., & Ramsbey, T. W. (1993). Premarital sexuality: A five-year follow-up study of attitudes and behavior by dating stage. *Adolescence, 28,* 67–80.

Rocheleau, B. (1995). Computer use by school age children: Trends, patterns and predictors. *Educational Computing Research, 1,* 1–17.

Rocigno, V. J., & Ainsworth-Darnell, J. W. (1999). Race, cultural capital, and educational resources: Persistent inequalities and achievement returns. *Sociology of Education, 72,* 158–160.

Rodin, J. (1993). Cultural psychosocial determinants of weight concerns. *Annals of Internal Medicine, 119,* 643–645.

Rodkin, P. C., Farmer, T. W., Pearl, R., & Van Acker, R. (2000). Heterogeneity of popular boys: Antisocial and prosocial configurations. *Developmental Psychology, 36,* 14–24.

Rodriguez, C., & Moore, N. B. (1995). Perceptions of pregnant/parenting teens: Reframing issues for an integral approach to pregnancy problems. *Adolescence, 30,* 685–706.

Rogers, K. B. (1998). Using current research to make "good" decisions about grouping. *NASSP Bulletin, 82,* 38–47.

Rohner, R., & Pettengill, S. (1985). Perceived parental acceptance-rejection and parental control among Korean adolescents. *Child Development, 56,* 524–528.

Rohner, R. P., & Veneziano, R. A. (2001). The importance of father love: History and contemporary evidence. *Review of General Psychology, 5,* 382–405.

Rojewski, J. W. (1999). Occupational and educational aspirations and attainment of young adults with and without LD 2 years after high school completion. *Journal of Learning Disabilities, 32,* 533–552.

Rojewski, J. W., & Yang, B. (1997). Longitudinal analysis of select influences on adolescents' occupational aspirations. *Journal of Vocational Behavior, 51,* 375–410.

Ronfeldt, H. M., Kimerling, R., & Arias, I. (1998). Satisfaction with relationship power and the perpetration of dating violence. *Journal of Marriage and the Family, 60,* 70–79.

Roper Starch Worldwide Inc. (1999). *The America Online/Roper Starch Youth Cyberstudy.* Retrieved July 18, 2002, from http://corp.aol.com/press/roper.html

Ropp, K. L. (1992, December). No-win situations for athletes. *FDA Consumer,* pp. 8–12.

Rosales, I. & Zigler, E. F. (1989). Role taking and self-image disparity: A further test of cognitive-developmental thought. *Psychological Reports, 64,* 41–42.

Roscoe, B., Diana, M. S., & Brooks, R. H. (1987). Early, middle, and late adolescents' views on dating and factors influencing partner selection. *Adolescence, 22,* 59–68.

Rose, L. C., & Gallup, A. M. (2002, September). The 33rd annual Phi Delta Kappan/Gallup Poll on the public's attitude toward public schools. *Phi Delta Kappan, 83,* 41–59.

Rose, L. C., Gallup, A. M., & Elam, S. M. (1997). The 29th annual Phi Delta Kappan/Gallup Poll of the public's attitudes toward the public schools. *Phi Delta Kappan, 79,* 41–57.

Rose, S., & Frieze, I. H. (1989). Young singles' scripts for a first date. *Gender and Society, 3,* 258–267.

Rose, S., & Frieze, I. H. (1993). Young singles' contemporary dating scripts. *Sex Roles, 28,* 499–512.

Rose, V. L. (1998, May 1). ACOG issues report on sexual assault. *American Family Physician, 57,* 1144–1146.

Rosenbaum, J. E. (1996). Policy uses of research on the high school-to-work transition. *Sociology of Education, 69,* 102–122.

Rosenbaum, J. E., & Kariya, T. (1989). From high school to work: Market and institutional mechanisms in Japan. *American Journal of Sociology, 94,* 1334–1336.

Rosenbaum, J. E., & Kariya, T. (1991). Do school achievements affect the early jobs of high school graduates in the United States and Japan? *Sociology of Education, 64,* 78–95.

Rosenberg, B. G., & Hyde, J. S. (1993). The only child: Is there only one kind? *Journal of Genetic Psychology, 154,* 269–283.

Rosenblum, G. D., & Lewis, M. (1999). The relations among body image, physical attractiveness, and body mass in adolescence. *Child Development, 70,* 50–64.

Rosenthal, R., & Jacobson, L. (1968). *Pygmalion in the classroom: Teacher expectation and pupils' intellectual development.* New York: Holt, Rinehart & Winston.

Rosnow, R. L., Rotheram-Borus, M. J., Ceci, S. J., Blanck, P. D., & Koocher, G. P. (1993). The institutional review board as a mirror of scientific and ethical standards. *American Psychologist, 48,* 821–826.

Roth, W. F. (1999, November). Computers can individualize learning and raise group-interaction skills. *Education Digest, 65,* 27–31.

Rothenberg, D. (1998, February). How the web destroys student research papers. *Education Digest,* 59–61.

Rotheram-Borus, M. J. (1989). Ethnic differences in adolescents' identity status and associated behavior problems. *Journal of Adolescence, 12,* 361–374.

Rotheram-Borus, M. J., & Koopman, C. (1991). Sexual risk behavior, AIDS knowledge, and beliefs about AIDS among predominantly minority gay and bisexual male adolescents. *AIDS Education and Prevention, 3,* 305–312.

Rothstein, L. E. (1995). *Special education law* (2nd ed.). White Plains, NY: Longman.

Rourke, B. P., & Del Dotto, J. E. (2001). Learning disabilities: A neuropsychological perspective. In C. E. Walker & M. C. Roberts (Eds.), *Handbook of clinical child psychology* (3rd ed., pp. 576–602). New York Wiley.

Rowe, R., & Snizek, W. E. (1995). Gender differences in work values: Perpetuating the myth. *Work and Occupations, 22,* 215–229.

Roye, C., & Balk, S. (1996). The relationship of partner support to outcomes for teenage mothers and their children: A review. *Journal of Adolescent Health, 19,* 86–93.

Rubin, A. M. (1995, July 21). Using pop culture to fight teen violence. *Chronicle of Higher Education,* p. A5.

Rubin, Z. (1980). *Children's friendships.* Cambridge: Harvard University Press.

Ruble, D. N. (1988). Sex role development. In M. H. Bornstein & M. E. Lamb (Eds.), *Social, emotional and personality development* (2nd ed., pp. 411–451). Hillsdale, NJ: Erlbaum.

Ruble, D. N., & Martin, C. L. (1998). Gender development. In W. Damon (Ed.), W. Damon, & N. Eisenberg (Vol. Eds.), *Handbook of child psychology* (5th ed., Vol. 3, pp. 933–1016). New York: Wiley.

Rudin, M. R. (1990). Cults and Satanism: Threats to teens. *National Association of Secondary School Principals Bulletin, 74,* 46–52.

Rudolph, K. D., & Hammen, C. (1999). Age and gender as determinants of stress exposure, generation, and reactions in youngsters: A transactional perspective. *Child Development, 70,* 660–677.

Ruhm, C. J. (1995). The extent and consequences of high school employment. *Journal of Labor Research, 3,* 293–303.

Ruittenbeck, H. M. (1964). *The individual and the crowd: A study of identity in America.* New York: New American Library.

Rumberger, R. W. (1987). High school dropouts: A review of the issues and evidence. *Review of Educational Research, 87,* 101–121.

Russell, C. (1997, November). What's wrong with kids? *American Demographics,* 32–36.

Rutter, M. (1978). Family, school and area influences in the genesis of conduct disorders. In L. A. Hersov & M. Berger (Eds.), *Aggression and antisocial behavior in childhood and adolescence.* New York: Pergamon Press.

Rutter, M. (1979). Maternal deprivation, 1972–1978: New findings, new concepts, new approaches. *Child Development, 50,* 283–305.

Rutter, M. (1985). Resilience in the face of adversity: Protective factors and resistance to psychiatric disorder. *British Journal of Psychiatry, 147,* 589–611.

Rutter, M. (1987). Prosocial resilience and protective mechanisms. *American Journal of Orthopsychiatry, 57,* 47–61.

Rutter, M., & Rutter, M. (1993). *Developing minds.* New York: Basic Books.

Rutter, M., Silberg, J., O'Connor, T., & Simnoff, E. (1999). Genetics and child psychiatry: II. Empirical research findings. *Journal of Child Psychology and Psychiatry, 40,* 19–55.

Ryan, A. M. (2001). The peer group as a context for the development of young adolescent motivation and achievement. *Child Development, 72,* 1135–1150.

Ryan, K. (1981). *Questions and answers on moral education.* Bloomington, IN: Phi Delta Kappa Educational Foundation.

Ryan, K. (1986, November). The new moral education. *Phi Delta Kappan,* 228–233.

Ryan, R. M., & Lynch, J. H. (1989). Emotional autonomy versus detachment: Revising the vicissitudes of adolescence and young adulthood. *Child Development, 60,* 340–356.

Rybash, J. M., Roodin, P. A., & Hoyer, W. J. (1995). *Adult development and aging* (3rd ed.). Dubuque, IA: Brown & Benchmark.

Rycek, R. F., Stuhr, S. L., McDermott, J., Benker, J., & Swartz, M. D. (1998). Adolescent egocentrism and cognitive functioning during late adolescence. *Adolescence, 33,* 746–751.

Sacco, W. P., & Beck, A. T. (1995). Cognitive theory and therapy. In E. E. Beckham & W. R. Leber (Ed.), *Handbook of depression* (2nd ed., pp. 95–104). New York: Wiley.

Sadker, M., & Sadker, D. (1985). Sexism in the schoolroom in the '80s. *Psychology Today, 19,* 54–57.

Sadker, M., & Sadker, D. (1994). *Failing at fairness: How America's schools cheat girls.* New York: Macmillan.

Safe Schools. (2002). *School violence prevention.* Retrieved November 23, 2002, from http://www.mentalhealth.org/schoolviolence

Safyer, A. W., Hawkins, B., & Colan, N. B. (1995). The impact of work on adolescent development. *Families in Society, 76,* 38–45.

Salem, S. S. (1993, November 27). Rap music mirrors its environment. *Billboard, 105,* 6.

Salmivalli, C. (2001). Aggression and violent behavior. *Aggression and Violent Behavior, 6,* 375–393.

Salmon, G., James, A., & Smith, D. M. (1998). Bullying in schools: Self-reported anxiety, depression, and self-esteem in secondary school children. *British Medical Journal, 317,* 924–926.

Salovey, P., & Mayer, J. D. (1990). Emotional intelligence. *Imagination, cognition, and personality, 9,* 185–211.

Salovey, P., & Mayer, J. (1997). *Emotional development and emotional intelligence.* New York: Basic Books.

Salpeter, J. (1999). New technology high school: Preparing students for the digital age. *Technology and Learning, 19,* 46–52.

Sammons, W. A. H., & Lewis, J. (2001). Helping children survive divorce. *Contemporary Pediatrics, 18,* 103–118.

Sanchez, H. G. (2001). Risk factor model for suicide assessment and intervention. *Professional Psychology: Research and Practice, 32,* 351–358.

Sanchez-Jankowski, M. S. (1991). *Islands in the street: Gangs and American urban society.* Berkeley, CA: University of California Press.

Sanders, C. E., Field, T. M., Diego, M., & Kaplan, M. (2000). The relationship of internet use to depression and social isolation among adolescents. *Adolescence, 35,* 237–242.

Sanderson, C. A., & Cantor, N. (1995). Social dating goals in late adolescence: Implications for safer sexual activity. *Journal of Personality and Social Psychology, 68,* 1121–1134.

Sandler, I. N., Tein, J. Y., & West, S. G. (1994). Coping, stress, and the psychological symptoms of children of divorce: A cross-sectional and longitudinal study. *Child Development, 65,* 1744–1763.

Sands, R., Tricker, J., Sherman, C., Armatas, C., & Maschette, W. (1997). Disordered eating patterns, body image, self-esteem, and physical activity in preadolescent school children. *International Journal of Eating Disorders, 21,* 159–166.

Sante, L. (1991). *Low life: Lures and snares of old New York.* New York: Vintage.

Santelli, J. S., Lowry, R., Brener, N. D., & Robin, L. (2000). The association of sexual behaviors with socioeconomic status, family structure, and race/ethnicity among US adolescents. *American Journal of Public Health, 90,* 1582–1588.

Sartor, C. E., & Youniss, J. (2002). The relationship between positive parental involvement and identity achievement during adolescence. *Adolescence, 37,* 221–225.

Satterfield, J. H., & Schell, A. (1997). A prospective study of hyperactive boys with conduct problems and normal boys: Adolescent and adult criminality. *Journal of the American Academy of Child and Adolescent Psychiatry, 36,* 1726–1735.

Saudino, K. J., & Plomin, R. (1996). Tester-rated temperament at 14, 20, and 24 months: Environmental change and genetic continuity. *British Journal of Developmental Psychology, 14,* 129–144.

Savage, L. B. (1998). Eliciting critical thinking skills through questioning. *The Clearing House, 71,* 291–294.

Savage, M. P., & Scott, L. B. (1998). Physical activity and rural middle school adolescents. *Journal of Youth and Adolescence, 27,* 245–252.

Savin-Williams, R. C. (1988). Theoretical perspectives accounting for adolescent homosexuality. *Journal of Adolescent Health Care, 9,* 95–105.

Savin-Williams, R. C., & Berndt, T. J. (1990). Friendship and peer relations. In S. S. Feldman & G. R. Elliott (Eds.), *At the threshold: The developing adolescent* (pp. 277–307). Cambridge: Harvard University Press.

Savin-Williams, R. C., & Dube, E. M. (1998). Parental reactions to their child's disclosure of a gay/lesbian identity. *Family Relations, 47,* 7–13.

Savin-Williams, R. C., & Small, S. A. (1986). The timing of puberty and its relationship to adolescent and parent perceptions of family interactions. *Developmental Psychology, 22,* 342–348.

Scarr, S. (1981). *Race, social class, and individual differences in IQ.* Hillsdale, NJ: Erlbaum.

Scarr, S., & McCartney, K. (1983). How people make their own environments: A theory of genotype-environment effects. *Child Development, 54,* 424–435.

Schaal, B., Tremblay, R. E., Soussignan, R., & Susman, E. J. (1996). Male testosterone linked to high social dominance but low physical aggression in early adolescence. *Journal of the American Academy of Child and Adolescent Psychiatry, 35,* 1322–1330.

Schachter, J. (1989). Why we need a program for the control of chlamydia trachomatis. *New England Journal of Medicine, 320,* 802–803.

Schaeffer, R. T., & Lamm, R. P. (1995). *Sociology* (5th ed.). New York: McGraw-Hill.

Schaffer, H. R. (1996). *Social development.* Oxford: Blackwell.

Schaie, K. W. (1994). The course of adult intellectual development. *American Psychologist, 49,* 304–313.

Scheel, K. R., & Westefeld, J. S. (1999). Heavy metal music and adolescent suicidality: An empirical investigation. *Adolescence, 34,* 253–266.

Schiedel, D. G., & Marcia, J. E. (1985). Ego identity, intimacy, sex role orientation and gender. *Developmental Psychology, 21,* 149–160.

Schiller, K. S. (1999). Effects of feeder patterns on students' transition to high school. *Sociology of Education, 72,* 216–233.

Schimel, J., Arndt, J., Pyszcynski, T., & Greenberg, J. (2000). Intrinsic self reduces defensiveness. *Journal of Personality and Social Psychology, 80,* 35–52.

Schlegel, A., & Barry, H., III. (1991). *Adolescence: An anthropological inquiry.* New York: Free Press.

Schmidt, G., Klusmann, D., Zeitzchel, U., & Lange, C. (1994). Changes in adolescents' sexuality between 1970 and 1990 in West Germany. *Archives of Sexual Behavior, 23,* 489–513.

Schmidt, P. (1994, September). Idea of "gender gap" under attack. *Education Week,* pp. 1, 16.

Schneider, W., Gruber, H., Gold, A., & Opwis, K. (1993). Chess expertise and memory for chess positions in children and adults. *Journal of Experimental Child Psychology, 56,* 328–349.

Schofield, J. W. (1991). School desegregation and intergroup relations: A review of the literature. *Review of Research in Education, 17,* 335–409.

School vouchers. (1999). *CQ Researcher, 9,* 291–300.

Schooler, J. (1997, May/June). Sharing the facts. *Adoptive Families, 30,* 49.

Schooler, J. (1998, May/June). See how they grow. *Adoptive Families, 30,* 51.

Schouten, F. (2002, October 17). Middle school getting edged to the back. *USA Today,* p. 12D.

Schuckit, M. A. (1986). Genetic and clinical implications of alcoholism and affective disorder. *American Journal of Psychiatry, 143,* 140–153.

Schuckit, M. A. (1987). Biological vulnerability to alcoholism. *Journal of Consulting and Clinical Psychology, 55,* 301–309.

Schuckit, M. A., Tsuang, J. W., Antheneilli, R. M., Tipp, J. E., & Nurnberger, J. I. (1996). Alcohol challenges in young men from alcohol pedigrees and control families: A report from the COGA project. *Journal of the Studies of Alcoholism, 57,* 368–377.

Schultz, D. A. (1984). *Human sexuality.* Englewood Cliffs, NJ: Prentice Hall.

Schunk, D. (1996). *Learning theories* (2nd ed.). Englewood Cliffs, NJ: Merrill.

Schunk, D. H., & Ertmer, P. A. (1999). Self-regulatory processes during computer skill acquisition goal and self-evaluative influences. *Journal of Educational Psychology, 91,* 251–260.

Schuster, M. A., Bell, R. M., Berry, T., & Kanouse, W. F. (1998). Impact of a high school condom availability program on sexual attitudes and behaviors. *Family Planning Perspectives, 30,* 67–73.

Schutte, N. S., Malouff, J. M., Post-Gorden, J. C., & Rodasta, A. L. (1988). Effects of playing video games on children's aggressive and other behaviors. *Journal of Applied Social Psychology, 18,* 454–460.

Schwartz, J. (1997, December). Kids take responsibility. *American Demographics, 27.*

Schwartz, R. H., & Weaver, A. B. (1998). Rohypnol: The date rape drug. *Clinical Pediatrics, 37,* 321.

Schwarz, J. C., Barton-Henry, M. L., & Prjzinsky, T. (1985). Assessing child-rearing behaviors: A comparison of ratings made by mother, father, child and sibling on the CRPBI. *Child Development, 56,* 462–479.

Scott, C. G., Murray, G. C., Mertens, C., & Dustin, E. R. (1996). Student self-esteem and the school system: Perceptions and implications. *Journal of Educational Research, 89,* 286–294.

Scott, D. (1995). The effect of video games on feelings of aggression. *The Journal of Psychology, 129,* 121–123.

Scott, D., & Willits, F. K. (1989). Adolescent and adult leisure patterns: A 37-year follow-up study. *Leisure Sciences, 11,* 323–335.

Scott, D., & Willits, F. K. (1998). Adolescent and adult leisure patterns: A reassessment. *Journal of Leisure Research, 30,* 319–331.

Scribner, S., & Cole, M. (1981). *The psychology of literacy.* Cambridge: Harvard University Press.

Sebald, H. (1986). Adolescents' shifting orientation toward parents and peers: A curvilinear trend over recent decades. *Journal of Marriage and the Family, 48,* 5–13.

Sebald, H. (1989). Adolescents' peer orientation: Changes in the support system during the past three decades. *Adolescence, 96,* 937–945.

Segal, B. M., & Stewart, J. C. (1996). Substance use and abuse in adolescence: An overview. *Human Development, 26,* 193–210.

Seidman, E., Aber, J. L., Allen, L., & French, S. E. (1996). The impact of the transition to high school on the self-system and perceived social context of poor urban youth. *American Journal of Community Psychology, 24,* 489–515.

Seidman, E., Allen, L., Aber, J. L., Mitchell, C., & Feinman, J. (1994). The impact of school transitions in early adolescence on the self-system and perceived social context of poor urban youth. *Child Development, 65,* 507–522.

Seidman, L. J., Biederman, J., Monuteaux, M. C., Doyle, A. E., & Faraone, S. V. (2001). Learning disabilities and executive dysfunction with attention-deficit/hyperactivity disorder. *Neuropsychology, 15,* 544–556.

Seidman, S. (1999). Revisiting sex-role stereotyping in MTV videos. *International Journal of Instructional Media, 26,* 11–22.

Seifert, S. A. (1999). Substance use and sexual assault. *Substance Use and Misuse, 34,* 934–945.

Seiffge-Krenke, L., & Shulman, S. (1990). Coping styles in adolescence. *Journal of Cross-Cultural Psychology, 21,* 351–377.

Seligman, M. E. P. (1974). Depression and learned helplessness. In R. J. Friedman & M. M. Katz (Eds.), *The psychology of depression: Contemporary theory and research.* Washington, DC: Winston-Wiley.

Seligman, M. E. P., & Csikszentmihalyi, M. (2000). Positive psychology: An introduction. *American Psychologist, 55,* 5–14.

Seligman, M. E. P., & Peterson, C. (1986). A learned helplessness perspective on childhood depression: Theory and research. In M. Rutter, C. E. Izard, & P. B. Read (Eds.), *Depression in young people: Developmental and clinical perspectives* (pp. 223–249). New York: Guilford Press.

Sellers, D. E., McGraw, S. A., & McKinlay, J. B. (1994). Does the promotion and distribution of condoms increase teen sexual activity? Evidence from an HIV prevention program for Latino youth. *American Journal of Public Health, 84,* 1952–1959.

Sellers, R. (1998, January/February). Nine global trends in religion. *Futurist, 32,* 20–26.

Selman, R. L. (1980). *The growth of interpersonal understanding: Developmental and clinical analysis.* New York: Academic Press.

Selman, R. L. (1989). Fostering intimacy and autonomy. In W. Damon (Ed.), *Child development today and tomorrow* (pp. 408–435). Jossey-Bass: San Francisco.

Serbin, L. A., Powlishta, K. K., & Gulko, J. (1993). The development of sex typing in middle childhood. *Monographs of the Society for Research in Child Development, 58*(2, Serial No. 232).

Serniclaes, W., Sprenger-Charolles, L., Carre, R., & Demonet, J. F. (2001). Perceptual discrimination of speech sounds in developmental dyslexia. *Journal of Speech, Language, and Hearing Research, 4,* 384–395.

Sev'er, A. (1999). Sexual harassment: Where we were, where we are and prospects for the new millennium: Introduction to special issue. *The Canadian Review of Sociology and Anthropology, 36,* 469–485.

Shafer, G. (2001, March). Vouchers, lies, and public schools. *The Humanist, 61,* 3.

Shanahan, M. J., Elder, G. H., Burchinal, M., & Conger, R. D. (1996). Adolescent paid labor and relationships with parents: Early work-family linkages. *Child Development, 67,* 2183–2200.

Shanker, A. (1988, July 10). Convention plots new course: A charter for change. *The New York Times, 4,* p. 7.

Shanker, A. (1997). Educational reform and basic standards. *Forum For Applied Research and Public Policy, 12,* 78–83.

Shantz, C. U. (1983). Social cognition. In J. H. Flavell & E. M. Markman (Eds.), *Handbook of child psychology* (4th ed., Vol. 3, pp. 495–556). New York: Wiley.

Shapiro, T., & Kalogerakis, A. (1997). Identity consolidation in adolescence. In L. T. Flaherty & R. M. Searles (Eds.), *Handbook of child and adolescent psychiatry* (Vol. 3, pp. 149–154). New York: Wiley.

Sharabany, R., Gershoni, R., & Hofman, J. E. (1981). Girlfriend, boyfriend: Age and sex differences in intimate friendships. *Developmental Psychology, 17,* 800–808.

Sharp, D. (1996, October 4). New Orleans puts its curfew in good light. *USA Today,* p. A4.

Shaver, J. P., & Strong, W. (1976). *Facing value decisions: Rationale-building for teachers.* Belmont, CA: Wadsworth.

Shaver, P., & Brennan, K. A. (1992). Attachment styles and the "Big Five" personality traits: Their connections with each other and with romantic relationship outcomes. *Personality and Social Psychology Bulletin, 18,* 536–545.

Shaver, P. R., Wu, S., & Schwartz, J. C. (1991). Cross-cultural similarities and differences in emotion and its representation: A prototype approach. In M. S. Clark (Ed.), *Review of personality and social psychology* (Vol. 13, pp. 175–212). Beverly Hills, CA: Sage.

Shaw, M. E. (1998). Adolescent breakfast skipping: An Australian study. *Adolescence, 132,* 851–861.

Shaw, S. F., McGuire, J. M., & Brinckerhoff, L. C. (1994). College and university programming. In P. J. Gerber & H. B. Reiff (Eds.). *Learning disabilities in adulthood: Persisting problems and evolving issues* (pp. 141–151). Stoneham, MA: Butterworth-Heinemann.

Shedler, J., & Block, J. (1990). Adolescent drug use and psychological health: A longitudinal perspective. *American Psychologist, 45,* 612–630.

Shek, D. T. L. (1998). A longitudinal study of the relations between adolescent-parent conflict and adolescent psychological well-being. *Journal of Genetic Psychology, 159,* 53–68.

Sheley, J. F., & Wright, J. D. (1993). *Gun acquisition and possession in selected juvenile samples: Research in brief* [NCJ 145326]. Washington, DC: U.S. Department of Justice, National Institute of Justice, and Office of Juvenile Justice and Delinquency Prevention.

Sheperd, D. (1996, September). The proliferation of juvenile curfews. *American Bar Association Criminal Justice Section Newsletter,* pp. 1–3.

Shepherdson, N. (2000, May). Life's a beach 101. *American Demographics, 22,* 56–64.

Shepperd, J. A., Arkin, R. M., & Slaughter, J. (1995). Constraints on excuse making: The deterring effects of shyness and anticipated retest. *Personality and Social Psychology Bulletin, 21,* 1061–1074.

Sher, K. J., Bartholow, B. D., & Wood, M. D. (2000). *Journal of Consulting and Clinical Psychology, 68,* 818–829.

Sheras, P. L. (2001). Depression and suicide in adolescence. In C. E. Walker & M. C. Roberts (Eds.), *Handbook of clinical child psychology* (3rd ed., pp. 657–673). New York: Wiley.

Sherman, B. L., & Dominick, J. R. (1986). Violence and sex in music videos: TV and rock 'n' roll. *Journal of Communication, 36,* 79–93.

Shetowsky, B. (1983). Ego identity development and obesity in adolescent girls. *Adolescence, 71,* 550–559.

Shew, M. L., Hellerstedt, W. L., Sieing, R. E., Smith, A. E., & Fee, R. M. (2000). Prevalence of home pregnancy testing among females. *American Journal of Public Health, 90,* 974–976.

Shields, C. M. (2002). A comparison study of student attitudes and perceptions in homogeneous and heterogeneous classrooms. *Roeper Review, 24,* 115–120.

Shiveley, J. M., & van Fossen, P. J. (1999). Critical thinking and the Internet: Opportunities for the social studies classroom. *Social Studies, 90,* 42–47.

Short, E. J., Schatschneider, C. W., & Friebert, S. E. (1993). Relationship between memory and metamemory performance: A comparison of specific and general strategy knowledge. *Journal of Educational Psychology, 85,* 412–423.

Shriner, J. G. (2000). Legal perspectives on school outcomes assessment for students with disabilities. *Journal of Special Education, 33,* 232–247.

Shrum, W., & Cheek, N. H. (1987). Social structure during the school years: Onset of the degrouping process. *American Sociological Review, 52,* 218–223.

Shrum, W., Cheek, N. H., & Hunter, S. M. (1988). Friendship in school: Gender and racial homophily. *Sociology of Education, 61,* 227–239.

Shulman, S., Laursen, B., Kalman Z., & Karpovsky, S. (1997). Adolescent intimacy revisited. *Journal of Youth and Adolescence, 26,* 597–617.

Shure, M. (2000). Bullies and their victims: A problem-solving approach to prevention. *The Brown University Child and Adolescent Behavior Letter, 16,* 1–3.

Shweder, R. A., Mahapatra, M., & Miller, J. G. (1987). Culture and moral development. In J. Kagan & S. Lamb (Eds.), *The emergence of morality in young children* (pp. 1–83). Chicago: University of Chicago Press.

Shweder, R. A., & Miller, G. (1991). The social construction of the person. In R. Shweder (Ed.), *Culture theory: Essays on mind, self, and emotion* (pp. 156–185). Cambridge: Harvard University Press.

Sickmund, M., Snyder, H. N., & Poe-Yamagata, E. (1997). *Juvenile offenders and victims: 1997 update on violence.* Washington, DC: Office of Juvenile Justice and Delinquency Prevention.

Sidney, S., Beck, J. E., Tekawa, I. S., Quesenberry, C. P., & Freiedman, G. D. (1997). Marijuana use and mortality. *American Journal of Public Health, 87,* 585–590.

Siegel, J., & Shaughnessy, M. F. (1995). There's a first time for everything: Understanding adolescence. *Adolescence, 30,* 217–222.

Siegel, L. J., & Senna, J. J. (2000). *Juvenile delinquency* (7th ed.). Belmont, CA: Wadsworth.

Signorella, M. L., Bigler, R. S., & Liben, L. S. (1993). Developmental differences in children's gender schemata about others: A meta-analytic review. *Developmental Review, 13,* 147–183.

Signorielli, N. (1991). *A sourcebook on children and television.* New York: Greenwood.

Signorielli, N. (1993). Television and adolescents' perceptions about work. *Youth and Society, 24,* 314–341.

Silberg, J. (1999). The influence of genetic factors and life stress on depression among adolescent girls. *Journal of the American Medical Association, 281,* 1970–1972.

Silitsky, D. (1996). Correlates of psychosocial adjustment in adolescents from divorced families. *Journal of Divorce and Remarriage, 26,* 151–169.

Silverman, R., & Zigmond, N. (1983). Self-concept in learning disabled adolescents. *Journal of Learning Disabilities, 16,* 478–490.

Silvern, S. B., & Williamson, P. A. (1987). The effects of video game play on young children's aggression, fantasy, and prosocial behavior. *Journal of Applied Developmental Psychology, 8,* 453–462.

Simmons, R. G., & Blyth, D. A. (1987). *Moving into adolescence: The impact of pubertal change and school context* (pp. 139–147). New York: Aldine De Gruyter.

Simmons, R. G., Blyth, D. A., Van Cleave, E. F., & Bush, D. M. (1979). Entry into early adolescence: The impact of school structure, puberty, and early dating on self-esteem. *American Sociological Review, 38,* 553–568.

Simmons, R. G., Rosenberg, F., & Rosenberg, M. (1973). Disturbance in self-image at adolescence. *American Sociological Review, 38,* 553–568.

Simonelli, C. J., & Ingram, K. M. (1998). Psychological distress among men experiencing physical and emotional abuse in heterosexual dating relationships. *Journal of Interpersonal Violence, 6,* 667–682.

Simons, R. L., Burgeson, R., & Reef, M. H. (1988). Cumulative change at entry to adolescence. In M. Gunar & W. A. Collins (Eds.), *Minnesota symposia on child psychology, 21,* 123–150.

Simpson, L., Douglas, S., & Schimmel, J. (1998). Tween consumers: Catalog clothing purchase behavior. *Adolescence, 33,* 637–645.

Singer, S. J., Levine, M., & Jou, S. (1993). Heavy metal music preference, delinquent friends, social control, and delinquency. *Journal of Research in Crime and Delinquency, 30,* 317–329.

Singh, K. (1998). Part-time employment in high school and its effect on academic achievement. *Journal of Educational Research, 91,* 131–140.

Singh, K., & Ozturk, M. (2000). Effect of part-time work on high school mathematics and science course taking. *The Journal of Educational Research, 94,* 67–74.

Singh, S., & Darroch, J. E. (1999). Trends in sexual activity among adolescent American women: 1982–1995. *Family Planning Perspectives, 31,* 212–219.

Singh, S., & Darroch, J. E. (2000). Adolescent pregnancy and childbearing: Levels and trends in developed countries. *Family Planning Perspectives, 32,* 14–23.

Singleton, N., & Rhoads, D. S. (1982). Meal and snack patterns of students. *Journal of School Health, 52,* 529–534.

Skeels, H. M. (1966). Adult status of children with contrasting early life experiences: A follow-up study. *Monographs of the Society for Research in Child Development, 31*(3).

Skinner, B. F. (1953). *Science and human behavior.* New York: Macmillan.

Skinner, B. F. (1974). *About behaviorism.* New York: Knopf.

Skinner, M. E. (1998). Promoting self-advocacy among college students with learning disabilities. *Intervention in School and Clinic, 33,* 278–283.

Skorikov, V. B., & Vondracek, F. W. (1997). Longitudinal relationships between part-time work and career development in adolescents. *The Career Development Quarterly, 45,* 221–235.

Skovholt, T. M., & Morgan, J. I. (1981). Career development: An outline of issues for men. *Personnel and Guidance Journal, 60*, 231–237.

Slaby, R. G., & Guerra, N. G. (1988). Cognitive mediators of aggression: I. Assessment. *Developmental Psychology, 24*, 580–588.

Slavin, R. (1984). Students motivating students to excel: Cooperative incentives, cooperative tasks and student achievement. *Elementary School Journal, 85*, 52–63.

Slavin, R. (1990). *Cooperative learning: theory, research and practice.* Englewood Cliffs, NJ: Prentice Hall.

Slavin, R. E. (1995, November). Detracking and its detractors: Flawed evidence, flawed values. *Phi Delta Kappan, 77*, 220–222.

Slavin, R. E., & Cooper, R. (1999). Improving intergroup relations: Lessons learned from cooperative learning. *Journal of Social Issues, 55*, 647–654.

Slonim, M. B. (1991). *Children, culture and ethnicity.* New York: Garland.

Smetana, J. G. (1988). Concepts of self and social convention: Adolescents' and parents' reasoning about hypothetical and actual family conflicts. In M. R. Gunnar & W. A. Collins (Eds.), *Development during the transition to adolescence: Minnesota symposia on child psychology.* Hillsdale, NJ: Erlbaum.

Smetana, J. G. (1989). Adolescents' and parents' reasoning about actual family conflict. *Child Development, 60*, 1052–1067.

Smetana, J. G. (1995). Context, conflict, and constraint in adolescent-parent authority relationships. In M. Killen & D. Hart (Eds.), *Morality in everyday life: Developmental perspective.* Cambridge, England: Cambridge University Press.

Smetana, J. G. (1996). Adolescent-parent conflict: Implications for adaptive and maladaptive development. In D. Cicchetti & S. L. Toth (Eds.), *Rochester symposium on developmental psychopathology* (pp. 1–46). Rochester, NY: University of Rochester Press.

Smetana, J. G. (2000). Middle-class African American adolescents' and parents' conceptions of parental authority and parenting practices: A longitudinal investigation. *Child Development, 71*, 1672–1686.

Smetana, J. G., Abernathy, A., & Harris, A. (2000). Adolescent-parent interactions in middle-class African American families: Longitudinal change and contextual variation. *Journal of Family Psychology, 14*, 458–474.

Smetana, J. G., & Asquith, P. (1994). Adolescents' and parents' conceptions of parental authority and personal autonomy. *Child Development, 65*, 1147–1162.

Smetana, J. G., Yau, J., & Hanson, S. (1991). Conflict resolution in families with adolescents. *Journal of Research on Adolescence, 1*, 189–206.

Smetana, J. G., Yau, J., Restrepo, A., & Braeges, J. L. (1991). Conflict and adaptation in adolescence: Adolescent-parent conflict. In M. E. Colten & S. Gore (Eds.), *Adolescent stress: Causes and consequences.* New York: Aldine de Gruyter.

Smith, A. E., Jussim, L, Eccles, J., Van Noy, M., Madon, S., & Palumbo, P. (1998). Self- fulfilling prophecies, perceptual biases, and accuracy at the individual and group levels. *Journal of Experimental Social Psychology, 34*, 530–533.

Smith, A. M. A., Rosenthal, D. A., & Reichler, H. (1996). High schoolers' masturbatory practices: Their relationship to sexual intercourse and personal characteristics. *Psychological Reports, 79*, 499–509.

Smith, B. L., Handley, P., & Eldredge, D. A. (1998). Sex differences in exercise motivation and body image satisfaction among college students. *Perceptual and Motor Skills, 86*, 723–732.

Smith, C., & Carlson, B. E. (1997). Stress, coping, and resilience in children and youth. *Social Service Review, 71*, 231–257.

Smith, C., & Shornberry, T. P. (1995). The relationship between childhood maltreatment and adolescent involvement in delinquency. *Criminology, 33*, 451–481.

Smith, P. K. (1995). Grandparenthood. In M. H. Bornstein (Ed.), *Handbook of parenting* (Vol. 3, pp. 89–112), Mahwah, NJ: Erlbaum.

Smith, S. (1988). Preparing the learning disabled adolescent for adulthood. *Childhood Today, 17*, 4–6.

Smith, S. S. (1999). Teens now less likely to have second baby, new study shows. *Public Health Reports, 114*, 282.

Smith, T. E. (1992). Time use and change in academic achievement: A longitudinal follow-up. *Journal of Youth and Adolescence, 21*, 725–747.

Smith, T. E. C. (1987). *Introduction to education.* St. Paul, MN: West.

Smithmyer, C. M., Hubbard, J. A., & Simons, R. F. (2000). Proactive and reactive aggression in delinquent adolescents: Relations to aggression outcome expectancies. *Journal of Clinical Child Psychology, 29*, 86–93.

Smollar, J., & Youniss, J. (1985). Adolescent-parent relations in adolescents whose parents are divorced. *Journal of Early Adolescence, 5*, 120–144.

Snary, J. (1985). Cross-cultural universality of social-moral development: A critical review. *Psychological Bulletin, 97*, 202–232.

Snyder, H. (2002). *Juvenile arrests 2000.* Washington, DC: Office of Juvenile Justice and Delinquency Prevention.

Snyder, H. N., Sickmund, M., & Poe-Yamagata, E. (1996). *Juvenile offenders and victims: 1996 update on violence.* Washington, DC: Office of Juvenile Justice and Delinquency Prevention.

Sobal, J., Nicolopoulos, V., & Lee, J. (1995). Attitudes about overweight and dating among secondary school students. *International Journal of Obesity, 19*, 376–381.

Sobol, S. Z., Nelson, M. L., Fisher, C., Gunzerath, L., Brody, C. L., Hu, S., et al. (1999). A genetic association for cigarette smoking behavior. *Health Psychology, 18*, 7–13.

Society for Research in Child Development (SRCD). (1990). Ethical standards for research with children. *Developments*, 5–6.

Sohn, E. (2001). The young and the virtueless. *U. S. News & World Report, 130*, p. 5.

Solomon, J. C., & Marx, J. (1995). "To grandmother's house we go": Health and school adjustment of children raised solely by grandparents. *The Gerontologist, 35*, 386–394.

Son, L. K., & Metcalfe, J. (2000). Metacognitive and control strategies in study-time allocation. *Journal of Experimental Psychology. Learning, Memory, and Cognition, 26*, 204–221.

Sonenstein, F. L., Ku, L., Lindberg, L. D., Turner, C. F., & Pleck, I. H. (1998). Changes in sexual behavior and condom use among teenaged men: 1988 to 1998. *American Journal of Public Health, 88*, 956–959.

Sonenstein, F. L., Pleck, J. H., & Ku, L. C. (1991). Levels of sexual activity among adolescent males in the United States. *Family Planning Perspectives, 21*, 152–158.

Sonis, W., Comite, F., Bloue, J., Pescovitz, O. H., Rahn, C. W., Hench, K. D., et al. (1985). Behavior problems and social competence in girls with true precocious puberty. *Journal of Pediatrics, 106*, 156–160.

Sorenson, E. (1997). A national profile of nonresident fathers and their ability to pay child support. *Journal of Marriage and the Family, 59*, 785–797.

Spaide, D. (1995). *Teaching your kids to care: How do discover and develop the spirit of charity in your children.* New York: Citadel.

Spearman, C. (1904). General intelligence, objectively determined and measured. *American Journal of Psychology, 15*, 201–293.

Spence, J. H., Helmreich, R., & Stapp, J. (1975). Ratings of self and peers on sex-role attribution and their relationship to self-esteem and concept of masculinity and femininity. *Journal of Personality and Social Psychology, 32*, 29–38.

Spencer, M. B. (1991). Minority development of identity. In M. Lerner (Ed.), *Encyclopedia of adolescence* (pp. 525–528). New York: Wiley.

Spencer, M. B., Dupress, D., Swanson, D. P., & Cunningham, M. (1998). The influence of physical maturation and hassles on African American adolescents' learning behaviors. *Journal of Comparative Family Studies, 27*, 189–200.

Spencer, M. B., & Markstrom-Adams, C. (1990). Identity processes among racial and ethnic minority children. *Child Development, 61*, 290–311.

Spergel, I. A., Chance, R., Ehrensaft, K., Regulus, T., Kane, C., Laseter, R., et al. (1994). *Gang suppression and intervention: Community models* [NCJ 148202]. Washington, DC: U.S. Department of Justice, Office of Justice Programs, Office of Juvenile Justice and Delinquency Prevention.

Spilka, B. (1991a). Adolescents and cults. In M. Lerner (Ed.), *Handbook of adolescence* (pp. 184–186). New York Wiley.

Spilka, B. (1991b). Religion and adolescence. In R. M. Lerner, A. C. Petersen, & J. Brooks-Gunn (Eds.), *Encyclopedia of adolescence* (pp. 926–929). New York: Garland.

Spivack, M., & Shure, G. (1982). The cognition of social adjustment: Interpersonal cognitive problem-solving thinking. In B. Lahey & A. Kazdin (Eds.), *Advances in clinical child psychology* (Vol. 5, pp. 323–372). New York: Plenum.

Sprafkin, J. N., Gadow, K. D., & Abelman, R. (1992). *Television and the exceptional child: A forgotten audience.* Hillsdale, NJ: Erlbaum.

Sprafkin, J. N., Watkins, L. T., & Gadow, K. D. (1990). Efficacy of television literacy curriculum for emotionally disturbed and learning disabled children. *Journal of Applied Developmental Psychology, 11*, 225–244.

Spruijt, E., & de Goede, M. (1997). Transitions in family structure and adolescent well-being. *Adolescence, 32,* 897–911.

Stack, S., Gundlach, J., & Reeves, J. L. (1994). The heavy metal subculture and suicide. *Suicide and Life-Threatening Behavior, 24,* 15–23.

Stangor, C., & Lange, J. E. (1994). Mental representation of social groups: Advances in understanding stereotypes and stereotyping. *Advances in Experimental Social Psychology, 26,* 357–416.

Stapleton, K. R. (1998). From the margins to mainstream: the political power of hip-hop. *Media, Culture & Society, 20,* 219–234.

Stapley, J., & Hovland, J. (1989). Beyond depression: Gender differences in normal adolescents' emotional experiences. *Sex Roles, 20,* 295–308.

Stark, E. (1986, May). Friends through it all. *Psychology Today,* pp. 54–60.

Steel, L. (1991). Early work experience among white and non-white youths: Implications for subsequent enrollment and employment. *Youth and Society, 22,* 419–447.

Steele, C. M. (1997). A threat in the air: How stereotypes shape intellectual identity and performance. *American Psychologist, 6,* 613–629.

Steele, C. M., & Aronson, J. (1995). Stereotype threat and the intellectual test performance of African Americans. *Journal of Personality and Social Psychology, 69,* 797– 811.

Steele, J., & Barling, J. (1996). Influence of maternal gender-role beliefs and role satisfaction on daughters' vocational interests. *Sex Roles, 34,* 637–648.

Stein, J. A., Newcomb, M. D., & Bentler, P. M. (1993). Differential effects of parents and grandparent drug use on behavior problems of male and female children. *Developmental Psychology, 29,* 31–43.

Stein, Z. A. (1995). Editorial: More on women and prevention of HIV infection. *American Journal of Public Health, 85,* 1485–1487.

Steinbach, S. (1997, November 1). Retailer survey examines vid's effect on R&B sales. *Billboard, 109,* 91.

Steinberg, L., Brown, B., & Dornbusch, S. (1996). *Beyond the classroom: Why school reform has failed and what parents need to do.* New York: Simon & Schuster.

Steinberg, L., & Dornbusch, S. (1992). Negative correlates of part-time employment during adolescence: Replication and elaboration. *Developmental Psychology, 27,* 304–314.

Steinberg, L., Dornbusch, S. M., & Brown, B. B. (1992). Ethnic differences in adolescent achievement: An ecological perspective. *American Psychologist, 47,* 723–739.

Steinberg, L. D., Fegley, S., & Dornbusch, S. M. (1993). Negative impact of part-time work on adolescent adjustment: Evidence from a longitudinal study. *Developmental Psychology, 29,* 171–180.

Steinberg, L., Greenberger, E., Garduque, L., & McAuliffe, S. (1982). Students in the labor force: Some costs and benefits to schooling and learning. *Evaluation and Policy Analysis, 4,* 363–372.

Steinberg, L., & Silverberg, S. B. (1986). The vicissitudes of autonomy in early adolescence. *Child Development, 57,* 841–851.

Stephens, R. S., Roffman, R. A., & Simpson, E. E. (1993). Adult marijuana users seeking treatment. *Journal of Consulting and Clinical Psychology, 61,* 1100–1104.

Stephenson, A. L., Henry, C., & Robinson, L. C. (1996). Family characteristics and adolescence substance abuse. *Adolescence, 31,* 59–77.

Sternberg, R. J. (1985). *Beyond IQ: A triarchic theory of human intelligence.* Cambridge, England: Cambridge University Press.

Sternberg, R. J. (1986). A triangular theory of love. *Psychological Review, 93,* 119–135.

Sternberg, R. J. (1988). *The triarchic mind: A new theory of human intelligence.* New York: Viking.

Sternberg, R. J. (1997). The concept of intelligence and its role in lifelong learning and success. *American Psychologist, 52,* 1030–1038.

Sternberg, R. J. (2000). Identifying and developing creative giftedness. *Roeper Review, 23,* 60–72.

Sternberg, R. J., & Dobson, D. M. (1987). Resolving interpersonal conflict: An analysis of stylistic consistency. *Journal of Personality and Social Psychology, 52,* 794–802.

Sternberg, R. J., & Grajek, S. (1984). The nature of love. *Journal of Personality and Social Psychology, 47,* 312–319.

Stets, J. (1991). Psychological aggression in dating relationships: The role of interpersonal control. *Journal of Family Violence, 6,* 97–114.

Stevens, L. M. (2001, December 26). Adolescent suicide. *Journal of the American Medical Association, 286,* 3194.

Stevenson, H. W. (1991). The development of prosocial behavior in large-scale collective societies: China and Japan. In R. A. Hinde & J. Groebel (Eds.), *Cooperation and prosocial behaviour* (pp. 89–105). Cambridge University Press.

Stevenson, H. W., Chen, C. & Lee, S. Y. (1993). Mathematics achievement of Chinese, Japanese and American children: Ten years later. *Science, 259,* 53–58.

Stevenson, H., Chen, C., & Uhal, D. (1990). Beliefs and achievement: A study of black, white, and Hispanic children. *Child Development, 61,* 508–523.

Stevens-Simon, C., Kelly, L., & Singer, D. (1998). Absence of negative attitudes towards childbearing among pregnant teenagers: A risk factor for rapid repeat pregnancy. *Archives of Pediatrics and Adolescent Medicine, 150,* 1037–1044.

Stewart, B. L. (2002, Summer). Charter schools: Opportunities to extend educational models: A positive view. *Education, 122,* 777–785.

Stice, E., & Barrera, M., Jr. (1995). A longitudinal examination of the reciprocal relations between perceived parenting and adolescents' substance use and externalizing behaviors. *Developmental Psychology, 31,* 322–334.

Stice, E., Killen, J. D., Hayward, C., & Taylor, C. B. (1998). Age of onset for binge eating and purging during late adolescence: A 4-year survival analysis. *Journal of Abnormal Psychology, 107,* 671–675.

Stiles, D. A., Gibbons, J. L., & Schnellmann, J. (1987). The smiling sunbather and the chivalrous football player: Young adolescents' images of the ideal woman and man. *Journal of Early Adolescence, 7,* 411–427.

Stimpson, D., Jensen, L. C., & Neff, W. (1991). Cross-cultural gender differences in preference for a caring morality. *Journal of Social Psychology, 132,* 317–322.

Stockard, J., & McGee, J. (1990). Children's occupational preferences: The influence of sex and perceptions of occupational characteristics. *Journal of Vocational Behavior, 36,* 287–303.

Stocker, C., & Dunn, J. (1991). Sibling relationships in adolescence. In R. M. Lerner, A. C. Petersen, & J. Brooks-Gunn (Eds.), *Encyclopedia of adolescence* (pp. 1046–1047). New York: Garland.

Stokley, V. (1999, January 22). A tale of two schools. *National Catholic Reporter,* pp. 2–5.

Stoller, C. L., Offer, D., Howard, K. I., & Koenig, L. (1996). Psychiatrists' concept of adolescent self-image. *Journal of Youth and Adolescence, 25,* 273–283.

Stone, J. R., & Mortimer, J. L. (1998). The effect of adolescent employment on vocational development: Public and educational policy implications. *Journal of Vocational Behavior, 53,* 184–214.

Stone, N., & Ingham, R. (2002). Factors affecting British teenagers' contraceptive use at first intercourse: The importance of partner communication. *Perspectives on Sexual and Reproductive Health, 34,* 191–198.

Stone, W. L., & La Greca, A. M. (1990). The social status of children with learning disabilities: A reexamination. *Journal of Learning Disabilities, 23,* 32–37.

Stoneman, B. (1998, January). Teen spending keeps climbing. *American Demographics,*

Stoudemire, A. (1998). *Human behavior: An introduction for medical students* (3rd ed.). Philadelphia: Lippincott-Raven.

Stouthamer-Loeber, M., & Loeber, R. (1988). Parents as intervention agents for children with conduct problems and juvenile offenders. *Children and Youth Services, 11,* 127–148.

Strachen, A., & Jones, D. (1982). Changes in identification during adolescence: A personal construct theory approach. *Journal of Personality Assessment, 46,* 139–148.

Strasburger, V. C. (1990). Television and adolescents: Sex, drugs, rock'n' roll. *Adolescent Medical State Art Review, 1,* 161–194.

Strasburger, V. C. (1993). Adolescents and the media: Five crucial issues. *Adolescent Medicine, 4,* 479–493.

Strasburger, V. C. (1995). *Adolescents and the media: Medical and psychological impact.* Thousand Oaks, CA: Sage.

Street, S., Kromrey, J. D., & Kimmel, E. (1995). University faculty gender roles perceptions. *Sex Roles, 32,* 407–422.

Strein, W. (1988). Classroom-based elementary school affective education programs: A critical review. *Psychology in the Schools, 25,* 288–296.

Strong, B., & DeVault, C. (1995). *The marriage and family experience* (6th ed.). St. Paul, MN: West.

Struckman-Johnson, C., & Struckman-Johnson, D. (1994). Men pressured and forced into sexual experiences. *Archives of Sexual Behavior, 23,* 93–114.

Stryker, J. (1997, June 16). Abstinence or else? *The Nation, 264,* pp. 19–22.

Study: Ecstasy may cause long-term impairment in memory. (October 22, 2001). *Alcohol & Drug Abuse Weekly, 13,* p. 7.

Stumpf, H., & Stanley, J. (1996). Gender related differences on the Board's Advanced Placement and Achievement tests, 1982–1992. *Journal of Educational Psychology, 88,* 353–364.

Stunkard, A. J., Harris, J. R., Pedersen, N. L., & McClearn, G. E. (1990). The body mass index of twins who have been reared apart. *New England Journal of Medicine, 322,* 1483–1487.

Stunkard, A. J., Soresen, T. I. A., Hanis, C., Teasdale, T. W., Chakraborty, R., Schutt, W. J., & Schulsinger, F. (1986). An adoption study of human obesity. *New England Journal of Medicine, 314,* 193–198.

Subrahmanyam, K., Greenfield, P., Kraut, R., & Gross, E. (2001). The impact of computer use on children's and adolescents' development. *Journal of Applied Developmental Psychology, 22,* 7–30.

Sui-Chu, E. H., & Williams, J. D. (1996). Effects of parental involvement on eight-grade achievement. *Sociology of Education, 69,* 126–141.

Sullivan, H. S. (1953). *The interpersonal theory of psychiatry.* New York: Norton.

Summers, P., Forehand, R., Armistead, L., & Tannenbaum, L. (1998). Parental divorce during early adolescence in Caucasian families: The role of family process variables in predicting the long-term consequences for early adult psychosocial adjustment. *Journal of Consulting and Clinical Psychology, 66,* 327–336.

Sun, D., Anderson, M., Shah, A., & Julliard, K. (1998). Early adolescents' perceptions of cigarette smoking: A cross-sectional survey in a junior high school. *Adolescence, 33,* 805–810.

Sund, A. M., & Wichstrom, L. (2002). Insecure attachment as a risk factor for future depressive symptoms in early adolescence. *Journal of the American Academy of Child and Adolescent Psychiatry, 41,* 1478–1486.

Super, D. E. (1953). A theory of vocational development. *American Psychologist, 8,* 185–190.

Super, D. E. (1972). Vocational development theory: Persons, positions, and processes. In J. M. Whiteley & A. Resnikoff (Eds.), *Perspectives on vocational development* (p. 17). Washington, DC: American Personnel and Guidance Association.

Super, D. E. (1984). Career and life development. In D. Brown & L. Brooks (Eds.), *Career choice and development* (pp. 192–234). San Francisco: Jossey-Bass.

Super, D. E., & Overstreet, P. L. (1960). *The vocational maturity of ninth grade boys.* New York: Teachers College, Columbia University.

Super, D. E., Savickas, M. L., & Super, C. M. (1996). The life-span, life-space approach to careers. In D. Brown, L. Brooks, & Associates (Eds.), *Career choice and development* (3rd ed., pp. 121–170). San Francisco: Jossey-Bass.

Surby, M. (1998). Parent and offspring strategies in the transition to adolescence. *Human Nature, 9,* 67–94.

Surgeon General. (2001). *Youth violence: A report to the Surgeon General.* Washington, DC: U.S. Public Health Service.

Surveys call attention to parental role in drug prevention. (1998, September 7). *Alcoholism & Drug Abuse Weekly, 10,* pp. 2–3.

Susman, E. J. (1997). Modeling developmental complexity in adolescence: Hormones and behavior in context. *Journal of Research on Adolescence, 7,* 286–306.

Susman, E. J., & Dorn, L. D. (1991). Hormones and behavior in adolescence. In R. M. Lerner, A. C. Petersen, & J. Brooks-Gunn (Eds.), *Encyclopedia of adolescence* (pp. 513–517). New York: Wiley.

Susman, E. J., Inoff-Germain, G., Nottelmann, E. D., Loriaux, D. L., Cutler, G. B., Jr., & Chrousos, G. P. (1987). Hormones, emotions, dispositions, and aggressive attributes in young adolescents. *Child Development, 58,* 1114–1134.

Susman, E. J., Nottelman, E. D., Dorn, L. D., Gold, P. W., & Chrousos, G. P. (1989). The physiology of stress and behavioral development. In D.

S. Palermo (Ed.), *Coping with uncertainty: Behavioral and developmental perspectives* (pp. 17–37). Hillsdale, NJ: Erlbaum.

Sussman, S., Stacy, A. W., Dent, C. W., Simon, T. R., & Johnson, C. A. (1996). Marijuana use: Current issues and new research directions. *Journal of Drug Issues, 26,* 695–733.

Swain, R. C., Oetting, E. R., Edwards, R. W., & Beauvais, F. (1989). Links from emotional distress to adolescent drug use: A path model. *Journal of Consulting and Clinical Psychology, 57,* 227–231.

Swann, W. (1987). Identity negotiation: Where two roads meet. *Journal of Personality and Social Psychology, 52,* 881–889.

Swanson, H. L. (1994). Short-term memory and working memory: Do both contribute to our understanding of academic achievement in children and adults with learning disabilities? *Journal of Learning Disabilities, 27,* 34–50.

Swanson, H. L. (2001). Searching for the best model for instructing students with learning disabilities. *Focus on Exceptional Children, 34,* 1–15.

Swanson, J. M., Cantwell, D., Lerner, M., McBurnett, K., & Hanna, G. (1991). Effects of stimulant medication on learning in children with ADHD. *Journal of Learning Disabilities, 24,* 219–230.

Sweet, J., & Bumpasss, L. (1988). *National survey of families and households, 1988.* Madison, WI: Center for Demography and Ecology, University of Wisconsin.

Szalavitz, M. (2002, February 2). Dare to change: The American public supports a tough stance on drugs, even though it doesn't work. The only way things can change is if the media start confronting some unpalatable facts. *New Scientist, 173,* 44–46.

Szapocznik, J., & Kutines, W. (1980). Acculturation, biculturalism, and adjustment among Cuban Americans. In A. M. Padilla (Ed.), *Acculturation: Theory, models, and some new findings* (pp. 136–161). Boulder, CO: Westview Press.

Tang, M., Fouad, N. A., & Smith, P. L. (1999). Asian Americans' career choices: A path model to examine factors influencing their career choices. *Journal of Vocational Behavior, 54,* 142–157.

Tang, S., & Zuo, J. (2000). Dating attitudes and behaviors of American and Chinese college students. *The Social Science Journal, 37,* 67–76.

Tanner, J. M. (1970). Physical growth. In P. H. Mussen (Ed.), *Carmichael's manual of child development* (3rd ed., pp. 77–155). New York: Wiley.

Tanner, J. M. (1990). *Fetus into man.* Cambridge: Harvard University Press.

Tapscott, D. (1998). *Growing up digital.* New York: McGraw Hill.

Tarter, R. E., Blackson, T., Martin, C., Loeber, R., & Moss, H. B. (1993). Characteristics and correlates of child discipline practices in substance abuse and normal families. *The American Journal of Addiction, 2,* 18–25.

Tarver-Behring, S., Barkley, R. A., & Karlsson, J. (1985). The mother-child interactions of hyperactive boys and their normal siblings. *American Journal of Orthopsychiatry, 55,* 202–209.

Taylor, E., Chadwick, O., Heptinstall, E., & Danckaerts, M. (1996). Hyperactivity and conduct problems as risk factors for adolescent development. *Journal of the American Academy of Child and Adolescent Psychiatry, 35,* 1213–1226.

Taylor, S. E., & Brown, J. D. (1988). Illusion and well-being: A social psychological perspective on mental health. *Psychological Bulletin, 116,* 21–27.

Teare, J. F., Garrett, C. R., Coughlin, D. D., Shanahan, D. L., & Daly, D. L. (1995). America's children in crisis: Adolescent requests for support from a national telephone hotline. *Journal of Applied Developmental Psychology, 54,* 1032–1039.

Tebbi, C. K., Richards, M. E., Cummings, K. M., Zevon, M. A., & Mallon, J. C. (1988). The role of parent-adolescent concordance in compliance with cancer chemotherapy. *Adolescence, 23,* 599–611.

Teen spending keeps climbing. (1998, January). *Forecast, 18,* pp. 1–3.

Teicher, M. H., & Ito, Y. (1996). Objective measurement of hyperactivity and attentional disorders. *Journal of the American Academy of Child and Adolescent Psychiatry, 35,* 334–343.

Tellegen, A., Lykken, D. T., Bouchard, T. J., Wilcox, K., Segal, N., & Rich, A. (1988). Personality similarity in twins reared together and apart. *Journal of Personality and Social Psychology, 54,* 1031–1039.

Temple, L. (1997, June 2). Today's girls taller—and standing taller too. *USA Today,* pp. 1C & 6C.

Temple, L. (1998, March 30). Drinking in tradition: College students keep alcohol in core curriculum. *USA Today*, pp. D1, D6.

Thatcher, N. S. (1999, February 24). Truth, statistics and entertainment. *Education Week*, p. 51.

Thies, K. M. (1999, December). Identifying the educational implications of chronic illness in school children. *Journal of School health, 69*, 392–400.

Thomas, A., & Chess, S. (1991). Temperament in adolescence and its functional significance. In R. M. Lerner, A. C. Petersen, & J. Brooks-Gunn (Eds.), *Encyclopedia of adolescence* (pp. 1131–1140). New York: Wiley.

Thomas, A., Chess, S., & Birch, H. G. (1970, August). The origins of personality. *Scientific American*, 102–109.

Thomas, S. B. (2000). College students and disability law. *Journal of Special Education, 33*, 248–262.

Thompson, C. J. (1995, Fall). A contextualist proposal for conceptualization and study of marketing ethics. *Journal of Public Policy and Marketing, 14*, 177–192.

Thompson, R. A. (1998). Early sociopersonality development. In W. Damon (Ed./Vol. Ed.) & N. Eisenberg (Vol. Ed.), *Handbook of child psychology* (5th ed., Vol. 3, pp. 25–104). New York: Wiley.

Thomsen, S. R., Weber, M. M., & Brown, L. B. (2002). The relationship between reading beauty and fashion magazines and the use of pathogenic dieting methods among adolescent females. *Adolescence, 37*, 1–18.

Thomson, E., McLanahan, S. S., & Curtin, R. B. (1992). Family structure, gender, and parental socialization. *Journal of Marriage and the Family, 54*, 368–378.

Thornberry, T. P., & Burch, J. H. (1997). *Gang members and delinquent behavior bulletin* [NCJ 1651544]. Washington, DC: U.S. Department of Justice, Office of Justice Programs, office of Juvenile Justice and Delinquency Prevention.

Thornburg, H. D., & Glider, P. (1984). Dimensions of early adolescent social perceptions and preferences. *Journal of early Adolescence, 4*, 387–406.

Thorne, A., & Michaelieu, Q. (1996). Situating adolescent gender and self-esteem with personal memories. *Child Development, 67*, 1374–1390.

Thornton, A. (1990). The courtship process and adolescent sexuality. *Journal of Family Issues, 11*, 239–273.

Thorpe, M. F., Pittenger, D. J., & Reed, B. D. (1999). Cheating the researcher: A study of the relation between personality measures and self-reported cheating. *College Student Journal, 33*, 49–59.

Thun, M. J., Apicella, L. F., & Henley, S. J. (2000, August 9). Smoking vs. other risk factors as the cause of smoking-attributable deaths. *Journal of the American Medical Association, 284*, 706–712.

Thurstone, L. (1938). *Primary mental abilities*. Chicago: University of Chicago Press.

Tiggemann, M., & Pickering, A. S. (1996). Role of television in adolescent work dissatisfaction and drive for thinness. *International Journal of Eating Disorders, 20*, 199–203.

Toby, J. (1999, June 28). Obsessive compulsion: The folly of mandatory high-school attendance. *National Review*, 30–33.

Toch, T. (1998, April 27). The new education bazaar. *U. S. News and World Report, 35*, 35–46.

Toch, T., Bennefield, R. M., & Bernstein, A. (1996, April 1). The case for tough standards. *U. S. News and World Report*, pp. 52–56.

Tokar, D. M., & Jome, L. M. (1998). Masculinity, vocational interests, and career choice traditionality: Evidence for a fully mediated model. *Journal of Counseling Psychology, 45*, 424–435.

Tolan, P., & Guerra, N. (1994). *What works in reducing adolescent violence: An empirical review of the field*. Chicago, Illinois: Center for the Study and Prevention of Violence, 1994.

Tolan, P. H., & Thomas, P. (1995). The implications of age of onset for delinquency risk: II. Longitudinal data. *Journal of Abnormal Psychology, 23*, 157–181.

Toledo-Dreves, V., Zabin, L. S., & Emerson, M. R. (1995). Durations of adolescent sexual relationships before and after conception. *Journal of Adolescent Health, 17*, 163–172.

Tomal, A. (2000). Parental involvement laws, religion, and abortion rates. *Gender Issues, 18*, 33–41.

Tomlin, A. M., & Passman, R. H. (1989). Grandmothers' responsibility in raising two-year-olds facilitates their grandchildren's adaptive behavior: A preliminary intrafamilial investigation of mothers' and maternal grandmothers' effects. *Psychology and Aging, 4*, 119–121.

Took, K. J., & Weiss, D. S. (1994). The relationship between heavy metal and rap music on adolescent turmoil: Real or artifact. *Adolescence, 29*, 613–622.

Torabi, M. R., Bailey, W. J., & Majd-Jabbari, M. (1993). Cigarette smoking as a predictor of alcohol and other drug use by children and adolescents: Evidence of the "Gateway Drug Effect." *Journal of School Health, 63*, 302–306.

Toro, P. A., Weissberg, R. P., Guare, J., & Liebenstein, N. L. (1990). A comparison of children with and without learning disabilities on social problem-solving skill, school behavior, and family background. *Journal of Learning Disabilities, 23*, 115–119.

Toups, M. L., & Holmes, W. R. (2002). Effectiveness of abstinence-based sex education curricula: A review. *Counseling and Values, 46*, 237–241.

Townsend, M. H., Wallick, M. M., Pleak, R. R., & Cambre, K. M. (1997). Gay and lesbian issues in child and adolescent psychiatry training as reported by training directors. *Journal of the American Academy of Child and Adolescent Psychiatry, 36*, 764–768.

Tracey, T. J., Leong, F. T. L., & Glidden, C. (1986). Help seeking and problem perception among Asian Americans. *Journal of Counseling Psychology, 59*, 49–58.

Tracking down mom: Should adopted children have the right to uncover their birth parents? More states are trying to open the records. (1999, February 22). *Time, 153*, 64–65.

Trad, P. V. (1999). Assessing patterns that prevent teenage pregnancy. *Adolescence, 34*, 221–241.

Trapani, C. (1990). *Transition goals for adolescents with learning disabilities*. Boston: Little Brown.

Travis, R., & Kohli, V. (1995). The birth order factor: Ordinal position, social strata, and educational achievement. *The Journal of Social Psychology, 135*, 499–507.

Tremblay, R. E., Schaal, B., Boulerice, B., Arseneault, L., Soussignan, R. G., Paquette, D., & Laurent, D. (1998). Testosterone, physical aggression, dominance, and physical development in early adolescence. *International Journal of Behavioral Development, 22*, 753–777.

Triandis, H. (1989). The self and social behavior in differing cultural contexts. *Psychological Review, 96*, 506–520.

Troiden, R. R. (1989). The formation of homosexual identities. *Journal of Homosexuality, 17*, 43–73.

Tubman, J. G., & Lerner, R. M. (1994). Affective experiences of parents and their children from adolescence to young adulthood: Stability of affective experiences. *Journal of Adolescence, 17*, 81–98.

Tubman, J. G., Windle, M., & Windle, R. C. (1996). The onset and cross-temporal patterning of sexual intercourse in middle adolescence: Prospective relations with behavioral and emotional problems. *Child Development, 67*, 327–343.

Tucker, C. M., Herman, K. C., Pedersen, T., Vogel, D., & Reinke, W. M. (2000). Student-generated solutions to enhance the academic success of African American youth. *Child Study Journal, 30*, 205–222.

Turiel, E. (1990). Moral judgment, action, and development. In D. Schrader (Ed.), *The legacy of Lawrence Kohlberg* (pp. 31–51). San Francisco: Jossey-Bass.

Turiel, E. (1998). The development of morality. In W. Damon (Ed. in Chief) & N. Eisenberg (Vol. Ed.), *Handbook of child psychology* (5th ed., pp. 863–932). New York: Wiley.

Tur-Kaspa, H., & Bryan, T. (1995). Teachers' ratings of the social competence and school adjustment of students with LD in elementary and junior high school. *Journal of Learning Disabilities, 28*, 44–52.

Turner, P. J., & Gervai, J. (1995). Teachers' ratings of the social competence and school adjustment of students with LD in elementary and junior high school. *Developmental Psychology, 31*, 759–772.

Turner, S. L., Hamilton, H., Jacobs, M., Angood, L. M., &Y Dwyer, D. H. (1997). The influence of fashion magazines on the body image satisfaction of college women: An exploratory analysis. *Adolescence, 32*, 603–615.

Turow, J. (2001). Family boundaries, commercialism, and the Internet: A framework for research. *Journal of Applied Developmental Psychology, 22*, 73–86.

Twenge, J. M., & Crocker, J. (2002). Race and self-esteem: Meta-analyses comparing Whites, Blacks, Hispanics, Asians, and American Indians and comments on Gray-Little and Hafdahl, 2000. *Psychological Bulletin, 128*, 374–408.

Udry, J. R., Billy, J. O., Morris, N. M., Groff, T. R., & Raj, M. S. (1985). Serum androgenic hormones motivate sexual behavior in adolescent boys. *Fertility and Sterility, 43,* 90–94.

U.S. Bureau of Labor Statistics. (1999). *BLS releases new 1998–2008 employment projections.* Washington, DC: Department of Labor. (USDL 99–339).

U.S. Census Bureau. (2001). *Statistical Abstract of the United States, 2001.* Washington, DC: Author.

U.S. Department of Commerce. (2000). *Statistical abstract of the United States.* Washington, DC: Author.

U.S. Department of Education. (1993). *National excellence: A case for developing America's talent.* Washington, DC: Author.

U.S. Department of Education. (1995). *The educational progress of black students.* Washington, DC: Author.

U.S. Department of Education. (1998). *Digest of Educational Statistics.* Washington, DC: Author.

U.S. Department of Education. (2001a). *Digest of educational statistics.* Washington, DC: Author.

U.S. Department of Education. (2001b, January). *Revised sexual harassment guidance: Harassment of students by school employees, other students, or third parties.* Washington, DC: U.S. Department of Education, Office for Civil Rights. Retrieved August 1, 2002, from http://www.ed.gov/ offices/OCR/shguide/shguide.pdf

U.S. Department of Justice. (1997). *National Crime Victimization Survey: Changes in Criminal Victimization, 1994–1995.* Washington, DC: Author.

U.S. Department of Labor. (1999). *Highlights of women's earnings in 1998* (Report 928). U.S. Department of Labor: Bureau of Labor Statistics.

U.S. Department of Labor. (2001, August). *Highlights of women's earnings in 2000* (Report 952). Washington, DC: Author.

United States Department of Transportation. (2000). *Determine why there are fewer young alcohol-impaired drivers* [Report number DOT HS 809 348]. Washington, DC: Author.

U.S. teen birth rate falls to new record low in 2001. (2002, July 7). *Medical Letter on the CDC & FDA,* p. 2.

Upchurch, D. M., Levy-Storms, L., Sucoff, C. A., & Aneshensel, C. S. (1998). Gender and ethnic differences in timing of first sexual intercourse. *Family Planning Perspective, 30,* 121–128.

Upchurch, R. L., & Lochhead, J. (1987). Computers and higher-order thinking skills. In V. Richardson-Koehler (Ed.), *Educators' handbook* (pp. 139–165). New York: Longman.

Urberg, K. A. (1999). Introduction: Some thoughts about studying the influence of peers on children and adolescents. *Merrill-Palmer Quarterly, 45,* 1–5.

Urberg, K. A., Degirmencioglu, S. M., & Pilgrim, C. (1997). Close friend and group influence on adolescent cigarette smoking and alcohol use. *Developmental Psychology, 33,* 834–844.

Urberg, K. A., Degirmencioglu, S. M., & Tolson, J. M. (1998). Adolescent friendship selection and termination: The role of similarity. *Journal of Social and Personal Relationships, 15,* 703–710.

Urberg, K. A., Degirmencioglu, S. M., Tolson, J. M., & Halliday-Scher, K. (1995). The structure of adolescent peer networks. *Developmental Psychology, 31,* 540–547.

Urdan, T. C., & Maehr, M. L. (1995). Beyond a two-goal theory of motivation and achievement: A case for social goals. *Review of Educational Research, 65,* 213–243.

USDHHS. (1996). *Trends in the well-being of American's children and youth, 1996.* Washington, DC: Author.

USDHHS. (1998). *Health, United States, 1998* (DSSH Publication No. PHS 98-1232). Washington, DC: U.S. Government Printing Office.

Valde, G. A. (1996). Identity closure: A fifth identity status. *Journal of Genetic Psychology, 157,* 245–254.

Valdivieso, R., & Nicolau, S. (1994). Look me in the eye: A Hispanic cultural perspective on school reform. In R. J. Rossi (Ed.), *Schools and students at risk: Context and framework for positive change* (pp. 95–115). New York: Teachers College Press.

Vallacher, R. R. (1980). An introduction to self-theory. In D. M. Wegner & R. R. Vallacher (Eds.), *The self in social psychology* (pp. 3–30). New York: Oxford University Press.

Vallerand, R. J., Fortier, M. S., & Guay, F. (1997). Self-determination and persistence in a real-life setting: Toward a motivational model of high school dropout. *Journal of Personality and Social Psychology, 72,* 1161–1176.

Valois, R. F., & Dunham, A. C. (1998). Association between employment and sexual risk-taking behaviors among public high school adolescents. *Journal of Child and Family Studies, 7,* 147–159.

Vandell, D. L., & Bailey, M. D. (1992). Conflicts between siblings. In C. U. Shatz & W. W. Hartup (Eds.), *Conflict in child and adolescent development* (pp. 242–269). Cambridge: Cambridge University Press.

Van den Broeck, W. (2002). The misconception of the regression-based discrepancy operationalization in the definition and research of learning disabilities. *Journal of Learning Disabilities, 35,* 194–205.

Vander Ven, T. M., Cullen, F. T., Carrozza, M. A., & Wright, J. P. (2001). Home alone: The impact of maternal employment on delinquency. *Social Problems, 48,* 236–255.

vanGulden, H., & Bartels-Rabb, L. (1997). Inherited lustfulness. *Adoptive Families, 30,* 51.

vanGulden, H., & Bartels-Rabb, L. (1998). Oh, those perfect parents. *Adoptive Families, 31,* 48.

van Kammen, W. B., & Loeber, R. (1994). Are fluctuations in delinquent activities related to the onset and offset of juvenile illegal drug use and drug dealing? *Journal of Drug Issues, 29,* 9–24.

Van Schie, G. M., & Wiegman, O. (1997). Children and video games: Leisure activities, aggression, social integration, and school performance. *Journal of Applied Social Psychology, 27,* 1175–1194.

Varley, C. K. (2002). Don't overlook depression in youth. *Contemporary Pediatrics, 19,* 70–77.

Varma, A. (2000). Impact of watching international television programs on adolescents in India: A research note. *Journal of Comparative Family Studies, 31,* 117–123.

Vasquez-Nuttal, E., Romero-Garcia, I., & De Leon, B. (1987). Sex roles and perceptions of femininity and masculinity of Hispanic women: A review of the literature. *Psychology of Women Quarterly, 11,* 409–425.

Vaughn, C., & Long, W. (1999). Surrender to win: How adolescent drug and alcohol users change their lives. *Adolescence, 133,* 9–23.

Venturelli, P. J. (2000). Drugs in schools: Myths and realities. *The Annals of the American Academy of Political and Social Science, 567,* 72–88.

Vergari, S. (1999). Charter schools in the United States: The question of autonomy. *Educational Policy, 9,* 331–358.

Vernberg, E. M. (1990). Psychological adjustment and experience with peers during early adolescence: Reciprocal, incidental, or unidirectional relationships? *Journal of Abnormal Child Psychology, 18,* 187–198.

Viadero, D. (1996, February 24). Teen culture seen impeding school reform. *Education Week,* pp. 1, 10.

Viadero, D. (2000, March 22). Lags in minority achievement defy traditional explanations. *Education Week,* pp. 1, 18.

Vigil, J. D., & Long, J. (1990). Emic and etic perspectives on gang culture: The Chicano Case. In C. R. Huff (Ed.), *Gangs in America* (pp. 146–162). Newbury Park, CA: Sage.

Villani, S. (2001). Impact of media on children and adolescents: A 10-year review of the research. *Journal of the American Academy of Child and Adolescent Psychiatry, 40,* 392–401.

Viney, W. (1993). *A history of psychology: Ideas and context.* Boston: Allyn & Bacon.

Vink, T., Hoinney, A., van Elburg A. A., van Goozen, S. H. M., Sandkul, L. A., Sinke, R. J., et al. (2001). Association between an agouti-related protein gene polymorphism and anorexia nervosa. *Molecular Psychiatry, 6,* 325–328.

Visher, E. B., & Visher, J. S. (1990). *Old loyalties, new ties: Therapeutic strategies with stepfamilies.* New York: Brunner/Mazel.

Vitz, P. C. (1990). The use of stories in moral development: New psychological reasons for an old education method. *American Psychologist, 45,* 709–720.

Vivian, D., & Langinrichsen-Roholing, J. (1994). Are bidirectionally violent couples mutually victimized? A gender-sensitive comparison. *Violence and Victims, 9,* 197–124.

Voeller, B. (1980). Society and the gay movement. In J. Marmor (Ed.), *Homosexual behavior.* New York: Basic Books.

Volling, B. L., & Belskiy, J. (1992). The contribution of mother-child and father-child relationships to the quality of sibling interaction: A longitudinal study. *Child Development, 63,* 1209–1222.

Vroegh, K. S. (1997). Transracial adoptees: Developmental status after 17 years. *American Journal of Orthopsychiatry, 67,* 568–575.

Vygotsky, L. (1962). *Thought and language.* Cambridge: MIT Press.

Vygotsky, L. S. (1978). *Mind in society.* Cambridge: Harvard University Press.

Wade, N. A., Birkhead, G. S., Warren, B. L., Charbonneau, T. T., French, P. T., Wang, L., et al., (1998). Abbreviated regimens of zidovudine prophylaxis and perinatal transmission of the human immunodeficiency virus. *New England Journal of Medicine, 339,* 1409–1414.

Wagner, R. K., Torgesen, J. K., & Rashotte, C. A. (1994). Development of reading-related phonological processing abilities: New evidence of bidirectional causality from a latent variable longitudinal study. *Developmental Psychology, 30,* 73–87.

Wagner, T. (1996, October 9). Creating community consensus on core values. *The Counseling Psychologist, 24,* 360–399. Retrieved February 12, 2003, from http://www.edweek.org/ew/vol-16/06wagner.h16

Wainryb, C. (1993). The application of moral judgments to other cultures: Relativism and universality. *Child Development, 64,* 924–933.

Waite, B. M., Hillbrand, M., & Foster, H. G. (1992). Reduction of aggressive behavior after removal of music television. *Hospital Community Psychiatry, 43,* 173–175.

Walden, E. L., & Thompson, S. A. (1981). A review of some alternative approaches to drug management of hyperactivity in children. *Journal of Learning Disabilities, 4,* 213–217.

Waldman, A. (1999). Heavy homecoming. *Billboard, 111,* 4–8.

Waldner-Haugrud, L. K., & Magruder, B. (1996). Homosexual identity expression among lesbian and gay adolescents. *Youth and Society, 27,* 313–333.

Walker, C. (1996, May). Can TV save the planet? *American Demographics,* 42–48.

Walker, J. H., Kozma, E. J., & Green, R. P. (1989). *American education: Foundations and policy.* St. Paul, MN: West.

Walker, L. J. (1984). Sex differences in the development of moral reasoning: A critical review. *Child Development, 53,* 1330–1336.

Walker, L. J. (1991). Sex differences in moral reasoning. In W. M. Kurtines & J. L. Gewirtz (Eds.), *Handbook of moral behavior and development: Vol. 2. Research* (pp. 333–364). Hillsdale, NJ: Erlbaum.

Walker, L. J., de Vries, B., & Trevethan, S. D. (1987). Moral stages and moral orientations in real-life and hypothetical dilemmas. *Child Development, 58,* 960–966.

Walker, L. J., Hennig, K. H., & Krettenauer, T. (2000). Parent and peer contexts for children's moral reasoning development. *Child Development, 71,* 1033–1043.

Wallace-Broscious, A., Serafica, F. C., & Osipow, S. H. (1994). Adolescent career development: Relationships to self-concept and identity status. *Journal of Research on Adolescence, 4,* 127–149.

Wallerstein, J. S. (1987). Children of divorce: Report of a ten-year-follow-up of early latency-age children. *American Journal of Orthopsychiatry, 57,* 199–211.

Wallerstein, J. S., & Blakeslee, S. (1989). *Second changes: Men, women, and children a decade after divorce.* New York: Ticknor & Fields.

Wallerstein, J. S., Corbin, S. B., & Lewis, J. M. (1988). Children of divorce: A 10-year-study. In E. M. Hetherington & J. D. Arasteh (Eds.), *Impact of divorce, single parenting, and stepparenting on children* (pp. 197–215). Hillsdale, NJ: Erlbaum.

Wallerstein, J., Lewis, J., & Blakeslee, S. (2000). *The unexpected legacy of divorce: A 25 year landmark study.* New York: Hyperion.

Wallis, J. R., & Barrett, P. M. (1998). Adolescent adjustment and the transition to high school. *Journal of Child and Family Studies, 7,* 43–58.

Walls, R. T. (2000). Vocational cognition: Accuracy of 3rd, 6th, 9th, and 12th grade students. *Journal of Vocational Behavior, 56,* 137–144.

Walsh, J. (2002, May). Shyness and social phobia: A social work perspective on a problem in living. *Health and Social Work, 27,* 137–145.

Walsh, W. B., & Betz, N. E. (2001). *Tests and assessment* (4th ed.). Upper Saddle River, NJ: Prentice-Hall.

Walsh, Y., & Bor, R. (1996). Psychological consequences of involvement in a new religious movement or cult. *Counseling Psychology Quarterly, 9,* 47–60.

Walters, G. (1992). A meta-analysis of gene-crime relationship. *Criminology, 30,* 595–613.

Walters, G. D. (1996). Addiction and identity: Exploring the possibility of a relationship. *Psychology of Addictive Behaviors, 10,* 9–17.

Walters, K., & Bowen, G. L. (1997). Peer group acceptance and academic performance among adolescents participating in a dropout prevention program. *Child and Adolescent Social Work Journal, 14,* 413–426.

Wan, C., Fan, C., Lin, G., & Jing, O. (1994). Comparison of personality traits of only and sibling children in Beijing. *Journal of Genetic Psychology, 155,* 377–389.

Wang, M. Q., & Yesalis, C. E. (1994). Desire for weight gain and potential risks of adolescent males using anabolic steroids. *Perceptual and Motor Skills, 78,* 267–275.

Ward, I. M., & Rivadeneyra, R. (1999). Contributions of entertainment television to adolescents' sexual attitudes and expectations: The role of viewing amount versus viewer involvement. *The Journal of Sex Research, 36,* 237–249.

Ward, L. M. (1995). Talking about sex: Common themes about sexuality in prime-time television programs children and adolescents view most. *Journal of Youth and Adolescence, 24,* 595–615.

Ward, S. L. (1991). Moral development in adolescence. In M. Lerner (Ed.), *Handbook of adolescence* (pp. 663–667). New York Wiley.

Ware, N., & Lee, V. (1988). Sex differences in choices of college science majors. *American Educational Research Journal, 25,* 593–614.

Wark, G. R., & Krebs, D. L. (1996). Gender and dilemma differences in real-life moral judgment. *Developmental Psychology, 32,* 220–230.

Warren, M. P., Brooks-Gunn, J., Fox, R., Lancelot, C., Newman, D., & Hamilton, W. G. (1991). Lack of bone accretion and amenorrhea in young dancers: Evidence for a relative osteopenia in weight bearing bones. *Journal of Clinical Endocrinology and Metabolism, 72,* 847–853.

Wass, H., Miller, M. D., & Redditt, C. A. (1991). Adolescents and destructive themes in rock music: A follow up. *Omega, 23,* 199–205.

Wasserman, G. A., Rauh, V. A., Brunelli, S. A., Garcia-Castro, M., & Necos, B. (1990).

Waterman, A. S. (1982). Identity development from adolescence to adulthood: An extension of theory and review of research. *Developmental Psychology, 18,* 341–358.

Waterman, A. S. (1984). Identity formation: Discovery or creation? *Journal of Early Adolescence, 4,* 329–341.

Waterman, A. S., & Archer, S. L. (1990). A life-span perspective on identity formation: Developments in form, function, and process. In P. B. Baltes, D. L. Featherman, R. M. Lerner (Eds.), *Life-span development and behavior* (Vol. 10, pp. 29–57). Hillsdale, NJ: Erlbaum.

Waterman, A. S., & Waterman, C. K. (1971). A longitudinal study of changes in ego identity status during the freshman year at college. *Developmental Psychology, 5,* 167–173.

Waters, E., & Deane, K. E. (1982). Theories, models, recent data and some tasks for comparative developmental analysis. In L. Hoffman, R. Gandelman, & R. Schiffman (Eds.), *Parenting: Its causes and consequences* (pp. 19–54). Hillsdale, NJ: Erlbaum.

Waters, E., Merrick, S., Treboux, D., Crowell, J., & Albersheim, L. (2000). Attachment security in infancy and early adulthood: A twenty-year longitudinal study. *Child Development, 71,* 684–689.

Waters, E., Weinfield, N. S., & Hamilton, C. E. (2000). The stability of attachment from infancy to early adulthood: General discussion. *Child Development, 71,* 703–706.

Watt, H. M. G. (2000, Summer). Measuring attitudinal change in mathematics and English over the 1st year of junior high school: A multidimensional analysis. The *Journal of Experimental Education, 68,* 331–342.

Wattleton, F. (1987). American teens: Sexually active, sexually illiterate. *Journal of School Health, 57,* 379–380.

Waugh, R. F., Godfrey, J. R., Evans, E. D., & Craig, D. (1995). Measuring students' perceptions about cheating in six countries. *Australian Journal of Psychology, 47,* 73–80.

Weaver, J. B. (1991). Exploring the links between personality and media preferences. *Personality and Individual Differences, 12,* 1293–1299.

Wechsler, D. (1991). *Manual for the Wechsler Intelligence Scale for Children–III.* San Antonio, TX: Psychological Corp.

Weiner, B. (1979). A theory of motivation for some classroom experiences. *Journal of Educational Psychology, 71,* 3–25.

Weiner, B. (1985). An attributional theory of achievement motivation and emotion. *Psychological Review, 92,* 548–573.

Weiner, B. (1999). Motivation: An overview. In A. Kazdin (Ed.), *Encyclopedia of psychology*. Washington, DC: Oxford University Press.

Weiner, B., & Graham, S. (1999). Attribution in personality psychology. In L. A. Pervin & O. P. John (Eds.), *Handbook of personality: Theory and research* (pp. 605–628). New York: Guilford.

Weiner, B., Graham, S., Taylor, S. E., & Meyer, W. U. (1983). Social cognition in the classroom. *Educational Psychologist, 18*, 109–124.

Weiner, B., Russell, D., & Lerman, D. (1979). The cognition-emotion process in achievement-related contexts. *Journal of Personality and Social Psychology, 37*, 1211–1220.

Weinfield, N. S., Sroufe, L. A., & Egeland, B. (2000). Attachment from infancy to early adulthood in a high-risk sample: Continuity, discontinuity, and their correlates. *Child Development, 71*, 695–702.

Weinraub, M., & Gringlas, M. B. (1995). Single parenting. In M. H. Bornstein (Ed.), *Handbook of parenting* (Vol. 3, pp. 65–87). Mahwah, NJ: Erlbaum.

Weinstein, R. S. (1989). Perceptions of classroom processes and student motivation: Children's views of self-fulfilling prophecies. In C. Ames & R. Ames (Eds.), *Research on motivation in education* (Vol. 3, pp. 187–221). San Diego: Academic Press.

Weisfeld, G. (1999). *Evolutionary principles of human adolescence*. New York: Basic Books.

Weiss, B., Dodge, K., Bates, J., & Petit, G. (1992). Some consequences of early harsh discipline: Child aggression and a maladaptive social information processing style. *Child Development, 63*, 1321–1335.

Weiss, G. (1990). Hyperactivity in childhood. *New England Journal of Medicine, 323*, 1413–1414.

Weiss, G., Hichtman, L., Milroy, T., & Perlman, T. (1985). Psychiatric status of hyperactives as adults. *Journal of American Academy of Child Psychiatry, 24*, 211–220.

Weiss, M. (1989). Psychological development in adults who experienced parental divorce during adolescence. *Australian Journal of Sex, Marriage, and Family, 9*, 144–149.

Weissberg, R. P., & Greenberg, M. T. (1998). School and community competence-enhancement and prevention programs. In W. Damon (Ed.), I. E. Sigel & K. A. Renninger (Vol. Eds.), *Handbook of child psychology* (5th ed., Vol. 4, pp. 877–954). New York: Wiley.

Weissman, H. (1993, July 26). Former teen mag junkie: There are fine lines between the different magazines for teen girls. *Mediaweek, 3*, 22.

Weissman, J., Bulakowski, C., & Jumisko, M. (1998). A study of white, black, and Hispanic students' transition to a community college. *Community College Review, 26*, 19–36.

Weissman, M. M., Wolk, S., Goldstein, R. B., Moreau, D., Adams, P., Greenwald, S., et al. (1999, May 12). Depressed adolescents grown up. *Journal of the American Medical Association, 281*, 1707–1712.

Weist, M. D., Freedman, A. H., Paskewitz, D. A., Proescher, E. J., & Flaherty, L. T. (1995). Urban youth under stress: Empirical identification of protective factors. *Journal of Youth and Adolescence, 24*, 705–722.

Weithorn, L. A., & Campbell, S. B. (1982). The competency of children and adolescents to make informed treatment decisions. *Child Development, 53*, 1589–1598.

Wellner, A. S. (2002). Diversity in America. *American Demographics, 24*, S1–S20.

Wells, A., & Hakanen, E. (1991). The emotional use of popular music by adolescents. *Journalism Quarterly, 68*, 445–454.

Wells, L. E., & Rankin, J. H. (1991). Families and delinquency: A meta-analysis of the impact of broken homes. *Social Problems, 38*, 71–93.

Welsh-Ross, M. K., & Schmidt, C. R. (1996). Gender-schema development and children's constructive story memory: Evidence for a developmental model. *Child Development, 67*, 820–835.

Wenar, C. (1994). *Developmental psychopathology* (3rd ed.). New York: McGraw Hill.

Werner, E. E. (1993). Risk, resilience, and recovery: Perspectives from the Kauai Longitudinal Study. *Development and Psychopathology, 5*, 503–515.

Werner, E. E., & Smith, R. S. (1982). *Vulnerable but invincible: A longitudinal study of resilient children and youth*. New York: Adams-Banister Co.

Werner-Wilson, R. J. (1998). Gender differences in adolescent sexual attitudes: The influence of individual and family factors. *Adolescence, 31*, 519–526.

Wertleib, D., Weigel, C., Springer, T., & Fedstein, M. (1987). Temperament as a moderator of children's stressful experiences. *American Journal of Orthopsychiatry, 57*, 234–245.

West, P. (1994, October 12). Report links increased enrollments in math, science to reforms of 80s. *Education Week*, p. 12.

Wester, S. R., Crown, C. L., Quatman, G. L., & Heesacker, M. (1997). The influence of sexually violent rap music on attitudes of men with little prior exposure. *Psychology of Women Quarterly, 21*, 497–508.

Whalen, H., Henker, R., Buhrmester, D., Hinshaw, S. P., Huber, A., & Laski, K. (1989). Does stimulant medication improve the peer status of hyperactive children? *Journal of Consulting and Clinical Psychology, 57*, 545–549.

Whitbeck, L. B., Conger, R. D., & Kao, M. Y. (1993). The influence of parental support, depressed affect, and peers on the sexual behaviors of adolescent girls. *Journal of Family Issues, 14*, 261–278.

Whitbourne, J. (2002, March). The dropout dilemma: One in four college freshmen drop out. What is going on here? What does it take to stay in? *Careers & Colleges, 22*, 26–31.

White, B. H., & Kurpius, S. E. R. (2002). Effects of victim sex and sexual orientation on perceptions of rape. *Sex Roles, 38*, 191–201.

White, H. R., & Hansell, S. (1998). Acute and long-term effects of drug use on aggression from adolescence into adulthood. *Journal of Drug Issues, 28*, 837–858.

White, J. L. (1989). *The troubled adolescent*. New York: Pergamon.

White, J. W., & Koss, M. P. (1991). Courtship violence: Incidence in a national sample of higher education students. *Violence and Victims, 6*, 247–256.

White, L. A. (2001, Spring). A re-investigation of sex-role stereotyping in MTV music videos. *Women and Language, 24*, 45.

White, M. J., Kruczek, T. A., & Brown, M. T. (1989). Occupational sex stereotypes among college students. *Journal of Vocational Behavior, 34*, 289–298.

White, S. D., & De Blassie, R. (1992). Adolescent sexual behavior. *Adolescence, 27*, 183–191.

White, S. H. (1994). G. Stanley Hall: From philosophy to developmental psychology. In R. D. Parke, J. Ornstein, J. Reiser, & C. Zahn-Waxler (Eds.), *A century of developmental psychology* (pp. 204–225). Washington, DC: American Psychological Association.

Whiteley, B. E., Jr. (1993). Reliability and aspects of the construct validity of Sternberg's triangular love scale. *Journal of Social and Personal Relationships, 10*, 475–480.

Whiting, B. B., & Edwards, C. P. (1988). *Children of different worlds*. Cambridge: Harvard University Press.

Whiting, B. B., & Whiting, W. M. (1991). Adolescence in preindustrial world. In R. M. Lerner, A. C. Petersen, & J. Brooks-Gunn (Eds.), *Encyclopedia of adolescence* (pp. 814–829). New York: Wiley.

Whiting, J., Burbank, V., & Ratner, M. (1986). The duration of maidenhood across cultures. In J. Lancaster & B. Hamburg (Eds.), *School-age pregnancy and parenthood: Biosocial dimensions* (pp. 273–302). New York: Aldine.

Whitley, B. E., Jr. (1998). Factors associated with cheating among college students: A review. *Research in Higher Education, 39*, 235–274.

Whitman, F. L., Diamond, M., & Martin, J. (1993). Homosexual orientation in twins: A report on 61 pairs and three triplet sets. *Archives of Sexual Behavior, 22*, 187–206.

Whitney, E. N., & Rolfes, S. R. (2002). *Understanding nutrition* (9th ed.). Belmont, CA: Wadsworth.

Wicks-Nelson, R., & Israel, A. C. (2000). *Behavior disorders of childhood* (4th ed.). Upper Saddle River, NJ: Prentice Hall.

Wiemann, C. M., Berenson, A. B., Garcia-del Pino, L., & McCombs, S. L. (1997). Factors associated with adolescents' risk for late entry into prenatal care. *Family Planning Perspectives, 29*, 273–276.

Wierson, M., Forehand, R., Fauber, R., & McCombs, A. (1989). Buffering young male adolescents against negative parental divorce influences: The role of good parent-adolescent relationships. *Child Study Journal, 19*, 101–115.

Wigfield, A., Eccles, J. S., Mac Iver, D., Reuman, D. A., & Midgley, C. (1991). Transitions during early adolescence: Changes in children's domain-specific self-perceptions and general self-esteem across the transition to junior high school. *Developmental Psychology, 27*, 552–565.

Wilcox, S., & Udry, J. R. (1986). Autism and accuracy in adolescent perceptions of friends' sexual attitudes and behavior. *Journal of Applied Social Psychology, 16,* 361–374.

Will, J. C., Denny, C., Serdula, M., & Muneta, B. (1999). Trends in body weight among American Indians: Findings from a telephone survey, 1985 through 1996. *American Journal of Public Health, 89,* 395–398.

Willemsen, T. M. (1998). Widening the gender gap: Teenage magazines for girls and boys. *Sex Roles, 38,* 851–862.

Williams, H. B. (1979). Not quite the TV generation. *American Demographics,* pp. 6–7.

Williams, K. D. (1996). Cooperative learning: A new direction. *Education, 117,* 39–43.

Wilson, G. T., & Fairburn, C. G. (1993). Cognitive treatments for eating disorders. *Journal of Consulting and Clinical Psychology, 61,* 261–269.

Wilson, J. Q., & Hernstein, R. (1985). *Crime and human nature.* New York: Simon & Schuster.

Wilson, M. D., & Joffe, A. (1995). Adolescent health. *Journal of the American Medical Association, 273,* 1657–1659.

Wilson, R. S. (1977). Mental development in twins. In A. Oliverio (Ed.), *Genetics, environment, and intelligence.* Amsterdam, the Netherlands: Elsevier.

Wilson, R. S. (1983). The Louisville twin study: Developmental synchronies in behavior. *Child Development, 54,* 298–316.

Wilson, R., & Brown, D. (1992). African Americans and career development: Focus on education. In D. Brown & C. W. Minor (Eds.), *Career needs in a diverse workforce: Implications of the NCDA Gallup Survey* (pp. 11–26). Alexandria, VA: National Career Development Association.

Wilson, S. M., & Medora, N. P. (1990). Gender comparisons of college students' attitudes toward sexual behavior. *Adolescence, 25,* 615–627.

Winefield, A. H., & Tiggemann, M. (1990). Employment status and psychological well-being: A longitudinal study. *Journal of Applied Psychology, 75,* 455–459.

Winkel, M., Novak, D. M., & Hopson, H. (1987). Personality factors, subject gender, and the effects of aggressive video games on aggression in adolescents. *Journal of Research in Personality, 21,* 211–223.

Winstanley, M. R., Meyers, S. A., & Florsheim, P. (2002). Psychosocial correlates of intimacy achievement among adolescent fathers-to-be. *Journal of Youth and Adolescence, 31,* 91–101.

Wintre, M., Hicks, R., McVey, G., & Fox, J. (1988). Age and sex differences in choice of consultant for various types of problems. *Child Development, 59,* 1046–1055.

Wirt, J. G., Muraskin, L. D., Goodwin, D. A., & Meyer, R. H. (1989). *National assessment of vocational education.* Washington, DC: U.S. Department of Education.

Wohlwill, J. F. (1980). Cognitive development in childhood. In O. G. Brim, Jr. & J. Kagan (Eds.), *Constancy and change in human development* (pp. 359–445). Cambridge: Harvard University Press.

Wolfson, A. R., & Carskadon, M. A. (1998). Sleep schedules and daytime functioning in adolescents. *Child Development, 69,* 875–887.

Wong, E. H., & Wiest, D. J. (1999). Adolescent depression: Links to academic coping and perceived autonomy support. *Education, 119,* 668–698.

Wood, R., & Synovitz, L. B. (2001). Addressing the threats of MDMA (Ecstasy): Implications for school health professionals, parents, and community members. *Journal of School Health, 71,* 38–45.

Wood, W., Wong, F. Y., & Chachere, J. G. (1991). Effects of media violence on viewers' aggression in unconstrained social interaction. *Psychological Bulletin, 109,* 371–389.

Woodard, E. H., & Gridina, N. (2000). *Media in the home, 2000: The fifth annual survey of parents and children.* The Annenberg Public Policy Center, Survey Series Number 7. Retrieved July 18, 2002, from http://www.appcpenn.org/mediainhome/survey/survey7.pdf

Woodside, D. B., Shekter-Wolfson, L. F., Garfinkel, P. E., & Olsted, M. P. (1995). Family interactions in bulimia nervosa: Study design, comparisons to established population norms and changes over the course of an intensive day hospital treatment program. *International Journal of Eating Disorders, 17,* 105–115.

Woodyard, C. (1998, October 6). Generation Y. *USA Today,* 1A, 2A. (epi)

Wright, K. N., & Wright, K. E. (1995). *Family life, delinquency and crime: A policymaker's guide.* Washington, DC: Office of Juvenile Justice and Delinquency Prevention. Department of Justice.

Wright, L. S., Frost, C. J., & Wisecarver, S. J. (1997). Church attendance, meaningfulness of religion and depressive symptomatology among adolescents. *Journal of Youth and Adolescence, 22,* 559–569.

Wright, S. A., & Piper, E. S. (1986). Families and cults: Familial factors related to youth leaving or remaining in deviant religious groups. *Journal of Marriage and the Family, 48,* 15–26.

Wroblewski, R., & Huston, A. C. (1987). Televised occupational stereotypes and their effects on early adolescents: Are they changing? *Journal of Early Adolescence, 7,* 283–297.

Wulff, D. M. (1997). *Psychology of religion* (2nd ed.). New York: Wiley.

Wurthnow, R., & Gluck, C. (1973). Religious loyalty, defection, and experimentation among college youth. *Journal of the Scientific Study of Religion, 12,* 157–180.

Wyatt, G. E. (1989). Reexamining factors predicting Afro-American and white women's age at first coitus. *Archives of Sexual Behavior, 18,* 271–298.

Wygant, S. A. (1997). Moral reasoning about real-life dilemmas: Paradox in research using the Defining Issues Test. *Personality and Social Psychology Bulletin, 23,* 1022–1030.

Wyman, P. A., Cowen, E. L., Work, W. C., Hoyt-Meyers, L., Magnus, K. B., & Fagen, D. B. (1999). Caregiving and developmental factors differentiating young at-risk urban children showing resilient versus stress-affected outcomes: A replication and extension. *Child Development, 70,* 645–659.

Wynne, E., & Ryan, K. (1992). *Reclaiming our schools: Teaching character, academics and discipline.* Upper Saddle River, NJ: Merrill.

Yamamoto, T., & Ishii, S. (1995). Developmental and environmental psychology: A microgenetic developmental approach to transition from a small elementary school to a big junior high school. *Environment and Behavior, 27,* 33–42.

Yang, B., Ollendick, T. H., Dong, Q., Xia, Y, & Lin, L. (1995). Only children and children with siblings in the People's Republic of China: Levels of fear, anxiety, and depression. *Child Development, 66,* 1301–1311.

Yang, D. J. (2000, January 17). Craving your next Web fix. *U.S. News & World Report, 128,* 41.

Yarnold, B. M. (1998). Steroid use among Miami's public school students, 1992. *Psychological Reports, 82,* 19–25.

Yates, E. L. (2002, July 18). Fighting tobacco use among Blacks: Pilot projects at NCC, Morgan States train students to be better informed on tobacco issues. *Black Issues in Higher Education, 19,* 12–14.

Yau, J., & Smetana, J. G. (1993). Chinese-American adolescents' reasoning about cultural conflicts. *Journal of Adolescent Research, 8,* 419–438.

Yew, W. (1987). Immigrant families. *Challenge, 26,* 1–3.

Yoshika, T., Kojo, K. & Kaku, H. (1982). A study in the development of social presentation in children. *Japanese Journal of Educational Psychology, 30,* 120–127.

Yoshikawa, H. (1994). Prevention as cumulative protection: Effects of early family support and education on chronic delinquency and its risks. *Psychological Bulletin, 115,* 28–54.

Young, K. S., & Rogers, R. C. (1998). *The relationship between depression and Internet addiction.* Retrieved July 18, 2002, from www.netaddiction.com/articles/cyberpsychology.htm

Youniss, J., & Smallar, S. (1985). *Adolescent relations with mothers, fathers, and friends.* Chicago: University of Chicago Press.

Zabin, L. S., Emerson, M. R., Ringers, P. A., & Sedivy, V. (1996). Adolescents with negative pregnancy test results: An accessible at-risk group. *Journal of the American Medical Association, 275,* 113–117.

Zabin, L. S., Hirsch, M. B., Smith, E. A., & Hardy, J. B. (1984). Adolescent sexual attitudes and behavior. Are they consistent? *Family Planning Perspectives, 16,* 181–185.

Zabriski, A. L., & Coie, J. D. (1996). A comparison of aggressive-rejected and nonaggressive-rejected children's interpretations of self-directed and other-directed rejection. *Child Development, 67,* 1048–1070.

Zacijek-Farber, M. L. (1998, August 1). Promoting good health in adolescents with disabilities. *Health and Social Work, 23,* 203–214.

Zametkin, A. J., Alter, M. R., & Yemini, T. (2001). Suicide in teenagers: Assessment, management, and prevention. *Journal of the American Medical Association, 286,* 3120–3125.

Zern, D. S. (1997). A longitudinal study of adolescents' attitudes about assistance in the development of moral values. *The Journal of Genetic Psychology, 158,* 79–96.

Zhang, L., Welte, J. W., & Wieczorek, W. F. (1999). The influence of parental drinking and closeness on adolescent drinking. *Journal of Studies on Alcohol, 60,* 245–257.

Zheng, Y. P., & Lin, K. M. (1994). A nationwide study of stressful life events in mainland China. *Psychosomatic Medicine, 56,* 296–305.

Zillmann, D., & Mundorf, N. (1987). Image effects in the appreciation of video rock. *Communication Research, 14,* 316–334.

Zimbardo, P. G. (1977). *Shyness: What it is, what to do about it.* Reading, MA: Addison-Wesley.

Zimmerman, B. J., Bandura, A., & Martinez-Pons, M. (1992). Self-motivation for academic attainment: The role of self-efficacy beliefs and personal goal setting. *American Educational Research Journal, 29,* 663–676.

Zimmerman, B. J., Bonner, S., & Kovach, R. (1996). *Developing self-regulated learners.* Washington, DC: American Psychological Association.

Zimmerman, B. J., & Martinez-Pons, M. (1990). Student differences in self-regulated learning: Relating grade, sex and giftedness of self-efficacy and strategy use. *Journal of Educational Psychology, 82,* 51–59.

Zito, M., Safer, D. J., dosReis, S., Gardner, J. F., Soeken, K., Boles, M., & Lynch, F. (2002). Rising prevalence of antidepressants among US youths. *Pediatrics, 109,* 721–729.

Zmiles, H., & Lee, V. E. (1991). Adolescent family structure and educational progress. *Developmental Psychology, 27,* 314–320.

Zollo, P. (1999). Not quite the TV generation. *American Demographics, 21,* 35–36.

Zuckerman, M. (1994). *Behavioral expressions and biosocial bases of sensation seeking.* New York: Cambridge University Press.

Zuckerman, M. J., & Rodger, W. (2000, March 16). Linking online kids with real-world ethics. *USA Today,* pp. D1, D2.

Zunker, V. G. (1998). *Career counseling: Applied concepts of life planning* (5th ed.). Pacific Grove, CA: Brooks Cole.

Name Index

Abernathy, A., 138
Abramovich, R., 57, 161
Abramowitz, A. J., 491
Abrams, L. A., 166
Abramson, L. Y., 469, 470, 472
Abramson, S. Y., 470
Acebo, C., 89
Achenbach, T. M., 70
Acock, A. C., 173, 175
Adamczyk-Robinette, S. L., 146
Adams, G. R., 318, 322
Adams, K. C., 506
Adams, S., 290
Adcock, A. G., 379
Adelson, J., 123, 323
Adeyanju, M., 84
Adler, J., 15
Adler, N., 87
Adler, P., 329
Adler, P. A., 329
Adolfsson, R., 509
Agresti, A. A., 361
Aguirre-Deandreis, A. L., 221
Aiken, L. S., 372
Ainsworth, M. D. S., 140
Ainsworth-Darnell, J. W., 241
Alain, M., 472
Albrecht, S. L., 403
Alessi, N., 278
Alexander, C. S., 133
Alexander, K. L., 248
Alfieri, T., 329
Alipuria, L. L., 337
Allen, J. G., 322
Allen, J. P., 141, 148, 249, 249n
Allen, M. G., 216, 219
Allen, S., 407, 408
Allgood-Merten, B., 310
Allison, B. N., 322
Alloy, L. B., 469
Allport, G. W., 301
Almeida, D. M., 85, 158, 455
Aloise-Young, P. A., 501
Alsaker, F. D., 1, 69, 70, 79, 81, 307
Alspaugh, J. W., 217
Alter, M. R., 474
Althaus, F., 359
Alvidrez, J., 240
Aman, C. J., 488
Amato, P. R., 168, 171
Ambronsini, P. J., 473
Ambrosini, P. J., 490
Ames, C., 236, 237
Anastopoulos, A. D., 488, 491
Anderson, A. F., 46
Anderson, C. A., 269, 270
Anderson, E. R., 169, 172
Anderson, M., 516
Anderson, M. L., 2
Andersson, T., 81
Andrade, M. M., 90
Andrews, J., 310, 484
Andrews, K., 511
Aneshensel, C. S., 205, 206
Angold, A., 467
Angst, F., 474
Angst, J., 474

Angus, D. L., 7
Anthony, J. C., 514
Apfel, H., 163
Apicella, L. F., 498
Applebaum, M. L., 116
Araujo, K., 351
Arbona, C., 436, 437
Archer, J., 224, 225, 235
Archer, S. L., 32, 33, 322, 325, 326
Arcus, D., 75
Arenson, J. D., 376
Argys, L. M., 241
Arias, I., 206, 207
Arkin, R. M., 465
Armistead, L., 166, 170
Armstead, P., 396
Arnett, J. J., 4, 5, 6, 15, 51, 133, 138, 173, 275, 276, 279, 283, 455
Aro, H., 81
Aron, A., 346
Aronson, J., 119
Arthur, C., 268, 272
Aseltine, R. H., 187, 243
Asher, S. R., 182, 193, 196
Asquith, P., 153, 154, 203
Astone, N. M., 173, 175
Atkin, C. K., 48
Attanucci, J., 391
Attie, I., 82
Aumiller, K., 195, 523
Aviles, R. M. D., 246
Axelrod, L., 484

Babad, E., 240
Bach, A., 366, 367
Bachman, J., 496, 497n, 499, 513
Bachman, J. G., 151, 307, 309, 399, 419, 420, 422
Bachrach, C. A., 372
Baddeley, A. D., 111
Badger, K., 391
Bagga, A., 78
Bagley, C. A., 336
Bagshaw, D., 197
Bagwell, C. L., 184
Bahr, S. J., 401
Bailey, C. E., 398
Bailey, J. M., 360, 361
Bailey, M. D., 161
Bailey, W. J., 502
Baird, A. A., 66
Baird, T. L., 359
Bakalar, J. B., 505
Baker, E., 501
Baker, L. A., 162
Baker, R. C., 391
Bakken, L., 324
Baldwin, D. C., 405
Baldwin, D. R., 455
Balk, S., 376
Ball, R. A., 524
Ballantine, J., 146
Ballard, M. E., 273, 276
Baltes, P. B., 32, 103
Bandalos, D. L., 438
Bandura, A., 37–38, 38, 232, 234, 436, 439

Bangert-Drowns, R. L., 514
Banks, T., 521
Barabasz, A., 488
Barabasz, M., 488
Baranowski, M. D., 374
Barber, B. K., 154
Barclay, L. C., 313
Barenboim, C., 130
Barkley, R. A., 488, 489
Barling, J., 167, 430
Barnes, 149, 150
Barnes, G. M., 510, 511
Barnett, M. A., 268
Barnow, S., 510
Baron, R. M., 240
Barone, A., 221
Barone, C., 221
Barr, S. L., 84, 477
Barrera, M., 183, 456, 511
Barrett, M. E., 206
Barrett, P. M., 221
Barringer, F., 418
Barron, J., 364
Barron, K. E., 234
Barry, H., 155, 455
Bar-Tal, D., 404
Bartels-Rabb, L., 150, 151
Barth, R. P., 359, 371
Bartholomew, K., 350
Bartholow, B. D., 508
Bartini, M., 197
Bartle-Haring, S., 322
Bartolovic, M., 454
Barton-Henry, M. L., 147
Basow, S. A., 329, 334
Bates, J. E., 148
Bathurst, K., 158
Battin, S. R., 524
Battin-Pearson, S., 247
Bauer, G., 411
Bauman, K. E., 189, 190, 512
Baumeister, R. F., 311, 313, 318, 319–320
Baumrind, D., 57, 138, 143, 145, 146, 148
Beal, C. R., 330
Beamish, P. M., 473
Beaty, L. A., 362, 363
Beck, A., 470
Beck, K. H., 360
Becker, J., 334
Becker, J. B., 68
Bedard, C., 528
Begley, S., 312
Behrens, J. T., 485
Beidel, D. C., 466
Belitz, J., 403
Bell, A., 360–361
Bell, R. Z., 11
Bellamy, C., 385
Bellet, W., 338
Belsky, J., 79, 162
Bem, S. L., 333, 465
Bengtson, V. L., 162, 163
Bennefield, R., 223, 224, 243
Bennett, K., 12
Benson, P. L., 151, 399, 400, 401

Bentler, P. M., 510
Berg, F., 87
Berger, E. P., 170–171, 172
Berger, T., 343
Bergman, B., 244
Berko, E. G., 483
Berman, M., 261, 262, 263
Bernard, H. S., 321, 323
Bernbaum, S. A., 360
Berndt, T. J., 179, 180, 183, 184, 187, 200, 207, 208, 209, 210, 404
Bernstein, A., 223
Bersoff, D. M., 155
Bethke, T., 207
Betz, M., 431
Betz, N., 116, 426, 431
Beunen, G., 61
Bevis, C., 407
Beyer, B., 105
Beyth-Marom, R., 128, 133
Bezilla, R., 138, 399
Bidgood, B. A., 85
Biederman, J., 489
Biener, L., 501
Bierman, K. L., 195, 199, 523
Bieschke, K. J., 436
Bigbee, M. A., 197
Biggar, H., 454, 461n
Bigler, R. S., 329
Bilchik, S., 12, 526
Billmann-Mahecha, E., 398
Binder, A., 274
Binet, A., 115
Bingham, C. R., 352, 357
Binion, V. J., 334
Birch, H. G., 75
Birmaher, B., 466, 471
Biro, F. M., 371
Bishop, J., 444, 445
Bishop, J. A., 183
Bjerregaard, B., 517, 524
Bjorklund, D. F., 111, 117, 131
Bjornsen, C. A., 3, 4n
Blackman, L. S., 118
Blair, J., 227
Blake, J., 165
Blakeslee, S., 167, 169
Blanchard, L., 111
Blanton, H., 372
Blasi, A., 390
Blatt, S. J., 324
Blinn-Pike, L., 157, 343
Block, C. R., 524
Block, J., 170, 307, 311, 505, 508, 510
Block, J. H., 170
Bloom, A., 277
Blos, P., 1, 3, 32, 181, 301, 318
Blum, C. R., 436
Blyth, D., 81, 160, 181, 187, 303, 307, 308, 309
Boarini, D., 485
Bochner, S., 324
Boden, J. M., 313
Bogenschneider, K., 498, 501
Boggess, S., 359
Boice, M. M., 70

Boivin, M., 187
Bond, M., 325
Bong, M., 235
Bonner, S., 114
Bookwala, J., 206, 207
Boot, B. P., 508
Booth, K., 171–172
Bor, R., 403
Borders, D., 431, 433
Bores-Rangel, E., 436
Borich, C., 115
Borow, H., 436
Borzekowski, D. L. G., 262
Bosworth, K., 412
Botvin, E. M., 501, 515
Botvin, G. J., 501
Bouchard, C., 61
Bouchard, T. J., 117
Bowen, G. L., 248
Bower, A., 517
Bower, B., 264
Bowlby, J., 140
Bowman, D. H., 228, 242
Boyd, D. A., 482
Boyes, M., 314, 392, 407, 408
Boyle, M., 467
Braaten, S., 526
Bracey, G. W., 222, 223, 243, 442
Bradfford, L. J., 360
Brage, D., 467, 468, 472
Brantley, J. C., 483
Bray, J. H., 172, 173, 174
Brehm, S. S., 51
Brember, L., 305, 307
Brengelman, D., 309
Brennan, K. A., 141
Brewer, D. J., 241
Brewster, K. L., 401
Brightman, J., 399
Brillon, L., 18
Brinckerhoff, L. C., 487
Brislin, R., 324
Brittain, C. V., 211
Broadbear, J. T., 125
Brockett, J. E., 375
Brody, C. J., 419
Brody, G. H., 152, 160, 502
Brohmers, S., 207
Broman, S. H., 117
Bromley, D. C., 130
Bronfenbrenner, U., 39, 42, 166
Bronstein, P., 170
Brook, J. S., 206, 505, 509, 512
Brooks, F., 197
Brooks, R. B., 304, 315
Brooks, R. H., 345
Brooks-Gunn, J., 1, 62, 63, 65, 69, 70, 79, 81, 82, 118, 146, 152, 157, 247, 330, 359, 375
Brophy, J., 236
Brouilette, L., 248
Brown, A. L., 107
Brown, B. B., 179, 180, 182, 189, 191, 193, 206, 208, 209, 211, 212, 213, 226, 229, 329
Brown, B. R., 371
Brown, D., 440
Brown, E., 258, 263, 264
Brown, E. F., 273, 274, 280
Brown, J. D., 311
Brown, J. E., 88
Brown, J. H., 171
Brown, L. B., 291
Brown, L. K., 359
Brown, L. M., 329, 330

Brown, M. T., 426, 430
Brownell, K. D., 88
Browning, K., 520, 523
Bruch, M., 479
Bruner, A. B., 498
Bryan, A. D., 372
Bryan, T., 484
Bryant, J., 283
Buchanan, C. M., 68, 69, 70, 71, 334
Bucher, K. T., 219, 231
Buchman, D. D., 267, 268, 271
Buchner, K. T., 216
Budd, J., 430
Buerkel-Rothfuss, N., 284
Buhrmester, D., 160, 161, 181, 182, 184, 187, 200
Buis, J. M., 131
Bukowski, W. B., 183, 187
Bulakowski, C., 244
Bulcroft, K. A., 175
Bulcroft, R. A., 175
Bullock, J. R., 197
Bumpass, L., 138
Burbank, V., 2
Burch, J., 525
Burcham, B., 488
Burchinal, M., 162
Burdman, P., 338
Burgeson, R., 183
Buriel, R., 159, 166
Burke, S., 379
Burmeister, D., 345
Burnett, G., 524
Burnett, P. C., 454
Burnette, E., 335
Burns, A., 171, 184
Burton, L. M., 163
Bush, G. W., 242
Bush, P. J., 179
Bushman, B. J., 311
Buss, A. H., 75
Buss, K. A., 75
Butler, D. L., 115, 484
Byrnes, J. P., 99

Caeti, T. J., 12
Cairns, R. B., 28, 35, 186, 189, 205, 208, 247, 407
Calfin, M. S., 278
Calfras, K., 89
Calhoun, C., 16
Calhoun, T., 502
Callan, V. J., 149
Calvert, S. L., 270
Camarena, P. M., 187
Cameron, G., 85
Cameron, J., 125
Campbell, R., 274
Campbell, S. B., 127
Campbell, S. M., 372
Cantor, N., 181, 203
Cantu, C. L., 336
Cardock, A. L., 500
Carducci, B. J., 464, 465
Carey, K. B., 359
Carey, M. P., 359
Carlock, C. J., 297
Carlson, B. E., 453, 458
Carlson, L., 488
Carlton-Ford, S., 309
Carmody, D. C., 175
Carney, D., 279
Carpendale, J. I. M., 390, 392
Carpenter, K., 476
Carr, R. V., 419, 421

Carrera, M. A., 378
Carroll, J. T., 278
Carroll, M., 49, 500
Carroll, R. L., 273
Carruth, B., 88
Carskadon, M. A., 89, 90, 91
Carver, V. C., 353, 359
Case, R., 112
Casey-Cannon, S., 197, 198
Cash, T. F., 85, 86, 87
Cashion, B. G., 402
Casper, L. M., 356
Casper, R. C., 85
Caspi, A., 81, 82, 465
Cassell, C., 378
Cassidy, L., 379
Catalano, R. F., 502
Catania, A. C., 37
Cauffman, E., 86, 477
Caya, M. L., 161
Chachere, J. G., 282
Chadwick, B. A., 138, 150, 403
Chaffee, S. H., 48
Chamberland, C., 248
Chambliss, L. N., 455
Chand, I. P., 152
Chandler, M., 314, 392
Chang, M., 266, 267
Chao, R. K., 147
Chapin, J. R., 283
Chapman, J. W., 485
Charney, D. A., 381
Chase-Lansdale, L., 375, 376
Chassin, L., 183, 300, 456, 499, 511, 512
Chatman, C., 240
Chatterjee, C., 228
Chavira, V., 337
Cheek, N. H., 189, 190
Chen, C., 224, 234
Chen, K., 502, 506
Chen, X., 148, 165
Chen, Y. R., 468
Cheng, K., 261
Chess, S., 75, 76
Chilcoat, H. D., 514
Childress, A. C., 87
Chilman, C. S., 352
Ching, C. L., 379
Chiras, S., 68
Choi, C. Y., 165
Chou, E. L., 439
Chou, K. L., 402, 403, 404, 406
Christensen, L., 57
Christenson, P., 274, 278
Christiansen, K. O., 521
Christie, K., 219
Chubb, N. H., 304, 307, 309
Church, M. A., 234, 236
Churchill, L. R., 55
Chusmir, L. H., 434
Cicchetti, D., 58
Cillessen, A. H. N., 195
Cipriani, D. C., 72
Claes, M., 276
Clark, C. L., 502
Clark, D. B., 466
Clark, J. J., 164
Clark, M. L., 206
Clark, R. M., 225
Clarke, G. N., 473
Clarke, M., 276
Clarkin, A. J., 32
Clasen, D. R., 206, 208, 209, 329

Clayton-Matthews, A., 85
Cleeton, E. C., 517
Clingempeel, W. G., 168, 173
Cloninger, C. R., 509
Coard, S. I., 373, 374
Coates, S., 273, 276
Coatsworth, J. D., 459
Coblenz, A., 206
Coccaro, E. F., 520
Coffey, P., 206
Cohen, K. M., 362
Cohen, P., 468, 512
Cohen, S., 455
Cohn, L., 87
Coie, J. D., 195, 282, 523
Colan, N. B., 421
Cole, A. K., 140
Cole, D. A., 227, 307
Cole, M., 105
Coleman, H. L. K., 338
Coleman, J. S., 181, 206
Coleman, M., 345–346
Coles, R., 355, 359
Coley, R. L., 171, 376
Colin, V. L., 140, 141
Colletti, J., 273
Collins, N. L., 350
Collins, R., 141, 351
Collins, W. A., 152, 153, 154, 181, 187, 205
Colvin, C. R., 311, 313
Comer, R. J., 362
Compas, B. E., 205, 454, 455, 456
Comstock, G., 282, 283
Confucius, 70
Conger, R. D., 81, 238, 356
Conley, T. D., 392
Connors, L. J., 238
Conoley, C. W., 431
Conrad, J., 194
Consroe, P., 504
Constant, D., 264
Constantine, M. G., 437
Constantino, J. N., 70
Conte, C., 224, 225
Conte, R., 484
Conway, F., 403
Coogan, J. C., 85
Cooksey, E. C., 354
Cooley, C. H., 298
Cooley, M. L., 375
Cooper, C. R., 149, 150, 157, 181, 336
Cooper, H., 420
Cooper, H. M., 240, 241
Cooper, J., 269
Cooper, M. L., 141, 351
Cooper, P. J., 468
Cooper, R., 106
Cooper, S., 433
Copeland, E. J., 336
Corbin, S. B., 167
Corbine, J., 2
Corcoran, M. E., 376
Corey, G., 473
Corley, R., 404
Cornwell, G. T., 358
Costa, P. T., 328
Costello, E. J., 467
Couglin, C., 169
Covington, M. V., 234
Cowan, G., 188
Cowan, P. A., 117
Cowen, C. P., 117
Cox, F. D., 201

Cox, M., 172
Cox, R., 172
Cradler, J., 224
Craft, R. S., 391
Crain, R. M., 307, 310
Crain, W., 36, 103
Cravatta, M., 21
Crawford, H. J., 372
Crick, N. R., 197, 521
Crider, D. M., 152
Crocker, J., 310
Crockett, L. J., 352, 357
Cronbach, L. J., 423
Cropley, A. J., 125
Crosbie-Burnett, M., 172, 173
Cross, B., 298, 305
Cross, H. J., 322
Cross, W., 310
Crothers, M., 443
Crouter, A. C., 39, 166
Crowell, A., 12
Csikszentmihalyi, M., 23, 69, 70, 71, 125, 179, 180, 181, 232
Cuban, L., 225
Cuijpers, P., 473
Culp, R. E., 375
Cummings, M. R., 72, 74
Cummins, R. A., 351
Cunningham, B., 442
Curran, C. P., 370, 372
Curran, P. J., 511, 512
Curry, G. D., 524
Curtner-Smith, M. E., 198, 211
Custis, L. L., 203
Cyranowski, J. M., 472
Czajka-Narins, M., 85

Dabbs, J. M., 521
Dahl, R. E., 66
Damarin, F. L., 426
D'Amico, R., 420
Damon, W., 300, 409
Daniels, D., 162
Dare, C., 478
Darling, C. A., 356
Darroch, J. E., 351, 354, 373
Dasen, P., 101
Dasgupta, S. D., 205
David, C., 170
Davidson, J. K., 356
Davies, J., 305, 307
Davies, P. T., 472
Davis, B., 519
Davis, C. G., 473
Davis, K. E., 349, 351
Davis, R., 479, 480
Davis, S., 286, 287
Davis, S. F., 396
Davis, W., 132
Davison, G. C., 363
Dawkins, M. P., 529
Dawson, L. D., 502
Day, J., 257, 261, 263
Day, S. X., 425, 426
Dean, K. C., 401
Deane, K. E., 140
DeAngelis, T., 477, 479, 509, 514
Deater-Deckard, K., 148
DeBlassie, A. M., 246
DeBlassie, R., 246, 356
de Bois-Reymond, M., 209
DeBro, S. C., 372
deCharms, R., 236
Decker, S. H., 524
de Gaston, J. F., 346, 353

Degirmencioglu, S. M., 187
de Goede, M., 168, 173, 175
De Groot, E. V., 114
De Haan, L., 400
de Joy, D. M., 207
Dekovic, M., 154, 209, 317, 318, 323
DeLamater, J., 344
Delaney, C. H., 2, 3
Delaney, P., 277, 279
Del Dotto, J. E., 484
De Leon, B., 334
Delgado-Gaitan, C., 18
Delisle, J. R., 432
de Man, A. E., 474
Demaria, T. P., 470
Demo, D. H., 173, 175, 307
Demont, J., 244
Dempsey, P., 378
DePaul, G. J., 489
Derzon, M. W., 525
Desiderato, L. L., 372
Detzer, M. J., 344
DeVault, C., 360, 362
deVries, K. H., 390
Diamond, M., 360
Diana, M. S., 345
Dickinson, A., 269, 270
Dickover, R. E., 368
DiClemente, R. J., 321, 359, 379
Diener, E., 70
Dietz, T. L., 267
Dill, C. A., 470
Dill, K. E., 270
Dilorio, C., 364
Dinh, K. T., 500
Di Saia, J., 277
Dishion, T. J., 141, 147, 195, 210, 511, 514
Dittus, P., 352, 364
Dlliot, E. S., 237
Dobash, R. P., 207
Dobson, D. M., 157
Dodge, K. A., 148, 199, 282, 521
Dodrill, C. B., 481
Dolan, C. V., 72
Dolcini, M. M., 133
Dollinger, S. J., 485
Dominick, J. R., 269, 270, 271, 277
Donahue, M. J., 399, 401
Donaldson, S. I., 512, 514
Dondero, G. M., 249
Donelson, E., 399
Donovan, J. M., 321
Donovan, P., 367
Doress, I., 403
Dorman, S. M., 268
Dorn, L. D., 70
Dornbusch, S. M., 146, 147, 148, 175, 226, 229, 421
Douglas, S., 258
Douvan, E., 323
Dowdy, B. B., 154, 157, 201
Downey, J., 85, 361
Downs, A. C., 332
Doyle, J. A., 328
Draper, P., 79
Drinkard, J., 188
Dronkers, J., 173
Drummond, R. J., 424, 440
Dube, E. M., 362
DuBois, D. L., 184
Dubow, E. F., 23, 375
Duckworth, E., 100

Duffy, M., 290
Dufresne, A., 112
Duggan, A., 376
Duke, D. L., 249
Duke, P., 89
Duke-Duncan, P., 85
Dukes, R. L., 336
Dumont, M., 456
Duncan, G. J., 118
Duncan, O. D., 238
Duncan, P. D., 81, 82, 85
Dunham, A. C., 421
Dunkle, M. E., 128
Dunlap, R., 171
Dunn, H., 78
Dunn, J., 160
Dunphy, D. C., 190
Duran, R. P., 119, 224
DuRant, R. H., 277, 500
Durkin, K., 182, 192
Durndell, A., 431
Dweck, C. S., 234
Dwyer, J., 84, 89

East, P. L., 161, 377
Eccles, J. S., 68, 139, 149, 181, 218, 227, 234, 238, 240, 241, 334, 430
Edelbrock, C. S., 70
Eder, D., 191, 192, 193, 194
Edmonds, P., 515
Edmondson, B., 19
Edwards, A., 426
Edwards, C. P., 147
Egan, S. K., 521
Egli, E. A., 272
Egolf, B., 457
Eicher, S. A., 191, 208, 209, 329
Eidelberg, L., 394
Eisele, J., 85
Eisenberg, N., 7, 160, 184, 305, 332, 402, 404, 406, 407, 408, 409
Eisenberg-Berg, N., 393
Eisenberger, R., 125
Eisenbud, L., 333
Eisler, I., 478
Eklin, C. H., 401
Elam, S. M., 222
Elder, G. H., 7–8, 81, 162, 465
Eldredge, D. A., 85, 89
Elia, J., 490
Elias, B. J., 89
Elias, M., 138, 152, 173, 207
Elkin, I., 473
Elkind, D., 131–132
Ellenbogen, S., 248
Ellickson, P. L., 524
Elliot, A. J., 234, 235, 236
Elliott, D., 420
Elliott, D. S., 523
Elliott, L., 151
Elliott, S. N., 484
Ellis, A. W., 484
Ellis, B. J., 79
Ellis, P., 346
Elshtain, J. B., 402
Elster, A. B., 376
Emerson, M. R., 377
Emery, R. E., 164, 167, 170
Emler, N., 297, 413
Emmons, S., 85, 86
Emslie, G. J., 474
England, E. M., 191, 200
Ennett, S., 189, 190
Ennis, R., 123
Ensign, J., 164, 168

Entwisle, D. R., 248
Epperson, D. L., 429
Epstein, J. L., 183, 185, 239
Epstein, L. H., 88, 89
Epstein, R., 125
Erb, T. O., 219
Erhardt, D., 491
Erickson, J., 400
Erikson, E., 28, 32–34, 36, 37, 203, 316, 317, 318, 319, 321, 322, 323, 337, 385, 398, 417
Erkanli, A., 467
Eron, L. D., 198, 283
Ertl, M., 206
Ertmer, P. A., 113
Esbensen, F., 524, 525
Escamilla, G., 500
Eshel, Y., 185, 187
Eshleman, J. R., 402
Estrada, 404
Etaugh, C., 227
Eure, C. R., 374
Evans, E. D., 290, 329
Evans, G. D., 516
Evans, K. M., 419, 427
Evans, M. D. R., 168
Evans, S. L., 375
Eveleth, P. B., 78, 79
Even, B., 433

Fabes, R. A., 305
Fabos, B., 274
Fagot, B. I., 145
Fahy, T. A., 478
Fairburn, C. G., 478, 479, 480
Falbo, T., 165
Fanshawe, J. P., 454
Farber, P., 242
Farmer, H., 417, 432
Farrell, M. P., 510
Farrington, D. P., 519, 522
Farrington, J., 287, 288, 460n
Fashola, O. S., 226
Fassa, N., 426
Fassinger, R. E., 431
Fauth, J. M., 314
Fay, R., 360
Federman, J., 282, 283
Feeney, J. A., 141
Fegley, S., 309, 402, 413, 421
Feingold, A., 328
Feiring, C., 181, 200, 201, 206, 315, 345
Feldlaufer, H., 218
Feldman, S., 143, 147, 154
Feldman, S. S., 181, 200, 201, 205, 206, 351
Felice, M. E., 373
Fennema, E., 234
Fergusson, D. M., 512
Ferrari, M., 112, 121
Fertman, C., 304, 307
Fichner-Rathus, L., 57
Fiedman, B. L., 392
Field, T., 145
Fielder, E. D., 242
Filozof, M., 310
Fine, M. A., 161, 173, 175
Finn, J. D., 248
Fiqua, D. R., 436
Firestone, I. J., 411
Firestone, W. A., 365
Fischer, E. F., 347
Fischer, J. L., 187
Fischer, K. W., 300, 302

Fischoff, B., 132
Fishbein, W., 473
Fisher, C. B., 42, 57
Fisher, L. A., 512
Fisher, S., 272
Fishman, M., 498
Fitch, S. A., 322
Flannery, D. J., 71, 522
Flavell, J. H., 98, 130
Flay, B. R., 500
Fleming, J., 467
Fleming, J. S., 232, 237
Fleming, R., 368
Fletcher, A. C., 146, 186
Flick, L., 274
Fling, S., 270
Flores, L. Y., 438
Florsheim, P., 376
Floyd, F. J., 362
Flum, H., 319, 322
Folkman, S., 453, 462
Ford, C. M., 269
Ford, D., 224
Fordham, S., 226, 337
Forehand, R., 158, 164, 170, 454, 460, 461n
Forgan, J. W., 485
Forgatch, M. S., 168
Forness, S. R., 490
Forrest, J. D., 366
Forrest, L., 391
Fortier, M. S., 248
Foshee, V. A., 146, 148, 149, 207
Foster, E. M., 376, 420
Foster, G. D., 85
Foster, H. G., 279
Foster-Clark, F. S., 181, 187
Fouad, N. A., 439
Fowler, J., 398, 400
Francis, L. J., 305, 395, 400
Franklyn-Stokes, A., 396
Franks, B. A., 129
Franz, C., 407
Franzoi, S. L., 194
Frary, R. B., 84
Fraser, A. M., 375
Frazer, W., 291
Frazier, H., 241
Freedland, J., 84, 89
Freedman, D. S., 79
Freize, I. H., 203
French, D. C., 194, 197
French, S. A., 87
Freud, A., 30–31, 70
Freud, S., 28, 29–30, 34, 36, 181, 394
Frey, D., 297
Friebert, S. E., 112
Fried, C. B., 277
Friedland, M. T., 483
Friedman, A. S., 529
Friedman, M. A., 88
Friedman, R. C., 361
Friedman, W. J., 392
Friedrich, W. N., 344
Frieze, I. H., 202n
Fritsch, E. J., 12
Fritz, G. K., 476
Frost, C. J., 401
Frost, J. J., 366
Fry, A. F., 110–111
Fu, V. R., 19
Fuligni, A. J., 139, 149, 153, 181, 208, 210, 223
Fuller-Thompson, E., 163

Fullerton, C. S., 304
Funder, D. C., 311
Funk, J. B., 267, 268, 271
Furby, L., 128
Furman, W., 141, 160, 161, 165, 181, 182, 184, 187, 199, 200, 345, 351
Furnham, A., 85
Furstenberg, F., 173, 247, 284, 359, 375, 376, 377

Gable, R. A., 482
Gable, S. L., 235
Gabrielli, W. F., 521
Gaddis, A., 65
Gadow, K. D., 283
Gadzella, B. M., 123, 126
Gahlinger, P. M., 502, 504, 507, 508
Gainor, K. A., 436
Galambos, N. L., 85, 158, 167
Gallup, A. M., 222
Gallup, G. H., 399
Galotti, K. M., 128, 392
Gamoran, A., 241
Ganong, H. L., 345–346
Garbarino, J., 527, 528
Garber, J., 79, 469, 470
Garcia-Coll, C., 18, 19, 374
Gard, C., 465
Gardner, H., 120–121
Gardyn, R., 264, 265
Gargiulo, J., 80, 81
Garmon, L. C., 390
Garner, A., 290
Garner, D. M., 480
Garovich-Szabo, L., 327
Garrett, J. T., 439
Garrett, M. W., 439
Garry, E. M., 527
Garty, Y., 426
Gaskill, F. W., 483
Gati, J., 426
Gatto, L., 276, 280
Gauvin, L., 88
Gavin, L. A., 141
Gavora, J., 367
Gawel, R., 267
Gay, J., 323
Ge, X., 81, 82
Gebhard, U., 398
Gehring, T., 143, 146
Gelfand, D. M., 404
Geller, B., 473
Gelman, D., 362
Gerber, P. J., 483, 487
Gerbner, G., 258, 285
Geronimus, A. T., 375
Gerrard, M., 168, 372, 500
Gershman, E. S., 196
Gershoni, R., 184
Gerton, J., 338
Gervai, J., 328–329
Gerwels, D., 426
Giacopassi, D., 498
Giancola, P. R., 502, 520
Gibb, G. D., 271
Gibbons, F. X., 500
Gibbons, J. L., 329, 330
Giesdorn, J., 249
Gil, V. E., 46
Gilbert, J., 8
Giles-Sims, J., 172, 173
Gilligan, C., 323, 329, 330, 331, 391, 392, 405
Gillock, K., 220

Gim-Chung, R. H., 439
Gimpel, G. A., 199
Ginorio, A., 228
Ginott, H., 415
Ginsberg, R., 487
Giordano, P. C., 183, 185
Girus, J. S., 456, 472
Gjerde, P. F., 170
Gladstone, T. R. G., 470
Glasgow, K. L., 238
Glei, D., 152
Glidden, C., 438
Glider, P., 217
Glover, R. W., 443, 446, 447
Gluck, C., 400
Godenne, G. D., 310
Goede, M., 172
Goldberg, C., 279
Goldberg, D., 88
Goldenberg, R. L., 375
Goldsmith, H. H., 74, 75
Goldstein, A. P., 199
Goldstein, S., 272
Goleman, D., 122–123
Golish, T. D., 173
Golub, S., 64
Gonzales, M., 287
Gonzalez, J., 133
Gonzalez, N. A., 225
Good, T., 240
Goodman, G. S., 167, 168, 172
Goodman, J. B., 409
Goodnow, J. J., 154, 184, 407
Goodyer, I. M., 468
Gordon, A. S., 206
Gordon, C. M., 359
Gordon, D. H., 99
Gore, S., 243
Gorman, D. M., 512
Gorsuch, R. A., 398
Gosselin, M. J., 472
Gotcher, M. J., 290
Gottfredson, G. D., 430
Gottfried, A. E., 158, 232, 237
Gottfried, A. W., 158, 232, 237
Gottman, J., 170, 184, 187
Gowen, K., 197, 198
Gowen, L. K., 200, 205
Graber, J., 477
Graber, J. A., 1, 79, 82
Grace, N. C., 157
Graef, R., 69
Graf, M., 469
Graham, J., 282
Graham, P. J., 161
Graham, S., 198, 393, 487, 518, 521
Grajek, S., 347
Grannemann, B. D., 313
Grant, B. F., 502
Grant, K. E., 456
Graves, W. L., 374
Grayson, C., 456, 472
Green, R. P., 216
Green, S., 198
Greenbaum, B., 487
Greenberg, J. S., 201, 345, 362
Greenberg, M. T., 374
Greenberger, E., 142, 419, 420, 422
Greene, K., 283
Greenfield, P. M., 118
Greenlee, S. P., 426
Greeson, L. E., 279
Gregory, A., 409
Gregory, R. J., 120

Gresham, E. M., 484
Gresham, F. M., 313
Gridina, N., 255, 256n, 262, 269, 279, 281
Grier, L. K., 411
Griffin, N., 300
Griffiths, M. D., 268, 271, 272, 283
Grigal, M., 482
Grigorenko, E. L., 117
Grimley, D. M., 368, 371
Gringlas, M. B., 168, 171
Grinspoon, L., 505
Grodzinsky, G., 489
Groer, M. W., 455
Grossman, J. B., 527
Grotevant, H. D., 6, 9, 23, 32, 138, 149, 150, 181, 298, 317, 318, 327, 336
Grube, E., 357
Grube, J. W., 357
Grusec, J. E., 407
Guay, F., 248
Guerra, N. G., 521, 527
Guest, C. L., 443
Guetzloe, E., 527
Guilford, J. P., 125
Guilkey, D., 354
Guillen, E. O., 477
Guisinger, S., 324
Guiton, G., 437
Guitteau, J., 268
Gulko, J., 333
Gullone, E., 84, 133
Gump, L. S., 391
Gundlach, J., 274
Gundry, L. K., 126
Gunsalus, C., 106
Gunter, B., 285
Guo, G., 247
Guthrie, J. F., 84
Gutman, L. M., 238
Guttmacher, S., 358
Gwartney-Gibbs, P. A., 207

Haager, D., 484
Haas, R., 171
Hackett, G., 426, 431, 436, 438
Haffner, D. W., 364
Hagan, M. S., 172
Hagborg, W. J., 485
Haggerty, R. J., 457
Hakanen, E., 273
Hale, S., 111
Haley, B., 273
Hall, C. W., 487
Hall, G. S., 7, 29, 165, 454–455
Hall, J. E., 483
Hall, P. D., 275
Hall, W., 508
Hallinan, M. T., 241
Halpern, C. T., 206
Halpern, D. F., 123, 125
Halteman, W., 196
Halverson, C. F., 333
Hamachek, D. E., 33
Hamalainen, M., 525
Hamer, D. H., 68
Hamilton, C. E., 141
Hamm, J. V., 185
Hammen, C., 471, 472
Hammer, T. J., 330
Hammermeister, J., 257, 259
Hammersmith, S., 361
Handee, W. R., 280

Handler, A., 359
Handley, P., 85, 89
Hankin, B. L., 470, 472
Hanmer, T. J., 391
Hannahy, M. E., 404
Hannon, R., 379
Hansell, S., 181, 190, 529
Hansen, C., 489
Hansen, C. H., 275, 277, 278
Hansen, D. M., 420
Hansen, E. J., 231
Hansen, K., 426
Hansen, R. D., 275, 277, 278
Hansford, B. C., 305
Hanson, G. M. B., 269
Hanson, T. L., 173
Harackiewicz, J. M., 234
Harakka, T., 205
Hardy, J., 376
Hardy, J. B., 118
Harmin, M., 409
Harold, R. D., 238
Harris, A., 138
Harris, J. C., 89, 90
Harris, J. D., 184
Harris, J. J., III, 224
Harris, L., 284
Harris, S. M., 455
Harris, Y. R., 366
Harrison, A. O., 19
Hart, D., 300, 309, 402, 413
Hart, E. R., 107
Harter, S., 298, 300, 301, 302, 303, 305, 306n, 307, 309, 310, 317, 326, 331
Hartman, B. W., 436
Hartmus, D. M., 379
Hartshorne, H., 407
Hartup, W. W., 181, 182, 183, 184, 185, 186, 187, 190, 209
Harvey, K., 89
Harvey, S. M., 353
Harwood, R. L., 17, 19
Hasbrouck, J. E., 282
Hatch, D. D., 483
Hatcher, P. J., 484
Hatfield, E., 348
Hattie, J. A., 305, 315
Haugaard, J. J., 167
Hauser, S. T., 336
Havighurst, R., 33–34, 51
Haviland, J., 70
Haviland, J. M., 99
Haviland, M. G., 426
Haviland, W. A., 2, 324
Hawkins, B., 421
Hawkins, J. A., 184
Hawkins, J. D., 502, 511, 519, 521, 522, 523, 526
Hawley, P., 430, 433
Hayes, D. S., 196
Hayes, R., 429
Hayes, T. J., 438
Haynie, D. L., 198
Hayward, C., 82, 197, 198
Hazier, R. J., 197
Healy, J. M., 224, 225
Hearn, J. C., 444
Heath, A. C., 509
Heaton, T. B., 138, 150
Hechtman, L., 489
Heimer, K., 175
Heinrich, R., 2

Helmreich, R., 328
Helweg, C. C., 129
Hemmens, C., 12
Hempelman, K. A., 10
Hendee, W. R., 273, 274
Henderson, S., 430
Hendry, J., 2
Henley, S. J., 498
Hennig, K. H., 409
Hennigan, K. M., 501
Henry, B., 520
Henry, C., 512
Henry, C. S., 407
Henry, P. E., 85, 87
Henry, T., 227, 251
Henshaw, S., 366, 372
Herbert, W., 409
Herdt, G., 68
Herek, G. M., 362
Herkenham, M., 504
Herman, M. A., 150
Herman-Giddens, M. E., 79
Herman-Stahl, M., 455, 458
Hernandez, D. J., 20
Hernandez, J. T., 321
Heron, A., 51, 101
Herrenhohl, E. C., 457
Herrenhohl, R. C., 457
Hershberger, S. L., 360
Hertsgaard, D., 85
Hertzler, A. A., 84
Hesketh, B., 324, 430
Hess, L. E., 166, 167
Hesse-Biber, S., 85
Hetherington, E. M., 168, 169, 170, 172, 173
Hicks, K. L., 86
Hickson, L., 118
Higgins, B. S., 374
Higgins, E. T., 329
Higginson, J. G., 46
Hill, C. I., 400
Hill, J., 160
Hill, J. P., 6, 141, 145, 157, 329, 392
Hillbrand, M., 279
Hilsman, R., 469, 470
Hilton, N. Z., 207
Himaki, W. C., 203
Hines, A. M., 168
Hinshaw, S. P., 491
Hippensteele, S., 381
Ho, M. K., 19
Hochschild, A., 324–325
Hockenberry-Eaton, M., 364
Hodgson, L. G., 162
Hoffer, T. B., 241, 242
Hoffman, J., 374
Hoffman, M., 390, 394, 395
Hoffman, S. D., 375–376
Hofman, J. E., 184
Hogan, D. P., 358
Hogan, R., 313
Hogarty, P. S., 116
Hoge, D., 307, 309
Hogue, A., 186
Holden, G. W., 522
Holder, H. B., 484
Holland, B., 278
Holland, J., 424–426, 430, 431, 433
Hollier, E. A., 173
Holmbeck, G. N., 6, 139, 141, 154, 157
Holmes, D. S., 57
Holmes, M. M., 379

Holmes, W. R., 365
Holstein, C. B., 390
Holton, L., 279
Holtzen, D. W., 361
Hoover, J. H., 197
Hoover-Dempsey, K., 238
Hopmeyer, A., 192–193
Hops, H., 519
Hops, R., 310
Hopson, H., 270
Horn, J. L., 485
Horowitz, L., 350
Horsey, C. S., 248
Horwitz, S. M., 375, 378
Horwood, L. J., 512
Hotchkiss, L., 436
Hotelling, K., 391
Hotz, V. J., 376
Houston, T., 498
Howell, J. C., 524, 525
Hoyer, W. J., 101
Hoyle, S. G., 184
Hoyt, K. B., 449
Hoza, B., 187
Hsia, J., 438
Hsu, F., 347
Hubbard, J. A., 517, 518n
Hubbs-Tait, L., 390
Hudley, C., 393, 518, 521
Huesmann, R. L., 521
Huffman, G. B., 475
Hughes, J. N., 282
Hughes, V., 227
Hulme, C., 484
Hunt, N., 271
Hunter, E., 402, 403
Hunter, F. T., 139, 144, 149, 187
Hunter, S. M., 190
Huntsinger, C. S., 238
Hurrell, R. M., 379
Huston, A. C., 282, 329, 441
Huston, M., 228
Hutchings, B., 521
Hutt, 351
Huttunen, A., 198
Hyde, J. S., 165, 166, 354, 392
Hymel, S., 199

Ianni, F., 413
Iannotti, R. J., 179
Iheanacho, S. L., 310.
Ihinger-Tallman, M., 172
Inbertditzen, H. M., 183
Ingersoll, G., 81
Ingram, K. M., 206
Inhelder, B., 96, 98, 99, 314
Ireland, D., 362
Irwin, C., 87
Irwin, C. E., 87
Isaac, J. D., 430
Isay, R. A., 361
Ishii, S., 217
Israel, A. C., 466, 477, 483, 488
Ito, Y., 66

Jaccard, J., 352, 364
Jackson, C., 146, 148, 149, 158
Jackson, L. A., 276, 280
Jacobson, L., 223, 240
Jacobson, L. J., 377
Jacobson, N. S., 470
Jacoby, T., 435, 437
Jadack, R. A., 390, 392

Jaffee, S., 392
James, A., 198
James, C., 255
James, W., 298, 305
James, W. H., 206
Janda, L. H., 85
Jani, S., 137
Jankowiak, W. R., 347
Janosz, M., 247
Jarvis, P. A., 420
Jencks, C., 118
Jenkins, J., 161
Jenkins, J. M., 161
Jenkins, J. R., 484
Jensen, L., 346, 391
Jensen, L. C., 391
Jepsen, D. A., 440
Jessor, R., 512
Ji, G., 165
Jiao, S., 165
Jing, Q., 165
Jipping, T. L., 278
Joekler, N., 490
Joffe, A., 84
Johnson, A., 400, 401
Johnson, B. E., 379
Johnson, H. C., 521
Johnson, J., 276, 280
Johnson, M. K., 418
Johnson, M. P., 207
Johnson, R. L., 86
Johnson, S., 502
Johnston, C., 488
Johnston, L. D., 151, 496, 497, 498, 499, 501, 502, 507, 513
Johnston, S. G., 170
Joiner, G. W., 85
Jome, L. M., 429, 435
Jonah, B. A., 3
Jones, B., 49, 500
Jones, D., 303
Jones, J., 402
Jones, J. T., 278
Jones, K. H., 477
Jordan, W. J., 248
Jory, B., 139
Jose, P. E., 238
Joshi, P., 282
Jou, S., 274
Jumisko, M., 244
Jung, J., 456
Juntunen, C. L., 439, 440
Jussim, L., 240, 241
Juvonen, J., 198

Kaeser, L., 364
Kagan, J., 75
Kahlbaugh, P., 99
Kahn, J. H., 429
Kahne, J., 305
Kail, R., 111
Kaku, H., 325
Kalat, J. W., 65, 472, 490
Kalichman, S. C., 372
Kalogerakis, A., 317
Kandel, D., 211
Kandel, D. B., 186, 203, 502, 506, 511
Kane, C., 525
Kane, P., 165
Kang, S., 445
Kann, L., 516
Kantor, H., 445, 446, 448
Kantrowitz, B., 21, 374, 399

Kao, M. Y., 356
Kaplan, D., 379
Kaplan, D. S., 247
Kaplan, H. B., 247
Kaplan, P., 297, 523
Kaplan, P. S., 100, 111, 118, 240, 433, 482, 483
Kardia, S. L. R., 509
Kariya, T., 447
Karlsson, J., 488
Karniol, R., 406
Karraker, K. H., 374–375
Kaschak, D. G., 282
Kasendorf, E., 336
Kashani, J. H., 466
Kashubeck, S., 85
Kaslow, N. J., 470
Kassin, S. M., 51
Kassinove, H., 470
Kastenbaum, G. I., 271
Katchadourian, H., 78, 343
Katic, A., 474
Katz, J., 206
Katz, K. D., 367
Katz, L. F., 170
Kaufman, N. J., 498
Kaufmann, K., 169
Kavale, K. A., 490
Kawachi, I., 500
Keating, D. P., 101, 102, 110, 124
Keefe, K., 187, 208
Kehily, 291, 292
Keith, B., 168
Keith, J. B., 355
Keller, S., 16
Kelley, J., 168
Kelley, M., 364
Kelley, M. L., 18, 157
Kelly, J. A., 372
Kelly, J. B., 168
Kelly, L., 373–374
Keltikangas-Jarvinen, L., 205
Kempton, T., 161
Kendler, K. S., 477
Kendrick, C., 160
Kennedy, W. A., 117
Kenon, M., 274
Kernis, M. H., 312
Kerns, K. A., 140, 141
Kerr, B., 227, 430, 431
Kerr, M., 147
Kershner, R., 379
Kessler, R. C., 455
Keyser, B. B., 125
Khalsa, H. K., 456
Kickul, J. R., 126
Kidwell, J. S., 318, 319, 321
Kiesler, S., 264
Kilbourne, 403
Killen, J. D., 87
Kilpatrick, D. G., 509
Kim, K. J., 11
Kimerling, R., 206
Kimmel, E., 328
King, K. A., 475n, 476
King, N. M. P., 55
King, S. L., 85
King, V., 162
Kinnaird, K. L., 168
Kinney, D. A., 191, 193, 194, 195, 221
Kirby, D., 364, 365, 366, 368, 378
Kirchler, E., 183
Kirkpatrick, L. A., 351

Kirkpatrick, S. W., 484
Kistner, J., 485
Kitayama, S., 324
Kite, M. E., 328
Kittleson, M. J., 353
Kivett, V. R., 163
Klaczynski, P. A., 98, 99, 314
Klebanov, P. K., 118
Klein, A. G., 43
Klein, D. F., 489
Klein, J. D., 257, 280
Kleiner, C., 385
Kleinfeld, J., 228
Klepac, L., 140
Klepinger, D. H., 374
Klerman, L. V., 375
Klesges, R. C., 499, 514
Kless, S. J., 329
Kliewer, W., 154, 157, 201
Knox, D., 203, 353, 370
Knox, M., 309
Kobasigawa, A., 112
Kobus, K., 220
Koegel, H. M., 439
Koestner, R., 232, 235, 407
Koff, E., 63, 64, 81
Kohlberg, L., 387, 390, 391, 392, 397, 398, 399, 408, 410–411
Kohli, V., 165
Kohn, A., 305
Kojo, K., 325
Koopman, C., 355
Kopp, C., 39n
Korenfeld, D., 404
Koss, M. P., 206
Kossen, S., 449
Kost, K., 366
Kostanski, M., 84, 133
Kotchick, B. A., 454, 461n
Kotesky, R. L., 400
Kouri, E. M., 505
Kovach, R., 114
Kowal, A., 162
Kowaleski-Jones, L., 359
Kozberg, S. F., 128
Kozma, E. J., 216
Krakow, J. B., 39n
Kramer, L., 162
Kramer, R., 388
Kramer, T. L., 187
Kraut, R., 260, 264, 265
Krebs, D. L., 390, 392
Kreinen, T., 364
Kreitler, H., 127
Kreitler, S., 127
Kremar, M., 283
Krettenauer, T., 409
Kroeger, E., 51
Kroger, J., 324, 325
Kromrey, J. D., 328
Kruczek, T. A., 430
Kruesi, M. J., 521
Kruger, A. C., 409
Krumboltz, J. D., 436
Krunstal, F., 150
Ksir, C., 506
Ku, L., 354, 368
Kubey, R., 270, 273
Kubiszyn, T., 115
Kuck, D. L., 379
Kuffel, S. W., 206
Kuhn, D., 123
Kuklinski, M. R., 240
Kulkarni, S., 78

Kunkel, D., 282, 285
Kunz, J. P., 376
Kurdek, L. A., 161, 173, 175, 184
Kurman, J., 185, 187
Kurpius, S. E. R., 379
Kurth, S., 431
Kurtz, D. A., 336
Kusel, S. J., 197
Kutines, W., 156

Labouvie-Vief, G., 102
Lacey, E. P., 353
Lacombe, A. C., 323
Lacourse, E., 276
LaFramboise, T., 338
La Greca, A. M., 484
Lam, C. M., 16
Lam, M., 153
Lamb, J. M., 454
Lamborn, S. D., 146
Lamm, R. P., 2
Lammers, C., 356
Lamp-Petraitis, C., 70, 71
Landry, D. J., 364, 365
Lane, E., 55
Lange, J. E., 327
Lange, R. E., 242
Langhinrichsen-Roholing, J., 206
Langley, J., 206
Langlois, J. H., 332
Laosa, L. M., 118, 119
Lapsley, D. K., 102, 133
Lara, J., 248
Larrabee, M. J., 419, 427
Larsen, R., 70
Larson, D., 164
Larson, J., 456, 472
Larson, M. S., 285
Larson, R., 85, 179, 180, 181, 270, 273
Larson, R. W., 23, 52, 69, 70, 71
Larson, S. L., 238
Last, C. G., 489
Laursen, B., 153, 187, 188, 205
Lavery, B., 133
Lawton, M., 526
Lazarus, R. S., 453, 462
Leadbeater, B., 102
Leahy, R. L., 308
Leary, M. R., 50, 54, 57
LeBlanc, R. S., 111
Lebra, T., 324
Lee, J. A., 87, 348–349
Lee, P. A., 368, 371
Lee, S. Y., 234
Lee, V., 431
Lee, V. E., 247
Leff, S., 197
Leggett, E. L., 234
Lehman, W. E., 206
Leitenberg, H., 344
Leiter, R. A., 10
Leland, N. L., 359, 371
Lemery, K. S., 75
Lennon, R., 406
Lenox, K., 195
Lent, R. W., 436
Leong, F. T. L., 438, 439
Lepper, M. R., 270, 271
Lerman, C., 509
Lerner, J. V., 76, 151, 166, 167, 430
Lerner, R. M., 42, 139, 152
Leshner, A. L., 495, 503
Lesko, N., 9

Lesser, G. S., 203, 211
Lesser, T. M., 321
Lester, J. N., 449
Leung, K., 325
Leung, S. A., 431, 432
Levine, E., 84
Levine, M., 274
Levine, R., 347, 348n
Levy, M. B., 349
Lewin, L. M., 519
Lewin, T., 228
Lewinsohn, P. M., 87, 310, 468, 469, 473
Lewis, A. C., 224, 242, 442
Lewis, C. C., 128
Lewis, D. R., 444, 445, 447, 448
Lewis, J., 171
Lewis, J. M., 167
Lewis, M., 86, 181
Lewis, R. G., 19
Li, D., 148
Li, S. A., 456
Li, Z., 165
Liben, L. S., 329
Lickona, T., 411
Liebert, R. M., 259
Liem, J. H., 161
Lieu, T. A., 83
Light, D., 16
Light, H. K., 85
Lightbody, P., 431
Lin, C. C., 19
Lin, K. M., 456
Lin, Q, 242
Lin, S., 270, 271
Lindauer, P., 106
Lindeman, M., 205
Lindenberger, U., 32, 103
Lindsay, M. K., 374
Lingeman, R., 402
Lipman, A. J., 469
Lipsey, M. W., 514, 525
Little, J. K., 329
Little, M., 368, 369, 370
Liu, M., 148
Livesley, W. J., 130
Livingstone, S., 287
Lochhead, J., 224
Lockwood, D., 526
Loeber, R., 211, 511, 519, 520, 523, 529
Lohr, M. J., 191
Long, J., 524, 525
Long, W., 46
Looker, E. D., 431
Lopez, F. G., 434
LoPresto, C. T., 344
Lord, C., 385
Lovell, S., 366, 367
Lovitt, T. C., 485
Lowry, D., 284
Luce, T., 497
Lueptow, L. B., 327
Lueptow, M. B., 327
Lukas, S. E., 505
Luker, K., 365
Lundberg, S., 374
Lurie, S. J., 508
Luster, T., 225, 375
Luthar, S. S., 23, 458
Luzzo, D. A., 426, 438
Lynch, J. H., 139
Lynch, J. P., 524
Lynch, L. M., 444

Lynch, M. E., 329, 392
Lynskey, M. T., 512
Lyons, N., 330
Lyons, N. P., 391
Lytle, L. J., 324, 331
Lytton, H., 332
Lyubomirsky, S., 472–473

Ma, H. K., 390, 406
Maag, J. W., 485
Maccoby, E. E., 145
MacEwen, K. E., 167
MacGavin, L., 188
MacGregor, M. W., 426
Mackie, D., 269
MacKinnon-Lewis, C. E., 211
Madden, P. F., 509
Madon, S., 240
Maehr, M. L., 232, 234
Magnussen, D., 81
Magruder, B., 361, 362
Mahapatra, M., 395
Mahoney, J. L., 247
Mail, P. D., 502
Majd-Jabbari, M., 502
Makepeace, J. M., 206
Males, M. A., 511, 512, 517
Malik, S., 205, 206, 207
Malina, R. M., 61
Malinowski, C. I., 390
Manber, R., 89
Mancuso, J., 89
Manis, F. R., 110
Manning, A., 513
Manning, M. L., 216, 219, 231
Manning, W., 419
Mannuzza, S., 44, 489
Manosevitz, M., 173
Manzo, B. V., 225, 242
Marchant, G. J., 146
Marcia, J., 318, 320, 321
Marcotte, D., 468, 472, 473
Mare, R., 241
Mares, M. L., 286, 287
Maresh, S. E., 430, 431
Marini, M. M., 418
Markovits, H., 98
Markstrom-Adams, C., 322, 335, 337
Markus, H., 324
Marohn, R. C., 297
Marold, D. B., 303
Marr, L., 368, 369, 370, 371
Marshall, J., 417
Marshall, R., 443, 446, 447
Marshall, S. K., 318
Marshall, S. P., 227
Marsiglio, W., 362, 376
Martin, C. L., 328, 329, 332, 333, 334
Martin, C. R., 274
Martin, D., 360
Martin, G., 276
Martin, J., 206, 360
Martin, J. A., 145
Martinez, R. O., 336
Martinez-Pons, M., 38, 113
Marttunen, M. J., 475
Marx, J., 163
Masi, F. A., 422
Masten, A. S., 23, 457, 459
Matlin, M. W., 517
Matsuba, M. K., 394
Matsueda, R. L., 175

Mattay, V. S., 490
Matthews, C. G., 481
Matthews, S. H., 162
Mauldon, J., 365
May, M. A., 407
Mayer, J. D., 121, 123
Mayes, L. C., 510
Maynard, R., 373
Mazza, J. J., 474, 475
McAdoo, H. P., 18, 225
McAndrew, F. T., 455, 456, 457
McCabe, D. L., 405
McCabe, M. P., 168, 171, 351
McCain, A. P., 157
McCall, R. B., 116
McCammon, S., 370
McCarthy, J., 307, 309
McCartney, K., 74, 75
McClanahan, S. S., 173
McClelland, S., 244
McClintock, M. K., 68
McClure, R. F., 272
McCoy, J. K., 354
McCracken, R. S., 428, 431
McCrae, R. R., 328
McCrone, W. P., 483
McElhaney, K. B., 148
McElroy, S. W., 376
McFarlane, A., 468
McGee, J., 430
McGee, P. A., 431
McGee, R., 305
McGraw, S. A., 354
McGregor, H. A., 235
McGregor, I. S., 508
McGue, M., 510
McGuigan, K. A., 524
McGuire, J. M., 487
McHale, S. M., 150, 472
McIlhaney, J. S., 369, 370
McIntire, W. G., 404
McIntosh, R., 484
McKinlay, J. B., 354
McLanahan, S. S., 171–172, 173, 175
McLellan, J. A., 422
McLeod, J. M., 48
McLoed, J. D., 455
McLoyd, V. C., 238
McMahon, R. J., 141, 147
McManus, M. A., 83
McNamara, J. R., 206
McNamara, M. S., 150
McNeal, R. B., 246, 247
McPartland, J. M., 248
McWhirter, E. H., 427, 436, 438, 443
McWhorter, J. F., 338
Mead, G. H., 298
Mead, M., 155
Means, S., 292
Mears, F. G., 272
Mednick, S. A., 521
Medora, N. P., 353
Meece, J. L., 236
Meeus, W., 154, 209, 317, 318, 322, 323
Megan, Z., 142
Meier, R. F., 379
Melan, E., 198
Mellanby, A., 291
Mellin, E. A., 473
Mellin, L. M., 87
Melton, G. B., 10

Mendelson, B. K., 88, 310
Mendelson, M. J., 88, 310
Menesini, E., 198
Meredith, W., 467, 468, 472
Merrell, J., 497
Merrell, K. W., 199
Merrick, S., 140, 141
Merrill, S. A., 255, 273
Meschke, L. L., 356
Metcalfe, J., 112
Mettetal, G., 187
Meyer, E. C., 18
Meyer, H. A., 232
Meyer, K. A., 420
Meyers, L. S., 272
Meyers, S. A., 376
Michael, R. T., 355, 356
Michaelieu, Q., 304, 310
Midgley, C., 218
Midlarsky, E., 404, 407
Mihalic, S. W., 420
Mildrum, N. K., 126
Miller, B. C., 354, 356, 373, 379
Miller, D. B., 338
Miller, G., 324
Miller, J. G., 155, 395
Miller, J. Y., 502
Miller, L., 430
Miller, M. D., 275
Miller, M. J., 426
Miller, P. H., 104
Miller, R. B., 162, 163
Miller, S., 22, 442
Miller, S. A., 44, 50, 56, 58
Miller-Johnson, S., 523, 527
Mills, A., 357
Millstein, S. G., 208
Minkel, W., 124
Minkler, M., 163
Minor, B., 243
Minor, C. W., 440
Minuchin, P., 478
Mirel, J. E., 7, 8
Mitchell, L. K., 436
Moffitt, T., 116, 117
Moffitt, T. E., 82, 520
Mogelonsky, M., 418
Mok, T. A., 203
Molenaar, C. M., 72
Monahan, S. C., 162
Monson, B. H., 379
Monson, T. C., 521
Monsour, A., 300, 301, 302
Montemayor, R., 152
Montgomery, M. S., 485
Montgomery, R. L., 132
Moore, K., 152, 284
Moore, K. A., 150, 162, 354, 373
Moore, N. B., 366
Moore, S. M., 64, 84, 133
Morash, M. A., 321
Morath, R. A., 422
Morgan, C., 430, 431
Morgan, J. I., 433
Morgan, K. L., 465
Morgan, R. L., 106
Morgan, S. P., 375
Morlock, H., 268
Morris, K., 508
Morris, P. A., 39
Morris, T., 89
Morrison, D. M., 359
Morrison, F. J., 110

Morrow, K. B., 187
Morrow, R. D., 19
Mortimer, J. T., 420, 421, 422
Moseley, M., 405
Moshman, D., 97, 127, 129
Mott, F. L., 359
Mounts, N., 208
Muise, J. G., 111
Mullen, J., 243
Mullis, A. K., 426
Mullis, R. L., 426
Mundorf, N., 277
Munley, P. H., 417
Munoz, K. A., 84
Muñoz-Plaza, C., 362
Muram, D., 379
Murphy, J. J., 359
Murphy, P. A., 517
Murphy, S. T., 285
Murray, B., 228, 377, 514
Mussen, P. H., 160, 393, 409
Must, A., 68
Musty, R. E., 504
Muuss, P. H., 391, 392, 478, 479
Muzzonigro, P. G., 361
Myers, R. S., 89

Nada-Raja, S., 206, 305
Nagel, K. L., 477
Nagy, S., 379
Nalin, J., 12
Nansel, T. R., 197, 198
Narasimham, G., 98
Nathan, J., 242
Natvig, G. K., 455
Nauta, M. M., 429, 432
Nazarro, J. N., 19
Neale, J. M., 363
Neeleman, J., 401
Neff, W., 391
Neher, L. S., 169
Neimark, E. D., 101
Neisser, U., 118
Nelson, F. L., 475
Nelson, W. L., 170
Ness, M. E., 273
Neufeld, J., 206
Neumann, H., 440
Neumarker, K. J., 477
Neumark-Sztainer, D., 85
Neuwirth, S., 484
Nevers, P., 398
Nevid, J. S., 57
Newacheck, P. W., 83
Newcomb, A. F., 184, 193, 195, 196
Newcomb, M. D., 510
Newman, B. M., 191
Newman, B. S., 361
Newman, D. L., 76
Newman, P. R., 191
Newstead, S. E., 396, 406
Nguyen, N., 88
Niblock, S. B., 379
Nicholls, J. G., 236
Nicholopoulos, V., 87
Nichols, P. I., 117
Nicklas, T. A., 84
Nicolau, S., 246
Nielsen, S., 477
Nieman, D. C., 86
Nigg, J. T., 74
Nightingale, E. O., 208
Nigolean, K., 268
Nisbett, R. E., 118

Nishina, A., 198
Nissim, R., 404
Nitz, K., 76, 373, 378
Nogata, D. K., 336
Nolen-Hoeksema, S., 456, 472–473
Noller, P., 141, 149
Nomura, C., 512
Noom, M. J., 154
Norman, D. A., 230
Norman, M. M., 224, 225
Norman, N. M., 500
Norris, S., 123
Norton, M. C., 379
Nottelmann, E. D., 69, 217
Nousiainen, S., 158
Novacek, J., 313
Novak, D. M., 270
Novy, D. M., 437
Nyberg, K. L., 241

Oakes, J., 437
Obeidallah, D. A., 472
O'Brien, K. M., 431, 438
O'Connell, L., 431
O'Connor, R. E., 484
O'Donnell, K., 139, 154, 157
Offer, D., 138
Offord, D. R., 467
Ogbar, J. O. G., 74, 279
Ogbu, J. U., 18, 226, 440
Oh, W., 374
Ohan, J. L., 488
Ohler, J., 224, 225
Okagaki, L., 407
O'Keefe, M., 207
O'Leary, G., 491
O'Leary, K. D., 206, 207
Oliver, M. B., 354
Oliver, R., 197
Ollendick, T. H., 196
Olson, 149, 150
Olson, L., 251
Olson, T. D., 354
Olszewski-Kubilius, P., 126
Olweus, D., 70, 198, 307
O'Malley, P. M., 151, 307, 309, 496, 497n, 499, 513
O'Neal, G., 502
O'Neil, D. M., 8
Oosterwegel, A., 315
Oppenheimer, L., 315
Orlofsky, J. L., 321, 322
Orr, D., 81
Orvaschel, H., 466
Oser, F., 411, 413
Osgood, D. W., 524, 525
Oshman, H. P., 173
Osipow, S. H., 417
Osterman, P., 443
Overstreet, P. L., 424
Overton, W. F., 98, 99
Ozturk, M., 421

Pace, B., 198
Pachter, L. M., 17
Padilla, A. M., 359
Page, R. M., 257, 465
Paik, H., 282, 283
Paikoff, R. L., 69, 70, 146, 152, 157
Painter, K., 505
Palincsar, A. S., 107
Palmonari, A., 183
Palos, P. A., 364
Panzarine, S., 376
Parish, T. S., 168, 482

Park, S. Y., 75
Park, T., 359
Parke, R. D., 158, 159, 166
Parker, J. G., 182, 184, 196
Parker, K. D., 502
Parkhurst, J. T., 192–193
Parks, P. S. M., 87
Parnell, D., 447
Partridge, S., 171
Pasley, K., 172
Passman, R. H., 162
Pastore, M., 266
Pattatucci, A. M., 68
Pattee, L., 193
Patterson, G. R., 168, 195, 511
Paul, J., 361
Paul, P., 251, 257, 277
Paulhus, D. L., 465
Paulson, S. E., 146, 147, 152, 158, 166, 229
Pawlby, S. J., 205, 357
Pearce, C., 276
Pearson, P. R., 395, 400
Pearson, T. C., 381
Peck, B. M., 247
Pellegrini, A. D., 197, 198
Penland, E., 123, 126
Pennington, B. F., 488
Pentz, M. A., 199
Peplau, L. A., 372
Perlman, T., 489
Perry, C. L., 87
Perry, C. M., 404
Perry, D. G., 197, 521
Perry, L. C., 197
Perry, R. P., 243
Perry, T. B., 183, 184
Perry, W. B., 102
Personick, V. A., 418
Peskin, H., 81
Pestrak, V. A., 360
Petersen, A. C., 1, 7, 62, 85, 187, 208, 455, 458
Peterson, C., 469
Peterson, G. W., 510
Peterson, J., 284
Peterson, K. L., 132
Peterson, K. S., 168, 355
Peterson, L., 404
Peterson, P. E., 223
Petrie, G., 106
Petrill, S. A., 117
Petro, K. D., 191, 200
Pettengill, S., 156
Pettit, G. S., 148
Phares, V., 138
Philliber, S., 378
Phillips, C. A., 271
Phillips, M., 118
Phinney, J. A., 336–337
Piaget, J., 28, 34–36, 95–101, 103, 107, 109, 130, 182, 314, 387, 388, 398, 408
Pick, S., 364
Pickering, A. S., 280
Piercy, F. P., 398
Pignatti, B., 198
Pike, A., 72–73, 77
Pillard, R. C., 360
Pino, R. W., 379
Pintrich, P. R., 114
Piotrkowski, C. C., 430
Piper, B., 151
Piper, E. S., 403
Pirkle, J. L., 501

Pirog-Good, M., 376, 377
Pittenger, D. J., 406
Plas, J. M., 338
Pleck, J. H., 354, 368
Plomin, R., 72, 73, 75, 77, 78, 117, 471, 488, 509, 520, 521
Plopper, B. L., 273
Plotnick, R. D., 374
Plunkett, S. W., 407
Pobeni, J. L., 183
Poe-Yamagata, E., 12, 522
Polit, D. F., 165
Polite, C., 426
Pollack, S., 378
Pomerleau, O. F., 509
Pope, A. W., 195
Pope, H. G., 505
Porter, J. N., 403
Portes, P. R., 168, 171
Posner, J. K., 227
Poston, D. L., Jr., 165
Potvin, L., 88
Powell, D., 117
Power, C., 411
Powlishta, K. K., 333
Preboth, M., 499, 502
Presson, C. C., 499
Price, L. A., 483
Printz, B. L., 455, 456, 458
Pritchard, M. E., 85
Prjzinsky, T., 147
Provost, M. A., 456
Pulkkinen, L., 525
Puskar, K. R., 454
Putnam, R., 265

Quadrel, M., 132
Quatman, T., 154, 201, 309
Quinn, S. C., 362
Quint, E. H., 378
Quinton, D., 357

Raab, M., 367
Rabin, J., 378
Rainey, L. M., 431, 433
Raloff, J., 280
Ramey, S. L., 162
Ramsbey, T. W., 353n, 354
Randall, J., 466
Rangarajan, A., 373
Rankin, J. H., 522
Rapoport, J. L., 490
Rapping, E., 285
Rapson, R. L., 348
Rasheed, S., 443
Rashotte, C. A., 484
Raskin, S., 313
Raths, L. E., 409
Rathunde, K., 150
Rathus, S. A., 57
Ratner, M., 2
Ravesloot, J., 209
Raviv, A., 404
Raviv, D., 485
Ray, O., 506
Ray, W. J., 48, 49
Read, D. A., 409
Read, M. H., 87
Read, S. J., 350
Rea-Holloway, M., 343
Reardon, 425
Reardon, R. C., 433, 434
Redditt, C. A., 275
Reddy, D. M., 368
Reed, B. D., 406

Reef, M. H., 183
Rees, D. I., 241
Reese-Weber, M., 157
Reeves, J. L., 274
Reggio, P., 504
Rehman, S. N., 278
Reid, J. B., 195
Reid, J. R., 511
Reid, M., 162
Reiff, H. B., 487
Reiff, M. I., 356, 526
Reilly, S. S., 278
Reinemer, M., 419
Reis, E. M., 118
Reisine, T., 506
Reisman, J. R., 185
Reiss, D., 73
Reiter, E. L., 330
Reiter, E. O., 62, 63, 65, 70
Remez, L., 355
Rendleman, R., 468, 472
Renk, K., 138
Rennison, C. M., 378
Repinski, J., 181, 187
Rest, J., 396
Retschitzki, J., 101
Rey, J., 516
Reyes, O., 220
Reynolds, J. R., 274, 277, 279
Reynolds, W. M., 464
Rhoads, D. S., 85
Rice, M. L., 360
Rich, M., 277
Richards, C. L., 364
Richards, M., 71, 200
Richards, M. H., 85
Richardson, 403
Richardson, J. L., 514
Richardson, R. A., 158
Richardson, S., 168, 171
Richins, M., 291
Rickert, V. I., 262
Rieble-Aubourg, S., 445
Rierdan, J., 63, 64, 81
Rigby, K., 197
Riggs, D. S., 207
Riley, R. W., 222
Rindfuss, R., 354
Ritchie, K. L., 522
Ritter, P. L., 226
Rivadeneyra, R., 259, 283
Roberts, C. R., 468
Roberts, D. F., 262, 274
Roberts, R. E., 468, 472
Roberts, R. J., Jr., 488
Robins, R. W., 307
Robinson, A. B., 392
Robinson, B. E., 361, 362
Robinson, D., 433
Robinson, L. A., 499, 514
Robinson, L. C., 512
Robinson, N., 302, 306n
Roche, J. P., 353, 354
Rocheleau, B., 266
Rockwell, S. C., 283
Rodger, W., 224
Rodin, J., 85
Rodkin, P. C., 194
Rodriguez, C., 366
Roehlkepartain, E. C., 151, 401
Roffman, R. A., 506
Rogers, A. G., 330
Rogers, C., 303
Rogers, K. B., 241
Rogers, R. C., 267

Rogosch, F., 183
Rohner, R., 148, 156
Rojewski, J. W., 436, 485
Rolfes, S. R., 84
Roll, S., 391
Rollins, B., 510
Romero-Garcia, I., 334
Romig, C., 324, 331
Romney, D. M., 332
Rompa, D., 372
Ronfeldt, H. M., 206, 207
Roodin, P. A., 101
Rook, K. S., 161
Ropp, K. L., 88
Rosales, I., 304
Roscigno, V. J., 241
Roscoe, B., 132, 345
Rose, L. C., 222
Rose, S., 202n, 203
Rose, V. L., 379
Rosenbaum, J. E., 443, 444, 445, 447
Rosenberg, B. G., 165, 166
Rosenberg, F., 307
Rosenberg, M., 307
Rosenblum, G. D., 86
Rosenthal, R., 240
Rosenthal, S. L., 371
Rosnow, R. L., 57
Ross, H., 333
Ross, J. L., 307
Roth, D. L., 89
Roth, W. F., 224
Rothenberg, D., 52
Rotheram-Borus, M. J., 321, 355
Rothlisberg, B. A., 146
Rothstein, L. E., 118
Rounds, J., 425, 426
Rounds, K. A., 362
Rourke, B. P., 484
Rowe, R., 430
Roye, C., 376
Rubin, A. M., 526
Rubin, K. H., 165
Rubin, L. R., 329, 334
Rubin, Z., 182
Ruble, D. N., 328, 329, 332, 333, 334
Rudin, M. R., 403
Rudolph, K. D., 472
Ruhm, C. J., 422
Ruittenbeck, H. M., 316
Rumberger, R. W., 246, 247
Russell, C., 8
Russell, R. C., 381
Rutter, M., 101, 140, 304, 458, 460, 471
Ryan, A. M., 186
Ryan, C. W., 424, 440
Ryan, K., 409, 411, 412, 413
Ryan, R. M., 139
Rybash, J. M., 101
Rycek, R. F., 133
Ryu, S., 421

Sacco, W. P., 470
Sadker, D., 228
Sadker, M., 228
Safyer, A. W., 421
Sager, D. W., 407
Salem, S. S., 277
Salmivalli, C., 311, 313
Salmon, G., 198
Salovey, P., 121, 123
Salpeter, J., 242
Samios, M., 206
Sammons, W. A. H., 171

Sanchez, H. G., 474
Sanchez-Huckles, J., 18
Sanchez-Jankowski, M. S., 524
Sanders, C. E., 265
Sanders, S. G., 376
Sanderson, C. A., 181, 203
Sandler, H. M., 238
Sandler, I. N., 170
Sands, R., 87
Sandvik, E., 70
Sansone, C., 430
Sante, L., 524
Santelli, J. S., 373
Sarafica, F. C., 438
Sargiani, P. A., 187
Sartor, C. E., 339
Satterfield, J. H., 489
Saudino, K. J., 72, 73, 75, 77, 78
Savage, L. B., 124
Savage, M. P., 88
Savickas, M. L., 423
Savin-Williams, R. C., 82, 180, 183, 184, 200, 208, 211, 307, 360, 362
Scales, W., 487
Scanlan, A., 257
Scarr, S., 74, 75, 118
Schaal, B., 70
Schacht, A., 403
Schacht, C., 370
Schaeffer, R. T., 2
Schaffer, H. R., 146
Schander, P. R., 379
Schatschneider, C. W., 112
Scheel, K. R., 276
Scheidt, P., 197, 198
Schel, M. J., 431
Schell, A., 489
Scherman, A., 164
Schiedel, D. G., 322, 323
Schiefele, U., 234
Schiller, K. S., 221
Schilmoeller, G. L., 374
Schimel, J., 258, 311
Schlegel, A., 155, 455
Schmidt, C. R., 333
Schmidt, G., 351
Schmidt, J., 278
Schmidt, P., 228
Schneider, W., 111
Schnellmann, J., 330
Schofield, J. W., 186
Schonert-Reichl, K. A., 138
Schooler, J., 150–151
Schouten, F., 219
Schrauben, B., 114
Schuckit, M. A., 510
Schulenberg, J., 400, 419, 420, 422
Schultz, J. B., 322
Schunk, D., 111
Schunk, D. H., 113
Schuster, M. A., 365
Schutte, N. S., 269
Schwartz, J., 8
Schwartz, J. C., 347
Schwartz, R. H., 379
Schwarz, J. C., 147
Scott, C. G., 297
Scott, D., 257, 269, 270, 271
Scott, L. B., 88
Scribner, S., 105
Scullard, M. G., 426
Scully, S., 87
Sebald, H., 211
Segal, B. M., 509
Segal, S., 173

Seidman, E., 217, 219, 220, 221, 307
Seidman, L. J., 488
Seidman, S., 277, 278
Seifert, S. A., 379
Seiffge-Krenke, L., 205
Seitz, V., 163
Seligman, M. E. P., 23, 469, 470
Sellers, D. E., 365, 368
Sellers, R., 402
Selman, R., 130–132, 185, 188
Seltzer, V., 378
Senna, J., 517, 522
Sepielli, P., 8
Serafica, F. C., 417, 439
Serbin, L. A., 333
Serniclaes, W., 484
Sev'er, A., 381
Shafer, G., 243
Shaffer, S. D., 488
Shanahan, M. J., 420, 421
Shanker, A., 241, 251
Shantz, C. U., 129
Shapiro, T., 317
Sharabany, R., 184, 200
Sharma, A. R., 151
Sharp, D., 12
Shaughnessey, M. F., 14
Shaver, J. P., 389
Shaver, P. R., 141, 347, 349, 350, 351
Shaw, M. E., 84
Shaw, S. F., 487
Shedler, J., 505, 510
Shek, D. T. L., 138
Sheley, J. F., 524
Shendler, J., 508
Sheperd, D., 12
Shepherdson, N., 287
Shepperd, J. A., 465
Sher, K. J., 508
Sheras, P. L., 475
Sherman, B. L., 277
Sherman, M. F., 344
Sherman, N. C., 344
Shermis, M. D., 455
Shestowsky, B., 88
Shew, M. L., 373
Shields, C. M., 242
Shirk, S. R., 308
Shively, J. M., 124
Shkodriani, G. M., 329
Shoffner, D., 455
Shorr, S. I., 185
Short, E. J., 112
Short, J. L., 169
Shriner, J. G., 482
Shulman, S., 184, 185, 205
Shure, G., 518
Shure, M., 197
Shurm, W., 189, 190
Shweder, R. A., 324, 395
Sickmund, M., 12, 522
Sidney, S., 506
Siegel, J., 14
Siegel, J., 522
Siegel, L. J., 517
Siegel, M., 501
Siegelman, J., 403
Signorella, M. L., 329
Signorielli, N., 285, 441
Silbereisen, R. K., 356, 472
Silberg, J., 473
Silitsky, D., 171
Silverberg, S. B., 142, 208, 211
Silverman, R., 485
Silvern, S. B., 269

Simmons, R. G., 81, 217, 303, 307, 308, 309
Simmons, R. L., 183
Simon, S. B., 409
Simonelli, C. J., 206
Simons, R. F., 517, 518n
Simons-Morton, B., 197, 198
Simpson, D. D., 206
Simpson, E. E., 506
Simpson, L., 258
Sinclair, R., 184
Singer, D., 373–374
Singer, M. I., 522
Singer, S. J., 274, 275
Singh, K., 419, 421
Singh, S., 351, 354, 373
Singleton, N., 85
Skeels, H. M., 117
Skeen, P., 361
Skinner, B. F., 36
Skinner, M. E., 486
Skinner, M. L., 168
Skorikov, V. B., 419, 420, 423
Skovholt, T. M., 433
Slaby, R., 527
Slaby, R. G., 521
Slaughter, J., 465
Slavin, R. E., 106, 226, 242
Sleeman, E., 85
Slocum, T. A., 484
Slonim, M. B., 19
Small, S. A., 82
Smart, L., 313
Smetana, J. G., 138, 153, 203
Smith, A. E., 241
Smith, B. L., 85, 89
Smith, C., 453, 459, 517, 524
Smith, C. P., 390
Smith, D. M., 198
Smith, J. D., 227
Smith, M. A., 161, 163
Smith, P. K., 18, 162
Smith, P. L., 439
Smith, R. S., 458, 459
Smith, S., 485
Smith, S. S., 373
Smith, T. E., 422
Smith, T. E. C., 216
Smithmyer, C. M., 517, 518n
Smollar, J., 139, 158, 181, 184, 187, 188
Smoot, D. L., 195, 523
Smyer, M. A., 169
Snary, J., 404
Snidman, N., 75
Snizek, W. E., 430
Snyder, H. N., 522
Sobal, J., 87
Sobol, S. Z., 509
Sohn, E., 385
Sollie, D. L., 187
Solomon, J. C., 163
Son, L. K., 112
Sonenstein, F. L., 354, 358, 368
Sonis, W., 69
Sorel, E., 402
Sorenson, E., 172
Sorenson, S. B., 205, 206
Spaide, D., 412
Spearman, C., 119–120
Speece, D. L., 107
Spence, J. H., 328
Spencer, M. B., 81, 335, 336, 337
Spergel, I. A., 525
Spigner, C., 353

Spilka, B., 100, 402, 403
Spivack, M., 518
Spohrer, J. C., 230
Sprafkin, J., 259, 283
Springer, T., 426
Sproull, L., 264
Spruijt, E., 168, 172, 173, 175
Spruill, K. L., 487
Sputa, C. L., 147, 152, 158
Srebnik, D., 344
Sroufe, L. A., 141
Stack, S., 274, 276
Stangor, C., 327
Stanley, J., 429
Stanley-Hagan, M. M., 169, 172, 173
Stapleton, K. R., 277
Stapley, J., 70
Stapp, J., 328
Stark, E., 430
Stassen, H. H., 474
Stattin, H., 147
Staudinger, U. M., 32, 103
Steele, C. M., 119
Steele, J., 430
Steele, L., 421
Stein, J., 297
Stein, J. A., 510
Stein, Z. A., 372
Steinbach, S., 277
Steinberg, L., 79, 86, 142, 186, 208, 211, 226, 229, 421, 477
Steinberg, L. D., 419, 420, 422, 423
Steingard, R. J., 474
Stephens, J. A., 231
Stephens, R. S., 506
Stephenson, A. L., 512
Sterk, H. M., 290
Stern, W., 115
Sternberg, R. J., 112, 121, 123, 126, 157, 346, 347
Stets, J., 206
Stevens, L. M., 475
Stevenson, H. W., 223, 224, 234, 409
Stevens-Simon, C., 373–374
Stewart, B. L., 242
Stewart, J. C., 509
Stice, E., 478, 511, 512
Stiles, D. A., 329, 330
Stimpson, D., 391
Stockard, J., 207, 430
Stocker, C., 302, 306n
Stokes, G., 355, 359
Stokley, V., 242
Stoller, C. L., 6
Stone, C. A., 485
Stone, J. R., 420, 422
Stone, W. L., 484
Stoneman, B., 257
Stouhamer-Loeber, M., 211, 519
Strachen, A., 303
Strasburger, V. C., 277, 280, 282
Street, S., 328
Strein, W., 315
Strey, J., 162
Strimple, R. E., 322
Strong, B., 360, 362
Strong, W., 389
Strouse, 284
Struckman-Johnson, C., 378
Struckman-Johnson, D., 378
Stryker, J., 354, 365, 368
Stumpf, H., 429
Stunkard, A. J., 73

Sturdivant, L., 353
Subrahmanyam, K., 260, 262, 266
Sugland, B. W., 373
Sui-Chu, E. H., 238
Sullivan, H. S., 181–182, 349
Summers, P., 170
Summers, T., 89
Sun, D., 47, 500
Sun, R., 358
Sund, A. M., 141
Super, C. M., 423
Super, D. E., 423–424
Surbey, M., 79
Susman, E. J., 69, 70, 79
Sussman, S., 505, 506
Svrakic, N. M., 509
Swain, C., 368
Swain, R. C., 512
Swaney, 425
Swanger, A., 314
Swann, W., 303
Swanson, H. L., 484, 490
Sweet, J., 138
Synder, E., 360
Synder, H. N., 12
Synovitz, L. B., 507, 508
Szalavitz, M., 512
Szapocznik, J., 156

Taber, S., 4
Taipale, V., 81
Tam, T., 502
Tan, S. L., 270
Tang, M., 439
Tang, S., 204
Tanner, J. M., 61, 62, 63n, 78, 79
Tapscott, D., 225, 260, 261
Tarter, R. E., 511
Tarver, S., 337
Tarver-Behring, S., 488
Taska, L. S., 315
Taylor, E., 489
Taylor, H. F., 2
Taylor, R. W., 12
Taylor, S. E., 311
Taylor, W., 89
Teare, J. F., 138
Teasdale, J. D., 470
Tebbi, C. K., 481
Tedeschi, J. T., 500
Teicher, M. H., 66
Tein, J. Y., 170
Tellegen, A., 520
Temple, L., 79, 502
Terracciano, A., 328
Thiel, K., 160
Thomas, A., 75, 76
Thomas, A. M., 170
Thomas, D. L., 403
Thomas, K., 2
Thomas, P., 519
Thomas, S. B., 482, 486, 487
Thomas, S. P., 455
Thompson, C. J., 389, 390
Thompson, D. N., 131
Thompson, R. A., 141
Thompson, S. A., 491
Thomsen, S. R., 291
Thomson, E., 172
Thornberry, T. P., 525
Thornburg, H. D., 217
Thorne, A., 304, 310
Thornton, A., 201, 345, 355
Thorpe, M. F., 406
Thun, M. J., 498

Thurstone, L., 120
Tiggemann, M., 280, 449
Titman, P., 85
Toby, J., 246
Toch, T., 223, 242
Tokar, D. M., 429, 435
Tolan, P. H., 519
Toledo-Dreves, V., 377
Tolson, J. M., 187
Tom, D. Y. H., 240
Tomasello, M., 409
Tomlin, A. M., 162
Took, K. J., 274, 275
Torabi, M. R., 502
Torgeson, J. K., 484
Toro, P. A., 484
Toth, S. L., 58
Toups, M. L., 365
Towles, D., 284
Townsend, M. H., 361
Tracey, T. J., 438
Trad, P. V., 374
Travis, R., 165
Tremblay, R. E., 70
Trevethan, T., 390
Trevino, L. K., 405
Triandis, H., 324, 325
Trickett, E. J., 221
Troiden, R. R., 362
Trueba, H. T., 18
Tryon, W. W., 57
Tseng, V., 153
Tubman, J. G., 139, 152, 356
Tucker, C. M., 227
Tuffin, K., 430
Turiel, E., 389, 391, 392, 394
Tur-Kaspa, H., 484
Turner, P. J., 328–329
Turner, R. A., 351
Turner, S. L., 87
Turner, T. M., 194
Turow, J., 266
Twenge, J. M., 310

Udry, J. R., 210, 343
Uhal, D., 224
Unger, D. C., 375
Upchurch, R. L., 224
Urberg, K. A., 179, 185, 186, 187, 189
Urdan, T. C., 234
Ursano, R. J., 304

Vachon, R., 98
Valde, G. A., 321, 326
Valdivieso, R., 246
Vallacher, R. R., 302
Vallerand, R. J., 248
Valois, R. F., 421
Vandell, D. L., 161, 227
Van den Broeck, W., 483
Vander Ven, T. M., 166
Vandiver, M., 498
van Fossen, P. J., 124
van Gulden, H., 150, 151
van Kammen, W. B., 529
Van Schie, G. M., 270, 271, 272
van Winkle, B., 524
Varley, C. K., 468, 473
Varma, A., 289
Vasquez-Nuttall, E., 334
Vaughn, C., 46
Vaughn, S., 484, 485
Vazsonyi, A. T., 522
Veneziano, R. A., 148, 158

Venturelli, P. J., 503
Vergari, S., 242
Verma, S., 52
Vernberg, E. M., 182
Viadero, D., 226, 229
Viera, C., 89
Vigil, J. D., 524, 525
Villani, S., 255, 256, 259
Villeneuve, M., 276
Viney, W., 32
Vink, T., 477
Visher, E. B., 174
Visher, J. S., 174
Vitz, P. C., 392
Vivian, D., 206
Voeller, B., 362
Vogt, R. A., 85
Volling, B. L., 162
Vondracek, F. W., 419, 420, 423
Vroegh, K. S., 151
Vuchinich, S., 169
Vygotsky, L., 95, 103–105, 107, 109, 111, 129, 130

Wadden, T. A., 85
Wade, N. A., 371
Wagner, R. K., 484
Wagner, T., 61, 409, 411, 412
Wainryb, C., 392
Waite, B. M., 279
Walden, E. L., 491
Waldman, A., 274
Waldner-Haugrud, L. K., 361, 362
Walker, C., 288
Walker, J. H., 216
Walker, J. S., 400
Walker, L. J., 390, 394, 409
Walker, R. R., 18
Walkup, J. T., 468, 472
Wallace-Broscious, A., 417, 423
Wallerstein, J. S., 167, 168, 169
Wallis, J. R., 221
Walls, R. T., 423
Walsh, W. B., 116, 426
Walsh, Y., 403
Walters, G., 521
Walters, G. D., 267
Walters, K., 248
Walters, L. H., 361
Walz, C., 524
Wan, C., 165
Wan, K. C., 325
Wang, M. Q., 87
Wanner, R. A., 168
Ward, I. M., 259, 283, 284n
Ward, R. H., 375
Ward, S. L., 389, 391, 392, 393, 394
Ware, N., 431
Wark, G. R., 390
Warren, M. P., 69, 79
Wass, H., 275
Wasserman, G. A., 18
Waterman, A. S., 32, 33, 317, 322, 323
Waterman, C. K., 322
Waters, E., 140
Waters, E. S., 140
Watkins, B. A., 282, 283
Watson, C. M., 309
Watt, H. M. G., 217
Waugh, R. F., 396
Weaver, A. B., 379
Weaver, J. B., 283
Webb, P. M., 455
Weber, M. M., 291

Webster, R. E., 487
Wechsler, D., 116, 119
Weed, S., 346
Wehner, E. A., 345, 351
Weinberg, M., 360–361
Weinberger, J., 407
Weiner, B., 233, 234
Weinfield, N. S., 141
Weinfurt, K. P., 179
Weinraub, M., 168, 171
Weinrich, J. D., 360
Weinstein, L., 271
Weinstein, R. S., 240
Weisfeld, G., 101
Weiss, B., 146
Weiss, D., 489
Weiss, D. S., 274, 275
Weiss, G., 489, 491
Weissberg, R. P., 374
Weissman, H., 290, 291
Weissman, J., 244
Weissman, M. M., 467
Weithorn, L. A., 127
Weitzman, L. M., 428, 431
Wellner, A. S., 22
Wells, A., 273
Wells, D., 426
Wells, L. E., 522
Welsh-Ross, M. K., 333
Welte, J. W., 512
Wenar, C., 477, 478, 479
Werner, E. E., 458, 459
Werner-Wilson, R. J., 355
West, P., 223
West, S. G., 170, 372
Westbay, L., 346
Westefeld, J. S., 276
Wester, K., 522
Wester, S. R., 275, 276
Whalen, H., 490
Whitbeck, L. B., 356
Whitbourne, J., 244
White, B. H., 379

White, D. R., 88
White, H. R., 529
White, J. L., 195
White, J. W., 206
White, L. A., 277
White, M. J., 430
White, S. D., 356
White, S. H., 29
Whiteley, B. E., Jr., 347
Whiteman, M., 206
Whitesell, N. R., 303
Whiting, B. B., 2, 147
Whiting, J., 2
Whiting, W. M., 2
Whitley, B. E., Jr., 405
Whitman, F. L., 360
Whitney, E. N., 84
Whorton, J. E., 106
Wichstrom, L., 141
Wicks-Nelson, R., 466, 477, 483, 488
Wieczorek, W. F., 512
Wiegman, O., 270, 271, 272
Wicmann, C. M., 374
Wierson, M., 166, 171
Wiest, D. J., 471
Wigfield, A., 227, 234, 307, 308
Wilcox, S., 210
Will, J. C., 88
Willemsen, T. M., 290, 291, 292
Willets, F. K., 152
Williams, D., 401
Williams, H. B., 19
Williams, J. D., 238
Williams, K. D., 106
Williams, L. L., 522
Williams, R. A., 279
Williams, S., 305
Williamson, G., 455
Williamson, L., 337
Williamson, P. A., 269
Willits, F. K., 257
Wilson, D. B., 514
Wilson, G. T., 479

Wilson, M. D., 84
Wilson, R., 440
Wilson, R. S., 117
Wilson, S. M., 353
Windle, M., 356, 472, 511
Windle, R. C., 356
Winebrenner, S., 242
Winfield, A. H., 449
Wingert, P., 21
Winkel, M., 270
Winstanley, M. R., 376
Winstead, B. A., 85
Wintre, M., 211
Wirt, J. G., 444, 445
Wisecarver, S. J., 401
Wohlwill, J. F., 116
Wolfson, A. R., 89, 90
Wong, E. H., 471
Wong, F. Y., 282
Wood, R., 507, 508
Wood, W., 282
Woodard, E. H., 255, 256n, 262, 269, 279, 281
Woodside, D. B., 478
Woodyard, C., 536
Wright, J. D., 419, 524
Wright, K., 146
Wright, K. E., 522, 525
Wright, K. N., 522, 525
Wright, L. S., 401
Wright, S. A., 403
Wroblewski, R., 441
Wu, S., 347
Wulff, D. M., 401
Wurthnow, R., 400
Wygant, S. A., 392
Wyman, P. A., 458
Wynne, E., 413

Yamaguchi, K., 502
Yamamoto, T., 217
Yando, T., 268
Yang, B., 165, 436

Yang, D. J., 267
Yarnold, B. M., 88
Yau, J., 156
Yemini, T., 474
Yesalis, C. E., 87
Yew, W., 156
Yoshida, T., 325
Yoshikawa, H., 521
Yost, P. R., 401
Young, K. S., 267
Young, R. D., 300
Youniss, J., 139, 144, 158, 181, 184, 187, 188, 339

Zabin, L. S., 356, 373, 377
Zabriski, A. L., 523
Zacijek-Farber, M. L., 46
Zametkin, A. J., 474, 475
Zaragoza, N., 484
Zarco, E. P., 465
Zehms, D., 43
Zeifman, D., 205
Zern, D. S., 412
Zhang, L., 512
Zheng, Y. P., 456
Zigler, E. F., 304
Zigmond, N., 485
Zilbert, E. E., 444
Zillmann, D., 277
Zimbardo, P. G., 464, 465
Zimmerman, B. J., 38, 113, 114
Zito, M., 473
Zmiles, H., 247
Zollo, P., 273
Zucker, K. J., 361
Zuckerman, M., 283
Zuckerman, M. J., 224, 235
Zunker, 425n
Zuo, J., 204
Zusman, M. E., 203, 353

Subject Index

Ability-attainment gap, 427
Abortion, 366–367
Abstractions, 100, 302
Abstract symbolic thought, 99–100
Academic achievement
  attention-deficit/hyperactivity disorder and, 488–490
  disengagement and, 228–229
  eating habits and, 85
  education level of parents and, 117–118, 225
  employment and, 420–421
  fatigue and, 90–91
  gender and, 227–228
  in high school, 221, 223–229
  intelligence tests and, 115
  learner-centered education and, 230–231
  learning disabilities and, 484–486
  in middle school, 217–219
  motivation and, 231–237
  parental role and, 229, 237–239
  school choice and, 242–243
  self-esteem and, 305, 459
  standardized tests to measure, 251
  teacher expectations and, 239–241
  tracking and, 241–242
  working mothers and, 166
Accidents, motor vehicle, 502
Accommodation, 96
Achievement tests
  predictive power of, 115
  use of, 251
Acquaintance rape, 378, 379
Acquired immune deficiency syndrome (AIDS), 370–371
Active effects, 74
Active parental consent, 55
Activism, 405
Acute illness, 480
Adaptation, 95, 96
Addiction
  explanation of, 495
  to Internet, 266–267
  to video games, 272
Adolescence
  change in views of, 7–8
  contextual view of, 14–16
  discontinuous vs. continuous development during, 28
  emphasis on balanced and positive view of, 23–24
  explanation of, 1, 6
  historical background of research on, 7
  information processing in, 110–112
  myths regarding, 6–7, 9, 211–213

theoretical approaches to, 27–29 (*See also* Theories; *specific theories*)
as time of choices, firsts, and transitions, 13–14
Adolescence: Its Psychology and Its Relations to Physiology, Anthropology, Sociology, Sex, Crime, Religion, and Education (Hall), 29
Adolescent culture
  value of academic achievement and, 228–229
  views of, 211–213
Adolescent mothers
  extended families of, 377
  issues facing, 375–376
  overview of, 374–375
Adolescent-parent relationship. *See also* Families; Parental influence; Parents
  adolescent dating and, 203–205
  changing nature of, 138–139
  development of, 141–143
  divorce and, 168–169
  emotional autonomy and, 139–141
  explanation of, 137–138
  peer influence and, 210–211
  in perspective, 175
  power and cohesiveness and, 143–145
Adolescent pregnancy
  concern about, 21
  poverty and, 373, 376
  programs to prevent, 377–378
  risk for, 373–374
  school programs to avoid dropping out and, 248
  statistics regarding, 372–373
Adolescents
  adult view of, 8–10
  changes in experience of, 19–23
  with chronic illness, 480–481
  as consumers, 257–258
  demographic information for, 21–22
  with disabilities, 482–487
  group membership influences on, 16–19 (*See also* Peer groups; Peer pressure)
  with jobs, 419–423
  legal status of, 10–12
  popular, 183, 192–194, 199
  psychologists' view of, 11, 13
  as research participants, 54–56
  rites of passage for, 1–3
  road to autonomy for, 3–4
  socialization of, 4–6
  stereotypes of, 6–7, 9 (*See also* Stereotypes)
  stress-resilient, 457–460

unpopular, 194–197
views of self held by, 8
Adopted children, 150–151
Adoption studies
  of aggression, 521
  explanation of, 73–74
Adrenal hormones, 61, 68
Adult Attachment Interview, 140–141
Adults. *See also* Fathers; Mothers; Parents
  with learning disabilities, 487
  view of adolescents by, 8–10
Advertising
  to adolescents, 259
  cigarette, 500, 501, 514, 515
  magazine, 290–291
  television, 287–288
African Americans. *See also* Minority groups
  academic achievement among, 223, 224
  adolescent pregnancy and motherhood among, 372–373, 375
  body image and, 85
  career choice among, 435–438, 440
  cigarette smoking and, 499
  contraceptive use and, 359
  demographic information for, 21
  dropout trends among, 246, 247
  family conflict and, 153, 154
  family structure and environment and, 18
  gang membership among, 524
  as grandparents, 163
  growth trends in, 79
  identity formation and, 336–338
  intelligence tests and, 118, 119
  parenting styles and, 148
  peer influences on, 226
  self-esteem and, 310, 311
  sexual activity and, 354
  in single-parent families, 171
  stress among, 456
  subculture identity influences for, 17
  suicide among, 474
  transition to college and, 244
Agape, 349
Aggression. *See also* Crime; Violence
  attention-deficit/hyperactivity disorder and, 488
  biological factors for, 520–521
  bullying as, 197–198
  cognitive factors and, 521
  cultivation theory and, 259
  early vs. late, 519
  gangs and, 524–525
  gender and, 521–523, 527–529

Aggression (*continued*)
   peer pressure and, 523
   proactive, 517, 518
   reactive, 517–518
   relational, 197
   in romantic relationships, 205–207
   self-esteem and, 311–312
   as stable characteristic, 519–520
   television violence and, 282–283
   testosterone and, 70–71, 334, 521
   unpopularity and, 194–195
   video games and, 269–271
Alcoholism, 509–510
Alcohol use. *See also* Drug use/abuse
   genetics and, 509–510
   overview of, 501–502
   by parents, 511
Altruistic behavior, 402–403. *See also*
   Prosocial behavior
American Association of University
   Women, 227, 228
American Council on Education, 381
American Indians. *See* Native Americans
American Psychiatric Association, 463,
   473
American Psychological Association, 54,
   56, 57
Americans with Disabilities Act (ADA),
   483
Amotivational syndrome, 505
Amphetamine psychosis, 507
Amygdala, 66
Anabolic steroids, 87–88, 508
Anal stage, 31
Androgyny, 328
Anonymity, 217
Anorexia nervosa
   explanation of, 87, 477–478
   treatment options for, 478–480
Antidepressants, 473–474, 479
Anti-Gang and Youth Violence Act of
   1996, 12
Anxiety
   eating disorders and, 479
   explanation of, 464
   self-esteem and, 305
   shyness and, 464–465
   social phobia and, 465–466
   in students with learning disabilities,
   485
Anxious/ambivalent attachment, 140
Anxious attachment, 140
Anxious/avoidant attachment, 140
Anxious disorganized/disoriented
   attachment, 140
Apprenticeship, 445–446
Asceticism, 31
Asian Americans. *See also* Minority
   groups
   academic achievement among,
   239–224
   career choice and, 438–439
   demographic information for, 21
   diversity of background of, 19

family conflict and, 155–157
family structure and environment and,
   19
gang membership among, 524
identity formation and, 336
intelligence tests and, 118
obedience and, 153
parenting style and, 147–148, 156, 239
subculture identity influences for, 17
Assimilation
   cognitive development and, 96
   explanation of, 96
   minority groups and, 337–338
Athletes
   puberty and, 79
   steroid use among, 87–88
Attachment, 140–141
Attachment theory
   emotional autonomy and, 139–141
   love and, 349–351
Attention, 110–111
Attention-deficit/hyperactivity disorder
   (ADHD)
   brain development and, 66
   explanation of, 488
   life with, 489
   longitudinal studies on, 44
   symptoms of, 488
   treatment of, 490–491
Attention span, 110, 111
Attributions
   depression and, 469–470
   explanation of, 233–234
Attrition, 44
Authoritarian parenting
   culture and, 147
   effects of, 148, 210, 522
   explanation of, 145, 146
   in stepfamilies, 174
Authoritative parenting
   academic achievement and, 238
   advantages of, 146–147, 210
   explanation of, 146
   in stepfamilies, 173
Automaticity, 112
Autonomy
   in adolescence, 3–4
   behavioral, 3
   conflict and, 138
   vs. doubt, 33
   emotional, 3, 139–141
   in middle school, 218, 232
   parenting style and, 210
   socialization practices and, 5
Average adolescents, 192
Avoidance, conflict, 205

Bar/bat mitzvahs, 2
Behavior. *See also* Risky behavior
   genetic influences on, 71–72, 74–78
   hormones and, 69–71
   moral, 390, 393
   prosocial, 271, 304–305, 402–406 (*See
      also* Prosocial behavior)

relationship between health and, 84
religious beliefs and, 401
showing false, 302–303
stress and, 455
Behavioral approach
   depression and, 468–469
   explanation of, 36–37
   strengths and weaknesses of, 41
Behavioral autonomy, 3
Behavior theory, 393
Bellotti v. Baird, 12
Binge drinking, 502. *See also* Alcohol use
Biological factors. *See also* Physical devel-
      opment; Puberty
   for aggression, 520–521
   explanation of, 67–68
   gender roles and, 334–335
   hormones and behavior and, 69–71,
   334
   puberty and, 68
Biological parents, 150, 151. *See also* Parents
Bisexuals, 360. *See also* Homosexuality
Board of Education v. Megens, 128
Body image
   eating disorders and, 477, 478
   eating habits and, 86–88
   explanation of, 85–86
   self-esteem and, 303, 310
Brain
   aggression and damage to, 520–521
   physical development of, 65–67
Breakfast, 84–85
Breaking Ranks (Carnegie Corporation),
   251
Breast development, 62, 64–65
Broad socialization
   effects of, 5–6
   explanation of, 4
   media influence and, 16
Bulimia
   explanation of, 87, 478
   treatment options for, 478–480
Bullying, 197–198

Cancer
   genital herpes and, 370
   genital warts and, 369
   marijuana and, 505
Career and technical education programs, 442, 444–445
Career choice. *See also* Employment
   factors involved in, 426–427
   females and, 426, 428–433
   for high school graduates, 442–448
   life-span, life-space approach to,
   423–424
   males and, 426, 433–435
   minority groups and, 435–442
   personality characteristics and,
   424–426
   in perspective, 449, 536
   for students who do not attend college, 442–448

Caregivers, 140
Case studies
  explanation of, 46–47
  strengths and weaknesses of, 53
Categorical approach, 463
Causal attribution, 233
Censorship, 278, 279
Cerebral cortex, 66
Character education, 411, 415
Charter schools, 242
Chat rooms, 263, 265
Cheating, 385
Child abuse, 206
Child Custody Protection Act, 367
Child-rearing strategies. *See also* Parenting style
  African American, 18
  Asian American, 19
  gender roles and, 332–333
  Latino, 19
  Native American, 19
  prosocial behavior and, 408
  in sociocentric cultures, 325
Children. *See also* Adolescents; Infants
  of adolescent mothers, 375
  adopted, 150–151
  attachment in, 140
  empathy in, 394–395
  meaning of friendship for, 184
  prosocial behavior in, 403–404
  raised by grandparents, 163–164
  rejected or neglected, 192–197
  in stepfamilies, 172–174
  stress in, 454, 460
China, 223, 395
Chlamydia, 368–369
Chronic illness, 480–481
Chronosystem, 42
Cigarette smoking. *See also* Drug use/abuse
  advertising and, 500, 501, 514, 515
  genetics and, 509
  image of, 500–501
  by parents, 511
  patterns of, 499–500
  perception of dangers of, 497–498
  programs to prevent, 514–515
  trends in, 498–499
Cliques
  explanation of, 182–183, 189
  membership in, 190
Club drugs, 507–508. *See also* Drug use/abuse
Cocaine. *See also* Drug use/abuse
  perception of dangers of, 497–498
  use of, 506
Cognitive appraisal, 453
Cognitive-behavioral therapy (CBT), 473, 480
Cognitive development. *See also* Intelligence
  gender roles and, 333–334
  information-processing approaches to, 35, 41, 109–115

intelligence and, 115–123 (*See also* Intelligence)
  in perspective, 133–135
  Piaget's developmental approach to, 34–35, 40, 96–103
  Vygotsky's sociocultural approach to, 103–107
Cognitive restructuring, 480
Cognitive skills. *See also* Intelligence; Social cognition
  creativity as, 125–126
  critical thinking as, 123–125
  decision making as, 126–129
  stress and, 459
Cohesiveness, 143–145
Cohort effect, 20, 22
Collectivist cultures, 324–325
Colleges/universities
  self-esteem and, 310
  students with disabilities attending, 482–483
  students with learning disabilities in, 485–486
  transition to, 243–244
Combinational logic, 99, 102
Commission on Skills in the American Workforce, 443
Commitment
  explanation of, 347
  identity and, 319–320
Communication. *See also* Conflict
  with friends, 187
  gender differences in, 158–159
  generation gap and, 151–152
  with parents, 149–150, 159, 187
  with peers, 149
Communities
  adolescents as part of, 15
  moral education in, 412–413
  violence in, 523–526
Companionate love, 347
Comparisons, psychological, 130
Competency, 128
Comprehensive Community Wide Gang Prevention, Intervention and Suppression program, 525
Compromise, 205
Computer use. *See also* Internet; Video games; World Wide Web
  adolescents and, 260–264
  dangers related to, 264–267
  in schools, 224–225
Concordance rate, 72
Concrete operations stage, 97
Condoms. *See* Contraceptives
Conduct disorder, 519
Confidentiality, 57–58
Confirmation ceremonies, 2
Conflict. *See also* Communication
  adaptive nature of, 157
  divorce and, 170, 172
  Freudian theory and, 29, 30, 32
  between friends, 187–188
  gender roles and, 324–325

management of, 157–158, 526
  with parents, 137–138, 141, 188, 203–204
  reasons for, 152–154
  in romantic relationships, 205–207
  between siblings, 160, 161
  in stepfamilies, 173
  in various cultures, 155–157
Conformity, 145–148, 173
Conjunctive faith, 399
Conservation, 97
Consumers, 257–258
Consummate love, 347
Contextual view of adolescence, 14–16
Continuous development, 28
Contraceptives
  availability in schools of, 364–365
  parental consent or parents' right know about distribution of, 367–368
Contraceptive use
  adolescent pregnancy and, 373
  inconsistency in, 359–360
  parental influence and, 360, 364
  statistics regarding, 358–359
  vulnerability as reason for, 372
Control function, 144–145
Controversial adolescents, 192
Conventional moral reasoning, 388
Convergent thinking, 125–126
Cooperative learning, 106
Coping with Depression Course, 473
Correlations, 48, 53
Crack. *See also* Drug use/abuse
  explanation of, 495
  use of, 506
Creativity, 125, 126
Crime. *See also* Aggression; Violence
  aggressive behavior and, 519
  bullies and, 198
  curfews and, 12
  gangs and, 524
  juvenile justice system and, 10
  trends in, 516, 517
Crisis, 318
Critical thinking
  in adolescents, 123–124
  explanation of, 123
  instruction in, 125
Criticism, 150
Cross-cultural research, 51–52
Cross-sectional designs
  explanation of, 43–45
  strengths and weaknesses of, 53
Crowds
  explanation of, 182–183, 190–191
  interaction in, 180
  membership in, 191
  movement between, 192
Cultivation theory
  explanation of, 258–259
  television viewing and, 283
Cults, 402–403
Cultural pluralism, 22

Culture
  academic achievement and, 223
  adolescent, 211–213, 228–229
  alcohol use and, 502
  Americanization of adolescents and,
    156–157
  body image and, 85–86
  career choice theory and, 426
  dating norms and, 204–205
  family conflict and, 153–157
  family structure and, 18
  gender roles and, 334
  individualistic, 324
  intelligence and, 118–119
  love and, 347–348
  morality and, 395–396
  parental involvement in schools and,
    238–239
  parenting style and, 147–149
  research and, 51–52
  rites of passage and, 2
  romantic relationships and, 205
  social interaction and, 103
  socialization and, 4–6
  values and attitudes and, 16
Culture wars, 279
Curfews, 11–12

Daily hassles, 456
Data collection. *See* Research methods
Date rape, 378, 379
Date rape drugs, 379
Dating. *See also* Romantic relationships
  explanation of, 200–201, 345–346
  functions of, 345
  interracial, 201, 203
  parental reaction to, 203–205
  process of, 201, 203
  roles in, 203
  scripts for hypothetical, 202
  violence in, 205–207
Deception, 55–57
Decision making
  competency in, 128
  developmental trends in, 127–129
  explanation of, 126–127
  role in family, 139
Deep processing, 235
Defense mechanisms, 30
Dehydroepiandrosterone (DHEA), 68
Dehydroepiandrosterone sulfate
    (DHEAS), 68
De-idealization, 32
Delinquency. *See also* Aggression; Crime;
    Violence
  parental supervision and, 522–523
  programs to prevent, 526–527
Demandingness
  drug use and, 510
  explanation of, 145
  parenting style and, 147–149
Dependence, Internet, 266–267
Dependent variables, 48–49

Depression
  Beck's theory of, 470–471
  biological factors related to, 471–472
  causes of, 468–472
  early maturation and, 82
  eating disorders and, 479
  explanation of, 466–467
  gender differences in, 71, 472–473
  heavy metal music and, 276
  hormones and, 69
  parental factors related to, 356, 471
  prevalence of, 467–468
  self-esteem and, 305
  suicide and, 474
  symptoms of, 467
  treatment for, 473–474
Desensitization, 259
De-tracking, 241–242
Developmental approaches
  explanation of, 33–34
  Piaget's theory, 95–103, 107, 108
  strengths and weaknesses of, 40
  Vygotsky's sociocultural theory,
    103–108
Developmental tasks, 34
Deviation IQ, 115
*Diagnostic and Statistical Manual of Mental
    Disorders*, 4th Edition Revised
    (DSM-IV-TR) (American Psychiatric
    Association), 463, 467, 495, 519
Dieting, 86–87
Differentiation, 299
Digital divide, 262
Dimensional approach, 463
Disabilities. *See also* Chronic illness
  explanation of, 463
  higher education for students with,
    482–483
  learning, 482–487 (*See also* Learning
    disabilities)
  legal protections for individuals with,
    483
  statistics for adolescents with, 482
Disclosure, 55–56
Discontinuous development, 28
Discrimination, 17, 336. *See also* Preju-
    dice; Stereotypes
Disease. *See* Illness
Disengagement
  academic achievement and, 228–229,
    250
  dropouts and, 247
Disorders, 463–464. *See also* Eating disor-
    ders; Internalizing disorders; *specific
    disorders*
Divergent thinking, 126
Divorce. *See also* Single-parent families;
    Stepfamilies
  adolescents and, 169–171
  changes brought by, 167–168
  effects of, 168–169
  trends in, 20–21, 164
Dizygotic twins, 72–73

Dopamine, 509
Driver's license, 2
Dropouts
  employment and, 420
  factors influencing, 246–248
  models to explain, 248
  overview of, 245–246
  programs to reach potential, 248–250
Drugs, 495
Drug use/abuse
  alcohol and, 501–502
  cigarette smoking and, 498–501
  club drugs and, 507–508
  cocaine and crack and, 506
  dangers of, 497–498
  explanation of, 495
  family relations and, 510–511
  gateway drug effect theory and,
    502–503
  heroin and, 506
  individual characteristics and, 508–510
  marijuana and, 504–506
  methamphetamine and, 506–507
  peer pressure and, 511–512, 523
  in perspective, 529–531
  programs to prevent, 512–516
  protective factors against, 512
  trends in, 496
  violence and, 506, 529–531
Dual system (Germany), 446
Dyslexia, 483–484
Dysthymic disorder, 467. *See also* Depres-
    sion

Early adolescence, 1
Early maturation
  in females, 81–82
  in males, 80–81
Eating disorders
  anorexia nervosa and, 87, 477–478
  bulimia and, 87, 478
  explanation of, 87, 479
  treatment options for, 478–480
  trends in, 476–477
Eating habits
  body image and, 86–88
  health and, 84–85
Eclecticism, 43
Ecological theory
  explanation of, 39, 42–43, 238
  strengths and weaknesses of, 41
Ecosystem, 39, 42
Ecstasy (MDMA), 507–508
Education. *See also* Academic achieve-
    ment
  character, 411, 415
  drug prevention, 512–515
  learner-centered, 230–231
  moral, 409–413
  Piaget's ideas applied to, 100–101
  sex, 364–381 (*See also* Sex education)
  sociocultural theory applied to,
    100–101

twentieth-century views of, 7, 8
vocational, 442, 444–445
Ego, 30, 31
Egocentrism, 131–133
Ego goals, 234–235
Ego ideal, 30, 394
Ego identity, 316
Ego undercontrol, 508
Ejaculation, 65
Elaborative rehearsal, 111
Elementary schools
  academic achievement in, 227
  study of teacher expectations in, 240
  transition from, 217
E-mail, 264, 265
Emotion
  brain development and expression of, 66
  hormones and, 69–71
  moodiness and, 70
  morality and, 394–395
Emotional autonomy
  attachment theory and, 139–141
  components of, 139
  explanation of, 3, 139
Emotional intelligence, 121–123
Emotion-focused coping, 462
Empathy
  explanation of, 386
  morality and, 394–395
  prosocial behavior and, 403–406
Employment. *See also* Career choice
  of adolescents, 419–423
  adolescents' view of, 417–418
  contemporary nature of, 418–419
  maternal, 166–167
  overview of, 417
  transition between school and, 442–443
  twentieth-century changes in views of, 7
Entertainment, 263, 265
Environmental influences
  in academic achievement, 237
  on intelligence, 117–118
  pubertal timing and, 79–80
  in siblings, 77–78
Equilibration, 34, 96
Eros, 348
Estrogen, 68, 69
Ethics. *See* Research ethics
Ethnic groups. *See* Minority groups; *specific groups*
Evocative effects, 74, 75
Exclusion, 331
Expectations, 154
Experimental studies
  explanation of, 48–49
  strengths and weaknesses of, 53
Exploration
  explanation of, 318
  identity and, 318–320
  minority groups and, 336

Externalizing disorders, 463–464, 519
External locus of control, 436
Extrinsic motivation, 232, 251

False behavior, 302–303
Families. *See also* Grandparents; Parental influence; Parents; Siblings
  aggression and, 522–523
  changes in twenty-first century, 20, 535–536
  cohesive, 407–408
  cohesiveness of, 143–145
  depression and interactions with, 471
  with divorced parents, 171
  drug use and, 510–512, 514
  multigenerational, 18
  single-child, 165–166
  single-parent, 20–21, 163, 164, 171–172, 175, 201, 345–346
  as source of stress, 455, 458, 461
  step-, 172–174
  time spent with, 179–180
Fantasy, 283–285
Fathers. *See also* Families; Mothers; Parents
  adolescent, 376–377
  attitudes toward maternal employment by, 167
  divorce and, 169
  interaction with, 158–159
  role of, 158
Fatigue
  effects of, 90–91
  hormones and, 69
Fatuous love, 347
Females. *See also* Gender; Gender roles
  academic achievement and, 227–228
  aggression and, 521, 523
  balancing work and family by, 431–433
  body image and, 85–86
  as bullies, 197
  career choice and, 428–433
  crime and, 517
  dating violence and, 206
  depression in, 71, 472–473
  early maturation in, 81–82
  eating disorders and, 477, 478
  eating habits and, 84–87
  friendship and, 187
  gender roles and voice of, 330–331
  growth spurt for, 61–63
  growth trends in, 79
  hormones in, 68
  identity formation and, 323–326
  interpersonal goals of, 429–431
  intimacy and, 322
  magazines for, 290–292
  in male-dominated professions, 429–430
  moral reasoning and, 391–392
  music and, 273
  occupational stereotypes and, 430
  parental recognition of autonomy for, 3, 4

prosocial behavior in, 405–406
puberty in, 62–65, 68, 78–79, 85 (See *also* Puberty)
rites of passage for, 2
self-esteem and, 309, 310
sexuality and, 352–355
shyness in, 465
stereotypes of, 275–278, 281
stereotypes of careers for, 430
stress and, 455–456
suicide and, 474
video games and, 269
Financial concerns
  divorce and, 169, 170
  parenting practices and, 238
First Amendment, 12
Firstborn children, 166
Follicle-stimulating hormone (FSH), 68
Forbidden fruit theory, 278
Formal operations stage
  abstract-symbolic thought in, 99–100
  combinational logic in, 99
  critique of, 101
  explanation of, 34–35, 97
  going beyond, 101–102
  hypothetical-deductive logic in, 98–99, 314
  sense of self and, 314–315
  separating real from possible in, 97–98
  thinking about thinking in, 100
Fourteenth Amendment, 12
Freudian theory, 30–32
Friendship. *See also* Peer groups
  benefits of, 183–184
  cliques and, 189–190
  communication, conflict and, 187–188
  conceptions of, 184–185
  cross-gender, 181 (*See also* Romantic relationships)
  formation of, 185–187
  gender and, 187
  peers and, 183
Frustration—self-esteem model, 248
Full inclusion, 482

Gang Resistance Education and Training (GREAT) Program, 525
Gangs, 524–525
Gateway drug effect theory, 502–503
Gays, 360. *See also* Homosexuality
Gender. *See also* Females; Males
  academic achievement and, 223, 227–228
  aggression and, 521–523, 527–529
  body image and, 85–86
  career choice and, 426–435
  crime and, 517
  dating roles and, 203
  depression and, 472–473
  eating disorders and, 477, 478
  eating habits and, 86–87
  emotions and, 71

Gender (*continued*)
 experiences and expectations and, 16–17
 friendship and, 187
 identity formation and, 323–326
 intimacy and, 322
 moral reasoning and, 390–392
 prosocial behavior and, 405–406
 religious beliefs and, 399
 self-esteem and, 309–310
 sexuality and, 352–355
 shyness and, 465
 stress and, 455–456
 suicide and, 474
 teacher interaction and, 227
 video games and, 268
Gender roles. *See also* Sex typing
 biological factors and, 334–335
 cognitive view of, 333–334
 conflict and, 324–325
 continuing evolution of, 535
 culture and, 334
 explanation of, 327
 learning theory approach to, 332–333
 role models and, 333
 sex typing and, 328–330
 stereotypes and, 327–330
 voice and, 330–331
Gender schema theory, 333
Generational forgetting, 513
Generation gap
 explanation of, 151–152, 213
 technology use and, 260–261
Genetics
 adoption studies and, 73–74
 aggression and, 521
 alcohol and, 509–510
 anorexia and, 477
 behavior and, 72, 74
 depression and, 471–472
 homosexuality and, 360, 361
 influence of, 67, 71–72
 intelligence and, 117
 misunderstandings about, 72
 siblings and, 76–78
 smoking and, 509
 temperament and, 75–76
 twin studies and, 72–73
Genital stage, 31
Genital warts, 369
Genotype/environment interaction model, 74
Germany, 445–448
Gesuii tribe of Kenya, 70
GHB, 507
Glamour, 290
Goal setting, 234–236
Gonadotropin-releasing hormone, 68
Gonadotropins, 68, 69
Gonads, 68
Gonorrhea, 369
Goodness-of-fit model, 76
Graduation rate, 227
Grandparents, 162–164. *See also* Families

Graphic organizers, 105, 106
Great Depression, 7
Group membership
 influences of, 16–18
 interpersonal relationships and, 180–181
Growth spurts, 61–62

Hazelwood v. Kuhlmeier, 128
Health. *See also* Illness
 body image and, 85–88
 cigarette smoking and, 498
 eating habits and, 86–88
 Internet use for information on, 263
 leisure activities and, 257
 music videos and, 280
 nutrition and, 84–85
 obesity and, 88
 physical activity and, 88–89
 rating adolescent, 83–84
 relationship between behavior and, 84
 sleep and, 89–91
 television advertising and, 287–288
Heavy metal music, 274–276, 279
Height, 78, 79
Heritability
 adoption studies and, 73–74
 explanation of, 72
 twins studies and, 72–73
Heroin, 506
Herpes simplex, 370
High school graduates, 443–444
High school graduation, 2–3
High schools
 academic achievement in, 221, 223–229
 changes in, 21
 dealing with problems in, 250–251
 evaluation of, 222–223
 involvement of students in, 221
 students with learning disabilities in, 485–486
 transition to, 220–221
Hispanics. *See* Latinos
HIV/AIDS, 370–371
Hobbies, 458
HomeNet, 260, 264
Homework, 266
Homosexuality
 dating and, 200
 disclosure of, 361–362
 myths about, 362–363
 origins of, 360–361
 statistics regarding, 360
 stereotypes of, 361
 tolerance toward, 363
Hormones
 behavior and, 69–71
 explanation of, 68
 sex typing and, 334
Hostile environment sexual harassment, 380
Human immunodeficiency virus (HIV), 370–371
Humanistic psychology, 23

Human papillomavirus (HPV), 369
Hypothalamus, 68
Hypothesis, 52
Hypothetical-deductive logic
 decision making and, 127
 explanation of, 98–99
 sense of self and, 314

Ice, 507
Id, 30
Identification, 394
Identity
 culture and, 324–325
 explanation of, 298, 316–318
 exploration period and, 318–319
 interpersonal vs. intrapersonal, 323
 psychosocial theory and, 32–33
 racial/ethnic, 17–18, 335–339
Identity achievement, 322–323
Identity crisis, 319
Identity diffusion, 321
Identity foreclosure, 320–321
Identity formation
 among minority groups, 17–18, 335–339
 commitment and exploration process of, 318–320
 explanation of, 317, 335
 four identity statuses approach to, 320–323
 gender and, 323–326
 in perspective, 339–340
 theories of, 318
Identity moratorium, 321
Identity status
 concerns about, 326–327
 identity achievement and, 322–323
 identity diffusion and, 321
 identity foreclosure and, 320–321
 identity moratorium and, 321
Illness. *See also* Health; *specific illnesses*
 acute, 480
 chronic, 480–481
 stress and, 455
Imaginary audience, 132, 133
Immanent justice, 396
Inclusion, 331
Incomplete disclosure, 55–56
Independent variables, 48
Individualistic cultures, 324, 325
Individualized Education Program (IEP), 482
Individuals with Disabilities Education Act (IDEA), 481, 482
Individuation, 32
Individuative-reflective faith, 399
Indulgent parenting. *See* Permissive parenting
Infants. *See also* Children
 of adolescent mothers, 375
 attachment in, 140
 empathy in, 394
Information processing
 attention and, 110, 111

automaticity and, 112
explanation of, 109–110, 114
memory and, 111–112
metacognition and, 112–113
self-regulation and, 113–115
speed of, 110–111
strategy use and, 112
Information-processing theory
explanation of, 35, 109–110
strengths and weaknesses of, 41
Informed consent, 54–56
Intellectualization, 31
Intelligence. *See also* Cognitive development; Cognitive skills
analytic, 121
creative, 121
culture and, 118–119
environmental factors and, 117–118
genetics and, 117
as measured by intelligence tests, 119
practical, 121
psychometric approach to, 115
stress and, 459
Intelligence quotient (IQ), 115
Intelligence tests
in adolescence, 116–117
controversies over, 117–123
explanation of, 115–116
performance of only children on, 165
predictive power of, 115
Stanford-Binet and Wechsler, 115, 116
Intelligence theories
emotional, 121–123
multiple, 120–121
triarchic, 121
types of, 119–120
Intercourse. *See also* Sexual behavior
motives for, 355–357
statistics regarding, 354–355
Internalizing disorders
depression and, 466–474
explanation of, 463, 464, 476, 519
shyness and, 464–465
social phobia and, 465–466
suicide and, 474–476
Internal locus of control, 436, 458
Internet. *See also* World Wide Web
adolescent use of, 255, 260–262
classroom use of, 224, 225
dangerous liaisons offered on, 265
evaluating information on, 124
homework issues and, 266
influence of, 21
as influence on thinking style, 266
overuse of, 266–267
as research tool, 52, 54
social responsibility and, 264–265
various uses of, 262–264
Interpersonal identity, 323
Interpersonal relationships
changes in, 179–181
success with peers and, 183
Intimacy
contraceptive use and, 360

explanation of, 346
as function of families, 144
isolation vs., 322
views of, 349–351
Intrapersonal identity, 323
Intrinsic motivation
explanation of, 232, 236, 251
home environment and, 237
Intuitive-projective faith, 398–399
Inverse correlations, 48
Isolation, 264, 322

Japan
academic achievement in, 223
apprenticeship programs in, 447
employment of high school graduates in, 445
Jews, 2, 524
Josephson Institute of Ethics, 385
Junior high schools, 215, 221. *See also* Middle schools
Juvenile Justice and Delinquency and Prevention Act of 1974, 10

Ketamine, 507
Korea, 223
Kota people, 2

Larry v. Riles, 118
Late adolescence, 1
Late maturation
in females, 81–82
in males, 80–81
Latency stage, 31
Latinos. *See also* Minority groups
academic achievement among, 224, 226, 227
career choice among, 435–438, 440
contraceptive use and, 359
demographic information for, 21, 22
diversity among, 19
dropout trends among, 246, 247
family conflict and, 153, 154
family structure and environment and, 18–19
gang membership among, 524
intelligence tests and, 118
parental involvement in schools and, 238–239
rites of passage for, 2
self-esteem and, 310, 311
sexual activity and, 354
stress among, 456
subculture identity influences for, 17
suicide among, 474
transition to college and, 244
Learned helplessness, 469–470
Learner-centered education, 230–231
Learning disabilities
explanation of, 482–484
secondary and postsecondary education and, 485–487
social and emotional functioning of adolescents with, 484–485

Learning theory, 332–333
Least restrictive environment, 482
Legal status, adolescent, 10–11
Leisure activities, 257
Lesbians, 360. *See also* Homosexuality
Liaisons, 189
Libido, 30
Life events stress, 456
Locus of control, 436, 458
Loneliness, 468, 472
Longitudinal designs
explanation of, 44–45
strengths and weaknesses of, 53
for temperament studies, 75–76
Long-term memory, 110, 111
Louisville Twin Study, 117
Love. *See also* Romantic relationships
components of, 346–347
culture and, 347–348
intimacy and, 346, 349–351
link between sex and, 346, 351
styles of, 348–349
Ludus, 348
Luteinizing hormone (LH), 68
Lying, 385

Machismo, 19
Macrosystem, 42
Magazines
advertising in, 290–291
for females, 290–292
for males, 291–292
overview of, 289–290
Magnet schools, 242
Maidenhood, 2
Maintenance rehearsal, 111
Major depressive disorder, 467. *See also* Depression
Males. *See also* Gender; Gender roles
academic achievement and, 227–228
aggression and, 521–523, 527–529
body image and, 85–87
as bullies, 197
career choice and, 433–435
crime and, 517
dating violence and, 206, 207
depression in, 472
early maturation in, 80–81
eating disorders and, 477
eating habits and, 86, 87
friendship and, 187
growth spurt for, 61–63
hormones in, 68
identity formation and, 323–326
intimacy and, 322
late maturation in, 81
magazines for, 291–292
moral reasoning and, 391–392
music and, 273
parental recognition of autonomy for, 3, 4
prosocial behavior in, 405–406
puberty in, 65, 68, 85 (*See also* Puberty)
rites of passage for, 2

Males (*continued*)
  self-esteem and, 309, 310
  sexuality and, 352–355
  shyness in, 465
  stereotypes of careers for, 433
  stress and, 455, 456
  suicide and, 474
  video games and, 269
Mania, 349
Marginality, 337
Marijuana. *See also* Drug use/abuse
  dependency and, 505–506
  health effects and, 504, 505
  use of, 504, 509
Marriage
  arranged, 347
  remarriage, 172–174
Masai tribe, 2
Mastery goals, 234–236
Masturbation, 65, 344
Maternal employment, 166–167
Mathematics, 218, 228
Maturation. *See also* Puberty
  cognitive development and, 96
  explanation of, 34
  in females, 81–82
  in males, 80–81
Maturity
  pseudo-, 421–422
  vocational, 424
Media. *See also* Internet; Movies; Music;
    Television; Video games
  adolescents as influence on, 257–258
  advertising and, 287–288, 500, 501
  censorship, warning labels and rating
    systems for, 278–279
  cohort effect and, 260–261
  cultivation theory and, 258–259
  desensitization and, 259
  influence of, 15–16, 21, 258–259,
    278–279, 288–289, 292–293
  magazines and, 289–292
  music on radio and, 273
  music videos and, 277–281
  in perspective, 292–293
  precautions regarding effects of,
    256
  sexual behavior and, 283–285, 357
  short- and long-term effects on, 259
  television and movies and, 281–289
  trends in use of, 255
Memory
  explanation of, 111–112
  long-term, 110, 111
  sensory, 109, 111
  short-term, 109–111
Menarche, 61, 62, 64, 78, 79. *See also* Men-
    struation; Puberty
Menstruation
  environmental influences and, 79
  explanation of, 63–64
  as rite of passage, 2
  trends in start of, 78–79

Mental retardation, 117
Mesosystem, 39
Metacognitive skills
  in adolescents, 112–113
  critical thinking and, 123
  explanation of, 110
Methamphetamine, 506–507. *See also*
    Drug use/abuse
Microsystem, 39
Middle adolescence, 1
Middle schools
  academic achievement in, 217–219
  explanation of, 215–216
  needs of adolescents and, 218–219
  self-esteem and, 307–309
  teacher training and, 219–220
  transition to, 216–218, 221
Minority groups. *See also* African Amer-
    icans; Asian Americans; Latinos;
    Native Americans; *specific
    groups*
  academic achievement among,
    224–227
  assimilation and, 337–338
  bicultural competence and, 338–339
  career choice and, 426, 435–442
  demographic information for, 21–22
  dropout trends among, 246
  family conflict in, 153, 154
  identity formation among, 17–18,
    335–339
  intelligence tests and, 118–119
  parental involvement in schools and,
    238
  parenting style and, 147, 148, 156
  peer influences on, 226
  portrayed on television and in movies,
    285–286
  poverty among, 17, 226, 227, 435–439
  self-esteem and, 310–311
  subculture identity influences of, 17
  suicide among, 474
Mobility, 226
Monitoring the Future Study, 496, 507
Monozygotic twins, 72–73
Moodiness, 70
Moral behavior
  explanation of, 393
  influences on, 407–409
  moral reasoning and, 390
Moral development
  approaches to, 386
  education to promote, 409–413
  influences on, 407–409
  moral reasoning and, 389–390
  in perspective, 413–415
Moral dilemmas, 410–411
Moral education
  home and community involvement in,
    412–413
  moral dilemmas approach to,
    410–411
  problems with, 413

  teaching approach to, 411–412
  values clarification courses and, 409
Morality
  culture and, 395–396
  emergence of, 407–408
  empathy and, 394–395
  Freud and, 394
  stages of applying, 396–398
Moral realism, 387
Moral reasoning
  conventional, 388
  development of, 389–390
  explanation of, 386
  gender and, 390–392
  Kohlberg's theory of, 387–390, 392
  moral behavior and, 390
  Piaget's theory of, 387
  postconventional, 388–389
  preconventional, 388
  prosocial behavior and, 403–405
Moral relativism, 387
Morals, 385
Mothers. *See also* Families; Fathers; Par-
    ents
  adolescent, 374–377
  education level of, 117–118, 225
  employment rate for, 20
  interaction with, 158–159
  role of, 158
  working, 166–167
Motivation
  attribution theory and, 233–234
  explanation of, 231–232
  extrinsic, 232, 251
  goal setting and self-evaluation and,
    234–236
  intrinsic, 232, 236, 237, 251
  self-consistency, 501
  self-enhancement, 501
  structures that support, 236–237
Motor vehicle accidents, 502
Movies
  cultivation theory and, 258–259
  extent of viewing, 281
  fantasy and sexual behavior in,
    283–285
  influence of global, 288–289
  stereotypes in, 285–286
  violence in, 282–283
Multiple intelligences theory, 120–121
Multitasking, 266
Music
  antifemale bias and, 276
  cultivation theory and, 259
  influence of, 278–279
  international reach of, 288
  meaning of, 273
  as source of controversy, 273–277
Music Television (MTV), 277, 288
Music videos
  criticisms of, 277–278
  cultivation theory and, 259
  effects of, 278–281

health consequences of, 280
overview of, 277
Myelinization, 65
Mythic-literal faith, 399

Narcissism, 312
Narrow socialization, 4, 5
National Assessment of Education Programs, 223
National Commission on Excellence in Education, 223
National Institute of Mental Health, 473
National Institute on Drug Abuse, 496
National Television Violence Study, 282, 283
A Nation at Risk (National Commission on Excellence in Education), 21, 223
Native Americans. *See also* Minority groups
    alcohol use among, 502
    career choice among, 435, 436, 439–440
    cigarette smoking among, 499
    demographic information for, 21
    family structure and environment and, 19
    identity formation and, 336
    rites of passage for, 2
    self-esteem and, 310, 311
    subculture identity influences for, 17
    suicide among, 474
Negative correlations, 48
Neglected adolescents
    consequences for, 196–197
    explanation of, 192, 195
Neurotransmitters, 471–472
Niche picking, 74
Nomination technique, 192
Nonshared environmental influences, 77–78
Nontraditional occupations
    females in, 428–429
    males in, 434–435
    role models for, 432
Normative discontent, 85
Nurturance function, 144–145
Nutrition, 84–85

Obesity, 86, 88
Object permanence, 96–97
Obscenity, 278
Observation, 46, 53
Occupational choice. *See* Career choice; Employment
Occupational self-efficacy, 426
Only children, 165–166
Operant conditioning, 36
Operational definitions, 46
Operations, 96
Oppositional defiant disorder, 519
Oral stage, 31
Organization, cognitive development and, 95, 96

Paired-comparison technique, 192
Parental consent
    abortion and, 366–367
    for contraceptives and sexual information to adolescents, 367–368
    for research participants, 55, 57
Parental influence
    aggression and, 522–523, 527
    in career choice, 439
    in contraceptive use, 360, 364
    on depression, 471
    disengagement from educational process and, 229
    drug use and, 510–512, 514
    eating disorders and, 477–478
    in moral development, 407–408
    in sexual behavior, 356–357
Parenting style. *See also* Child-rearing strategies
    academic achievement and, 229, 237–239
    for adolescents, 146–147
    authoritarian, 145–148, 174, 210, 522
    authoritative, 146–147, 173, 210, 238
    culture and, 147–149, 156
    drug use and, 510–511
    explanation of, 145
    minority groups and, 147, 148, 156, 239
    permissive, 145, 146, 210
    rejecting/neglecting, 146, 522
    in stepfamilies, 173–174
    stress resilience and, 459–460
Parents. *See also* Adolescent-parent relationship; Families
    of adopted children, 150, 151
    communication with, 149–150
    conflict management and, 157–158
    of depressed adolescents, 471
    drug use by, 511
    early- vs. late-maturation and relationship to, 82
    education level of, 117–118, 225
    identity formation and, 339
    involvement in educational process, 229
    knowledge of media content and, 279
    legal rights of, 11
    noncustodial, 171
    qualities of good, 142–143
    reaction to dating by, 203–205
    recognition of autonomy by, 3
    self-esteem and relationship with, 315
    sex education by, 364
    step-, 172–174
    unequal treatment of siblings by, 162
Participation-identification model, 248
Passion, 347
Passive effects, 74
Passive parental consent, 55
Peer groups. *See also* Cliques; Crowds; Friendship
    academic achievement and, 226
    communication in, 149

conformity to, 210–211
    coping with divorce and, 169
    eating habits and, 85
    friendships and, 183
    functions of, 8, 181–182
    in high school, 221
    influence of, 14–15, 21, 179
    interpersonal relationships and, 179–181
    levels of relationships in, 182–183
    moral behavior and, 408–409
Peer pressure
    adolescent-parent relationship and, 210–211
    aggression and, 523
    drug use and, 511–512, 523
    dynamics of, 207–208
    explanation of, 207
    extent of, 208–210
    sexual behavior and, 355–356
Pelvic inflammatory disease (PID), 368–369
Performance-approach goals, 235–236
Performance-avoidance goals, 235–237
Performance goals, 234–235
Permissive parenting
    effects of, 210
    explanation of, 145, 146
Personal fable, 132–133
Personality
    occupational choice and, 424–426
    stress and, 458
    violence and, 520
Personalizing, 470
Phallic stage, 31
Phonological awareness, 484
Physical abuse, 206, 509, 522
Physical activity, 88–89
Physical appearance. *See* Body image
Physical development. *See also* Health
    biological bases for behavior and, 67–78
    environmental factors and pubertal timing and, 79–80
    in perspective, 91–93
    psychological reactions to pubertal timing and, 80–82
    during puberty, 61–67 (*See also* Puberty)
    secular trend and, 78–79
Piaget's developmental approach
    assimilation and accommodation and, 96
    critique of, 101, 107
    early cognitive development stages and, 96–97
    educational application of, 100–101
    explanation of, 95, 108, 109
    formal operations stage and, 97–101
    going beyond formal operations and, 101–103
    influences on, 96
    schemata and operations and, 96

Piaget's moral reasoning theory, 387
Piers-Harris Self-Concept Scale, 43–44
Pituitary gland, 68
Planned Parenthood v. Casey, 366
Popular adolescents. *See also* Unpopular
    adolescents
    characteristics of, 192–194, 199
    measurement of, 192
    self-esteem and, 183
Population, 47
Positive correlations, 48
Positive psychology, 22, 23
Postconventional moral reasoning,
    388–389
Postformal operational reasoning,
    101–103
Postsecondary schools. *See* Colleges/uni-
    versities
Posttraumatic stress syndrome, 379
Poverty
    academic achievement and, 225, 226
    adolescent pregnancy and, 373, 376
    among minority groups, 17, 226, 227,
        435–439
    career choice and, 435
    identity formation and, 336
    intelligence tests and, 117, 118
    nutrition and, 85
    in single-parent families, 171–172
    stress and, 456
    violence and, 523, 525
Power, 143–145
Pragma, 349
Preconventional moral reasoning, 388
Predatory violence, 518
Prefrontal cortex, 65–66
Pregnancy. *See* Adolescent pregnancy
Prejudice, 17, 18. *See also* Discrimination;
    Stereotypes
Preoperational stage, 97
Primary prevention, 527
Primary sex characteristics
    explanation of, 61, 68
    hormones and, 68, 69
Privacy rights, 10–11
Privately shy, 464
Privatization of entertainment, 265
Proactive aggression, 517, 518
Problem-directed coping, 462
Procedural checklists, 105, 106
Process scaffolding, 105, 106
Prosocial behavior
    activism and volunteering and, 405
    developmental trends in, 403–405
    explanation of, 402–403
    gender and, 405–406
    influences on, 407–409
    self-esteem and, 304–305
    video games and, 271
Protective factors
    against drug use/abuse, 512
    against violence, 525–526, 528–529
Protestants, 2

Prozac, 473, 474
Pseudomaturity, 421–422
Psychoanalytic theory, 29–32, 40
Psychologists, 11, 13
Psychology, 22–23
Psychosexual stages, 30, 31
Psychosocial theory
    explanation of, 32–33
    strengths and weaknesses of, 40
Puberty
    biological basis of, 68
    brain development during, 65–67
    consequences of early and late, 80–82
    emotional swings during, 70
    environmental factors and timing of,
        79–80
    explanation of, 1, 6, 61, 343–344
    female development during, 62–65
    growth spurt during, 61–62
    male development during, 65
    rites of passage and, 2
    secular trend and, 78–79
    weight gain during, 85
Publicly shy, 464
Putting Parents First Act (PPFA), 367

Quasi-experimental studies
    explanation of, 49–50
    strengths and weaknesses of, 53
Questionnaires
    explanation of, 47–48
    strengths and weaknesses of, 53, 57
Quid pro quo sexual harassment, 380
Quinceañera, 2

Radio, 273
Rape, 278–279
Rap music, 274, 276–279
Rating scale technique, 192
Reactive aggression, 517–518
Reciprocal interaction, 11
Reciprocal teaching, 107
Reflective thinking, 100
Refusal skills, 513–514
Rehabilitation Act of 1973, 482–483
Rehearsal, 111
Reinforcement, 36
Reinforcers, 36
Rejected adolescents
    consequences for, 196–197
    explanation of, 192, 194–195
Rejecting/neglecting parenting, 146, 522
Relational aggression, 197
Relational violence, 518
Relativistic reasoning, 102
Releasing factors, 68
Religious beliefs
    adolescents and, 399–401
    cults and, 402–403
    development of, 398–399
    rites of passage and, 2
    spirituality vs., 398
    values and behavior and, 401

Remarriage
    changes following, 172–173
    parenting styles and, 173–174
Required helpfulness, 459
Research
    assessment of, 50–51
    background of adolescence, 7
    cross-cultural, 51–52
    Internet as tool for, 52, 54
Research designs
    cross-sectional, 43–44
    explanation of, 43
    longitudinal, 44–45
    sequential, 45
    strengths and weaknesses of, 53
    use of, 45–46
Research ethics
    confidentiality and, 57–58
    deception and, 56–57
    informed consent and, 54–56
    standards for, 54, 56
Research methods
    case study, 46–47
    correlations, 48
    experimental, 48–49
    observation, 46, 95
    quasi-experimental, 49–50
    questionnaire and survey, 47–48
    strengths and weaknesses of, 53
Resilience
    explanation of, 23
    to stress, 23, 457–463
Responsiveness
    drug use and, 510
    explanation of, 145
    parenting style and, 147–149, 157
    in stepfamilies, 173
Restrictiveness, 148
Risky behavior
    alcohol use and, 502
    contraceptive use and, 359
    music lyrics and, 275–276
    music videos and, 280
    personal fable and, 132, 133
    shyness and, 465
    stress and, 455
Ritalin, 490
Rite of passage, 1–3, 6
Rohypnol, 507
Role confusion
    explanation of, 316–317
    identity vs., 318
Role models
    career choice and, 432, 437–439
    gender roles and, 333
    identity formation and, 336
    media presentation of, 16
Roman Catholics, 2
Romantic love, 347
Romantic relationships. *See also* Dating;
    Love
    conflict in, 205
    dating and, 200–205

depression following end of, 468
explanation of, 200, 345
physical violence in, 205–207
Rumination, 456, 473

Safe Dates Program, 207
Sample, 47
Scaffolding, 105, 106
Schema, 96, 470
Schools. *See also* Colleges/universities;
    Elementary schools; High schools;
    Middle schools
    academic requirements in, 21,
        251
    accommodations with students with
        disabilities in, 482–483
    changes in, 21
    charter, 242
    influence and structure of, 15
    instilling values in, 385
    magnet, 242
    sex education in, 364–368
    technology use in, 224–225
    violence in, 21, 516, 527
School-to-Work Opportunities Act of
    1994, 443
Science, 228
Scripts, dating, 202, 203
Secondary prevention, 527
Secondary schools, 222, 485–486. *See also*
    High school
Secondary sex characteristics
    explanation of, 61, 344
    in females, 64–65, 78–79
    hormones and, 68, 69
    in males, 68
Sects, 402
Secular trend, 78–79
Secure attachment, 140, 141
Selection bias, 50
Selective attention, 110, 111
Self
    as cognitive construct, 298–299
    explanation of, 297
    personal experiences and, 299
    preoccupation with, 301
    real and ideal, 303–304
    social nature of, 298
Self-concept
    of academic ability, 308
    cognitive functioning and, 313, 314
    culture and, 324
    developmental changes in, 300–302
    explanation of, 297, 298, 305
    false selves and, 302–303
    identity and, 317
    in perspective, 339–340
    real and ideal, 303–304
    stability of, 303
    in students with learning disabilities,
        485
Self-consistency motivation, 501
Self-Directed Search (SDS), 426

Self-efficacy
    career choice and, 436–437, 439, 442
    explanation of, 37–38
    occupational, 426
    school programs to improve, 315
    stress and, 458
Self-enhancement motivation, 501
Self-esteem
    adolescent orientations to, 305–307
    aggression and, 311–312
    baseline inflated, 313
    causes of inflated, 313
    cognitive development and, 313–315
    culture and, 324
    depression and, 467
    drug use and, 509
    explanation of, 297–298, 304, 316
    friendships and, 183–184
    in high school students, 221
    homosexuals and, 362
    improvement of, 315–316
    in males, 433–434
    in minority adolescents, 310–311
    physical appearance and, 303
    prosocial behavior and, 304–305
    secure attachment and, 141
    shyness and, 465
    stress and, 458–459
    trends in, 307–310
    unstable, 312–313
    weight and, 85, 88
Self-fulfilling prophecy, 50, 240
Self-other understanding stages, 130–131
Self-regulated learners
    explanation of, 110
    strategies used by, 113–114
    teaching skills to become, 114–115
Self-regulation
    importance of, 122, 123
    stress and, 459
Sensorimotor stage, 96
Sensory memory, 109, 111
Sequential designs, 45, 53
Seventeen, 290
Sex
    link between love and, 346, 351
    revolution in attitudes toward,
        352–354
Sex characteristics
    in females, 62–65, 78–79
    primary, 61, 68
    secondary, 61, 64–65, 68, 78–79, 344
Sex education
    on adolescent pregnancy, 372–378
    on forced sexual behavior, 378–379
    at home, 364
    parental consent or parents' right to
        know issues and, 367–368
    in schools, 364–368
    on sexual harassment, 379–381
    on sexually transmitted diseases,
        368–372
Sex hormones, 68

Sex typing. *See also* Gender roles
    biological differences and, 334
    culture and, 334
    explanation of, 327
    function of, 328–330
Sexual assault, 278–279
Sexual attraction, 68
Sexual behavior. *See also* Intercourse
    contraceptive use and, 358–360
    evolution of adolescent, 354–355
    family influence and, 356–357
    forced, 378–379
    media and, 283–285, 357
    motives for, 355–357
    peer pressure and, 355–356
    statistics regarding, 354–355
Sexual harassment
    categories of, 380
    explanation of, 379–380
    rate of, 380–381
Sexuality
    alcohol and, 280
    dating and, 345 (*See also* Dating)
    Freudian view of, 30
    intimacy and, 349
    masturbation and, 344
    in music lyrics, 274, 275, 277
    in music videos, 277–279
    in perspective, 381
    physical changes in, 343–344
    puberty and, 343–344 (*See also*
        Puberty)
    on television and in movies, 283–285
Sexually transmitted infections (STI)
    AIDS as, 370–371
    chlamydia as, 368–369
    explanation of, 21, 368
    genital warts as, 369
    gonorrhea as, 369
    herpes simplex as, 370
    prevention of, 371–372
    syphilis as, 369
Sexual orientation. *See* Homosexuality
Shared environmental influences, 77–78
Short-term memory
    explanation of, 109–110
    transfer to, 111
Shyness
    explanation of, 464–465
    social phobia vs., 466
Siblings. *See also* Families
    genetic influences on, 76–78
    patterns of interaction with, 160–162
    unequal parental treatment of, 162
Similarity, 185–186
Single-child families, 165–166
Single-parent families
    achievement of children raised in, 163,
        164
    characteristics of, 171–172, 175
    dating among adolescents from, 201,
        345–346
    statistics for, 20–21

Skillstreaming method, 199
Sleep, 89–91
Sleeper effect, 51
Smoking. *See* Cigarette smoking
Social cognition
    adolescent egocentrism and, 131–133
    explanation of, 129–130, 132
    perception of others and, 130
    taking perspective of other individuals
        and, 130–131
Social dominance, 193
Socialization
    broad, 4–6, 16
    explanation of, 4–6, 11
    friendship formation and, 186–187
    gender roles and, 331
    narrow, 4–6
Social learning theory
    explanation of, 37–38, 393
    strengths and weaknesses of, 38, 41
Social phobia
    eating disorders and, 479
    explanation of, 465–466
Social skills
    computer use and, 264–265
    methods for enhancing, 199–200
    of only children, 165
    peer groups and, 182
    popularity and, 195
    programs to teach, 315–316, 486, 526
    stress and, 458
    of students with learning disabilities,
        484–486
    video games and, 271
    violence and, 526, 527
Social support, 458
Social transmission, 34, 96
Society for Research in Child Develop-
    ment, 54, 56
Sociocentric cultures, 324, 325
Sociocultural theory
    explanation of, 103, 108, 109
    influence on education of, 104–107
    social interaction and transmission of
        skills and, 103
    zone of proximal development and,
        103–104
Sociometric techniques, 192
Spirituality, 398, 401. *See also* Religious
    beliefs
Stage theories, 28
Standardized tests, 115, 251. *See also*
    Intelligence tests
Stanford-Binet Intelligence Test, 116
Stepfamilies, 172–173
Stereotypes
    of adolescents, 6–7, 9
    of cigarette smokers, 500–501
    gender, 275–278, 327–328
    of homosexuals, 361
    of minority groups, 18
    in music lyrics, 275, 276
    in music videos, 277–278, 281
    occupational, 430, 433

    in television and in movies, 285–286
    in video games, 267
Stereotype threat, 119
Steroids, 87–88
Storge, 349
Stress
    in adolescents, 454–455
    among minority groups, 456
    explanation of, 453–454
    gender and, 455–456
    methods for coping with, 461–463
    personality and, 458
    pubertal timing and, 79, 82
    reasons for concern about, 455
    suicide and, 475
    warning signs for, 460
Stressors
    delayed-action effect of, 460
    explanation of, 453
    family risk factors and, 461
    interpersonal, 454, 455
    nature of, 456–457
Stress resilience
    explanation of, 23
    factors for, 457–459
    guidelines for, 461–463
    long-term outcomes for, 460
    model for, 459–460
Striatum, 66
Strong ties, 264, 265
Subcultures
    explanation of, 16
    identity influences of, 17
    research in other, 51–52
Substance dependence, 495
Substance use/abuse. *See* Drug
    use/abuse
Substitution effect, 259
Suicide
    heavy metal music and, 276
    prevalence of, 474
    prevention of, 476
    reasons for, 474–475
    risk factors for, 475
Sunk costs problem, 125
Superego, 30, 31, 394
Supreme Court, U.S.
    abortion and, 366
    adolescent decision-making compe-
        tence and, 128
    rights for juveniles and, 10–12
Surface processing, 236
Surveys
    explanation of, 47–48
    strengths and weaknesses of, 53
Symbols, 97
Synthetic-conventional faith, 399
Syphilis, 369

Tainted fruit theory, 278
Talk shows, 286–287
Teachers
    in elementary schools, 227
    expectations of, 239–241

    interaction with males and females by,
        227–228
    in middle schools, 219–220
Team accelerated instruction (TAI), 106
Technology. *See also* Computer use;
        Internet; Video games; World Wide
        Web
    comfort level with, 260–261
    in schools, 224–225
    societal change resulting from,
        534–535
Tech-prep system, 447, 448
Teen, 290
Teen Outreach, 249–250
Television
    advertising on, 287–288
    aggressive behavior and, 271
    careers depicted on, 441
    cultivation theory and, 258–259
    extent of viewing, 281
    fantasy and sexual behavior on,
        283–285
    international reach of, 288–289
    stereotypes on, 285–286
    talk shows on, 286–287
    V-chip for, 279
    violence on, 282–283
Temperament
    characteristics of, 75
    longitudinal studies of, 75–76
    stress and, 458
Terrorist attacks of September 11, 2001,
    20, 536–537
Testicles, 65
Testosterone
    aggression and, 70–71, 334, 521
    explanation of, 68, 87
    sexual interest and, 343
Texas Adoption Project, 74
Theoretical approaches
    behavioral, 36–37
    biological, 29
    cognitive development, 34–35
    developmental task, 33–34
    ecological, 39, 42–43
    information-processing, 35
    psychoanalytic, 29–32
    psychosocial, 32–33
    social learning, 37–38
    strengths and weaknesses of, 40–41
Theories
    differences between, 28
    elements of good, 28, 29
    explanation of, 27–28
Tobacco. *See* Cigarette smoking
Tolerance, 495
Tracking, 241–242
Transitions, 13–14
Treatment of Depression Collaborative
    Research Program (National Insti-
    tute of Mental Health), 473
Triarchic theory of intelligence, 121
Trust vs. mistrust, 33
Twins, 72–73

Twin studies
  on aggression, 521
  drawbacks of, 74
  explanation of, 72–73
  on intelligence, 117

Unconscious, 29
Unemployment
  adolescent, 448–449
  among Native Americans, 439
Universalizing faith, 399
Universities. *See* Colleges/universities
Unpopular adolescents
  aggression and, 194–195
  characteristics of, 194, 199
  consequences for, 196–197
  neglected adolescents as, 195
  reasons for dislike of, 195–196
  rejected adolescents as, 194–195

Values, 411–412
Values clarification courses, 409
Victims, of bullying, 197
Video games
  aggression and, 269–273
  gender and, 268
  overuse of, 271–272
  overview of, 267–268
  social skills and, 271
Vietnam War, 20
Violence. *See also* Aggression
  aggressiveness and, 519–520
  biological factors and, 520–521

cognitive factors and, 521
community factors and, 523–524
drug use and, 506, 529–531
exposure to, 206, 509
family processes and relationships
  and, 522–523
gangs and, 524–525
against homosexuals, 362
media and, 258–259
in music lyrics, 274–277
in music videos, 277–280
overview of, 516–517
peer factors and, 523
personality and, 520
in perspective, 529–531
poverty and, 523, 525
predatory, 518
prediction of, 524–525
programs to prevent, 518, 525–527
protective factors against, 525–526,
  528–529
relational, 518
in romantic relationships, 205–207
in schools, 21
self-esteem and, 311–312
on television and in movies, 282–283
types of, 517–519
in video games, 267, 269–271
vulnerability and, 527–529
Vocational choice. *See also* Career choice;
  Employment
  apprenticeship and, 445–448
  career and technical education pro-
    grams and, 444–445

employers and high school graduates
  and, 443–444
transition between school and work
  and, 442–443
Vocational development, 423–424
Vocational education programs, 442,
  444–445
Vocational maturity, 424
Volunteering, 405
Voucher plan, 243

Wadadika Paiute, 2
Warning labels, 278–279
Weak ties, 264
Wechsler Adult Intelligence Scale
  (WAIS), 116
Wechsler Intelligence Scale for Children
  (WISC), 116
Weight
  obesity and, 88
  obsession with, 86–87
  puberty and, 85
Withdrawal, 495
World Wide Web. *See also* Internet
  classroom use of, 224, 225
  evaluating information on, 124
  influence of, 21

YM, 290
Youth Charter, 413

Zone of proximal development, 103–104